DISCOVERING
LITERATURE

C O M P A C T   E D I T I O N

HANS P. GUTH
Santa Clara University

GABRIELE L. RICO
San Jose State University

PRENTICE HALL
Upper Saddle River, New Jersey 07458

Library of Congress Cataloging-in-Publication Data
Guth, Hans Paul
    Discovering literature / Hans P. Guth, Gabriele L. Rico. —
Compact ed.
        p.   cm.
    Includes index.
    ISBN 0-13-083556-0
    1. English language—Rhetoric.   2. Literature—Collections.
3. College readers.   I. Rico, Gabriele L.   II. Title.
    [PE1417.G866   2000]
    808—dc21   98-54727
                                                            CIP

Editorial Director: Charlyce Jones-Owen
Editor-in-Chief: Leah Jewell
Acquisition Editor: Carrie Brandon
Editorial Assistant: Gianna Caradonna
*AVP, Director of Manufacturing and
    Production:* Barbara Kittle
Sr. Managing Editor: Bonnie Biller
Production Liaison: Fran Russello
Project Manager: Joseph Barron/P. M.
    Gordon Associates, Inc.
Manufacturing Manager: Nick Sklitsis
Prepress and Manufacturing Buyer:
    Mary Ann Gloriande

Art Director: Jayne Conte
Cover Designer: Bruce Kenselaar
Cover Art: Photodisk
Director, Image Resource Center: Melinda
    Lee Reo
Manager, Rights and Permissions: Kay
    Dellosa
Image Specialist: Beth Boyd
Marketing Manager: Brandy Dawson
Copy Editor: Sue Gleason
Permissons Editor: Frederick T. Courtright

This book was set in 10.5/12 Garamond by Lithokraft II
and was printed and bound by Courier Companies, Inc.
The cover was printed by Phoenix Color Corp.

Acknowledgments appear on pages 1207–1216,
which constitute an extension of the copyright page.

© 2000 by Prentice-Hall, Inc.
Upper Saddle River, New Jersey 07458

Printed in the United States of America

10 9 8 7 6 5 4 3 2 1

ISBN 0-13-083556-0

Prentice-Hall International (UK) Limited, *London*
Prentice-Hall of Australia Pty. Limited, *Sydney*
Prentice-Hall Canada Inc., *Toronto*
Prentice-Hall Hispanoamericana, S.A., *Mexico*
Prentice-Hall of India Private Limited, *New Delhi*
Prentice-Hall of Japan, Inc., *Tokyo*
Pearson Education Asia Pte. Ltd., *Singapore*
Editora Prentice-Hall do Brasil, Ltda., *Rio de Janeiro*

The Promise
of *Discovering Literature*

Our aim in working on this compact edition of *Discovering Literature* has been

⋇ to initiate a new generation of students into their rich literary heritage

⋇ to bring the classics to life and make them relevant to the lives of today's students

⋇ to show the continuity between the past and the classics of today and tomorrow

⋇ to show that imaginative literature crosses borders of time, ethnicity, and gender

⋇ to show students how literature illuminates and enhances life

⋇ to highlight key concepts and make them accessible to the common reader

⋇ to explore the range of the readers' response

⋇ to bring the students' own imagination and creativity into play

⋇ to validate the students' writing and thinking about imaginative literature

⋇ to explore new resources for the study of literature in the electronic age

Brief Contents

FICTION

POETRY

DRAMA

Contents

FICTION

POETRY

13   PATTERN   The Whole Poem   *339*

14   IMAGE   The Open Eye   *361*

DRAMA

26 PREVIEW   The Magic of the Stage   *655*

27 CONFLICT   The Heart of Drama   *672*

28 GREEK TRAGEDY   The Embattled Protagonist   *733*

Writing about Literature
Writing Workshops at a Glance

Subtitles in parentheses indicate a special rhetorical or pedagogical focus. Note boldface for documented papers requiring library work, parenthetical documentation, and a list of Works Cited.

FICTION

POETRY

DRAMA

Preface

To the Instructor

Everything is new under the sun.
CZESLAW MILOSZ

Silence is the real crime against humanity.
NADYEZHDA MANDELSHTAM

In this compact edition of *Discovering Literature,* we have culled from the rich resources of the full-length book the materials most likely to help the teacher construct a course focused on the needs of today's students. We have focused on helping teachers design a course that will engage students' attention and help them become active, responsive readers and writers.

LITERATURE FOR TODAY'S READERS

We have aimed at making *Discovering Literature* the most accessible and motivating of the major anthologies. Basically, we want to help teachers turn reluctant readers—or nonreaders—into readers. Our goal is to help students discover the power of literature to illuminate and enhance lives. We provide materials designed to elicit your students' personal responses and to validate student writing. We believe that responding to imaginative literature will give students a fuller sense of what it means to be human.

Discovering the Heritage   We aim at helping students discover the richness of their literary heritage. Classics speak from beyond gulfs of time and distance to succeeding generations. We try to give students a way in to the reading of Sophocles' *Antigone,* Shakespeare's *Hamlet,* Emily Dickinson, John Steinbeck, John Donne, Gwendolyn Brooks, or Flannery O'Connor. Stressing the continuity between the present and the past, this book integrates treatment of the classics with the best current writing. "Juxtapositions" show the treatment of the same theme by authors of a different time, culture, or gender.

Rethinking the Canon   Each generation rediscovers the classics, discovers tomorrow's classics, and rethinks its list of canonical works. Among today's classics in this edition are stories by Louise Erdrich, Toni Morrison, and Sandra Cisneros. New voices in poetry include Alberto Ríos, Rita Dove, Yusef Komunyakaa, and Bethlyn Madison Webster. Strong new entries in the drama section include plays by David Henry Hwang and David Mamet.

Gender and Ethnic Balance   Imaginative literature transcends boundaries of gender, ethnicity, race, or sexual orientation. This book introduces students to the rich multicultural diversity of the American tradition and of world literature. Among the poets in this volume, women from earlier periods include Juana Inés de la Cruz, the Countess of Dia, and Marie de Pisan. New selections include poems by Janice Mirikitani, Chitra Divakaruni, Maya Angelou, and Martín Espada.

The Relevance of Criticism   *Discovering Literature* examines contemporary criticism for its relevance to the student reader's response to literature. It shares with your students current rereadings and reevaluations of classic texts. It gives students a sense of the range of critical responses as readers examine texts from the vantage point of such divergent perspectives as formalist, Marxist, psychoanalytic, or feminist theory. The book represents feminist and minority writers who ask us to listen to the unheard voices of the present and the past.

The Creative Dimension   A drily analytic approach to imaginative literature is a contradiction in terms. This book privileges critics who help us honor the power of literature to educate the emotions and to stir the imagination. If students are to enter into the spirit of poem or play, our teaching needs to engage their imaginative faculties. *Discovering Literature* encourages students to cease being passive readers and instead to bring their own imagination into play. The "Creative Dimension" strand encourages students to discover their own creativity.

Validating Student Writing   Writing about literature makes students more intelligent and more responsive readers. *Discovering Literature* provides guidelines for writing and model papers with each chapter. Writing workshops repeatedly take students through major stages in the writing process, from preliminary exploration and note taking through shaping and drafting to rethinking and revising in response to feedback from instructor and peers. A wealth of motivated, well-developed student writing provides model papers for class discussion of writing strategies and for peer review.

A TEACHING TEXT

We aim to give teachers a text that will help them reach the students in today's classroom. The following are special teaching features of this book:

Motivating the Student Reader Reviewers of an earlier edition praised its "invitation to students" and its ability to encourage reading. Headnotes go beyond routine biography or literary history to put selections in a living context and raise the student reader's expectations. We have strengthened the sequence of selections to help student and teacher move consistently from the inviting or accessible to the more challenging.

Rethinking Critical Terminology We introduce critical terms where they help illuminate the literature—asking students to see critical terminology as a tool rather than as a barrier. We have worked hard to clarify definitions that tell insiders what they already know but that remain opaque for the outsider. We have been wary of technical jargon—of literature taught for the sake of theory. In this text, criticism and critical theory serve the literary enterprise.

Restoring Earlier Texts We have cautiously modernized punctuation (and sometimes spelling) where needed to make poems of earlier periods intelligible and enjoyable for a new generation. Where obsolete printers' conventions or dysfunctional marks impede the modern reader, we update punctuation to help today's student follow the syntax of a poem by John Donne or the magnificent rhythms of a poem by John Keats. Modernizing is somewhat of a misnomer here, since poets like Donne and Whitman wrote English that was eminently modern in their time.

Inviting Shakespeare Edition We aim at offering students a more inviting, intelligible, and motivating introduction to Shakespeare than competing books. In the glossed (rather than footnoted) student edition of *Hamlet,* the marginal glosses replace the thicket of conventional footnotes at the bottom of the page. Close at hand and available at a glance, the glosses illuminate difficult passages and provide the closest modern meaning in the context of a line.

Demystifying Research *Discovering Literature* initiates students into library research and sets up an ample choice of research paper projects on literary topics. The text provides guidelines and models of documented papers for each genre—short story, poetry, and drama. Pointed instructions demystify for students the current MLA documentation style, clarifying the rationale while giving a wealth of sample entries. New sections discuss online research and the evolving style for documenting online sources.

ACKNOWLEDGMENTS

We owe a large debt to our own teachers who guided and inspired us and introduced us to the world of imaginative literature. We cherish the friendship and good example of colleagues who believe in the potential of their students and know how to make the printed page come to life in the classroom. We have enjoyed joining in the dialogue with critics and theorists who have in recent decades made the teaching of literature a heady intellectual undertaking.

We are thankful to reviewers and to users of the book who shared with us their reactions, questions, and concerns. We want to thank especially the reviewers of the compact edition: Barbara A. Farrelly, University of Dayton; Myrna A. Goldberg, Montgomery College; Troy D. Nordman, Butler County Community College; Anita Obermeier, Arizona State University; and William Provost, University of Georgia.

Our largest debt of gratitude is to our students, whose intelligence, curiosity, and imagination have kept alive our faith in the power of literature and in the human enterprise. Of the many students who have allowed us to use or adapt their work, we want to thank especially Debbie Nishimura, Andrea Sandke, Olivia Nunez, Francia Stephens, Mike deAngelis, Dea Nelson, Kam Chieu, Greg Grewell, Joanna Wright, Merritt Ireland, Linda Spencer, Elizabeth Kerns, Conrad Mangrum, Joyce Halenar, Marilyn Johnson, Michael Guth, John Newman, Judith Gardner, Pamela Cox, Rita Frakas, Barbara Hill, Melody Brune, Paul Francois, Ruth Randall, Katheryn Crayton-Shay, Dorothy Overstreet, Bill Irwin, Ruth Veerkamp, Martha Kell, Kevin McCabe, Thomas Perez-Jewell, Janelle Ciraulo, Irina Raicu, Joyce Sandoval, Catherine Hooper, Gail Bowman, Todd Marvin, Catherine Russell, and Simone Rico.

HANS P. GUTH
GABRIELE L. RICO

Introduction

The Promise of Literature

The person who writes out of an inner need is trying to order his corner of the universe; very often the meaning of an experience or an emotion becomes clear only in this way.

MAXINE KUMIN

Reading and writing aren't sacred yet people have been killed as if they were.

ADRIENNE RICH

Why read literature? Imaginative literature invites you to share in human experience. Poets, storytellers, and playwrights make you more aware of how other human beings think and feel. Literature holds the mirror up to life, but it is more active than a mirror. Unlike a mirror, it selects and shapes what it sees. It finds a pattern; it finds meaning. Readers who love imaginative literature know that it enriches their lives. It helps them understand what it means to be human.

Each poem is different. Each story or play creates its own world. Nevertheless, guidelines like the following can help you make the most of your reading:

The Ideal Reader   What does it take to be a good reader? The English novelist Virginia Woolf said the ideal reader was the "author's fellow-worker and accomplice." She wanted you to be on the writer's side—trying to respond to whatever the author had to say. She wanted you to be willing to check out what is different or new. She wished you to listen to characters long enough to discover that in some ways they are like you or like people you care about. She expected you to be a receptive reader—ready to try out new visions, new ways of looking at life.

Using Your Imagination   Poets say that it takes two poets to make a poem. First, the poet-author writes the poem. Then the poet-reader re-creates the poem in the theater of the mind, seeing its sights with the mind's eye. To help a poem come to life, you have to use your imagination. Let a story or poem take you to its own world of shapes, colors, textures, or sounds. Let it call up the sights, sounds, and smells of an apple market in Michigan. Imagine yourself watching a father building a fire to fight the bitter morning cold on a winter Sunday.

The World of Feelings   Literature stirs our emotions. We do not just register the movements of people like a surveillance camera. We do not merely record sights and sounds and events like a camcorder. Instead, we become involved. We share in the hopes and fears of others. A poem makes us angry or makes us glad. A story bothers us or puzzles us or fills us with anxiety; it may leave us frustrated, or it may leave us happy. Imaginative literature activates the empathy, or imaginative sympathy, that makes us share in the range of human emotions. You need to be willing to get into the spirit of a poem or a story, to relive the tensions or conflicts of a play.

Crossing the Boundaries   Literature crosses the borders. The Greek playwright Sophocles wrote his *Antigone* 2500 years ago. In the play, a young woman has to choose between what the law commands and what her own conscience tells her to do. In Yukio Mishima's "Swaddling Clothes," a story set in modern Japan, the wife cares about a baby born into poverty, with no family or hope of a decent education. Her callous husband jokes about the mother and the child with his friends. If we subtract from the story the Japanese setting—with its Imperial Palace and cherry blossoms—the basic contrast could be played out in Glendale, California, or Buffalo, New York.

The Personal Connection   Readers go back to literature that has something to say to them personally. A poem or a story has a strong hold on them when it speaks to something in their own experience or personality. Many readers, for instance, are fascinated by stories about growing up, about being initiated into the adult world. When they read a story like Alice Munro's "Boys and Girls," they identify with a character caught between conflicting role models or rival influences—whether father or mother, school against church, or traditional gender roles versus the individual's true potential.

Literature and Creativity   Creativity is everyone's birthright. There is a poet buried in every one of us. How else could we respond to song and poem and story? You will often make a story, poem, or play truly your own if you try an imaginative or creative response. You may choose to re-create in your own way a key image in a poem, following the train of associations it sets in motion. Or you may want to re-create a haunting overall impression that a story imprinted on your mind. You are likely to get more fully into the spirit of a play if you look at its world through the eyes of a character—perhaps starting an imaginary monologue with "I, Antigone, . . ." or "I, Hamlet, . . ." or "I, Ophelia, . . ." You may want to join a group in a miniproduction or adaptation of a scene from a play.

Writing about Literature   When you write about literature, you write to sort out your own thoughts and feelings and to share your findings with others. Both you as the writer and your reader learn something from a well-worked-out paper. When you keep a reading log or journal, you have a chance to record revealing details, striking quotations, first impressions, tentative conclusions, or personal reactions. When you prepare a more structured paper, you reread, you take notes, you reconsider. You sort out and organize your responses. Just as people who read well become better writers, people who write about what they read become better readers.

Don't be discouraged when a challenging short story or poem seems baffling at first reading. Think about it. Come back to it again. Listen to what others have to say about it. One definition of a classic is that it has rich meanings that unfold on second or third reading. Remember that the selections you read in this book are here because they have given pleasure to others before you—stimulating their imagination, making them think and feel, and giving them joy.

Fiction

A story really isn't any good unless it successfully
hangs on and expands in the mind.

1 Preview

The World of Fiction

We are story-telling animals. As our primitive ancestors sat around the fire carving spearheads and eating blackberries, they told stories which in time were woven into a tapestry of myth and legend.

SAM KEEN

FOCUS ON FICTION

What is the appeal of a good story? The Greek writer Nikos Kazantsakis tells a brief story that has in it essential elements of the storyteller's art:

> There was a smell of fig trees in the air. A little old woman who was walking past stopped next to me. She lifted up some leaves covering a basket she was carrying. She picked out two of the figs in the basket and offered them to me. "Do you know me from somewhere, granny?" I asked. She looked at me, surprised. "No, my lad. Do I have to know you to give you something? You are a human being. So am I. Isn't that enough?"

This story does in miniature what other stories take longer to do for their readers. It takes us on a flight of the imagination to a setting; it takes us to a time and a place. We come to know two characters, who become real to us as human beings. Something happens that is worth remembering, worth telling. As we imagine ourselves in the traveler's place, we are likely to be moved by what the old woman said. The figs become a symbol—they represent the nourishment that sustains life, but they are also a token of the fellow feeling or bonding that helps us survive. In the hurry of everyday life, this incident stands out. It is complete and self-contained, with a meaning of its own. It makes a good story.

Every story is different. It makes its own rules; it creates its own world. Nevertheless, as readers, we become aware of questions that arise in our minds again and again. A preview of key questions that readers and critics may ask about a story might look like this:

3

Setting   *Where are we? Where is the story taking us?* What kind of world, what kind of reality, does it create for us? Storytellers take us to a world of their creation. The story takes us to a place, a time, a situation. Often the place becomes so vivid that we forget we are not in a real place but merely in an imagined setting, a country of the mind. Ask yourself: Could this story be happening anywhere? You will be reading a different story depending on whether you watch white officials in colonial Africa, or tenant farmers scraping together a living in the backwoods, or a young woman growing up in an old-fashioned patriarchal family.

Character   *Who are the people?* What is their history or their current situation? What are their motives, needs, or desires? What explains the way they act? In a traditional story, the storyteller places believable characters in a vividly imagined setting and then puts them in motion. How well do you get to know them? You may know them from what the author says about them—or, more exactly, from what the narrator, the person telling the story, says. You learn about them what *other* characters in the story tell you. You watch characters in action—reaching conclusions about their motives, their problems, their ambitions, their desires. You know them from listening to them—talking mentally to themselves or engaging in dialogue with others in the story.

Plot   *What is happening and why?* What story line gives shape to the story as a whole? What is the situation? Is there a central conflict or a central problem, and how is it going to be resolved? Is there a turning point, a turning of the tide? What needs or wants create an unfinished agenda? What obstacles create suspense? Stories vary in how much overt action they incorporate. Sometimes much of the story is in the thoughts and feelings taking place in a character's mind.

Point of View   *Whose eyes are looking at the world?* Who is telling the story? From what point of view? What kind of window is the story opening on the world around us? What is included, what left out? What special insights or privileged information are we able to share? What biases may cloud our vision? What blind spots do we need to take into account?

Symbol   *What in the story has a meaning beyond itself?* What objects, people, or events seem to have a special significance beyond their literal meaning? What in the story acquires a symbolic meaning—the way a handshake might symbolize brotherhood, or the way a new shoot on a tree might stand for rebirth or renewal? A river might at first seem merely a means of transportation, but it might slowly begin to suggest the steady, slow flow of time, which can never be stopped or reversed.

Theme   *What is the meaning of the story as a whole?* What issues does it raise; what ideas does it explore? For instance, does it act out an optimistic or pessimistic view of human nature? Even a lighthearted story is likely to have a point, although that point may not be spelled out in so many words. We call the implied point, the implied comment, the *theme* of the story. Authors used to feel free to spell out the moral of the tale. Most writers today are wary of spelling out the theme of a story too directly. They do not want to preach or editorialize. They want us to live through the experience of the story to discover what it has to say. What we witness raises questions, and the story as a whole suggests possible answers.

Style   *How does the author use language?* Is the language rich in striking images? Or does the writer use the minimum language needed to tell the story? Does the story appeal to our emotions, making us share in joy and sadness? Does it make us experience bitterness and passionate disappointment? Or does the story keep us detached—maintaining an ironic tone, making us look at events with a wry, knowing smile? Much of the impact of a story is not just in what is said but in how it is said.

The following story takes us to a setting and introduces us to a set of characters. It makes us watch a minidrama that meant something to the author. Where are we? Who are the people? What happens in the story? From whose point of view is the story told? Does anything in the story seem to have symbolic significance? What did the events in the story mean to the author? What do they mean to you?

Sandra Cisneros   *(born 1954)*

Sandra Cisneros is a widely published Chicana, or Mexican-American, writer, born of a Mexican father and a Mexican-American mother in Chicago. Her stories recreate in loving detail the environment where many working-class Americans live. In the following story, she uses a few more or less self-explanatory Spanish phrases and references to Mexican history. La Virgen de Guadalupe is the Virgin Mary of Guadalupe. The first PRI elections, which brought Mexico's traditional ruling party to power, disillusioned many of the more radical supporters of the Mexican revolution.

Mericans   *1991*

We're waiting for the awful grandmother who is inside dropping pesos into *la ofrenda* box before the altar to La Divina Providencia. Lighting votive candles and genuflecting. Blessing herself and kissing her thumb. Running a crystal rosary between her fingers. Mumbling, mumbling, mumbling.

There are so many prayers and promises and thanks-be-to-God to be given in the name of the husband and the sons and the only daughter who never attend mass. It doesn't matter. Like La Virgen de Guadalupe, the awful grandmother intercedes on their behalf. For the grandfather who hasn't believed in anything since the first PRI elections. For my father, El Periquín, so skinny he needs his sleep. For Auntie Light-skin, who only a few hours before was breakfasting on brain and goat tacos after dancing all night in the pink zone. For Uncle Fat-face, the blackest of the black sheep—*Always remember your Uncle Fat-face in your prayers*. And Uncle Baby—*You go for me, Mamá—God listens to you*.

The awful grandmother has been gone a long time. She disappeared behind the heavy leather outer curtain and the dusty velvet inner. We may stay near the church entrance. We must not wander over to the balloon and punch-ball vendors. We cannot spend our allowance on fried cookies or Familia Burrón comic books or those clear cone-shaped suckers that make everything look like a rainbow when you look through them. We cannot run off and have our picture taken on the wooden ponies. We must not climb the steps up the hill behind the church and chase each other through the cemetery. We have promised to stay right where the awful grandmother left us until she returns.

There are those walking to church on their knees. Some with fat rags tied around their legs and others with pillows, one to kneel on, and one to flop ahead. There are women with black shawls crossing and uncrossing themselves. There are armies of penitents carrying banners and flowered arches while musicians play tinny trumpets and tinny drums.

La Virgen de Guadalupe is waiting inside behind a plate of thick glass. There's also a gold crucifix bent crooked as a mesquite tree when someone once threw a bomb. La Virgen de Guadalupe on the main altar because she's a big miracle, the crooked crucifix on a side altar because that's a little miracle.

But we're outside in the sun. My big brother Junior hunkered against the wall with his eyes shut. My little brother Keeks running around in circles.

Maybe and most probably my little brother is imagining he's a flying feather dancer, like the ones we saw swinging high up from a pole on the Virgin's birthday. I want to be a flying feather dancer too, but when he circles past me he shouts, "I'm a B-Fifty-two bomber, you're a German," and shoots me with an invisible machine gun. I'd rather play flying feather dancers, but if I tell my brother this, he might not play with me at all.

"*Girl*. We can't play with a *girl*." *Girl*. It's my brothers' favorite insult now instead of "sissy." "You *girl*," they yell at each other. "You throw that ball like a *girl*."

I've already made up my mind to be a German when Keeks swoops past again, this time yelling, "I'm Flash Gordon. You're Ming the Merciless and the Mud People." I don't mind being Ming the Merciless, but I don't like being the Mud People. Something wants to come out of the corners of my eyes, but I don't let it. Crying is what *girls* do.

I leave Keeks running around in circles—"I'm the Lone Ranger, you're   10
Tonto." I leave Junior squatting on his ankles and go look for the awful
grandmother.

Why do churches smell like the inside of an ear? Like incense and the
dark and candles in blue glass? And why does holy water smell of tears? The
awful grandmother makes me kneel and fold my hands. The ceiling high
and everyone's prayers bumping up there like balloons.

If I stare at the eyes of the saints long enough, they move and wink at
me, which makes me a sort of saint too. When I get tired of winking saints,
I count the awful grandmother's mustache hairs while she prays for Uncle
Old, sick from the worm, and Auntie Cuca, suffering from a life of troubles
that left half her face crooked and the other half sad.

There must be a long, long list of relatives who haven't gone to church.
The awful grandmother knits the names of the dead and the living into one
long prayer fringed with the grandchildren born in that barbaric country
with its barbarian ways.

I put my weight on one knee, then the other, and when they both grow fat
as a mattress of pins, I slap them each awake. *Micaela, you may wait outside
with Alfredito and Enrique.* The awful grandmother says it all in Spanish,
which I understand when I'm paying attention. "What?" I say, though it's neither proper nor polite. "What?" which the awful grandmother hears as
"¿Guat?" But she only gives me a look and shoves me toward the door.

After all that dust and dark, the light from the plaza makes me squinch   15
my eyes like if I just came out of the movies. My brother Keeks is drawing
squiggly lines on the concrete with a wedge of glass and the heel of his
shoe. My brother Junior squatting against the entrance, talking to a lady
and man.

They're not from here. Ladies don't come to church dressed in pants.
And everybody knows men aren't supposed to wear shorts.

"*¿Quieres chicle?*" the lady asks in a Spanish too big for her mouth.

"*Gracias.*" The lady gives him a whole handful of gum for free, little cellophane cubes of Chiclets, cinnamon and aqua and the white ones that
don't taste like anything but are good for pretend buck teeth.

"*Por favor,*" says the lady. "*¿Un foto?*" pointing to her camera.

"*Sí.*"   20

She's so busy taking Junior's picture, she doesn't notice me and Keeks.

"Hey, Michele, Keeks. You guys want gum?"

"But you speak English!"

"Yeah," my brother says, "we're Mericans."

We're Mericans, we're Mericans, and inside the awful grandmother prays.   25

The Receptive Reader

1. Where are we? What details does the writer use to help you visualize the
place, to bring it to life?

2. Like many Americans, the people in this story live in a place between two
languages or two cultures. Which people and which details in the story best
represent the two poles?

3. How do the young people in the story relate to their bilingual or cultural context? Are they "americanized"?

The Personal Response

Do you recognize the place? (Does it resemble any setting familiar to you?) Does the place become real for you? Why or why not? Do the people become real for you? Do they remind you of anyone you know?

WRITING ABOUT LITERATURE

1   Keeping a Short Story Journal (Materials for Writing)

The Writing Workshop   Writing about literature can make you a more attentive, a more thoughtful reader. When you keep a short story **journal,** you record your impressions and reactions as you read. You have a chance to register your questions, to record tentative conclusions, and to do some preliminary sorting out of your thinking. You try to formulate your personal responses, puzzling over contradictory or unexpected reactions on your part. You experiment with creative responses to what you have read, such as quickly sketched re-creations of a haunting image, a prevailing mood, a turning point in a story.

Writing weekly or biweekly entries in a reading journal or reading log gives you a chance to do some extensive prewriting for more structured papers, to accumulate a rich fund of materials for more formal writing tasks. Here are some possible kinds of entries for your journal:

Thinking about Previous Reading   In one of your first journal entries, you may want to look back over your previous experiences as a reader. What kind of reading has shaped your expectations? For instance, what kind of story made a lasting impression on you, and why? You may write about a story you loved or admired but also about a story that upset or disturbed you. Perhaps you will choose a work of literature that did not mean much at the time but that in retrospect has acquired a special meaning.

First Impressions   You will often find it helpful to record your initial impressions after your first reading. You may want to sort out and put into words your first reactions and your preliminary understanding of a story. Take time to gather your thoughts, to pull together what seems most significant. Include any questions the story may have raised in your mind. Here is one reader's first reaction to a story by the Canadian author Alice Munro:

Alice Munro's "Boys and Girls" takes place in Canada where the head of a small family raises silver foxes for furs. Of the two children, the girl tells the story, making pertinent observations on life on the fox farm and on the other members of the family. Life is seen entirely through her eyes. Foxes are slaughtered and their skins prepared for sale. Old injured horses are killed for food for the foxes. What it means to be a boy and what it means to be a girl become major issues in the story. (Is it significant that both the foxes and the horses are given male and female names?) Gender roles flip-flop in the story as the narrator prides herself on doing "man's work" as her father's helper while her mother grumbles about not getting enough help from her in the kitchen. Stereotypes are constantly challenged, but in the end they seem to triumph as the girl realizes she is "only a girl."

Running Commentary   An excellent way to make the most of your reading is to prepare a running commentary. You jot down your observations, queries, and comments as you read along. You include striking details, quotable quotations, and puzzlers to be checked out later. What at first was a puzzling detail may acquire fuller meaning as the author sounds the same note again and again. The following running commentary traces one reader's growing understanding of Ernest Hemingway's "Hills like White Elephants." The story takes the reader into a world of thinking and feeling different from the macho world of bullfights, big-game hunting, and deep-sea fishing that for many of his readers is the stereotypical Hemingway setting.

A man and a woman (American) are at a railroad station somewhere in Spain. Everything is hot and dry.

There seems to be some kind of communication problem, or a misunderstanding of some sort that is unresolved between them. The woman says the hills remind her of "white elephants" but later says that the man "wouldn't have" seen one, so he couldn't know what they look like. He doesn't have the spirit of adventure or the imagination?

Why does everything taste like licorice? The exotic drinks—Anis del Toro and absinth—both taste like licorice to the woman: "the things you've waited so long for" taste like licorice. A note of bitterness, discontent?

There seems to be a pointlessness in their lives: "all we do is . . . look at things and try new drinks."

They start talking about an operation. The man keeps saying it's "an awfully simple operation." The operation is "just to let the air in"—ha! The man pretends he wouldn't mind if the girl didn't go through with the abortion: "If you don't want to you don't have to." Actually, he sees it as very important: "the only thing that bothers us." She feels, "once they take it away, you never get it back." But she also knows that if she decides against the abortion he will not be happy.

The girl knows she really has no choice despite the man's words. She cannot listen to him any more; she drives home the word PLEASE seven times when she tells him to stop talking. She says, "I'll scream."

Clustering   Many writers use clustering to start and organize the flow of ideas. For a story to work, it has to engage with what we already know. What images and feelings does a story activate in the reader's mind? What associations with a central term does the reader bring to the story? **Clustering** is a prewriting technique that lets you explore a network of images, memories, or associations. With strands of ideas branching out from a central stimulus word, you can follow the different chains of associations the central idea brings into play. The idea is to sketch in freely, spontaneously, what a key word or key term brings to mind.

In a story like Bernard Malamud's "The Magic Barrel" or Shirley Jackson's "The Lottery," tradition plays a central role—tradition and the way the characters in the story live up to it, fight it, or make it suit their purposes. A cluster like the following might map the network of associations that a reader brings to the story. Notice that in this cluster a pattern is taking shape: the cluster graphically shows thinking in progress. It shows the writer thinking about the two-sided nature of tradition, a force for good and evil.

Sample Cluster

The following passage lays out the material and traces the pattern that the cluster has generated:

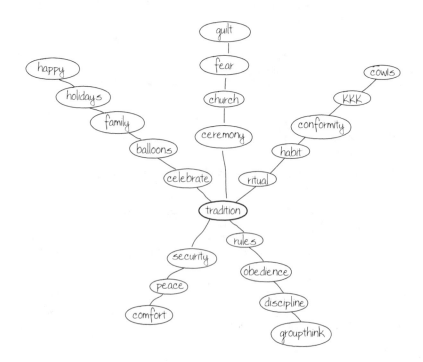

Tradition to many of us means first of all nostalgic memories of Christmas or Easter or Passover, happy hours spent with family and friends, birthday celebrations with balloons and ice cream cake and candles. In the traditional family, there is a sense of security—of knowing what to do, of relying on the tried and true. However, we also feel the weight of tradition—feeling guilty about not going to mass, feeling fear of retribution for our sins and backslidings. The inherent danger in tradition is the reliance on groupthink. Blind obedience to traditional rules and regulations can lead to unquestioned acceptance of cruel or idiotic practices. When we look at the dual nature of tradition, we see interlocking elements that can suddenly cover the face of love with a cowl of enmity and violence.

Focusing on Character   In other journal entries, you may go beyond the note-taking state to start to organize your thinking. For instance, in a **capsule portrait** of a character, you pull together traits illustrated in the incidents of the story. You integrate crucial hints about the character that may be scattered over quite a few pages. What kind of person does the author show you? What are key traits, and how are they related? Is there a trait that provides the clue to the character as a whole? Does the character change or grow in the course of the story? Here is a sample of such a character portrait:

The central character in Alice Munro's story "Boys and Girls" is struggling to adjust to the fact that she is slowly changing from a girl to a young woman. In the beginning, she is her Daddy's helper around the fox farm where her father raises foxes for their pelts. Oblivious to the stereotypical female gender role, she helps her father care for the animals, rakes up the grass or weeds he has cut, and does other traditional "male" chores. However, she begins to realize that as a female she is expected to do some things and not others; in particular, she is expected to help her mother in the kitchen, a place she detests. She rebels against her expected role, trying to stay out of the kitchen and close to the outdoors she loves. Her grandmother's comments, such as "Girls don't slam doors like that" or "Girls keep their knees together when they sit down," lead her to continue to slam doors and to sit as awkwardly as possible. Her rebellious behavior shows her strong will, stubbornness, and nonconformity, and, most of all, her spirit. Her spiritedness is mirrored in her daydreams of performing heroic rescues. She has a zest for constant excitement in life, and when her life doesn't supply it, she creates her own, as when she dares her three-year-old little brother to climb the barn ladder to the top beam. As she gets older, her old spirit carries over when she allows Flora, the horse scheduled to be shot for meat for the foxes, to escape through the gate. This scene shows her developing her own person, her own opinions, her own values. Despite the ending of the story, where she seems to be submitting herself to her expected gender roles, I believe that the strong spirit she has exhibited throughout the story will never leave her.

Focusing on Theme   You may frequently want to sum up for yourself the impact or meaning of a story as a whole. What idea or ideas stay with the reader at the end of the story? What seems to give the story its special quality or particular force? Here is a sample entry:

"The Open Boat," by Stephen Crane, is a late 19th to early 20th century story. Crew members and a newspaper correspondent in a lifeboat struggle for days in the stormy shark-infested sea, with their hopes for rescue or an easy landfall repeatedly dashed. In the end one of them drowns; the others make it to shore. This is an early modern view: There is no loving or benevolent nature. The shipwrecked sailors undergo a terrible ordeal, but they do not conclude that nature was out to punish them, nor do they feel that nature is loving or maternal. Birds were made to survive on the ocean; they are part of nature. The only way for human beings to survive is to work together—practice brotherhood. Since they are not at home in nature, they must make their home within it with the help of others. They need solidarity. Nature is alien and inhospitable; it couldn't care less.

For Class Interaction   You may want to share one or more early journal entries with your classmates. For instance, you might want to discuss with them what made a story especially meaningful to you, or what expectations you brought to it, or what made it difficult for you to read or enjoy.

2 Setting

Landscapes of the Mind

*Here I am, where I ought to be. A writer must have
a place where he or she feels this, a place to love
and be irritated with.*

LOUISE ERDRICH

FOCUS ON SETTING

One of the first questions we ask of a story is: Where is the story taking us? By establishing the setting, a writer lets us know where we are, makes us realize what time it is. Often the setting plays a major role in shaping the characters, the action, or the theme of a story. A *New York Times* reviewer said about the stories in Bobbie Ann Mason's *Shiloh and Other Stories* (1982),

> Mason's setting was Kentucky—not the old Kentucky of small towns and gracious farms, but that proud territory of the new South speckled with shopping malls and subdivisions, fast-food franchises and drive-in movies, a shiny new place, vacuumed clean of history and tradition. Reeling from the swiftness of the transition, Mason's characters all seemed to wander about in a fog, either spacing out in front of the television or passively drifting away from their families and friends, aware, however dimly, that they had misplaced something important along the way.

Here are ways the setting may help give shape to a story as a whole:

The Setting as Mirror The setting may mirror a prevailing mood. It may signal or reinforce prevailing emotions. An arid landscape, for instance, may mirror despair, spiritual desolation. Barren hills, scrubby vegetation, and dusty dirt roads may provide a fitting setting for emotionally dried-up characters. However, you cannot always expect a direct connection between the setting and the people who play their roles in it. The setting may be ironic, as when a character feels depressed in a springtime setting. Our sense of **irony** makes us respond with a grim smile when things do not turn out the we way we would like or expect.

The Setting as Mold   The setting of a story often shapes character. It helps make people what they are. Someone growing up on a farm, with its chores, dependence on rain and sun, and closeness to living things, is likely to have a different outlook, a different definition of life, than someone growing up in a neighborhood where the only open spaces are parking lots. A story may show its characters as creatures of the setting, reflecting its mood, living out its mores or approved ways of acting and thinking. On the other hand, a story may show a character rebelling against a stifling environment, struggling to break free.

The Setting as Escape   Escape literature takes us to imaginary settings where we act out daydreams. The story may take us to a mansion in the pre–Civil War South to make us witness scenes of flaming passion. It may take us to ancient Rome to appall us with scenes of treachery and depravity. However, a faraway setting may not really provide an escape; it may be the destination of a journey of discovery. In a strange setting, we may encounter facets of our own personality denied an outlet in our ordinary world.

The Alien Setting   Much modern literature circles back to the loss of roots, the loss of home. You may find yourself in a setting that is inhospitable, like an alien planet. You may identify with the exile, the undesirable, the refugee. In much early twentieth-century fiction, you encounter the eternal tourist, the expatriate—the person in exile from his or her own country.

SETTINGS: THE SENSE OF PLACE

Some writers are especially effective at creating a compelling environment—a world that we can imaginatively enter and reenter. In reading the following stories, pay special attention to the role the setting plays in the story as a whole.

James Joyce   *(1882–1941)*

"This race and this country and this life produced me," he said. "I shall express myself as I am."
                    JAMES JOYCE, *A PORTRAIT OF THE ARTIST*
                                        AS A YOUNG MAN

James Joyce (1882–1941) was one of the Irish writers who helped shape twentieth-century literature. Like other artists and intellectuals of his time, Joyce worked most of his life in self-imposed exile from his native country. Born in a suburb of Dublin, he left Dublin at the age of twenty-two, and he returned only twice for brief visits. However, the city of his birth and its people are in almost everything he wrote.

Joyce was the son of an outgoing but spendthrift father and a devoutly Catholic mother. At the age of six, he entered a school run by Jesuit priests; he later enrolled at the Jesuit order's Belvedere College in Dublin. However, he decided against entering the priesthood. He similarly distanced himself from the passionate, intolerant nationalism that was the legacy of Ireland's struggle against British colonial rule. Family, church, and country came to seem to him like nets thrown to restrain the free exercise of the creative spirit. As he said in his largely autobiographical first novel, *A Portrait of the Artist as a Young Man* (1916), "I will not serve that in which I no longer believe."

Joyce barely survived by teaching English and doing clerical work, first in Zurich (Switzerland) and later in Trieste (Italy) and Paris. He wrote constantly, developing the **stream-of-consciousness** technique that revolutionized much of modern fiction. Human beings do not think in complete sentences, carry on coherent logical conversations with themselves, or make rational decisions after lining up the pros and cons. Instead, their mental world is a shifting sequence of sensations, thoughts, and feelings. In Joyce's masterpiece, *Ulysses* (1922), a thread of external events alternates with stretches of **interior monologue,** immersing the readers in a stream of impressions, reminiscences, and half-formulated thoughts.

The following classic short story is from an early collection, *Dubliners* (1914). Compared with Joyce's later work, these stories have a straightforward, conventional story line. However, like his later work, they focus on the private thoughts, emotions, and daydreams of his characters. A few references in this story might puzzle today's reader. One of the books mentioned early in the story told the life story of Vidocq, a legendary French detective. The Freemasons, members of a private fraternal organization, were viewed with suspicion by people with traditional religious views. The florin was a British silver coin worth two shillings. A *café chantant* was a French coffeehouse with musical entertainment.

Araby   *1914*

North Richmond Street, being blind, was a quiet street except at the hour when the Christian Brothers' School set the boys free. An uninhabited house of two stories stood at the blind end, detached from its neighbors in a square ground. The other houses of the street, conscious of decent lives within them, gazed at one another with brown imperturbable faces.

The former tenant of our house, a priest, had died in the back drawing-room. Air, musty from having been long enclosed, hung in all the rooms, and the waste room behind the kitchen was littered with old useless papers. Among these I found a few paper-covered books, the pages of which were curled and damp: *The Abbot,* by Walter Scott, *The Devout Communicant* and *The Memoirs of Vidocq.* I liked the last best because its leaves were yellow. The wild garden behind the house contained a central apple-tree and a few straggling bushes under one of which I found the late tenant's rusty bicycle-pump. He had been a very charitable priest; in his will he had left all his money to institutions and the furniture of his house to his sister.

When the short days of winter came dusk fell before we had well eaten our dinners. When we met in the street the houses had grown somber. The space of sky above us was the color of ever-changing violet and toward it the lamps of the street lifted their feeble lanterns. The cold air stung us and we played till our bodies glowed. Our shouts echoed in the silent street. The career of our play brought us through the dark muddy lanes behind the houses where we ran the gauntlet of the rough tribes from the cottages, to the back doors of the dark dripping gardens where odors arose from the ashpits, to the dark odorous stables where a coachman smoothed and combed the horse or shook music from the buckled harness. When we returned to the street light from the kitchen windows had filled the areas. If my uncle was seen turning the corner we hid in the shadow until we had seen him safely housed. Or if Mangan's sister came out on the doorstep to call her brother in to his tea we watched her from our shadow peer up and down the street. We waited to see whether she would remain or go in and, if she remained, we left our shadow and walked up to Mangan's steps resignedly. She was waiting for us, her figure defined by the light from the half-opened door. Her brother always teased her before he obeyed and I stood by the railings looking at her. Her dress swung as she moved her body, and the soft rope of her hair tossed from side to side.

Every morning I lay on the floor in the front parlor watching her door. The blind was pulled down to within an inch of the sash so that I could not be seen. When she came out on the doorstep my heart leaped. I ran to the hall, seized my books and followed her. I kept her brown figure always in my eye and, when we came near the point at which our ways diverged, I quickened my pace and passed her. This happened morning after morning. I had never spoken to her, except for a few casual words, and yet her name was like a summons to all my foolish blood.

Her image accompanied me even in places the most hostile to romance.   5
On Saturday evenings when my aunt went marketing I had to go to carry some of the parcels. We walked through the flaring streets, jostled by drunken men and bargaining women, amid the curses of laborers, the shrill litanies of shop-boys who stood on guard by the barrels of pigs' cheeks, the nasal chanting of street-singers, who sang a *come-all-you* about O'Donovan Rossa, or a ballad about the troubles in our native land. These noises converged in a single sensation of life for me: I imagined that I bore my chalice safely through a throng of foes. Her name sprang to my lips at moments in strange prayers and praises which I myself did not understand. My eyes were often

full of tears (I could not tell why) and at times a flood from my heart seemed to pour itself out into my bosom. I thought little of the future. I did not know whether I would ever speak to her or not or, if I spoke to her, how I could tell her of my confused adoration. But my body was like a harp and her words and gestures were like fingers running upon the wires.

One evening I went into the back drawing-room in which the priest had died. It was a dark rainy evening and there was no sound in the house. Through one of the broken panes I heard the rain impinge upon the earth, the fine incessant needles of water playing in the sodden beds. Some distant lamp or lighted window gleamed below me. I was thankful that I could see so little. All my senses seemed to desire to veil themselves and, feeling that I was about to slip from them, I pressed the palms of my hands together until they trembled, murmuring: *"O love! O love!"* many times.

At last she spoke to me. When she addressed the first words to me I was so confused that I did not know what to answer. She asked me was I going to *Araby*. I forgot whether I answered yes or no. It would be a splendid bazaar, she said she would love to go.

"And why can't you?" I asked.

While she spoke she turned a silver bracelet round and round her wrist. She could not go, she said, because there would be a retreat that week in her convent. Her brother and two other boys were fighting for their caps and I was alone at the railings. She held one of the spikes, bowing her head towards me. The light from the lamp opposite our door caught the white curve of her neck, lit up her hair that rested there and, falling, lit up the hand upon the railing. It fell over one side of her dress and caught the white border of a petticoat, just visible as she stood at ease.

"It's well for you," she said.   10

"If I go," I said, "I will bring you something."

What innumerable follies laid waste my waking and sleeping thoughts after that evening! I wished to annihilate the tedious intervening days. I chafed against the work of school. At night in my bedroom and by day in the classroom her image came between me and the page I strove to read. The syllables of the word *Araby* were called to me through the silence in which my soul luxuriated and cast an Eastern enchantment over me. I asked for leave to go to the bazaar on Saturday night. My aunt was surprised and hoped it was not some Freemason affair. I answered few questions in class. I watched my master's face pass from amiability to sternness; he hoped I was not beginning to idle. I could not call my wandering thoughts together. I had hardly any patience with the serious work of life which, now that it stood between me and my desire, seemed to me child's play, ugly monotonous child's play.

On Saturday morning I reminded my uncle that I wished to go to the bazaar in the evening. He was fussing at the hallstand, looking for the hat-brush, and answered me curtly:

"Yes, boy, I know."

As he was in the hall I could not go into the front parlor and lie at the   15
window. I left the house in bad humor and walked slowly toward the school. The air was pitilessly raw and already my heart misgave me.

When I came home to dinner my uncle had not yet been home. Still it was early. I sat staring at the clock for some time and, when its ticking began to irritate me, I left the room. I mounted the staircase and gained the upper part of the house. The high cold empty gloomy rooms liberated me and I went from room to room singing. From the front window I saw my companions playing below in the street. Their cries reached me weakened and indistinct and, leaning my forehead against the cool glass, I looked over at the dark house where she lived. I may have stood there for an hour, seeing nothing but the brown-clad figure cast by my imagination, touched discreetly by the lamplight at the curved neck, at the hand upon the railings and at the border below the dress.

When I came downstairs again I found Mrs. Mercer sitting at the fire. She was an old garrulous woman, a pawn-broker's widow, who collected used stamps for some pious purpose. I had to endure the gossip of the tea-table. The meal was prolonged beyond an hour and still my uncle did not come. Mrs. Mercer stood up to go: she was sorry she couldn't wait any longer, but it was after eight o'clock and she did not like to be out late, as the night air was bad for her. When she had gone I began to walk up and down the room, clenching my fists. My aunt said:

"I'm afraid you may put off your bazaar for this night of Our Lord."

At nine o'clock I heard my uncle's latchkey in the halldoor. I heard him talking to himself and heard the hallstand rocking when it had received the weight of his overcoat. I could interpret these signs. When he was midway through his dinner I asked him to give me the money to go to the bazaar. He had forgotten.

"The people are in bed and after their first sleep now," he said.   20

I did not smile. My aunt said to him energetically:

"Can't you give him the money and let him go? You've kept him late enough as it is."

My uncle said he was very sorry he had forgotten. He said he believed in the old saying: "All work and no play makes Jack a dull boy." He asked me where I was going and, when I had told him a second time he asked me did I know *The Arab's Farewell to his Steed*. When I left the kitchen he was about to recite the opening lines of the piece to my aunt.

I held a florin tightly in my hand as I strode down Buckingham Street toward the station. The sight of the streets thronged with buyers and glaring with gas recalled to me the purpose of my journey. I took my seat in a third-class carriage of a deserted train. After an intolerable delay the train moved out of the station slowly. It crept onward among ruinous houses and over the twinkling river. At Westland Row Station a crowd of people pressed to the carriage doors; but the porters moved them back, saying that it was a special train for the bazaar. I remained alone in the bare carriage. In a few minutes the train drew up beside an improvised wooden platform. I passed out on to the road and saw by the lighted dial of a clock that it was ten minutes to ten. In front of me was a large building which displayed the magical name.

I could not find any sixpenny entrance and, fearing that the bazaar would   25
be closed, I passed in quickly through a turnstile, handing a shilling to a weary-looking man. I found myself in a big hall girdled at half its height by a gallery. Nearly all the stalls were closed and the greater part of the hall

was in darkness. I recognized a silence like that which pervades a church after a service. I walked into the center of the bazaar timidly. A few people were gathered about the stalls which were still open. Before a curtain, over which the words *Café Chantant* were written in colored lamps, two men were counting money on a salver. I listened to the fall of the coins.

Remembering with difficulty why I had come I went over to one of the stalls and examined porcelain vases and flowered tea-sets. At the door of the stall a young lady was talking and laughing with two young gentlemen. I remarked their English accents and listened vaguely to their conversation.

"O, I never said such a thing!"

"O, but you did!"

"O, but I didn't!"

"Didn't she say that?"   30

"Yes. I heard her."

"O, there's a . . . fib!"

Observing me the young lady came over and asked me did I wish to buy anything. The tone of her voice was not encouraging; she seemed to have spoken to me out of a sense of duty. I looked humbly at the great jars that stood like eastern guards at either side of the dark entrance to the stall and murmured:

"No, thank you."

The young lady changed the position of one of the vases and went back   35 to the two young men. They began to talk of the same subject. Once or twice the young lady glanced at me over her shoulder.

I lingered before her stall, though I knew my stay was useless, to make my interest in her wares seem the more real. Then I turned away slowly and walked down the middle of the bazaar. I allowed the two pennies to fall against the sixpence in my pocket. I heard a voice call from one end of the gallery that the light was out. The upper part of the hall was now completely dark.

Gazing up into the darkness I saw myself as a creature driven and derided by vanity; and my eyes burned with anguish and anger.

The Receptive Reader

1. What striking details help the setting come to life for you? Which seem to set the tone or point forward to the rest of the story?

2. What striking images help you understand the boy's feelings? What images give his devotion a quasi-religious quality? (What are the associations of the word *chalice;* what feelings does it bring into play?)

3. Is the boy able to share his feelings with anyone? If not, why not?

4. What is the role of the uncle in the story?

5. Is it a coincidence that the climactic high point of the story takes place in a bazaar—a special annual event?

6. As we watch crucial scenes in the story, we at times have to sense the boy's feelings rather than having them explained in so many words by the author. What are some examples?

The Personal Response

Is the boy merely infatuated? Should he have known better? Is he acting "immature"?

The Creative Dimension

Writers sometimes describe how a short story took shape from a striking, teasing image in the writer's mind. Sometimes after we finish reading, what stays with us is a haunting image that seems to sum up something essential in the story. The following student-written passage re-creates a key moment in Joyce's "Araby." What does the writer capture in the story? Write your own re-creation of a haunting image or key moment in Joyce's story or in another story in this chapter.

> We played in
>   the cold, short winter evenings
>   colored violet with dusk.
>   We made a career
>   of playing long in
>   the streets
>   and alleys with shadows
>   our bodies small and cold
>   and glowing
>   In the street the lamps
>   lined up,
>   illuminating
>   a playmate's sister strolling
>   towards us,
>   soft smooth hair,
>   swinging skirt.

Bobbie Ann Mason   *(born 1940)*

Mason was part of a group of writers (informally called the literary "brat pack") who became known in the eighties. Their trademark was a determination to be true to the trivial, undramatic realities of ordinary life. The stories in her collection *Shiloh and Other Stories* (1982) are set in Paducah, in rural Kentucky, where she grew up. She takes her readers to a New South where the struggles with the North are ancient history. Her characters are part of a new working class of truck drivers, retail clerks, and Tupperware sales representatives, who bake zucchini bread and make casseroles from potatoes and mushroom soup, and who pass their free time building model log cabins from Lincoln Logs or making wall hangings of an Arizona sunset. These characters are steeped in American popular culture—talk shows, shopping malls, made-for-TV movies.

Against this setting, Mason plays off plots where, "with no decisive snap of the thread, human relationships become unraveled" (Francis

King); where "restless women strain against the confines of marriage" (Robert Towers); and where the men are sometimes "silent and transient" (Anatole Broyard). As David Quammen said in the *New York Times Book Review*, Mason "examines in her various truck drivers and sales clerks the dawning recognition—in some cases only a vague worry—of having missed something, something important, some alternate life more fruitful than the life that's been led." What has struck reviewers of her stories is that she does not treat these "unremarkable" people with condescension but with "complete respect." They are capable of moments of insight or self-understanding; they try "so hard, and with such optimism, to keep up with change" (Anne Tyler).

Shiloh   *1982*

Leroy Moffitt's wife, Norma Jean, is working on her pectorals. She lifts three-pound dumbbells to warm up, then progresses to a twenty-pound barbell. Standing with her legs apart, she reminds Leroy of Wonder Woman.

"I'd give anything if I could just get these muscles to where they're real hard," says Norma Jean. "Feel this arm. It's not as hard as the other one."

"That's 'cause you're right-handed," says Leroy, dodging as she swings the barbell in an arc.

"Do you think so?"

"Sure."   5

Leroy is a truckdriver. He injured his leg in a highway accident four months ago, and his physical therapy, which involves weights and a pulley, prompted Norma Jean to try building herself up. Now she is attending a body-building class. Leroy has been collecting temporary disability since his tractor-trailer jackknifed in Missouri, badly twisting his left leg in its socket. He has a steel pin in his hip. He will probably not be able to drive his rig again. It sits in the backyard, like a gigantic bird that has flown home to roost. Leroy has been home in Kentucky for three months, and his leg is almost healed, but the accident frightened him and he does not want to drive any more long hauls. He is not sure what to do next. In the meantime, he makes things from craft kits. He started by building a miniature log cabin from notched Popsicle sticks. He varnished it and placed it on the TV set, where it remains. It reminds him of a rustic Nativity scene. Then he tried string art (sailing ships on black velvet), a macramé owl kit, a snap-together B-17 Flying Fortress, and a lamp made out of a model truck, with a light fixture screwed in the top of the cab. At first the kits were diversions, something to kill time, but now he is thinking about building a full-scale log house from a kit. It would be considerably cheaper than building a regular house, and besides, Leroy has grown to appreciate how things are put together. He has begun to realize that in all the years he was on the road he never took time to examine anything. He was always flying past scenery.

"They won't let you build a log cabin in any of the new subdivisions," Norma Jean tells him.

"They will if I tell them it's for you," he says, teasing her. Ever since they were married, he has promised Norma Jean he would build her a new home one day. They have always rented, and the house they live in is small and nondescript. It does not even feel like a home, Leroy realizes now.

Norma Jean works at the Rexall drugstore, and she has acquired an amazing amount of information about cosmetics. When she explains to Leroy the three stages of complexion care, involving creams, toners, and moisturizers, he thinks happily of other petroleum products—axle grease, diesel fuel. This is a connection between him and Norma Jean. Since he has been home, he has felt unusually tender about his wife and guilty over his long absences. But he can't tell what she feels about him. Norma Jean has never complained about his traveling; she has never made hurt remarks, like calling his truck a "widow-maker." He is reasonably certain she has been faithful to him, but he wishes she would celebrate his permanent homecoming more happily. Norma Jean is often startled to find Leroy at home, and he thinks she seems a little disappointed about it. Perhaps he reminds her too much of the early days of their marriage, before he went on the road. They had a child who died as an infant, years ago. They never speak about their memories of Randy, which have almost faded, but now that Leroy is home all the time, they sometimes feel awkward around each other, and Leroy wonders if one of them should mention the child. He has the feeling that they are waking up out of a dream together—that they must create a new marriage, start afresh. They are lucky they are still married. Leroy has read that for most people losing a child destroys the marriage—or else he heard this on *Donahue*. He can't always remember where he learns things anymore.

At Christmas, Leroy bought an electric organ for Norma Jean. She used to   10
play the piano when she was in high school. "It don't leave you," she told him once. "It's like riding a bicycle."

The new instrument had so many keys and buttons that she was bewildered by it at first. She touched the keys tentatively, pushed some buttons, then pecked out "Chopsticks." It came out in an amplified fox-trot rhythm, with marimba sounds.

"It's an orchestra!" she cried.

The organ had a pecan-look finish and eighteen preset chords, with optional flute, violin, trumpet, clarinet, and banjo accompaniments. Norma Jean mastered the organ almost immediately. At first she played Christmas songs. Then she bought *The Sixties Songbook* and learned every tune in it, adding variations to each with the rows of brightly colored buttons.

"I didn't like these old songs back then," she said. "But I have this crazy feeling I missed something."

"You didn't miss a thing," said Leroy.   15

Leroy likes to lie on the couch and smoke a joint and listen to Norma Jean play "Can't Take My Eyes Off You" and "I'll Be Back." He is back again. After fifteen years on the road, he is finally settling down with the woman he loves. She is still pretty. Her skin is flawless. Her frosted curls resemble pencil trimmings.

Now that Leroy has come home to stay, he notices how much the town has changed. Subdivisions are spreading across western Kentucky like an oil slick. The sign at the edge of town says "Pop: 11,500"—only seven hundred more than it said twenty years before. Leroy can't figure out who is living in all the new houses. The farmers who used to gather around the courthouse square on Saturday afternoons to play checkers and spit tobacco juice have gone. It has been years since Leroy has thought about the farmers, and they have disappeared without his noticing.

Leroy meets a kid named Stevie Hamilton in the parking lot at the new shopping center. While they pretend to be strangers meeting over a stalled car, Stevie tosses an ounce of marijuana under the front seat of Leroy's car. Stevie is wearing orange jogging shoes and a T-shirt that says CHATTAHOOCHEE SUPER-RAT. His father is a prominent doctor who lives in one of the expensive subdivisions in a new white-columned brick house that looks like a funeral parlor. In the phone book under his name there is a separate number, with the listing "Teenagers."

"Where do you get this stuff?" asks Leroy. "From your pappy?"

"That's for me to know and you to find out," Stevie says. He is slit-eyed   20 and skinny.

"What else you got?"

"What you interested in?"

"Nothing special. Just wondered."

Leroy used to take speed on the road. Now he has to go slowly. He needs to be mellow. He leans back against the car and says, "I'm aiming to build me a log house, soon as I get time. My wife, though, I don't think she likes the idea."

"Well, let me know when you want me again," Stevie says. He has a cig-   25 arette in his cupped palm, as though sheltering it from the wind. He takes a long drag, then stomps it on the asphalt and slouches away.

Stevie's father was two years ahead of Leroy in high school. Leroy is thirty-four. He married Norma Jean when they were both eighteen, and their child Randy was born a few months later, but he died at the age of four months and three days. He would be about Stevie's age now. Norma Jean and Leroy were at the drive-in, watching a double feature (*Dr. Strangelove* and *Lover Come Back*), and the baby was sleeping in the back seat. When the first movie ended, the baby was dead. It was the sudden infant death syndrome. Leroy remembers handing Randy to a nurse at the emergency room, as though he were offering her a large doll as a present. A dead baby feels like a sack of flour. "It just happens sometimes," said the doctor, in what Leroy always recalls as a nonchalant tone. Leroy can hardly remember the child anymore, but he still sees vividly a scene from *Dr. Strangelove* in which the President of the United States was talking in a folksy voice on the hot line to the Soviet premier about the bomber accidentally headed toward Russia. He was in the War Room, and the world map was lit up. Leroy remembers Norma Jean standing catatonically beside him in the hospital and himself thinking: Who is this strange girl? He had forgotten who she was. Now scientists are saying that crib death is caused by a virus. Nobody knows anything, Leroy thinks. The answers are always changing.

When Leroy gets home from the shopping center, Norma Jean's mother, Mabel Beasley, is there. Until this year, Leroy has not realized how much time she spends with Norma Jean. When she visits, she inspects the closets and then the plants, informing Norma Jean when a plant is droopy or yellow.

Mabel calls the plants "flowers," although there are never any blooms. She always notices if Norma Jean's laundry is piling up. Mabel is a short, overweight woman whose tight, brown-dyed curls look more like a wig than the actual wig she sometimes wears. Today she has brought Norma Jean an off-white dust ruffle she made for the bed; Mabel works in a custom-upholstery shop.

"This is the tenth one I made this year," Mabel says. "I got started and couldn't stop."

"It's real pretty," says Norma Jean.

"Now we can hide things under the bed," says Leroy, who gets along   30 with his mother-in-law primarily by joking with her. Mabel has never really forgiven him for disgracing her by getting Norma Jean pregnant. When the baby died, she said that fate was mocking her.

"What's that thing?" Mabel says to Leroy in a loud voice, pointing to a tangle of yarn on a piece of canvas.

Leroy holds it up for Mabel to see. "It's my needlepoint," he explains. "This is a *Star Trek* pillow cover."

"That's what a woman would do," says Mabel. "Great day in the morning!"

"All the big football players on TV do it," he says.

"Why, Leroy, you're always trying to fool me. I don't believe you for one   35 minute. You don't know what to do with yourself—that's the whole trouble. Sewing!"

"I'm aiming to build a log house," says Leroy. "Soon as my plans come."

"Like *heck* you are," says Norma Jean. She takes Leroy's needlepoint and shoves it into a drawer. "You have to find a job first. Nobody can afford to build now anyway."

Mabel straightens her girdle and says, "I still think before you get tied down y'all ought to take a little run to Shiloh."

"One of these days, Mama," Norma Jean says impatiently.

Mabel is talking about Shiloh, Tennessee. For the past few years, she has   40 been urging Leroy and Norma Jean to visit the Civil War battleground there. Mabel went there on her honeymoon—the only real trip she ever took. Her husband died of a perforated ulcer when Norma Jean was ten, but Mabel, who was accepted into the United Daughters of the Confederacy in 1975, is still preoccupied with going back to Shiloh.

"I've been to kingdom come and back in that truck out yonder," Leroy says to Mabel, "but we never yet set foot in that battleground. Ain't that something? How did I miss it?"

"It's not even that far," Mabel says.

After Mabel leaves, Norma Jean reads to Leroy from a list she has made. "Things you could do," she announces. "You could get a job as a guard at Union Carbide, where they'd let you set on a stool. You could get on at the lumberyard. You could do a little carpenter work, if you want to build so bad. You could—"

"I can't do something where I'd have to stand up all day."

"You ought to try standing up all day behind a cosmetics counter. It's   45 amazing that I have strong feet, coming from two parents that never had strong feet at all." At the moment Norma Jean is holding on to the kitchen counter, raising her knees one at a time as she talks. She is wearing two-pound ankle weights.

"Don't worry," says Leroy. "I'll do something."

"You could truck calves to slaughter for somebody. You wouldn't have to drive any big old truck for that."

"I'm going to build you this house," says Leroy. "I want to make you a real home."

"I don't want to live in any log cabin."

"It's not a cabin. It's a house."   50

"I don't care. It looks like a cabin."

"You and me together could lift those logs. It's just like lifting weights."

Norma Jean doesn't answer. Under her breath, she is counting. Now she is marching through the kitchen. She is doing goose steps.

Before his accident, when Leroy came home he used to stay in the house with Norma Jean, watching TV in bed and playing cards. She would cook fried chicken, picnic ham, chocolate pie—all his favorites. Now he is home alone much of the time. In the mornings, Norma Jean disappears, leaving a cooling place in the bed. She eats a cereal called Body Buddies, and she leaves the bowl on the table, with the soggy tan balls floating in a milk puddle. He sees things about Norma Jean that he never realized before. When she chops onions, she stares off into a corner, as if she can't bear to look. She puts on her house slippers almost precisely at nine o'clock every evening and nudges her jogging shoes under the couch. She saves bread heels for the birds. Leroy watches the birds at the feeder. He notices the peculiar way goldfinches fly past the window. They close their wings, then fall, then spread their wings to catch and lift themselves. He wonders if they close their eyes when they fall. Norma Jean closes her eyes when they are in bed. She wants the lights turned out. Even then, he is sure she closes her eyes.

He goes for long drives around town. He tends to drive a car rather care-   55
lessly. Power steering and an automatic shift make a car feel so small and inconsequential that his body is hardly involved in the driving process. His injured leg stretches out comfortably. Once or twice he has almost hit something, but even the prospect of an accident seems minor in a car. He cruises the new subdivisions, feeling like a criminal rehearsing for a robbery. Norma Jean is probably right about a log house being inappropriate here in the new subdivisions. All the houses look grand and complicated. They depress him.

One day when Leroy comes home from a drive he finds Norma Jean in tears. She is in the kitchen making a potato and mushroom-soup casserole, with grated-cheese topping. She is crying because her mother caught her smoking.

"I didn't hear her coming. I was standing here puffing away pretty as you please," Norma Jean says, wiping her eyes.

"I knew it would happen sooner or later," says Leroy, putting his arm around her.

"She don't know the meaning of the word 'knock,'" says Norma Jean. "It's a wonder she hadn't caught me years ago."

"Think of it this way," Leroy says. "What if she caught me with a joint?"   60

"You better not let her!" Norma Jean shrieks. "I'm warning you, Leroy Moffitt!"

"I'm just kidding. Here, play me a tune. That'll help you relax."

Norma Jean puts the casserole in the oven and sets the timer. Then she plays a ragtime tune, with horns and banjo, as Leroy lights up a joint and lies on the couch, laughing to himself about Mabel's catching him at it. He thinks of Stevie Hamilton—a doctor's son pushing grass. Everything is funny. The whole town seems crazy and small. He is reminded of Virgil Mathis, a boastful policeman Leroy used to shoot pool with. Virgil recently led a drug bust in a back room at a bowling alley, where he seized ten thousand dollars' worth of marijuana. The newspaper had a picture of him holding up the bags of grass and grinning widely. Right now, Leroy can imagine Virgil breaking down the door and arresting him with a lungful of smoke. Virgil would probably have been alerted to the scene because of all the racket Norma Jean is making. Now she sounds like a hard-rock band. Norma Jean is terrific. When she switches to a Latin-rhythm version of "Sunshine Superman," Leroy hums along. Norma Jean's foot goes up and down, up and down.

"Well, what do you think?" Leroy says, when Norma Jean pauses to search through her music.

"What do I think about what?"   65

His mind has gone blank. Then he says, "I'll sell my rig and build a house." That wasn't what he wanted to say. He wanted to know what she thought—what she *really* thought—about them.

"Don't start in on that again," says Norma Jean. She begins playing "Who'll Be the Next in Line?"

Leroy used to tell hitchhikers his whole life story—about his travels, his hometown, the baby. He would end with a question: "Well, what do you think?" It was just a rhetorical question. In time, he had the feeling that he'd been telling the same story over and over to the same hitchhikers. He quit talking to hitchhikers when he realized how his voice sounded—whining and self-pitying, like some teenage-tragedy song. Now Leroy has the sudden impulse to tell Norma Jean about himself, as if he had just met her. They have known each other so long they have forgotten a lot about each other. They could become reacquainted. But when the oven timer goes off and she runs to the kitchen, he forgets why he wants to do this.

The next day, Mabel drops by. It is Saturday and Norma Jean is cleaning. Leroy is studying the plans of his log house, which have finally come in the mail. He has them spread out on the table—big sheets of stiff blue paper, with diagrams and numbers printed in white. While Norma Jean runs the vacuum, Mabel drinks coffee. She sets her coffee cup on a blueprint.

"I'm just waiting for time to pass," she says to Leroy, drumming her fingers on the table.   70

As soon as Norma Jean switches off the vacuum, Mabel says in a loud voice, "Did you hear about the datsun dog that killed the baby?"

Norma Jean says, "The word is 'dachshund.'"

"They put the dog on trial. It chewed the baby's legs off. The mother was in the next room all the time." She raises her voice. "They thought it was neglect."

Norma Jean is holding her ears. Leroy manages to open the refrigerator and get some Diet Pepsi to offer Mabel. Mabel still has some coffee and she waves away the Pepsi.

"Datsuns are like that," Mabel says. "They're jealous dogs. They'll tear a   75
place to pieces if you don't keep an eye on them."

"You better watch out what you're saying, Mabel," says Leroy.

"Well, facts is facts."

Leroy looks out the window at his rig. It is like a huge piece of furniture gathering dust in the backyard. Pretty soon it will be an antique. He hears the vacuum cleaner. Norma Jean seems to be cleaning the living room rug again.

Later, she says to Leroy, "She just said that about the baby because she caught me smoking. She's trying to pay me back."

"What are you talking about?" Leroy says, nervously shuffling blueprints.   80

"You know good and well," Norma Jean says. She is sitting in a kitchen chair with her feet up and her arms wrapped around her knees. She looks small and helpless. She says, "The very idea, her bringing up a subject like that! Saying it was neglect."

"She didn't mean that," Leroy says.

"She might not have *thought* she meant it. She always says things like that. You don't know how she goes on."

"But she didn't really mean it. She was just talking."

Leroy opens a king-sized bottle of beer and pours it into two glasses,   85
dividing it carefully. He hands a glass to Norma Jean and she takes it from him mechanically. For a long time, they sit by the kitchen window watching the birds at the feeder.

Something is happening. Norma Jean is going to night school. She has graduated from her six-week body-building course and now she is taking an adult-education course in composition at Paducah Community College. She spends her evenings outlining paragraphs.

"First you have a topic sentence," she explains to Leroy. "Then you divide it up. Your secondary topic has to be connected to your primary topic."

To Leroy, this sounds intimidating. "I never was any good in English," he says.

"It makes a lot of sense."

"What are you doing this for, anyhow?"   90

She shrugs. "It's something to do." She stands up and lifts her dumbbells a few times.

"Driving a rig, nobody cared about my English."

"I'm not criticizing your English."

Norma Jean used to say, "If I lose ten minutes' sleep, I just drag all day." Now she stays up late, writing compositions. She got a B on her first paper—a how-to theme on soup-based casseroles. Recently Norma Jean has been cooking unusual foods—tacos, lasagna, Bombay chicken. She doesn't play the organ anymore, though her second paper was called "Why

Music Is Important to Me." She sits at the kitchen table, concentrating on her outlines, while Leroy plays with his log house plans, practicing with a set of Lincoln Logs. The thought of getting a truckload of notched, numbered logs scares him, and he wants to be prepared. As he and Norma Jean work together at the kitchen table, Leroy has the hopeful thought that they are sharing something, but he knows he is a fool to think this. Norma Jean is miles away. He knows he is going to lose her. Like Mabel, he is just waiting for time to pass.

One day, Mabel is there before Norma Jean gets home from work, and 95 Leroy finds himself confiding in her. Mabel, he realizes, must know Norma Jean better than he does.

"I don't know what's got into that girl," Mabel says. "She used to go to bed with the chickens. Now you say she's up all hours. Plus her a-smoking. I like to died."

"I want to make her this beautiful home," Leroy says, indicating the Lincoln Logs. "I don't thinks she even wants it. Maybe she was happier with me gone."

"She don't know what to make of you, coming home like this."

"Is that it?"

Mabel takes the roof off his Lincoln Log cabin. "You couldn't get *me* in a 100 log cabin," she says. "I was raised in one. It's no picnic, let me tell you."

"They're different now," says Leroy.

"I tell you what," Mabel says, smiling oddly at Leroy.

"What?"

"Take her on down to Shiloh. Y'all need to get out together, stir a little. Her brain's all balled up over them books."

Leroy can see traces of Norma Jean's features in her mother's face. 105 Mabel's worn face has the texture of crinkled cotton, but suddenly she looks pretty. It occurs to Leroy that Mabel has been hinting all along that she wants them to take her with them to Shiloh.

"Let's all go to Shiloh," he says. "You and me and her. Some Sunday."

Mabel throws up her hands in protest. "Oh, no, not me. Young folks want to be by theirselves."

When Norma Jean comes in with groceries, Leroy says excitedly, "Your mama here's been dying to go to Shiloh for forty-five years. It's about time we went, don't you think?"

"I'm not going to butt in on anybody's second honeymoon," Mabel says.

"Who's going on a honeymoon, for Christ's sake?" Norma Jean says loudly. 110

"I never raised no daughter of mine to talk that-a-way," Mabel says.

"You ain't seen nothing yet," says Norma Jean. She starts putting away boxes and cans, slamming cabinet doors.

"There's a log cabin at Shiloh," Mabel says. "It was there during the battle. There's bullet holes in it."

"When are you going to *shut up* about Shiloh, Mama?" asks Norma Jean.

"I always thought Shiloh was the prettiest place, so full of history," Mabel 115 goes on. "I just hoped y'all could see it once before I die, so you could tell me about it." Later, she whispers to Leroy, "You do what I said. A little change is what she needs."

*   *   *

"Your name means 'the king,'" Norma Jean says to Leroy that evening. He is trying to get her to go to Shiloh, and she is reading a book about another century.

"Well, I reckon I ought to be right proud."

"I guess so."

"Am I still king around here?"

Norma Jean flexes her biceps and feels them for hardness. "I'm not fool-   120
ing around with anybody, if that's what you mean," she says.

"Would you tell me if you were?"

"I don't know."

"What does *your* name mean?"

"It was Marilyn Monroe's real name."

"No kidding!"   125

"Norma comes from the Normans. They were invaders," she says. She closes her book and looks hard at Leroy. "I'll go to Shiloh with you if you'll stop staring at me."

On Sunday, Norma Jean packs a picnic and they go to Shiloh. To Leroy's relief, Mabel says she does not want to come with them. Norma Jean drives, and Leroy, sitting beside her, feels like some boring hitchhiker she has picked up. He tries some conversation, but she answers him in monosyllables. At Shiloh, she drives aimlessly through the park, past bluffs and trails and steep ravines. Shiloh is an immense place, and Leroy cannot see it as a battleground. It is not what he expected. He thought it would look like a golf course. Monuments are everywhere, showing through the thick clusters of trees. Norma Jean passes the log cabin Mabel mentioned. It is surrounded by tourists looking for bullet holes.

"That's not the kind of log house I've got in mind," says Leroy apologetically.

"I know *that*."

"This is a pretty place. Your mama was right."   130

"It's O.K.," says Norma Jean. "Well, we've seen it. I hope she's satisfied."

They burst out laughing together.

At the park museum, a movie on Shiloh is shown every half hour, but they decide that they don't want to see it. They buy a souvenir Confederate flag for Mabel, and then they find a picnic spot near the cemetery. Norma Jean has brought a picnic cooler, with pimiento sandwiches, soft drinks, and Yodels. Leroy eats a sandwich and then smokes a joint, hiding it behind the picnic cooler. Norma Jean has quit smoking altogether. She is picking cake crumbs from the cellophane wrapper, like a fussy bird.

Leroy says, "So the boys in gray ended up in Corinth. The Union soldiers zapped 'em finally, April 7, 1862."

They both know that he doesn't know any history. He is just talking   135
about some of the historical plaques they have read. He feels awkward, like a boy on a date with an older girl. They are still just making conversation.

"Corinth is where Mama eloped to," says Norma Jean.

They sit in silence and stare at the cemetery for the Union dead and, beyond, at a tall cluster of trees. Campers are parked nearby, bumper to bumper, and small children in bright clothing are cavorting and squealing.

Norma Jean wads up the cake wrapper and squeezes it tightly in her hand. Without looking at Leroy, she says, "I want to leave you."

Leroy takes a bottle of Coke out of the cooler and flips off the cap. He holds the bottle poised near his mouth but cannot remember to take a drink. Finally he says, "No, you don't."

"Yes, I do."

"I won't let you."   140

"You can't stop me."

"Don't do me that way."

Leroy knows Norma Jean will have her own way. "Didn't I promise to be home from now on?" he says.

"In some ways, a woman prefers a man who wanders," says Norma Jean. "That sounds crazy, I know."

"You're not crazy."   145

Leroy remembers to drink from his Coke. Then he says, "Yes, you *are* crazy. You and me could start all over again. Right back at the beginning."

"We *have* started all over again," says Norma Jean. "And this is how it turned out."

"What did I do wrong?"

"Nothing."

"Is this one of those women's lib things?" Leroy asks.   150

"Don't be funny."

The cemetery, a green slope dotted with white markers, looks like a subdivision site. Leroy is trying to comprehend that his marriage is breaking up, but for some reason he is wondering about white slabs in a graveyard.

"Everything was fine till Mama caught me smoking," says Norma Jean, standing up. "That set something off."

"What are you talking about?"

"She won't leave me alone—*you* won't leave me alone." Norma Jean 155 seems to be crying, but she is looking away from him. "I feel eighteen again. I can't face that all over again." She starts walking away. "No, it *wasn't* fine. I don't know what I'm saying. Forget it."

Leroy takes a lungful of smoke and closes his eyes as Norma Jean's words sink in. He tries to focus on the fact that thirty-five hundred soldiers died on the grounds around him. He can only think of that war as a board game with plastic soldiers. Leroy almost smiles, as he compares the Confederates' daring attack on the Union camps and Virgil Mathis's raid on the bowling alley. General Grant, drunk and furious, shoved the Southerners back to Corinth, where Mabel and Jet Beasley were married years later, when Mabel was still thin and good-looking. The next day, Mabel and Jet visited the battleground, and then Norma Jean was born, and then she married Leroy and they had a baby, which they lost, and now Leroy and Norma Jean are here at the same battleground. Leroy knows he is leaving out a lot. He is leaving out the insides of history. History was always just names and dates to him. It occurs to him that building a house out of logs is similarly empty—too simple. And the real inner workings of a marriage, like most of history, have escaped him. Now he sees that building a log house is the dumbest idea he could have had. It was clumsy of him to think Norma Jean would want a log house. It was a crazy idea. He'll have to think of something else, quickly. He will wad the blueprints into tight balls and fling them into the lake. Then he'll get moving again. He opens his eyes. Norma Jean has moved away and is walking through the cemetery, following a serpentine brick path.

Leroy gets up to follow his wife, but his good leg is asleep and his bad leg still hurts him. Norma Jean is far away, walking rapidly toward the bluff by the river, and he tries to hobble toward her. Some children run past him, screaming noisily. Norma Jean has reached the bluff, and she is looking out over the Tennessee River. Now she turns toward Leroy and waves her arms. Is she beckoning to him? She seems to be doing an exercise for her chest muscles. The sky is unusually pale—the color of the dust ruffle Mabel made for their bed.

The Receptive Reader

1. This story takes us to a working-class *setting,* with such class markers as the characters' working-class language. Where does their language become most noticeable, or where does it become an issue, in the story? Attitudes toward the working class have traditionally ranged from snobbish contempt to solidarity for the aspirations of common people. What is the attitude of the author?

2. Some southern readers feel particularly at home in this story. To you, what if anything is southern about the setting and about this story as a whole?

3. Mason is a fanatic for apparently trivial *realistic detail*—about Leroy's job, his accident, his therapy; about Norma Jean's job at the drugstore, her bodybuilding exercises, her classes at the college; about their trip to Shilo, and so forth. What to you are striking examples of these apparent trivia? What do they do for the story as a whole?

4. Mason makes the setting real by striking uses of *figurative language*—language using imaginative comparisons. What images and feelings does she bring into play when she says that Leroy's rig parked in the back was like a big bird come home to roost? What are other striking examples of imaginative comparisons?

5. How ordinary are the lives of these people? What are some of the ordinary everyday things that make their lives average? Do extraordinary things happen to them?

6. The *dialogue* in this story is very sparse. What are occasions in the story where you expect them to say more about their lives or their feelings than they do? Are their feelings "frozen," as one student reader said?

7. What role does Mabel, Leroy's mother-in-law, play as a *minor character* in the story? What is her relationship with Leroy? with her daughter? How does the author use her to develop or round out the setting of the story?

8. Readers are likely to detect symbolic meanings or overtones in details and incidents in this story. What are the possible symbolic meanings of the parked rig, the "nondescript" rented home, the electronic organ, the change in

the cooking, Mabel's hair, the log cabin Leroy wants to build, the trip to the battlefield?

9. When did you first decide that the marriage was going to break up? For you, was the breakup a foregone conclusion? Who or what is to blame?

10. Both *major characters*, Leroy and Norma Jean, change or develop in the course of this story. How do they change or grow? Do they develop in the same direction or along parallel lines? Do they understand what is happening to them? (How much self-realization is there in this story?)

The Personal Response

Anne Tyler, a fellow writer reviewing Mason's stories for *The New Republic,* said that it was "heartening to find male characters portrayed sympathetically, with an appreciation for the fact that they can feel as confused and hurt and lonely as the female characters." What are your personal feelings toward the two major characters in "Shiloh"? Do you feel closer to Leroy or to Norma Jean? Why?

Yukio Mishima   *(1925–1970)*

Yukio Mishima (pen name of Kimitake Hiraoka) was a prolific writer of novels, plays, and stories. He was a flamboyant media personality who became a cult figure in Japan and a legend in the West. He was alienated from westernized, materialistic modern Japan and became obsessed with Japanese history and traditional Japanese values. He set out to revive and reenact the code and ritual of the samurai warriors of Japan's feudal, aristocratic past, with traditions akin to the code of chivalry of the European Middle Ages. He studied the martial arts— boxing, karate, and sword fighting; he created the Shield Society, a private army of a hundred dedicated followers. In a final spectacular rejection of the decadent present, he committed *seppuku,* or public ritual suicide, in 1970.

Translations of Mishima's best-known works include *Confessions of a Mask* (1958), *The Sailor Who Fell from Grace with the Sea* (1965), and *Sun and Steel* (1970). In *The Sailor Who Fell from Grace,* a boy who disapproves of the lover of his widowed mother joins with a band of his fellows in an effort to terminate the love affair and the lover. Mishima's short stories were collected in *Death and Midsummer and Other Stories* (1966). Some of his best-known stories celebrate the ecstasy of married love, loyalty to the Empire, and ceremonial suicide. He once spoke of "my heart's leaning toward Death, Night, and Blood." The following story will take you to a different world—not merely a different geographical setting but a different world of thought and feeling.

Swaddling Clothes   *1966*

TRANSLATED BY IVAN MORRIS

He was always busy, Toshiko's husband. Even tonight he had to dash off to an appointment, leaving her to go home alone by taxi. But what else could a woman expect when she married an actor—an attractive one? No doubt she had been foolish to hope that he would spend the evening with her. And yet he must have known how she dreaded going back to their house, unhomely with its Western-style furniture and with the bloodstains still showing on the floor.

Toshiko had been oversensitive since girlhood: that was her nature. As the result of constant worrying she never put on weight, and now, an adult woman, she looked more like a transparent picture than a creature of flesh and blood. Her delicacy of spirit was evident to her most casual acquaintance.

Earlier that evening, when she had joined her husband at a night club, she had been shocked to find him entertaining friends with an account of "the incident." Sitting there in his American-style suit, puffing at a cigarette, he had seemed to her almost a stranger.

"It's a fantastic story," he was saying, gesturing flamboyantly as if in an attempt to outweigh the attractions of the dance band. "Here this new nurse for our baby arrives from the employment agency, and the very first thing I notice about her is her stomach. It's enormous—as if she had a pillow stuck under her kimono! No wonder, I thought, for I soon saw that she could eat more than the rest of us put together. She polished off the contents of our rice bin like that. . . ." He snapped his fingers. "'Gastric dilation'—that's how she explained her girth and her appetite. Well, the day before yesterday we heard groans and moans coming from the nursery. We rushed in and found her squatting on the floor, holding her stomach in her two hands, and moaning like a cow. Next to her our baby lay in his cot, scared out of his wits and crying at the top of his lungs. A pretty scene, I can tell you!"

"So the cat was out of the bag?" suggested one of their friends, a film   5
actor like Toshiko's husband.

"Indeed it was! And it gave me the shock of my life. You see, I'd completely swallowed that story about 'gastric dilation.' Well, I didn't waste any time. I rescued our good rug from the floor and spread a blanket for her to lie on. The whole time the girl was yelling like a stuck pig. By the time the doctor from the maternity clinic arrived, the baby had already been born. But our sitting room was a pretty shambles!"

"Oh, that I'm sure of!" said another of their friends, and the whole company burst into laughter.

Toshiko was dumbfounded to hear her husband discussing the horrifying happening as though it were no more than an amusing incident which they chanced to have witnessed. She shut her eyes for a moment and all at once she saw the newborn baby lying before her: on the parquet floor the infant lay, and his frail body was wrapped in bloodstained newspapers.

Toshiko was sure that the doctor had done the whole thing out of spite. As if to emphasize his scorn for this mother who had given birth to a bastard under such sordid conditions, he had told his assistant to wrap the baby in some loose newspapers, rather than proper swaddling. This callous treatment of the newborn child had offended Toshiko. Overcoming her disgust at the entire scene, she had fetched a brand-new piece of flannel from her cupboard and, having swaddled the baby in it, had lain him carefully in an armchair.

This all had taken place in the evening after her husband had left the 10 house. Toshiko had told him nothing of it, fearing that he would think her oversoft, oversentimental; yet the scene had engraved itself deeply in her mind. Tonight she sat silently thinking back on it, while the jazz orchestra brayed and her husband chatted cheerfully with his friends. She knew that she would never forget the sight of the baby, wrapped in stained newspapers and lying on the floor—it was a scene fit for a butchershop. Toshiko, whose own life had been spent in solid comfort, poignantly felt the wretchedness of the illegitimate baby.

I am the only person to have witnessed its shame, the thought occurred to her. The mother never saw her child lying there in its newspaper wrappings, and the baby itself of course didn't know. I alone shall have to preserve that terrible scene in my memory. When the baby grows up and wants to find out about his birth, there will be no one to tell him, so long as I preserve silence. How strange that I should have this feeling of guilt! After all, it was I who took him up from the floor, swathed him properly in flannel, and laid him down to sleep in the armchair.

They left the night club and Toshiko stepped into the taxi that her husband had called for her. "Take this lady to Ushigomé," he told the driver and shut the door from the outside. Toshiko gazed through the window at her husband's smiling face and noticed his strong, white teeth. Then she leaned back in the seat, oppressed by the knowledge that their life together was in some way too easy, too painless. It would have been difficult for her to put her thoughts into words. Through the rear window of the taxi she took a last look at her husband. He was striding along the street toward his Nash car, and soon the back of his rather garish tweed coat had blended with the figures of the passers-by.

The taxi drove off, passed down a street dotted with bars and then by a theater, in front of which the throngs of people jostled each other on the pavement. Although the performance had only just ended, the lights had already been turned out and in the half dark outside it was depressingly obvious that the cherry blossoms decorating the front of the theater were merely scraps of white paper.

Even if that baby should grow up in ignorance of the secret of his birth, he can never become a respectable citizen, reflected Toshiko, pursuing the same train of thoughts. Those soiled newspaper swaddling clothes will be the symbol of his entire life. But why should I keep worrying about him so much? Is it because I feel uneasy about the future of my own child? Say twenty years from now, when our boy will have grown up into a fine, carefully educated young man, one day by a quirk of fate he meets the other boy, who then will also have turned twenty. And say that the other boy, who has been sinned against, savagely stabs him with a knife. . . .

It was a warm, overcast April night, but thoughts of the future made   15
Toshiko feel cold and miserable. She shivered on the back seat of the car.

No, when the time comes I shall take my son's place, she told herself
suddenly. Twenty years from now I shall be forty-three. I shall go to that
young man and tell him straight out about everything—about his newspaper swaddling clothes, and about how I went and wrapped him in flannel.

The taxi ran along the dark wide road that was bordered by the park and
by the Imperial Palace moat. In the distance Toshiko noticed the pinpricks
of light which came from the blocks of tall office buildings.

Twenty years from now that wretched child will be in utter misery. He
will be living a desolate, hopeless, poverty-stricken existence—a lonely rat.
What else could happen to a baby who has had such a birth? He'll be wandering through the streets by himself, cursing his father, loathing his mother.

No doubt Toshiko derived a certain satisfaction from her somber thoughts:
she tortured herself with them without cease. The taxi approached Han-
zomon and drove past the compound of the British Embassy. At that point
the famous rows of cherry trees were spread out before Toshiko in all their
purity. On the spur of the moment she decided to go and view the blossoms
by herself in the dark night. It was a strange decision for a timid and unad-
venturous young woman, but then she was in a strange state of mind and
she dreaded the return home. That evening all sorts of unsettling fancies
had burst open in her mind.

She crossed the wide street—a slim, solitary figure in the darkness. As a   20
rule when she walked in the traffic Toshiko used to cling fearfully to her
companion, but tonight she darted alone between the cars and a moment
later had reached the long narrow park that borders the Palace moat. Chi-
dorigafuchi, it is called—the Abyss of the Thousand Birds.

Tonight the whole park had become a grove of blossoming cherry trees.
Under the calm cloudy sky the blossoms formed a mass of solid whiteness.
The paper lanterns that hung from wires between the trees had been put
out; in their place electric light bulbs, red, yellow, and green, shone dully
beneath the blossoms. It was well past ten o'clock and most of the flower-
viewers had gone home. As the occasional passers-by strolled through the
park, they would automatically kick aside the empty bottles or crush the
waste paper beneath their feet.

Newspapers, thought Toshiko, her mind going back once again to those
happenings. Bloodstained newspapers. If a man were ever to hear of that
piteous birth and know that it was he who had lain there, it would ruin his
entire life. To think that I, a perfect stranger, should from now on have to
keep such a secret—the secret of a man's whole existence. . . .

Lost in these thoughts, Toshiko walked on through the park. Most of the
people still remaining there were quiet couples; no one paid her any attention. She noticed two people sitting on a stone bench beside the moat, not
looking at the blossoms, but gazing silently at the water. Pitch black it was,
and swathed in heavy shadows. Beyond the moat the somber forest of the
Imperial Palace blocked her view. The trees reached up, to form a solid
dark mass against the night sky. Toshiko walked slowly along the path
beneath the blossoms hanging heavily overhead.

On a stone bench, slightly apart from the others, she noticed a pale object—not, as she had at first imagined, a pile of cherry blossoms, nor a garment forgotten by one of the visitors to the park. Only when she came closer did she see that it was a human form lying on the bench. Was it, she wondered, one of those miserable drunks often to be seen sleeping in public places? Obviously not, for the body had been systematically covered with newspapers, and it was the whiteness of those papers that had attracted Toshiko's attention. Standing by the bench, she gazed down at the sleeping figure.

It was a man in a brown jersey who lay there, curled up on layers of   25
newspapers, other newspapers covering him. No doubt this had become his normal night residence now that spring had arrived. Toshiko gazed down at the man's dirty, unkempt hair, which in places had become hopelessly matted. As she observed the sleeping figure wrapped in its newspapers, she was inevitably reminded of the baby who had lain on the floor in its wretched swaddling clothes. The shoulder of the man's jersey rose and fell in the darkness in time with his heavy breathing.

It seemed to Toshiko that all her fears and premonitions had suddenly taken concrete form. In the darkness the man's pale forehead stood out, and it was a young forehead, though carved with the wrinkles of long poverty and hardship. His khaki trousers had been slightly pulled up; on his sockless feet he wore a pair of battered gym shoes. She could not see his face and suddenly had an overmastering desire to get one glimpse of it.

She walked to the head of the bench and looked down. The man's head was half buried in his arms, but Toshiko could see that he was surprisingly young. She noticed the thick eyebrows and the fine bridge of his nose. His slightly open mouth was alive with youth.

But Toshiko had approached too close. In the silent night the newspaper bedding rustled, and abruptly the man opened his eyes. Seeing the young woman standing directly beside him, he raised himself with a jerk, and his eyes lit up. A second later a powerful hand reached out and seized Toshiko by her slender wrist.

She did not feel in the least afraid and made no effort to free herself. In a flash the thought had struck her. Ah, so the twenty years have already gone by! The forest of the Imperial Palace was pitch dark and utterly silent.

The Receptive Reader

1. What is strange and what is familiar about the *setting?* What expectations (or what stereotypes) do you bring to the Japanese setting of the story? How much of an effort of the imagination is necessary for you to get into the spirit of this story?

2. The author makes a point of the westernized or americanized ways of Toshiko's husband. What are revealing details? What contrast is Mishima setting up between the husband and the wife as *key characters?* What role does that contrast play in the story as a whole? What is the author's attitude toward the husband?

3. What are Toshiko's feelings about the illegitimate child? Does she reflect the expected attitudes of her culture? Are there parallels in American culture or social mores to the attitude toward unwed mothers and children born out of wedlock that play a strong role in this story? (Are our attitudes more enlightened or just different?)

4. Is the ending a **surprise ending,** or has the author prepared you for it? Does the story as a whole lead up to it? How? Do you react to it as something that really happened or as a dream, a nightmare?

5. Some of the details in this story are not just mentioned in passing. They come up again, providing a kind of link or a continuing strand. What is the role of recurrent details like the cherry blossoms or newspapers in this story?

6. One editor said that "this fiercely condensed" story, focused on a "single, overpowering incident," "explodes in a burst of revelation or illumination" (Irving Howe). For you, what is that revelation? Does this story have a point? Does it have a *theme*—some key idea acted out or implied in the story as a whole?

The Personal Response

Does the story as a whole remain strange or alien for you? How do you relate to Toshiko as the central character? How do you relate to the story as a whole?

The Range of Interpretation

Mishima's story invites a wide range of reactions. In your judgment, which of the following student responses best gets into the spirit of the story? How or why does the student writer seem to do justice to the author's intention? How are these responses different from your own interpretation of the story?

1.   This story is very disturbing. Although it is set in Japan, the story reflects stereotypical sex roles reminding me of many couples I know. The husband is domineering and shallow, and Toshiko is the stereotypically passive, dependent "oversensitive" wife. Under the quiet stereotypical surface, Toshiko is a warm, caring person. But whereas she is a keen observer of her culture (her gloomy prediction for the baby reveals this), she lives her whole life in her fears and feelings. While the husband is vain and self-absorbed, Toshiko spends her life alone in the private world of her fears. She feels great warmth toward the child, but she knows that it will suffer greatly as the result of its dishonorable beginnings. What we see in Toshiko is the constant battle waged between the traditional role and the emergence of the more modern woman. She is alienated from her callous, self-centered husband, and she assumes responsibility for the harsh treatment that society has in store for the newborn child.

2.   This story is very fatalistic. The child, because of its illegitimate birth, is doomed to "utter misery." I expected Toshiko to come to a tragic end. I could empathize with Toshiko somewhat because of her culture and beliefs, but I wanted to stop her from feeling so guilty and destroying her life. It is as if Toshiko created the ending in the park. She is determined to sacrifice herself. At times I wanted to reach into the story and stop her from being so guilt-ridden and oversensitive. As a woman, it made me angry that she would destroy herself.

3.   On the literal level, this story leaves many questions unresolved. The abrupt, surprising ending leaves me wondering whether it is real—is it a dream? a nightmare? If the derelict in the park literally attacked the woman, was the result death? rape? Symbolically, in the context of the story as a whole, Toshiko is taking the place of her own son. She is sacrificing herself in his stead, so that she rather than he will be the target of the dispossessed child's anger and resentment when it returns to exact vengeance. In spite of the difference in cultures, the story made me hear echoes of my own Catholic upbringing. The incident where Toshiko wrapped the child in swaddling clothes mirrored the birth of Christ in a manger where Mary wrapped him in swaddling clothes. The ending where Toshiko is willing to give up her life so that her son may live parallels Christ's willingness to give up his life so that his people may have eternal life.

WRITING ABOUT LITERATURE

2   Exploring the Setting (The Structured Paper)

The Writing Workshop   As you develop a paper focused on setting or on another facet of the storyteller's art, you first of all build up a rich backlog of material. You scribble comments in the margins of what you read (not in library copies!). You take ample reading notes. You compare notes and impressions with classmates or friends. However, the second major step is to bring your material under control. Early in the process of gathering the material, you may begin to focus on a key question that you will want to answer or a key issue that you may want to explore. You start pulling together quotations and details that bear on the same point. This process of sorting out, of pulling your material into shape, will provide the ground plan or working outline for your first draft. You then refine or adjust your plan as necessary as you revise your paper.

What are some basic requirements for the finished paper that will be the result of this process of focusing, shaping, and revising? Each paper is different. However, the following guidelines are meant to alert you to needs that arise again and again in student papers.

✗ *Avoid generic titles.*   Although you may not hit on the right title until late in the process of writing your paper, remember that the title will be the first thing to strike your reader. Titles should not be perfunctory and interchangeable—good perhaps for filing the paper under the author's name or the name of the story, but not enough to hook the reader into reading your essay. A good title is informative (it helps map the territory), but it should also be beckoning. Your title should be specific and attractive enough to invite the reader. It need not be a "grabber," but it should be alive. It should suggest a topic, a point of view, a program, a style.

TOO INTERCHANGEABLE:	Joyce's "Araby"
TOO INFORMAL?	A Boy and His Bubble
FORMAL:	The Dark Infatuation of Joyce's "Araby"

◢ *Take your reader into the world of the story.*   Help your reader get into the spirit by starting with a revealing quotation or a crucial incident:

"Your name means 'the king,'" Norma Jean informs her husband Leroy in Bobbie Ann Mason's "Shiloh," but Leroy, a disabled truck driver, model-kit hobbyist, and occasional joint smoker, is more like the palace groundkeeper than the king.

◢ *Bring your paper into focus.*   The first page is crucial. What is your central focus? What is your overall plan? After a brief pointed introduction, use your opening paragraphs to set directions. Try to provide a preview or program. Sketch out or hint at your overall scheme. Avoid a program that is too general—too open and interchangeable:

WEAK: In this story, certain elements of the setting underscore and highlight the problems of the main characters.

(What certain elements? This is too vague: No one is going to say "I am all excited—I am going to be told about certain elements!")

Instead, for a short paper, try to sketch out a three-point or four-point program that provides a road map for your reader. Create expectations that your paper as a whole is going to fulfill. For instance, in writing about Mason's "Shiloh," you might plan to show how three main characters relate differently to their setting:

The characters in Mason's story relate differently to their Southern setting: Leroy, the husband, is stranded in the present; Mabel, the mother-in-law, is living in the past; Norma Jean, the wife, has a future.

This statement provides a **thesis,** summing up the central idea of the paper. However, it also implies an itinerary. It alerts the reader to how the thesis is going to be followed up as the writer looks at each of the major characters in turn.

◢ *Wean yourself from a mere plot summary.*   Follow a logical rather than a merely chronological order. Sometimes, especially for a story with a complicated plot, an initial tracing of the story line can help writer and reader get their bearings. But avoid a mere "read-along-with-me" effect—make sure your readers do not think your paper as a whole will merely retell the story. Show that you have tied things together, that you can bring together evidence from different parts of the story. Show that you can pull out relevant quotations or incidents that bear on a key question or key point. (If you follow the order of the story, look at each segment from the angle that is the issue. Use each stage in the story to make a point that is part of your overall argument.)

✗ *Weave in rich authentic detail.*   Remember that any point worth making is worth following up with examples and support. Provide ample telling detail and show its significance in the story. For instance, in "Shiloh," the organ is rich in electronic wizardry—and Norma Jean masters it "almost immediately" (a hint of her ability to adjust to what is new?). Early in your paper, start weaving in telling, revealing short quotations. For instance, you might use the following interchange between Leroy and Norma Jean when you try to show the reader how these two are "slowly drifting apart":

> "We *have* started all over again," says Norma Jean. "And this is how it turned out."
> "What did I do wrong?"
> "Nothing."

Use specific details and apt quotations to show your command of the material. Build up a rich texture of supporting detail to counteract the thin, anemic, overgeneral effect of improvised, hastily written prose.

✗ *Strengthen logical connections.*   Avoid lame **transitions** like *also* or *another.* When you find yourself writing "another important aspect of the setting is . . . ," ask yourself: How is this feature of the setting *related* to the others—how is it part of the whole picture?

Perhaps you have made a point of Leroy's inability to communicate. (He wants to talk about their marriage but instead lamely repeats that he will build his wife a house.) You now want to move on to a second point: "Leroy's anachronistic behavior is *another problem* in the Moffitt marriage." (His playing with the plans for model log houses points to the past, not the future.) What is the logical connection between the two points? What is the connection in the larger context of the story? Perhaps you could strengthen the connection with a transition like the following:

TRANSITION: Having no way to voice his feelings articulately with words, he builds model log houses because he has no other way to express himself. However, this preoccupation with symbols of the past only serves to widen the gap between him and his wife. . . .

✗ *Aim at a strong conclusion.*   Revise a conclusion that is merely a lame recapitulation of points already clear. Try bringing your paper full circle by picking up an image, incident, or keynote from the beginning of the paper. Use the opportunity to drive home a key point. Or use the opportunity to branch out, showing larger implications, showing a personal connection. One student paper started: "'Shiloh' by Bobbie Ann Mason presents a dull yet strikingly real vision of America." The following conclusion drives home the central point and highlights the connection between the story and our own lives:

> "Shiloh" is a perfect portrayal of life in the 1990s. It is realistic, poignant, and depressing. It is ordinary, sometimes, dismal, but rarely extravagant. That is left for Oprah and Geraldo to display on television. We see ourselves in the couple—our drive to succeed and prosper in Norma Jean and our love of the couch in Leroy.

Study the following sample paper. What role does the setting of the story play in the paper? How well does the paper live up to the requirements sketched above?

Sample Student Paper

Muscle Building in the New South

Bobbie Ann Mason's short story "Shiloh" is a bleak portrait of a marriage at the point of dissolution—a picture of two people poised at the brink of what for the woman is a new life of personal growth and freedom but what is for the man the loss of most in his life that he thought secure. Mason uses physical detail—the way the characters relate to their bodies and to their physical setting—to mirror the wife's upward spiral and the husband's decline. They both find themselves in a new world that is different from the old South represented by Leroy's mother-in-law. But for one of them this new world means disillusionment and stagnation; for the other it means opportunity.

Leroy Moffitt is a truck driver from Kentucky, who is at home recovering from an accident in which his leg was badly injured. It is the first time since the early days of his marriage that he has been at home for any length of time, and he begins to feel that he has missed much of his married life. He realizes "that in all the years he was on the road he never took time to examine anything. He was always flying past scenery." Now his years of flying past the scenery of his life are over, and he for the first time is experiencing what it is like to stay in one place. Having a chance to watch his wife for more than hurried intervals, he finds that she is a different person from the woman he married.

His injured leg symbolizes Leroy's new slowing down, his new lack of mobility. It was badly twisted in its socket when his truck jackknifed in the road, and he now has a steel pin in his hip. Although he is healing, he is scared to go back on the road; he has moved from an extremely fast-paced, always-moving lifestyle to one in which he can walk only with difficulty. His career and his marriage have shuddered painfully to a standstill. He finds himself in a setting where much of what he does merely helps to pass the time: building small-scale model log houses, expecting his wife to play old favorites on a state-of-the-art electronic piano.

Leroy's new immobility is reflected even in Leroy's drug of choice. Where before he took drugs that were suited to his fast, mobile lifestyle, he now uses drugs of a more mellow nature: "Leroy used to take speed on the road. Now he has to go slowly. He needs to be mellow." The weed he buys allows him to dull and slow down his perception of his surroundings. He buys his joints from a source who represents the downside of the New South—a son of a doctor, whose drug-dealing symbolizes the rejection of his goal-oriented doctor father.

While Leroy is slowing down, however, his wife Norma Jean is speeding up. After fifteen years of staying home while her husband traveled, she is physically and symbolically stepping out into a new world. She is trying to move beyond the drugstore job—beyond the feeling of going nowhere experienced by people who are trapped in an average existence. She is taking steps toward personal improvement and intellectual growth—steps which are reflected in her new attention to her body. Early in the story, we see her working out with dumbbells, improving her muscle tone and physical appearance: "I'd give anything if I could just get these muscles to where they're real hard," she says impatiently. Leroy, with some foreboding, sees the potential for improvement in her, thinking that as she stood with her legs apart she reminded him of "Wonder Woman." Norma Jean wears ankle weights, lifts barbells, and flexes her arm to test the size of her biceps—testing, symbolically, her emotional and intellectual strength as she nears the point of breaking away from Leroy.

As she is improving herself physically, she improves herself intellectually with night classes and reading. As Leroy notes, "she stays up late, writing compositions." Norma Jean breaks out of confining old habits: She quits smoking; she cooks unusual foods, walking around the kitchen with ankle weights attached. Although she is still living in their house, her mind and body are already in a different place.

The differences in Leroy's and Norma Jean's emotional and intellectual needs lead to the final breakup in a setting full of hints of forgotten conflicts, the Civil War battleground at Shiloh. When Norma Jean walks away from Leroy, he is physically unable to follow her, for "his good leg is asleep and his bad leg still hurts him." She moves quickly, widening the chasm where their marriage used to be. In our last glimpse of Leroy and Norma Jean, she is waving her arms in some sort of "exercise for her chest muscles," testing her wings, perhaps, before moving upward and away from her old life.

Questions

How well does the introduction get you into the spirit of the story? Where does the central idea or thesis come into focus? Where does the program or agenda for the paper as a whole become clear to the reader? Where does the writer do a good job of relating specific details to the concerns of the paper as a whole? What use does the paper make of quotations? What transitions effectively move the reader from point to point? How does the conclusion wrap up the paper? How does it hark back to earlier parts of the paper; what does it add that is new? Where do you agree and where would you take issue with the paper?

3 Character

The Buried Self

I don't invent characters because the Almighty has already invented millions, just as experts at finger-prints do not create fingerprints but learn how to read them.

ISAAC BASHEVIS SINGER

FOCUS ON CHARACTER

How do you come to understand the characters in a short story? Storytellers create characters and set them in motion. They know we are fascinated with the variety of people in our world. We are willing to hear about their hopes and fears, their goals and self-doubts. As we learn about them, we may begin to care, taking sides and becoming involved. An author may give us a capsule portrait as advance notice of what we may expect. However, in much modern fiction, we see character unfold. We see people act out (and hear them talk out) who they are. The author may let us watch a character from outside, letting us draw our own conclusions. Or the author may take us inside the character's mind, letting us overhear private thoughts and feelings.

As you study character in fiction, bear in mind features like the following:

Probing Motivation   When you pay close attention to character, you find yourself going from the *what* to the *why*. You go from people's words and actions to their motives. Why do people talk and act the way they do? Be prepared to think about a character's **motivation.** Look for clues to behavior that may seem puzzling on the surface. For instance, characters who act spiteful or hostile may not be by temperament hostile people. They may be venting pent-up frustrations. They may have been driven to the edge by a series of adverse events. Their hostility may be "nothing personal"; they may be "mad at the world."

Flat and Round Characters   **Flat characters** have a one-track personality: the miser is always a Scrooge; the whiner always finds fault. Such one-dimensional characters are common in popular fiction and sometimes make for the easy laugh. **Round characters** have the combination of traits that make real people complicated. They may be loyal to a person or a cause—but they may be having private doubts after seeing disturbing shortcomings. They may have been raised in an atmosphere of rah-rah patriotism but discover unsuspected sympathies for a prisoner of war—the enemy. Be prepared to recognize divided loyalties and mixed emotions.

The Developing Character   Characters may prove capable of growth, of development. A story may chronicle a stage in a character's spiritual journey. Stories like Alice Munro's "Boys and Girls" are stories of **initiation.** They reenact rites of passage. You may see characters moving from childhood to adolescence, from the happy protected childhood world to the limitations of the adult world. A story may focus on an important turn in the road of a character's life. After a crucial challenge or disillusionment, a central character may become a different person.

Person and Persona   Many modern writers go beyond the surface, beyond the stereotype. They probe for the hidden personality, the buried self, beneath the public **persona.** They explore the contrast between the image and the real person. They may contrast the face someone presents to the outside world (perfect hostess, Mr. Personality) and private insecurities or vendettas. They may make us discover the private frustrations or fantasy life of a person who seems a cowed average individual nine to five.

The Dynamics of Interaction   Sometimes, a single character emerges from the background—giving a solo performance. More typically, a character's personality is revealed in interaction with others. We often see characters as part of a web of relationships, of "interpersonal relations." In the Alice Munro story, the girl who is at the center of the story is influenced by two conflicting role models, her father and her mother. Often the true nature of an individual comes to the surface in a fateful encounter.

THE RANGE OF CHARACTERIZATION

You would have me, when I describe horse thieves,
say: "Stealing horses is evil." But that has been
known for ages without my saying so. Let the jury
judge them; it's my job simply to show what sort of
people they are.

ANTON CHEKHOV

In some stories, the characters stay pale. They may seem inter-changeable with others of their time or their setting. They seem repre-sentative of their stage in life or of their class. In other stories, however, the mystery of personality is at the center of the story. The story tries to make us understand a complex human being. It probes a character's motives, explores surface contradictions, or ponders a change of heart. To a large extent, the character is the story. In the stories that follow, character plays a central role.

Raymond Carver   *(1939–1988)*

Carver has an acute sense of the singularity, the
endearing oddity, of each human being; to each
person he grants a measure of dignity because, if
nothing else at all, this person has the sure distinc-
tion that no one else is exactly like him—no
human life can be replicated; therefore each, how-
ever flawed, is precious.

JONATHAN YARDLEY

Raymond Carver has been praised for his intentional "blue-collar real-ism and unsophistication" (John Barth). Carver had himself worked at blue-collar jobs in the towns of the Pacific Northwest, the setting of many of his stories. He himself, like some of his characters, had done battle against alcoholism. His characters are often unskilled and unem-ployed and yet of sufficient human interest to the author. He often gives a voice to the feelings or point of view of people of few words, "speak-ing the thoughts of those who cannot themselves speak" (John Clute). One reviewer thought of him as the kind of writer "who turned banal-ity's pockets out and found all their contents beautiful" (Marilynne Robinson).

Carver is one of a group of contemporary writers tending toward a **minimalist** stance (though he himself disliked the label). Like other minimalist writers, he kept his stories to the essential minimum, writing on the theory that "less is more," being suspicious of all showy effects.

He once said, "I cut my work to the marrow, not just the bone." Carver seems to enjoy teasing the reader with the puzzle of personality. His narrator, as in the following story, may be someone listening to another character, piecing together the pieces of the puzzle, wanting to say (as does Carver's reader), "Tell me more."

The Third Thing That Killed My Father Off   1977

I'll tell you what did my father in. The third thing was Dummy, that Dummy died. The first thing was Pearl Harbor. And the second thing was moving to my grandfather's farm near Wenatchee. That's where my father finished out his days, except they were probably finished before that.

My father blamed Dummy's death on Dummy's wife. Then he blamed it on the fish. And finally he blamed himself—because he was the one that showed Dummy the ad in the back of *Field and Stream* for live black bass shipped anywhere in the U.S.

It was after he got the fish that Dummy started acting peculiar. The fish changed Dummy's whole personality. That's what my father said.

I never knew Dummy's real name. If anyone did, I never heard it. Dummy it was then, and it's Dummy I remember him by now. He was a little wrinkled man, baldheaded, short but very powerful in the arms and legs. If he grinned, which was seldom, his lips folded back over brown, broken teeth. It gave him a crafty expression. His watery eyes stayed fastened on your mouth when you were talking—and if you weren't, they'd go to someplace queer on your body.

I don't think he was really deaf. At least not as deaf as he made out. But   5
he sure couldn't talk. That was for certain.

Deaf or no, Dummy'd been on as a common laborer out at the sawmill since the 1920s. This was the Cascade Lumber Company in Yakima, Washington. The years I knew him, Dummy was working as a cleanup man. And all those years I never saw him with anything different on. Meaning a felt hat, a khaki workshirt, a denim jacket over a pair of coveralls. In his top pockets he carried rolls of toilet paper, as one of his jobs was to clean and supply the toilets. It kept him busy, seeing as how the men on nights used to walk off after their tours with a roll or two in their lunchboxes.

Dummy carried a flashlight, even though he worked days. He also carried wrenches, pliers, screwdrivers, friction tape, all the same things the millwrights carried. Well, it made them kid Dummy, the way he was, always carrying everything. Carl Lowe, Ted Slade, Johnny Wait, they were the worst kidders of the ones that kidded Dummy. But Dummy took it all in stride. I think he'd gotten used to it.

My father never kidded Dummy. Not to my knowledge, anyway. Dad was a big, heavy-shouldered man with a crew-haircut, double chin, and a belly of real size. Dummy was always staring at that belly. He'd come to the filing room where my father worked, and he'd sit on a stool and watch my dad's belly while he used the big emery wheels on the saws.

*   *   *

Dummy had a house as good as anyone's.

It was a tarpaper-covered affair near the river, five or six miles from   10
town. Half a mile behind the house, at the end of a pasture, there lay a
big gravel pit that the state had dug when they were paving the roads
around there. Three good-sized holes had been scooped out, and over the
years they'd filled with water. By and by, the three ponds came together to
make one.

It was deep. It had a darkish look to it.

Dummy had a wife as well as a house. She was a woman years younger
and said to go around with Mexicans. Father said it was busybodies that
said that, men like Lowe and Wait and Slade.

She was a small stout woman with glittery little eyes. The first time I saw
her, I saw those eyes. It was when I was with Pete Jensen and we were on
our bicycles and we stopped at Dummy's to get a glass of water.

When she opened the door, I told her I was Del Fraser's son. I said, "He
works with—" And then I realized. "You know, your husband. We were on
our bicycles and thought we could get a drink."

"Wait here," she said.   15

She came back with a little tin cup of water in each hand. I downed mine
in a single gulp.

But she didn't offer us more. She watched us without saying anything.
When we started to get on our bicycles, she came over to the edge of the
porch.

"You little fellas had a car now, I might catch a ride with you."

She grinned. Her teeth looked too big for her mouth.

"Let's go," Pete said, and we went.   20

There weren't many places you could fish for bass in our part of the
state. There was rainbow mostly, a few brook and Dolly Varden in some of
the high mountain streams, and silvers in Blue Lake and Lake Rimrock. That
was mostly it, except for the runs of steelhead and salmon in some of the
freshwater rivers in late fall. But if you were a fisherman, it was enough to
keep you busy. No one fished for bass. A lot of people I knew had never
seen a bass except for pictures. But my father had seen plenty of them
when he was growing up in Arkansas and Georgia, and he had high hopes
to do with Dummy's bass, Dummy being a friend.

The day the fish arrived, I'd gone swimming at the city pool. I remember
coming home and going out again to get them since Dad was going to give
Dummy a hand—three tanks Parcel Post from Baton Rouge, Louisiana.

We went in Dummy's pickup, Dad and Dummy and me.

These tanks turned out to be barrels, really, the three of them crated in
pine lath. They were standing in the shade out back of the train depot, and
it took my dad and Dummy both to lift each crate into the truck.

Dummy drove very carefully through town and just as carefully all the   25
way to his house. He went right through his yard without stopping. He
went on down to within feet of the pond. By that time it was nearly dark,
so he kept his headlights on and took out a hammer and a tire iron from
under the seat, and then the two of them lugged the crates up close to the
water and started tearing open the first one.

The barrel inside was wrapped in burlap, and there were these nickel-sized holes in the lid. They raised it off and Dummy aimed his flashlight in.

It looked like a million bass fingerlings were finning inside. It was the strangest sight, all those live things busy in there, like a little ocean that had come on the train.

Dummy scooted the barrel to the edge of the water and poured it out. He took his flashlight and shined it into the pond. But there was nothing to be seen anymore. You could hear the frogs going, but you could hear them going anytime it newly got dark.

"Let me get the other crates," my father said, and he reached over as if to take the hammer from Dummy's coveralls. But Dummy pulled back and shook his head.

He undid the other two crates himself, leaving dark drops of blood on   30
the lath where he ripped his hand doing it.

From that night on, Dummy was different.

Dummy wouldn't let anyone come around now anymore. He put up fencing all around the pasture, and then he fenced off the pond with electrical barbed wire. They said it cost him all his savings for that fence.

Of course, my father wouldn't have anything to do with Dummy after that. Not since Dummy ran him off. Not from fishing, mind you, because the bass were just babies still. But even from trying to get a look.

One evening two years after, when Dad was working late and I took him his food and a jar of iced tea, I found him standing talking with Syd Glover, the millwright. Just as I came in, I heard Dad saying, "You'd reckon the fool was married to them fish, the way he acts."

"From what I hear," Syd said, "he'd do better to put that fence round his   35
house."

My father saw me then, and I saw him signal Syd Glover with his eyes.

But a month later my dad finally made Dummy do it. What he did was, he told Dummy how you had to thin out the weak ones on account of keeping things fit for the rest of them. Dummy stood there pulling at his ear and staring at the floor. Dad said, Yeah, he'd be down to do it tomorrow because it had to be done. Dummy never said yes, actually. He just never said no, is all. All he did was pull on his ear some more.

When Dad got home that day, I was ready and waiting. I had his old bass plugs out and was testing the treble hooks with my finger.

"You set?" he called to me, jumping out of the car. "I'll go to the toilet, you put the stuff in. You can drive us out there if you want."

I'd stowed everything in the back seat and was trying out the wheel   40
when he came back out wearing his fishing hat and eating a wedge of cake with both hands.

Mother was standing in the door watching. She was a fair-skinned woman, her blonde hair pulled back in a tight bun and fastened down with a rhinestone clip. I wonder if she ever went around back in those happy days, or what she ever really did.

I let out the handbrake. Mother watched until I'd shifted gears, and then, still unsmiling, she went back inside.

It was a fine afternoon. We had all the windows down to let the air in. We crossed the Moxee Bridge and swung west onto Slater Road. Alfalfa fields stood off to either side, and farther on it was cornfields.

Dad had his hand out the window. He was letting the wind carry it back. He was restless, I could see.

It wasn't long before we pulled up at Dummy's. He came out of the house wearing his hat. His wife was looking out the window. 45

"You got your frying pan ready?" Dad hollered out to Dummy, but Dummy just stood there eyeing the car. "Hey, Dummy!" Dad yelled. "Hey, Dummy, where's your pole, Dummy?"

Dummy jerked his head back and forth. He moved his weight from one leg to the other and looked at the ground and then at us. His tongue rested on his lower lip, and he began working his foot into the dirt.

I shouldered the creel. I handed Dad his pole and picked up my own.

"We set to go?" Dad said. "Hey, Dummy, we set to go?"

Dummy took off his hat and, with the same hand, he wiped his wrist 50 over his head. He turned abruptly, and we followed him across the spongy pasture. Every twenty feet or so a snipe sprang up from the clumps of grass at the edge of the old furrows.

At the end of the pasture, the ground sloped gently and became dry and rocky, nettle bushes and scrub oaks scattered here and there. We cut to the right, following an old set of car tracks, going through a field of milkweed that came up to our waists, the dry pods at the tops of the stalks rattling angrily as we pushed through. Presently, I saw the sheen of water over Dummy's shoulder, and I heard Dad shout, "Oh, Lord, look at that!"

But Dummy slowed down and kept bringing his hand up and moving his hat back and forth over his head, and then he just stopped flat.

Dad said, "Well, what do you think, Dummy? One place good as another? Where do you say we should come onto it?"

Dummy wet his lower lip.

"What's the matter with you, Dummy?" Dad said. "This your pond, ain't it?" 55

Dummy looked down and picked an ant off his coveralls.

"Well, hell," Dad said, letting out his breath. He took out his watch. "If it's all right with you, we'll get to it before it gets too dark."

Dummy stuck his hands in his pockets and turned back to the pond. He started walking again. We trailed along behind. We could see the whole pond now, the water dimpled with rising fish. Every so often a bass would leap clear and come down in a splash.

"Great God," I heard my father say.

We came up to the pond at an open place, a gravel beach kind of. 60

Dad motioned to me and dropped into a crouch. I dropped too. He was peering into the water in front of us, and when I looked, I saw what had taken him so.

"Honest to God," he whispered.

A school of bass was cruising, twenty, thirty, not one of them under two pounds. They veered off, and then they shifted and came back, so densely spaced they looked like they were bumping up against each other. I could see their big, heavy-lidded eyes watching us as they went by. They flashed away again, and again they came back.

They were asking for it. It didn't make any difference if we stayed squatted or stood up. The fish just didn't think a thing about us. I tell you, it was a sight to behold.

We sat there for quite a while, watching that school of bass go so innocently about their business, Dummy the whole time pulling at his fingers and looking around as if he expected someone to show up. All over the pond the bass were coming up to nuzzle the water, or jumping clear and falling back, or coming up to the surface to swim along with their dorsals sticking out.   65

Dad signaled, and we got up to cast. I tell you, I was shaky with excitement. I could hardly get the plug loose from the cork handle of my pole. It was while I was trying to get the hooks out that I felt Dummy seize my shoulder with his big fingers. I looked, and in answer Dummy worked his chin in Dad's direction. What he wanted was clear enough, no more than one pole.

Dad took off his hat and then put it back on and then he moved over to where I stood.

"You go on, Jack," he said. "That's all right, son—you do it now."

I looked at Dummy just before I laid out my cast. His face had gone rigid, and there was a thin line of drool on his chin.

"Come back stout on the sucker when he strikes," Dad said. "Sons of bitches got mouths hard as doorknobs."   70

I flipped off the drag lever and threw back my arm. I sent her out a good forty feet. The water was boiling even before I had time to take up the slack.

"Hit him!" Dad yelled. "Hit the son of a bitch! Hit him good!"

I came back hard, twice. I had him, all right. The rod bowed over and jerked back and forth. Dad kept yelling what to do.

"Let him go, let him go! Let him run! Give him more line! Now wind in! Wind in! No, let him run! Woo-ee! Will you look at that!"

The bass danced around the pond. Every time it came up out of the water, it shook its head so hard you could hear the plug rattle. And then he'd take off again. But by and by I wore him out and had him in up close. He looked enormous, six or seven pounds maybe. He lay on his side, whipped, mouth open, gills working. My knees felt so weak I could hardly stand. But I held the rod up, the line tight.   75

Dad waded out over his shoes. But when he reached for the fish, Dummy started sputtering, shaking his head, waving his arms.

"Now what the hell's the matter with you, Dummy? The boy's got hold of the biggest bass I ever seen, and he ain't going to throw him back, by God!"

Dummy kept carrying on and gesturing toward the pond.

"I ain't about to let this boy's fish go. You hear me, Dummy? You got another thing coming if you think I'm going to do that."

Dummy reached for my line. Meanwhile, the bass had gained some strength back. He turned himself over and started swimming again. I yelled and then I lost my head and slammed down the brake on the reel and started winding. The bass made a last, furious run.   80

That was that. The line broke. I almost fell over on my back.

"Come on, Jack," Dad said, and I saw him grabbing up his pole. "Come on, goddamn the fool, before I knock the man down."

That February the river flooded.

It had snowed pretty heavy the first weeks of December, and turned real cold before Christmas. The ground froze. The snow stayed where it was. But toward the end of January, the Chinook wind struck. I woke up one morning to hear the house getting buffeted and the steady drizzle of water running off the roof.

It blew for five days, and on the third day the river began to rise.   85

"She's up to fifteen feet," my father said one evening, looking over his newspaper. "Which is three feet over what you need to flood. Old Dummy going to lose his darlings."

I wanted to go down to the Moxee Bridge to see how high the water was running. But my dad wouldn't let me. He said a flood was nothing to see.

Two days later the river crested, and after that the water began to subside.

Orin Marshall and Danny Owens and I bicycled out to Dummy's one morning a week after. We parked our bicycles and walked across the pasture that bordered Dummy's property.

It was a wet, blustery day, the clouds dark and broken, moving fast   90 across the sky. The ground was soppy wet and we kept coming to puddles in the thick grass. Danny was just learning how to cuss, and he filled the air with the best he had every time he stepped in over his shoes. We could see the swollen river at the end of the pasture. The water was still high and out of its channel, surging around the trunks of trees and eating away at the edge of the land. Out toward the middle, the current moved heavy and swift, and now and then a bush floated by, or a tree with its branches sticking up.

We came to Dummy's fence and found a cow wedged in up against the wire. She was bloated and her skin was shiny-looking and gray. It was the first dead thing of any size I'd ever seen. I remember Orin took a stick and touched the open eyes.

We moved on down the fence, toward the river. We were afraid to go near the wire because we thought it might still have electricity in it. But at the edge of what looked like a deep canal, the fence came to an end. The ground had simply dropped into the water here, and the fence along with it.

We crossed over and followed the new channel that cut directly into Dummy's land and headed straight for his pond, going into it lengthwise and forcing an outlet for itself at the other end, then twisting off until it joined up with the river farther on.

You didn't doubt that most of Dummy's fish had been carried off. But those that hadn't been were free to come and go.

Then I caught sight of Dummy. It scared me, seeing him. I motioned to   95 the other fellows, and we all got down.

Dummy was standing at the far side of the pond near where the water was rushing out. He was just standing there, the saddest man I ever saw.

* * *

"I sure do feel sorry for old Dummy, though," my father said at supper a few weeks after. "Mind, the poor devil brought it on himself. But you can't help but be troubled for him."

Dad went on to say George Laycock saw Dummy's wife sitting in the Sportsman's Club with a big Mexican fellow.

"And that ain't the half of it—"

Mother looked up at him sharply and then at me. But I just went on eat-   100
ing like I hadn't heard a thing.

Dad said, "Damn it to hell, Bea, the boy's old enough!"

He'd changed a lot, Dummy had. He was never around any of the men anymore, not if he could help it. No one felt like joking with him either, not since he'd chased Carl Lowe with a two-by-four stud after Carl tipped Dummy's hat off. But the worst of it was that Dummy was missing from work a day or two a week on the average now, and there was some talk of his being laid off.

"The man's going off the deep end," Dad said. "Clear crazy if he don't watch out."

Then on a Sunday afternoon just before my birthday, Dad and I were cleaning the garage. It was a warm, drifty day. You could see the dust hanging in the air. Mother came to the back door and said, "Del, it's for you. I think it's Vern."

I followed Dad in to wash up. When he was through talking, he put the   105
phone down and turned to us.

"It's Dummy," he said. "Did in his wife with a hammer and drowned himself. Vern just heard it in town."

When we got out there, cars were parked all around. The gate to the pasture stood open, and I could see tire marks that led on to the pond.

The screen door was propped ajar with a box, and there was this lean, pock-faced man in slacks and sports shirt and wearing a shoulder holster. He watched Dad and me get out of the car.

"I was his friend," Dad said to the man.

The man shook his head. "Don't care who you are. Clear off unless you   110
got business here."

"Did they find him?" Dad said.

"They're dragging," the man said, and adjusted the fit of his gun.

"All right if we walk down? I knew him pretty well."

The man said, "Take your chances. They chase you off, don't say you wasn't warned."

We went on across the pasture, taking pretty much the same route we   115
had the day we tried fishing. There were motorboats going on the pond, dirty fluffs of exhaust hanging over it. You could see where the high water had cut away the ground and carried off trees and rocks. The two boats had uniformed men in them, and they were going back and forth, one man steering and the other man handling the rope and hooks.

An ambulance waited on the gravel beach where we'd set ourselves to cast for Dummy's bass. Two men in white lounged against the back, smoking cigarettes.

One of the motorboats cut off. We all looked up. The man in back stood up and started heaving on his rope. After a time, an arm came out of the water. It looked like the hooks had gotten Dummy in the side. The arm went back down and then it came out again, along with a bundle of something.

It's not him, I thought. It's something else that has been in there for years.

The man in the front of the boat moved to the back, and together the two men hauled the dripping thing over the side.

I looked at Dad. His face was funny the way it was set.   120

"Women," he said. He said, "That's what the wrong kind of woman can do to you, Jack."

But I don't think Dad really believed it. I think he just didn't know who to blame or what to say.

It seemed to me everything took a bad turn for my father after that. Just like Dummy, he wasn't the same man anymore. That arm coming up and going back down in the water, it was like so long to good times and hello to bad. Because it was nothing but that all the years after Dummy drowned himself in that dark water.

Is that what happens when a friend dies? Bad luck for the pals he left behind?

But as I said, Pearl Harbor and having to move back to his dad's place 125 didn't do my dad one bit of good, either.

The Receptive Reader

1. How do we learn what we come to know about Dummy? Who is the *narrator*—what kind of person tells us the story? What is his role in the story? Is he a major or a minor character? What is his vantage point? What are his limitations?

2. How does the author make Dummy come to life in the early sections of the story? What is Dummy's problem? Can you visualize his physical appearance? How much and what kind of *descriptive detail* do you get?

3. How do Dummy's coworkers treat him, and how are we expected to feel about them?

4. What is the relationship between the narrator's father and Dummy? Who is the true *central character* in the story? Does the story have a hero?

5. As the story unfolds, how much insight do we get into Dummy's personality or character? Do you understand the way Dummy acts about the fish, the pond, the flood? (How important are the fish in the story as a whole?)

6. What role does Dummy's wife play in the story? Is she playing a bit part? Is she expendable?

7. A central *irony* in the story is that Dummy is the character who seems to have urgent things to say to the others, but he is unable to communicate through language. How *does* he communicate? What is he trying to tell the others?

8. What is the role of humor in the story? What is the tone of the references to the father's death in the title, at the beginning, and in the conclusion? Do they color the story as a whole?

The Personal Response

For you, is Dummy an eccentric—an isolated invidivual, a person with special personal problems all of his own? Is he someone "acting peculiar"? Or does his story have a more general human meaning?

The Creative Dimension

Assume Dummy could have been a more articulate or eloquent character. Write an extended suicide note that he might have written to explain himself to his friends.

Alice Munro   *(born 1931)*

Alice Munro is one of several Canadian writers who became widely known in the United States in the 1970s and 1980s. She grew up in southwestern Ontario, and many of her stories take us to rural settings—the countryside and small towns of eastern Canada. During the harsh winters, snowdrifts would curl around the houses "like sleeping whales." Her father was a farmer, and when she writes in the first person as a girl growing up on a farm, it is tempting to equate the "I" telling the story with the author.

Her first collection of short stories, *Dance of the Happy Shades,* was published in 1968 and received the Canadian Governor General's Literary Award. She published her second collection of stories, *Something I've Been Meaning to Tell You,* in 1972. Her novel *Lives of Girls and Women* appeared in 1971.

Munro has a special gift for creating a sense of place. In her story "Thanks for the Ride," she takes us to a town where the signs in Pop's Café (between fly-specked and slightly yellowed cutouts of strawberry sundaes and tomato sandwiches) say things like "Don't ask for information—if we knew anything, we wouldn't be here." In such settings, she places characters who are often undergoing a rite of passage. They may be at a turning point in their lives, moving from childhood to adolescence, or from the confused passions of adolescence to the world of adult responsibilities. Her characters are often people who are still spontaneous and innocent but who encounter people more knowing and perhaps more defeated than they are. Such a story may become a story of **initiation,** as the hero or heroine discovers the limitations, the invisible walls, that mark off his or her world.

In the following story, there is much nostalgic re-creation of the golden world of childhood. But at the center of the story is a young woman at the crossroads. Who is this young woman? What are the contradictory influences that help shape her identity? Viewed as a rite of passage, her story is a passage from what to what? Where is she headed at the end of the story?

The Ave referred to in a song mentioned early in the story is short for the Catholic prayer Ave Maria, or Hail Mary. Orangemen's Day (July 12) is a Protestant holiday dedicated to the memory of William of Orange, who replaced the Catholic James II as king of England in 1689. Judy Canova was a popular entertainer of the 1930s and 1940s.

Boys and Girls   *1968*

*It is difficult to stand forth in one's growing if one
is not permitted to live through the states of one's
unripeness, clumsiness, unreadiness, as well as
one's grace and aptitude.*

                         M. C. RICHARDS

My father was a fox farmer. That is, he raised silver foxes, in pens; and in the fall and early winter, when their fur was prime, he killed them and skinned them and sold their pelts to the Hudson's Bay Company or the Montreal Fur Traders. These companies supplied us with heroic calendars to hang, one on each side of the kitchen door. Against a background of cold blue sky and black pine forests and treacherous northern rivers, plumed adventurers planted the flags of England or of France; magnificent savages bent their backs to the portage.

For several weeks before Christmas, my father worked after supper in the cellar of our house. The cellar was whitewashed, and lit by a hundred-watt bulb over the worktable. My brother Laird and I sat on the top step and watched. My father removed the pelt inside-out from the body of the fox, which looked surprisingly small, mean and ratlike, deprived of its arrogant weight of fur. The naked, slippery bodies were collected in a sack and buried at the dump. One time the hired man, Henry Bailey, had taken a swipe at me with this sack, saying, "Christmas present!" My mother thought that was not funny. In fact she disliked the whole pelting operation—that was what the killing, skinning, and preparation of the furs was called—and wished it did not have to take place in the house. There was the smell. After the pelt had been stretched inside-out on a long board my father scraped away delicately, removing the little clotted webs of blood vessels, the bubbles of fat; the smell of blood and animal fat, with the strong primitive odor of the fox itself, penetrated all parts of the house. I found it reassuringly seasonal, like the smell of oranges and pine needles.

Henry Bailey suffered from bronchial troubles. He would cough and cough until his narrow face turned scarlet, and his light blue, derisive eyes filled up with tears; then he took the lid off the stove, and, standing well back, shot out a great clot of phlegm—hsss—straight into the heart of the flames. We admired him for this performance and for his ability to make his stomach growl at will, and for his laughter, which was full of high whistlings and gurglings and involved the whole faulty machinery of his chest. It was sometimes hard to tell what he was laughing at, and always possible that it might be us.

After we had been sent to bed we could still smell fox and still hear Henry's laugh, but these things, reminders of the warm, safe, brightly lit downstairs world, seemed lost and diminished, floating on the stale cold air upstairs. We were ˄fraid at night in the winter. We were not afraid of *outside* though this was the time of year when snowdrifts curled around our house like sleeping whales and the wind harassed us all night, coming up from the buried fields, the frozen swamp, with its old bugbear chorus of threats and misery. We were afraid of *inside,* the room where we slept. At this time the upstairs of our house was not finished. A brick chimney went up one wall. In the middle of the floor was a square hole, with a wooden railing around it; that was where the stairs came up. On the other side of the stairwell were the things that nobody had any use for any more—a soldiery roll of linoleum, standing on end, a wicker baby carriage, a fern basket, china jugs and basins with cracks in them, a picture of the Battle of Balaclava, very sad to look at. I had told Laird, as soon as he was old enough to understand such things, that bats and skeletons lived over there; whenever a man escaped from the county jail, twenty miles away, I imagined that he had somehow let himself in the window and was hiding behind the linoleum. But we had rules to keep us safe. When the light was on, we were safe as long as we did not step off the square of worn carpet which defined our bedroom-space; when the light was off no place was safe but the beds themselves. I had to turn out the light kneeling on the end of my bed, and stretching as far as I could to reach the cord.

In the dark we lay on our beds, our narrow life rafts, and fixed our eyes   5 on the faint light coming up the stairwell, and sang songs. Laird sang "Jingle Bells," which he would sing any time, whether it was Christmas or not, and I sang "Danny Boy." I loved the sound of my own voice, frail and supplicating, rising in the dark. We could make out the tall frosted shapes of the windows now, gloomy and white. When I came to the part, *When I am dead, as dead I well may be*—a fit of shivering caused not by the cold sheets but by pleasurable emotion almost silenced me. *You'll kneel and say an Ave there above me*—What was an Ave? Every day I forgot to find out.

Laird went straight from singing to sleep. I could hear his long, satisfied, bubbly breaths. Now for the time that remained to me, the most perfectly private and perhaps the best time of the whole day, I arranged myself tightly under the covers and went on with one of the stories I was telling myself from night to night. These stories were about myself, when I had grown a little older; they took place in a world that was recognizably mine, yet one that presented opportunities for courage, boldness and self-sacrifice, as mine never did. I rescued people from a bombed building (it discouraged me that the real war had gone on so far away from Jubilee). I shot two rabid wolves who were menacing the schoolyard (the teachers cowered terrified at my back). I rode a fine horse spiritedly down the main street of Jubilee, acknowledging the townspeople's gratitude for some yet-to-be-worked-out piece of heroism (nobody ever rode a horse there, except King Billy in the Orangemen's Day parade). There was always riding and shooting in these stories, though I had only been on a horse twice—bareback because we did not own a saddle—and the second time I had slid right around and dropped under the horse's feet; it had stepped placidly over me. I really was learning to shoot, but I could not hit anything yet, not even tin cans on fence posts.

Alive, the foxes inhabited a world my father made for them. It was surrounded by a high guard fence, like a medieval town, with a gate that was padlocked at night. Along the streets of this town were ranged large, sturdy pens. Each of them had a real door that a man could go through, a wooden ramp along the wire, for the foxes to run up and down on, and a kennel—something like a clothes chest with airholes—where they slept and stayed in winter and had their young. There were feeding and watering dishes attached to the wire in such a way that they could be emptied and cleaned from the outside. The dishes were made of old tin cans, and the ramps and kennels of odds and ends of old lumber. Everything was tidy and ingenious; my father was tirelessly inventive and his favorite book in the world was *Robinson Crusoe.* He had fitted a tin drum on a wheelbarrow, for bringing water down to the pens. This was my job in summer, when the foxes had to have water twice a day. Between nine and ten o'clock in the morning, and again after supper, I filled the drum at the pump and trundled it down through the barnyard to the pens, where I parked it, and filled my watering can and went along the streets. Laird came too, with his little cream and green gardening can, filled too full and knocking against his legs and slopping water on his canvas shoes. I had the real watering can, my father's, though I could only carry it three-quarters full.

The foxes all had names, which were printed on a tin plate and hung beside their doors. They were not named when they were born, but when they survived the first year's pelting and were added to the breeding stock. Those my father had named were called names like Prince, Bob, Wally and Betty. Those I had named were called Star or Turk, or Maureen or Diana. Laird named one Maud after a hired girl we had when he was little, one Harold after a boy at school, and one Mexico, he did not say why.

Naming them did not make pets out of them, or anything like it. Nobody but my father ever went into the pens, and he had twice had blood-poisoning from bites. When I was bringing them their water they prowled up and down on the paths they had made inside their pens, barking seldom—they saved that for nighttime, when they might get up a chorus of community frenzy—but always watching me, their eyes burning, clear gold, in their pointed, malevolent faces. They were beautiful for their delicate legs and heavy, aristocratic tails and the bright fur sprinkled on dark down their backs—which gave them their name—but especially for their faces, drawn exquisitely sharp in pure hostility, and their golden eyes.

Besides carrying water I helped my father when he cut the long grass,   10 and the lamb's quarter and flowering money-musk, that grew between the pens. He cut with the scythe and I raked into piles. Then he took a pitchfork and threw fresh-cut grass all over the top of the pens, to keep the foxes cooler and shade their coats, which were browned by too much sun. My father did not talk to me unless it was about the job we were doing. In this he was quite different from my mother, who, if she was feeling cheerful, would tell me all sorts of things—the name of a dog she had had when she was a little girl, the names of boys she had gone out with later on when she was grown up, and what certain dresses of hers had looked like—she could not imagine now what had become of them. Whatever thoughts and stories my father had were private, and I was shy of him and would never ask him questions. Nevertheless I worked willingly under his eyes, and with a feeling of pride. One time a feed salesman came down into the pens to talk to him and my father said, "Like to have you meet my new hired man." I turned away and raked furiously, red in the face with pleasure.

"Could of fooled me," said the salesman. "I thought it was only a girl."

After the grass was cut, it seemed suddenly much later in the year. I walked on stubble in the earlier evening, aware of the reddening skies, the entering silences, of fall. When I wheeled the tank out of the gate and put the padlock on, it was almost dark. One night at this time I saw my mother and father standing talking on the little rise of ground we called the gangway, in front of the barn. My father had just come from the meathouse; he had his stiff bloody apron on, and a pail of cut-up meat in his hand.

It was an odd thing to see my mother down at the barn. She did not often come out of the house unless it was to do something—hang out the wash or dig potatoes in the garden. She looked out of place, with her bare lumpy legs, not touched by the sun, her apron still on and damp across the stomach from the supper dishes. Her hair was tied up in a kerchief, wisps of it falling out. She would tie her hair up like this in the morning, saying she did not have time to do it properly, and it would stay tied up all day. It was true, too; she really did not have time. These days our back porch was piled with baskets of peaches and grapes and pears, bought in town, and onions and tomatoes and cucumbers grown at home, all waiting to be made into jelly and jam and preserves, pickles and chili sauce. In the kitchen there was a fire in the stove all day, jars clinked in boiling water, sometimes a cheesecloth bag was strung on a pole between two chairs straining blue-black grape pulp for jelly. I was given jobs to do and I would sit at the table peeling peaches that had been soaked in the hot water, or cutting up onions, my eyes smarting and streaming. As soon as I was done I ran out of the house, trying to get out of earshot before my mother thought of what she wanted me to do next. I hated the hot dark kitchen in summer, the green blinds and the flypapers, the same old oilcloth table and wavy mirror and bumpy linoleum. My mother was too tired and preoccupied to talk to me, she had no heart to tell about the Normal School Graduation Dance; sweat trickled over her face and she was always counting under her breath, pointing at jars, dumping cups of sugar. It seemed to me that work in the house was endless, dreary and peculiarly depressing; work done out of doors, and in my father's service, was ritualistically important.

I wheeled the tank up to the barn, where it was kept, and I heard my mother saying, "Wait till Laird gets a little bigger, then you'll have a real help."

What my father said I did not hear. I was pleased by the way he stood listening, politely as he would to a salesman or a stranger, but with an air of wanting to get on with his real work. I felt my mother had no business down here and I wanted him to feel the same way. What did she mean about Laird? He was no help to anybody. Where was he now? Swinging himself sick on the swing, going around in circles, or trying to catch caterpillars. He never once stayed with me till I was finished.

15

"And then I can use her more in the house," I heard my mother say. She had a dead-quiet, regretful way of talking about me that always made me uneasy. "I just get my back turned and she runs off. It's not like I had a girl in the family at all."

I went and sat on a feed bag in the corner of the barn, not wanting to appear when this conversation was going on. My mother, I felt, was not to be trusted. She was kinder than my father and more easily fooled, but you could not depend on her, and the real reasons for the things she said and did were not to be known. She loved me, and she sat up late at night making a dress of the difficult style I wanted, for me to wear when school started, but she was also my enemy. She was always plotting. She was plotting now to get me to stay in the house more, although she knew I hated it (*because* she knew I hated it) and keep me from working for my father. It seemed to me she would do this simply out of perversity, and to try her power. It did not occur to me that she could be lonely, or jealous. No grown-up could be; they were too fortunate. I sat and kicked my heels monotonously against a feed bag, raising dust, and did not come out till she was gone.

At any rate, I did not expect my father to pay any attention to what she said. Who could imagine Laird doing my work—Laird remembering the padlock and cleaning out the watering dishes with a leaf on the end of a stick, or even wheeling the tank without it tumbling over? It showed how little my mother knew about the way things really were.

I have forgotten to say what the foxes were fed. My father's bloody apron reminded me. They were fed horsemeat. At this time most farmers still kept horses, and when a horse got too old to work, or broke a leg or got down and would not get up, as they sometimes did, the owner would call my father, and he and Henry went out to the farm in the truck. Usually they shot and butchered the horse there, paying the farmer from five to twelve dollars. If they had already too much meat on hand, they would bring the horse back alive, and keep it for a few days or weeks in our stable, until the meat was needed. After the war the farmers were buying tractors and gradually getting rid of horses altogether, so it sometimes happened that we got a good healthy horse, that there was just no use for any more. If this happened in the winter we might keep the horse in our stable till spring, for we had plenty of hay and if there was a lot of snow—and the plow did not always get our road cleared—it was convenient to be able to go to town with a horse and cutter.

The winter I was eleven years old we had two horses in the stable. We   20
did not know what names they had had before, so we called them Mack and Flora. Mack was an old black workhorse, sooty and indifferent. Flora was a sorrel mare, a driver. We took them both out in the cutter. Mack was slow and easy to handle. Flora was given to fits of violent alarm, veering at cars and even at other horses, but we loved her speed and high-stepping, her general air of gallantry and abandon. On Saturdays we went down to the stable and as soon as we opened the door on its cosy, animal-smelling darkness Flora threw up her head, rolled her eyes, whinnied despairingly and pulled herself through a crisis of nerves on the spot. It was not safe to go into her stall; she would kick.

This winter also I began to hear a great deal more on the theme my mother had sounded when she had been talking in front of the barn. I no longer felt safe. It seemed that in the minds of the people around me there was a steady undercurrent of thought, not to be deflected, on this one subject. The word *girl* had formerly seemed to be innocent and unburdened, like the word *child;* now it appeared that it was no such thing. A girl was not, as I had supposed, simply what I was; it was what I had to become. It was a definition, always touched with emphasis, with reproach and disappointment. Also it was a joke on me. Once Laird and I were fighting, and for the first time ever I had to use all my strength against him; even so, he caught and pinned my arm for a moment, really hurting me. Henry saw this, and laughed, saying, "Oh, that there Laird's gonna show you, one of these days!" Laird was getting a lot bigger. But I was getting bigger too.

My grandmother came to stay with us for a few weeks and I heard other things. "Girls don't slam doors like that." "Girls keep their knees together when they sit down." And worse still, when I asked some questions, "That's none of girls' business." I continued to slam the doors and sit as awkwardly as possible, thinking that by such measures I kept myself free.

When spring came, the horses were let out in the barnyard. Mack stood against the barn wall trying to scratch his neck and haunches, but Flora trotted up and down and reared at the fences, clattering her hooves against the rails. Snow drifts dwindled quickly, revealing the hard gray and brown earth, the familiar rise and fall of the ground, plain and bare after the fantastic landscape of winter. There was a great feeling of opening-out, of release. We just wore rubbers now, over our shoes; our feet felt ridiculously light. One Saturday we went out to the stable and found all the doors open, letting in the unaccustomed sunlight and fresh air. Henry was there, just idling around looking at his collection of calendars which were tacked up behind the stalls in a part of the stable my mother had probably never seen.

"Come to say goodbye to your old friend Mack?" Henry said. "Here, you give him a taste of oats." He poured some oats into Laird's cupped hands and Laird went to feed Mack. Mack's teeth were in bad shape. He ate very slowly, patiently shifting the oats around in his mouth, trying to find a stump of a molar to grind it on. "Poor old Mack," said Henry mournfully. "When a horse's teeth's gone, he's gone. That's about the way."

"Are you going to shoot him today?" I said. Mack and Flora had been in the stable so long I had almost forgotten they were going to be shot.   25

Henry didn't answer me. Instead he started to sing in a high, trembly, mocking-sorrowful voice, *Oh, there's no more work, for poor Uncle Ned, he's gone where the good darkies go.* Mack's thick, blackish tongue worked diligently at Laird's hand. I went out before the song was ended and sat down on the gangway.

I had never seen them shoot a horse, but I knew where it was done. Last summer Laird and I had come upon a horse's entrails before they were buried. We had thought it was a big black snake, coiled up in the sun. That was around in the field that ran up beside the barn. I thought that if we went inside the barn, and found a wide crack or a knothole to look through, we would be able to see them do it. It was not something I wanted to see; just the same, if a thing really happened, it was better to see it, and know.

My father came down from the house, carrying the gun.

"What are you doing here?" he said.

"Nothing."

"Go on up and play around the house."

He sent Laird out of the stable. I said to Laird, "Do you want to see them shoot Mack?" and without waiting for an answer led him around to the front door of the barn, opened it carefully, and went in. "Be quiet or they'll hear us," I said. We could hear Henry and my father talking in the stable, then the heavy, shuffling steps of Mack being backed out of his stall.

In the loft it was cold and dark. Thin, crisscrossed beams of sunlight fell through the cracks. The hay was low. It was a rolling country, hills and hollows, slipping under our feet. About four feet up was a beam going around the walls. We piled hay up in one corner and I boosted Laird up and hoisted myself. The beam was not very wide; we crept along it with our hands flat on the barn walls. There were plenty of knotholes, and I found one that gave me the view I wanted—a corner of the barnyard, the gate, part of the field. Laird did not have a knothole and began to complain.

I showed him a widened crack between two boards. "Be quiet and wait. If they hear you you'll get us in trouble."

My father came in sight carrying the gun. Henry was leading Mack by the halter. He dropped it and took out his cigarette papers and tobacco; he rolled cigarettes for my father and himself. While this was going on Mack nosed around in the old, dead grass along the fence. Then my father opened the gate and they took Mack through. Henry led Mack way from the path to a patch of ground and they talked together, not loud enough for us to hear. Mack again began searching for a mouthful of fresh grass, which was not to be found. My father walked away in a straight line, and stopped short at a distance which seemed to suit him. Henry was walking away from Mack too, but sideways, still negligently holding on to the halter. My father raised the gun and Mack looked up as if he had noticed something and my father shot him.

Mack did not collapse at once but swayed, lurched sideways and fell, first on his side; then he rolled over on his back and, amazingly, kicked his legs for a few seconds in the air. At this Henry laughed, as if Mack had done a trick for him. Laird, who had drawn a long, groaning breath of surprise when the shot was fired, said out loud, "He's not dead." And it seemed to me it might be true. But his legs stopped, he rolled on his side again, his muscles quivered and sank. The two men walked over and looked at him in a business-like way; they bent down and examined his forehead where the bullet had gone in, and now I saw his blood on the brown grass.

"Now they just skin him and cut him up," I said. "Let's go." My legs were a little shaky and I jumped gratefully down into the hay. "Now you've seen how they shoot a horse," I said in a congratulatory way, as if I had seen it many times before. "Let's see if any barn cat's had kittens in the hay." Laird jumped. He seemed young and obedient again. Suddenly I remembered how, when he was little, I had brought him into the barn and told him to climb the ladder to the top beam. That was in the spring, too, when the hay was low. I had done it out of a need for excitement, a desire for something to happen so that I could tell about it. He was wearing a little bulky brown

30

35

and white checked coat, made down from one of mine. He went all the way up just as I told him, and sat down on the top beam with the hay far below him on one side, and the barn floor and some old machinery on the other. Then I ran screaming to my father, "Laird's up on the top beam!" My father came, my mother came, my father went up the ladder talking very quietly and brought Laird down under his arm, at which my mother leaned against the ladder and began to cry. They said to me, "Why weren't you watching him?" but nobody ever knew the truth. Laird did not know enough to tell. But whenever I saw the brown and white checked coat hanging in the closet, or at the bottom of the rag bag, which was where it ended up, I felt a weight in my stomach, the sadness of unexorcised guilt.

I looked at Laird, who did not even remember this, and I did not like the look on this thin, winter-pale face. His expression was not frightened or upset, but remote, concentrating. "Listen," I said, in an unusually bright and friendly voice, "you aren't going to tell, are you?"

"No," he said absently.

"Promise."   40

"Promise," he said. I grabbed the hand behind his back to make sure he was not crossing his fingers. Even so, he might have a nightmare; it might come out that way. I decided I had better work hard to get all thoughts of what he had seen out of his mind—which, it seemed to me, could not hold very many things at a time. I got some money I had saved and that afternoon we went into Jubilee and saw a show, with Judy Canova, at which we both laughed a great deal. After that I thought it would be all right.

Two weeks later I knew they were going to shoot Flora. I knew from the night before, when I heard my mother ask if the hay was holding out all right, and my father said, "Well, after tomorrow there'll just be the cow, and we should be able to put her out to grass in another week." So I knew it was Flora's turn in the morning.

This time I didn't think of watching it. That was something to see just one time. I had not thought about it very often since, but sometimes when I was busy, working at school, or standing in front of the mirror combing my hair and wondering if I would be pretty when I grew up, the whole scene would flash into my mind: I would see the easy, practiced way my father raised the gun, and hear Henry laughing when Mack kicked his legs in the air. I did not have any great feeling of horror and opposition, such as a city child might have had; I was too used to seeing the death of animals as a necessity by which we lived. Yet I felt a little ashamed, and there was a new wariness, a sense of holding-off, in my attitude to my father and his work.

It was a fine day, and we were going around the yard picking up tree branches that had been torn off in winter storms. This was something we had been told to do, and also we wanted to use them to make a teepee. We heard Flora whinny, and then my father's voice and Henry's shouting, and we ran down to the barnyard to see what was going on.

The stable door was open. Henry had just brought Flora out, and she had   45
broken away from him. She was running free in the barnyard, from one end to the other. We climbed up on the fence. It was exciting to see her running, whinnying, going up on her hind legs, prancing and threatening like a

horse in a Western movie, an unbroken ranch horse, though she was just an old driver, an old sorrel mare. My father and Henry ran after her and tried to grab the dangling halter. They tried to work her into a corner, and they had almost succeeded when she made a run between them, wild-eyed, and disappeared around the corner of the barn. We heard the rails clatter down as she got over the fence, and Henry yelled, "She's into the field now!"

That meant she was in the long L-shaped field that ran up by the house. If she got around the center, heading towards the lane, the gate was open; the truck had been driven into the field this morning. My father shouted to me, because I was on the other side of the fence, nearest the lane, "Go shut the gate!"

I could run very fast. I ran across the garden, past the tree where our swing was hung, and jumped across a ditch into the lane. There was the open gate. She had not got out, I could not see her up on the road; she must have run to the other end of the field. The gate was heavy. I lifted it out of the gravel and carried it across the roadway. I had it halfway across when she came in sight, galloping straight toward me. There was just time to get the chain on. Laird came scrambling through the ditch to help me.

Instead of shutting the gate, I opened it as wide as I could. I did not make any decision to do this, it was just what I did. Flora never slowed down; she galloped straight past me, and Laird jumped up and down, yelling, "Shut it, shut it!" even after it was too late. My father and Henry appeared in the field a moment too late to see what I had done. They only saw Flora heading for the township road. They would think I had not got there in time.

They did not waste any time asking about it. They went back to the barn and got the gun and the knives they used, and put these in the truck; then they turned the truck around and came bouncing up the field toward us. Laird called to them, "Let me go too, let me go too!" and Henry stopped the truck and they took him in. I shut the gate after they were all gone.

I supposed Laird would tell. I wondered what would happen to me. I   50
had never disobeyed my father before, and I could not understand why I had done it. Flora would not really get away. They would catch up with her in the truck. Or if they did not catch her this morning somebody would see her and telephone us this afternoon or tomorrow. There was no wild country here for her to run to, only farms. What was more, my father had paid for her, we needed the meat to feed the foxes, we needed the foxes to make our living. All I had done was make more work for my father who worked hard enough already. And when my father found out about it he was not going to trust me any more; he would know that I was not entirely on his side. I was on Flora's side, and that made me no use to anybody, not even to her. Just the same, I did not regret it; when she came running at me and I held the gate open, that was the only thing I could do.

I went back to the house, and my mother said, "What's all the commotion?" I told her that Flora had kicked down the fence and got away. "Your poor father," she said, "now he'll have to go chasing over the countryside. Well, there isn't any use planning dinner before one." She put up the ironing board. I wanted to tell her, but thought better of it and went upstairs and sat on my bed.

Lately I had been trying to make my part of the room fancy, spreading the bed with old lace curtains, and fixing myself a dressing table with some leftovers of cretonne for a skirt. I planned to put up some kind of barricade between my bed and Laird's, to keep my section separate from his. In the sunlight, the lace curtains were just dusty rags. We did not sing at night any more. One night when I was singing Laird said, "You sound silly," and I went right on but the next night I did not start. There was not so much need to anyway, we were no longer afraid. We knew it was just old furniture over there, old jumble and confusion. We did not keep to the rules. I still stayed awake after Laird was asleep and told myself stories, but even in these stories something different was happening, mysterious alterations took place. A story might start off in the old way, with a spectacular danger, a fire or wild animals, and for a while I might rescue people; then things would change around, and instead, somebody would be rescuing me. It might be a boy from our class at school, or even Mr. Campbell, our teacher, who tickled girls under the arms. And at this point the story concerned itself at great length with what I looked like—how long my hair was, and what kind of dress I had on; by the time I had these details worked out the real excitement of the story was lost.

It was later than one o'clock when the truck came back. The tarpaulin was over the back, which meant there was meat in it. My mother had to heat dinner up all over again. Henry and my father had changed from their bloody overalls into ordinary working overalls in the barn, and they washed their arms and necks and faces at the sink, and splashed water on their hair and combed it. Laird lifted his arm to show off a streak of blood. "We shot old Flora," he said, "and cut her up in fifty pieces."

"Well I don't want to hear about it," my mother said. "And don't come to my table like that."

My father made him go and wash the blood off.   55

We sat down and my father said grace and Henry pasted his chewing gum on the end of his fork, the way he always did; when he took it off he would have us admire the pattern. We began to pass the bowls of steaming, overcooked vegetables. Laird looked across the table at me and said proudly, distinctly, "Anyway it was her fault Flora got away."

"What?" my father said.

"She could of shut the gate and she didn't. She just open' it up and Flora run out."

"Is that right?" my father said.

Everybody at the table was looking at me. I nodded, swallowing food   60
with great difficulty. To my shame, tears flooded my eyes.

My father made a curt sound of disgust. "What did you do that for?"

I did not answer. I put down my fork and waited to be sent from the table, still not looking up.

But this did not happen. For some time nobody said anything, then Laird said matter-of-factly, "She's crying."

"Never mind," my father said. He spoke with resignation, even good humor, the words which absolved and dismissed me for good. "She's only a girl," he said.

I didn't protest that, even in my heart. Maybe it was true.   65

The Receptive Reader

1. What about the physical *setting* of this story is most real? What striking images or imaginative comparisons help bring the setting to life? How would you expect the physical world of the story to influence a person's character? How do you think watching the work with the foxes and horses would affect a person's outlook?

2. Like many adolescents, the girl in this story faces a *conflict* between different models that she might choose to follow. What kind of role model is her father? How would you describe the kind of person or temperament? How does she feel about his work? What scenes or incidents do most to illuminate her relationship with her father?

3. What kind of role model is the mother? What is the girl's relationship with the mother and what she stands for? What makes the father and the mother in this story *polar opposites?* What details for you most strikingly bring the opposition between the father's and the mother's influence into focus?

4. The setting in which people grow up often sets limits to what they can be or become. What are these limits in this story? How do we become aware of them? Can you point to a key phrase or to a *thematic passage*—spelling out a key idea acted out in the story as a whole?

5. The story reaches its *climax,* or high point, when Flora, the horse about to be shot, gets away. Why does the girl relate to Flora differently than she did to Mack, the other horse in the story? What is the girl's role in the climactic episode? Why does she do what she does? How does her behavior here change the way she thinks of her father and of herself?

6. What is the role of the *minor characters* in this story? What are the roles of Henry and of the grandmother? In this story of growing up, how does the role of Laird, the girl's younger brother, change? What facets of the girl's character are shown in her relationship with her brother?

7. If you read this story as a story of *initiation,* of passing from one stage to another, how would you sum up the girl's starting point and the stage she reaches at the end of the story?

The Personal Response

Do you think of the girl as defeated by the end of the story? What do you think are her prospects for the future? What facets of her character would you consider in making a prediction?

The Creative Dimension

In a **monologue,** one person is talking without interruption by others. Write a monologue in which you imagine yourself in the place of one of the characters in the story. From that person's point of view, look at one of the *other* characters in the story. For instance, look at

- the younger brother as seen through the eyes of the girl (or vice versa)
- the father as seen through the eyes of the girl
- the girl as seen through the eyes of her mother
- the mother as seen through the eyes of her daughter

Compare and contrast Joyce's "Araby" and Munro's "Boys and Girls" as stories of initiation. How do the two authors treat the theme of growing up?

Louise Erdrich   *(born 1954)*

History has a way of intruding upon the present.
                                            DEE BROWN

Louise Erdrich ranks high among widely published writers who in recent decades have introduced a new generation to Native American life. She has been praised for "conveying unflinchingly the funkiness, humor, and great unspoken sadness of the Indian reservations, and a people exiled to a no-man's-land between two worlds" (Peter Matthiessen). In her prize-winning poems and stories, she writes with great empathy about people who were stripped of their way of life, their religion, and their self-respect and who experienced the failures of forced assimilation.

Erdrich was born in Little Falls, Minnesota, of Chippewa and German-American descent. She grew up on a reservation in North Dakota where her grandfather had been tribal chair and where her father was a teacher. She studied at Dartmouth College and Johns Hopkins University. She has been actively involved in Native American issues, ranging from the litigation of land claims to the effects of alcoholism on the unborn.

In her widely read *Love Medicine* (1984), Erdrich wove together stories about the lives of two reservation families. In the following selection from the book, she tells the story of two brothers, with the younger brother trying to understand and help an older brother who went to Vietnam and was never the same after his return. Erdrich continued writing the history of the fictional families in these stories in *Beet Queen* (1986) and *Tracks* (1988).

The Red Convertible   *1984*
Lyman Lamartine

I was the first one to drive a convertible on my reservation. And of course it was red, a red Olds. I owned that car along with my brother Henry Junior. We owned it together until his boots filled with water on a windy night and he bought out my share. Now Henry owns the whole car, and his younger brother Lyman (that's myself), Lyman walks everywhere he goes.

How did I earn enough money to buy my share in the first place? My one talent was I could always make money. I had a touch for it, unusual in a Chippewa. From the first I was different that way, and everyone recognized it. I was the only kid they let in the American Legion Hall to shine shoes, for example, and one Christmas I sold spiritual bouquets for the mission door to door. The nuns let me keep a percentage. Once I started, it seemed the more money I made the easier the money came. Everyone encouraged it. When I was fifteen I got a job washing dishes at the Joliet Café, and that was where my first big break happened.

It wasn't long before I was promoted to busing tables, and then the short-order cook quit and I was hired to take her place. No sooner than you know it I was managing the Joliet. The rest is history. I went on managing. I soon became part owner, and of course there was no stopping me then. It wasn't long before the whole thing was mine.

After I'd owned the Joliet for one year, it blew over in the worst tornado ever seen around here. The whole operation was smashed to bits. A total loss. The fryalator was up in a tree, the grill torn in half like it was paper. I was only sixteen. I had it all in my mother's name, and I lost it quick, but before I lost it I had every one of my relatives, and their relatives, to dinner, and I also bought that red Olds I mentioned, along with Henry.

The first time we saw it! I'll tell you when we first saw it. We had gotten   5
a ride up to Winnipeg, and both of us had money. Don't ask me why, because we never mentioned a car or anything, we just had all our money. Mine was cash, a big bankroll from the Joliet's insurance. Henry had two checks—a week's extra pay for being laid off, and his regular check from the Jewel Bearing Plant.

We were walking down Portage anyway, seeing the sights, when we saw it. There it was, parked, large as life. Really as *if* it was alive. I thought of the word *repose,* because the car wasn't simply stopped, parked, or whatever. That car reposed, calm and gleaming, a FOR SALE sign in its left front window. Then, before we had thought it over at all, the car belonged to us and our pockets were empty. We had just enough money for gas back home.

We went places in that car, me and Henry. We took off driving all one whole summer. We started off toward the Little Knife River and Mandaree in Fort Berthold and then we found ourselves down in Wakpala somehow, and then suddenly we were over in Montana on the Rocky Boy, and yet the summer was not even half over. Some people hang on to details when they travel, but we didn't let them bother us and just lived our everyday lives here to there.

I do remember this one place with willows. I remember I laid under those trees and it was comfortable. So comfortable. The branches bent down all around me like a tent or a stable. And quiet, it was quiet, even though there was a powwow close enough so I could see it going on. The air was not too still, not too windy either. When the dust rises up and hangs in the air around the dancers like that, I feel good. Henry was asleep with his arms thrown wide. Later on, he woke up and we started driving again. We were somewhere in Montana, or maybe on the Blood Reserve—it could have been anywhere. Anyway it was where we met the girl.

All her hair was in buns around her ears, that's the first thing I noticed about her. She was posed alongside the road with her arm out, so we stopped. That girl was short, so short her lumber shirt looked comical on her, like a nightgown. She had jeans on and fancy moccasins and she carried a little suitcase.

"Hop on in," says Henry. So she climbs in between us.   10

"We'll take you home," I says. "Where do you live?"

"Chicken," she says.

"Where the hell's that?" I ask her.

"Alaska."

"Okay," says Henry, and we drive.   15

We got up there and never wanted to leave. The sun doesn't truly set there in summer, and the night is more a soft dusk. You might doze off, sometimes, but before you know it you're up again, like an animal in nature. You never feel like you have to sleep hard or put away the world. And things would grow up there. One day just dirt or moss, the next day flowers and long grass. The girl's name was Susy. Her family really took to us. They fed us and put us up. We had our own tent to live in by their house, and the kids would be in and out of there all day and night. They couldn't get over me and Henry being brothers, we looked so different. We told them we knew we had the same mother, anyway.

One night Susy came in to visit us. We sat around in the tent talking of this and that. The season was changing. It was getting darker by that time, and the cold was even getting just a little mean. I told her it was time for us to go. She stood up on a chair.

"You never seen my hair," Susy said.

That was true. She was standing on a chair, but still, when she unclipped her buns the hair reached all the way to the ground. Our eyes opened. You couldn't tell how much hair she had when it was rolled up so neatly. Then my brother Henry did something funny. He went up to the chair and said, "Jump on my shoulders." So she did that, and her hair reached down past his waist, and he started twirling, this way and that, so her hair was flung out from side to side.

"I always wondered what it was like to have long pretty hair," Henry   20
says. Well we laughed. It was a funny sight, the way he did it. The next morning we got up and took leave of those people.

On to greener pastures, as they say. It was down through Spokane and across Idaho then Montana and very soon we were racing the weather right along under the Canadian border through Columbus, Des Lacs, and then we were in Bottineau County and soon home. We'd made most of the trip, that summer, without putting up the car hood at all. We got home just in time, it turned out, for the army to remember Henry had signed up to join it.

I don't wonder that the army was so glad to get my brother that they turned him into a Marine. He was built like a brick outhouse anyway. We liked to tease him that they really wanted him for his Indian nose. He had a nose big and sharp as a hatchet, like the nose on Red Tomahawk, the Indian who killed Sitting Bull, whose profile is on signs all along the North Dakota highways. Henry went off to training camp, came home once during Christmas, then the next thing you know we got an overseas letter from him. It was 1970, and he said he was stationed up in the northern hill country. Whereabouts I did not know. He wasn't such a hot letter writer, and only got off two before the enemy caught him. I could never keep it straight, which direction those good Vietnam soldiers were from.

I wrote him back several times, even though I didn't know if those letters would get through. I kept him informed all about the car. Most of the time I had it up on blocks in the yard or half taken apart, because that long trip did a hard job on it under the hood.

I always had good luck with numbers, and never worried about the draft myself. I never even had to think about what my number was. But Henry was never lucky in the same way as me. It was at least three years before Henry came home. By then I guess the whole war was solved in the government's mind, but for him it would keep on going. In those years I'd put his car into almost perfect shape. I always thought of it as his car while he was gone, even though when he left he said, "Now it's yours," and threw me his key.

"Thanks for the extra key," I'd said. "I'll put it up in your drawer just in case I need it." He laughed.

When he came home, though, Henry was very different, and I'll say this: the change was no good. You could hardly expect him to change for the better, I know. But he was quiet, so quiet, and never comfortable sitting still anywhere but always up and moving around. I thought back to times we'd sat still for whole afternoons, never moving a muscle, just shifting our weight along the ground, talking to whoever sat with us, watching things. He'd always had a joke, then, too, and now you couldn't get him to laugh, or when he did it was more the sound of a man choking, a sound that stopped up the throats of other people around him. They got to leaving him alone most of the time, and I didn't blame them. It was a fact: Henry was jumpy and mean.

I'd bought a color TV set for my mom and the rest of us while Henry was away. Money still came very easy. I was sorry I'd ever bought it though, because of Henry. I was also sorry I'd bought color, because with black-and-white the pictures seem older and farther away. But what are you going to do? He sat in front of it, watching it, and that was the only time he was completely still. But it was the kind of stillness that you see in a rabbit when it freezes and before it will bolt. He was not easy. He sat in his chair gripping the armrests with all his might, as if the chair itself was moving at a high speed and if he let go at all he would rocket forward and maybe crash right through the set.

Once I was in the room watching TV with Henry and I heard his teeth click at something. I looked over, and he'd bitten through his lip. Blood was going down his chin. I tell you right then I wanted to smash that tube to pieces. I went over to it but Henry must have known what I was up to. He rushed from his chair and shoved me out of the way, against the wall. I told myself he didn't know what he was doing.

My mom came in, turned the set off real quiet, and told us she had made something for supper. So we went and sat down. There was still blood going down Henry's chin, but he didn't notice it and no one said anything, even though every time he took a bite of his bread his blood fell onto it until he was eating his own blood mixed in with the food.

*   *   *

While Henry was not around we talked about what was going to happen   30
to him. There were no Indian doctors on the reservation, and my mom
couldn't come around to trusting the old man, Moses Pillager, because he
courted her long ago and was jealous of her husbands. He might take
revenge through her son. We were afraid that if we brought Henry to a regular hospital they would keep him.

"They don't fix them in those places," Mom said; "they just give them
drugs."

"We wouldn't get him there in the first place," I agreed, "so let's just forget about it."

Then I thought about the car.

Henry had not even looked at the car since he'd gotten home, though
like I said, it was in tip-top condition and ready to drive. I thought the car
might bring the old Henry back somehow. So I bided my time and waited
for my chance to interest him in the vehicle.

One night Henry was off somewhere. I took myself a hammer. I went out   35
to that car and I did a number on its underside. Whacked it up. Bent the tail
pipe double. Ripped the muffler loose. By the time I was done with the car
it looked worse than any typical Indian car that has been driven all its life
on reservation roads, which they always say are like government promises—full of holes. It just about hurt me, I'll tell you that! I threw dirt in the
carburetor and I ripped all the electric tape off the seats. I made it look just
as beat up as I could. Then I sat back and waited for Henry to find it.

Still, it took him over a month. That was all right, because it was just getting warm enough, not melting, but warm enough to work outside.

"Lyman," he says, walking in one day, "that red car looks like shit."

"Well it's old," I says. "You got to expect that."

"No way!" says Henry. "That car's a classic! But you went and ran the piss
right out of it, Lyman, and you know it don't deserve that. I kept that car in
A-one shape. You don't remember. You're too young. But when I left, that
car was running like a watch. Now I don't even know if I can get it to start
again, let alone get it anywhere near its old condition."

"Well you try," I said, like I was getting mad, "but I say it's a piece of   40
junk."

Then I walked out before he could realize I knew he'd strung together
more than six words at once.

After that I thought he'd freeze himself to death working on that car. He
was out there all day, and at night he rigged up a little lamp, ran a cord out
the window, and had himself some light to see by while he worked. He was
better than he had been before, but that's still not saying much. It was easier
for him to do the things the rest of us did. He ate more slowly and didn't jump
up and down during the meal to get this or that or look out the window. I
put my hand in the back of the TV set, I admit, and fiddled around with it
good, so that it was almost impossible now to get a clear picture. He didn't
look at it very often anyway. He was always out with that car or going off
to get parts for it. By the time it was really melting outside, he had it fixed.

I had been feeling down in the dumps about Henry around this time. We had always been together before. Henry and Lyman. But he was such a loner now that I didn't know how to take it. So I jumped at the chance one day when Henry seemed friendly. It's not that he smiled or anything. He just said, "Let's take that old shitbox for a spin." Just the way he said it made me think he could be coming around.

We went out to the car. It was spring. The sun was shining very bright. My only sister, Bonita, who was just eleven years old, came out and made us stand together for a picture. Henry leaned his elbow on the red car's windshield, and he took his other arm and put it over my shoulder, very carefully, as though it was heavy for him to lift and he didn't want to bring the weight down all at once.

"Smile." Bonita said, and he did.

45

That picture. I never look at it anymore. A few months ago, I don't know why, I got his picture out and tacked it on the wall. I felt good about Henry at the time, close to him. I felt good having his picture on the wall, until one night when I was looking at television. I was a little drunk and stoned. I looked up at the wall and Henry was staring at me. I don't know what it was, but his smile had changed, or maybe it was gone. All I know is I couldn't stay in the same room with that picture. I was shaking. I got up, closed the door, and went into the kitchen. A little later my friend Ray came over and we both went back into that room. We put the picture in a brown bag, folded the bag over and over tightly, then put it way back in a closet.

I still see that picture now, as if it tugs at me, whenever I pass that closet door. The picture is very clear in my mind. It was so sunny that day Henry had to squint against the glare. Or maybe the camera Bonita held flashed like a mirror, blinding him, before she snapped the picture. My face is right out in the sun, big and round. But he might have drawn back, because the shadows on his face are deep as holes. There are two shadows curved like little hooks around the ends of his smile, as if to frame it and try to keep it there—that one, first smile that looked like it might have hurt his face. He has his field jacket on and the worn-in clothes he'd come back in and kept wearing ever since. After Bonita took the picture, she went into the house and we got into the car. There was a full cooler in the trunk. We started off, east, toward Pembina and the Red River because Henry said he wanted to see the high water.

The trip over there was beautiful. When everything starts changing, drying up, clearing off, you feel like your whole life is starting. Henry felt it, too. The top was down and the car hummed like a top. He'd really put it back in shape, even the tape on the seats was very carefully put down and glued back in layers. It's not that he smiled again or even joked, but his face looked to me as if it was clear, more peaceful. It looked as though he wasn't thinking of anything in particular except the bare fields and windbreaks and houses we were passing.

The river was high and full of winter trash when we got there. The sun was still out, but it was colder by the river. There were still little clumps of dirty snow here and there on the banks. The water hadn't gone over the banks yet, but it would, you could tell. It was just at its limit, hard swollen, glossy like an old gray scar. We made ourselves a fire, and we sat down and watched the current go. As I watched it I felt something squeezing inside me and tightening and trying to let go all at the same time. I knew I was not just feeling it myself; I knew I was feeling what Henry was going through at that moment. Except that I couldn't stand it, the closing and opening. I jumped to my feet. I took Henry by the shoulders and I started shaking him. "Wake up," I says, "wake up, wake up, wake up!" I didn't know what had come over me. I sat down beside him again.

His face was totally white and hard. Then it broke, like stones break all   50
of a sudden when water boils up inside them.

"I know it," he says. "I know it. I can't help it. It's no use."

We start talking. He said he knew what I'd done with the car. It was obvious it had been whacked out of shape and not just neglected. He said he wanted to give the car to me for good now, it was no use. He said he'd fixed it just to give it back and I should take it.

"No way," I says. "I don't want it."

"That's okay," he says, "you take it."

"I don't want it, though," I says back to him, and then to emphasize, just   55
to emphasize, you understand, I touch his shoulder. He slaps my hand off.

"Take that car," he says.

"No," I say. "Make me," I say, and then he grabs my jacket and rips the arm loose. That jacket is a class act, suede with tags and zippers. I push Henry backwards, off the log. He jumps up and bowls me over. We go down in a clinch and come up swinging hard, for all we're worth, with our fists. He socks my jaw so hard I feel like it swings loose. Then I'm at his rib cage and land a good one under his chin so his head snaps back. He's dazzled. He looks at me and I look at him and then his eyes are full of tears and blood and at first I think he's crying. But no, he's laughing. "Ha! Ha!" he says. "Ha! Ha! Take good care of it."

"Okay," I says. "Okay, no problem. Ha! Ha!"

I can't help it, and I start laughing, too. My face feels fat and strange, and after a while I get a beer from the cooler in the trunk, and when I hand it to Henry he takes his shirt and wipes my germs off. "Hoof-and-mouth disease," he says. For some reason this cracks me up, and so we're really laughing for a while, and then we drink all the rest of the beers one by one and throw them in the river and see how far, how fast, the current takes them before they fill up and sink.

"You want to go on back?" I ask after a while. "Maybe we could snag a   60
couple nice Kashpaw girls."

He says nothing. But I can tell his mood is turning again.

"They're all crazy, the girls up here, every damn one of them."

"You're crazy too," I say, to jolly him up. "Crazy Lamartine boys!"

He looks as though he will take this wrong at first. His face twists, then clears, and he jumps up on his feet. "That's right!" he says. "Crazier 'n hell. Crazy Indians!"

I think it's the old Henry again. He throws off his jacket and starts spring-   65
ing his legs up from the knees like a fancy dancer. He's down doing something

between a grass dance and a bunny hop, no kind of dance I ever saw before, but neither has anyone else on all this green growing earth. He's wild. He wants to pitch whoopee! He's up and at me and all over. All this time I'm laughing so hard, so hard my belly is getting tied up in a knot.

"Got to cool me off!" he shouts all of a sudden. Then he runs over to the river and jumps in.

There's boards and other things in the current. It's so high. No sound comes from the river after the splash he makes, so I run right over. I look around. It's getting dark. I see he's halfway across the water already, and I know he didn't swim there but the current took him. It's far. I hear his voice, though, very clearly across it.

"My boots are filling," he says.

He says this in a normal voice, like he just noticed and he doesn't know what to think of it. Then he's gone. A branch comes by. Another branch. And I go in.

By the time I get out of the river, off the snag I pulled myself onto, the sun is down. I walk back to the car, turn on the high beams, and drive it up the bank. I put it in first gear and then I take my foot off the clutch. I get out, close the door, and watch it plow softly into the water. The headlights reach in as they go down, searching, still lighted even after the water swirls over the back end. I wait. The wires short out. It is all finally dark. And then there is only the water, the sound of it going and running and going and running and running. 70

The Receptive Reader

1. What kind of person is the brother telling the story? What is his relationship to his older brother? What details or incidents do most to help you imagine or understand the narrator?

2. What happened to Henry in the army? How do you find out? Why do you think you get the clues to what happened to him in bits and pieces?

3. How does the car come to play a central role in the story? Does it have a symbolic meaning?

4. What contribution, if any, do minor characters make to this story?

5. What is happening at the end of the story? Were you puzzled by the way the two brothers act? Why do the two brothers fight? What are their motives?

6. Does this story tend to confirm or to counteract prejudices or preconceptions about reservation life?

The Personal Response

Would you have acted differently than the younger brother in the story? Do you think he understood his older brother?

The Creative Dimension

This is a story in which much that is important remains unsaid. Imagine that a counselor or close friend could have gotten the older brother to talk more freely about his thoughts and feelings. What might he have said?

Making Connections—For Discussion or Writing

Do you find the central characters in the stories by Carver, Munro, and Erdrich puzzling or easy to understand? Do they seem complicated or relatively simple to you? Is one of them more complex than the others?

WRITING ABOUT LITERATURE

3   Tracing Character (Focus on Prewriting)

The Writing Workshop   A paper about a central character may show us a character as a complex human being. It may trace the growth of a character. It may center on the interaction of two or more characters in a story. In working on your paper, imagine yourself in a writing workshop situation. In a workshop format, you take your paper through overlapping stages in the writing process. You make time for **prewriting** activities that lead up to your first draft: note taking, pushing toward a thesis, structuring your paper.

Running Commentary   The following is part of a running commentary on the Munro story. These reading notes seize on striking details; they record verbatim quotations that could be useful in helping get a reader into the prevailing mood of the story. These notes already include much material related to the girl narrator's search for identity:

Senses predominate. Penetrating smell of foxes, dead flesh, blood. Beauty of live foxes contrasts with scraping particles of fat and blood from the inside of the dead skin. Naked slippery dead carcasses look "surprisingly small, mean, and ratlike." When alive, foxes have faces "drawn exquisitely sharp in pure hostility" and "golden eyes."

Death and blood are taken rather casually by the men. There is something alarming about the coldness of the term "fox farm." There is a hierarchy of value? Horses are killed to feed foxes, who provide furs and money. Life is seen entirely through the eyes of the young girl telling the story, naturally inclined toward "male activities." The work done "in her father's service" was important like a ritual. Her little brother tags timidly along, obeying her.

The narrator is treated like a boy and acts like one, and she is introduced by her father as "the new hired man." The salesman responds that he thought it was "only a girl." The girl wants to possess the characteristic masculine strengths and virtues.

The mother is constantly invoking the female stereotype, implying that when her daugher helps the father with "male" duties, the help is not real. She is eager to get her daughter into the house to help with girl work. ("It is not like I had a girl in the family at all.")

Pushing Toward a Thesis   Early in your note taking, the central question is likely to emerge: In the world of Munro's story, what does it mean to be a girl? What does it mean to be a boy? Some people easily take to the role society has sketched out for them. They fit the mold. But the girl in this story is an independent, adventurous, imaginative spirit. The following paragraph sums up what might become the unifying overall idea of a paper:

> Children search for their identities and constantly run up against the wall of gender stereotypes to which they are made to conform. *The girl in the story reluctantly conforms to the stereotypes that will deny a part of her personality.* In her innocence, the girl in the story identifies with the outdoor work of her father, "red in the face with pleasure" when her father seems to praise and accept her as a co-worker. Her daydreams are about heroic rescues in which she plays the hero's part. However, her mother and grandmother conspire to drive home what is expected of a girl. It seems that after a last act of futile rebellion the invisible walls of the predestined gender roles will close in on her.

Structuring the Paper   How will your paper be laid out? Since this is a story of initiation, your paper as a whole might follow the pattern of a spiritual journey. You may move from the girl's innocent identification with the father's work and *male* values to the weight of traditional stereotypes about the *female* role You prepare a **scratch outline** like the following:

> —spirited imaginative character—the prank played on kid brother, leadership etc. daydreams: "courage, boldness, and self-sacrifice"
> —the lure of the father's job
> —the mother and grandmother as voices of the stereotype
> —the climactic rebellion
> —pivotal role of younger brother—he will overtake her by virtue of the mere fact of being born male; he has the advantage

Look at the way this kind of prewriting fed into a first draft of a paper. What use did the student make of her prewriting? How nearly finished is this paper? What suggestions or advice would you give the student writer when she is ready to prepare a final draft?

Sample First Draft

A Story of Initiation

Alice Munro's story "Boys and Girls" introduces us to a spirited, imaginative young girl. She plays scary pranks on her kid brother, making him climb to the top beam of the barn. She also experiences the fears of childhood, as she and the brother try to mark off a "safe" zone among the scary shadows of the unfinished loft where they sleep, singing "Jingle Bells" and "Danny Boy" to ward off fear of the dark. Above all, she admires her father, who runs a fox farm for the pelts of the animals. As her father's helper and Girl Friday, she is used to the penetrating smell of the foxes. She responds to the beauty of the live foxes who have faces "drawn exquisitely sharp in pure hostility" and "golden eyes." She is just as used to the naked slippery dead carcasses that look "surprisingly small, mean, and ratlike." However, in the course of the story, the girl has to leave this world of her childhood behind, growing up to discover her true destined role in a "man's world."

Children search for their identities and constantly run up against the wall of gender stereotypes to which they are made to conform. The girl in the story reluctantly conforms to the stereotypes that will deny a part of her personality. In her innocence, the girl in the story identifies with the outdoor work of her father, "red in the face with pleasure" when her father seems to praise and accept her as a co-worker. Her daydreams are about heroic rescues in which she plays the hero's part. However, her mother and grandmother conspire to drive home what is expected of a girl. It seems that after a last act of futile rebellion the invisible walls of the predestined gender roles will close in on her.

Life is seen entirely through the eyes of the young girl telling the story. As a child, she seems naturally inclined toward "male activities." The work done "in her father's service" is important to her like a ritual. (Her little brother tags timidly along, obeying her.) The narrator is treated like a boy and acts like one, and she is introduced by her father as "the new hired man." The salesman he is talking to responds that he thought it was "only a girl," a hint of the disillusionment that lies ahead. In her innocence, the narrator values and espouses those traditionally male qualities admired by the world, and she strives to cultivate those strengths within herself, as yet unburdened by the weight of stereotypes.

However, the mother increasingly represents the weight of the adult world, invoking the female stereotype, implying that when her daughter helps the father with "male" duties, the help is not real. The mother is eager to get her daughter into the house to help with girl work. ("It is not like I had a girl in the family at all.") The girl "hated the hot dark kitchen in summer"; work in the house was endless, dreary, and "particularly depressing."

The horses that are kept to provide meat for the foxes give an interesting twist to the gender issue, because there are a male and a female. The male, Mack, is slow and docile, while the female, Flora, is spirited, temperamental, and rebellious. When Flora's turn comes to be killed and butchered to feed the foxes, the narrator, in a dramatic act of rebellion against the way things are, lets her escape through the open gate that her father asks her to close. In trying to free the horse, she is making a last symbolic attempt to free herself. But she fails, both literally and symbolically. Flora is free for only a few hours longer. And the narrator, who is "only a girl," cannot free herself from the stereotype society has imposed on her, except for a few brief childhood years.

Questions

What, to you, are the strengths and possible weaknesses of this paper? How clear is the overall pattern of the paper? In her final draft, what details or what features do you think the student should add to round out the character?

4 Plot

The Chain of Events

There has to be a tension, a sense that something is imminent, that certain things are in relentless motion, or else, most often, there simply won't be a story.

RAYMOND CARVER

FOCUS ON PLOT

A traditional short story puts characters in a setting and then sets them in motion. You focus on **plot** when you trace what happens as a result. The plot is the story line, the sequence of actions or events that gives direction to the story as a whole. Frank O'Connor's classic "Guests of the Nation" takes us to the war between the Irish and the English that led to the founding of the Irish Free State in 1922, after centuries of English rule. We spend our time with two young soldiers in the Irish Republican Army who are guarding two English prisoners. Security is lax, since with their English accents and khaki tunics the prisoners would not get far if they had a mind to escape. The foursome play cards, argue about capitalism and communism, about priests and love of country. One of the Englishmen becomes a helpmate to the lady of the house, doing chores and running errands for her. However, the grim realities of the war catch up with us: the English have executed Irish rebels, and the two English hostages will be shot in retaliation.

Where are we as readers in this story? Maybe we can keep cool and refuse to become involved. It's not *our* war; the hostages have long been dead and buried. More likely, however, we will be drawn into the story. When word comes down from headquarters to kill the hostages, we are likely to say: "No, you cannot do that!" We are likely to argue and agonize and prevaricate. The chances are we will finally do as told; and, like the narrator in the story, we will never again be quite the same. We will not know what to say when the lady of the house asks: "What did ye do with them?"

77

When tracing the plot of a story, you ask yourself: "How does the story take shape? What sets it in motion? What keeps it going? What brings it to a satisfying close?" Look for features like the following when thinking about plot:

The Unstable Situation   Look for a situation that has in it the seeds of a story. Are there signs of an agenda to be attended to, a score to be settled? The initial setting up, or **exposition,** creates a situation that has the seed of further developments in it. Think about where the story might be headed. Perhaps a new element disturbs the status quo: a stranger arrives; an outsider marries into the family; a distant relative comes close. As in the O'Connor story, a looming threat that everyone has pushed out of mind may finally overtake the people in the story.

The Potential of Character   Size up characters for what they might do. What actions do they seem capable of; what events might they precipitate? Their motives—their motivation—is their potential for action: "what sets them in motion." An accident-prone character is "an accident waiting to happen." A character with seething resentment is a time bomb waiting to go off. A lonely character may take steps to make human contact, with sad and funny results.

The Looming Conflict   Look for sources of conflict. Are rivals in love or ambition likely to face off like the **protagonist** (the first or chief contender) and the **antagonist** (the worthy opponent) in ancient Greek drama? Or is a conflict simmering that will be treated in a lower key? People may find themselves at cross-purposes without articulating loud grievances. Mason's "Shiloh" develops a conflict between the opposed, diverging needs of a couple; the conflict plays itself out without fireworks or fanfare.

External/Internal Action   Keep your eye on the central action or progression of events. Does the story line focus on **external** physical action—quarrels, journeys, acts of defiance, suicides? The characters may have mountains to scale or pursuers to evade. Or is the action of the story mainly **internal,** psychological—as in much modern fiction? A character may experience a change in perspective, learning something about others. A character may reach a moment of self-realization, facing up to something important about himself or herself.

Tracking the Narrative   Do not expect stories to follow a standard formula. With a **loose** narrative structure, events may come to pass in leisurely fashion, in chronological order. Things just seem to happen— "and then this," "and then that." In Carver's "The Third Thing That Killed My Father Off," we see the central character develop an interest in a hobby that interferes with his performance at work. An apparent mis-understanding leads to the alienation of old friends. Unexpected natural events intervene. In other stories, there may be a **tight** narrative struc-ture, with events marching on from cause to effect. In John Steinbeck's story "Flight," a proud young boy is provoked into a fatal brawl and then is hunted down methodically by the friends of the man he killed. The result is a compact, tightly plotted story. **Flashbacks** may break up the chronological sequence of events. In a Faulkner story like "A Rose for Emily," you may have to reconstruct the actual chain of events from partial clues, gradually filling in the missing pieces of the puzzle.

PLOTTING THE STORY

A plot is a narrative of events, the emphasis falling on causality. "The king died and then the queen died" is a story. "The king died, and then the queen died of grief" is a plot.

E. M. FORSTER

The following three selections are by authors who write gripping sto-ries. They entice readers into a story and then lock in their interest until the story reaches its satisfying conclusion. However, these writers use very different techniques, ranging from the more traditional to the more modern. Try to chart the plot, the story line, as you read.

Bernard Malamud　　*(1914–1986)*

A bad reading of my work would indicate that I'm writing about losers. That would be a very bad reading. One of my most important themes is a man's hidden strength.

BERNARD MALAMUD

Bernard Malamud was born and went to school in Brooklyn. He went to the College of the City of New York and Columbia University. He taught high school evening classes for years before he could make a liv-ing as a writer and university teacher. He knew the cultural heritage of the American Jewish community, and he wrote about Jewish everyday life in *The Assistant* (1956), about a struggling neighborhood grocer and the down-and-out stranger he befriends. *The Fixer* (1966) told the story of a Jew accused of ritual murder in Czarist Russia. Malamud's fiction is colored by the tragic view of life of a people who underwent centuries of persecution. In the depths of loneliness and bitterness, Leo Finkle, the rabbinical student in Malamud's story "The Magic Barrel," reminds himself "that he was yet a Jew and that a Jew suffered." However, inter-meshing with this mournful strand is a zany sense of humor, as likely to target one's own shortcomings as those of others.

What is the plot? Malamud's "The Magic Barrel" has the kind of straightforward plot that delights lovers of spontaneous storytelling. A young rabbinical student, shy and lonely, enlists the services of a traditional matchmaker or marriage broker in his search for a suitable wife. The young man's quest for happiness leads him through a series of tragicomic adventures that seem to doom him to disappointment. The story leads up to a surprise ending. Is it a happy ending? The answer depends on the reader's point of view.

However, while the official plot is played out toward its conclusion, much of what the characters publicly say and do plays to a counterpoint of private thoughts and feelings. Parallel to the overt action a spiritual journey takes place—a journey toward self-discovery. Leo learns things about himself that, before, he did not care to admit. He reexamines his life, his history, his vocation. What does he learn? How does his character develop or grow in the course of the story?

The Magic Barrel   1958

Not long ago there lived in uptown New York, in a small, almost meager room, though crowded with books, Leon Finkle, a rabbinical student in the Yeshivah University. Finkle, after six years of study, was to be ordained in June and had been advised by an acquaintance that he might find it easier to win himself a congregation if he were married. Since he had no present prospects of marriage, after two tormented days of turning it over in his mind, he called in Pinye Salzman, a marriage broker, whose two-line advertisement he had read in the *Forward*.

The matchmaker appeared one night out of the dark fourth-floor hallway of the graystone rooming house, grasping a black, strapped portfolio that had been worn thin with use. Salzman, who had been long in the business, was of slight but dignified build, wearing an old hat and an overcoat too short and tight for him. He smelled frankly of fish, which he loved to eat, and although he was missing a few teeth, his presence was not displeasing, because of an amiable manner curiously contrasted by mournful eyes. His voice, his lips, his wisp of beard, his bony fingers were animated, but give him a moment of repose, and his mild blue eyes soon revealed a depth of sadness, a characteristic that put Leo a little at ease although the situation, for him, was inherently tense.

He at once informed Salzman why he had asked him to come, explaining that his home was in Cleveland, and that but for his parents, who had married comparatively late in life, he was alone in the world. He had for six years devoted himself entirely to his studies, as a result of which, quite understandably, he had found himself without time for a social life and the company of young women. Therefore he thought it the better part of trial and error—of embarrassing fumbling—to call in an experienced person to advise him in these matters. He remarked in passing that the function of the marriage broker was ancient and honorable, highly approved in the Jewish community, because it made practical the necessary without hindering joy. Moreover, his own parents had been brought together by a matchmaker. They had made, if not a financially profitable marriage—since neither had possessed any worldly goods to speak of—at least a successful one in the sense of their everlasting devotion to one another. Salzman listened in embarrassed surprise, sensing a sort of apology. Later, however, he experienced a glow of pride in his work, an emotion that had left him years ago, and he heartily approved of Finkle.

The two men went to their business. Leo had led Salzman to the only clear place in the room, a table near a window that overlooked the lamplit city. He seated himself at the matchmaker's side but facing him, attempting by an act of will to suppress the unpleasant tickle in his throat. Salzman eagerly unstrapped his portfolio and removed a loose rubber band from a thin packet of much-handled cards. As he flipped through them, a gesture and sound that physically hurt Leo, the student pretended not to see and gazed steadfastly out the window. Although it was still February, winter was on its last legs, signs of which he had for the first time in years begun to notice. He now observed the round white moon, moving high in the sky through a cloud-menagerie, and watched with half-open mouth as it penetrated a huge hen and dropped out of her like an egg laying itself. Salzman, though pretending through eyeglasses he had just slipped on, to be engaged in scanning the writing on the cards, stole occasional glances at the young man's distinguished face, noting with pleasure the long, severe scholar's nose, brown eyes heavy with learning, sensitive yet ascetic lips, and a certain almost hollow quality of the dark cheeks. He gazed around at shelves upon shelves of books and let out a soft but happy sigh.

When Leo's eyes fell upon the cards, he counted six spread out in Salzman's hand.   5

"So few?" he said in disappointment.

"You wouldn't believe me how much cards I got in my office," Salzman replied. "The drawers are already filled to the top, so I keep them now in a barrel, but is every girl good for a new rabbi?"

Leo blushed at this, regretting all he had revealed of himself in a curriculum vitae he had sent to Salzman. He had thought it best to acquaint him with his strict standards and specifications, but in having done so now felt he had told the marriage broker more than was absolutely necessary.

He hesitantly inquired, "Do you keep photographs of your clients on file?"

"First comes family, amount of dowry, also what kind promises," Salzman replied, unbuttoning his tight coat and settling himself in the chair. "After comes pictures, rabbi."   10

"Call me Mr. Finkle. I'm not a rabbi yet."

Salzman said he would, but instead called him doctor, which he changed to rabbi when Leo was not listening too attentively.

Salzman adjusted his horn-rimmed spectacles, gently cleared his throat and read in an eager voice the contents on the top card:

"Sophie P. Twenty-four years. Widow for one year. No children. Educated high school and two years college. Father promises eight thousand dollars. Has a wonderful wholesale business. Also real estate. On mother's side comes teachers, also one actor. Well known on Second Avenue."

Leo gazed up in surprise. "Did you say a widow?"   15

"A widow don't mean spoiled, rabbi. She lived with her husband maybe four months. He was a sick boy, she made a mistake to marry him."

"Marrying a widow has never entered my mind."

"This is because you have no experience. A widow, specially if she is young and healthy like this girl, is a wonderful person to marry. She will be thankful to you the rest of her life. Believe me, if I was looking now for a bride, I would marry a widow."

Leo reflected, then shook his head.

Salzman hunched his shoulders in an almost imperceptible gesture of   20
disappointment. He placed the card down on the wooden table and began to read another:

"Lily H. High-school teacher. Regular. Not a substitute. Has savings and new Dodge car. Lived in Paris one year. Father is successful dentist thirty-five years. Interested in professional man. Well Americanized family. Wonderful opportunity.

"I know her personally," said Salzman. "I wish you could see this girl. She is a doll. Also very intelligent. All day you could talk to her about books and theater and what not. She also knows current events."

"I don't believe you mentioned her age?"

"Her age?" Salzman said, raising his brows in surprise. "Her age is thirty-two years."

Leo said after a while, "I'm afraid that seems a little too old."   25

Salzman let out a laugh. "So how old are you, rabbi?"

"Twenty-seven."

"So what is the difference, tell me, between twenty-seven and thirty-two? My own wife is seven years older than me. So what did I suffer?—Nothing. If Rothschild's daughter wants to marry you, would you say on account of her age, no?"

"Yes," Leo said dryly.

Salzman shook off the no in the yes. "Five years don't mean a thing. I   30
give you my word that when you will live with her for one week, you will forget her age. What does it mean five years—that she lived more and knows more than somebody who is younger? On this girl, God bless her, years are not wasted. Each one that it comes makes better the bargain."

"What subject does she teach in high school?"

"Languages. If you heard the way she reads French, you will think it is music. I am in the business twenty-five years, and I recommend her with my whole heart. Believe me, I know what I'm talking, rabbi."

"What's on the next card?" Leo said abruptly.

Salzman reluctantly turned up the third card:

"Ruth K. Nineteen years. Honor student. Father offers thirteen thousand   35
dollars cash to the right bridegroom. He is a medical doctor. Stomach specialist with marvelous practice. Brother-in-law owns own garment business. Particular people."

Salzman looked up as if he had read his trump card.

"Did you say nineteen?" Leo asked with interest.

"On the dot."

"Is she attractive?" He blushed. "Pretty?"

Salzman kissed his fingertips. "A little doll. On this I give you my word. 40
Let me call the father tonight and you will see what means pretty."

But Leo was troubled. "You're sure she's that young?"

"This I am positive. The father will show you the birth certificate."

"Are you positive there isn't something wrong with her?" Leo insisted.

"Who says there is wrong?"

"I don't understand why an American girl her age should go to a mar- 45
riage broker."

A smile spread over Salzman's face.

"So for the same reason you went, she comes."

Leo flushed. "I am pressed for time."

Salzman, realizing he had been tactless, quickly explained. "The father
came, not her. He wants she should have the best, so he looks around himself. When we will locate the right boy, he will introduce him and encourage. This makes a better marriage than if a young girl without experience
takes for herself. I don't have to tell you this."

"But don't you think this young girl believes in love?" Leo spoke 50
uneasily.

Salzman was about to guffaw, but caught himself and said soberly, "Love
comes with the right person, not before."

Leo parted dry lips but did not speak. Noticing that Salzman had
snatched a quick glance at the next card, he cleverly asked, "How is her
health?"

"Perfect," Salzman said, breathing with difficulty. "Of course, she is a little lame on her right foot from an auto accident that it happened to her
when she was twelve years, but nobody notices on account she is so brilliant and also beautiful."

Leo got up heavily and went to the window. He felt curiously bitter and
upbraided himself for having called in the marriage broker. Finally, he
shook his head.

"Why not?" Salzman persisted, the pitch of his voice rising. 55

"Because I hate stomach specialists."

"So what do you care what is his business? After you marry her, do you
need him? Who says he must come every Friday night to your house?"

Ashamed of the way the talk was going, Leo dismissed Salzman, who
went home with melancholy eyes.

Though he had felt only relief at the marriage broker's departure, Leo was
in low spirits the next day. He explained it as arising from Salzman's failure
to produce a suitable bride for him. He did not care for his type of clientele.
But when Leo found himself hesitating over whether to seek out another
matchmaker, one more polished than Pinye, he wondered if it could be—
his protestations to the contrary, and although he honored his father and
mother—that he did not, in essence, care for the matchmaking institution?
This thought he quickly put out of his mind yet found himself still upset. All
day he ran around in a fog—missed an important appointment, forgot to
give out his laundry, walked out of a Broadway cafeteria without paying
and had to run back with the ticket in his hand; had even not recognized

his landlady in the street when she passed with a friend and courteously called out, "A good evening to you, Doctor Finkle." By nightfall, however, he had regained sufficient calm to sink his nose into a book and there found peace from his thoughts.

Almost at once there came a knock on the door. Before Leo could say   60
enter, Salzman, commercial cupid, was standing in the room. His face was gray and meager, his expression hungry, and he looked as if he would expire on his feet. Yet the marriage broker managed, by some trick of the muscles, to display a broad smile.

"So good evening. I am invited?"

Leo nodded, disturbed to see him again, yet unwilling to ask him to leave.

Beaming still, Salzman laid his portfolio on the table. "Rabbi, I got for you tonight good news."

"I've asked you not to call me rabbi. I'm still a student."

"Your worries are finished. I have for you a first-class bride."   65

"Leave me in peace concerning this subject." Leo pretended lack of interest.

"The world will dance at your wedding."

"Please, Mr. Salzman, no more."

"But first must come back my strength," Salzman said weakly. He fumbled with the portfolio straps and took out of the leather case an oily paper bag, from which he extracted a hard seeded roll and a small smoked whitefish. With one motion of his hand he stripped the fish out of its skin and began ravenously to chew. "All day in a rush," he muttered.

Leo watched him eat.   70

"A sliced tomato you have maybe?" Salzman hesitantly inquired.

"No."

The marriage broker shut his eyes and ate. When he had finished, he carefully cleaned up the crumbs and rolled up the remains of the fish in the paper bag. His spectacled eyes roamed the room until he discovered, amid some piles of books, a one-burner gas stove. Lifting his hat, he humbly asked, "A glass of tea you got, rabbi?"

Conscience-stricken, Leo rose and brewed the tea. He served it with a chunk of lemon and two cubes of lump sugar, delighting Salzman.

After he had drunk his tea, Salzman's strength and good spirits were   75
restored.

"So tell me, rabbi," he said amiably, "you considered any more the three clients I mentioned yesterday?"

"There was no need to consider."

"Why not?"

"None of them suits me."

"What, then, suits you?"   80

Leo let it pass because he could give only a confused answer.

Without waiting for a reply, Salzman asked, "You remember this girl I talked to you—the high-school teacher?"

"Age thirty-two?"

But, surprisingly, Salzman's face lit in a smile. "Age twenty-nine."

Leo shot him a look. "Reduced from thirty-two?"   85

"A mistake," Salzman avowed. "I talked today with the dentist. He took me to his safety deposit box and showed me the birth certificate. She was twenty-nine last August. They made her a party in the mountains where she went for her vacation. When her father spoke to me the first time, I forgot to write the age and I told you thirty-two, but now I remember this was a different client, a widow."

"The same one you told me about? I thought she was twenty-four?"

"A different. Am I responsible that the world is filled with widows?"

"No, but I'm not interested in them, nor for that matter, in schoolteachers."

Salzman passionately pulled his clasped hands to his breast. Looking at   90
the ceiling he exclaimed, "Jewish children, what can I say to somebody that he is not interested in high-school teachers? So what then you are interested?"

Leo flushed but controlled himself.

"In who else you will be interested," Salzman went on, "if you not interested in this fine girl that she speaks four languages and has personally in the bank ten thousand dollars? Also her father guarantees further twelve thousand. Also she has a new car, wonderful clothes, talks on all subjects, and she will give you a first-class home and children. How near do we come in our life to paradise?"

"If she's so wonderful, why wasn't she married ten years ago?"

"Why," said Salzman with a heavy laugh. "—Why? Because she is *par-tikler*. This is why. She wants only the *best*."

Leo was silent, amused at how he had trapped himself. But Salzman had   95
aroused his interest in Lily H., and he began seriously to consider calling on her. When the marriage broker observed how intently Leo's mind was at work on the facts he had supplied, he felt positive they would soon come to an agreement.

Late Saturday afternoon, conscious of Salzman, Leo Finkle walked with Lily Hirschorn along Riverside Drive. He walked briskly and erectly, wearing with distinction the black fedora he had that morning taken with trepidation out of the dusty hatbox on his closet shelf, and the heavy black Saturday coat he had thoroughly whisked clean. Leo also owned a walking stick, a present from a distant relative, but had decided not to use it. Lily, petite and not unpretty, had on something signifying the approach of spring. She was *au courant,* animatedly, with all subjects, and he weighed her words and found her surprisingly sound—score another for Salzman, whom he uneasily sensed to be somewhere around, hiding perhaps high in a tree along the street, flashing the lady signals; or perhaps a cloven-hoofed Pan, piping nuptial ditties as he danced his invisible way before them, strewing wild buds on the walk and purple summer grapes in their path, symbolizing fruit of a union, of which there was yet none.

Lily startled Leo by remarking, "I was thinking of Mr. Salzman, a curious figure, wouldn't you say?"

Not certain what to answer, he nodded.

She bravely went on, blushing, "I for one am grateful for his introducing us. Aren't you?"

He courteously replied, "I am."   100

"I mean," she said with a little laugh—and it was all in good taste, or at least gave the effect of being not in bad—"do you mind that we came together so?"

He was not afraid of her honesty, recognizing that she meant to set the relationship aright, and understanding that it took a certain amount of experience in life, and courage, to want to do it quite that way. One had to have some sort of past to make that kind of beginning.

He said that he did not mind. Salzman's function was traditional and honorable—valuable for what it might achieve, which, he pointed out, was frequently nothing.

Lily agreed with a sigh. They walked on for a while, and she said after a long silence, again with a nervous laugh, "Would you mind if I asked you something a little bit personal? Frankly, I find the subject fascinating." Although Leo shrugged, she went on half embarrassedly, "How was it that you came to your calling? I mean, was it a sudden passionate inspiration?"

Leo, after a time, slowly replied, "I was always interested in the Law."   105

"You saw revealed in it the presence of the Highest?"

He nodded and changed the subject. "I understand you spent a little time in Paris, Miss Hirschorn?"

"Oh, did Mr. Salzman tell you, Rabbi Finkle?" Leo winced, but she went on, "It was ages and ages ago and almost forgotten. I remember I had to return for my sister's wedding."

But Lily would not be put off. "When," she asked in a trembly voice, "did you become enamored of God?"

He stared at her. Then it came to him that she was talking not about Leo   110 Finkle, but a total stranger, some mystical figure, perhaps even passionate prophet that Salzman had conjured up for her—no relation to the living or dead. Leo trembled with rage and weakness. The trickster had obviously sold her a bill of goods, just as he had him, who'd expected to become acquainted with a young lady of twenty-nine, only to behold, the moment he laid eyes upon her strained and anxious face, a woman past thirty-five and aging very rapidly. Only his self-control, he thought, had kept him this long in her presence.

"I am not," he said gravely, "a talented religious person," and in seeking words to go on, found himself possessed by fear and shame. "I think," he said in a strained manner, "that I came to God not because I love Him, but because I did not."

This confession he spoke harshly because its unexpectedness shook him.

Lily wilted. Leo saw a profusion of loaves of bread sailing like ducks high over his head, not unlike the loaves by which he had counted himself to sleep last night. Mercifully, then, it snowed, which he would not put past Salzman's machinations.

He was infuriated with the marriage broker and swore he would throw him out of the room the moment he reappeared. But Salzman did not come that night, and when Leo's anger had subsided, an unaccountable despair grew in its place. At first he thought this was caused by his disappointment in Lily, but before long it became evident that he had involved himself with Salzman without a true knowledge of his own intent. He gradually realized—

with an emptiness that seized him with six hands—that he had called in the broker to find him a bride because he was incapable of doing it himself. This terrifying insight he had derived as a result of his meeting and conversation with Lily Hirschorn. Her probing questions had somehow irritated him into revealing—to himself more than her—the true nature of his relationship with God, and from that it had come upon him, with shocking force, that apart from his parents, he had never loved anyone. Or perhaps it went the other way, that he did not love God so well as he might, because he had not loved man. It seemed to Leo that his whole life stood starkly revealed and he saw himself, for the first time, as he truly was—unloved and loveless. This bitter but somehow not fully unexpected revelation brought him to a point of panic controlled only by extraordinary effort. He covered his face with his hands and wept.

The week that followed was the worst of his life. He did not eat, and lost 115 weight. His beard darkened and grew ragged. He stopped attending lectures and seminars and almost never opened a book. He seriously considered leaving the Yeshivah, although he was deeply troubled at the thought of the loss of all his years of study—saw them like pages from a book strewn over the city—and at the devastating effect of this decision upon his parents. But he had lived without knowledge of himself, and never in the Five Books and all the Commentaries—*mea culpa*—had the truth been revealed to him. He did not know where to turn, and in all this desolating loneliness there was no *to whom,* although he often thought of Lily but not once could bring himself to go downstairs and make the call. He became touchy and irritable, especially with his landlady, who asked him all manner of questions; on the other hand, sensing his own disagreeableness, he waylaid her on the stairs and apologized abjectly, until mortified, she ran from him. Out of this, however, he drew the consolation that he was yet a Jew and that a Jew suffered. But gradually, as the long and terrible week drew to a close, he regained his composure and some idea of purpose in life: to go on as planned. Although he was imperfect, the ideal was not. As for his quest of a bride, the thought of continuing afflicted him with anxiety and heartburn, yet perhaps with this new knowledge of himself he would be more successful than in the past. Perhaps love would now come to him and a bride to that love. And for this sanctified seeking who needed a Salzman?

The marriage broker, a skeleton with haunted eyes, returned that very night. He looked, withal, the picture of frustrated expectancy—as if he had steadfastly waited the week at Miss Lily Hirschorn's side for a telephone call that never came.

Casually coughing, Salzman came immediately to the point: "So how did you like her?"

Leo's anger rose and he could not refrain from chiding the matchmaker: "Why did you lie to me, Salzman?"

Salzman's pale face went dead white, as if the world had snowed on him.

"Did you not state that she was twenty-nine?" Leo insisted.   120

"I give you my word—"

"She was thirty-five. At *least* thirty-five."

"Of this I would not be too sure. Her father told me—"

"Never mind. The worst of it was that you lied to her."

"How did I lie to her, tell me?"   125

"You told her things about me that weren't true. You made me out to be more, consequently less than I am. She had in mind a totally different person, a sort of semimystical Wonder Rabbi."

"All I said, you was a religious man."

"I can imagine."

Salzman sighed. "This is my weakness that I have," he confessed. "My wife says to me I shouldn't be a salesman, but when I have two fine people that they would be wonderful to be married, I am so happy that I talk too much." He smiled wanly. "This is why Salzman is a poor man."

Leo's anger went. "Well, Salzman, I'm afraid that's all."   130

The marriage broker fastened hungry eyes on him.

"You don't want any more a bride?"

"I do," said Leo, "but I have decided to seek her in a different way. I am no longer interested in an arranged marriage. To be frank, I now admit the necessity of premarital love. That is, I want to be in love with the one I marry."

"Love?" said Salzman, astounded. After a moment he said, "For us, our love is our life, not for the ladies. In the ghetto they—"

"I know, I know," said Leo. "I've thought of it often. Love, I have said to   135
myself, should be a by-product of living and worship rather than its own end. Yet for myself I find it necessary to establish the level of my need and to fulfill it."

Salzman shrugged but answered, "Listen, rabbi, if you want love, this I can find for you also. I have such beautiful clients that you will love them the minute your eyes will see them."

Leo smiled unhappily. "I'm afraid you don't understand."

But Salzman hastily unstrapped his portfolio and withdrew a manila packet from it.

"Pictures," he said, quickly laying the envelope on the table.

Leo called after him to take the pictures away, but as if on the wings of   140
the wind, Salzman had disappeared.

March came. Leo had returned to his regular routine. Although he felt not quite himself yet—lacked energy—he was making plans for a more active social life. Of course it would cost something, but he was an expert in cutting corners; and when there were no corners left he could make circles rounder. All the while Salzman's pictures had lain on the table, gathering dust. Occasionally as Leo sat studying, or enjoying a cup of tea, his eyes fell on the manila envelope, but he never opened it.

The days went by, and no social life to speak of developed with a member of the opposite sex—it was difficult, given the circumstances of his situation. One morning Leo toiled up the stairs to his room and stared out the window at the city. Although the day was bright, his view of it was dark. For some time he watched the people in the street below hurrying along and then turned with a heavy heart to his little room. On the table was the packet. With a sudden relentless gesture he tore it open. For a half-hour he stood there, in a state of excitement, examining the photographs of the ladies Salzman had included. Finally, with a deep sigh he put them down. There were six, of varying degrees of attractiveness, but look at them long enough and they all became Lily Hirschorn: all past their prime, all starved behind bright smiles, not a true personality in the lot. Life, despite their anguished struggles and frantic yoohooings, had passed them by; they were photographs in a briefcase that stank of fish. After a while, however, as Leo attempted to return the pictures into the envelope, he found another in it, a small snapshot of the type taken by a machine for a quarter. He gazed at it a moment and let out a cry.

Her face deeply moved him. Why, he could at first not say. It gave him the impression of youth—all spring flowers—yet age—a sense of having been used to the bone, wasted; this all came from the eyes, which were hauntingly familiar, yet absolutely strange. He had a strong impression that he had met her before, but try as he might he could not place her, although he could almost recall her name, as if he had read it written in her own handwriting. No, this couldn't be; he would have remembered her. It was not, he affirmed, that she had an extraordinary beauty—no, although her face was attractive enough; it was that *something* about her moved him. Feature for feature, even some of the ladies of the photographs could do better; but she leaped forth to the heart—had lived, or wanted to—more than just wanted, perhaps regretted it—had somehow deeply suffered: it could be seen in the depths of those reluctant eyes, and from the way the light enclosed and shone from her, and within her, opening whole realms of possibility: this was her own. Her he desired. His head ached and eyes narrowed with the intensity of his gazing, then, as if a black fog had blown up in the mind, he experienced fear of her and was aware that he had received an impression, somehow, of filth. He shuddered, saying softly, it is thus with us all. Leo brewed some tea in a small pot and sat sipping it, without sugar, to calm himself. But before he had finished drinking, again with excitement he examined the face and found it good: good for him. Only such a one could truly understand Leo Finkle and help him to seek whatever he was seeking. How she had come to be among the discards in Salzman's barrel he could never guess, but he knew he must urgently go find her.

Leo rushed downstairs, grabbed up the Bronx telephone book, and searched for Salzman's home address. He was not listed, nor was his office. Neither was he in the Manhattan book. But Leo remembered having written down the address on a slip of paper after he had read Salzman's advertisement in the "personals" column of the *Forward*. He ran up to his room and tore through his papers, without luck. It was exasperating. Just when he needed the matchmaker he was nowhere to be found. Fortunately Leo remembered to look in his wallet. There on a card he found his name written and a Bronx address. No phone number was listed, which, Leo now recalled, was the reason he had originally communicated with Salzman by letter. He got on his coat, put a hat on over his skull cap and hurried to the subway station. All the way to the far end of the Bronx he sat on the edge of his seat. He was more than once tempted to take out the picture and see if the girl's face was as he remembered it, but he refrained, allowing the snapshot to remain in his inside coat pocket, content to have her so close. When the train pulled into the station, he was waiting at the door and bolted out. He quickly located the street Salzman had advertised.

The building he sought was less than a block from the subway, but it was 145
not an office building, nor even a loft, nor a store in which one could rent
office space. It was an old and grimy tenement. Leo found Salzman's name
in pencil on a soiled tag under the bell and climbed three dark flights to his
apartment. When he knocked, the door was opened by a thin, asthmatic,
gray-haired woman, in felt slippers.

"Yes?" she said, expecting nothing. She listened without listening. He could
have sworn he had seen her somewhere before but knew it was illusion.

"Salzman—does he live here? Pinye Salzman," he said, "the matchmaker?"

She stared at him a long time. "Of course."

He felt embarrassed. "Is he in?"

"No." Her mouth was open, but she offered nothing more.   150

"This is urgent. Can you tell me where his office is?"

"In the air." She pointed upward.

"You mean he has no office?" Leo said.

"In his socks."

He peered into the apartment. It was sunless and dingy, one large room   155
divided by a half-open curtain, beyond which he could see a sagging metal
bed. The nearer side of the room was crowded with rickety chairs, old
bureaus, a three-legged table, racks of cooking utensils, and all the appara-
tus of a kitchen. But there was no sign of Salzman or his magic barrel, probably also a figment of his imagination. An odor of frying fish made Leo
weak to the knees.

"Where is he?" he insisted, "I've got to see your husband."

At length she answered, "So who knows where he is? Every time he thinks
a new thought he runs to a different place. Go home, he will find you."

"Tell him Leo Finkle."

She gave no sign that she had heard.

He went downstairs, deeply depressed.   160

But Salzman, breathless, stood waiting at his door.

Leo was overjoyed and astounded. "How did you get here before me?"

"I rushed."

"Come inside."

They entered. Leo fixed tea and a sardine sandwich for Salzman.   165

As they were drinking, he reached behind him for the packet of pictures
and handed them to the marriage broker.

Salzman put down his glass and said expectantly, "You found maybe
somebody you like?"

"Not among these."

The marriage broker turned sad eyes away.

"Here's the one I like." Leo held forth the snapshot.   170

Salzman slipped on his glasses and took the picture into his trembling
hand. He turned ghastly and let out a miserable groan.

"What's the matter?" cried Leo.

"Excuse me. Was an accident this picture. She is not for you."

Salzman frantically shoved the manila packet into his portfolio. He thrust
the snapshot into his pocket and fled down the stairs.

Leo, after momentary paralysis, gave chase and cornered the marriage 175
broker in the vestibule. The landlady made hysterical outcries, but neither
of them listened.

"Give me back the picture, Salzman."

"No." The pain in his eyes was terrible.

"Tell me where she is then."

"This I can't tell you. Excuse me."

He made to depart, but Leo, forgetting himself, seized the matchmaker 180
by his tight coat and shook him frenziedly.

"Please," sighed Salzman. *"Please."*

Leo ashamedly let him go. "Tell me who she is," he begged. "It's very
important for me to know."

"She is not for you. She is a wild one—wild, without shame. This is not
a bride for a rabbi."

"What do you mean wild?"

"Like an animal. Like a dog. For her to be poor was a sin. This is why she 185
is dead now."

"In God's name, what do you mean?"

"Her I can't introduce to you," Salzman cried.

"Why are you so excited?"

"Why he asks," Salzman said, bursting into tears. "This is my baby, my
Stella, she should burn in hell."

Leo hurried up to bed and hid under the covers. Under the covers he 190
thought his whole life through. Although he soon fell asleep he could not
sleep her out of his mind. He woke, beating his breast. Though he prayed
to be rid of her, his prayers went unanswered. Through days of torment he
struggled endlessly not to love her; fearing success, he escaped it. He then
concluded to convert her to goodness, himself to God. The idea alternately
nauseated and exalted him.

He perhaps did not know that he had come to a final decision until he
encountered Salzman in a Broadway cafeteria. He was sitting alone at a rear
table sucking the bony remains of a fish. The marriage broker appeared
haggard, and transparent to the point of vanishing.

Salzman looked up at first without recognizing him. Leo had grown a
pointed beard, and his eyes were weighted with wisdom.

"Salzman," he said, "love has at last come to my heart."

"Who can love from a picture?" mocked the marriage broker.

"It is not impossible." 195

"If you can love her, then you can love anybody. Let me show you some
new clients that they just sent me their photographs. One is a little doll."

"Just her I want," Leo murmured.

"Don't be a fool, doctor. Don't bother with her."

"Put me in touch with her, Salzman," Leo said humbly. "Perhaps I can do
her a service."

Salzman had stopped chewing, and Leo understood with emotion that it 200
was now arranged.

Leaving the cafeteria, he was, however, afflicted by a tormenting suspicion that Salzman had planned it all to happen this way.

*   *   *

Leo was informed by letter that she would meet him on a certain corner, and she was there one spring night, waiting under a street lamp. He appeared, carrying a small bouquet of violets and rosebuds. Stella stood by the lamppost, smoking. She wore white with red shoes, which fitted his expectations, although in a troubled moment he had imagined the dress red, and only the shoes white. She waited uneasily and shyly. From afar he saw that her eyes—clearly her father's—were filled with desperate innocence. He pictured, in hers, his own redemption. Violins and lit candles revolved in the sky. Leo ran forward with the flowers outthrust.

Around the corner, Salzman, leaning against a wall, chanted prayers for the dead.

The Receptive Reader

1. What kind of story is this? What kind of story do the title and the *beginning* lead you to expect? Are your expectations fulfilled or disappointed by the rest of the story?

2. What is the *conflict* between the traditional view of love and romantic love in this story? How central is this conflict to the plot? How is the conflict resolved?

3. What are hints or touches that require you to read between the lines? Where are you most aware of the comic contrast between what the characters say and what they really think or know? What are striking examples of the contrast between make-believe and reality?

4. What role does Salzman play in the story as a whole? How essential is he to the plot? What are Finkle's mixed feelings about the "commercial cupid"?

5. What makes Salzman a *comic* figure? (What features do you recognize in his use of English?) How would you describe the kind of humor that pervades this story? What are striking examples?

6. Where in this story does Finkle experience *self-discovery* or self-revelation? What does he discover about himself? What role does this self-examination play in the story as a whole?

7. How believable is the *ending?*

The Personal Response

How essential is an understanding of Jewish culture or tradition to the reader's appreciation of this story? For you, does the author's ethnic background limit or enhance the appeal of the story? Why (or why not)?

Shirley Jackson   *(1919–1965)*

I hoped, by setting a particularly brutal ancient rite in the present and in my own village, to shock the story's readers with a graphic dramatization of the pointless violence and general inhumanity in their own lives.

SHIRLEY JACKSON

Shirley Jackson, a native of San Francisco, attended Syracuse University and settled in Vermont. She is a master of the modern horror story where evil surfaces in ordinary everyday surroundings. Her story "The Lottery" is one of the great controversial stories of modern times. When first published in *The New Yorker* in 1948, it raised a tempest of protest. The story takes you to a village where you watch the preparations for a traditional ritual, in which one of the villagers is going to meet a terrible fate. The proceedings might remind you of accounts of ceremonial sacrifices to a vegetation god to ensure a rich harvest. ("Lottery in June, corn be heavy soon" is a folk saying in the village.)

Many of its original readers hated this story. It generated batches of hate mail, making the author feel grateful that many in her own town did not know she was a writer. Two facets of the story were particularly disturbing: first, the people in the story were not a prehistoric tribe acting out primitive rituals. This was a village that had a post office, a bank, and a school; the villagers talked about tractors and taxes. (Jackson said she had in mind North Bennington, the town where she lived with her husband, who taught at Bennington College.) Second, the people selected to play the central role in the ritual were selected by lot—without the benefit of due process or trial by jury.

What explains the climate of fear in Jackson's story? We might try to see the story in its historical context: totalitarian regimes in Hitler's Germany and in Stalin's Russia had been persecuting artists, intellectuals, dissidents—a whole range of supposed "antisocial elements" and "enemies of the people." Because their grandparents held the Jewish faith, people whose families had lived in Germany for centuries were denied the right to live. In Stalinist Russia, young people whose family had owned a farm or a store were of the wrong social class. They had no right to go to school, to join the army, to make a living. Closer to home, during the Great Depression, families had been losing their farms or businesses and turned into hoboes. They were the random victims of an economic tailspin that threw millions out of work.

What happens in Jackson's story is irrational, but it seems inevitable. We see it coming but find it impossible to stop, like a freight train. The story has a concentrated impact created by a tightly crafted, linear plot. She once said about the writing of short stories, "no scene and no character can be allowed to wander off by itself; there must be some furthering of the story in every sentence."

The Lottery   *1948*

The morning of June 27th was clear and sunny, with the fresh warmth of a full-summer day; the flowers were blossoming profusely and the grass was richly green. The people of the village began to gather in the square, between the post office and the bank, around ten o'clock; in some towns there were so many people that the lottery took two days and had to be started on June 26th, but in this village, where there were only about three hundred people, the whole lottery took less than two hours, so it could begin at ten o'clock in the morning and still be through in time to allow the villagers to get home for noon dinner.

The children assembled first, of course. School was recently over for the summer, and the feeling of liberty sat uneasily on most of them; they tended to gather together quietly for a while before they broke into boisterous play, and their talk was still of the classroom and the teacher, of books and reprimands. Bobby Martin had already stuffed his pockets full of stones, and the other boys soon followed his example, selecting the smoothest and roundest stones; Bobby and Harry Jones and Dickie Delacroix—the villagers pronounced this name "Dellacroy"—eventually made a great pile of stones in one corner of the square and guarded it against the raids of the other boys. The girls stood aside, talking among themselves, looking over their shoulders at the boys, and the very small children rolled in the dust or clung to the hands of their older brothers or sisters.

Soon the men began to gather, surveying their own children, speaking of planting and rain, tractors and taxes. They stood together, away from the pile of stones in the corner, and their jokes were quiet and they smiled rather than laughed. The women, wearing faded house dresses and sweaters, came shortly after their menfolk. They greeted one another and exchanged bits of gossip as they went to join their husbands. Soon the women, standing by their husbands, began to call to their children, and the children came reluctantly, having to be called four or five times. Bobby Martin ducked under his mother's grasping hand and ran, laughing, back to the pile of stones. His father spoke up sharply, and Bobby came quickly and took his place between his father and his oldest brother.

The lottery was conducted—as were the square dances, the teenage club, the Halloween program—by Mr. Summers, who had time and energy to devote to civic activities. He was a round-faced, jovial man and he ran the coal business, and people were sorry for him, because he had no children and his wife was a scold. When he arrived in the square, carrying the black wooden box, there was a murmur of conversation among the villagers, and he waved and called, "Little late today, folks." The postmaster, Mr. Graves, followed him, carrying a three-legged stool, and the stool was put in the center of the square and Mr. Summers set the black box down on it. The villagers kept their distance, leaving a space between themselves and the stool, and when Mr. Summers said, "Some of you fellows want to give me a hand?" there was a hesitation before two men, Mr. Martin and his oldest son, Baxter, came forward to hold the box steady on the stool while Mr. Summers stirred up the papers inside it.

The original paraphernalia for the lottery had been lost long ago, and the black box now resting on the stool had been put into use even before Old Man Warner, the oldest man in town, was born. Mr. Summers spoke frequently to the villagers about making a new box, but no one liked to upset even as much tradition as was represented by the black box. There was a story that the present box had been made with some pieces of the box that had preceded it, the one that had been constructed when the first people settled down to make a village here. Every year, after the lottery, Mr. Summers   5 began talking again about a new box, but every year the subject was allowed to fade off without anything's being done. The black box grew shabbier each year; by now it was no longer completely black but splintered badly along one side to show the original wood color, and in some places faded or stained.

Mr. Martin and his oldest son, Baxter, held the black box securely on the stool until Mr. Summers had stirred the papers thoroughly with his hand. Because so much of the ritual had been forgotten or discarded, Mr. Summers had been successful in having slips of paper substituted for the chips of wood that had been used for generations. Chips of wood, Mr. Summers had argued, had been all very well when the village was tiny, but now that the population was more than three hundred and likely to keep on growing, it was necessary to use something that would fit more easily into the black box. The night before the lottery, Mr. Summers and Mr. Graves made up the slips of paper and put them in the box, and it was then taken to the safe of Mr. Summers' coal company and locked up until Mr. Summers was ready to take it to the square next morning. The rest of the year, the box was put away, sometimes one place, sometimes another; it had spent one year in Mr. Graves's barn and another year underfoot in the post office, and sometimes it was set on a shelf in the Martin grocery and left there.

There was a great deal of fussing to be done before Mr. Summers declared the lottery open. There were the lists to make up—of heads of families, heads of households in each family, members of each household in each family. There was the proper swearing-in of Mr. Summers by the postmaster, as the official of the lottery; at one time, some people remembered, there had been a recital of some sort, performed by the official of the lottery, a perfunctory, tuneless chant that had been rattled off duly each year; some people believed that the official of the lottery used to stand just so when he said or sang it, others believed that he was supposed to walk among the people, but years and years ago this part of the ritual had been allowed to lapse. There had been, also, a ritual salute, which the official of the lottery had had to use in addressing each person who came up to draw from the box, but this also had changed with time, until now it was felt necessary only for the official to speak to each person approaching. Mr. Summers was very good at all this; in his clean white shirt and blue jeans, with one hand resting carelessly on the black box, he seemed very proper and important as he talked interminably to Mr. Graves and the Martins.

Just as Mr. Summers finally left off talking and turned to the assembled villagers, Mrs. Hutchinson came hurriedly along the path to the square, her sweater thrown over her shoulders, and slid into place in the back of the crowd. "Clean forgot what day it was," she said to Mrs. Delacroix, who stood next to her, and they both laughed softly. "Thought my old man was out back stacking wood," Mrs. Hutchinson went on, "and then I looked out the window and the kids was gone, and then I remembered it was the twenty-seventh and came a-running." She dried her hands on her apron, and Mrs. Delacroix said, "You're in time, though. They're still talking away up there."

Mrs. Hutchinson craned her neck to see through the crowd and found her husband and children standing near the front. She tapped Mrs.

Delacroix on the arm as a farewell and began to make her way through the crowd. The people separated good-humoredly to let her through; two or three people said, in voices just loud enough to be heard across the crowd, "Here comes your Missus, Hutchinson," and "Bill, she made it after all." Mrs. Hutchinson reached her husband, and Mr. Summers, who had been waiting, said cheerfully, "Thought we were going to have to get on without you, Tessie." Mrs. Hutchinson said, grinning, "Wouldn't have me leave m'dishes in the sink, now, would you, Joe?" and soft laughter ran through the crowd as the people stirred back into position after Mrs. Hutchinson's arrival.

"Well, now," Mr. Summers said soberly, "guess we better get started, get   10
this over with, so's we can go back to work. Anybody ain't here?"

"Dunbar," several people said, "Dunbar, Dunbar."

Mr. Summers consulted his list. "Clyde Dunbar," he said. "That's right. He's broke his leg, hasn't he? Who's drawing for him?"

"Me, I guess," a woman said, and Mr. Summers turned to look at her. "Wife draws for her husband," Mr. Summers said. "Don't you have a grown boy to do it for you, Janey?" Although Mr. Summers and everyone else in the village knew the answer perfectly well, it was the business of the official of the lottery to ask such questions formally. Mr. Summers waited with an expression of polite interest while Mrs. Dunbar answered.

"Horace's not but sixteen yet," Mrs. Dunbar said regretfully. "Guess I gotta fill in for the old man this year."

"Right," Mr. Summers said. He made a note on the list he was holding.   15
Then he asked, "Watson boy drawing this year?"

A tall boy in the crowd raised his hand. "Here," he said. "I'm drawing for m'mother and me." He blinked his eyes nervously and ducked his head as several voices in the crowd said things like "Good fellow, Jack," and "Glad to see your mother's got a man to do it."

"Well," Mr. Summers said, "guess that's everyone. Old Man Warner make it?"

"Here," a voice said, and Mr. Summers nodded.

A sudden hush fell on the crowd as Mr. Summers cleared his throat and looked at the list. "All ready?" he called. "Now, I'll read the names—heads of families first—and the men come up and take a paper out of the box. Keep the paper folded in your hand without looking at it until everyone has had a turn. Everything clear?"

The people had done it so many times that they only half listened to the   20
directions; most of them were quiet, wetting their lips, not looking around. Then Mr. Summers raised one hand high and said, "Adams." A man disengaged himself from the crowd and came forward. "Hi, Steve," Mr. Summers said, and Mr. Adams said, "Hi, Joe." They grinned at one another humorlessly and nervously. Then Mr. Adams reached into the black box and took out a folded paper. He held it firmly by one corner as he turned and went hastily back to his place in the crowd, where he stood a little apart from his family, not looking down at his hand.

"Allen," Mr. Summers said. "Anderson. . . . Bentham."

"Seems like there's no time at all between lotteries any more," Mrs. Delacroix said to Mrs. Graves in the back row. "Seems like we got through with the last one only last week."

"Time sure goes fast," Mrs. Graves said.

"Clark. . . . Delacroix."

"There goes my old man," Mrs. Delacroix said. She held her breath while   25
her husband went forward.

"Dunbar," Mr. Summers said, and Mrs. Dunbar went steadily to the box
while one of the women said, "Go on, Janey," and another said, "There she
goes."

"We're next," Mrs. Graves said. She watched while Mr. Graves came
around from the side of the box, greeted Mr. Summers gravely, and selected
a slip of paper from the box. By now, all through the crowd there were men
holding the small folded papers in their large hands, turning them over and
over nervously. Mrs. Dunbar and her two sons stood together, Mrs. Dunbar
holding the slip of paper.

"Harburt. . . . Hutchinson."

"Get up there, Bill," Mrs. Hutchinson said, and the people near her
laughed.

"Jones."   30

"They do say," Mrs. Adams said to Old Man Warner, who stood next to
him, "that over in the north village they're talking of giving up the lottery."

Old Man Warner snorted. "Pack of crazy fools," he said. "Listening to the
young folks, nothing's good enough for *them*. Next thing you know, they'll
be wanting to go back to living in caves, nobody work any more, live *that*
way for a while. Used to be a saying about 'Lottery in June, corn be heavy
soon.' First thing you know, we'd all be eating stewed chickweed and
acorns. There's *always* been a lottery," he added petulantly. "Bad enough to
see young Joe Summers up there joking with everybody."

"Some places have already quit lotteries," Mrs. Adams said.

"Nothing but trouble in *that*," Old Man Warner said stoutly. "Pack of
young fools."

"Martin." And Bobby Martin watched his father go forward. "Over-   35
dyke. . . . Percy."

"I wish they'd hurry," Mrs. Dunbar said to her older son. "I wish they'd
hurry."

"They're almost through," her son said.

"You get ready to run tell Dad," Mrs. Dunbar said.

Mr. Summers called his own name and then stepped forward precisely
and selected a slip from the box. Then he called, "Warner."

"Seventy-seventh year I been in the lottery," Old Man Warner said as he   40
went through the crowd. "Seventy-seventh time."

"Watson." The tall boy came awkwardly through the crowd. Someone
said, "Don't be nervous, Jack," and Mr. Summers said, "Take your time, son."

"Zanini."

After that, there was a long pause, a breathless pause, until Mr. Summers,
holding his slip of paper in the air, said, "All right, fellows." For a minute,
no one moved, and then all the slips of paper were opened. Suddenly, all
the women began to speak at once, saying, "Who is it?," "Who's got it?," "Is
it the Dunbars?," "Is it the Watsons?" Then the voices began to say, "It's
Hutchinson. It's Bill," "Bill Hutchinson's got it."

"Go tell your father," Mrs. Dunbar said to her older son.

People began to look around to see the Hutchinsons. Bill Hutchinson   45
was standing quiet staring down at the paper in his hand. Suddenly, Tessie
Hutchinson shouted to Mr. Summers, "You didn't give him time enough to
take any paper he wanted. I saw you. It wasn't fair."

"Be a good sport, Tessie," Mrs. Delacroix called, and Mrs. Graves said,
"All of us took the same chance."

"Shut up, Tessie," Bill Hutchinson said.

"Well, everyone," Mr. Summers said, "that was done pretty fast, and now
we've got to be hurrying a little more to get done in time." He consulted his
next list. "Bill," he said, "you draw for the Hutchinson family. You got any
other households in the Hutchinsons?"

"There's Don and Eva," Mrs. Hutchinson yelled. "Make *them* take their
chance!"

"Daughters draw for their husbands' families, Tessie," Mr. Summers said   50
gently. "You know that as well as anyone else."

"It wasn't *fair*," Tessie said.

"I guess not, Joe," Bill Hutchinson said regretfully. "My daughter draws
with her husband's family, that's only fair. And I've got no other family
except the kids."

"Then, as far as drawing for families is concerned, it's you," Mr. Summers
said in explanation, "and as far as drawing for households is concerned,
that's you, too. Right?"

"Right," Bill Hutchinson said.

"How many kids, Bill?" Mr. Summers asked formally.   55

"Three," Bill Hutchinson said. "There's Bill, Jr., and Nancy, and little
Dave. And Tessie and me."

"All right, then," Mr. Summers said. "Harry, you got their tickets back?"

Mr. Graves nodded and held up the slips of paper. "Put them in the box,
then," Mr. Summers directed. "Take Bill's and put it in."

"I think we ought to start over," Mrs. Hutchinson said, as quietly as she
could, "I tell you it wasn't *fair*. You didn't give him time enough to choose.
*Every*body saw that."

Mr. Graves had selected the five slips and put them in the box, and he   60
dropped all the papers but those onto the ground, where the breeze caught
them and lifted them off.

"Listen, everybody," Mrs. Hutchinson was saying to the people around her.

"Ready, Bill?" Mr. Summers asked, and Bill Hutchinson, with one quick
glance around at his wife and children, nodded.

"Remember," Mr. Summers said, "take the slips and keep them folded
until each person has taken one. Harry, you help little Dave." Mr. Graves
took the hand of the little boy, who came willingly with him up to the box.
"Take a paper out of the box, Davy," Mr. Summers said. Davy put his hand
into the box and laughed. "Take just *one* paper," Mr. Summers said. "Harry,
you hold it for him." Mr. Graves took the child's hand and removed the
folded paper from the tight fist and held it while little Dave stood next to
him and looked up at him wonderingly.

"Nancy next," Mr. Summers said. Nancy was twelve, and her school
friends breathed heavily as she went forward, switching her skirt, and took
a slip daintily from the box. "Bill, Jr.," Mr. Summers said, and Billy, his face

red and his feet over-large, nearly knocked the box over as he got a paper out. "Tessie," Mr. Summers said. She hesitated for a minute, looking around defiantly, and then set her lips and went up to the box. She snatched a paper out and held it behind her.

"Bill," Mr. Summers said, and Bill Hutchinson reached into the box and   65
felt around, bringing his hand out at last with the slip of paper in it.

The crowd was quiet. A girl whispered, "I hope it's not Nancy," and the sound of the whisper reached the edges of the crowd.

"It's not the way it used to be," Old Man Warner said clearly. "People ain't the way they used to be."

"All right," Mr. Summers said. "Open the papers. Harry, you open little Dave's."

Mr. Graves opened the slip of paper and there was a general sigh through the crowd as he held it up and everyone could see that it was blank. Nancy and Bill, Jr. opened theirs at the same time, and both beamed and laughed, turning around to the crowd and holding their slips of paper above their heads.

"Tessie," Mr. Summers said. There was a pause, and then Mr. Summers   70
looked at Bill Hutchinson, and Bill unfolded his paper and showed it. It was blank.

"It's Tessie," Mr. Summers said, and his voice was hushed. "Show us her paper, Bill."

Bill Hutchinson went over to his wife and forced the slip of paper out of her hand. It had a black spot on it, the black spot Mr. Summers had made the night before with the heavy pencil in the coal-company office. Bill Hutchinson held it up, and there was a stir in the crowd.

"All right, folks," Mr. Summers said. "Let's finish quickly."

Although the villagers had forgotten the ritual and lost the original black box, they still remembered to use stones. The pile of stones the boys had made earlier was ready; there were stones on the ground with the blowing scraps of paper that had come out of the box. Mrs. Delacroix selected a stone so large she had to pick it up with both hands and turned to Mrs. Dunbar. "Come on," she said. "Hurry up."

Mrs. Dunbar had small stones in both hands, and she said, gasping for   75
breath, "I can't run at all. You'll have to go ahead and I'll catch up with you."

The children had stones already, and someone gave little Davy Hutchinson a few pebbles.

Tessie Hutchinson was in the center of a cleared space by now, and she held her hands out desperately as the villagers moved in on her. "It isn't fair," she said. A stone hit her on the side of the head.

Old Man Warner was saying, "Come on, come on, everyone." Steve Adams was in the front of the crowd of villagers, with Mrs. Graves beside him.

"It isn't fair, it isn't right," Mrs. Hutchinson screamed, and then they were upon her.

The Receptive Reader

1. The story is told in straightforward *chronological* fashion. As you read along, do you feel nevertheless that essential information is missing? What is being withheld and why? Why does the author tell the story the way she does?

2. Why do you think the author goes into such detail about the procedure, the preparations, the box used, and its history? What details stand out?

3. How did you expect the story to come out? When were you sure of the outcome? Does the author provide any *foreshadowing* or early hints of what is to come?

4. *Tradition* becomes a key force in this story. What role does it play in the story as a whole? What is its influence, its power? Who speaks up for it? Does anyone question it?

5. Jackson is a master of *irony*—of contradictions between what we might innocently expect and what happens in grim reality. What is ironic about the organizer, Mr. Summers—his other activities, his behavior during the ritual? Is there any humor in the way the author portrays him, and if so what kind?

6. How does the author lead up to the *climactic* event? How does she first introduce the victim and why? Why do you think the author puts in a second drawing—somewhat like a run-off election?

7. This story is often read as a study in mass psychology. What are the reactions of the crowd as the story approaches its climactic ending? Do they provide a comment on or insights into mob psychology?

8. How does the victim react? Is she right when she says the drawing was not fair? What are your feelings as you watch her reaction?

9. Where are you in this story? Do you identify with the victims? the instigators? the bystanders? Or do you stay aloof, like an observer from a distant planet? (How do your reactions compare with those of your classmates?)

The Personal Response

Do you object to or resent the story? How do you explain the reactions of hostile readers? Does our society today have similar rituals? Can you think of any parallel situation from your own observation, experience, reading, or viewing?

The Range of Interpretation

The following passage is from Lenemaja Friedman's book *Shirley Jackson* (1975). What evidence from the story would you cite when supporting or taking issue with her view?

> Jackson views man's nature as basically evil, and she indicates that, in his relationship with his fellow beings, man does not hesitate to lie, cheat, and steal—even to kill when it suits his purposes to do so. As in "The Lottery," he may be persuaded that the evil committed is for the common good; but he nevertheless has the herd instinct and does not oppose the harmful mores of his community. And, sadly enough, man does not improve with age; the grandmothers are as guilty of hypocrisy and wrongdoing as the younger members of society. (p. 76)

The Creative Dimension

Have you ever felt unsatisfied at the end of a story? Have you felt unwilling to let the matter rest where the author concluded the story? Or have you felt the need for a modern update? Use your imagination—write a sequel or update to a story you have read. Study the following update as an example. How well does it get into the spirit of the original?

Winning the Lottery

Over the years, many of the old buildings have been torn down to make room for Seven Elevens and a large SUPER-mart with a cafeteria. Young women come in for the latest cosmetic or fashion magazine. There's even an aisle for the devout; it has Bibles and plastic Virgins that customers can attach to the dashboards of their cars. People are remodeling, improving, and accessorizing their homes, their bodies, and their televisions. The annual lottery has been moved to the large SUPER-mart parking lot. This year, it's— Mr. Stanfield! He was a pretty good man, and he watched television regularly too. The crowd moves to his home and dismantles it piece by piece. Pictures of his family are distributed, clothing passed around, and patterned dishes lovingly packed in bubble wrap. He wanders slowly down the road, past the store where he used to rent movies and the station where he used to put gas in his car. He ambles slowly in the single pair of sneakers he was allowed to keep; of course it's taboo for anyone to give him a ride. He dejectedly holds on to a hand-lettered sign that says he'll work for food, but he knows it's against the rules for anyone to help him. Every morning he leaves the old cardboard that's his cover during the nights under the overpass and stands in line at the Bureau with the other lottery winners of years past. The lone window opens for a short span at ten. The person working the window tells the waiting line of winners that the forms they need to get sustenance stamps were delayed at the printers but that they can expect them any day.

William Faulkner   *(1897–1962)*

INTERVIEWER: *Some people say they can't understand your writing, even after they read it two or three times. What approach would you suggest to them?*

FAULKNER: *Read it four times.*

William Faulkner was one of the great experimenters in early twentieth-century fiction. His many-layered sentences sprawl across paragraph breaks, and his stories slowly emerge from the broken-mirror effects of his narrative technique. Nevertheless, he became one of the most widely read, translated, and discussed writers of modern times. His best-known novels—*The Sound and the Fury* (1929), *As I Lay Dying* (1931), *Sanctuary* (1931), *Absalom! Absalom!* (1936), *Intruder in the Dust* (1948), *Requiem for a Nun* (1951)—have been read around the world.

Faulkner's fiction immerses us in the memories and traumas of the Old South. Many of his stories and novels were part of an ongoing saga of the people of his fictitious Yoknapatawpha County, modeled on Lafayette County in northern Mississippi, where he lived in Oxford, home of the University of Mississippi. As a child, Faulkner lived with a kindly but determined Scottish great-grandfather who made each child in the house recite a memorized Bible verse before breakfast. Faulkner served briefly in the Royal Canadian Flying Corps in World War I and lived in New Orleans for a time, working for a newspaper and trying to make a living as a writer. He returned to Mississippi in 1926 and eventually became a writer in residence at the university. He received the Nobel Prize for Literature in 1950.

Faulkner's characters are often embittered by seeing their values threatened in an uprooted modern world. They are often country people trying to live "off here to themselves"—to keep their distance from a new world of neon lights, quick, easy money, and shiny automobiles. Often the characters in his stories are stubbornly independent—a thorn in the side to state officials, tax collectors, and government agents trying to "interfere with how a man farmed his own land, raised his own cotton."

At the same time, Faulkner's characters are caught in the traditional class structure of the South. His own great-grandfather had become wealthy and famous in Mississippi before the Civil War. He became a colonel in the Confederate army and was killed years later in a duel. Many of Faulkner's characters belong to clans—the Sartorises, the Compsons, the Sutpens, the McCaslins—that represent the old social aristocracy of the South, often still living in antebellum, prewar mansions with their columned porticoes. However, often the offspring of the old families are beset by debts and by social upstarts, such as Flem Snopes, one of the "litter" of a family of poor white tenant farmers—pushy, unscrupulous, advancing his fortunes with dubious money-making schemes.

Faulkner broke up traditional plot structure. He told his stories in indirect, or oblique, ways, forcing us to puzzle out what is happening (the way we are often forced to in real life). He frequently uses **flashbacks,** in which glimpses of the past slowly begin to explain or illuminate the present. The stories often lead up to a **climax**—a climactic event or revelation.

A Rose for Emily   *1931*

I

When Miss Emily Grierson died, our whole town went to her funeral: the men through a sort of respectful affection for a fallen monument, the women mostly out of curiosity to see the inside of her house, which no one save an old manservant—a combined gardener and cook—had seen in at least ten years.

It was a big, squarish frame house that had once been white, decorated with cupolas and spires and scrolled balconies in the heavily lightsome style of the seventies, set on what had once been our most select street. But garages and cotton gins had encroached and obliterated even the august names of that neighborhood; only Miss Emily's house was left, lifting its stubborn and coquettish decay above the cotton wagons and the gasoline pumps—an eyesore among eyesores. And now Miss Emily had gone to join the representatives of those august names where they lay in the cedar-bemused cemetery among the ranked and anonymous graves of Union and Confederate soldiers who fell at the battle of Jefferson.

Alive, Miss Emily had been a tradition, a duty, and a care; a sort of hereditary obligation upon the town, dating from that day in 1894 when Colonel Sartoris, the mayor—he who fathered the edict that no Negro woman should appear on the streets without an apron—remitted her taxes, the dispensation dating from the death of her father on into perpetuity. Not that Miss Emily would have accepted charity. Colonel Sartoris invented an involved tale to the effect that Miss Emily's father had loaned money to the town, which the town, as a matter of business, preferred this way of repaying. Only a man of Colonel Sartoris' generation and thought could have invented it, and only a woman could have believed it.

When the next generation, with its more modern ideas, became mayors and aldermen, this arrangement created some little dissatisfaction. On the first of the year they mailed her a tax notice. February came, and there was no reply. They wrote her a formal letter, asking her to call at the sheriff's office at her convenience. A week later the mayor wrote her himself, offering to call or to send his car for her, and received in reply a note on paper of an archaic shape, in a thin, flowing calligraphy in faded ink, to the effect that she no longer went out at all. The tax notice was also enclosed, without comment.

They called a special meeting of the Board of Aldermen. A deputation   5 waited upon her, knocked at the door through which no visitor had passed since she ceased giving china-painting lessons eight or ten years earlier. They were admitted by the old Negro into a dim hall from which a stairway mounted into still more shadow. It smelled of dust and disuse—a close, dank smell. The Negro led them into the parlor. It was furnished in heavy, leather-covered furniture. When the Negro opened the blinds of one window, they could see that the leather was cracked; and when they sat down, a faint dust rose sluggishly about their thighs, spinning with slow motes in the single sun-ray. On a tarnished gilt easel before the fireplace stood a crayon portrait of Miss Emily's father.

They rose when she entered—a small, fat woman in black, with a thin gold chain descending to her waist and vanishing into her belt, leaning on an ebony cane with a tarnished gold head. Her skeleton was small and spare; perhaps that was why what would have been merely plumpness in another was obesity in her. She looked bloated, like a body long submerged in motionless water, and of that pallid hue. Her eyes, lost in the fatty ridges of her face, looked like two small pieces of coal pressed into a lump of dough as they moved from one face to another while the visitors stated their errand.

She did not ask them to sit. She just stood in the door and listened quietly until the spokesman came to a stumbling halt. Then they could hear the invisible watch ticking at the end of the gold chain.

104   PLOT

Her voice was dry and cold. "I have no taxes in Jefferson. Colonel Sartoris explained it to me. Perhaps one of you can gain access to the city
records and satisfy yourselves."

"But we have. We are the city authorities, Miss Emily. Didn't you get a
notice from the sheriff, signed by him?"

"I received a paper, yes," Miss Emily said. "Perhaps he considers himself   10
the sheriff. . . . I have no taxes in Jefferson."

"But there is nothing on the books to show that, you see. We must go by
the—"

"See Colonel Sartoris. I have no taxes in Jefferson."

"But, Miss Emily—"

"See Colonel Sartoris." (Colonel Sartoris had been dead almost ten years.)
"I have no taxes in Jefferson. Tobe!" The Negro appeared. "Show these
gentlemen out."

II

So she vanquished them, horse and foot, just as she had vanquished their   15
fathers thirty years before about the smell. That was two years after her
father's death and a short time after her sweetheart—the one we believed
would marry her—had deserted her. After her father's death she went out
very little; after her sweetheart went away, people hardly saw her at all. A
few of the ladies had the temerity to call, but were not received, and the
only sign of life about the place was the Negro man—a young man then—
going in and out with a market basket.

"Just as if a man—any man—could keep a kitchen properly," the ladies
said; so they were not surprised when the smell developed. It was another
link between the gross, teeming world and the high and mighty Griersons.

A neighbor, a woman, complained to the mayor, Judge Stevens, eighty
years old.

"But what will you have me do about it, madam?" he said.

"Why, send her word to stop it," the woman said. "Isn't there a law?"

"I'm sure that won't be necessary," Judge Stevens said. "It's probably just a   20
snake or a rat that nigger of hers killed in the yard. I'll speak to him about it."

The next day he received two more complaints, one from a man who
came in diffident deprecation. "We really must do something about it,
Judge. I'd be the last one in the world to bother Miss Emily, but we've got
to do something." That night the Board of Aldermen met—three graybeards
and one younger man, a member of the rising generation.

"It's simple enough," he said. "Send her word to have her place cleaned
up. Give her a certain time to do it in, and if she don't . . ."

"Dammit, sir," Judge Stevens said, "will you accuse a lady to her face of
smelling bad?"

So the next night, after midnight, four men crossed Miss Emily's lawn and
slunk about the house like burglars, sniffing along the base of the brick-
work and at the cellar openings while one of them performed a regular
sowing motion with his hand out of a sack slung from his shoulder. They
broke open the cellar door and sprinkled lime there, and in all the out-
buildings. As they recrossed the lawn, a window that had been dark was
lighted and Miss Emily sat in it, the light behind her, and her upright torso

motionless as that of an idol. They crept quietly across the lawn and into the shadow of the locusts that lined the street. After a week or two the smell went away.

That was when people had begun to feel really sorry for her. People in   25
our town, remembering how old lady Wyatt, her great-aunt, had gone completely crazy at last, believed that the Griersons held themselves a little too high for what they really were. None of the young men were quite good enough for Miss Emily and such. We had long thought of them as a tableau, Miss Emily a slender figure in white in the background, her father a spraddled silhouette in the foreground, his back to her and clutching a horsewhip, the two of them framed by the back-flung front door. So when she got to be thirty and was still single, we were not pleased exactly, but vindicated; even with insanity in the family she wouldn't have turned down all of her chances if they had really materialized.

When her father died, it got about that the house was all that was left to her; and in a way, people were glad. At last they could pity Miss Emily. Being left alone, and a pauper, she had become humanized. Now she too would know the old thrill and the old despair of a penny more or less.

The day after his death all the ladies prepared to call at the house and offer condolence and aid, as is our custom. Miss Emily met them at the door, dressed as usual and with no trace of grief on her face. She told them that her father was not dead. She did that for three days, with the ministers calling on her, and the doctors, trying to persuade her to let them dispose of the body. Just as they were about to resort to law and force, she broke down, and they buried her father quickly.

We did not say she was crazy then. We believed she had to do that. We remembered all the young men her father had driven away, and we knew that with nothing left, she would have to cling to that which had robbed her, as people will.

III

She was sick for a long time. When we saw her again, her hair was cut short, making her look like a girl, with a vague resemblance to those angels in colored church windows—sort of tragic and serene.

The town had just let the contracts for paving the sidewalks, and in the   30
summer after her father's death they began the work. The construction company came with niggers and mules and machinery, and a foreman named Homer Barron, a Yankee—a big, dark, ready man, with a big voice and eyes lighter than his face. The little boys would follow in groups to hear him cuss the niggers, and the niggers singing in time to the rise and fall of picks. Pretty soon he knew everybody in town. Whenever you heard a lot of laughing anywhere about the square, Homer Barron would be in the center of the group. Presently we began to see him and Miss Emily on Sunday afternoons driving in the yellow-wheeled buggy and the matched team of bays from the livery stable.

At first we were glad that Miss Emily would have an interest, because the ladies all said, "Of course a Grierson would not think seriously of a Northerner, a day laborer." But there were still others, older people, who said that even grief could not cause a real lady to forget *noblesse oblige*—without calling it *noblesse oblige*. They just said, "Poor Emily. Her kinsfolk should come to her." She had some kin in Alabama; but years ago her father had fallen out with them over the estate of old lady Wyatt, the crazy woman, and there was no communication between the two families. They had not even been represented at the funeral.

And as soon as the old people said, "Poor Emily," the whispering began. "Do you suppose it's really so?" they said to one another. "Of course it is. What else could . . ." This behind their hands; rustling of craned silk and satin behind jalousies closed upon the sun of Sunday afternoon as the thin, swift clop-clop-clop of the matched team passed: "Poor Emily."

She carried her head high enough—even when we believed that she was fallen. It was as if she demanded more than ever the recognition of her dignity as the last Grierson; as if it had wanted that touch of earthiness to reaffirm her imperviousness. Like when she bought the rat poison, the arsenic. That was over a year after they had begun to say "Poor Emily," and while the two female cousins were visiting her.

"I want some poison," she said to the druggist. She was over thirty then, still a slight woman, though thinner than usual, with cold, haughty black eyes in a face the flesh of which was strained across the temples and about the eyesockets as you imagine a lighthouse-keeper's face ought to look. "I want some poison," she said.

"Yes, Miss Emily. What kind? For rats and such? I'd recom—"   35

"I want the best you have. I don't care what kind."

The druggist named several. "They'll kill anything up to an elephant. But what you want is—"

"Arsenic," Miss Emily said. "Is that a good one?"

"Is . . . arsenic? Yes, ma'am. But what you want—"

"I want arsenic."   40

The druggist looked down at her. She looked back at him, erect, her face like a strained flag. "Why, of course," the druggist said. "If that's what you want. But the law requires you to tell what you are going to use it for."

Miss Emily just stared at him, her head tilted back in order to look him eye for eye, until he looked away and went and got the arsenic and wrapped it up. The Negro delivery boy brought her the package; the druggist didn't come back. When she opened the package at home there was written on the box, under the skull and bones: "For rats."

IV

So the next day we all said, "She will kill herself"; and we said it would be the best thing. When she had first begun to be seen with Homer Barron, we had said, "She will marry him." Then we said, "She will persuade him yet," because Homer himself had remarked—he liked men, and it was known that he drank with the younger men in the Elks' Club—that he was not a marrying man. Later we said, "Poor Emily" behind the jalousies as they passed on Sunday afternoon in the glittering buggy, Miss Emily with her head high and Homer Barron with his hat cocked and a cigar in his teeth, reins and whip in a yellow glove.

Then some of the ladies began to say that it was a disgrace to the town and a bad example to the young people. The men did not want to interfere, but at last the ladies forced the Baptist minister—Miss Emily's people were Episcopal—to call upon her. He would never divulge what happened during that interview, but he refused to go back again. The next Sunday they again drove about the streets, and the following day the minister's wife wrote to Miss Emily's relations in Alabama.

So she had blood-kin under her roof again and we sat back to watch developments. At first nothing happened. Then we were sure that they were to be married. We learned that Miss Emily had been to the jeweler's and ordered a man's toilet set in silver, with the letters H.B. on each piece. Two days later we learned that she had bought a complete outfit of men's clothing, including a nightshirt, and we said, "They are married." We were really glad. We were glad because the two female cousins were even more Grierson than Miss Emily had ever been.

So we were not surprised when Homer Barron—the streets had been finished some time since—was gone. We were a little disappointed that there was not a public blowing-off, but we believed that he had gone on to prepare for Miss Emily's coming, or to give her a chance to get rid of the cousins. (By that time it was a cabal, and we were all Miss Emily's allies to help circumvent the cousins.) Sure enough, after another week they departed. And, as we had expected all along, within three days Homer Barron was back in town. A neighbor saw the Negro man admit him at the kitchen door at dusk one evening.

And that was the last we saw of Homer Barron. And of Miss Emily for some time. The Negro man went in and out with the market basket, but the front door remained closed. Now and then we would see her at a window for a moment, as the men did that night when they sprinkled the lime, but for almost six months she did not appear on the streets. Then we knew that this was to be expected too; as if that quality of her father which had thwarted her woman's life so many times had been too virulent and too furious to die.

When we next saw Miss Emily, she had grown fat and her hair was turning gray. During the next few years it grew grayer and grayer until it attained an even pepper-and-salt iron-gray, when it ceased turning. Up to the day of her death at seventy-four it was still that vigorous iron-gray, like the hair of an active man.

From that time on her front door remained closed, save for a period of six or seven years, when she was about forty, during which she gave lessons in china-painting. She fitted up a studio in one of the downstairs rooms, where the daughters and granddaughters of Colonel Sartoris' contemporaries were sent to her with the same regularity and in the same spirit that they were sent on Sundays with a twenty-five-cent piece for the collection plate. Meanwhile her taxes had been remitted.

The newer generation became the backbone and the spirit of the town, and the painting pupils grew up and fell away and did not send their children to her with boxes of color and tedious brushes and pictures cut from the ladies' magazines. The front door closed upon the last one and remained closed for good. When the town got free postal delivery, Miss Emily alone refused to let them fasten the metal numbers above her door and attach a mailbox to it. She would not listen to them.

Daily, monthly, yearly we watched the Negro grow grayer and more stooped, going in and out with the market basket. Each December we sent her a tax notice, which would be returned by the post office a week later, unclaimed. Now and then we would see her in one of the downstairs windows—she had evidently shut up the top floor of the house—like the carven torso of an idol in a niche, looking or not looking at us, we could never tell which. Thus she passed from generation to generation—dear, inescapable, impervious, tranquil, and perverse.

And so she died. Fell ill in the house filled with dust and shadows, with only a doddering Negro man to wait on her. We did not even know she was sick; we had long since given up trying to get any information from the Negro. He talked to no one, probably not even to her, for his voice had grown harsh and rusty, as if from disuse.

She died in one of the downstairs rooms, in a heavy walnut bed with a curtain, her gray head propped on a pillow yellow and moldy with age and lack of sunlight.

V

The Negro met the first of the ladies at the front door and let them in, with their hushed, sibilant voices and their quick, curious glances, and then he disappeared. He walked right through the house and out the back and was not seen again.

The two female cousins came at once. They held the funeral on the second day, with the town coming to look at Miss Emily beneath a mass of bought flowers, with the crayon face of her father musing profoundly above the bier and the ladies sibilant and macabre; and the very old men—some in their brushed Confederate uniforms—on the porch and the lawn, talking of Miss Emily as if she had been a contemporary of theirs, believing that they had danced with her and courted her perhaps, confusing time with its mathematical progression, as the old do, to whom all the past is not a diminishing road, but, instead, a huge meadow which no winter ever quite touches, divided from them now by the narrow bottleneck of the most recent decade of years.

Already we knew that there was one room in that region above stairs which no one had seen in forty years, and which would have to be forced. They waited until Miss Emily was decently in the ground before they opened it.

The violence of breaking down the door seemed to fill this room with pervading dust. A thin, acrid pall as of the tomb seemed to lie everywhere upon this room decked and furnished as for a bridal: upon the valance curtains of faded rose color, upon the rose-shaded lights, upon the dressing table, upon the delicate array of crystal and the man's toilet things backed with tarnished silver, silver so tarnished that the monogram was obscured. Among them lay a collar and tie, as if they had just been removed, which, lifted, left upon the surface a pale crescent in the dust. Upon the chair hung the suit, carefully folded; beneath it the two mute shoes and the discarded socks.

The man himself lay in the bed.

For a long while we just stood there, looking down at the profound and fleshless grin. The body had apparently once lain in the attitude of an embrace, but now the long sleep that outlasts love, that conquers even the grimace of love, had cuckolded him. What was left of him, rotted beneath what was left of the nightshirt, had become inextricable from the bed in which he lay; and upon him and upon the pillow beside him lay that even coating of the patient and biding dust.

Then we noticed that in the second pillow was the indentation of a head. 60 One of us lifted something from it, and leaning forward, that faint and invisible dust dry and acrid in the nostrils, we saw a long strand of iron-gray hair.

The Receptive Reader

1. Faulkner said that the seed of this story was a picture in his mind "of the strand of hair on the pillow. . . . Simply a picture of a strand of hair on the pillow in the abandoned house." How does the strand of hair sum up what happened in this story or what is important in this story?

2. How and why does Faulkner's story depart from straightforward chronological storytelling? Where and how does Faulkner introduce the plot elements most essential to your understanding of the story? Can you reconstruct from the author's *flashbacks* a chronological sequence of events?

3. What is the keynote in Faulkner's treatment of the *setting*—Miss Emily's house, her street, the town?

4. How essential to the story is Faulkner's treatment of tradition and the Old South? What is Faulkner's attitude toward Colonel Sartoris' generation and the "next generation with its more modern ideas"? What is the meaning of *noblesse oblige,* and what is the role of this concept in the story?

5. What picture emerges of Miss Emily as the *main character?* Is there a central clue to her personality? Is she a creature of her environment? What explains the attitude of the townspeople toward her?

6. Faulkner is known for a *style* rich in unusual words, provocative images, and emotional overtones. What is the meaning of *coquettish, macabre, impervious, perverse?* How are these words related to the prevailing mood of the story? What is the effect on the reader of comparing Emily to a "carven torso of an idol in a niche"? What other striking imaginative comparisons play a role in the story?

7. One student wrote: "Time does not pass in linear chronological fashion in this story; the plot does not move forward through the traditional build-up of tension to climax and denouement. However, in its indirect and apparently meandering way, the story leads to a much more startling climax than could have been possible in a classic short-story format." Can you show whether the student was right?

The Personal Response

As you read the story, do you feel you are expected to admire Miss Emily, condemn her, or write her off as an eccentric? What are your feelings about her? Poetic justice is meted out to a character in poetry or fiction when he or she is justly punished for an offense, whether or not it was punishable according to law. Is Homer Barron the victim of poetic justice?

Making Connections—For Discussion or Writing

✘ Compare and contrast the Old South of Faulkner's "A Rose for Emily" with the New South of Mason's "Shiloh." What is the relationship between the setting and the characters in each story?

✘ Compare and contrast Jackson's "The Lottery" and Faulkner's "A Rose for Emily" as modern horror stories. How does their use of horror differ from its use in popular entertainment? What use do the two authors make of the grotesque—a mixture of terror and dark humor?

WRITING ABOUT LITERATURE

4   Charting the Plot (Focus on Revision)

The Writing Workshop   In writing about a story, you will often focus on how the parts serve the story as a whole. In writing about plot, for instance, do not just retell the story. Consider guidelines like the following:

✘ *Avoid mere plot summaries*   Use them only if they are needed to help the readers find their bearings. (Summaries can be useful for giving an initial overview—they can make the reader see the overall line of development in a complex or multilayered story.)

✘ *Look at what sets a story in motion.*   Look at key characters and their unmet needs, unfulfilled desires, or hidden agendas. Look at a situation that has in it potential sources of conflict: festering resentments, fatal misunderstandings.

✘ *Identify major stages.*   Make sure your readers get a sense of the overall development of the story. Highlight turning points. Show how a story builds to a climactic event. Show how a conflict plays itself out and reaches a resolution.

✘ *Disentangle major threads.*   Look for **polarities**—the possible play of polar opposites, such as the romantic and the realistic strands in Malamud's "The Magic Barrel."

✘ *Look for features that reinforce the overall pattern.*   Look for examples of **foreshadowing**—for early hints of what is to come. Look for **recurrence** of key elements, for passages that echo earlier issues or concerns.

Instructor's Comments and Revision   Learn to respond to feedback from an instructor or editor as you revise a first draft. Study the samples of instructors' comments in the material that follows. Look at rewrites of passages in response to an instructor's comments.

✘ *Pay special attention to comments on your opening paragraphs.* Does the focus of your paper become clear enough? Does your reader get a preview of your overall approach? Should you spell out your main point or **thesis** more fully or more clearly early in your paper? (Remember that in real life many readers don't go on beyond the opening of an essay if they find it unfocused, murky, or confusing.)

✗ *Respond to suggestions for strengthening your overall plan.* Consider whether reshuffling material might make for a stronger progression—for instance, from the fairly obvious to the controversial or new.

✗ *Respond to advice for improving the flow of material.* Respond to suggestions for building up a rich texture of comment, quotation, and interpretation.

ORIGINAL: After his first meeting with Salzman, the strange little matchmaker, Leo expresses doubts about the wisdom of having a bride chosen by someone else. Malamud writes,

> Leo was in low spirits. . . . He explained it as arising from Salzman's failure to produce a suitable bride for him. He did not care for his type of clientele. But when Leo found himself hesitating over whether to seek out another matchmaker, one more polished than Pinye, he wondered if it could be—his protestations to the contrary, and although he honored his father and mother—that he did not, in essence, care for the matchmaking institution? This thought he quickly put out of his mind.

COMMENT: You are probably using too many block quotations ("chunk quotations"—because they can make your paper seem chunky or lumpy). Save them to clinch an argument or highlight a major turning point? Try to work short, apt quotations into the flow of your argument.

REVISED: The first meeting with Salzman, the strange little matchmaker, does not go well. Leo is disheartened and expresses doubts about the wisdom of having a bride chosen by someone else. He entertains notions of hiring another matchmaker, someone "more polished than Pinye." But when Leo examines his deeper feelings, he wonders "if it could be—his protestations to the contrary, and although he honored his father and mother—that he did not, in essence, care for the matchmaking institution?" Although Leo has not yet realized it, this question is the beginning of the conflict between his traditional upbringing and his romantic nature. Although he "quickly put this thought out of his mind," it has planted a niggling suspicion that reaches full bloom as the story progresses.

✗ *Pay special attention to comments on weak transitions.* Where did the reader fail to see a logical connection that you thought was there? Be sure to respond to questions like "Why is this in here at this point? How are these two sections of your paper *related?* How does this fit into your overall plan?"

✗ *Respond to suggestions for strengthening your conclusion.*

ORIGINAL: . . . Jackson's "The Lottery" showed how people will do all kinds of crazy things, even things they don't really want to do, in the name of tradition.

COMMENT: Perfunctory or lame conclusion? What *is* the force of tradition? Why does it seem to carry such weight?

REVISED: . . . Jackson's "The Lottery" shows how tradition is like a subliminal force—because of it, people will do all kinds of crazy things, even things they don't really want to. We witness the peer pressure involved in tradition, forcing people to do something just because everyone else is doing it, and no one else is questioning it. As the story shows, human beings have a strong need to belong and be accepted by their society. This need causes them to want to conform, blindly and almost unconsciously, to the rules that their society has set up. Even stronger than tradition itself are the peer pressure and the human need for acceptance that fuels it.

Sample Student Paper

Study the following sample student paper. Does it make you more conscious of the role of plot in giving shape to a story as a whole?

Magic and Reality

"The Magic Barrel." In its very title, Bernard Malamud hints at the paradoxical nature of his short story. "The Magic Barrel" prepares us, the readers, to expect a fairy tale; it asks us to enter imaginatively into a world where miracles are possible. On the other hand, "The Magic Barrel" also gives us pause. "The Magic Barrel"? A rounded wooden vessel used to store wine or fish, magical? Had Malamud chosen "The Magic Well" or "The Magic Chalice" as his title, we would have been less puzzled, less intrigued. Adept at creating dualities and contrasts, Malamud invests his plot with "magic" elements as well as with sobering, realistic ones, just as he does his title. Malamud's plot introduces us to the lonely young scholar and the eccentric, enigmatic matchmaker, both likely inhabitants of a fairy-tale world. However, it also reveals conditions all too familiar to many in their everyday reality: the desperate lovelessness of the scholar and the harsh poverty of the matchmaker. As the plot is unveiled, Bernard Malamud's story is both like and unlike a fairy tale, ultimately a story in which fantasy and reality blend.

As "The Magic Barrel" begins, we are introduced to a person who is well suited to the world of the fairy tale: Leo Finkle, a rabbinical student, lives in a room which is "small, almost meager . . . though crowded with books." Leo has been studying for six years and is about to be ordained. From the first words of the story, Leo appears to be the stereotypical poor, lonely scholar, possessing little in the way of worldly goods but rich in spirituality, a kind of inner prosperity. We would wish a devoted companion for such a worthy, lonely fellow, and we are not disappointed. Leo, the author tells us, has decided to enlist the services of Pinye Salzman, a professional matchmaker, or "commercial cupid" as Malamud calls him. Malamud prepares the reader for a traditional romantic story, and he does not disappoint. The plot follows Leo as he listens without satisfaction to the descriptions of Salzman's clients, and as he meets, without enthusiasm, one of the eligible women. It follows Leo after he decides he must have romantic love before marriage, and after he finds a small, displaced photograph in an envelope of snapshots loaned to him by Salzman to help him in his quest. In true romantic style, Leo chases around the city attempting to locate the matchmaker (and so the woman) as frantically as Prince Charming's courtiers tried to locate the owner of the lone glass slipper. In true romantic style, Leo finds he has fallen for the one woman he should not have, Stella, the "shameless" daughter Salzman considers dead, a woman whose picture found its way into the matchmaker's envelope only by mistake (a marvelous, unlikely coincidence). In true romantic style, Leo pursues her anyway, and, with the power of wishful thinking triumphing over probability fairy-tale style, he finds her. Leo's discovery of his need for romantic love and the actions he takes to fulfill that need are suited to the world of fairy tales.

However, Malamud's plot not only explores the romantic occurrences in Leo's life, it also explores the more mundane, realistic ones. If Leo is not Prince Charming, he is at least a close relative. He is, however, also very human. The plot takes him through experiences that belong in the potentially painful real world rather than in the fairy-tale world. Leo has been studying diligently to become a rabbi for six years, but we also learn that his motives were not particularly admirable. "I think," Leo confesses to Lily Hirschorn, startling himself as much as the reader, "that I came to God not because I love Him, but because I did not." After this revelation, Leo experiences the worst week of his life. "With shocking force," he realizes that apart from his parents, he had never loved anyone. "It seemed to Leo that his whole life stood starkly revealed and he saw himself, for the first time, as he truly was—unloved and loveless." This young student stops eating and begins to lose weight. As his health suffers, he stops attending class. Malamud eventually allows Leo to "regain his composure," but this section of the plot takes the student about as far down as a human can go. The romantic events in Leo's life may predominate in the story, but they do not create an unrealistic story. Leo earns his romance the hardest way possible.

Malamud's most ambiguous scene occurs at the end of "The Magic Barrel." On one hand, it is the most romantic moment. On the other, it is curious and ambiguous. In this scene, after he has extracted some cooperation from Salzman, Leo succeeds in meeting Stella, the love of his life. She seems a bit wild, but not in an incorrigible way. She stands by a lamppost, smoking, but she waits "uneasily and shyly," her eyes filled with "desperate innocence." Experiencing "violins and lit candles" revolving in the sky, Leo rushes toward her, a bouquet of flowers outstretched in his hands. This moment, the most romantic in the story, is love found. However, its ambiguity lies in Salzman's presence and actions. The matchmaker stands "around the corner . . . leaning against a wall," chanting "prayers for the dead." Salzman could be blessing the union in the only way he knows how while steadfastly opposing Stella's earlier lifestyle, thus contributing to a romantic ending. Conversely, he could be offering his last prayers to a daughter whom he is deserting. He could be saying a farewell to one who he thinks is making her biggest and final error in an already "wicked" life, contributing to a modern, realistic ending. Malamud's plot follows the fairy-tale romantic events in Leo's life as well as the soberingly realistic ones. In his ambiguous ending, the author illustrates both views in one stroke.

Bernard Malamud's "The Magic Barrel" navigates between fantasy and reality. Some of Leo's acts, such as finding the woman of his dreams in a displaced photograph, desperately searching for her, then finding her, are very romantic, befitting a fairy tale. Other events in Leo's life, such as his realization that he is "unloved and loveless" and his ensuing crisis, belong in the realm of reality, not the fairy tale. In choosing to craft his plot to encompass both realms, Malamud creates a story that satisfies both the romantic and the pragmatist in us, the readers. He reminds us that fairy tales were created by real people; they are based on real life, not separate from it. Romantic happenings and happy endings can be and should be a part of everyday reality.

Questions

Does this paper add something to your own reading and understanding of the story? What is the overall thesis of this paper? How well do you think it fits the story? How well does the student writer use evidence to support it? Where do you want to disagree or take issue? How do you react to the ending of the paper?

5 Point of View

Windows on the World

The author is the central intelligence through whose eyes and mind we see the story.

MARTHA COX

FOCUS ON POINT OF VIEW

When reading a short story, we look at the world through the eyes of the writer. Whatever reality the story creates for us is a selection. We attend to what the author has brought into focus; we look at it from his or her angle of vision. No objective reality exists "out there" that is the same for everyone. What we call reality is our perception of reality—a picture we have constructed in our minds. We read a story in part to share imaginatively in a writer's perception of reality. We share in a writer's vision of the world.

Much modern fiction keeps us aware of the angle of vision. Who is the **narrator** observing the events—observing them from what angle? In much nineteenth-century fiction, the author could pretend to be God—to know everything. The all-knowing author seemed to be able to read the minds of all the different characters in a story, to be in several places at once to observe dispersed events. But much modern fiction opts for a more **limited** point of view. In a modern story, we are often aware of the person through whose eyes and ears we register details and events. We may take in only what a participant or an observer at the scene would actually have witnessed. We then become more conscious of the window that a story opens on the world.

When you study point of view, you ask: From what vantage point does the person telling the story look at the world?

The Omniscient Author The traditional **omniscient,** all-knowing author had access to the private thoughts and feelings of everyone in a novel or a story. A nineteenth-century novelist like George Eliot (pen name of Marian Evans) knew what went on in the minds and hearts of her several characters. Of course, what the omniscient author chose to tell the readers was a limited selection—the author merely *acted* as if she "knew all."

The Intruding Author   Some authors serve the reader as guides to their fictional world. The **intruding** author feels free to comment, to chat with us as the readers, to take us into his or her confidence. We are very much aware of the author's presence as the narrator. Every so often the author steps into the story from the outside, interrupting it to turn to us and offer asides, philosophical reflections, a personal view of life.

Third-Person Objective   In many stories, there is no "I, the storyteller" and no "you, the reader." The story talks about its characters in the third person: *she* did so-and-so; *he* did such-and-such. What the characters think and feel is seen from the outside. In much early modern fiction, the stance of the author was: We are not mind readers; we can never enter totally into someone else's world of thinking and feeling. We *can* try to be impartial observers, faithful to what we see and hear. In a Hemingway story, for instance, the author often assumes the stance of the honest witness, the incorruptible reporter. In such an **objective** narrative, there is a minimum of editorializing, judging, or preaching.

First-Person Autobiographical   In many deeply felt stories, we sense that the authors are speaking in thinly disguised form about their own childhood, their own families, their own conflicts or alienation. The "I" speaking in the story is talking about scenes and people from personal experience—perhaps with names and dates altered. Such writing may have a **confessional** tone; the writer may be unburdening his or her heart. However, we have to remember that the autobiographical material is fictionalized—shaped by the creative imagination. The "I" speaking to us in the story then becomes a **persona**—an assumed identity. (A persona was originally the mask actors wore on the classical Greek stage. Through it the sound of their voices came forth to reach the spectator—it "sounded through.") The distance between person and persona varies greatly from story to story.

First-Person Observer   The fictionalized "I" will play different roles in different stories. We may see the story through the eyes of someone at the center of the action. However, we may also see events through the eyes of someone on the sidelines who is not a major player. This person then becomes our scout, our reliable source, our "chosen interpreter." The person becomes our **reflector**—anything that happens in the story will reach us by way of his or her perceptions. A special **irony** may make us smile at the naive narrator who seems to know less than an alert reader. Mark Twain's Huckleberry Finn in the classic of the same name watches the world with wide-open, innocent eyes—

recognizing human duplicity or vindictiveness long after the more knowing reader.

Interior Monologue James Joyce and other early moderns experimented with the **stream-of-consciousness** technique. We enter into the mind of the narrator, sharing in a flow of thought and feeling. We listen in on the **interior monologue.** The narrative is not linear but moves by leaps and bounds of association. We may be distracted by bodily sensations (like the feel of a wet bar of soap in a trouser pocket). We may be sent off on a tangent by a scent, or by a remark that rekindles a long-forgotten memory. Like our own private thoughts and feelings, the narrator's flow of thought is likely to circle back sooner or later to the hopes, anxieties, or traumas that really matter. In a story like Tillie Olsen's "I Stand Here Ironing," we follow a more focused, *edited* interior monologue. We share in the private thoughts of the narrator. However, her memories, thoughts, and feelings are focused on the hardships, struggles, and regrets related to the bringing up of her oldest child.

WORLDS OF THOUGHT AND FEELING

There are both outer space and inner space to be explored.

NIKKI GIOVANNI

The following stories take us into a central character's personal world. They make us look at the world as seen through one character's eyes. Since the central characters in these stories are very different people, each takes us into a different universe of thought and feeling. However, in addition, the point of view from which the author chooses to tell the story varies, with the later stories taking us a step closer to sharing in the character's personal, private thoughts and emotions.

Anton Chekhov   *(1860–1904)*

Stories of youth and adolescence often adopt a distinctive, limited point of view. They see the world through the eyes of people less experienced, less knowing than we are. The following story is by Anton Chekhov, a nineteenth-century Russian writer whose grandfather had been a serf and who became famous as a playwright and as a writer of short stories. Chekhov's plays—*The Seagull, The Cherry Orchard, Three Sisters*—are still part of the modern repertory. The story that follows looks at the world from the perspective of youth. How and how well does the author control the point of view? What does the reader gain, and what does the reader lose, by looking at the world from a limited perspective?

Vanka   *1886*

Vanka Zhukov, a nine-year-old boy, who had been apprenticed to Alyahin the shoemaker these three months, did not go to bed on Christmas Eve. After his master and mistress and the journeymen had gone to midnight Mass, he got an inkpot and a penholder with a rusty nib out of the master's cupboard and, having spread out a crumpled sheet of paper, began writing. Before he formed the first letter he looked fearfully at the doors and windows several times, shot a glance at the dark icon, at either side of which stretched shelves filled with lasts, and heaved a broken sigh. He was kneeling before a bench on which his paper lay.

"Dear Granddaddy, Konstantin Makarych," he wrote. "And I am writing you a letter. I wish you a merry Christmas and everything good from the Lord God. I have neither father nor mother, you alone are left me."

Vanka shifted his glance to the dark window on which flickered the reflection of his candle and vividly pictured his grandfather to himself. Employed as a watchman by the Zhivaryovs, he was a short, thin, but extraordinarily lively and nimble old man of about sixty-five whose face was always crinkled with laughter and who had a toper's eyes. By day he slept in the servants' kitchen or cracked jokes with the cook; at night, wrapped in an ample sheepskin coat, he made the rounds of the estate, shaking his clapper. The old bitch, Brownie, and the dog called Wriggles, who had a black coat and a long body like a weasel's, followed him with hanging heads. This Wriggles was extraordinarily deferential and demonstrative, looked with equally friendly eyes both at his masters and at strangers, but did not enjoy a good reputation. His deference and meekness concealed the most Jesuitical spite. No one knew better than he how to creep up behind you and suddenly snap at your leg, how to slip into the icehouse, or how to steal a hen from a peasant. More than once his hind legs had been all but broken, twice he had been hanged, every week he was whipped till he was half dead, but he always managed to revive.

At the moment Grandfather was sure to be standing at the gates, screwing up his eyes at the bright-red windows of the church, stamping his felt boots, and cracking jokes with the servants. His clapper was tied to his belt. He was clapping his hands, shrugging with the cold, and, with a senile titter, pinching now the housemaid, now the cook.

"Shall we have a pinch of snuff?" he was saying, offering the women his   5
snuffbox.

They each took a pinch and sneezed. Grandfather, indescribably delighted, went off into merry peals of laughter and shouted:

"Peel it off, it has frozen on!"

The dogs too are given a pinch of snuff. Brownie sneezes, wags her head, and walks away offended. Wriggles is too polite to sneeze and only wags his tail. And the weather is glorious. The air is still, clear, and fresh.

The night is dark, but one can see the whole village with its white roofs and smoke streaming out of the chimneys, the trees silvery with hoarfrost, the snowdrifts. The entire sky is studded with gaily twinkling stars and the Milky Way is as distinctly visible as though it had been washed and rubbed with snow for the holiday. . . .

Vanka sighed, dipped his pen into the ink and went on writing:

"And yesterday I got it hot. The master pulled me out into the courtyard   10
by the hair and gave me a hiding with a knee-strap because I was rocking the baby in its cradle and happened to fall asleep. And last week the mistress ordered me to clean a herring and I began with the tail, and she took the herring and jabbed me in the mug with it. The helpers make fun of me, send me to the pothouse for vodka and tell me to steal pickles for them from the master, and the master hits me with anything that comes handy. And there is nothing to eat. In the morning they give me bread, for dinner porridge, and in the evening bread again. As for tea or cabbage soup, the master and mistress bolt it all themselves. And they tell me to sleep in the entry, and when the baby cries I don't sleep at all, but rock the cradle. Dear Granddaddy, for God's sake have pity on me, take me away from here, take me home to the village, it's more than I can bear. I bow down at your feet and I will pray to God for you forever, take me away from here or I'll die."

Vanka puckered his mouth, rubbed his eyes with his black fist, and gave a sob.

"I will grind your snuff for you," he continued, "I will pray to God for you, and if anything happens, you may thrash me all you like. And if you think there's no situation for me, I will beg the manager for Christ's sake to let me clean boots, or I will take Fedka's place as a shepherd boy. Dear Granddaddy, it's more than I can bear, it will simply be the death of me. I thought of running away to the village, but I have no boots and I am afraid of the frost. And in return for this when I grow big, I will feed you and won't let anybody do you any harm, and when you die I will pray for the repose of your soul, just as for my Mom's.

"Moscow is a big city. The houses are all the kind the gentry live in, and there are lots of horses, but no sheep, and the dogs are not fierce. The boys here don't go caroling, carrying the star at Christmas, and they don't let anyone sing in the choir, and once in a shop window I saw fishing-hooks for sale all fitted up with a line, for every kind of fish, very fine ones, there was even one hook that will hold a forty-pound sheatfish. And I saw shops where there are all sorts of guns, like the master's at home, so maybe each one of them is a hundred rubles. And in butchers' shops there are woodcocks and partridge and hares, but where they shoot them the clerks won't tell.

"Dear Granddaddy, when they have a Christmas tree with presents at the master's, do get a gilt walnut and put it away in the little green chest. Ask the young lady, Olga Ignatyevna, for it, say it's for Vanka."

Vanka heaved a broken sigh and again stared at the window. He recalled   15
that it was his grandfather who always went to the forest to get the Christmas tree for the master's family and that he would take his grandson with him. It was a jolly time! Grandfather grunted, the frost crackled, and, not to be outdone, Vanka too made a cheerful noise in his throat. Before chopping down the Christmas tree, Grandfather would smoke a pipe, slowly take a

pinch of snuff, and poke fun at Vanka who looked chilled to the bone. The young firs draped in hoarfrost stood still, waiting to see which of them was to die. Suddenly, coming out of nowhere, a hare would dart across the snowdrifts like an arrow. Grandfather could not keep from shouting: "Hold him, hold him, hold him! Ah, the bob-tailed devil!"

When he had cut down the fir tree, Grandfather would drag it to the master's house, and there they would set to work decorating it. The young lady, Olga Ignatyevna, Vanka's favorite, was the busiest of all. When Vanka's mother, Pelageya, was alive and a chambermaid in the master's house, the young lady used to give him goodies, and, having nothing with which to occupy herself, taught him to read and write, to count up to a hundred, and even to dance the quadrille. When Pelageya died, Vanka had been relegated to the servants' kitchen to stay with his grandfather, and from the kitchen to the shoemaker's.

"Do come, dear Granddaddy," Vanka went on. "For Christ's sake, I beg you, take me away from here. Have pity on me, an unhappy orphan, here everyone beats me, and I am terribly hungry, and I am so blue, I can't tell you how, I keep crying. And the other day the master hit me on the head with a last, so that I fell down and it was a long time before I came to. My life is miserable, worse than a dog's—I also send greetings to Alyona, one-eyed Yegorka and the coachman, and don't give my harmonica to anyone. I remain, your grandson, Ivan Zhukov, dear Granddaddy, do come."

Vanka twice folded the sheet covered with writing and put it into an envelope he had bought for a kopeck the previous day. He reflected a while, then dipped the pen into the ink and wrote the address:

To Grandfather in the village

Then he scratched himself, thought a little, and added: *Konstantin Maka-rych*. Glad that no one had interrupted him at his writing, he put on his cap and, without slipping on his coat, ran out into the street with nothing over his shirt.

The clerks at the butchers' whom he had questioned the day before had told him that letters were dropped into letter boxes and from the boxes they were carried all over the world in troikas with ringing bells and drunken drivers. Vanka ran to the nearest letter box and thrust the precious letter into the slit.

An hour later, lulled by sweet hopes, he was fast asleep. In his dream he   20 saw the stove. On the stove sat grandfather, his bare legs hanging down, and read the letter to the cooks. Near the stove was Wriggles, wagging his tail.

The Receptive Reader

1. What would you include in a *capsule portrait* of Vanka?

2. Why do you think Chekhov does not include any specific reference to the boy's mistreatment until we have read one-third of the story?

3. What details in the story keep reminding us of Vanka's limited *point of view?* (Does anything get into the story that should really be beyond the central character's ken?)

4. Where is the author in this story, and why does he adopt this limited perspective? What is the appeal for the reader—what do you gain (or lose) from looking at the world through Vanka's eyes?

The Creative Dimension

Write a letter that you might have written when you were nearer Vanka's age. Write about a topic that seemed important at the time; address your letter to someone who was then important in your life.

Tillie Olsen   *(born 1912)*

We must not speak of women writers in our century (as we cannot speak of women in any area of recognized human achievement) without speaking also of the invisible, the as-innately-capable: the born to wrong circumstances—diminished, excluded, foundered, silenced.

TILLIE OLSEN

Tillie Olsen came to be widely admired for giving voice to the story of the unheard, the silenced, in American society. Writing about the Great Depression of the thirties, she wrote with bitter eloquence about the working-class experience—poverty, illness, hunger, unemployment, soul-deadening jobs. A native of Omaha, Nebraska, with only a high school education, she herself lived through grey poverty to write powerful stories shaking up our complacency. Her story "Tell Me a Riddle" won the O. Henry Award as the best short story of the year in 1961. She has since received prestigious grants and honors and lectured at universities including Amherst and Stanford.

Women readers and women writers made her a revered figure in the women's movement. They identified with the heroic struggle of a "family wage earner at dull and time-sapping menial jobs" (Nolan Miller)—a woman who "held down a job, raised four children, and still somehow managed to become and remain a writer," surviving a "grueling obstacle race" that cost her "twenty years of her writing life" (Margaret Atwood). In her collection *Silences* (1978), Olsen collected and reprinted the testimony of writers, and especially women from Virginia Woolf to Katherine Mansfield, about the social and psychological forces that hobble the creative spirit, forcing many who are not white, male, or affluent into silence.

In the following story, we look through the eyes of a mother at a daughter who was "the child of anxious, not proud love." What world do we see through the narrator's eyes? (The WPA referred to in the story is the Works Progress Administration, begun in 1935 to provide federally funded jobs for the unemployed during the Great Depression.)

I Stand Here Ironing   *1961*

I stand here ironing, and what you asked me moves tormented back and forth with the iron.

"I wish you would manage the time to come in and talk with me about your daughter. I'm sure you can help me understand her. She's a youngster who needs help and whom I'm deeply interested in helping."

"Who needs help.". . . Even if I came, what good would it do? You think because I am her mother I have a key, or that in some way you could use me as a key? She has lived for nineteen years. There is all that life that has happened outside of me, beyond me.

And when is there time to remember, to sift, to weigh, to estimate, to total? I will start and there will be an interruption and I will have to gather it all together again. Or I will become engulfed with all I did or did not do, with what should have been and what cannot be helped.

She was a beautiful baby. The first and only one of our five that was   5 beautiful at birth. You do not guess how new and uneasy her tenancy in her now-loveliness. You did not know her all those years she was thought homely, or see her poring over her baby pictures, making me tell her over and over how beautiful she had been—and would be, I would tell her—and was now, to the seeing eye. But the seeing eyes were few or nonexistent. Including mine.

I nursed her. They feel that's important nowadays. I nursed all the children, but with her, with all the fierce rigidity of first motherhood, I did like the books then said. Though her cries battered me to trembling and my breasts ached with swollenness, I waited till the clock decreed.

Why do I put that first? I do not even know if it matters, or if it explains anything.

She was a beautiful baby. She blew shining bubbles of sound. She loved motion, loved light, loved color and music and textures. She would lie on the floor in her blue overalls patting the surface so hard in ecstasy her hands and feet would blur. She was a miracle to me, but when she was eight months old I had to leave her daytimes with the woman downstairs to whom she was no miracle at all, for I worked or looked for work and for Emily's father, who "could no longer endure" (he wrote in his good-bye note) "sharing want with us."

I was nineteen. It was the pre-relief, pre-WPA world of the depression. I would start running as soon as I got off the streetcar, running up the stairs, the place smelling sour, and awake or asleep to startle awake, when she saw me she would break into a clogged weeping that could not be comforted, a weeping I can hear yet.

After a while I found a job hashing at night so I could be with her days,   10 and it was better. But it came to where I had to bring her to his family and leave her.

It took a long time to raise the money for her fare back. Then she got chicken pox and I had to wait longer. When she finally came, I hardly knew her, walking quick and nervous like her father, looking like her father, thin, and dressed in a shoddy red that yellowed her skin and glared at the pockmarks. All the baby loveliness gone.

She was two. Old enough for nursery school they said, and I did not know then what I know now—the fatigue of the long day, and the lacerations of group life in the kinds of nurseries that are only parking places for children.

Except that it would have made no difference if I had known. It was the only place there was. It was the only way we could be together, the only way I could hold a job.

And even without knowing, I knew. I knew the teacher that was evil because all these years it has curdled into my memory, the little boy hunched in the corner, her rasp, "why aren't you outside, because Alvin hits you? that's no reason, go out, scaredy." I knew Emily hated it even if she did not clutch and implore "don't go Mommy" like the other children, mornings.

She always had a reason why we should stay home. Momma, you look   15 sick. Momma, I feel sick. Momma, the teachers aren't there today, they're sick. Momma, we can't go, there was a fire there last night. Momma, it's a holiday today, no school, they told me.

But never a direct protest, never rebellion. I think of our others in their three-, four-year-oldness—the explosions, the tempers, the denunciations, the demands—and I feel suddenly ill. I put the iron down. What in me demanded that goodness in her? And what was the cost, the cost to her of such goodness?

The old man living in the back once said in his gentle way: "You should smile at Emily more when you look at her." What *was* in my face when I looked at her? I loved her. There were all the acts of love.

It was only with the others I remembered what he said, and it was the face of joy, and not of care or tightness or worry I turned to them—too late for Emily. She does not smile easily, let alone almost always as her brothers and sisters do. Her face is closed and sombre, but when she wants, how fluid. You must have seen it in her pantomimes, you spoke of her rare gift for comedy on the stage that rouses laughter out of the audience so dear they applaud and applaud and do not want to let her go.

Where does it come from, that comedy? There was none of it in her when she came back to me that second time, after I had had to send her away again. She had a new daddy now to learn to love, and I think perhaps it was a better time.

Except when we left her alone nights, telling ourselves she was old   20 enough.

"Can't you go some other time, Mommy, like tomorrow?" she would ask. "Will it be just a little while you'll be gone? Do you promise?"

The time we came back, the front door open, the clock on the floor in the hall. She rigid awake. "It wasn't just a little while. I didn't cry. Three times I called you, just three times, and then I ran downstairs to open the door so you could come faster. The clock talked loud. I threw it away, it scared me what it talked."

She said the clock talked loud again that night I went to the hospital to have Susan. She was delirious with the fever that comes before red measles, but she was fully conscious all the week I was gone and the week after we were home when she could not come near the new baby or me.

She did not get well. She stayed skeleton thin, not wanting to eat, and night after night she had nightmares. She would call for me, and I would rouse from exhaustion to sleepily call back: "You're all right, darling, go to sleep, it's just a dream," and if she still called, in a sterner voice, "now go to sleep, Emily, there's nothing to hurt you." Twice, only twice, when I had to get up for Susan anyhow, I went in to sit with her.

Now when it is too late (as if she would let me hold and comfort her like   25
I do the others) I get up and go to her at once at her moan or restless stirring. "Are you awake, Emily? Can I get you something?" And the answer is always the same: "No, I'm all right, go back to sleep, Mother."

They persuaded me at the clinic to send her away to a convalescent home in the country where "she can have the kind of food and care you can't manage for her, and you'll be free to concentrate on the new baby." They still send children to that place. I see pictures on the society page of sleek young women planning affairs to raise money for it, or dancing at the affairs, or decorating Easter eggs or filling Christmas stockings for the children.

They never have a picture of the children so I do not know if the girls still wear those gigantic red bows and the ravaged looks on the every other Sunday when parents can come to visit "unless otherwise notified"—as we were notified the first six weeks.

Oh it is a handsome place, green lawns and tall trees and fluted flower beds. High up on the balconies of each cottage the children stand, the girls in their red bows and white dresses, the boys in white suits and giant red ties. The parents stand below shrieking up to be heard and the children shriek down to be heard, and between them the invisible wall: "Not to Be Contaminated by Parental Germs or Physical Affection."

There was a tiny girl who always stood hand in hand with Emily. Her parents never came. One visit she was gone. "They moved her to Rose Cottage," Emily shouted in explanation. "They don't like you to love anybody here."

She wrote once a week, the labored writing of a seven-year-old. "I am   30
fine. How is the baby. If I write my leter nicly I will have a star. Love." There never was a star. We wrote every other day, letters she could never hold or keep but only hear read—once. "We simply do not have room for children to keep any personal possessions," they patiently explained when we pieced one Sunday's shrieking together to plead how much it would mean to Emily, who loved so to keep things, to be allowed to keep her letters and cards.

Each visit she looked frailer. "She isn't eating," they told us.

(They had runny eggs for breakfast or mush with lumps, Emily said later, I'd hold it in my mouth and not swallow. Nothing ever tasted good, just when they had chicken.)

It took us eight months to get her released home, and only the fact that she gained back so little of her seven lost pounds convinced the social worker.

I used to try to hold and love her after she came back, but her body would stay stiff, and after a while she'd push away. She ate little. Food sickened her, and I think much of life too. Oh she had physical lightness and brightness, twinkling by on skates, bouncing like a ball up and down up and down over the jump rope, skimming over the hill; but these were momentary.

She fretted about her appearance, thin and dark and foreign-looking at a   35
time when every little girl was supposed to look or thought she should look
a chubby blonde replica of Shirley Temple. The doorbell sometimes rang
for her, but no one seemed to come and play in the house or be a best
friend. Maybe because we moved so much.

There was a boy she loved painfully through two school semesters.
Months later she told me how she had taken pennies from my purse to buy
him candy. "Licorice was his favorite and I brought him some every day, but
he still liked Jennifer better'n me. Why, Mommy?" The kind of question for
which there is no answer.

School was a worry to her. She was not glib or quick in a world where
glibness and quickness were easily confused with ability to learn. To her
overworked and exasperated teachers she was an overconscientious "slow
learner" who kept trying to catch up and was absent entirely too often.

I let her be absent, though sometimes the illness was imaginary. How different from my now-strictness about attendance with the others. I wasn't
working. We had a new baby, I was home anyhow. Sometimes, after Susan
grew old enough, I would keep her home from school, too, to have them
all together.

Mostly Emily had asthma, and her breathing, harsh and labored, would fill
the house with a curiously tranquil sound. I would bring the two old dresser
mirrors and her boxes of collections to her bed. She would select beads and
single earrings, bottle tops and shells, dried flowers and pebbles, old postcards and scraps, all sorts of oddments; then she and Susan would play
Kingdom, setting up landscapes and furniture, peopling them with action.

Those were the only times of peaceful companionship between her and   40
Susan. I have edged away from it, that poisonous feeling between them,
that terrible balancing of hurts and needs I had to do between the two, and
did so badly, those earlier years.

Oh there are conflicts between the others too, each one human, needing, demanding, hurting, taking—but only between Emily and Susan, no,
Emily toward Susan that corroding resentment. It seems so obvious on the
surface, yet it is not obvious. Susan, the second child, Susan, golden- and
curly-haired and chubby, quick and articulate and assured, everything in
appearance and manner Emily was not; Susan, not able to resist Emily's
precious things, losing or sometimes clumsily breaking them; Susan telling
jokes and riddles to company for applause while Emily sat silent (to say to
me later: that was *my* riddle, Mother, I told it to Susan); Susan, who for all
the five years' difference in age was just a year behind Emily in developing
physically.

I am glad for that slow physical development that widened the difference
between her and her contemporaries, though she suffered over it. She was
too vulnerable for that terrible world of youthful competition, of preening
and parading, of constant measuring of yourself against every other, of
envy, "If I had that copper hair," "If I had that skin. . . ." She tormented herself enough about not looking like the others, there was enough of the
unsureness, the having to be conscious of words before you speak, the constant caring—what are they thinking of me? without having it all magnified
by the merciless physical drives.

Ronnie is calling. He is wet and I change him. It is rare there is such a cry now. That time of motherhood is almost behind me when the ear is not one's own but must always be racked and listening for the child cry, the child call. We sit for a while and I hold him, looking out over the city spread in charcoal with its soft aisles of light. *"Shoogily,"* he breathes and curls closer. I carry him back to bed, asleep. *Shoogily.* A funny word, a family word, inherited from Emily, invented by her to say: *comfort.*

In this and other ways she leaves her seal, I say aloud. And startle at my saying it. What do I mean? What did I start to gather together, to try and make coherent? I was at the terrible, growing years. War years. I do not remember them well. I was working, there were four smaller ones now, there was not time for her. She had to help be a mother, and housekeeper, and shopper. She had to set her seal. Mornings of crisis and near hysteria trying to get lunches packed, hair combed, coats and shoes found, everyone to school or Child Care on time, the baby ready for transportation. And always the paper scribbled on by a smaller one, the book looked at by Susan then mislaid, the homework not done. Running out to that huge school where she was one, she was lost, she was a drop; suffering over the unpreparedness, stammering and unsure in her classes.

There was so little time left at night after the kids were bedded down.   45
She would struggle over books, always eating (it was in those years she developed her enormous appetite that is legendary in our family) and I would be ironing, or preparing food for the next day, or writing V-mail to Bill, or tending the baby. Sometimes, to make me laugh, or out of her despair, she would imitate happenings or types at school.

I think I said once: "Why don't you do something like this in the school amateur show?" One morning she phoned me at work, hardly understandable through the weeping: "Mother, I did it. I won, I won; they gave me first prize; they clapped and clapped and wouldn't let me go."

Now suddenly she was Somebody, and as imprisoned in her difference as she had been in anonymity.

She began to be asked to perform at other high schools, even in colleges, then at city and statewide affairs. The first one we went to, I only recognized her that first moment when thin, shy, she almost drowned herself into the curtains. Then: Was this Emily? The control, the command, the convulsing and deadly clowning, the spell, then the roaring, stamping audience, unwilling to let this rare and precious laughter out of their lives.

Afterwards: You ought to do something about her with a gift like that—but without money or knowing how, what does one do? We have left it all to her, and the gift has as often eddied inside, clogged and clotted, as been used and growing.

She is coming. She runs up the stairs two at a time with her light grace-   50
ful step, and I know she is happy tonight. Whatever it was that occasioned your call did not happen today.

"Aren't you ever going to finish the ironing, Mother? Whistler painted his mother in a rocker. I'd have to paint mine standing over an ironing board." This is one of her communicative nights and she tells me everything and nothing as she fixes herself a plate of food out of the icebox.

She is so lovely. Why did you want me to come in at all? Why were you concerned? She will find her way.

She starts up the stairs to bed. "Don't get me up with the rest in the morning." "But I thought you were having midterms." "Oh, those," she comes back in, kisses me, and says quite lightly, "in a couple of years when we'll all be atom-dead they won't matter a bit."

She has said it before. She *believes* it. But because I have been dredging the past, and all that compounds a human being is so heavy and meaningful in me, I cannot endure it tonight.

I will never total it all. I will never come in to say: She was a child seldom   55
smiled at. Her father left me before she was a year old. I had to work her first six years when there was work, or I sent her home and to his relatives. There were years she had care she hated. She was dark and thin and foreign-looking in a world where the prestige went to blondeness and curly hair and dimples, she was slow where glibness was prized. She was a child of anxious, not proud, love. We were poor and could not afford for her the soil of easy growth. I was a young mother, I was a distracted mother. There were other children pushing up, demanding. Her younger sister seemed all that she was not. There were years she did not want me to touch her. She kept too much in herself, her life was such she had to keep too much in herself. My wisdom came too late. She has much to her and probably little will come of it. She is a child of her age, of depression, of war, of fear.

Let her be. So all that is in her will not bloom—but in how many does it? There is still enough left to live by. Only help her to know—help make it so there is cause for her to know—that she is more than this dress on the ironing board, helpless before the iron.

The Receptive Reader

1. Who is the *you* addressed in the story?

2. How do the physical conditions, the circumstances of her life, shape the narrator's outlook? What physical details are especially telling or have a possible symbolic meaning?

3. Early in the story, we catch glimpses of the teacher, of Emily's father, and of the old man who lives in the back. What role do these people on the periphery of the story play in the narrator's world and her view of the world?

4. What is the narrator's attitude toward *institutions?* Why do they loom so large in the story? What are striking details? Is the narrator's attitude one-sided?

5. What picture of Emily as the oldest child emerges in this story? What are key points the narrator wants us to see or understand about Emily as a person? What makes the child—and the mother's relationship with her—*complex* rather than simple?

6. Although it is told in a low key, without melodrama or eloquent indictments, there are powerful undercurrents of *emotion* running in this story. What are they? Where are they harshest—or most frankly described?

7. What kind of summing up does the *ending* of the story provide? What attitude toward life or view of the world emerges here? Is it of one piece with the story as a whole?

8. How do you think the situation or the child might have looked when seen from a *different* point of view? For instance, what might have been the perspective of a teacher or social worker? Does the narrator acknowledge different points of view?

The Personal Response

How do you relate to the narrator in the story? Do you think of her as a bitter person? an angry person? a defeated person? How do you relate to the daughter in the story? What do you think the future holds for her?

Making Connections—For Discussion or Writing

Critics reading literature from a Marxist perspective emphasize the role of social class in shaping people's lives. Compare the perspectives on American working-class life in Bobbie Ann Mason's "Shiloh," in Raymond Carver's "The Third Thing That Killed My Father Off," and Tillie Olsen's "I Stand Here Ironing."

Katherine Anne Porter   *(1890–1980)*

The truth is, I have never written a story in my life that didn't have a very firm foundation in actual human experience—somebody else's experience quite often, but an experience that became my own by hearing the story, by witnessing the thing, by hearing just a word perhaps. It doesn't matter, it just takes a little—a tiny seed. Then it takes root, and it grows.

KATHERINE ANNE PORTER

Katherine Anne Porter became known as a writer more interested in a character's state of mind than in external action. She published *Flowering Judas,* her first collection of short stories, in 1930. Born in Texas, she drew on her experiences as a young girl growing up in the South and as an observer of revolutionary turmoil in Mexico. She is best known for her novellas (long short stories or short novels) "Noon Wine" (1937) and "Pale Horse, Pale Rider" (1939). She traveled widely, and she drew on her observations of Europe in the thirties and forties in her novel *Ship of Fools* (1962). This novel, made into a movie with José Ferrer, Oskar Werner, and Simone Signoret, followed a group of travelers on a voyage to Germany in 1931, when anti-Semitism was on the rise and ominous signs pointed toward the Nazi takeover in 1933.

"The Jilting of Granny Weatherall" is a short story that takes us inside the consciousness of the main character. We follow the stream of observations, memories, and rationalizations as they pass through the character's mind. Instead of following external action from cause to effect, or from action to reaction, we follow the **stream of consciousness.** In most of the story, we hear the main character thinking to herself; we listen to the **interior monologue.** We move on two levels: we get glimpses of the outer, or surface, reality of the sickroom. But we also participate in the inner reality of the central character's observations, thoughts, and feelings. As often with the stream-of-consciousness technique, some of the stream of thoughts and emotions seems trivial or routine. But eventually the character's thinking circles back to what really matters.

The Jilting of Granny Weatherall   1929

She flicked her wrist neatly out of Doctor Harry's pudgy careful fingers and pulled the sheet up to her chin. The brat ought to be in knee breeches. Doctoring around the country with spectacles on his nose! "Get along now, take your schoolbooks and go. There's nothing wrong with me."

Doctor Harry spread a warm paw like a cushion on her forehead where the forked green vein danced and made her eyelids twitch. "Now, now, be a good girl, and we'll have you up in no time."

"That's no way to speak to a woman nearly eighty years old just because she's down. I'd have you respect your elders, young man."

"Well, Missy, excuse me." Doctor Harry patted her cheek. "But I've got to warn you, haven't I? You're a marvel, but you must be careful or you're going to be good and sorry."

"Don't tell me what I'm going to be. I'm on my feet now, morally speaking. It's Cornelia. I had to go to bed to get rid of her."   5

Her bones felt loose, and floated around in her skin, and Doctor Harry floated like a balloon around the foot of the bed. He floated and pulled down his waistcoat and swung his glasses on a cord. "Well, stay where you are, it certainly can't hurt you."

"Get along and doctor your sick," said Granny Weatherall. "Leave a well woman alone. I'll call for you when I want you. . . . Where were you forty years ago when I pulled through milk-leg and double pneumonia? You weren't even born. Don't let Cornelia lead you on," she shouted, because Doctor Harry appeared to float up to the ceiling and out. "I pay my own bills, and I don't throw my money away on nonsense!"

She meant to wave good-by, but it was too much trouble. Her eyes closed of themselves, it was like a dark curtain drawn around the bed. The pillow rose and floated under her, pleasant as a hammock in a light wind. She listened to the leaves rustling outside the window. No, somebody was swishing newspapers: no, Cornelia and Doctor Harry were whispering together. She leaped broad awake, thinking they whispered in her ear.

"She was never like this, *never* like this!" "Well, what can we expect?" "Yes, eighty years old. . . ."

Well, and what if she was? She still had ears. It was like Cornelia to whisper around doors. She always kept things secret in such a public way. She was always being tactful and kind. Cornelia was dutiful; that was the trouble with her. Dutiful and good: "So good and dutiful," said Granny, "that I'd like to spank her." She saw herself spanking Cornelia and making a fine job of it.   10

"What'd you say, Mother?"

Granny felt her face tying up in hard knots.

"Can't a body think, I'd like to know?"

"I thought you might want something."

"I do. I want a lot of things. First off, go away and don't whisper."   15

She lay and drowsed, hoping in her sleep that the children would keep out and let her rest a minute. It had been a long day. Not that she was tired. It was always pleasant to snatch a minute now and then. There was always so much to be done, let me see: tomorrow.

Tomorrow was far away and there was nothing to trouble about. Things were finished somehow when the time came; thank God there was always a little margin over for peace: then a person could spread out the plan of life and tuck in the edges orderly. It was good to have everything clean and folded away, with the hair brushes and tonic bottles sitting straight on the white embroidered linen: the day started without fuss and the pantry shelves laid out with rows of jelly glasses and brown jugs and white stone-china jars with blue whirligigs and words painted on them: coffee, tea, sugar, ginger, cinnamon, allspice: and the bronze clock with the lion on top nicely dusted off. The dust that·lion could collect in twenty-four hours! The box in the attic with all those letters tied up, well, she'd have to go through that tomorrow. All those letters—George's letters and John's letters and her letters to them both—lying around for the children to find afterwards made her uneasy. Yes, that would be tomorrow's business. No use to let them know how silly she had been once.

While she was rummaging around she found death in her mind and it felt clammy and unfamiliar. She had spent so much time preparing for death there was no need for bringing it up again. Let it take care of itself now. When she was sixty she had felt very old, finished, and went around making farewell trips to see her children and grandchildren, with a secret in her mind: This is the very last of your mother, children! Then she made her will and came down with a long fever. That was all just a notion like a lot of other things, but it was lucky too, for she had once for all got over the idea of dying for a long time. Now she couldn't be worried. She hoped she had better sense now. Her father had lived to be one hundred and two years old and had drunk a noggin of strong hot toddy on his last birthday. He told reporters it was his daily habit, and he owed his long life to that. He had made quite a scandal and was very pleased about it. She believed she'd just plague Cornelia a little.

"Cornelia! Cornelia!" No footsteps, but a sudden hand on her cheek. "Bless you, where have you been?"

"Here, Mother."   20

"Well, Cornelia, I want a noggin of hot toddy."

"Are you cold, darling?"

"I'm chilly, Cornelia. Lying in bed stops the circulation. I must have told you that a thousand times."

Well, she could just hear Cornelia telling her husband that Mother was getting a little childish and they'd have to humor her. The thing that most annoyed her was that Cornelia thought she was deaf, dumb, and blind. Little hasty glances and tiny gestures tossed around her and over her head saying, "Don't cross her, let her have her way, she's eighty years old," and she sitting there as if she lived in a thin glass cage. Sometimes Granny almost made up her mind to pack up and move back to her own house where nobody could remind her every minute that she was old. Wait, wait, Cornelia, till your own children whisper behind your back!

In her day she had kept a better house and had got more work done. She wasn't too old yet for Lydia to be driving eighty miles for advice when one of the children jumped the track, and Jimmy still dropped in and talked things over: "Now, Mammy, you've a good business head, I want to know what you think of this? . . ." Old. Cornelia couldn't change the furniture around without asking. Little things, little things! They had been so sweet when they were little. Granny wished the old days were back again with the children young and everything to be done over. It had been a hard pull, but not too much for her. When she thought of all the food she had cooked, and all the clothes she had cut and sewed, and all the gardens she had made—well, the children showed it. There they were, made out of her, and they couldn't get away from that. Sometimes she wanted to see John again and point to them and say, Well, I didn't do so badly, did I? But that would have to wait. That was for tomorrow. She used to think of him as a man, but now all the children were older than their father, and he would be a child beside her if she saw him now. It seemed strange and there was something wrong in the idea. Why, he couldn't possibly recognize her. She had fenced in a hundred acres once, digging the post holes herself and clamping the wires with just a negro boy to help. That changed a woman. John would be looking for a young woman with the peaked Spanish comb in her hair and the painted fan. Digging post holes changed a woman. Riding country roads in the winter when women had their babies was another thing: sitting up nights with sick horses and sick negroes and sick children and hardly ever losing one. John, I hardly ever lost one of them! John would see that in a minute, that would be something he could understand, she wouldn't have to explain anything!

It made her feel like rolling up her sleeves and putting the whole place to rights again. No matter if Cornelia was determined to be everywhere at once, there were a great many things left undone on this place. She would start tomorrow and do them. It was good to be strong enough for everything, even if all you made melted and changed and slipped under your hands, so that by the time you finished you almost forgot what you were working for. What was it I set out to do? she asked herself intently, but she could not remember. A fog rose over the valley, she saw it marching across the creek swallowing the trees and moving up the hill like an army of ghosts. Soon it would be at the near edge of the orchard, and then it was time to go in and light the lamps. Come in, children, don't stay out in the night air.

Lighting the lamps had been beautiful. The children huddled up to her and breathed like little calves waiting at the bars in the twilight. Their eyes followed the match and watched the flame rise and settle in a blue curve, then they moved away from her. The lamp was lit, they didn't have to be scared and hang on to mother any more. Never, never, never more. God, for all my life I thank Thee. Without Thee, my God, I could never have done it. Hail, Mary, full of grace.

25

I want you to pick all the fruit this year and see that nothing is wasted. There's always someone who can use it. Don't let good things rot for want of using. You waste life when you waste good food. Don't let things get lost. It's bitter to lose things. Now, don't let me get to thinking, not when I am tired and taking a little nap before supper. . . .

The pillow rose about her shoulders and pressed against her heart and the memory was being squeezed out of it: oh, push down the pillow, somebody: it would smother her if she tried to hold it. Such a fresh breeze blowing and such a green day with no threats in it. But he had not come, just the same. What does a woman do when she has put on the white veil and set out the white cake for a man and he doesn't come? She tried to remember. No, I swear he never harmed me but in that. He never harmed me but in that . . . and what if he did? There was the day, the day, but a whirl of dark smoke rose and covered it, crept up and over into the bright field where everything was planted so carefully in orderly rows. That was hell, she knew hell when she saw it. For sixty years she had prayed against remembering him and against losing her soul in the deep pit of hell, and now the two things were mingled in one and the thought of him was a smoky cloud from hell that moved and crept in her head when she had just got rid of Doctor Harry and was trying to rest a minute. Wounded vanity, Ellen, said a sharp voice in the top of her mind. Don't let your wounded vanity get the upper hand of you. Plenty of girls get jilted. You were jilted, weren't you? Then stand up to it. Her eyelids wavered and let in streamers of blue-gray light like tissue paper over her eyes. She must get up and pull the shades down or she'd never sleep. She was in bed again and the shades were not down. How could that happen? Better turn over, hide from the light, sleeping in the light gave you nightmares. "Mother, how do you feel now?" and a stinging wetness on her forehead. But I don't like having my face washed in cold water!

Hapsy? George? Lydia? Jimmy? No, Cornelia, and her features were   30
swollen and full of little puddles. "They're coming, darling, they'll all be here soon." Go wash your face, child, you look funny.

Instead of obeying, Cornelia knelt down and put her head on the pillow. She seemed to be talking but there was no sound. "Well, are you tongue-tied? Whose birthday is it? Are you going to give a party?"

Cornelia's mouth moved urgently in strange shapes. "Don't do that, you bother me, daughter."

"Oh, no, Mother. Oh, no. . . ."

Nonsense. It was strange about children. They disputed your every word. "No what, Cornelia?"

"Here's Doctor Harry."   35

"I won't see that boy again. He just left five minutes ago."

"That was this morning, Mother. It's night now. Here's the nurse."

"This is Doctor Harry, Mrs. Weatherall. I never saw you look so young and happy!"

"Ah, I'll never be young again—but I'd be happy if they'd let me lie in peace and get rested."

She thought she spoke up loudly, but no one answered. A warm weight   40
on her forehead, a warm bracelet on her wrist, and a breeze went on whispering, trying to tell her something. A shuffle of leaves in the everlasting

hand of God, He blew on them and they danced and rattled. "Mother, don't mind, we're going to give you a little hypodermic." "Look here, daughter, how do ants get in this bed? I saw sugar ants yesterday." Did you send for Hapsy too?

It was Hapsy she really wanted. She had to go a long way back through a great many rooms to find Hapsy standing with a baby on her arm. She seemed to herself to be Hapsy also, and the baby on Hapsy's arm was Hapsy and himself and herself, all at once, and there was no surprise in the meeting. Then Hapsy melted from within and turned flimsy as gray gauze and the baby was a gauzy shadow, and Hapsy came up close and said, "I thought you'd never come," and looked at her very searchingly and said, "You haven't changed a bit!" They leaned forward to kiss, when Cornelia began whispering from a long way off, "Oh, is there anything you want to tell me? Is there anything I can do for you?"

Yes, she had changed her mind after sixty years and she would like to see George. I want you to find George. Find him and be sure to tell him I forgot him. I want him to know I had my husband just the same and my children and my house like any other woman. A good house too and a good husband that I loved and fine children out of him. Better than I hoped for even. Tell him I was given back everything he took away and more. Oh, no, oh, God, no, there was something else besides the house and the man and the children. Oh, surely they were not all? What was it? Something not given back. . . . Her breath crowded down under her ribs and grew into a monstrous frightening shape with cutting edges; it bored up into her head, and the agony was unbelievable: Yes, John, get the doctor now, no more talk, my time has come.

When this one was born it should be the last. The last. It should have been born first, for it was the one she had truly wanted. Everything came in good time. Nothing left out, left over. She was strong, in three days she would be as well as ever. Better. A woman needed milk in her to have her full health.

"Mother, do you hear me?"

"I've been telling you—"   45

"Mother, Father Connolly's here."

"I went to Holy Communion only last week. Tell him I'm not so sinful as all that."

"Father just wants to speak to you."

He could speak as much as he pleased. It was like him to drop in and inquire about her soul as if it were a teething baby, and then stay on for a cup of tea and a round of cards and gossip. He always had a funny story of some sort, usually about an Irishman who made his little mistakes and confessed them, and the point lay in some absurd thing he would blurt out in the confessional showing his struggles between native piety and original sin. Granny felt easy about her soul. Cornelia, where are your manners? Give Father Connolly a chair. She had her secret comfortable understanding with a few favorite saints who cleared a straight road to God for her. All as surely signed and sealed as the papers for the new Forty Acres. Forever . . . heirs and assigns forever. Since the day the wedding cake was not cut, but thrown out and wasted. The whole bottom dropped out of the world, and there she was blind and sweating with nothing under her feet and the walls falling away. His hand had caught her under the breast, she had not fallen, there was the freshly polished floor with the green rug on it, just as before. He had cursed like a sailor's parrot and said, "I'll kill him for you." Don't lay a hand on him, for my sake leave something to God. "Now, Ellen, you must believe what I tell you. . . ."

So there was nothing, nothing to worry about any more, except some-   50
times in the night one of the children screamed in a nightmare, and they both hustled out shaking and hunting for the matches and calling, "There, wait a minute, here we are!" John, get the doctor now, Hapsy's time has come. But there was Hapsy standing by the bed in a white cap. "Cornelia, tell Hapsy to take off her cap. I can't see her plain."

Her eyes opened very wide and the room stood out like a picture she had seen somewhere. Dark colors with the shadows rising toward the ceiling in long angles. The tall black dresser gleamed with nothing on it but John's picture, enlarged from a little one, with John's eyes very black when they should have been blue. You never saw him, so how do you know how he looked? But the man insisted the copy was perfect, it was very rich and handsome. For a picture, yes, but it's not my husband. The table by the bed had a linen cover and a candle and a crucifix. The light was blue from Cornelia's silk lampshades. No sort of light at all, just frippery. You had to live forty years with kerosene lamps to appreciate honest electricity. She felt very strong and she saw Doctor Harry with a rosy nimbus around him.

"You look like a saint, Doctor Harry, and I vow that's as near as you'll ever come to it."

"She's saying something."

"I heard you, Cornelia. What's all this carrying-on?"

"Father Connolly's saying—"   55

Cornelia's voice staggered and bumped like a cart in a bad road. It rounded corners and turned back again and arrived nowhere. Granny stepped up in the cart very lightly and reached for the reins, but a man sat beside her and she knew him by his hands, driving the cart. She did not look in his face, for she knew without seeing, but looked instead down the road where the trees leaned over and bowed to each other and a thousand birds were singing a Mass. She felt like singing too, but she put her hand in the bosom of her dress and pulled out a rosary, and Father Connolly murmured Latin in a very solemn voice and tickled her feet. My God, will you stop that nonsense? I'm a married woman. What if he did run away and leave me to face the priest by myself? I found another a whole world better. I wouldn't have exchanged my husband for anybody except Saint Michael himself, and you may tell him that for me with a thank you in the bargain.

Light flashed on her closed eyelids, and a deep roaring shook her. Cornelia, is that lightning? I hear thunder. There's going to be a storm. Close all the windows. Call the children in. . . . "Mother, here we are, all of us." "Is that you, Hapsy?" "Oh, no, I'm Lydia. We drove as fast as we could." Their faces drifted above her, drifted away. The rosary fell out of her hands and Lydia put it back. Jimmy tried to help, their hands fumbled together, and Granny closed two fingers around Jimmy's thumb. Beads wouldn't do, it must be something alive. She was so amazed her thoughts ran round and round. So, my dear Lord, this is my death and I wasn't even thinking about it. My children have come to see me die. But I can't, it's not time. Oh, I always hated surprises. I wanted to give Cornelia the amethyst set—Cornelia, you're to have the amethyst set, but Hapsy's to wear it when she wants, and, Doctor Harry, do shut up. Nobody sent for you. Oh, my dear Lord, do wait a minute. I meant to do something about the Forty Acres, Jimmy doesn't need it and Lydia will later on, with that worthless husband of hers. I meant to finish the altar cloth and send six bottles of wine to Sister Borgia for her dyspepsia. I want to send six bottles of wine to Sister Borgia, Father Connolly, now don't let me forget.

Cornelia's voice made short turns and tilted over and crashed. "Oh, Mother, oh, Mother, oh, Mother. . . ."

"I'm not going, Cornelia. I'm taken by surprise. I can't go."

You'll see Hapsy again. What about her? "I thought you'd never come."   60 Granny made a long journey outward, looking for Hapsy. What if I don't find her? What then? Her heart sank down and down, there was no bottom to death, she couldn't come to the end of it. The blue light from Cornelia's lampshade drew into a tiny point in the center of her brain, it flickered and winked like an eye, quietly it fluttered and dwindled. Granny lay curled down within herself, amazed and watchful, staring at the point of light that was herself; her body was now only a deeper mass of shadow in an endless darkness and this darkness would curl around the light and swallow it up. God, give a sign!

For the second time there was no sign. Again no bridegroom and the priest in the house. She could not remember any other sorrow because this grief wiped them all away. Oh, no, there's nothing more cruel than this—I'll never forgive it. She stretched herself with a deep breath and blew out the light.

The Receptive Reader

1. In how much of this story do we look at the world from Granny Weatherall's *point of view?* How much is inner reality, or stream-of-consciousness? What is the alternative strand of things happening that the main character does not fully take in? How much of the story is the outer reality of the sickroom?

2. What kinds of memories and concerns take up the early pages of the story? What are striking examples of the blending of present and past?

3. When does the narrative begin to close in on the events alluded to in the title? How are you able to piece together the story of what happened sixty years earlier? What is the central character's attitude toward those events? What role did the jilting play in her life as a whole? Why do you think the author approaches this central topic in such a roundabout way?

4. Look at the *minor characters.* What role does Cornelia play in the story? What role do Granny's husband and family play in the story as a whole? What role does Hapsy play in Granny's thoughts and feelings as the end approaches?

5. Does this story have a *plot?* Does any action or development take place parallel to the physical events of the sickroom? How does the ending tie major concerns of the story together?

6. How would you sum up in one sentence the attitude toward life implied in this story?

The Personal Response

How would you describe the central character in the story? What kind of person emerges from the story as a whole? What kind of life has she had? How do you relate to her as the reader? How do you think the author *expected* you to feel toward the central character? (Does she seem to steer the reader's feelings or reactions?)

WRITING ABOUT LITERATURE

5　Sharing a Point of View (Focus on Peer Response)

The Writing Workshop　What window does a story open on the world? Through whose eyes do we see the people and events, and what difference does it make? In writing a paper about point of view, ask yourself questions like the following:

✘ What is the narrator's relation to the events of the story? Are we listening to a casual observer? to a reliable impartial witness? to a person with an axe to grind? Does the story read like self-justification? like nostalgic reenactment of the past?

✘ How does the point of view limit your vision as the reader? (What is left out that you might want to know?) How does it steer your reactions? (Do you anywhere resist what the narrator apparently expects you to think or feel?)

✘ How might the events of the story look if seen from a different point of view? Try to imagine what the story would be like if told from the perspective of someone else in the story.

✘ Does the narrator take in more of what happens than someone else might—or less? Do you at times feel that you know (or suspect) more than the narrator does? Are you expected to question the perceptions of the narrator?

Focus on Peer Response　When you work on papers about the stories you read, bringing the topic into focus, gathering material, and pulling it into shape will absorb much of your attention. But sooner or later, you will begin to focus on what happens when your writing reaches the reader. In many writing classes, student writers have a chance to learn from **peer response.** When your writing is critiqued by your peers, you become more audience-conscious. You become more aware of how readers react. You become more conscious of what will help and what may hinder your reader.

When you in turn participate in peer response, you formulate your reactions to the writing of fellow students, trying to help them revise and strengthen their papers. Remember the golden rule of peer criticism: Respond unto others as you would have them respond unto you. Try to avoid mere fault-finding. Respond to both strengths and weaknesses, showing that you are basically on the writer's side. In responding to the paper of a fellow student, try to see details in the context of the paper as a whole. How do they affect the overall effectiveness of the paper? What can the writer do to make the paper more effective? Try to answer questions like the following:

✗ *What is the writer trying to do?*   What seems to be the general purpose? How well has it been achieved?

✗ *Does the paper get off to a good start?*   Do the title and the opening lines capture the attention of the reader? Do they channel it in the right direction?

✗ *Does the paper have a strong central idea or thesis?*   Is it spelled out clearly enough—at the beginning or, sometimes, toward the end of the paper? Does the writer keep it in view or lose sight of it as the paper develops?

✗ *What is the general strategy or master plan?*   Does it become clear enough to the reader? Or does the reader need more of a preview or program early in the paper? Does the reader run into apparent detours or digressions? Should the organization be streamlined? Should major sections of the paper be reshuffled?

✗ *Are key points well developed?*   Is there a rich supporting texture of short quotable quotes and striking authentic detail? Where do you feel a lack of support or follow-through? Are any points merely mentioned in passing and then dropped?

✗ *How effective are the transitions from one point to the next?*   Does the paper show the connection between major parts? Does it signal turning points or steps in an argument? Does the paper need stronger logical links?

✗ *Does the conclusion merely rehash points already made?*   Or does it do a needed job of pulling together different parts of an argument? Does it add anything to show the larger meaning or implications of the author's points? Does it leave readers with a striking quotation or telling incident to remember?

✗ *How well does the paper communicate its points?*   Where would you put in the margin "well put" or "well said" or "good touch"? Where are readers likely to stumble over garbled or incomplete sentences or over missing commas? Where are they likely to be confused by words that are near misses or just plain wrong? Where are big words or shifting, confusing terms used without definition? Where is the wording too disrespectful or slangy—and where too stiff or pretentious? Where do you hear clichés rather than the writer's own voice?

✗ *Does the paper show any personal involvement or commitment?* Does it sound too much like an "assignment"? Is there a personal connection?

Peer Responses to a Draft

Study the following sample student paper and the excerpts from peer responses that follow it. How carefully have the authors of the peer responses read the paper? How do these readers compare with your own vision of an ideal responsive reader for your own writing?

Creating an Empathetic Audience: A Skillful Use of Point of View

Point of view is a useful author's tool. If used skillfully, it can allow the reader to learn much about a character from a few carefully placed clues. This type of story-telling avoids preachy didacticism and allows the reader to form personal opinions about the character that are not influenced by other characters' thoughts or actions. Tillie Olsen's "I Stand Here Ironing" is an example of a first-person narrative in which the main character is speaking mostly about her nineteen-year-old daughter, Emily, but the reader still learns much about the narrator herself. Also, by telling the story from the mother's point of view, Olsen allows the reader to feel empathy for a character who might otherwise inspire anger or disgust.

If this story were told from the troubled Emily's point of view, one can only imagine the vision of the mother that would emerge. A fly on the wall in the counselor's office who confronts Emily's mother at the beginning of the story might have heard Emily describe her mother in a negative light. Emily might tell the counselor, "My mother never smiled at me; she only smiled at my younger sister, Susan, who was prettier. She sent me away all the time—first to my father's family, then to a day school, then to an awful convalescent hospital. She never had time for me; she always worked. She was never there when I needed her." And so on, until all the mother's evils were categorized and the reader feels nothing but anger at the seemingly heartless mother and sympathy for Emily. But by telling the story from the mother's point of view, Olsen uncovers the flip side of the situation, allowing the woman to respond to her daughter's allegations and explain her actions, thus letting the reader empathize with her and gain a better understanding of her. In this way, Olsen also makes a point about the difficulties a single woman can face raising a child and how, oftentimes, innocent lives can be sacrificed and lost in the daily struggle to survive.

The narrator begins the story by describing how difficult it was for her in the early years after her husband left her, describing the hectic pace of her life as she tried to scrape up the daily necessities. "I would start running as soon as I got off the streetcars, running up the stairs, . . ." She describes how she had to send her daughter away to her husband's family, and then later, once she was finally able to bring her back, how she had to send her to nursery school during the day. The narrator guiltily admits that she knew the nursery was evil, but "it was the only place there was." It was the only way we could be together, the only way I could hold a job. The first-person narrative of the story allows her readers this insight into the woman's actions. It allows them to learn that such actions, although they may seem cruel, were the only alternative the woman had as she desperately tried to support herself and her child.

Later in the story, the narrator explains how she had to send Emily away again—this time because she did not get well after a bout with the red measles. "They persuaded me at the clinic to send her away to a convalescent home in the country," she says. They told her Emily would receive "the kind of food and care you can't manage for her." The narrator discusses with heartwrenching guilt the "ravaged looks" of the girls in the home and how she desperately tried to get Emily back. If her readers did not have this insight into the woman's feelings, they might believe she was a careless or apathetic mother who found it easier to stick her child into a gruesome home rather than take proper care of her.

The narrator does admit, however, that she made many mistakes with Emily. She rarely smiled at Emily when she was a child, she never held and loved Emily as she did the other children, and she denied Emily the affection she showered on Susan, the second child. She knows these and other things made life harder on Emily than it was on the other children. The narrator admits her error, but knows in her heart that sometimes such happenings are inevitable. "I was at the terrible, growing years. War years. I do not remember them well. I was working, there were four smaller ones now, there was not time for her. She had to help be a mother, and housekeeper, and shopper." Through comments such as these, the reader learns that the narrator, very young herself, was also having a rough time making ends meet. And although it does seem a heavy burden to fall on Emily's small shoulders, placed in the context of an impoverished woman struggling to feed six mouths with one paycheck, Emily's burden becomes one of necessity, not of cruelty. The story's first-person point of view allows the reader the indulgence of pity for Emily and her difficult youth, yet also allows empathy for the mother. Because the reader is privy to the narrator's side of the situation, Emily's hardship is lessened in the face of the family's fierce struggle to survive.

Tillie Olsen's use of first-person narrative in "I Stand Here Ironing" permits the reader to step into the shoes of a poor working-class mother and her daily fight for survival. It permits those of us who have never experienced such hardship to ask ourselves "What would I do if . . . ?" The answer might shock us: we might do the exact thing the narrator was forced to do, which was to rely on a child to perform chores beyond her, in essence robbing that child of the playtime essential to healthy growth. The narrator Olsen creates is universal: a character struggling to survive despite overwhelming odds. And, although that character makes mistakes, these are forgiven in the face of the struggle. The situation Olsen creates is also universal, telling the often unavoidable fate of the children born into such conditions, whose own personalities are lost in the cycle of poverty and the fight for survival.

Peer Responses

I.   While reading this essay, I started on a very negative slant, but the author won me over. The paper starts slowly and actually somewhat awkwardly. To begin with, the title, for me, is too long and general. It gives no hint of what the major focus of the story is. Then the first three sentences are solely generalizations about point of view in general. Then, finally, the writer introduces the story that will be the major subject of the essay. So I stop to wonder—is the author writing about point of view, using this story as a convenient example, or is she writing about how point of view makes this story what it is? It is a subtle difference, but it significantly affects how one approaches the story. Both the title and the beginning talk about point of view in very general terms, and that hardly draws the reader in. However, once the author starts writing about Tillie Olsen and her story, she does an excellent job of following up and using quotes effectively to support her thesis: In this story, point of view creates a receptive, empathetic reader. She keeps this central idea in focus well throughout her essay.

2.   The writer hints at her thesis in the title and then spells it out at the end of her first paragraph. The main point is that the first-person narrative—the point of view used in "I Stand Here Ironing"—lets the reader get inside the skin of the character and helps readers understand and empathize with her. The paper shows good use of counterpoint in the second paragraph: One key element that works well in this paper is that the writer balances the narrator's point of view with the projected point of view of the daughter. The reader is made to see how the story might have been completely different if told from the perspective of the daughter. The paper leads up effectively to an awareness of the universal nature of the narrator's predicament and her guilt. The ending shows great strength, making up for some of the mechanical quality of the beginning. As for the title, something more imaginative, perhaps drawn from the inner core of the story, would be better.

3.   We get a good idea of the importance of point of view in this paper. The author gets right to the point and stays there. The purpose of the paper is to justify the mother's actions and decisions. I feel more attention could have been paid to how the mother actually felt about Emily. She may have resented ever having her. Often a parent will like one child and dislike another. Some phrases slip into clichés: "making ends meet"; "despite overwhelming odds."

Questions

1. Where are the student responses in substantial *agreement* on the strengths and weaknesses of this paper?

2. How do the responses *differ?* If you were the author of the paper, whose judgment would you be inclined to trust, and why?

3. What revised or improved *title* would you suggest that would be snappier and more informative at the same time?

4. What *opening quotation* chosen from the story might get the reader's attention and lead up effectively to the writer's thesis?

6 Symbol

The Eloquent Image

Symbolism adds a new value to an object or an act, without thereby violating its immediate or "historical" validity. . . . seen in this light the universe is no longer sealed off, nothing is isolated inside its own existence: everything is linked by a system of correspondences and assimilations.

MIRCEA ELIADE

FOCUS ON SYMBOLS

Symbols are images that have a meaning beyond themselves. In a short story, a symbol is a detail, a character, or an incident that has a meaning beyond its literal role in the narrative. As we read, the mind's eye takes in images—vividly imagined details, shapes, textures. But often we sense that there is more than meets the eye. Something tells us: The sun in this story is not just a physical fact. It leaves the landscape parched; it dries up the sources of life-giving water. It becomes overpowering, threatening. It means something—it tells us something, if only we knew how to read between the lines.

As you interpret the language of symbols, keep points like the following in mind:

Shared Symbols   Some symbols come into a story from a shared language of symbols. Much in human experience has traditional symbolic associations: the dawn with hope, the dark forest with evil, clay with death, water with fertility. Light is often the symbol for knowledge, fighting the darkness of ignorance.

Personal Symbols   Some symbols have a special personal meaning for the writer. Their meaning may come into focus as they return again and again in the writer's work. The icy heights of snow-capped mountains may become a writer's symbol for a freezing up of the emotional life, for his characters' inability to relate to other people.

141

The Range of Associations   Literary symbols are rich in associations. They have more possible layers of meaning than simple signs. The skull and bones that say "poison" have a clear, unequivocal message. But literary symbols do not simply signal "Danger" or "All Clear." An ancient symbol in Western culture is the garden. It brings with it a wealth of associations: the Garden of Eden was a scene of innocence and happiness, before the fall of Adam. The garden is a symbol of nature, seen as fruitful and life-sustaining. Like the Garden of Eden, it may be the cultivated spot in the surrounding wilderness. It may suggest the oasis in the desert. It may suggest a retreat from the intrigues of office or business— we retreat there to "cultivate our own garden."

Ambiguous Symbols   Symbols may be ambiguous. In Melville's great American classic *Moby Dick,* the mythic white whale seems paradoxically double-faced. To the obsessed Captain Ahab, the whale is evil. It stands for everything that is destructive in nature—and the whale does in the end send his ship and his crew to the bottom of the sea. But at other times, the whale seems to stand for good. It stands for everything that is beautiful in nature—as it floats through the calm sea, shedding "enticings."

Symbols in Context   Symbols acquire their full meaning in the context of a story. In Nathaniel Hawthorne's novel *The Scarlet Letter,* the letter *A* for adultery, embroidered on the sinner's gown, may at first seem a matter of historical interest. We can say, "This is how the Puritans identified an adulteress." However, as we watch her and her innocent child, the scarlet letter begins to haunt us; it makes us think. The author used it as the title of the whole novel: *The Scarlet Letter.* As we finish the novel, that scarlet letter is likely to have been burned into our consciousness. It becomes a symbol of our consciousness of guilt, of our doubts about who is truly guilty. We begin to imagine it carried by others—like the Puritan minister Dimmesdale—who is guilty but not publicly stigmatized.

THE CENTRAL SYMBOL

*In the short story the action is usually small, while
the meanings are large.*

THOMAS A. GULLERSON

Often a **central symbol** becomes the focal point of a story. A central symbol focuses our attention. It provides a tangible object for our emotions—since we find it hard to anchor our feelings to disembodied ideas. A central symbol becomes the hub for meanings and associations. It may slowly evolve, acquiring its full meaning only as the story as a whole takes shape. In each of the following stories, a rich central symbol helps give shape to the story as a whole.

Mary Robison   *(born 1949)*

Mary Robison, the author of the following **short short** (an exceptionally short short story), has been described as a runaway at sixteen, another child of the sixties dropping out from a society that seemed to have lost its meaning. In the story that follows, we focus on a single significant day in the life of a couple. We learn something about the setting of their lives, about them as people, about their relationship. But details of setting, character, and plot are almost crowded out by something the wife brought home from the store: Halloween pumpkins. They are the first and last things we see in the story. The people work on them and talk about them for most of the story. They loom large. What do they mean? What role do they play? For what do they serve as symbols?

Yours   *1983*

Allison struggled away from her white Renault, limping with the weight of the last of the pumpkins. She found Clark in the twilight on the twig-and-leaf-littered porch behind the house.

He wore a wool shawl. He was moving up and back in a padded glider, pushed by the ball of his slippered foot.

Allison lowered a big pumpkin, let it rest on the wide floorboards.

Clark was much older—seventy-eight to Allison's thirty-five. They were married. They were both quite tall and looked something alike in their facial features. Allison wore a natural-hair wig. It was a thick blond hood around her face. She was dressed in bright-dyed denims today. She wore durable clothes, usually, for she volunteered afternoons at a children's day-care center.

She put one of the smaller pumpkins on Clark's long lap. "Now, nothing surreal," she told him. "Carve just a *regular* face. These are for kids."

In the foyer, on the Hepplewhite desk, Allison found the maid's chore list with its cross-offs, which included Clark's supper. Allison went quickly through the day's mail: a garish coupon packet, a bill from Jamestown Liquors, November's pay-TV program guide, and the worst thing, the funniest, an already opened, extremely unkind letter from Clark's relations up North. "You're an old fool," Allison read, and, "You're being cruelly deceived." There was a gift check for Clark enclosed, but it was uncashable, signed, as it was, "Jesus H. Christ."

Late, late into this night, Allison and Clark gutted and carved the pumpkins together, at an old table set on the back porch, over newspaper after soggy newspaper, with paring knives and with spoons and with a Swiss Army knife Clark used for exact shaping of tooth and eye and nostril. Clark had been a doctor, an internist, but also a Sunday watercolorist. His four pumpkins were expressive and artful. Their carved features were suited to

5

the sizes and shapes of the pumpkins. Two looked ferocious and jagged. One registered surprise. The last was serene and beaming.

Allison's four faces were less deftly drawn, with slits and areas of distortion. She had cut triangles for noses and eyes. The mouths she had made were just wedges—two turned up and two turned down.

By one in the morning they were finished. Clark, who had bent his long torso forward to work, moved back over to the glider and looked out sleepily at nothing. All the lights were out across the ravine.

Clark stayed. For the season and time, the Virginia night was warm. Most   10
leaves had been blown away already, and the trees stood unbothered. The moon was round above them.

Allison cleaned up the mess.

"Your jack-o'-lanterns are much, much better than mine," Clark said to her.

"Like hell," Allison said.

"Look at me," Clark said, and Allison did.

She was holding a squishy bundle of newspapers. The papers reeked   15
sweetly with the smell of pumpkin guts.

"Yours are *far* better," he said.

"You're wrong. You'll see when they're lit," Allison said.

She went inside, came back with yellow vigil candles. It took her a while to get each candle settled, and then to line up the results in a row on the porch railing. She went along and lit each candle and fixed the pumpkin lids over the little flames.

"See?" she said.

They sat together a moment and looked at the orange faces.   20

"We're exhausted. It's good night time," Allison said. "Don't blow out the candles. I'll put in new ones tomorrow."

That night, in their bedroom, a few weeks earlier in her life than had been predicted, Allison began to die. "Don't look at me if my wig comes off," she told Clark. "Please."

Her pulse cords were fluttering under his fingers. She raised her knees and kicked away the comforter. She said something to Clark about the garage being locked.

At the telephone, Clark had a clear view out back and down to the porch. He wanted to get drunk with his wife once more. He wanted to tell her, from the greater perspective he had, that to own only a little talent, like his, was an awful, plaguing thing; that being only a little special meant you expected too much, most of the time, and liked yourself too little. He wanted to assure her that she had missed nothing.

He was speaking into the phone now. He watched the jack-o'-lanterns.   25
The jack-o'-lanterns watched him.

The Receptive Reader

1. How do you learn about the situation in which the two characters find themselves? What clues are especially important?

2. What role does the age difference between the two people play in the story? Is it treated differently from what you might have expected? How?

3. When do you first suspect that the pumpkins have a special significance? (What kind of fruit are they; what associations with them do you bring to the story?) What role do they play in the story as a whole? Does it matter that they are carved differently? What do you think they symbolize?

The Personal Response

This story deals with age, illness, and death. How does it treat these topics? Do you think the story as a whole is affirmative toward life or disillusioned or depressing?

The Creative Dimension

Fiction stimulates the reader's imagination. For instance, you may want to re-create an impression that lingered in your memory. You may want to evoke a haunting image that in some way seems to sum up the story. Look at the following student-written response to Mary Robison's "Yours." Does it add to or enhance your own reading of the story?

Pumpkins in orange October,
    their sweet soggy smell
    rises from carved insides
    on wet news
Their fierce pumpkin faces, lit by candles,
    glow till morning,
    the live flame softening their shells
Pumpkin, a child's toy,
    not for May or December,
    but for late October, ushering in
    November and a Thanksgiving of sorts
Pumpkins from the brittle vine
    the last sweet
    harvest

John Steinbeck   *(1902–1968)*

Much of Steinbeck's fiction takes us to Steinbeck Country—California's agricultural Salinas Valley and scenic Monterey Bay, stretching south to the rugged coast of Big Sur. This area, where Steinbeck grew up and went to school, sets the scene for books like *Tortilla Flat* (1935), *Of Mice and Men* (1937), *Cannery Row* (1945), and *East of Eden* (1952). Many characters he places in this setting are social outcasts, poor people, derelicts, migrant workers, and the people who befriend them.

Steinbeck's work was part of the tradition of naturalistic fiction, represented earlier by Americans like Stephen Crane and Jack London. After decades of Victorian high-mindedness, **naturalism** late in the nineteenth century had set out to correct the balance—to recognize the physical and instinctual nature of people. It tried to be more honest about their suppressed (or repressed) physical and emotional needs. Some of Steinbeck's best-known work was part of the literature of **social protest** of the thirties and forties. In the depths of the Great Depression, Steinbeck became famous with his novel *The Grapes of Wrath* (1939). Made into a movie starring Henry Fonda, Steinbeck's mythical novel proved to have a powerful hold on the imagination of millions around the world. Steinbeck told the story of the "Okies" (rural Americans from Oklahoma and other parts of the dust bowl of the thirties) who were driven from their farms by dust storms and laissez-faire (let-market-forces-do-their-work) economics.

Feminist critics have in recent years taken a fresh look at the "strong women" in Steinbeck's fiction. They may be women who have a strength of will missing in their husbands; they seem to have more energy and vitality than is needed for their tasks. They "must somehow express themselves meaningfully within the narrow possibilities open to women in a man's world" (Marilyn H. Mitchell).

The Chrysanthemums   *1937*

The high grey-flannel fog of winter closed off the Salinas Valley from the sky and from all the rest of the world. On every side it sat like a lid on the mountains and made of the great valley a closed pot. On the broad, level land floor the gang plows bit deep and left the black earth shining like metal where the shares had cut. On the foothill ranches across the Salinas River, the yellow stubble fields seemed to be bathed in pale cold sunshine, but there was no sunshine in the valley now in December. The thick willow scrub along the river flamed with sharp and positive yellow leaves.

It was a time of quiet and of waiting. The air was cold and tender. A light wind blew up from the southwest so that the farmers were mildly hopeful of a good rain before long; but fog and rain do not go together.

Across the river, on Henry Allen's foothill ranch there was little work to be done, for the hay was cut and stored and the orchards were plowed up to receive the rain deeply when it should come. The cattle on the higher slopes were becoming shaggy and rough-coated.

Elisa Allen, working in her flower garden, looked down across the yard and saw Henry, her husband, talking to two men in business suits. The three of them stood by the tractor shed, each man with one foot on the side of the little Fordson. They smoked cigarettes and studied the machine as they talked.

Elisa watched them for a moment and then went back to her work. She   5
was thirty-five. Her face was lean and strong and her eyes were as clear as water. Her figure looked blocked and heavy in her gardening costume, a man's black hat pulled low down over her eyes, clodhopper shoes, a figured print dress almost completely covered by a big corduroy apron with four big pockets to hold the snips, the trowel and scratcher, the seeds and the knife she worked with. She wore heavy leather gloves to protect her hands while she worked.

She was cutting down the old year's chrysanthemum stalks with a pair of short and powerful scissors. She looked down toward the men by the tractor shed now and then. Her face was eager and mature and handsome; even her work with the scissors was over-eager, over-powerful. The chrysanthemum stems seemed too small and easy for her energy.

She brushed a cloud of hair out of her eyes with the back of her glove, and left a smudge of earth on her cheek in doing it. Behind her stood the neat white farm house with red geraniums close-banked around it as high as the windows. It was a hard-swept looking little house, with hard-polished windows, and a clean mud-mat on the front steps.

Elisa cast another glance toward the tractor shed. The strangers were getting into their Ford coupe. She took off a glove and put her strong fingers down into the forest of new green chrysanthemum sprouts that were growing around the old roots. She spread the leaves and looked down among the close-growing stems. No aphids were there, no sowbugs or snails or cutworms. Her terrier fingers destroyed such pests before they could get started.

Elisa started at the sound of her husband's voice. He had come near quietly, and he leaned over the wire fence that protected her flower garden from cattle and dogs and chickens.

"At it again," he said. "You've got a strong new crop coming." 　10

Elisa straightened her back and pulled on the gardening glove again. "Yes. They'll be strong this coming year." In her tone and on her face there was a little smugness.

"You've got a gift with things," Henry observed. "Some of those yellow chrysanthemums you had this year were ten inches across. I wish you'd work out in the orchard and raise some apples that big."

Her eyes sharpened. "Maybe I could do it, too. I've a gift with things, all right. My mother had it. She could stick anything in the ground and make it grow. She said it was having planters' hands that knew how to do it."

"Well, it sure works with flowers," he said.

"Henry, who were those men you were talking to?" 　15

"Why, sure, that's what I came to tell you. They were from the Western Meat Company. I sold those thirty head of three-year-old steers. Got nearly my own price, too."

"Good," she said. "Good for you."

"And I thought," he continued, "I thought how it's Saturday afternoon, and we might go into Salinas for dinner at a restaurant, and then to a picture show—to celebrate, you see."

"Good," she repeated. "Oh, yes. That will be good."

Henry put on his joking tone. "There's fights tonight. How'd you like to 　20 go to the fights?"

"Oh, no," she said breathlessly. "No, I wouldn't like fights."

"Just fooling, Elisa. We'll go to a movie. Let's see. It's two now. I'm going to take Scotty and bring down those steers from the hill. It'll take us maybe two hours. We'll go in town about five and have dinner at the Cominos Hotel. Like that?"

"Of course I'll like it. It's good to eat away from home."

"All right, then. I'll go get up a couple of horses."

She said, "I'll have plenty of time to transplant some of these sets, I guess."   25

She heard her husband calling Scotty down by the barn. And a little later she saw the two men ride up the pale yellow hillside in search of the steers.

There was a little square sandy bed kept for rooting the chrysanthemums. With her trowel she turned the soil over and over, and smoothed it and patted it firm. Then she dug ten parallel trenches to receive the sets. Back at the chrysanthemum bed she pulled out the little crisp shoots, trimmed off the leaves of each one with her scissors and laid it on a small orderly pile.

A squeak of wheels and plod of hoofs came from the road. Elisa looked up. The country road ran along the dense bank of willows and cottonwoods that bordered the river, and up this road came a curious vehicle, curiously drawn. It was an old springwagon, with a round canvas top on it like the cover of a prairie schooner. It was drawn by an old bay horse and a little grey-and-white burro. A big stubble-bearded man sat between the cover flaps and drove the crawling team. Underneath the wagon, between the hind wheels, a lean and rangy mongrel dog walked sedately. Words were painted on the canvas, in clumsy, crooked letters. "Pots, pans, knives, sisors, lawn mores, Fixed." Two rows of articles, and the triumphantly definitive "Fixed" below. The black paint had run down in little sharp points beneath each letter.

Elisa, squatting on the ground, watched to see the crazy, loose-jointed wagon pass by. But it didn't pass. It turned into the farm road in front of her house, crooked old wheels skirling and squeaking. The rangy dog darted from between the wheels and ran ahead. Instantly the two ranch shepherds flew out at him. Then all three stopped, and with stiff and quivering tails, with taut straight legs, with ambassadorial dignity, they slowly circled, sniffing daintily. The caravan pulled up to Elisa's wire fence and stopped. Now the newcomer dog, feeling out-numbered, lowered his tail and retired under the wagon with raised hackles and bared teeth.

The man on the wagon seat called out, "That's a bad dog in a fight when   30
he gets started."

Elisa laughed. "I see he is. How soon does he generally get started?"

The man caught up her laughter and echoed it heartily. "Sometimes not for weeks and weeks," he said. He climbed stiffly down, over the wheel. The horse and the donkey drooped like unwatered flowers.

Elisa saw that he was a very big man. Although his hair and beard were greying, he did not look old. His worn black suit was wrinkled and spotted with grease. The laughter had disappeared from his face and eyes the moment his laughing voice ceased. His eyes were dark, and they were full of the brooding that gets in the eyes of teamsters and of sailors. The calloused hands he rested on the wire fence were cracked, and every crack was a black line. He took off his battered hat.

"I'm off my general road, ma'am," he said. "Does this dirt road cut over across the river to the Los Angeles highway?"

Elisa stood up and shoved the thick scissors in her apron pocket. "Well,   35
yes, it does, but it winds around and then fords the river. I don't think your team could pull through the sand."

He replied with some asperity, "It might surprise you what them beasts can pull through."

"When they get started?" she asked.

He smiled for a second. "Yes. When they get started."

"Well," said Elisa, "I think you'll save time if you go back to the Salinas road and pick up the highway there."

He drew a big finger down the chicken wire and made it sing. "I ain't in   40 any hurry, ma'am. I go from Seattle to San Diego and back every year. Takes all my time. About six months each way. I aim to follow nice weather."

Elisa took off her gloves and stuffed them in the apron pocket with the scissors. She touched the under edge of her man's hat, searching for fugitive hairs. "That sounds like a nice kind of a way to live," she said.

He leaned confidentially over the fence. "Maybe you noticed the writing on my wagon. I mend pots and sharpen knives and scissors. You got any of them things to do?"

"Oh, no," she said quickly. "Nothing like that." Her eyes hardened with resistance.

"Scissors is the worst thing," he explained. "Most people just ruin scissors trying to sharpen 'em, but I know how. I got a special tool. It's a little bobbit kind of thing, and patented. But it sure does the trick."

"No. My scissors are all sharp."   45

"All right, then. Take a pot," he continued earnestly, "a bent pot, or a pot with a hole. I can make it like new so you don't have to buy no new ones. That's a saving for you."

"No," she said shortly. "I tell you I have nothing like that for you to do."

His face fell to an exaggerated sadness. His voice took on a whining undertone. "I ain't had a thing to do today. Maybe I won't have no supper tonight. You see I'm off my regular road. I know folks on the highway clear from Seattle to San Diego. They save their things for me to sharpen up because they know I do it so good and save them money."

"I'm sorry," Elisa said irritably. "I haven't anything for you to do."

His eyes left her face and fell to searching the ground. They roamed   50 about until they came to the chrysanthemum bed where she had been working. "What's them plants, ma'am?"

The irritation and resistance melted from Elisa's face. "Oh, those are chrysanthemums, giant whites and yellows. I raise them every year, bigger than anybody around here."

"Kind of a long-stemmed flower? Looks like a quick puff of colored smoke?" he asked.

"That's it. What a nice way to describe them."

"They smell kind of nasty till you get used to them," he said.

"It's a good bitter smell," she retorted, "not nasty at all."   55

He changed his tone quickly. "I like the smell myself."

"I had ten-inch blooms this year," she said.

The man leaned farther over the fence. "Look. I know a lady down the road a piece, has got the nicest garden you ever seen. Got nearly every kind of flower but no chrysanthemums. Last time I was mending a copper-bottom washtub for her (that's a hard job but I do it good), she said to me, 'If you ever run acrost some nice chrysantheums I wish you'd try to get me a few seeds.' That's what she told me."

Elisa's eyes grew alert and eager. "She couldn't have known much about chrysanthemums. You *can* raise them from seed, but it's much easier to root the little sprouts you see there."

"Oh," he said. "I s'pose I can't take none to her, then."   60

"Why yes you can," Elisa cried. "I can put some in damp sand, and you can carry them right along with you. They'll take root in the pot if you keep them damp. And then she can transplant them."

"She'd sure like to have some, ma'am. You say they're nice ones?"

"Beautiful," she said. "Oh, beautiful." Her eyes shone. She tore off the battered hat and shook out her dark pretty hair. "I'll put them in a flower pot, and you can take them right with you. Come into the yard."

While the man came through the picket gate Elisa ran excitedly along the geranium-bordered path to the back of the house. And she returned carrying a big red flower pot. The gloves were forgotten now. She kneeled on the ground by the starting bed and dug up the sandy soil with her fingers and scooped it into the bright new flower pot. Then she picked up the little pile of shoots she had prepared. With her strong fingers she pressed them into the sand and tamped around them with her knuckles. The man stood over her. "I'll tell you what to do," she said. "You remember so you can tell the lady."

"Yes, I'll try to remember."   65

"Well, look. These will take root in about a month. Then she must set them out, about a foot apart in good rich earth like this, see?" She lifted a handful of dark soil for him to look at. "They'll grow fast and tall. Now remember this: In July tell her to cut them down, about eight inches from the ground."

"Before they bloom?" he asked.

"Yes, before they bloom." Her face was tight with eagerness. "They'll grow right up again. About the last of September the buds will start."

She stopped and seemed perplexed. "It's the budding that takes the most care," she said hesitantly. "I don't know how to tell you." She looked deep into his eyes, searchingly. Her mouth opened a little, and she seemed to be listening. "I'll try to tell you," she said. "Did you ever hear of planting hands?"

"Can't say I have, ma'am."   70

"Well, I can only tell you what it feels like. It's when you're picking off the buds you don't want. Everything goes right down into your fingertips. You watch your fingers work. They do it themselves. You can feel how it is. They pick and pick the buds. They never make a mistake. They're with the plant. Do you see? Your fingers and the plant. You can feel that, right up your arm. They know. They never make a mistake. You can feel it. When you're like that you can't do anything wrong. Do you see that? Can you understand that?"

She was kneeling on the ground looking up at him. Her breast swelled passionately.

The man's eyes narrowed. He looked away self-consciously. "Maybe I know," he said. "Sometimes in the night in the wagon there—"

Elisa's voice grew husky. She broke in on him, "I've never lived as you do, but I know what you mean. When the night is dark—why, the stars are sharp-pointed, and there's quiet. Why, you rise up and up! Every pointed star gets driven into your body. It's like that. Hot and sharp and—lovely."

Kneeling there, her hand went out toward his legs in the greasy black 75 trousers. Her hesitant fingers almost touched the cloth. Then her hand dropped to the ground. She crouched low like a fawning dog.

He said, "It's nice, just like you say. Only when you don't have no dinner, it ain't."

She stood up then, very straight, and her face was ashamed. She held the flower pot out to him and placed it gently in his arms. "Here. Put it in your wagon, on the seat, where you can watch it. Maybe I can find something for you to do."

At the back of the house she dug in the can pile and found two old and battered aluminum saucepans. She carried them back and gave them to him. "Here, maybe you can fix these."

His manner changed. He became professional. "Good as new I can fix them." At the back of his wagon he set a little anvil, and out of an oily tool box dug a small machine hammer. Elisa came through the gate to watch him while he pounded out the dents in the kettles. His mouth grew sure and knowing. At a difficult part of the work he sucked his under-lip.

"You sleep right in the wagon?" Elisa asked. 80

"Right in the wagon, ma'am. Rain or shine I'm dry as a cow in there."

"It must be nice," she said. "It must be very nice. I wish women could do such things."

"It ain't the right kind of a life for a woman."

Her upper lip raised a little, showing her teeth. "How do you know? How can you tell?" she said.

"I don't know, ma'am," he protested. "Of course I don't know. Now 85 here's your kettles, done. You don't have to buy no new ones."

"How much?"

"Oh, fifty cents'll do. I keep my prices down and my work good. That's why I have all them satisfied customers up and down the highway."

Elisa brought him a fifty-cent piece from the house and dropped it in his hand. "You might be surprised to have a rival some time. I can sharpen scissors, too. And I can beat the dents out of little pots. I could show you what a woman might do."

He put his hammer back in the oily box and shoved the little anvil out of sight. "It would be a lonely life for a woman, ma'am, and a scarey life, too, with animals creeping under the wagon all night." He climbed over the singletree, steadying himself with a hand on the burro's white rump. He settled himself in the seat, picked up the lines. "Thank you kindly, ma'am," he said. "I'll do like you told me; I'll go back and catch the Salinas road."

"Mind," she called, "if you're long in getting there, keep the sand damp." 90

"Sand, ma'am? . . . Sand? Oh, sure. You mean around the chrysanthemums. Sure I will." He clucked his tongue. The beasts leaned luxuriously into their collars. The mongrel dog took his place between the back wheels. The wagon turned and crawled out the entrance road and back the way it had come, along the river.

Elisa stood in front of her wire fence watching the slow progress of the caravan. Her shoulders were straight, her head thrown back, her eyes half-closed, so that the scene came vaguely into them. Her lips moved silently, forming the words "Good-bye—good-bye." Then she whispered, "That's a bright direction. There's a glowing there." The sound of her whisper startled her. She shook herself free and looked about to see whether anyone had been listening. Only the dogs had heard. They lifted their heads toward her from their sleeping in the dust, and then stretched out their chins and settled asleep again. Elisa turned and ran hurriedly into the house.

In the kitchen she reached behind the stove and felt the water tank. It was full of hot water from the noonday cooking. In the bathroom she tore off her soiled clothes and flung them into the corner. And then she scrubbed herself with a little block of pumice, legs and thighs, loins and chest and arms, until her skin was scratched and red. When she had dried herself she stood in front of a mirror in her bedroom and looked at her body. She tightened her stomach and threw out her chest. She turned and looked over her shoulder at her back.

After a while she began to dress, slowly. She put on her newest under-clothing and her nicest stockings and the dress which was the symbol of her prettiness. She worked carefully on her hair, penciled her eyebrows and rouged her lips.

Before she was finished she heard the little thunder of hoofs and the   95
shouts of Henry and his helper as they drove the red steers into the corral. She heard the gate bang shut and set herself for Henry's arrival.

His step sounded on the porch. He entered the house calling, "Elisa, where are you?"

"In my room, dressing. I'm not ready. There's hot water for your bath. Hurry up. It's getting late."

When she heard him splashing in the tub, Elisa laid his dark suit on the bed, and shirt and socks and tie beside it. She stood his polished shoes on the floor beside the bed. Then she went to the porch and sat primly and stiffly down. She looked toward the river road where the willow-line was still yellow with frosted leaves so that under the high grey fog they seemed a thin band of sunshine. This was the only color in the grey afternoon. She sat unmoving for a long time. Her eyes blinked rarely.

Henry came banging out of the door, shoving his tie inside his vest as he came. Elisa stiffened and her face grew tight. Henry stopped short and looked at her. "Why—why, Elisa. You look so nice!"

"Nice? You think I look nice? What do you mean by 'nice'?"   100

Henry blundered on. "I don't know. I mean you look different, strong and happy."

"I am strong? Yes, strong. What do you mean 'strong'?"

He looked bewildered. "You're playing some kind of a game," he said helplessly. "It's a kind of a play. You look strong enough to break a calf over your knee, happy enough to eat it like a watermelon."

For a second she lost her rigidity. "Henry! Don't talk like that. You didn't know what you said." She grew complete again. "I'm strong," she boasted. "I never knew before how strong."

Henry looked down toward the tractor shed, and when he brought his 105
eyes back to her, they were his own again. "I'll get out the car. You can put
on your coat while I'm starting."

Elisa went into the house. She heard him drive to the gate and idle down
his motor, and then she took a long time to put on her hat. She pulled it
here and pressed it there. When Henry turned the motor off she slipped
into her coat and went out.

The little roadster bounced along on the dirt road by the river, raising the
birds and driving the rabbits into the brush. Two cranes flapped heavily
over the willow-line and dropped into the river-bed.

Far ahead on the road Elisa saw a dark speck. She knew.

She tried not to look as they passed it, but her eyes would not obey. She
whispered to herself sadly, "He might have thrown them off the road. That
wouldn't have been much trouble, not very much. But he kept the pot," she
explained. "He had to keep the pot. That's why he couldn't get them off the
road."

The roadster turned a bend and she saw the caravan ahead. She swung 110
full around toward her husband so she could not see the little covered
wagon and the mismatched team as the car passed them.

In a moment it was over. The thing was done. She did not look back.

She said loudly, to be heard above the motor, "It will be good, tonight, a
good dinner."

"Now you're changed again," Henry complained. He took one hand from
the wheel and patted her knee. "I ought to take you in to dinner oftener. It
would be good for both of us. We get so heavy out on the ranch."

"Henry," she asked, "could we have wine at dinner?"

"Sure we could. Say! That will be fine."   115

She was silent for a while; then she said, "Henry, those prize fights, do
the men hurt each other very much?"

"Sometimes a little, not often. Why?"

"Well, I've read how they break noses, and blood runs down their chests.
I've read how the fighting gloves get heavy and soggy with blood."

He looked around at her. "What's the matter, Elisa? I didn't know you
read things like that." He brought the car to a stop, then turned to the right
over the Salinas River bridge.

"Do any women ever go to the fights?" she asked.   120

"Oh, sure, some. What's the matter, Elisa? Do you want to go? I don't
think you'd like it, but I'll take you if you really want to go."

She relaxed limply in the seat. "Oh, no. No. I don't want to go. I'm sure
I don't." Her face was turned away from him. "It will be enough if we can
have wine. It will be plenty." She turned up her coat collar so he could not
see that she was crying weakly—like an old woman.

The Receptive Reader

1. What is the meaning of the chrysanthemums as the central, gradually
evolving *symbol* in the story? How much of a continuing thread do they provide
for the story as a whole? What role do they play at the high point of the story?
Were you surprised when you saw the flowers in the road?

2. When flowers are used as symbols, they activate a whole range of memories, associations, *connotations*. Cluster the word *flower*. What chains of association and patterns of thought does it bring to mind? Which of these do you think are especially relevant to this story?

3. What telling or revealing *details*—dress, the weather, features of the physical setting, the boxing, the wine—might be charged with symbolic significance?

4. Critics have found much sexual imagery, symbolism, or allusion in the encounter between Elisa and the tinker. What are striking examples? What is significant in the description of his arrival? What is strange or paradoxical about their relationship?

5. What is the role of the husband in this story? What kind of person is he? What kind of marriage do he and Elisa have? What are striking details or images that bring the nature of their relationship into focus?

6. What is the role of traditional assumptions about men's work and women's work, or about men's interests and women's interests, in this story? Do you see in the heroine an "ambiguous combination of feminine and masculine traits" (Marilyn Mitchell)?

7. Would you call the sight of the discarded flowers in the road the *climax,* or high point, of the story? Where does the story go afterwards? What impact have the developments of the story had on Eliza? How does the story end?

8. Critics have singled out Steinbeck as one of the few male authors of his time who went beyond stereotypical portraits of women. Do you think they are right? How might this story have been different if it had been written by a woman?

The Personal Response

How do you relate to Elisa as the *central character?* Do you find her sympathetic? strong? weak? strange? (Support your answer in detail.)

JUXTAPOSITIONS

The Range of Interpretation

In the following two critical excerpts, compare a traditional reading of the story by a male critic with a rereading of this and another story from a feminist point of view.

Stanley Renner

Stanley Renner, in "The Real Woman in 'The Chrysanthemums,'" claims that "the story's evidence does not support the view that Elisa is a woman kept from fulfillment by male domination." For him, the story is shaped by traditional male complaints "against the sexual unresponsiveness of the female, against an ambivalent female sexuality that both invites and repels male admiration, against the sexual delicacy of the female, who, repelled by sexual reality, holds out for indulgences of her emotional and spiritual yearnings":

The Real Woman in "The Chrysanthemums"

Unlike men, women incline more toward romantic fantasies of sex than the act of love itself. Clearly Elisa romanticizes the tinker. In ironic mockery of Elisa's great and perverse capacity for romanticizing reality, Steinbeck makes everything about the tinker the utter antithesis of her fastidious tidiness, which symbolizes her delicate sexual sensibility. Unshaven, unwashed, his clothes "wrinkled and spotted with grease," he represents everything she furiously purges from her garden and scrubs out of her house. Yet she fantasizes sexual intercourse with him when he gratifies her hunger for romance because it is only a fantasy: he will presently climb back into his slovenly wagon and ride away into the romantic sunset. Henry, clean and reliable if a bit stodgy and clumsy, is reality pressing against Elisa's fence seeking an actual sexual relationship. But in rejecting reality, albeit unideal, as reality always is, for a patently falsified romantic fantasy, she defeats her own impulses toward a fuller life.

From *Modern Fiction Studies,* Summer 1985

Marilyn H. Mitchell

Contrasting with Renner's perspective focusing on male dissatisfaction and complaints, Marilyn H. Mitchell, in "Steinbeck's Strong Women: Feminine Identity in the Short Stories," claims that Steinbeck shows women who "are trapped between society's definition of the masculine and the feminine and are struggling against the limitations of the feminine." Steinbeck is using them "to refute outmoded conceptions of what a woman should be" and aims to show "the real human beauty beneath Elisa's rough and somewhat masculine exterior":

Steinbeck's Strong Women and "The Chrysanthemums"

Two of John Steinbeck's more intricate and memorable stories are "The Chrysanthemums" and "The White Quail." Both examine the psychology and sexuality of strong women who must somehow express themselves meaningfully within the narrow possibilities open to women in a man's world. In each case the woman chooses a traditional feminine activity, gardening, as a creative outlet. . . . Steinbeck reveals fundamental differences between the way women see themselves and the way they are viewed by men. For example, both husbands relate primarily to the physical attributes of their wives, making only meager attempts to comprehend their personalities. Consequently, a gulf of misunderstanding exists between the marriage partners, which creates verbal as well as sexual blocks to communication. In each marriage, at least one of the spouses is aware of some degree of sexual frustration, although dissatisfaction is never overtly articulated. Furthermore, the propensity of the men to see their wives as dependent inferiors, while the women perceive themselves as being equal if not superior partners, creates a strain within the marriage which is partially responsible for the isolation of each of the characters.

Both Elisa Allen of "The Chrysanthemums" and Mary Teller in "The White Quail" display a strength of will usually identified with the male but which, in these cases, the husbands are not shown to have. . . . Elisa Allen demonstrates a very earthly sensuality in "The Chrysanthemums," though not in the presence of her husband, indicating that their failure as a couple may be as much his fault as hers.

From *Southwest Review,* Summer 1976

The Receptive Reader

Is there any common basis for these two approaches to the story? How and why do they disagree? Who do you think is more nearly right, and why?

Making Connections—For Discussion or Writing

Compare and contrast the treatment of unfulfilled desire in Katherine Anne Porter's "The Jilting of Granny Weatherall" and in John Steinbeck's "The Chrysanthemums." Does it make a difference that one of the stories is by a female author and the other by a male author?

Charlotte Perkins Gilman   *(1860–1935)*

Charlotte Perkins Gilman was a leading feminist and social activist at the turn of the century. She grew up in a family that included prominent suffragists (advocates of a woman's right to vote); one of her great-aunts was the abolitionist Harriet Beecher Stowe, author of *Uncle Tom's Cabin*. In her *Women and Economics* (1898) and other writings, Gilman argued that the traditional conception of women's roles was the result of social custom; it was culturally conditioned rather than anchored in biology. She made revolutionary proposals for freeing women for work outside the home.

Born and raised in Connecticut, Gilman moved to California after separating from her first husband, and she edited and published feminist publications there. She helped organize the California Women's Congresses of 1894 and 1895 and was one of the founders of the Women's Peace Party. Besides writing nonfiction, she wrote novels and short stories that dramatized her belief in women's capacity for independence and self-realization.

Gilman's much-anthologized "The Yellow Wallpaper" chronicles a young woman's descent into insanity. The story has been read as a clinical study of the escalation of mental illness—as if we were watching the patient from the *outside,* somewhat the way the husband-physician does in the story. However, the author makes us see everything in her story from the *inside*. We see everything from the point of view of the patient. Gilman herself had suffered from severe postpartum depression after the birth of a daughter in 1884. She was treated by a specialist who prescribed a "rest cure"—bed rest and no physical exertion or intellectual stimulation. (This is the Weir Mitchell mentioned by the patient's husband in the story.) The treatment, Gilman said later, drove her "so near the borderline of mental ruin" that she "could see over."

The Yellow Wallpaper   1892

It is very seldom that mere ordinary people like John and myself secure ancestral halls for the summer.

A colonial mansion, a hereditary estate, I would say a haunted house, and reach the height of romantic felicity—but that would be asking too much of fate!

Still I will proudly declare that there is something queer about it.

Else, why should it be let so cheaply? And why have stood so long untenanted?

John laughs at me, of course, but one expects that in marriage.   5

John is practical in the extreme. He has no patience with faith, an intense horror of superstition, and he scoffs openly at any talk of things not to be felt and seen and put down in figures.

John is a physician, and *perhaps*—(I would not say it to a living soul, of course, but this is dead paper and a great relief to my mind—) *perhaps* that is one reason I do not get well faster.

You see he does not believe I am sick!

And what can one do?

If a physician of high standing, and one's own husband, assures friends   10
and relatives that there is really nothing the matter with one but temporary nervous depression—a slight hysterical tendency—what is one to do?

My brother is also a physician, and also of high standing, and he says the same thing.

So I take phosphates or phosphites—whichever it is, and tonics, and journeys, and air, and exercise, and am absolutely forbidden to "work" until I am well again.

Personally, I disagree with their ideas.

Personally, I believe that congenial work, with excitement and change, would do me good.

But what is one to do?   15

I did write for a while in spite of them; but it *does* exhaust me a good deal—having to be so sly about it, or else meet with heavy opposition.

I sometimes fancy that in my condition if I had less opposition and more society and stimulus—but John says the very worst thing I can do is to think about my condition, and I confess it always makes me feel bad.

So I will let it alone and talk about the house.

The most beautiful place! It is quite alone, standing well back from the road, quite three miles from the village. It makes me think of English places that you read about, for there are hedges and walls and gates that lock, and lots of separate little houses for the gardeners and people.

There is a *delicious* garden! I never saw such a garden—large and shady, full of box-bordered paths, and lined with long grape-covered arbors with seats under them.

There were greenhouses, too, but they are all broken now.

There was some legal trouble, I believe, something about the heirs and coheirs; anyhow, the place has been empty for years.

That spoils my ghostliness, I am afraid, but I don't care—there is something strange about the house—I can feel it.

I even said so to John one moonlight evening, but he said what I felt was a *draught,* and shut the window.

I get unreasonably angry with John sometimes. I'm sure I never used to be so sensitive. I think it is due to this nervous condition.

But John says if I feel so, I shall neglect proper self-control; so I take pains to control myself—before him, at least, and that makes me very tired.

I don't like our room a bit. I wanted one downstairs that opened on the piazza and had roses all over the window, and such pretty old-fashioned chintz hangings! but John would not hear of it.

He said there was only one window and not room for two beds, and no near room for him if he took another.

He is very careful and loving, and hardly lets me stir without special direction.

I have a schedule prescription for each hour in the day; he takes all care from me, and so I feel basely ungrateful not to value it more.

He said we came here solely on my account, that I was to have perfect rest and all the air I could get. "Your exercise depends on your strength, my dear," said he, "and your food somewhat on your appetite; but air you can absorb all the time." So we took the nursery at the top of the house.

It is a big, airy room, the whole floor nearly, with windows that look all ways, and air and sunshine galore. It was nursery first and then playroom and gymnasium, I should judge; for the windows are barred for little children, and there are rings and things in the walls.

The paint and paper look as if a boys' school had used it. It is stripped off—the paper—in great patches all around the head of my bed, about as far as I can reach, and in a great place on the other side of the room low down. I never saw a worse paper in my life.

One of those sprawling flamboyant patterns committing every artistic sin.

It is dull enough to confuse the eye in following, pronounced enough to constantly irritate and provoke study, and when you follow the lame uncertain curves for a little distance they suddenly commit suicide—plunge off at outrageous angles, destroy themselves in unheard of contradictions.

The color is repellent, almost revolting; a smouldering unclean yellow, strangely faded by the slow-turning sunlight.

It is a dull yet lurid orange in some places, a sickly sulphur tint in others.

No wonder the children hated it! I should hate it myself if I had to live in this room long.

There comes John, and I must put this away,—he hates to have me write a word.

I

We have been here two weeks, and I haven't felt like writing before,   40
since that first day.

I am sitting by the window now, up in this atrocious nursery, and there
is nothing to hinder my writing as much as I please, save lack of strength.

John is away all day, and even some nights when his cases are serious.

I am glad my case is not serious!

But these nervous troubles are dreadfully depressing.

John does not know how much I really suffer. He knows there is no *rea-*   45
son to suffer, and that satisfies him.

Of course it is only nervousness. It does weigh on me so not to do my
duty in any way!

I meant to be such a help to John, such a real rest and comfort, and here
I am a comparative burden already!

Nobody would believe what an effort it is to do what little I am able,—
to dress and entertain, and order things.

It is fortunate Mary is so good with the baby. Such a dear baby!

And yet I *cannot* be with him, it makes me so nervous.   50

I suppose John never was nervous in his life. He laughs at me so about
this wallpaper!

At first he meant to repaper the room, but afterwards he said that I was
letting it get the better of me, and that nothing was worse for a nervous
patient than to give way to such fancies.

He said that after the wallpaper was changed it would be the heavy bedstead, and then the barred windows, and then that gate at the head of the
stairs, and so on.

"You know the place is doing you good," he said, "and really, dear, I
don't care to renovate the house just for a three months' rental."

"Then do let us go downstairs," I said, "there are such pretty rooms there."   55

Then he took me in his arms and called me a blessed little goose, and
said he would go down cellar, if I wished, and have it whitewashed into the
bargain.

But he is right enough about the beds and windows and things.

It is as airy and comfortable room as any one need wish, and, of course,
I would not be so silly as to make him uncomfortable just for a whim.

I'm really getting quite fond of the big room, all but that horrid paper.

Out of one window I can see the garden, those mysterious deep-shaded   60
arbors, the riotous old-fashioned flowers, and bushes and gnarly trees.

Out of another I get a lovely view of the bay and a little private wharf
belonging to the estate. There is a beautiful shaded lane that runs down
there from the house. I always fancy I see people walking in these numerous paths and arbors, but John has cautioned me not to give way to fancy in
the least. He says that with my imaginative power and habit of story-making,
a nervous weakness like mine is sure to lead to all manner of excited fancies, and that I ought to use my will and good sense to check the tendency.
So I try.

I think sometimes that if I were only well enough to write a little it would
relieve the press of ideas and rest me.

But I find I get pretty tired when I try.

It is so discouraging not to have any advice and companionship about my work. When I get really well, John says we will ask Cousin Henry and Julia down for a long visit; but he says he would as soon put fireworks in my pillow-case as to let me have those stimulating people about now.

I wish I could get well faster.   65

But I must not think about that. This paper looks to me as if it *knew* what a vicious influence it had!

There is a recurrent spot where the pattern lolls like a broken neck and two bulbous eyes stare at you upside down.

I get positively angry with the impertinence of it and the everlastingness. Up and down and sideways they crawl, and those absurd, unblinking eyes are everywhere. There is one place where two breadths didn't match, and the eyes go all up and down the line, one a little higher than the other.

I never saw so much expression in an inanimate thing before, and we all know how much expression they have! I used to lie awake as a child and get more entertainment and terror out of blank walls and plain furniture than most children could find in a toy-store.

I remember what a kindly wink the knobs of our big, old bureau used to   70
have, and there was one chair that always seemed like a strong friend.

I used to feel that if any of the other things looked too fierce I could always hop into that chair and be safe.

The furniture in this room is no worse than inharmonious, however, for we had to bring it all from downstairs. I suppose when this was used as a playroom they had to take the nursery things out, and no wonder! I never saw such ravages as the children have made here.

The wallpaper, as I said before, is torn off in spots, and it sticketh closer than a brother—they must have had perseverance as well as hatred.

Then the floor is scratched and gouged and splintered, the plaster itself is dug out here and there, and this great heavy bed which is all we found in the room, looks as if it had been through the wars.

But I don't mind it a bit—only the paper.   75

There comes John's sister. Such a dear girl as she is, and so careful of me! I must not let her find me writing.

She is a perfect and enthusiastic housekeeper, and hopes for no better profession. I verily believe she thinks it is the writing which made me sick!

But I can write when she is out, and see her a long way off from these windows.

There is one that commands the road, a lovely shaded winding road, and one that just looks off over the country. A lovely country, too, full of great elms and velvet meadows.

This wallpaper has a kind of subpattern in a different shade, a particu-   80
larly irritating one, for you can only see it in certain lights, and not clearly then.

But in the places where it isn't faded and where the sun is just so—I can see a strange, provoking, formless sort of figure, that seems to skulk about behind that silly and conspicuous front design.

There's sister on the stairs!

II

Well, the Fourth of July is over! The people are all gone and I am tired out. John thought it might do me good to see a little company, so we just had mother and Nellie and the children down for a week.

Of course I didn't do a thing. Jennie sees to everything now.

But it tired me all the same.   85

John says if I don't pick up faster he shall send me to Weir Mitchell in the fall.

But I don't want to go there at all. I had a friend who was in his hands once, and she says he is just like John and my brother, only more so!

Besides, it is such an undertaking to go so far.

I don't feel as if it was worth while to turn my hand over for anything, and I'm getting dreadfully fretful and querulous.

I cry at nothing, and cry most of the time.   90

Of course I don't when John is here, or anybody else, but when I am alone.

And I am alone a good deal just now. John is kept in town very often by serious cases, and Jennie is good and lets me alone when I want her to.

So I walk a little in the garden or down that lovely lane, sit on the porch under the roses, and lie down up here a good deal.

I'm getting really fond of the room in spite of the wallpaper. Perhaps *because* of the wallpaper.

It dwells in my mind so!   95

I lie here on this great immovable bed—it is nailed down, I believe—and follow that pattern about by the hour. It is as good as gymnastics, I assure you. I start, we'll say, at the bottom, down in the corner over there where it has not been touched, and I determine for the thousandth time that I *will* follow that pointless pattern to some sort of a conclusion.

I know a little of the principle of design, and I know this thing was not arranged on any laws of radiation, or alternation, or repetition, or symmetry, or anything else that I ever heard of.

It is repeated, of course, by the breadths, but not otherwise.

Looked at in one way each breadth stands alone, the bloated curves and flourishes—a kind of "debased Romanesque" with *delirium tremens* go waddling up and down in isolated columns of fatuity.

But, on the other hand, they connect diagonally, and the sprawling out- 100 lines run off in great slanting waves of optic horror, like a lot of wallowing seaweeds in full chase.

The whole thing goes horizontally, too, at least it seems so, and I exhaust myself in trying to distinguish the order of its going in that direction.

They have used a horizontal breadth for a frieze, and that adds wonderfully to the confusion.

There is one end of the room where it is almost intact, and there, when the crosslights fade and the low sun shines directly upon it, I can almost fancy radiation after all,—the interminable grotesques seem to form around a common center and rush off in headlong plunges of equal distraction.

It makes me tired to follow it. I will take a nap I guess.

III

I don't know why I should write this.   105
I don't want to.
I don't feel able.
And I know John would think it absurd. But I *must* say what I feel and think in some way—it is such a relief!
But the effort is getting to be greater than the relief.
Half the time now I am awfully lazy, and lie down ever so much.   110
John says I mustn't lose my strength, and has me take cod liver oil and lots of tonics and things, to say nothing of ale and wine and rare meat.
Dear John! He loves me very dearly, and hates to have me sick. I tried to have a real earnest reasonable talk with him the other day, and tell him how I wish he would let me go and make a visit to Cousin Henry and Julia.
But he said I wasn't able to go, nor able to stand it after I got there; and I did not make out a very good case for myself, for I was crying before I had finished.
It is getting to be a great effort for me to think straight. Just this nervous weakness I suppose.
And dear John gathered me up in his arms, and just carried me upstairs 115 and laid me on the bed, and sat by me and read to me till it tired my head.
He said I was his darling and his comfort and all he had, and that I must take care of myself for his sake, and keep well.
He says no one but myself can help me out of it, that I must use my will and self-control and not let any silly fancies run away with me.
There's one comfort, the baby is well and happy, and does not have to occupy this nursery with the horrid wallpaper.
If we had not used it, that blessed child would have! What a fortunate escape! Why, I wouldn't have a child of mine, an impressionable little thing, live in such a room for worlds.
I never thought of it before, but it is lucky that John kept me here after 120 all, I can stand it so much easier than a baby, you see.
Of course I never mention it to them any more—I am too wise,—but I keep watch of it all the same.
There are things in that paper that nobody knows but me, or ever will.
Behind that outside pattern the dim shapes get clearer every day.
It is always the same shape, only very numerous.
And it is like a woman stooping down and creeping about behind that 125 pattern. I don't like it a bit. I wonder—I begin to think—I wish John would take me away from here!

IV

It is so hard to talk with John about my case, because he is so wise, and because he loves me so.
But I tried it last night.
It was moonlight. The moon shines in all around just as the sun does.
I hate to see it sometimes, it creeps so slowly, and always comes in by one window or another.

John was asleep and I hated to waken him, so I kept still and watched 130
the moonlight on that undulating wallpaper till I felt creepy.

The faint figure behind seemed to shake the pattern, just as if she wanted
to get out.

I got up softly and went to feel and see if the paper *did* move, and when
I came back John was awake.

"What is it, little girl?" he said. "Don't go walking about like that—you'll
get cold."

I thought it was a good time to talk, so I told him that I really was not
gaining here, and that I wished he would take me away.

"Why, darling!" said he, "our lease will be up in three weeks, and I can't 135
see how to leave before.

"The repairs are not done at home, and I cannot possibly leave town just
now. Of course if you were in any danger, I could and would, but you really
are better, dear, whether you can see it or not. I am a doctor, dear, and I
know. You are gaining flesh and color, your appetite is better, I feel really
much easier about you."

"I don't weigh a bit more," said I, "nor as much; and my appetite may be
better in the evening when you are here, but it is worse in the morning
when you are away!"

"Bless her little heart!" said he with a big hug, "she shall be as sick as she
pleases! But now let's improve the shining hours by going to sleep, and talk
about it in the morning!"

"And you won't go away?" I asked gloomily.

"Why, how can I, dear? It is only three weeks more and then we will take 140
a nice little trip of a few days while Jennie is getting the house ready. Really
dear you are better!"

"Better in body perhaps—" I began, and stopped short, for he sat up
straight and looked at me with such a stern, reproachful look that I could
not say another word.

"My darling," said he, "I beg of you, for my sake and for our child's sake,
as well as for your own, that you will never for one instant let that idea
enter your mind! There is nothing so dangerous, so fascinating, to a temperament like yours. It is a false and foolish fancy. Can you not trust me as
a physician when I tell you so?"

So of course I said no more on that score, and we went to sleep before
long. He thought I was asleep first, but I wasn't, and lay there for hours trying to decide whether that front pattern and the back pattern really did
move together or separately.

V

On a pattern like this, by daylight, there is a lack of sequence, a defiance
of law, that is a constant irritant to a normal mind.

The color is hideous enough, and unreliable enough, and infuriating 145
enough, but the pattern is torturing.

You think you have mastered it, but just as you get well underway in following, it turns a back-somersault and there you are. It slaps you in the face,
knocks you down, and tramples upon you. It is like a bad dream.

The outside pattern is a florid arabesque, reminding one of a fungus. If you can imagine a toadstool in joints, an interminable string of toadstools, budding and sprouting in endless convolutions—why, that is something like it.

That is, sometimes!

There is one marked peculiarity about this paper, a thing nobody seems to notice but myself, and that is that it changes as the light changes.

When the sun shoots in through the east window—I always watch for 150
that first long, straight ray—it changes so quickly that I never can quite believe it.

That is why I watch it always.

By moonlight—the moon shines in all night when there is a moon—I wouldn't know it was the same paper.

At night in any kind of light, in twilight, candlelight, lamplight, and worst of all by moonlight, it becomes bars! The outside pattern I mean, and the woman behind it is as plain as can be.

I didn't realize for a long time what the thing was that showed behind, that dim subpattern, but now I am quite sure it is a woman.

By daylight she is subdued, quiet. I fancy it is the pattern that keeps her 155
so still. It is so puzzling. It keeps me quiet by the hour.

I lie down ever so much now. John says it is good for me, and to sleep all I can.

Indeed he started the habit by making me lie down for an hour after each meal.

It is a very bad habit I am convinced, for you see I don't sleep.

And that cultivates deceit, for I don't tell them I'm awake—O no!

The fact is I am getting a little afraid of John.   160

He seems very queer sometimes, and even Jennie has an inexplicable look.

It strikes me occasionally, just as a scientific hypothesis,—that perhaps it is the paper!

I have watched John when he did not know I was looking, and come into the room suddenly on the most innocent excuses, and I've caught him several times *looking at the paper!* And Jennie too. I caught Jennie with her hand on it once.

She didn't know I was in the room, and when I asked her in a quiet, a very quiet voice, with the most restrained manner possible, what she was doing with the paper—she turned around as if she had been caught stealing, and looked quite angry—asked me why I should frighten her so!

Then she said that the paper stained everything it touched, that she had 165
found yellow smooches on all my clothes and John's, and she wished we would be more careful!

Did not that sound innocent? But I know she was studying that pattern, and I am determined that nobody shall find it out but myself!

VI

Life is very much more exciting now than it used to be. You see I have something more to expect, to look forward to, to watch. I really do eat better, and am more quiet than I was.

John is so pleased to see me improve! He laughed a little the other day, and said I seemed to be flourishing in spite of my wallpaper.

I turned it off with a laugh. I had no intention of telling him it was *because* of the wallpaper—he would make fun of me. He might even want to take me away.

I don't want to leave now until I have found it out. There is a week more, 170 and I think that will be enough.

VII

I'm feeling ever so much better! I don't sleep much at night, for it is so interesting to watch developments; but I sleep a good deal in the daytime.

In the daytime it is tiresome and perplexing.

There are always new shoots on the fungus, and new shades of yellow all over it. I cannot keep count of them, though I have tried conscientiously.

It is the strangest yellow, that wallpaper! It makes me think of all the yellow things I ever saw—not beautiful ones like buttercups, but old foul, bad yellow things.

But there is something else about that paper—the smell! I noticed it the 175 moment we came into the room, but with so much air and sun it was not bad. Now we have had a week of fog and rain, and whether the windows are open or not, the smell is here.

It creeps all over the house.

I find it hovering in the dining-room, skulking in the parlor, hiding in the hall, lying in wait for me on the stairs.

It gets into my hair.

Even when I go to ride, if I turn my head suddenly and surprise it—there is that smell!

Such a peculiar odor, too! I have spent hours in trying to analyze it, to 180 find what it smelled like.

It is not bad—at first, and very gentle, but quite the subtlest, most enduring odor I ever met.

In this damp weather it is awful, I wake up in the night and find it hanging over me.

It used to disturb me at first. I thought seriously of burning the house—to reach the smell.

But now I am used to it. The only thing I can think of that it is like is the *color* of the paper! A yellow smell.

There is a very funny mark on this wall, low down, near the mopboard. 185 A streak that runs round the room. It goes behind every piece of furniture, except the bed, a long, straight, even *smooch,* as if it had been rubbed over and over.

I wonder how it was done and who did it, and what they did it for. Round and round and round—round and round and round!—it makes me *dizzy!*

VIII

I really have discovered something at last.

Through watching so much at night, when it changes so, I have finally found out.

The front pattern *does* move—and no wonder! The woman behind shakes it!

Sometimes I think there are a great many women behind, and sometimes only one, and she crawls around fast, and her crawling shakes it all over. 190

Then in the very bright spots she keeps still, and in the very shady spots she just takes hold of the bars and shakes them hard.

And she is all the time trying to climb through. But nobody could climb through that pattern—it strangles so; I think that is why it has so many heads.

They get through, and then the pattern strangles them off and turns them upside down, and makes their eyes white!

If those heads were covered or taken off it would not be half so bad.

IX

I think that woman gets out in the daytime!   195

And I'll tell you why—privately—I've seen her!

I can see her out of every one of my windows!

It is the same woman, I know, for she is always creeping, and most women do not creep by daylight.

I see her in that long shaded lane, creeping up and down. I see her in those dark grape arbors, creeping all around the garden.

I see her on that long road under the trees, creeping along, and when a 200 carriage comes she hides under the blackberry vines.

I don't blame her a bit. It must be very humiliating to be caught creeping by daylight!

I always lock the door when I creep by daylight. I can't do it at night, for I know John would suspect something at once.

And John is so queer now, that I don't want to irritate him. I wish he would take another room! Besides, I don't want anybody to get that woman out at night but myself.

I often wonder if I could see her out of all the windows at once.

But, turn as fast as I can, I can only see out of one at one time.   205

And though I always see her, she *may* be able to creep faster than I can turn!

I have watched her sometimes away off in the open country, creeping as fast as a cloud shadow in a high wind.

X

If only that top pattern could be gotten off from the under one! I mean to try it, little by little.

I have found out another funny thing, but I shan't tell it this time! It does not do to trust people too much.

There are only two more days to get this paper off, and I believe John is 210 beginning to notice. I don't like the look in his eyes.

And I heard him ask Jennie a lot of professional questions about me. She had a very good report to give.

She said I slept a good deal in the daytime.

John knows I don't sleep very well at night, for all I'm so quiet!

He asked me all sorts of questions, too, and pretended to be very loving and kind.

As if I couldn't see through him!   215

Still, I don't wonder he acts so, sleeping under this paper for three months.

It only interests me, but I feel sure John and Jennie are secretly affected by it.

XI

Hurrah! This is the last day, but it is enough. John to stay in town over night, and won't be out until this evening.

Jennie wanted to sleep with me—the sly thing! but I told her I should undoubtedly rest better for a night all alone.

That was clever, for really I wasn't alone a bit! As soon as it was moon- 220 light and that poor thing began to crawl and shake the pattern, I got up and ran to help her.

I pulled and she shook, I shook and she pulled, and before morning we had peeled off yards of that paper.

A strip about as high as my head and half around the room.

And then when the sun came and that awful pattern began to laugh at me, I declared I would finish it today!

We go away tomorrow, and they are moving all my furniture down again to leave things as they were before.

Jennie looked at the wall in amazement, but I told her merrily that I did 225 it out of pure spite at the vicious thing.

She laughed and said she wouldn't mind doing it herself, but I must not get tired.

How she betrayed herself that time!

But I am here, and no person touches this paper but me,—not *alive!*

She tried to get me out of the room—it was too patent! But I said it was so quiet and empty and clean now that I believed I would lie down again and sleep all I could; and not to wake me even for dinner—I would call when I woke.

So now she is gone, and the servants are gone, and the things are gone, 230 and there is nothing left but that great bedstead nailed down, with the canvas mattress we found on it.

We shall sleep downstairs tonight, and take the boat home tomorrow.

I quite enjoy the room, now it is bare again.

How those children did tear about here!

This bedstead is fairly gnawed!

But I must get to work.   235

I have locked the door and thrown the key down into the front path.

I don't want to go out, and I don't want to have anybody come in, till John comes.

I want to astonish him.

I've got a rope up here that even Jennie did not find. If that woman does get out, and tries to get away, I can tie her!

But I forgot I could not reach far without anything to stand on!   240

This bed will *not* move!

I tried to lift and push it until I was lame, and then I got so angry I bit off a little piece at one corner—but it hurt my teeth.

Then I peeled off all the paper I could reach standing on the floor. It sticks horribly and the pattern just enjoys it! All those strangled heads and bulbous eyes and waddling fungus growths just shriek with derision!

I am getting angry enough to do something desperate. To jump out of the window would be admirable exercise, but the bars are too strong even to try.

Besides I wouldn't do it. Of course not. I know well enough that a step 245 like that is improper and might be misconstrued.

I don't like to *look* out of the windows even—there are so many of those creeping women, and they creep so fast.

I wonder if they all come out of that wallpaper as I did?

But I am securely fastened now by my well-hidden rope—you don't get *me* out in the road there!

I suppose I shall have to get back behind the pattern when it comes night, and that is hard!

It is so pleasant to be out in this great room and creep around as I please! 250

I don't want to go outside. I won't, even if Jennie asks me to.

For outside you have to creep on the ground, and everything is green instead of yellow.

But here I can creep smoothly on the floor, and my shoulder just fits in that long smooch around the wall, so I cannot lose my way.

Why there's John at the door!

It is no use, young man, you can't open it!   255

How he does call and pound!

Now he's crying for an axe.

It would be a shame to break down that beautiful door!

"John dear!" said I in the gentlest voice, "the key is down by the front steps, under a plantain leaf!"

That silenced him for a few moments.   260

Then he said—very quietly indeed, "Open the door, my darling!"

"I can't," said I. "The key is down by the front door under a plantain leaf!"

And then I said it again, several times, very gently and slowly, and said it so often that he had to go and see, and he got it of course, and came in. He stopped short by the door.

"What is the matter?" he cried. "For God's sake, what are you doing!"

I kept on creeping just the same, but I looked at him over my shoulder. 265

"I've got out at last," said I, "in spite of you and Jennie! And I've pulled off most of the paper, so you can't put me back!"

Now why should that man have fainted? But he did, and right across my path by the wall, so that I had to creep over him every time!

The Receptive Reader

1. At the beginning, the narrator refers to her husband, John, and herself as "ordinary people." What makes the setting and the people at the beginning of the story seem ordinary? What kind of ordinary person does the narrator seem to be? When do you notice the first hints of something extraordinary?

2. What and how do you learn about the narrator's illness? What and how do you learn about the treatment proposed by the doctor-husband?

3. What is the husband-physician's attitude toward his wife? What is her attitude toward him? How does it change in the course of the story?

4. How does the wallpaper become an obsessive preoccupation in this story? How does its appearance slowly change and shift? How does its meaning change or evolve as the *central symbol* in the story? What are some major stages?

5. Who is the woman behind the wallpaper? How does your perception of her change and evolve? What is the significance of the smudge (running the length of the wallpaper) that the woman begins to perceive?

6. What is the symbolic contrast between the garden and the enclosed, confined room? (Why does the woman herself throw the key away?)

7. What, for you, is the symbolic meaning of the way the story ends? Can the ending be read as a kind of liberation?

8. Feminist critics have found a special significance in the fact that the narrator has to do her writing secretly, against the wishes of her husband. What symbolic significance do you think they find in his prohibition?

The Personal Response

For you, what does the story as a whole say about the author's view of mental illness and her view of the relation between women and male physicians? Is the story still thought provoking to current readers, or have changes in the modern world made the questions it raises obsolete?

WRITING ABOUT LITERATURE

6   Decoding Symbols (Two Readings of a Story)

The Writing Workshop   Writing about symbols tests your ability to be a responsive reader—to respond fully to the way imaginative literature acts out or embodies meanings. You cannot be literal-minded if strong, richly charged symbols are to bring into play the emotions and attitudes they are likely to carry. Here is the kind of advice a writing teacher might give you after studying papers focused on the role symbols play in short fiction:

▮ *Explore the full range of possible associations of a symbol.*   Literary symbols tend not to be one-track, one-dimensional signals that simply say "Danger" or "Evil lurks here." A serpent may symbolize danger. It may symbolize guile (the snake in the grass). It may stand for the alien or otherness (since reptiles represent a very different life from our own mammalian existence). It may represent danger that has a strange paradoxical attraction or beauty.

The following cluster traces some of the possible associations of flowers as familiar recurrent symbols carrying rich traditional freight. Many of these associations may be activated by a story like Steinbeck's "The Chrysanthemums," where flowers play a central role at turning points in the story. (Which of these associations do you think are relevant to Steinbeck's story?)

✗ *Trace the full meaning of a gradually evolving central symbol.* A symbol is not likely to come into a story with its symbolic value ready-made, like the monetary value of a dollar bill. In Gilman's "The Yellow Wallpaper," we at first look at the twisted pattern of the paper the way an interior designer might wonder at its strange design. But gradually we—or rather the narrator through whose eyes we see everything in the story—read more and more human meaning into its strange shapes. They come to life, making the narrator participate in the struggle of whatever seems imprisoned behind its bars. It is as if each time we look at the paper we discover a new and frightening dimension, leading to an escalation of apprehension and terror. We have to read and ponder the story as a whole to sense what the wallpaper comes to stand for as the story heads for its frightening conclusion.

✗ *Look for secondary symbols that echo the major theme of a story.* In addition to considering the chrysanthemums in Steinbeck's story, readers have scrutinized the pots and pans in need of mending as a possible symbol; they have wondered about the symbolic meaning of the fog that closes off the valley:

> "The high grey-flannel fog of winter closed off the Salinas Valley from the sky and from all the rest of the world," Steinbeck begins. This introductory sentence points to one of the basic themes of the story. Something (in this case, the fog) is keeping something or someone "closed off"—held in, cut off. The fog covers the valley. Similarly, Elisa's situation closes in on her, keeps her trapped, holds her back. Neither her husband nor the itinerant tinker understands the energy and care she puts into the chrysanthemums, and her ability and potential go unrecognized and unappreciated; they are kept under wraps, "closed off." The fog is the lid that keeps the sun from penetrating; Elisa's circumstances put the "lid" on her vital energy and desires.

▮ *Look for contrasts or polarities.*   Often the play of opposites helps organize a story. In Steinbeck's "The Chrysanthemums," a key contrast juxtaposes the farm family that stays fogbound and the tinker who follows "the nice weather." The conventional cattle-tending chores of the predictable, unimaginative husband contrast with the mismatched team pulling the strange wagon of the unconventional traveler. In Gilman's "The Yellow Wallpaper," the central symbol is the wallpaper, but a major polarity that helps organize the narrative plays off the colors green and yellow and what they symbolize in the story.

▮ *Look for the personal connection.*   How does the use of symbols in a story touch your own life, your own experience? What symbols have a special personal meaning for you—as the way Elisa dresses in the chrysanthemums story had for the student writer of the following passage?

> Steinbeck's story dealt with feminine emotions that can be very hard to understand. I was struck by the contrast between Elisa's mannish "working clothes" (her shapeless outfit, her heavy gloves) and the makeup and dress she puts on after her encounter with the tinker. Much of her thinking revolved around whether the men in her world would respect her work and desire her at the same time. Her change of clothes symbolizes the fact that in the male world the woman has to play a dual role. She has to be a man's equal to survive in the world of work, yet on the other hand she is expected to be feminine and seductive. Today a woman has to look more like a man by wearing a dark "power" suit and practically no makeup to compete with men, or she may not be taken seriously. In a recent sitcom episode, I watched a sterile-looking businesswoman teaching a fashionable female how to dress for business success. Her pupil donned a blue suit, a buttoned white shirt, and a bandage-type thing to hide her breasts. Steinbeck's story points up this unresolved conflict: It is a sad but honest account of how women are taken advantage of when they expose their feminine selves.

Two Readings of a Story   The language of symbols may be universal, but it also by its very nature fosters a range of interpretation. Writers relying heavily on symbols are the least likely to spell out the meaning or the moral of a story in so many words. Where do the two following readings of "The Yellow Wallpaper" seem to agree? Where do they differ in emphasis or interpretation? Which is closer to your own reading of the story? Which do you learn from the most?

Sample Student Paper 1

"The Yellow Wallpaper": A Woman's Struggle with Madness

"I've got out at last . . . and I've pulled off most of the paper, so you can't put me back!" declares the narrator of "The Yellow Wallpaper" at the end of her futile struggle with madness. By peeling off the yellow wallpaper and releasing the woman the narrator sees trapped behind its "conspicuous front design," the narrator peels off the façade of normalcy she is trapped behind and releases her own madness. This façade is created by a "very careful and loving" husband, who refuses to believe his wife is ill, and is perpetuated by the medical conventions of the time that dismiss her mental illness as "a slight hysterical tendency."

In his effort to help his wife get over her "temporary nervous depression," John takes her to a house in the country which is "quite alone, standing well back from the road, quite three miles from the village." He feels that this quiet atmosphere along with "perfect rest" is just what she needs. In fact, she is "absolutely forbidden to work" and has "a scheduled prescription for each hour of the day." The narrator, on the other hand, feels "that congenial work, with excitement and change, would do me good." However, because her husband is "a physician of high standing," she feels he must know what is best for her. When they first move into the house, she wants a room "downstairs that opened on the piazza and had roses all over the window, and such pretty old-fashioned chintz hangings" but "John would not hear of it." He insists they take "the nursery at the top of the house" even though "the windows are barred, . . . the floor is scratched and gouged and splintered, the plaster itself is dug out here and there," and the room is covered in a "horrid paper"—"one of those sprawling flamboyant patterns committing every artistic sin" and colored "repellent, almost revolting . . . unclean yellow." He also insists that she stop writing, which she feels "would relieve the press of ideas and rest me." She does manage to write a bit "in spite of them," but it is too exhausting "having to be so sly about it."

Consequently, with no outlet for her "imaginative power and habit of storymaking," she develops a grotesque fascination with the yellow wallpaper. At first the paper is just irritating, "dull enough to confuse the eye in following, pronounced enough to constantly irritate and provoke study." But, as the narrator studies the wallpaper more and more, she begins to see hideous images in the pattern. "The pattern lolls like a broken neck and two bulbous eyes . . . those absurd, unblinking eyes are everywhere." She dwells on this pattern and soon sees "a kind of subpattern in a different shade . . . that seems to sulk behind" the front design. The wallpaper so disturbs the narrator that she tries to have "a real earnest and reasonable talk" with her husband about her condition. He tells her that she is getting better, but she replies, "Better in body, perhaps." He dismisses her concern for her mental state as "a false and foolish fancy." He tells her that she must not give in to her feelings, and that only she can help herself get better. She must use her "will and self-control and not let any silly fancies run away with her."

It is at this point in the story, after the narrator tries, unsuccessfully, to share her fears for her sanity, that she can no longer control the madness she has been struggling to contain. This madness takes the form of the woman behind the wallpaper. "I didn't realize for a long time what the thing was that showed behind, that dim subpattern, but now I am quite sure it is a woman" (483). The narrator describes the woman as "subdued, quiet," and the narrator believes "it is the pattern that keeps her so still." The narrator is, in fact, describing herself, so quiet and subdued, and the pattern keeping her that way is her life.

As the narrator's illness progresses, she begins to identify more and more with the woman behind the wallpaper. She sees the woman creeping around everywhere: "in that long shaded lane . . . in those dark grape arbors . . . on that long road under the trees, creeping along, and when a carriage comes she hides." The narrator sympathizes with this woman for she, too, is creeping around. "I always lock the door when I creep by daylight," the narrator writes.

Ultimately, her madness takes complete control and her one purpose in life is to help the woman escape from the wallpaper. Piece by piece, the narrator peels off the wallpaper as she peels away at her own sanity, until the woman is able to escape from behind the paper, and the narrator is able to escape into her own madness. The narrator wonders "if they all come out of the wallpaper as I did?"

No less obvious than the symbolism of the yellow wallpaper is the irony of the story. A loving husband, a physician no less, prescribes a treatment of rest and relaxation he feels will improve his wife's slightly depressed condition; however, instead of helping her, he unwittingly drives her to insanity. His mistake was in not taking her condition seriously, not accepting that she was, indeed, very ill. We want to say, "Poor woman, if she existed today, she could have been helped." Maybe, and maybe not. Situations similar to the narrator's do exist today. The modern term for John is "enabler." Just as John, by pretending nothing was seriously wrong, enabled his wife to succumb to her illness, many spouses and families of alcoholics enable them to continue being alcoholics by not admitting they have a problem. They, too, are trapped behind the façades of normalcy they create. This is only one example. We are all "enablers" in one way or another. By ignoring the problems that exist all around us, and refusing to admit they are real problems, we perpetuate those problems. Only by admitting a problem exists, whether in the family or in society, can we truly begin to find a solution.

Sample Student Paper 2

Yellow Women

Gilman's "The Yellow Wallpaper" is a tragic story of a woman's attempt to recover from post-partum depression. This story represents through symbolism the characteristic attitude towards woman and of women during the late 1800's and early 1900's. Gilman writes honestly of the isolated and confused feelings women were feeling. The woman in "The Yellow Wallpaper" goes through three periods of change throughout the story. The story begins with the description of the woman as being sick, but there are no signs of mental illness, and she is aware of her environment and even believes she is not really sick. Then there is a curious change in her character, and she appears to be disillusioned and on the verge of becoming mentally insane. And in the end she does go over the edge, and her character is literally lost. There are factors which cause these changes; I will explore these three major changes in her life as well as the use of powerful symbolism.

The woman in this story is taken to a summer house to rest and recuperate. Her husband, John, who is also her doctor, treats her as a child, and she says that "perhaps that is one reason I do not get well faster." She is apparently suffering from the baby blues, which is a depression some women experience after giving birth to a child. However, her husband sticks her in an atrocious nursery with barred windows and a wallpaper that she describes as

> dull enough to confuse the eye in following, pronounced enough to constantly irritate and provoke study, and when you follow the lame uncertain curves for a little distance they suddenly commit suicide—plunge off at outrageous angles, destroy themselves in unheard of contradictions.

Her description of the wallpaper represents her feelings about the paper, but it also symbolizes the feelings she has about herself. This confusing pattern could be a typical categorization of women, whereas a typical pattern for men might be straight and neat lines that meet at edges and appear to have an overall meaning. I say this because, in the story, John apparently knows all and has prescribed his wife's life as he sees fit. In a description of John's sister, the woman says she is "a perfect and enthusiastic housekeeper, and hopes for no better profession." This heartless description lacks praise for her sister-in-law's profession; it also symbolizes the status of women in the time the story was written.

Her husband, who calls her "his little girl" and his "blessed goose," forbids her to work until she is well; she disagrees, believing "congenial work, with excitement and change," would do her good. She believes she could recover from her baby blues if only she were able to keep active and do other things than sit alone in a nursery and stare at the wallpaper. She even asks her husband to have company for companionship, but he tells her, "he would as soon put fireworks in my pillow case as to let me have those stimulating people about now." She might not even have progressed to her second stage if it were not for her husband, brother, and sister-in-law constantly reminding her of how tired and sick she is.

Her second stage begins when she becomes "fond" of the wallpaper. She is losing contact with the outside world, instead spending her time trying, in a painstaking effort, to understand the overall pattern of the wallpaper. She sees a figure that looks like a "woman stooping down and creeping about behind that pattern." She also goes on to say, "I don't like it a bit. . . . I wish John would take me away from here." She is herself the woman "creeping" through the wallpaper. The woman creeping symbolizes women who are not allowed to stand tall and free and speak their minds. She "creeps" at night when her husband is asleep and, when she is caught "creeping," her husband tells her to get back in bed. Her husband, who has good intentions, keeps on assuring her that she is getting better, and when she disagrees with him by saying, "Better in body perhaps," he looks at her with such a "stern, reproachful" stare that she does not dare say another word.

She is alone in her own little world with no real support from anyone. She cannot be blamed for her condition and eventually insanity takes over her body. Here is another example of how the wallpaper symbolizes women:

> The front pattern does move—and no wonder! The woman behind shakes it! Sometimes I think there are a great many women behind, . . . And she is all the time trying to climb through. But nobody could climb through that pattern—it strangles so; I think that is why it has so many heads.

She realizes she is not the only woman who is lost but also many other women. This realization pushes her to her mental limit, and she tries to peel all of the wallpaper off so that the "strangled heads" can be free. She feels secure and safe in the room "creeping" and she says, "I don't want to go outside. . . . For outside you have to creep on the ground, and everything is green instead of yellow." She has no desire to live in the "green" world, and she chooses the "yellow" familiar world instead. She even locks herself in the room and throws away the key. This act symbolizes an instance of control over her own life. Comfortable in her "creeping" role, she does not want anyone to bother her. She is now mentally insane.

The woman in "The Yellow Wallpaper" represents many women, even today, in the late 20th century. There are many women who do not take advantage of their freedom, many who are also servants in life. I have seen this to be so in my grandmother's as well as in my mother's marriage. However, the wallpaper women are hiding behind is slowly being peeled off by both men and women.

Questions

1. Do these two papers agree in their estimate of the relation between the woman and her physician husband?

2. How do the two papers compare in their interpretation of key symbolic elements: the wallpaper pattern, the woman behind the paper, the creeping, the peeling off of the paper?

3. Do both papers interpret the symbolism of the colors green and yellow, and do they agree in their interpretation?

4. How do the two papers compare in their view of what the story means to today's women?

The Personal Response

After reading the second paper, one student reader wrote the following comment. Where do you agree or disagree with it, and why?

I remember that when first reading the story I was totally overpowered by it. This is a fascinating, disturbing paper that has made me see this terrible story in a new way. The "yellow women" designated by this student writer are not just victims to her; they are also "yellow," i.e. chicken, afraid, able only to escape via insanity. There's a strange implication—and judgment of—learned helplessness. Without quite saying it, this writer attempts to say that the flight into insanity is as much a cop-out as it is the oppressor's unknowing way of forcing insanity on the female. I get an ambiguous picture: the male isn't being deliberately patronizing; he is just as much a victim of the cultural norm as the female is. Conversely, the female plays as big a part in her insanity as the male. She could "choose" the green way—partly because she knows where the "green way" is: downstairs, near the roses and the entrance to the garden—and in her writing. A key word in this paper is "choose." The implication is that she can't buck convention enough to stand up for herself, so she retreats into the "yellow" room on the second floor, giving up the organic living greenness and groundedness in earth and reality of the first floor where she could heal naturally from a natural disequilibrium. If this writer does what I think she's doing, she has become aware of a double tragedy often missed: the pathetic ignorance of men as well as women in roles they wear because they know no other.

7 Theme

The Search for Meaning

Invention, not preaching, enchants the modern reader and sustains the illusion of reality.

ANN CHARTERS

FOCUS ON THEME

Imaginative literature has the power to make you think. A story that has a strong impact is likely to raise questions to which the story as a whole suggests answers. It is likely to make you rethink some facet of human life. When you try to put the human meaning of a story into your own words, you formulate its **theme.** You try to state the idea or ideas that the story as a whole seems to act out.

Keep the following in mind when reading for theme:

The Overt Theme   Writers of earlier generations felt free to spell out the meaning of a story in a **thematic passage.** They might put these in the mouth (or in the mind) of an observer or of a key character. In his "The Blue Hotel" (1898), a story set in Nebraska in the Old West, Stephen Crane traces the events leading up to a barroom brawl in which a man is killed. From the beginning, our attention centers on the strange behavior of a recent arrival, the Swede. He is subject to neurotic fears, he covers up his apprehensions with bluster and bravado, and he is a constant source of irritation to the small group of men spending the night in the hotel. A long evening of drinking and random quarreling comes to a head when the Swede accuses a loudmouthed local boy of cheating at poker and batters him in a bloody fight. Flushed with liquor and his sense of victory, the Swede checks out of the hotel and stumbles on to a saloon. He there picks a fight with a gambler who refuses to drink with him, and the trouble-making Swede is killed in the ensuing brawl.

The locals feel that the Swede only got what he deserved; he had it coming. However, Crane wants us to learn something else from this story, and he puts it in the mouth of one of his characters. The "Easterner" has been mostly a silent observer and at times a calming influence in the

176

story. He finally says to a local cowboy who accuses the Swede of acting like a jackass:

> You're a bigger jackass than the Swede by a million majority. Now let
> me tell you one thing. . . . Johnnie *was* cheating. I saw him. . . . And
> I refused to stand up and be a man. I let the Swede fight it out alone.
> And you—you were simply puffing around the place and wanting to
> fight. . . . We are all in it! . . . Every sin is the result of collaboration.
> We, five of us, have collaborated in the murder of this Swede.

Evil is the result of collaboration. Crane's theme in this story is a general statement, but it is not a glib generalization. It is an earned generalization—not brought into the story from the outside. It is anchored in
the lived experience of the story.

The Implied Theme   Most twentieth-century writers would have preferred not to sum up the theme of Crane's story in so many words. They
would have preferred to have the reader *think* about the role collaboration plays in causing evil. Modern writers have been reluctant to preach
or to editorialize. As a result, the themes of modern fiction tend to be
implied rather than spelled out. They are ideas organically embedded in
image, action, and emotion.

The Fear of Abstraction   In writing and thinking about theme, beware
of large abstractions. Part of the modern temper has been a suspicion of
big words, hasty generalizations, and premature abstractions. **Abstractions** (from a Latin word meaning "pulling away") draw us away from
the nitty-gritty of unsorted detail to the larger labels and categories that
we need to find our way in a multilayered world. But abstract terms
cover much; they are "umbrella" terms. They easily become foggy or
misleading. Be prepared to ask: "Freedom"—to do what? "Love of
humanity"—what part or what features of it?

The Simplified Theme   Beware of oversimplification. Some readers
look for an overly simple message. If you were to look for a common
denominator for stories by Faulkner, Jackson, and Hawthorne in this
volume, you might start by saying their authors agree that "evil lurks in
the human heart." However, the questions each story raises and the possible answers it leads us to explore are more complex than that. Like
other writers who have wrestled with the problem of how to explain
evil in our world, each of these authors has arrived at a somewhat different answer.

Avoiding Clichés   Beware of clichés. "All you need is love" makes a
marvelous popular song. But it is too sweeping (and too obviously

untrue) to serve as an insight that we carry away from a gripping story. If you bring a ready-made phrase to a story from outside, it may not carry the authentic stamp of honest feeling, of lived experience. Be wary of greeting-card phrases—phrases we take down ready-made from the rack when we find it hard to put our own honest feeling and thinking into words.

You may encounter two related meanings of the term *theme*. It may mean simply a focus of attention, an area of concern. In this sense, one great modern theme is alienation—the feeling of uprootedness, the loss of a sense of home. However, in many critical discussions, the theme is what a story as a whole says *about* alienation. The story as a whole may be making a statement about the roots of alienation. Or it may say something about our ways of coping with it. It may make us think about how alienation explains the people we are or the people we encounter.

THE THINKING READER

The concepts of beauty and ugliness are mysterious to me. Many people write about them. In mulling over them, I try to get underneath them and see what they mean, understand the impact they have on what people do. I also write about love and death. The problem I face as a writer is to make my stories mean something. You can have wonderful, interesting people, a fascinating story, but it's not about anything. It has no real substance.

TONI MORRISON

Thinking readers have always looked in literature for an interpretation of experience. They listen to writers who help them make sense of life—or of some corner of it. They remember writers who were guideposts or beacons in times of bewilderment, of confusion. Each of the following stories puts its characters into situations that confront them with searching questions. What are these questions in each story? What answers does the story as a whole suggest? What ideas—about people, about human nature, about evil—are at the heart of each story?

Alice Walker   *(born 1944)*

Her deepest concern is with individuals and how their relationships are affected by their confrontations with wider political and moral issues.

CAROL RUMENS

Alice Walker's novel *The Color Purple* (1982) established her as a dominant voice in the quest for a new black identity. Often her heroines are women in the African-American community struggling to emerge from a history of oppression and abuse. They find strength in bonding with other women, and they turn to the African past in the search for alternatives to our rapacious technological civilization. A recurrent feature in her fiction are black males representing a generation of men who "had failed women—and themselves." Walker's more recent novel, *The Temple of My Familiar* (1989), has been called a book of "amazing, overwhelming" richness, with characters "pushing one another towards self-knowledge, honesty, engagement" (Ursula K. Le Guin).

Born in Eatonton, Georgia, Walker knew poverty and racism at close quarters as the child of sharecroppers in the Deep South. While a student at Spelman College in Atlanta, she joined in the rallies, sit-ins, and freedom marches of the civil rights movement, which, she said later, "broke the pattern of black servitude in this country." She worked as a case worker for the New York City Welfare Department and as an editor for *Ms.* magazine. She has written and lectured widely on the relationship between black men and women, between black and white women, and between her writing and the work of African-American writers— Jean Toomer, Zora Neale Hurston—who were her inspiration. She has taught creative writing and black literature at colleges including Jackson State College, Wellesley, and Yale.

Many of Walker's essays, articles, and reviews were collected in her *In Search of Our Mothers' Gardens* (1983). In the title essay, she paid tribute to women of her mother's and grandmother's generations, who channeled the creative and spiritual energies that were denied other outlets into their rich gardens and into the "fanciful, inspired, and yet simple" quilts they fashioned from "bits and pieces of worthless rags." In the following story, the older generation tries to hold onto its hard-won pride, while members of a younger generation assert their independence from the past by adopting Muslim names and African greetings.

Everyday Use   *1973*
For Your Grandmamma

I will wait for her in the yard that Maggie and I made so clean and wavy yesterday afternoon. A yard like this is more comfortable than most people know. It is not just a yard. It is like an extended living room. When the hard clay is swept clean as a floor and the fine sand around the edges lined with tiny, irregular grooves, anyone can come and sit and look up into the elm tree and wait for the breezes that never come inside the house.

Maggie will be nervous until after her sister goes: she will stand hopelessly in corners, homely and ashamed of the burn scars down her arms and legs, eyeing her sister with a mixture of envy and awe. She thinks her sister has held life always in the palm of one hand, that "no" is a word the world never learned to say to her.

You've no doubt seen those TV shows where the child who has "made it" is confronted, as a surprise, by her own mother and father, tottering in weakly from backstage. (A pleasant surprise, of course: What would they do if parent and child came on the show only to curse out and insult each other?) On TV mother and child embrace and smile into each other's faces. Sometimes the mother and father weep, the child wraps them in her arms and leans across the table to tell how she would not have made it without their help. I have seen these programs.

Sometimes I dream a dream in which Dee and I are suddenly brought together on a TV program of this sort. Out of a dark and soft-seated limousine I am ushered into a bright room filled with many people. There I meet a smiling, gray, sporty man like Johnny Carson who shakes my hand and tells me what a fine girl I have. Then we are on the stage and Dee is embracing me with tears in her eyes. She pins on my dress a large orchid, even though she has told me once that she thinks orchids are tacky flowers.

In real life I am a large, big-boned woman with rough, man-working   5 hands. In the winter I wear flannel nightgowns to bed and overalls during the day. I can kill and clean a hog as mercilessly as a man. My fat keeps me hot in zero weather. I can work outside all day, breaking ice to get water for washing; I can eat pork liver cooked over the open fire minutes after it comes steaming from the hog. One winter I knocked a bull calf straight in the brain between the eyes with a sledge hammer and had the meat hung up to chill before nightfall. But of course all this does not show on television. I am the way my daughter would want me to be: a hundred pounds lighter, my skin like an uncooked barley pancake. My hair glistens in the hot bright lights. Johnny Carson has much to do to keep up with my quick and witty tongue.

But that is a mistake. I know even before I wake up. Who ever knew a Johnson with a quick tongue? Who can even imagine me looking a strange white man in the eye? It seems to me I have talked to them always with one foot raised in flight, with my head turned in whichever way is farthest from them. Dee, though. She would always look anyone in the eye. Hesitation was no part of her nature.

"How do I look, Mama?" Maggie says, showing just enough of her thin body enveloped in pink skirt and red blouse for me to know she's there, almost hidden by the door.

"Come out into the yard," I say.

Have you ever seen a lame animal, perhaps a dog run over by some careless person rich enough to own a car, sidle up to someone who is ignorant enough to be kind to them? That is the way my Maggie walks. She has been like this, chin on chest, eyes on ground, feet in shuffle, ever since the fire that burned the other house to the ground.

Dee is lighter than Maggie, with nicer hair and a fuller figure. She's a   10 woman now, though sometimes I forget. How long ago was it that the other house burned? Ten, twelve years? Sometimes I can still hear the flames and feel Maggie's arms sticking to me, her hair smoking and her dress falling off her in little black papery flakes. Her eyes seemed stretched open, blazed open by the flames reflected in them. And Dee. I see her standing off under the sweet gum tree she used to dig gum out of; a look of concentration on her face as she watched the last dingy gray board of the house fall in toward the red-hot brick chimney. Why don't you do a dance around the ashes? I'd wanted to ask her. She had hated the house that much.

I used to think she hated Maggie, too. But that was before we raised the money, the church and me, to send her to Augusta to school. She used to read to us without pity; forcing words, lies, other folks' habits, whole lives upon us two, sitting trapped and ignorant underneath her voice. She washed us in a river of make-believe, burned us with a lot of knowledge we didn't necessarily need to know. Pressed us to her with the serious way she read, to shove us away at just the moment, like dimwits, we seemed about to understand.

Dee wanted nice things. A yellow organdy dress to wear to her graduation from high school; black pumps to match a green suit she'd made from an old suit somebody gave me. She was determined to stare down any disaster in her efforts. Her eyelids would not flicker for minutes at a time. Often I fought off the temptation to shake her. At sixteen she had a style of her own: and knew what style was.

I never had an education myself. After second grade the school was closed down. Don't ask me why: in 1927 colored asked fewer questions than they do now. Sometimes Maggie reads to me. She stumbles along good naturedly but can't see well. She knows she is not bright. Like good looks and money, quickness passed her by. She will marry John Thomas (who has mossy teeth in an earnest face) and then I'll be free to sit here and I guess just sing church songs to myself. Although I never was a good singer. Never could carry a tune. I was always better at a man's job. I used to love to milk till I was hooked in the side in '49. Cows are soothing and slow and don't bother you, unless you try to milk them the wrong way.

I have deliberately turned my back on the house. It is three rooms, just like the one that burned, except the roof is tin; they don't make shingle roofs any more. There are no real windows, just some holes cut in the sides, like the portholes in a ship, but not round and not square, with rawhide holding the shutters up on the outside. This house is in a pasture, too, like the other one. No doubt when Dee sees it she will want to tear it down. She wrote me once that no matter where we "choose" to live, she will manage to come see us. But she will never bring her friends. Maggie and I thought about this and Maggie asked me, "Mama, when did Dee ever *have* any friends?"

She had a few. Furtive boys in pink shirts hanging about on washday after school. Nervous girls who never laughed. Impressed with her they worshiped the well-turned phrase, the cute shape, the scalding humor that erupted like bubbles in lye. She read to them.   15

When she was courting Jimmy T she didn't have much time to pay to us, but turned all her faultfinding power on him. He *flew* to marry a cheap city girl from a family of ignorant flashy people. She hardly had time to recompose herself.

* * *

When she comes I will meet—but there they are!

Maggie attempts to make a dash for the house, in her shuffling way, but I stay her with my hand. "Come back here," I say. And she stops and tries to dig a well in the sand with her toe.

It is hard to see them clearly through the strong sun. But even the first glimpse of leg out of the car tells me it is Dee. Her feet were always neat-looking, as if God himself had shaped them with a certain style. From the other side of the car comes a short, stocky man. Hair is all over his head a foot long and hanging from his chin like a kinky mule tail. I hear Maggie suck in her breath. "Uhnnnh," is what it sounds like. Like when you see the wriggling end of a snake just in front of your foot on the road. "Uhnnnh."

Dee next. A dress down to the ground, in this hot weather. A dress so   20
loud it hurts my eyes. There are yellows and oranges enough to throw back the light of the sun. I feel my whole face warming from the heat waves it throws out. Earrings gold, too, and hanging down to her shoulders. Bracelets dangling and making noises when she moves her arm up to shake the folds of the dress out of her armpits. The dress is loose and flows, and as she walks closer, I like it. I hear Maggie go "Uhnnnh" again. It is her sister's hair. It stands straight up like the wool on a sheep. It is black as night and around the edges are two long pigtails that rope about like small lizards disappearing behind her ears.

"Wa-su-zo-Tean-o!" she says, coming on in that gliding way the dress makes her move. The short stocky fellow with the hair to his navel is all grinning and he follows up with "Asalamalakim, my mother and sister!" He moves to hug Maggie but she falls back, right up against the back of my chair. I feel her trembling there and when I look up I see the perspiration falling off her chin.

"Don't get up," says Dee. Since I am stout it takes something of a push. You can see me trying to move a second or two before I make it. She turns, showing white heels through her sandals, and goes back to the car. Out she peeks next with a Polaroid. She stoops down quickly and lines up picture after picture of me sitting there in front of the house with Maggie cowering behind me. She never takes a shot without making sure the house is included. When a cow comes nibbling around the edge of the yard she snaps it and me and Maggie *and* the house. Then she puts the Polaroid in the back seat of the car, and comes up and kisses me on the forehead.

Meanwhile Asalamalakim is going through motions with Maggie's hand. Maggie's hand is as limp as a fish, and probably as cold, despite the sweat, and she keeps trying to pull it back. It looks like Asalamalakim wants to shake hands but wants to do it fancy. Or maybe he don't know how people shake hands. Anyhow, he soon gives up on Maggie.

"Well," I say. "Dee."

"No, Mama," she says. "Not 'Dee,' Wangero Leewanika Kemanjo!"   25

"What happened to 'Dee'?" I wanted to know.

"She's dead," Wangero said. "I couldn't bear it any longer, being named after the people who oppress me."

"You know as well as me you was named after your aunt Dicie," I said. Dicie is my sister. She named Dee. We called her "Big Dee" after Dee was born.

"But who was *she* named after?" asked Wangero.

"I guess after Grandma Dee," I said.   30

"And who was she named after?" asked Wangero.

"Her mother," I said, and saw Wangero was getting tired. "That's about as far back as I can trace it," I said. Though, in fact, I probably could have carried it back beyond the Civil War through the branches.

"Well," said Asalamalakim, "there you are."

"Uhnnnh," I heard Maggie say.

"There I was not," I said, "before 'Dicie' cropped up in our family, so   35
why should I try to trace it that far back?"

He just stood there grinning, looking down on me like somebody inspecting a Model A car. Every once in a while he and Wangero sent eye signals over my head.

"How do you pronounce this name?" I asked.

"You don't have to call me by it if you don't want to," said Wangero.

"Why shouldn't I?" I asked. "If that's what you want us to call you, we'll call you."

"I know it might sound awkward at first," said Wangero.   40

"I'll get used to it," I said. "Ream it out again."

Well, soon we got the name out of the way. Asalamalakim had a name twice as long and three times as hard. After I tripped over it two or three times he told me to just call him Hakim-a-barber. I wanted to ask him was he a barber, but I didn't really think he was, so I didn't ask.

"You must belong to those beef-cattle peoples down the road," I said. They said "Asalamalakim" when they met you, too, but they didn't shake hands. Always too busy: feeding the cattle, fixing the fences, putting up salt-lick shelters, throwing down hay. When the white folks poisoned some of the herd the men stayed up all night with rifles in their hands. I walked a mile and a half just to see the sight.

Hakim-a-barber said, "I accept some of their doctrines, but farming and raising cattle is not my style." (They didn't tell me, and I didn't ask, whether Wangero (Dee) had really gone and married him.)

We sat down to eat and right away he said he didn't eat collards and pork   45
was unclean. Wangero, though, went on through the chitlins and corn bread, the greens and everything else. She talked a blue streak over the sweet potatoes. Everything delighted her. Even the fact that we still used the benches her daddy made for the table when we couldn't afford to buy chairs.

"Oh, Mama!" she cried. Then turned to Hakim-a-barber. "I never knew how lovely these benches are. You can feel the rump prints," she said, running her hands underneath her and along the bench. Then she gave a sigh and her hand closed over Grandma Dee's butter dish. "That's it!" she said. "I knew there was something I wanted to ask you if I could have." She jumped up from the table and went over in the corner where the churn stood, the milk in it clabber by now. She looked at the churn and looked at it.

"This churn top is what I need," she said. "Didn't Uncle Buddy whittle it out of a tree you all used to have?"

"Yes," I said.

"Uh huh," she said happily. "And I want the dasher, too."

"Uncle Buddy whittle that, too?" asked the barber.   50

Dee (Wangero) looked up at me.

"Aunt Dee's first husband whittled the dash," said Maggie so low you almost couldn't hear her. "His name was Henry, but they called him Stash."

"Maggie's brain is like an elephant's," Wangero said, laughing. "I can use the churn top as a centerpiece for the alcove table," she said, sliding a plate over the churn, "and I'll think of something artistic to do with the dasher."

When she finished wrapping the dasher the handle stuck out. I took it for a moment in my hands. You didn't even have to look close to see where hands pushing the dasher up and down to make butter had left a kind of sink in the wood. In fact, there were a lot of small sinks; you could see where thumbs and fingers had sunk into the wood. It was beautiful light yellow wood, from a tree that grew in the yard where Big Dee and Stash had lived.

After dinner Dee (Wangero) went to the trunk at the foot of my bed and 55
started rifling through it. Maggie hung back in the kitchen over the dishpan. Out came Wangero with two quilts. They had been pieced by Grandma Dee and then Big Dee and me had hung them on the quilt frames on the front porch and quilted them. One was in the Lone Star pattern. The other was Walk Around the Mountain. In both of them were scraps of dresses Grandma Dee had worn fifty and more years ago. Bits and pieces of Grandpa Jarrell's Paisley shirts. And one teeny faded blue piece, about the size of a penny matchbox, that was from Great Grandpa Ezra's uniform that he wore in the Civil War.

"Mama," Wangero said sweet as a bird. "Can I have these old quilts?"

I heard something fall in the kitchen, and a minute later the kitchen door slammed.

"Why don't you take one or two of the others?" I asked. "These old things was just done by me and Big Dee from some tops your grandma pieced before she died."

"No," said Wangero. "I don't want those. They are stitched around the borders by machine."

"That'll make them last better," I said. 60

"That's not the point," said Wangero. "These are all pieces of dresses Grandma used to wear. She did all this stitching by hand. Imagine!" She held the quilts securely in her arms, stroking them.

"Some of the pieces, like those lavender ones, come from old clothes her mother handed down to her," I said, moving up to touch the quilts. Dee (Wangero) moved back just enough so that I couldn't reach the quilts. They already belonged to her.

"Imagine!" she breathed again, clutching them closely to her bosom.

"The truth is," I said, "I promised to give them quilts to Maggie, for when she marries John Thomas."

She gasped like a bee had stung her. 65

"Maggie can't appreciate these quilts!" she said. "She'd probably be backward enough to put them to everyday use."

"I reckon she would," I said. "God knows I been saving 'em for long enough with nobody using 'em. I hope she will!" I didn't want to bring up how I had offered Dee (Wangero) a quilt when she went away to college. Then she had told me they were old-fashioned, out of style.

"But they're *priceless!*" she was saying now, furiously; for she has a temper. "Maggie would put them on the bed and in five years they'd be in rags. Less than that!"

"She can always make some more," I said. "Maggie knows how to quilt."

Dee (Wangero) looked at me with hatred. "You just will not understand. The point is these quilts, *these* quilts!"

"Well," I said, stumped. "What would *you* do with them?"

"Hang them," she said. As if that was the only thing you *could* do with quilts.

Maggie by now was standing in the door. I could almost hear the sound her feet made as they scraped over each other.

"She can have them, Mama," she said, like somebody used to never winning anything, or having anything reserved for her. "I can 'member Grandma Dee without the quilts."

I looked at her hard. She had filled her bottom lip with checkerberry snuff and it gave her face a kind of dopey, hangdog look. It was Grandma Dee and Big Dee who taught her how to quilt herself. She stood there with her scarred hands hidden in the folds of her skirt. She looked at her sister with something like fear but she wasn't mad at her. This was Maggie's portion. This was the way she knew God to work.

When I looked at her like that something hit me in the top of my head and ran down to the soles of my feet. Just like when I'm in church and the spirit of God touches me and I get happy and shout. I did something I never had done before: hugged Maggie to me, then dragged her on into the room, snatched the quilts out of Miss Wangero's hands and dumped them into Maggie's lap. Maggie just sat there on my bed with her mouth open.

"Take one or two of the others," I said to Dee.

But she turned without a word and went out to Hakim-a-barber.

"You just don't understand," she said, as Maggie and I came out to the car.

"What don't I understand?" I wanted to know.

"Your heritage," she said. And then she turned to Maggie, kissed her, and said, "You ought to try to make something of yourself, too, Maggie. It's really a new day for us. But from the way you and Mama still live you'd never know it."

She put on some sunglasses that hid everything above the tip of her nose and her chin.

Maggie smiled; maybe at the sunglasses. But a real smile, not scared. After we watched the car dust settle I asked Maggie to bring me a dip of snuff. And then the two of us sat there just enjoying, until it was time to go in the house and go to bed.

The Receptive Reader

1. What is the self-image of the mother? How does her sense of her real self contrast with her daydreams? How does her initial self-portrait as the *narrator* and central character point forward to what happens later in the story?

2. What is the contrasting history of the two siblings? How does one serve as a *foil* to the other? What is most significant in their earlier history?

3. What is the mother's view of Dee and her companion? How would you spell out the mother's attitude implied at various points in the story? What touches seem satirical and why? Is everything in the story seen from the mother's *point of view?*

4. How does the confrontation over the quilts bring things to a head? What do the quilts symbolize? How does the climactic ending resolve the central conflict in this story? How does it turn the tables on Dee's use of terms like *backward* and *heritage?*

5. How would you spell out in so many words the *theme* of this story? (How does the title hint at the central theme?)

6. What in the story helps especially to bring the theme to life for you and keep it from becoming an abstract idea?

The Personal Response

Do you identify with the narrator in this story? Is there another side to the story? Could you say something in defense of Dee?

The Creative Dimension

Write a passage in which one or the other of the daughters tells her side of the story. Or rewrite the ending the way you would have preferred the story to come out.

Nathaniel Hawthorne   *(1804–1864)*

A dreamer may dwell so long among fantasies that the things without him will seem as real as those within.

NATHANIEL HAWTHORNE

Nathaniel Hawthorne was born in Salem, Massachusetts, and lived there for many years at his mother's house after finishing college. An ancestor had been a member of the court that sentenced the witches at the Salem trials in 1692. As a student and at first little-read writer, Hawthorne immersed himself in the history of colonial New England. When he married after a brief stint at a socialistic commune (Brook Farm), he settled at Concord, in the heart of historical New England.

Until he went to Liverpool in England as an American consul, Hawthorne lived in the heartland of American Puritanism. Here ministers like Cotton Mather and Jonathan Edwards had preached the Puritan dogma of the depravity of humankind. They had painted in vivid colors the ever-powerful temptation of sin, the fear and trembling of sinners in the hands of an angry God, and the ever-lurking presence of the devil. Hawthorne's Puritanical ancestors had left England to escape persecution as dissenters from the established Anglican church. In the New World, they set up a religious commonwealth where prayer and attendance at church services were rigidly enforced and where Quakers and other independent spirits were persecuted in turn.

Much of Hawthorne's fiction made his readers rethink and reexamine the Puritan past. His novel *The Scarlet Letter* (1850) has left readers around the world with unforgettable images of Hester Prynne, wearing the scarlet *A* branding her as an adulteress; her love child, Pearl, at play in the forest; and the child's father, the Puritan minister Dimmesdale, in the spiritual agonies of guilt.

The following much-analyzed story is set in Puritan New England at the time of King William III, who ruled in England from 1689 to 1702. Salem Village, established only forty years before, was on the edge of the wilderness, with heathen natives in the forests. The King Philip mentioned in the story was Metacomet, leader of the last organized Native American resistance in southern New England. The people in the story, too humble to be called gentlemen and ladies, are called Goodman Brown and Goody (short for Goodwife) Cloyse or Goody Cory. These women were among the victims of the Salem witch-hunt that took the lives of twenty men and women. Much of the learning of the Puritan divines had been concerned with witchcraft and with the devil's power to create delusions and apparitions. At a witches' Sabbath, the devil himself would preside at rituals that were a blasphemous perversion of the rites of the church.

Young Goodman Brown   *1835*

Young Goodman Brown came forth at sunset into the street at Salem village; but put his head back, after crossing the threshold, to exchange a parting kiss with his young wife. And Faith, as the wife was aptly named, thrust her own pretty head into the street, letting the wind play with the pink ribbons of her cap while she called to Goodman Brown.

"Dearest heart," whispered she, softly and rather sadly, when her lips were close to his ear, "prithee put off your journey until sunrise and sleep in your own bed tonight. A lone woman is troubled with such dreams and such thoughts that she's afeard of herself sometimes. Pray tarry with me this night, dear husband, of all nights in the year."

"My love and my Faith," replied Goodman Brown, "of all nights in the year, this one night must I tarry away from thee. My journey, as thou callest it, forth and back again, must needs be done 'twixt now and sunrise. What, my sweet, pretty wife, dost thou doubt me already, and we but three months married?"

"Then God bless you!" said Faith, with the pink ribbons; "and may you find all well when you come back."

"Amen!" cried Goodman Brown. "Say thy prayers, dear Faith, and go to   5
bed at dusk, and no harm will come to thee."

So they parted; and the young man pursued his way until, being about to turn the corner by the meeting-house, he looked back and saw the head of Faith still peeping after him with a melancholy air, in spite of her pink ribbons.

"Poor little Faith!" thought he, for his heart smote him. "What a wretch am I to leave her on such an errand! She talks of dreams, too. Methought as she spoke there was trouble in her face, as if a dream had warned her what work is to be done tonight. But no, no; 'twould kill her to think it. Well, she's a blessed angel on earth; and after this one night I'll cling to her skirts and follow her to heaven."

With this excellent resolve for the future, Goodman Brown felt himself justified in making more haste on his present evil purpose. He had taken a dreary road, darkened by all the gloomiest trees of the forest, which barely stood aside to let the narrow path creep through, and closed immediately behind. It was all as lonely as could be; and there is this peculiarity in such a solitude, that the traveller knows not who may be concealed by the innumerable trunks and the thick boughs overhead; so that with lonely footsteps he may yet be passing through an unseen multitude.

"There may be a devilish Indian behind every tree," said Goodman Brown to himself; and he glanced fearfully behind him as he added, "What if the devil himself should be at my very elbow!"

His head being turned back, he passed a crook of the road, and, looking 10 forward again, beheld the figure of a man, in grave and decent attire, seated at the foot of an old tree. He arose at Goodman Brown's approach and walked onward side by side with him.

"You are late, Goodman Brown," said he. "The clock of the Old South was striking as I came through Boston, and that is full fifteen minutes agone."

"Faith kept me back a while," replied the young man, with a tremor in his voice, caused by the sudden appearance of his companion, though not wholly unexpected.

It was now deep dusk in the forest, and deepest in that part of it where these two were journeying. As nearly as could be discerned, the second traveller was about fifty years old, apparently in the same rank of life as Goodman Brown, and bearing a considerable resemblance to him, though perhaps more in expression than features. Still they might have been taken for father and son. And yet, though the elder person was as simply clad as the younger, and as simple in manner too, he had an indescribable air of one who knew the world, and who would not have felt abashed at the governor's dinner table or in King William's court, were it possible that his affairs should call him thither. But the only thing about him that could be fixed upon as remarkable was his staff, which bore the likeness of a great black snake, so curiously wrought that it might almost be seen to twist and wriggle itself like a living serpent. This, of course, must have been an ocular deception, assisted by the uncertain light.

"Come, Goodman Brown," cried his fellow-traveller, "this is a dull place for the beginning of a journey. Take my staff, if you are so soon weary."

"Friend," said the other, exchanging his slow pace for a full stop, "having 15 kept covenant by meeting thee here, it is my purpose now to return whence I came. I have scruples touching the matter thou wot'st of."

"Sayest thou so?" replied he of the serpent, smiling apart. "Let us walk on, nevertheless, reasoning as we go; and if I convince thee not thou shalt turn back. We are but a little way in the forest yet."

"Too far! too far!" exclaimed the goodman, unconsciously resuming his walk. "My father never went into the woods on such an errand, nor his father before him. We have been a race of honest men and good Christians since the days of the martyrs; and shall I be the first of the name of Brown that ever took this path and kept—"

"Such company, thou wouldst say," observed the elder person, interpreting his pause. "Well said, Goodman Brown! I have been as well acquainted with your family as with ever a one among the Puritans; and that's no trifle to say. I helped your grandfather, the constable, when he lashed the Quaker woman so smartly through the streets of Salem; and it was I that brought your father a pitch-pine knot, kindled at my own hearth, to set fire to an Indian village, in King Philip's war. They were my good friends, both; and many a pleasant walk have we had along this path, and returned merrily after midnight. I would fain be friends with you for their sake."

"If it be as thou sayest," replied Goodman Brown, "I marvel they never spoke of these matters; or, verily, I marvel not, seeing that the least rumor of the sort would have driven them from New England. We are a people of prayer, and good works to boot, and abide no such wickedness."

"Wickedness or not," said the traveller with the twisted staff, "I have a   20 very general acquaintance here in New England. The deacons of many a church have drunk the communion wine with me; the selectmen of divers towns make me their chairman; and a majority of the Great and General Court are firm supporters of my interest. The governor and I, too—But these are state secrets."

"Can this be so?" cried Goodman Brown, with a stare of amazement at his undisturbed companion. "Howbeit, I have nothing to do with the governor and council; they have their own ways, and are no rule for a simple husbandman like me. But, were I to go on with thee, how should I meet the eye of that good old man, our minister, at Salem village? Oh, his voice would make me tremble both Sabbath day and lecture day."

Thus far the elder traveller had listened with due gravity; but now burst into a fit of irrepressible mirth, shaking himself so violently that his snake-like staff actually seemed to wriggle in sympathy.

"Ha! ha! ha!" shouted he again and again; then composing himself, "Well, go on, Goodman Brown, go on; but, prithee, don't kill me with laughing."

"Well, then, to end the matter at once," said Goodman Brown, considerably nettled, "there is my wife, Faith. It would break her dear little heart; and I'd rather break my own."

"Nay, if that be the case," answered the other, "e'en go thy ways, Good-   25 man Brown. I would not for twenty old women like the one hobbling before us that Faith should come to any harm."

As he spoke he pointed his staff at a female figure on the path, in whom Goodman Brown recognized a very pious and exemplary dame, who had taught him his catechism in youth, and was still his moral and spiritual adviser, jointly with the minister and Deacon Gookin.

"A marvel, truly, that Goody Cloyse should be so far in the wilderness at nightfall," said he. "But with your leave, friend, I shall take a cut through the woods until we have left this Christian woman behind. Being a stranger to you, she might ask whom I was consorting with and whither I was going."

"Be it so," said his fellow-traveller. "Betake you to the woods, and let me keep the path."

Accordingly the young man turned aside, but took care to watch his companion, who advanced softly along the road until he had come within a staff's length of the old dame. She, meanwhile, was making the best of her way, with singular speed for so aged a woman, and mumbling some indistinct words—a prayer, doubtless—as she went. The traveller put forth his staff and touched her withered neck with what seemed the serpent's tail.

"The devil!" screamed the pious old lady.   30

"Then Goody Cloyse knows her old friend?" observed the traveller, confronting her and leaning on his writhing stick.

"Ah, forsooth, and is it your worship indeed?" cried the good dame. "Yea, truly it is, and in the very image of my old gossip, Goodman Brown, the grandfather of the silly fellow that now is. But—would your worship believe it?—my broomstick hath strangely disappeared, stolen, as I suspect, by that unhanged witch, Goody Cory, and that, too, when I was all anointed with the juice of smallage, and cinquefoil, and wolf's bane—"

"Mingled with fine wheat and the fat of a new-born babe," said the shape of old Goodman Brown.

"Ah, your worship knows the recipe," cried the old lady, cackling aloud. "So, as I was saying, being all ready for the meeting, and no horse to ride on, I made up my mind to foot it; for they tell me there is a nice young man to be taken into communion tonight. But now your good worship will lend me your arm, and we shall be there in a twinkling."

"That can hardly be," answered her friend. "I may not spare you my arm,   35 Goody Cloyse; but here is my staff, if you will."

So saying, he threw it down at her feet, where, perhaps, it assumed life, being one of the rods which its owner had formerly lent to the Egyptian magi. Of this fact, however, Goodman Brown could not take cognizance. He had cast up his eyes in astonishment, and, looking down again, beheld neither Goody Cloyse nor the serpentine staff, but his fellow-traveller alone, who waited for him as calmly as if nothing had happened.

"That old woman taught me my catechism," said the young man; and there was a world of meaning in this simple comment.

They continued to walk onward, while the elder traveller exhorted his companion to make good speed and persevere in the path, discoursing so aptly that his arguments seemed rather to spring up in the bosom of his auditor than to be suggested by himself. As they went, he plucked a branch of maple to serve for a walking stick, and began to strip it of the twigs and little boughs, which were wet with evening dew. The moment his fingers touched them they became strangely withered and dried up as with a week's sunshine. Thus the pair proceeded, at a good free pace, until suddenly, in a gloomy hollow of the road, Goodman Brown sat himself down on the stump of a tree and refused to go any farther.

"Friend," said he, stubbornly, "my mind is made up. Not another step will I budge on this errand. What if a wretched old woman do choose to go to the devil when I thought she was going to heaven: is that any reason why I should quit my dear Faith and go after her?"

"You will think better of this by and by," said his acquaintance, compos-   40
edly. "Sit here and rest yourself a while; and when you feel like moving
again, there is my staff to help you along."

Without more words, he threw his companion the maple stick, and was
as speedily out of sight as if he had vanished into the deepening gloom. The
young man sat a few moments by the roadside, applauding himself greatly,
and thinking with how clear a conscience he should meet the minister in his
morning walk, nor shrink from the eye of good old Deacon Gookin. And
what calm sleep would be his that very night, which was to have been
spent so wickedly, but so purely and sweetly now, in the arms of Faith!
Amidst these pleasant and praiseworthy meditations, Goodman Brown
heard the tramp of horses along the road, and deemed it advisable to conceal himself within the verge of the forest, conscious of the guilty purpose
that had brought him thither, though now so happily turned from it.

On came the hoof tramps and the voices of the riders, two grave old
voices, conversing soberly as they drew near. These mingled sounds
appeared to pass along the road, within a few yards of the young man's
hiding-place; but, owing doubtless to the depth of the gloom at that particular spot, neither the travellers nor their steeds were visible. Though their
figures brushed the small boughs by the wayside, it could not be seen that
they intercepted, even for a moment, the faint gleam from the strip of bright
sky athwart which they must have passed. Goodman Brown alternately
crouched and stood on tiptoe, pulling aside the branches and thrusting
forth his head as far as he durst without discerning so much as a shadow. It
vexed him the more, because he could have sworn, were such a thing possible, that he recognized the voices of the minister and Deacon Gookin, jogging along quietly, as they were wont to do, when bound to some
ordination or ecclesiastical council. While yet within hearing, one of the riders stopped to pluck a switch.

"Of the two, reverend sir," said the voice like the deacon's, "I had rather
miss an ordination dinner than tonight's meeting. They tell me that some of
our community are to be here from Falmouth and beyond, and others from
Connecticut and Rhode Island, besides several of the Indian powwows,
who, after their fashion, know almost as much deviltry as the best of us.
Moreover, there is a goodly young woman to be taken into communion."

"Mighty well, Deacon Gookin!" replied the solemn old tones of the minister. "Spur up, or we shall be late. Nothing can be done, you know, until I
get on the ground."

The hoofs clattered again; and the voices, talking so strangely in the   45
empty air, passed on through the forest, where no church had ever been
gathered or solitary Christian prayed. Whither, then, could these holy men be
journeying so deep into the heathen wilderness? Young Goodman Brown
caught hold of a tree for support, being ready to sink down on the ground,
faint and overburdened with the heavy sickness of his heart. He looked up
to the sky, doubting whether there really was a heaven above him. Yet there
was the blue arch, and the stars brightening in it.

"With heaven above and Faith below, I will yet stand firm against the
devil!" cried Goodman Brown.

While he still gazed upward into the deep arch of the firmament and had lifted his hands to pray, a cloud, though no wind was stirring, hurried across the zenith and hid the brightening stars. The blue sky was still visible, except directly overhead, where this black mass of cloud was sweeping swiftly northward. Aloft in the air, as if from the depths of the cloud, came a confused and doubtful sound of voices. Once the listener fancied that he could distinguish the accents of townspeople of his own, men, and women, both pious and ungodly, many of whom he had met at the communion table, and had seen others rioting at the tavern. The next moment, so indistinct were the sounds, he doubted whether he had heard aught but the murmur of the old forest, whispering without a wind. Then came a stronger swell of those familiar tones, heard daily in the sunshine at Salem village, but never until now from a cloud of night. There was one voice, of a young woman, uttering lamentations, yet with an uncertain sorrow, and entreating for some favor, which, perhaps, it would grieve her to obtain; and all the unseen multitude, both saints and sinners, seemed to encourage her onward.

"Faith!" shouted Goodman Brown, in a voice of agony and desperation; and the echoes of the forest mocked him, crying, "Faith! Faith!" as if bewildered wretches were seeking her all through the wilderness.

The cry of grief, rage, and terror was yet piercing the night, when the unhappy husband held his breath for a response. There was a scream, drowned immediately in a louder murmur of voices, fading into far-off laughter, as the dark cloud swept away, leaving the clear and silent sky above Goodman Brown. But something fluttered lightly down through the air and caught on the branch of a tree. The young man seized it, and beheld a pink ribbon.

"My Faith is gone!" cried he, after one stupefied moment. "There is no good on earth; and sin is but a name. Come, devil; for to thee is this world given."   50

And, maddened with despair, so that he laughed loud and long, did Goodman Brown grasp his staff and set forth again, at such a rate that he seemed to fly along the forest path rather than to walk or run. The road grew wilder and drearier and more faintly traced, and vanished at length, leaving him in the heart of the dark wilderness, still rushing onward with the instinct that guides mortal man to evil. The whole forest was peopled with frightful sounds—the creaking of the trees, the howling of wild beasts, and the yell of Indians; while sometimes the wind tolled like a distant church bell, and sometimes gave a broad roar around the traveller, as if all Nature were laughing him to scorn. But he was himself the chief horror of the scene, and shrank not from its other horrors.

"Ha! ha! ha!" roared Goodman Brown when the wind laughed at him. "Let us hear which will laugh loudest. Think not to frighten me with your deviltry. Come witch, come wizard, come Indian powwow, come devil himself, and here comes Goodman Brown. You may as well fear him as he fear you."

In truth, all through the haunted forest there could be nothing more frightful than the figure of Goodman Brown. On he flew among the black pines, brandishing his staff with frenzied gestures, now giving vent to an inspiration of horrid blasphemy, and now shouting forth such laughter as set all the echoes of the forest laughing like demons around him. The fiend in his own shape is less hideous than when he rages in the breast of man. Thus sped the demoniac on his course, until, quivering among the trees, he saw a red light before him, as when the felled trunks and branches of a clearing have been set on fire, and throw up their lurid blaze against the sky, at the hour of midnight. He paused, in a lull of the tempest that had driven him onward, and heard the swell of what seemed a hymn, rolling solemnly from a distance with the weight of many voices. He knew the tune; it was a familiar one in the choir of the village meeting-house. The verse died heavily away, and was lengthened by a chorus, not of human voices, but of all the sounds of the benighted wilderness pealing in awful harmony together. Goodman Brown cried out, and his cry was lost to his own ear by its unison with the cry of the desert.

In the interval of silence he stole forward until the light glared full upon his eyes. At one extremity of an open space, hemmed in by the dark wall of the forest, arose a rock, bearing some rude, natural resemblance either to an altar or a pulpit, and surrounded by four blazing pines, their tops aflame, their stems untouched, like candles at an evening meeting. The mass of foliage that had overgrown the summit of the rock was all on fire, blazing high into the night and fitfully illuminating the whole field. Each pendent twig and leafy festoon was in a blaze. As the red light arose and fell, a numerous congregation alternately shone forth, then disappeared in shadow, and again grew, as it were, out of the darkness, peopling the heart of the solitary woods at once.

"A grave and dark-clad company," quoth Goodman Brown.   55

In truth they were such. Among them, quivering to and fro between gloom and splendor, appeared faces that would be seen next day at the council board of the province, and others which, Sabbath after Sabbath, looked devoutly heavenward, and benignantly over the crowded pews, from the holiest pulpits in the land. Some affirm that the lady of the governor was there. At least there were high dames well known to her, and wives of honored husbands, and widows, a great multitude, and ancient maidens, all of excellent repute, and fair young girls, who trembled lest their mothers should espy them. Either the sudden gleams of light flashing over the obscure field bedazzled Goodman Brown, or he recognized a score of the church members of Salem village famous for their especial sanctity. Good old Deacon Gookin had arrived, and waited at the skirts of that venerable saint, his revered pastor. But, irreverently consorting with these grave, reputable, and pious people, these elders of the church, these chaste dames and dewy virgins, there were men of dissolute lives and women of spotted fame, wretches given over to all mean and filthy vice, and suspected even of horrid crimes. It was strange to see that the good shrank not from the wicked, nor were the sinners abashed by the saints. Scattered also among their pale-faced enemies were the Indian priests, or powwows, who had often scared their native forest with more hideous incantations than any known to English witchcraft.

"But where is Faith?" thought Goodman Brown; and, as hope came into his heart, he trembled.

Another verse of the hymn arose, a slow and mournful strain, such as the pious love, but joined to words which expressed all that our nature can conceive of sin, and darkly hinted at far more. Unfathomable to mere mortals is the lore of fiends. Verse after verse was sung; and still the chorus of the desert swelled between like the deepest tone of a mighty organ; and with the final peal of that dreadful anthem there came a sound, as if the roaring wind, the rushing streams, the howling beasts, and every other voice of the unconverted wilderness were mingling and according with the voice of guilty man in homage to the prince of all. The four blazing pines threw up a loftier flame, and obscurely discovered shapes and visages of horror on the smoke wreaths above the impious assembly. At the same moment the fire on the rock shot redly forth and formed a glowing arch above its base, where now appeared a figure. With reverence be it spoken, the figure bore no slight similitude, both in garb and manner, to some grave divine of the New England churches.

"Bring forth the converts!" cried a voice that echoed through the field and rolled into the forest.

At the word, Goodman Brown stepped forth from the shadow of the   60
trees and approached the congregation, with whom he felt a loathful brotherhood by the sympathy of all that was wicked in his heart. He could have well-nigh sworn that the shape of his own dead father beckoned him to advance, looking downward from a smoke wreath, while a woman, with dim features of despair, threw out her hand to warn him back. Was it his mother? But he had no power to retreat one step, nor to resist, even in thought, when the minister and good old Deacon Gookin seized his arms and led him to the blazing rock. Thither came also the slender form of a veiled female, led between Goody Cloyse, that pious teacher of the catechism, and Martha Carrier, who had received the devil's promise to be queen of hell. A rampant hag was she. And there stood the proselytes beneath the canopy of fire.

"Welcome, my children," said the dark figure, "to the communion of your race. Ye have found thus young your nature and your destiny. My children, look behind you!"

They turned; and flashing forth, as it were, in a sheet of flame, the fiend worshippers were seen; the smile of welcome gleamed darkly on every visage.

"There," resumed the sable form, "are all whom ye have reverenced from youth. Ye deemed them holier than yourselves, and shrank from your own sin, contrasting it with their lives of righteousness and prayerful aspirations heavenward. Yet here are they all in my worshipping assembly. This night it shall be granted you to know their secret deeds: how hoary-bearded elders of the church have whispered wanton words to the young maids of their households; how many a woman, eager for widows' weeds, has given her husband a drink at bedtime and let him sleep his last sleep in her bosom; how beardless youths have made haste to inherit their fathers' wealth; and how fair damsels—blush not, sweet ones—have dug little graves in the garden, and bidden me, the sole guest, to an infant's funeral. By the sympathy of your human hearts for sin ye shall scent out all the places—whether in church, bedchamber, street, field, or forest—where crime has been committed, and shall exult to behold the whole earth one stain of guilt, one mighty blood spot. Far more than this. It shall be yours to penetrate, in every bosom, the deep mystery of sin, the fountain of all wicked arts, and which inexhaustibly supplies more evil impulses than human power—than my power at its utmost—can make manifest in deeds. And now, my children, look upon each other."

They did so; and, by the blaze of the hell-kindled torches, the wretched man beheld his Faith, and the wife her husband, trembling before that unhallowed altar.

"Lo, there ye stand, my children," said the figure, in a deep and solemn   65
tone, almost sad with its despairing awfulness, as if his once angelic nature could yet mourn for our miserable race. "Depending upon one another's hearts, ye had still hoped that virtue were not all a dream. Now are ye unde-ceived. Evil is the nature of mankind. Evil must be your only happiness. Welcome again, my children, to the communion of your race."

"Welcome," repeated the fiend worshippers, in one cry of despair and triumph.

And there they stood, the only pair, as it seemed, who were yet hesitat-ing on the verge of wickedness in this dark world. A basin was hollowed, naturally, in the rock. Did it contain water, reddened by the lurid light? or was it blood? or, perchance, a liquid flame? Herein did the shape of evil dip his hand and prepare to lay the mark of baptism upon their foreheads, that they might be partakers of the mystery of sin, more conscious of the secret guilt of others, both in deed and thought, than they could now be of their own. The husband cast one look at his pale wife, and Faith at him. What polluted wretches would the next glance show them to each other, shud-dering alike at what they disclosed and what they saw!

"Faith! Faith!" cried the husband, "look up to heaven, and resist the wicked one."

Whether Faith obeyed he knew not. Hardly had he spoken when he found himself amid calm night and solitude, listening to a roar of the wind which died heavily away through the forest. He staggered against the rock, and felt it chill and damp; while a hanging twig, that had been all on fire, besprinkled his cheek with the coldest dew.

The next morning young Goodman Brown came slowly into the street of   70
Salem village, staring around him like a bewildered man. The good old min-ister was taking a walk along the graveyard to get an appetite for breakfast and meditate his sermon, and bestowed a blessing, as he passed, on Good-man Brown. He shrank from the venerable saint as if to avoid an anathema. Old Deacon Gookin was at domestic worship, and the holy words of his prayer were heard through the open window. "What God doth the wizard pray to?" quoth Goodman Brown. Goody Cloyse, that excellent old Chris-tian, stood in the early sunshine at her own lattice, catechizing a little girl who had brought her a pint of morning's milk. Goodman Brown snatched away the child as from the grasp of the fiend himself. Turning the corner by the meeting-house, he spied the head of Faith, with the pink ribbons, gaz-ing anxiously forth, and bursting into such joy at the sight of him that she skipped along the street and almost kissed her husband before the whole village. But Goodman Brown looked sternly and sadly into her face, and passed on without a greeting.

Had Goodman Brown fallen asleep in the forest and only dreamed a wild dream of a witch-meeting?

Be it so if you will; but, alas! it was a dream of evil omen for young Goodman Brown. A stern, a sad, a darkly meditative, a distrustful, if not a desperate man did he become from the night of that fearful dream. On the Sabbath day, when the congregation were singing a holy psalm, he could not listen because an anthem of sin rushed loudly upon his ear and drowned all the blessed strain. When the minister spoke from the pulpit with power and fervid eloquence, and, with his hand on the open Bible, of the sacred truths of our religion, and of saint-like lives and triumphant deaths, and of future bliss or misery unutterable, then did Goodman Brown turn pale, dreading lest the roof should thunder down upon the gray blasphemer and his hearers. Often, waking suddenly at midnight, he shrank from the bosom of Faith; and at morning or eventide, when the family knelt down at prayer, he scowled and muttered to himself, and gazed sternly at his wife, and turned away. And when he had lived long, and was borne to his grave a hoary corpse, followed by Faith, an aged woman, and children and grandchildren, a goodly procession, besides neighbors not a few, they carved no hopeful verse upon his tombstone, for his dying hour was gloom.

The Receptive Reader

1. As the story opens, what are major steps and key details in Young Goodman Brown's journey into the forest? What is strange, what is frightening, and what is funny about the journey? Where does it go counter to our naive expectations, creating the effect of *irony?*

2. Much critical discussion of this story has focused on the role of Brown's "aptly named" wife, Faith. What is her role in the story? When is she real? When is she a *symbol?* Could she be both? (What is the role of the pink ribbon?)

3. What happens at the witches' Sabbath? How does it end? What question or questions does it leave open?

4. How are we as readers expected to react to Brown's transformation after his experience in the forest?

5. How would you sum up in a sentence or two what the story as a whole says about sin or about evil? How does your statement of the *theme* compare with statements of the theme by your classmates?

The Range of Interpretation

Hawthorne has a reputation for **ambiguity,** intentionally leaving his stories ambiguous and open-ended. Critics have read widely differing meanings into "Young Goodman Brown." Which of the following interpretations is to you most convincing? What evidence from the story would support it?

✗ Is Young Goodman Brown's journey into the forest an evil dream (perhaps inspired by the devil)?

✗ Is his journey a dream vision telling him the truth about human nature?

✗ Is his journey a symbolic acting out of his own paranoid fears and suspicions about others?

✗ Is his journey a symbolic acting out of his own sinful nature, his secret inclination toward evil?

✗   Is Hawthorne's vision of evil in this story a re-creation of a historical cycle that his generation had left behind? Or is it his own view?

Making Connections—For Discussion or Writing

Two other stories about evil lurking behind a genteel or reassuring surface are Shirley Jackson's "The Lottery" and William Faulkner's "A Rose for Emily." What is similar, or what is different, about the vision of evil in these three stories? Which do you find most persuasive? which least?

WRITING ABOUT LITERATURE

7.   Tracing a Recurrent Theme (Comparison and Contrast)

The Writing Workshop   A crucial part of your task as a writer is to make connections. When you compare stories by two different writers, you become more aware of each author's distinct way of looking at the world. You may want to try your hand at tracing the same or a similar theme in two stories by different authors. See what you can learn from such a paper about comparison and contrast as a major organizational strategy.

When you try to show the connections between several stories, the overall plan of your paper will be more complex than usual. How will you make your readers' eyes travel between the two stories to make them see the connections you want them to see? How will you go about highlighting similarities and differences? How are you going to lay out your material?

Let us assume you are writing about the vision of evil in Hawthorne's "Young Goodman Brown" and Jackson's "The Lottery." You have tentatively mapped out three areas where the stories seem to converge in their vision of how evil enters our world. Both stories take us into a world that is superficially benign—people seem superficially dignified, harmless, friendly, or virtuous. But these apparently harmless or well-meaning people are observed to engage in strange rituals—puzzling, disturbing observances that seem like part of an ancient tribal religion. Finally, the community as a whole seems implicated—*all* seem in some way involved in evil.

What plan of organization will allow you to show these three features in both of the stories? Here are organizing strategies you might consider:

✗ You might try a **point-by-point** comparison. The first third of your paper might show that in both stories there is a reassuring façade of normalcy that hides evil from the casual observer (point A). Then the second third of your paper might show that in both stories we witness strange quasi-religious rituals—as if evil were not something that happens casually or almost by accident. It is built into the traditions of the community (point B). Finally, the last third of your paper might show that evil does not seem the work of isolated individuals—a "criminal element." The whole community seems implicated in one way or another (point C). With a point-by-point comparison there is little danger that your readers will miss the connections.

✗ You might feel that in a point-by-point comparison your readers would not get enough of a sense of the characteristic atmosphere of each story as a whole. You might then try a **parallel-order** comparison. You discuss each story separately, but each time you run through the three key points in the same order: first the reassuring benign surface, then the strange traditional rituals, and finally the involvement in evil of the whole community. As you go through the second story, you might nudge your reader into realizing that you are in fact lining up the major points in the same order for easy cross-reference.

✗ You might decide to start by showing *similarities* between the two stories—especially if they are likely to be readily noticed by the reader. You might then go on to show a crucial *difference* your readers might have overlooked. (Conversely, you might point out differences first but then go on to important features that two superficially very different stories have in common.)

The following student paper compares and contrasts two short stories treating a similar or related theme. What is the writer's organizing strategy? Does it become clear to the reader? How successful is the writer in carrying it out?

Sample Student Paper

Two Women's Passions

John Steinbeck's "The Chrysanthemums" and Alice Walker's "Everyday Use" explore obstacles that women, both white and black, have had to face. Women often find that they are taken for granted; their intelligence, creative abilities, even the hard labor that they do often go unappreciated. Facing this reality, women find themselves pulled in conflicting directions. On the one hand, there is the strong desire to be attractive to men. Yet by pursuing the traditional ideal of femininity, they may be stifling their true being: their true passions about independence and their struggle toward their own reality.

Elisa in "The Chrysanthemums" is a housewife who has a particular talent in working with flowers. Because this is normally considered "women's work," there is no one restricting her from becoming passionate about it, so she does. Perhaps she puts her energy into her garden only because of her discontent with the rest of her life, where there is little outlet for her energy and strength. Like Elisa's chrysanthemums, the handmade quilts in "Everyday Use" also represent a passion in a woman's life. These quilts were pieced together by the woman and other women in her family from scraps of old dresses, shirts, and even a "teeny faded blue piece

. . . that was from Great Grandpa Ezra's uniform that he wore in the Civil War." More than Elisa's flowers, however, these quilts were objects of everyday life, in "everyday use" as bed covers and sources of warmth. They represent a tradition of making do with limited resources, making the best of what you have, in a setting where there is little room for waste or extravagance.

In both stories, the women struggle with the desire to be attractive to men and the harsh realities these longings produce. Elisa finds herself spilling her passions to an old, dirty tinker who shows some false interest in her flowers. She begins by telling him of the budding process and of how to plant the seeds, and his encouraging nods and grunts lead her to continue. She talks passionately of night-time and the stars—"driven into your body. . . . Hot and sharp—and lovely." Apparently even this poor excuse for a man holds her attention enough for Elisa to reach out to him, hoping to find some connection to make her less isolated and trapped in her restricted existence. Unfortunately, the encounter turns into a humbling experience for her, as in the end the tinker is only looking for some pots to mend and cares little for the passions of a sexually frustrated housewife.

The black woman in "Everyday Use" wishes to be attractive as well, although for her this attractiveness would be a way of gaining her daughter's approval. Ideally, she would be "the way my daughter would want me to be: a hundred pounds lighter, my skin like an uncooked barley pancake," giving the quick-witted Johnny Carson "much to do to keep up with my quick and witty tongue." She realizes, however, that this image is far from reality:

> In real life I am a large, big-boned woman with rough, man-working hands. In the winter I wear flannel nightgowns to bed and overalls during the day. I can kill and clean a hog as mercilessly as a man.

She knows too that in reality she has trouble looking white men (let alone a famous white comedian) in the eye; instead she has "talked to them always with one foot raised in flight." This fear or lack of confidence is part of her nature even though this woman is surviving on her own, feeding and educating her children with no help from a man.

Both women are patronized by others who care little for their passions and want to use them only for their own ends. The tinker in Steinbeck's story seems to listen with strong interest when Elisa goes on about the stars while he is actually waiting for the appropriate moment to ask for work. The mother in Walker's story is patronized by her daughter Dee, who goes through her mother's house looking for black artifacts that would be interesting objects to exhibit in her own home.

Today's reader is waiting for these women to leave their humiliation behind or to express their anger, to turn on those who condescend to them. Elisa's rebellion is weak and indirect at best. After seeing the chrysanthemums the tinker has discarded lying in the road, Elisa turns to her husband and asks him about some boxing matches, imagining them bloody and gory. Her interest in going to one surprises her husband, but he invites her to go. But she almost immediately draws back:

> . . . She relaxed limply in the seat. "Oh, no. No. I don't want to go. I'm sure I don't." Her face was turned away from him. "It will be enough if we can have wine. It will be plenty." She turned up her coat collar so he could not see that she was crying weakly—like an old woman.

The mother in "Everyday Use" is more assertive in regaining her pride. Despite her daughter Dee's claim that the mother knew nothing of her heritage, she did not give in to her daughter's request for the quilts. The mother had promised the quilts to Maggie, Dee's younger sister, and despite Dee's protest that Maggie would ruin them by using them every day, their mother "dragged" Maggie into the room, "snatched the quilts" out of Dee's hand, and "dumped them into Maggie's lap." In this seemingly insignificant incident, the mother stood up for what she believed in.

In these stories, we get glimpses of women's needs and passions but also of the strength and wisdom women have. Perhaps in the future they will be able to channel their passion into science, politics, art, and our changing world rather than into 10-inch chrysanthemums and patchwork quilts.

Questions

How does the writer set up an overall perspective for comparing the two stories? What is the organizing strategy? Does this paper tend to break up into two separate miniessays? What does the writer do to make the reader see the connections between the two stories? How successful is the paper in tracing similarities? Does it do justice to how the stories are different?

8 Style

The Writer's Voice

Great writers leave their mark by the originality of
their style, stamping it with an imprint that imposes
a new face on the coins of language.

JEAN-JOSEPH GOUX

FOCUS ON STYLE

What is style? **Style** is the writer's personal way of using language to create his or her reality. It is a distinctive manner of choosing words and putting sentences together. It is a writer's own way of moving from one idea to another. When you discuss style, you take a close look at the texture of sentences or paragraphs. However, just as often you will focus on the larger elements of style. You will be tracing the writer's way of weaving images and events into a larger pattern.

Style is more than a matter of style. It makes a statement of its own. The following two passages come from short stories at opposite poles of the spectrum of prose style. The first is from Ernest Hemingway's "Big Two-Hearted River," a story about a camping trip to Michigan's Upper Peninsula, a trout fisher's paradise.

He came down a hillside covered with stumps into a meadow. At the edge of the meadow flowed the river. Nick was glad to get to the river. He walked upstream through the meadow. His trousers were soaked with the dew as he walked. After the hot day, the dew had come quickly and heavily. The river made no sound. It was too fast and too smooth. At the edge of the meadow, before he mounted to a piece of high ground to make camp, Nick looked down the river at the trout rising. They were rising to insects come from the swamp on the other side of the stream when the sun went down. The trout jumped out of the water to take them. While Nick walked through the little stretch of meadow along the stream, trout had jumped high out of the water. Now as he looked down the river, the insects must be settling on the surface, for the trout were feeding steadily all down the stream. As far down the long stretch as he could see, the trout were rising, making circles all down the surface of the water, as though it were starting to rain.

This passage shows an unadorned modern style that aims at doing justice to reality. It does without grand gestures, without emoting. There are the bare-fact sentences that became the hallmark of the Hemingway style: "At the edge of the meadow flowed the river. . . . The river made no sound. It was too fast and too smooth." The words are simple, direct—and make the scene real for us: *soaked, dew, mist, jumped, feeding, stream*. The author does not come between us and the outdoor setting. The sentences that tell us about his state of mind are like minimal bulletins: "Nick was glad to get to the river." However, this style of deliberate **understatement** does not keep us from responding to the fresh, startling beauty of the unspoiled natural scene. It does not keep us from responding to the lovely image of the trout rising from below to feed on the insects settled on the surface of the water and making circles everywhere "as though it were starting to rain."

Fifty or a hundred years before Hemingway, the dominant style expressed emotion much more freely. A master at arousing the emotions of the audience was Edgar Allan Poe, who wrote the following passage in his short story "The Black Cat":

> With my aversion to this cat, however, its partiality for myself seemed to increase. It followed my footsteps with a pertinacity which it would be difficult to make the reader comprehend. Whenever I sat, it would crouch beneath my chair or spring upon my knees, covering me with its loathsome caresses. If I arose to walk, it would get between my feet and thus nearly throw me down, or, fastening its long and sharp claws in my dress, clamber in this manner to my breast. At such time, although I longed to destroy it with a blow, I was yet withheld from so doing, partly by a memory of my former crime, but chiefly—let me confess it at once—by absolute *dread* of the beast.

There are no bare-bones sentences here. Several sentences start with preambles like "If I . . ." or "Whenever I . . ." and then work their way through layers of mixed or complicated emotions. (The narrator would love to strangle the cat but is held back by his guilt feelings about having done the same to an earlier specimen.) The language is elevated, **formal**—deliberately above the trivial talk of every day: *partiality* for *kindness, pertinacity* for *stubbornness, comprehend* for *understand*. Does the language signal that the events of this story are more important, more momentous, more ominous than what ordinary cat fanciers are likely to experience? The whole passage builds up to a climax of "absolute *dread.*" No reluctance here to use superlatives (or to italicize for emphasis). Poe's style thrives on **hyperbole**—he is willing to exaggerate, to enhance, to pull out the stops.

How do you become more sensitive to the texture of what you read? You can try to place elements of a writer's style on a spectrum, or on a scale, ranging from one extreme to the other. The two poles do not necessarily represent good and bad, although writers and critics often have strong preferences one way or the other.

Abstract and Concrete Some prose remains general or **abstract,** whereas other prose becomes **concrete:** it engages in rich, specific detail with the sensory surface of life—with what we can see, hear, smell, touch, feel. Hemingway was a stickler for detail (like many of his characters, who are often perfectionists, sticklers for doing something exactly the right way). In his story about the camping trip, he makes us see the water *swirl* (rather than wash) around the logs of the bridge; he makes us see and hear the wings of grasshoppers *whirr.* The current raises a mist of sand in *spurts* from the bottom of the creek.

Denotation and Connotation Some words point and identify. The word *glass* simply points to an object that holds liquid for drinking. The word in itself says nothing about whether the person who used it was thirsty, or likes to drink, or prefers a glass to a mug or a stein. Other words, however, bring into play attitudes or emotions. When James Joyce in "Araby" uses the word *chalice,* it calls up a range of feelings associated with religious ritual: otherworldliness, devotion, religious exaltation. The objective, emotionally neutral meaning of a word is its **denotation.** The denotation of *knife* is simply an instrument for cutting. The range of attitudes or emotions a word brings into play is its **connotation.** The word *knife* may suggest menace, threat, treachery, as when someone is knifed in the back.

Literal and Figurative Figurative language uses imaginative comparisons to carry meanings that otherwise might be hard to put into words. In the following passage from a story by Sandra Cisneros, her characters use exuberant imaginative comparisons to convey the feeling of being in love:

> Rachel says love is like a big black piano being pushed off the top of a three-story building and you're waiting on the bottom to catch it. But Lourdes says it's not that way at all. It's like a top, like all the colors in the world are spinning so fast they're not colors anymore and all that's left is a white hum.
>
> "One Holy Night"

Metaphors are imaginative comparisons that do not come with a sign that says: "This is a comparison!" There is no term such as *like* or *as if* to alert us that someone is speaking on an as-if basis. **Similes** are figurative expressions that *do* provide the *like* or *as if* that signals the comparison. (In Bobbie Ann Mason's "Shiloh," Norma Jean picks up "cake crumbs from the cellophane wrapper, *like a fussy bird*.") In imaginative writing, metaphors are often rich and provocative. Patricia Hampl, talking about her own writing, said, "Our most ancient metaphor says life is a journey." Writing about her experience, she "is the traveler who goes on foot, living the journey, taking in mountains, enduring deserts, marveling at the lush green places." As she writes, she moves "through it all faithfully, not so much a survivor with a harrowing tale to tell as a pilgrim, seeking, wondering."

Formal and Informal   Formal language can make events seem important and characters dignified. (When overdone, it can make characters seem pompous.) Informal language can put the reader at ease, but when it shades over into slang it easily becomes disrespectful or insulting. If the formal or informal way of talking appears in **dialogue,** it helps create character—dignified, stodgy, tough, or laid back. If it is used by the narrator, it will color the tone of the story as a whole. ("Ain't noboby gonna beat me at nuthin," says the tough city-kid narrator at the end of Toni Cade Bambara's "The Lesson.")

Simple and Complex   Varied sentence length (the short and the long of it) is a major source of sentence variety. An arresting short sentence after a series of long and involved sentences, full of ifs and buts, may focus our attention and highlight an important thought or detail. It catches us up short. Sentences with elaborate **parallelism**—repetition of grammatically similar elements—can create a strong rhythm, building up emotion, hammering home a point, leading up to climactic finale.

Sentimental and Ironic   Popular fiction has often catered to the readers' love of **sentimentality,** making them cry at the undeserved sufferings of the innocent and at unsuspected evidence of goodness in the guilty. Serious modern prose has tended to deny the reader the warm gush of self-approving feelings. A pervasive feature of much modern fiction is a lively sense of **irony**—a refusal to be taken in. Irony heightens the sad and comic contrast between expectation and event, between ideal and reality. The ironic tone may range from amused tolerance and indulgence of human foibles to cutting, sardonic exposure of stupidity and greed.

THE CHALLENGE TO CONVENTION

We are what we imagine.
        N. SCOTT MOMADAY

We most easily notice a writer's style when it is different. Much modern fiction has experimented with new ways of storytelling. It has often done without a conventional story line—without suspense or a tightly scripted plot. It has bypassed surface realism and linear cause-and-effect thinking. It has journeyed in the inner space of private obsessions and hidden feelings.

Ernest Hemingway   *(1899–1961)*

Ernest Hemingway is one of the two or three most widely read American authors around the world. Like many of his generation, he witnessed the butchery of World War I (1914–1918), when seven million died on the battlefields and in the trenches. He served as an American volunteer driving an ambulance on the Italian front, and the experience left him radically disillusioned with the windbag oratory of politicians. It left him and many of his generation distrustful of language, disgusted with big words. His short stories and novels—including *The Sun Also Rises* (1926), *A Farewell to Arms* (1929), *For Whom the Bell Tolls* (1940), and *The Old Man and the Sea* (1953)—often focus on shell-shocked survivors searching for a definition of manhood without "all that talking."

For later readers, the Hemingway legend began to overshadow his work as a writer. The public remembered his life as an expatriate in France and Cuba—deep-sea fisherman, great white hunter, bullfight aficionado. However, far from being strutting macho males, the men in his fiction are often emotionally impaired characters who have lost their bearings in a cynical, violent modern world.

Hemingway set the direction for the style of much early modern fiction with his suspicion of cheap words or stylistic embellishments. Most of what is important in the following story we have to read between the lines. Many of Hemingway's stories are set in Italy or Spain. In the following story, the Ebro is a river in Spain, and *reales* are Spanish coins.

Hills like White Elephants   1927

The hills across the valley of the Ebro were long and white. On this side there was no shade and no trees and the station was between two lines of rails in the sun. Close against the side of the station there was the warm shadow of the building and a curtain, made of strings of bamboo beads, hung across the open door into the bar, to keep out flies. The American and the girl with him sat at a table in the shade, outside the building. It was very hot and the express from Barcelona would come in forty minutes. It stopped at this junction for two minutes and went on to Madrid.

"What should we drink?" the girl asked. She had taken off her hat and put it on the table.

"It's pretty hot," the man said.

"Let's drink beer."

"Dos cervezas," the man said into the curtain.   5

"Big ones?" a woman asked from the doorway.

"Yes. Two big ones."

The woman brought two glasses of beer and two felt pads. She put the felt pads and the beer glasses on the table and looked at the man and the girl. The girl was looking off at the line of hills. They were white in the sun and the country was brown and dry.

"They look like white elephants," she said.

"I've never seen one," the man drank his beer.   10

"No, you wouldn't have."

"I might have," the man said. "Just because you say I wouldn't have doesn't prove anything."

The girl looked at the bead curtain. "They've painted something on it," she said. "What does it say?"

"Anis del Toro. It's a drink."

"Could we try it?"   15

The man called "Listen" through the curtain. The woman came out from the bar.

"Four reales."

"We want two Anis del Toro."

"With water?"

"Do you want it with water?"

"I don't know," the girl said. "Is it good with water?"   20

"It's all right."

"You want them with water?" asked the woman.

"Yes, with water."

"It tastes like licorice," the girl said and put the glass down.   25

"That's the way with everything."

"Yes," said the girl. "Everything tastes of licorice. Especially all the things you've waited so long for, like absinthe."

"Oh, cut it out."

"You started it," the girl said. "I was being amused. I was having a fine time."

"Well, let's try and have a fine time."   30

"All right. I was trying. I said the mountains looked like white elephants. Wasn't that bright?"

"That was bright."

"I wanted to try this new drink. That's all we do, isn't it—look at things and try new drinks?"

"I guess so."

The girl looked across at the hills.   35

"They're lovely hills," she said. "They don't really look like white elephants. I just meant the coloring of their skin through the trees."

"Should we have another drink?"

"All right."

The warm wind blew the bead curtain against the table.

"The beer's nice and cool," the man said.   40

"It's lovely," the girl said.

"It's really an awfully simple operation, Jig," the man said. "It's not really an operation at all."

The girl looked at the ground the table legs rested on.

"I know you wouldn't mind it, Jig. It's really not anything. It's just to let the air in."   45

The girl did not say anything.

"I'll go with you and I'll stay with you all the time. They just let the air in and then it's all perfectly natural."

"Then what will we do afterward?"

"We'll be fine afterward. Just like we were before."

"What makes you think so?"

"That's the only thing that bothers us. It's the only thing that's made us   50 unhappy."

The girl looked at the bead curtain, put her hand out and took hold of two of the strings of beads.

"And you think then we'll be all right and be happy."

"I know we will. You don't have to be afraid. I've known lots of people that have done it."

"So have I," said the girl. "And afterward they were all so happy."

"Well," the man said, "if you don't want to you don't have to. I wouldn't   55 have you do it if you didn't want to. But I know it's perfectly simple."

"And you really want to?"

"I think it's the best thing to do. But I don't want you to do it if you don't really want to."

"And if I do it you'll be happy and things will be like they were and you'll love me?"

"I love you now. You know I love you."

"I know. But if I do it, then it will be nice again if I say things are like   60 white elephants, and you'll like it?"

"I'll love it. I love it now but I just can't think about it. You know how I get when I worry."

"If I do it you won't ever worry?"

"I won't worry about that because it's perfectly simple."

"Then I'll do it. Because I don't care about me."

"What do you mean?"   65

"I don't care about me."

"Well, I care about you."

"Oh, yes. But I don't care about me. And I'll do it and then everything will be fine."

"I don't want you to do it if you feel that way."

The girl stood up and walked to the end of the station. Across on the   70 other side, were fields of grain and trees along the banks of the Ebro. Far away, beyond the river, were mountains. The shadow of a cloud moved across the field of grain and she saw the river through the trees.

"And we could have all this," she said. "And we could have everything and every day we make it more impossible."

"What did you say?"

"I said we could have everything."

"We can have everything."

"No, we can't."

"We can have the whole world."

"No, we can't."

"We can go everywhere."

"No, we can't. It isn't ours any more."

"It's ours."

"No, it isn't. And once they take it away, you never get it back."

"But they haven't taken it away."

"We'll wait and see."

"Come on back in the shade," he said. "You mustn't feel that way."

"I don't feel any way," the girl said. "I just know things."

"I don't want you to do anything that you don't want to do—"

"Nor that isn't good for me," she said. "I know. Could we have another beer?"

"All right. But you've got to realize—"

"I realize," the girl said. "Can't we maybe stop talking?"

They sat down at the table and the girl looked across at the hills on the dry side of the valley and the man looked at her and at the table.

"You've got to realize," he said, "that I don't want you to do it if you don't want to. I'm perfectly willing to go through with it if it means anything to you."

"Doesn't it mean anything to you? We could get along."

"Of course it does. But I don't want anybody but you. I don't want any one else. And I know it's perfectly simple."

"Yes, you know it's perfectly simple."

"It's all right for you to say that, but I do know it."

"Would you do something for me now?"

"I'd do anything for you."

"Would you please please please please please please please stop talking?"

He did not say anything but looked at the bags against the wall of the station. There were labels on them from all the hotels where they had spent nights.

"But I don't want you to," he said, "I don't care anything about it."

"I'll scream," the girl said.

The woman came out through the curtains with two glasses of beer and put them down on the damp felt pads. "The train comes in five minutes," she said.

"What did she say?" asked the girl.

"That the train is coming in five minutes."

The girl smiled brightly at the woman, to thank her.

"I'd better take the bags over to the other side of the station," the man said. She smiled at him.

"All right. Then come back and we'll finish the beer."

He picked up the two heavy bags and carried them around the station to the other tracks. He looked up the tracks but could not see the train. Coming back, he walked through the barroom, where people waiting for the train were drinking. He drank an Anis at the bar and looked at the people. They were all waiting reasonably for the train. He went out through the bead curtain. She was sitting at the table and smiled at him.

"Do you feel better?" he asked.

"I feel fine," she said. "There's nothing wrong with me. I feel fine." 110

The Receptive Reader

1. As you first listen to the conversation of the two characters in this story, what makes the *dialogue* seem trivial or empty? (How does their style of talking echo their lifestyle?)

2. The woman's comparing the hills to white elephants is touched on several times in the story. (And it gave the story its title.) Do the hills or other elements of the story have a *symbolic* significance?

3. When do you first realize that these two people are talking about an important *choice?* How does the man talk about it? (What does it mean to him?) How does the woman talk about it? (What does it mean to her?) How does the woman react to the man's attitude?

4. Hemingway, as one of the first great moderns, was wary of emotionalism and melodrama. Where in the story are you most aware of the emotions and tensions beneath the understated, "cool" surface?

5. Does this story reach a *conclusion?* Has anything changed or been accomplished by the end? (Where do you think these two people are headed? What is ahead for them?)

The Personal Response

Eloquent pleas for sympathy are not part of the Hemingway style. Do you find yourself taking sides? If so, how and why?

Franz Kafka   *(1883–1924)*

Kafka's fictions all seem to be awakenings into an incomprehensible world, which he truly wants to understand.

FREDERICK R. KARL

Franz Kafka's strange, dreamlike stories and novels make us ponder the great twentieth-century themes. Kafka was the prophet of alienation—homelessness, rootlessness—and the anxiety it generates. He foresaw a totalitarian future in which the individual is helpless when struggling against a faceless, all-pervading bureaucratic authority. Kafka made *angst*—a feverish, all-pervading anxiety—a household world.

Kafka was the first great prophet of the **absurd.** Although we are forever anxiously trying to make sense of the world, we come to suspect that we are living in an irrational universe. We find ourselves in a reality that we cannot really understand or bring under control. Depending on our perspective, we may respond with madcap absurdist humor or with a pervading feeling of loss and alienation. Kafka was one of the first great masters of the **surreal:** in his stories, as in a dream, logical connections are missing. Haunting images pull us into a world in which our yearnings, traumas, and anxieties are acted out.

Kafka grew up as a German-speaking Jew in Prague, a Czech city that was still part of the Austrian empire. Acutely aware of the anti-Semitic society around him, Kafka hated the feeling of needing police protection from hate-filled thugs. At the same time, many Jews, including Kafka, felt that their people had a special mission to point the way for humanity—to help humanize our species.

Kafka wrote his best-known works—*The Judgment, Metamorphosis, The Trial, The Castle, Amerika*—between 1912 and his death from tuberculosis in 1924. He worked in an insurance office, dealing with workmen's compensation. Kafka published only his short stories during his lifetime, and even these only reluctantly. He instructed his friend Max Brod to burn all unpublished work (including the great novels) in case of Kafka's death. These instructions Brod decided he could not in good conscience carry out.

Kafka's narratives have been called "anti-fairy tales." In a fairy tale, the hero often sets out alone on a quest and overcomes obstacles in his search for good fortune. In a Kafka story, the hero is likely to get bogged down in the struggle. Critics have differed widely on what these stories say about the human condition.

The Country Doctor   *1919*

TRANSLATED BY WILLA MUIR AND EDWIN MUIR

I was in great perplexity; I had to start on an urgent journey; a seriously ill patient was waiting for me in a village ten miles off; a thick blizzard of snow filled all the wide spaces between him and me; I had a gig, a light gig with big wheels, exactly right for our country roads; muffled in furs, my bag of instruments in my hand, I was in the courtyard all ready for the journey; but there was no horse to be had, no horse. My own horse had died in the night, worn out by the fatigues of this icy winter; my servant girl was now running round the village trying to borrow a horse; but it was hopeless, I knew it, and I stood there forlornly, with the snow gathering more and more thickly upon me, more and more unable to move. In the gateway the girl appeared, alone, and waved the lantern; of course, who would lend a horse at this time for such a journey? I strode through the courtway once more; I could see no way out; in my confused distress I kicked at the dilapidated door of the yearlong uninhabited pigsty. It flew open and flapped to and fro on its hinges. A steam and smell as of horses came out of it. A dim stable lantern was swinging inside from a rope. A man, crouching on his hams in that low space, showed an open blue-eyed face. "Shall I yoke up?" he asked, crawling out on all fours. I did not know what to say and merely stooped down to see what else was in the sty. The servant girl was standing beside me. "You never know what you're going to find in your own house," she said, and we both laughed. "Hey there, Brother, hey there, Sister!" called the groom, and two horses, enormous creatures with powerful flanks, one after the other, their legs tucked close to their bodies, each well-shaped head lowered like a camel's, by sheer strength of buttocking squeezed out through the door hole which they filled entirely. But at once they were standing up, their legs long and their bodies steaming thickly. "Give him a hand," I said, and the willing girl hurried to help the groom with the harnessing. Yet hardly was she beside him when the groom clipped hold of her and pushed his face against hers. She screamed and fled back to me; on her cheek stood out in red the marks of two rows of teeth. "You brute," I yelled in fury, "do you want a whipping?" but in the same moment reflected that the man was a stranger; that I did not know where he came from, and that of his own free will he was helping me out when everyone else had failed me. As if he knew my thoughts he took no offense at my threat but, still busied with the horses, only turned round once toward me. "Get in," he said then, and indeed everything was ready. A magnificent pair of horses, I observed, such as I had never sat behind, and I climbed in happily. "But I'll drive, you don't know the way," I said. "Of course," said he, "I'm not coming with you anyway, I'm staying with Rose." "No," shrieked Rose, fleeing into the house with a justified presentiment that her fate was inescapable; I heard the door chain rattle as she put it up; I heard the key turn in the lock; I could see, moreover, how she put out the lights in the entrance hall and in further flight all through the rooms to keep herself from being discovered. "You're coming with me," I said to the groom, "or I won't go, urgent as my journey is. I'm not thinking of paying for it by handing the girl over to you." "Gee up!" he said; clapped his hands; the gig whirled off like a log in a freshet; I could just hear the door of my house splitting and bursting as the groom charged at it and then I was deafened and blinded by a storming rush that steadily buffeted all my senses. But this only for a moment, since, as if my patient's farmyard had opened out just before my courtyard gate, I was already there; the horses had come quietly to a standstill; the blizzard had stopped; moonlight all around; my patient's parents hurried out of the house, his sister behind them; I was almost lifted out of the gig; from their confused ejaculations I gathered not a word; in the sickroom the air was almost unbreathable; the neglected stove was smoking; I wanted to push open a window; but first I had to look at my patient. Gaunt, without any fever, not cold, not warm, with vacant eyes, without a shirt, the youngster heaved himself up from under the feather bedding, threw his arms around my neck, and whispered in my ear: "Doctor, let me die." I glanced round the room; no one had heard it; the parents were leaning forward in silence waiting for my verdict; the sister had set a chair for my handbag; I opened the bag and hunted among my instruments; the boy kept clutching at me from his bed to remind me of his entreaty; I picked up a pair of tweezers, examined them in the candlelight and laid them down again. "Yes," I thought blasphemously, "in cases like this the gods are helpful, send the missing horse, add to it a second because of the urgency, and to crown everything bestow even a groom—" And only now did I remember Rose again; what was I to do, how could I rescue her, how could I pull her away from under that groom at ten miles' distance, with a team of horses I couldn't control. These horses, now, they had somehow slipped the reins loose, pushed the windows open from outside, I did not know how; each of them had stuck a head in at a window and, quite unmoved by the startled cries of the family, stood eyeing the patient. "Better go back at once," I thought, as if the horses were summoning me to the return journey, yet I permitted the patient's sister, who fancied that I was dazed by the heat, to take my fur coat from me. A glass of rum was poured out for me, the old man clapped me on the shoulder, a familiarity justified by this offer of his treasure. I shook my head; in the narrow confines of the old man's thoughts I felt ill; that was my only reason for refusing the drink. The mother stood by the bedside and cajoled me toward it; I yielded, and, while one of the horses whinnied loudly to the ceiling, laid my head to the boy's breast, which shivered under my wet beard. I confirmed what I already knew; the boy was quite sound, something a little wrong with his circulation, saturated with coffee by his solicitous mother, but sound and best turned out of bed with one shove. I am no world reformer and so I let him lie. I was the district doctor and did my duty to the uttermost, to the point where it became almost too much. I was badly paid and yet generous and helpful to the poor. I had still to see that Rose was all right, and then the boy might have his way and I wanted to die too. What was I doing there in that endless winter! My horse was dead, and not a single person in the village would lend me another. I had to get my team out of the pigsty; if they hadn't chanced to be horses I should have had to travel with swine. That was how it was. And I nodded to the family. They knew nothing about it, and, had they known, would not have believed it. To write prescriptions is easy, but to come to an understanding with people is hard. Well, this should be the end of my visit, I had once more been called out needlessly, I was used to that, the whole district made my life a torment with my night bell, but that I should have to sacrifice Rose this time as well, the pretty girl who had lived in my house for years almost without my noticing her—that sacrifice was too much to ask, and I had somehow to get it reasoned out in my head with the help of what craft I could muster, in order not to let fly at this family, which with the best will in the world could not restore Rose to me. But as I shut my bag and put an arm out for my fur coat, the family meanwhile standing together, the father sniffing at the glass of rum in his hand, the mother, apparently disappointed in me—why, what do people expect?—biting her lips with tears in her eyes, the sister fluttering a blood-soaked towel, I was somehow ready to admit conditionally that the boy might be ill after all. I went toward him, he welcomed me smiling as if I were bringing him the most nourishing invalid broth—ah, now both horses were whinnying together; the noise, I suppose, was ordained by heaven to assist my examination of the patient—and this time I discovered that the boy was indeed ill. In his right side, near the hip, was an open wound as big as the palm of my hand. Rose-red, in many variations of shade, dark in the hollows, lighter at the edges, softly granulated, with irregular clots of blood, open as a surface mine to the daylight. That was how it looked from a distance. But on a closer inspection there was another complication. I could not help a low whistle of surprise. Worms, as thick and as long as my little finger, themselves rose-red and blood-spotted as well, were wriggling from their fastness in the interior of the wound toward the light, with small white heads and many little legs. Poor boy, you were past helping. I had discovered your great wound; this blossom in your side was destroying you. The family was pleased; they saw me busying myself; the sister told the mother, the mother the father, the father told several guests who were coming in, through the moonlight at the open door, walking on tiptoe, keeping their balance with outstretched arms. "Will you save me?" whispered the boy with a sob, quite blinded by the life within his wound. That is what people are like in my district. Always expecting the impossible from the doctor. They have lost their ancient beliefs; the parson sits at home and unravels his vestments, one after another; but the doctor is supposed to be omnipotent with his merciful surgeon's hand. Well, as it pleases them; I have not thrust my services on them; if they misuse me for sacred ends, I let that happen to me too; what better do I want, old country doctor that I am, bereft of my servant girl! And so they came, the family and the village elders, and stripped my clothes off me; a school choir with the teacher at the head of it stood before the house and sang these words to an utterly simple tune:

> Strip his clothes off, then he'll heal us,
> If he doesn't, kill him dead!
> Only a doctor, only a doctor.

Then my clothes were off and I looked at the people quietly, my fingers in my beard and my head cocked to one side. I was altogether composed and equal to the situation and remained so, although it was no help to me, since they now took me by the head and feet and carried me to the bed. They laid me down in it next to the wall, on the side of the wound. Then they all left the room; the door was shut; the singing stopped; clouds covered the moon; the bedding was warm around me; the horses' heads in the opened windows wavered like shadows. "Do you know," said a voice in my ear, "I have very little confidence in you. Why, you were only blown in here, you didn't come on your own feet. Instead of helping me, you're cramping me on my deathbed. What I'd like best is to scratch your eyes out." "Right," I said, "it is a shame. And yet I am a doctor. What am I to do? Believe me, it is not too easy for me either." "Am I supposed to be content with this apology? Oh, I must be, I can't help it. I always have to put up with things. A fine wound is all I brought into the world; that was my sole endowment." "My young friend," said I, "your mistake is: you have not a wide enough view. I have been in all the sickrooms, far and wide, and I tell you: your wound is not so bad. Done in a tight corner with two strokes of the ax. Many a one proffers his side and can hardly hear the ax in the forest, far less that it is coming nearer to him." "Is that really so, or are you deluding me in my fever?" "It is really so, take the word of honor of an official doctor." And he took it and lay still. But now it was time for me to think of escaping. The horses were still standing faithfully in their places. My clothes, my fur coat, my bag were quickly collected; I didn't want to waste time dressing; if the horses raced home as they had come, I should only be springing, as it were, out of this bed into my own. Obediently a horse backed away from the window; I threw my bundle into the gig; the fur coat missed its mark and was caught on a hook only by the sleeve. Good enough. I swung myself onto the horse. With the reins loosely trailing, one horse barely fastened to the other, the gig swaying behind, my fur coat last of all in the snow. "Gee up!" I said, but there was no galloping; slowly, like old men, we crawled through the snowy wastes; a long time echoed behind us the new but faulty song of the children:

O be joyful, all you patients,
The doctor's laid in bed beside you!

Never shall I reach home at this rate; my flourishing practice is done for; my successor is robbing me, but in vain, for he cannot take my place; in my house the disgusting groom is raging; Rose is the victim; I do not want to think about it any more. Naked, exposed to the frost of this most unhappy of ages, with an earthly vehicle, unearthly horses, old man that I am, I wander astray. My fur coat is hanging from the back of the gig, but I cannot reach it, and none of my limber pack of patients lifts a finger. Betrayed! Betrayed! A false alarm on the night bell once answered—it cannot be made good, not ever.

The Perceptive Reader

1. How far into the story can you read while assuming it to be a realistic narrative of events? What are your first clues that this story is going to be *surreal,* like a dream?

2. What is the role of the *groom?* How is he different from the doctor, who is supposedly his employer? What is the doctor's attitude toward him?

3. What is the possible *symbolism* of the horses? the pigsty?

4. What is the role of *Rose?* (Could she be a "mother figure"? Could she be for the doctor an object of unacknowledged sexual desire?)

5. What do you make of the doctor's first declaring the patient healthy and then finding the incurable wound? (Could the wound be the wound in the side of Christ on the cross?)

6. What is the doctor's interaction with the patient's family? How do they treat him?

7. The doctor seems very inadequate as the modern physician-healer who is supposed to perform the miracles of modern medicine. Could he be a *satirical* portrait of the overreaching pride—or hubris—of modern science?

8. Why is the *priest* sitting at home "unraveling his vestments"?

9. Although the events of the story are surreal, the doctor often uses *trite sayings* that sound as if things were normal. Why? What are striking examples?

The Personal Response

Although many critics approach Kafka with deadly earnestness, other readers have marveled at the mixture of the sad and comic in his fiction. Kafka read some of his stories to his friends with tears of laughter streaming down his face. Does anything about this story strike you as comical?

Making Connections—For Discussion or Writing

Compare the dream element in "Young Goodman Brown" and "The Country Doctor." In what ways are the two stories like dreams?

JUXTAPOSITIONS

Playing the Role

Each of the two stories that follow was written by a writer with a sharp eye for how people act and a quick ear for how people talk. Both authors are alert observers of someone's personal *style*. In both stories, young people without money come downtown to the pricey avenues of Manhattan. They come into stores that they know are not for them. The focus is on their manner: their style of behavior, their style of talking. What is similar, what is different, about the point of view from which we see the events of each story? What do the young people in the stories have in common? What is similar or different about the way they act and talk? Do the stories differ in theme—in what each story as a whole has to say?

Dorothy Parker   *(1893–1967)*

Dorothy Parker, who got her start in the publishing world by working for *Vogue* and *Vanity Fair,* became legendary in the twenties and thirties for her devastating wit. One interviewer said about her, "Her sentences are punctuated with observations phrased with lethal force." Parker was an early regular contributor to *The New Yorker.* She wrote plays for the New York stage and worked on screenplays in Hollywood. She was for a time one of the most widely quoted, praised, and criticized women in the United States.

The Standard of Living   1926

Annabel and Midge came out of the tea room with the arrogant slow gait of the leisured, for their Saturday afternoon stretched ahead of them. They had lunched, as was their wont, on sugar, starches, oils, and butter-fats. Usually they ate sandwiches of spongy new white bread greased with butter and mayonnaise; they ate thick wedges of cake lying wet beneath ice cream and whipped cream and melted chocolate gritty with nuts. As alternates, they ate patties, sweating beads of inferior oil, containing bits of bland meat bogged in pale, stiffening sauce; they ate pastries, limber under rigid icing, filled with an indeterminate yellow sweet stuff, not still solid, not yet liquid, like salve that has been left in the sun. They chose no other sort of food, nor did they consider it. And their skin was like the petals of wood anemones, and their bellies were as flat and their flanks as lean as those of young Indian braves.

Annabel and Midge had been best friends almost from the day that Midge had found a job as stenographer with the firm that employed Annabel. By now, Annabel, two years longer in the stenographic department, had worked up to the wages of eighteen dollars and fifty cents a week; Midge was still at sixteen dollars. Each girl lived at home with her family and paid half her salary to its support.

The girls sat side by side at their desks, they lunched together every noon, together they set out for home at the end of the day's work. Many of their evenings and most of their Sundays were passed in each other's company. Often they were joined by two young men, but there was no steadiness to any such quartet; the two young men would give place, unlamented, to two other young men, and lament would have been inappropriate, really, since the newcomers were scarcely distinguishable from their predecessors. Invariably the girls spent the fine idle hours of their hot-weather Saturday afternoons together. Constant use had not worn ragged the fabric of their friendship.

They looked alike, though the resemblance did not lie in their features. It was in the shape of their bodies, their movements, their style, and their adornments. Annabel and Midge did, and completely, all that young office workers are besought not to do. They painted their lips and their nails, they darkened their lashes and lightened their hair, and scent seemed to shimmer from them. They wore thin, bright dresses, tight over their breasts and high on their legs, and tilted slippers, fancifully strapped. They looked conspicuous and cheap and charming.

Now, as they walked across to Fifth Avenue with their skirts swirled by   5
the hot wind, they received audible admiration. Young men grouped lethargically about newsstands awarded them murmurs, exclamations, even—the ultimate tribute—whistles. Annabel and Midge passed without the condescension of hurrying their pace; they held their heads higher and set their feet with exquisite precision, as if they stepped over the necks of peasants.

Always the girls went to walk on Fifth Avenue on their free afternoons, for it was the ideal ground for their favorite game. The game could be played anywhere, and, indeed, was, but the great shop windows stimulated the two players to their best form.

Annabel had invented the game; or rather she had evolved it from an old one. Basically, it was no more than the ancient sport of what-would-you-do-if-you-had-a-million dollars? But Annabel had drawn a new set of rules for it, had narrowed it, pointed it, made it stricter. Like all games, it was the more absorbing for being more difficult.

Annabel's version went like this: You must suppose that somebody dies and leaves you a million dollars, cool. But there is a condition to the bequest.

It is stated in the will that you must spend every nickel of the money on yourself.

There lay the hazard of the game. If, when playing it, you forgot, and listed among your expenditures the rental of a new apartment for your family, for example, you lost your turn to the other player. It was astonishing how many—and some of them among the experts, too—would forfeit all their innings by such slips.

It was essential, of course, that it be played in passionate seriousness. 10 Each purchase must be carefully considered and, if necessary, supported by argument. There was no zest to playing wildly. Once Annabel had introduced the game to Sylvia, another girl who worked in the office. She explained the rules to Sylvia and then offered her the gambit "What would be the first thing you'd do?" Sylvia had not shown the decency of even a second of hesitation. "Well," she said, "the first thing I'd do, I'd go out and hire somebody to shoot Mrs. Gary Cooper, and then . . ." So it is to be seen that she was no fun.

But Annabel and Midge were surely born to be comrades, for Midge played the game like a master from the moment she learned it. It was she who added the touches that made the whole thing cozier. According to Midge's innovations, the eccentric who died and left you the money was not anybody you loved, or, for the matter of that, anybody you even knew. It was somebody who had seen you somewhere and had thought, "That girl ought to have lots of nice things. I'm going to leave her a million dollars when I die." And the death was to be neither untimely nor painful. Your benefactor, full of years and comfortably ready to depart, was to slip softly away during sleep and go right to heaven. These embroideries permitted Annabel and Midge to play their game in the luxury of peaceful consciences.

Midge played with a seriousness that was not only proper but extreme. The single strain on the girls' friendship had followed an announcement once made by Annabel that the first thing she would buy with her million dollars would be a silver-fox coat. It was as if she had struck Midge across the mouth. When Midge recovered her breath, she cried that she couldn't imagine how Annabel could do such a thing—silver-fox coats were common! Annabel defended her taste with the retort that they were not common, either. Midge then said that they were so. She added that everybody had a silver-fox coat. She went on, with perhaps a slight loss of head, to declare that she herself wouldn't be caught dead in silver fox.

For the next few days, though the girls saw each other as constantly, their conversation was careful and infrequent, and they did not once play their game. Then one morning, as soon as Annabel entered the office, she came to Midge and said that she had changed her mind. She would not buy a silver-fox coat with any part of her million dollars. Immediately on receiving the legacy, she would select a coat of mink.

Midge smiled and her eyes shone. "I think," she said, "you're doing absolutely the right thing."

Now, as they walked along Fifth Avenue, they played the game anew. It 15 was one of those days with which September is repeatedly cursed; hot and glaring, with slivers of dust in the wind. People drooped and shambled, but the girls carried themselves tall and walked a straight line, as befitted young heiresses on their afternoon promenade. There was no longer need for them to start the game at its formal opening. Annabel went direct to the heart of it.

"All right," she said. "So you've got this million dollars. So what would be the first thing you'd do?"

"Well, the first thing I'd do," Midge said, "I'd get a mink coat." But she said it mechanically, as if she were giving the memorized answer to an expected question.

"Yes," Annabel said, "I think you ought to. The terribly dark kind of mink." But she, too, spoke as if by rote. It was too hot; fur, no matter how dark and sleek and supple, was horrid to the thoughts.

They stepped along in silence for a while. Then Midge's eye was caught by a shop window. Cool, lovely gleamings were there set off by chaste and elegant darkness.

"No," Midge said, "I take it back. I wouldn't get a mink coat the first   20
thing. Know what I'd do? I'd get a string of pearls. Real pearls."

Annabel's eyes turned to follow Midge's.

"Yes," she said, slowly. "I think that's kind of a good idea. And it would make sense, too. Because you can wear pearls with anything."

Together they went over to the shop window and stood pressed against it. It contained but one object—a double row of great, even pearls clasped by a deep emerald around a little pink velvet throat.

"What do you suppose they cost?" Annabel said.

"Gee, I don't know." Midge said. "Plenty, I guess."   25

"Like a thousand dollars?" Annabel said.

"Oh, I guess like more," Midge said. "On account of the emerald."

"Well, like ten thousand dollars?" Annabel said.

"Gee, I wouldn't even know," Midge said.

The devil nudged Annabel in the ribs. "Dare you to go in and price   30
them," she said.

"Like fun!" Midge said.

"Dare you," Annabel said.

"Why, a store like this wouldn't even be open this afternoon," Midge said.

"Yes, it is so, too," Annabel said. "People just came out. And there's a doorman on. Dare you."

"Well," Midge said. "But you've got to come too."   35

They tendered thanks, icily, to the doorman for ushering them into the shop. It was cool and quiet, a broad, gracious room with paneled walls and soft carpet. But the girls wore expressions of bitter disdain, as if they stood in a sty.

A slim, immaculate clerk came to them and bowed. His neat face showed no astonishment at their appearance.

"Good afternoon," he said. He implied that he would never forget it if they would grant him the favor of accepting his soft-spoken greeting.

"Good afternoon," Annabel and Midge said together, and in like freezing accents.

"Is there something—?" the clerk said.   40

"Oh, we're just looking," Annabel said. It was as if she flung the words down from a dais.

The clerk bowed.

"My friend and myself merely happened to be passing," Midge said, and stopped, seeming to listen to the phrase. "My friend here and myself," she went on, "merely happened to be wondering how much are those pearls you've got in your window."

"Ah, yes," the clerk said. "The double rope. That is two hundred and fifty thousand dollars, Madam."

"I see," Midge said.   45

The clerk bowed. "An exceptionally beautiful necklace," he said. "Would you care to look at it?"

"No, thank you," Annabel said.

"My friend and myself merely happened to be passing," Midge said.

They turned to go; to go, from their manner, where the tumbrel awaited them. The clerk sprang ahead and opened the door. He bowed as they swept by him.

The girls went on along the Avenue and disdain was still on their faces.   50

"Honestly!" Annabel said. "Can you imagine a thing like that?"

"Two hundred and fifty thousand dollars!" Midge said. "That's a quarter of a million dollars right there!"

"He's got his nerve!" Annabel said.

They walked on. Slowly the disdain went, slowly and completely as if drained from them, and with it went the regal carriage and tread. Their shoulders dropped and they dragged their feet; they bumped against each other, without notice or apology, and caromed away again. They were silent and their eyes were cloudy.

Suddenly Midge straightened her back, flung her head high, and spoke,   55
clear and strong.

"Listen, Annabel," she said. "Look. Suppose there was this terribly rich person, see? You don't know this person, but this person has seen you somewhere and wants to do something for you. Well, it's a terribly old person, see? And so this person dies, just like going to sleep, and leaves you ten million dollars. Now, what would be the first thing you'd do?"

The Receptive Reader

1. How well do you come to know the young women? What is their style? How do they dress, act, and talk?

2. What does the game the two young women play tell you about them?

3. Parker was known for her sharp tongue and malicious *wit*. Do these show in the style of this story?

4. What is the author's attitude toward the two young women? How do you think she expects you to react to them?

The Personal Response

Does this story strike you as being based on real life? Do you think this story is out of date?

Toni Cade Bambara   *(born 1939)*

Toni Cade Bambara became known for the stories collected in *Gorilla, My Love* (1972) and *The Sea Birds Are Still Alive* (1977). Her novel *If Blessing Comes* was published in 1987. Born in New York City and holding degrees from Queens and City College, she has had an active career as a dancer, teacher, critic, editor, lecturer, civil rights activist, and writer. Anne Tyler has said about the echoes of street talk in Bambara's fiction, "Everything these people say, you feel, ordinary, real-life people are saying right now on any street corner. It's only that the rest of us didn't realize it was sheer poetry they were speaking."

The Lesson   1972

Back in the days when everyone was old and stupid or young and foolish and me and Sugar were the only ones just right, this lady moved on our block with nappy hair and proper speech and no makeup. And quite naturally we laughed at her, and laughed the way we did at the junk man who went about his business like he was some big-time president and his sorry-ass horse his secretary. And we kinda hated her too, hated the way we did the winos who cluttered up our parks and pissed on our handball walls and stank up our hallways and stairs so you couldn't halfway play hide-and-seek without a goddamn gas mask. Miss Moore was her name. The only woman on the block with no first name. And she was black as hell, cept for her feet, which were fish-white and spooky. And she was always planning these boring-ass things for us to do, us being my cousin, mostly, who lived on the block cause we all moved North the same time and to the same apartment then spread out gradual to breathe. And our parents would yank our heads into some kinda shape and crisp up our clothes so we'd be presentable for travel with Miss Moore, who always looked like she was going to church, though she never did. Which is just one of the things the grownups talked about when they talked behind her back like a dog. But when she came calling with some sachet she'd sewed up or some ginger-bread she'd made or some book, why then they'd all be too embarrassed to turn her down and we'd get handed over all spruced up. She'd been to college and said it was only right that she should take responsibility for the young ones' education, and she not even related by marriage or blood. So they'd go for it. Specially Aunt Gretchen. She was the main gofer in the family. You got some ole dumb shit foolishness you want somebody to go for, you send for Aunt Gretchen. She been screwed into the go-along for so long, it's a blood-deep natural thing with her. Which is how she got saddled with me and Sugar and Junior in the first place while our mothers were in a la-de-da apartment up the block having a good ole time.

So this one day Miss Moore rounds us all up at the mailbox and it's puredee hot and she's knockin herself out about arithmetic. And school suppose to let up in summer I heard, but she don't never let up. And the starch in my pinafore scratching the shit outta me and I'm really hating this nappy-head bitch and her goddamn college degree. I'd much rather go to the pool or to the show where it's cool. So me and Sugar leaning on the mailbox being surly, which is a Miss Moore word. And Flyboy checking out what everybody brought for lunch. And Fat Butt already wasting his peanut-butter-and-jelly sandwich like the pig he is. And Junebug punchin on Q.T.'s arm for potato chips. And Rosie Giraffe shifting from one hip to the other waiting for somebody to step on her foot or ask her if she from Georgia so she can kick ass, preferably Mercedes'. And Miss Moore asking us do we know what money is, like we a bunch of retards. I mean real money, she say, like it's only poker chips or monopoly papers we lay on the grocer. So right away I'm tired of this and say so. And would much rather snatch Sugar and go to the Sunset and terrorize the West Indian kids and take their hair ribbons and their money too. And Miss Moore files that remark away for next week's lesson on brotherhood, I can tell. And finally I say we oughta get to the subway cause it's cooler and besides we might meet some cute boys. Sugar done swiped her mama's lipstick, so we ready.

So we heading down the street and she's boring us silly about what things cost and what our parents make and how much goes for rent and how money ain't divided up right in this country. And then she gets to the part about we all poor and live in the slums, which I don't feature. And I'm ready to speak on that, but she steps out in the street and hails two cabs just like that. Then she hustles half the crew in with her and hands me a five-dollar bill and tells me to calculate 10 percent tip for the driver. And we're off. Me and Sugar and Junebug and Flyboy hangin out the window and hollering to everybody, putting lipstick on each other cause Flyboy a faggot anyway, and making farts with our sweaty armpits. But I'm mostly trying to figure how to spend this money. But they all fascinated with the meter ticking and Junebug starts laying bets as to how much it'll read when Flyboy can't hold his breath no more. Then Sugar lays bets as to how much it'll be when we get there. So I'm stuck. Don't nobody want to go for my plan, which is to jump out at the next light and run off to the first bar-b-que we can find. Then the driver tells us to get the hell out cause we there already. And the meter reads eighty-five cents. And I'm stalling to figure out the tip and Sugar say give him a dime. And I decide he don't need it bad as I do, so later for him. But then he tries to take off with Junebug foot still in the door so we talk about his mama something ferocious. Then we check out that we on Fifth Avenue and everybody dressed up in stockings. One lady in a fur coat, hot as it is. White folks crazy.

"This is the place," Miss Moore say, presenting it to us in the voice she uses at the museum. "Let's look in the windows before we go in."

"Can we steal?" Sugar asks very serious like she's getting the ground rules   5
squared away before she plays. "I beg your pardon," say Miss Moore, and we fall out. So she leads us around the windows of the toy store and me and Sugar screamin, "This is mine, that's mine, I gotta have that, that was made for me, I was born for that," till Big Butt drowns us out.

"Hey, I'm goin to buy that there."

"That there? You don't even know what it is, stupid."

"I do so," he say punchin on Rosie Giraffe. "It's a microscope."

"Whatcha gonna do with a microscope, fool?"

"Look at things."   10

"Like what, Ronald?" ask Miss Moore. And Big Butt ain't got the first notion. So here go Miss Moore gabbing about the thousands of bacteria in a drop of water and the somethinorother in a speck of blood and the million and one living things in the air around us is invisible to the naked eye. And what she say that for? Junebug go to town on that "naked" and we rolling. Then Miss Moore ask what it cost. So we all jam into the window smudgin it up and the price tag say $300. So then she ask how long'd take for Big Butt and Junebug to save up their allowances. "Too long," I say. "Yeh," adds Sugar, "outgrown it by that time." And Miss Moore say no, you never outgrow learning instruments. "Why, even medical students and interns and," blah, blah, blah. And we ready to choke Big Butt for bringing it up in the first damn place.

"This here costs four hundred eighty dollars," says Rosie Giraffe. So we pile up all over her to see what she pointin out. My eyes tell me it's a chunk of glass cracked with something heavy, and different-color inks dripped into the splits, then the whole thing put into a oven or something. But for $480 it don't make sense.

"That's a paperweight made of semi-precious stones fused together under tremendous pressure," she explains slowly, with her hands doing the mining and all the factory work.

"So what's a paperweight?" asks Rosie Giraffe.

"To weigh paper with, dumbbell," say Flyboy, the wise man from the East.   15

"Not exactly," say Miss Moore, which is what she say when you warm or way off too. "It's to weigh paper down so it won't scatter and make your desk untidy." So right away me and Sugar curtsy to each other and then to Mercedes who is more the tidy type.

"We don't keep paper on top of the desk in my class," say Junebug, figuring Miss Moore crazy or lyin one.

"At home, then," she say. "Don't you have a calendar and pencil case and a blotter and a letter-opener on your desk at home where you do your homework?" And she know damn well what our homes look like cause she nosys around in them every chance she gets.

"I don't even have a desk," say Junebug. "Do we?"

"No. And I don't get no homework neither," says Big Butt.   20

"And I don't even have a home," say Flyboy like he do at school to keep the white folks off his back and sorry for him. Send this poor kid to camp posters, is his specialty.

"I do," says Mercedes. "I have a box of stationery on my desk and a picture of my cat. My godmother bought the stationery and the desk. There's a big rose on each sheet and the envelopes smell like roses."

"Who wants to know about your smelly-ass stationery," say Rosie Giraffe fore I can get my two cents in.

"It's important to have a work area all your own so that . . ."

"Will you look at this sailboat, please," say Flyboy, cuttin her off and   25 pointin to the thing like it was his. So once again we tumble all over each other to gaze at this magnificent thing in the toy store which is just big enough to maybe sail two kittens across the pond if you strap them to the posts tight. We all start reciting the price tag like we in assembly. "Hand-crafted sailboat of fiberglass at one thousand one hundred ninety-five dollars."

"Unbelievable," I hear myself say and am really stunned. I read it again for myself just in case the group recitation put me in a trance. Same thing. For some reason this pisses me off. We look at Miss Moore and she lookin at us, waiting for I dunno what.

"Who'd pay all that when you can buy a sailboat set for a quarter at Pop's, a tube of glue for a dime, and a ball of string for eight cents? It must have a motor and a whole lot else besides," I say. "My sailboat cost me about fifty cents."

"But will it take water?" say Mercedes with her smart ass.

"Took mine to Alley Pond Park once," say Flyboy. "String broke. Lost it. Pity."

"Sailed mine in Central Park and it keeled over and sank. Had to ask my   30 father for another dollar."

"And you got the strap," laugh Big Butt. "The jerk didn't even have a string on it. My old man wailed on his behind."

Little Q.T. was staring hard at the sailboat and you could see he wanted it bad. But he too little and somebody'd just take it from him. So what the hell. "This boat for kids, Miss Moore?"

"Parents silly to buy something like that just to get all broke up," say Rosie Giraffe.

"That much money it should last forever," I figure.

"My father'd buy it for me if I wanted it."   35

"Your father, my ass," say Rosie Giraffe getting a chance to finally push Mercedes.

"Must be rich people shop here," say Q.T.

"You are a very bright boy," say Flyboy. "What was your first clue?" And he rap him on the head with the back of his knuckles, since Q.T. the only one he could get away with. Though Q.T. liable to come up behind you years later and get his licks in when you half expect it.

"What I want to know is," I says to Miss Moore though I never talk to her, I wouldn't give the bitch that satisfaction, "is how much a real boat costs? I figure a thousand'd get you a yacht any day."

"Why don't you check that out," she says, "and report back to the group?"   40 Which really pains my ass. If you gonna mess up a perfectly good swim day least you could do is have some answers. "Let's go in," she say like she got something up her sleeve. Only she don't lead the way. So me and Sugar turn the corner to where the entrance is, but when we get there I kinda hang back. Not that I'm scared, what's there to be afraid of, just a toy store. But I feel funny, shame. But what I got to be shamed about? Got as much right to go in as anybody. But somehow I can't seem to get hold of the door, so I step away from Sugar to lead. But she hangs back too. And I look at her and she looks at me and this is ridiculous. I mean, damn, I have never ever been shy about doing nothing or going nowhere. But then Mercedes steps up and then Rosie Giraffe and Big Butt crowd in behind and shove, and next thing we all stuffed into the doorway with only Mercedes squeezing past us, smoothing out her jumper and walking right down the aisle. Then the rest of us tumble in like a glued-together jigsaw done all wrong. And people lookin at us. And it's like the time me and Sugar crashed into the Catholic church on a dare. But once we got in there and everything so hushed and holy and the candles and the bowin and the handkerchiefs on all the drooping heads, I just couldn't go through with the plan. Which was for me to run up to the altar and do a tap dance while Sugar played the nose flute and messed around in the holy water. And Sugar kept givin me the elbow. Then later teased me so bad I tied her up in the shower and turned it on and locked her in. And she'd be there till this day if Aunt Gretchen hadn't finally figured I was lyin about the boarder takin a shower.

Same thing in the store. We all walkin on tiptoe and hardly touchin the games and puzzles and things. And I watched Miss Moore who is steady watchin us like she waitin for a sign. Like Mama Drewery watches the sky and sniffs the air and takes note of just how much slant is in the bird formation. Then me and Sugar bump smack into each other, so busy gazing at the toys, specially the sailboat. But we don't laugh and go into our fat-lady bump-stomach routine. We just stare at that price tag. Then Sugar run a finger over the whole boat. And I'm jealous and want to hit her. Maybe not her, but I sure want to punch somebody in the mouth.

"Watcha bring us here for, Miss Moore?"

"You sound angry, Sylvia. Are you mad about something?" Givin me one of them grins like she tellin a grown-up joke that never turns out to be funny. And she's lookin very closely at me like maybe she planning to do my portrait from memory. I'm mad, but I won't give her that satisfaction. So I slouch around the store bein very bored and say, "Let's go."

Me and Sugar at the back of the train watchin the tracks whizzin by large then small then getting gobbled up in the dark. I'm thinkin about this tricky toy I saw in the store. A clown that somersaults on a bar then does chin-ups just cause you yank lightly at his leg. Cost $35. I could see me askin my mother for a $35 birthday clown. "You wanna who that costs what?" she'd say, cocking her head to the side to get a better view of the hole in my head. Thirty-five dollars could buy new bunk beds for Junior and Gretchen's boy. Thirty-five dollars and the whole household could go visit Granddaddy Nelson in the country. Thirty-five dollars would pay for the rent and the piano bill too. Who are these people that spend that much for performing clowns and $1000 for toy sailboats? What kinda work they do and how they live and how come we ain't in on it? Where we are is who we are, Miss Moore always pointin out. But it don't necessarily have to be that way, she always adds then waits for somebody to say that poor people have to wake up and demand their share of the pie and don't none of us know what kind of pie she talking about in the first damn place. But she ain't so smart cause I still got her four dollars from the taxi and she sure ain't gettin it. Messin up my day with this shit. Sugar nudges me in my pocket and winks.

Miss Moore lines us up in front of the mailbox where we started from, seem like years ago, and I got a headache for thinkin so hard. And we lean all over each other so we can hold up under the draggy-ass lecture she always finishes us off with at the end before we thank her for borin us to tears. But she just looks at us like she readin tea leaves. Finally she say, "Well, what did you think of F.A.O. Schwarz?"

Rosie Giraffe mumbles, "White folks crazy."

45

"I'd like to go there again when I get my birthday money," says Mercedes, and we shove her out the pack so she has to lean on the mailbox by herself.

"I'd like a shower. Tiring day," say Flyboy.

Then Sugar surprises me by sayin, "You know, Miss Moore, I don't think all of us here put together eat in a year what that sailboat costs." And Miss Moore lights up like somebody goosed her. "And?" she say, urging Sugar on. Only I'm standin on her foot so she don't continue.

"Imagine for a minute what kind of society it is in which some people   50 can spend on a toy what it would cost to feed a family of six or seven. What do you think?"

"I think," say Sugar pushing me off her feet like she never done before, cause I whip her ass in a minute, "that this is not much of a democracy if you ask me. Equal chance to pursue happiness means an equal crack at the dough, don't it?" Miss Moore is besides herself and I am disgusted with Sugar's treachery. So I stand on her foot one more time to see if she'll shove me. She shuts up, and Miss Moore looks at me, sorrowfully I'm thinkin. And somethin weird is goin on, I can feel it in my chest.

"Anybody else learn anything today?" lookin dead at me. I walk away and Sugar has to run to catch up and don't even seem to notice when I shrug her arm off my shoulder.

"Well, we got four dollars anyway," she says.

"Uh hunh."

"We could go to Hascombs and get half a chocolate layer and then go to   55 the Sunset and still have plenty money for potato chips and ice cream sodas."

"Un hunh."

"Race you to Hascombs," she say.

We start down the block and she gets ahead which is O.K. by me cause I'm going to the West End and then over to the Drive to think this day through. She can run if she want to and even run faster. But ain't nobody gonna beat me at nuthin.

The Receptive Reader

1. In this story we see the children from uptown through the eyes of one of their own. How does this *point of view* shape the story as a whole? What do we take in of their behavior, their thinking, their sense of humor? Do you recognize a pattern or a type?

2. How does the tough street language the narrator and her friends speak differ from the genteel middle-class language used by other authors? What distinctive features do you recognize? Do you find the language offensive? Why or why not?

3. How is Miss Moore introduced to the reader? How do you feel about her at the beginning? How does her role change in the story? Does your estimate of her change?

4. The story reaches a *turning point* when the group comes to the store. What theme becomes overt at this point? (What is "the lesson" promised in the title?) Does the story get too preachy for you?

5. Where does the story go after the climactic episode in the toy store? How does it *end?* What does the ending do for the story as a whole?

6. What do you think is the relationship between the author and the first-person narrator in the story? (What do you think is the distance between the author as a person and the *persona* speaking in the story?)

The Personal Response

People who talk tough may be playing a role. Do you think there is a different personality behind the narrator's public persona?

The Creative Dimension

Write about a situation, real or imagined, in which a central character plays a public role—different from what he or she is when not observed by strangers or outsiders. The central character could be an imaginary third party (as in the Parker story), or you could be speaking in the first person as the narrator (as in the Bambara story). Re-create for your readers a manner of behaving, a style of talking. You may want to try your hand at an episode or vignette in which the punch line is "Ain't nobody gonna beat me at nuthing."

WRITING ABOUT LITERATURE

8   Responding to Style (Prewriting to Draft)

The Writing Workshop   Writing about an author's style requires you to pay close attention to word choice, sentence rhythms, key images, ways of expressing (or suppressing) emotion. However, as you read closely for detail, try to see how features of style serve the larger purposes of a story. You need to stay close to detail—but you have to go on to sort out and lay out your material in a pattern that makes sense.

From Prewriting to First Draft   Do you ever suffer from writer's block? Do you find yourself staring at a blank screen or blank sheet of paper? Go through some of the steps that other writers use to start the flow. Draw on the different prewriting techniques that help a substantial, purposeful paper take shape.

Brainstorming   Brainstorming allows you to bring up from hidden corners of your memory material that might prove relevant to your topic. Let us assume you have read Bret Harte's much-anthologized "The Outcasts of Poker Flat." You want to write about it as an example of the sentimentality that is a staple of American popular culture. You start by trying to call up and jotting down any phrases, catch words, quotations, images, or incidents connected with your key word. You leave sifting and editing for later. Sample:

Sentimentality: The word brings to mind true love and romance, life lovingly and beautifully portrayed, with death only a momentary transition to a better place. Every cloud has a silver lining. Life may be harsh and cruel, but redemption and salvation are the eventual outcome. Everything is loaded with sympathy, empathy, compassion, caring. There is some good in everyone. "Life is real; life is earnest." Live is invigorating, challenging.

Death is softened, described almost tenderly. Mother holds the hand of darling child dying of tuberculosis. Dying soldier props himself up on elbow to remember loved ones. The gentle easing from sleep to death. Nothing gory, bloody, sickening.

Hearts, flowers, sunsets, baby shoes. Make the reader feel good. Life may be cruel, but there is justice and beauty. Hallmark greeting cards.

Reading Notes   Focus your reading notes on questions of tone or style. Look for possible connections; try to be open to a possible pattern that might emerge. Sample notes:

appeal to our sympathy: the heartless, self-righteous towns people turn out the band of sinners in the dead of winter

(Holman and Harmon on sentimentality in *A Handbook of Literature:* "an optimistic overemphasis on the goodness of humanity")

finding goodness in unexpected places: Oakhurst, the gambler, gives up his horse to the Duchess, trading for her "sorry mule"; later, Oakhurst decides to stay with his "weaker and more pitiable companions"

the naive young "innocents": "they unaffectedly exchanged a kiss, so honest and sincere that it might have been heard above the swaying pines"; note: the naive purity of the innocents softens the hardened sinners

Mother Shipton, notorious for her coarse language and violent oaths, becomes the hooker with the heart of gold who starves herself so that the virginal Piney may eat an additional portion of the rations and so have a chance to live

final good deed: Oakhurst piles firewood by the cabin before he dies with a flourish, "handing in his checks"

softening of death: the Duchess and Piney (sin and innocence) die "locked in each other's arms," with the "younger and purer pillowing the head of her soiled sister upon her virgin breast"; they "fall asleep"; the fatal blizzard becomes a flurry of soft flakes—"feathery drifts of snow" cover the dead

saving touches of grim realism: Uncle Billy is a true rascal and hard-bitten cynic (and he survives when the others die); the hypocritical citizens of Poker Flat are satirized for their self-righteousness

Structuring Your Paper   Look at the way the following paper plays off two different facets of an author's style in an "on-the-one-hand" and "on-the-other-hand" pattern:

The Sentimental Sinners of Poker Flat

(Introduction: defining the key term)

Driven out of town by the moral majority, "The Outcasts of Poker Flat" perish (with one exception) in an early snowstorm that traps them in the mountains. Two prostitutes, a gambler, and a drunk—these, along with two innocents, are the main characters of Bret Harte's sentimental tale. In sentimental writing, the tender emotions, such as love and pity, are superabundant, and evil exists mainly to stimulate our pity for the victims and our moral indignation. We feel tender pity for the innocent victims and we feel a warm glow of emotion when evildoers repent or show an unexpected noble side.

(Thesis: a sentimental story saved from mawkishness)

Bret Harte's characters do indeed act their parts in a story that has most of the elements of nineteenth-century sentimentality. Nevertheless, somehow the story does not leave us with that sickeningly sweet, cloying sensation that a truly sentimental narrative often produces. Harte's skillful use of humor rescues "The Outcasts" from complete mawkishness.

(First major point: the sentimental side of the story)

The story is indeed sentimental. A group of characters who are extremely unlikely candidates for sainthood nevertheless exhibit heroic virtue and selflessness. Their ordeal, rather than demonstrating the baseness of human nature, shows humanity's basic goodness. The only appearance of anything less than virtuous is in Uncle Billy, the drunk. He steals away in the night with the mules, stranding the others in the snowstorm. The rest of the group are inspired to attain a saintly goodness. There is no fighting over food or shelter; each individual is concerned only for the others. . . .

(Further follow-up of first point—clinching examples)

The real heroics, though, come from the greatest "sinners," in true sentimental fashion. The gambler, Oakhurst, although he is known to be "a coolly desperate man," never "thought of deserting his weaker and more pitiable companions." Mother Shipton, the legendary prostitute with a heart of gold, starves herself to save the young virgin. . . .

(Turning point of the essay—Harte's saving humor)

However, Harte's story as a whole is more successful and more enjoyable than this description would suggest. Humor is the key to Harte's success. Harte's wry humor—a Western, often ironic brand—runs throughout the story, setting it apart from other sentimental writing and allowing a modern reader to appreciate it. The beginning of the story sets the tone: The community of Poker Flat, having lately suffered the loss of "several thousand dollars, two valuable horses," and (almost as an afterthought) "a prominent citizen," is experiencing "a spasm of virtuous reaction." The real reason the townspeople are after Oakhurst is not simply that he is a gambler but that he is a better one than they are—and they want their money back. Oakhurst himself is presented as a worldly-wise character who looks at life with dry ironic humor: "With him life was at best an uncertain game, and he recognized the usual percentage in favor of the dealer." . . .

(Conclusion—sentimental ending with a final humorous touch)

The ending of the story is the closest approach to cloying sentimentality. The virgin and the prostitute huddle together in the snow and freeze to death in each other's arms. However, the story does not end there but with a final touch of humor. Oakhurst has left his own epitaph, scribbled on the deuce of clubs and pinned to a tree with a knife. In keeping with his character, it reads: "Beneath this tree lies the body of John Oakhurst, who struck a streak of bad luck . . . and handed in his checks on the 7th December, 1850."

Questions

Where or how is the initial definition of sentimentality echoed later in the paper? How would you state the central thesis in your own words? How and how well is the program it implies implemented in the paper? Where do you agree and where do you disagree with the student author?

9 A Writer in Depth

Flannery O'Connor

No writer is a pessimist; the very act of writing is an optimistic act.

FLANNERY O'CONNOR

FOCUS ON THE WRITER

Sometimes we read a story strictly on its own terms. We let it create its own world. In practice, however, we often do not read an anonymous, unsigned story. We read James Joyce or Alice Walker or Flannery O'Connor. Reading a new story by a familiar writer, we may feel like a traveler recognizing landmarks. We find our bearings more easily than in reading an unknown author. We recognize the writer's voice. We respond to a familiar solemn or ironic tone, to a familiar mood of foreboding or expectation. We are already attuned to the author's way of looking at places and people.

At the same time, critics and biographers take us beyond the individual work in front of us by placing it in a larger context. They help us see it in relation to the author's life and work. A religious upbringing, a traumatic childhood, bouts with illness—all these may help explain a writer's way of looking at the world. As you come to know the life and work of an author, you bring expectations to a story, and you can take pleasure in seeing them fulfilled. At the same time, you need to remain flexible enough to see a side of the author that you did not notice before.

FLANNERY O'CONNOR: AUTHOR AND WORK

With the serious writer, violence is never an end in itself. It is the extreme situation that best reveals what we are essentially, and I believe these are the times when writers are more interested in what we are essentially than in the tenor of our daily lives.

FLANNERY O'CONNOR

230

When Flannery O'Connor (1924–1964) was asked to name the most important influences on her life, she replied they were probably "being a Catholic and a Southerner and a writer." O'Connor was a devout Catholic in the Baptist South, and she attended Catholic schools before she went to Georgia Women's College. Readers of her fiction encounter a central paradox: her characters live in a violent world in which evil seems to triumph. But her stories are written by an author who believes in redemption. She believed in divine grace, in the supremacy of God's mercy. She once said that a writer of fiction is "concerned with ultimate mystery as we find it embodied in the concrete world of sense experience."

O'Connor grew up in Savannah and Milledgeville, Georgia, in the segregated South, in a landscape dotted with sharecroppers' shacks. When a southern novelist was asked why the South had produced so many of America's best writers, he pointed to the lost war that made the southern experience different from that of the North. O'Connor commented on his reply that he

> didn't mean by that simply that a lost war makes good subject matter. What he was saying was that we had our Fall. We have gone into the modern world with an inburnt knowledge of human limitations and with a sense of mystery which could not have developed in our first state of innocence—as it has not sufficiently developed in the rest of the country.

O'Connor was a master of the **grotesque**—the mixture of the frightening and the comic. She had a sharp eye for the laughable, for the absurd. But in her fiction, horror and comedy mingle. We watch with a sense of unease, fear, and puzzlement as her parables of antagonism and violence unfold. It is as if she had some implied vision of humankind in harmony with God's purposes by which our imperfect, sinful human reality is judged and found wanting—and laughable. She said:

> Whenever I am asked why Southern writers particularly have a penchant for writing about freaks, I say it is because we are still able to recognize one. To be able to recognize a freak, you have to have some conception of the whole man, and in the South the general conception of man is still, in the main, theological.

Even the good, in O'Connor's view, had traits of the freakish, the grotesque, because "in us the good is something under construction."

O'Connor suffered from a debilitating hereditary illness (lupus), and she was on crutches during most of her writing life. Some of her best work was not published until after her early death at age thirty-nine. The following widely read story may be the first O'Connor story you encounter.

As you start reading it, what about it seems familiar, reassuring, or easy to understand? Where or how does it become strange or perturbing? Overall, how do you react to the story?

A Good Man Is Hard to Find   *1955*

The grandmother didn't want to go to Florida. She wanted to visit some of her connections in east Tennessee and she was seizing every chance to change Bailey's mind. Bailey was the son she lived with, her only boy. He was sitting on the edge of his chair at the table, bent over the orange sports section of the *Journal.* "Now look here, Bailey," she said, "see here, read this," and she stood with one hand on her thin hip and the other rattling the newspaper at his bald head. "Here this fellow that calls himself The Misfit is aloose from the Federal Pen and headed toward Florida and you read here what it says he did to these people. Just you read it. I wouldn't take my children in any direction with a criminal like that aloose in it. I couldn't answer to my conscience if I did."

Bailey didn't look up from his reading so she wheeled around then and faced the children's mother; a young woman in slacks, whose face was as broad and innocent as a cabbage and was tied around with a green headkerchief that had two points on the top like rabbit's ears. She was sitting on the sofa, feeding the baby his apricots out of a jar. "The children have been to Florida before," the old lady said. "You all ought to take them somewhere else for a change so they would see different parts of the world and be broad. They never have been to east Tennessee."

The children's mother didn't seem to hear her, but the eight-year-old boy, John Wesley, a stocky child with glasses, said, "If you don't want to go to Florida, why dontcha stay at home?" He and the little girl, June Star, were reading the funny papers on the floor.

"She wouldn't stay at home to be queen for a day," June Star said without raising her yellow head.

"Yes, and what would you do if this fellow, The Misfit, caught you?" the   5
grandmother asked.

"I'd smack his face," John Wesley said.

"She wouldn't stay at home for a million bucks," June Star said. "Afraid she'd miss something. She has to go everywhere we go."

"All right, Miss," the grandmother said. "Just remember that the next time you want me to curl your hair."

June Star said her hair was naturally curly.

The next morning the grandmother was the first one in the car, ready to   10
go. She had her big black valise that looked like the head of a hippopotamus in one corner, and underneath it she was hiding a basket with Pitty Sing, the cat, in it. She didn't intend for the cat to be left alone in the house for three days because he would miss her too much and she was afraid he might brush against one of the gas burners and accidentally asphyxiate himself. Her son, Bailey, didn't like to arrive at a motel with a cat.

She sat in the middle of the back seat with John Wesley and June Star on either side of her. Bailey and the children's mother and the baby sat in the front and they left Atlanta at eight forty-five with the mileage on the car at 55890. The grandmother wrote this down because she thought it would be interesting to say how many miles they had been when they got back. It took them twenty minutes to reach the outskirts of the city.

The old lady settled herself comfortably, removing her white cotton gloves and putting them up with her purse on the shelf in front of the back window. The children's mother still had on slacks and still had her head tied up in a green kerchief, but the grandmother had on a navy blue straw sailor hat with a bunch of white violets on the brim and a navy blue dress with a small white dot in the print. Her collar and cuffs were white organdy trimmed with lace and at her neckline she had pinned a purple spray of cloth violets containing a sachet. In case of an accident, anyone seeing her dead on the highway would know at once that she was a lady.

She said she thought it was going to be a good day for driving, neither too hot nor too cold, and she cautioned Bailey that the speed limit was fifty-five miles an hour and that the patrolmen hid themselves behind billboards and small clumps of trees and sped out after you before you had a chance to slow down. She pointed out interesting details of the scenery: Stone Mountain; the blue granite that in some places came up to both sides of the highway; the brilliant red clay banks slightly streaked with purple; and the various crops that made rows of green lace-work on the ground. The trees were full of silver-white sunlights and the meanest of them sparkled. The children were reading comic magazines and their mother had gone back to sleep.

"Let's go through Georgia fast so we won't have to look at it much," John Wesley said.

"If I were a little boy," said the grandmother, "I wouldn't talk about my   15 native state that way. Tennessee has the mountains and Georgia has the hills."

"Tennessee is just a hillbilly dumping ground," John Wesley said, "and Georgia is a lousy state too."

"You said it," June Star said.

"In my time," said the grandmother, folding her thin veined fingers, "children were more respectful of their native states and their parents and everything else. People did right then. Oh look at the cute little pickaninny!" she said and pointed to a Negro child standing in the door of a shack. "Wouldn't that make a picture, now?" she asked and they all turned and looked at the little Negro out of the back window. He waved.

"He didn't have any britches on," June Star said.

"He probably didn't have any," the grandmother explained. "Little nig-   20 gers in the country don't have things like we do. If I could paint, I'd paint that picture," she said.

The children exchanged comic books.

The grandmother offered to hold the baby and the children's mother passed him over the front seat to her. She set him on her knee and bounced him and told him about the things they were passing. She rolled her eyes and screwed up her mouth and stuck her leathery thin face into his smooth bland one. Occasionally he gave her a faraway smile. They passed a large cotton field with five or six graves fenced in the middle of it, like a small island. "Look at the graveyard!" the grandmother said, pointing it out. "That was the old family burying ground. That belonged to the plantation."

"Where's the plantation?" John Wesley asked.

"Gone With the Wind," said the grandmother. "Ha. Ha."

When the children finished all the comic books they had brought, they opened the lunch and ate it. The grandmother ate a peanut butter sandwich and an olive and would not let the children throw the box and the paper napkins out the window. When there was nothing else to do they played a game by choosing a cloud and making the other two guess what shape it suggested. John Wesley took one the shape of a cow and June Star guessed a cow and John Wesley said, no, an automobile, and June Star said he didn't play fair, and they began to slap each other over the grandmother.

The grandmother said she would tell them a story if they would keep quiet. When she told a story, she rolled her eyes and waved her head and was very dramatic. She said once when she was a maiden lady she had been courted by a Mr. Edgar Atkins Teagarden from Jasper, Georgia. She said he was a very good-looking man and a gentleman and that he brought her a watermelon every Saturday afternoon with his initials cut in it, E.A.T. Well, one Saturday, she said, Mr. Teagarden brought the watermelon and there was nobody at home and he left it on the front porch and returned in his buggy to Jasper, but she never got the watermelon, she said, because a nigger boy ate it when he saw the initials, E.A.T.! This story tickled John Wesley's funny bone and he giggled and giggled but June Star didn't think it was any good. She said she wouldn't marry a man that just brought her a watermelon on Saturday. The grandmother said she would have done well to marry Mr. Teagarden because he was a gentleman and had bought Coca-Cola stock when it first came out and that he had died only a few years ago, a very wealthy man.

They stopped at The Tower for barbecued sandwiches. The Tower was a part-stucco and part-wood filling station and dance hall set in a clearing outside of Timothy. A fat man named Red Sammy Butts ran it and there were signs stuck here and there on the building and for miles up and down the highway saying, TRY RED SAMMY'S FAMOUS BARBECUE. NONE LIKE FAMOUS RED SAMMY'S! RED SAM! THE FAT BOY WITH THE HAPPY LAUGH. A VETERAN! RED SAMMY'S YOUR MAN!

Red Sammy was lying on the bare ground outside The Tower with his head under a truck while a gray monkey about a foot high, chained to a small chinaberry tree, chattered nearby. The monkey sprang back into the tree and got on the highest limb as soon as he saw the children jump out of the car and run toward him.

Inside, The Tower was a long dark room with a counter at one end and tables at the other and dancing space in the middle. They all sat down at a broad table next to the nickelodeon and Red Sam's wife, a tall burnt-brown woman with hair and eyes lighter than her skin, came and took their order. The children's mother put a dime in the machine and played "The Tennessee Waltz," and the grandmother said that tune always made her want to dance. She asked Bailey if he would like to dance but he only glared at her. He didn't have a naturally sunny disposition like she did and trips made him nervous. The grandmother's brown eyes were very bright. She swayed her head from side to side and pretended she was dancing in her chair. June Star said play something she could tap to so the children's mother put in another dime and played a fast number and June Star stepped out onto the dance floor and did her tap routine.

"Ain't she cute?" Red Sam's wife said, leaning over the counter. "Would   30 you like to come be my little girl?"

"No, I certainly wouldn't," June Star said. "I wouldn't live in a broken-down place like this for a million bucks!" and she ran back to the table.

"Ain't she cute?" the woman repeated, stretching her mouth politely.

"Aren't you ashamed?" hissed the grandmother.

Red Sam came in and told his wife to quit lounging on the counter and hurry up with these people's order. His khaki trousers reached just to his hip bones and his stomach hung over them like a sack of meal swaying under his shirt. He came over and sat down at a table nearby and let out a combination sigh and yodel. "You can't win," he said. "You can't win," and he wiped his sweating red face off with a gray handkerchief. "These days you don't know who to trust," he said. "Ain't that the truth?"

"People are certainly not nice like they used to be," said the grandmother.   35

"Two fellers come in here last week," Red Sammy said, "driving a Chrysler. It was an old beat-up car but it was a good one and these boys looked all right to me. Said they worked at the mill and you know I let them fellers charge the gas they bought? Now why did I do that?"

"Because you're a good man!" the grandmother said at once.

"Yes'm, I suppose so," Red Sam said as if he were struck with this answer.

His wife brought the orders, carrying the five plates all at once without a tray, two in each hand and one balanced on her arm. "It isn't a soul in this green world of God's that you can trust," she said. "And I don't count nobody out of that, not nobody," she repeated, looking at Red Sammy.

"Did you read about that criminal, The Misfit, that's escaped?" asked the   40 grandmother.

"I wouldn't be a bit surprised if he didn't attack this place right here," said the woman. "If he hears about it being here, I wouldn't be none surprised to see him. If he hears it's two cent in the cash register, I wouldn't be a tall surprised if he . . ."

"That'll do," Red Sam said. "Go bring these people their Co'-Colas," and the woman went off to get the rest of the order.

"A good man is hard to find," Red Sammy said. "Everything is getting terrible. I remember the day you could go off and leave your screen door unlatched. Not no more."

He and the grandmother discussed better times. The old lady said that in her opinion Europe was entirely to blame for the way things were now. She said the way Europe acted you would think we were made of money and Red Sam said it was no use talking about it, she was exactly right. The children ran outside into the white sunlight and looked at the monkey in the lacy chinaberry tree. He was busy catching fleas on himself and biting each one carefully between his teeth as if it were a delicacy.

They drove off again into the hot afternoon. The grandmother took cat   45 naps and woke up every few minutes with her own snoring. Outside of Toombsboro she woke up and recalled an old plantation that she had visited in this neighborhood once when she was a young lady. She said the house had six white columns across the front and that there was an avenue of oaks leading up to it and two little wooden trellis arbors on either side in front where you sat down with your suitor after a stroll in the garden. She recalled exactly which road to turn off to get to it. She knew that Bailey would not be willing to lose any time looking at an old house, but the more she talked about it, the more she wanted to see it once again and find out if the little twin arbors were still standing. "There was a secret panel in this house," she said craftily, not telling the truth but wishing that she were, "and the story went that all the family silver was hidden in it when Sherman came through but it was never found . . ."

"Hey!" John Wesley said. "Let's go see it! We'll find it! We'll poke all the woodwork and find it! Who lives there? Where do you turn off at? Hey Pop, can't we turn off there?"

"We never have seen a house with a secret panel!" June Star shrieked. "Let's go to the house with the secret panel! Hey, Pop, can't we go see the house with the secret panel!"

"It's not far from here, I know," the grandmother said. "It wouldn't take over twenty minutes."

Bailey was looking straight ahead. His jaw was as rigid as a horseshoe. "No," he said.

The children began to yell and scream that they wanted to see the house 50 with the secret panel. John Wesley kicked the back of the front seat and June Star hung over her mother's shoulder and whined desperately into her ear that they never had any fun even on their vacation, that they could never do what THEY wanted to do. The baby began to scream and John Wesley kicked the back of the seat so hard that his father could feel the blows in his kidney.

"All right!" he shouted and drew the car to a stop at the side of the road. "Will you all shut up? Will you all just shut up for one second? If you don't shut up, we won't go anywhere."

"It would be very educational for them," the grandmother murmured.

"All right," Bailey said, "but get this. This is the only time we're going to stop for anything like this. This is the one and only time."

"The dirt road that you have to turn down is about a mile back," the grandmother directed. "I marked it when we passed."

"A dirt road," Bailey groaned. 55

After they had turned around and were headed toward the dirt road, the grandmother recalled other points about the house, the beautiful glass over the front doorway and the candle lamp in the hall. John Wesley said that the secret panel was probably in the fireplace.

"You can't go inside this house," Bailey said. "You don't know who lives there."

"While you all talk to the people in front, I'll run around behind and get in a window," John Wesley suggested.

"We'll all stay in the car," his mother said.

They turned onto the dirt road and the car raced roughly along in a swirl 60 of pink dust. The grandmother recalled the times when there were no paved roads and thirty miles was a day's journey. The dirt road was hilly and there were sudden washes in it and sharp curves on dangerous embankments. All at once they would be on a hill, looking down over the blue tops of trees for miles around, then the next minute, they would be in a red depression with the dust-coated trees looking down on them.

"This place had better turn up in a minute," Bailey said, "or I'm going to turn around."

The road looked as if no one had traveled on it in months.

"It's not much farther," the grandmother said and just as she said it, a horrible thought came to her. The thought was so embarrassing that she turned red in the face and her eyes dilated and her feet jumped up, upsetting her valise in the corner. The instant the valise moved, the newspaper top she had over the basket under it rose with a snarl and Pitty Sing, the cat, sprang onto Bailey's shoulder.

The children were thrown to the floor and their mother, clutching the baby, was thrown out the door onto the ground; the old lady was thrown into the front seat. The car turned over once and landed right-side-up in a gulch on the side of the road. Bailey remained in the driver's seat with the cat—gray-striped with a broad white face and an orange nose—clinging to his neck like a caterpillar.

As soon as the children saw they could move their arms and legs, they 65 scrambled out of the car, shouting, "We've had an ACCIDENT!" The grandmother was curled up under the dashboard, hoping she was injured so that Bailey's wrath would not come down on her all at once. The horrible thought she had had before the accident was that the house she had remembered so vividly was not in Georgia but in Tennessee.

Bailey removed the cat from his neck with both hands and flung it out the window against the side of a pine tree. Then he got out of the car and started looking for the children's mother. She was sitting against the side of the red gutted ditch, holding the screaming baby, but she only had a cut down her face and a broken shoulder. "We've had an ACCIDENT!" the children screamed in a frenzy of delight.

"But nobody's killed," June Star said with disappointment as the grandmother limped out of the car, her hat still pinned to her head but the broken front brim standing up at a jaunty angle and the violet spray hanging off the side. They all sat down in the ditch, except the children, to recover from the shock. They were all shaking.

"Maybe a car will come along," said the children's mother hoarsely.

"I believe I have injured an organ," said the grandmother, pressing her side, but no one answered her. Bailey's teeth were clattering. He had on a yellow sport shirt with bright blue parrots designed in it and his face was as yellow as the shirt. The grandmother decided that she would not mention that the house was in Tennessee.

The road was about ten feet above and they could see only the tops of the 70 trees on the other side of it. Behind the ditch they were sitting in there were more woods, tall and dark and deep. In a few minutes they saw a car some distance away on top of a hill, coming slowly as if the occupants were watching them. The grandmother stood up and waved both arms dramatically to attract their attention. The car continued to come on slowly, disappeared around a bend and appeared again, moving even slower, on top of the hill they had gone over. It was a big black battered hearselike automobile. There were three men in it.

It came to a stop over them and for some minutes, the driver looked down with a steady expressionless gaze to where they were sitting, and didn't speak. Then he turned his head and muttered something to the other two and they got out. One was a fat boy in black trousers and a red sweat shirt with a silver stallion embossed on the front of it. He moved around on the right side of them and stood staring, his mouth partly open in a kind of loose grin. The other had on khaki pants and a blue striped coat and a gray hat pulled down very low, hiding most of his face. He came around slowly on the left side. Neither spoke.

The driver got out of the car and stood by the side of it, looking down at them. He was an older man than the other two. His hair was just beginning to gray and he wore silver-rimmed spectacles that gave him a scholarly look. He had a long creased face and didn't have on any shirt or undershirt. He had on blue jeans that were too tight for him and was holding a black hat and a gun. The two boys also had guns.

"We've had an ACCIDENT!" the children screamed.

The grandmother had the peculiar feeling that the bespectacled man was someone she knew. His face was as familiar to her as if she had known him all her life but she could not recall who he was. He moved away from the car and began to come down the embankment, placing his feet carefully so that he wouldn't slip. He had on tan and white shoes and no socks, and his ankles were red and thin. "Good afternoon," he said. "I see you all had you a little spill."

"We turned over twice!" said the grandmother.   75

"Oncet," he corrected. "We seen it happen. Try their car and see will it run, Hiram," he said quietly to the boy with the gray hat.

"What you got that gun for?" John Wesley asked. "Whatcha gonna do with that gun?"

"Lady," the man said to the children's mother, "would you mind calling them children to sit down by you? Children make me nervous. I want all you all to sit down right together there where you're at."

"What are you telling us what to do for?" June Star asked.

Behind them the line of woods gaped like a dark open mouth. "Come   80 here," said their mother.

"Look here now," Bailey began suddenly, "we're in a predicament! We're in . . ."

The grandmother shrieked. She scrambled to her feet and stood staring. "You're The Misfit!" she said. "I recognized you at once!"

"Yes'm," the man said, smiling slightly as if he were pleased in spite of himself to be known, "but it would have been better for all of you, lady, if you hadn't of reckernized me."

Bailey turned his head sharply and said something to his mother   85 that shocked even the children. The old lady began to cry and The Misfit reddened.

"Lady," he said, "don't you get upset. Sometimes a man says things he don't mean. I don't reckon he meant to talk to you thataway."

"You wouldn't shoot a lady, would you?" the grandmother said and removed a clean handkerchief from her cuff and began to slap at her eyes with it.

The Misfit pointed the toe of his shoe into the ground and made a little hole and then covered it up again. "I would hate to have to," he said.

"Listen," the grandmother almost screamed, "I know you're a good man. You don't look a bit like you have common blood. I know you must come from nice people!"

"Yes mam," he said, "finest people in the world." When he smiled he 90 showed a row of strong white teeth. "God never made a finer woman than my mother and my daddy's heart was pure gold," he said. The boy with the red sweat shirt had come around behind them and was standing with his gun at his hip. The Misfit squatted down on the ground. "Watch them children, Bobby Lee," he said. "You know they make me nervous." He looked at the six of them huddled together in front of him and he seemed to be embarrassed as if he couldn't think of anything to say. "Ain't a cloud in the sky," he remarked, looking up at it. "Don't see no sun but don't see no cloud neither."

"Yes, it's a beautiful day," said the grandmother. "Listen," she said, "you shouldn't call yourself The Misfit because I know you're a good man at heart. I can just look at you and tell."

"Hush!" Bailey yelled. "Hush! Everybody shut up and let me handle this!" He was squatting in the position of a runner about to spring forward but he didn't move.

"I pre-chate that, lady," The Misfit said and drew a little circle in the ground with the butt of his gun.

"It'll take a half a hour to fix this here car," Hiram called, looking over the raised hood of it.

"Well, first you and Bobby Lee get him and that little boy to step over 95 yonder with you," The Misfit said, pointing to Bailey and John Wesley. "The boys want to ask you something," he said to Bailey. "Would you mind stepping back in them woods there with them?"

"Listen," Bailey began, "we're in a terrible predicament! Nobody realizes what this is," and his voice cracked. His eyes were as blue and intense as the parrots in his shirt and he remained perfectly still.

The grandmother reached up to adjust her hat brim as if she were going to the woods with him but it came off in her hand. She stood staring at it and after a second she let it fall on the ground. Hiram pulled Bailey up by the arm as if he were assisting an old man. John Wesley caught hold of his father's hand and Bobby Lee followed. They went off toward the woods and just as they reached the dark edge, Bailey turned and supporting himself against a gray naked pine trunk, he shouted, "I'll be back in a minute, Mamma, wait on me!"

"Come back this instant!" his mother shrilled but they all disappeared into the woods.

"Bailey Boy!" the grandmother called in a tragic voice but she found she was looking at The Misfit squatting on the ground in front of her. "I just know you're a good man," she said desperately. "You're not a bit common!"

"Nome, I ain't a good man," The Misfit said after a second as if he had   100
considered her statement carefully, "but I ain't the worst in the world neither. My daddy said I was a different breed of dog from my brothers and sisters. 'You know,' Daddy said, 'it's some that can live their whole life out
without asking about it and it's others has to know why it is, and this boy
is one of the latters. He's going to be into everything!'" He put on his black
hat and looked up suddenly and then away deep into the woods as if he
were embarrassed again. "I'm sorry I don't have on a shirt before you
ladies," he said, hunching his shoulders slightly. "We buried our clothes that
we had on when we escaped and we're just making do until we can get better. We borrowed these from some folks we met," he explained.

"That's perfectly all right," the grandmother said. "Maybe Bailey has an
extra shirt in his suitcase."

"I'll look and see terrectly," The Misfit said.

"Where are they taking him?" the children's mother screamed.

"Daddy was a card himself," The Misfit said. "You couldn't put anything
over on him. He never got in trouble with the Authorities though. Just had
the knack of handling them."

"You could be honest too if you'd only try," said the grandmother. "Think   105
how wonderful it would be to settle down and live a comfortable life and
not have to think about somebody chasing you all the time."

The Misfit kept scratching in the ground with the butt of his gun as if
he were thinking about it. "Yes'm, somebody is always after you," he
murmured.

The grandmother noticed how thin his shoulder blades were just behind
his hat because she was standing up looking down on him. "Do you ever
pray?" she asked.

He shook his head. All she saw was the black hat wiggle between his
shoulder blades. "Nome," he said.

There was a pistol shot from the woods, followed closely by another.
Then silence. The old lady's head jerked around. She could hear the wind
move through the tree tops like a long satisfied insuck of breath. "Bailey
Boy!" she called.

"I was a gospel singer for a while," The Misfit said. "I been most every-   110
thing. Been in the arm service, both land and sea, at home and abroad,
been twict married, been an undertaker, been with the railroads, plowed
Mother Earth, been in a tornado, seen a man burnt alive oncet," and he
looked up at the children's mother and the little girl who were sitting close
together, their faces white and their eyes glassy; "I even seen a woman
flogged," he said.

"Pray, pray," the grandmother began, "pray, pray . . ."

"I never was a bad boy that I remember of," The Misfit said in an almost
dreamy voice, "but somewheres along the line I done something wrong and
got sent to the penitentiary. I was buried alive," and he looked up and held
her attention to him by a steady stare.

"That's when you should have started to pray," she said. "What did you
do to get sent to the penitentiary that first time?"

"Turn to the right, it was a wall," The Misfit said, looking up again at the
cloudless sky. "Turn to the left, it was a wall. Look up it was a ceiling, look

down it was a floor. I forget what I done, lady. I set there and set there, trying to remember what it was I done and I ain't recalled it to this day. Oncet
in a while, I would think it was coming to me, but it never come."

"Maybe they put you in by mistake," the old lady said vaguely.   115

"Nome," he said. "It wasn't no mistake. They had the papers on me."

"You must have stolen something," she said.

The Misfit sneered slightly. "Nobody had nothing I wanted," he said. "It
was a head-doctor at the penitentiary said what I had done was kill my
daddy but I known that for a lie. My daddy died in nineteen ought nineteen
of the epidemic flu and I never had a thing to do with it. He was buried in
the Mount Hopewell Baptist churchyard and you can go there and see for
yourself."

"If you would pray," the old lady said, "Jesus would help you."

"That's right," The Misfit said.   120

"Well then, why don't you pray?" she asked trembling with delight
suddenly.

"I don't want no hep," he said. "I'm doing all right by myself."

Bobby Lee and Hiram came ambling back from the woods. Bobby Lee
was dragging a yellow shirt with bright blue parrots in it.

"Throw me that shirt, Bobby Lee," The Misfit said. The shirt came flying
at him and landed on his shoulder and he put it on. The grandmother
couldn't name what the shirt reminded her of. "No, lady," The Misfit said
while he was buttoning up, "I found out the crime don't matter. You can do
one thing or you can do another, kill a man or take a tire off his car, because
sooner or later you're going to forget what it was you done and just be punished for it."

The children's mother had begun to make heaving noises as if she   125
couldn't get her breath. "Lady," he asked, "would you and that little girl like
to step off yonder with Bobby Lee and Hiram and join your husband?"

"Yes, thank you," the mother said faintly. Her left arm dangled helplessly
and she was holding the baby, who had gone to sleep, in the other. "Hep
that lady up, Hiram," The Misfit said as she struggled to climb out of the
ditch, "and Bobby Lee, you hold onto that little girl's hand."

"I don't want to hold hands with him," June Star said. "He reminds me of
a pig."

The fat boy blushed and laughed and caught her by the arm and pulled
her off into the woods after Hiram and her mother.

Alone with The Misfit, the grandmother found that she had lost her
voice. There was not a cloud in the sky nor any sun. There was nothing
around her but woods. She wanted to tell him that he must pray. She
opened and closed her mouth several times before anything came out.
Finally she found herself saying, "Jesus, Jesus," meaning, Jesus will help
you, but the way she was saying it, it sounded as if she might be cursing.

"Yes'm," The Misfit said as if he agreed. "Jesus thrown everything off bal-   130
ance. It was the same case with Him as with me except He hadn't committed any crime and they could prove I had committed one because they had
the papers on me. Of course," he said, "they never shown me my papers.
That's why I sign myself now. I said long ago, you get you a signature and
sign everything you do and keep a copy of it. Then you'll know what you

done and you can hold up the crime to the punishment and see do they match and in the end you'll have something to prove you ain't been treated right. I call myself The Misfit," he said, "because I can't make what all I done wrong fit what all I gone through in punishment."

There was a piercing scream from the woods, followed closely by a pistol report. "Does it seem right to you, lady, that one is punished a heap and another ain't punished at all?"

"Jesus!" the old lady cried. "You've got good blood! I know you wouldn't shoot a lady! I know you come from nice people! Pray! Jesus, you ought not to shoot a lady. I'll give you all the money I've got!"

"Lady," The Misfit said, looking beyond her far into the woods, "there never was a body that give the undertaker a tip."

There were two more pistol reports and the grandmother raised her head like a parched old turkey hen crying for water and called, "Bailey Boy, Bailey Boy!" as if her heart would break.

"Jesus was the only One that ever raised the dead," The Misfit continued, 135 "and He shouldn't have done it. He thrown everything off balance. If He did what He said, then it's nothing for you to do but throw away everything and follow Him, and if He didn't then it's nothing for you to do but enjoy the few minutes you got left the best way you can—by killing somebody or burning down his house or doing some other meanness to him. No pleasure but meanness," he said and his voice had become almost a snarl.

"Maybe He didn't raise the dead," the old lady mumbled, not knowing what she was saying and feeling so dizzy that she sank down in the ditch with her legs twisted under her.

"I wasn't there so I can't say He didn't," The Misfit said. "I wisht I had of been there," he said, hitting the ground with his fist. "It ain't right I wasn't there because if I had of been there I would of known. Listen lady," he said in a high voice, "if I had of been there I would of known and I wouldn't be like I am now." His voice seemed about to crack and the grandmother's head cleared for an instant. She saw the man's face twisted close to her own as if he were going to cry and she murmured, "Why, you're one of my babies. You're one of my own children!" She reached out and touched him on the shoulder. The Misfit sprang back as if a snake had bitten him and shot her three times through the chest. Then he put his gun down on the ground and took off his glasses and began to clean them.

Hiram and Bobby Lee returned from the woods and stood over the ditch, looking down at the grandmother who half sat and half lay in a puddle of blood with her legs crossed under her like a child's and her face smiling up at the cloudless sky.

Without his glasses, The Misfit's eyes were red-rimmed and pale and defenseless-looking. "Take her off and throw her where you thrown the others," he said, picking up the cat that was rubbing itself against his leg.

"She was a talker, wasn't she?" Bobby Lee said, sliding down the ditch 140 with a yodel.

"She would of been a good woman," The Misfit said, "if it had been somebody there to shoot her every minute of her life."

"Some fun!" Bobby Lee said.

"Shut up, Bobby Lee," The Misfit said. "It's no real pleasure in life."

The Receptive Reader

1. What kind of person is the grandmother? What roles (or how many roles) does she play as a *central character* in the development of the story? At how many points in the story does she play a major or minor part? Does she symbolically represent the past—the "Old South"? Is there a conflict between the generations?

2. What is your reaction to the other members of the family as *minor characters* in the story? Are they comical? strange? ordinary? repellent?

3. What role does the *episode,* or interlude, at the "fat man's" barbecue play in the story?

4. How or why did these characters meet their fate? How would you summarize the *plot* or story line?

5. Is there anything representative or *symbolic* about what happens to these people?

6. What is the Misfit's story (and how much of it do you believe)? What are his manners? (Do you find them surprising or *ironic?*) What is the gist of the climactic conversation between the Misfit and the grandmother? Does it suggest a *theme;* does it have thematic implications?

7. Where would you draw the line between the comic and the tragic in this story? How does it illustrate the mixed genre critics call the *grotesque?*

8. Does this story change your idea about "senseless violence"? How?

The Personal Response

How true to the spirit of the story, or how far off, is the personal reaction in the following journal entry?

> Maybe the Misfit was like Lucifer, the misfit Angel. Lucifer didn't see things God's way, so God cast him out of heaven and punished him. Did Lucifer become evil because of the punishment not fitting the crime? Or was Lucifer just inherently evil? If he was inherently evil, he wouldn't have been an angel in the first place. I think those who jailed the misfit turned him from just different to bad. I wasn't terribly sorry to see that family go, especially those rancid children. The mother was harmless, but I had real sympathy only for the Misfit, the baby, and the cat, Pitty Sing. Maybe O'Connor made the family so nasty and annoying to act as a foil for the Misfit, who really was a pitiful man.

The Creative Dimension

O'Connor's stories leave readers with haunting images or the memory of striking incidents. Critics puzzle over key phrases ("good country people"), provocative sentences ("a good man is hard to find"), symbolic gestures, climactic exchanges, violent confrontations. Focus on a haunting image, incident, gesture, or saying in O'Connor's stories. Re-create it, following the train of ideas, images, or associations it calls up in your mind.

As you start reading the following story by the same author, do you find yourself in familiar territory? Do its characters seem in some way akin to those in the preceding story? Does this second story raise issues or explore questions that seem related to those in the first?

Everything That Rises Must Converge   *1965*

Her doctor had told Julian's mother that she must lose twenty pounds on account of her blood pressure, so on Wednesday nights Julian had to take her downtown on the bus for a reducing class at the Y. The reducing class was designed for working girls over fifty, who weighed from 165 to 200 pounds. His mother was one of the slimmer ones, but she said ladies did not tell their age or weight. She would not ride the buses by herself at night since they had been integrated, and because the reducing class was one of her few pleasures, necessary for her health, and *free,* she said Julian could at least put himself out to take her, considering all she did for him. Julian did not like to consider all she did for him, but every Wednesday night he braced himself and took her.

She was almost ready to go, standing before the hall mirror, putting on her hat, while he, his hands behind him, appeared pinned to the door frame, waiting like Saint Sebastian for the arrows to begin piercing him. The hat was new and had cost her seven dollars and a half. She kept saying, "Maybe I shouldn't have paid that for it. No, I shouldn't have. I'll take it off and return it tomorrow. I shouldn't have bought it."

Julian raised his eyes to heaven. "Yes, you should have bought it," he said. "Put it on and let's go." It was a hideous hat. A purple velvet flap came down on one side of it and stood up on the other; the rest of it was green and looked like a cushion with the stuffing out. He decided it was less comical than jaunty and pathetic. Everything that gave her pleasure was small and depressed him.

She lifted the hat one more time and set it down slowly on top of her head. Two wings of gray hair protruded on either side of her florid face, but her eyes, sky-blue, were as innocent and untouched by experience as they must have been when she was ten. Were it not that she was a widow who had struggled fiercely to feed and clothe and put him through school and who was supporting him still, "until he got on his feet," she might have been a little girl that he had to take to town.

"It's all right, it's all right," he said. "Let's go." He opened the door himself and started down the walk to get her going. The sky was a dying violet and the houses stood out darkly against it, bulbous liver-colored monstrosities of a uniform ugliness though no two were alike. Since this had been a fashionable neighborhood forty years ago, his mother persisted in thinking they did well to have an apartment in it. Each house had a narrow collar of dirt around it in which sat, usually, a grubby child. Julian walked with his hands in his pockets, his head down and thrust forward and his eyes glazed with the determination to make himself completely numb during the time he would be sacrificed to her pleasure.

The door closed and he turned to find the dumpy figure, surmounted by the atrocious hat, coming toward him. "Well," she said, "you only live once and paying a little more for it, I at least won't meet myself coming and going."

5

"Some day I'll start making money," Julian said gloomily—he knew he never would—"and you can have one of those jokes whenever you take the fit." But first they would move. He visualized a place where the nearest neighbors would be three miles away on either side.

"I think you're doing fine," she said, drawing on her gloves. "You've only been out of school a year. Rome wasn't built in a day."

She was one of the few members of the Y reducing class who arrived in hat and gloves and who had a son who had been to college. "It takes time," she said, "and the world is in such a mess. This hat looked better on me than any of the others, though when she brought it out I said, 'Take that thing back. I wouldn't have it on my head,' and she said, 'Now wait till you see it on,' and when she put it on me, I said, 'We-ull,' and she said, 'If you ask me, that hat does something for you and you do something for the hat, and besides,' she said, 'with that hat, you won't meet yourself coming and going.'"

Julian thought he could have stood his lot better if she had been selfish,   10 if she had been an old hag who drank and screamed at him. He walked along, saturated in depression, as if in the midst of his martyrdom he had lost his faith. Catching sight of his long, hopeless, irritated face, she stopped suddenly with a grief-stricken look, and pulled back on his arm. "Wait on me," she said. "I'm going back to the house and take this thing off and tomorrow I'm going to return it. I was out of my head. I can pay the gas bill with that seven-fifty."

He caught her arm in a vicious grip. "You are not going to take it back," he said. "I like it."

"Well," she said, "I don't think I ought . . ."

"Shut up and enjoy it," he muttered, more depressed than ever.

"With the world in the mess it's in," she said, "it's a wonder we can enjoy anything. I tell you, the bottom rail is on the top."

Julian sighed.   15

"Of course," she said, "if you know who you are, you can go anywhere." She said this every time he took her to the reducing class. "Most of them in it are not our kind of people," she said, "but I can be gracious to anybody. I know who I am."

"They don't give a damn for your graciousness," Julian said savagely. "Knowing who you are is good for one generation only. You haven't the foggiest idea where you stand now or who you are."

She stopped and allowed her eyes to flash at him. "I most certainly do know who I am," she said, "and if you don't know who you are, I'm ashamed of you."

"Oh hell," Julian said.

"Your great-grandfather was a former governor of this state," she said.   20 "Your grandfather was a prosperous land-owner. Your grandmother was a Godhigh."

"Will you look around you," he said tensely, "and see where you are now?" and he swept his arm jerkily out to indicate the neighborhood, which the growing darkness at least made less dingy.

"You remain what you are," she said. "Your great-grandfather had a plantation and two hundred slaves."

"There are no more slaves," he said irritably.

"They were better off when they were," she said. He groaned to see that she was off on that topic. She rolled onto it every few days like a train on an open track. He knew every stop, every junction, every swamp along the way, and knew the exact point at which her conclusion would roll majestically into the station: "It's ridiculous. It's simply not realistic. They should rise, yes, but on their own side of the fence."

"Let's skip it," Julian said.   25

"The ones I feel sorry for," she said, "are the ones that are half white. They're tragic."

"Will you skip it?"

"Suppose we were half white. We would certainly have mixed feelings."

"I have mixed feelings now," he groaned.

"Well let's talk about something pleasant," she said. "I remember going to   30
Grandpa's when I was a little girl. Then the house had double stairways that went up to what was really the second floor—all the cooking was done on the first. I used to like to stay down in the kitchen on account of the way the walls smelled. I would sit with my nose pressed against the plaster and take deep breaths. Actually the place belonged to the Godhighs but your grandfather Chestny paid the mortgage and saved it for them. They were in reduced circumstances," she said, "but reduced or not, they never forgot who they were."

"Doubtless that decayed mansion reminded them," Julian muttered. He never spoke of it without contempt or thought of it without longing. He had seen it once when he was a child before it had been sold. The double stairways had rotted and been torn down. Negroes were living in it. But it remained in his mind as his mother had known it. It appeared in his dreams regularly. He would stand on the wide porch, listening to the rustle of oak leaves, then wander through the high-ceilinged hall into the parlor that opened onto it and gaze at the worn rugs and faded draperies. It occurred to him that it was he, not she, who could have appreciated it. He preferred its threadbare elegance to anything he could name and it was because of it that all the neighborhoods they had lived in had been a torment to him— whereas she had hardly known the difference. She called her insensitivity "being adjustable."

"And I remember the old darky who was my nurse, Caroline. There was no better person in the world. I've always had a great respect for my colored friends," she said. "I'd do anything in the world for them and they'd . . ."

"Will you for God's sake get off that subject?" Julian said. When he got on a bus by himself, he made it a point to sit down beside a Negro, in reparation as it were for his mother's sins.

"You're mighty touchy tonight," she said. "Do you feel all right?"

"Yes I feel all right," he said. "Now lay off."   35

She pursed her lips. "Well, you certainly are in a vile humor," she observed. "I just won't speak to you at all."

They had reached the bus stop. There was no bus in sight and Julian, his hands still jammed in his pockets and his head thrust forward, scowled down the empty street. The frustration of having to wait on the bus as well as ride on it began to creep up his neck like a hot hand. The presence of his mother was borne in upon him as she gave a pained sigh. He looked at her bleakly. She was holding herself very erect under the preposterous hat, wearing it like a banner of her imaginary dignity. There was in him an evil urge to break her spirit. He suddenly unloosened his tie and pulled it off and put it in his pocket.

She stiffened. "Why must you look like *that* when you take me to town?" she said. "Why must you deliberately embarrass me?"

"If you'll never learn where you are," he said, "you can at least learn where I am."

"You look like a—thug," she said.   40

"Then I must be one," he murmured.

"I'll just go home," she said. "I will not bother you. If you can't do a little thing like that for me . . ."

Rolling his eyes upward, he put his tie back on. "Restored to my class," he muttered. He thrust his face toward her and hissed, "True culture is in the mind, the *mind*," he said, and tapped his head, "the mind."

"It's in the heart," she said, "and in how you do things and how you do things is because of who you *are*."

"Nobody in the damn bus cares who you are."   45

"I care who I am," she said icily.

The lighted bus appeared on top of the next hill and as it approached, they moved out into the street to meet it. He put his hand under her elbow and hoisted her up on the creaking step. She entered with a little smile, as if she were going into a drawing room where everyone had been waiting for her. While he put in the tokens, she sat down on one of the broad front seats for three which faced the aisle. A thin woman with protruding teeth and long yellow hair was sitting on the end of it. His mother moved up beside her and left room for Julian beside herself. He sat down and looked at the floor across the aisle where a pair of thin feet in red and white canvas sandals were planted.

His mother immediately began a general conversation meant to attract anyone who felt like talking. "Can it get any hotter?" she said and removed from her purse a folding fan, black with a Japanese scene on it, which she began to flutter before her.

"I reckon it might could," the woman with the protruding teeth said, "but I know for a fact my apartment couldn't get no hotter."

"It must get the afternoon sun," his mother said. She sat forward and   50
looked up and down the bus. It was half filled. Everybody was white. "I see we have the bus to ourselves," she said. Julian cringed.

"For a change," said the woman across the aisle, the owner of the red and white canvas sandals. "I come on one the other day and they were thick as fleas—up front and all through."

"The world is in a mess everywhere," his mother said. "I don't know how we've let it get in this fix."

"What gets my goat is all those boys from good families stealing automobile tires," the woman with the protruding teeth said. "I told my boy, I said you may not be rich but you been raised right and if I ever catch you in any such mess, they can send you on to the reformatory. Be exactly where you belong."

"Training tells," his mother said. "Is your boy in high school?"

"Ninth grade," the woman said.   55

"My son just finished college last year. He wants to write but he's selling typewriters until he gets started," his mother said.

The woman leaned forward and peered at Julian. He threw her such a malevolent look that she subsided against the seat. On the floor across the aisle there was an abandoned newspaper. He got up and got it and opened it out in front of him. His mother discreetly continued the conversation in a lower tone but the woman across the aisle said in a loud voice, "Well that's nice. Selling typewriters is close to writing. He can go right from one to the other."

"I tell him," his mother said, "that Rome wasn't built in a day."

Behind the newspaper Julian was withdrawing into the inner compartment of his mind where he spent most of his time. This was a kind of mental bubble in which he established himself when he could not bear to be a part of what was going on around him. From it he could see out and judge but in it he was safe from any kind of penetration from without. It was the only place where he felt free of the general idiocy of his fellows. His mother had never entered it but from it he could see her with absolute clarity.

The old lady was clever enough and he thought that if she had started   60
from any of the right premises, more might have been expected of her. She lived according to the laws of her own fantasy world, outside of which he had never seen her set foot. The law of it was to sacrifice herself for him after she had first created the necessity to do so by making a mess of things. If he had permitted her sacrifices, it was only because her lack of foresight had made them necessary. All of her life had been a struggle to act like a Chestny without the Chestny goods, and to give him everything she thought a Chestny ought to have; but since, said she, it was fun to struggle, why complain? And when you had won, as she had won, what fun to look back on the hard times! He could not forgive her that she had enjoyed the struggle and that she thought *she* had won.

What she meant when she said she had won was that she had brought him up successfully and had sent him to college and that he had turned out so well—good looking (her teeth had gone unfilled so that his could be straightened), intelligent (he realized he was too intelligent to be a success), and with a future ahead of him (there was of course no future ahead of him). She excused his gloominess on the grounds that he was still growing up and his radical ideas on his lack of practical experience. She said he didn't yet know a thing about "life," that he hadn't even entered the real world—when already he was as disenchanted with it as a man of fifty.

The further irony of all this was that in spite of her, he had turned out so well. In spite of going to only a third-rate college, he had, on his own initiative, come out with a first-rate education; in spite of growing up dominated by a small mind, he had ended up with a large one; in spite of all her foolish views, he was free of prejudice and unafraid to face facts. Most miraculous of all, instead of being blinded by love for her as she was for him, he had cut himself emotionally free of her and could see her with complete objectivity. He was not dominated by his mother.

The bus stopped with a sudden jerk and shook him from his meditation. A woman from the back lurched forward with little steps and barely escaped falling in his newspaper as she righted herself. She got off and a large Negro got on. Julian kept his paper lowered to watch. It gave him a certain satisfaction to see injustice in daily operation. It confirmed his view that with a few exceptions there was no one worth knowing within a radius of three hundred miles. The Negro was well dressed and carried a briefcase. He looked around and then sat down on the other end of the seat where the woman with the red and white canvas sandals was sitting. He immediately unfolded a newspaper and obscured himself behind it. Julian's mother's elbow at once prodded insistently into his ribs. "Now you see why I won't ride on these buses by myself," she whispered.

The woman with the red and white canvas sandals had risen at the same time the Negro sat down and had gone further back in the bus and taken the seat of the woman who had got off. His mother leaned forward and cast her an approving look.

Julian rose, crossed the aisle, and sat down in the place of the woman   65
with the canvas sandals. From this position, he looked serenely across at his mother. Her face had turned an angry red. He stared at her, making his eyes the eyes of a stranger. He felt his tension suddenly lift as if he had openly declared war on her.

He would have liked to get in conversation with the Negro and to talk with him about art or politics or any subject that would be above the comprehension of those around them, but the man remained entrenched behind his paper. He was either ignoring the change of seating or had never noticed it. There was no way for Julian to convey his sympathy.

His mother kept her eyes fixed reproachfully on his face. The woman with the protruding teeth was looking at him avidly as if he were a type of monster new to her.

"Do you have a light?" he asked the Negro.

Without looking away from his paper, the man reached in his pocket and handed him a packet of matches.

"Thanks," Julian said. For a moment he held the matches foolishly. A NO   70
SMOKING sign looked down upon him from over the door. This alone would not have deterred him; he had no cigarettes. He had quit smoking some months before because he could not afford it. "Sorry," he muttered and handed back the matches. The Negro lowered the paper and gave him an annoyed look. He took the matches and raised the paper again.

His mother continued to gaze at him but she did not take advantage of his momentary discomfort. Her eyes retained their battered look. Her face seemed to be unnaturally red, as if her blood pressure had risen. Julian allowed no glimmer of sympathy to show on his face. Having got the advantage, he wanted desperately to keep it and carry it through. He would have liked to teach her a lesson that would last her a while, but there seemed no way to continue the point. The Negro refused to come out from behind his paper.

Julian folded his arms and looked stolidly before him, facing her but as if he did not see her, as if he had ceased to recognize her existence. He visualized a scene in which, the bus having reached their stop, he would remain in his seat and when she said, "Aren't you going to get off?" he would look at her as a stranger who had rashly addressed him. The corner they got off on was usually deserted, but it was well lighted and it would not hurt her to walk by herself the four blocks to the Y. He decided to wait until the time came and then decide whether or not he would let her get off by herself. He would have to be at the Y at ten to bring her back, but he could leave her wondering if he was going to show up. There was no reason for her to think she could always depend on him.

He retired again into the high-ceilinged room sparsely settled with large pieces of antique furniture. His soul expanded momentarily but then he became aware of his mother across from him and the vision shriveled. He studied her coldly. Her feet in little pumps dangled like a child's and did not quite reach the floor. She was training on him an exaggerated look of reproach. He felt completely detached from her. At that moment he could with pleasure have slapped her as he would have slapped a particularly obnoxious child in his charge.

He began to imagine various unlikely ways by which he could teach her a lesson. He might make friends with some distinguished Negro professor or lawyer and bring him home to spend the evening. He would be entirely justified but her blood pressure would rise to 300. He could not push her to the extent of making her have a stroke, and moreover, he had never been successful at making any Negro friends. He had tried to strike up an acquaintance on the bus with some of the better types, with ones that looked like professors or ministers or lawyers. One morning he had sat down next to a distinguished-looking dark brown man who had answered his questions with a sonorous solemnity but who had turned out to be an undertaker. Another day he had sat down beside a cigar-smoking Negro with a diamond ring on his finger, but after a few stilted pleasantries, the Negro had rung the buzzer and risen, slipping two lottery tickets into Julian's hand as he climbed over him to leave.

He imagined his mother lying desperately ill and his being able to secure 75 only a Negro doctor for her. He toyed with that idea for a few minutes and then dropped it for a momentary vision of himself participating as a sympathizer in a sit-in demonstration. This was possible but he did not linger with it. Instead, he approached the ultimate horror. He brought home a beautiful suspiciously Negroid woman. Prepare yourself, he said. There is nothing you can do about it. This is the woman I've chosen. She's intelligent, dignified, even good, and she's suffered and she hasn't thought it *fun*. Now persecute us, go ahead and persecute us. Drive her out of here, but remember, you're driving me too. His eyes were narrowed and through the indignation he had generated, he saw his mother across the aisle, purple-faced, shrunken to the dwarf-like proportions of her moral nature, sitting like a mummy beneath the ridiculous banner of her hat.

He was tilted out of his fantasy again as the bus stopped. The door opened with a sucking hiss and out of the dark a large, gaily dressed, sullen-looking colored woman got on with a little boy. The child, who might have been four, had on a short plaid suit and a Tyrolean hat with a blue feather in it. Julian hoped that he would sit down beside him and that the woman would push in beside his mother. He could think of no better arrangement.

As she waited for her tokens, the woman was surveying the seating possibilities—he hoped with the idea of sitting where she was least wanted.
There was something familiar-looking about her but Julian could not place
what it was. She was a giant of a woman. Her face was set not only to meet
opposition but to seek it out. The downward tilt of her large lower lip was
like a warning sign: DON'T TAMPER WITH ME. Her bulging figure was encased
in a green crepe dress and her feet overflowed in red shoes. She had on a
hideous hat. A purple velvet flap came down on one side of it and stood up
on the other; the rest of it was green and looked like a cushion with the
stuffing out. She carried a mammoth red pocketbook that bulged throughout as if it were stuffed with rocks.

To Julian's disappointment, the little boy climbed up on the empty seat
beside his mother. His mother lumped all children, black and white, into the
common category, "cute," and she thought little Negroes were on the whole
cuter than little white children. She smiled at the little boy as he climbed on
the seat.

Meanwhile the woman was bearing down upon the empty seat beside
Julian. To his annoyance, she squeezed herself into it. He saw his mother's
face change as the woman settled herself next to him and he realized with
satisfaction that this was more objectionable to her than it was to him. Her
face seemed almost gray and there was a look of dull recognition in her
eyes, as if suddenly she had sickened at some awful confrontation. Julian
saw that it was because she and the woman had, in a sense, swapped sons.
Though his mother would not realize the symbolic significance of this, she
would feel it. His amusement showed plainly on his face.

The woman next to him muttered something unintelligible to herself. He   80
was conscious of a kind of bristling next to him, a muted growling like that
of an angry cat. He could not see anything but the red pocketbook upright
on the bulging green thighs. He visualized the woman as she had stood
waiting for her tokens—the ponderous figure, rising from the red shoes
upward over the solid hips, the mammoth bosom, the haughty face, to the
green and purple hat.

His eyes widened.

The vision of the two hats, identical, broke upon him with the radiance
of a brilliant sunrise. His face was suddenly lit with joy. He could not
believe that Fate had thrust upon his mother such a lesson. He gave a loud
chuckle so that she would look at him and see that he saw. She turned her
eyes on him slowly. The blue in them seemed to have turned a bruised purple. For a moment he had an uncomfortable sense of her innocence, but it
lasted only a second before principle rescued him. Justice entitled him to
laugh. His grin hardened until it said to her as plainly as if he were saying
aloud: Your punishment exactly fits your pettiness. This should teach you a
permanent lesson.

Her eyes shifted to the woman. She seemed unable to bear looking at
him and to find the woman preferable. He became conscious again of the
bristling presence at his side. The woman was rumbling like a volcano
about to become active. His mother's mouth began to twitch slightly at one
corner. With a sinking heart, he saw incipient signs of recovery on her face
and realized that this was going to strike her suddenly as funny and was

going to be no lesson at all. She kept her eyes on the woman and an amused smile came over her face. The little Negro was looking up at her with large fascinated eyes. He had been trying to attract her attention for some time.

"Carver!" the woman said suddenly. "Come heah!"

When he saw that the spotlight was on him at last, Carver drew his feet   85
up and turned himself toward Julian's mother and giggled.

"Carver!" the woman said. "You heah me? Come heah!"

Carver slid down from the seat but remained squatting with his back against the base of it, his head turned slyly around toward Julian's mother, who was smiling at him. The woman reached a hand across the aisle and snatched him to her. He righted himself and hung backwards on her knees, grinning at Julian's mother. "Isn't he cute?" Julian's mother said to the woman with the protruding teeth.

"I reckon he is," the woman said without conviction.

His mother yanked him upright but he eased out of her grip and shot across the aisle and scrambled, giggling wildly, onto the seat beside his love.

"I think he likes me," Julian's mother said, and smiled at the woman. It was   90
the smile she used when she was being particularly gracious to an inferior. Julian saw everything lost. The lesson had rolled off her like rain on a roof.

The woman stood up and yanked the little boy off the seat as if she were snatching him from contagion. Julian could feel the rage in her at having no weapon like his mother's smile. She gave the child a sharp slap across his leg. He howled once and then thrust his head into her stomach and kicked his feet against her shins. "Behave," she said vehemently.

The bus stopped and the Negro who had been reading the newspaper got off. The woman moved over and set the little boy down with a thump between herself and Julian. She held him firmly by the knee. In a moment he put his hands in front of his face and peeped at Julian's mother through his fingers.

"I see yoooooooo!" she said and put her hand in front of her face and peeped at him.

The woman slapped his hand down. "Quit yo' foolishness," she said, "before I knock the living Jesus out of you!"

Julian was thankful that the next stop was theirs. He reached up and   95
pulled the cord. The woman reached up and pulled it at the same time. Oh my God, he thought. He had the terrible intuition that when they got off the bus together, his mother would open her purse and give the little boy a nickel. The gesture would be as natural to her as breathing. The bus stopped and the woman got up and lunged to the front, dragging the child, who wished to stay on, after her. Julian and his mother got up and followed. As they neared the door, Julian tried to relieve her of her pocketbook.

"No," she murmured, "I want to give the little boy a nickel."

"No!" Julian hissed. "No!"

She smiled down at the child and opened her bag. The bus door opened and the woman picked him up by the arm and descended with him, hanging at her hip. Once in the street she set him down and shook him.

Julian's mother had to close her purse while she got down the bus step but as soon as her feet were on the ground, she opened it again and began to rummage inside. "I can't find but a penny," she whispered, "but it looks like a new one."

"Don't do it!" Julian said fiercely between his teeth. There was a street- 100 light on the corner and she hurried to get under it so that she could better see into her pocketbook. The woman was heading off rapidly down the street with the child still hanging backward on her hand.

"Oh little boy!" Julian's mother called and took a few quick steps and caught up with them just beyond the lamppost. "Here's a bright new penny for you," and she held out the coin, which shone bronze in the dim light.

The huge woman turned and for a moment stood, her shoulders lifted and her face frozen with frustrated rage, and stared at Julian's mother. Then all at once she seemed to explode like a piece of machinery that had been given one ounce of pressure too much. Julian saw the black fist swing out with the red pocketbook. He shut his eyes and cringed as he heard the woman shout, "He don't take nobody's pennies!" When he opened his eyes, the woman was disappearing down the street with the little boy staring wide-eyed over her shoulder. Julian's mother was sitting on the sidewalk.

"I told you not to do that," Julian said angrily. "I told you not to do that!"

He stood over her for a minute, gritting his teeth. Her legs were stretched out in front of her and her hat was on her lap. He squatted down and looked her in the face. It was totally expressionless. "You got exactly what you deserved," he said. "Now get up."

He picked up her pocketbook and put what had fallen out back in it. He 105 picked the hat up off her lap. The penny caught his eye on the sidewalk and he picked that up and let it drop before her eyes into the purse. Then he stood up and leaned over and held his hands out to pull her up. She remained immobile. He sighed. Rising above them on either side were black apartment buildings, marked with irregular rectangles of light. At the end of the block a man came out of a door and walked off in the opposite direction. "All right," he said, "suppose somebody happens by and wants to know why you're sitting on the sidewalk?"

She took the hand and, breathing hard, pulled heavily up on it and then stood for a moment, swaying slightly as if the spots of light in the darkness were circling around her. Her eyes, shadowed and confused, finally settled on his face. He did not try to conceal his irritation. "I hope this teaches you a lesson," he said. She leaned forward and her eyes raked his face. She seemed trying to determine his identity. Then, as if she found nothing familiar about him, she started off with a headlong movement in the wrong direction.

"Aren't you going on to the Y?" he asked.

"Home," she muttered.

"Well, are we walking?"

For answer she kept going. Julian followed along, his hands behind him. 110 He saw no reason to let the lesson she had had go without backing it up with an explanation of its meaning. She might as well be made to understand what had happened to her. "Don't think that was just an uppity Negro woman," he said. "That was the whole colored race which will no longer take your condescending pennies. That was your black double. She can wear the same hat as you, and to be sure," he added gratuitously (because he thought it was funny), "it looked better on her than it did on you. What all this means," he said, "is that the old world is gone. The old manners are obsolete and your graciousness is not worth a damn." He thought bitterly of the house that had been lost for him. "You aren't who you think you are," he said.

She continued to plow ahead, paying no attention to him. Her hair had come undone on one side. She dropped her pocketbook and took no notice. He stooped and picked it up and handed it to her but she did not take it.

"You needn't act as if the world had come to an end," he said, "because it hasn't. From now on you've got to live in a new world and face a few realities for a change. Buck up," he said, "it won't kill you."

She was breathing fast.

"Let's wait on the bus," he said.

"Home," she said thickly.   115

"I hate to see you behave like this," he said. "Just like a child. I should be able to expect more of you." He decided to stop where he was and make her stop and wait for a bus. "I'm not going any farther," he said, stopping. "We're going on the bus."

She continued to go on as if she had not heard him. He took a few steps and caught her arm and stopped her. He looked into her face and caught his breath. He was looking into a face he had never seen before. "Tell Grandpa to come get me," she said.

He stared, stricken.

"Tell Caroline to come get me," she said.

Stunned, he let her go and she lurched forward again, walking as if one 120 leg were shorter than the other. A tide of darkness seemed to be sweeping her from him. "Mother!" he cried. "Darling, sweetheart, wait!" Crumpling, she fell to the pavement. He dashed forward and fell at her side, crying, "Mamma, Mamma!" He turned her over. Her face was fiercely distorted. One eye, large and staring, moved slightly to the left as if it had become unmoored. The other remained fixed on him, raked his face again, found nothing and closed.

"Wait here, wait here!" he cried and jumped up and began to run for help toward a cluster of lights he saw in the distance ahead of him. "Help, help!" he shouted, but his voice was thin, scarcely a thread of sound. The lights drifted farther away the faster he ran and his feet moved numbly as if they carried him nowhere. The tide of darkness seemed to sweep him back to her, postponing from moment to moment his entry into the world of guilt and sorrow.

The Receptive Reader

1. What kind of person is Julian's mother? What kind of attitudes and mental habits shape her personality? (How are they revealed in such telling details as the hat, the to-do about the seating in the bus, the coin for the black child?) What are her true feelings about her son? Is there any one dominant trait that provides a clue to her character?

2. O'Connor is a master of mixed feelings and contradictory emotions. What kind of person is Julian? What is his basic conflict with his mother? What are the central themes of his mental monologues? Which incidents are most revealing of his character? What would you identify as his most characteristic trait or problem? Are there any contradictions in his personality? (Are we supposed to like him or identify with his point of view?)

3. This story takes us to the South in a period of *transition*. Black or African Americans are still called "Negroes" (or, more politely, "colored"). Buses have recently been integrated, with no more relegation of colored people to the back of the bus. What is the role of black people in this story? What kind of person is the mother of the little boy? Is the author's portrait of her unflattering or favorable?

4. Can you find any passages that would serve as *capsule portraits* of the major characters?

5. What is the significance of the *ending*?

6. Does this story reinforce or does it counteract stereotypes about southerners and African Americans?

The Personal Response

In this story, do you find yourself taking sides between Julian's mother and her son? What side are you on, and why? Do you think the author expects you to like Julian or identify with his point of view?

The Creative Dimension

Flannery O'Connor is a writer who keeps very tight control over her characters, with every detail meaningful and very little left to chance. Suppose one of the characters—Julian's mother, Julian, or the black woman (or maybe the child)—had a chance to have a last word, talking freely about what they felt deep down. Choose one of these, and write what you think they might say.

JUXTAPOSITIONS

A Range of Sources

With a puzzling, provocative author like Flannery O'Connor, readers may turn for help to a range of **secondary sources.** They may look for guidance in the author's own comments in conversations, lectures, or letters. They may look for helpful hints in tributes by fellow writers or in expert testimony by literary critics.

Author Testimony   O'Connor herself lectured and wrote extensively about the writing and teaching of literature. (She did, however, once say, "asking me to lecture about story-writing is like asking a fish to lecture on swimming.") The following is her interpretation of one of her stories from a reading she presented to a college audience.

Flannery O'Connor

On "A Good Man Is Hard to Find"   *1963*

This is the story of a family of six which, on its way driving to Florida, gets wiped out by an escaped convict who calls himself the Misfit. The family is made up of the Grandmother and her son, Bailey, and his children, John Wesley and June Star and the baby, and there is also the cat and the children's mother. The cat is named Pitty Sing, and the Grandmother is taking him with them, hidden in a basket.

Now I think it behooves me to try to establish with you the basis on which reason operates in this story. Much of my fiction takes its character from a reasonable use of the unreasonable, though the reasonableness of my use of it may not always be apparent. The assumptions that underlie this use of it, however, are those of the central Christian mysteries. These are assumptions to which a large part of the modern audience takes exception. About this I can only say that there are perhaps other ways than my own in which this story could be read, but none other by which it could have been written. Belief, in my own case anyway, is the engine that makes perception operate.

The heroine of this story, the Grandmother, is in the most significant position life offers the Christian. She is facing death. And to all appearances she, like the rest of us, is not too well prepared for it. She would like to see the event postponed. Indefinitely.

I've talked to a number of teachers who use this story in class and who tell their students that the Grandmother is evil, that in fact, she's a witch, even down to the cat. One of these teachers told me that his students, and particularly his Southern students, resisted this interpretation with a certain bemused vigor, and he didn't understand why. I had to tell him that they resisted it because they all had grandmothers or great-aunts just like her at home, and they knew, from personal experience, that the old lady lacked comprehension, but that she had a good heart. The Southerner is usually tolerant of those weaknesses that proceed from innocence, and he knows that a taste for self-preservation can be readily combined with the missionary spirit.

This same teacher was telling his students that morally the Misfit was several cuts above the Grandmother. He had a really sentimental attachment to the Misfit. But then a prophet gone wrong is almost always more interesting than your grandmother, and you have to let people take their pleasures where they find them.

It is true that the old lady is a hypocritical old soul; her wits are no match for the Misfit's, nor is her capacity for grace equal to his; yet I think the unprejudiced reader will feel that the Grandmother has a special kind of triumph in this story which instinctively we do not allow to someone altogether bad.

I often ask myself what makes a story work, and what makes it hold up as a story, and I have decided that it is probably some action, some gesture of a character that is unlike any other in the story, one which indicates where the real heart of the story lies. This would have to be an action or a gesture which was both totally right and totally unexpected; it would have to be one that was both in character and beyond character; it would have to suggest both the world and eternity. The action or gesture I'm talking about would have to be on . . . the level which has to do with the Divine life and our participation in it. It would be a gesture that transcended any neat allegory that might have been intended or any pat moral categories a reader could make. It would be a gesture which somehow made contact with mystery.

There is a point in this story where such a gesture occurs. The Grandmother is at last alone, facing the Misfit. Her head clears for an instant and she realizes, even in her limited way, that she is responsible for the man before her and joined to him by ties of kinship which have their roots deep in the mystery she has been merely prattling about so far. And at this point, she does the right thing, she makes the right gesture. . . .

I don't want to equate the Misfit with the devil. I prefer to think that, however unlikely this may seem, the old lady's gesture, like the mustard seed, will grow to be a great crow-filled tree in the Misfit's heart, and will be enough of a pain to him there to turn him into the prophet he was meant to become. But that's another story.

From *Mystery and Manners,* edited by Sally and Robert Fitzgerald

The Receptive Reader

Does this account by the author change your understanding of the story?

Author Correspondence   Readers often turn to an author's published **letters** for insights into the writer's personality and work. The following is an excerpt from a review by Joyce Carol Oates of a volume of O'Connor's letters. Oates said, "it will be no surprise to admirers of Flannery O'Connor's enigmatic, troubling, and highly idiosyncratic fiction to learn that there were, behind the near-perfect little rituals of violence and redemption she created, not one but several Flannery O'Connors."

Joyce Carol Oates
A Self-Portrait in Letters   *1987*

It must be said of the letters that they give life to a wonderfully warm, witty, generous, and complex personality, surely one of the most gifted of contemporary writers. At the same time they reveal a curiously girlish, childlike, touchingly timid personality. . . . The letters give voice, on one side, to a hilariously witty observer of the grotesque, the vulgar, and the merely silly in this society, and in the rather limited world of the Catholic imagination; and then they reveal a Catholic intellectual so conservative and docile that she will write to a priest-friend for permission to read Gide and Sartre (at that time on the Church's Index of forbidden writers). . . .

The first letter in the collection was written in 1948, when Flannery was "up north" at Yaddo, the writers' colony in Saratoga Springs. The last letter, a heartbreaking one, was written just before her death on August 3, 1964, when she knew she was dying of complications following an operation for the removal of a tumor. The years between 1948 and 1964 were rich, full ones, despite the fact that Flannery's debilitating condition (lupus) kept her at home, and frequently bedridden, for long periods of time. She was not at all a solitary, reclusive person; she had a wide circle of friends, and clearly loved seeing them, and writing to them often. . . .

She always knew that the process of creation was subjected to no rules, and that, as an artist, she "discovered" the truth of her stories in the writing of them. She enjoyed writing—perhaps it is not an exaggeration to say that she lived for it, and in it. Easily exhausted, she forced herself to work two or three hours every day, in the morning, and managed by this discipline to write about one story a year during the worst periods. During the final year of her life, 1964, when everything seemed to go wrong she was completing the volume that would be her finest achievement, "Everything That Rises Must Converge," which would be published, to wide critical acclaim, after her death. One cannot imagine an ailing person less given to self-pity. When, as a fairly young woman, she learned she would probably be on crutches the rest of her life, she says merely, "So, so much for that. I will henceforth be a structure with flying buttresses. . . ." Writing to a friend in 1964, she says she must submit to an operation because "I have a large tumor and if they don't make haste and get rid of it, they will have to remove me and leave it." It is only near the very end of her life that she says, briefly, to the same friend: "Prayers requested. I am sick of being sick."

From "Flannery O'Connor: A Self-Portrait
in Letters" in *Antaeus,* Autumn 1987

The Receptive Reader

Which details or comments in this review do most to round out your mental picture of O'Connor? Which are most enlightening or thought provoking?

Tribute by a Fellow Writer   Alice Walker, author of *The Color Purple,* grew up in a sharecropper's shack a few miles from where O'Connor lived for a time in a house built by slaves. Walker discovered the "dazzling perfection" of O'Connor's writing while taking a course on southern writers up North. Walker appreciated O'Connor's work because she wrote about southern white women with "not a whiff of magnolia" hovering in the air and about "black folks without melons and superior racial patience." Walker says, "as a college student in the sixties I read her books endlessly, scarcely conscious of the difference between her racial and economic background and my own, but put them away in anger when I discovered that, while I was reading O'Connor—Southern, Catholic, and white—there were other women writers—some Southern, some religious, all black—I had not been allowed to know." Later, after discovering black writers like Zora Neale Hurston and Jean Toomer, Walker came to look at O'Connor's fiction from a new perspective.

Alice Walker
Beyond the Peacock   *1975*

Whether one "understands" her stories or not, one knows her characters are new and wondrous creations in the world and that none of her stories—not even the earliest ones in which her consciousness of racial matters had not evolved sufficiently to be interesting or to differ much from the insulting and ignorant racial stereotyping that preceded it—could have been written by anyone else. As one can tell . . . a Picasso from a Hallmark card, one can tell an O'Connor story from any story laid next to it. Her Catholicism did not in any way limit (by defining it) her art. After her great stories of sin, damnation, prophecy and revelation, the stories one reads casually in the average magazine seem to be about love and roast beef. . . .

She destroyed the last vestiges of sentimentality in white Southern writing; she caused white women to look ridiculous on pedestals, and she approached her black characters—as a mature artist—with unusual humility and restraint. She also cast spells and worked magic with the written word.

From *In Search of Our Mother's Gardens*

The Receptive Reader

How did you react to the references to black people in O'Connor's stories? Can you relate Walker's comments to the stories you have read?

The Critic's Voice   Many critics take their clue from O'Connor's Catholicism in looking in her "startling dramas" for hints of divine love or redemption—for religious overtones that are implied rather than spelled out. The critic who wrote the following excerpt said that love is "at the very core of Flannery O'Connor's fiction."

Richard Giannone
The Mystery of Love   *1989*

There is no reason to contest the fact that human dereliction sets O'Connor's narratives in motion and directs their course and outcome. What we need to look for is the gift of grace, the exultant salute to the eternal that she avows in her lectures and correspondence and that brings her anguished conflicts to a higher resolution. "It is a sign of maturity not to be scandalized and to try to find explanations in charity." O'Connor candidly challenges us to take a charitable view of her work, and scarcely anyone has met that challenge.

A shift in the locus of inquiry will bring about a change in our perception of O'Connor. She will emerge as more than an astute recorder of casual disasters. A quiet, patient smile of controlled abandonment to love shines through all of her fictional violence. And an unexpected contour will emerge from her art. . . . To the undiscerning or the psychologically oriented,

O'Connor's unrelenting exposure of human fault might seem like obsession or preacherly harangue; for O'Connor, however, the sight of inner wretchedness precedes the experience of love. . . . The guilt and punishment that her characters bring upon themselves have no independent reality of their own, but are the dark shadows of the grace and life that O'Connor finds in existence. . . .

Her strange choices for heroes—nihilists, petty tyrants, and killers—turn out to be wanderers in love. Their encounter with the mystery of their existence, the adventurer of love whom O'Connor calls God, brings the quest to a close. All the endings take both protagonist and reader by surprise. O'Connor believes, and in powerful action shows, unfathomable reality to suggest the overwhelming boldness of divine love invading human life. Her fundamental understanding of this mysterious incursion is that love is not a human right or a mental deduction but a divine revelation, a gift of plenitude found within the human heart. "I believe love to be efficacious in the loooong run" she writes to a friend. O'Connor's fiction enacts her belief.

From *Flannery O'Connor and the Mystery of Love*

The Receptive Reader

Does this critic make you reexamine the role of the author's religious convictions in her stories? How?

WRITING ABOUT LITERATURE

9   One Author in Depth (Integrating Sources)

The Writing Workshop   When you are puzzled or provoked by your reading, you may turn to other work by the same author to see if you can find a pattern. You look for clues to familiar preoccupations or a recurrent theme. In addition, you may want to turn to personal testimony by the author—in letters, in lectures, in conversations with friends. You may be able to get help from biographers who focus on the relationship between the author and the work. Your exploration may lead to a paper in which you look for the common thread or a recurrent issue in several works by the same author.

In a paper drawing on a range of sources, your task will be to write a unified paper while integrating diverse materials. Ask yourself: What am I trying to do in this paper? Here are accounts of what gave purpose and direction to some sample projects:

✗ A student writer was intrigued by the fact that both the talkative grandmother in "A Good Man Is Hard to Find" and the mother in "Everything That Rises Must Converge" seem to live in the past, holding on to genteel traditions and to concepts of good breeding that no longer fit the realities of the South. The student found a third O'Connor story that spells out the same underlying theme even more directly: in "A Late

Encounter with the Enemy," a teacher has been taking summer classes for years to earn a belated teaching credential. She plans to have her grandfather present at her graduation. He is a Confederate general, 104 years old, and she wants him to shame the upstarts by having him there to represent the "old traditions! Dignity! Honor! Courage! My kin!" The irony of the story is that the supposed general was actually a foot soldier in the war, who was given his general's uniform by a movie company promoting *Gone with the Wind.*

✘ In a paper discussing stories by Flannery O'Connor, a student writer focused on the "moment of revelation" (the *epiphany*) when a character "suddenly accepts into his or her consciousness key facts or conditions of his or her life. " For instance, at the end of "A Good Man Is Hard to Find," the Misfit rejects the grandmother's last frantic appeal to spare her life because "I know you come from nice people." She urges him to pray and reaches out to touch him: "Why you're one of my babies. You're one of my own children!" The student writer quoted O'Connor as explaining the ending to an audience to whom she was reading this story: The grandmother realizes, "even in her limited way, that she is responsible for the man before her and joined to him by ties of kinship which have their roots deep in the mystery she has been merely prattling about so far." The paper found a similar pattern of a climactic final insight or realization in two other stories.

Writing an Integrated Paper   A paper tracing a common thread in several stories by the same author tests your ability to integrate material. Keep your paper from seeming stitched together—with too many of the seams showing. Consider guidelines like the following:

✘ *Push toward a unifying thesis.*   Note the weak *also* in the following opening paragraph of a first draft. (How are the two points raised there related?)

FIRST DRAFT   O'Connor's stories shock the reader because, as she herself says, "No matter how well we are able to soften the grotesque by humor or compassion, there is always an intensity about it that creates a general discomfort." O'Connor writes about the mixture of the frightening and the comical that we call the grotesque. The conflict between good and evil is also central to O'Connor's themes. These themes are evident in several of her stories. . . .

A more integrated trial thesis might read like this:

SECOND DRAFT   O'Connor's stories shock the reader because, as she herself says, "No matter how well we are able to soften the grotesque by humor or compassion, there is always an intensity about it that creates a general discomfort." O"Connor's preoccupation with the grotesque is rooted in one of her most basic themes: the struggle between good and evil. *When evil erupts into our ordinary world, it is frightening, but it is also comical because it is so different from what we expect or what should be.*

✗ *Chart your overall strategy.* For instance, you may decide to explore the role of violence in each of three stories, tracing important continuities and key differences as you examine *each story* in turn. You then have to make sure to keep important connections in view as you leave one story behind and move on to the next. Instead, you might plot your essay to move not from story to story but from point to point. You may set up three or four key features of the archetypal southern lady found in many of O'Connor's stories and take up *each feature* in turn. You might identify such common character traits as nostalgia for a more genteel past, outdated condescending views on race, and unrealistic expectations of the current crop of white people merely because they are white. You would then take each of these up in turn and show that each can be found in all three or four major characters you are examining.

✗ *Use brief characteristic quotations to take your reader into the author's world.* Suppose you are trying to show in a lesser-known story by O'Connor the familiar blend of the threatening and strange with the zany and comical. A web of specific references and short apt quotations will create the familiar atmosphere:

> Enoch in "Enoch and the Gorilla" is isolated from others. When he had opened "a nutty surprise" that his father had brought for him from the penitentiary, a "coiled piece of steel had sprung out at him and broken off the ends of his two front teeth." The waitress who instead of filling his order begins to fry bacon for herself bids him farewell by saying "Any way I don't see you will be all right with me." When Enoch lines up with the children waiting to shake hands with a man in a gorilla suit promoting a gorilla movie, the gorilla's hand is "the first hand that had been extended to Enoch since he had come to the city." This handshake changes Enoch's life; he attacks the hapless gorilla to take over the suit so that he can "see people waiting to shake his hand."

✗ *Test a critic's opinion against your own first-hand reading.* Do not just accept the critic's say-so as gospel. Show why the critic's comment is helpful; show why you agree or disagree. The following passage does a good job of working a critical quotation into the student writer's own text:

> Susanne M. Paulson, in *Flannery O'Connor: A Study of the Short Fiction,* says, "both the Misfit and the grandmother derive from the same human family tainted by sin and suffering in the material world." O'Connor is indeed

showing the reader that the Misfit is not an alien being but might be one of our neighbors or our own family. The Misfit himself says, "I been most everything. Been in the arm service . . . twict married, been an undertaker, been with the railroads." He says, "I was a gospel singer for a while." We could have encountered him anywhere in familiar everyday reality.

✖ *Pay special attention to transitions.* You will need strong ties and cross-references between the several different stories you are discussing. Suppose you are moving on from the story about the Misfit to the story about Enoch and the gorilla. Avoid a lame transition like "We see similar themes in another O'Connor story." Provide the missing link between the two sections of your paper. Show a strong thematic connection by highlighting a major shared element:

TRANSITION   Like the Misfit in "A Good Man Is Hard to Find," Enoch in "Enoch and the Gorilla" is also a "misfit" in his world.

What is the focus of the following student paper? How successful is it in integrating material from several different stories? How successful is it in defining and making meaningful a key term in critical discussions of O'Connor's work?

Sample Student Paper

Flannery O'Connor's Grotesques

The grotesque: absurdly incongruous; departing markedly from the natural, the expected, or the typical . . . a combination of horror and humor.

This definition of the word *grotesque* perfectly describes the life of Flannery O'Connor. After all, isn't it absurd and unexpected that, as a young woman of twenty-five, her bones were so weak from lupus that she was forced to hobble around on crutches like a woman of eighty? Or ironic that she would eventually die from complications of an abdominal operation that was supposed to help improve her condition? And despite the horror O'Connor undoubtedly had to deal with during her illness, she still held a positive outlook on life, writing shortly before her relapse and death in 1964, "I intend to survive this." This absurdity, this incongruity, this grotesqueness that seemed to dominate the path of her life has carried over into O'Connor's writing, as can be seen in the short stories "A Good Man Is Hard to Find," "Everything That Rises Must Converge," and "Enoch and the Gorilla." In each of these stories lurk characteristics of the grotesque—descriptions and comparisons that seem unnatural or incongruous, ideas that are absurd or unexpected, and that same ironic combination of horror and positive humor that haunted O'Connor throughout her illness.

Perhaps it was her own physical illness that caused O'Connor's fascination with physical deformity. Many brief descriptions in her stories reflect this fascination, such as in "Everything That Rises Must Converge," when Julian turned his stricken mother over and saw that "her face was fiercely distorted. One eye, large and staring, moved slightly to the left as if it had become unmoored." This sense of grotesque distortion is also evident in the description of Enoch putting on the gorilla suit in "Enoch and the Gorilla." O'Connor portrays the act as a weird metamorphosis, as if the boy were actually turning into a gorilla:

> In the uncertain light, one of his lean white legs could be seen to disappear and then the other, one arm and then the other: a black heavier shaggier figure replaced his. For an instant, it had two heads, one light and one dark. . . .

Likewise, the comparisons O'Connor draws between two objects often seem unnatural or incongruous. In "A Good Man Is Hard to Find," the mother's face is described as "broad and innocent as a cabbage," which I found to be a peculiar comparison. Similarly, in "Enoch and the Gorilla," Enoch's broken umbrella is compared to "an instrument for some specialized kind of torture that had gone out of fashion," which I thought was a warped, distorted way of viewing a common household object.

The descriptions and comparisons were not the only hints of distortion or unnaturalness. In fact, some of O'Connor's main story ideas contain elements of the unnatural or the unexpected, sometimes to the point of absurdity. In "A Good Man Is Hard to Find," the whole idea of the grandmother trying to talk a hardened criminal out of killing her on the basis that she is "a good lady" and of "good blood" is absurd. The situation becomes even more ridiculous when the grandmother and the Misfit begin very nonchalantly to discuss the weather, or when the grandmother, showing her good breeding and southern hospitality, kindly offers him one of her own son's shirts to wear, despite the fact that he is just about to have her son killed and is planning to own the shirt the son had been wearing.

Also unexpected and absurd is the Misfit's exceedingly calm and polite manner. In fact, when he notices that the mother is getting very uneasy and anxious, he politely asks her, "Lady, would you and that little girl like to step off yonder with Bobby Lee and Hiram and join your husband?" to which the mother answers in obvious relief, "Yes, thank you." Ever the gentleman, he orders his men to "Hep that lady up."

Although the Misfit's gentlemanly mannerisms are very surprising, perhaps the most unexpected part of the story occurs when the grandmother has been talking to the Misfit for a while. Suddenly feeling as if she were beginning to understand him, she declares, "Why, you're one of my babies. You're one of my own children!" Ironically it is at this moment of understanding and intimacy that the Misfit chooses to kill her.

Despite the grim ending of this and the other two stories, there is evidence of an ironic blending of humor with horror. In "A Good Man Is Hard to Find," the images of the cat jumping onto Bailey's shoulder, "clinging like a caterpillar," and the children scrambling out of the overturned car shouting, "'We've had an ACCI-DENT!'" are humorous. In fact, even after we realize the mother has suffered serious injury, the accident still seems funny in a sick sort of way.

Similarly, in "Enoch and the Gorilla," Enoch's nervous introduction to Gonga the Gorilla is hilarious, although we know how hurt and humiliated Eoch must have felt afterwards:

> "My name is Enoch Emery," he mumbled. "I attended the Rodemill Boys' Bible Academy. I work at the city zoo. I seen two of your pictures. I'm only eighteen years old but I already work for he city. My daddy made me come . . ." and his voice cracked . . . "You go take a jump," a surly voice inside the ape-suit said.

In "Everything That Rises Must Converge," the humor found in Julian's rebellious fantasies in which he "brought home a beautiful suspiciously Negroid woman" or "imagined his mother lying desperately ill and his being able to secure only a Negro doctor for her" lies on the surface of a pain that lurks underneath, the pain of his and his mother's strained relationship. The humor is there, but the underlying pain and horror make it feel warped and distorted.

This warping of reality, this distortion of common things, this grotesqueness, is something O'Connor shows an affinity for and a talent in using. Through her manipulation of unnatural comparisons, unexpected and absurd ideas, and humor laced with horror, she shows how even her most self-righteous characters are not clean of the grotesque. Despite the grandmother's "good blood," she too was grotesque in her absurd conversation with the Misfit. Even bright, young, non-prejudiced, socially aware Julian was tainted with the grotesque because of the delight he took in destroying his mother's comfortable little dreamworld in which she and her ancestors had a special identity. O'Connor has a knack for using distortion to create a confusing environment for her characters in which the line between the "good" and "evil" characters is very finely drawn. As one critic put it, "the real grotesques are the self-justified, the apparent grotesques may be the blessed."

Questions

How would you sum up the student writer's definition of the key term? What is the writer's strategy for structuring the paper? How adequate or convincing are the examples? What questions does the paper leave unanswered?

10 Perspectives

The Reader's Response

Writing disappears unless there is a response to it.
BARBARA CHRISTIAN

FOCUS ON CRITICAL PERSPECTIVES

Literature is not dead letters on a page. It is not really a self-contained text that is the same for all. Living literature is created by a human being and recreated in the mind of the reader, listener, or spectator. Critical discussions of literature may focus our attention on different facets of this interaction:

✘ *We may focus on the work itself.* Much of the time we encounter literature as **text** on the printed page. (We may also be listening to it— at readings or on tape, sometimes with stories or poems read by the original author.) We try to do justice to "what is there"—to respond to what the author has put in the story, the poem, the play.

✘ *We may focus on the writer.* For the **author,** the crucial experience is in the joy and challenge of creation. The excitement is in making the story, the poem, or the play take shape. At the same time, we need to see the work in context: The writer is a human being enmeshed in the needs, passions, and loyalties of human existence. The writer's perspective is influenced by race or ethnic background, gender, and social class. In the process of creation, writers are influenced by tradition, by their reading of other authors. The way writers write reflects how they observe or rebel against the conventions of their craft. It reflects how they exploit the opportunities and deal with the limitations of language.

✘ *We may focus on the reader.* For the reader, literature comes to life in the interaction between the text and its audience. What readers bring to a story or a poem shapes what they see. Readers do not come to their reading with an idling, empty mind. Critics stressing **reader response** focus on how the experience, expectations, and needs that readers bring to a story shape their reading of the text. A story is words on a page until the reader's imagination brings it to life in the theater of the

266

mind. Readers experience and reconstruct a story or a poem in accordance with their own vital concerns and interests. They provide the "missing bridges" between the world of the story and their own personal experience (Wolfgang Iser).

Here are agendas that help explain how a critic responds to a work of literature:

Author Biography   How much need we know about the author? **Author biography** aims at a full accounting of the author's life and times. It studies the setting of the artist's work. We should see John Steinbeck, for instance, in the context of the California fishing and farming region that was his home. We need to see his sympathy with the down-and-out against the background of the Great Depression of the thirties. Millions were losing their jobs, their homes, and their sense of self-worth. An era of poverty and despair helps explain his ties with the Communist party, "in dubious battle" (the title of one of his books) against the capitalist system that had failed a generation of American workers and farmers.

Today's biographers often go beyond an author's public image—the warm-hearted storyteller, the loving parent. Practicing the art of the **exposé,** they probe the personal problems behind the public persona. Best-selling author biographies dwell on childhood traumas or failed personal relationships.

Formalist Criticism   Can we read a poem or a story as a self-contained complete whole? Instead of focusing on the author's life and times, the **New Criticism** (originally new in the forties and fifties) focused on the work itself. It focused on a story or poem as a finely crafted finished artifact, repaying close study of its verbal texture, imagery, or pattern. Critics paying close attention to form and technique are often called **formalists,** a label implying that *too much* attention is being paid to form rather than to the larger meanings.

Rather than studying the background, the author, or the times, critics in this tradition let the work speak for itself. Instead of bringing information to a story from the outside, readers read *out of* the story what it had to say about current politics, contemporary religion, or whatever. In practice, this approach meant above all **close reading** of the text itself. In a New Critical reading of a short story or poem, every word or every detail counts. Critics paid detailed attention to image, symbol, irony, and point of view. They disliked fiction with a simple-minded message, steering readers instead to fiction that was challenging, subtle, and complex. Critical favorites were authors like William Faulkner, whose "A Rose for Emily" is an early example of his reliance on multilayered symbols, weighty hints and allusions, intermeshing flashbacks, and sudden revelations.

Psychoanalytic Criticism   Does close formal analysis slight the connection between literature and life? Literature that moves us powerfully speaks to our needs, desires, and traumas as thinking, feeling human beings. **Psychoanalytic** critics, or critics influenced by psychoanalysis, early claimed that a story grips the readers' imagination when it engages with deep-seated concerns, agendas, or traumas in their own personal experience. The **symbolic action** of the story takes them through a process of recognizing their own psychological burdens and trying to cope with them. Often these are rooted in traumatic early childhood experiences or family conflicts—repressed or thwarted love for the mother, rebellion against a domineering father, or sibling rivalry. Seen from the perspective of Freudian psychology, the neuroses or maladjustments of adult life are rooted in what happened to people in their earliest formative childhood years.

In the tradition of the depth psychology of the Austrian neurologist Sigmund Freud (1856–1939) and his followers, psychoanalytic critics assume a basic similarity between the world of dreams and the world created by the imagination of a great artist. In both, according to Freud, repressed material beyond the grasp of the conscious intellect rises from the unconscious. It lets us know things about ourselves that we did not suspect. With a writer like Kafka, the psychoanalytic critic has a head start: many of Kafka's stories have the feverish, oppressive quality of an anxiety dream, a nightmare that we find hard to shake off.

Myth Criticism   Does literature speak to knowledge deeply embedded in the collective unconscious? **Myth** critics looked for the echoes of myths and archetypes anchored in the collective racial memory of the human species. Stories that have a powerful hold on the reader activate unconscious memories of basic patterns of human life. Archetypes are "the psychic residue" of numberless experiences "deeply implanted in the memory of the race." Although they may seem strange on the surface, there is "that within us which leaps at the sight of them, a cry of the blood which tells us we have known them always" (Gilbert Murray). In much imaginative literature, followers of the Swiss psychologist Carl Jung (1875–1961) trace patterns of initiation into adulthood or rituals of death and rebirth that find a profound echo in our "racial memory."

Marxist Criticism   What are the social responsibilities of writers and artists? **Marxist** critics focus on how literature mirrors, distorts, or tries to change social and economic reality. They look at the way a writer's assumptions and loyalties are shaped by social class and economic status. They study the way the power structure of a society tries to use and at times suppress literature for its own purposes. Much criticism indebted to a Marxist perspective examines the way literary works deal with patterns of power and powerlessness, domination and oppression, wealth and exploitation.

The German Jewish political scientist Karl Marx (1818–1883), coauthor of the *Communist Manifesto,* made economic relations and social class the key to his analysis of bourgeois society. Marxist critics look for the social and political implications of a writer's work. To what social class does the author belong? Does a writer accept or attack the existing class structure? Much traditional literature mirrors or serves a society of wealth and status. Openly or by implication, it endorses the privileged status of a feudal aristocracy or of the bourgeois middle class. A writer who keeps quiet about the injustices of his society endorses and supports them by implication. Artists and writers lend the prestige of culture to unjust social systems.

In a story like Tillie Olsen's "I Stand Here Ironing," the grinding poverty and the impersonality of the institutions shape the mother's and the daughter's lives. Although the story has a stark, documentary quality, like other working-class literature it appeals to our social conscience; it indicts a system that grinds honest working people into the dust.

Feminist Criticism   How does literature mirror, perpetuate, or challenge the condition of women? **Feminist** critics heighten our awareness of how literature reflects or questions traditional gender roles. They have asked readers to reread literary classics from the perspective of the woman reader. How have traditional assumptions about what it means to be male or female shaped the literature of the past? How have these assumptions shaped the way scholars or critics have interpreted the classics of our literary heritage? Today many readers reread traditional texts with a heightened awareness of how they mirror traditional patterns of disenfranchisement or oppression. They reread the novels of some of the great women novelists of the past, like Charlotte Brontë's *Jane Eyre,* with an eye on how they anticipate the struggle of later generations for equality and liberation.

Feminist critics have a special interest in female authors and their neglect or recognition in a male-dominated culture. They have championed or rediscovered writers like Edith Wharton, Kate Chopin, and Zora Neale Hurston, who were slighted by critics putting a premium on stylistic experiment or technical sophistication. Feminists find special relevance in a story like Charlotte Perkins Gilman's "The Yellow Wallpaper," which chronicles the experience of a woman driven to the brink of madness by a domineering, insensitive male medical establishment.

Deconstructionism   **Deconstructionists** show the strong influence of French intellectuals of the sixties and seventies and their radical critique of traditional society and culture. Jacques Derrida, pioneer of deconstructionism, made it his aim to "disrupt," to undermine traditional notions of structure and objective truth. He insisted on the inherent, insoluble contradictions of our available think schemes, including his own. All systems of concepts are suspect; they can be used at best in a provisional, experimental way to see what they will yield in a given situation.

Deconstructionist critics probe beyond the finished surface of a story. Having been written by a human being with unresolved conflicts and contradictory emotions, a story may disguise rather than reveal the underlying anxieties or perplexities of the author. Below the surface, unresolved tensions or contradictions may account for the true dynamics of the story. A story may have one message for the ordinary unsophisticated reader and another for a reader who responds to its subtext, its subsurface ironies. Readers who deconstruct a text will be "resistant" readers. They will not be taken in by what a story says on the surface but will try "to penetrate the disguises" of the text. They may be especially attracted to works that used to be considered flawed because they seemed unfinished or contradictory.

Multicultural Perspectives   As late as 1970, the African American poet Ishmael Reed could say that "in this country art is what white people do." However, he also said, "it may turn out that the great restive underground language arising from the American slums and fringe communities is the real American poetry and prose, that can tell you the way things are happening now." In the years since, publishers, teachers, and critics have recognized a wide range of authors from minority backgrounds. They have tried to honor the true diversity of America's rich multicultural tradition. Among writers widely published and discussed are African-American writers like Alice Walker, Toni Morrison, Terry McMillan, and August Wilson; Spanish-American (Latino/Latina) authors like Victor Villaseñor, Sandra Cisneros, and Gary Soto; Asian-American authors like Tam Lin, Maxine Hong Kingston, Frank Chin, and David Henry Whang; and Native American authors like Louise Erdrich, Joy Harjo, and Leslie Marmon Silko.

Critics responding to the full multicultural range of imaginative literature have broadened their assumptions and criteria to reckon with the influence of nonwhite, non-Western traditions. They probe the way current fiction or poetry reflects minority experience. For instance, studying the fiction of Morrison or Walker, they may deal with the legacy of racism, the rediscovery of African roots, antagonism between black women and black men, or the role of the Black Muslim movement in the African-American community.

CONTEXTS FOR READING

Critics present differing personal readings of a story or poem. They may build their interpretation on a close analysis of details that other readers may have overlooked. In interviews and critical biographies, they probe an author's intentions and the relation between the author's life and work. In recent years, especially, critics have placed works of literature in the context of the larger culture. They may involve the reader in sexual politics, the class struggle, or theories about the workings of language.

Toni Cade Bambara

Interviewers have extensively questioned well-known current writers. The following excerpts are from a long interview Claudia Tate conducted with Toni Cade Bambara and included in the book *Black Women Writers at Work*. In this part of the interview, Bambara talks to the interviewer about being a woman and a writer, being a black writer in a white-dominated society, and balancing the personal motives and political challenges of being a writer.

Trying to Stay Centered   1985

C.T.:   How does being black and female constitute a particular perspective in your work?

BAMBARA: As black and woman in a society systematically orchestrated to oppress each and both, we have a very particular vantage point and, therefore, have a special contribution to make to the collective intelligence, to the literatures of this historical moment. I'm clumsy and incoherent when it comes to defining that perspective in specific and concrete terms, worse at assessing the value of my own particular pitch and voice in the overall chorus. I leave that to our critics, to our teachers and students of literature. I'm a nationalist; I'm a feminist, at least that. That's clear, I'm sure, in the work. My story "Medley" could not have been written by a brother, nor could "A Tender Man" have been written by a white woman. Those two stories are very much cut on the bias, so to speak, by a seamstress on the inside of the cloth. I am about the empowerment and development of our sisters and of our community. That sense of caring and celebration is certainly reflected in the body of my work and has been consistently picked up by other writers, reviewers, critics, teachers, students. But as I said, I leave that hard task of analysis to the analysts. I do my work and I try not to blunder.

C.T.:   How do you fit writing into your life?

BAMBARA: Up until recently, I had never fully appreciated the sheer anguish of that issue. I never knew what the hell people were talking about when they asked, "How do you manage to juggle the demands of motherhood, teaching, community work, writing and the rest?" Writing had never been a central activity in my life. It was one of the things I did when I got around to it or when the compulsion seized me and sat me down. The short story, the article, the book review, after all, are short-term pieces. I would simply commandeer time, space, paper and pen, close the door, unplug the phone, get ugly with would-be intruders and get to work for a few days. Recently, however, working on a novel and a few movie scripts—phew! I now know what that question means and I despair. I had to renegotiate a great many relationships that fell apart around me; the novel took me out of action for nearly a year. I was unfit to work—couldn't draft a simple office memo, couldn't keep track of time, blew meetings, refused to answer the door, wasn't interested in hanging out in any way, shape, or form. My daughter hung in there, screened calls, learned to iron her own clothes and generally kept out of my sight. My mama would look at me funny every now and then, finding that days had gone by and I hadn't gotten around to combing my hair or calling her to check in and just chat. Short stories are a piece of time. The novel is a way of life.

I have no shrewd advice to offer developing writers about this business of snatching time and space to work. I do not have anything profound to offer mother-writers or worker-writers except to say that it will cost you something. Anything of value is going to cost you something. I'm not much of a caretaker, for example, in relationships. I am not consistent about giving vibrancy and other kinds of input to a relationship. I don't always remember the birthdays, the anniversaries. There are periods when I am the most attentive and thoughtful lover in the world, and periods, too, when I am just unavailable. I have never learned, not yet anyway, to apologize for or continually give reassurance about what I'm doing. I'm not terribly accountable or very sensitive to other people's sense of being beat back, cut out, blocked, shunted off.

I've had occasion, as you can well imagine, to talk about just this thing with sister writers. How do the children handle your "absence"—standing at the stove flipping them buckwheats but being totally elsewhere? How does your man deal with the fact that you are just not there and it's nothing personal? Atrocity tales, honey, and sad. I've known playwrights, artists, filmmakers—brothers I'm talking about—who just do not understand, or maybe pretend not to understand, that mad fit that gets hold of me and makes me prefer working all night and morning at the typewriter to playing poker or going dancing. It's a trip. But some years ago, I promised myself a period of five years to tackle this writing business in a serious manner. It's a priority item now—to master the craft, to produce, to stick to it no matter how many committee meetings get missed.

My situation isn't nearly as chary as others I know. I'm not a wife, and my daughter couldn't care less what the house looks like so long as the hamper isn't overflowing. I'm not a husband; I do not have the responsibility of trying to live up to "provider." I'm not committed to any notion of "career." Also, I'm not addicted to anything—furniture, cars, wardrobe, etc.—so there's no sense of sacrifice or foolishness about how I spend my time in non-money-making pursuits. Furthermore, I don't feel obliged to structure my life in respectably routine ways; that is to say, I do not mind being perceived as a "weirdo" or whatever. My situation is, perhaps, not very characteristic; I don't know. But to answer the question—I just flat out announce I'm working, leave me alone and get out of my face. When I "surface" again, I try to apply the poultices and patch up the holes I've left in relationships around me. That's as much as I know how to do . . . so far.

C.T.:   What determines your responsibility to yourself and to your audience?

BAMBARA: I start with the recognition that we are at war, and that war is not simply a hot debate between the capitalist camp and the socialist camp over which economic/political/social arrangement will have hegemony in the world. It's not just the battle over turf and who has the right to utilize resources for whomsoever's benefit. The war is also being fought over the truth: what is the truth about human nature, about the human potential? My responsibility to myself, my neighbors, my family and the human family is to try to tell the truth. That ain't easy. There are so few truth-speaking traditions in this society in which the myth of "Western civilization" has claimed the allegiance of so many. We have rarely been encouraged and equipped to appreciate the fact that the truth works, that it releases the Spirit and that it is a joyous thing. We live in a part of the world, for example, that equates criticism with assault, that equates social responsibility with naive idealism, that defines the unrelenting pursuit of knowledge and wisdom as fanaticism.

I do not think that literature is *the* primary instrument for social transformation, but I do think it has potency. So I work to tell the truth about people's lives; I work to celebrate struggle, to applaud the tradition of struggle in our community, to bring to center stage all those characters, just ordinary folks on the block, who've been waiting in the wings, characters we thought we had to ignore because they weren't pimp-flashy or hustler-slick or because they didn't fit easily into previously acceptable modes or stock types. I want to lift up some usable truths—like the fact that the simple act of corn-rowing one's hair is radical in a society that defines beauty as blonde tresses blowing in the wind; that staying centered in the best of one's own cultural tradition is hip, is sane, is perfectly fine despite all claims to universality-through-Anglo-Saxonizing and other madnesses.

It would be dishonest, though, to end my comments there. First and foremost I write for myself. Writing has been for a long time my major tool for self-instruction and self-development. I try to stay honest through pencil and paper. I run off at the mouth a lot. I've a penchant for flamboyant performance. I exaggerate to the point of hysteria. I cannot always be trusted with my mouth open. But when I sit down with the notebooks, I am absolutely serious about what I see, sense, know. I write for the same reason I keep track of my dreams, for the same reason I meditate and practice being still—to stay in touch with me and not let too much slip by me. We're about building a nation; the inner nation needs building, too. I would be writing whether there were a publishing industry or not, whether there were presses or not, whether there were markets or not.

The Receptive Reader

What is Bambara's attitude toward critics? What for her is the connection between being black and being a woman? What for her are the special challenges and demands of being a woman and a writer? How does she cope with them? What is her view of the political responsibilities or potential of literature? What is the personal meaning her writing has for her?

Stanley Kozikowski

The **New Criticism,** or formalism, became influential in the forties and fifties and dominated the teaching of literature for decades. It asked readers to concentrate on the literary text in front of them and give it an intense close reading. In a New Critical reading of a short story or poem, every detail is potentially significant, contributing to the meaning of the whole. Like the author of the following critical analysis, critics influenced by this tradition find symbolic significance, unsuspected double meanings, and thematic echoes in words and objects that the casual reader might overlook.

Symbolism in "Hills like White Elephants"   *1994*

Recent observations about the bamboo curtain in Hemingway's "Hills like White Elephants," particularly those of Sherlyn Abdoo, draw suggestive reference to the richly and immensely detailed pattern of Hemingway's story. The pivotal image of the curtained doorway, I would add, is even more powerfully implicated in the story's highly imaginative structure of contrasting meanings than is already assumed to be the case. The image, as it is signaled in the figural consciousness of "the girl" and in the literal awareness of "the man" helps the reader to reformulate the events of the story into a new coherence.

Hills are like white elephants for Jig because they carry ambivalent evocations of the child within her—like a white elephant, an unwanted gift, a seemingly remote but immense problem. They ominously suggest the pallid skin tone of a stillborn infant, but they also evoke that which is "bright," "lovely," beautiful with the promise of life, and intrinsically of value, as was the highly esteemed Siamese white elephant. Stirring Jig's acute apprehension and her cherished affections, the apparently distant hills attract to the "very hot" and "dry" Ebro plain and the train station an uncomfortable but refreshing "warm wind" that blows through the bamboo curtain. To this bimodal breeze, the American man and Jig respond differently: He feels it as a simple, quick remedy to a removable annoyance. She experiences it, in her ambivalence, as a "lovely" invigoration, at the very moment that she has looked upon the "lovely hills," which are like white elephants—fearfully unwanted but precious.

To the American man, as distant from metaphor as he is from the hills, the "wind" of the hills simply defines casually and literally what an abortion is: As "the warm wind blew the bead curtain against the table," he is quick to say, "I know you wouldn't mind it, Jig. It's really not anything. It's just to let the air in. . . . I'll go with you. . . . They just let the air in and then it's perfectly natural."

Jig's reaction, delayed but deliberate, and consistent with her sense of what the hills are like, is signaled in the doorway. The wind through the bamboo curtain illustrates for her the sweet past and the bitter present. The curtain, painted with the words "Anis del Toro," signifies the sweet-now-bitter anise-seed of the bull. In the very drinks that both have, it conveys to the man, with doltish literalism, "a drink," but to Jig, a licorice taste grown as bitter as wormwood—the very taste evoking "all the things you've waited so long for, like absinthe." Jig, again figuratively, thus experiences what life—precious and unwanted—is "like." The breeze, the moving beaded curtain, and the evocative drink—like hills like white elephants—connote to Jig the sweet promise of seeding and the bitter termination of birthing. The same objects convey to the man an easy sense of exit, excision, and getting on with other things. Ever opposite, his ironic and brutal, but now figurative, words, "Oh, cut it out," are answered by Jig's sharp but now literal, "You started it"—a remarkable counterpoint of clauses, playing off his dour, unimaginative indelicacy against her superb delicacy of self-awareness.

Just as Jig holds the two strings of bamboo beads blown into her hand, she maintains full literal possession of her self and her child, as we see in the story's culminating design. But Jig nevertheless has an abortion of sorts, one precisely like hills like white elephants: Having taken "the [not their] two bags"—"Two heavy bags" to the other side of the station, symbolically the mother and child, the man then goes into the bar from that other side, drinks "an Anis at the bar," and finally, with an astonishing irony to which he is oblivious, struts "out through the bead curtain" to the table outside, where Jig and he had sat previously, and where Jig, now smiling, remains seated. Conveyed out from the barroom, through the breezy doorway, through which the "air" gets "let in" from the other side, "the man" (appropriately nameless, mere reiterated "seed" from "bull"—Anis del Toro—but now like an aerated fetus himself) is ironically terminated, expelled—in her (now triumphantly ironic figural) consciousness—from any further relationship with Jig. Clearly, Jig and her child have now come out literally "fine" after this "awfully simple operation." He, metaphorically, goes "out through the bead curtain" and out of their lives.

Reasonably, Jig's name, which among its various meanings denotes a device that separates waste from precious ore (*OED*), symbolizes her excision of the identityless "man"—his bull and seed—from her and her precious child's lives. Moreover, Jig's literally precise "nothing wrong with me" addresses numerous ambivalent references to "things" in the story—the man's naming the child within as an "only thing" and Jig's perception of the child as "everything." With splendid verbal and situational irony, Hemingway's American man, aborted from Jig's world, becomes the very "nothing"—the white elephant—that he had urged Jig to renounce and remove from their lives moments before. We may now fathom Jig's "smile" as she grasps how indeed things can be like other things—hills can be like white elephants, and lovers, too—in Hemingway's bravely and imaginatively affecting tale.

From *The Explicator*

The Receptive Reader

According to this reading, how do details of the setting and the words and movements of the characters mirror the major symbolic action of the story? For instance, what does this reader make of the white elephants, the breeze, the moving beaded curtain, the drink? How does he show that the man and the woman in the story read their setting and their situation in very different ways? What for this reader is the heart of the story?

Sandra M. Gilbert and Susan Gubar

In 1985, Sandra M. Gilbert and Susan Gubar published a comprehensive anthology of literature in English by women. Their book was designed to help rediscover women writers neglected or ignored in the patriarchal, male-dominated literary tradition. In an earlier book, *The Madwoman in the Attic* (1979), they had traced images of imprisonment and escape in the work of the great English and American women writers of the nineteenth century. They discussed recurrent symbolic uses of madness as an escape from the intolerable restrictions society imposed on women and women writers. In the following excerpt, the two authors read Charlotte Perkins Gilman's "The Yellow Wallpaper" from a **feminist** perspective. The story becomes a "paradigmatic" tale that "seems to tell *the* story" that all literary women could tell if they were to give voice to their experience as women and writers.

Enclosure and Escape: Gilman's "The Yellow Wallpaper"   *1979*

As if to comment on the unity of all these points—on, that is, the anxiety-inducing connections between what women writers tend to see as their parallel confinements in texts, houses, and maternal female bodies—Charlotte Perkins Gilman brought them all together in 1890 in a striking story of female confinement and escape, a paradigmatic tale which (like *Jane Eyre*) seems to tell *the* story that all literary women would tell if they could speak their "speechless woe." "The Yellow Wallpaper," which Gilman herself called "a description of a case of nervous breakdown," recounts in the first person the experiences of a woman who is evidently suffering from a severe postpartum psychosis. Her husband, a censorious and paternalistic physician, is treating her according to methods by which S. Weir Mitchell, a famous "nerve specialist," treated Gilman herself for a similar problem. He has confined her to a large garret room in an "ancestral hall" he has rented, and he has forbidden her to touch pen to paper until she is well again, for he feels, says the narrator, "that with my imaginative power and habit of story-making, a nervous weakness like mine is sure to lead to all manner of excited fancies, and that I ought to use my will and good sense to check the tendency."

The cure, of course, is worse than the disease, for the sick woman's mental condition deteriorates rapidly. "I think sometimes that if I were only well enough to write a little it would relieve the press of ideas and rest me," she remarks, but literally confined in a room she thinks is a one-time nursery because it has "rings and things" in the walls, she is literally locked away from creativity. The "rings and things," although reminiscent of children's gymnastic equipment, are really the paraphernalia of confinement, like the gate at the head of the stairs, instruments that definitively indicate her imprisonment. Even more tormenting, however, is the room's wallpaper: a sulphurous yellow paper, torn off in spots, and patterned with "lame uncertain curves" that "plunge off at outrageous angles" and "destroy themselves in unheard of contradictions." Ancient, smoldering, "unclean" as the oppressive structures of the society in which she finds herself, this paper surrounds the narrator like an inexplicable text, censorious and overwhelming as her physician husband, haunting as the "hereditary estate" in which she is trying to survive. Inevitably she studies its suicidal implications—and inevitably, because of her "imaginative power and habit of story-making," she revises it, projecting her own passion for escape into its otherwise incomprehensible hieroglyphics. "This wallpaper," she decides, at a key point in her story,

has a kind of subpattern in a different shade, a particularly irritating one, for you can only see it in certain lights, and not clearly then.
    But in the places where it isn't faded and where the sun is just so—I can see a strange, provoking, formless sort of figure, that seems to skulk about behind that silly and conspicuous front design.

As time passes, this figure concealed behind what corresponds (in terms of what we have been discussing) to the facade of the patriarchal text becomes clearer and clearer. By moonlight the pattern of the wallpaper "becomes bars! The outside pattern I mean, and the woman behind it is as plain as can be." And eventually, as the narrator sinks more deeply into what the world calls madness, the terrifying implications of both the paper and the figure imprisoned behind the paper begin to permeate—that is, to *haunt*—the rented ancestral mansion in which she and her husband are immured. The "yellow smell" of the paper "creeps all over the house," drenching every room in its subtle aroma of decay. And the woman creeps too—through the house, in the house, and out of the house, in the garden and "on that long road under the trees." Sometimes, indeed, the narrator confesses, "I think there are a great many women" both behind the paper and creeping in the garden, "and sometimes only one, and she crawls around fast, and her crawling shakes [the paper] all over. . . . And she is all the time trying to climb through. But nobody could climb through that pattern—it strangles so; I think that is why it has so many heads."

Eventually it becomes obvious to both reader and narrator that the figure creeping through and behind the wallpaper is both the narrator and the narrator's double. By the end of the story, moreover, the narrator has enabled this double to escape from her textual/architectural confinement: "I pulled and she shook, I shook and she pulled, and before morning we had peeled off yards of that paper." Is the message of the tale's conclusion mere madness? Certainly the righteous Doctor John—whose name links him to the anti-hero of Charlotte Brontë's *Villette*—has been temporarily defeated, or at least momentarily stunned. "Now why should that man have fainted?" the narrator ironically asks as she creeps around her attic. But John's unmasculine swoon of surprise is the least of the triumphs Gilman imagines for her madwoman. More significant are the madwoman's own imaginings and creations, mirages of health and freedom with which her author endows her like a fairy godmother showering gold on a sleeping heroine. The woman from behind the wallpaper creeps away, for instance, creeps fast and far on the long road, in broad daylight. "I have watched her sometimes away off in the open country," says the narrator, "creeping as fast as a cloud shadow in a high wind."

Indistinct and yet rapid, barely perceptible but inexorable, the progress of that cloud shadow is not unlike the progress of nineteenth-century literary women out of the texts defined by patriarchal poetics into the open spaces of their own authority. That such an escape from the numb world behind the patterned walls of the text was a flight from dis-ease into health was quite clear to Gilman herself. When "The Yellow Wallpaper" was published she sent it to Weir Mitchell whose strictures had kept her from attempting the pen during her own breakdown, thereby aggravating her illness, and she was delighted to learn, years later, that "he had changed his treatment of nervous prostration since reading" her story. "If that is a fact," she declared, "I have not lived in vain." Because she was a rebellious feminist besides being a medical iconoclast, we can be sure that Gilman did not think of this triumph of hers in narrowly therapeutic terms. Because she knew, with Emily Dickinson, that "Infection in the sentence breeds," she knew that the cure for female despair must be spiritual as well as physical, aesthetic as well as social. What "The Yellow Wallpaper" shows she knew, too, is that even when a supposedly "mad" woman has been sentenced to imprisonment in the "infected" house of her own body, she may discover that, as Sylvia Plath was to put it seventy years later, she has "a self to recover, a queen."

The Receptive Reader

1. What is the connection between *patriarchal* and *paternalistic?*

2. What is the parallel Gilbert and Gubar trace between the way women are treated traditionally in literary texts by male authors, between the way women are treated literally in the home, and between the way their lives are traditionally defined by "maternal female bodies"?

3. How do the two critics trace the theme of imprisonment and escape in Gilman's story? What parts of the story does this discussion make you see in a new light?

Making Connections—For Discussion and Writing

How do Bambara in the interview and Gilbert and Gubar in this excerpt see the connection between literature and life?

Wilfred L. Guerin

Freud, the pioneering Austrian psychoanalyst, helped shape the thinking of many modern readers. He influenced the way they think and talk about human psychology—even if they disagree with major points of his theory. They may quarrel with his making sexual energy (or libido) an all-pervasive human motive, or with his tracing mental illness to traumatic childhood events, or with his skepticism about women's memories of sexual abuse. Much of our modern vocabulary for talking about human sexuality goes back to Freud nevertheless. Freud himself had looked to art and imaginative literature for evidence of the workings of the unconscious. Critics draw on the Freudian perspective especially when dealing with the literature that moves in the border country between waking and dream, or the conscious intellect and buried unconscious motives.

"Young Goodman Brown": Id versus Superego   *1992*

The theme of innocence betrayed is central to Nathaniel Hawthorne's "Young Goodman Brown," the tale of the young bridegroom who leaves his wife Faith to spend a night with Satan in the forest. The events of that terrifying night are a classic traumatic experience for the youth. At the center of the dark wilderness he discovers a witches' Sabbath involving all the honored teachers, preachers, and friends of his village. The climax is reached when his own immaculate bride is brought forth to stand by his side and pledge eternal allegiance to the Fiend of Hell. Following this climactic moment in which the hero resists the diabolical urge to join the fraternity of evil, he wakes to find himself in the deserted forest wondering if what has happened was dream or reality. Regardless of the answer, he is a changed man. He returns in the morning to the village and to his Faith, but he is never at peace with himself again. Henceforth he can never hear the singing of a holy hymn without also hearing the echoes of the anthem of sin from that terrible night in the forest. He shrinks even from the side of Faith. His dying hour is gloom, and no hopeful epitaph is engraved upon his tombstone.

Aside from the clearly intended allegorical meanings discussed elsewhere in this book, it is the story's underlying psychological implications that concern us here. We start with the assumption that, through symbolism and technique, "Young Goodman Brown" means more than it says. In this respect our task is one of extrapolation, an inferring of the unknown from the known. Our first premise is that Brown's journey is more than a physical one; it is a psychological one as well. To see what this journey means in psychological terms, we need to examine the setting, the time and place. Impelled by unmistakably libidinal force, the hero moves from the village of Salem into the forest. The village is a place of light and order, both social and spiritual order. Brown leaves Faith behind in the town at sunset and returns to Faith in the morning. The journey into the wilderness is taken in the night: "My journey . . . forth and back again," explains the young man to his wife, "must needs be done 'twixt now and sunrise." It is in the forest, a place of darkness and unknown terrors, that Brown meets the Devil. On one level, then, the village may be equated with consciousness, the forest with the dark recesses of the unconscious. But, more precisely, the village, as a place of social and moral order (and inhibition) is analogous to Freud's superego, conscience, the morally inhibiting agent of the psyche; the forest, as a place of wild, untamed passions and terrors, has the attributes of the Freudian id. As mediator between these opposing forces, Brown himself resembles the poor ego, which tries to effect a healthy balance and is shattered because it is unable to do so.

Why can't he reconcile these forces? Is his predicament that of all human beings, as is indicated by his common, nondistinctive surname? If so, are we all destined to die in gloom? Certainly, Hawthorne implies, we cannot remain always in the village, outside the forest. And sooner or later, we must all confront Satan. Let us examine this diabolical figure for a moment. When we first see him (after being prepared by Brown's expressed fear, "What if the devil himself should be at my very elbow!"), he is "seated at the foot of an old tree"—an allusion to the "old tree" of forbidden fruit and the knowledge of sin. He is described as "bearing a considerable resemblance" to the hero himself. He is, in short, Brown's own alter ego, the dramatic projection of a part of Brown's psyche, just as Faith is the projection of another part of his psyche. The staff Satan is carrying, similar to the maple stick he later gives to Brown, is like a "great black snake . . . a living serpent"—a standard Freudian symbol for the uncontrollable phallus. As he moves on through the forest, Brown encounters other figures, the most respected of his moral tutors: old Goody Cloyse, Deacon Gookin, and, at last, even Faith herself, her pink ribbon reflecting the ambiguity that Brown is unable to resolve, for pink is the mixture of white (for purity) and red (for passion). Thoroughly unnerved—then maddened—by disillusionment, Brown capitulates to the wild evil in this heart of darkness and becomes "himself the chief horror of the scene, [shrinking] not from its other horrors." That the whole lurid scene may be interpreted as the projection of Brown's formerly repressed impulses is indicated in Hawthorne's description of the transformed protagonist:

> In truth, all through the haunted forest there could be nothing more frightful than the figure of Goodman Brown. On he flew among the black pines, brandishing his staff with frenzied gestures, now giving vent to an inspiration of horrid blasphemy, and now shouting forth such laughter as set all the echoes of the forest laughing like demons around him. *The fiend in his own shape is less hideous than when he rages in the breast of man.* (italics added)

Though Hawthorne implies that Brown's problem is that of Everyman, he does not suggest that all humans share Brown's gloomy destiny. Like Freud, Hawthorne saw the dangers of an overactive suppression of libido and the consequent development of a tyrannous superego, though he thought of the problem in his own terms as an imbalance of head versus heart. Goodman Brown is the tragic victim of a society that has shut its eyes to the inevitable "naturalness" of sex as a part of humankind's physical and mental constitution, a society whose moral system would suppress too severely natural human impulses.

Among Puritans the word "nature" was virtually synonymous with "sin." In Hawthorne's *The Scarlet Letter,* little Pearl, illegitimate daughter of Hester Prynne and the Reverend Mr. Arthur Dimmesdale, is identified throughout as the "child of nature." In his speech to the General Court in 1645, Governor John Winthrop defined "natural liberty"—as distinguished from "civil liberty"—as a "liberty to do evil as well as good . . . the exercise and maintaining of [which] makes men grow more evil, and in time to be worse than brute beasts. . . ." Hawthorne, himself a descendant of Puritan witch hunters and a member of New England society, the moral standards of which had been strongly conditioned by its Puritan heritage, was obsessed with the nature of sin and with the psychological results of violating the taboos imposed by this system. Young Goodman Brown dramatizes the neurosis resulting from such a violation.

After his night in the forest he becomes a walking guilt complex, burdened with anxiety and doubt. Why? Because he has not been properly educated to confront the realities of the external world or of the inner world, because from the cradle on he has been indoctrinated with admonitions against tasting the forbidden fruit, and because sin and Satan have been inadvertently glamorized by prohibition, he has developed a morbid compulsion to taste of them. He is not necessarily evil; he is, like most young people, curious. But because of the severity of Puritan taboos about natural impulses, his curiosity has become an obsession. His dramatic reactions in the forest are typical of what happens in actual cases of extreme repression. Furthermore, the very nature of his wilderness fantasy substantiates Freud's theory that our repressed desires express themselves in our dreams, that dreams are symbolic forms of wish fulfillment. Hawthorne, writing more than a generation before Freud, was a keen enough psychologist to be aware of many of the same phenomena Freud was to systematize through clinical evidence.

In *Handbook of Critical Approaches to Literature,* third edition

The Receptive Reader

Does Guerin's synopsis, or brief overview of the story, include the most important points? What clues does Guerin find in the story to its symbolic, nonliteral meanings? How does Guerin show the role in the story of two key terms of Freudian psychology: the Freudian superego and the Freudian id? What does the critic mean when he says, "sooner or later, we must all confront Satan"? (How is the devil "Brown's own alter ego"?) What is the role of Brown's wife Faith in this Freudian analysis? What, according to Guerin, is Hawthorne's comment on a repressive society?

WRITING ABOUT LITERATURE

10   Examining Critical Perspectives (Documented Paper)

The Writing Workshop   For a paper based on library research, you may be asked to study in depth one important critical approach to a much-discussed story. Or, instead of studying one critical perspective in depth, you may be asked to compare two or more different critical approaches. Some sample projects:

✗ Much has been written on Nathaniel Hawthorne's richly symbolic and ambiguous "Young Goodman Brown." You might focus on critics' differing views of the relationship between Hawthorne's story and the role of sin and guilt in the Puritan tradition of New England. Was Hawthorne himself profoundly influenced by that tradition? Or was he critical of it, distancing himself from it?

✗ A classic short story like John Steinbeck's "The Chrysanthemums" or Charlotte Gilman's "The Yellow Wallpaper" will reveal new or unexpected depth when a new generation of critics looks at it from a fresh perspective. You might contrast a more traditional approach to such a story with a recent rereading from a feminist perspective.

✗ You may want to choose a Kafka story—like "A Country Doctor," "Metamorphosis," or "The Judgment." Your paper might focus on the definition of a key term. For example, you might focus on the "Jewish" Kafka; or on Kafka as the prophet of totalitarianism; or on the Freudian Kafka.

Finding Promising Leads   To work up material for your paper, you are likely to begin by checking in electronic or printed indexes for books, collections of critical articles, and individual articles in periodicals. For a writer like Kafka, Hawthorne, or O'Connor, most college libraries will have a wide range of critical and scholarly sources. Beginning with Angel Flores' *The Kafka Problem* (1946), there have been over fifty collections of critical articles on Kafka, including critical anthologies like the following:

Ronald Gray, *Kafka: A Collection of Critical Essays*

Heinz Politzer, *Franz Kafka*

Angel Flores, *The Kafka Debate*

J. P. Stern, *The World of Franz Kafka*

Kenneth Hughes, *Kafka: An Anthology of Marxist Criticism*

Ruth V. Gross, *Critical Essays on Franz Kafka*

In addition, by searching for sources with Kafka's name in the title, you might be able to locate books like Anthony Northey's *Kafka's Relatives* or articles like John Felstiner's "Looking for Kafka" (in *Stanford* for December 1991).

Scholars and students are increasingly doing much of their research on the computer. Working on a Kafka paper, you may want to check out the **website** of the Kafka Society of America <http://www.temple.edu/kafka/index.html>. Headquartered at Temple University, the society publishes a journal and organizes presentations of papers at scholarly conventions. You may want to check out the entries on Kafka in current **online encyclopedias,** like the *Britannica Online* or the Microsoft *Encarta.* You may ask your favorite **search engine** to find entries under "Kafka AND Critic." With a ballyhooed new translation of Kafka's *Castle* getting much media attention, you will be calling up literally hundreds of entries. (According to news reports, thousands of people turned out at New York's Town Hall for a panel discussion of Kafka occasioned by the new translation.)

Taking Notes   During your exploratory reading, you need to look sources over quickly, deciding whether they will be helpful. But you also have to slow down and close in when you hit upon promising materials. Remember:

✘ *Copy direct quotations accurately, word for word.*   Enclose all quoted material in quotation marks to show material copied verbatim. (Include the *closing* quotation mark to show where the quotation ends.)

✘ *Tag your notes.*   Start your notes with a tag or **descriptor.** (Indicate the subtopic or section of your paper where a quotation or piece of information will be useful.)

✘ *Include all the publishing data you will need later to identify your sources.*   Include exact page numbers for your quotations. (Also note *inclusive* page numbers for a whole article or story.) Sample notes might look like this:

Self-contained quotation

KAFKA THE WRITER

"'A Country Doctor' reveals much about Kafka's attitude toward being a writer . . . what qualifies him to be a writer, what people expected of him as a writer, what he could accomplish, what would be his ultimate fate."

Peter Mailloux, *A Hesitation Before Birth: The Life of Franz Kafka* (Newark: U of Delaware P, 1989), 392.

Partial quotation

SYMBOLS—horses

Critic John Hibberd believes Kafka's "unearthly" horses "represent the power of inspiration that promised Kafka fulfillment but carried him away to a devastating reminder of his helplessness."

John Hibberd, *Kafka in Context* (New York: Studio Vista, 1975), 84.

Distinguish clearly between **paraphrase** and direct firsthand quotation. When you paraphrase, you put someone else's ideas in your own words. You can thus highlight what seems most important to you and condense other parts. Even when you paraphrase, be sure to use quotation marks for striking phrases that you keep in the exact wording of the author. For instance, in summing up briefly a critic's view of Kafka's doctor, put in quotation marks a striking reference to the doctor himself as "the patient, the smitten victim."

Note finer points: use **single quotation marks** for a phrase that appears as a quote-within-a-quote: "Freudian critics are fascinated by Kafka's 'unearthly horses.'" Use the **ellipsis**—three spaced periods—to show an omission (see Mailloux quotation above). Use four periods when the periods include the period at the end of a sentence. **Square brackets** show that you have inserted material into the original quotation: "He became engaged [to Felice Bauer], broke off the engagement, became engaged again."

Pushing Toward a Thesis   While taking notes, you begin to follow up tentative patterns and promising connections. You start looking for a unifying thread. You look for recurrent issues; you look for a note that in your materials is struck again and again. The following might be your tentative thesis:

TRIAL THESIS: Critics again and again find a connection between the hesitations and ineffectualness of the country doctor and Kafka's own hesitations and doubts as a writer.

Using a Working Outline   Sketch out a **working outline** as soon as you have a rough idea how your material is shaping up. At first, your plan might be very tentative. A working outline is not a final blueprint; its purpose is to help you visualize a possible pattern and to help you refine it as you go along. Suppose you are moving toward a paper showing how different critical approaches make the reader notice and concentrate on different key images in a story. At an intermediate stage, your working outline might look like this:

WORKING OUTLINE: —Freudian emphasis on sexual overtones
the buttocking horses
the animalistic groom
Rose as victim
—Marxist emphasis on the doctor's social role
ineffectualness of the doctor
doctor vs. priest
immobilized doctor at the end
—religious critic's emphasis on religious symbols
wound in the side of the boy (allusion to Christ on the cross?)
jeering, hostile patients (Christ reviled?)

Drafting and Revising   In your first draft, you concentrate on feeding into your paper the evidence you have collected. Feel free to work on later sections of the paper first—concentrating on key segments and filling in the connecting threads later. In a first draft, you lay out all your material so you can step back and see how it hangs together. You can then decide what is already in good shape and what needs work.

Would major changes in strategy be advisable? A reordering of major sections might be necessary to correct awkward backtrackings. Do you need to strengthen the evidence for major points? Should you play down or take out material that distracts from your major arguments? In your first draft, quotations are likely to be chunky—you may need to weave them into the paper more smoothly during revision.

Documenting the Paper   When you draw on a range of sources—for instance, a range of critical interpretations of a story—you may be asked to provide **documentation.** In a documented paper, you fully identify your sources, furnishing complete publishing information and exact page numbers. Accurate documentation shows that your readers are welcome to go to the sources you have drawn on—to check your use of them and to get further information from them if they wish. Unless instructed otherwise, follow the current style of documentation of the Modern Language Association (MLA). This current style has done away with footnotes (though it still provides for **explanatory notes** at the end of a paper).

The current MLA style requires you to remember three simple principles:

✗ *Identify your sources briefly in your text.*   Generally, introduce a quotation by saying something like "Lucy M. Freibert says in her article on Margaret Atwood's *The Handmaid's Tale, . . .*"

✗ *Give page references in parentheses in your text.*   For instance, type (89) or (280–82). If you have not mentioned the author, this is the place to give his or her last name: (Freibert 280–82). If you are using more than one source by the same author, you may also have to specify briefly which one (Freibert, "Control," 280–82). Tag author or title in parentheses only if you have not already given the information in your running text.

✗ *Describe each source fully in a final alphabetical listing of Works Cited.*   This used to be the bibliography (literally the "book list"), but it now often includes *non*print sources—interviews, lectures, PBS broadcasts, videotapes, Internet sources, CD-ROMs. Here is a typical entry for an article in a critical journal. This entry includes volume number (a volume usually covers all issues for one year), date, and the complete page numbers for the whole article (not just the material you have quoted):

Shumaker, Conrad. "'Too Terribly Good to be Printed': Charlotte Gilman's 'The Yellow Wallpaper.'" *American Literature* 57 (1985): 588–99.

Study sample entries for your alphabetical listing of "Works Cited." Remember a few pointers:

✗ Use <u>underlining</u> (for italics) for the title of a *whole* publication. For instance, italicize or underline the title of a book-length study, a collection or anthology of stories or essays, a periodical that prints critical articles, or a newspaper that prints reviews. However, use quotation marks for titles of short stories or critical articles that are *part* of a collection.

✗ Leave one space after periods marking off chunks of information in the entry. Indent the second and following lines of each entry five spaces.

✗ Use *ed.* for editor; *trans.* for translator.

✗ Abbreviate the names of publishing houses (Prentice for Prentice-Hall, Inc; Southern Illinois UP for Southern Illinois University Press). Abbreviate the names of the months: Dec., Apr., Mar.

Primary sources: Listing of short stories, letters, interviews

Cheever, John. *The Stories of John Cheever.* New York: Knopf, 1978.
[Collected stories of the author. The publisher's name is short for Alfred A. Knopf.]

O'Connor, Flannery. *Everything That Rises Must Converge.* New York: Farrar, 1965.
[A selection of the author's stories, named after the title story. Name of publisher is short for Farrar, Straus and Giroux.]

Achebe, Chinua. "Dead Men's Path." *The Story and Its Writer: An Introduction to Short Fiction.* Ed. Ann Charters. 3rd ed. Boston: Bedford, 1991. 10–12.
[A story reprinted in an anthology, with editor's name and number of edition and with inclusive page numbers for the story.]

Cheever, Benjamin, ed. *The Letters of John Cheever.* New York: Simon, 1988.
[Author's correspondence, edited by his son.]

Faulkner, William. Interview. *Writers at Work: The* Paris Review *Interviews.* Ed. Malcolm Cowley. New York: Viking-Compass, 1959. 122–41.
[Compass was an imprint, or special line of books, of Viking Press. The title of the *Paris Review* is roman—straight type—to set it off from italicized book title.]

Tan, Amy. Lecture. *Visiting Author Series.* Santa Clara, 12 Jan. 1992.
[Talk by an author as part of a lecture series]

Secondary sources: Listing of critical studies, articles, or reviews

Abel, Darrel. *The Moral Picturesque: Studies in Hawthorne's Fiction.* West Lafayette: Purdue UP, 1988.
[Book with subtitle, published by a university press.]

Emrich, Wilhelm. *Franz Kafka: A Critical Study of His Writings.* Trans. Sheema Zeben Buehne. New York: Ungar, 1968.
[Book with translator's name.]

Cady, Edwin H., and Louis J. Budd, ed. Introduction. *On Hawthorne: The Best from American Literature.* Durham: Duke UP, vi–x.
[Introduction to a collection with two editors—only the first typed with last name first. Page number for prefaces and the like are given in small roman numerals. Use roman type (not italics) for title within title.]

Freibert, Lucy M. "Control and Creativity: The Politics of Risk in Margaret Atwood's *The Handmaid's Tale.*" *Critical Essays on Margaret Atwood.* Ed. Judith McCombs. Boston: Hall, 1988. 280–91.
[Article in a collection, with inclusive page numbers. Note "Ed." for the editor who assembled the collection.]

Davenport, Mary. "Today's Minimalist Fiction." *New York Times* 15 May 1991, late ed. , sec. 2: 1+.
[Newspaper article, with edition and section specified. Article starts on page 1 and continues later in the newspaper.]

Shumaker, Conrad. "'Too Terribly Good to be Printed': Charlotte Gilman's 'The Yellow Wallpaper.'" *American Literature* 57 (1985): 588–99.
[Journal article, with volume number and inclusive page numbers. Note quotation in title—single quotation marks; note that title of story is quoted in title of article—single quotation marks. Sometimes number of volume *and* issue may be needed when pages are not numbered consecutively throughout a single volume: *Fiction Review* 14. 3 (1992): 17–21.]

The Art of the Story. Narr. Pat Evans. Writ. and prod. Jeremiah Phelps. KCBM, San Benito. 17 Nov. 1991.
[A television program with names of narrator and writer-producer. Should be listed alphabetically under "Art."]

Electronic sources: Online, CD-ROM, e-mail

Guidelines for documenting electronic sources are being updated as new technology evolves and users make it serve their purposes. The following guidelines are based on the section on electronic sources in the *MLA Style Manual* (Second Edition, 1998). For most of your entries, start with as much of the usual publishing information as is available—including authors, titles, and dates. However, include the **access date**—the date you accessed the source or site. The date of access will often follow the date the material was published or posted. (The access date can tell your reader how recently the material was available.)

For material from the net, include the **Internet address**—the URL (uniform resource locator). Put it between angled brackets. Typically, the electronic address will start with the access mode, usually **<http:// ....>.** (Other access modes include *telnet* and *ftp.*) The address will then go on to the relevant path and specific file names (often beginning with **www.** for World Wide Web) Try to have the whole URL on the same line, or else try to have a break only after a period or slash. Make sure that dots, slashes, colons, capitals, and spacing are exactly right. (Do not add hyphens or final periods.)

For material from other electronic sources, specify the **medium,** such as CD-ROM, diskette, or magnetic tape. Here are sample entries:

Coates, Steve. "A Dead Language Comes to Life on the Internet." *New York Times on the Web* 28 Oct. 1996. 20 Apr.1997 <http://www.nytimes.com/ web/doscroot/library/cyber/week/1028Latin.html>
[Newspaper online]

McCalla, John. "Kafka's Hot and He's Also Funny." *Penn News* 2 Apr. 1998. 13 Oct. 1998 <http://www.upenn.edu/pennnews/current/1998/ 040298/Kafka.html>
[Newsletter online]

L., Harold. Rev. of *The Castle: A New Translation,* by Franz Kafka. Trans. Mark Harman. *Philadelphia Inquirer* 26 Apr. 1998. 13 Oct. 1998. <http:// www.phillynews.com/inquirer/98/Apr/26/books/KAFKA26.tml>
[Book review online]

"Kafka." *Britannica Online.* Vers. 97.1.1. Mar. 1997. Encyclopaedia Britannica. 7 Apr. 1997. <http://www.eb.com/>
[Reference work online, with version number and date]

Fresca, Dolores. "Kafka and Patriarchy." *The World of Kafka.* CD-ROM. New York: Klamm Publications, 1999.
[Collection of Kafka materials on CD-ROM]

Minusco, Sarah. E-mail to the author. 5 Apr. 2000.
[Give dates for e-mail to you or to others]

Study the example of a documented paper that concludes this chapter. How successful was the student author in finding contemporary sources? How well does the paper support its main points? How clear or adequate are parenthetical documentation and the entries in the Works Cited? Are there unusual situations or entries?

A note on format: the following sample typewritten page is the opening page of the paper formatted according to the guidelines of the MLA (Modern Language Association). Double-space your typescript throughout, including your title and your final list of works cited. Leave standard margins—an inch on each side, half an inch at the top and bottom. Use running heads (your last name and page number) at the top of each page, flush right. Use half an inch for paragraph indentation, an additional half-inch for block quotations.

Sample Research Paper Page

Nansen 1

Pat L. Nansen

Professor Holton

English 2

18 May 1997

The Psychoanalytic Kafka: Dream and Reality

Once, when Kafka was visiting his good friend Max Brod, he accidentally woke up Brod's father, who was sleeping on the couch. Instead of just simply apologizing, Kafka slowly tiptoed out of the room, whispering, "Please consider me a dream" (Baumer 2). When we look at Kafka the writer, this incident acquires symbolic meaning. Dreams fascinated Kafka, and he was obsessed with chronicling "his dreamlike inner existence," which threatened to crowd out ordinary daylight reality. He said in a diary entry for August 6, 1914:

> The taste for describing my dreamlike inner existence has pushed everything else in the background, where it has atrophied in a terrifying way and does not cease to atrophy. Nothing else can satisfy me. (qtd. in Baumer 3)

In a letter to Max Brod in 1922, Kafka called this exploration of the inner self "this descent to the dark powers, this unleashing . . . of dubious embraces and everything else that may be happening below." He said that a writer who "writes stories in the sunlight" above "no longer knows anything" about this hidden subconscious reality (qtd. in Baumer 7). For Kafka, "the dream reveals the reality" while "conception"—our ability to understand—"lags behind" (qtd. in Hamalian 12). It is this search for a deeper truth buried in our subsconscious. . . .

Sample Documented Paper

The Psychoanalytic Kafka: Dream and Reality

Once, when Kafka was visiting his good friend Max Brod, he accidentally woke up Brod's father, who was sleeping on the couch. Instead of just simply apologizing, Kafka slowly tiptoed out of the room, whispering, "Please consider me a dream" (Baumer 2). When we look at Kafka the writer, this incident acquires symbolic meaning. Dreams fascinated Kafka, and he was obsessed with chronicling "his dreamlike inner existence," which threatened to crowd out ordinary daylight reality. He said in a diary entry for August 6, 1914:

> The taste for describing my dreamlike inner existence has pushed everything else in the background, where it has atrophied in a terrifying way and does not cease to atrophy. Nothing else can satisfy me. (qtd. in Baumer 3)

In a letter to Max Brod in 1922, Kafka called this exploration of the inner self "this descent to the dark powers, this unleashing . . . of dubious embraces and everything else that may be happening below." He said that a writer who "writes stories in the sunlight" above "no longer knows anything" about this hidden subconscious reality (qtd. in Baumer 7). For Kafka, "the dream reveals the reality" while "conception"—our ability to understand—"lags behind" (qtd. in Hamalian 12). It is this search for a deeper truth buried in our subconscious and revealed in dreams that made Franz Kafka, in the words Peter Dow Webster, "the psychologist's perfect dreamer" (ll8). The psychoanalytical theory concerning dreams, first introduced by Freud, assumes that dreams tell us the real truth about ourselves, especially about our subconscious fears and desires. Our dreams keep coming back to our innermost preoccupations and dilemmas. In Kafka's case, in the words of Ruth Gross, these include "power and impotence," "marriage versus bachelorhood," and "success versus failure" (577).

Kafka"s "A Country Doctor" has a typical dreamlike sequence of events, with time and space distorted in such a way that the events cannot be literally happening. The story reveals Kafka's innermost struggle with a choice he made in his own life and the subconscious feelings surrounding that choice. In a letter to Brod, Kafka wrote that "in order to devote himself to literature, the writer must sacrifice fulfillment in life" (qtd. in Sokel 1158). Kafka had a strong desire for marriage and family, but because of his fears and hesitancies—and because of his exclusive devotion to his mission as a writer—his various engagements and romantic involvements ended in failure. In his own words, "The price to pay for this 'life as a writer' is rigid, uncompromising aloneness, a radical isolation from the outside world, from other people and—most painfully—from his beloved" (qtd. in Beug 125).

The dreamlike images and plot of "A Country Doctor" encourage us to see the story as an exploration of Kafka's own ambivalent feelings toward major choices in his own life. As suggested in one critical interpretation, when the country doctor heeds "the call of the 'nightbell' summoning him to the bedside of a patient," the call of the bell "can be understood as a translation into sensory terms of Kafka's call to literature, which he understood as an art of healing and self-preservation, a 'doctor's' art" (Sokel 1158).

However, when the doctor tries to respond to the call, he finds out his horse has died from overexertion. Rose, the servant girl he has just begun to notice, is unable to borrow a horse—"no horse to be had, no horse." In his dilemma, the doctor turns "absentmindedly" to his forgotten pigsty and in doing so releases the animal-like groom and a team of unearthly horses (Kafka 137). He allows the groom to take Rose; contrary to what the doctor says, he does in fact leave Rose behind. She is the price for the groom's aid. "The 'unearthly horses' transport the doctor away from life, woman, and home" (Sokel 1158). This scene seems to mirror Kafka's continual withdrawal from the various women in his life when they would press him for a commitment. Whenever a relationship became too serious, he would back away, claiming that his fanatical dedication to his writing "would condemn his spouse to monastic loneliness" (Sokel 1153).

As Kafka writes about the journey between the two houses, the doctor's and the patient's, he mirrors his own ambivalence toward his writer's art and the sacrifices he has made on behalf of that art. In the story, the two houses graphically represent the two poles of the doctor's existence. In his own house, the doctor abandons the possibility of fulfillment through love; in the other house, the house of the patient, he dedicates himself to his art, exploring "the congenital wound of mortality"—the wound in the young patient's side (Sokel 1158).

The doctor's ambivalence is such that he cannot be content at either pole. At home, he sacrifices the young woman to his mission, but at his destination he regrets the price he has paid and wants to return. Thoughts of Rose begin to haunt him: "And only now did I remember Rose again: what was I to do, how could I rescue her, how could I pull her away from under that groom at ten miles distance, with a team of horses I couldn't control" (Kafka 139). This pull in contradictory directions mirrors Kafka's own problem. He would make every effort to discourage a woman's hope for the future. However, in the case of Felice Bauer, for instance, the moment she showed signs of heeding his warning, he would return to the role of ardent wooer. As much as Kafka desired marriage and family, he was also fearful and would become "oppressed by the actual prospect of marriage" (Sokel 1154).

At the end of the story, the doctor is seen escaping the patient's house. While it took the doctor only seconds to arrive at the house of the sick boy, now it is taking him forever to get home: "Never shall I reach home at this rate; my flourishing practice is done for; my successor is robbing me . . ." (Kafka 143). The doctor is shown riding aimlessly between the houses—the distance between them has become immeasurable, and he cannot stay at either place.

Kafka's tendency to explore the subconscious in a dreamlike fashion is strongly evident in "The Country Doctor." As readers, we cannot be quite sure whether, in fact, his story is an actual dream (where the subconscious is revealed and dominates) or whether it is based on actual events with subconscious thoughts quickly intruding on the conscious mind. Kafka has chosen a country doctor to portray his own inner struggles as an author who must deal with the choices he has made. In this sense, we are all country doctors and have to deal with our own internal voices speaking to our consciousness. Kafka is not alone. What career mother leaving home and a sick child does not experience a twinge of guilt as her guilt feelings about her choices rise to the surface? What student working late into the night does not have visions of responsiblities denied or postponed—the dinner not cooked, the phone calls not returned?

Works Cited

Baumer, Franz. *Franz Kafka.* New York: Unger, 1971.
Beug, Joachim. "The Cunning of a Writer." *The World of Franz Kafka.* Ed. J.P. Stern. New York: Holt, 1980. 122–33.

Gross, Ruth V. "Fallen Bridge, Fallen Women, Fallen Text." *The Literary Review* 26.4 (1983): 577–87.

Hamalian, Leo. Introduction. *Franz Kafka: A Collection of Criticism.* Ed. Leo Hamalian. New York, McGraw, 1981. 1–17

Kafka, Franz. *The Metamorphosis, the Penal Colony, and Other Stories.* Trans. Willa and Edwin Muir. New York: Schocken, 1975.

Sokel, Walter H. "Franz Kafka." *European Writers: The Twentieth Century.* Ed. George Stade. New York: Scribner's, 1989. Vol. 9. 1151–77.

Webster, Peter Dow. "'Dies Irae' in the Unconscious, or the Significance of Franz Kafka." *Franz Kafka: A Collection of Criticism.* Ed. Leo Hamalian. New York: McGraw, 1981. 118–25.

Questions

How convincing is the parallel between the doctor as healer and the writer who provides spiritual comfort and healing? In addition to the lines quoted in this paper, are there other references to Rose while the doctor is in the patient's house?

11 Other Voices/Other Visions

A World of Stories

Kate Chopin   *(1851–1904)*

Kate Chopin was rediscovered by feminist editors and critics who championed her as an early rebel against the conventions of a sexually repressed society. She came from a wealthy St. Louis family. Her husband, as had been her mother, was from a French Louisiana background, and she wrote her popular early stories about New Orleans and plantation life. In her novel *The Awakening* (1899) and other fiction, Chopin dealt with topics that were to become major themes of feminist literature: a woman's right to rebel against a stifling marriage, to reject the traditional ideal that a woman should "sacrifice herself for her children," and to have the same freedom to fulfill her emotional and sexual needs that men were taking for granted.

The Story of an Hour   *1891*

Knowing that Mrs. Mallard was afflicted with a heart trouble, great care was taken to break to her as gently as possible the news of her husband's death.

It was her sister Josephine who told her, in broken sentences, veiled hints that revealed in half concealing. Her husband's friend Richards was there, too, near her. It was he who had been in the newspaper office when intelligence of the railroad disaster was received, with Brently Mallard's name leading the list of "killed." He had only taken the time to assure himself of its truth by a second telegram, and had hastened to forestall any less careful, less tender friend in bearing the sad message.

She did not hear the story as many women have heard the same, with a paralyzed inability to accept its significance. She wept at once, with sudden, wild abandonment, in her sister's arms. When the storm of grief had spent itself she went away to her room alone. She would have no one follow her.

There stood, facing the open window, a comfortable, roomy armchair. Into this she sank, pressed down by a physical exhaustion that haunted her body and seemed to reach into her soul.

She could see in the open square before her house the tops of trees that 5 were all aquiver with the new spring life. The delicious breath of rain was in the air. In the street below a peddler was crying his wares. The notes of a distant song which some one was singing reached her faintly, and count-less sparrows were twittering in the eaves.

There were patches of blue sky showing here and there through the clouds that had met and piled above the other in the west facing her window.

She sat with her head thrown back upon the cushion of the chair quite motionless, except when a sob came up into her throat and shook her, as a child who has cried itself to sleep continues to sob in its dreams.

She was young, with a fair, calm face, whose lines bespoke repression and even a certain strength. But now there was a dull stare in her eyes, whose gaze was fixed away off yonder on one of those patches of blue sky. It was not a glance of reflection, but rather indicated a suspension of intel-ligent thought.

There was something coming to her and she was waiting for it, fearfully. What was it? She did not know; it was too subtle and elusive to name. But she felt it, creeping out of the sky, reaching toward her through the sounds, the scents, the color that filled the air.

Now her bosom rose and fell tumultuously. She was beginning to recog-   10
nize this thing that was approaching to possess her, and she was striving to beat it back with her will—as powerless as her two white slender hands would have been.

When she abandoned herself a little whispered word escaped her slightly parted lips. She said it over and over under her breath: "Free, free, free!" The vacant stare and the look of terror that had followed it went from her eyes. They stayed keen and bright. Her pulses beat fast, and the coursing blood warmed and relaxed every inch of her body.

She did not stop to ask if it were not a monstrous joy that held her. A clear and exalted perception enabled her to dismiss the suggestion as trivial.

She knew that she would weep again when she saw the kind, tender hands folded in death; the face that had never looked save with love upon her, fixed and gray and dead. But she saw beyond that bitter moment a long procession of years to come that would belong to her absolutely. And she opened and spread her arms out to them in welcome.

There would be no one to live for during those coming years; she would live for herself. There would be no powerful will bending her in that blind persistence with which men and women believe they have a right to impose a private will upon a fellow creature. A kind intention or a cruel intention made the act seem no less a crime as she looked upon it in that brief moment of illumination.

And yet she had loved him—sometimes. Often she had not. What did it   15
matter! What could love, the unsolved mystery, count for in face of this pos-session of self-assertion which she suddenly recognized as the strongest impulse of her being.

"Free! Body and soul free!" she kept whispering.

Josephine was kneeling before the closed door with her lips to the key-hole, imploring for admission. "Louise, open the door! I beg; open the door—you will make yourself ill. What are you doing, Louise? For heaven's sake open the door."

"Go away. I am not making myself ill." No; she was drinking in a very elixir of life through that open window.

Her fancy was running riot along those days ahead of her. Spring days, and summer days, and all sorts of days that would be her own. She breathed a quick prayer that life might be long. It was only yesterday she had thought with a shudder that life might be long.

She arose at length and opened the door to her sister's importunities. 20 There was a feverish triumph in her eyes, and she carried herself unwittingly like a goddess of Victory. She clasped her sister's waist, and together they descended the stairs. Richards stood waiting for them at the bottom.

Some one was opening the front door with a latchkey. It was Brently Mallard who entered, a little travel-stained, composedly carrying his grip-sack and umbrella. He had been far from the scene of accident, and did not even know there had been one. He stood amazed at Josephine's piercing cry; at Richards' quick motion to screen him from the view of his wife.

But Richards was too late.

When the doctors came they said she had died of heart disease—of joy that kills.

Ursula K. Le Guin   *(born 1929)*

Ursula K. Le Guin was born in Berkeley and educated at Radcliffe and Columbia. She has written eloquently in defense of the environment, passenger trains, abortion rights, and the cultural traditions of Native Americans. She is admired as an author of travel literature, essays on feminist issues, and science fiction. Her science fiction does not focus on space age gadgets and aliens from outer space but instead raises questions about human nature and human destiny. The novels of her *Earthsea Trilogy* (1968–1972) and her later novels made her a favorite of thoughtful readers.

The Ones Who Walk Away from Omelas   1973
Variations on a Theme by William James

With a clamor of bells that set the swallows soaring, the Festival of Summer came to the city Omelas, bright-towered by the sea. The rigging of the boats in harbor sparkled with flags. In the streets between houses with red roofs and painted walls, between old moss-grown gardens and under avenues of trees, past great parks and public buildings, processions moved. Some were decorous: old people in long stiff robes of mauve and grey, grave master workmen, quiet, merry women carrying their babies and chatting as they walked. In other streets the music beat faster, a shimmering of gong and tambourine, and the people went dancing, the procession was a dance. Children dodged in and out, their high calls rising like the swallows' crossing flights over the music and the singing. All the processions wound toward the north side of the city, where on the great water-meadow called the Green Fields boys and girls, naked in the bright air, with mud-stained feet and ankles and long, lithe arms, exercised their restive horses before the race. The horses wore no gear at all but a halter without bit.

Their manes were braided with streamers of silver, gold, and green. They flared their nostrils and pranced and boasted to one another; they were vastly excited, the horse being the only animal who has adopted our ceremonies as his own. Far off to the north and west the mountains stood up half encircling Omelas on her bay. The air of morning was so clear that the snow still crowning the Eighteen Peaks burned with white-gold fire across the miles of sunlit air, under the dark blue of the sky. There was just enough wind to make the banners that marked the racecourse snap and flutter now and then. In the silence of the broad green meadows one could hear the music winding through the city streets, farther and nearer and ever approaching, a cheerful faint sweetness of the air that from time to time trembled and gathered together and broke out into the great joyous clanging of the bells.

Joyous! How is one to tell about joy? How describe the citizens of Omelas?

They were not simple folk, you see, though they were happy. But we do not say the words of cheer much any more. All smiles have become archaic. Given a description such as this one tends to make certain assumptions. Given a description such as this one tends to look next for the King, mounted on a splendid stallion and surrounded by his noble knights, or perhaps in a golden litter borne by great-muscled slaves. But there was no king. They did not use swords, or keep slaves. They were not barbarians. I do not know the rules and laws of their society, but I suspect that they were singularly few. As they did without monarchy and slavery, so they also got on without the stock exchange, the advertisement, the secret police, and the bomb. Yet I repeat that these were not simple folk, not dulcet shepherds, noble savages, bland utopians. They were not less complex than us. The trouble is that we have a bad habit, encouraged by pedants and sophisticates, of considering happiness as something rather stupid. Only pain is intellectual, only evil interesting. This is the treason of the artist: a refusal to admit the banality of evil and the terrible boredom of pain. If you can't lick 'em, join 'em. If it hurts, repeat it. But to praise despair is to condemn delight, to embrace violence is to lose hold of everything else. We have almost lost hold, we can no longer describe a happy man, nor make any celebration of joy. How can I tell you about the people of Omelas? They were not naïve and happy children—though their children were, in fact, happy. They were mature, intelligent, passionate adults whose lives were not wretched. O miracle! but I wish I could describe it better. I wish I could convince you. Omelas sounds in my words like a city in a fairy tale, long ago and far away, once upon a time. Perhaps it would be best if you imagined it as your own fancy bids, assuming it will rise to the occasion, for certainly I cannot suit you all. For instance, how about technology? I think that there would be no cars or helicopters in and above the streets; this follows from the fact that the people of Omelas are happy people. Happiness is based on a just discrimination of what is necessary, what is neither necessary nor destructive, and what is destructive. In the middle category, however—that of the unnecessary but undestructive, that of comfort, luxury, exuberance, etc.—they could perfectly well have central heating, subway trains, washing machines, and all kinds of marvelous devices not yet invented here, floating light-sources, fuelless power, a cure for the common cold. Or they could have none of that: it doesn't matter. As you like it. I incline to think that people from towns up and down the coast have been coming in to Omelas during the last days before the Festival on very fast little trains and double-decked trams, and that the train station of Omelas is actually the handsomest building in town, though plainer than the magnificent Farmers' Market. But even granted trains, I fear that Omelas so far strikes some of you as goody-goody. Smiles, bells, parades, horses, bleh. If so, please add an orgy. If an orgy would help, don't hesitate. Let us not, however, have temples from which issue beautiful nude priests and priestesses already half in ecstasy and ready to copulate with any man or woman, lover or stranger, who desires union with the deep godhead of the blood, although that was my first idea. But really it would be better not to have any temples in Omelas—at least, not manned temples. Religion yes, clergy no. Surely the beautiful nudes can just wander about, offering themselves like divine soufflés to the hunger of the needy and the rapture of the flesh. Let them join the processions. Let tambourines be struck above the copulations, and the glory of desire be proclaimed upon the gongs, and (a not unimportant point) let the offspring of these delightful rituals be beloved and looked after by all. One thing I know there is none of in Omelas is guilt. But what else should there be? I thought at first there were no drugs, but that is puritanical. For those who like it, the faint insistent sweetness of *drooz* may perfume the ways of the city, *drooz* which first brings a great lightness and brilliance to the mind and limbs, and then after some hours a dreamy languor, and wonderful visions at last of the very arcana and inmost secrets of the Universe, as well as exciting the pleasure of sex beyond all belief; and it is not habit-forming. For more modest tastes I think there ought to be beer. What else, what else belongs in the joyous city? The sense of victory, surely, the celebration of courage. But as we did without clergy, let us do without soldiers. The joy built upon successful slaughter is not the right kind of joy; it will not do; it is fearful and it is trivial. A boundless and generous contentment, a magnanimous triumph felt not against some outer enemy but in communion with the finest and fairest in the souls of all men everywhere and the splendor of the world's summer: this is what swells the hearts of the people of Omelas, and the victory they celebrate is that of life. I really don't think many of them need to take *drooz*.

Most of the procession have reached the Green Fields by now. A marvelous smell of cooking goes forth from the red and blue tents of the provisioners. The faces of small children are amiably sticky; in the benign grey beard of a man a couple of crumbs of rich pastry are entangled. The youths and girls have mounted their horses and are beginning to group around the starting line of the course. An old woman, small, fat, and laughing, is passing out flowers from a basket, and tall young men wear her flowers in their shining hair. A child of nine or ten sits at the edge of the crowd, alone, playing on a wooden flute. People pause to listen, and they smile, but they do not speak to him, for he never ceases playing and never sees them, his dark eyes wholly rapt in the sweet, thin magic of the tune.

He finishes, and slowly lowers his hands holding the wooden flute.   5

As if that little private silence were the signal, all at once a trumpet sounds from the pavilion near the starting line: imperious, melancholy, piercing.

The horses rear on their slender legs, and some of them neigh in answer. Sober-faced, the young riders stroke the horses' necks and soothe them, whispering, "Quiet, quiet, there my beauty, my hope. . . ." They begin to form in rank along the starting line. The crowds along the racecourse are like a field of grass and flowers in the wind. The Festival of Summer has begun.

Do you believe? Do you accept the festival, the city, the joy? No? Then let me describe one more thing.

In a basement under one of the beautiful public buildings of Omelas, or perhaps in the cellar of one of its more spacious private homes, there is a room. It has one locked door, and no window. A little light seeps in dustily between cracks in the boards, secondhand from a cobwebbed window somewhere across the cellar. In one corner of the little room a couple of mops, with stiff, clotted, foul-smelling heads, stand near a rusty bucket. The floor is dirt, a little damp to the touch, as cellar dirt usually is. The room is about three paces long and two wide: a mere broom closet or disused tool room. In the room a child is sitting. It could be a boy or a girl. It looks about six, but actually is nearly ten. It is feeble-minded. Perhaps it was born defective, or perhaps it has become imbecile through fear, malnutrition, and neglect. It picks its nose and occasionally fumbles vaguely with its toes or genitals, as it sits hunched in the corner farthest from the bucket and the two mops. It is afraid of the mops. It finds them horrible. It shuts its eyes, but it knows the mops are still standing there; and the door is locked; and nobody will come. The door is always locked; and nobody ever comes, except that sometimes—the child has no understanding of time or interval—sometimes the door rattles terribly and opens, and a person, or several people, are there. One of them may come in and kick the child to make it stand up. The others never come close, but peer in at it with frightened, disgusted eyes. The food bowl and the water jug are hastily filled, the door is locked, the eyes disappear. The people at the door never say anything, but the child, who has not always lived in the tool room, and can remember sunlight and its mother's voice, sometimes speaks. "I will be good," it says. "Please let me out. I will be good!" They never answer. The child used to scream for help at night, and cry a good deal, but now it only makes a kind of whining, "eh-haa, eh-haa," and it speaks less and less often. It is so thin there are no calves to its legs; its belly protrudes; it lives on a half-bowl of corn meal and grease a day. It is naked. Its buttocks and thighs are a mass of festered sores, as it sits in its own excrement continually.

They all know it is there, all the people of Omelas. Some of them have come to see it, others are content merely to know it is there. They all know that it has to be there. Some of them understand why, and some do not, but they all understand that their happiness, the beauty of their city, the tenderness of their friendships, the health of their children, the wisdom of their scholars, the skill of their makers, even the abundance of their harvest and the kindly weathers of their skies, depend wholly on this child's abominable misery.

This is usually explained to children when they are between eight and twelve, whenever they seem capable of understanding; and most of those who come to see the child are young people, though often enough an adult comes, or comes back, to see the child. No matter how well the matter has been explained to them, these young spectators are always shocked and   10 sickened at the sight. They feel disgust, which they had thought themselves superior to. They feel anger, outrage, impotence, despite all the explanations. They would like to do something for the child. But there is nothing they can do. If the child were brought up into the sunlight out of the vile place, if it were cleaned and fed and comforted, that would be a good thing, indeed; but if it were done, in that day and hour all the prosperity and beauty and delight of Omelas would wither and be destroyed. Those are the terms. To exchange all the goodness and grace of every life in Omelas for that single, small improvement: to throw away the happiness of thousands for the chance of the happiness of one: that would be to let guilt within the walls indeed.

The terms are strict and absolute; there may not even be a kind word spoken to the child.

Often the young people go home in tears, or in a tearless rage, when they have seen the child and faced this terrible paradox. They may brood over it for weeks or years. But as time goes on they begin to realize that even if the child could be released, it would not get much good of its freedom: a little vague pleasure of warmth and food, no doubt, but little more. It is too degraded and imbecile to know any real joy. It has been afraid too long ever to be free of fear. Its habits are too uncouth for it to respond to humane treatment. Indeed, after so long it would probably be wretched without walls about it to protect it, and darkness for its eyes, and its own excrement to sit in. Their tears at the bitter injustice dry when they begin to perceive the terrible justice of reality, and to accept it. Yet it is their tears and anger, the trying of their generosity and the acceptance of their helplessness, which are perhaps the true source of the splendor of their lives. Theirs is no vapid, irresponsible happiness. They know that they, like the child, are not free. They know compassion. It is the existence of the child, and their knowledge of its existence, that makes possible the nobility of their architecture, the poignancy of their music, the profundity of their science. It is because of the child that they are so gentle with children. They know that if the wretched one were not there snivelling in the dark, the other one, the flute-player, could make no joyful music as the young riders line up in their beauty for the race in the sunlight of the first morning of summer.

Now do you believe in them? Are they not more credible? But there is one more thing to tell, and this is quite incredible.

At times one of the adolescent girls or boys who go to see the child does not go home to weep or rage, does not, in fact, go home at all. Sometimes also a man or woman much older falls silent for a day or two, and then leaves home. These people go out into the street, and walk down the street alone. They keep walking, and walk straight out of the city of Omelas, through the beautiful gates. They keep walking across the farmlands of Omelas. Each one goes alone, youth or girl, man or woman. Night falls; the traveler must pass down village streets, between the houses with yellow-lit windows, and on out into the darkness of the fields. Each alone, they go west or north, toward the mountains. They go on. They leave Omelas, they walk ahead into the darkness, and they do not come back. The place they go toward is a place even less imaginable to most of us than the city of happiness. I cannot describe it at all. It is possible that it does not exist.

But they seem to know where they are going, the ones who walk away from Omelas.

Toni Morrison   *(born 1931)*

In 1993, Toni Morrison was awarded the Nobel Prize for literature, the first American woman to be so honored in fifty-five years. Born near Cleveland, Ohio, as the child of sharecroppers, she studied and taught at Howard University and went on to a prestigious professorship at Princeton University. Her novels—*The Bluest Eye* (1970), *Sula* (1973), *Song of Solomon* (1977), *Tar Baby* (1981), *Jazz* (1992)—have reached large audiences and are widely taught and studied in college courses. Her novel *Beloved* (1987) told the story of an escaped slave haunted by the memory of the baby daughter she killed to keep her out of slave catchers' hands. Morrison became a widely respected voice on race as a challenge and obsession in American life and literature. In the following self-contained narrative that is part of the novel *Sula,* a black woman, "with heavy misgiving," takes the archetypal journey back to the Old South. In New Orleans, people still know Creole, a dialect going back to French colonial times: *Vrai?* (Is that true?); *chère* (dear); *Comment t'appelle?* (What's your name?), or *'Voir* (see you). The Elysian Fields, a street named after the posh Champs Elysées in Paris, runs through the poor part of town.

1920   *1973*

It had to be as far away from the Sundown House as possible. And her grandmother's middle-aged nephew who lived in a Northern town called Medallion was the one chance she had to make sure it would be. The red shutters had haunted both Helene Sabat and her grandmother for sixteen years. Helene was born behind those shutters, daughter of a Creole whore who worked there. The grandmother took Helene away from the soft lights and flowered carpets of the Sundown House and raised her under the dolesome eyes of a multicolored Virgin Mary, counseling her to be constantly on guard for any sign of her mother's wild blood.

So when Wiley Wright came to visit his Great Aunt Cecile in New Orleans, his enchantment with the pretty Helene became a marriage proposal—under the pressure of both women. He was a seaman (or rather a lakeman, for he was a ship's cook on one of the Great Lakes lines), in port only three days out of every sixteen.

He took his bride to his home in Medallion and put her in a lovely house with a brick porch and real lace curtains at the window. His long absences were quite bearable for Helene Wright, especially when, after some nine years of marriage, her daughter was born.

Her daughter was more comfort and purpose than she had ever hoped to find in this life. She rose grandly to the occasion of motherhood—grateful, deep down in her heart, that the child had not inherited the great beauty that was hers: that her skin had dusk in it, that her lashes were substantial but not undignified in their length, that she had taken the broad flat nose of Wiley (although Helene expected to improve it somewhat) and his generous lips.

Under Helene's hand the girl became obedient and polite. Any enthusiasms that little Nel showed were calmed by the mother until she drove her daughter's imagination underground.   5

Helene Wright was an impressive woman, at least in Medallion she was. Heavy hair in a bun, dark eyes arched in a perpetual query about other people's manners. A woman who won all social battles with presence and a conviction of the legitimacy of her authority. Since there was no Catholic church in Medallion then, she joined the most conservative black church. And held sway. It was Helene who never turned her head in church when latecomers arrived; Helene who established the practice of seasonal altar flowers; Helene who introduced the giving of banquets of welcome to returning Negro veterans. She lost only one battle—the pronunciation of her name. The people in the Bottom refused to say Helene. They called her Helen Wright and left it at that.

All in all her life was a satisfactory one. She loved her house and enjoyed manipulating her daughter and her husband. She would sigh sometimes just before falling asleep, thinking that she had indeed come far enough away from the Sundown House.

So it was with extremely mixed emotions that she read a letter from Mr. Henri Martin describing the illness of her grandmother, and suggesting she come down right away. She didn't want to go, but could not bring herself to ignore the silent plea of the woman who had rescued her.

It was November. November, 1920. Even in Medallion there was a victorious swagger in the legs of white men and a dull-eyed excitement in the eyes of colored veterans.

Helene thought about the trip South with heavy misgiving but decided   10
that she had the best protection: her manner and her bearing, to which she would add a beautiful dress. She bought some deep-brown wool and three-fourths of a yard of matching velvet. Out of this she made herself a heavy but elegant dress with velvet collar and pockets.

Nel watched her mother cutting the pattern from newspapers and moving her eyes rapidly from a magazine model to her own hands. She watched her turn up the kerosene lamp at sunset to sew far into the night.

The day they were ready, Helene cooked a smoked ham, left a note for her lake-bound husband, in case he docked early, and walked head high and arms stiff with luggage ahead of her daughter to the train depot.

It was a longer walk than she remembered, and they saw the train steaming up just as they turned the corner. They ran along the track looking for the coach pointed out to them by the colored porter. Even at that they made a mistake. Helene and her daughter entered a coach peopled by some twenty white men and women. Rather than go back and down the three wooden steps again, Helene decided to spare herself some embarrassment and walked on through to the colored car. She carried two pieces of luggage and a string purse; her daughter carried a covered basket of food.

As they opened the door marked COLORED ONLY, they saw a white conductor coming toward them. It was a chilly day but a light skim of sweat glistened on the woman's face as she and the little girl struggled to hold the door open, hang on to their luggage and enter all at once. The conductor let his eyes travel over the pale yellow woman and then stuck his little finger into his ear, jiggling it free of wax. "What you think you doin', gal?"

Helene looked up at him.   15

So soon. So soon. She hadn't even begun the trip back. Back to her grandmother's house in the city where the red shutters glowed, and already she had been called "gal." All the old vulnerabilities, all the old fears of being somehow flawed gathered in her stomach and made her hands tremble. She had heard only that one word; it dangled above her wide-brimmed hat, which had slipped, in her exertion, from its carefully leveled placement and was now tilted in a bit of a jaunt over her eye.

Thinking he wanted her tickets, she quickly dropped both the cowhide suitcase and the straw one in order to search for them in her purse. An eagerness to please and an apology for living met in her voice. "I have them. Right here somewhere, sir. . . ."

The conductor looked at the bit of wax his fingernail had retrieved. "What was you doin' back in there? What was you doin' in that coach yonder?"

Helene licked her lips. "Oh . . . I . . ." Her glance moved beyond the white man's face to the passengers seated behind him. Four or five black faces were watching, two belonging to soldiers still in their shit-colored uniforms and peaked caps. She saw their closed faces, their locked eyes, and turned for compassion to the gray eyes of the conductor.

"We made a mistake, sir. You see, there wasn't no sign. We just got in the   20
wrong car, that's all. Sir."

"We don't 'low no mistakes on this train. Now git your butt on in there."

He stood there staring at her until she realized that he wanted her to move aside. Pulling Nel by the arm, she pressed herself and her daughter into the foot space in front of a wooden seat. Then, for no earthly reason, at least no reason that anybody could understand, certainly no reason that Nel understood then or later, she smiled. Like a street pup that wags its tail at the very doorjamb of the butcher shop he has been kicked away from only moments before, Helene smiled. Smiled dazzlingly and coquettishly at the salmon-colored face of the conductor.

Nel looked away from the flash of pretty teeth to the other passengers. The two black soldiers, who had been watching the scene with what appeared to be indifference, now looked stricken. Behind Nel was the bright and blazing light of her mother's smile; before her the midnight eyes of the soldiers. She saw the muscles of their faces tighten, a movement under the skin from blood to marble. No change in the expression of the eyes, but a hard wetness that veiled them as they looked at the stretch of her mother's foolish smile.

As the door slammed on the conductor's exit, Helene walked down the aisle to a seat. She looked about for a second to see whether any of the men would help her put the suitcases in the overhead rack. Not a man moved. Helene sat down, fussily, her back toward the men. Nel sat opposite, facing both her mother and the soldiers, neither of whom she could look at. She felt both pleased and ashamed to sense that these men, unlike her father, who worshiped his graceful, beautiful wife, were bubbling with a hatred for her mother that had not been there in the beginning but had been born with the dazzling smile. In the silence that preceded the train's heave, she looked deeply at the folds of her mother's dress. There in the fall of the heavy brown wool she held her eyes. She could not risk letting them travel upward for fear of seeing that the hooks and eyes in the placket of the dress had come undone and exposed the custard-colored skin underneath. She stared at the hem, wanting to believe in its weight but knowing that custard was all that it hid. If this tall, proud woman, this woman who was very particular about her friends, who slipped into church with unequaled elegance, who could quell a roustabout with a look, if *she* were really custard, then there was a chance that Nel was too.

It was on that train, shuffling toward Cincinnati, that she resolved to be on guard—always. She wanted to make certain that no man ever looked at her that way. That no midnight eyes or marbled flesh would ever accost her and turn her into jelly. 25

For two days they rode; two days of watching sleet turn to rain, turn to purple sunsets, and one night knotted on the wooden seats (their heads on folded coats), trying not to hear the snoring soldiers. When they changed trains in Birmingham for the last leg of the trip, they discovered what luxury they had been in through Kentucky and Tennessee, where the rest stops had all had colored toilets. After Birmingham there were none. Helene's face was drawn with the need to relieve herself, and so intense was her distress she finally brought herself to speak about her problem to a black woman with four children who had got on in Tuscaloosa.

"Is there somewhere we can go to use the restroom?"

The woman looked up at her and seemed not to understand. "Ma'am?" Her eyes fastened on the thick velvet collar, the fair skin, the high-tone voice.

"The restroom," Helene repeated. Then, in a whisper, "The toilet."

The woman pointed out the window and said, "Yes ma'am. Yonder." 30

Helene looked out of the window halfway expecting to see a comfort station in the distance; instead she saw gray-green trees leaning over tangled grass. "Where?"

"Yonder," the woman said. "Meridian. We be pullin' in direc'lin." Then she smiled sympathetically and asked, "Kin you make it?"

Helene nodded and went back to her seat trying to think of other things—for the surest way to have an accident would be to remember her full bladder.

At Meridian the women got out with their children. While Helene looked about the tiny stationhouse for a door that said COLORED WOMEN, the other woman stalked off to a field of high grass on the far side of the track. Some white men were leaning on the railing in front of the stationhouse. It was not only their tongues curling around toothpicks that kept Helene from asking information of them. She looked around for the other woman and, seeing just the top of her head rag in the grass, slowly realized where "yonder" was. All of them, the fat woman and her four children, three boys and a girl, Helene and her daughter, squatted there in the four o'clock Meridian sun. They did it again in Ellisville, again in Hattiesburg, and by the time they reached Slidell, not too far from Lake Pontchartrain, Helene could not only fold leaves as well as the fat woman, she never felt a stir as she passed the muddy eyes of the men who stood like wrecked Dorics under the station roofs of those towns.

The lift in spirit that such an accomplishment produced in her quickly   35 disappeared when the train finally pulled into New Orleans.

Cecile Sabat's house leaned between two others just like it on Elysian Fields. A Frenchified shotgun house, it sported a magnificent garden in the back and a tiny wrought-iron fence in the front. On the door hung a black crepe wreath with purple ribbon. They were too late. Helene reached up to touch the ribbon, hesitated, and knocked. A man in a collarless shirt opened the door. Helene identified herself and he said he was Henri Martin and that he was there for the settin'-up. They stepped into the house. The Virgin Mary clasped her hands in front of her neck three times in the front room and once in the bedroom where Cecile's body lay. The old woman had died without seeing or blessing her granddaughter.

No one other than Mr. Martin seemed to be in the house, but a sweet odor as of gardenias told them that someone else had been. Blotting her lashes with a white handkerchief, Helene walked through the kitchen to the back bedroom where she had slept for sixteen years. Nel trotted along behind, enchanted with the smell, the candles and the strangeness. When Helene bent to loosen the ribbons of Nel's hat, a woman in a yellow dress came out of the garden and onto the back porch that opened into the bedroom. The two women looked at each other. There was no recognition in the eyes of either. Then Helene said, "This is your . . . grandmother, Nel." Nel looked at her mother and then quickly back at the door they had just come out of.

"No. That was your great-grandmother. This is your grandmother. My mother . . ."

Before the child could think, her words were hanging in the gardenia air. "But she looks so young."

The woman in the canary-yellow dress laughed and said she was forty-   40 eight, "an old forty-eight."

Then it was she who carried the gardenia smell. This tiny woman with the softness and glare of a canary. In that somber house that held four Virgin Marys, where death sighed in every corner and candles sputtered, the gardenia smell and canary-yellow dress emphasized the funeral atmosphere surrounding them.

The woman smiled, glanced in the mirror and said, throwing her voice toward Helene, "That your only one?"

"Yes," said Helene.

"Pretty. A lot like you."

"Yes. Well. She's ten now."   45

"Ten? Vrai? Small for her age, no?"

Helene shrugged and looked at her daughter's questioning eyes. The woman in the yellow dress leaned forward. "Come. Come, chère."

Helene interrupted. "We have to get cleaned up. We been three days on the train with no chance to wash or . . ."

"Comment t'appelle?"

"She doesn't talk Creole."

"Then you ask her."

"She wants to know your name, honey."

With her head pressed into her mother's heavy brown dress, Nel told her and then asked, "What's yours?"

"Mine's Rochelle. Well. I must be going on." She moved closer to the mirror and stood there sweeping hair up from her neck back into its halo-like roll, and wetting with spit the ringlets that fell over her ears. "I been here, you know, most of the day. She pass on yesterday. The funeral tomorrow. Henri takin' care." She struck a match, blew it out and darkened her eyebrows with the burnt head. All the while Helene and Nel watched her. The one in a rage at the folded leaves she had endured, the wooden benches she had slept on, all to miss seeing her grandmother and seeing instead that painted canary who never said a word of greeting or affection or . . .

Rochelle continued, "I don't know what happen to de house. Long time   55
paid for. You be thinkin' on it? Oui?" Her newly darkened eyebrows queried Helene.

"Oui." Helene's voice was chilly. "I be thinkin' on it."

"Oh, well. Not for me to say . . ."

Suddenly she swept around and hugged Nel—a quick embrace tighter and harder than one would have imagined her thin soft arms capable of.

"'Voir! 'Voir!" and she was gone.

In the kitchen, being soaped head to toe by her mother, Nel ventured an   60
observation. "She smelled so nice. And her skin was so soft."

Helene rinsed the cloth. "Much handled things are always soft."

"What does 'vwah' mean?"

"I don't know," her mother said. "I don't talk Creole." She gazed at her daughter's wet buttocks. "And neither do you."

When they got back to Medallion and into the quiet house they saw the note exactly where they had left it and the ham dried out in the icebox.

"Lord, I've never been so glad to see this place. But look at the dust. Get   65
the rags, Nel. Oh, never mind. Let's breathe awhile first. Lord, I never thought I'd get back here safe and sound. Whoo. Well it's over. Good and over. Praise His name. Look at that. I told that old fool not to deliver any milk and there's the can curdled to beat all. What gets into people? I told him not to. Well, I got other things to worry 'bout. Got to get a fire started. I left it ready so I wouldn't have to do nothin' but light it. Lord, it's cold. Don't just sit there, honey. You could be pulling your nose . . ."

Nel sat on the red-velvet sofa listening to her mother but remembering the smell and the tight, tight hug of the woman in yellow who rubbed burned matches over her eyes.

Late that night after the fire was made, the cold supper eaten, the surface dust removed, Nel lay in bed thinking of her trip. She remembered clearly the urine running down and into her stockings until she learned how to squat properly; the disgust on the face of the dead woman and the sound of the funeral drums. It had been an exhilarating trip but a fearful one. She had been frightened of the soldiers' eyes on the train, the black wreath on the door, the custard pudding she believed lurked under her mother's heavy dress, the feel of unknown streets and unknown people. But she had gone on a real trip, and now she was different. She got out of bed and lit the lamp to look in the mirror. There was her face, plain brown eyes, three braids and the nose her mother hated. She looked for a long time and suddenly a shiver ran through her.

"I'm me," she whispered. "Me."

Nel didn't know quite what she meant, but on the other hand she knew exactly what she meant.

"I'm me. I'm not their daughter. I'm not Nel. I'm me. Me."   70

Each time she said the word *me* there was a gathering in her like power, like joy, like fear. Back in bed with her discovery, she stared out the window at the dark leaves of the horse chestnut.

"Me," she murmured. And then, sinking deeper into the quilts, "I want . . . I want to be . . . wonderful. Oh, Jesus, make me wonderful."

The many experiences of her trip crowded in on her. She slept. It was the last as well as the first time she was ever to leave Medallion.

For days afterward she imagined other trips she would take, alone though, to faraway places. Contemplating them was delicious. Leaving Medallion would be her goal. But that was before she met Sula, the girl she had seen for five years at Garfield Primary but never played with, never knew, because her mother said Sula's mother was sooty. The trip, perhaps, or her new found me-ness, gave her the strength to cultivate a friend in spite of her mother.

When Sula first visited the Wright house, Helene's curdled scorn turned   75
to butter. Her daughter's friend seemed to have none of the mother's slack-ness. Nel, who regarded the oppressive neatness of her home with dread, felt comfortable in it with Sula, who loved it and would sit on the red-velvet sofa for ten to twenty minutes at a time—still as dawn. As for Nel, she pre-ferred Sula's woolly house, where a pot of something was always cooking on the stove; where the mother, Hannah, never scolded or gave directions; where all sorts of people dropped in; where newspapers were stacked in the hallway, and dirty dishes left for hours at a time in the sink, and where a one-legged grandmother named Eva handed you goobers from deep inside her pockets or read you a dream.

Edgar Allan Poe   *(1809–1849)*

Edgar Allan Poe's poems and stories have enjoyed immense popular-ity. He was a master at catering to popular taste in writing the detective story, the ghost story, and the horror story. Losing early his actress mother and alcoholic father and befriended for a time by a rich foster parent, he led a troubled life, doing battle with poverty, gambling, alcoholism, nothing jobs in publishing, and a moralistic establishment with little sympathy for the down-and-out. During sober intervals, spectacular suc-cesses like *The Raven* poem gained him recognition and critical acclaim. Stories like "The Murders of the Rue Morgue," "The Black Cat," and "The Pit and the Pendulum" have been read by millions around the world.

The Black Cat   *1843*

For the most wild yet most homely narrative which I am about to pen, I neither expect nor solicit belief. Mad indeed would I be to expect it, in a case where my very senses reject their own evidence. Yet, mad am I not— and very surely do I not dream. But tomorrow I die, and today I would unburden my soul. My immediate purpose is to place before the world, plainly, succinctly, and without comment, a series of mere household events. In their consequences, these events have terrified—have tortured— have destroyed me. Yet I will not attempt to expound them. To me, they have presented little but horror—to many they will seem less terrible than *baroques*. Hereafter, perhaps, some intellect may be found which will reduce my phantasm to the commonplace—some intellect more calm, more logical, and far less excitable than my own, which will perceive, in the cir- cumstances I detail with awe, nothing more than an ordinary succession of very natural causes and effects.

From my infancy I was noted for the docility and humanity of my dispo- sition. My tenderness of heart was even so conspicuous as to make me the jest of my companions. I was especially fond of animals, and was indulged by my parents with a great variety of pets. With these I spent most of my time, and never was so happy as when feeding and caressing them. This peculiarity of character grew with my growth, and, in my manhood, I derived from it one of my principal sources of pleasure. To those who have cherished an affection for a faithful and sagacious dog, I need hardly be at the trouble of explaining the nature or the intensity of the gratification thus derivable. There is something in the unselfish and self-sacrificing love of a brute, which goes directly to the heart of him who has had frequent occa- sion to test the paltry friendship and gossamer fidelity of mere *Man*.

I married early, and was happy to find in my wife a disposition not uncongenial with my own. Observing my partiality for domestic pets, she lost no opportunity of procuring those of the most agreeable kind. We had birds, gold-fish, a fine dog, rabbits, a small monkey, and a *cat*.

This latter was a remarkably large and beautiful animal, entirely black, and sagacious to an astonishing degree. In speaking of his intelligence, my wife, who at heart was not a little tinctured with superstition, made frequent allusion to the ancient popular notion, which regarded all black cats as witches in disguise. Not that she was ever *serious* upon this point—and I mention the matter at all for no better reason than that it happens, just now, to be remembered.

Pluto—this was the cat's name—was my favorite pet and playmate. I alone fed him, and he attended me wherever I went about the house. It was even with difficulty that I could prevent him from following me through the streets.   5

Our friendship lasted, in this manner, for several years, during which my general temperament and character—through the instrumentality of the Fiend Intemperance—had (I blush to confess it) experienced a radical alteration for the worse. I grew, day by day, more moody, more irritable, more regardless of the feelings of others. I suffered myself to use intemper- ate language to my wife. At length, I even offered her personal violence. My pets, of course, were made to feel the change in my disposition. I not only neglected, but ill-used them. For Pluto, however, I still retained sufficient regard to restrain me from maltreating him, as I made no scruple of maltreating the rabbits, the monkey, or even the dog, when, by accident, or through affection, they came in my way. But my disease grew upon me—for what disease is like Alcohol!—and at length even Pluto, who was now becoming old, and consequently somewhat peevish—even Pluto began to experience the effects of my ill temper.

One night, returning home, much intoxicated, from one of my haunts about town, I fancied that the cat avoided my presence. I seized him; when, in his fright at my violence, he inflicted a slight wound upon my hand with his teeth. The fury of a demon instantly possessed me. I knew myself no longer. My original soul seemed, at once, to take its flight from my body; and a more than fiendish malevolence, gin-nurtured, thrilled every fibre of my frame. I took from my waistcoat-pocket a penknife, opened it, grasped the poor beast by the throat, and deliberately cut one of its eyes from the socket! I blush, I burn, I shudder, while I pen the damnable atrocity.

When reason returned with the morning—when I had slept off the fumes of the night's debauch—I experienced a sentiment half of horror, half of remorse, for the crime of which I had been guilty; but it was, at best, a feeble and equivocal feeling, and the soul remained untouched. I again plunged into excess, and soon drowned in wine all memory of the deed.

In the meantime the cat slowly recovered. The socket of the lost eye presented, it is true, a frightful appearance, but he no longer appeared to suffer any pain. He went about the house as usual, but, as might be expected, fled in extreme terror at my approach. I had so much of my old heart left, as to be at first grieved by this evident dislike on the part of a creature which had once so loved me. But this feeling soon gave place to irritation. And then came, as if to my final and irrevocable overthrow, the spirit of PER-VERSENESS. Of this spirit philosophy takes no account. Yet I am not more sure that my soul lives, than I am that perverseness is one of the primitive impulses of the human heart—one of the indivisible primary faculties, or sentiments, which give direction to the character of Man. Who has not, a hundred times, found himself committing a vile or a stupid action, for no other reason than because he knows he should *not?* Have we not a perpetual inclination, in the teeth of our best judgment, to violate that which is *Law,* merely because we understand it to be such? This spirit of perverseness, I say, came to my final overthrow. It was this unfathomable longing of the soul *to vex itself*—to offer violence to its own nature—to do wrong for the wrong's sake only—that urged me to continue and finally to consummate the injury I had inflicted upon the unoffending brute. One morning, in cold blood, I slipped a noose about its neck and hung it to the limb of a tree;—hung it with the tears streaming from my eyes, and with the bitterest remorse at my heart;—hung it *because* I knew that it had loved me, and *because* I felt it had given me no reason of offence;—hung it *because* I knew that in so doing I was committing a sin—a deadly sin that would so jeopardize my immortal soul as to place it—if such a thing were possible—even beyond the reach of the infinite mercy of the Most Merciful and Most Terrible God.

On the night of the day on which this most cruel deed was done, I was   10
aroused from sleep by the cry of fire. The curtains of my bed were in
flames. The whole house was blazing. It was with great difficulty that my
wife, a servant, and myself, made our escape from the conflagration. The
destruction was complete. My entire worldly wealth was swallowed up, and
I resigned myself thenceforward to despair.

I am above the weakness of seeking to establish a sequence of cause and
effect, between the disaster and the atrocity. But I am detailing a chain of
facts—and wish not to leave even a possible link imperfect. On the day succeeding the fire, I visited the ruins. The walls, with one exception, had fallen
in. This exception was found in a compartment wall, not very thick, which
stood about the middle of the house, and against which had rested the head
of my bed. The plastering had here, in great measure, resisted the action of
the fire—a fact which I attributed to its having been recently spread. About
this wall a dense crowd were collected, and many persons seemed to be
examining a particular portion of it with very minute and eager attention.
The words "strange!" "singular!" and other similar expressions, excited my
curiosity. I approached and saw, as if graven in *bas-relief* upon the white
surface, the figure of a gigantic *cat*. The impression was given with an accuracy truly marvellous. There was a rope about the animal's neck.

When I first beheld this apparition—for I could scarcely regard it as less—
my wonder and my terror were extreme. But at length reflection came to my
aid. The cat, I remembered, had been hung in a garden adjacent to the
house. Upon the alarm of fire, this garden had been immediately filled by
the crowd—by some one of whom the animal must have been cut from the
tree and thrown, through an open window, into my chamber. This had probably been done with the view of arousing me from sleep. The falling of other
walls had compressed the victim of my cruelty into the substance of the
freshly-spread plaster; the lime of which, with the flames, and the *ammonia*
from the carcass, had then accomplished the portraiture as I saw it.

Although I thus readily accounted to my reason, if not altogether to my
conscience, for the startling fact just detailed, it did not the less fail to make
a deep impression upon my fancy. For months I could not rid myself of the
phantasm of the cat; and, during this period, there came back into my spirit
a half-sentiment that seemed, but was not, remorse. I went so far as to
regret the loss of the animal, and to look about me, among the vile haunts
which I now habitually frequented, for another pet of the same species, and
of somewhat similar appearance, with which to supply its place.

One night as I sat, half stupefied, in a den of more than infamy, my attention was suddenly drawn to some black object, reposing upon the head of
one of the immense hogsheads of gin, or of rum, which constituted the
chief furniture of the apartment. I had been looking steadily at the top of
this hogshead for some minutes, and what now caused me surprise was the
fact that I had not sooner perceived the object thereupon. I approached it,
and touched it with my hand. It was a black cat—a very large one—fully as
large as Pluto, and closely resembling him in every respect but one. Pluto
had not a white hair upon any portion of his body; but this cat had a large,
although indefinite splotch of white, covering nearly the whole region of
the breast.

Upon my touching him, he immediately arose, purred loudly, rubbed   15
against my hand, and appeared delighted with my notice. This, then, was
the very creature of which I was in search. I at once offered to purchase it
of the landlord; but this person made no claim to it—knew nothing of it—
had never seen it before.

I continued my caresses, and when I prepared to go home, the animal
evinced a disposition to accompany me. I permitted it to do so; occasionally
stooping and patting it as I proceeded. When it reached the house it domesticated itself at once, and became immediately a great favorite with my wife.

For my own part, I soon found a dislike to it arising within me. This was
just the reverse of what I had anticipated; but—I know not how or why it
was—its evident fondness for myself rather disgusted and annoyed me. By
slow degrees these feelings of disgust and annoyance rose into the bitterness of hatred. I avoided the creature; a certain sense of shame, and the
remembrance of my former deed of cruelty, preventing me from physically
abusing it. I did not, for some weeks, strike, or otherwise violently ill use it;
but gradually—very gradually—I came to look upon it with unutterable
loathing, and to flee silently from its odious presence, as from the breath of
a pestilence.

What added, no doubt, to my hatred of the beast, was the discovery, on
the morning after I brought it home, that, like Pluto, it also had been
deprived of one of its eyes. This circumstance, however, only endeared it to
my wife, who, as I have already said, possessed, in a high degree, that
humanity of feeling which had once been my distinguishing trait, and the
source of many of my simplest and purest pleasures.

With my aversion to this cat, however, its partiality for myself seemed to
increase. It followed my footsteps with a pertinacity which it would be difficult to make the reader comprehend. Whenever I sat, it would crouch
beneath my chair, or spring upon my knees, covering me with its loathsome
caresses. If I arose to walk it would get between my feet and thus nearly
throw me down, or, fastening its long and sharp claws in my dress, clam-
ber, in this manner, to my breast. At such times, although I longed to
destroy it with a blow, I was yet withheld from so doing, partly by a memory of my former crime, but chiefly—let me confess it at once—by absolute
dread of the beast.

This dread was not exactly a dread of physical evil—and yet I should be
at a loss how otherwise to define it. I am almost ashamed to own—yes,
even in this felon's cell, I am almost ashamed to own—that the terror and   20
horror with which the animal inspired me, had been heightened by one of
the merest chimeras it would be possible to conceive. My wife had called
my attention, more than once, to the character of the mark of white hair,
of which I have spoken, and which constituted the sole visible difference between the strange beast and the one I had destroyed. The reader
will remember that this mark, although large, had been originally very
indefinite; but, by slow degrees—degrees nearly imperceptible, and which
for a long time my reason struggled to reject as fanciful—it had, at length,
assumed a rigorous distinction of outline. It was now the representation of
an object that I shudder to name—and for this, above all, I loathed, and
dreaded, and would have rid myself of the monster *had I dared*—it was

now, I say, the image of a hideous—of a ghastly thing—of the GALLOWS!—
oh, mournful and terrible engine of Horror and of Crime—of Agony and
of Death!

And now was I indeed wretched beyond the wretchedness of mere
Humanity. And *a brute beast*—whose fellow I had contemptuously
destroyed—*a brute beast* to work out for *me*—for me, a man fashioned in
the image of the High God—so much of insufferable woe! Alas! neither by
day nor by night knew I the blessing of rest any more! During the former
the creature left me no moment alone, and in the latter I started hourly from
dreams of unutterable fear to find the hot breath of *the thing* upon my face,
and its vast weight—an incarnate nightmare that I had no power to shake
off—incumbent eternally upon my *heart!*

Beneath the pressure of torments such as these the feeble remnant of the
good within me succumbed. Evil thoughts became my sole intimates—the
darkest and most evil of thoughts. The moodiness of my usual temper
increased to hatred of all things and of all mankind; while from the sudden,
frequent, and ungovernable outbursts of a fury to which I now blindly
abandoned myself, my uncomplaining wife, alas, was the most usual and
the most patient of sufferers.

One day she accompanied me, upon some household errand, into the
cellar of the old building which our poverty compelled us to inhabit. The
cat followed me down the steep stairs, and, nearly throwing me headlong,
exasperated me to madness. Uplifting an axe, and forgetting in my wrath
the childish dread which had hitherto stayed my hand, I aimed a blow at
the animal, which, of course, would have proved instantly fatal had it
descended as I wished. But this blow was arrested by the hand of my wife.
Goaded by the interference into a rage more than demoniacal, I withdrew
my arm from her grasp and buried the axe in her brain. She fell dead upon
the spot without a groan.

This hideous murder accomplished, I set myself forthwith, and with
entire deliberation, to the task of concealing the body. I knew that I could
not remove it from the house, either by day or by night, without the risk of
being observed by the neighbors. Many projects entered my mind. At one
period I thought of cutting the corpse into minute fragments, and destroying them by fire. At another, I resolved to dig a grave for it in the floor of
the cellar. Again, I deliberated about casting it in the well in the yard—about
packing it in a box, as if merchandise, with the usual arrangements, and so
getting a porter to take it from the house. Finally I hit upon what I considered a far better expedient than either of these. I determined to wall it up
in the cellar, as the monks of the Middle Ages are recorded to have walled
up their victims.

For a purpose such as this the cellar was well adapted. Its walls were   25
loosely constructed, and had lately been plastered throughout with a
rough plaster, which the dampness of the atmosphere had prevented from
hardening. Moreover, in one of the walls was a projection, caused by a false
chimney, or fireplace, that had been filled up and made to resemble the rest
of the cellar. I made no doubt that I could readily displace the bricks at this
point, insert the corpse, and wall the whole up as before, so that no eye
could detect any thing suspicious.

And in this calculation I was not deceived. By means of a crowbar I easily dislodged the bricks, and, having carefully deposited the body against the inner wall, I propped it in that position, while with little trouble I relaid the whole structure as it originally stood. Having procured mortar, sand, and hair, with every possible precaution, I prepared a plaster which could not be distinguished from the old, and with this I very carefully went over the new brick-work. When I had finished, I felt satisfied that all was right. The wall did not present the slightest appearance of having been disturbed. The rubbish on the floor was picked up with the minutest care. I looked around triumphantly, and said to myself: "Here at least, then, my labor has not been in vain."

My next step was to look for the beast which had been the cause of so much wretchedness; for I had, at length, firmly resolved to put it to death. Had I been able to meet with it at the moment, there could have been no doubt of its fate; but it appeared that the crafty animal had been alarmed at the violence of my previous anger, and forbore to present itself in my present mood. It is impossible to describe or to imagine the deep, the blissful sense of relief which the absence of the detested creature occasioned in my bosom. It did not make its appearance during the night; and thus for one night, at least, since its introduction into the house, I soundly and tranquilly slept; aye, *slept* even with the burden of murder upon my soul.

The second and the third day passed, and still my tormentor came not. Once again I breathed as a free man. The monster, in terror, had fled the premises for ever! I should behold it no more! My happiness was supreme! The guilt of my dark deed disturbed me but little. Some few inquiries had been made, but these had been readily answered. Even a search had been instituted—but of course nothing was to be discovered. I looked upon my future felicity as secured.

Upon the fourth day of the assassination, a party of the police came, very unexpectedly, into the house, and proceeded again to make rigorous investigation of the premises. Secure, however, in the inscrutability of my place of concealment, I felt no embarrassment whatever. The officers bade me accompany them in their search. They left no nook or corner unexplored. At length, for the third or fourth time, they descended into the cellar. I quivered not in a muscle. My heart beat calmly as that of one who slumbers in innocence. I walked the cellar from end to end. I folded my arms upon my bosom, and roamed easily to and fro. The police were thoroughly satisfied and prepared to depart. The glee at my heart was too strong to be restrained. I burned to say if but one word, by way of triumph, and to render doubly sure their assurance of my guiltlessness.

"Gentlemen," I said at last, as the party ascended the steps, "I delight to   30
have allayed your suspicions. I wish you all health and a little more courtesy. By the bye, gentlemen, this—this is a very well-constructed house," (in the rabid desire to say something easily, I scarcely knew what I uttered at all),—"I may say an *excellently* well-constructed house. These walls—are you going, gentlemen?—these walls are solidly put together"; and here, through the mere frenzy of bravado, I rapped heavily with a cane which I held in my hand, upon that very portion of the brick-work behind which stood the corpse of the wife of my bosom.

But may God shield and deliver me from the fangs of the Arch-Fiend! No sooner had the reverberation of my blows sunk into silence, than I was answered by a voice from within the tomb!—by a cry, at first muffled and broken, like the sobbing of a child, and then quickly swelling into one long, loud, and continuous scream, utterly anomalous and inhuman—a howl—a wailing shriek, half of horror and half of triumph, such as might have arisen only out of hell, conjointly from the throats of the damned in their agony and of the demons that exult in the damnation.

Of my own thoughts it is folly to speak. Swooning, I staggered to the opposite wall. For one instant the party on the stairs remained motionless, through extremity of terror and awe. In the next a dozen stout arms were toiling at the wall. It fell bodily. The corpse, already greatly decayed and clotted with gore, stood erect before the eyes of the spectators. Upon its head, with red extended mouth and solitary eye of fire, sat the hideous beast whose craft had seduced me into murder, and whose informing voice had consigned me to the hangman. I had walled the monster up within the tomb.

Poetry

When I began to read nursery rhymes for myself, and, later, to read other verses and ballads, I knew I had discovered the most important things that could be ever. There they were, seemingly lifeless, made only of black and white, but out of them, out of their own being, came love and terror and pity and pain and wonder and all the other vague abstractions that made our ephemeral lives dangerous, great, and bearable.

DYLAN THOMAS

12   Preview

The Voice of Poetry

The poet, lacking the impediment of speech with which the rest of us are afflicted, gazes, records, diagnoses, and prophesies.

RICHARD SELZER

FOCUS ON POETRY

Poets are in love with words. The gift of language makes us human, and poets make the fullest use of it. Poetry is language at its best: poets activate its full potential, using more of it and using it to better advantage than we usually do. They often seem to write with a heightened sense of awareness, with a special intensity—"in a fine frenzy," in Shakespeare's words. Listen to the human voice speaking in a poem. That voice may be speaking about anything in human experience, real or imagined. Here is a modern American poet speaking to you about the pain of separation.

W. S. Merwin   *(1927–1995)*

Separation   *1963*

Your absence has gone through me
Like thread through a needle.
Everything I do is stitched with its color.

What makes this a poem rather than ordinary prose?

✗ Out of the flow of experience, the poet has brought something into *focus*. For a moment, we stop hurrying to whatever we were doing next. We stop to pay attention. We linger for a while—to contemplate, to take something in.

✗ What we take in is not just talk. We are helped to *imagine* what separation is like. The poem gives us something to visualize, to take in

317

with the mind's eye. It is as if our days, like a piece of embroidery, were stitched through with a continuing thread—of missing the other person. A sewing needle does not jab the fabric once and then think about something else. It does its work by making one stitch after the other, stitching in the thread that will hold the fabric together or that will shape a pattern in a piece of embroidered material.

✗ The poem does not just give us information to feed into a data bank. We are not expected to record the message with no more emotion than a fax machine. The poet assumes that we are capable of caring one way or the other. We are capable of entering imaginatively into the poet's *feelings,* of sharing his sense of loss.

✗ Finally, the poem is printed as lines of verse. These measure out or mark off units of thought. They lay out the message in a satisfying *pattern* (that we can take in at a glance). When we finish reading, we have the satisfying sense of having taken in a complete whole.

THE POET'S LANGUAGE

Poems demand your attention. They use a language richer in meaning than ordinary talk. As you read and study poems, you respond to recurrent features of the poet's language:

Image   What does the poem make you see? Poets think in images. The images in a poem bring an experience to life by appealing to your senses—by making you see, hear, smell, taste, and touch. A dictionary might define *presentiment* as a sudden fleeting feeling of anxiety—a sudden, passing sense of foreboding. It is a "premonition that something hurtful is going to happen." Unlike a dictionary definition, the following poem does not *state* this idea; it brings it to life. It gives you something to see, to visualize.

Emily Dickinson   *(1830–1886)*

Presentiment   *1863*

Presentiment—Is that long Shadow—on the Lawn—
Indicative that Suns go down—
The Notice to the startled Grass
That Darkness—is about to pass—

The poem starts with a striking image: on a sunny day, we all of a sudden notice the dark shadow on the lawn that annnounces (or is an indication of) the coming of evening. Like the grass, we may be startled, afraid of darkness. We may share in a shuddery feeling. We are reminded that "suns go down"; like them, sunny parts of our lives must sooner or later alternate with darkness. Although there are feelings and thoughts in this poem, they come to us through the poet's use of vivid imagery.

Metaphor   How does the poem make imaginative connections? The most basic device poets use to go beyond ordinary literal speech is the **metaphor.** It "carries us beyond" literal meanings to something else. Metaphors are imaginative comparisons carrying meanings that might remain pale or incomplete when spelled out in literal terms. The poet Gregory Orr says, "Like any other man / I was born with a knife / in one hand / and a wound in the other." He does not mean that literally at birth he had a knife and a wound. He means that he, like all of us, was born with the ability and perhaps the genetic inclination to kill. At the same time, he, like all of us, was born capable of being harmed, of becoming in turn a victim.

A poet may trace a metaphor into its various ramifications, following up related similarities. Look at the **extended metaphor** in the following poem by a leading figure of the Harlem Renaissance of the thirties and forties:

Countee Cullen   *(1903–1946)*

For My Grandmother   *1927*

This lovely flower fell to seed;
Work gently sun and rain;
She held it as her dying creed
That she would grow again.

The central metaphor in this poem compares the grandmother to a flower. But the poet extends the metaphor beyond the flower in bloom to its whole life cycle: the flower grows from a seed, helped by sun and rain; it then decays and in turn leaves a seed. We cherish it because of its loveliness, but it is also subject to death and decay. However, the seed the flower leaves behind carries the promise of renewed growth— of rebirth and new life.

The Receptive Reader
1. Are the sun and the rain in this poem literal or metaphorical, or both?
2. When speaking of renewed growth, was the poet thinking of resurrection and eternal life? Or was he thinking of the grandchildren who were the "seed" representing continued life?

Symbol   What in the poem has a meaning beyond itself? A **symbol** carries a literal meaning and yet at the same time has a larger significance.

The following poem, one of the best-loved and most often discussed in the English language, is often read for its symbolic meaning.

Robert Frost   *(1874–1963)*

Stopping by Woods on a Snowy Evening   *1923*

Whose woods these are I think I know.
His house is in the village, though;
He will not see me stopping here
To watch his woods fill up with snow.

My little horse must think it queer   5
To stop without a farmhouse near
Between the woods and frozen lake
The darkest evening of the year.

He gives his harness bells a shake
To ask if there is some mistake.   10
The only other sound's the sweep
Of easy wind and downy flake.

The woods are lovely, dark and deep.
But I have promises to keep,
And miles to go before I sleep,   15
And miles to go before I sleep.

In this poem, we find ourselves on a deserted rural road in the winter, away from the nearest village or farmhouse, with the driver of the horse-drawn vehicle stopping to look at the woods filling up with snow. It is cold enough for the lake to have frozen over, and the evening is getting very dark, so the normal thing would be to hurry on home. (The horse certainly seems to think so, wondering "if there is some mistake.")

But something strange happens in this poem: it is very quiet; the wind is an "easy wind." The snowflakes are "downy"—soft like the feathers in a down-filled pillow beckoning toward rest. The snow-covered woods look "lovely." It would be tempting not to go on—to go to sleep in the soft snow. It would be restful to push out of mind whatever cares, responsibilities, or pressures are waiting in the village. While ordinarily we would be afraid to die in the freezing cold, to a harried person death could begin to seem restful and beautiful. In the end, tempting as the thought may be of dropping out, of going to "sleep," the speaker in the poem is kept going by the thought of "promises to keep." There are still "miles to go," as the speaker says twice, "miles to go."

If we read the woods in Frost's poems not as a place for a temporary rest but as a beckoning toward the final long rest of death, we are reading them as a symbol. A symbol has a literal reality and at the same a larger meaning. The woods in the Frost poem are literally there; we may choose to give them a larger symbolic significance.

The Receptive Reader

1. What kind of "promises" do you think the speaker had in mind?

2. Critics have argued over whether or not the dark woods in this poem are a symbol of death. What would be your answer, and how would you support it?

3. What is the effect of the poet's repeating the last line?

Rhyme   Does the poem use the echo effect of rhyme? Rhyme and meter are formal features of much traditional poetry, but they became optional during the twentieth century. **Rhyme** is an echo effect produced when a poet repeats the same sounds at the end of two or more lines: "The grizzly bear whose potent HUG / Was feared by all is now a RUG (Arthur Guiterman).

Rhyme keeps alive the delight in repetition, in finding recurrent patterns, of children who recite "Hickory-dickory-DOCK / The mouse ran up the CLOCK." At the same time, rhyme helps a poet create patterns by marking off regular intervals, by measuring off lines of verse. Rhyme can help a poet give shape to a **stanza,** a set of related lines with a pattern that may be repeated in other such stanzas in the same poem. In the following opening stanza of a song from a Shakespeare play (*Cymbeline* 4.2), we see an interlaced rhyme scheme: The first and third lines rhyme (*sun/done*). So do the second and fourth, as well as the fifth and sixth (giving us a pattern of ababcc):

William Shakespeare   *(1564–1616)*

Fear No More the Heat of the Sun

Fear no more the heat o' the SUN,	a
Nor the furious winter's RAGES.	b
Thou thy worldly task hast DONE,	a
Home art gone, and ta'en thy WAGES.	b
Golden lads and girls all MUST,	c
As chimney-sweepers, come to DUST.	c

Most poets of the last century have done without rhyme. They have moved from traditional form, with rhyme and an underlying regular beat, or meter, toward more open form. They lay out their poems and give shape to them by other means.

Meter   Does the poem have a regular rhythm, or meter? In much traditional poetry, **meter** regulates the free-flowing rhythms of ordinary speech. It sets up a regular underlying beat—the kind that in music might make you tap your feet or clap your hands. Much modern poetry has moved toward freer, more irregular rhythms—hard to chart, or **scan,** as a regular beat.

Meter has an enticing and sometimes hypnotic effect. It mirrors basic rhythms of life: the lub-DUB, lub-DUB, lub-DUB of the heart; the one-two, one-two of walking or running; the in-out of deep breathing. The following lines from the poem by Robert Frost that you read earlier have an exceptionally regular beat. Each second syllable has a stronger stress than the first. The exceptions are the fourth word in the first and second lines and the second word in the third line. These variations keep the basic four-beat line from becoming monotonous, like the tick-tack of a metronome:

> Whose WOODS these <u>are</u> I THINK I KNOW.
> His HOUSE is <u>in</u> the VILLAGE THOUGH.
> He <u>will</u> not SEE me STOPPING HERE
> To WATCH his WOODS fill UP with SNOW.

To chart the basic meter, we can cut up the line into four pairs of syllables, each with an *unstressed* or weak syllable first and a *stressed* or emphasized syllable second:

> To WATCH | his WOODS | fill UP | with SNOW.

Each of these four segments is called a **foot.** A foot with only two syllables and the stress last is an **iambic** foot, and the "DETROIT-DETROIT-DETROIT" meter it sets up is called iambic meter. The following poem is by Alfred, Lord Tennyson, poet-sage of the Victorian Age (roughly the mid-nineteenth century). Read the poem out loud or hear it read out loud. Which lines come closest to a regular four-beat iambic meter? What makes the second and third lines different?

Alfred, Lord Tennyson   *(1809–1892)*

The Eagle   *1851*

He clasps the crag with crooked hands;
Close to the sun in lonely lands,
Ringed with the azure° world, he stands.   *deep sky-blue*

The wrinkled sea beneath him crawls;
He watches from his mountain walls,   5
And like a thunderbolt he falls.

The first line of the poem, like the fourth, has a very regular beat:

He CLASPS | the CRAG | with CROOK | ed HANDS

But at the beginning of the second line (and also of the third), the stress pattern is reversed. This reversal, or inversion, sets up the kind of counter-rhythm that keeps meter from becoming too mechanical:

CLOSE to | the SUN | in LONE | ly LANDS

The Receptive Reader

1. How should this poem sound when read aloud? Listen as several classmates read the poem. Which of them comes closest to the right balance—making the reader sense the underlying rhythm without making it mechanical or obtrusive?

2. Although almost extinct, the eagle is everywhere in traditional lore and public symbols. What images, ideas, or associations does the eagle bring to mind? Are any of them echoed in Tennyson's poem? Is there anything new or different about the way Tennyson asks us to imagine the eagle in this poem?

Rhythm   How does the poem use the natural rhythms of language? Even in Tennyson's time, poets were experimenting with less regular rhythms. Here is an example of **free verse** by the American poet Walt Whitman, the "poet of democracy." Whitman's free verse has a strong rhythm, but it does not have an easily charted regular beat. Some lines are short, but others go on and on. Whitman saw himself as the prophet of new national spirit, and we can imagine that we are hearing the poet chant these lines. In the words of one student reader, "The almost chanting, yet not mesmerizingly regular rhythm elevates the tone of the poem and gives it almost oracular power."

Walt Whitman   *(1819–1892)*

A Noiseless Patient Spider   *1881*

A noiseless patient spider
I marked where on a little promontory° it stood isolated,   *outcropping*
Marked how to explore the vacant vast surrounding
It launched forth filament, filament, filament out of itself,
Ever unreeling them, ever tirelessly speeding them.   5

And you O my soul where you stand,
Surrounded, detached, in measureless oceans of space,
Ceaselessly musing, venturing, throwing, seeking the spheres to
    connect them,
Till the bridge you will need be formed, till the ductile°   *easily bent*
    anchor hold,
Till the gossamer thread you fling catch somewhere, O my soul.   10

This poem focuses on the parallel between "the noiseless patient spider" and the human soul. The spider stands "isolated" as if on a cliff jutting out into the sea, encircled by the "vacant vast surrounding." Similarly, the soul finds itself "detached, in measureless oceans of space"— in the vast spaces our thoughts can travel. The spider spins and launches forth "filament, filament, filament," hoping they will catch at points beyond the empty space to allow it to anchor its net. Similarly, the human soul, "ceaselessly musing, venturing, throwing, seeking," launches forth the thoughts that will allow it to connect with what gives meaning to our lives.

Here is how you might mark the stresses that account for the rhythm of the first three lines.

A NOISEless PATient SPIDer
I MARKed where on a LITTle PROMONtory it STOOD ISolated,
MARKed how to EXPLORE the VACANT VAST surROUNDing

The Receptive Reader

1. How well do you respond to the *rhythm* of Whitman's verse? Can you chart the major stressed syllables in the rest of the poem? Do you and your classmates agree on the rhythmic patterns of the lines?

2. What ideas or associations do spiders usually bring to mind? What is *different* about the way Whitman looks at the spider in this poem?

3. What is the connection between the spider and the poet's *soul?* What is the "bridge" the soul will need? What is the "gossamer thread" the soul flings in this poem?

4. Why does the poet start with the *image* of the patient spider—rather than with the central idea of the poem? What does the poet lose or gain by not letting us know till halfway through the poem that it is addressed to his soul?

Open Form   What gives the poem its unique shape? Much later poetry has a less strong, less chanting rhythm than Whitman's poems. Modern poets have used the full range of **open form,** which allows them to give each poem its own individual shape and rhythm. What gives the following poem its unique shape? Gwendolyn Brooks is best known for eloquent poems about the injustices suffered by black Americans, although many of her poems are loving portraits of people she cherished.

Gwendolyn Brooks   *(born 1917)*

truth   *1949*

And if sun comes
How shall we greet him?
Shall we not dread him,

Shall we not fear him
After so lengthy a   5
Session with shade?

Though we have wept for him,
Though we have prayed
All through the night-years—
What if we wake one shimmering morning to   10
Hear the fierce hammering
Of his firm knuckles
Hard on the door?

Shall we not shudder?—
Shall we not flee   15
Into the shelter, the dear thick shelter
Of the familiar
Propitious° haze?   *promising good fortune*

Sweet is it, sweet is it
To sleep in the coolness   20
Of snug unawareness.

The dark hangs heavily
Over the eyes.

The Receptive Reader

1. This poem does not use traditional rhyme and meter. What guides you in reading the poem with the right rhythm? Point out examples of the poet's repeating phrases or sentence frames. Can you show how this repetition sets up patterns that help make the poem a unified whole? What is the effect of the frequent repetition or echoing on you as the reader?

2. Traditional guidelines for rhyme ruled out the repetition of identical words at the end of lines. It occurs in contemporary poetry—where does it occur in this poem? Pairs of words that do not rhyme but more distantly sound alike are **half-rhymes** or **slant rhymes.** Where do you find these in the poem?

3. How are the images and feelings associated with the sun in this poem different from more familiar or predictable ones? How are the images and feelings associated with the dark, its opposite, different from what we might expect?

4. What "fierce" and feared or dreaded truths do you think the poet had in mind? What kind of "night-years" may the poet have been thinking about?

Theme   What does the poem say as a whole? Poems do not usually hand on ideas ready-made. A poem may imply or suggest ideas; it may play them off or act them out. When we look for the statement made by a poem as a whole, we are looking for its **theme.** The theme is the answer the poem as a whole seems to give to the questions it raises.

The following poem is exceptionally direct in the message it addresses to its readers. A Spanish scholar, playwright, and poet who has been called "the first poetic figure of the New World" here takes up a theme to which she repeatedly returned in her poems. She wrote at a time when conventions of courtship required the male lover to pursue or "importune" the lady, who was expected to be reluctant or disdainful, and who was then blamed for being cruel and cold.

Juana Inés de la Cruz   *(1651–1695)*

Ignorant Men   *1692*

TRANSLATED BY JUDITH THURMAN

Ignorant men who disclaim
women with no reason,
you do not see you are the reason
for what you blame.

Importuning her disdain   5
with such pressing desire,
why is it goodness you then require,
who have caused her shame?

What humour° can be so rare   *state of mind*
that carelessly will blur   10
a mirror, and then aver°   *claim*
that it's not clear?

Critics: In your sight
no woman can win:
Keep you out, and she's too tight;   15
she's too loose if you get in.
          From *A Satirical Romance*

The Receptive Reader

1. How does this poem lead up to its central message? What makes the mirror image effective?

2. Do you think this message by a seventeenth-century poet has lost its timeliness? Or does it still speak to the modern reader? Do you think the poet's indictment of men is justified?

3. Do you think women today speak this frankly to men?

4. Do you think this poem is addressed only to men—or also to women?

5. Write a journal entry as a reply to or comment on this poem.

Making Connections—For Discussion or Writing

Which of the poems in this group speaks to you most directly as a reader? Which is least meaningful for you? Which lives up best to what you expect poetry to be?

CLOSE READING AND THE PERSONAL RESPONSE

May God us keep
From single vision.
WILLIAM BLAKE

What is your role as the reader? A poem is not like an art object in a glass case in a museum, with a sign that says, "Do not touch the artifacts." A successful poem does something for you as the reader: It may open a new perspective. It may shake you up; it may move you to laughter or to tears. The poem ceases to be just words on a page when it triggers this kind of interaction between the poet and you as the reader.

Give the following short poem a careful line-by-line reading. Then look at one student reader's close reading of the poem. What did you miss that the student reader noticed? What in turn did you notice that she apparently missed?

Linda Pastan   *(born 1932)*

Sometimes in Winter   *1991*

when I look into
the fragile faces
of those I love,

I long to be
one of those people who skate   5
over the surface

of their lives, scoring
the ice with patterns
of their own making,

people who have   10
no children,
who are attached

to earth only by
silver blades moving
at high speed,   15

who have learned to use
the medium of the cold
to dance in.

Compare the reading in the following sample student paper with your own reading of the poem:

Sample Student Paper

Dancing in the Medium of the Cold

In the poem "Sometimes in Winter," we are asked to explore the relationship between life and ice-skating. Taken out of context, the metaphor of life as skating over ice might not appear to be entirely serious. But the images that are used in this poem make us think seriously about the comparison. The comparison is followed up in a chain of related words and images: winter, cold, a surface that can be scored but not penetrated, patterns sketched in the ice, silver blades speeding across the ice.

On the surface, the sight of the "silver blades moving / at high speed" across the ice is very appealing. The skaters score "the ice with patterns / of their own making." They seem in charge, in control, deciding for themselves whether they want to score in the ice a figure 8 or some other kind of graceful loop. What a relief it would be to be a free-floating skater and not to have to worry about the needs and demands of others who depend on us.

However, the person speaking to us in the poem cannot be like an ice-skater skimming over the surface of life. For her, love means attachment. Looking into the "fragile" faces of those she loves, she sees how vulnerable they are. The speaker implies that love for children holds her to the earth when she says that people who have no children are attached to the earth only by "silver blades moving / at high speed." Is this connection enough to hold a person to the earth for very long? What happens to the ice-skater when this tenuous connection is severed? Does she fly off the earth? Does she cease to exist? That is what the metaphor implies. People who are not attached to loved ones are not fully participating in life; they only glide over the surface. They dance on top of life, but they do not enter into it.

The speaker in the poem says that she longs to be one of the people who skate over the surface of life, but the metaphor she uses belies or contradicts that claim. She may be attracted to the speed and flash of the ice-skater, but the images we see make us realize that the flash is all on the surface. The skaters are adapting to the medium in which they live; they are surrounded by the cold, so they have learned to dance (live) in it. If they were allowed to choose all over again, might they not say that they long to be attached to the earth by something more than silver blades moving at high speed?

Bickering, emergency phone calls, and disrupted schedules make life in close contact with others very different from skating gracefully over the ice. But could we stand "the medium of the cold" if we severed our ties?

The Receptive Reader

Does this reading explain why there is so much ice and cold in this poem? What do the "silver blades" make you see or feel? Were you surprised by the use of the word *fragile* at the beginning of the poem? (Does the student writer do enough to explain how it makes us feel?) How do you explain that the skaters are "dancing"?

The two responses that follow the next poem by an Irish poet are by the same reader. The first response is again the kind of close reading that tries to do justice to the poem in front of us on the page. The second response, however, goes a step further. The reader asked: What does this poem mean to me personally? Is there any personal connection between this poem and something in my own life? Study the two different dimensions of this reader's response. How are they different? How are they related?

Seamus Heaney   *(born 1939)*

Valediction   *1966*

Lady with the frilled blouse
And simple tartan skirt,
Since you have left the house
Its emptiness has hurt
All thought. In your presence   5
Time rode easy, anchored
On a smile; but absence
Rocked love's balance, unmoored
The days. They buck and bound
Across the calendar   10
Pitched from the quiet sound
Of your flower-tender
Voice. Need breaks on my strand;°   *beach, shore*
You've gone, I am at sea.
Until you resume command   15
Self is in mutiny.

Look at the way the following reading pulls out and interprets significant details in the poem:

CLOSE READING: The poem "Valediction" describes the emotional experience of a man whose female companion (probably his wife) has left him. The poet uses a central metaphor to explain the speaker's emotional state, a metaphor he develops in a variety of ways, to describe exactly how the man in the poem is affected by her absence.

The metaphor in the poem is that of a boat on a lake or an ocean. When the "lady with the frilled blouse / And simple tartan skirt" was present, the boat was "anchored" secure in its mooring. "Time rode easy," suggesting the placid setting and the speaker's previously peaceful state of mind. With her absence, however, the calmness is lost: "love's balance," which existed in her presence, is "rocked," and the days "unmoored." Time is no longer safe at anchor but cast off, wild. The days now "buck" and "bound" as the boat pitches in the water; there is nothing smooth about the man's existence any more.

Meanwhile, the waves have started to break on the beach. The waves are the man's "need," the beach his "strand." With the lady gone, the speaker is truly "at sea." He can only visualize calm in his life once more if she will return to "command" the boat that is the speaker himself. Until that time the boat is doomed to be "in mutiny," that is, beyond his control, at the mercy of time and the waves.

The Receptive Reader

What details in the poem follow up the contrast between the calm before and the turmoil after the woman's departure? Were you surprised by the phrase "resume command"? What do you think it shows about the relationship between the two people? Did this reader miss any significant details in this poem?

Look at the way the following response by the same reader relates the poem to the reader's own experience. A paper anchored in close reading but going on to the personal connection would answer both basic questions: What does this poem mean—to perhaps a majority of perceptive readers? And what does the poem mean to me?

PERSONAL RESPONSE: It is easy to identify with a poem that carries such an obvious central metaphor. It uses the boat rocked by waves as the metaphor for an event disturbing the equilibrium of someone's life. While I have never experienced what it is like to have the most important person in my life walk out on me, curiously enough, I dreamed about this happening to me just a few nights ago. In my dream I was in college, and J. had just left me. (As is common with dreams, there was no obvious reason for this occurrence.)

I experienced total and utter despair. Although several close friends and family were with me, they were unable, even unwilling, to help me through the experience. I was truly "at sea." I started out into the streets, attempting to find my way "home" to J. A wind started to roar towards me, hindering my steps, and the flat road suddenly became a hill. My last impression before awaking involved a clear realization that I never would succeed in reaching the crest of the hill and passing over to the other side.

Thinking about this dream, I have become aware that I fear greatly this absence that Heaney describes in his poem. I find myself believing that I would act like the man he describes and like the person I appeared to be in my dream. Fortunately for me, I have the warning ahead of time—never to take your loved ones for granted.

The Receptive Reader

How do you explain this reader's dream? What is the connection between the dream and the poem? Did this poem bring any personal associations or memories to your mind? How did you personally react to the poem?

THE CREATIVE DIMENSION

One way of "getting into" a poem is to allow it to trigger a creative response, to bring your own creativity into play. When a poem moves you in a special way, it may trigger a creative effort of your own—a poem, a prose passage, a drawing, a photograph. Such a creative response or **re-creation** may sum up a personal impression. It may pursue a train of thought set in motion by something in the original poem. It may focus on a haunting image or take off from a provocative phrase. It may talk back to the original poem. One basic function of poetry is to keep alive the poet in each of us. We are not likely to become good readers of poetry if we seldom use our own imagination.

One way to get into the spirit of a poem is to write a similar poem of your own. This way you get to know the poem "from the inside"—the way a person playing an instrument or acting a part in amateur performance ceases to be a passive spectator. The following is a poem that invites imitation—not a dutiful copying but a playing with the same basic format and tone:

Wallace Stevens   *(1879–1955)*

Disillusionment of Ten O'Clock   *1923*

The houses are haunted
By white night-gowns.
None are green,
Or purple with green rings,
Or green with yellow rings,   5
Or yellow with blue rings.
None of them are strange,
With socks of lace
And beaded ceintures.°   *fancy sashes*
People are not going   10
To dream of baboons and periwinkles.°   *cone-shaped snails*
Only, here and there, an old sailor,
Drunk and asleep in his boots,
Catches tigers
In red weather.   15

The Receptive Reader

1. Why is this poet "disillusioned"? About what?

2. What is funny about the idea of these houses being "haunted"? Why does the color of people's nightgowns matter in this poem? The critic Irving Howe said that the nightgowns are the "uniform of ordinariness and sober nights." What did he mean?

3. Why do *dreams* matter in this poem? What do the people's dreams and their nightgowns have in common?

4. Does the poet share the conventional attitude toward *drunks?* Howe said that the sailor is the one person in this poem who "stands outside the perimeter of busy dullness." What did he mean?

The Creative Dimension

We know that a student has understood and appreciated the Wallace Stevens poem when we see the following student-written re-creation. How or how well does the student poem capture the mood and intention of the original? How close is it to the original in pattern or form? Try your hand at a similar creative effort, inspired by this or another poem you have read.

Disenchantment at the Dance

The dance is crowded
With blue denim.
There are no dresses
Of shiny, red satin
Or shimmering silk.
No bright feathered hats
No rhinestone buttons.
People aren't dancing
The foxtrot or cha cha.
Only, once in a while,
A few underclassmen
In T-shirts and jeans
Clap their hands
Shuffle their feet.

In the following unrhymed modern poem, the layout of the lines on the page guides us in setting up the pauses that shape the rhythm of the poem as a whole. Have you ever felt like leaving a message that might begin "This is just to say"?

William Carlos Williams   *(1883–1963)*

This Is Just to Say   1934

I have eaten
the plums
that were in
the icebox

and which   5
you were probably
saving
for breakfast

Forgive me
they were delicious   10
so sweet
and so cold

The Creative Dimension

Look at the following student-written response to the Williams poem. How or how well did the student reader get into the spirit of the original poem? Then write a "This-is-just-to-say" message of your own.

This is just to say

I used
the last of
the gas
in your car

you will probably be in
a rush tomorrow
and won't have
time
to refill the
tank

I'm sorry
but I had
no money
and I so
detest the
smell of gas
on my
hands

WRITING ABOUT LITERATURE

12   Keeping a Poetry Journal (Suggestions for Writing)

The Writing Workshop   Keeping a poetry journal helps you become a more responsive, more thoughtful reader. Your journal can also be the place where you do much of the **prewriting** for more structured formal papers. In writing a paper, you will be able to turn to your journal for tentative ideas, relevant evidence, and background information

✶ Your journal gives you a chance to formulate your *overall impression* of a poem. You may start with first impressions, trying to organize them into some preliminary pattern. You may try to get down and organize some of the free-floating associations and reactions that the poem activates on first reading. Keeping a journal will get you into the habit of thinking about the significance, shape, and tone of a poem as a whole.

✶ Your journal enables you to keep a rough record of what you take in as you read. You may want to use part of your journal for a *running commentary,* highlighting striking passages, key images, or notes struck more than once in a poem. In your journal, you can focus on a question that bothers you or on puzzling details. Your journal then serves as the record of your close reading of a poem, as you get involved in the way it takes shape and as you try to do justice to nuances and shades of meaning.

✶ Your journal gives you a chance to formulate your *personal response.* Some poems move us strongly. They strike a powerful chord. We seem to be listening to a kindred spirit. Other poems are impressive or thought-provoking, but we read them from a respectful distance. Still other poems we fight, because they seem to be looking at our world through the wrong end of the telescope. Or they may make us confront topics or issues we have been trying to avoid. In your journal, you can begin to explain and justify to yourself your own personal interaction with a poem.

The following sample entries from student journals illustrate possible topics and formats for your own journal. Note that the entries show evidence of careful firsthand reading—weaving into the text quoted words and phrases, half lines and whole lines, from the poems being discussed.

Focus on Words   A large part of careful close reading is trying to decode fully the shades of meaning, the overtones, and the associations of the poet's words. In a short poem, each word counts. (It has been estimated that the weight-per-word is five to ten times in a poem what it would be in ordinary casual prose.) The author of the following journal entry "read out" of the poet's choice of words considerably more than their bare dictionary meaning:

William Carlos Williams in "The Dance" makes us see the peasants making merry in a painting by Breughel, a sixteenth-century Flemish painter of peasant life. Right away we see that the people in the painting are big, beefy, corpulent, solid peasant types. The poet uses the word *round* several times ("the dancers go round, they go round and / around"). The poet compares their bellies to the "thick-sided glasses whose wash they impound."

Williams uses words like *squeal* and *blare* and *tweedle* to decribe the music of the bagpipes. These words are not normally used to describe music;

in fact, they have connotations of being really annoying sounds. *Squeal* brings to mind pictures of stuck pigs, angry children, or the air being let out of tires. *Blare* makes us hear the horns of frustrated drivers, the sound a donkey makes, unwelcome stereos at 3 a.m., or a charging elephant. *Tweedle* to me is an annoying, monotonous sound that alternates between two high-pitched notes, back and forth, back and forth. The choice of these words gives us an idea that the dancers are not a noble bunch. These are people whose children probably don't wear shoes; these dancers dance to loud music and drink and belch and don't give a second thought. Just from these word choices, I see big bellies that shirts don't quite cover. I see women with enormous hips. Food in enormous quantities is being eaten, perhaps without utensils or even plates. Faces are being wiped on sleeves, not napkins or towels. These people are hard workers, and they celebrate hard, with great happiness.

Focus on Metaphor   Often a poem comes into focus for us as we begin to see the full meaning of a central metaphor or organizing symbol. The following journal entry traces in detail the possible ramifications of a haunting central image:

Spiders usually bring associations of haunted, spooky places inhabited by ghosts, witches, and skeletons. Spiders are often thought of as cruel beings who suck the blood out of poor trapped helpless bugs. On the other hand, spiders also bring visions of beautiful, sparkling, intricate webs. In his poem "A Noiseless Patient Spider," Walt Whitman takes us way beyond the ordinary associations. He sees the spider sympathetically as it noiselessly and patiently performs the simple life-supporting fucntion of sending out its web in search of its needs. So Whitman can easily slip into the parallel search of each person (not just poets!). "Ceaselessly musing, venturing, throwing," we search for the ideas, beliefs, values, or mission that can be the anchor of our lives. The "gossamer threads" that the soul flings are the searching thoughts, the trial and error, the seeking that each person performs to find a happy or at least bearable environment in which the mind and heart can live. The bridge each soul seeks to build will take it to a meaning that imposes order on the universe, which without it remains an incomprehensible, dangerous place.

The Reader's Background   A poem is a ransaction between the poet and the reader. A poem is not sufficient onto itself. It activates and shapes what the reader brings to the poem—in the way of memories, associations, overtones of words, shared values, or cultural heritage. The student author of the following entry was able to get into the spirit of a poem because it stimulated a range of relevant associations. She was able to make the right connections:

In his poem "Pied Beauty," G. M. Hopkins writes about beauty that is not smooth and boring but instead dappled, freckled, "counter, original, spare, strange." The poem cites as an example different occupations or trades with their "gear and tackle and trim." I thought right away of a friend who was a rock climber—he had a fascinating variety of ropes, clips, wedges, "helpers," with the ropes and slings in bright, varied colors. I also thought of painters or roofers, with their trucks loaded down with various gear—ladders, paint cans with paint dripping down the sides, plastic coverings, drop cloths spattered with paint. Hopkins looked with wonder and delight at asymmetrical things that to him became a symbol of the color and variety of God's creation.

The student who wrote the following entry felt he had a special way into a poem because of his regional background:

An image is the picture that is worth a thousand words. But do images communicate equally effectively with different readers? If the reader does not have the background that a poet assumes, does the significance of the poem suffer? I cannot help feeling that something is lost if people are not aware of what it takes to rise on a bitter cold winter morning as "imaged" in Robert Hayden's poem "Those Winter Sundays." In the "blueblack cold," the father, with cracked hands that ached from his weekday labor, made the "banked fires blaze"—but "no one ever thanked him" for this labor of love. As an Easterner transplanted to Southern California, I know it is difficult to explain bitter cold, or the glory of thunderstorms, or the bite of the air on a crisp autumn day. Here there is no weather. Spirits cannot be brought down by yearning for a weekend that is then rained out—two months in a row. Spirits cannot be raised by the first sight of buds on the trees, the first call of spring birds. There are no major mood swings.

The Personal Response How we as readers experience a poem depends on our private agendas, emotional needs, and moral values. A poem can have a powerful impact on us if it gives voice and directions to what we already strongly feel:

In his poem "London," William Blake takes us to an eighteenth-century city where we hear the "infant's cry of fear," "the hapless soldier's sigh," and the "youthful harlot's curse" among soot-blackened churches and castles whose walls are figuratively covered with blood. Every day my own point of view toward today's cities comes closer to Blake's. Cities today are filled with poverty, violence, and hunger. I cannot walk to school without seeing the lines of people in the naturalization offices, the children waiting in line at the rescue mission, or the homeless and mentally challenged sleeping on the grass outside Grace Baptist Church. I honestly don't know why I get so upset about all the poverty in the city. I guess I feel so guilty because of all the advantages I have had. And when I see the children lining up to get at least one real meal, the guilt sets in.

The Creative Dimension A poem may serve as a stimulus or catalyst for a creative effort of your own that spins off from the original. The student author of the following entry had read Thomas Hardy's end-of-the-century poem "The Darkling Thrush" (Chapter 13—the century being the nineteenth century. She wrote the following farewell poem for the twentieth century:

An Epitaph for the Twentieth Century by 438-11-7322

Nine digits we're linked to
from birth
A number that stays with us
till our last day on earth

Without a number
You can have no card
Without a card
All business retards

Whether you're a king, queen, or jack
Hinges on where your card fits into the stack

In the future they'll remark:
Humankind gave the digit a high place
and did much to erase
Fingerprint and face.

How to Cite Poetry   In writing your journal entries, practice the conventions that you will have to observe in more formal papers.

✘ Put the title of the poem in quotation marks; *italicize* (<u>underscore</u> on an old-fashioned typewriter) the book or collection in which it appears.

Judy Grahn's poem "Paris and Helen" appears in her collection *The Queen of Wands*.

✘ When you run in lines of poetry as part of your own text, use a **slash** (with a space on either side) to show line breaks in the original poem:

Asked to let anger out of its cage, the speaker in the poem says that anger, once loose, "may / turn on me, maul / my face, draw blood."

✘ Normally set off three or more lines of verse as a **block quotation**—indent and center on page, *no* quotation marks. (You may choose to set off even a single line or two lines to make them stand out.)

The rose plays a somewhat unusual role in the opening lines of Gwendolyn Brooks' poem "A Song in the Frontyard":
> I've stayed in the front yard all my life.
> I want to peek at the back
> Where it's rough and untended and hungry weeds grow.
> A girl gets sick of a rose.

✘ Use double quotation marks for ordinary quotations; use **single quotation marks** for a quote-within-a-quote:

In her introduction to Janet Lewis' *Poems Old and New: 1918–1978*, Helen Trimpi says that Lewis' poetry has a drive "toward balance—to 'bind despair and joy / into a stable whole'—in life as well as in music and art."

13 Pattern

The Whole Poem

*The person who writes out of an inner need is
trying to order his corner of the universe; very
often the meaning of an experience or an emotion
becomes clear only in this way.*

MAXINE KUMIN

FOCUS ON PATTERN

Poetry, like its sister arts, springs from our impulse to give shape to experience. A poem opens, moves forward, and comes to a close. It has an overall pattern; it has a design. When we read attentively, we sense how the poem takes shape. As we read and reread, we begin to see how details work in **context**—in a web of meanings. Parts that seemed puzzling at first may slowly fall into place. They become part of the whole.

Each poem is different. However, organizing strategies like the following may help a poet shape a poem as a whole:

The Central Question A poem may directly or indirectly ask a question. It may focus our attention on something for us to ponder, to be concerned about. It may seem to raise an issue and then work toward an answer. The answer the poem points to may not be the last word on the issue. It will not suit everyone. But it can give us a sense that the poet finished what he or she started.

The Play of Polarities A poem may play off opposites. When we see clearly defined polar opposites, we call them **polarities.** Polarities help us organize our thoughts; they help us draw our mental maps. They are built into the texture of our lives: man and woman, night and day, land and sea, arrival and departure, storm and calm. We chart our course between opposite poles: work and play, success and failure, dependence and independence. The following passage from the King James Bible (Ecclesiastes 3:1–8) rehearses age-old polarities that are constants in human experience. Which of these opposed pairs from biblical times still play a major role in our lives? For those that seem dated or obsolete, what would be a modern counterpart?

339

Ecclesiastes 3:1–8

To every thing there is a season, and a time to every purpose under the
    heaven:
A time to be born, and a time to die; a time to plant, and a time to pluck
    up that which is planted;
A time to kill, and a time to heal; a time to break down, and a time to
    build up;
A time to weep, and a time to laugh; a time to mourn, and a time to dance;
A time to cast away stones, and a time to gather stones together; a time to   5
    embrace, and a time to refrain from embracing;
A time to get, and a time to lose; a time to keep, and a time to cast away;
A time to rend, and a time to sew; a time to keep silence, and a time to
    speak;
A time to love, and a time to hate; a time of war, and a time of peace.

Contrasting Perspectives   A poem may play off contrasting points of
view. In some early poems about love, the pleas of the male lover alternate with the doubts and misgivings expressed by the woman. The
poem reads like a **dialogue,** with two people having their say. Or a
poem may juxtapose one person's feelings about another at the beginning and at the end of a relationship.

Travels of the Mind   A poem may move from one kind of reality to
another. It may move from the present back to the past or onward to the
future. It may move between dream and waking, playing off our everyday world against the world of daydream or nightmare. It may move
between surface appearance and underlying reality.

When a poem has reached its destination, when it has had its say, we
feel a satisfying sense of completeness. We say that the poem has
achieved **closure.** Something worth our attention has been accomplished or completed. Many readers have found the following poem
beautifully finished, complete in itself. The poet takes us on a journey
of the mind—a journey from one state of mind to another. The poem
focuses on a need. The poem as a whole then fills that need.

Wendell Berry   *(born 1934)*

The Peace of Wild Things   *1968*

When the despair of the world grows in me
and I wake in the night at the least sound
in fear of what my life and my children's life may be,
I go and lie down where the wood drake°   *male duck with brilliant plumage*
rests in his beauty on the water, and the   5
    great heron feeds.
I come into the peace of wild things
who do not tax their lives with forethought

of grief. I come into the presence of still water.
And I feel above me the day-blind stars
waiting with their light. For a time   10
I rest in the grace of the world, and am free.

The Receptive Reader

1. What is the need the speaker in the poem feels while lying awake in the dark of night? How does the poem provide the needed antidote?

2. For you, what are the key contrasts between the speaker's human world and the world of the "wild things" of nature? What does the speaker mean by "forethought of grief"?

3. How are the stars "day-blind"? For the speaker, do you think the stars were comforting or distant and cold?

4. The word *grace* has several possible meanings, from "gracefulness" to "divine grace." What does the word mean in the context of the last line?

The Personal Response

What do you think are the fears that keep the speaker in the poem awake at night? Do you think people can find ways to escape from "forethought" or worry about the future?

THE POWER OF ATTENTION

A poem is a momentary stay against confusion.
ROBERT FROST

How do poems organize the flow of experience? First of all, poems focus our attention. Too often we are hurried, unable to pay undivided attention to any one thing. The poet asks us to slow down, to stop for a closer look. The poem, for a time, brings part of our human reality into **focus.** For instance, it may ask us to focus on a place, a person, or an event in order to fix a moment in time. The following poem is like a freeze-frame capturing a picture that, though mute, has something to say to us. What does the poem invite you to see? What does it make you feel? Does it make you think?

William Carlos Williams   *(1883–1963)*

Between Walls   *1934*

the back wings
of the

hospital where
nothing

will grow lie   5
cinders

in which shine
the broken

pieces of a green
bottle   10

The Receptive Reader

1. Why do you think the poet bypassed the rest of the building and of the
hospital grounds to focus your attention where he does?

2. Some of the key words in this poem are *hospital, nothing,* and *cinders.*
Why are they key words? How does the poem make them stand out?

3. What is the lone touch of *color* in these lines? What does it make you feel
or think?

4. This poem uses bare-minimum lines, with no chance for lush rhythms to
develop. Why?

The following poem is by a poet who became well known in the
eighties. What do you see in the frame the poet sets up in the poem? Is
there a movement or a mental journey to give a pattern to the poem as
a whole?

Sharon Olds   *(born 1942)*

The Possessive   *1980*

My daughter—as if I
owned her—that girl with the
hair wispy as a frayed bellpull

has been to the barber, that knife grinder,
and had the edge of her hair sharpened.   5

Each strand now cuts
both ways. The blade of new bangs
hangs over her red-brown eyes
like carbon steel.

       All the little   10
spliced ropes are sliced. The curtain of
dark paper-cuts veils the face that
started from next to nothing in my body—

My body. My daughter. I'll have to find
another word. In her bright helmet   15
she looks at me as if across a
great distance. Distant fires can be
glimpsed in the resin light of her eyes:

the watch fires of an enemy, a while before
the war starts.   20

This poem focuses on a crucial stage in the relationship between mother and daughter: The distance seems to be growing between mother and child. We come in at a turning point when the daughter is moving from a nonthreatening wispy-hair or curly-hair stage to a new helmetlike hairdo, with bangs that remind the mother of sharpened blades, hinting at future hostility and aggressiveness, The poem leaves us with the uneasy sense of a coming confrontation. Parent and child are headed for a future where they will be like two armies, each waiting around its campfires on the evening before battle.

The Receptive Reader

1. How does hair become an issue in this poem? (What exactly did the barber do to the girl's hair?)

2. How many words in the poem remind you of *weapons* used to fend off or hurt an enemy?

3. Possessive pronouns show where or to whom something belongs: *my* daughter, *your* son, *her* briefcase. Where and how does a possessive pronoun become an issue in this poem?

The Personal Response

Long hair, bald heads, ethnic hair styles—why or how does hair become an issue in the confrontation between the generations? Do adults overreact to the hairstyles of the young?

The Creative Dimension

Often what lingers in the mind after we read a poem is something that appeals strongly to the visual imagination—a central image or a key metaphor (or a web of related metaphors). What did the student-author of the following re-creation carry away from the poem? Do a similar brief re-creation of a central image or metaphor in this or in an earlier poem in this chapter.

> My daughter has pulled on a helmet
> as protection from sharp words.
> She hears nothing but feels
> >   all.
> Her eyes look out from behind the blades
> of her new bangs.
> Behind their curtain
> she prepares for battle.

The following poem again focuses on a significant moment. A poet from the Southwest, who published a book of poems called *Hijo del Pueblo*—Son of the Pueblo—remembers an encounter that acquires a new meaning in retrospect. What is that meaning?

Leroy V. Quintana   *(born 1944)*

Legacy II   *1976*

Grandfather never went to school
spoke only a few words of English,
a quiet man; when he talked
talked about simple things

planting corn or about the weather   5
sometimes about herding sheep as a child.
One day pointed to the four directions
taught me their names

          El Norte
Poniente   Oriente   10
          El Sur

He spoke their names as if they were
one of only a handful of things
a man needed to know

Now I look back   15
only two generations removed
realize I am nothing but a poor fool
who went to college

trying to find my way back
to the center of the world   20
where Grandfather stood
that day

The Receptive Reader

1. *El Norte* and *El Sur* are Spanish for "North" and "South"; *Poniente* means
"West" ("where the sun sets"), and *Oriente* means "East" ("where the sun rises").
Poems that use the physical arrangement of words on a page to mirror meaning are often called **concrete poetry.** How does the arrangement of the Spanish names on the page help the poet make the main point of the poem?

2. How are we supposed to feel about or toward the grandfather who is at
the center of this poem?

3. How does the treatment of the grandfather-grandson relationship compare with the treatment of the mother-daughter relationship in the poem by
Sharon Olds?

The Personal Response

A central issue in our growing up is how we accept or reject the heritage of
family tradition, regional ties, or ethnic roots. Write about your relation to one
major part of your own legacy.

The following poem observes a familiar traditional pattern: it focuses
on a scene from the natural world. This scene then inspires feelings and

reflections. Thomas Hardy, an English poet and novelist who had become well known by the 1880s and 1890s, wrote the first of the two poems on the last day of the nineteenth century. During the preceding decades, there had been much questioning of traditional religious faith. What was the poet's end-of-century mood? (The thrush is a small bird known as an excellent singer.)

Thomas Hardy   *(1840–1928)*

The Darkling Thrush   *1900*

I leant upon a coppice° gate	*grove of small trees*
When Frost was specter-gray,	
And Winter's dregs made desolate	
The weakening eye of day.	
The tangled bine-stems° scored the sky	*shoots of climbers* 5
Like strings of broken lyres,°	*small (poet's) harps*
And all mankind that haunted nigh°	*near*
Had sought their household fires.	

The land's sharp features seemed to be
    The Century's corpse outleant,   10
His crypt the cloudy canopy,°   *raised cloth covering*
    The wind his death-lament.
The ancient pulse of germ and birth
    Was shrunken hard and dry,
And every spirit upon earth   15
    Seemed fervorless° as I.   *without passion*

At once a voice arose among
    The bleak twigs overhead
In a full-hearted evensong°   *sung evening prayer*
    Of joy illimited;°   *unlimited* 20
An aged thrush, frail, gaunt, and small,
    In blast-beruffled plume,°   *feathers, plumage*
Had chosen thus to fling his soul
    Upon the growing gloom.

So little cause for carolings   25
    Of such ecstatic sounds
Was written on terrestrial° things   *earthly*
    Afar or nigh around,
That I could think there trembled through
    His happy good-night air   30
Some blessed Hope, whereof he knew
    And I was unaware.

The Receptive Reader

1. Take a close look at the poet's *language*. What is "the weakening eye of day"? What is the "cloudy canopy"? What is the "ancient pulse of germ and birth"? How was the bird's plumage "blast-beruffled"?

2. Where did you expect this poem to lead you as the reader? What details help make the *setting* unpromising for what happens later in the poem?

3. Where does this poem leave you? What makes the thrush in this poem a good *symbol* for hope?

4. Which words in the poem have religious overtones or *connotations*? Do you think the poet is religious?

The Creative Dimension

Assume today is the last day of another century, a hundred years after Hardy wrote his poem. Write your own epitaph for the *twentieth* century.

THE SHAPE OF THE POEM

To know one thing, you must know its opposite just
as much; else you don't know that one thing.

HENRY MOORE

Each poem has its own unique shape. There is no standard formula to guide the poet's creative imagination. Nevertheless, when we look at a finished poem, we often see shaping forces at work that we recognize. The ability to focus, to concentrate, takes us a first big step toward bringing order into miscellaneous experience. A second organizing strategy that poets employ is intentional, purposeful **repetition.** Repetition can be thoughtless or mechanical; it then grates on our ears. Repetition is purposeful when used to highlight, to emphasize. It can line up like and like, or confront like and unlike. In the following poem, the poet repeats exactly the way each set of lines, each stanza, is laid out on the page. What are the uses of repetition in the poem?

Dorothy Parker   *(1893–1967)*

Solace   *1931*

There was a rose that faded young;
I saw its shattered beauty hung
    Upon a broken stem.
I heard them say, "What need to care
With roses budding everywhere?"   5
    I did not answer them.

There was a bird, brought down to die;
They said, "A hundred fill the sky—
    What reason to be sad?"
There was a girl, whose lover fled;   10
I did not wait, the while they said:
    "There's many another lad."

This poem, like much poetry traditional in form, uses repetition at the most basic level to create sound patterns pleasing to the ear. End rhymes, in an interlaced rhyme scheme, mark off lines of similar length and help punctuate the poet's words. Lines with a recurrent underlying iambic meter (there WAS a ROSE that FADED YOUNG) alternate with a three-beat line (UPON a BROKEN STEM). These formal features serve to reinforce a pattern of repetition that helps guide our thoughts and feelings in the poem as whole. The same sentence frame—"*There was a* rose"; "*There was a* bird"; "*There was a* girl"—introduces each of the three parts of the poem. These sentences are **parallel** in grammatical form—a signal to the reader that the three scenarios they introduce might also be parallel in content or in meaning.

The Receptive Reader

1. What is the same basic story that is repeated in the three parts of the poem? What is the reaction of the speaker in the poem?

2. Can you trace the close similarity in the way each parallel minievent is patterned beyond the first half of the opening lines?

The Personal Response

Are you inclined to side with the "I" or the "they" of the poem?

Repetition sets up the routine of our lives. Other basic patternings are similarly rooted in common human experience. For instance, we often see a sequence of events build up to a **climactic** high point. Clouds slowly darken the sky until a climactic thunderstorm releases crashing thunder and pouring rain. Tensions in a marriage slowly build up until they explode in a divorce. Other poems hinge on a pivotal *but* that provides the turning point. We go from point to **counterpoint,** from statement to counterstatement.

Look for the uses of repetition and the play of point and counterpoint in the following lines from a longer poem by New England's first poet.

Anne Bradstreet   *(about 1612–1672)*

From *The Vanity of All Worldly Things*   *1650*

As he said "vanity!" so "vain!" say I,
"Oh! vanity, O vain all under sky."
Where is the man can say,° "Lo, I have found   *who can say*
On brittle earth a consolation sound"?
What is 't in honor to be set on high?°   *raised to high station*   5
No, they like beasts and sons of men shall die,
And whilst they live, how oft doth turn their fate;
He's now a captive that was king of late.°   *only recently*
What is 't in wealth great treasures to obtain?

No, that's but labor, anxious care, and pain.   10
He heaps up riches, and he heaps up sorrow,
It's his today, but who's his heir tomorrow?
What then? Content in pleasure canst thou find?
More vain than all, that's but to grasp the wind.
The sensual senses for a time they please,   15
Meanwhile the conscience rage, who shall appease?
What is 't in beauty? No, that's but a snare,
They're foul° enough today that once were fair.   *ugly*
What is 't in flowering youth or manly age?
The first is prone to vice, the last to rage.   20
Where is it then, in wisdom, learning, arts?
Sure, if on earth, it must be in those parts;
Yet these the wisest man of men did find
But vanity, vexation of mind.

The Receptive Reader

1. The poet's first line takes up the words of the preacher who repeated the biblical "Vanity of vanities; all is vanity." Can you show that the parts making up this excerpt are *parallel* both in wording and in meaning?

2. What examples of *point and counterpoint* can you find in these lines?

3. Religion in Bradstreet's time was often more demanding than in ours. How much of her outlook is strange and how much is familiar to you as a modern reader?

The Creative Dimension

We call a heightened and compressed playing off of opposites an **antithesis**. (*Thesis* and *antithesis* are the original Greek words for "statement" and "counterstatement.") Study the following examples of antithesis. For each, write one or more imitations (close or approximate) of your own.

1. To err is human; to forgive, divine. (Alexander Pope)
   SAMPLE IMITATION: To whine is childish; to ask, adult.
2. There are a thousand hacking at the branches of evil to one who is striking at the root. (Henry David Thoreau)
   SAMPLE IMITATION: There are a thousand correcting with red ink to one who writes an encouraging word.
3. It is a miserable state of mind to have few things to desire and many things to fear. (Sir Francis Bacon)

JUXTAPOSITIONS

The Daily Cycle

At times, the patterning that gives shape to a poem seems to be directly inspired by the patterns of nature or of ordinary human life.

Both of the following poems follow the daily cycle from dawn through noon to dusk and night. One makes us trace it in wonder and awe, as if we were the first people on earth. The other plays variations on it that are part serious, part tongue in cheek. The first poem is by a poet of Kiowa ancestry who grew up in Oklahoma and often draws in his poems on the legends and ways of the tribal life of the past.

N. Scott Momaday   *(born 1934)*

New World   *1976*

1.
First Man,
behold:
the earth
glitters   5
with leaves;
the sky
glistens
with rain.   2.
Pollen   At dawn   10
is borne   eagles
on winds   hie and
that low   hover
and lean   above   3.
upon   the plain   At noon   15
mountains.   where light   turtles
Cedars   gathers   enter
blacken   in pools.   slowly
the slopes—   Grasses   into   4.
and pines.   shimmer   the warm   At dusk   20
                 and shine.   dark loam.   the gray
                 Shadows   Bees hold   foxes
                 withdraw   the swarm.   stiffen
                 and lie   Meadows   in cold;
                 away   recede   blackbirds 25
                 like smoke.   through planes are fixed
                                of heat   in the
                                and pure   branches.
                                distance.   Rivers
                                               follow   30
                                               the moon,
                                               the long
                                               white track
                                               of the
                                               full moon. 35

The Receptive Reader

1. For people living closer to nature than we do, each stage of the day (like each stage in the cycle of the seasons) had its own characteristic feel or atmosphere. What is the morning feeling in this poem? How do the details selected by the poet conjure up the feeling of high noon? What is striking about the visual images that bring up dusk?

2. How does the sense of an immemorial cycle that gives shape to this poem affect you as a reader? What feelings are you left with as you finish the poem?

The Creative Dimension

What are the three (four? five?) stages of the day in your own present-day world? Bring them to life for your reader in a poem or prose passage.

The second poem is by an English poet of the early seventeenth century who rewrote conventions and crossed established boundaries. He was one of the **metaphysical** poets of his time, passionate, but at the same forever analyzing and rationalizing their emotions. What use does the poet make of the familiar stages of the daily cycle? How does he impose his own perspective and priorities?

John Donne   *(1572–1631)*

A Lecture upon the Shadow   *1635*

Stand still, and I will read to thee
A lecture, love, in Love's philosophy.
    These three hours that we have spent
    Walking here, two shadows went
Along with us, which we ourselves produced;   5
    But, now° the sun is just above our head,   *now that*
    We do those shadows° tread,   *on those shadows*
And to brave clearness all things are reduced.
    So, whilst our infant loves did grow,
    Disguises did and shadows flow   10
From us and our cares,° but now 't is not so.   *our fears*

That love hath not attained the highest degree
Which is still diligent lest others° see.   *so others won't*

Except° our loves at this noon stay,   *Unless*
We shall new shadows make the other way.   15
    As the first were made to blind
    Others, these which come behind
Will work upon ourselves, and blind our eyes.
    If our loves faint and westwardly decline,
    To me thou falsely thine,   20

And I to thee mine, actions shall disguise.
　　The morning shadows wear away,
　　But these grow longer all the day;
But oh, love's day is short, if love decay.

Love is a growing or full constant light,   25
And his first minute after noon is night.

The Receptive Reader

1. The shadow cast by the sun becomes the central *metaphor* in this poem. What were the shadows in the morning? (What were the "cares" and "disguises" of the morning?) What happens to the shadows at high noon? What is the crucial difference between the morning shadows and the shadows after noon?

2. How does this poem ask you to revise your usual sense of the daily cycle? What familiar associations of dawn, noon, and night does the poem preserve? How does it depart from them?

The Personal Response

How do you react to the student-written response that follows? How does it compare with your own response to the poem?

> I like the beginning of this poem much more than the end. As the sun moves through the sky, the shadows cast according to the position of the sun change, just as love in a relationship is different when it is young and when it is tried and true. At first, we hide behind shadows or façades instead of showing our true selves, but after a while we can put our disguises away just as at noon we can walk on our shadows. However, in the afternoon, love might grow weary and turn false, with the afternoon shadows pointing forward to the night and the end of love. The reason I would rather focus on the first half of the poem is that I think love should continue to grow and build on itself. If love grows weary, making "new shadows" the other way, I don't think it was love in the first place. I have never heard a parent say: "I have fallen out of love with my children; I think I will find a more suitable child elsewhere." Would that be true love?

POEMS FOR FURTHER STUDY

In reading the following poems, pay special attention to features that give shape to the poem as a whole. For instance, where does the poem focus your attention? Is there a playing off of opposites? Is there a movement from then to now, or from question to answer? What makes the poem a complete, finished whole?

Marge Piercy   *(born 1936)*

Simple Song   *1968*

When we are going toward someone we say
You are just like me
your thoughts are my brothers
word matches word
how easy to be together.   5

When we are leaving someone we say:
how strange you are
we cannot communicate
we can never agree
how hard, hard and weary to be together.   10

We are not different nor alike
But each strange in his leather body
sealed in skin and reaching out clumsy hands
and loving is an act
that cannot outlive   15
the open hand
the open eye
the door in the chest standing open.

The Receptive Reader

1. What is simple about this "simple song"?

2. What does the poet mean by "your thoughts are my brothers"? (Or by "word matches word"?) What are we supposed to think or feel when we are told that we are in a "leather body" and "sealed in skin"? What is the role or significance of the open hand, the open eye, the open door?

3. How does this poem use *parallelism* to line up opposites and to bond things that are similar?

4. How would you chart the overall *development* or shape of this poem?

The Creative Dimension

Some poems leave an exceptionally clear or compelling pattern imprinted on our minds. Choose one such poem. Can you sum up the pattern as briefly as the student-author did in the following response to the Piercy poem? (Can you do so without oversimplifying?)

When we agree
I like you
we are one.
When we disagree
I don't like you
we are separate.
You are my enemy.

Gary Soto   *(born 1952)*

We are beginning to see the work of **bilingual** poets—American poets who speak English as a second language or who are part of the first generation in their family to speak mainly English while another language is still the language of the home. The following poem is by a Chicano poet who grew up in a Mexican-American neighborhood in Fresno, California. A listener at one of Soto's poetry readings said that he "was funny, and humble, and touching, and completely terrific."

Oranges   *1985*

The first time I talked
With a girl, I was twelve,
Cold, and weighted down
With two oranges in my jacket.
December. Frost cracking   5
Beneath my steps, my breath
Before me, then gone,
As I walked toward
Her house, the one whose
Porch light burned yellow   10
Night and day, in any weather.
A dog barked at me, until
She came out pulling
At her gloves, face bright
With rouge. I smiled,   15
Touched her shoulder, and led
Her down the street, across
A used car lot and a line
Of newly planted trees,
Until we were breathing   20
Before a drugstore. We
Entered, the tiny bell
Bringing a saleslady
Down a narrow aisle of goods.
I turned to the candies   25
Tiered like bleachers
And asked what she wanted—
Light in her eyes, a smile
Starting at the corners
Of her mouth. I fingered   30
A nickel in my pocket,
And when she lifted a chocolate
That cost a dime,
I didn't say anything.
I took the nickel from   35
My pocket, then an orange,

And set them quietly on
The counter. When I looked up,
The lady's eyes met mine,
And held them, knowing   40
Very well what it was all
About.
      Outside,
A few cars hissing past,
Fog hanging like old   45
Coats between the trees.
I took my girl's hand
In mine for two blocks,
Then released it to let
Her unwrap the chocolate.   50
I peeled my orange
That was so bright against
The grey of December
That, from some distance,
Someone might have thought   55
I was making a fire in my hands.

The Receptive Reader

1. This poet has an uncanny gift for recalling the small revealing details that conjure up scenes from the past. What are striking examples in this poem?

2. How does this poem develop and take shape? What is the overall pattern? What are major stages or high points? What helps the reader experience a sense of completion?

3. Gary Soto is known for poems presenting candid and bittersweet childhood memories in understated and wrily humorous fashion. How does this poem show these qualities?

Robert Frost   *(1874–1963)*

Fire and Ice   *1923*

Some say the world will end in fire,
Some say in ice.
From what I've tasted of desire
I hold with those who favor fire.
But if I had to perish twice   5
I think I know enough of hate
To say that for destruction ice
Is also great
And would suffice.

1. How is Frost playing off opposites in this poem? How well do fire and ice fit the emotions for which they serve as symbols in this poem?

2. How does the rhyme scheme in this poem serve to highlight the polar opposites?

Where have you encountered the destructiveness of desire as a theme in your reading or viewing?

Adrienne Rich   *(born 1929)*

Novella   *1967*

Two people in a room, speaking harshly.
One gets up, goes out to walk.
(That is the man.)
The other goes out into the next room
and washes the dishes, cracking one.   5
(That is the woman.)
It gets dark outside.
The children quarrel in the attic.
She has no blood left in her heart.
The man comes back to a dark house.   10
The only light is in the attic.
He has forgotten his key.
He rings at his own door
and hears sobbing on the stairs.
The lights go on in the house.   15
The door closes behind him.
Outside, separate as minds,
the stars too come alight.

1. From what perspective or vantage point are we watching the scene unfolding in this poem?

2. Many of the sentences in this poem are spare and factual. What are striking examples? Where and how do the powerful emotions involved in what we observe shine through?

3. A **novella** is a story that is shorter and more pointed than a full-length novel. Does the poet expect us to read this poem as the story of two specific individuals? Or are the people in this poem representative or even archetypal—standing for an age-old, often repeated pattern?

4. The final two lines bring the poem to a close by serving as a summing up and last word. How?

WRITING ABOUT LITERATURE

13   *The Whole Paper (From Notes to Revision)*

The Writing Workshop   How does a successful paper about a poem take shape? Think of your writing as a process that starts with your first reading of a poem and ends with a revised final draft. Be prepared to take a paper through overlapping stages: careful reading, note taking, thinking about the poem, planning your strategy, preparing a rough first draft, working on a more polished revision, final editing, and proofreading. Remember that false starts and blind alleys are part of a writer's day. Be prepared to change direction as necessary. Always go back to the poem itself as your main source of ideas and evidence.

Reading Notes   Suppose you are working on a paper about Marge Piercy's "Simple Song." Allow time for the preliminary note-taking stage. Many readers find it useful to jot down a running commentary as they work their way through a poem. Here they note key phrases and striking images, questions that arise in the reader's mind, or possible clues to the poet's intention or the larger meaning of the poem. Your **reading notes** for the poem might look like this:

> title: why "Simple Song"? Words in the poem are very simple (none need to be looked up in a dictionary)
>
> (line 5) it's "easy to be together" because they don't really see who's there
>
> second stanza is exactly parallel in layout to the first—but now we exit from the relationship
>
> (line 7) "how strange you are"—the other person was not really known to begin with
>
> (line 10) last lines in first and second stanzas are parallel: "how easy . . ."; "how hard . . ." But the same line in second stanza is longer, more drawn-out
>
> ("how hard, hard and weary . . .") to make the point of how hard and weary it is to stay together when love is gone
>
> (line 12) "leather body"—leather used as a protection since early times; it's tough, more impenetrable than human skin
>
> (line I7) the "open eye"—we really see others for what they are?
>
> (line 18) "door in the chest standing open"—willingness to let someone in

Reading Journal   A journal entry will often record your interpretation of a poem—the way you make sense of it—and your more personal reaction. It may also note your queries—your attempts to puzzle out difficult passages, your tentative answers to unsolved questions. In your paper, you will then be able to draw on some of the more unstructured and informal material in your journal. A journal entry for the Piercy poem might look as follows:

> I felt in reading this poem that most people operate exactly the way the first ten lines of this poem describe. In the early stages of courtship, all is euphoria. People focus on everything they can share and agree on. They say, "how easy to be together." Then they slowly let down their guard. They let their differences come to the surface; they become impatient with each other. They start calling each other weird and "strange." Getting along becomes "hard, hard and weary." Although this poem seems to talk mainly about romantic or sexual relationships, I believe the pattern applies to friendships as well.

Planning the Paper   Even while taking notes and recording tentative reactions, you will be thinking about how to lay out your material in a paper. You will be pushing toward an overall impression or keynote—a key idea or ideas what will make your details add up. You will be sketching out a master plan—the major stages through which you will take your reader. Give special thought to the following way stations in the itinerary to be traveled by your reader:

✗ *Introduction.*   What is going to be your lead? How are you going to attract and focus the attention of your reader? You may want to lead your readers into the poem from a biographical fact, such as a revealing detail about the poet's war experience or family history that could serve to illuminate the poem. You may want to start with a striking quote from the poet, illuminating his or her intention. You may want to dramatize the setting or the time, vividly re-creating the context of the poem.

✗ *Overview.*   What will be your central focus? If possible, let a graphic, vivid introduction lead your readers directly to your main point. State it as your **thesis** and then devote your paper to developing and supporting it. A thesis sums up in a short, memorable statement what the paper as a whole is trying to prove. (Sometimes, however, you will prefer to raise a question to be pondered by the reader and to be answered by the paper as a whole.) Give the kind of preview or overview here that will point your readers in the right direction. Often a thesis statement broadly hints at the major stages in the writer's master plan. It furnishes the reader with a capsule itinerary for the journey ahead.

✗ *Plan.*   How are you going to follow up your thesis? For the body of a short paper, try sketching out a three-step or four-point plan. Make sure that you arrive at a clear agenda: first this, next this, then that. Highlight the transitions from one major point or stage to the next, so your readers will not get lost in detail. Signal turning points, crucial objections, clinching arguments. Provide links like "on the other hand"; "readers hostile to easy answers may object . . ."; "however, such objections will carry much less weight when we realize. . . ."

Often the way the poem itself takes shape will provide a tentative blueprint for all or part of your paper. The "Simple Song" poem swings from the extreme of euphoria, of being blissfully and uncritically in love, to the opposite extreme of sour disappointment and failure to communicate. We may well look to the third and last part of the poem for some middle ground, or for some lesson to be learned, or for some sort of answer. The paper, like the poem, could go from point to counterpoint and then toward some kind of resolution.

✗ *Follow-up.*   Whatever your claims or generalizations, each general statement you make is a promise to your readers. You are saying in effect, "This is what I claim, and here is the evidence to support it." Much of your text should show a rich texture of quotation, explication (close careful explanation), and interpretation. Choose brief, revealing quotations—but don't rip them out of context, omitting essential ifs and buts. Explain what your quotations say and how they say it; explore their overtones and implications. Relate them to the larger context of the poem: what role do they play in the poem as a whole?

✗ *Conclusion.*   End on a strong note. Pull together essentials of your argument. Put them in perspective: put them in the context of today, or of your own experience, or of the readers' lives. Or relate the individual poem to the larger patterns of the poet's work. Aim for a wrap-up or a clincher sentence that your readers will remember.

✗ *Title.*   Writers are often content with a dull working title while drafting a paper ("Structure in Marge Piercy's 'Simple Song'"). Then, first things last, they hit on the title that is both informative and provocative. An effective title does justice to the topic but also beckons to the reader. A thought-provoking quote can attract the reader's attention. A play on a key word or an allusion to a figure from myth or legend can make a title stand out.

Read the following student paper to see how it lives up to the criteria sketched in these guidelines.

Sample Student Paper

The Real Act of Love

In her introduction to *Circle on the Water,* a book of her selected poems, Marge Piercy writes that a poem should "function for us in the ordinary chaos of our lives." Her intention in writing her poems is to "give voice to something in the experience of life. . . . To find ourselves spoken for in art gives dignity to our pain, our anger, our lust, our losses."

Her poem "Simple Song" achieves these goals for me. The poem asks us to face the most terrifying and difficult of human activities: loving another person and opening ourselves to love in return. The title promises us a "simple song." The simplicity promised in the title is carried out in the three-part structure of the poem and conveyed in its simple language. By focusing on the essentials of a very complex issue, the poem helps us see first the lacking sense of reality and second the inevitable alienation that defeats us when we "reach out" to others. It then takes us to a third stage that explains the dilemma and may offer a way out.

The poem filters out all intermediate stages to focus on the two phases that are like turning points in our lives: "going toward" and "leaving." The first group of five lines makes us feel the sweetness and newness of someone we have just met. This is the state of falling in love when we feel totally in harmony with the other person. We say, "You are just like me / your thoughts are my brothers / word matches word / how easy to be together." We feel we have found the perfect soulmate, who thinks and speaks like us.

However, anyone with experience can already forecast the exact opposite stage. In the next set of five lines, we are leaving. The other person has become "strange": "we cannot communicate / we can never agree / how hard, hard and weary to be together." Here we have a feeling of loss, a feeling of confusion and defeat as for some reason we stop loving. The lines in this second stanza are arranged in parallel fashion to those in the first; they serve as a mirror image to those in the first. "You are just like me" turns into "how strange you are." "Word matches word" turns into "we cannot communicate." These contrasting lines give us a clue that maybe our "going toward" was not a clear-eyed move but at least in part self-deception. It did not make allowance for hard times or unexpected problems. Did we know the person whom we told "your thoughts are my brothers" in any real sense?

The last stanza moves beyond the dilemma that confronts us in the first two stanzas and points toward a possible solution to our confusion and pain. The first three lines of the stanza say, "We are not different nor alike / But each strange in his leather body / sealed in skin and reaching out clumsy hands." Our problem is not that we are different from each other. We are all "strange." We are each in a leather body, which sounds tough, isolated from human touch like an animal. To be "sealed in skin" sounds sterile, like being put in a vacuum plastic pouch. We are impenetrable, isolated human beings, groping for contact with "clumsy hands." But we are too thick-skinned to let in another in order to know the soft-skinned person inside the leather covering.

The last five lines may be pointing to a course between the polar opposites of uncritical acceptance and resentful rejection. The poem says, "loving is an act / that cannot outlive the open hand / the open eye / the door in the chest standing open." The image of the open hand may imply an opening up of our fist to show what's there and let the other person see who we really are. But it may also imply the willingness to accept what the other person has to offer, without illusions that we create about the other person in our minds. The "open eye" implies willingness to see others as they really are, to see that rarely does "word match word" and that it is not "easy to be together" on a continuous basis. We have to risk the open door if we do not want to be satisfied with the less fearful business of having someone fill a temporary need for companionship.

The type of love in the first stanza cannot last because it makes us imagine a perfect merging of people who are really unique and strange. When we exaggerate everything we have in common, we already program ourselves for the disappointment acted out in the second stanza. I read a book recently that talks about a "matching game"—trying to build a relationship on everything that makes two people alike. The real key is to teach our "clumsy hands" to be more accepting of what makes us different. This way we can be in love with a real person rather than with a creation of our own minds.

Questions

How effectively do title and introduction lead toward the main point of the paper? What overview or preview does the paper provide—how effectively does it prepare you for what is to come? How clear does the structure or shape of the poem become to the reader? What important details stand out, and how well does the writer explain them? What does the conclusion do that the rest of the paper has not already done? Where do you agree and where do you part company with the student writer?

14 Image

The Open Eye

Great literature, if we read it well, opens us up to the world. It makes us more sensitive to it, as if we acquired eyes that could see through things and ears that could hear smaller sounds.

DONALD HALL

FOCUS ON IMAGE

Poets take you into a world of images. An **image** is a vividly imagined detail that speaks to your sense of sight, hearing, smell, taste, or touch. Poets expect you to read their poems with open eyes and willing ears. They write with a heightened awareness, asking you take in more of the world around you than people do who see only the stretch of asphalt in front of their cars.

The Visual Imagination Poets tend to have a highly developed visual imagination. "This morning," Javier Gálvez says, "the sun broke / my window / and came in laughing." To be receptive readers of poetry, we need to be able to say at this point, "Yes, I can see it! The morning sun is so strong and so cheerful—it is as if it were breaking the glass and spilling laughter into my room!"

Images and Ideas For many poets, insisting on concrete images, anchored in firsthand observation, has been a safeguard against second-hand ideas. Poets are likely to speak in vivid images even when making a general point about life or about people. They are likely to remind us that the poem and a prose translation, or paraphrase, are not the same. Look at the relation between image and idea in the following lines by the poet Kenneth Rexroth, who became known as a voice of the "beat generation":

The trout is taken when he
Bites an artificial fly.
Confronted with fraud, keep your
Mouth shut, and don't volunteer.

How is fraud like fishing for trout? What would be lost if this poet had given us only the last two lines? The trout is without guile, going about its legitimate business as nature prompts it. People producing the artificial fly used in trout fishing invest great ingenuity and resourcefulness in producing something to fool an unsuspecting victim. By dramatizing the relationship between the perpetrator and the victim of fraud, the poet makes us "see it feelingly"; we know how it feels to be hooked.

Visual and Other Images   By *image,* we usually mean a picture we see with the mind's eye. However, we also use the word for any detail that speaks to our senses, whether of sight, hearing, smell, taste, or touch. Most poetic images are visual images—something we can see the way we look in a mirror and see an image of ourselves. However, others are sound images, like the rustling of leaves or the pounding of the surf. Still others are taste images—like the sourness of a lemon that makes the mouth pucker. Still others might be touch images, like the sensation we feel when run our fingers over the rough bark of a tree.

THE RANGE OF IMAGES

The images we grasp with our senses make poetry **concrete**—they bring our eyes and ears and nerve ends into play. Concrete, sensory details take us into a world of sights, sounds, smells, tastes, and sensations. The following poem is by a poet who revels in the sights and sounds and smells of the apple harvest. Does he succeed in making you share in the experience?

Peter Meinke   *(born 1932)*

Sunday at the Apple Market   *1977*

Apple-smell everywhere!
Haralson   McIntosh   Fireside   Rome
old ciderpresses weathering in the shed
old ladders tilting at empty branches
boxes and bins of apples by the cartload
yellow and green and red   5
piled crazy in the storehouse barn
miraculous profusion, the crowd

around the testing table laughing rolling
the cool applechunks in their mouths   10
dogs barking at children in the appletrees
couples holding hands, so many people
out in the country carrying bushels
and baskets and bags and boxes of apples
to their cars, the smell of apples   15
making us for one Sunday afternoon free
and happy as people must have been meant to be.

The Receptive Reader

1. Apples are everywhere in this poem. Where in this poem do you see, smell, or taste apples? What are striking realistic details that only an observer who knows the scene well could have noticed? Which images in this poem stay with you after you finish reading?

2. Some poems early strike a *keynote* that sets the tone and recurs through the poem like the tolling of a bell. What is the keynote in this poem, and how does it echo through the poem?

The Personal Response

Why does the apple market become a symbol of happiness for the poet? Are you the kind of person who would have shared in the happy feeling? Why or why not?

The following poem centers on a memorable visual image. It asks you focus on and take in a striking sight. If you let it, the central image in this poem will etch itself on your memory. It will start a chain of association activating disturbing thought and feelings. It may come back to haunt you at unexpected moments.

William Stafford   *(1914–1992)*

At the Bomb Testing Site   *1960*

At noon in the desert a panting lizard
waited for history, its elbows tense,
watching the curve of a particular road
as if something might happen.

It was looking for something farther off   5
than people could see, an important scene
acted in stone for little selves
at the flute end of consequences.

There was just a continent without much on it
under a sky that never cared less.   10
Ready for a change, the elbows waited.
The hands gripped hard on the desert.

This poem begins and ends with the sight the poet calls up before our eyes. The panting watchful lizard, its elbows tense, grips the desert floor hard with its hands, surrounded by the empty desert (like a "continent without much on it"), under the empty, uncaring, cloudless sky. This is a striking image, and the poet takes the time to let it sink in. At the same time, there is more to the lizard than meets the eye. Our first hint is that the panting lizard "waited for history." We *are* at a bomb testing site. Something disastrous might happen to the desert life at any moment. The lizard, part of life that has existed on this earth for untold millions of years, might presently perish in the blinding flash of a nuclear holocaust. A chain of associations and forebodings will take each of us to our own personal version of the distant "important scene" at the "flute end of consequences"—where our common history will be channeled as toward the end of a flute, toward its final destination.

The Receptive Reader

1. Does it make any difference to the poem as a whole that the time is noon? that the lizard is watching a curve in the road? Why is the "important scene" in the future acted out for "little selves"?

2. The poem does not preach; the image of the lizard is mute and eloquent at the same time. For you, what is its message?

3. For many people, lizards, like other reptiles, seem alien, remote from human beings in the chain of evolution. For you, does the lizard make a good central image for this poem? Why or not? (What for you would have been a better choice?)

Look for the striking visual images in the following poem. What does the poem invite you see? What does it make you feel? Does it ask you to think?

Mary Oliver   *(born 1935)*

The Black Snake   *1979*

When the black snake
flashed onto the morning road,
and the truck could not swerve—
death, that is how it happens.

Now he lies looped and useless   5
as an old bicycle tire.
I stop the car
and carry him into the bushes.

He is as cool and gleaming
as a braided whip, he is as beautiful and quiet   10
as a dead brother.
I leave him under the leaves

and drive on, thinking,
about *death:* its suddenness,
its terrible weight,   15
its certain coming. Yet under

reason burns a brighter fire, which the bones
have always preferred.
It is the story of endless good fortune.
It says to oblivion: not me!   20

It is the light at the center of every cell.
It is what sent the snake coiling and flowing forward
happily all spring through the green leaves before
he came to the road.

The speaker in this poem is thinking about what keeps us going in
face of the knowledge that disaster may strike. Death may lurk at any
turn in the road. (The one thing sure about death is its "certain coming.") However, the person speaking does her thinking in vivid images.
The poem focuses on the black snake—which has to become real for
us if the poem is to carry its true weight. We need to imagine the snake
as it moves "happily through the green leaves" until it meets sudden
death in the road. Perhaps then we will be ready to say with the poet:
"That's how it happens." The snake apparently is not some alien creature "out there." *We* are like the snake, moving through life merrily until
of a sudden something terrible overtakes us. We feel the "terrible
weight" of that knowledge.

The Receptive Reader

1. What graphic images make you see the way the snake moved when it was
alive? What images help you see the way it looked after it had been hit?

2. How is what "reason" says in this poem different from what people know
(or prefer to believe) in their "bones"? What striking image helps you visualize
the intense vital energy of that knowledge?

3. What is "the light at the center of every cell"? What do you know about
cells that can help you understand this phrase and its role in the poem?

The Personal Response

As you look back over the poem, are you likely to remember the image of
the dead snake or the image of the live snake moving "happily all spring
through the green leaves"? Which for you is stronger in the poem—the experience of death or the affirmation of life?

The American poet Theodore Roethke had a special gift for using the image-making language of poetry to re-create the rich texture of sensory experience. In the following poem, Roethke uses visual images, but he also uses images that speak strongly to other senses. What does the poem make you see? And how does the poet go *beyond* visual images to include other kinds of sensory detail? What sensations and feelings does the boy experience?

Theodore Roethke   *(1908–1963)*

My Papa's Waltz   *1948*

The whiskey on your breath
Could make a small boy dizzy;
But I hung on like death:
Such waltzing was not easy.

We romped until the pans   5
Slid from the kitchen shelf;
My mother's countenance
Could not unfrown itself.

The hand that held my wrist
Was battered on one knuckle;   10
At every step you missed
My right ear scraped a buckle.

You beat time on my head
With a palm caked hard by dirt,
Then waltzed me off to bed   15
Still clinging to your shirt.

The Receptive Reader

1. What does this poem make you see? What details in the poem bring senses *other* than sight into play?

2. What helps you put yourself in the boy's place? Where and how do *you* share in what the boy sensed and felt?

The Range of Interpretation

Many readers find that this poem makes them relive the experience but does not tell them what to make of it. Whether the boy in the poem felt a sickening fear or a mad dizzy joy is for our own emotional antennas to pick up. Critics have read the poem different ways—depending on their negative or positive reactions to the father. *Romp* is usually an approving word; it makes us think of a happy, boisterous, energetic kind of running or dancing. Do you think the boy liked the romp in this poem? As he looks back, how does the speaker in the poem feel about his father? Is he critical of the father? Or is he expressing feelings of love for him? How do *you* feel about the father?

IMAGES AND FEELINGS

*If . . . it makes my whole body so cold no fire can
ever warm me, I know that is poetry. If I feel physically as if the top of my head were taken off, I
know that is poetry.*

EMILY DICKINSON

Poets vary greatly in how fully they signal their emotions. Often, like
Theodore Roethke in "My Papa's Waltz," they let the experience speak
for itself. Contrast the Roethke poem with another father-son poem by
Robert Hayden, who in other poems has written eloquently about the
African-American heritage. In this poem, the poet makes us suffer the
bitter cold by appealing to our senses of sight and touch. We can visualize the "blueblack cold" and feel the "cracked hands that ached."
When the blazing fire drives out the icy cold, our sense of hearing is
brought into play: as the blazing wood shifts and splits, we seem to
"hear the cold splintering, breaking." What feelings does the poet
express in response to the scenes he dramatizes in this poem? What was
his relationship with his father when he was a boy? How does he feel
about his father now?

Robert Hayden   *(1913–1980)*

Those Winter Sundays   1962

Sundays too my father got up early,
and put his clothes on in the blueblack cold,
then with cracked hands that ached
from labor in the weekday weather made
banked fires blaze. No one ever thanked him.   5

I'd wake and hear the cold splintering, breaking.
When the rooms were warm, he'd call,
and slowly I would rise and dress,
fearing the chronic angers of that house.

Speaking indifferently to him,   10
who had driven out the cold
and polished my good shoes as well.
What did I know, what did I know
of love's austere and lonely offices?

The Receptive Reader

1. What do you learn about the boy's family situation as he grew up? As the
poet steers your emotions in this poem, what are your feelings toward the
lonely father?

2. The word *austere* means being self-denying but at the same time being proud to be so, holding aloof. How does this key word fit into the poem?

3. Why does the poet repeat the question "What did I know?" in the next to the last line of the poem?

The Creative Dimension

Most of us can think of an occasion or person that we did not appreciate properly. We remember lost opportunities, occasions for regret. Write a passage or poem on the theme of "What did I know, what did I know."

Making Connections—For Discussion of Writing

Look at poems that center on parent-child relations, like Sharon Olds's "The Possessive," Theodore Roethke's "My Papa's Waltz," and Robert Hayden's "Those Winter Sundays." Are there recurrent concerns? Or do the poems offer very different perspectives?

Both of the following poems take you to a place to which the poet has strong emotional ties. What images make the setting real for you? How do the poets communicate their feelings? Can you share in the feelings expressed in these poems?

William Stafford   *(1914–1992)*

One Home   *1963*

Mine was a Midwest home—you can keep your world.
Plain black hats rode the thoughts that made our code.
We sang hymns in the house; the roof was near God.

The light bulb that hung in the pantry made a wan light,
but we could read by it the names of preserves—   5
outside, the buffalo grass, and the wind in the night.

A wildcat sprang at Grandpa on the Fourth of July
when he was cutting plum bushes for fuel,
before Indians pulled the West over the edge of the sky.

To anyone who looked at us we said, "My friend";   10
liking the cut of a thought, we could say, "Hello."
(But plain black hats rode the thoughts that made our code.)

The sun was over our town; it was like a blade.
Kicking cottonwood leaves we ran toward storms.
Wherever we looked the land would hold us up.   15

The Receptive Reader

1. What striking images put us in the Midwest that was the poet's home? Where do the poet's feelings about the land show? Where do his feelings about the people show? How?

2. The poem is divided into stanzas, or sets of lines each of which follows a similar pattern, like the verses of a song. Can you show that each stanza (or almost each stanza) focuses on one dimension or aspect of the Midwestern tradition or mentality that is the subject of this poem?

3. In some songlike poems, the same line comes back in each stanza as a refrain. In this poem, a key line is repeated only once. Why is it important enough for the poet to repeat it?

4. This poem makes some limited, low-key use of rhyme. Where and how? The poem also uses lines of roughly similar length, with a steady underlying beat. Can you find some lines that have a clear five-beat rhythm? Why is it not surprising that this poet would like a style that is low-key but has a steady underlying beat?

The second poem about a favorite place takes us to the now empty and fenced-in lots under a raised freeway in California, with the small houses gone and the fruit trees and vegetable patches running wild. The Hispanic poet talking here about childhood scenes slides from English into Spanish (the language of her childhood) and back, moving easily between two languages like other bilingual Americans.

Lorna Dee Cervantes   *(born 1954)*

Freeway 280   *1981*

Las casitas° near the gray cannery	*the little houses*
nestled amid wild abrazos° of climbing roses	*hugs*
and man-high red geraniums	
are gone now. The freeway conceals it	
all beneath a raised scar.	5
But under the fake windsounds of the open lanes,	
in the abandoned lots below, new grasses sprout,	
wild mustard remembers, old gardens	
come back stronger than they were,	
trees have been left standing in their yards.	10
Albaricoqueros, cerezos, nogales° . . .	*apricot, cherry, and walnut*
Viejitas° come here with paper bags to gather greens.	*little old women*
Espinaca, verdolagas, yerbabuena° . . .	*spinach, purslane, mint*

I scramble over the wire fence	
that would have kept me out.	15
Once, I wanted out, wanted the rigid lanes	
to take me to a place without sun,	
without the smell of tomatoes burning	
on swing shift in the greasy summer air.	

Maybe it's here   20
en los campos extranos de esta ciudad°   *in the strange fields of this city*
where I'll find it, that part of me
mown under
like a corpse
or a loose seed.   25

The Receptive Reader

1. What is the "raised scar"? What are the "windsounds," and why are they "fake"? How does the poet feel about the freeway?

2. How did the poet feel about this setting when she grew up there? What role did the cannery play in her childhood or adolescence?

3. What are her feelings as she returns to this setting? What does she mean when she says that "wild mustard remembers"?

4. Students of language use the term *code-switching* for shifting from one language, or linguistic code, to the other. At what points in the poem does the poet shift back to the Spanish of her childhood? Can you speculate why? What might have been lost if she had used the literal English translations here printed in the margin?

The Personal Response

Do you think the part of the poet (or of her past) that was "mown under" will prove a "corpse" or a "seed"? What images of continuing growth earlier in this poem might help you answer this question?

The Creative Dimension

Most people have intense personal associations—positive or negative—with a childhood setting that may haunt them in their dreams. Write a poem or prose passage about a childhood setting or favorite place recalled in vivid memories or revisited in a dream.

JUXTAPOSITIONS

Writing to Commemorate

One of the earliest functions of poetry was to keep alive the memory of the dead. The two following poems take us to the Vietnam War Memorial in Washington D.C., which records on an unadorned granite wall the names of Americans who died in Vietnam. The wall cuts into a hillside, with sections starting close to the ground and then gradually rising to full height, with name after name after name cut into the black stone. What does each poet see? What thoughts and feelings go through each poet's mind? How are the two poems similar and alike?

Alberto Rios   *(born 1952)*

The Vietnam Wall   *1988*

I
Have seen it
And I like it: The magic,
The way like cutting onions
It brings water out of nowhere.   5
Invisible from one side, a scar
Into the skin of the ground
From the other, a black winding
Appendix line.
       A dig.   10
       An archaeologist can explain.
The walk is slow at first,
Easy, a little black marble wall
Of a dollhouse,
A smoothness, a shine   15
The boys in the street want to give.
One name. And then more
Names, long lines, lines of names until
They are the shape of the U.N. Building
Taller than I am: I have walked   20
Into a grace.
And everything I expect has been taken away, like that, quick:
       The names are not alphabetized.
       They are in the order of dying,
       An alphabet of—somewhere—screaming.   25
I start to walk out. I almost leave
But stop to look up names of friends,
My own name. There is somebody
Severiano Ríos.
Little kids do not make the same noise   30
Here, junior high school boys don't run
Or hold each other in headlocks.
No rules, something just persists
Like pinching on St. Patrick's Day
Every year for no green.   35
       No one knows why.
Flowers are forced
Into the cracks
Between sections.
Men have cried   40
At this wall.
I have
Seen them.

The Receptive Reader

1. What details in the poem are realistic details remembered by an alert observer? How do the details help you reenact the poet's walk past the monument?

2. Where and how does this poet convey the powerful emotional effect the sight of the monument had on him, as it has on many of its observers?

3. The speaker in the poem says, "everything I expect has been taken away." How did what he saw and experienced go counter to ordinary expectations?

4. Many sentences in this poem are short, matter-of-fact: "One knows why." "I have seen them." Why do you think the poem uses this matter-of-fact style in talking about a subject that inspires powerful emotions?

5. What do you think you are most likely to remember when you think of this poem?

What did the author of the following poem see and feel at the memorial? How was his experience similar to or different from that of the other poet?

Jeffrey Harrison   *(born 1957)*

Reflection on the Vietnam War Memorial   *1987*

Here is, the back porch of the dead.
You can see them milling around in there,
    screened in by their own names,
    looking at us in the same
vague and serious way we look at them.   5

An underground house, a roof of grass—
one version of the underworld. It's all
    we know of death, a world
    like our own (but darker, blurred).
inhabited by beings like ourselves.   10

The location of the name you're looking for
can be looked up in a book whose resemblance
    to a phone book seems to claim
    some contact can be made
through the simple act of finding a name.   15

As we touch the name the stone absorbs our grief.
It takes us in—we see ourselves inside it.
    And yet we feel it as a wall
    and realize the dead are all
just names now, the separation final.   20

The Receptive Reader

1. At times in this poem, the wall seems almost transparent; at other times, it becomes a real wall. How are the thoughts and feelings the wall inspires different at the beginning and at the end of the poem?

2. The poet keeps coming back to the names—the names on the wall, the entries in the book guiding visitors in finding a name. How does each mention make you see the names in a somewhat different light?

The Personal Response

Do you think your own feelings and attitudes would have resembled those of the first poet or the second? Or would your reactions have been different from either? How and why?

POEMS FOR FURTHER STUDY

In reading the following poems, pay special attention to imagery that brings a scene or a natural setting to life for the reader. How does it appeal to the senses? What does it do for the reader?

Dana Gioia   *(born 1950)*

California Hills in August   1982

I can imagine someone who found
these fields unbearable, who climbed
the hillside in the heat, cursing the dust,
cracking the brittle weeds underfoot,
wishing a few more trees for shade.   5

An Easterner especially, who would scorn
the meagreness of summer, the dry
twisted shapes of black elm,
scrub oak, and chaparral—a landscape
August has already drained of green.   10

One who would hurry over the clinging
thistle, foxtail, golden poppy,
knowing everything was just a weed,
unable to conceive that these trees
And sparse brown bushes were alive.   15

And hate the bright stillness of the noon,
without wind, without motion,
the only other living thing
a hawk, hungry for prey, suspended
in the blinding, sunlit blue.   20

And yet how gentle it seems to someone
raised in a landscape short of rain—
the skyline of a hill broken by no more
trees than one can count, the grass,
the empty sky, the wish for water.   25

The Receptive Reader

1. What is the task the poet set himself in this poem? Why does he make us look at the landscape familiar to him through the eyes of the *outsider?*

2. What images or details make the landscape real for you? Were you surprised when the poem reached its turning point at the beginning of the last stanza?

3. What phrase or phrases would you nominate as the key to the characteristic quality of the landscape in this poem?

4. Do your sympathies lie with the easterner or the westerner in this poem?

John Keats   *(1795–1821)*

To Autumn   *1819*

Season of mists and mellow fruitfulness,
    Close bosom friend of the maturing sun;
Conspiring with him how to load and bless
    With fruit the vines that round the thatch eaves° run;   *of thatched roofs*
To bend with apples the mossed cottage trees,   5
    And fill all fruit with ripeness to the core;
        To swell the gourd, and plump the hazel shells
With a sweet kernel; to set budding more,
And still more, later flowers for the bees,
Until they think warm days will never cease,   10
        For summer has over-brimmed° their clammy cells.   *filled to overflowing*

Who hath not seen thee oft amid thy store?
    Sometimes whoever seeks abroad may find
    Thee sitting careless on a granary floor,
    Thy hair soft-lifted by the winnowing wind;   15
Or on a half-reaped furrow sound asleep,
    Drowsed with the fume of poppies, while thy hook
        Spares the next swath and all its twinèd° flowers: *intertwined*
And sometimes like a gleaner thou dost keep
    Steady thy laden head across a brook;   20
    Or by a cider-press with patient look
        Thou watchest the last oozings hours by hours.

Where are the songs of Spring? Aye, where are they?
    Think not of them, thou hast thy music too—
While barrèd° clouds bloom the soft-dying day,   *streaked*   25
    And touch the stubble-plains with rosy hue;

Then in a wailful choir the small gnats mourn
    Among the river sallows,° borne aloft   *low willow trees*
        Or sinking as the light wind lives or dies;
And full-grown lambs loud bleat from hilly bourn;°   *field* 30
    Hedge crickets sing; and now with treble soft
    The redbreast whistles from a garden-croft;°   *small plot*
        And gathering swallows twitter in the skies.

The Receptive Reader

1. Readers have long turned to Keats's poetry for its rich sensuous imagery. How much of Keats's *harvest imagery* does the modern reader still recognize? (Can you visualize the reaper cutting a swath through the wheat interspersed with flowers; can you visualize the wind winnowing the grain—by blowing the lighter chaff away as the grain is thrown into the air?)

2. What words and images in this poem help create the prevailing *mood*—the rich harvest mood of things coming to fruition, offering a feast to the senses? (Which images are visual images? Which are sound images? Which involve sensations—touch, taste?) What does Keats's way of looking at the nuts, the bees, or the cider press contribute to the characteristic feeling that pervades the poem?

3. Why are the swallows gathering? Is it a mere coincidence that Keats mentions them last in the poem?

The Personal Response

Keats, like other Romantic poets of the early nineteenth century, saw the healing influence of nature as an antidote to the ills of city civilization. Can you get into the spirit of his nature poetry? Is your own relationship with nature similar or different?

T. S. Eliot   *(1888–1965)*

Preludes   *1917*

I
The winter evening settles down
With smell of steaks in passageways.
Six o'clock.
The burnt-out ends of smoky days.
And now a gusty shower wraps   5
The grimy scraps
Of withered leaves about your feet
And newspapers from vacant lots;
The showers beat
On broken blinds and chimney-pots,   10
And at the corner of the street
A lonely cab-horse steams and stamps.
And then the lighting of the lamps.

II
The morning comes to consciousness
Of faint stale smells of beer   15
From the sawdust-trampled street
With all its muddy feet that press
To early coffee-stands.
With the other masquerades
That time resumes,   20
One thinks of all the hands
That are raising dingy shades
In a thousand furnished rooms.

III
You tossed a blanket from the bed,
You lay upon your back, and waited;   25
You dozed, and watched the night revealing
The thousand sordid images
Of which your soul was constituted;
They flickered against the ceiling.
And when all the world came back   30
And the light crept up between the shutters
And you heard the sparrows in the gutters,
You had such a vision of the street
As the street hardly understands;
Sitting along the bed's edge, where   35
You curled the papers from your hair,
Or clasped the yellow soles of feet
In the palms of both soiled hands.

IV
His soul stretched tight across the skies
That fade behind a city block,   40
Or trampled by insistent feet
At four and five and six o'clock;
And short square fingers stuffing pipes,
And evening newspapers, and eyes
Assured of certain certainties,   45
The conscience of a blackened street
Impatient to assume the world.

I am moved by fancies that are curled
Around these images, and cling:
The notion of some infinitely gentle   50
Infinitely suffering thing.

Wipe your hand across your mouth, and laugh;
The worlds revolve like ancient women
Gathering fuel in vacant lots.

The Receptive Reader

1. T. S. Eliot was a leader in the early modern rebellion against the conventionally beautiful or superficially pretty in poetry. How many of the images make this poem head in the opposite direction? Which are most striking or memorable for you, and why?

2. How does the "you" adressed in the poem relate to the "sordid" images shown in this poem? How does the "I" that is speaking? How do you?

The Creative Dimension

Much modern poetry explores negative or mixed emotions about the urban landscape or cityscape in which most of us live. Write a passage or poem packed with images that project your own feelings about the city or about the American small town. How do you react to the following example?

After the first rain, the city's smells only reek louder and damper: damp wool, wet newspapers, the oily dirty street. The smell of yesterday's meatloaf wafts from the neighboring apartment when I open the window to smell the wet cement. Today will be like yesterday. I open a thousand locks on the front door and lock a thousand behind me.

WRITING ABOUT LITERATURE

14   Looking at Imagery (Using Detail)

The Writing Workshop   You need to read a poem with an open eye and a willing ear. One of your first questions will be: What does the poet want me to see and hear? What does the poet want me to visualize, to imagine? You have to be receptive to the signals that are designed to call up vivid images on your mental screen. In preparing a paper on the imagery of a poem, ask yourself questions like the following:

✗ How does the poet make the *setting* real for you? Where is the poem taking you? What revealing details bring the place, the people, or the situation to life?

✗ What *key images* are striking or revealing? What sights seem to stand out? Why are they important in the poem as a whole? Quote phrases, half-lines, or lines to make your reader see key images and how they come back or find an echo at other points in the poem.

✗ Does the poem appeal to more than your sense of sight? Does it bring *other senses* into play—your hearing, your sense of smell, or your sense of touch? One way to organize your paper might be to sort out the different kinds of imagery.

✖ What *emotions* do the images in the poem stir in the reader? What attitudes do they bring into play? Do they trigger contradictory feelings or mixed emotions? One way to organize your paper might be to look first at images that steer the reader's reactions one way and then at images that point in a different direction.

✖ Is the poem unified by a prevailing *mood?* Or does it move through stages as images shift or as the associations and implications of key images change? One way to organize your paper might be to mark off major stages in the way the poem shapes the reader's thoughts and feelings.

Study the following student paper focused on a poem's imagery. How does the writer set her paper in motion? Is there a preview or hint of her general strategy? Does the paper follow up what you took to be the writer's overall plan? What use does she make of short, apt quotations? How does she wind up her paper?

Sample Student Paper

At Peter Meinke's Apple Market

"Apple-smell everywhere!" So starts Peter Meinke's poem, "Sunday at the Apple Market." Apples of all kinds (Haralson, McIntosh, Fireside, Rome), apple smells, and the paraphernalia of the apple harvest are everywhere in this poem— in "miraculous profusion." The poet could simply have said, "The apple market was busy Sunday afternoon with lots of people buying tons of apples of different colors and kinds." Instead, Peter Meinke assaults our senses with a feast of concrete imagery. We can choose to let this poem simply "be," as Archibald MacLeish says—to let it simply exist and speak for itself. Or we can choose to look behind the images to find a larger meaning. Either way, we cannot help relishing the rich sensuous quality of its "being."

Poems often display vivid visual and auditory imagery, and this poem does so in exceptional profusion. We see yellow, green, and red apples "piled crazy in the storehouse barn (7), apples in "bushels / and baskets and bags and boxes" (13–14), "apples by the cartload" (5). We hear "the crowd / around the testing table laughing" and the "dogs barking at children in the appletrees."

However, this poem appeals to all the senses; indeed, apple smell is everywhere from the beginning to the "smell of apples" at the end (l5). We experience taste along with smell as the people around the testing table roll "the cool applechunks in their mouths" (10) or as we recall the juice made by the "old cider-presses weathering in the shed" (3). We can imagine ourselves holding hands as the couples do in the poem; we carry the weight of bushels, baskets, bags, and boxes.

Why is the crowd laughing; why are the people happy? We see them at the apple market at the time of harvest, of ripeness and fruition. All the previous stages, from winter and pruning of the trees through blossom time, have led up to this stage of fullness and culmination. We can imagine the harvest cycle as parallel to our own journey through life, since all the stages of our own growth are represented: We see the children in the apple trees; we see the couples holding hands; we see the children's parents carrying apples back to their cars. We can enjoy a sense of cycle that leads up to this moment when we enjoy the fruits of our journey through life.

However, the poem does not stop there. Contrasting with the dominating concrete images of the ample harvest are hints of a further stage in the cycle. The "old ciderpress weathering in the shed" (3) suggests fermentation and aging. The "old ladders tilting at the empty branches" (4) foreshadow the end of fertility, with the coming of barrenness and decay—the inevitable continuation of the process we experience at the high point of the cycle in this poem. We see "so many people out in the country" on this Sunday to capture and carry back with them this happy moment of fulfillment that cannot last. For "one Sunday afternoon" these people are "free / and happy as people must have been meant to be" (15–16).

Reading the poem, I was struck by the image of the dogs barking at the children in the apple trees. It brought to mind a time when my grandparents' orchard was for me a "free and happy" world of its own. I remember a Sunday when I was hiding from my cousins in my grandmother's apple tree, stifling giggles on a high branch, my Sunday dress torn on the rough bark. I wrote a brief poem recalling the experience; it ends as follows:

In Sunday black and white like spotted puppies
they sniff and search under apple carts
and behind the stacked up empty wooden crates.
Behind heavy leaves red apples hide.
I hide, too.

Questions

1. How does the student writer set the scene or the tone? How well does she get into the spirit of the poem?

2. Does she provide the evidence needed to support her conclusions?

3. How do you react to the way she winds up her paper?

4. Is your response to the poem different from that of the student writer? Do you disagree with any of her conclusions?

15 Metaphor

Making Connections

When we attempt to express living experience with words, logical speech quickly becomes permeated with symbols and metaphors.

CHARLES M. JOHNSTON

FOCUS ON METAPHOR

Poets use striking imaginative comparisons to go beyond the resources of literal speech. When they take us into a world of vivid visual images, there is often more to the image than meets the eye.

The *as if* of Metaphor   Diane Wakoski says in "Meeting an Astronomer,"

We drive the same highways
in the dark, not seeing each other,
                            only the lights.

As we visualize the car lights we encounter when driving at night, we know we are not on a real highway. We could be at home, in a classroom, or in a hallway on the way to work. But it is *as if* the people we encounter were drivers whose faces we cannot see and whose thoughts we cannot read—because the only thing we can see is their lights. The car lights are examples of **metaphor,** language used imaginatively to carry ideas and feelings that otherwise might be hard to put into words.

Metaphor and Simile   A metaphor is a brief, compressed comparison that talks about one thing as if it were another. The comparison is implied, not spelled out. It comes into the poem unannounced, without the words *like* or *as* to signal that something is not literally a road but only in some ways like a road. However, a **simile,** a close cousin of metaphor, signals the comparison by words such as *like* or *as if.* When Shakespeare says "My reason, *the physician* to my love," he is using metaphor. When he says "My love is *as a fever,* longing still," he is using a simile.

380

The Web of Metaphor   Often, several related metaphors work together. In Linda Pastan's "After an Absence," the alien uncharted territory, the beckoning garden in the desert, the life-giving water, and the sand in the parched mouth are all metaphors offering contrasting perspectives on marriage:

> I had even forgotten how married love
> is a territory more mysterious
> the more it is explored, like one of those terrains
> you read about, a garden in the desert
> where you stoop to drink, never knowing
> if your mouth will fill with water or sand.

Familiar and Fresh Metaphors   Poetic metaphors range from the easily accessible to the more challenging. Many of the metaphors of ordinary speech are well established: we turn to a *dog-eared* page, watch tempers *boil,* or give someone a *fish-eyed* stare. Some familiar metaphors may once have been fresh and appealing, but they have become overused, losing their tread like a bald tire, turning into **clichés:** *the tip of the iceberg, a window of opportunity.* By contrast, poetic metaphors are often fresh and thought-provoking. They forge new connections; they discover unexpected, revealing similarities. When the American poet Carl Sandburg asks us to

> Remember all paydays of lilacs and songbirds

no familiar connection between paydays and songbirds guides us. We have to work out the implied equation ourselves. It sounds as if the poet had in mind the sense of reward and elation that workers might feel on payday. That elation corresponds to the joy brought by the rich blooms of the lilac and the song of birds.

The following poem does not talk about ideas; it acts them out in vivid images. These images have a meaning beyond what meets the eye. As readers, we have to decode the metaphors.

Linda Pastan   *(born 1932)*

Anger   1985

You tell me
that it's all right
to let it out of its cage,
though it may claw someone,
even bite.   5
You say that letting it out

may tame it somehow.
But loose it may
turn on me, maul
my face, draw blood.   10
Ah, you think you know so much,
you whose anger is a pet dog,
its canines dull with disuse.
But mine is a rabid thing, sharpening its teeth
on my very bones,   15
and I will never let it go.

The Receptive Reader

1. What is the *central metaphor* in this poem? Into how many details can you trace this central metaphor? Which details are especially graphic or concrete?

2. Where and how does the metaphor branch out into two opposite variations?

3. Where do you stand on the question raised by this poem?

The Creative Dimension

How do *you* visualize anger? Write an imaginative response to this poem, using your own central metaphor instead of the one used by the poet. Or do the same for another poem with a striking central metaphor. How do you react to the following student-written sample?

I watch you,
you who say,
"Be emotional; it's all right."
But you sit with the emotion
clamped to your leg
like a steel trap on a rabbit.
You struggle to get free
without chance of success.
I watch you
trying to gnaw it loose
as the rabbit would.

THE LANGUAGE OF METAPHOR

Without metaphor, language would lose its life-blood and stiffen into a conventional system of signs.

ERNST CASSIRER

The English eighteenth-century poet William Blake says, "The tigers of wrath are wiser than the horses of instruction." We need no nudging to make us realize that these animals are not literally there. They are brought in by way of comparison. Reading such metaphors, we mentally fill in the possible connections: righteous anger is fiery *like* a tiger and moves us to swift action. Compared with the powerful welling up of passion, instruction is more plodding, like the horses pulling a brewery wagon. It makes us do what we are told, as horses do what pleases their masters. It is not likely to move us to generous or passionate endeavor.

Both an image on the literal level and a metaphor may appeal strongly to our visual imagination. The difference is that the metaphor makes us visualize something that we could not literally interact with or see. When the poet Adrien Stoutenburg says, "The strawberry's leaves / Are a green hand spread open," we are looking at real leaves but not at a real hand. We are looking at small leaves that together form a kind of hand holding up the ripening strawberry. Metaphor (from a Greek word meaning "to carry over") carries us over from the normal surface meaning of a word to something else. It exploits similarities and makes connections between things we might otherwise keep apart.

Often, the poet will develop a metaphor beyond a single word. Such an **extended metaphor** traces the ramifications of the implied comparison. It follows up related similarities. A single extended metaphor may give shape to a poem as a whole, but often a poem moves through several related, interacting metaphors. The following poem is built around three related metaphors: the house, the horse, and the dog. Look at the way these metaphors work together. What do they make you see? What feelings do they bring into play? How do they challenge more familiar ways of looking at our bodies?

May Swenson   *(1919–1989)*

Question   *1954*

Body my house
my horse my hound
What will I do
When you are fallen

Where will I sleep   5
How will I ride
What will I hunt

Where can I go without my mount
all eager and quick
How will I know   10
in thicket ahead
is danger or treasure
When Body my good
bright dog is dead

How will it be   15
to lie in the sky
without roof or door
and wind for an eye
with cloud for shift°   *woman's shirt or chemise*
how will I hide?   20

In this poem, three meshing metaphors make us reexamine the way we feel about our bodies. First, the poet calls the body "my house," reminding us that it puts up the roof and walls giving us shelter and the doors barring intruders. It offers us a place to sleep, to hide; it offers refuge and protection.

When the poet calls the body "my horse," we are asked to imagine not a tired nag but a spirited mount—"all eager and quick"—ready to carry us to adventure. We are not rooted like a tree. Life is movement, motion, activity—but only if we can depend on the body to carry us into action. Finally, the poet calls the body "my hound"—a "good bright dog" that like a hunting dog serves its master well. It alerts us to danger (lurking "in thicket ahead") or hunts down "treasure." We depend on our bodies to keep us alert, prepared to deal with the threats and promises of every day.

The Receptive Reader

1. How is the way this poem looks at the body different from other, more familiar ways of looking at our bodies? Do you share the feelings or sympathize with the attitudes that the metaphors in this poem suggest?

2. For you, what is the connecting *thread* that links the three metaphors? What do they have in common?

3. What tone does the *title* set for the poem? What is the poet's "question"? Does the poem suggest an answer?

The Creative Dimension

Explore your own possible metaphors for the body. Complete the line "My body my . . ." in your own way, writing your own body poem or passage about the body. How well does the central metaphor work in the following example?

Body

You ship of a fool!
Why do I worry about
    sprung planks
    leaky decks
    spent rigging
    peeling paint?
The rats left a long time ago,
and you're still afloat!

What is the central metaphor in the following poem? How does the poet develop it into an extended metaphor? Which of the similarities between hope and "the thing with feathers" seem most fitting? Which seem most strange? Which to you are most thought-provoking or revealing?

Motorists driving through the Midwest see silos rising over the wheat fields—grain elevators "blocks long, a cathedral of high and mighty cylinders of white" (Ursula K. Le Guin). To an observer with a vivid imagination, they suggest comparisons, like those in the following poem.

Rita Dove   *(born 1952)*

Silos   *1989*

Like martial swans in spring paraded against the city sky's
shabby blue, they were always too white and
suddenly there.
They were never fingers, never xylophones, although once
a stranger said they put him in mind of Pan's pipes   5
and all the lost songs of Greece. But to the townspeople
they were like cigarettes, the smell chewy and bitter
like a field shorn of milkweed, or beer brewing, or
a fingernail scorched over a flame.

No, no, exclaimed the children. They're a fresh packet of chalk,   10
dreading math work.

They were masculine toys. They were tall wishes. They
were the ribs of the modern world.

The Receptive Reader

1. Which of the imaginative comparisons in this poem are to you the most fitting? Which are the most unexpected or far-ranging? (What is a xylophone? What kind of pipes did Pan, the ancient Greek god of shepherds, play?)

2. Is this poem all playful? Does it have a serious point?

METAPHOR, SIMILE, PERSONIFICATION

Metaphor is one kind of nonliteral language under the larger umbrella heading of **figurative** language. Like a metaphor, a **simile** is a brief, compressed imaginative comparison. Unlike a metaphor, a simile uses the words *as* or *like* or *as if* to advertise that a comparison will follow. These signals alert us to look for the similarities that the poet had in mind: "My love is like a red, red rose"; "My love is like a silken tent." A simile says outright that something is like something else. Sometimes similes are considered merely a special kind of metaphor—a metaphor announced rather than implied.

Love poems through the centuries have used metaphor and simile to express feelings that might otherwise be hard to put into words. A famous simile opens the following poem by the Scottish poet Robert Burns. Look at what the two similes in the opening stanza (group of four related lines) do for the poem as a whole. Note that *fair* in this poem means "beautiful"—as in much early love poetry.

Robert Burns   *(1759–1796)*

A Red, Red Rose   *1796*

O my luve's like a red, red rose
That's newly sprung in June;
O my luve's like the melodie
That's sweetly played in tune.

As fair art thou, my bonny lass,°   *my dear girl*   5
So deep in luve am I;
And I will luve thee still, my dear,
Till a' the seas gang dry°—   *run (go) dry*

Till a'° the seas gang dry, my dear,   *all*
And the rocks melt wi' the sun: 10
O I will luve thee still, my dear,
While the sands o' life shall run.

And fare thee weel, my only luve,
And fare thee weel awhile!
And I will come again, my luve,   15
Though it were a thousand mile.

The opening simile here draws on the rich traditional associations of the rose. For instance, its rich, red color is pleasing to the eye (and often associated with passion). People who love roses treasure the delicate petals and the fresh scent on a June morning. The second simile likens the poet's love to a melody "sweetly played in tune"—soothing the nerves frazzled by the jangling noises of everyday. The poet then tells his readers what many of them want to hear: A love like the poet's is not a casual, passing encounter. It will last forever, longer than the rocks and the sea. Any separation will be only for "awhile."

The Receptive Reader

1. How, or how well, do the two opening *similes* work together?

2. What explains the "sands of life" *metaphor?* Sand (on beaches) does not usually "run." What traditional device used sand to measure time?

3. Much traditional love poetry used *hyperbole,* or extreme exaggeration—for instance, to praise the beauty of the beloved to the skies. What instances of hyberbole can you find in this poem?

The Personal Response

To you, does Burns's love poem seem timeless or out of date? Would you consider sending it to someone? If someone sent it to you, what might be your response?

In the thirties and forties, Langston Hughes came to be considered the "poet laureate" or unofficial voice of black America. Each simile in the following poem sets up a different scenario for what might happen if a dream is deferred or hope denied.

Langston Hughes   *(1902–1967)*

Dream Deferred   *1951*

What happens to a dream deferred?
Does it dry up
Like a raisin in the sun?
Or fester like a sore—
And then run?   5
Does it stink like rotten meat?
Or crust and sugar over—
like a syrupy sweet?

Maybe it just sags
like a heavy load.   10

Or does it explode?

The Receptive Reader

1. Which similes in this poem fit exceptionally well? Which of the alternative scenarios can you most vividly imagine? Which seems to you most likely?
2. How does the poem build up to its ending? What makes it especially dramatic?

The bolder a poet's similes, the more they are likely to stimulate our imagination. The following poem focuses on the big bird—"the great gull"—that came from the sea. What images and feelings are brought into the poem by two key similes: "like a high priest" and "like a merchant prince"?

Howard Nemerov   *(born 1920)*

The Great Gull   *1951*

Restless, rising at dawn
I saw the great gull come from the mist
To stand upon the lawn.
And there he shook his savage wing
To quiet, and stood like a high priest   5
Bird-masked, mantled in gray.
Before his fierce austerity
My thought bowed down, imagining
The wild sea-lanes he wandered by
And the wild waters where he slept   10
Still as a candle in the crypt.
Noble, and not courteous,
He stared upon my green concerns.
Then, like a merchant prince
Come to some poor province,   15
Who, looking all about, discerns
No spice, no treasure house,
Nothing that can be made
Delightful to his haughty trade,
And so spreads out his sail,   20
Leaving to savage men
Their miserable regimen;°   *rigidly ordered life*
So did he rise, making a gale
About him with his wings,
And fought his huge freight into air   25
And vanished seaward with a cry—
A strange tongue but the tone clear.

The poet is fascinated by the large seabird that came out of the ocean
fog to stand on the lawn, stashing its large wings for an at-rest position
until it finally unfolds them again for takeoff. First, the bird "shook his
savage wing / To quiet"; later, it spread out its wings like a sail, creating
a miniature storm like a gale at sea, "fighting" its way into the air to lift
the "huge freight" of its body. The poet's carefully trimmed lawn (his
"green concerns") must seem petty and tame to this "savage," "fierce,"
and "haughty" bird from the "wild sea-lanes" and "wild waters." The
poet uses several similes to help us share his feelings about this majestic wild bird. For instance, he compares the bird to a high priest, wearing a bird mask and mantle of gray (like its coat of gray feathers),
expecting us to bow down to it as to a priest in a strange pagan ritual.

The Receptive Reader

1. The second simile compares the bird to a "merchant prince." How
would such a person be different from an ordinary merchant? What would such

a merchant prince be looking for and where? What would be disappointing about the "poor province" the gull actually found? What does this second simile have in common with the first?

2. A third simile makes us imagine the bird sleeping on the waters "Still as a candle in a crypt." What images and feelings does this simile bring into the poem? How is it related to the other two similes?

3. For you, what is the connecting thread that links the three similes? How do they work together; how are they related?

The Personal Response

What animal would *you* choose to represent untamed savage nature? Do you think a sea animal would be a better choice than a land animal? Why?

Personification is a metaphor or a simile that treats something non-human as if it were human. It is figurative language that makes things or animals act human. Personification can make the world around us mirror our own state of mind. When a blues singer sings, "The sky is crying / Look at the tears roll down the street," the whole world seems to share the singer's sadness and loneliness. The metaphors in the following poem make us think of both the frost and the flower as if they were human beings, acting out a grim minidrama.

Emily Dickinson   *(1830–1886)*

Apparently with no Surprise   1884

Apparently with no surprise
to any happy Flower
The Frost beheads it at its play—
In accidental power—
The blonde Assassin passes on—   5
The Sun proceeds unmoved
To measure off another Day
For an approving God.

As we read this poem, our first hint that the poet is speaking metaphorically is the the word *happy* applied to the flower. Flowers are not literally happy or unhappy. They have no feelings, just as they do not "play" (any more than they go about serious business). These metaphors are each an example of personification. It is *as if* the flower had been happily and innocently at play when it was attacked by the frost. It is *as if* the killer frost were an executioner who "beheads" the condemned victim. It is *as if* the frost were an "assassin," thus adding the idea of treachery to the brutality of the victim's execution.

The Receptive Reader

1. Dickinson's poems often have puzzling, provocative phrases tucked away in them. Why "accidental power"? Why "blonde assassin"? Is the scene being watched by an "approving God"?

2. What contrast does the poem set up between the work of the killer frost and the sun proceeding on its course?

3. Does this poem stir your feelings? Do you shudder at the swift destruction of the helpless flower? Do you feel a twinge of terror at seeing it destroyed? Why or why not?

JUXTAPOSITIONS

The Range of Metaphor

Poets vary in how boldly they explore new metaphorical connections. Love poems of earlier centuries featured fanciful extended metaphors called **conceits.** These were elaborately developed, setting up an analogy and then tracing it in careful detail. Such conceits were an expected ornament of the love sonnets written by the Italian fourteenth-century poet Petrarch and his many followers. The **sonnet** is an elaborately crafted fourteen-line poem with an interlaced rhyme scheme and iambic meter. In the following example by one of Petrarch's English translators, the lover's "enemy" steering the ship is also called "my lord." Both of these terms early love poets applied to the haughty, disdainful "cruel" lady to whom they addressed their "plaints." What is the central conceit or extended metaphor in the poem? How is it developed?

Thomas Wyatt   *(1503–1542)*

My Galley Charged with Forgetfulness   *before 1540*

My galley charged with forgetfulness	
Thorough° sharp seas in winter nights doth pass	*through*
'Tween rock and rock; and eke° mine enemy, alas,	*also*
That is my lord, steereth with cruelness;	
And every oar a thought in readiness,	5
As though that death were light in such a case.	
An endless wind doth tear the sail apace	
Of forced sighs and trusty fearfulness	
A rain of tears, a cloud of dark disdain,	
Hath done the wearied cords great hinderance;	10
Wreathed with error and eke with ignorance,	
The stars be hid° that led me to this pain;	*are hidden*
Drowned is reason that should me consort,°	*stay with me*
And I remain despairing of the port.	

The Receptive Reader

1. A conceit often follows the basic metaphor into every conceivable detail. (In this poem, once we are on the ship, we stay on the ship.) Why is it winter and night? What are the oars, the wind, the rain, the cloud, the harbor? Who or what drowned? What are the rocks?

2. What is the *keynote* of this poem? What are the prevailing emotions? Why do you think generations of readers related to this kind of love poetry (and still do)?

In the more conventional kind of conceit, the poet stays on the track prescribed by the dominating metaphor. By contrast, the metaphors in a Shakespearean sonnet often keep developing and shifting. They may start as elaborate conceits, but then they escalate, following up new and unexpected associations. What are the three key metaphors in the following sonnet? How do they develop; how do they mesh? (Note that the word *choir* in the fourth line stands for the part of a church reserved for the choir.)

William Shakespeare   *(1564–1616)*

Sonnet 73   *before 1598*

That time of year thou mayst in me behold
When yellow leaves, or none, or few, do hang
Upon those boughs which shake against the cold,
Bare ruined choirs, where late the sweet birds sang.
In me thou seest the twilight of such day   5
As after sunset fadeth in the west;
Which by and by° black night doth take away,   *gradually*
Death's second self, that seals up all in rest.
In me thou seest the glowing of such fire
That on the ashes of his youth doth lie,   10
As the deathbed whereon it must expire,
Consumed with that which it was nourished by.
This thou perceivest, which makes thy love more strong,
To love that well which thou must leave ere long.°   *before long*

The much-analyzed first metaphor in this sonnet makes us think of approaching age as the late autumn of the speaker's life, when we see the bare branches of the tree shaken by cold winds, with only a few last withered yellow leaves clinging to the boughs. But the metaphor shifts and develops: the bare wood of the branches apparently makes the poet think of the wooden pews where the choirboys or choristers used to sit in church (where they sang the way the "sweet birds" sang in the tree). Now the church is in ruins, like many of the great abbey churches of England after the Protestant Reformation had shut down the monasteries. Both the tree and the church used to be filled with sweet song, but they are now fitting metaphors for the approaching decay and loneliness of age. They are likely to make us long for the rich growth and sweet birdsong of summers past.

The Receptive Reader

1. What is the *second* major metaphor, developed in the second set of four lines (or quatrain) in the sonnet? What parallels or connections make it especially fitting or expressive? How does it shift to acquire a further dimension? (How is night "Death's second self"?)

2. What is the metaphor in the *third* set of four lines? (What was "Consumed with that which it was nourished by," and how?) Can you see more than one parallel or connection between this third major metaphor and the other two?

3. Many Shakespearean sonnets provide a "turning" in the final couplet, or set of two lines—an answer to a central question, or a *counterpoint* to an earlier assertion. How does this sonnet fit this pattern?

Making Connections—For Discussion or Writing

We are often told that our language today is deficient in the language of the emotions. Look at Gary Soto's "Oranges," Robert Burns's "A Red, Red Rose," and the sonnets by Thomas Wyatt and Shakespeare. Does the language of love in any of these poems have something to teach to today's lovers?

POEMS FOR FURTHER STUDY

Pay special attention to the workings of metaphor, simile, or personification in the following poems.

William Shakespeare   *(1564–1616)*

Sonnet 29   *before 1598*

When, in disgrace with Fortune and men's eyes,
I all alone beweep my outcast state,
And trouble deaf heaven with my bootless° cries,   *useless*
And look upon myself and curse my fate,
Wishing me like to one more rich in hope,   5
Featured like him, like him with friends possessed,
Desiring this man's art and that man's scope,
With what I most enjoy contented least;
Yet in these thoughts myself almost despising,
Haply I think on thee, and then my state°   *condition* 10
(Like to the lark at break of day arising
From sullen earth) sings hymns at heaven's gate;
For thy sweet love remembered such wealth brings
That then I scorn to change my state with kings.

The Receptive Reader

1. In the first eight lines, or *octave,* of this sonnet, what is literal statement? What is metaphor? (What image or associations does the reference to Fortune bring to mind?)

2. Lines 11 and 12 combine simile, metaphor, and personification. How? As Shakespeare's use of figurative language often does, the lark simile seems to escalate, shifting to a further and bolder metaphor in midflight. How, and with what effect on the reader?

3. Sonnets often reach a turning point at the end of the octave; Shakespeare's sonnets especially often lead up to a concluding couplet that leaves us with a thought to remember. How does this sonnet illustrate both of these features?

Sylvia Plath   *(1932–1963)*

Metaphors   *1960*

I'm a riddle in nine syllables,
An elephant, a ponderous° house,   *very weighty*
A melon strolling on two tendrils.
O red fruit, ivory, fine timbers!
This loaf's big with its yeasty rising.   5
Money's new-minted in this fat purse.
I'm a means, a stage, a cow in calf.
I've eaten a bag of green apples,
Boarded the train there's no getting off.

The Receptive Reader

1. Where in your reading of the poem did you first guess at the answer to the riddle? What in the poem did most to confirm your guess?

2. Why "nine syllables"? Why a poem of nine lines of nine syllables each? (The title has nine letters, but this may be just a coincidence.)

3. Why green apples? Which metaphors in the poem seem to be most expressive or to fit the speaker's condition best?

4. What are the speaker's feelings? Which of the metaphors do most to reveal her attitude? Is there humor in the poem, and what kind?

The Personal Response

The situation in which the speaker in this poem finds herself has often inspired mixed emotions or contradictory feelings. Have you observed or perhaps personally shared these? Write about the mixed emotions.

John Donne   *(1572–1631)*

A Valediction: Forbidding Mourning   *1611*

As virtuous men pass mildly away,
And whisper to their souls to go,
Whilst some of their sad friends do say
The breath goes now, and some say no:

So let us melt, and make no noise,   5
No tear floods, nor sigh-tempests move;
'Twere profanation° of our joys   *it would make something*
To tell the laity our love.   *sacred common*

Moving of the earth° brings harms and fears;   *earthquakes*
Men reckon what it did and meant;   10
But trepidation of the spheres,°   *trembling of the heavenly spheres*
Though greater far, is innocent.

Dull sublunary° lovers' love   *below the moon, earthbound*
(Whose soul is sense) cannot admit
Absence, because it doth remove   15
Those things which elemented° it.   *gave it substance*

But we, by a love so much refined
That ourselves know not what it is,
Inter-assured° of the mind,   *mutually sure*
Care less eyes, lips, and hands to miss.   20

Our two souls, therefore, which are one,
Though I must go, endure not yet
A breach, but an expansion,
Like gold° to airy thinness beat.   *like gold leaf*

If they be two, they are two so   25
As stiff twin compasses are two:
Thy soul, the fixed foot, makes no show
To move, but doth if the other do.

And though it in the center sit,
Yet when the other far doth roam,   30
It leans and harkens after it,
And grows erect as that comes home.

Such wilt thou be to me, who must,
Like the other foot, obliquely° run;   *at a wide angle*
Thy firmness makes my circle just,°   *makes it perfect*   35
And makes me end where I begun.

The Receptive Reader

1. According to Izaak Walton, a contemporary biographer, Donne wrote this
farewell poem for his wife before leaving on a journey to France. What is the

connection between the parting of the spouses and the death scene described in the first stanza? (Why do you think Donne's contemporaries believed that good, virtuous people would have a "mild" or gentle death?)

2. If outsiders are the "laity," what does the implied comparison make the two people in love?

3. Donne's contemporaries believed that the heavens were perfect (reflecting the perfection of God). Everything "sublunary"—below the moon, on this earth—was *im*perfect, subject to decay and death. Furthermore, the planets moving in orbit around the earth in the geocentric, earth-centered Ptolemaic view of the universe were attached to spheres of crystal. At times these moved or shook, accounting for apparent irregularities in the astronomers' calculations. How does Donne draw on these contemporary beliefs in this poem?

4. Probably the best-known example of figurative language in English literature is the comparison of the two people in love to the pair of "twin compasses" used in geometry classes to draw a circle. What does this device look like? How does it work? How does Donne put it to work in this poem?

The Personal Response

Critics (and presumably lovers) have been divided on whether to welcome into love poetry comparisons drawn from areas like astronomy, geometry, and medicine. How would you vote on this issue, and why?

WRITING ABOUT LITERATURE

15 *Writing About Metaphor (Organizing the Paper)*

The Writing Workshop   In reading a poem, we have to be alert to metaphor and simile. We have to respond to imaginative comparisons that make us see one thing while making us think of another. For instance, in John Donne's "A Valediction: Forbidding Mourning," we are asked to visualize "gold to airy thinness beat"—gold hammered incredibly thin by the goldsmith's art, so that an ounce or less of the metal will yield enough gold leaf to gild a whole column or an altar in a church. But in reading the poem, we are expected to make the connection between the gold leaf we see and the love uniting the speaker in the poem and his wife. Their love (precious like gold) also is infinitely malleable or "stretchable," so that instead of the journey's causing a "breach" or break, their love will merely expand (enduring an "expansion") to bridge the distance.

When you prepare a paper that focuses on the workings of metaphor, consider the following guidelines:

✘ Look for imaginative comparisons *spelled out or implied*. Similes are easy to recognize because the *as* or *like* or *as if* is part of the text

("*As* virtuous men pass mildly away . . ."). Metaphors do not carry such a label; the *as if* is merely implied. They are easiest to recognize when something is clearly not literally true. "Tear-floods" and "sigh-tempests" are not literally floods and tempests.

✗ Look for *sustained* or *extended metaphors* that the poet traces into their ramifications. The poet comparing his love to a ship lost at sea is likely to show more than one way in which being in love is like being on a drifting ship.

✗ Look for *central metaphors* that help organize the poem as a whole. A poem may be built around the metaphor of the ice skaters, who are like people moving quickly across the surface of their lives, dancing on the ice. Often a poem builds up to a culminating metaphor that stays with us after we finish reading.

✗ Respond to the *range of associations* of key metaphors. With most poetic metaphors, there is no simple one-to-one relationship between figurative and literal meaning. Try to do justice to what is left out in a simple prose paraphrase of a metaphorical line. Explore the images it conjures up; respond to the emotions it brings into play.

✗ Look for the *connections* between the metaphors in a poem. For instance, they may be variations on a theme, reinforcing or driving home a central concern of the poet. Or they may reflect polarities that set up the basic tension or challenge in a poem. Or they may be part of an escalating series of metaphors that lead up to a new way of seeing or feeling.

When writing a paper about a poem rich in metaphor and simile, you may want to start with reading notes that take stock of the imaginative comparisons in the poem. Here are sample reading notes for John Donne's "A Valediction: Forbidding Mourning":

Reading Notes

The parting of the lovers is compared to a death: "As virtuous men pass mildly away . . . so let us melt, and make no noise." Virtuous people who are dying have nothing to fear in the afterlife and therefore die in peace. A journey separating the lovers is in some ways like the separation caused by death, but it should be like a virtuous person's death—without fear and emotional upheaval.

The noisy mourning of others is compared to floods ("tear-floods") and tempests ("sigh-tempests").

Telling others of the speaker's intimate, private love (through loud display of grief) would be like priests revealing the mysteries of their faith to "the laity," that is, to lay people—to unappreciative, unprepared outsiders. The lovers would then "profane" the mysteries of their love—desecrating something sacred by taking it down to the level of ordinary reality.

The upheavals in the lives or ordinary lovers are earthquakes ("moving of the earth"). But any disturbance in the more refined loves of the two people in this poem is "a trepidation of the spheres"—it is like the far off trembling in the crystal spheres of the heavens, which is "innocent" or harmless as far as actual damage in the world around us is concerned.

The "souls" of ordinary clods are not really soul but sense—they stay on the level of sense perception and sensual feeling; they don't really have a "soul."

True love is like gold—it can be stretched incredibly thin like gold leaf without breaking.

The souls of the two lovers are joined like twin compasses. One leg, "the fixed foot," is planted firmly in the center. The other "travels," describing a perfect circle, returning to its point of origin. The farther the moving leg extends from the fixed center, the more the stationary leg needs to incline or lean toward it (it "harkens after it"). But at the same time the stationary leg keeps the moving leg from roaming too far, from going off on a tangent. In fact the firmness of the "fixed foot" (the person who stayed home) makes sure the absent lover comes full circle.

Organizing the Paper   How would you organize this material? The metaphors and similes in Donne's poem are each bold and original in their own right. You often need to make the required mental leap from what you see to what it means. At the same time, the metaphors shift rapidly, and you need to be alert if you are not to be left behind. To write a unified paper, you will have to aim at working out an overall framework or perspective. You will have to try to fit the rapidly shifting individual metaphors into an overall pattern.

The student author of the following paper uses the idea of the journey—which is the subject of the poem—as the organizing principle for the paper.

Model Student Paper

Thou Shalt Not Cry When I Am Gone

In a favorite scene in yesterday's romantic movies, someone is boarding a train, going off to war or to some far-off assignment or tour of duty. The person left behind is fighting back tears as the train slowly pulls out of the station. The traveler is trying to stay calm, forestalling the "tear-floods" and "sigh-tempests" that John Donne dreads in his farewell poem, "A Valediction: Forbidding Mourning." Scheduled to leave on a journey to France, Donne pleads with his wife Anne More to accept his departure in a spirit of calm acceptance, confident that the strength of their love will triumph over their physical separation.

In arguing against mourning and emotional upheaval, Donne takes us on a journey through a sequence of bold unexpected images, each one a metaphor or a simile for the love between him and his wife. Finally we reach the circle drawn by the twin compasses in the final stanzas as the metaphor for a perfect love that will bring him back to the starting point of his journey, making "me end where I begun."

The structure of the poem, a progression from one striking metaphor or simile to another, is the more appropriate when we consider that the poem was presented to his wife before he departed on a journey.

The journey begins with an unexpected analogy between the impending separation of the lovers and death. The poet says "So let us melt"—go quietly, like snow that melts in the March sun, making "no noise" (5). The startling comparison is between their parting and the death of "virtuous men," who "pass mildly away / And whisper to their souls to go" (1–2). Virtuous men and their friends have no need to mourn unduly at their passing—after all, their virtue in this life has assured them of glory and reward in the life to come. Similarly, the poet and his love have no need for noise at their separation—"no tear-floods, nor sigh-tempests" (6). There is no need to weep and sigh, since the beauty and strength of their love will survive their separation.

Their love is in fact almost sacred. It would be profaned if it should be made known to others, who could not comprehend love on such a high spiritual plane. Since it is almost holy, the lovers should not cheapen or defile it through such ordinary demonstration of grief as weeping or lamenting. Like priests, they should guard their sacred mysteries from "profanation" by the laity (7–8).

We next move to a larger circle than the temple where love is protected from the uninitiated. Even the earth is not adequate to contain true love. For more common lovers, the earthquake of separation would bring "harms and fears" (9). But the love between the poet and his wife is above the reach of such earthly upheavals. It is as if their love resided in the heavens, among the crystal spheres of the Ptolemaic universe. Even when there is "trepidation" or trembling of the spheres, it is "innocent"—it will cause no harm here below. Donne remains in the Ptolemaic universe for another verse or two: Ordinary earth-bound lovers are caught up in the physical presence of the other person, which like all material things in this "sublunary" sphere below the moon is subject to change and decay. Their "soul is sense"; the only outlet for what soul they have is through the five senses. Their love hinges on the physical act of love, which cannot be consummated in the absence of the beloved. More refined lovers don't need the presence of the physical body; they "care less" if they have to miss "eyes, lips, and hands" (13–20).

The love of these two exceptional lovers is like gold—not just because it is precious, but because gold can be beaten into a layer of the thinnest gold leaf that stretches incredibly far—perhaps even from England to France without a "breach" or breaking. However, the culminating metaphor is that of the twin compasses, which "are two" only in the sense that there are two legs joined permanently at the top. The "fixed foot" of the stay-at-home "leans and harkens" after the other that "far doth roam" (25–30). As the foot that actually draws the circle travels around the stationary part, that part must incline at the right angle. (It cannot just forget about the "roaming" part.)

Together, the twin compasses create a circle, to Donne's contemporaries the most perfect shape in the universe. The firmness of the "other foot" enables the poet to come full circle; it makes his journey "end where I begun" (36).

Questions

1. How well does this paper read the metaphors in the poem? (In the poem, which are metaphors, and which are similes?) Where or how does the paper help you understand Donne's figurative language? Do you disagree with any of the interpretations? Did the student writer miss anything important?

2. Which of the metaphors or similes in this poem seem to you particularly unexpected or strange? Which make the most sense after the reader has a chance to think about them?

3. One reader thought the poem "terribly romantic," since the poet wants the love between him and his wife to be perfect, better than anyone else's. At the opposite end of the spectrum, another reader found the poet to be romantic on the surface but really insensitive, lecturing a silent, passive partner about what she should feel and think. Where do you stand? How do you respond to the poem?

16 Symbol

A World of Meanings

Symbols are the bridging language between the visible and the invisible world.

ANGELIS ARRIEN

FOCUS ON SYMBOLS

A **symbol** is something that you can see but that has taken on a meaning beyond itself. It is literally there, but it has taken on a larger meaning. The speaker in Paul Goodman's "Haiku" is a person who actually grows roses—and these then take on for him a symbolic meaning:

Sprayed with strong poison
my roses are crisp this year
In the crystal vase

In this poem, we are made to visualize actual roses—in a crystal vase. They have been sprayed with actual pest killer or fungicide. Why did the poet mention these details? They push us beyond the ordinary reaction of "How nice to have roses." The roses have been produced at a price. They become a symbol of beauty that is produced at the cost of using potentially lethal toxic agents.

Conventional Symbols Poets often use or adapt traditional symbols. We all know the language of symbols that are current in our culture: the dove of peace prevails when nations sheathe the sword. The daily bread sustains life; it becomes the staff of life. The raised fist calls to armed struggle. Hands joined in a handshake proclaim human brotherhood. Chains used to shackle prisoners become a symbol of slavery and oppression. A broken chain, in turn, becomes a symbol of freedom. Poets may make use of such conventional symbols, but they will also often give new symbolic significance to objects and events. Rather than bring the meaning of a symbol *into* the poem from the outside, we have to read the meaning of the symbol *out of* the poem.

400

The Network of Associations   Powerful symbols activate a network of associations. A plow was the peasant's basic tool—needed to break the sod and start the planting cycle that would lead to the bounty of the harvest. Over the centuries, the plow became a symbol for the steady toil required to feed humankind. It reminds us to honor the labor that staves off famine. It admonishes the privileged, who squander in thoughtless luxury what the workers in the fields gain toiling from sunup to sundown. As William Langland says in the medieval poem *Piers Plowman,*

> Some were following the plow, with no time for pleasure,
> Sowing the seed, sweating at their labor,
> Winning the wealth that the worthless waste in luxury.

Symbol and Metaphor   What is the difference between symbol and metaphor? The roses in Goodman's poem are literally there. They are part of the scene the poet asks us to visualize. Metaphors bring images into a poem that are not literally a part of what we see. When Laura St. Martin in a poem called "The Ocean" says, "the ocean is a strange / midnight lover," we are asked to imagine a real ocean, but not a literal human lover. The ocean, to the person swimming at night, is in some ways *like* a lover—caressing, passionate, changeable. There is no human lover in this ocean at this time. The lover in this poem is metaphorical.

THE LANGUAGE OF SYMBOLS

What the bee knows
Tastes in the honey
Sweet and sunny.
O wise bee. O rose.
       JOHN FANDEL, "TRIBUTE"

   A poem will often center on a unifying symbol. Often these symbols are rooted in age-old human experience, drawing on a community of shared meanings. For instance, green is a potently symbolic color: since the dawn of history, the first budding green life of April, after the barrenness and ice of winter, has served as a symbol of rebirth, of the triumph of life over death. In the depth of winter, a sprig of evergreen (or a whole tree) can symbolize our faith that burgeoning life will return to the barren, frozen land. Poets draw on this common fund of symbolic meanings. In reading the following poem, we soon realize that the frogs in the basement of the abandoned house are more than a footnote in the speaker's childhood memories. The "green chorus" of the green frogs, who had "slept in an icy bed" all winter, comes back to life in the spring, "pouring / out of their green throats."

David Wagoner   *(born 1926)*

The Other House   *1983*

As a boy, I haunted an abandoned house
Whose basement was always full of dark-green water
Or dark-green ice in winter,
Where frogs came back to life and sang each spring.

On broken concrete under the skeleton   5
Of a roof, inside ribbed walls, I listened alone
Where the basement stairs went down
Under the water, down into their music.

During storms, our proper house would be flooded too.
The water would spout from drains, through the foundation   10
And climb the basement stairs
But silently, and would go away silently,

As silent as my father and mother were
All day and during dinner and after
And after the radio   15
With hardly a murmur all the way into sleep.

All winter, the frogs slept in an icy bed,
Remembering how to sing when it melted.
If I made a sound, they stopped
And listened to me sing nothing, singing nothing.   20

But gradually, finally April would come pouring
Out of their green throats in a green chorus
To chorus me home toward silence.
Theirs was the only home that sang all night.

The Receptive Reader

1. Would you call the sound the frogs make "music"? What makes the "other house" an unlikely or unpromising setting for songs celebrating the return of spring? Do the frogs and the setting undercut the symbolism of spring and renewal for you?

2. The poet does not take us to the boy's own "proper house" till the third stanza. Why? What is the key to the polar opposition of what the two houses stand for? How is this polarity central to the poem as a whole?

3. Is there anything symbolic about the frogs' falling silent when they heard the boy?

4. Do you think the boy has been permanently influenced by his parents? Do you agree with the following student reaction to the poem?

There is no renewal in spring-green trees if it does not resonate on the inside. A soul that cannot sing at the melting of the snows is winter-cold, ice-hard, regardless of the sun's warmth. A dark mysterious center that sings without sunlight breathes more life than this proper emptiness. The coldness of the silent parent is visited upon the son, perhaps for always, so his soul can never vibrate with mysterious yearnings, never feel the spring-green trees.

The Personal Response

In your own growing up, how much "silence" has there been and how much "song"?

The Creative Dimension

When we read a poem that has a strong impact on us, a haunting image or central symbol may linger in our minds. Look at the way the following student-written passage re-creates the lasting impression the poem left in the student's mind. Then do your own re-creation of a lasting impression left in your mind by this poem or by another poem in this chapter.

In spring,
after the ice melts
and the drains fill
the concrete cracks
of the basement floor
with green water,
the frogs are born
to keep me company
and fill my silent nights
with songs.

The following poem focuses our attention on the rose and on water, which are both rich in symbolic overtones and associations. The rose, often a deep red or blood red, has long stood for passion or for beauty. The more arid the country, the more water is likely to be worshiped as the source of life, making the desert bloom, creating an oasis in a wasteland of rock or sand. What are the symbolic meanings of the rose and of water in this poem?

Denise Levertov   *(1923–1997)*

To One Steeped in Bitterness   1964

Nail the rose
              to your mind's door
like a rat, a thwarted chickenhawk.
Yes, it has had its day.

And the water   5
              poured for you
which you disdain to drink,
yes, throw it away.

Yet the fierce rose
                    stole nothing   10
from your cooped heart,
nor plucked your timid eye;

and from inviolate rock
                    the liquid light
was drawn, that's dusty now   15
and your lips dry.

In this poem, we see a number of symbolic objects and symbolic gestures. We can imagine someone being offered a rose or a drink of water.
We can also imagine the person turning these down. In the poem, as in
real life, both of these gestures invite symbolic interpretation. Both the
water and the disdainful gesture that throws it out are likely to mean
something beyond themselves. They reveal an attitude, a state of mind.
The gesture of pouring the water may mean friendship or hospitality.
The gesture of refusing it may symbolize bitterness and hostility.

The Receptive Reader

1. What is likely to be the symbolic meaning of the rose? We are asked to
imagine it nailed to the "mind's door" by the bitter, hostile person being
addressed in the poem. The person "steeped in bitterness," with a "cooped
heart," would nail the rose to the barn door (the way ranchers nail varmints they
consider their natural enemies). Why?

2. What is likely to be the symbolic meaning of the water? The person
steeped in bitterness disdainfully rejects the offered water, which is like "liquid
light," and which would bring much-needed liquid to dry, parched lips. What
would the parched soul be thirsting for?

The following poem was written by a famous English poet of the
Romantic Age, an era of both revolution and reaction. The title of the
poem names an Egyptian pharaoh who, like other early Egyptian rulers,
commissioned colossal statues of himself.

Percy Bysshe Shelley   *(1792–1822)*

Ozymandias   *1818*

I met a traveler from an antique land
Who said: "Two vast and trunkless legs of stone
Stand in the desert . . . Near them on the sand,
Half-sunk, a shattered visage° lies, whose frown,   *face*
And wrinkled lip, and sneer of cold command,   5
Tell that its sculptor well those passions read
Which yet survive, stamped on these lifeless things,
The hand that mocked them, and the heart that fed:

And on the pedestal these words appear:
'My name is Ozymandias, king of kings: 10
Look on my works, ye Mighty, and despair!'
Nothing beside remains. Round the decay
Of that colossal wreck, boundless and bare
The lone and level sands stretch far away."

The Receptive Reader

1. According to the poem, what did the pharaoh want the statue he commissioned to symbolize? What does the statue symbolize for the poet?

2. Shelley, like other Romantics, was a rebel against tyrannical authority. How does this commitment show in the poem?

PUBLIC AND PRIVATE SYMBOLS

All poems say the same thing, and each poem is unique.

OCTAVIO PAZ

Some poets develop a symbolic language of their own that may at first seem private or obscure. However, it gradually becomes meaningful as we learn more about the poet or read several poems by the same poet. We learn the poet's symbolic language; we gradually feel less like strangers in the poet's world of meanings. The English poet William Blake was a precursor of the Romantic movement. For him, all experience was shot through with symbolic meanings—he was able "to see a world in a grain of sand / And a heaven in a wild flower." Breaking with eighteenth-century standards of rationality and restraint, he used bold, unusual symbols to celebrate the divine energies at work in the universe. The following is Blake's most famous poem. What do you think would be the poet's answers to the questions he asks in this poem?

William Blake   *(1757–1827)*

The Tyger   *1794*

Tyger! Tyger! burning bright
In the forests of the night,
What immortal hand or eye
Could frame thy fearful symmetry?

In what distant deeps or skies   5
Burnt the fire of thine eyes?
On what wings dare he aspire?
What the hand, dare° seize the fire?   *hand that dares*

And what shoulder, & what art,
Could twist the sinews of thy heart?   10
And when thy heart began to beat,
What dread hand? & what dread feet?

What the hammer? what the chain?
In what furnace was thy brain?
What the anvil? what dread grasp   15
Dare its deadly terrors clasp?

When the stars threw down their spears,
And water'd heaven with their tears,
Did he smile his work to see?
Did he who made the lamb make thee?   20

Tyger! Tyger! burning bright
In the forests of the night,
What immortal hand or eye
Dare frame thy fearful symmetry?

The Receptive Reader

1. How does Blake make us see the tiger as beautiful and terrifying at the same time?

2. How does Blake make us imagine the process of creation? (What associations do the images in the fourth stanza—the anvil, the furnace, the forge—bring into play?) How is his vision of the process different from what we might conventionally expect?

3. How has the lamb traditionally been used as a symbol of goodness? How has the tiger traditionally been used as a symbol of evil? How is Blake's use of these symbols different? Is the tiger evil or sinister in this poem?

4. What is the answer to the questions the poet asks in this poem?

Adrienne Rich has been called "perhaps the leading American feminist poet of her generation" (Eric Mendelsohn). In her poems as in her essays and editorial work, she played a pioneering role in exploring a new language of thought and feeling for women breaking out of a traditional patriarchal mold. What new or different meanings do familiar symbols assume in the following poem?

Adrienne Rich   *(born 1929)*

Aunt Jennifer's Tigers   *1951*

Aunt Jennifer's tigers prance across a screen,
Bright topaz denizens of a world of green.
They do not fear the men beneath the tree;
They pace in sleek chivalric certainty.

Aunt Jennifer's fingers fluttering through her wool   5
Find even the ivory needle hard to pull.
The massive weight of Uncle's wedding band
Sits heavily upon Aunt Jennifer's hand.

When Aunt is dead, her terrified hands will lie
Still ringed with ordeals she was mastered by.   10
The tigers in the panel that she made
Will go on prancing, proud and unafraid.

The Receptive Reader

1. What do the tigers represent in Aunt Jennifer's world? What does the wedding band represent? How do these two symbols function as *polar opposites* in this poem?

2. What is the range of meaning your dictionary gives for words like *topaz, denizen, chivalric, ordeal?* What do these words mean in the context of this poem?

3. In a later reprinting of this poem, the poet changed the words *prance* (line l) and *prancing* (line 12) to *stride* and *striding.* What difference does the change make? Why do you think the poet might have wanted to change the words?

4. How have the central symbols in this poem changed from more traditional meanings and associations?

Making Connections—For Discussion or Writing

How are Blake's tiger and Rich's tigers related in their symbolic meanings or associations? In what ways are they similar? In what ways are they different?

The Irish poet William Butler Yeats stands out among poets using a highly individual symbolic language. In his earlier poetry, he had drawn inspiration from the lore of Ireland. In his later years, he repeatedly used symbols from the rich religious art of Byzantium (later Constantinople and now Istanbul), the fabled capital of the eastern part of the Roman Empire during the early Christian era. Byzantine art was famous for precious materials and finely crafted artifice. It was legendary for the ornamental patterns of its mosaics; for its carved ivory, its enamel work, and the work of its goldsmiths. Shortly before he wrote the following poem, Yeats had seen spectacular examples of Byzantine mosaics depicting saints and prophets (the "sages" mentioned in the third stanza) in a church at Ravenna in northern Italy.

In the poem, the poet takes us on a symbolic voyage. We travel from a country of the young to "the holy city of Byzantium"—a place more attuned to the spiritual needs of the aging speaker in the poem. What special fascination does the "artifice" of the Greek artists of Byzantium hold for the poet?

William Butler Yeats   *(1865–1939)*

Sailing to Byzantium   *1927*

1

That is no country for old men. The young
In one another's arms, birds in the trees
—Those dying generations—at their song,
The salmon-falls, the mackerel-crowded seas,
Fish, flesh, or fowl, commend all summer long   5
Whatever is begotten, born, and dies.
Caught in that sensual music all neglect
Monuments of unaging intellect.

2

An aged man is but a paltry thing,
A tattered coat upon a stick, unless   10
Soul clap its hands and sing, and louder sing
For every tatter in its mortal dress,
Nor is there singing school but studying
Monuments of its own magnificence;
And therefore I have sailed the seas and come   15
To the holy city of Byzantium.

3

O sages standing in God's holy fire
As in the gold mosaic of a wall,
Come from the holy fire, perne in a gyre,°   *turn with a spiral motion*
And be the singing masters of my soul.   20
Consume my heart away, sick with desire
And fastened to a dying animal
It knows not what it is; and gather me
Into the artifice of eternity.

4

Once out of nature, I shall never take   25
My bodily form from any natural thing,
But such a form as Grecian° goldsmiths make   *Greek*
Of hammered gold and gold enameling
To keep a drowsy Emperor awake;
Or set upon a golden bough to sing   30
To lords and ladies of Byzantium
Of what is past, or passing, or to come.

Much of the early part of the poem revolves around a polar opposition of youth and age. The speaker in the poem finds himself out of place in a country of the young that is full of "sensual music." To the aging speaker in the poem, fastened to his decaying body as "to a dying animal" (line 22), there is no comfort in the surface vitality of a life caught up in the world of the senses. The second stanza focuses on the central paradox of the poem: the body decays, leaving the physical person little more than a scarecrow, "a tattered coat upon a stick." However, the intellect survives; the soul is still capable of song and artistic creation. Here is the answer to the decay of the body: the soul can metaphorically "clap its hands" and create immortal music. The "singing school" for the soul, teaching it to triumph over decay, is the work of artists that have gone before.

The Receptive Reader

1. We are conditioned to think positively of youth and burgeoning nature. What turns the speaker away from them?

2. Much of this poem revolves around related *polarities:* the opposition of youth and age, of intellect and the body, and of nature and art. What striking details help flesh out each of these polarities?

3. Why do the salmon fighting their way up the "salmon-falls" provide the poet with an especially appropriate *symbol* for life in the natural world?

4. What vision of art or "artifice" is developed in the final two stanzas? How will "artifice" provide the answer to age and decay? What makes the artifacts of Byzantine art apt symbols for the poet's way of transcending or overcoming age?

5. In this poem, Yeats uses a finely crafted interlaced rhyme scheme called **ottava rima** (or "set of eight"). Why is it more appropriate to this poem than free-flowing free verse would be?

The Personal Response

Do you think art should celebrate the vitality of life or help us triumph over its imperfections?

JUXTAPOSITIONS

Symbol and Allegory

In an **allegory,** symbols work together in a set pattern. Symbolic figures or objects play their roles like actors in a drama. The author of the first of the following two poems belonged to the Pre-Raphaelites, a group of English painters and writers who turned to medieval art and religion for inspiration. In her poem, the road, the hill, the inn, the darkness at end of day, the traveler, and the other wayfarers all play their assigned roles in the poet's allegorical vision of our spiritual journey to our final destination. In the earlier allegorical poem by the English poet William Blake, what is the meaning of the symbolic details? What role does each play in the allegory?

Christina Rossetti   *(1830–1894)*

Uphill   1858

Does the road wind uphill all the way?
    Yes, to the very end.
Will the day's journey take the whole long day?
    From morn to night, my friend.

But is there for the night a resting place?   5
    A roof for when the slow dark hours begin.
May not the darkness hide it from my face?
    You cannot miss that inn.

Shall I meet other wayfarers at night?
    Those who have gone before.   10
Then must I knock, or call when just in sight?
    They will not keep you standing at that door.

Shall I find comfort, travel-sore and weak?
    Of labor you shall find the sum.
Will there be beds for me and all who seek?   15
    Yea, beds for all who come.

The Receptive Reader

Who are the two speakers in this poem? What is the meaning of each of the symbolic details in this allegory? What makes this poem earnest and uplifting in the Victorian nineteenth-century manner?

William Blake   *(1757–1827)*

A Poison Tree   1794

I was angry with my friend:
I told my wrath, my wrath did end.
I was angry with my foe:
I told it not, my wrath did grow.

And I watered it in fears,   5
Night and morning with my tears:
And I sunned° it with smiles,   *gave it sunlight*
And with soft deceitful wiles.

And it grew both day and night,
Till it bore an apple bright.   10
And my foe beheld it shine,
And he knew that it was mine.

And into my garden stole
When the night had veiled the pole:
In the morning glad I see   15
My foe outstretched beneath the tree.

The Receptive Reader

1. Much medieval poetry had preached against wrath as one of the seven deadly sins. Is this poem a warning against wrath?

2. What makes this poem simple and almost childlike in its form and its symbolism? Does the simple form undercut the serious question the poem raises?

The Personal Response

Are you aware of any trends in pop psychology that relate to the issue of whether to hold in or release negative emotions?

POEMS FOR FURTHER STUDY

In reading the following poems, pay special attention to objects or figures that may have symbolic significance. How does the poet use or change familiar symbols? What images, emotions, or ideas does the symbol bring into play? What role does a symbol play in the poem as a whole?

Lorna Dee Cervantes   *(born 1954)*

Refugee Ship   *1981*

Like wet cornstarch, I slide
past my grandmother's eyes. Bible
at her side, she removes her glasses.
The pudding thickens.
Mama raised me without language,   5

I'm orphaned from my Spanish name.
The words are foreign, stumbling
on my tongue. I see in the mirror
My reflection: bronzed skin, black hair.

I feel I am a captive   10
aboard the refugee ship.
The ship that will never dock.
El barco que nunca atraca.

The Receptive Reader

1. Do the cornstarch and the Bible in this poem have possible symbolic meanings?

2. How could the speaker in the poem have been raised "without language" and be "orphaned" from her Spanish name?

3. What did the mirror tell her?

4. The last line repeats in Spanish the previous line about the refugee ship "that will never dock." Why are some refugee ships not allowed to dock or their passengers not allowed to reach land? What makes the refugee ship a symbol of the speaker's own journey? What makes it a symbol of the experience of untold millions of refugees in the modern world?

The Creative Dimension

Sometimes a poem is for us like a mirror in which we see our own faces. Look at what one student saw in the mirror of the Cervantes poem. Then write your own response to a poem that seems like a mirror for a part of your self.

> The refugee ship reminds me of the girl I see in the mirror every day. The speaker feels left out of the culture in which she grew up. In the Hispanic culture, there is a certain pressure from the family to retain one's culture. Maybe the poet is a refugee because she forgot all her tradition. Now she sees the Hispanic only in her appearance, not in her head.

Matthew Arnold   *(1822–1888)*

Dover Beach   *1867*

The sea is calm tonight.
The tide is full, the moon lies fair
Upon the straits; on the French coast the light
Gleams and is gone; the cliffs of England stand,
Glimmering and vast, out in the tranquil bay.   5
Come to the window, sweet is the night-air!
Only, from the long line of spray
Where the sea meets the moon-blanched° land,   *pale under the moon*
Listen! you hear the grating roar
Of pebbles which the waves draw back, and fling,   10
At their return, up the high strand,
Begin, and cease, and then again begin,
With tremulous cadence° slow, and bring   *regular rhythm*
The eternal note of sadness in.

Sophocles° long ago   *Greek playwright*   15
Heard it on the Aegean,° and it brought   *sea circling Greece*
Into his mind the turbid° ebb and flow   *murky*
Of human misery; we
Find also in the sound a thought,
Hearing it by this distant northern sea.   20

The Sea of Faith
Was once, too, at the full, and round° earth's shore   *around*
Lay like the folds of a bright girdle° furled.   *sash circling waist*
But now I only hear
Its melancholy, long, withdrawing roar,   25

Retreating, to the breath
Of the night-wind, down the vast edges drear
And naked shingles° of the world.   *pebble-strewn beaches*

Ah, love, let us be true
To one another! for the world, which seems   30
To lie before us like a land of dreams,
So various, so beautiful, so new,
Hath really neither joy, nor love, nor light,
Nor certitude, nor peace, nor help for pain;
And we are here as on a darkling plain   35
Swept with confused alarms of struggle and flight,
Where ignorant armies clash by night.

The Receptive Reader

Matthew Arnold, influential Victorian lecturer and critic, was part of an ide-
alistic generation beset by religious doubts. What is the *central symbol* in this
poem? What gives it its special power or hold on the imagination? How is it followed up or reinforced in the poem? What is the poet's answer to the religious
soul-searching of his time?

John Keats   *(1795–1821)*

Bright Star   *1819*

Bright star, would° I were steadfast as thou art—   *I wish*
    Not in lone splendor hung aloft the night°   *high in night sky*
And watching, with eternal lids apart,
    Like nature's patient, sleepless Eremite,°   *religious hermit*
The moving waters at their priestlike task   5
    Of pure ablution° round earth's human shores,   *cleansing*
Or gazing on the new soft fallen mask
    Of snow upon the mountains and the moors—
No—yet still steadfast, still unchangeable,
    Pillowed upon my fair love's ripening breast,   10
To feel forever its soft fall and swell.
    Awake forever in a sweet unrest,
Still, still to hear her tender-taken breath,
And so live ever—or else swoon to death.

The Receptive Reader

1. Like the other Romantic poets of his generation, Keats intuitively and naturally imbued the physical universe around us with quasi-human life and feeling, at the same time endowing it with divine qualities inspiring religious awe.
How does personification help Keats achieve these ends in this poem? (What is
striking about images like the "eternal lids apart" or ebb and tide attending to
their task of "pure ablution"?)

2. The first eight lines (or octave) of this sonnet develops one set of symbolic associations for the star, and then the next six lines (sestet) *reject* these. Why? What is the basic symbolic meaning of the star in this poem? Why is it strange or unexpected when applied to human love?

Lucille Clifton   *(born 1936)*

my mama moved among the days   1969

My Mama moved among the days
like a dreamwalker in a field;
seemed like what she touched was hers
seemed like what touched her couldn't hold,
she got us almost through the high grass   5
then seemed like she turned around and ran
right back in
right back on in

The Receptive Reader

What is the symbolic meaning of the high grass? Why does the poet repeat the last line? How would you sum up the poet's attitude toward her mother?

WRITING ABOUT LITERATURE

16   Symbols in Context (Focus on Prewriting)

A short poem is like a cricket; it rubs parts of its small body together to produce a sound that is magnified far above that of larger bodies and leaves a loud, chirping sound reverberating in the ears of a listener, saying, "I am small, but I am alive."

STUDENT PAPER

The Writing Workshop   When you write about symbolic meanings, you try to be alert to possible symbolic overtones. Water, for instance, may become the symbol of spiritual regeneration in a wasteland of dried-up feeling, where a poet says: "In the desert of the heart / Let the healing fountain start" (W. H. Auden). Keep an eye on how a symbol works in the poem. Look for reinforcement of possible symbolic meanings in the **context** of the poem as a whole. Green, a color that in one poem may symbolize envy, may in another poem be a symbol of growth, standing for the bright, untamed vitality of nature. Ask yourself:

✗ Does a poem focus on *recurrent* elements with symbolic meanings? In Adrienne Rich's poem, "Aunt Jennifer's Tigers," the proud, unafraid tigers keep prancing and pacing throughout the poem.

✗ Does the poem play off symbolic elements against their *opposites,* the way Rich plays off the untamed tigers against the restraining heavy wedding band symbolizing an oppressive marriage?

✗ Does the poem *build up* to the poet's introduction of a central symbol?

Focus on Prewriting   The following might be part of your prewriting for a paper on Adrienne Rich's "Aunt Jennifer's Tigers."

Reading Notes

Here is a partial record of one student's close attention to key words and phrases:

"Aunt Jennifer's *tigers* prance across a screen"
   Rich uses the tigers to represent Aunt Jennifer's free and true spirit, that part of her which is suppressed by her marriage to Uncle. This symbol is close to Blake's "Tyger," which represents divine energy that animates all creation. In Rich, the tiger represents that same energy within Aunt Jennifer, and ultimately in all women. The tiger is feared but not despised. Its ferocity is tempered because of its feline, catlike grace that makes it seem both beautiful and terrible at the same time.

"Bright *topaz* denizens of a world of green
They pace in sleek *chivalric* certainty."
   The word *topaz* stands for a jewel, implying that the tigers are precious to the aunt. *Denizen* means "native inhabitant." These tigers are in their natural element, just as Aunt Jennifer wishes to be her true self. *Chivalric* seems to imply that like knights in armor the tigers are proud and sure in their role, not afraid of the men in their native teritory.

"The *massive* weight of Uncle's *wedding band*
Sits *heavily* upon Aunt Jennifer's hand."
   The wedding ring, traditionally a symbol of love, honor, and protection is transformed by words like *massive* and *heavily.* We get a mental picture of shackles and chains, not of wedding bells and love tokens.

Clustering   **Clustering** is a way of exploring the associations and connections of key words or concepts. In the more linear kind of free association, you jot ideas down more less in the order in which they come to mind. Clustering instead allows you to branch out from a common core, pursuing different lines of association that soon form a web of meaning. Clustering is more suited to sketch possible *connections* than other kinds of brainstorming and prewriting.

Since many related associations tend to cluster around a central symbol, clustering may prove a good way to map the possible range of associations of a symbol on which you mean to focus in a paper. Here is one student's cluster of the key word *green:*

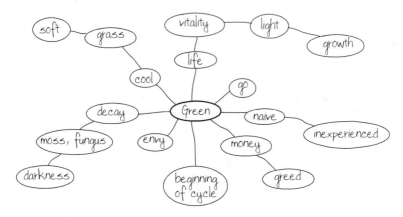

Here is the student writing up the results of the cluster:

The word *green* has many positive associations; in fact, I listed all of my positive ones before the negative ones. Green makes us think of grass, rich in color, soft to the touch. Green vegetation signifies life—a plant thriving with water and sunlight. Plants are green at the beginning of their life cycle. (They fall into the "sear and yellow leaf" at the end—see *Macbeth.*) With this comes vitality. On the possibly negative side, green represents envy, as well as the greed associated with money. Green can be found in moss and fungus, a note of contrast with the green grass. Green, because of its use with unripe early vegetation, also represents inexperience (one who "just fell off the turnip truck"; one who is not street-smart).

Background Notes   The tiger poem is one of the poet's earlier poems (Rich wrote it while she was a student). She wrote about Aunt Jennifer "with deliberate detachment" as a woman of a different generation, keeping a "cool" distance. In hindsight, she realized that she was weaving into this poem a part of herself she did not yet fully understand or recognize—her own role as a woman in a man's world. One student writer found the following illuminating statement by the poet in a collection of her essays:

In writing this poem, composed and apparently cool as it is, I thought I was creating a portrait of an imaginary woman. But this woman suffers from the opposition of her imagination, worked out in tapestry, and her life-style, "ringed with ordeals she was mastered by." It was important to me that Aunt Jennifer was a person as distinct from myself as possible—distanced by the formalism of the poem, by its objective, observant tone—even by putting the woman in a different generation.

On Lies, Secrets, and Silence, p. 40

A paper has a good chance of success when the writer at the beginning of the process of shaping and organizing has this kind of prewriting material at hand—a rich array of notes and tentative ideas to sort out and pull into shape.

Sample Student Paper

Tigers and Terrified Hands

"When Aunt is dead, her terrified hands will lie / Still ringed with ordeals she was mastered by. / The tigers in the panel that she made / Will go on prancing, proud and unafraid." So ends the lush and very focused poem "Aunt Jennifer's Tigers" by Adrienne Rich. With memorable symbolism, the poet illuminates the tragedy of a woman who has lived the greater part of her life as the subordinate member in an unbalanced marriage.

The tiger has been symbolically used many times, and readers may assume that the presence of a tiger represents evil or darkness. In this poem, however, the tigers have an entirely different symbolic meaning. Aunt Jennifer's tigers, those "topaz denizens of a world of green" (2) are the brilliant jewel-like embodiments of the faded shadows hiding in their creator's spirit. Their world of green, bursting with life, vitality, regeneration, receives its life-force from the crushed stirrings in Aunt Jennifer's defeated soul. Any shred of hope or victory or joy that somehow remains within her flows unconsciously through her fluttering fingers into the tapestry she so painfully sews. These wonderful tigers do not sidle or sneak or skulk; they stride "proud and unafraid" (12). With the natural confidence of knighthood, they "pace in sleek chivalric certainty" (4). And, perhaps most importantly, they "do not fear the men beneath the tree" (3). Aunt Jennifer stitches her defiance the only way she can, unconscious of her own vision.

Aunt Jennifer is the perfect foil for her creations, the gorgeous tigers. She is so fraught with anxiety, nervous confusion, exhausted resignation, fear, and defeat, that her fingers, which can only "flutter" through her wool (5), "find even the ivory needle hard to pull" (6). This shade of a woman is still weighed down by the "massive weight of Uncle's wedding band," which has doubtlessly drained her of any capacity for joy, celebration of life, or even peace. She is feeble, afraid, and "mastered." Even in death her "terrified hands will lie / Still ringed with ordeals she was mastered by" (9–10). She cannot escape the "ordeals" that were thrust upon her by her partner in marriage; the dominance and oppression that were her lot in marriage will always be part of who she was.

However, she has left a legacy. She has stitched a panel of glittering tigers that will "go on prancing, proud and unafraid" (l2). Other women will come after Aunt Jennifer, and they may be inspired by her tigers to hold their heads up proudly and assume their rightful places as equals, rejecting any subordinate or humiliating roles. The tigers, often symbols of vitality, power, pride, fearlessness, here are those and more: They are the irrepressible human spirit and symbols of hope for woman's future.

The readers are not told of the particular ordeals in her marriage that defeated Aunt Jennifer. But they can make guesses and poke around for possibilities. The word *mastered* itself, used to describe Aunt Jennifer's situation, implies a "master." It is not a wild or unlikely conjecture that Aunt Jennifer's husband resembled other males who played the role of "master of the house," such as the poet's own father. Rich has said about her father: "After your death I met you again as the face of patriarchy, could name at last precisely the principle you embodied; there was an ideology at last which let me dispose of you, identify the suffering you caused, hate you righteously as part of a system, the kingdom of the fathers." Aunt Jennifer's husband, in the poet's mind, represents the traditional power of the male. And as one who has stated that "the search for justice and compassion is the great wellspring for poetry in our time," Rich is drawing from that wellspring in her poem "Aunt Jennifer's Tigers."

Questions

1. How does the initial quotation bring the two central interacting symbols in the poem into focus? What sentence in the introduction serves as the *thesis* spelling out the aunt's role in her marriage?

2. The body of the paper has a clear *plan;* it is laid out in accordance with a simple design. We look first at the tigers and their symbolic implications: what, according to this paper, do they symbolize? We then look at the symbolic meaning of the wedding ring: for what does it serve as a symbol? We then *return* to the tigers and look at them as the aunt's legacy: how does it point forward to the life of a future generation?

3. The flow of the paper owes much to *transitions* that point up an organic or dynamic rather than mechanical sequence. (The writer does not start major sections by saying. "The first symbol means . . ." and "The second symbol means. . . .") What major links highlight logical connections between key sections of the paper?

4. Major paragraphs of this paper have a rich *texture* of brief quotations interwoven with explanation and interpretation. For instance, how does the writer spell out shades of meanings or overtones and associations when looking at the role of key words like *prance* or *chivalric* in the poem?

5. Having finished the close reading of the poem, the writer addresses a question in the minds of many readers: What is the connection between this poem and the poet's own life? How does the *conclusion* of the paper answer this question?

6. Where do you agree and where do you want to take issue with this writer?

17 Words

The Web of Language

After many years as a writer, I find myself falling in love with words. Maybe this is strange, like a carpenter suddenly discovering how much he likes wood.

J. RUTH GENDLER

FOCUS ON WORDS

Poets are in love with words. Language is their tool, but it is a tool that fascinates and challenges them. You yourself may have gone through a stage in your growing up when you were fascinated by new words, strange words, big words. When reading a poem, be prepared to slow down and respond fully to a single word. Take in its full meaning; savor its overtones and associations. See how an important word echoes or interacts with other words in a poem. As you become more word-conscious, you will note key features of the poet's use of language:

The Right Word   Poets are sticklers for the right word. They may spend hours fine-tuning a poem—trading an almost-right word for a word with the exact shade of meaning. When a poet refers to the "distant glitter / of the January sun," *glitter* is a better word than *blaze* or *glare*. It is colder, more frigid, less blinding, though bright. To be able to make the right choices, poets use more of the full range of language than ordinary talk.

The Range of Connotation   Poets have a keen ear for the emotional quality of words. Language is alive with threat, warning, pleading, rejection, and regret. We call the emotional overtones and attitudes that words carry the **connotations** of a word. We call the stripped-down, bare-facts meaning of a word its **denotation.** The following lines glow with the magic of words that have pleasing connotations—*slender, roses, music, blooms, flares, candle*—the more so since they are played off against the drab "grey streets":

419

When I with you so wholly disappear
into the mirror of your slender hand
grey streets of the city grow roses
and daisies, the music of flowers
blooms in our voices, the eye of
the grocer flares like a candle

> Peter Meinke, "When I with You"

The Register of Tone   Poets have a keen ear for differences in **tone.** When the opening lines of a poem set the tone, they establish the attitude that words suggest toward the subject or toward the reader. Many nineteenth-century poets cultivated a formal, solemn tone. For an elevated effect, they might use **archaic** language—language no longer in common use: *brethren* for brothers, *fain* or *lief* for gladly, and *ere* for before. At the other end of the scale, a poet may echo the folk speech of factory, pool hall, or down-home neighborhood. "We real cool" begins a famous poem by Gwendolyn Brooks.

The Texture of Sound   Poets have a keen ear for the sound of words. When words seem to sound out the sounds they describe, we call them **onomatopoeic,** or sound-mirroring, words. We hear a sound-mirroring effect in the hisssing of snakes, the buzzzing of bees, the rᴜᴍʙʟing of thunder, and the ᴄ-ʀ-ᴀ-ᴄ-ᴋ of a whip. Although sound seldom echoes sense this closely, the right word in a poem is often a word that sounds right. When G. M. Hopkins says that "Generations have ᴛʀᴏᴅ, have ᴛʀᴏᴅ," we seem to hear the heavy, slow, monotonous tread of successive generations. Poems are more than words on a page. Make use of opportunities to read them out loud and to hear them read aloud.

When the author of the following poem records his observations of bathtubs, he chooses the right words to help us share in his feelings and reactions. Some words in the poem carry special freight—like the name of Marat, the fiery French revolutionary who was murdered in his bathtub by the counterrevolutionary Charlotte Corday in 1793.

Jeffrey Harrison   *(born 1957)*

Bathtubs, Three Varieties   *1975*

First the old-fashioned kind, standing on paws,
like a domesticated animal—
I once had a whole flock of these
(seven—for good luck? I never asked
the landlord) under a walnut tree   5
in my backyard, like sheep in shade.

They collected walnuts in the fall
then filled up with snow, like thickening wool.

Modern tubs are more like ancient tombs.
And it is a kind of death we ask for   10
in the bath. Nothing theatrical
like Marat with his arm hanging out—
just that the boundary between the body
and the world dissolve, that we forget
ourselves, and that the tub become   15
the sarcophagus of dreams.

My bathtub in Japan was square, and deep.
You sat cross-legged like a Zen
monk in meditation, up to your neck
in water always a little too hot,   20
relaxed and yet attentive to the moment
(relaxation as a discipline)—
staring through a rising cloud of steam
at the blank wall in front of you.

The Receptive Reader

1. When do you use the word *flock*, when the word *herd?*

2. What is the difference between a *tomb* and a *grave?* Is every performance in a theater by definition *theatrical?* What is the difference between a *sarcophagus* and an ordinary coffin? What is the difference between *meditation* and ordinary thinking?

3. Would you consider it weird to think of "relaxation as a discipline"? Why or why not?

THE WILLING EAR

*I wanted to write poetry in the beginning because
I had fallen in love with words. The first poems I
knew were nursery rhymes, and before I could
read them for myself I had come to love them just
for the words of them, the words alone.*

DYLAN THOMAS

Although poems speak to the heart and the mind, they first of all please the ear. Words have a shape and texture of their own, and they combine in patterns that please (or grate upon) our ears. Children first fall in love with poetry because of its sound. (What is the meaning of "Hickory-dickory-dock / The mouse ran up the clock"?) The following poem makes us see the nighttime setting and share in night thoughts. However, it asks us first of all to relish the words and revel in the way they echo and play off one another in the poem. How should the poem sound when read aloud?

Reuel Denney   *(born 1913)*

Fixer of Midnight   *1961*

He went to fix the awning,
Fix the roping,
In the middle of the night,
On the porch;
He went to fix the awning,   5
In pajamas went to fix it,
Fix the awning,
In the middle of the moonlight,
On the porch;
He went to fix it yawning;   10
The yawning of this awning
In the moonlight
Was his problem of the night;
It was knocking,
And he went to fix its flight.   15
He went to meet the moonlight
In the porch-night
Where the awning was up dreaming
Dark and light.
It was shadowy and seeming;   20
In the night the unfixed awning,
In his nightmare,
Had been knocking dark and bright.
It seemed late
To stop it in its deep careening.   25
The yawner went to meet it,
Meet the awning,
By the moon of middle night,
On his porch;
And he went to fix it right.   30

The sounds in this poem echo and run together without a full stop till the end. We can listen to the sound the way we can listen to the comings and goings of the surf as it washes over rocks by the shore. However, even with this poem, we do not just let the sounds wash over us. We delight in the interplay of sound and meaning. We can imagine the wide open mouth of the sleepy "yawner" as the words y-A-A-W-W-n-i-n-g and A-A-W-W-ning echo through the poem. We can almost hear the "fixer" tiptoeing "in the middle of the night." We seem to hear the repeated KNOCK-KNOCK-KNOCKing of the careening awning echoing through the nightmare of the sleeper by the moon of middle night.

The Receptive Reader

Listen to more than one classmate read this poem aloud. How close do they come to how you think the poem is meant to sound?

Sound seems to dance out the meaning in the following poem inspired by a painting by the sixteenth-century Flemish painter Pieter Breughel. Breughel delighted in painting down-to-earth scenes of rural life, showing the peasants cavorting at weddings or at a country fair (the traditional Kermess). Look for the words that help you hear the sounds of the peasant music. Look for the words that help you see the peasants dance.

William Carlos Williams   *(1883–1963)*

The Dance   *1944*

In Breughel's great picture, The Kermess,
the dancers go round, they go round and
around, the squeal and the blare and the
tweedle of bagpipes, a bugle and fiddles
tipping their bellies (round as the thick-   5
sided glasses whose wash they impound)
their hips and their bellies off balance
to turn them. Kicking and rolling about
The Fair Grounds, swinging their butts, those
shanks must be sound to bear up under such   10
rollicking measures, prance as they dance
in Breughel's great picture, The Kermess.

Many of the words here seem exactly right for what they stand for. Blunt words like *bellies* (thick as the thick-sided glasses) and *butts* and *shanks* seem more right than would squeamish words when applied to the anatomy of these very physical, unpolished merrymakers. *Squeal* and *blare* and *tweedle* make us hear the rustic instruments (it's not the New York Philharmonic!). The word *squeal* seems to sound out the penetrating, high-pitched sound that pigs make when in distress; *tweedle* seems to tootle like a bagpipe that forever runs over the same limited range of sounds. The words for movements seem to roll and rollick just as the peasants do. *Prance* is indeed a prancing word, quite different from *slink* or *shuffle* or *slouch*. (To prance, we need room to high-step and half-lift our arms, proud of ourselves, feeling our oats.)

The Receptive Reader

1. Can you read this poem with the right rolling, rollicking rhythm? Can you read it so that your listeners can hear the underlying drumbeat of the peasant music? (Your class may want to audition several readings of this poem and vote for the best rendition.)

2. How would you describe a *blaring* sound? What is the difference between *violins* and *fiddles,* between *belly* and *abdomen?*

3. Where does the poet show that he is not *limited* to blunt, down-to-earth language? What does the poet mean when he says the revelers "impound" the wash of their thick-sided glasses?

The Personal Response

What kind of readers would love this poem? What kind of readers might get little out of it?

Maya Angelou, who played a prominent role in the civil rights movement and spent several years living in Ghana, has worked as singer, dancer, actor, and director. She delights large audiences as she recites, chants, or acts out poetry.

Maya Angelou   *(born 1928)*

Phenomenal Woman   *1978*

Pretty women wonder where my secret lies.
I'm not cute or built to suit a fashion model's size,
But when I start to tell them,
They think I'm telling lies.
I say,   5
It's in the reach of my arms,
The span of my hips,
The stride of my step,
The curl of my lips.
I'm a woman   10
Phenomenally.
Phenomenal woman,
That's me.

I walk into a room
Just as cool as you please,   15
And to a man,
The fellows stand or
Fall down on their knees.
Then they swarm around me,
A hive of honey bees.   20
I say,
It's the fire in my eyes,

And the flash of my teeth,
The wing in my waist,
And the joy in my feet.   25
I'm a woman
Phenomenally.
Phenomenal woman,
That's me.

Men themselves have wondered   30
What they see in me.
They try so much
But they can't touch
My inner mystery.
When I try to show them   35
They say they still can't see.
I say,
It's in the arch of my back,
The sun of my smile,
The ride of my breasts,   40
The grace of my style.
I'm a woman
Phenomenally.
Phenomenal woman,
That's me.   45

Now you understand
Just why my head's not bowed.
I don't shout or jump about
Or have to talk real loud.
When you see me passing   50
It ought to make you proud.
I say,
It's in the click of my heels,
It's the bend of my hair,
The palm of my hand,   55
The need for my care.
'Cause I'm a woman
Phenomenally.
Phenomenal woman,
That's me.   60
           From *And Still I Rise,* Random House, 1978

The Receptive Reader

1. Angelou throughout uses repetition of words and sentence patterns to create a strongly rhythmic, chanting effect. What are striking examples? How should this poem sound when read aloud?

2. The poem is rich in concrete words that make us visualize features and movements of the human body. What examples can you point out?

3. The word *phenomenal* keeps echoing through the poem. What does the poet mean by it? What other strongly charged words help give the poem its special impact?

4. How would you sum up the self-image of the person speaking in the poem? What stereotypes does the poem make fun of or reject?

The Personal Response

How do you react to people who "come on strong"?

THE RIGHT WORD

I try to make each and every word carry its full
measure and not just its meaning defined.

LUCILLE CLIFTON

Poets wrestle with both the sounds of words and their meanings. A short poem is a message that says much in little; the poet knows how to make every word count. Instead of three words that blur the point, a poet may find the one word that has the right shade of meaning. The following poem, though very short, has long been a favorite of readers:

William Carlos Williams   *(1883–1963)*

The Red Wheelbarrow   1923

so much depends
upon

a red wheel
barrow

glazed with rain   5
water

beside the white
chickens.

How does rainwater look on a surface like that of the wheelbarrow? If we said the water "coated" the surface, the objection might be that often a coat covers up what is underneath. "*Glazed* with rain / water" is right because it means coated with a shiny, transparent cover not hiding what is underneath.

The Creative Dimension

Write your own "So much depends" passage or poem.

Poets have a range of vocabulary that enables them to make the right choices. The following poem stays close to the tangible details that make up firsthand experience. In much of this poem, the poet's language serves as a mirror of "what was there." Many of the words are specific, accurate words that give a faithful accounting of sights and events. (Others bring in striking imaginative comparisons, like the simile that compares the pink swim bladder of the fish to a big peony.)

Elizabeth Bishop   *(1911–1979)*

The Fish   *1946*

I caught a tremendous fish
and held him beside the boat
half out of water, with my hook
fast in a corner of his mouth.
He didn't fight.   5
He hadn't fought at all.
He hung a grunting weight,
battered and venerable
and homely. Here and there
his brown skin hung in strips   10
like ancient wall-paper,
and its pattern of darker brown
was like wall-paper:
shapes like full-blown roses
stained and lost through age.   15
He was speckled with barnacles,
fine rosettes of lime,
and infested
with tiny white sea-lice,
and underneath two or three   20
rags of green weed hung down.
While his gills were breathing in
the terrible oxygen
—the frightening gills,
fresh and crisp with blood,   25
that can cut so badly—
I thought of the coarse white flesh
packed in like feathers,
the big bones and the little bones,
the dramatic reds and blacks   30
of his shiny entrails,
and the pink swim-bladder
like a big peony.
I looked into his eyes
which were far larger than mine   35

but shallower, and yellowed,
the irises backed and packed
with tarnished tinfoil
seen through the lenses
of old scratched isinglass.°   *fish gelatin*   40
They shifted a little, but not
to return my stare.
—It was more like the tipping
of an object toward the light.
I admired his sullen face,   45
the mechanism of his jaw,
and then I saw
that from his lower lip
—if you would call it a lip—
grim, wet, and weapon-like,   50
hung five old pieces of fish-line,
or four and a wire leader
with the swivel still attached,
with all their five big hooks
grown firmly in his mouth.   55
A green line, frayed at the end
where he broke it, two heavier lines,
and a fine black thread
still crimped from the strain and snap
when it broke and he got away.   60
Like medals with their ribbons
frayed and wavering,
a five-haired beard of wisdom
trailing from his aching jaw.
I stared and stared   65
and victory filled up the little rented boat,
from the pool of bilge
where oil had spread a rainbow
around the rusted engine
to the bailer rusted orange,   70
the sun-cracked thwarts,
the oarlocks on their strings,
the gunnels—until everything
was rainbow, rainbow, rainbow!
And I let the fish go.   75

   This poet uses **specific** words—*barnacles, gills*—to call things by
their right names. Many are **concrete** words that bring your senses into
play, calling up for you things you can see, hear, or touch. (Can you
visualize the fish "speckled with barnacles" and "infested / with tiny
white sea-lice"? the brown skin that "hung in strips"? Can you feel its
"grunting weight" as the fish hangs half out of water with a "hook / fast
in a corner of his mouth"?) Without the concrete words and without the

striking similes—the "tarnished tinfoil" of the irises, the "beard of wisdom"—the poet could not make her readers share as completely in the experience she relives here.

The Receptive Reader

1. How familiar are you with the *special language* of boaters and anglers? What are thwarts, oarlocks, gunnels?

2. How and where does the speaker in the poem show her *feelings* about the fish? Which details make the fish seem near-human? Which remind you that it is a fish?

3. What was the *rainbow* that the speaker saw spreading in the bilge at the bottom of the boat?

4. Were you ready for the *ending?* Were you prepared for what happened in the last line of the poem? Why or why not?

JUXTAPOSITIONS

Cityscapes

The following poems were written within ten years of each other. Two English poets here look at the city of London. However, they use language to steer the reader's reactions in very different directions. In reading these poems, explore especially the connotations of words—their emotional impact, overtones, and associations.

William Wordsworth   *(1770–1850)*

Composed upon Westminster Bridge, September 3, 1802   *1802*

Earth has not anything to show more fair:°   *more beautiful*
Dull would he be of soul who could pass by
A sight so touching in its majesty;
This City now doth, like a garment, wear
The beauty of the morning; silent, bare,   5
Ships, towers, domes, theaters, and temples lie
Open unto the fields, and to the sky;
All bright and glittering in the smokeless air.
Never did sun more beautifully steep
In his first splendor, valley, rock, or hill;   10
Never saw I, never felt, a calm so deep!
The river glideth at his own sweet will:
Dear God! the very houses seem asleep;
And all that mighty heart is lying still!

The Receptive Reader

Explore the associations and overtones of the many connotative words in this poem. What would be missing from the poem if the poet had said, "Dull would he be of brain" rather than "of soul"? What if he had said, "doth, like a coat, wear" instead of "like a garment" wear? What makes the words *domes* and *temples* different from the word *churches?* What if the poet had said "With his first rays" rather than "In his first splendor"? What would be different if the poet had said at the end "that mighty nerve center" rather than "that mighty heart"?

William Blake   *(1757–1827)*

London   *1794*

I wander through each chartered° street,   legally set up
Near where the chartered Thames does flow,
And mark in every face I meet
Marks of weakness, marks of woe.
In every cry of every man,   5
In every Infant's cry of fear,
In every voice, in every ban,°   announcement
The mind-forged manacles I hear.

How the chimney-sweeper's cry
Every blackening church appalls;   10
And the hapless soldier's sigh
Runs in blood down Palace walls.

But most through midnight streets I hear
How the youthful Harlot's curse
Blasts the new-born Infant's tear,   15
And blights with plagues the Marriage hearse.

The Receptive Reader

1. What words most directly describe the speaker's *emotions* when contemplating a city with maimed or penniless veterans, young prostitutes, and soot-covered churches? What would be different if the poet had used "mind-made bonds" rather than "mind-forged manacles"? What would be missing in the last line if he had said "damages" rather than "blights"?

2. What gives *metaphors* like "Runs in blood down Palace walls" and the "Marriage hearse" their special force?

3. How would you pinpoint the difference in perspective between this and Wordsworth's poem?

The Personal Response

If you were to write out your feelings about one of today's cities, would your point of view be closer to Wordsworth's or to Blake's?

THE LIMITS OF LANGUAGE

Everything which opens out to us a new world is
bound to appear strange at first.

EDITH SITWELL

Poets vary greatly in how far they will stretch the limits of language. Difficult but rewarding poets use language in original or intensely personal ways. First of all, the poet's vocabulary may include exotic gleanings brought back from excursions into ancient history, legend, or fabled places. The following poem delights readers who cherish words that, like rare coins, seldom see the light of common day:

John Masefield   *(1878–1967)*

Cargoes   *1902*

Quinquereme of Nineveh from distant Ophir,
Rowing home to haven in sunny Palestine,
With a cargo of ivory,
And apes and peacocks,
Sandalwood, cedarwood, and sweet white wine.   5

Stately Spanish galleon coming from the Isthmus,
Dipping through the Tropics by the palm-green shores,
With a cargo of diamonds,
Emeralds, amethysts,
Topazes, and cinnamon, and gold moidores.   10

Dirty British coaster with a salt-caked smoke-stack,
Butting through the Channel in the mad March days,
With a cargo of Tyne coal,
Road-rails, pig-lead,
Firewood, iron-ware, and cheap tin trays.   15

What is a quinquereme? The context of the poem tells us that it is an ancient ship being rowed to its home harbor, carrying rich, exotic cargo. (Some readers may remember the trireme; of ancient Rome, with three banks of galley slaves plying *three* levels of oars. The legendary ship in this poem then would have *five* levels of oars.) Nineveh is clearly a city in ancient Palestine, wealthy enough to outfit magnificent trading ships. (It is mentioned in the Bible as a great city.) Ophir sounds like a legendary faraway city of great wealth. (Poets mention it: "More than all of Ophir's gold / does the fleeting second hold.")

The second of the three ships in this poem—the elaborately ornamented Spanish galleon carrying rich loot from tropical Central America back to the Old World—takes us closer to what we know about history and geography. The "Isthmus" should be the isthmus of Panama—a thin strip of land that kept ships from reaching the Pacific from the Caribbean until the Panama Canal was built. We may not own emeralds, amethysts, and topazes, but we can at least revel in the marvelous exotic names of these priceless gems. If *quinquereme* has not sent us to the dictionary, *moidores* will. (The conquistadores melted down the golden artifacts of Aztecs and Incas to make gold coins—"money of gold" minted in Portugal and Brazil.)

By the third stanza, finally, we are within range of a more everyday vocabulary: the coal is from Newcastle-upon-Tyne. ("Carrying coals to Newcastle" was for a long time the equivalent of shipping hogs to Missouri.)

The Receptive Reader

1. One student reader called this poem a "three-sided prism," with each stanza reflecting a different view of the cargo ships that since time immemorial have plied the seas. How would you label the three different cargoes?

2. Which words in this poem are rich in *connotation*—in overtones or personal association—for you? For instance, what ideas or feelings do words like *Palestine, ivory, peacock, galleon,* or *emerald* bring to mind?

The Range of Interpretation

Where do you stand on the issue raised in the following excerpt from a student paper about this poem? What in the poem helps you make up your mind one way or the other?

The last stanza is particularly intriguing in its contrast with the other two. The "dirty British coaster" brings us forward in time to the grimy industrial age. The sooty words and leaden cargo describe a harshly realistic working vessel, whereas the other two ships were romanticized, idealized, and seen through a nostalgic haze. We could easily argue that the harshness of the final stanza gives us a negative view of the modern world. We get a glimpse here of the sordid materialism of our age.

However, we might easily argue the opposite as well. If the poet had cast the same realistic eye on the past as he did on the present, he might have picked slave ships or cattle boats, quite common in the ancient days, or he might have shown us the chained galley slaves rowing the splendid ancient ship. The dirty British coaster then would not come off so badly after all. In any case, Masefield suggests strength and power and working muscle in his description of the coaster "butting" stubbornly through the English Channel in ugly weather. This ship carries no glittering booty from "palm-green shores." It is a workaday mule of the seas. Its cargo represents the everyday needs served by the economy of an industrial nation. We should not look down on it but accept it as part of living everyday reality.

Some of the poets most admired by modern readers test the boundaries of language. The wording in a poem may be compressed, with much meaning packed into a compact phrase. For instance, in the following poem, the phrase "Fresh firecoal chestnut-falls" asks us to visualize chestnuts that have freshly fallen from the tree. They have split open their thick green covering on hitting the ground, revealing the intense reddish-brown of their skins. These seem to glow like coals on fire. This poem is about "all the lovely dappled, alternating, changing and shifting things in the world" that come from God (J. R. Watson). The poem is by a nineteenth-century Catholic priest whose intense and difficult poetry remained unpublished in his lifetime, but who delighted twentieth-century readers with his bold, unconventional use of language.

Gerard Manley Hopkins   *(1844–1889)*

Pied Beauty   *1877*

Glory be to God for dappled things—
    For skies of couple-color as a brinded° cow;   *streaked, flecked*
        For rose-moles all in stipple upon trout that swim;
Fresh firecoal chestnut-falls; finches' wings;
    Landscape plotted and pieced—fold,° fallow, and plow;   *pasture* 5
        And áll trádes, their gear and tackle and trim.
All things counter, original, spare, strange;
    Whatever is fickle, freckled (who knows how?)
        With swift, slow; sweet, sour; adazzle, dim;
He fathers-forth whose beauty is past change: 10
        Praise him.

The poet draws on a range of words for the "pied beauty" that he loves—and that he prefers to whatever is too smooth, too much of one piece. The word *pied* itself means showing two or more colors in blotches or splotches, like the hide of a horse. Then we have *dappled, stipple, plotted* (for land laid out in small strips and plots that alternates pasture, land lying fallow, and land under the plow). We have *pieced* (together), *freckled.* Everything here goes counter to boring smoothness and simplicity.

The Receptive Reader

1. What in the *wording* of this poem is most difficult for you? What are skies of "couple-color"? What do you make of the compressed phrase "fathers-forth"?

2. How would the gear and tackle of different trades meet Hopkins's criteria of beauty? Can you give examples of what he might have had in mind? What, for you, would be examples of things "counter, original, spare, strange"?

3. Is it strange that an unchanging God would create beauty that is variable and made up of contradictory elements?

4. How does the language of this poem live up to the poet's own standard of what is beautiful?

The Personal Response

The poet Richard Wilbur calls this poem a "celebration of the rich and quirky particularity of all things whatever." Can you relate to this taste for the "quirky" and irregular, or do you prefer beauty that is smooth and harmonious?

In the following poem, the English Romantic poet John Keats moves beyond everyday language to create a rich overlay of associations taking us beyond the ordinary. He compares his awe and excitement at discovering Chapman's sixteenth-century translation of Homer's *Iliad* to the excitement the Spanish conquerors of Mexico must have felt when they first saw the Pacific Ocean from Darien in Panama. Which words are unfamiliar or difficult for you? Which would you have to check in a dictionary?

John Keats   *(1795–1821)*

On First Looking into Chapman's Homer   *1816*

Much have I traveled in the realms of gold,
    And many goodly states and kingdoms seen;
    Round many western islands have I been
Which bards in fealty to Apollo hold.
Oft of one wide expanse had I been told   5
    That deep-browed Homer ruled as his demesne;
    Yet did I never breathe its pure serene
Till I heard Chapman speak out loud and bold:
Then felt I like some watcher of the skies
    When a new planet swims into his ken;   10
Or like stout Cortez when with eagle eyes
    He stared at the Pacific—and all his men
Looked at each other with a wild surmise—
    Silent, upon a peak in Darien.

The Receptive Reader

1. Each of the following is a simpler or more familiar word for a richer, *more connotative* word used by the poet. Parentheses enclose the overtones or associations added by the word Keats actually chose in the poem. Which word in the poem matches each of the following? (ancient, venerable) kingdom; (ancient, honored) poets; loyalty (to a feudal medieval overlord); (brilliant, divine) patron of poetry; (a lord's) lands; expanse (of calm, pure sky or sea); (sharply perceived) field of vision

2. What features make you recognize this poem as a *sonnet?* Where is its turning point? Can you argue that the poem follows a cumulative or climactic order?

Dylan Thomas, a Welsh poet, often seems impatient with plodding ordinary language, leaping ahead instead to make new connections. One reader said of him that he "strips from words their old, dull, used sleepiness, and gives them a refreshed and awakened meaning." Read the following poem the first time without puzzling over difficult phrases. Allow yourself to be carried along by the chanting rhythm. Then go back over the poem, looking at his plays on words and his strange tele-scopings or juxtapositions. Fern Hill is the name of a farm that Thomas's uncle and aunt rented as tenant farmers.

Dylan Thomas   *(1914–1953)*

Fern Hill   *1946*

Now as I was young and easy under the apple boughs
About the lilting house and happy as the grass was green,
    The night above the dingle° starry,   *wooded valley*
        Time let me hail and climb
      Golden in the heydays of his eyes,   5
And honored among wagons I was prince of the apple towns
And once below a time I lordly had the trees and leaves
        Trail with daisies and barley
    Down the rivers of the windfall light.

And as I was green and carefree, famous among the barns   10
About the happy yard and singing as the farm was home,
      In the sun that is young once only,
        Time let me play and be
      Golden in the mercy of his means,
And green and golden I was huntsman and herdsman, the calves   15
Sang to my horn, the foxes on the hills barked clear and cold,
        And the sabbath rang slowly
    In the pebbles of the holy streams.

All the sun long it was running, it was lovely, the hay
Fields high as the house, the tunes from the chimneys, it was air 20
      And playing, lovely and watery
        And fire green as grass.
      And nightly under the simple stars
As I rode to sleep the owls were bearing the farm away,
All the moon long I heard, blessed among stables, the night-jars°   *night birds* 25
      Flying with the ricks,° and the horses   *haystacks*
        Flashing into the dark.

And then to awake, and the farm, like a wanderer white
With the dew, come back, the cock on his shoulder: it was all
      Shining, it was Adam and maiden,   30
        The sky gathered again
      And the sun grew round that very day.
So it must have been after the birth of the simple light
In the first, spinning place, the spellbound horses walking warm
      Out of the whinnying green stable   35
        On to the fields of praise.

And honored among foxes and pheasants by the gay house
Under the new made clouds and happy as the heart was long,
    In the sun born over and over,
        I ran my heedless ways,   40
    My wishes raced through the house high hay
And nothing I cared, at my sky blue trades, that time allows
In all his tuneful turning so few and such morning songs
    Before the children green and golden
        Follow him out of grace,   45

Nothing I cared, in the lamb white days, that time would take me
Up to the swallow thronged loft by the shadow of my hand,
    In the moon that is always rising,
        Nor that riding to sleep
    I should hear him fly with the high fields   50
And wake to the farm forever fled from the childless land.
Oh as I was young and easy in the mercy of his means,
        Time held me green and dying
    Though I sang in my chains like the sea.

The Receptive Reader

1. Try to puzzle out telescoped phrases or strange juxtapositions in the early stanzas. For instance, what could have been "lilting" about the house? How did the child "hail and climb golden" in the heydays of Time? How was he "prince of the apple towns"? What is the connection between light and "rivers" and a "windfall"? Why in this poem is the sun "young once only"?

2. What is the *symbolic* meaning of the colors "green and golden," whose names echo through this poem?

3. What are key *images* and prevailing feelings in the poet's account of the first days after Creation? What is borrowed from and what is different from the account in Genesis?

4. What are the "chains" at the conclusion of the poem? Assuming the words are not meant literally, in what sense did Time hold the child "green and dying"?

Making Connections—For Discussion or Writing

Gerard Manley Hopkins's "Pied Beauty," William Wordsworth's "Composed upon Westminster Bridge," and Dylan Thomas's "Fern Hill" each project a vision of what is beautiful in the world in which we live. What is different or unique in each poet's vision? Is there a common thread?

POEMS FOR FURTHER STUDY

In the following poems pay special attention to the poet's word choice, or diction.

Margaret Atwood   *(born 1939)*

Dreams of the Animals   *1970*

Mostly the animals dream
of other animals   each
according to its kind

       (though certain mice and small rodents
       have nightmares of a huge pink   5
       shape with five claws descending)

: moles dream of darkness and delicate
mole smells

frogs dream of green and golden
frogs   10
sparkling like wet suns
among the lilies

red and black
striped fish, their eyes open
have red and black striped   15
dreams   defense, attack, meaningful
patterns
birds dream of territories
enclosed by singing.

Sometimes the animals dream of evil   20
in the form of soap and metal
but mostly the animals dream
of other animals.

There are exceptions:

       the silver fox in the roadside zoo   25
       dreams of digging out
       and of baby foxes, their necks bitten

       the caged armadillo
       near the train
       station, which runs   30
       all day in figure eights
       its piglet feet pattering,
       no longer dreams
       but is insane when waking;

       the iguana   35
       in the petshop window on St. Catherine Street
       crested, royal-eyed, ruling
       its kingdom of water-dish and sawdust

       dreams of sawdust

The Receptive Reader

1. What are the usual associations of the animals in this poem? How does the poem transform these associations or leave them behind? Look at the words that cluster around the names of the animals here. Which of the words have positive connotations, showing the poet's empathy or fellow-feeling? (Which of these words are especially *unusual* or unexpected?)

2. In this poem, what is the difference between the animals in the wild and those in captivity? What words especially drive home the contrast between the animals in the wild and their caged cousins?

The Personal Response

Disney cartoons have often made animals seem cute, harmless, and lovable. Disney wildlife films, however, have often taken an uncompromisingly honest look at life in the wild. Does Atwood make animals seem too lovable and human?

Gerard Manley Hopkins   *(1844–1889)*

The Windhover   *1877*
To Christ Our Lord

I caught this morning morning's minion,° king-	*beloved*
dom of daylight's dauphin,° dapple-dawn-drawn	*crown prince*
Falcon, in his riding	
Of the rolling level underneath him steady air, and striding	
High there, how he rung upon the rein of a wimpling° wing	*rippling* 5
In his ecstasy! then off, off forth on swing,	
As a skate's heel sweeps smooth on a bow-bend: the hurl	
and gliding	
Rebuffed the big wind. My heart in hiding	
Stirred for a bird,—the achieve of, the mastery of the thing!	10
Brute beauty and valor and act, oh, air, pride, plume here	
Buckle! AND the fire that breaks from thee then, a billion	
Times told lovelier, more dangerous, O my chevalier!°	*knight*
No wonder of it: shéer plód makes plow down sillion°	*furrow*
Shine, and black-blue embers, ah my dear,	15
Fall, gall themselves, and gash gold-vermilion.	

The Receptive Reader

1. Several of the words Hopkins applies to the falcon and to Christ suggest the glamor and pageantry of chivalry: a *minion* is a cherished, beloved court favorite; the *Dauphin* was the crown prince of medieval France; a *chevalier* is a knight who represents the chivalric virtues (*chevalier* and *chivalry* come from the same root). Where in the poem does Hopkins spell out the *connotations* that these words suggest?

2. When the poet celebrates the masterful, ecstatic flight of the falcon, what do *concrete* words like *riding, striding, sweep, hurl,* and *gliding* add to the meaning of the generic term *fly?* (What does each make you visualize? What associations or feelings does each carry with it?) What makes *rebuff* different from *resist?*

3. In the pivotal word *buckle,* the inspiring qualities of the falcon "come together" or are welded together (as the two ends of a belt are buckled or fastened). The two parts of the poem also meet: the splendor of God's creation and the billionfold "lovelier, more dangerous" splendor of "Our Lord." How do the two concluding images in the last three lines of the poem mirror the relationship between the "brute" creature and its creator?

4. In addition to the end rhyme that is traditional in a sonnet like this one, Hopkins uses **alliteration**—the repetition of the same sound at the beginning of several words in the same line ("this MORNing MORNing's MINion"). The telescoped phrase "dapple-dawn-drawn" allows the poet to complete the alliteration started by "DAYlight's DAUPHin." How would you spell out the meaning of the telescoped phrase in more ordinary language?

The Range of Interpretation

According to a recent introduction to Hopkins's poetry, some critics "have seen the poem as one of frustration and sadness." The poem is "concerned with the unbridgeable distance between the hawk, flying so freely and beautifully, and the poet, whose heart is 'in hiding'; the heart is hidden away as if afraid, locked up by the severe discipline of the priesthood and the demands of self-sacrifice which it makes." To other readers, the poem "does not seem to be a poem of frustration so much as a poem of enthusiasm and exultation. . . . The excitement is conveyed in the way in which the heart, while it may have been 'in hiding,' that is inactive, now 'Stirred for a bird'; as if the heart moved and leaped at the sight of the hawk" (J. R. Watson, *The Poetry of Gerard Manley Hopkins*). Which of these two interpretations would you be inclined to support? (What do *you* make of the phrase "my heart in hiding"?)

John Heaviside

A Gathering of Deafs   *1989*

By the turnstiles
in the station
where the L train greets
the downtown six there was
a congregation of deafs   5
passing forth
a jive wild
and purely physical
in a world dislocated
from the subway howling   10
hard sole shoe stampede
punk rock blasted radio

screaming, pounding, honking
they gather in community
lively and serene, engaging   15
in a dexterous conversation

An old woman
of her dead husband tells
caressing the air
with wrinkled fingers that demonstrate the story with   20
delicate, mellifluous motion
she placcs gentle configurations before the faces of the group

A young Puerto Rican
describes a fight with his mother emphasizing each word
with abrupt, staccato movements jerking his elbows   25
and twisting his wrists
teeth clenched and lips pressed
he concluded the story
by pounding his fist
into his palm   30

By the newsstand
two lovers express emotion
caressing the air
with syllables
graceful and slow   35
joining their thoughts
by the flow of fingertips

The Receptive Reader

1. In this student-written poem, what is right about words like *congregation, jive, community, dexterous, configuration?* How effective or expressive are the words setting up the contrast between the punk rock and the silent conversation of the deaf?

2. What is the difference between *mellifluous* and *staccato?* What words clustering around each of these help a reader unfamiliar with them?

3. What statement is the student poet making about the sign language of the deaf?

WRITING ABOUT LITERATURE

17   Responding to Connotations (Interpreting the Evidence)

The Writing Workshop   When studying a poem rich in connotative language, you will be paying special attention to emotional overtones and implied attitudes. How do emotionally charged words steer the reactions of the reader?

✖ *You may want to start by defining your key term.*   You may want to get the subject of connotative language clearly into focus, using brief striking illustrations.

✖ *Show that you have read carefully for implications.*   Show that you have gone through the poem line by line, paying special attention to key words or to recurrent words that echo in the poem.

✖ *Do not take words out of context.*   Is a word part of a network of similar or related terms? Are its associations or implications reinforced by what goes with it in the poem? Or are unusual associations negated or overruled by other words that strongly affect the tone or emotional quality of the poem?

✖ *Work out a clear overall plan.*   For instance, you may want to follow the overall pattern of the poem. (Is there perhaps an initial set of words with very similar connotations but then a turning, with the poem moving in a different or opposed direction?) Or you may sort out different kinds of connotative language or different effects of connotative language on the reader.

Study the model student paper examining connotative language in a poem. How carefully has the writer read the poem? What use does she make of evidence from the poem? Are any of the connotations she traces private or personal rather than widely shared associations? How convincing are her conclusions?

Sample Student Paper

Connotative Language: Harrison's Three Bathtubs

Dictionary meanings are usually denotative meanings; they give us exact, objective, limited definitions. When words take us beyond objective labeling to expand our associations, when they carry an overlay of emotional association, they have connotative meaning. For example, the word *house* denotes a structure with walls, floors, ceilings, and doors, and including bedrooms and a kitchen; *house* does not have the emotional overlay that the word *home* suggests. *Home* may recall the warmth of a featherbed in winter or the smell of newly mown grass in summer. It suggests a place that provides security and protection, an anchor in an uncertain world.

Connotative meanings may be personal and private. Abigail may be a beautiful name to many, but if we have known an Abigail who was cross and domineering, the word will have unpleasant associations for us. To work for the poet, a word must usually have more broadly shared layers of meaning. When Romeo calls Juliet's balcony the east and Juliet the sun, we know he is suggesting that, like the rising sun, Juliet is new, fresh, bright, warm, and central in his life.

In Jeffrey Harrison's "Bathtubs, Three Varieties," the poet relies on both the denotative and connotative meanings of words. In three stanzas, he describes three kinds of bathtubs: "an old-fashioned kind," "modern tubs," and his "bathtub in Japan." He does not flatly state his preference for one kind of bathtub over another, but if we focus on his word choices and the connotations of certain words, we may conclude that he does indeed have a preference.

In the first stanza, the speaker in the poem surprises us with not one but seven old-fashioned tubs under a walnut tree in his backyard. Parenthetically, he adds that he has not asked his landlord why they are there, but he associates seven with "good luck." Interior decorators call old-fashioned tubs claw-footed or lion-footed, but the speaker chooses to see this kind of tub as standing on "paws, / like a domesticated animal." Unlike lions' claws, paws are non-threatening and connote the softness of a cat's paws. Another reference to a domesticated animal, tame and trusting, reinforces this kind of feeling: Seven of these tubs make a "whole flock" of "sheep in shade"; the connotation here is of a gathering of domesticated animals in a pleasant, pastoral scene. When cold weather comes, the tubs fill with snow—normally cold and forbidding, but here compared to the thickening wool of the sheep; thus the snow sounds paradoxically warm and protecting. Earlier, the tubs were collecting walnuts, reminding us of the rich bounty of harvest time.

The second stanza, on modern tubs, presents a startling contrast. Here we have tubs "like ancient tombs," a bath that is a "kind of death," and a tub that becomes a "sarcophagus," or massive stone coffin. Our tub death is not even "theatrical," like the dramatic death in the French painter David's portrait of Marat, the French revolutionary hero stabbed in his bath.

In the third stanza, we find ourselves in a Japanese tub described as "square"— without the welcoming comfort of a circular or oval shape. We do not stretch out in this tub but sit "cross-legged like a Zen monk in meditation." We sit up to our necks in deep water "always a little too hot." We hear an echo here of the expressions "up to our necks in something" and "being in hot water," both of which have negative implications. This is a strange mixture of relaxation with "discipline," as we find ourselves staring "at the blank wall." This tub sounds uninviting for any but those stoic people who like a strenuous life.

For me, at least, the tubs in the first stanza suggest memories of peaceful contentment. There is something bleak and forbidding about the modern tomblike tub. And it would probably take special training in Zen to maintain the half-relaxed, half-disciplined attitude proper to the over-hot, steamy Japanese variety.

Questions

Do you agree with this student's reading of the poem? Why or why not? Did she overlook any significant details? Does she bring in personal associations that you would question? What parts of the paper are for you especially instructive or convincing?

18 Form

Rhyme, Meter, and Stanza

Let chaos storm!
Let cloud shapes swarm!
I wait for form.
ROBERT FROST, "PERTINAX"

FOCUS ON FORM

Poetry today moves between the poles of traditional form and the open form that became second nature to many modern poets. Traditional form is shaped by rhyme, meter, and stanza. Poets long wrote strongly metrical lines of verse, regularizing the natural rhythms of language: "With HOW / sad STEPS, / O MOON, / thou CLIMB'ST / the SKIES" (Sir Philip Sidney). Often such lines were linked by rhyme: SKIES/TRIES. Poems were often arranged in stanzas, or sets of lines, of similar shape. To read with an alert eye and attentive ear, you need to respond to features like the following:

Rhyme Poets exploit our delight in the echo effects of language. In the following poem, Ogden Nash, the heavyweight of light verse, uses traditional **end rhyme:** BLIND/KIND. He adds some internal rhyme (rhyme words in the *same* line) for good measure: PLUCK and LUCK. Traditionally, rhyme helps mark off lines. However, it also has a bonding effect by linking two or more lines in a poem.

Ogden Nash   *(1902–1971)*

The Hunter   1949

The hunter crouches in his BLIND
'Neath camouflage of every KIND,
And conjures up a quacking NOISE
To lend allure to his decoys.
This grown-up man, with PLUCK and LUCK,   5
Is hoping to outwit a DUCK.

Rhythm and Meter   Poets build on the natural rhythms of language. Some syllables are stressed or accentuated in ordinary speech: dePART, ACcident, interroGATION. By laying words and phrases with the same stress pattern end to end, poets set up the drumbeat of **meter.** Meter is exceptionally regular in the following opening lines of a Shakespeare sonnet:

> That tíme | of yéar | thou máyst | in mé | behóld
> When yél|low léaves, | or nóne, | or féw, | do háng
> Upón | those bóughs | which sháke | agáinst | the cóld.

Remember that meter provides the *underlying* beat, over which the actual lines may play variations.

Stanza Form   Poets appeal to our delight in recurrent patterns. Poets have often broken up a poem into **stanzas**—sets of lines following a similar pattern. Sometimes, each stanza repeats the same rhyme scheme, with perhaps the same alternation of shorter and longer lines. Can you show how the second stanza repeats the rhyme scheme in the following song lyrics?

American Folk Song   *Anonymous*

Black Is the Color   *traditional*

Black, black, black is the color of my true love's hair.
His lips are something wond'rous fair,
The purest eyes and the fairest hands,
I love the ground whereon he stands.
Black, black, black is the color of my true love's hair.   5

I love my love and well he knows
I love the ground whereon he goes.
And if my love no more I see,
My life would quickly fade away.
Black, black, black is the color of my true love's hair.   10

The Receptive Reader

1. What is haunting or appealing about the opening line that comes back twice as the refrain in this poem? What other line is repeated in slightly different form? (Why isn't this other line repeated exactly?)

2. There is much repetition in this poem. Does the poem nevertheless move on or go forward? From what to what?

3. In our culture, do you expect love lyrics to be written and sung by the male rather than the female lover? Does this folk song seem different in this respect? Why or why not?

Traditional and Open Form   **Open form** modifies or abandons traditional formal features, letting the poet give each poem its own unique pattern and rhythm. For a time, champions of modernism did battle with defenders of tradition, who scorned poets playing "tennis with the net down" (Robert Frost). The objection to traditional form has often been that it may become a straitjacket. A poet might feel hemmed in by the requirements of traditional meter and rhyme. Today, many poets use open form, whereas others make at least some use of traditional formal features. Some use either traditional or open form—on different occasions and for different purposes.

RHYME, ALLITERATION, FREE VERSE

Like meter, rhyme is a highly formal device. It is a
signal that language is going to be used in an
unusual, often a serious and memorable, way. . . .
Because it is out of the ordinary, rhyme attracts
our attention and prepares us for a completely
organized and unusually expressive language.

KARL SHAPIRO

Why rhyme? **Rhyme** bonds two or more lines by final syllables that start out differently but end alike. Children delight in the echo effects of rhyme: "Celery, RAW, / Develops the JAW, / But celery, STEWED, / Is more quietly CHEWED"—Ogden Nash. Beyond this simple pleasure, as elementary as the pleasure of hopping and skipping, rhyme serves as the most visible sign that the poem has a shape, a pattern. It is more patterned, more ordered, than ordinary disjointed experience.

Rhyme helps the poet measure off lengths of verse; it sets up recurrent points of rest. It thus helps set up a basic rhythm, like the rhythm of purposeful walking. At the same time, rhyme has a bonding effect, giving a sense of continuity, of meaningful forward movement. This effect of pulling things together or keeping them headed in the same direction is especially strong with **multiple** rhymes—more than two lines rhyming—as in the following opening lines of a Bob Dylan song:

Darkness at the break of noon	a
Shadows even the silver spoon	a
The hand made blade, the child's balloon	a
Eclipses both the sun and moon	a
To understand you know too soon,	a
There is no sense in trying.	b

Bob Dylan, "It's Alright Ma
(I'm Only Bleeding)"

In the eighteenth century, when the tidy packaging of ideas was the fashion, rhyme helped seal off sets of two lines in self-contained **closed couplets.**

> Good nature and good sense must ever join;
> To err is human; to forgive, divine.
>
>   Alexander Pope, "Essay on Criticism"

With later poets, we see fewer boxed-in lines where rhyme signals "end of a sentence, end of a line." Instead, we see spillovers where the unfinished sense pulls us over into the next line. Then the sentence may end halfway through the next line, causing a strong break *within* rather than between lines and setting up a counter-rhythm. Critics call the spillover from one line to the next **enjambment.** They call the strong break *within* a line a **caesura** (a "cut" that divides the line). In the following lines by the English Romantic poet Percy Bysshe Shelley, notice the spillover at the end of the second and third lines and the strong break in the third:

> We are as clouds that veil the midnight moon;
> How restlessly they speed, and gleam, and quiver, →
> Streaking the darkness radiantly! | | Yet soon →
> Night closes round, and they are lost forever.
>
>   "Mutability"

Like songbirds, rhymes are easier to listen to and enjoy than to classify. Rhyme watchers note variations from the simple **end rhymes** marking off lines of verse, in the *love/dove, moon/spoon* pattern:

✗ **Internal rhymes** multiply the echo effect of rhyme *within* a line:

> All is SEARED with trade; BLEARED, SMEARED with toil.
>
>   Gerard Manley Hopkins, "God's Grandeur"

✗ Most common are **single** (or **masculine**) rhymes—single-syllable rhymes. Only the beginning of the syllable varies, while the rest stays the same: *high/sky, leave/grieve, stone/own.* **Double (feminine)** rhymes match two-syllable words (or parts of words), with the first syllable stressed and the second unstressed: *ocean/motion, started/parted, (re)peated/ (de)feated.* More unusual are **triple** ryhmes—three-syllable rhymes, with stress on the first of the three *(beautiful/dutiful).*

✗ Some double rhymes are actually only **half-rhymes.** For instance, the vowel sounds in the first syllables of *merit* and *bear it* or *merit* and *spirit* are only similar, not alike. For poets who found traditional rhyme too predictable, such **slant rhymes** were a step toward a greater range of choice. In the following poem, which rhymes are slant rhymes?

Emily Dickinson   *(1830–1886)*

The Soul selects her own Society   *about 1862*

The Soul selects her own Society—
Then—shuts the Door—
To her divine Majority—
Present no more—

Unmoved—she notes the Chariots—pausing   5
At her low Gate—
Unmoved—an Emperor be kneeling
Upon her Mat—

I've known her—from an ample nation—
Choose One—   10
Then—close the Valves of her attention—
Like Stone—

The Receptive Reader

1. Which are conventional *full* rhymes? Which are slant rhymes?
2. A literal *paraphrase* of this poem might run like this:

> The human soul chooses friends or soulmates carefully and then shuts out any others, allowing no one else to join in. It will not be moved by others humbly asking to be admitted. I have known her to select only one from a large group and then pay absolutely no attention to anyone else.

How do the metaphors in the poem go beyond this bare-bones paraphrase? What do they make you see? What do they make you feel? What do they make you think?

✗ When only the internal vowel sounds of final syllables are similar or alike, the result is **assonance,** again a more distant echo than full rhyme. Assonance is a partial sound echo, as in *break/fade* or *mice/fight*.

✗ **Alliteration** is an echo effect that was once a key feature of poetry and that is still active in popular speech: "<u>s</u>afe and <u>s</u>ound," "<u>sp</u>ick and <u>sp</u>an," "<u>k</u>it and <u>c</u>aboodle." Alliteration was the precursor and the opposite of end rhyme. Traditionally, three or more stressed syllables in a line *started* with the same sound: "A <u>w</u>onder on the <u>w</u>ave—<u>w</u>ater turned bone" (from a riddle whose answer is "ice"). The words that alliterated started either with the same consonant or else with any vowel. The earliest poems in English used an alliterating four-beat line that sounded like this:

Leave <u>s</u>ORROW a<u>s</u>IDE / for it <u>s</u>EEMS more <u>w</u>ISE
To <u>f</u>IGHT for a <u>f</u>RIEND / than to <u>f</u>RET and <u>m</u>OURN.
We <u>a</u>LL in the <u>e</u>ND / go <u>o</u>UT of this <u>w</u>ORLD.

Let us ᴅᴏ great ᴅᴇᴇᴅꜱ / before ᴅᴇᴀᴛʜ ᴛᴀᴋᴇꜱ us.
That is ʙᴇꜱᴛ for the ʙʀᴀᴠᴇ / who are ʙᴏʀɴ to ᴅɪᴇ.

From *Beowulf*

In later times, partial alliteration—not following a regular pattern and perhaps stretching over more than a line—has enriched the texture of verse. Shakespeare at times uses alliteration to accentuate the highly individualized rhythm of his sonnets. Look for the repetition of initial consonants in the following example:

William Shakespeare   *(1564–1616)*

Sonnet 30   *before 1598*

When to the sessions of sweet silent thought
I summon up remembrance of things past,
I sigh the lack of many a thing I sought,
And with old woes new wail° my dear time's waste: *newly mourn*
Then can I drown an eye (unused to flow)   5
For precious friends hid in death's dateless° night,   *endless*
And weep afresh love's long since canceled woe,
And moan the expense° of many a vanished sight,   *the loss*
Then can I grieve at grievances foregone,°   *griefs long past*
And heavily from woe to woe tell o'er°   *tell over again* 10
The sad account of fore-bemoaned moan,
Which I new pay as if not paid before.
But if the while I think on thee, dear friend,
All losses are restored and sorrows end.

The Receptive Reader

1. Look at the repetition of the initial *s* in the first three lines. In reading the poem aloud, how much would you make the alliterating syllables stand out?

ᴡʜᴇɴ to | the ꜱᴇꜱꜱ|ions of | ꜱᴡᴇᴇᴛ ꜱɪ|lent ᴛʜᴏᴜɢʜᴛ
I ꜱᴜᴍᴍ|on ᴜᴘ | reᴍᴇᴍ|brance of | things ᴘᴀꜱᴛ,
I ꜱɪɢʜ | the ʟᴀᴄᴋ | of ᴍᴀɴ|y a ᴛʜɪɴɢ | I ꜱᴏᴜɢʜᴛ.

2. How many other examples of repeated initial consonants can you find? How important are the alliterating words in the poem?

3. Where is the *turning point* in this sonnet? How does the poem lead up to it?

During the last century, rhyme became increasingly optional. Today, some poets rely on rhyme; many more don't. Instead of making every line, or every second line, rhyme, they may use rhyme, if at all, at irregular intervals. The decline of rhyme, together with the appeal of rhythms freer and more variable than traditional meter, made possible the rise of **free verse**—poetry less governed by formal conventions—as the dominant mode of poetry.

JUXTAPOSITIONS

The Role of Rhyme

Do you find yourself shifting gears, so to speak, when reading the following three passages aloud? Point out any examples of full rhyme, single and double rhyme, half-rhyme, internal rhyme, assonance, or alliteration.

1. Durable bird pulls interminable worm,
    Coiled in subterranean caverns;
    Feeds on fossils of ferns and monsters.

    > Beatrice Janosco, "To a Tidelands Oil Pump"

2. Last night I saw the savage world
    And heard the blood beat up the stair;
    The fox's bark, the owl's shrewd pounce,
    The crying creatures—all were there,
    And men in bed with love and fear.

    > Elizabeth Jennings, "Song for a Birth or a Death"

3. I bring fresh showers for the thirsting flowers,
    From the seas and the streams;
    I bear light shade for the leaves when laid
    In their noonday dreams.
    From my wings are shaken the dews that waken
    The sweet buds every one,
    When rocked to rest on their mother's breast,
    As she dances about the sun.

    > Percy Bysshe Shelley, "The Cloud"

RHYTHM AND METER

Poetry is oral; it is not words, but words performed. . . . the "real" poem is not the scratches on the paper, but the sounds those scratches stand for.

JUDSON JEROME

Poetry is rhythmic, like breathing, walking, dancing. When the rhythm of successive lines becomes regular and predictable, we call it meter. **Meter** regularizes the natural rhythms of speech. The poet sets up an underlying recurring beat, over which the actual poem plays variations. The meter is the steadying beat of the metronome over which longer and shorter notes dance out the actual music of the verse.

In speech, **stress** (or accent) makes us raise our voices slightly and makes us seem to linger over the accented syllable. Stress makes one syllable stand out in words like reMAIN and dePART; or LISten and SUMmon; or PEDigree and destiNATion. It makes words (or stressed parts of words) stand out in phrases like "in the WOODS," "under the SUN," or "have to aGREE." In poems employing traditional meter, the stressed syllables set up a regular beat, as in the opening lines of the Beatles song:

> PICture yourSELF on a BOAT in a RIVer,
> With TANgerine TREES and MARmalade SKIES,
> SOMEbody CALLS you, you ANswer quite SLOWly,
> A GIRL with kaLEIdoscope EYES.
>
>   "Lucy in the Sky with Diamonds"

Meter is rhythm regular enough to be charted, or scanned. Scanning charts the underlying beat and its variations, the way a cardiogram charts the heartbeat and any irregularities. To make meter visible, we can use a special notation for stressed and unstressed syllables: a sharp accent (´) for strong stress; a flat accent (`) for weaker stress; no mark (or often a small half-circle resting on its curved side) for an unstressed syllable.

Read the following short poem first with exaggerated emphasis on the underlying beat ("The WAY a CROW / Shook DOWN on ME"). Then try to read it with enough variation in the *degree* of stress to bring your reading closer to the natural rhythms of speech. Note weaker or secondary stress alternating with strong stress in the first two lines:

Robert Frost   *(1874–1963)*

Dust of Snow   1923

The wày a crów
Shook dówn on mè
The dúst of snów
From a hémlock trée

Has gíven my héart   5
A chánge of móod
And sáved some párt
Of a dáy I had rúed.°   *viewed with regret*

The basic unit of our metrical currency is the **foot**—one stressed syllable, with one or more unstressed ones. Several feet together make up a line of verse. The Frost poem uses an unusually short line with only two feet: "The dúst | of snów." The traditional line of verse is a four-beat or five-beat line—made up of four or five feet:

Wórds are | like léaves; | and whére | they móst | abóund,
Much frúit | of sénse | benéath | is ráre | ly fóund.

Alexander Pope, "Essay on Criticism"

Different stress patterns account for different kinds of meter:

iambic	DeTROIT—DeTROIT—DeTROIT
trochaic	BOSTon—BOSTon—BOSTon
anapestic	New ROCHELLE—New ROCHELLE—New ROCHELLE
dactylic	BALtimore—BALtimore—BALtimore

✗ The most common meter of English poetry has been **iambic**—a "one-TWO | one-TWO | one-TWO" rhythm akin to the rhythm of walking. The iamb is a foot made up of two syllables, with the stressed one last: DeTROIT—DeTROIT—DeTROIT—DeTROIT. (The Greek name originally labeled a lame-footed person, whose gimpy gait made one foot come down harder than the other.) The following lines set up a prevailing iambic beat. Notice that words spill over from one foot to the next, preventing the meter from cutting the lines mechanically like slices of cheese:

I képt | my áns | wers smáll | and képt | them néar;
Big qués | tions brúised | my mínd | but stíll | I lét
Small áns | wers bé | a búl | wark tò | my féar.

Elizabeth Jennings, "Answers"

✗ The first line in the Pope couplet shows a common reversal (or **inversion**): "WORDS are | like leaves . . ." The stress has shifted to the first syllable. The result is a **trochaic** foot, or trochee, on the "BOSTon—BOSTon—BOSTon" model. A line of trochaic feet changes the metrical pattern from "clip-CLOP | clip-CLOP | clip-CLOP" to "CLIP-clop | CLIP-clop | CLIP-clop." Poems with an underlying trochaic beat throughout are rare. The most common assignment of the trochaic foot is to bring variation into a prevailing iambic pattern. A trochaic foot, starting out strong, can serve as an attention getter. (Is it only an accident that in Pope's couplet the most important word—namely, *Words*—is pulled to the front of the first line by trochaic inversion?)

Here is an example of a predominantly trochaic poem. In reading this poem aloud, can you make the listener aware of the trochaic pattern—without making it sound mechanical?

Percy Bysshe Shelley   *(1792–1822)*

To ——   *1824*

Músic, | whèn soft | vóices | díe,	trochaic
Víbrates | ìn the | mémo|ry.	trochaic
Odors, | whèn sweet | víolets | sícken,	trochaic
Líve with|ín the | sénse they | quícken.	trochaic
Róse leaves, | whèn the | róse is | déad,	trochaic
Are héaped | fòr the | belóv|ed's béd.	iambic
And só | thy thóughts, | when thóu | art góne,	iambic
Lóve it|sélf shall | slúmber | ón.	trochaic

✘ A third kind of foot may also serve as a bit player introducing variation into an iambic line. The **anapest** doubles up two unstressed syllables to lead up to the third and stressed syllable, on the "New Rochelle—New Rochelle—New Rochelle" model. The added unstressed syllable can have a "hurry up—hurry up—hurry up" effect. A predominantly anapestic line would look like this:

> *But his* wíngs \| *will not* rést \| *and his* féet \| *will not* stáy \| for us.
>
> Algernon Charles Swinburne, "At Parting"

More common is anapestic variation in an otherwise iambic line:

> The wóods \| *are prepár*\|*ing to* wáit \| out wínter.
> Gusts blów \| *with an* éarn\|*est of* áll \| there ís \| *to be* dóne
>
> Charles Tomlinson, "The View"

✘ A fourth kind of foot, reversing the pattern of the anapest, is nearly extinct in English. The **dactyl** doubles up two unstressed syllables after a stressed one, on the "BALtimore—BALtimore—BALtimore" model. A hundred years ago, a large popular audience read dactylic verse like the following. Listen for the doubling up of the unstressed syllables in Longfellow's six-beat line:

> Thís *is the* \| fórest *prim*\|*éval; but* \| whére *are the* \| héarts *that* \| be\|néath it
> Léaped *like the* \| róe, *when he* \| héars *in the* \| wóod*land the* \| vóice *of the* \| húntsman?
>
> Henry Wadsworth Longfellow, "Evangeline"

✗ The **spondee** is a variation that can strongly emphasize *part* of a line. It is *all* emphasis—it juxtaposes *two* stressed syllables, slowing down the reader. (This is the way many people pronounce HONG KONG.) A spondee often follows or comes before a set of two *un*stressed syllables, so that the total number of beats in a line need not change. The following are the opening lines of a sonnet John Milton wrote in 1655 about his blindness. The spondee in the second line propels us into the world of darkness in which he already lived when he dictated his most ambitious poems:

When I | consíd|er hòw | my líght | is spént
Ere hálf | my dáys | *in this* | DARK WORLD | and wíde . . .

Even in verse that is alive with variations and pauses, exceptionally regular lines may help maintain the underlying beat. Meter is the combined product of the chosen kind of foot multiplied by the *number* of feet per line. To label kinds of meter, we identify the kind of foot (iambic or trochaic, for instance) and then show the number of feet (for instance, pentameter—a five-beat line). Here are the Greek names we still use for lines of different length:

five-beat line	pentameter
four-beat line	tetrameter
three-beat line	trimeter
six-beat line	hexameter

✗ The five-beat line is by far the most common, whether rhymed as in the sonnet, or unrhymed as in the **blank verse** of Shakespeare's plays. As the pentagon is a building with five sides, so **pentameter** is a meter with five stressed syllables to the line. A five-beat line using predominantly iambic feet is in iambic pentameter. The iambic pentameter line often sounds natural and unforced; it seems to stay close to the natural speech patterns of English:

By dáy the bát is cóusin tò the móuse.
He líkes the áttic òf an áging hóuse
                    Theodore Roethke

✗ Three-beat or four-beat lines make up many songs and songlike poems. As a trilogy is a set of three books (or plays), so **trimeter** is meter with three stressed syllables to the line. **Tetrameter** is meter with four stressed syllables to the line. In folk song and ballad, tetrameter and trimeter often alternate in a four-line stanza:

They líghted dówn to táke a drínk	tetrameter
Of the spríng that rán so cléar,	trimeter
And dówn the spríng ran his góod heart's blóod,	tetrameter
And sóre she begán to féar.	trimeter
"Hold úp, hold úp, Lord Wílliam," she sáys,	tetrameter
"For I féar that yòu are sláin."	trimeter
"'Tis nóthing but the shádow of my scárlet clóak,	tetrameter
That shínes in the wáter so pláin."	trimeter

Anonymous, "The Douglas Tragedy"

✗ A six-beat line, or **hexameter,** was the line of Homer's epics. In the following lines, as often with hexameter, a slight break, marked here by a slash, divides the long lines into half-lines. How would you read these lines?

> I would that we were, my beloved, / white birds on the foam of the sea!
> We tire of the flame of the meteor, / before it can fade and flee;
> And the flame of the blue star of twilight, / hung low on the rim of the sky,
> Has awaked in our hearts, my beloved, / a sadness that may not die.

William Butler Yeats, "The White Birds"

When poetry started to break loose from traditional meter, poets wrote poems with varying length of line and with a harder-to-chart rhythm. In most of the **free verse** of the twentieth century, the rhythmic beat has been free-flowing and irregular.

JUXTAPOSITIONS

The Matter of Meter

In reading the following passages aloud, how do you have to shift gears to do justice to the different kinds of meter? What is the dominant meter in each of the passages as a whole or in individual lines? What variations are there?

1. Double, double, toil and trouble;
   Fire burn and cauldron bubble.

Shakespeare, *Macbeth*

2. My wife and I lived all alone,
   contention was our only bone.

I fought with her, she fought with me,
and things went on right merrily.

> Robert Creeley, "Ballad of the
> Despairing Husband"

3. It was many and many a year ago,
   In a kingdom by the sea,
   That a maiden there lived whom you may know
   By the name of Annabel Lee.

> Edgar Allan Poe, "Annabel Lee"

4. But yesterday the word of Caesar might
   Have stood against the world. Now lies he here,
   And none so poor to do him reverence.

> Shakespeare, *Julius Caesar*

5. Poplars are standing there still as death.

> Arna Bontemps, "Southern Mansion"

TRADITIONAL STANZA FORM

Scorn not the sonnet: Critic, you have frowned
Mindless of its just honors; with this key Shake-
speare unlocked his heart.

WILLIAM WORDSWORTH

Much traditional poetry is laid out in **stanzas**—sets of lines similar in shape. Traditional stanzas may repeat the same rhyme scheme, as if programmed to make lines rhyme according to the same formula. They may show the same alternation of longer and shorter lines, making lines expand or contract in the same sequence. Familiar stanza form harks back to a time when the history of song and poem was still one. We expect a songlike poem to have stanzas the way we expect a song to have successive verses, all sung to the same melody. Look at the rhyme scheme that is shared by both stanzas in each of the following songs. Look at how the final lines of the stanza come back as a **refrain** in the second song:

William Shakespeare   *(1564–1616)*

O Mistress Mine   1602

O mistress mine, where are you roaming?   a
O, stay and hear; your true love's coming   a
That can sing both high and low.   b

Trip no further, pretty sweeting,   c
Journeys end in lovers meeting,   c   5
Every wise man's son doth know.   b

What is love? 'Tis not hereafter;
Present mirth hath present laughter;
What's to come is still unsure.
In delay there lies no plenty;   10
Then come kiss me, sweet and twenty,
Youth's a stuff will not endure.

Under the Greenwood Tree   *1599*

Under the greenwood tree   a
Who loves to lie with me,   a
And turn his merry note   b
Unto the sweet bird's throat,   b
Come hither, come hither, come hither!   c   5
Here shall he see   a
No enemy   a
But winter and rough weather.   c

Who doth ambition shun,
And loves to live in the sun,   10
Seeking the food he eats,
And pleased with what he gets,
Come hither, come hither, come hither!
Here shall he see
No enemy   15
But winter and rough weather.
                    From *As You Like It*

The Receptive Reader

The repetition of an interlaced, intertwining rhyme scheme and of variation in sentence length help make the two stanzas in each song parallel. In each song, what is the pattern of the stanza?

Refrains come back and drive home a prevailing mood or idea in other songlike poems—the **popular ballads.** These anonymous folk ballads (many of them going back to the Middle Ages) were originally sung to record a notable exploit or calamity, often presented in stark outline, hitting home without embellishment. Some of the best-known early ballads follow a question-and-answer format in a pattern of **cumulative** repetition. The questioner persists in asking questions until the horrible truth is revealed. The following **literary ballad** picks up the question-and-answer style of earlier ballads. Once we become attuned to the pattern, we wait for the next question—and the next answer, as the poem builds up to its grim conclusion. Make sure you read this poem—or hear the poem read—aloud.

Melvin Walker La Follette   *(born 1930)*

The Ballad of Red Fox   *1959*

Yellow sun yellow
Sun yellow sun,
When, oh, when
Will red fox run?

When the hollow horn shall sound,   5
When the hunter lifts his gun
And liberates the wicked hound,
Then, oh, then shall red fox run.

Yellow sun yellow
Sun yellow sun, Where, oh, where   10
Will red fox run?

Through meadows hot as sulphur,
Through forests cool as clay,
Through hedges crisp as morning
And grasses limp as day.   15

Yellow sky yellow
Sky yellow sky,
How, oh, how
Will red fox die?

With a bullet in his belly,   20
A dagger in his eye,
And blood upon his red red brush
Shall red fox die.

The Receptive Reader

1. The questions in this poem provide a variable rather than completely identical *refrain*. How does it change?

2. To what extent do the answers in this poem follow the *rhyme* scheme of the traditional ballad stanza—a four-liner (or quatrain) rhyming abcb? A rhyming pattern can place special emphasis on key words in a poem. What rhymes make key words echo throughout this poem?

3. What do you think accounts for the continuing appeal of the old ballad style?

The Personal Response

In the battle between the hunter and the hunted, on which side is the poet? On which side are you?

The best-known and most widely practiced traditional stanza form is the **sonnet.** The sonnet is a single stanza of fourteen lines, although the early sonneteers repeated the same form again and again in sonnet sequences of over a hundred poems. Many early sonnets were poems of unrequited love, with the mournful, humble lover forever replaying his "plaint" to the cruel, disdainful lady. Soon, however, poets extended the form to other subjects.

Traditionally, the sonnet works with a five-beat iambic line; it therefore often has ten or eleven syllables to the line. When following the model of the Italian poet Petrarch, sonneteers rhyme the first eight lines (the **octave**) in an interlaced pattern: abbaabba. The remaining six lines (the **sestet**) may rhyme cdcdee or cdecde. Sonneteers imitating the Shakespearean sonnet group the fourteen lines somewhat differently: They have alternating rhymes in the first three **quatrains,** or groups of four (abab/cdcd/efef), followed by a concluding couplet (gg).

In a Petrarchan sonnet, a turning in the flow of thought may start at or near the break after the first eight lines. The remaining six lines then represent a kind of countertide. Where is the turn in the flow of ideas in John Milton's poem on his blindness?

John Milton   *(1608–1674)*

When I Consider How My Light Is Spent   *1655*

When I consider how my light is spent	
Ere° half my days, in this dark world and wide,	*before*
And that one talent which is death to hide	
Lodged with me useless, though my soul more bent	
To serve therewith my Maker, and present	5
My true account, lest he° returning chide;	*so he won't*
"Doth God exact day-labor, light denied?"°	*with sight denied*
I fondly° ask; but Patience to prevent	*foolishly*
That murmur, soon replies, "God doth not need	
Either man's work or his own gifts; who best	10
Bear his mild yoke, they serve him best. His state	
Is kingly. Thousands at his bidding speed	
And post° over land and ocean without rest:	*carry messages*
They also serve who only stand and wait.	

In Milton's sonnet, the first sentence runs through all but the last three lines of the fourteen-line poem. The underlying pattern is "When I think about my blindness . . . I ask a foolish rebellious question (does God expect a blind poet to continue his work?) . . . but Patience replies that God does not depend on any one person's labor or gifts." This long elaborate sentence puts the poet's whole situation—both the question it raises and the answer the poet has reached—before us. But after the first period, which comes almost at the end of the eleventh line, we stop short at a sentence that goes to the opposite extreme. It has four words.

It makes us take in and ponder the essence of the lesson the poet has learned: the majesty of God. "His state / Is kingly." His glory does not depend on our praise or service, however dedicated.

The Receptive Reader

1. What *rhyme* words fill in the typical Petrarchan rhyme scheme?

2. What lines come closest to perfect *iambic pentameter?* Where do you see clear examples of trochaic inversion at the beginning of a line?

3. What are some striking examples of *enjambment,* with the sense spilling over into the next line to give the poem a characteristically Miltonic sense of flow—of long, rich sentences moving forward regardless of line boundaries? (Where does a subsequent *caesura,* or cut within a line, help to set up a syncopating counter-rhythm?)

4. How does the poem as a whole lead up to its famous last line?

Conventionally, sonnets looked at love from the perspective of the lover yearning for a love that often seemed unattainable. How does the author of the following sonnet depart from this convention?

Edna St. Vincent Millay   *(1892–1950)*

I, Being Born a Woman and Distressed   1923

I, being born a woman and distressed
By all the needs and notions of my kind,
Am urged by your propinquity° to find   *nearness*
Your person fair, and feel a certain zest
To bear your body's weight upon my breast: 5
So subtle is the fume of life designed
To clarify the pulse and cloud the mind,
And leave me once again undone, possessed.
Think not for this, however, the poor treason
Of my stout blood against my staggering brain,   10
I shall remember you with love, or season
My scorn with pity,—let me make it plain:
I find this frenzy insufficient reason
For conversation when we meet again.

The Receptive Reader

1. What *formal* features of the traditional sonnet does this poem illustrate? What is the rhyme scheme?

2. What basic *polarities* help organize this poem? Where in this sonnet is there a turning or counter-tide, and what makes it central to the poem as a whole?

The Personal Response

Millay has been called "very much a revolutionary in all her sympathies, and a whole-hearted Feminist" (Floyd Dell). In most of the sonnet tradition, the woman was the silent audience and the silent partner in the love relationship. How do you react as the woman in this poem speaks up and talks back?

TRADITIONAL AND OPEN FORM

Of all the possible distinctions between verse and prose, the simplest, and most objective, is that verse uses the line as a unit. Prose goes right on . . . Verse turns.

JUDSON JEROME

Defenders of traditional form claim that it allows much creative freedom within the limits it sets up. The following sonnet was written by a leading poet of the English Romantic movement. The poem has fourteen lines and an interlaced rhyme scheme: "free—Nun—sun—(tranquili)ty; Sea—(a)wake—make—(everlasting)ly" (abbaacca). It has the traditional underlying five-beat meter (iambic pentameter): "The HO|ly TIME | is QUI|et AS | a NUN." However, its pattern, rhythm, and tone make it memorable and unique. It is different from any other sonnet. Like several other Wordsworth poems, this poem addresses a younger sister, who lived with him and shared his love of nature.

William Wordsworth   *(1770–1850)*

It Is a Beauteous Evening   *1807*

It is a beauteous° evening, calm and free,   *beautiful*
The holy time is quiet as a Nun
Breathless with adoration; the broad sun
Is sinking down in its tranquility;
The gentleness of heaven broods over the Sea: 5
Listen! the Mighty Being is awake,
And doth with his eternal motion make
A sound like thunder—everlastingly.
Dear Child! dear Girl! that walkest with me here,
If thou appear untouched by solemn thought,   10
Thy nature is not therefore less divine:
Thou liest in Abraham's bosom all the year,
And worshipst at the Temple's inner shrine,
God being with thee when we know it not.

This poem has a strong metrical pattern, but it is not monotonous. At key points, the poem reverses the iambic (DᴇTROIT—DᴇTROIT) pattern to stress the first syllable of a line: "ʙʀᴇᴀᴛʜless with adoration"; "ʟɪsᴛᴇɴ! the mighty being is awake." This variation emphasizes key words; it sets off key stages in the poem as a whole. Rhyme words do not neatly mark off sentences. At the end of the second line, we are pulled over into the third with only a minor pause. But then we come to a major break *within* the line, setting up a strong counter-rhythm: "The holy time is quiet as a Nun / Breathless with adoration; | | the broad sun . . ."

The Receptive Reader

1. Where else in this poem do strong breaks vary the rhythm? with what effect?

2. How should this poem *sound* when read aloud? How much should the reading make the listener aware of the meter—and of the line breaks following the rhyme words?

Widely admired twentieth-century poets have written some poems with a stricter traditional pattern, and some in a more open modern style. Study the following two examples by poets who move easily between traditional formal discipline and modern creative freedom. What can traditional form do that might be hard to achieve in a more open format? What is possible with open form that traditional form might make it hard for the poet to do?

Anne Sexton   *(1928–1974)*

Her Kind   *1960*

I have gone out, a possessed witch,
haunting the black air, braver at night;
dreaming evil, I have done my hitch
over the plain houses, light by light:
lonely thing, twelve-fingered, out of mind.   5
A woman like that is not a woman, quite.
I have been her kind.

I have found the warm caves in the woods,
filled them with skillets, carvings, shelves,
closets, silks, innumerable goods;   10
fixed the suppers for the worms and the elves:
whining, rearranging the disaligned.
A woman like that is misunderstood.
I have been her kind.

I have ridden in your cart, driver,   15
waved my nude arms at villages going by,
learning the last bright routes, survivor
where your flames still bite my thigh
and my ribs crack where your wheels wind.
A woman like that is not ashamed to die.   20
I have been her kind.

How do the formal features of this poem serve the poet's purpose? The poem is intense, concentrated, deliberate. It is like an incantation— the poem puts a spell (or a hex, as it were) on the reader. The poem is divided into three stanzas of identical shape, each laid out according to the same plan. Each stanza frames a striking, haunting picture. Within each stanza, the interlacing rhyme scheme knits the material together, as if all distracting detail had been left out. The threefold repetition of the stanza form makes us expect that each of the three will be part of the same story. This expectation is reinforced by **parallelism;** that is, closely similar sentence structure or wording. The opening lines are parallel in sentence pattern: "I have gone . . ."; "I have found . . ."; "I have ridden. . . ." So is the last-but-one line in each stanza ("A woman like that is . . ."). We sense that the perspective will remain the same: the speaker will continue to look at the witch not from the point of view of her persecutors but of someone who identifies with the outcast: "I have been her kind."

The Receptive Reader

1. How does the *rhyme scheme* bond the two weighty final lines of each stanza to the earlier lines? How does the rhyme scheme link stanza to stanza?

2. What *details* give this poem the intensity of a nightmare?

3. What role does the refrain play in this poem? What makes its repetition cumulative—how does the poem build up to a climax?

4. Women accused of being witches were for centuries the target of persecution and lynch justice. How does the poet want you to think of the women behind the caricatures and stereotypes?

The Creative Dimension

Have you ever identified with the outcast, the outsider, the underdog? Write a journal entry (poem or prose) in which the refrain might be "I have been her (his) kind."

In the following poem, what gives shape to the poem as a whole—in the absence of such traditional features as rhyme, meter, and stanza?

Sharon Olds   *(born 1942)*

I Go Back to May 1937   *1987*

I see them standing at the formal gates of their colleges,
I see my father strolling out
under the ochre sandstone arch, the
red tiles glinting like bent
plates of blood behind his head, I   5
see my mother with a few light books at her hip
standing at the pillar made of tiny bricks with the
wrought-iron gate still open behind her, its
sword-tips black in the May air,
they are about to graduate, they are about to get married,   10
they are kids, they are dumb, all they know is they are
innocent, they would never hurt anybody.
I want to go up to them and say Stop,
don't do it—she's the wrong woman,
he's the wrong man, you are going to do things   15
you cannot imagine you would ever do,
you are going to do bad things to children,
you are going to suffer in ways you never heard of,
you are going to want to die. I want to go
up to them there in the late May sunlight and say it,   20
her hungry pretty blank face turning to me,
her pitiful beautiful untouched body,
his arrogant handsome blind face turning to me,
his pitiful beautiful untouched body,
but I don't do it. I   25
want to live. I take them up like the male and female
paper dolls and bang them together
at the hips like chips of flint as if to
strike sparks from them. I say
Do what you are going to do, and I will tell about it.   30

What makes this poem an example of open form? There is no rhyme (although there are some echo effects like "at the *hips* like *chips*"). The lines are of irregular length, and the line breaks often come at strange points in the middle of a phrase (the / ¬ed tiles). There is no steady underlying drumbeat of meter. Compared with the Sexton poem, this poem seems more open-ended. The story of the speaker's parents, and her attempt to come to terms with it, are still in progress. We can still share in the impulse to tell her parents "No!" but then resolve to let human nature take its course. Key phrases like "I want to live" are not set off; they appear as natural stages in the flow of thought. **Parallelism** in this poem sets up open frames allowing the poet to multiply striking lifelike details (or urgent warnings). Open-ended parallel structure ("I see . . ."; "I see . . ."; "I see . . .") allows the poet to build up the details that make the campus scene come hauntingly to life, from the sandstone arch and glinting red tiles to the "few light books" at the mother's hip and the black "sword-tips" of the wrought-iron gate.

The Receptive Reader

1. What *line breaks* come at an unexpected place in a sentence or in the middle of a phrase, partly counteracting the pause traditionally signaled by the end of a line?

2. How does *parallel structure* serve for emphasis in the lines making us look at the faces and bodies of the parents? How do these lines sum up the mixed emotions of the speaker?

3. How does this poem achieve *closure,* leaving us with a satisfying sense of completeness?

The Personal Response

In recent years, the concern of (grown) children with the quality of the parenting they received has become a major focus in the media and in popular psychology. How would you sum up the attitude of the speaker in this poem toward her parents? How does it compare with your own attitudes?

JUXTAPOSITIONS

Close and Free Translation

Many translations use a more open form than the original poet did. It is hard to be faithful to the original meaning while at the same time reproducing features of poetic form, such as meter and rhyme. Study the following translations of a much-translated poem by a widely translated German poet. The first translation hews close to the regular iambic pentameter and the end rhymes of the original stanzas. (In the original, the first and third lines of each stanza also rhyme.) The second translation aims at getting close to the spirit of the original while abandoning traditional formal features.

Rainer Maria Rilke   *(1875–1926)*

The Panther   *1927*
Jardin des Plantes, Paris

TRANSLATED BY HANS P. GUTH

From pacing past the barriers of his cage
His tired gaze no longer seems to see.
All that exists: a thousand iron bars.
The world beyond the bars has ceased to be.

The supple tread of sinuous steps revolves   5
In circles of benumbing narrowness,
Like power dancing round a pedestal
Where a majestic will stands powerless.

And yet, at times, the veil that blunts his eye
Moves stealthily aside—an image enters,   10
Glides through the silence of his tautened limbs—
And ceases where his being centers.

Many translators of poetry are poets in their own right. They bring to the translator's task a special empathy, a special ability to get into the spirit of a fellow poet. This affinity shows when Robert Bly translates and comments on the same Rilke poem:

From seeing and seeing the seeing has become so exhausted
it no longer sees anything anymore.
The world is made of bars, a hundred thousand
bars, and behind the bars, nothing.

The lithe swinging of that rhythmical easy stride   5
that slowly circles down to a single point
is like a dance of energy around a hub,
in which a great will stands stunned and numbed.

At times the curtains of the eye lift
without a sound—then a shape enters,   10
slips through the tightened silence of the shoulders,
reaches the heart and dies.

The poet-translator said about this much-reprinted poem:

Rilke . . . watched a panther at the zoo, and his German lines, in rhythm and sound, embody movingly the repetitive, desperate walk of the panther. By the end of the poem he is somehow inside the panther's body. Each time the panther glimpses a shape, say a dog or a child, the image goes to the body's center, the place from which a leap begins; but no leap can take place. A leap can't take place, and so the image "reaches the heart, and dies."

The Receptive Reader
Where do the two translations seem very close, reflecting the common original? Where do they diverge and with what effect? What difference does the difference in form make to your response? What do you think is the key to the fascination this poem has had for readers and translators around the world?

POEMS FOR FURTHER STUDY

In reading the following poems, pay special attention to the way they use or modify traditional formal features, such as rhyme, meter, and stanza form.

Popular Ballad   *Anonymous*

Lord Randal   *traditional*

"O where have you been, Lord Randal, my son?
And where have you been, my handsome young man?"
"I have been at the greenwood; mother, make my bed soon,
For I'm wearied with hunting, and fain° would lie down."   *gladly*

"And who met you there, Lord Randal, my son?   5
And who met you there, my handsome young man?"
"O I met with my true-love; mother, make my bed soon,
For I'm wearied with hunting, and fain would lie down."

"And what did she give you, Lord Randal, my son?
And what did she give you, my handsome young man?"   10
"Eels fried in a pan; mother, make my bed soon,
For I'm wearied with hunting, and fain would like down."

"And who got your leavings, Lord Randal, my son?
And what became of them, my handsome young man?"
"My hawks and my hounds; mother, make my bed soon,   15
For I'm wearied with hunting, and fain would lie down."

"And what became of them, Lord Randal, my son?
And what became of them, my handsome young man?"
"They stretched their legs out and died; mother, make my bed soon,
For I'm wearied with hunting, and fain would lie down."   20

"O I fear you are poisoned, Lord Randal, my son!
I fear you are poisoned, my handsome young man!"
"O yes, I am poisoned; mother, make my bed soon,
For I'm sick at heart, and fain would lie down."

"What d' you leave to your mother, Lord Randal, my son?   25
What d' you leave to your mother, my handsome young man?"
"Four and twenty milk kine;° mother, make my bed soon,   *cattle*
For I'm sick at heart, and fain would lie down."

"What d' you leave to your sister, Lord Randal, my son?
What d' you leave to your sister, my handsome young man?"   30
"My gold and my silver; mother, make my bed soon,
For I'm sick at heart, and fain would lie down."

"What d' you leave to your brother, Lord Randal, my son?
What d' you leave to your brother, my handsome young man?"
"My houses and my lands; mother, make my bed soon,   35
For I'm sick at heart, and fain would lie down."

"What d' you leave to your true-love, Lord Randal, my son?
What d' you leave to your true-love, my handsome young man?"
"I leave her hell and fire; mother, make my bed soon,
For I'm sick at heart, and fain would lie down."   40

The Receptive Reader

When does the often-repeated *refrain* first turn ominous? How does this ballad use the pattern of *cumulative repetition* twice? How does the ballad strip the
story down to *essentials?* What do you think made this story survive through the
centuries?

Christine de Pisan   *(1363–1430)*

Marriage Is a Lovely Thing   *before 1400*

TRANSLATED BY JOANNA BANKIER

Marriage is a lovely thing
—my own example proves it—
for her whose husband is as kind
as he whom God has found for me.
Since day by day he has sustained me,   5
praised be He who guards his life
and keeps him safe for me,
          and surely my gentle one loves me well.

On the night of our union,
the first time we slept together   10
I could see how kind he was.
Nothing did that could have hurt me
and before the rising sun
had kissed me, oh a hundred times
but never urged against my will,   15
          and surely my gentle one loves me well.

And how sweet the words he spoke;
"Dearest Friend, God led me to you
to serve you courteously and well
as if he wished to raise me up."   20
Thus he mused all through the night
and his manner never faltered
but stayed the same, unwaveringly,
          and surely my gentle one loves me well.

O Prince, his love can drive me to distraction   25
when he assures me he's all mine
and of sweetness makes me burst.

The Receptive Reader

1. Like many other love poems of the Middle Ages, this poem has a *refrain* and a "send-off" (or *envoi*) of three lines. (The modern translator has not attempted to reproduce the rhymes of the original French poem.) What gives the refrain in this poem its special appeal or special force? How does the poem as a whole lead up to the send-off?

2. Christine de Pisan, a native of Italy living in France, was happily married for a few short years. After her husband's death, she became one of the first women in Europe to support herself by her writing. How is the treatment of love in this poem different from that in other early love lyrics you have read?

William Wordsworth   *(1770–1850)*

I Wandered Lonely as a Cloud   *1807*

I wandered lonely as a cloud
    That floats on high o'er vales and hills,
When all at once I saw a crowd,
    A host,° of golden daffodils;   *massed ranks*
Beside the lake, beneath the trees,   5
Fluttering and dancing in the breeze.

Continuous as the stars that shine
    And twinkle on the milky way,
They stretched in never-ending line
    Along the margin of a bay: 10
Ten thousand saw I at a glance,
Tossing their heads in sprightly dance.

The waves beside them danced; but they
    Outdid the sparkling waves in glee;
A poet could not but be gay,   15
    In such a jocund° company;   *joyful*
I gazed—and gazed—but little thought
What wealth the show to me had brought:

For oft, when on my couch I lie
    In vacant or in pensive° mood,   *thoughtful* 20
They flash upon that inward eye
    Which is the bliss of solitude;
And then my heart with pleasure fills,
And dances with the daffodils.

The Receptive Reader

How does the poet use rhyme, meter, stanza form? Does the poet make the experience re-enacted in this poem come to life for you as the reader? Can you follow, and sympathize with, the train of thought in the last stanza?

Thomas Nashe   *(1567–1601)*

A Litany in Time of Plague   *1592*

Adieu, farewell, earth's bliss;
This world uncertain is;
Fond° are life's lustful joys;   *foolish*
Death proves them all but toys;
None from his darts can fly;   5
I am sick; I must die.
      Lord, have mercy on us!

Rich men, trust not in wealth,
Gold cannot buy you health:
Physic° himself must fade;   *the physician's art*   10
All things to end are made;
The plague full swift goes by.
I am sick, I must die.
      Lord have mercy on us!

Beauty is but a flower   15
Which wrinkles will devour;
Brightness falls from the air;
Queens have died young and fair;
Dust hath closed Helen's° eye.   *Helen of Troy*
I am sick, I must die.   20
      Lord have mercy on us!

Strength stoops unto the grave,
Worms feed on Hector° brave;   *Trojan prince*
Swords may not fight with fate;
Earth still holds open her gate;   25
Come, come, the bells do cry.
I am sick, I must die.
      Lord have mercy on us!

Wit with his wantonness
Tastes death's bitterness;   30
Hell's executioner
Hath no ears for to hear
What vain art can reply.
I am sick, I must die.
      Lord, have mercy on us!   35

Haste, therefore, each degree,°   *rank*
To welcome destiny;
Heaven is our heritage,
Earth but a player's stage;
Mount we° unto the sky;   *let us mount*   40
I am sick, I must die.
            Lord, have mercy on us!

The Receptive Reader

1. A litany is a chantlike prayer with much *repetition.* What use does this prayer make of outright repetition? What use does it make of parallel structure?

2. What is the *rhyme scheme?* How does rhyme carry over from one stanza to the next? What is the central word to which the carry-over rhyme directs attention?

3. What is the underlying *meter* in the first five lines of each stanza? In what lines does it show most clearly? What is the major recurrent variation on this metrical pattern? How does the meter change in the refrain? How does the change in meter affect your reading of the poem?

The Personal Response

How remote or how understandable are the sentiments expressed in this poem for you as a modern reader?

WRITING ABOUT LITERATURE

18   Form and Meaning (First and Second Draft)

The Writing Workshop   Much writing about poetry aims at showing the connection between form and meaning. It traces the relationship between technical formal features and what the poem as a whole does for the reader. Writing about form and meaning, you may be focusing on how traditional formal features work in a poem. You may be focusing on how formal features are modified or replaced in much modern poetry. Remember the following guidelines:

✘ *See what use the poem makes of rhyme.*   Does it use traditional full rhymes throughout? part of the time? in strategic places? Is there an alternating rhyme scheme or other pattern that bonds a series of lines? Does the poem make use of half-rhymes or internal rhymes? Does rhyme serve to highlight important words? Does it help to segment the poem neatly into lines, or does the sense of a line frequently spill over into the next line (enjambment)?

✘ *Check if the poem sets up a strong underlying beat, or meter.*   (Be sure to read lines aloud.) Does it use the common iambic pentameter line? How regular are the lines? Is there much variation—with what effect? Is variation used for emphasis, or to speed up or slow down a line? If the poem uses free verse, is it strongly rhythmic—and does the rhythm give the lines an eloquent or hypnotic effect? Or is the rhythm of the lines closer to the casual pattern of ordinary speech? Is the poet's treatment of the subject or attitude toward the reader also casual?

✗ *Check whether the poem is divided into stanzas.*   Does the poet use a traditional stanza such as the four-line ballad stanza or the fourteen-line sonnet? If the first, does the poem have a songlike quality? Does it keep commentary out, ballad-style? Does it use a refrain? With what effect? If the second, does the poem have the ceremonial, carefully crafted quality of the traditional sonnet?

✗ *In a poem using open form, look for features that help give shape to the poem.*   Look for deliberate repetition for emphasis; parallel sentence structure tying together closely related parts of the poem; the echoing of words or phrases; the playing off of opposites.

The following are key sections from the first draft of a student paper that focuses on form and meaning. The comments are feedback from an instructor; they are designed to guide the writer in revising and strengthening the paper. Study the comments, and then see how the student writer has responded to them in the second draft of the paper.

First Draft

New England Discipline

COMMENT   Title too dry or uninformative? Use a title that conveys the spirit of the poem in more dramatic fashion?

In his sonnet, "New England," Edwin Arlington Robinson skillfully employs the powers of form and sound to intensify the meaning of the poem. Robinson fittingly uses the most demanding of poetic forms, the Petrarchan or Italian sonnet, to frame his objection to the New England tradition of emphasizing discipline and self-denial at the expense of love and joy. Robinson himself observes the strict discipline of the traditional fourteen lines, subdivided into octet (first eight lines) and sestet (remaining six lines) . . .

COMMENT   Excellent focus on the central concern of the poem and on its overall intention. To introduce your thesis more effectively, replace the somewhat interchangeable first sentence (it could fit many different poems)? Perhaps start with a striking quotation instead?

The first word of the poem appropriately forms an inversion of the iambic rhythm, a trochee: "Here's where the wind is always north-northeast" focusing the reader's attention quite forcibly on cold New England. The "always north-north-east" wind and the children in the next line who "learn to walk on frozen toes" start out the poem on a distinctly chilly note. New England is cold in more ways than one. Here it is so cold that "Joy shivers in the corner where she knits." Note that in this line the word *joy* forms a spondee with the following word, *shivers,* adding emphasis . . .

COMMENT   Good here and later on how formal features emphasize or highlight meaning. Try to explain more—and demonstrate the workings of the technical features a little more graphically?

Lines three to eight introduce a major contrast. They are like a simmering stew of lush, hothouse words that describe the opposite of traditional New England values—"those / Who boil elsewhere with such a lyric yeast / Of love that you will hear them at a feast / Where demons would appeal for some repose, / Still clamoring where the chalice overflows / And crying wildest who have drunk the least." Here all the bars are down—the words rush by and knock down the structure that contained them. The reader is flooded with a rush of passionate warmth and feeling, which the New Englander can only regard with "wonder [that] begets envy." Robinson has used enjambment to create this effect . . .

COMMENT   A good paragraph. Set off the group of five lines as a block quotation for easier reading (and for added emphasis). Use partial quotes to avoid awkward use of square brackets?

At the end of line eight, the sonnet takes its traditional turn in direction. The excursion into passion ends. The sestet, or concluding six lines, sums up the poet's rebellion against the traditional New England attitude toward life: "Passion here is a soilure of the wits, / We're told, and Love a cross for them to bear," it begins. . . .

Edwin Arlington Robinson, himself a New Englander with deep roots in the Puritan tradition, has written a memorable poem that utilized traditional form very effectively to deepen its message.

COMMENT   Your conclusion, like your introduction, seems too perfunctory and interchangeable. Develop the key point about the poet's own New England roots?

Second Draft

Shivering Joy, Comfortable Conscience

"Joy shivers in the corner where she knits / And conscience always has the rocking chair" (11–12). With such vivid images, Edwin Arlington Robinson in his sonnet "New England" explores the New England values of hard work, moral uprightness, and distrust of emotion. Robinson skillfully employs form and sound to enhance the meaning of the poem.

Fittingly, he uses the most highly disciplined and demanding of poetic forms, the sonnet, to explore and question the New England tradition of rigorous discipline and self-denial at the expense of such human passions as love and joy. Robinson's sonnet observes the traditional discipline of fourteen lines; a variation of the traditional Petrarchan rhyme scheme (abba/abba/cdcdcd); and the traditional iambic pentameter. Ironically, however, the traditional sonnet form here becomes a vehicle for questioning traditional attitudes that restrict the free development of the human spirit.

The very first word of the poem causes an inversion of the iambic rhythm, shifting the stress from the second syllable of the line to the first (a trochee). The first line reads: "*Here's* where | the wind | is all | ways North- | northeast," focusing the reader's attention forcibly on cold New England. The "always North-northeast" wind and the children in the next line who "learn to walk on frozen toes" start out the poem on a distinctly chilly note. The poet's native New England is cold in more ways than one, we are soon to learn. Here it is so cold that "Joy shivers in the corner where she knits" (11). In this line, the word *Joy,* stressed at the beginning of the line, forms a spondee with what would normally be the second and accented syllable of the first iambic foot: "*Joy shiv*|ers in | the cor|ner where | she knits." Several words in that line—*shivers, in, knits*—have the short *i* sound, suggesting smallness or diminution, which is apparently what the strict New Englanders, apprehensive that joy might get out of hand, would desire. And even joy must not sit idly wasting time—she sits in her designated cold corner, knitting, probably warm mittens or woollen socks needed for survival in the chill outdoors.

And now for the polar opposite: Lines 3 to 8 are a simmering stew of lush, hothouse words, describing those

> Who boil elsewhere with such a lyric yeast
> Of love that you will hear them at a feast
> Where demons would appeal for some repose,
> Still clamoring where the chalice overflows
> And crying wildest who have drunk the least. (4–8)

Here all the bars are down: The words rush unrestrainedly, seemingly of their own volition, and knock down the structure that has been carefully erected to contain them. The lines spill over (enjambment), as in "the lyric yeast / of love" (4–5). The reader is flooded with a rush of passionate warmth and feeling, which the New Englander can only regard with wonder that "begets an envy" (3).

At the end of line 8, however, the sonnet takes the traditional turn in direction. The excursion into passion ends. The sestet, or concluding six lines, reaffirms the dominance of a more restrictive view of life. "Passion here is a soilure of the wits, / We're told, and Love a cross for them to bear" (9–10). The key word at the beginning of these lines again is emphasized by trochaic inversion: "*Pas*sion | here is." In these final six lines, everything is again under control, with the thoughts arranged in neat rhyming couplets. Here we see Joy shivering in her corner, while the mistress of the house, Conscience, "always has the rocking chair." Conscience is perversely "cheerful"—note again the emphasis on this unexpected word through trochaic inversion: "*Cheer*ful | as when . . ." (13). She was apparently equally cheerful when she caused the death of the first cat to be killed not, as in the familiar saying, by curiosity but, New England style, by too much worry and care.

Edwin Arlington Robinson was himself a New Englander with deep roots in the Puritan tradition. He was related through his mother to Anne Bradstreet, Puritan

New England's first poet. In this poem, he uses the traditional sonnet form effectively to explore the New England tradition of stressing discipline and distrusting emotion.

Questions

1. Where and how does this student writer show examples of outward form serving as "a mirror to the sense"? How convincing are the examples in this paper?

2. Does this paper seem to capture Robinson's attitude toward the New England tradition? Does the paper seem prejudiced or too negative?

3. Why does the poet's use of traditional form seem ironic to the student writer?

4. When confronted with the polarity explored in this paper, where would you take your stand?

19 Persona

Masks and Faces

All writing is the assumption of a mask, a persona,
an implied author.

DAVID W. SMIT

FOCUS ON PERSONA

Who is speaking to you in a poem? The voice you hear may be different from that of the poet as a person. You may need to distinguish between the poet as a biographical person (whom you could interview and question about the poem) and the "I" addressing you in the poem—the **persona.** The distance between the poet and the persona speaking in the poem varies greatly from poem to poem:

The Personal Dimension   A poet may share with you real-life experiences and personal feelings. You hear the voice of the poet speaking to you as a person, taking you into his or her confidence, the way you might talk to someone you trust in a frank personal letter. A poem may be the poet's ways of working through painful experiences or personal traumas. It may reveal a side of the poet's personality that others might hide from public view. Highly personal poems taking you into the poet's confidence are sometimes called **confessional** poetry.

The Persona as Mask   A poem may present a guarded or edited version of the human being behind the poem. The poet may be revealing to you only one part of his or her personality. Or else the voice speaking in the poem may be an idealized version of the poet-as-a-person. The poet may be speaking to you in a public role, living up to a public image or speaking to you as the voice of a group or a movement. The persona speaking in the poem may be a disguise, a mask—designed to shield the real poet from prying eyes.

The Poet as Observer   A poet may adopt the stance of the detached observer. Many twentieth-century critics have encouraged poets to keep a distance from their material, to maintain an intellectual perspective. They have warned the poet not to be swept away by raw personal emotions.

The Imagined Persona   The persona may be an imaginary character very different from the poet. In the opening lines of a poem by C. K. Williams titled "Hood," a bully speaks to the person he used to bully. Most readers would assume that the poet is identifying not with the booted bully who made teachers and students cringe but with the victim:

> Remember me? I was the one
> In high school you were always afraid of.
> I kept cigarettes in my sleeve, wore
> engineer's boots, long hair, my collar
> up in back and there were always
> girls with me in the hallways.
> You were nothing. I had it in for you—
> when I peeled rubber at the lights
> you cringed like a teacher.

In the concluding lines, the poem enacts the comeuppance of the bully that is a favorite daydream of the people abused:

> And when I crashed and broke both lungs
> on the wheel, you were so relieved
> that you stroked the hard Ford paint
> And your hands shook.

If we remember being bullied ourselves, we are likely to sympathize with the bully's victim. We are likely to share the cringing—and the guilty feeling of relief when the bully crashed. Where is the poet in this poem? Maybe the poet is somewhat of a bully, but more likely the bully is a persona, an assumed identity.

THE AUTOBIOGRAPHICAL "I"

I am not a metaphor or symbol.
This you hear is not the wind in the trees,
Nor a cat being maimed in the street.
It is I being maimed in the street.
    CALVIN C. HERNTON, "THE DISTANT DRUM"

Poets using the **autobiographical "I"** share with us their personal experiences and feelings. The poet takes us into his or her confidence, revealing part of the self that may normally be hidden behind a non-committal façade. We are privileged to look beyond the outer shell that shields people from prying or ridicule. The more autobiographical the poem, the more the person speaking in the poem and the poet who wrote the poem become identical in the reader's mind.

Often an autobiographical poem takes us back to an earlier self. The following poem takes us to a childhood world of thought and feeling.

Rita Dove   *(born 1952)*

Flash Cards   1989

In math I was the whiz kid, keeper
of oranges and apples. *What you don't understand,*
master, my father said; the faster
I answered, the faster they came.
I could see one bud on the teacher's geranium,   5
one clear bee sputtering at the wet pane.
The tulip trees always dragged after heavy rain
so I tucked my head as my boots slapped home.

My father put up his feet after work
and relaxed with a highball and *The Life of Lincoln.*   10
After supper we drilled and I climbed the dark
before sleep, before a thin voice hissed
numbers as I spun on a wheel. I had to guess.
Ten, I kept saying, *I'm only ten.*

The Receptive Reader

1. Do you think this poem is based on the poet's real-life experience? Why or why not?

2. What lifelike details make the speaker's childhood experience real for you as the reader?

3. Why or how does the speaker in the poem spin "on a wheel" in her sleep? What gives a special twist to the number she keeps saying in her sleep?

4. Do you consider the experience that this poem reenacts a positive or a negative experience?

5. What kind of person do you think the poet is?

In classical Greece, the nine Muses were quasi-divine beings who inspired poets, musicians, historians, and followers of the other arts and sciences. The philosopher Plato called Sappho "the tenth Muse," and many Greeks considered her their most outstanding lyric poet. She lived on the island of Lesbos and is thought to have run a school for women there. Bookburners of a later age destroyed most of her poems but not her legendary reputation. A few whole poems and fragments of others survive. Gay women still call themselves lesbians in her honor.

Sappho   *(about 620–550 B.C.)*

Letter to Anaktoria   *sixth century* B.C.

TRANSLATED BY RICHMOND LATTIMORE

Like the very gods in my sight is he who
sits where can look in your eyes, who listens
close to you, to hear the soft voice, its sweetness
     murmur in love and

laughter, all for him. But it breaks my spirit;   5
underneath my breath all the heart is shaken.
Let me only glance where you are, the voice dies,
     I can say nothing,

but my lips are stricken to silence, under-
neath my skin the tenuous flame suffuses;   10
nothing shows in front of my eyes, my ears are
     muted in thunder.

And the sweat running upon me, fever
shakes my body, paler I turn than grass is;
I can feel that I have been changed, I feel that   15
     death has come near me.

The Receptive Reader
What kind of person is speaking in this poem? What is the situation? What are the mixed emotions the speaker feels toward the two people in this poem? Do her feelings seem strange or familiar? How would you expect to react to a poem written 2,500 years ago? How do you react to this poem?

The Creative Dimension
Write a poem or prose passage that re-creates what for you is the dominant emotion in this poem.

Intensely personal poetry often seems like a catharsis—a cleansing or purifying of painful memories and passionate grievances. In recent decades, minority authors have made the majority listen to the voices of those that Martin Luther King, Jr., called the "unheard." The following poem speaks for young Native Americans taken from their families to be made over in the white man's image. Of German and Chippewa heritage, the poet relives her experience with the forced assimilation of young people denied pride in their own past.

Louise Erdrich   *(born 1954)*

Indian Boarding School: The Runaways   *1984*

Home's the place we head for in our sleep.
Boxcars stumbling north in dreams
don't wait for us. We catch them on the run.
The rails, old lacerations that we love,
soot parallel across the face and break   5
just under Turtle Mountains. Riding scars
you can't get lost. Home is the place they cross.
The lame guard strikes a match and makes the dark
less tolerant. We watch through cracks in boards
as the land starts rolling, rolling till it hurts   10
to be here, cold in regulation clothes.
We know the sheriff's waiting at midrun
to take us back. His car is dumb and warm.
The highway doesn't rock, it only hums
like a wing of long insults. The worn-down welts   15
of ancient punishments lead back and forth.

All runaways wear dresses, long green ones,
the color you would think shame was. We scrub
the sidewalks down because it's shameful work.
Our brushes cut the stone in watered arcs   20
and in the soak frail outlines shiver clear
a moment, things us kids pressed on the dark
face before it hardened, pale, remembering
delicate old injuries, the spines of names and leaves.

The Receptive Reader

1. To you, does the poem seem like intensely felt *personal experience* or like an imaginary situation vividly imagined? If pressed to explain your answer, what would you say?

2. What *assumptions* about reservation life and Indian schools do you bring to this poem? How does this poem change or challenge them?

3. What is the *situation* of the runaways? What do they think, feel, and remember?

4. In this poem, much of what you see—the railroad tracks, the highway, work, a color—takes on *symbolic* significance. Where and how?

The Personal Response

When you read this poem, are you looking at the young runaways from the outside? Do you identify with the "we" speaking in the poem? Why or why not?

The speaker in the following poem shared the experience of young Japanese Americans who were confined with their parents in the Tule Lake relocation camp during World War II.

Janice Mirikitani   *(born 1938)*

For My Father

He came over the ocean
carrying Mt. Fuji on
his back/Tule Lake on his chest
hacked through the brush
of deserts   5
and made them grow
strawberries

     we stole berries
     from the stem
     we could not afford them   10
     for breakfast

his eyes held
nothing
as he whipped us
for stealing.   15

the desert had dried
his soul.

wordless
he sold
the rich,   20
full berries
to hakujin°   *white people*
whose children
pointed at our eyes

     they ate fresh   25
     strawberries
     on corn flakes.

Father,
i wanted to scream
at your silence.   30
Your strength
was a stranger
i could never touch.

iron
in your eyes   35
to shield
the pain
to shield desert-like wind
from patches

of strawberries   40
grown
from
tears.

The Receptive Reader

1. What details in the poem remind you of the poet's Japanese-American ancestry?

2. What is the story of the poet's father? What are the daughter's feelings about him? Do you come to understand him?

3. How do the strawberries serve as a central *symbol* in this poem?

THE PUBLIC PERSONA

The age
requires this task:
create
a different image;
re-animate
the mask.
        DUDLEY RANDALL

The "I" we hear in a poem may be speaking to us as the voice of a group, a commitment, or a cause. The editorial *we* may replace the singular *I*. It is as if the poet were speaking to us in an official capacity, assuming a public persona. Dylan Thomas was a Welsh poet whose chanting voice and powerful, cryptic poems converted a generation of listeners and readers to the cause of poetry. In the following poem, he speaks of his mission as a poet with a grand sweep, without diffidence or self-doubt. The persona he assumes in the poem is that of the charismatic bard, dramatizing and glorifying the poet's calling.

Dylan Thomas   *(1914–1953)*

In My Craft or Sullen Art   *1946*

In my craft or sullen art
Exercised in the still night
When only the moon rages
And the lovers lie abed
With all their griefs in their arms,   5
I labor by singing light
Not for ambition or bread
Or the strut and trade of charms
On the ivory stages

But for the common wages   10
Of their most secret heart.

Not for the proud man apart
From the raging moon I write
On these spindrift° pages   *sea spray*
Nor for the towering dead   15
With their nightingales and psalms
But for the lovers, their arms
Round the griefs of the ages,
Who pay no praise or wages
Nor heed my craft or art.   20

The Receptive Reader

1. Dylan Thomas's poetry was shot through with bold, provocative *metaphors*. Why or how could his art be "sullen," and what could he mean by "singing light"? How does he use metaphorically *bread, strut, ivory, common wages, spindrift pages, towering dead?*

2. Where and how often does the central word *art* appear in the poem, and with what effect? What other key word rhymes with it, and where in the poem? Why is *wages* also a key word in the poem? Where does it appear, and how many rhymes help it echo through the poem?

3. What is the *symbolic* role of the moon in this poem?

4. With what *tone* should this poem be read? What kind of person do you imagine the poet to be?

Among poets who have seen themselves as the conscience of their time, Walt Whitman created for himself a persona as the voice of a new continent and a new nation. In many of his poems, he is speaking to us as the prophet of the new American democracy. The following poem, a part of his *Song of Myself,* shows the kind of **empathy**—sharing the feelings of others—that could make him say, "I am the hounded slave," and "I do not ask the wounded person how he feels, I myself become the wounded person."

Walt Whitman   *(1819–1892)*

I Understand the Large Hearts of Heroes   *1855*

I understand the large hearts of heroes.
The courage of present times and all times,
How the skipper saw the crowded and rudderless wreck of the steamship,
    and Death chasing it up and down the storm,
How he knuckled tight and gave not back an inch, and was faithful of
    days and faithful of nights,
And chalked in large letters on a board, "Be of good cheer, we will not   5
    desert you";

How he followed with them and tacked with them three days and would
  not give it up,
How he saved the drifting company at last,
How the lank loose-gowned women looked when boated from the side of
  their prepared graves,
How the silent old-faced infants and the lifted sick, and the sharp-lipped
  unshaved men;
All this I swallow, it tastes good, I like it well, it becomes mine,   10
I am the man, I suffered, I was there.

The Receptive Reader

1. Whitman was fascinated with *people*—how they looked and talked and
moved, whether in developing the continent or in the agonies of civil war. What
striking, revealing details make this account of shipwreck and rescue come to
life for the reader?

2. What kind of *person* is speaking to you in this poem? Whitman has at
times been accused of striking heroic poses. Do you think he is sincere in this
poem? Why or why not?

Today, eloquent voices speak to us in the name of a larger group.
They help formulate a changed consciousness, a new sense of group
identity. They may speak for women in search of a new self-image.
They may speak for minority groups proud of their heritage. The following poem is by an American poet of West Indian descent who has
said that she speaks not only for the woman who inhabits her physical
self but "for all those feisty incorrigible black women who insist on
standing up and saying, 'I *am* and you cannot wipe me out, no matter
how irritating I am, how much you fear what I might represent.'"

Audre Lorde   *(1934–1992)*

Coal   1976

I
is the total black, being spoken
from the earth's inside.
There are many kinds of open
how a diamond comes into a knot of flame   5
how sound comes into a word, colored
by who pays what for speaking.

Some words are open like a diamond
on glass windows
singing out within the passing crash of sun.   10
Then there are words like stapled wagers
in a perforated book,—buy and sign and tear apart—
and come whatever wills all chances

the stub remains
an ill-pulled tooth with a ragged edge.   15
Some words live in my throat
breeding like adders. Others know sun
seeking like gypsies over my tongue
to explode through my lips
like young sparrows bursting from shell.   20
Some words
bedevil me.

Love is a word, another kind of open.
As the diamond comes into a knot of flame
I am Black because I come from the earth's inside   25
now take my word for jewel in the open light.

The Receptive Reader

1. Look at the bold provocative *metaphors* and *similes* in this poem. What is their meaning? What role do they play in the poem?

2. The word *open* becomes a key word in this poem. What role does it play? What meanings and associations cluster around it?

3. Some earlier black poets used a formal literary language, avoiding all echoes of *black English*. How is this poem different? What is the effect on the reader?

4. Who is the collective *I* speaking in this poem? What kind of collective self-image takes shape in this poem?

Making Connections—For Discussion or Writing

Compare and contrast the two poems by Whitman and Lorde. How do the two poets compare as voices of social awareness? How do they shape our self-image as members of society, as socially responsible beings?

IMAGINED SELVES

Aye! I am a poet and upon my tomb
Shall maidens scatter rose leaves
And men myrtles, ere the night
Slays day with her dark sword.
                                                        EZRA POUND

Sometimes the voice speaking in a poem is clearly distant or separate from the poet's autobiographical self. The "I" speaking may be an imaginary or historical character who has a special fascination for the poet. We may sense a special affinity or attraction, as we do in the following poem about Cassandra, the mad Trojan princess and priestess, who in the ancient Greek poems and plays about the siege of Troy speaks as the voice of impending doom. In her prophetic visions, Cassandra saw her native city in flames, with its towers crashing down. She also prophesied that Agamemnon, the Greek commander who carried her off as part of the spoils of war, would be murdered on his return to Greece by his wife and her lover.

Louise Bogan   *(1897–1970)*

Cassandra   *1968*

To me, one silly task is like another.
I bare the shambling tricks of lust and pride.
This flesh will never give a child its mother—
Song, like a wing, tears through my breast, my side,
And madness chooses out my voice again,   5
Again. I am the chosen no hand saves:
The shrieking heaven lifted over men,
Not the dumb earth, wherein they set their graves.

The Receptive Reader

1. What do you think is the special attraction the character of Cassandra had for the author as a woman and as a poet? What might make the legendary character a kind of *alter ego* for her—a "second self" or counterpart?

2. Why is it strange or contradictory that this poem should have a neat regular rhyme scheme and underlying iambic meter? Is it a coincidence that the word *again,* repeated at the beginning of the sixth line, breaks up the pattern of neatly marked off lines as it pulls us over into the new line?

What is the role the poet imagines for herself in the following poem? When Hitler drove many German artists and writers into exile, others, including this poet, went through a period of "emigration to the interior"—staying in Germany while trying to live intellectually and spiritually outside the mentality of the Nazi era. She was much honored by the West German literary establishment after the war. The following poem shows her affinity with an active women's movement in Germany.

Marie Luise Kaschnitz   *(1901–1974)*

Women's Program   *1972*

TRANSLATED BY LISEL MÜLLER

I give a talk on the radio
Toward morning when no one is listening
I offer my recipes

Pour milk into the telephone
Let your cats sleep   5

In the dishwashers
Smash the clocks in your washing machines
Leave your shoes behind

Season your peaches with paprika
And your soup meat with honey   10
Teach your children the alphabet of foxes
Turn the leaves in your gardens silver side up
Take the advice of the owl

When summer arrives put on your furs
Go meet the ones with the bagpipes   15
Who come from inside the mountains
Leave your shoes behind

Don't be too sure
Evening will come
Don't be too sure   20
That God loves you.

The Receptive Reader

1. What kind of person is speaking in this poem? (How close do you think the poet's personality is to the *persona* in the poem?)

2. What is the point and the motivation of the subversive advice given in this poem? (Does any of it seem particularly strange or particularly sensible?)

3. Where and how does the poet *allude* to the story of the Pied Piper of Hamlin? How does her use of the story depart from what you might expect?

In some poems, we listen to a **dramatic monologue,** or lengthy first-person speech, as it might be delivered by a character in a play. The best-known author of dramatic monologues is the English nineteenth-century poet Robert Browning, who lived for a time in Italy after eloping with his fellow poet Elizabeth Barrett, the semi-invalid daughter of a domineering father. In many of his monologues, we listen as artists, scholars, church dignitaries, or aristocrats of the Italian Renaissance reveal to us their ambitions and aspirations—or, as in the following poem, their passions and hidden motives. In the poem that follows, we listen to a sixteenth-century Duke of Ferrara whose last duchess died young and who is now talking to a representative of another aristocratic family about a second marriage.

Robert Browning   *(1812–1889)*

My Last Duchess   *1842*
Ferrara

That's my last duchess painted on the wall,
Looking as if she were alive. I call

That piece a wonder, now: Frà Pandolf's° hands   *Brother Pandolf's*
Worked busily a day, and there she stands.   *(a monk or friar)*
Will 't please you sit and look at her? I said   5
"Frà Pandolf" by design,° for never read   *on purpose*
Strangers like you that pictured countenance,°   *face*
The depth and passion of its earnest glance,
But to myself they turned (since none puts by
The curtain I have drawn for you, but I)   10
And seemed as they would ask me, if they durst,°   *dared*
How such a glance came there; so, not the first
Are you to turn and ask thus. Sir, 't was not
Her husband's presence only, called° that spot   *that called*
Of joy into the Duchess' cheek: perhaps   15
Frà Pandolf chanced to say "Her mantle laps
Over my lady's wrist too much," or "Paint
Must never hope to reproduce the faint
Half-flush that dies along her throat": such stuff
Was courtesy, she thought, and cause enough   20
For calling up that spot of joy. She had
A heart—how shall I say?—too soon made glad,
Too easily impressed; she liked whate'er
She looked on, and her looks went everywhere.
Sir, 't was all one! My favor° at her breast,   *love token*   25
The dropping of the daylight in the west,
The bough of cherries some officious° fool   *eager to serve*
Broke in the orchard for her, the white mule
She rode with round the terrace—all and each
Would draw from her alike the approving speech,   30
Or blush, at least. She thanked men—good! but thanked
Somehow—I know not how—as if she ranked
My gift of a nine-hundred-years-old name
With anybody's gift. Who'd stoop to blame
This sort of trifling? Even had you° skill   *if you had*   35
In speech—which I have not—to make your will
Quite clear to such an one, and say, "Just this
Or that in you disgusts me; here you miss,
Or there exceed the mark"—and if she let
Herself be lessoned so, nor plainly set   40
Her wit to yours, forsooth,° and made excuse   *in truth*
—E'en then would be some stooping; and I choose
Never to stoop. Oh sir, she smiled, no doubt,
Whene'er I passed her, but who passed without
Much the same smile? This grew; I gave commands;   45
Then all smiles stopped together. There she stands
As if alive. Will 't please you rise? We'll meet
The company below, then. I repeat,
The Count your master's known munificence°   *generosity*
Is ample warrant° that no just pretense°   *guarantee/demand*   50
Of mine for dowry will be disallowed;

Though his fair daughter's self, as I avowed
At starting, is my object. Nay, we'll go
Together down, sir. Notice Neptune, though,
Taming a sea-horse, thought a rarity,   55
Which Claus of Innsbruck cast in bronze for me.

The Receptive Reader

1. What is the *situation?* Where in the poem did you first suspect what happened to the duchess? When were you sure?

2. To judge from this monologue by her husband, what was the duchess like as a *person?* What was her offense? Do you consider her a frivolous or superficial person?

3. What is the key to the *persona* created by Browning in this poem? What is the duke's problem? Why didn't he explain how he felt to the duchess?

4. What is strange about the duke's speaking in a relaxed, polite conversational *tone?* Is it in keeping with his character? Many of his sentences start in the middle of a line and spill over into the next. (The technical term for this effect is *enjambment*—from the French word for "straddling.") How does the straddling effect contribute to the conversational tone?

5. What public persona has the duke created for himself—what *image* does he present to the world? (The Italian Renaissance was a golden age of the creative arts. What is the role of art in this poem?)

The Personal Response

Has the duke's mentality become extinct with the passing of the aristocratic society of his time? Do you think there could be any modern parallels to his mindset and behavior?

POEMS FOR FURTHER STUDY

In reading the following poems, pay special attention to questions like the following: Who is speaking? What kind of voice do you hear in the poem? What is the persona or assumed identity? How much distance do think there is between the persona and the person behind the poem?

Yusef Komunyakaa   *(born 1947)*

My Father's Love Letters   *1993*

On Fridays he'd open a can of Jax
After coming home from the mill,
& ask me to write a letter to my mother
Who sent postcards of desert flowers
Taller than men. He would beg,   5

Promising to never beat her
Again. Somehow I was happy
She had gone, & sometimes wanted
To slip in a reminder, how Mary Lou
Williams' "Polka Dots & Moonbeams"   10
Never made the swelling go down.
His carpenter's apron always bulged
With old nails, a claw hammer
Looped at his side & extension cords
Coiled around his feet.   15
Words rolled from under the pressure
Of my ballpoint: Love,
Baby, Honey, Please.
We sat in the quiet brutality
Of voltage meters & pipe threaders,   20
Lost between sentences . . .
The gleam of a five-pound wedge
On the concrete floor
Pulled a sunset
Through the doorway of his toolshed.   25
I wondered if she laughed
& held them over a gas burner.
My father could only sign
His name, but he'd look at blueprints
& say how many bricks   30
Formed each wall. This man,
Who stole rose & hyacinth
For his yard, would stand there
With eyes closed & fists balled,
Laboring over a simple word, almost   35
Redeemed by what he tried to say.

The Receptive Reader

1. What is the portrait of the father that emerges from this poem? What is his history? What is his problem, or what are his problems?

2. What are the son's mixed feelings or contradictory emotions about the father? Are the son's memories of the father completely negative?

Countee Cullen   *(1903–1946)*

Saturday's Child   *1925*

Some are teethed on a silver spoon,
With the stars strung for a rattle;
I cut my teeth as the black raccoon—
For implements of battle.

Some are swaddled in silk and down,   5
And heralded by a star;
They swathed my limbs in a sackcloth gown
On a night that was black as tar.

For some godfather and goddame°   *godmother*
The opulent° fairies be;   *living richly*   10
Dame Poverty gave me my name,
And Pain godfathered me.

For I was born on Saturday—
"Bad time for planting a seed,"
Was all my father had to say,   15
And, "One more mouth to feed."

Death cut the strings that gave me life,
And handed me to Sorrow,
The only kind of middle wife
My folks could beg or borrow.   20

The Receptive Reader

1. How do the stanza form and rhyme scheme help the poet line up the *opposites* that give shape to the poem as a whole?

2. What is the role of *personified abstractions* in this poem? (How did "Death cut the strings that gave me life"?)

3. What is the *persona* the poet creates for himself in this poem? How close do you think it is to the poet's real-life personality?

Denise Levertov   *(1923–1997)*

In Mind   *1964*

There's in my mind a woman
of innocence, unadorned but

fair-featured, and smelling of
apples or grass. She wears

a utopian smock or shift, her hair   5
is light brown and smooth, and she

is kind and very clean without
ostentation—
            but she has
no imagination.   10
            And there's a
turbulent moon-ridden girl

or old woman or both
dressed in opals and rags, feathers

and torn taffeta.   15
and who knows strange songs—

but she is not kind.

The Receptive Reader

Do you recognize the two different personalities in this poem? What are their
virtues and shortcomings? (Are they polar opposites?) Do you think two such
different personalities could dwell in the same mind?

Sylvia Plath   *(1932–1963)*

Mirror   *1961*

I am silver and exact. I have no preconceptions.
Whatever I see I swallow immediately
Just as it is, unmisted by love or dislike.
I am not cruel, only truthful—
The eye of a little god, four-cornered.   5
Most of the time I meditate on the opposite wall.
It is pink, with speckles. I have looked at it so long
I think it is a part of my heart. But it flickers.
Faces and darkness separate us over and over.
Now I am a lake. A woman bends over me,   10
Searching my reaches for what she really is.
Then she turns to those liars, the candles or the moon.
I see her back, and reflect it faithfully.
She rewards me with tears and an agitation of hands.
I am important to her. She comes and goes.   15
Each morning it is her face that replaces the darkness.
In me she has drowned a young girl, and in me an old woman
Rises toward her like a terrible fish.

The Receptive Reader

1. What touches early in the poem might make the mirror sound like a curious observer—with a limited or even naive perspective and no evil intentions?
(How is the mirror like the eye of a god—and why of "a little god"?)

2. How does the lake metaphor make the mirror seem more knowing and
more threatening? Why or how would "candles or the moon" be more likely to
prove liars than the mirror?

3. Do you think the mirror is cruel? Do you think the poet is being cruel?
Where is the poet in this poem?

The Creative Dimension

What story would your own mirror tell if it could speak?

Making Connections—For Discussion or Writing

Several poems in this chapter (as well as in other parts of this book) are the record of a poet exploring her identity as a woman or embarked on a search for self. Study several such poems, looking for shared themes, recurrent issues, or similar perspectives.

WRITING ABOUT LITERATURE

19　*Playing the Role (Imitation and Parody)*

The Writing Workshop　Poets with an especially unmistakable style seem to invite imitation. Their poems seem to cry out for **parody**—an imitation that lovingly or mockingly exaggerates characteristic traits. The poetry of Robert Browning has been much imitated and much parodied. What features of the original did the student capture who wrote the following dramatic monologue?

My Last Essay

That's my last essay pinned up on the wall,
Looking as if it's not survived. I call
That piece a wonder, now! Jim Bello's hand
Worked busily an hour, and thus its state.
Will 't please you stay and read of it? I said
"Jim Bello" by design, for never saw
Strangers like you such tattered manuscript
But to myself they turned in stunned surprise
And seemed as they would ask me, if they durst,
How such red marks came there; so not the first
Are you to turn and ask thus. Nay, 't was not
Just split infinitives that roused his ire—
"Support unclear," he muttered through his teeth
In reference to my cherished prose. He had
A mind—how shall I say?—too soon made mad,
Too easily overcome; he slashed what words
He looked on, and his looks went everywhere!
Yes, 't was all one. My pronoun reference fault,
Verb disagreement, too—and "Comma splice!"
So, friend you see my tattered work displayed,
Defiled with red disgracefully, I know.
But I retyped it, and the ms sold
To Murdoch's tabloid for an even thou'.
You caught that issue? Thanks!

A parody is a close imitation with a humorous twist, exaggerating characteristic features of the original. A parody may be gently spoofing, but it may also be cruel, holding up to ridicule what is overdone or outdated in its target. To parody something well takes a quick ear and careful attention. The following stanza is from a flip poem (written in 1601) by a would-be lover. The next stanza is from a student-written parody written almost four hundred years later.

> I care not for these ladies,
> That must be wooed and prayed:
> Give me kind Amaryllis,
> The wanton country maid.
>> Her when we court and kiss,
>> She cries, "Forsooth, let go!"
>> But when we come where comfort is,
>> She never will say no.
>>> Thomas Campion

The student who wrote the following rejoinder had a good ear, and she gets well into the spirit of the original poem:

> They care not for us ladies
> That want to be loved and pursued.
> They care for Amaryllis
> Who is impure and crude.
>> 'Cause when men seek a kiss,
>> Her cries have just begun.
>> No longer can she resist;
>> She pleads for more than one.
>>> Sharee Pearson, "Ladies"

20 Tone

The Language of the Emotions

*The poet sheds his blood in the ring and calls the
pools poems.*

GEORGE BARKER

FOCUS ON TONE

Poetry is an education in the language of the emotions. In the poet's
language, as in ordinary language, much of the message is in the **tone.**
Live language has a human coloring that conveys the feelings, attitudes,
and intentions of the speaker. "It's you again!" may be said in a tone of
welcome ("It's you again—how wonderful!"). But it may also be said in
a tone of disappointment ("It's you again—of all people!"). Tone in
poetry runs the gamut of human attitudes and emotions.

The Elegiac Tone   Much early poetry was poetry of mourning. Poets
lamented the death of heroes or the passing of the good things of
this earth. Chronicling the campaigns and voyages of his Bronze Age
warriors, Homer shows them weeping for their dead comrades. Walt
Whitman sets a mournful tone in the opening lines of his great **elegy**
on the death of President Lincoln:

> When lilacs last in the dooryard bloomed,
> And the great star early drooped in the western sky in the night,
> I mourned, and yet shall mourn with ever-returning spring.

Religious Poetry   Religious poetry through the ages has sung the
grandeur of God. The poet may speak in a tone of solemn religious
awe, as the seventeenth-century poet Henry Vaughan does in the opening lines of his poem "The World":

> I saw eternity the other night
> Like a great ring of pure and endless light,
>   All calm as it was bright;

And round beneath it, Time, in hours, days, years,
  Driven by the spheres,
Like a vast shadow moved, in which the world
  And all her train were hurled.

The Voice of Passion   In much traditional love poetry, the poet's emotional thermostat is set high, with the poem giving voice to yearning, ecstasy, or despair. Romantic love celebrates love as an overwhelming passion, promising fulfillment, giving meaning to otherwise meaningless lives. "How Do I Love Thee?" asked Elizabeth Barrett Browning in 1845.

I love thee with a love I seemed to lose
With my lost saints—I love thee with the breath,
Smiles, tears, of all my life!—and, if God choose,
I shall but love thee better after death.

The Ironic Counterpoint   Much of the best-known modern poetry has had an irreverent ironic tone. It has opted for dry wit or cool detachment rather than for an outpouring of emotion. Whenever something seems too beautiful to be true, we seem prepared for the ironic counterpoint. We seem ready for the revenge of reality on rosy projections. The following concluding stanza from a poem by Sylvia Plath is well attuned to the modern temper:

Droll, vegetarian, the water rat
Saws down a reed and swims from his limber grove,
While the students stroll or sit,
Hands laced, in a moony indolence° of love—   *carefree laziness*
Black-gowned, but unaware
How in such mild air
The owl shall stoop from his turret,° the rat   *small tower jutting from a castle*
  cry out.

The first few words of this stanza already hint at an unusual perspective: the water rat (which we might expect to be repulsive) is described as "droll"—amusing in a harmless, eccentric way—and "vegetarian," as if watching its health like a fellow human. The rat provides an ironic underside to the idyllic college setting where students stroll lazily in the "mild air," absorbed in moony thoughts of young love. They are ironically unaware of the life-and-death drama played out as the owl swoops down on the harmless-seeming, amusing rat. When we least suspect it, evil lurks, ready to strike and make us "cry out."

THE REGISTER OF EMOTIONS

Forgive me that I pitch your praise too low.
Such reticence my reverence demands.
For silence falls with laying on of hands.
Forgive me that my words come thin and slow.
        JOHN WAIN, "APOLOGY FOR UNDERSTATEMENT"

    Poems vary greatly in emotional intensity. Traditionally, poetry has been the voice of passion: the joy of mutual love and the sorrow of separation. Much twentieth-century poetry has been more sparing in its expression of emotions. Poets have tended to understate rather than to overstate their feelings. The following poem about a dream recalls more violent emotions than we encounter in much other modern poetry.

Louise Bogan   *(1897–1970)*

The Dream   *1941*

O God, in the dream the terrible horse began
To paw at the air, and make for me with his blows.
Fear kept for thirty-five years poured through his mane,
And retribution equally old, or nearly, breathed through his nose.

Coward complete, I lay and wept on the ground   5
When some strong creature appeared, and leapt for the rein.
Another woman, as I lay half in a swound°   *fainting fit*
Leapt in the air, and clutched at the leather and chain.

Give him, she said, something of yours as a charm.
Throw him, she said, some poor thing you alone claim.   10
No, no, I cried, he hates me; he's out for harm,
And whether I yield or not, it is all the same.

But, like a lion in a legend, when I flung the glove
Pulled from my sweating, my cold right hand,
The terrible beast, that no one may understand,   15
Came to my side, and put down his head in love.

The Receptive Reader

    1. What is the *prevailing tone* in this poem? What kind of a dream are you asked to share? What words and phrases openly label emotion? What images help project it? How many words refer to violent motion?

    2. How is this poem like a legend or *fairy tale?*

    3. How did you expect the poem to *end?* How did you react to the ending?

    4. Do you think that in our dreams emotions surface that we tend to subdue or suppress in our waking life?

The Personal Response
What nightmares, if any, do you have? Have they changed over the years?

Through the centuries, poets have celebrated romantic love as an overwhelming passion, carrying all before it. Poets in this tradition were given to **hyperbole**—frank overstatement, praising the angelic beauty of the beloved, idealizing the devotion of the lover. Many of Shakespeare's sonnets use the heightened, exalted language of idealized love.

William Shakespeare   *(1564–1616)*

Sonnet 18   *before 1598*

Shall I compare thee to a summer's day?	
Thou art more lovely and more temperate:	
Rough winds do shake the darling buds of May,	
And summer's lease hath all too short a date:°	*time span*
Sometimes too hot the eye of heaven shines,	5
And often is his gold complexion dimmed;	
And every fair° from fair sometimes declines,	*everything lovely*
By chance or nature's changing course untrimmed;°	*undone*
But thy eternal summer shall not fade,	
Nor lose possession of that fair thou owst;°	*you own* 10
Nor shall death brag thou wanderst in his shade,	
When in eternal lines° to time thou growst:	*lines of verse*
So long as men can breathe, or eyes can see,	
So long lives this, and this gives life to thee.	

The Receptive Reader
1. How does this sonnet employ *hyperbole?* (How, in fact, does it go hyperbole one better?) Normally, to compare the beloved to the days of early summer or to the dazzling beauty of the glorious sun would be considered high praise. Why does the poet consider these comparisons inadequate?

2. Sometimes the final six lines (the **sestet**) and sometimes the final couplet provide a major "turning" in a sonnet. Which is it here? What answer does this poem give to the questions raised earlier?

Early in the twentieth century, the richer chords of much traditional poetry began to give way to the sparer, understated tone that became the modern idiom. **Understatement** makes the poet play down personal feelings, letting the images of a poem speak for themselves. The following is an understated modern poem that lets a thought-provoking, disturbing incident speak for itself.

William Stafford   *(1914–1992)*

Traveling through the Dark   *1960*

Traveling through the dark I found a deer
dead on the edge of the Wilson River road.
It is usually best to roll them into the canyon:
that road is narrow; to swerve might make more dead.

By glow of the tail-light I stumbled back of the car   5
and stood by the heap, a doe, a recent killing;
she had stiffened already, almost cold.
I dragged her off; she was large in the belly.

My fingers touching the side brought me the reason—
her side was warm; her fawn lay there waiting,   10
alive, still, never to be born.
Beside that mountain road I hesitated.

The car aimed ahead its lowered parking lights;
under the hood purred the steady engine.
I stood in the glare of the warm exhaust turning red;   15
around our group I could hear the wilderness listen.

I thought hard for us all—my only swerving—
then pushed her over the edge into the river.

    This poem starts on a dry, matter-of-fact note: the deer is dead; the
road is narrow; best "to roll them into the canyon" to prevent further
accidents. But the side of the killed deer is still warm; she is large with
a fawn, "alive, still, never to be born." The speaker in the poem hesitates, but only for a time. Then he does the right thing. What are the
poet's feelings? Maybe the poet is sick at heart at the thought of a mindless machine barreling down the highway to destroy one of God's creatures. However, the poem does not say. We can "hear the wilderness
listen," and we also listen. But we hear no expressions of protest or
grief; the only sound we hear is the motor of the automobile "purring"
steadily in the background. Whatever he may feel, the speaker in the
poem does not wave his arms or shout "I hate you!" at the universe. We
know he "thought hard for us all." As one student reader said, "for a
brief moment, he makes us think of the impossible task of saving the
fawn." He hesitates for a time—that was his "only swerving" from acting
businesslike and sensible. We as readers are left to wrestle with the traumatic event.

The Receptive Reader

    1. Some readers have found the title of the poem to have more than a sim-
ple descriptive or factual significance. What could be its *symbolic* meaning?
    2. What details or phrases for you do most to *set the tone* of the poem?

3. Do you think the poet felt emotions that the poem does not express? Do you think he *should* have expressed them?

The Personal Response

Do you think different readers would react differently to this poem? How much depends on the reader's experience with similar situations and on the reader's mind-set or personality?

Poems may reflect a mood of fatalistic acceptance but also a mood of rebellion or defiance. Departing from the prevailing mode of wry understatement, the Welsh poet Dylan Thomas found a large audience for chanting, intensely emotional poems like the following:

Dylan Thomas   *(1914–1953)*

Do Not Go Gentle into That Good Night   *1952*

Do not go gentle into that good night,
Old age should burn and rave at close of day;
Rage, rage against the dying of the light.

Though wise men at their end know dark is right,
Because their words had forked no lightning they   5
Do not go gentle into that good night.

Good men, the last wave by, crying how bright
Their frail deeds might have danced in a green bay,
Rage, rage against the dying of the light.

Wild men who caught and sang the sun in flight,   10
And learn too late, they grieved it on its way,
Do not go gentle into that good night.

Grave men, near death, who see with blinding sight
Blind eyes could blaze like meteors and be gay,
Rage, rage against the dying of the light.   15

And you, my father, there on the sad height,
Curse, bless, me now with your fierce tears, I pray.
Do not go gentle into that good night.
Rage, rage against the dying of the light.

The Receptive Reader

1. How is the tone in this poem *different* from what you might expect in a poem about death?

2. The speaker in the poem does not address his own father directly till the *last stanza* of the poem. How does this last stanza affect your response to the poem? (How do you think your response to the poem might have been different if the father had been brought into the poem at the beginning?)

3. Thomas attracted a large following in the thirties and forties by writing with passionate intensity about the experiences of *ordinary people*. In this poem, what are striking examples of his writing about ordinary experience in heightened, intensely emotional language? How much of the heightened, passionate quality of his verse results from the playing off of extreme *opposites?*

4. This poem uses the traditional form of the *villanelle,* a set of three-line stanzas repeating the same rhyme scheme (aba), which is further reinforced by a fourth line added to the concluding stanza (rhyming abaa). What are the two opposed key words in the poem that the rhyme scheme keeps driving home? Two final lines alternate in the stanzas until they are juxtaposed in the concluding couplet. Why is this kind of insistent *repetition* more appropriate to Thomas's poem than it would be to a poem written in a more understated style?

The Personal Response

If wise men know that in the end "dark is right," is the "rage" the poet calls up futile? (Is it impious?)

Some of the earliest known poems are poems of mourning and lamentation. Like the following modern elegy, traditional elegies do not always maintain the same note of bitterness to the end. They often work their way through bitter grief to calm acceptance or to the joyful certainty of resurrection. How does the following poem come to terms with loss?

N. Scott Momaday   *(born 1934)*

Earth and I Gave You Turquoise   *1974*

Earth and I gave you turquoise
   when you walked singing
We lived laughing in my house
   and told old stories
You grew ill when the owl cried   5
We will meet on Black Mountain

I will bring corn for planting
   and we will make fire
Children will come to your breast
   You will heal my heart   10
I speak your name many times
The wild cane remembers you

My young brother's house is filled
   I go there to sing
We have not spoken of you   15
   but our songs are sad
When Moon Woman goes to you
I will follow her white way

Tonight they dance near Chinle
    by the seven elms 20
There your loom whispered beauty
    They will eat mutton
and drink coffee till morning
You and I will not be there

I saw a crow by Red Rock 25
    standing on one leg
It was the black of your hair
    The years are heavy
I will ride the swiftest horse
You will hear the drumming hooves 30

The Receptive Reader

Although Momaday places his poem in the setting of the tribal past, it speaks a language that transcends time and place. Which of the images and statements in the poem do most to help you share the speaker's emotions? Which do most to help you place yourself in the speaker's place? How does the speaker deal with his grief?

The Creative Dimension

The following re-creation captures the elegiac tone of Momaday's poem. For this or another poem in this chapter, do a similar re-creation that captures the tone of the original.

> We walked the earth together
> In my house we danced and drank coffee till morning
> I planted corn
> You wanted children
> But you became ill
> I thought love could heal you
> The years drag
> I'll dance no more
> But one day I'll speak your name
> And you'll come on a swift horse

THE USES OF IRONY

Snowy egrets stand
graceful, majestic, serene
among the beer cans
STUDENT HAIKU

Some poets filter out what is ugly or disappointing in life. Filtered poetry is like a portrait photographer who airbrushes blemishes, frowns, and signs of age. We are flattered by the retouched picture, but we know it tells only part of the truth. Many modern poets take naturally to irony as a way of bringing in a neglected or ignored part of the story. **Irony** produces a wry humorous effect by bringing in a part of the truth that we might have preferred to hide.

What is the irony in the following poem? One of his readers said of this Latino poet (North American of Puerto Rican ancestry) that he "brings to life his love for his people while etching haunting pictures that create lasting images" for his readers. What contradictory thoughts or mixed feelings do you think were in the poet's mind in front of the pawnshop window?

Martín Espada   *(born 1957)*

Latin Night at the Pawnshop   *1987*

Chelsea, Massachusetts
Christmas, 1987

The apparition of a salsa band
gleaming in the Liberty Loan
pawnshop window:

Golden trumpet.
silver trombone,   5
congas, maracas, tambourine,
all with price tags dangling
like the city morgue ticket
on a dead man's toe.

The Receptive Reader

1. What is sad and ironic about the name of the pawnshop? What is ironic about the time of year?

2 What for you is the central irony in this poem? How does the poet heighten it or drive it home?

3. What are the emotions created by the concluding simile?

Illness provides an ironic counterpoint to our hopes for a happy and fulfilled life. The author of the following poem, admired by fellow poets and fiercely loyal readers, struggled with and was finally defeated by mental illness.

Anne Sexton   *(1928–1975)*

Ringing the Bells   *1960*

And this is the way they ring
the bells in Bedlam
and this is the bell-lady
who comes each Tuesday morning

to give us a music lesson   5
and because the attendants make you go
and because we mind by instinct,
like bees caught in the wrong hive,
we are the circle of the crazy ladies
who sit in the lounge of the mental house   10
and smile at the smiling woman
who passes us each a bell,
who points at my hand
that holds my bell, E flat,
and this is the gray dress next to me   15
who grumbles as if it were special
to be old, to be old,
and this is the small hunched squirrel girl
on the other side of me
who picks at the hair over her lip,   20
who picks at the hairs over her lip all day,
and this is how the bells really sound,
as untroubled and clean
as a workable kitchen,
and this is always my bell responding   25
to my hand that responds to the lady
who points at me, E flat;
and although we are no better for it,
they tell you to go. And you do.

The Receptive Reader

1. Bedlam (originally Bethlehem) was the name of a notorious London insane asylum. In the dark ages of mental health care, people came there to gawk at the antics of the inmates. What is the irony in the poet's use of this name?

2. What is ironic about the music therapy she decribes? What is ironic about the smiles in this poem? What is ironic about the sound of the bells? (How are the patients like "bees caught in the wrong hive"?)

3. Why is there so much repetition, with everything running together without proper punctuation?

A contrast between what we expect and what really happens makes for **irony of situation.** When the ocean liner *Titanic,* touted as unsinkable, went down on her maiden voyage with a terrible loss of life, the English poet Thomas Hardy pondered the ironic contrast between boastful human vanity and the ship's inglorious end. A contrast between what we say and what we really mean makes for **verbal irony**—intentional irony in our use of language. The following poem, by a British-born poet who became an American citizen, is an extended exercise in verbal irony, starting with the title. Monuments to the Unknown Soldier commemorated the heroic war dead by honoring the remains of an unidentified soldier killed in action. As we read the following poem, we find that there is nothing heroic about the "unknown citizen," and it is not the poet's intention to honor him. What *is* the poet's intention?

W. H. Auden   *(1907–1973)*

The Unknown Citizen   1940
*(To JS/O7/M/378
This Marble Monument
Is Erected by the State)*

He was found by the Bureau of Statistics to be
One against whom there was no official complaint,
And all the reports of his conduct agree
That in the modern sense of an old-fashioned word, he was a saint,
For in everything he did he served the Greater Community.   5
Except for the War till the day he retired
He worked in a factory and never got fired,
But satisfied his employers, Fudge Motors Inc.
Yet he wasn't a scab° or odd in his views,   *strike breaker*
For his Union reports that he paid his dues,   10
(Our report on his Union shows it was sound)
And our Social Psychology workers found
That he was popular with his mates° and liked a drink.   *his friends*
The Press are convinced that he bought a paper every day
And that his reactions to advertisements were normal in every way.   15
Policies taken out in his name prove that he was fully insured,
And his Health-card shows he was once in a hospital but left it cured.
Both Producers Research and High-Grade Living declare
He was fully sensible to the advantages of the Installment Plan
And had everything necessary to the Modern Man,   20
A phonograph, a radio, a car and a frigidaire.
Our researchers into Public Opinion are content
That he held the proper opinions for the time of year;
When there was peace, he was for peace; when there was war he went.
He was married and added five children to the population,   25
Which our Eugenist° says was the right number for a   *population planner*
    parent of his generation,
And our teachers report that he never interfered with their education.
Was he free? Was he happy? The question is absurd:
Had anything been wrong, we should certainly have heard.

The Receptive Reader

1. The Unknown Soldier was anonymous because the remains could not be identified. Why does Auden give his Unknown Citizen no name but only a number?

2. What clues in the poem remind us that the poet is speaking ironically? For instance, what is wrong with holding "the proper opinions for the time of year"?

What is ironic about the citizen's attitude toward war? Why is what the teachers say about him a left-handed compliment? (Can you find other examples of mock compliments that are examples of verbal irony?)

3. Many of the institutions keeping tab on the citizenry apparently regarded JS/07/M/378 as a model citizen, if not a "saint." What is the poet's basic criticism of him? (What is the poet's basic criticism of the state?)

The Creative Dimension

Auden wrote this poem in 1940. What would you include in an updated portrait of the Unknown Citizen or the Unknown Consumer? Write your own ironic portrait of today's Unknown Citizen.

A poet with a strong sense of irony may play off popular stereotypes against the poet's perception of the truth. How does the following poem by Walt Whitman go counter to stereotypes current in periods of gay bashing or homophobia?

Walt Whitman   *(1819–1892)*

A Glimpse

A glimpse through an interstice caught,
Of a crowd of workmen and drivers in a bar-room around the stove late
    of a winter night, and I unremarked seated in a corner,
Of a youth who loves me and whom I love, silently approaching and seat-
    ing himself near, that he may hold me by the hand,
A long while amid the noises of coming and going, of drinking and oath
    and smutty jest,
There we two, content, happy in being together, speaking little, perhaps   5
    not a word.

The Receptive Reader

1. Who are the other people in the barroom? What ironic contrast does the poet set up between them and the two lovers?

2. The two people at the center of this poem spoke little, "perhaps not a word." How important is the spoken word in a love relationship?

THE CHALLENGE OF PARADOX

Although life is an affair of light and shadow, we never accept it as such. We are always reaching toward the light. From childhood we are given values which correspond only to an ideal world. The shadowy side of real life is ignored. Thus, we are unable to deal with the mixture of light and shadow of which life really consists.

MIGUEL SERRAN

A **paradox** is a seeming contradiction that makes sense on second thought. It is a paradox that many feel lonely in a crowd. They are alone in the midst of our crowded, congested cities. This apparent contradiction makes sense on second thought: the physical presence of others is not enough; we need to be with people who understand and who care. Irony and paradox both bring in a part of the truth that simple-minded people might ignore. But irony tends to undercut the simpler or more optimistic assumption. A paradox asks us to puzzle over the apparent contradiction and to balance off the conflicting points of view. We may have to live with the paradox.

Poets have found love a paradoxical emotion, combining attraction and rejection. It brings joy and pain, hope and despair. Love poetry in the Western world long followed the lead of the Italian fourteenth-century poet Petrarch. In the Petrarchan tradition, love was a paradoxical mixture of joy and sorrow. Love was a source of much joy, but it was often disappointed and therefore also the cause of much suffering. The following is a modern translation of a sonnet by Petrarch.

Francesco Petrarca   *(1304–1374)*

Or Che 'l Ciel e la Terra e 'l Vento Tace   *1369*

TRANSLATED BY HANS P. GUTH

Calm now are heaven and earth, and the winds asleep.
No birds now stir; wild beasts in slumber lie.
Night guides her chariot across the starry sky.
No wave now moves the waters of the deep.
I only keep vigil—I think, I burn, I weep.   5
She who destroys me dazzles my mind's eye.
At war with myself, raging and grieving, I
Long for the peace that's hers to give or keep.
From the same single fountain of life
Rise the bitter and sweet that feed my soul.   10
I am caressed and slashed by the same hand.
A martyr in a world of ceaseless strife,
I have died and risen a thousandfold.
So far am I from reaching the promised land.

The Receptive Reader

1. What is fitting, and what is *paradoxical,* about the nighttime setting?

2. What examples can you find of *opposed* concepts, clashing images, and mixed emotions?

3. Poets who made love into a religion often used the vocabulary of religious devotion. Where and how does this poem use *religious imagery?* What makes the religious images paradoxical?

In the following Shakespeare sonnet, a central paradox sets up many of the apparent contradictions in the poem. At first, the time of year seems to be winter—freezing, bare, and barren. A loved person is away, and everything seems dark and empty. But here is the paradox: it's actually summer, the season of birdsong and abundance. Why then is the speaker in the poem shivering and freezing? The answer is that it is summer outside but winter in the poet's soul.

William Shakespeare   *(1564–1616)*
Sonnet 97   *before 1598*

How like a winter hath my absence been
From thee, the pleasure of the fleeting° year!   *quickly passing*
What freezings have I felt, what dark days seen!
What old December's bareness everywhere!
And yet this time removed° was summer's time   *with you absent*   5
The teeming° autumn, big with rich increase,   *full of new life*
Bearing the wanton burthen of the prime,°   *giving birth to spring's*
Like widowed wombs after their lords' decease: *luxurious offspring*
Yet this abundant issue seemed to me
But hope of orphans and unfathered fruit;   10
For summer and his pleasures wait on thee,
And, thou away,° the very birds are mute.   *with you away*
Or, if they sing, 'tis° with so dull a cheer   *it is*
That leaves look pale, dreading the winter's near.

The Receptive Reader
1. As one student reader said, "In this poem, summer comes only when the loved person is there." In how many different ways is this *central paradox* followed up or echoed in this poem?

2. Where and how does the central metaphor shift from autumn to widowhood? What is the connection? What paradoxical emotions does the orphan metaphor bring into the poem?

3. How do the leaves in the last line illustrate *personification*—reading human qualities into the inanimate world? Where else does the poem use personification?

JUXTAPOSITIONS
Convention and Originality

Gather ye rosebuds while ye may
Old time is still a-flying
And this same flower that smiles today
Tomorrow will be dying.

ROBERT HERRICK,
"TO THE VIRGINS, TO MAKE MUCH OF TIME"

The seventeenth-century poet pleads with a reluctant partner: "Seize the day; make use of the passing day" (**carpe diem** in Latin). The rose "smiles today," but if we do not enjoy it now, it will have wilted by tomorrow. Therefore, "gather ye rosebuds while ye may." The two poems that follow depart from this convention, each in its own way. The first one, one of the best known poems in the English language, is Andrew Marvell's "To His Coy Mistress." (The title means "To His Reluctant Lady.") This poem has no rosebuds, no songbirds, and no conventional springtime setting in the English countryside. Then read a poem by the Countess of Dia, a French poet of the twelfth century, who looks at love and courtship from a female rather than the conventional male perspective.

In Marvell's poem, bold and paradoxical images roam from the Humber river in northern England to the river Ganges in India (then famous for its jewels and spices) and from there to "deserts of vast eternity." The poem ranges over vast stretches of time, from Noah's flood to the "conversion of the Jews," then not expected till the end of time. Paradoxically, the metaphors and similes in this poem are drawn from geography, biblical history, and botany—areas not conventionally associated with love.

Andrew Marvell   *(1621–1678)*

To His Coy Mistress   *before 1678*

Had we but world enough, and time,
This coyness, lady, were° no crime.   *would be*
We would sit down and think which way
To walk and pass our long love's day.
Thou by the Indian Ganges' side   5
Shouldst rubies find; I by the tide
Of Humber would complain.° I would   *write plaintive love songs*
Love you ten years before the flood,
And you should, if you please, refuse
Till the conversion of the Jews.   10

My vegetable love should grow
Vaster than empires and more slow;
An hundred years should go to praise
Thine eyes and on thy forehead gaze,
Two hundred to adore each breast,   15
But thirty thousand to the rest,
An age at least to every part,
And the last age should show your heart.
For, lady, you deserve this state,°   *this high station*
Nor would I love at lower rate.   20
    But at my back I always hear
Time's wingèd chariot hurrying near,
And yonder all before us lie
Deserts of vast eternity.
Thy beauty shall no more be found,   25
Nor, in thy marble vault, shall sound
My echoing song; then worms shall try
That long-preserved virginity,
And your quaint honor° turn to dust,   *deliberate virtue*
And into ashes all my lust.   30
The grave's a fine and private place,
But none, I think, do there embrace.
    Now therefore, while the youthful hue
Sits on thy skin like morning dew,
And while thy willing soul transpires°   *breathes forth*   35
At every pore with instant fires,
Now let us sport us while we may,
And now, like amorous birds of prey,
Rather at once our time devour
Than languish in his slow-chapped° power. *chewing with slow-moving jaws* 40
Let us roll all our strength and all
Our sweetness up into one ball,
And tear our pleasures with rough strife
Through the iron gates of life.
Thus, though we cannot make our sun   45
Stand still, yet we will make him run.

The Receptive Reader

1. Where and how does Marvell carry *hyperbole,* or poetic exaggeration, to new extremes?

2. What is paradoxical about a "vegetable love" growing slowly to vast size like a giant cabbage? On second thought, what might be desirable or welcome about the idea?

3. What images and associations do time and eternity usually bring to your mind? How are the metaphors Marvell uses different? (What were the original uses of a chariot?)

4. What is the effect of the poet's bringing graveyard imagery into a love poem? (Can you find a good example of *verbal irony* in this passage?)

5. When Marvell replaces the conventional songbirds with birds of prey, what is the effect on the way we think about love and lovers? How do these birds help him turn the tables on all-devouring time? Why does he make us imagine "the iron gates of life" rather than a meadow with spring flowers?

6. How does Marvell's use of the sun differ from Herrick's? (Why would lovers want to make the sun "stand still"? How would they make the sun "run" to keep up with them?)

The Creative Dimension

A student poet wrote in her "Reply of Your Coy Mistress":

We have the world, and we have the time;
To wait a while longer would be no crime.

Write your own personal reply or response to Marvell.

We tend to think of the early love poets, or troubadours, of southern France as male. However, many poems of women troubadours have come down to us. How does the following poem depart from the conventions of much male-oriented love poetry?

Countess of Dia   *(born about 1140)*

I Sing of That Which I Would Rather Hide   *before 1200*

TRANSLATED BY HANS P. GUTH

I sing of that which I would rather hide:
Where is the one who should be at my side
And whom I dearly love, come ebb or tide?
My kindness and sweet grace he has denied,
My beauty and good sense and goodly show.   5
I am betrayed, deceived, my love defied,
As if I were the lowest of the low.

Yet I take heart: I never brought you shame
Nor ever did the least to hurt your name.
My love surpasses loves of greater fame,   10
And I am pleased I beat you at love's game—
Outscored you when devotion was the test.
Your cold words and your slights all speak the same—
And yet you play the charmer with the rest.

The Receptive Reader

1. How is the *perspective* of the speaker in this poem different from that in traditional male-oriented poems of love and courtship? How much of this poem seems to belong to a different time, a different world? How much seems relevant or intelligible in our own time?

2. Modern translators of the southern French, or Provençal, poetry of the early Middle Ages often do not attempt to reproduce the finely crafted *stanza forms* and the intricate rhyme scheme of the originals. How do you think the rhyme scheme and the stanza form re-created here affect the reader's reactions to the poem?

POEMS FOR FURTHER STUDY

When reading the following poems, pay special attention to tone. What is the prevailing tone in each poem? What kind of voice is speaking to you in the poem? If the poem uses irony, is it gentle and teasing or bitter and sarcastic? If the poem uses paradox, what is the basic contradiction?

Sir John Suckling   *(1609–1642)*

Song   *1638*

Why so pale and wan, fond° lover?   *foolish*
　　Prithee,° why so pale?   *Please*
Will, when looking well can't move her,
　　Looking ill prevail?
Prithee, why so pale?   5

Why so dull and mute, young sinner?
　　Prithee, why so mute?
Will, when speaking well can't win her,
　　Saying nothing do 't?

Quit, quit, for shame; this will not move,°   *persuade*   10
　　This cannot take her.
If of herself she will not love,
　　Nothing can make her:
　　The devil take her

Sharon Olds   *(born 1942)*

Quake Theory   *1980*

When two plates of earth scrape along each other
like a mother and daughter
it is called a fault.

There are faults that slip smoothly past each other
an inch a year, with just a faint rasp   5
like a man running his hand over his chin,
that man between us,

and there are faults that get stuck at a bend for twenty years.
The ridge bulges up like a father's sarcastic forehead
and the whole thing freezes in place, the man between us.   10

When this happens, there will be heavy damage
to industrial areas and leisure residence
when the deep plates
finally jerk past
the terrible pressure of their contact.   15

                              The earth cracks
and innocent people slip gently in like swimmers.

The Receptive Reader

How does the earthquake metaphor affect the tone of this poem? In developing the implications of this central metaphor, how does the poet start in a low key and build up to a climax? (Where is the high point? How does the poet make it stand out?) What is the speaker's attitude toward the daughter? What is the speaker's attitude toward the father? Who are the "innocent people"?

Joy Harjo   *(born 1951)*

Leaving   *1983*

Four o'clock this morning there was a call.
She talked Indian, so it was probably her mother.
It was. Something not too drastic, tone of voice,
no deaths or car wrecks. But something. I was
out of the sheets, unwrapped from the blankets,   5
fighting to stay in sleep. Slipped in and out of her
voice, her voice on the line.
She came back to me. Lit cigarette blurred in the dark.
All lights off but that. Laid
down next to me, empty, these final hours   10
before my leaving.
Her sister was running away from her boyfriend and
was stranded in Calgary, Alberta. Needed money
and comfort for the long return back home.

I dreamed of a Canadian plain, and warm arms around me,   15
the soft skin of the body's landscape. And I dreamed
of bear, and a thousand mile escape homeward.

The Receptive Reader

1. What is the situation in this poem by a Native American poet? What is happening? What clues are there in the poem?

2. What is the prevailing tone in this poem about parting? What are the speaker's emotions? Are they what you would expect in this situation?

William Shakespeare   *(1564–1616)*

Sonnet 130   *before 1598*

My mistress' eyes are nothing like the sun;
Coral is far more red than her lips' red;
If snow be white, why then her breasts are dun;°   *grayish brown*
If hairs be wires, black wires grow on her head.
I have seen roses damasked,° red and white,   *multicolored*   5
But no such roses see I in her cheeks;
And in some perfumes there is more delight
Than in the breath that from my mistress reeks.
I love to hear her speak, yet well I know
That music hath a far more pleasing sound;   10
I grant I never saw a goddess go;
My mistress, when she walks, treads on the ground.
And yet, by heaven, I think my love as rare°   *marvelous*
As any she belied° with false compare.   *any woman misrepresented*

The Receptive Reader

1. How does this poem illustrate the idea that irony is the revenge of reality on poetic exaggeration?

2. Readers hostile to irony accuse it of undercutting our capacity for sincere emotion. Do you think it does so in this sonnet?

WRITING ABOUT LITERATURE

20   *Responding to Tone (Reading the Clues)*

The Writing Workshop   When you write about tone, you need to read between the lines. You need to have your antennae out for the emotional quality of a poem. Make your paper show that you have read for clues to the attitudes and feelings that seem built into a poem:

✘ *Pay special attention to the connotations of words.*   Look for a network of related words that might help set the tone of a poem. A poet might create a careless, joyful mood by the repeated use of synonyms or near-synonyms like *mirth, merry, jocund, revelry, good cheer, fiesta, frolic, joyous.*

✘ *Listen to the rhythm of the poem as it is read out loud.*   Is the poem slow-moving, deliberate, earnest? Is it skipping and cheerful? Is it urgent, driven by passionate indignation?

✗ *Look at the attitude the poem adopts toward the reader or listener.* Is the tone defiant? challenging? Does the poem take you into the speaker's confidence as if in a conspiratorial whisper?

✗ *Look for signs of humorous intention or irreverent wit.* When Lord Byron says about the high-toned philosophical speculations of a fellow poet, "I wish he would explain his explanations," we know that Byron's attitude will be less than worshipful.

✗ *Look for shifts in tone that help shape a poem as a whole.* A poem may move from a tone of bitterness and indignation to a more understanding and forgiving tone. An elegy may start with notes of deep mourning but is likely to work its way to the joyful certainty of resurrection.

How does the following student paper read the clues that help the poet set the tone?

Sample Student Paper

"Quake Theory," or Whose Fault Is It?

There is nothing quite as much fun as a punning wit. To utilize one word to mean two different things creates an effect like those optical illusions where we can see an old woman or a young girl . . . or again an old woman—this tickles the brain. And, tickled, we smile until, as in Sharon Olds's poem "Quake Theory," the serious message sinks in, and we realize this isn't fun anymore.

An initial metaphor is developed in the first stanza; it also sets up the pun: "When two plates of earth scrape along each other/ like a mother and daughter / it is called a fault." The word *fault* does double-time here as a description of a fracture in the earth and as a key word to alert us to the distance between a mother and her daughter. That distance can best be summed up in the question: "Whose fault is it?" What is the *it* that isn't working?

The poem does not enlighten us immediately. Instead it sounds for a moment as though it might drone along in a professorial manner, informing us of two different kinds of fault in two stanzas. ("There are faults that slip smoothly past each other / an inch a year.") We read along, smiling in anticipation of further developments in what may prove an extended joke. The tone is dry, almost too dry, but we have been trained by generations of deadpan comedians to expect lurking underneath the surface dryness the levity of a joke. Sharon Olds lures us in but then abruptly shifts gears to refer to "that man between us."

Just who is this man? The man, as Sharon Olds intended, is a discordant note in this poem. Not only does his introduction into the poem upset the flow of the poem, but he himself is an upsetting influence in the relationship between mother and daughter.

We read in the second stanza that a fault can be trouble-free with only a bit of friction—friction likened to what results when a man rubs his five-o'clock shadow (not just any man, but "that man between us"). However, in the third stanza, we read that a fault may also be blocked and build up tension "like a father's sarcastic forehead," and "the whole thing freezes in place, the man between us." With this ominous note, the poem no longer seems to point toward a humorous conclusion. The repeated references to "that man," ending each of the two stanzas, remind us that the central metaphor in this poem is the earthquake.

The point of view is that of the mother speaking to the daughter (or perhaps vice versa). The speaker is trying to describe their relationship, which remains in constant motion, "scraping" at times, building up tension at others. But there is also a third dynamic, "that man," the father. He is there benignly or as an active threat. but he is certainly there.

What is the result when the tension builds up between the two locked bodies? "There will be heavy damage . . . when the deep plates / finally jerk past / the terrible pressure of their contact." In keeping with the metaphor of the earthquake, the poem itself fractures at this point, skips a line, and then resumes:

> The earth cracks
> and innocent people slip gently in like swimmers.

What an odd analogy! We may assume that in a clash of wills or land masses, some who are bystanders will suffer, perhaps even be swallowed, but this image seems both deadly and harmless at the same time. To "slip gently in like swimmers" seems to belie the violence just described. But this is perhaps as it should be: In any family upset there are not necessarily bleeding victims left lying around afterwards. People are sucked under without a surface struggle or disturbance.

In this poem, we are carried along at first amused, then puzzled or disturbed, and then saddened at the end. We sense that things might have been different; there is regret here. But whose "fault" is it? It is neither the mother's nor the daughter's but, as in plate tectonics, the fault of the rift between them, the father.

Questions

1. How does this paper trace the shifts in tone in this poem? Does it discover nuances that you might have missed?

2. This student writer was especially sensitive to the relation between form and meaning, sound and sense. Where and how does the paper show the connection between meaning and outward shape or form?

3. How close is this writer's reaction to the poem to your own?

21 Theme

The Making of Meaning

For me the real issues of our time are the issues of every time—the hurt and wonder of loving; making in all its forms, children, loaves of bread, paintings, building; and the conservation of life of all people and all places, the jeopardizing of which no abstract doubletalk of "peace" or "implacable foes" can excuse.

SYLVIA PLATH

FOCUS ON THEME

Poems make us think. Poetry helps us find meanings in the flow of experience. Often a poem invites us to look at a familiar idea in a new light. When we focus on the **theme** of a poem, we try to sum up its meaning. We try to put into words what makes the poem thought-provoking. We look at the issues a poem seems to raise and the possible answers it suggests.

Theme as Heading   Poets and critics use the word *theme* in two somewhat different ways: the term may simply point to the general subject, to an area of concern. A collection may sort poems out under thematic headings like "Love," "Family," "Identity," "Alienation," and "Dissent." Such themes are large umbrella headings; individual poems will offer different perspectives. Under the heading of "Family," one poem might be mourning the lost golden world of childhood. Another poem might focus on the need for breaking the fetters the family clamps on the individual.

Theme as Statement   Often, however, the term *theme* stands for the statement that a poem as a whole makes *about* a subject. The theme then is what the poem as a whole says about identity, alienation, or dissent. The theme is the recurrent message or fresh insight that stays with us as we leave the poem behind. When we state the theme, we try to

516

formulate the ideas or insights that the poem as a whole makes us ponder or remember.

The Implied Theme   Some poets leave larger meanings implied—hinted at, suggested only. Most twentieth-century poets have been suspicious of large uplifting abstractions: happiness, patriotism, love. These are words that are easy to use and hard to live up to. **Abstractions** like these are labels for large areas of human experience. In themselves, they are neither good nor bad. However, they do abstract—they "draw us away," from specifics and individuals. They extrapolate the larger patterns that help us chart our way. Many modern poets have steered clear of them, afraid they might become *mere* abstractions, removing us from flesh-and-blood realities.

The Overt Theme   Other poets are less shy about spelling out key ideas in so many words. Poets of earlier ages, and some in our own time, draw explicit conclusions. They make statements. Even so, ideas in poetry are live ideas—anchored to what you can see and hear and feel. You cannot take them out of a poem the way you take candy out of a wrapper. The poet's ideas take shape before your eyes—embedded in graphic images, acted out in scenes and events that stir your emotions.

IDEA AND IMAGE

Poems are like dreams; in them you put what you
don't know you know.

ADRIENNE RICH

Poets vary greatly in how explicitly they verbalize the ideas acted out in their poems. Some poets let their images speak for themselves. Other poets speak for their images, serving as guides or interpreters. They spell out the message embedded in metaphor or symbol. In the following poem, what is the relation between idea and image? How does the poet take a large abstraction to the level of firsthand experience?

William Stafford   *(1914–1992)*

Freedom   *1969*

Freedom is not following a river.
Freedom is following a river
   though, if you want to.
It is deciding now by what happens now.
It is knowing that luck makes a difference.   5

No leader is free; no follower is free—
    the rest of us can often be free.
Most of the world are living by
creeds too odd, chancy, and habit-forming
    to be worth arguing about by reason.   10

If you are oppressed, wake up about
four in the morning; most places
you can usually be free some of the time
    if you wake up before other people.

What does this poem say about freedom? Much in our lives *restricts* our freedom. Apparently, being a leader and being a follower are both incompatible with making free choices. (Both leader and follower march with the main body of troops.) To be caught up in habitual creeds, to make today's decisions bound by yesterday's precedents, to be oppressed—all these limit the sphere of free choice. Nevertheless, there is a margin of freedom—if only in the early morning hours, before the mechanisms that constrain us kick in.

The Receptive Reader

1. What do you make of the concrete *images* in this poem? When or how would someone want to follow a river? What does freedom have to do with following or not following it? What does freedom have to do with getting up early?

2. Why do you think the speaker claims that part of freedom is "deciding now by what happens now"? What makes the speaker in the poem say that neither a "leader" nor a "follower" can be free? What is "habit-forming" about "creeds"? (And how do they limit your freedom?)

3. Does the poem provide any hints or guidelines on how to enlarge your margin of freedom?

4. How would you sum up in a sentence or two the *theme* of this poem—the statement the poem as a whole makes about freedom?

The Personal Response

How does the statement about freedom that the poem makes as a whole compare with the ideas you yourself associate with the word?

The following poem by the American poet Walt Whitman "makes a statement" about the speaker's alienation from coldly analytical science. However, it does so without verbalizing the poet's implied attitude. What is the poet's statement?

Walt Whitman   *(1819–1892)*

When I Heard the Learn'd Astronomer   *1865*

When I heard the learn'd astronomer,
When the proofs, the figures, were ranged in columns before me,
When I was shown the charts and diagrams, to add, divide, and
     measure them,
When I sitting heard the astronomer where he lectured with much
     applause in the lecture room,
How soon unaccountable I became tired and sick,   5
Till rising and gliding out I wandered off by myself,
In the mystical moist night air, and from time to time,
Looked up in perfect silence at the stars.

The Receptive Reader

1. The poem does not make an explicit assertion about the scientific temperament. But we can infer the poet's attitude from the brief scenario we see acted out. When the speaker in the poem attended an astronomy lecture, what made him feel "tired and sick"?

2. The speaker in the poem wandered off by himself. Once outside, he found the antidote. What was it? What does the poem say about two different ways to look at the stars?

The Personal Response

Do you sympathize with the poet's reponse to the astronomy lecture? Do you feel there is something to be said on the other side?

The title of the following seventeenth-century religious poem refers not to altars or incense but to a mechanical device made of wheels, blocks, and rope. A pulley was used to multiply human strength and lift heavy weights in the days before steam-powered or electricity-driven winches. What is different or unexpected about the relationship between God and humanity in the poem? What is the central paradox in this poem?

George Herbert   *(1593–1633)*

The Pulley   *1633*

When God at first made man,
Having a glass of blessings standing by,
"Let us," he said, "pour on him all we can:
Let the world's riches, which dispersèd° lie,   *lie scattered*
     Contract into a span."°   *short space*   5

So strength first made a way;
Then beauty flowed, then wisdom, honor, pleasure.
When almost all was out, God made a stay,°   *paused*
Perceiving that, alone of all his treasure,
    Rest in the bottom lay.   10

"For if I should," said he,
"Bestow° this jewel also on my creature,   *pass on to*
He would adore my gifts instead of me,
And rest in Nature, not the God of Nature;
    So both should losers be.   15

"Yet let him keep the rest,
But keep them with repining° restlessness: *yearning*
Let him be rich and weary, that at least,
If goodness lead him not, yet weariness
    May toss him to my breast."   20

The Receptive Reader

1. Herbert and other **metaphysical** poets of his time are known for bringing their learning and educated intelligence into their poems. They have often
been admired for their *wit*—in the more general sense of a quick mind or intellectual alertness. Part of this mental quickness is their willingness to use a play
on words, or *pun,* even when writing about solemn subjects. What does the
word *rest* mean when "*Rest* in the bottom lay"? (*Restlessness* later appears as its
opposite.) What does the word mean when God's creature is likely to "*rest* in
Nature, not the God of Nature"? How does the poet pun, or play on the word,
when God decides to let us "keep the *rest*"—everything except *rest?* (How does
the poet make this key word stand out in the poem?)

2. What is paradoxical about richly blessed creatures suffering from "repin-
ing restlessness"? Do you think it is true?

3. One student wrote that in this poem humanity is "deprived rather than
depraved." What did she mean?

THE COMMITTED POET

I am a poet
who yearns to dance on rooftops,
to whisper delicate lines about joy
and the blessings of human understanding.
I try. I go to my land, my tower of words and
bolt the door, but the typewriter doesn't fade out
the sounds of blasting and muffled outrage.

                          LORNA DEE CERVANTES,
                  "POEM FOR THE YOUNG WHITE MAN"

Should poems take sides? When we explore the ideas embedded in poems, we face the question of the poet's engagement or commitment. Should poets take a stand on the social and political issues of their time? Can they afford to testify on behalf of causes? Can poets serve party, ideology, or country? When poets write poems "for daily political use," their art becomes disposable, fading like the campaign posters of yesteryear. When poets follow a party line, they may seem to cease speaking to us in their own right as one human being to another.

Nevertheless, poets from John Milton to Gwendolyn Brooks and Adrienne Rich have found it hard to stay aloof from the political and ideological struggles of their time. Much modern poetry has been poetry of protest and of warning. At the same time, a poet's keeping *silent* about the political issues of the time has also been seen as a political statement. By not confronting the issues, a poem may seem to be condoning oppression or abuses.

Much twentieth-century poetry has focused on the ironic contrast between official war propaganda and the horrible realities of war. The following poem is by Wilfred Owen, a British officer who wrote about the "sorrowful dark hell" of the Great War—World War I—and who was killed on the western front a week before the armistice ended the war in 1918. The motto he quotes in the title of the poem (and again at the end) is a quotation from the Roman poet Horace. It was known to every British schoolboy of Owen's generation: *Dulce et decorum est pro patria mori*—"How sweet and fitting it is to die for one's country." Owen once said, "My subject is war and the pity of war. The poetry is in the pity."

Wilfred Owen   *(1893–1918)*

Dulce et Decorum Est   *1918*

Bent double, like old beggars under sacks,
Knock-kneed, coughing like hags, we cursed through sludge,
Till on the haunting flares we turned our backs
And toward our distant rest began to trudge.
Men marched asleep. Many had lost their boots   5
But limped on, blood-shod. All went lame; all blind;
Drunk with fatigue; deaf even to the hoots
Of tired, outstripped Five-Nines,° that dropped behind.   *gas shells*

Gas! Gas! Quick, boys!—An ecstasy of fumbling,
Fitting the clumsy helmets just in time;   10
But someone still was yelling out and stumbling,
And floundering like a man in fire or lime . . .
Dim through the misty panes and thick green light,

As under a green sea, I saw him drowning.
In all my dreams, before my helpless sight,   15
He plunges at me, guttering, choking, drowning.

If in some smothering dreams you too could pace
Behind the wagon that we flung him in,
And watch the white eyes writhing in his face,
His hanging face, like a devil's sick of sin;   20
If you could hear, at every jolt, the blood
Come gargling from his froth-corrupted lungs,
Obscene as cancer, bitter as the cud
Of vile, incurable sores on innocent tongues,—
My friend, you would not tell with such high zest   25
To children ardent for some desperate glory,
The old Lie: Dulce et decorum est
Pro patria mori.

The Receptive Reader

1. How does the picture the first stanza paints of the troops being withdrawn from the front lines for "rest" differ from the one you would expect to encounter on propaganda posters or in patriotic speeches? Why is there a bitter irony in the *timing* of the gas attack in this poem?

2. Many people have read about the use of poison gas by the belligerents in World War I. How does Owen drive the realities of chemical warfare home? From what *perspectives*—when and how—do you see the victim? What is the effect on you as the reader?

3. How and with what effect is the word *drowning* repeated in this poem? What gives the word *innocent* toward the end of the poem its special power? Who is guilty in this poem?

4. This poem owes its eloquence in part to the insistent piling on of related words and similar, *parallel* structures. Where and how?

5. What is the basic irony in this poem?

The Personal Response

Are we today too removed from the realities of war to share feelings like those expressed in this poem? Are our feelings too blunted from overexposure? How does the treatment of war in the media affect our feelings about war?

The following poem by an African-American writer pays tribute to Frederick Douglass, whose autobiography told the story of his rebellion against slavery. As a journalist and public speaker, Douglass became a leader of the antislavery movement in the United States. What makes the following poem in his honor eloquent?

Robert Hayden   *(1913–1980)*

Frederick Douglass   *1966*

When it is finally ours, this freedom, this liberty, this beautiful
and terrible thing, needful to man as air,
usable as earth; when it belongs at last to all,
when it is truly instinct, brain matter, diastole, systole,°   *phases of the heartbeat*
reflex action; when it is finally won, when it is more   5
than the gaudy mumbo jumbo of politicians:
this man, this Douglass, this former slave, this Negro
beaten to his knees, exiled, visioning a world
where none is lonely, none hunted, alien,
this man, superb in love and logic, this man   10
shall be remembered. Oh, not with statues' rhetoric,
nor with legends and poems and wreaths of bronze alone,
but with the lives grown out of his life, the lives
fleshing his dream of the beautiful, needful thing.

The Receptive Reader

1. What in this poem is different from the "gaudy mumbo jumbo of politicians" and conventional rhetoric in praise of liberty? What is strange or unexpected in the poet's description of freedom?

2. Is the poet speaking for a limited group? Is he speaking to a limited
group? Do you think the poem would speak eloquently to a white audience?
Why or why not?

The Personal Response

We are often told that modern audiences have few heroes. Write a tribute
(poem or prose passage) to someone you admire, trying to make it convincing
for the skeptical modern reader.

Poetry can be timely and timeless at the same time if readers sense
that the poet's long-range solidarity with suffering and deluded humanity is as strong as the commitment to the current struggle. Does the following poem take sides? Whose?

Denise Levertov   *(1923–1997)*

What Were They Like?   *1966*

1) Did the people of Vietnam
     use lanterns of stone?
2) Did they hold ceremonies
     to reverence the opening of buds?
3) Were they inclined to quiet laughter?   5
4) Did they use bone and ivory,
     jade and silver, for ornament?

5) Had they an epic poem?
6) Did they distinguish between speech and singing?

1) Sir, their light hearts turned to stone.   10
   It is not remembered whether in gardens
   stone lanterns illumined pleasant ways.
2) Perhaps they gathered once to delight in blossom,
   but after the children were killed
   there were no more buds.   15
3) Sir, laughter is bitter to the burned mouth.
4) A dream ago, perhaps. Ornament is for joy.
   All the bones were charred.
5) It is not remembered. Remember,
   most were peasants; their life   20
   was in rice and bamboo.
   When peaceful clouds were reflected in the paddies
   and the water buffalo stepped surely along terraces,
   maybe fathers told their sons old tales.
   When bombs smashed those mirrors   25
   there was time only to scream.
6) There is an echo yet
   of their speech which was like a song.
   It was reported their singing resembled
   the flight of moths in moonlight.   30
   Who can say? It is silent now.

The Receptive Reader

1. Who are the two speakers in this poem? What is the difference in their *points of view?* What kind of person is asking the questions? What kind of person is giving the answers?

2. Why do you think the poet used a *question-and-answer* format? What effect does it have on the reader?

3. The poem shifts easily from the factual questionnaire mode to the metaphorical language of the poet. What are memorable *metaphors,* and what role do they play in the poem?

The Personal Response

What for you is the message of this poem? What is your personal response?

JUXTAPOSITIONS

Poems of War

Much modern poetry has dealt with the subject of war. From what point of view are you asked to look at war in each of the following poems? Does the poet spell out the ideas or attitudes implied or embedded in the poem? What does the poem as a whole say about war?

Henry Reed   *(born 1914)*

Naming of Parts   *1946*

Today we have naming of parts. Yesterday,
We had daily cleaning. And tomorrow morning,
We shall have what to do after firing. But today,
Today we have naming of parts. Japonica
Glistens like coral in all of the neighboring gardens,   5
       And today we have naming of parts.

This is the lower sling swivel. And this
Is the upper sling swivel, whose use you will see,
When you are given your slings. And this is the piling swivel,
Which in your case you have not got. The branches   10
Hold in the gardens their silent, eloquent gestures,
       Which in our case we have not got.

This is the safety-catch, which is always released
With an easy flick of the thumb. And please do not let me
See anyone using his finger. You can do it quite easy   15
If you have any strength in your thumb. The blossoms
Are fragile and motionless, never letting anyone see
       Any of them using their finger.

And this you can see is the bolt. The purpose of this
Is to open the breech, as you see. We can slide it   20
Rapidly backwards and forwards: we call this
Easing the spring. And rapidly backwards and forwards
The early bees are assaulting and fumbling the flowers:
       They call it easing the Spring.

They call it easing the Spring: it is perfectly easy   25
If you have any strength in your thumb: like the bolt,
And the breech, and the cocking-piece, and the point of balance,
Which in our case we have not got; and the almond-blossom
Silent in all of the gardens and the bees going backwards and forwards,
       For today we have naming of parts.   30

The Receptive Reader

1. Much of the talking in this poem is done by the drill instructor. Is what he says a **caricature**—a comic distortion exaggerating key traits to make them ridiculous? Or does it sound to you like a fairly accurate rendering of what an instructor might say?

2. The technology of war and the world of nature provide a steady play of *point and counterpoint* in this poem. How? With what effect? What does the poem as a whole say about technology and nature?

3. What is this poet's attitude toward war?

Richard Eberhart   *(born 1904)*

The Fury of Aerial Bombardment   *1947*

You would think the fury of aerial bombardment
Would rouse God to relent; the infinite spaces
Are still silent. He looks on shock-pried faces.
History, even, does not know what is meant.

You would feel that after so many centuries   5
God would give man to repent; yet he can kill
As Cain could, but with multitudinous will,
No farther advanced than in his ancient furies.

Was man made stupid to see his own stupidity?
Is God by definition indifferent, beyond us all?   10
Is the eternal truth man's fighting soul
Wherein the Beast ravens° in its own avidity?   *prowls*

Of Van Wettering I speak, and Averill,
Names on a list, whose faces I do not recall
But they are gone to early death, who late in school   15
Distinguished the belt feed lever from the belt holding pawl.

The Receptive Reader

1. What questions does this poem raise about God's intentions? What questions does it raise about our human responsibilities? Why does the poet bring the *allusion* to Cain into the poem?

2. Like Reed's poem, this poem takes us to the schoolrooms of military training. (Eberhart himself was for a time an aerial gunnery instructor in World War II.) How is Eberhart's use of the training experience similar to or different from Reed's?

3. Does this poem answer the questions it raises?

POEMS FOR FURTHER STUDY

In reading the following poems, pay special attention to theme. What ideas or attitudes are expressed or implied in the poem? What statement does the poem as a whole have for the reader? Does the poem spell it out in so many words? How does the poem as a whole carry its message?

Bethlyn Madison Webster   *(born 1964)*

Stamps   *1995*

I'm watching the woman
who is watching my groceries
rolling along the conveyor belt.

She stands Cheerio-mouthed
in a pink and white dress   5
sporting a crisp, curled hairdo
and staring as much as she pleases
while I stand behind my husband,
hiding behind him and the baby.
She has seen him produce   10
a book of foodstamps
from his pocket, and I think she wants
to see how her tax dollars
are being wasted today.
Eggs, milk, peanut butter, bread   15
root beer and a bag of store brand
chocolate chips. She looks
at those the longest.
I want to tell her that we work
for ten cents above minimum.   20
I want to explain
that it's Friday, we're tired,
and our chocolate is none of her business.
Somehow, we're on display
along with the tabloids and gum.   25
With long pink-nailed fingertips,
she puts her stuff up now:
a big red rib-eye steak
a head of green lettuce,
the leafy kind, and a bottle of merlot.   30
Our total is rung
and my husband pays.
The checker lays the coupons upside-down,
like a blackjack hand,
and pounds them with a rubber stamp.   35

The Receptive Reader

1. What is the point of this poem? What are key phrases? What are telling or revealing details? Does the ending have a possible symbolic meaning?

2. Does the poet expect you to take sides? What side are you on in reading this poem?

Denise Levertov   *(1923–1997)*

The Mutes   *1966*

Those groans men use
passing a woman on the street
or on the steps of the subway
to tell her she is a female
and their flesh knows it,   5

are they a sort of tune,
an ugly enough song, sung
by a bird with a slit tongue

but meant for music?

Or are they the muffled roaring   10
of deafmutes trapped in a building that is
slowly filling with smoke?

Perhaps both.

Such men most often
look as if groan were all they could do,   15
yet a woman, in spite of herself,

knows it's a tribute:
if she were lacking all grace
they'd pass her in silence:

so it's not only to say she's   20
a warm hole. It's a word
in grief-language, nothing to do with
primitive, not an ur-language;°   *earliest human language*
language stricken, sickened, cast down

in decrepitude.° She wants to   *deterioration*   25
throw the tribute away, dis-
gusted, and can't,

it goes on buzzing in her ear,
it changes the pace of her walk,
the torn posters in echoing corridors   30

spell it out, it
quakes and gnashes as the train comes in.
Her pulse sullenly

had picked up speed,
but the cars slow down and   35
jar to a stop while her understanding

keeps on translating:
"Life after life after life goes by
without poetry
without seemliness   40
without love."

The Receptive Reader

1. What is the role in the poem of the bird metaphor? Why is the deafmute
metaphor central to the poem? What kind of counterpoint does the subway provide in the poem?

2. What, in your own words, is the theme the poet spells out in the last stanza? How does the poem as a whole lead up to it?

3. Does this poem express hostility toward men?

The Personal Response

What attitudes about sexual harassment are widespread among women? What reactions to current concerns about sexual harassment are widespread among men? How does the poem relate to either?

Alice Walker   *(born 1944)*

Women   *1970*

They were women then
My mamma's generation
Husky of voice—Stout of
Step
With fists as well as   5
Hands
How they battered down
Doors
And ironed
Starched white   10
Shirts
How they led
Armies
Headragged Generals
Across mined   15
Fields
Booby-trapped
Ditches
To discover books
Desks   20
A place for us
How they knew what we
Must know
Without knowing a page
Of it   25
Themselves.

The Receptive Reader

1. What is the role of the *military metaphor* in this poem? (Why "head-ragged" generals?) What was the campaign in which the women of the mother's generation participated? (What clue is provided by the shirts?)

2. What is the paradox that concludes the poem?

3. What, for you, is the prevailing *mood* or emotion in this poem?

WRITING ABOUT LITERATURE

21   Tracing a Common Theme (Comparison and Contrast)

The Writing Workshop   A **comparison-and-contrast** paper presents a special challenge to your ability to organize material. You will have to develop a strategy for laying out your material in such a way that your reader can see the points of comparison. The reader has to see the connections—whether similarities or striking differences setting apart things that seem similar on the surface. Consider some familiar strategies for organizing a comparison and contrast of two poems:

✘ *You may want to develop a **point-by-point** comparison.*   For instance, you may want to begin by showing how two poets share a distrust of "big words." This idea then provides the starting point both for your paper and for their poetic technique. You may go on to show how both poets rely on startling, thought-provoking images. Here you come to the heart of both your paper and of their way of writing poetry. You may conclude by showing how both nevertheless in the end spell out the kind of thought that serves as an *earned* conclusion, a generalization that the poem as a whole has worked out. Simplified, the scheme for such a point-by-point comparison might look like this:

Point 1—poem A and then B
Point 2—poem A and then B
Point e—poem A and then B

✘ *You may want to develop a **parallel-order** comparison.*   You show first the distrust of abstractions; then the bold, provocative images; and finally the poet's spelling out of the theme in poem A. You then take these three points up again in the same, or parallel, order for poem B. This way you may be able to give your reader a better sense of how each poem works on its own terms, as a self-contained whole. However, you will have to make a special effort to remind your readers of what in the second poem is parallel to or different from what you showed in the first.

✘ *You may want to start from a common base.*   You may want to emphasize similarities first. You may then want to go on to the significant differences. You might vary this strategy by starting with surface similarities that might deceive the casual observer. You then go on to essential distinctions.

How does the following student paper use or adapt these organizing strategies?

Sample Student Paper

Today We Have Naming of Parts

Disillusioned by the experience of World War II, Henry Reed in "Naming of Parts" and Richard Eberhart in "The Fury of Aerial Bombardment" condemn and reject the horror of war. Both poems condemn our failure to see war as it is, attack our indifference, and reflect postwar anti-war feeling. We shall see that Eberhart's poem takes the attack on indifference one step further than Reed's poem does.

Henry Reed's "Naming of Parts" satirically attacks the callousness of the military. By using impersonal, neutral words and phrases ("Today we have naming of parts. Yesterday / we had daily cleaning"), the speaker satirizes how precise and impersonal these lessons are. The trainee learns a process, without being taught or made aware how terrible and ugly practicing that process is. References to "the lower sling swivel," "the upper sling swivel," and the "slings" describe machinery. Such references to mechanical parts evoke neutral or even positive feelings, since most machines are used for the good of humanity. This technical language conceals the horror of using this particular machinery. Saying that "you can do it quite easy / If you have any strength in your thumb" obscures the possibility that it might be difficult emotionally to gun down a fellow human being.

Reed uses a comparison to nature at the end of each stanza. Jumping from the mechanics of the gun to the beauty of the garden in consecutive sentences presents a contrast between the gun and the flower, the one a symbol of death and the other a symbol of life. The references in the first two stanzas stress the innocence of nature. "Japonica / glistens like coral in all of the neighboring gardens" evokes an image of serenity and peace. The branches with "their silent, eloquent gestures" paint another image of bliss. The sterile descriptions of the gun and the beautiful descriptions of nature proceed in a point-counterpoint fashion.

Richard Eberhart's "The Fury of Aerial Bombardment" shares the theme of "Naming of Parts" in that both poems attack indifference to violence and suffering. By saying that "History, even, does not know what is meant," the poet seems to lament that even painful experience does not teach us to prevent the senselessness of war. We are "no farther advanced," making the poet ask: "Was man made stupid?" Here again, as in Reed's poem, technical, impersonal references to the "belt feed lever" and the "belt holding pawl" imply a criticism of the callousness with which people handle the subject of war. A lesson about a belt feed lever might be more instructive if the part were named the genocide lever, for instance.

However, "The Fury of Aerial Bombardment" contrasts with "Naming of Parts" because Eberhart goes beyond attacking human indifference by attacking divine indifference to the horrors of war. The poet questions why God has not intervened to stop the aerial bombardment. The answer, that "the infinite spaces/ Are still silent," is a criticism of God's looking passively upon "shock-pried faces." These are the faces of the people who have witnessed the horror of the bombing but to whom God offers no respite. The poet seems to expect a thinking, feeling entity to intervene, but no such intervention takes place. Men still kill with "multitudinous will." In the third stanza, the poet asks: "Is God by definition indifferent, beyond us all?"

Both of these poems were written half a century ago, yet their relevance remains undiminished today. In an age when we read daily of war and death, indifference is commonplace. The way in which a news reporter casually reads death tolls from current conflicts is reminiscent of the cold, sterile wording of "Naming of Parts."

The casual and callous projections of the cost in human lives of "winning" a nuclear war are another example of what is under attack in these poems. And people who ponder such atrocities as Auschwitz and Hiroshima have cause to question divine indifference, for the earth is long on suffering.

Questions

How convincing do the parallels between the two poems become in this paper? What are striking examples? How, according to this student writer, does the second poem go beyond the first? For you, do the two poems seem dated, or do they seem still relevant today?

22 Myth and Allusion

Recovered Memories

The mythic journey is as ancient as the human race itself.

JOHN A. ALLEN

FOCUS ON MYTH

Our modern world has rediscovered myth as a mirror of deep-seated human needs and feelings. **Myths** (from *mythos,* the Greek word for "tale") are stories about gods, godlike heroes, and monstrous adversaries. They are rooted in prehistoric oral tradition. People heard them in a spirit of religious awe, listening for clues to the nature of the mysterious universe in which they lived. Creation myths celebrated *genesis*—the creation of the earth, of man and woman, of sun and moon. In the dark of winter, myths of rebirth kept alive the faith in the return of spring. Many early cultures had myths about the titanic struggle between good and evil. Often myths were embedded in **rituals** that acted out a mythical story or celebrated a godlike champion or redeemer.

Myth and Archetype   Many ancient myths have parallels in diverse cultures. It is as if recurrent mythical patterns were part of our collective consciousness, wired into the collective memory of the human species. Many myths focus on **archetypal** experiences and needs that are constants in the lives of people from different times and places. In traditions from many sources, we see a mythical god-king undergo a ritual of death and mourning, followed by rebirth or resurrection. We witness a cycle of defeat, death, and triumphant return. In the words of Joseph Campbell, we see different incarnations of "a hero with a thousand faces."

The Earth Goddess Myth   Students of myth, from nineteenth-century anthropologists to today's feminist poets, have gone back beyond male-centered patriarchal god and heroes. They have reconstructed myths about the earth goddess that echo in the earliest lore of the Middle East, cradle of Western civilization. These myths give a voice to the need for

533

bonding and nurturing essential for human survival. They symbolize the human need for living in harmony with the generative forces in nature. Such earth goddesses were Ishtar of Mesopotamia (now Iraq) or Cybele of Asia Minor (now Turkey). The Babylonian Ishtar and the Greek Demeter may hark back to a phase of human culture centered on the worship of a life-giving and life-preserving feminine principle. In Greek myth, Demeter is the earth mother or "grain mother," goddess of the harvest, who sustains and nourishes all that lives on land, in the sea, and in the air.

The Prometheus Myth   Many cultures have myths about the fire-bringer—who brings the fire that symbolizes warmth, the hearth, survival, permanence, the light of knowledge. The firebringer in Greek mythology was Prometheus, who defied the king of the gods by returning to humanity the fire that Zeus had meant to deny them. To poets and artists of later generations, Prometheus became a symbol of aspiration, of rebellion, of determination "to defy power, which seems omnipotent" (Percy Bysshe Shelley, *Prometheus Unbound*). We still call people "Promethean" who are willing to test the boundaries, to reach for what was thought unattainable.

Myth and Allusion   Poets and artists discovered in myth and legend rich sources of symbol and allusion. An **allusion** is a brief mention that calls up a whole story, rich in overtones and associations. A single word, a single name, may activate a whole network of memories. When a poet alludes to Cassandra, we see with the mind's eye the Trojan princess to whom the god Apollo had given the gift of foreseeing the future—and the curse of not being believed. In her mad ravings, she foresaw the death of Hector, the Trojan champion; she saw Troy in flames, the towers falling down, the men killed, the women sold into slavery. But no one believed her. As Robinson Jeffers says in his poem "Cassandra," people truly "hate the truth"; they would sooner

Meet a tiger on the road.
Therefore the poets honey their truth with lying.

THE RANGE OF ALLUSION

People do gossip
And they say about
Leda, that she
Once found an egg
hidden under
wild hyacinths
SAPPHO

Allusion is a kind of shorthand. What does a writer mean when saying, "We are all Custer"? The short, cryptic statement has layers of meaning that we can peel away like the layers of an onion. George Armstrong Custer was an American general in command of the U.S. Seventh Cavalry. He attacked a large encampment of the Sioux, or Lakota, on the Little Big Horn in 1876. He was killed with most of his men in the last desperate battle the Lakota fought against the invaders. The allusion here, however, says more: as Americans, we are all implicated in a shared history. It is as if we rode with the U.S. cavalry against the Native American tribes, ravaged by the starvation and disease the white settlers had brought. We share the guilt for the massacre at Wounded Knee, where men, women, and children were gunned down.

Allusions in poetry assume a shared cultural tradition that allows the poet to play on a common knowledge of myth, legend, and history. One large source of allusion is **Greek mythology**—the body of myths and legends that poets inherited from the civilization of ancient Greece. The following example shows the central role allusion can play in a poem. The central figure is a balloon vendor who is literally lame. But the poet calls him "goat-footed"—a hint that we may be watching a half-human, half-animal mythic creature.

e. e. cummings   *(1894–1963)*

in Just-   *1923*

in Just-
spring   when the world is mud-
luscious the little
lame balloonman

whistles   far   and wee   5

and eddieandbill come
running from marbles and
piracies and it's
spring

when the world is puddle-wonderful   10

the queer
old balloonman whistles
far   and   wee
and bettyandisbel come dancing

from hop-scotch and jump-rope and   15

it's
spring
and

                    the
                         goat-footed   20
    balloonMan   whistles
    far
    and
    wee

   Who has goat's feet and whistles? Pan, Greek god of flocks and shepherds, often appears in works of art as a sensual being with horns, a
snub nose, and goat's feet. He is often shown dancing or playing the
shepherd's flute, which he had invented. Often, he is leading the dances
of the nymphs, or female woodland creatures. Pan is one of the many
lesser semidivine beings who, in Greek mythology, populate nature.
They turn it from an alien, savage place into a world full of breathing,
sensitive life. For cummings, the goat-footed balloonman (Pan in a modern disguise) becomes a fitting symbol of spring—of the spirit of joy,
mirth, frolic, holiday, or fiesta.

The Receptive Reader

   1. What is "luscious" about mud or "wonderful" about puddles?

   2. How should the poem *sound* when read aloud? Spring here is a time of
children dancing and skipping—as the poem itself skips over the printed page.
How does it "dance out" the dancing and skipping it describes?

   3. How does the poet use *repetition* and pauses to highlight, to focus our
attention?

   4. In ancient Greek times, Pan played his flute for grown-up beings. Why
aren't there any adults in this modern poem?

   5. Do you think this poem would work for readers who have never heard of
Pan? Why or why not?

   What kind of cultural literacy does the poet assume in the following
poem? What is the poet's range of allusion?

William Butler Yeats   *(1865–1939)*

Leda and the Swan   *1923*

A sudden blow: the great wings beating still
Above the staggering girl, her thighs caressed
By the dark webs, her nape caught in his bill,
He holds her helpless breast upon his breast.

How can those terrified vague fingers push   5
The feathered glory from her loosening thighs?
And how can body, laid in that white rush,
But feel the strange heart beating where it lies?

A shudder in the loins engenders there
The broken wall, the burning roof and tower   10
And Agamemnon dead.
                              Being so caught up,
So mastered by the brute blood of the air,
Did she put on his knowledge with his power
Before the indifferent beak could let her drop?   15

The terrifying swan is a mythic creature: Zeus, the king of the Greek
gods, residing on Mount Olympus, has assumed the shape of an animal.
The offspring of his union with Leda is going to be Helen, whose abduc-
tion by the Trojan prince Paris will launch the "thousand ships" of the
Greek war against Troy. The "broken wall, the burning roof and tower"
call up before our eyes the city of Troy being reduced to rubble and
ashes in defeat. In the aftermath of the war, Agamemnon, the leader of
the Greek forces, will return home after years of absence, to be murdered by his wife Clytemnestra and her lover Aegisthus.

The Receptive Reader

1. In the world of Greek myth, animals often do not have derogatory connotations. What are the connotations of the animal in Yeats's poem? Is the swan
mostly beast? human? divine?

2. Greek art and literature were more explicit about sex than later civilizations. What would you say to readers who may find this poem offensive?

Helen of Troy—the daughter of Zeus, who had made love to Leda in
the shape of a swan—was often blamed for the bloody conflict between
Greece and Troy. Helen had married Menelaus, king of Sparta, and she
incurred the hatred of her fellow-Greeks when she allowed the "fire-
brand" Trojan prince Paris to carry her away to Troy, thus causing the
bloody Trojan war. What two different ways of viewing Helen contend
in the following poem?

H. D. (Hilda Doolittle)   *(1886–1961)*

Helen   *1924*

All Greece hates
the still eyes in the white face,
the luster as of olives
where she stands,
And the white hands.   5

All Greece reviles
the wan face when she smiles,
hating it deeper still
when it grows wan and white,
remembering past enchantments   10
And past ills.

Greece sees unmoved,
God's daughter, born of love,
the beauty of cool feet
and slenderest knees,   15
could love indeed the maid,
only if she were laid,
white ash amid funereal cypresses.

The Receptive Reader

1. How does the poet emphasize and drive home the unrelenting hate felt for Helen by her countrymen and countrywomen?

2. What labels applied here to Helen and what descriptive details *counteract* these powerful negative feelings, and how? Explore the connotations—associations, implications—of words like *luster, enchantments, maid,* and of phrases like "God's daughter, born of love" and "beauty of cool feet / and slenderest knees."

3. Is the poet herself taking sides? As you read the poem, are you?

JUXTAPOSITIONS

The Sacrifice of Isaac

For many centuries, allusions to the Bible have been woven into the language of poets and artists. Old Testament themes like Cain's fratricide, Noah's flood, or David slaying Goliath are part of our collective memory. New Testament parables like those of the Good Samaritan help shape our thinking on subjects like charity and antiwelfare reform. The sacrifice of Isaac as the Lord's test of Abraham's obedience has long been a favorite subject for artists. Compare the Old Testament story with its use by a twentieth-century poet.

Genesis 22:1–3

And it came to pass after these things that God did tempt Abraham and
    said unto him, Abraham: and he said, Behold, here I am.
And he said, Take now thy son, thine only son Isaac, whom thou lovest,
    and get thee into the land of Moriah; and offer him there for a burnt
    offering upon one of the mountains which I will tell thee of.

And Abraham rose up early in the morning, and saddled his ass, and took
  two of his young men with him, and Isaac his son, and clave the
  wood for the burnt offering, and rose up, and went unto the place of
  which God had told him.
Then on the third day Abraham lifted up his eyes, and saw the place
  afar off.
And Abraham said unto his young men, Abide ye here with the ass; and
  I and the lad will go yonder and worship, and come again to you.
And Abraham took the wood of the burnt offering, and laid it upon Isaac
  his son; and he took the fire in his hand, and a knife; and they went
  both of them together.
And Isaac spake unto Abraham his father, and said, My father: and he
  said, Here am I, my son. And he said, Behold the fire and the wood:
  but where is the lamb for a burnt offering?
And Abraham said, My son, God will provide himself a lamb for a burnt
  offering: so they went both of them together.
And they came to the place which God had told him of; and Abraham
  built an altar there, and laid the wood in order, and bound Isaac his
  son, and laid him on the altar upon the wood.
And Abraham stretched forth his hand, and took the knife to slay his son.
And the angel of the Lord called unto him out of heaven, and said,
  Abraham, Abraham: and he said, Here am I.
And he said, Lay not thine hand upon the lad, neither do thou anything
  unto him: for now I know that thou fearest God, seeing thou hast not
  withheld thy son, thine only son from me.
And Abraham lifted up his eyes, and looked, and behold behind him a
  ram caught in a thicket by his horns: and Abraham went and took the
  ram, and offered him up for a burnt offering in the stead of his son.

Wilfred Owen wrote his adaptation of the biblical story during the
years of trench warfare in World War I, when Britain, France, and Germany were sacrificing the lives of hundreds of thousands of young men.
How far and how closely does the poet follow the biblical story? When
do you first realize that Owen has transposed the story from its ancient
setting? How does he change the climactic ending of the story?

Wilfred Owen   *(1893–1918)*

The Parable of the Old Men and the Young   1918

So Abram rose, and clave° the wood, and went,   *split*
And took the fire with him, and a knife.
And as they journeyed both of them together,
Isaac the first-born spake and said, My Father,
Behold the preparations, fire and iron,   5
But where the lamb for this burnt-offering?
Then Abram bound the youth with belts and straps,

And builded parapets° and trenches there,   *earthworks*
And stretched forth the knife to slay his son.
When lo! an angel called him out of heaven,   10
Saying, Lay not thy hand upon the lad,
Neither do anything to him. Behold,
A ram caught in a thicket by its horns;
Offer the Ram of Pride instead of him.
But the old man would not so, but slew° his son—   *killed*   15
And half the seed° of Europe, one by one.   *offspring*

The Receptive Reader

1. What are the *common* elements in both versions of the story?

2. How has the poet *changed* the meaning of the test undergone by Abraham? What does the "Ram of Pride" stand for? Who or what is the target of Owen's indictment?

3. What biblical *parables* do you know? How is this poem like a parable? Why does the poet's use of the biblical story give his indictment special force?

THE LANGUAGE OF MYTH

. . . still the heart doth need a language, still
Doth the old instinct bring back the old names.
                    SAMUEL TAYLOR COLERIDGE

To many modern readers, myths have seemed, in the words of the psychoanalyst Carl Jung, "still fresh and living" in the hidden recesses of their minds. Anthropologists and psychoanalysts have probed recurrent **archetypes**—symbolic embodiments of vital forces and life cycles that we encounter in many disguises and variations. The earliest religions may have centered on mother goddesses associated with the development of agriculture and worshiped in fertility cults.

Judy Grahn   *(born 1940)*

They Say She Is Veiled   *1982*

They say she is veiled
and a mystery. That is
one way of looking.
Another
is that she is where   5
she has always been,
exactly in place,
and it is we,

we who are mystified,
we who are veiled   10
and without faces.

The Receptive Reader

How does the poet play on the words *mystery* and *mystified?* What are the two ways "of looking" in this poem?

JUXTAPOSITIONS

The Icarus Myth

According to a universally known Greek myth, Daedalus fashioned wings for himself and his son Icarus, but as Icarus flew too close to the sun, the wax gluing the feathers in his wings melted and he perished in the sea. The myth is part of a web of stories taking place on the island of Crete. Daedalus was the Athenian inventor employed by King Minos to build the maze, or labyrinth, designed to pen in the Minotaur, a monstrous creature half man, half bull. When Minos refused Daedalus' request to let him and his son return to Athens, Daedalus constructed wings from feathers and wax so that father and son could make their escape through the air. The Roman poet Ovid (43 B.C.–A.D. 18) concludes his retelling of the myth as follows:

When the boy, too bold, too young, too ambitious in daring,
    Forced his way too high, leaving his father below,
So the bonds of the wings were loosened, the fastenings melted,
    Nor could the moving arms hold in the desert of air. . . .
All of the wax was gone: his arms were bare as he struggled
    Beating the void of the air, unsupported, unstayed.
"Father!" he cried as he fell, "Oh, father, father, I'm falling!"
    Till the green of the wave closed on the agonized cry,
While the father, alas, a father no longer, was calling,
    "Icarus, where do you fly, Icarus, where in the sky?
Icarus!" he would call—and saw the wings on the water.
    Now earth covers his bones; now that sea has his name.

                                      Translated by Rolfe Humphries

Different readers have used the traditional story as a prompt to construct their own private myths. Here are some of the readings:

✱ The myth acts out the age-old archetypes of impetuous, headstrong, ambitious youth and cautious, prudent, shell-shocked age.

✱ The myth focuses on the theme of overreaching, of overambitious, heedless pride that goes before a fall. In the words of a student reader, "each time we dare, we taunt the gods a little." The Greeks called arrogant human pride *hubris,* and they expected it to provoke the wrath of the gods.

✖ The myth glorifies the human capacity for aspiration, for "testing the boundaries." Flight has long been a symbol for our human capacity to struggle up from the mud and clay, even at the risk of failure.

✖ The myth focuses on the strongest kind of human love—the love of a parent for a child.

Look at the treatment of the Icarus myth in the following modern poems. What is the meaning of the myth for each poet?

Anne Sexton   *(1928–1974)*

To a Friend Whose Work Has Come to Triumph   1962

Consider Icarus, pasting those sticky wings on,
testing that strange little tug at his shoulder blade,
and think of that first flawless moment over the lawn
of the labyrinth. Think of the difference it made!
There below are the trees, as awkward as camels;   5
and here are the shocked starlings pumping past
and think of innocent Icarus who is doing quite well;
larger than a sail, over the fog and blast
of the plushy ocean he goes. Admire his wings!
Feel the fire at his neck and see how casually   10
he glances up and is caught, wondrously tunneling
into that hot eye. Who cares that he fell back into the sea?
See him acclaiming the sun and come plunging down
while his sensible daddy goes straight into town.

The Receptive Reader

1. Traditionally, people have listened to myths with grave attention. What details and imaginative comparisons give this poem a more irreverent or *ironic* modern twist?

2. What in the poem could lead a reader to conclude that nevertheless the myth has a serious meaning for the modern poet? What is the *theme* of this poem?

3. Both form and content of this poem play modern variations on traditional patterns. How does this fourteen-line poem live up to the requirements of the traditional *sonnet?* How does it depart from them?

The following poem gives us a retelling that takes us "down to earth" in its search for the reality behind the mythical tradition. The poem thus becomes a modern countermyth in which the ancient story becomes demythologized and the original heroes become modern antiheroes.

The tone is irreverent toward both gods and human beings. How much does the poem preserve of the spirit or appeal of the original myth?

David Wagoner   *(born 1926)*

The Return of Icarus   *1958*

He showed up decades later, crook-necked and hip-sprung,
Not looking for work but cadging food and wine as artfully
As a king, while our dogs barked themselves inside out
At the sight of his hump and a whiff of his goatskin.

We told him Daedalus was dead, worn out with honors   5
(Some of them fabulous), but especially for making
Wings for the two of them and getting them off the ground.
He said he remembered that time, but being too young a mooncalf,

He hadn't cared about those labyrinthine double-dealings
Except for the scary parts, the snorting and bellowing.   10
He'd simply let the wax be smeared over his arms
And suffered handfuls of half-stuck second-hand chicken feathers

And flapped and flapped, getting the heft of them, and taken
Off (to both their amazements), listening for his father's
Endless, garbled, and finally inaudible instructions   15
From further and further below, and then swooping

And banking and trying to hover without a tail and stalling
While the old man, a slow learner, got the hang of it.
At last, with the weight of his years and his genius,
Daedalus thrashed aloft and was gawkily airborne.   20

And they went zigzagging crosswing and downwind over the water,
Half-baked by the sirocco,° with Daedalus explaining   *hot wind*
Everything now: which way was up, how to keep your mouth
Shut for the purpose of breathing and listening,

How to fly low (having no choice himself) in case of Harpies,°   *monstrous birds* 25
And how to keep Helios,° beaming at a comfortable distance   *the sun*
By going no higher than the absolute dangling minimum
To avoid kicking Poseidon,° the old salt, square in the froth.   *god of the sea*

But Icarus saw the wax at his skinny quill-tips sagging,
And he couldn't get a word in edgewise or otherwise,   30
So he strained even higher, searching for ships or landfalls
While he still had time to enjoy his share of the view,

And in the bright, high-spirited silence, he took comfort
From his father's lack of advice, and Helios turned
Cool, not hot as Icarus rose, joining a wedge of geese   35
For an embarrassing, exhilarating moment northward,

And then he grew cold till the wax turned brittle as marble,
Stiffening his elbows and suddenly breaking
Away, leaving him wingless, clawing at nothing, then falling
Headfirst with a panoramic, panchromatic vista   40

Of the indifferent sun, the indifferent ocean, and a blurred
Father passing sideways, still chugging and flailing away
With rows of eagle feathers. When Icarus hit the water,
He took its salt as deeply as his own.

He didn't tell us how he'd paddled ashore or where   45
He'd been keeping himself or what in the world he'd been doing
For a living, yet he didn't seem bitter. "Too bad
You weren't around," we said, "there'd have been something in it

For you, probably—an apartment straddling an aqueduct,
Orchards, invitations, hecatombs° of women."   *crowds (as in*   50
"No hard feelings," he said. "Wings weren't my idea."   *communal tombs)*
And he told odd crooked stories to children for hours

About what lived under water, what lived under the earth,
And what still lived in the air, and why. A few days later
He slouched off on his game leg and didn't come back.   55
He didn't steal any chickens or girls' hearts

Or ask after his father's grave or his father's money
Or even kick the dogs. But he showed us calluses
Thicker than hooves on his soles and palms, and told us
That's how he'd stay in touch, keeping his feet on the ground.   60

The Receptive Reader

1. How does the first stanza signal that the ancient story is again being retold with a modern twist? How does it realign your perspective?

2. How does this retelling redraw the portrait of the father? How does it change your image of the father and our image of the young son? How does it reinterpret or refashion the relationship between father and son?

3. In the retelling of the flight, which parts of it are *humorous;* which seem serious?

4. For you, does the last line of the poem spell out the *theme* of the poem? Does it point a moral? Does it strike the keynote for the poem as a whole?

5. What is witty about the *allusion* in the father's "labyrinthine double-dealings" and the "snorting and bellowing"? What other references remind you that we are in the world of Greek mythology?

The Personal Response

Do this poet's changes in the story make the myth more believable or less?

The following modern sonnet strips the Icarus myth of many of its traditional trappings. There is no literal flight in this poem—no flying with false feathers like the original Icarus, nor flying in a metal bird that shears the clouds and becomes a menace to real birds. The flights here are "imaged" flights, journeys of the mind. Although our bodies are earthbound, our minds are capable of tremendous flights of the imagination, making us outsoar the highest reaches of heaven and making us plummet to deepest hell.

Vassar Miller   *(born 1924)*

The New Icarus   1956

Slip off the husk of gravity to lie
Bedded with wind; float on a whimsy, lift
Upon a wish: your bow's own arrow, rift
Newton's decorum—only when you fly.
But naked. No false-feathered fool, you try   5
Dalliance with heights, nor, plumed with metal, shift
And shear the clouds, imperiling lark and swift
And all birds bridal-bowered in the sky.

Your wreck of bone, barred their delight's dominions,
Lacking their formula for flight, holds imaged   10
Those alps of air no eagle's wing can quell.
With arms flung crosswise, pinioned to wooden pinions,
You in one motion, plucked and crimson-plumaged,
Outsoar all Heaven, plummeting all Hell.

The Receptive Reader

1. Examine the poet's graphic *metaphors*. What is exceptionally appropriate or fitting about the image she creates by the phrase "Slip off the husk of gravity"?

2. Look at the *paradoxical* metaphors—metaphors that at first glance seem contradictory or physically impossible: how could the person addressed be told to be "your bow's own arrow"? (We propel our imaginary selves on the imagined voyage with the force of our own will and desire; these serve as the bow shooting forth ourselves as the arrow.) What do you make of the paradoxical "plumed with metal" or "alps of air"? What sense do they make on second thought?

3. The *allusion* to Newton, master physicist and mathematician of the eighteenth century, makes us think of Newtonian science. We are expected to think of a mechanistic model of the universe, where everything behaves according to the strict laws of physics—as if in accordance with strict etiquette or "decorum." How would the new Icarus "rift / Newton's decorum"?

4. The *pun* in the phrase "pinioned (fastened, shackled) to wooden pinions (wings)" makes us imagine a person with arms flung wide and fastened to the wooden wings as to a cross. Are you prepared to agree with the student who wrote the following passage about the possible religious implications of the poem?

The new Icarus is Christ, whose "wreck of bone" finds salvation through suffering. Christ "pinioned to wooden pinions" and "crimson plumaged" reaches heights of love that ancient humanity (Icarus) or modern humanity, "plumed with metal" of modern airplanes, will never outsoar. Living the life of the spirit incurs a great risk, since it can bring suffering, a "plummeting" to "all Hell." However, although Christ lacks the birds' "formula for flight," he can go the eagle one better. He can rise from his "plucked" "wreck of bone" to "those alps of air no eagle's wing can quell." Despite being nailed to the cross, "pinioned to wooden pinions," he can "in one motion . . . outsoar all Heaven."

The following poem is one of several commenting on the painting "The Fall of Icarus" by the Flemish painter Pieter Breughel (about 1525–1569). How does the poem put the mythical story in perspective?

William Carlos Williams   *(1883–1963)*

Landscape with the Fall of Icarus   *1960*

According to Breughel
when Icarus fell
it was spring

a farmer was plowing
his field   5
the whole pageantry

of the year was
awake tingling
near

the edge of the sea   10
concerned with itself
sweating in the sun
that melted the wings' wax

unsignificantly
off the coast   15
there was

a splash quite unnoticed
this was
Icarus drowning

Making Connections—For Discussion or Writing

Explore the versions of the Icarus myth found in these poems. What do they show about the perennial or universal appeal of the myth? What do they show about the difference between more traditional and more modern perspectives? Which of the poems do you find most congenial or personally appealing and why?

Write your own personal version of the Icarus myth or of another myth that you have known for some time.

MODERN MYTHS

goddess of the silver screen
the only original American queen
JUDY GRAHN,
"HELEN IN HOLLYWOOD"

Although many myths are age-old, we see the myth-making faculty at work in our own time. The lone rider of the frontier assumed mythical proportions in the cowboy myth that is at the heart of American popular culture. Its central figure, like mythical heroes of the past, appears in countless permutations, from Buffalo Bill to space-age cowboys like "Star Trek's" Captain Kirk. To city dwellers hemmed in by city life, the cowboy seems to stimulate a collective memory of wide-open spaces, of depending on oneself, of being able to move on.

The Hollywood dream factory created mythical sex goddesses. Norma Jean Baker was turned into Marilyn Monroe, who became the daydream of every immature male: "Marilyn, who was every man's love affair . . . who was blonde and beautiful and had a little rinky-dink of a voice . . . which carried such ripe overtones of erotic excitement and yet was the voice of a little child" (Norman Mailer, *Marilyn*). After her death, admirers and defenders created the countermyth of the actress rebelling against the stereotype of the dumb blonde that denied her her own humanity—Marilyn "who tried, I believe, to help us see that beauty has a mind of its own" (Judy Grahn).

Sharon Olds   *(born 1942)*

The Death of Marilyn Monroe   1983

The ambulance men touched her cold
body, lifted it, heavy as iron,
onto the stretcher, tried to close the
mouth, closed the eyes, tied the
arms to the sides, moved a caught   5
strand of hair, as if it mattered,
saw the shape of her breasts, flattened by
gravity, under the sheet,
carried her, as if it were she,
down the steps.   10

These men were never the same. They went out
afterwards, as they always did,
for a drink or two, but they could not meet
each other's eyes.

              Their lives took   15
a turn—one had nightmares, strange
pains, impotence, depression. One did not
like his work, his wife looked
different, his kids. Even death
seemed different to him—a place where she   20
would be waiting,

And one found himself standing at night
in the doorway to a room of sleep, listening to
a woman breathing, just an ordinary
woman   25
breathing.

The Receptive Reader

1. What was the cause of Marilyn Monroe's death?

2. Why were the men in the poem "never the same"? What is the *mythic* or symbolic significance of Monroe in this poem?

3. Has popular entertainment left the *stereotype* of the Hollywood blonde behind?

4. Is the Marilyn Monroe myth alive?

The Creative Dimension

What is the keynote of this poem for you? What lasting impression does it leave in your mind? Look at the following re-creation by a fellow student, and then write your own.

Those ambulance men
shocked into recognition of death and tenuous life
shifted the body
prepared her for the journey
The body wasn't going anywhere special
they were
One to nightmares, strangeness
Another to dislike, to fear
The last to listening.

How does the following poem rewrite the cowboy myth?

e. e. cummings   *(1894–1963)*

Buffalo Bill's   *1923*

Buffalo Bill's
defunct
       who used to
       ride a watersmooth-silver
                    stallion   5
and break onetwothreefourfive pigeonsjustlikethat
                               Jesus
he was a handsome man
                and what i want to know is
how do you like your blueeyed boy   10
Mister Death

The Receptive Reader

Who was Buffalo Bill? What was his claim to fame? In what ways is he a symbol of his period in American history? What is the attitude toward him in this poem?

The Creative Dimension

A student wrote the "Portrait I" tribute shortly after e. e. cummings had died. How well did the student writer get into the spirit of the original? Try your hand at a similar portrait of someone more recently defunct.

   Portrait I

   e. e. someone
   buried by busy ones,
              used to
              wish yes aprils with a you
                     and a me
   and write onetwothreefourfive poemsjustlikethat
                        by dong and ding
   he was a perceptive man
                and what i want to know is
   where is he now when we need him
   Mister Death

POEMS FOR FURTHER STUDY

In reading the following poems, pay special attention to the poet's use of myth and allusion. What knowledge of myth, legend, or history does the poet assume? What is the role of an allusion in a poem as a whole?

William Wordsworth   *(1770–1850)*

The World Is Too Much with Us   *1807*

The world is too much with us; late and soon,
Getting and spending, we lay waste our powers;
Little we see in nature that is ours;
We have given our hearts away, a sordid boon.
This sea that bares her bosom to the moon,   5
The winds that will be howling at all hours,
And are up-gathered now like sleeping flowers,
For this, for everything, we are out of tune;
It moves us not.—Great God! I'd rather be
A pagan suckled in a creed outworn;   10
So might I, standing on this pleasant lea,°   *grassland*
Have glimpses that would make me less forlorn;
Have sight of Proteus rising from the sea;
Or hear old Triton blow his wreathèd horn.

The Receptive Reader

From a dictionary or other reference work, what can you find out about Proteus and Triton? What role do they play in the poem? What does the world of
Greek myth mean to the speaker in this sonnet?

Edna St. Vincent Millay   *(1892–1950)*

An Ancient Gesture   *1931*

I thought, as I wiped my eyes on the corner of my apron:
Penelope did this too.
And more than once: you can't keep weaving all day
And undoing it all through the night;
Your arms get tired, and the back of your neck gets tight;   5
And along towards morning, when you think it will never be light,
And your husband has been gone, and you don't know where, for years,
Suddenly you burst into tears;
There is simply nothing else to do.

And I thought, as I wiped my eyes on the corner of my apron: 10
This is an ancient gesture, authentic, antique,
In the very best tradition, classic, Greek;
Ulysses did this too.
But only as a gesture,—a gesture which implied
To the assembled throng that he was much too moved to speak.   15
He learned it from Penelope . . .
Penelope, who really cried.

The Receptive Reader

1. What is the story of Penelope and Ulysses?

2. In Homer, men weep over their slain comrades. What makes this poet suspicious of Ulysses' tears?

Donald Finkel   *(born 1929)*

The Sirens   *1959*

The news lapped at us out of all
Horizons: the ticking night full
Of gods; sensed, heard the tactile

Sea turn in his bed, prickling
Among derelicts. When the song   5
Was clear enough, we spread our hair,

Caught it. Under the comb the strands
Whipped into fresh harmonies, untangled
Again. The wind took it, and he heard.

The droll ship swung leeward;   10
Caught sight of him (rather, could
Have seen, busy with the fugue)

Yanking his bonds, the strings of his wide
Neck drawn like shrouds, his scream
Caught in the sail.   15
        Now in a sea

Of wheat he rows, reconstructing.
In his ridiculous, lovely mouth the strains
Tumble into place. Do you think
Wax could have stopped us, or chains?   20

The Receptive Reader

The sirens were mythical women whose song was so irresistible that mariners would steer their ships into the rocks of the sirens' island and perish. This poem alludes to the story of a famous traveler who passed by the island during his far-flung voyages. What is the story of Ulysses and the sirens? How does this poem reverse the usual perspective from which we see this story—and with what effect?

WRITING ABOUT LITERATURE

22   Reinterpreting Myth (Focus on Peer Review)

The Writing Workshop   Writers don't write in a vacuum. They live with feedback from friends, family, colleagues, editors, reviewers—or just plain readers. In a classroom, you can simulate such input by having your peers react to your writing as individuals or in a group. Such feedback helps make you more audience-conscious; it strengthens your sense of what happens when your writing reaches the reader.

In turn, when you act as a peer reviewer, you help alert other writers to the reader's needs. You help them see their writing through the reader's eyes. Remember that it is easy to lapse into a fault-finding mode. Although it is important to identify weaknesses, it is just as important to help writers develop what is promising and to help them build on their strengths. What can the writer do to improve, to make the writing more instructive, more effective? Here are sample passages with comments that might help a writer develop the full potential of a paper:

> Ovid, David Wagoner, and Vassar Miller offer vastly different interpretations of the classic myth. However, we are also able to see a few similarities.

COMMENT: What *are* these differences and similarities? Give us a hint to keep us interested? Give us more of a preview?

> In the biblical account, Abraham "bound Isaak his son, and laid him upon the altar upon the wood." Owen's poem says that "Abram bound the youth with belts and straps, / And builded parapets and trenches." Belts and straps, parapets and trenches are surely alien to people of biblical times who herded sheep for a living. These words denote the military.

COMMENT: Follow up and explain? Why does the poet use these "military" references? What kind of warfare and what war does he have in mind?

> The first thing that must be taken into consideration about this poem is its basis in the traditional biblical story. . . . Once the element of war and sacrifice has been introduced, the whole concept of sacrifice is looked at in respect to the ones that do the sacrificing as well as the ones being sacrificed. . . . Owen has successfully conveyed the personalities and situations involved with war and sacrifice.

COMMENT: Rewrite to avoid the wooden, impersonal passive? "The element of war and sacrifice *has been introduced*"—by whom? Try "Once the poet *has introduced* . . . he *looks* at

this theme . . ."? Cut down on jargony words like *basis,*
element, concept, situation? Rewrite chunky passages like
"looked at in respect to the ones that"?

Student Paper for Peer Review

Monroe: Quest of Beauty

Marilyn Monroe became something more than human even before her suicide in
the early 60s. Her image—celluloid clips, photo stills—keeps appearing in sometimes unlikely places. Sometimes her image reappears in another embodiment,
such as Madonna, and the casual observer will still think "Monroe" before recognition sets in. We know who she is, or was. Or at least we think we do.

Norman Mailer in *Marilyn,* one of a never-ending stream of books about the "goddess of the silver screen," said, "She was not the dark contract of the passionate
brunette depths that speak of blood, vows taken for life, and the furies of
vengeance . . . no, Marilyn suggested sex might be difficult or dangerous with others, but ice cream with her." Mailer said, "we think of Marilyn who was every man's
love affair" and whose "little rinky-dink voice" carried "ripe overtones of erotic
excitement and yet was the voice of a little child."

In her poem, "The Death of Marilyn Monroe," Sharon Olds describes the impact
that Marilyn's death had on the ambulance attendants who carried "her cold body"
to the ambulance. "These men were never the same." One had nightmares,
became impotent, suffered depresssion. One did not "like his work, his wife /
looked different, his kids." Death became a place "where she would be waiting."
Another

      found himself standing at night
in the doorway to a room of sleep, listening to
a woman breathing, just an ordinary
woman
breathing.

For these men, and all men and women, the death of Marilyn meant far more than
the tragedy of an individual; it was the death of a modern goddess, of a mythical
being.

To Judy Grahn, a feminist poet, Monroe, like Harlowe, Holiday, or Taylor, represents an older myth, that of Helen of Troy. In her poem, "Helen in Hollywood," she
says, "'That's the one,' we say in instant recognition, / because our breath is taken
away by her beauty, / or what we call her beauty." Helen herself, to Judy Grahn is
merely the human incarnation of a deity humanity has almost forgotten. This deity
goes by many names and lives in many cultures and is represented in our world by
the Hollywood star who

      writes in red red lipstick
on the window of her body,
long for me, oh need me!

We, her fans, crowd around her to share in her "luminescent glow," and we may
destroy her in the process:

We adore her. we imitate and rob her
adulate   envy
admire   neglect
scorn.   leave alone
invade, fill
ourselves with her.
we love her, we say
and if she isn't careful
we may even kill her.

She is our "leaping, laughing leading lady," who "sweeps eternally / down the steps / in her long round gown." But it is also she "who lies strangled / in the bell-tower"; it is she "who is monumentally drunk and suicidal." It is she who when "locked waiting in the hightower . . . leaps from her blue window."

For years after Marilyn's death, men would say (and women, too): "If only she had met me, I could have saved her!" Something in her flawed beauty, in her vulnerability, made her personal to millions of people. She became the best celluloid representation of the goddess of beauty, approachable and accepting of everyone's gifts. She taught us the power of sexual awareness, the power of our sexual selves. Everyone was welcome at her well. To Sharon Olds, not to have Marilyn as a symbol in our lives is the price the ambulance crew paid. It is not to have connection; it is not to have sexual, social, or family bonds. It is to stand alone in the dark, doubting and seeking reaffirmation of the reality of a loved person in our lives, "listening to / a woman breathing, just an ordinary / woman breathing."

Questions

1. Should the writer have brought out her *thesis* earlier or more clearly in the paper? What would you suggest as a possible thesis statement early in the paper? Compare your suggestions with those of your classmates.

2. Could the relation between Mailer, Olds, and Grahn have been clarified more to make the overall *pattern* or drift of the paper clearer to the reader? What is the connection? What is the overall pattern?

3. Do you feel anywhere in the essay a need for additional *explanation* or discussion of the quoted passages?

4. Do you need additional *quotations?* Do you need more of a sense of the overall *intention* and pattern of a source? Where or why?

5. Do you have suggestions for strengthening *beginning and end*—title, introduction, conclusion?

6. What is your personal *reaction* to this writer's interpretation of the Monroe myth? Does it need more explanation or justification? How do you think other readers will react?

7. "Helen in Hollywood" appears in Judy Grahn's *Queen of Wands,* along with other Helen poems. Does this paper make you want to read the whole poem by Judy Grahn or more of her poetry? Why or why not?

23 Three Poets in Depth

Dickinson, Frost, Brooks

Experiment escorts us last—
His pungent company
Will not allow an Axiom
An Opportunity
                    EMILY DICKINSON

FOCUS ON THE POET

Lovers of poetry do not usually read a poem in isolation. They reread a poem by a favorite poet, or they read a poem in a new collection by a known poet, or they read a poem by a new poet they have heard discussed. Reading a new or unfamiliar poem by a familiar poet, they are already attuned to the poet's way of looking at the world. They recognize the poet's style, the poet's personal voice. Reading a favorite poet, they recognize themes that have loomed large in the poet's personal experience or poetic career. They recognize political or ideological commitments that have shaped the poet's sense of mission.

This chapter will focus in turn on three kinds of investigation that can help you understand and appreciate poems:

The Poet's Voice   As faithful readers, we become attuned to a poet's unmistakable personal idiom or style. The best-loved poets have an inimitable, personal way of looking at the world and sharing with us what they see. Reading a poet like Emily Dickinson, Robert Frost, or Gwendolyn Brooks, we treasure the poet's personal voice, the way we welcome a cherished face. Being attuned to a poet's style, we find our bearings in reading a difficult or challenging passage. One poem helps us understand another; we interpret a difficult passage by way of cross-reference to a similar passage elsewhere. We see the connections; we trace familiar threads.

Author Biography   How does a poem become more meaningful when we see it in the context of the poet's life? Who is the biographical person

555

behind the persona speaking in a poem? Who is the person behind the mask a particular poem may create? Reading biographical material helps us read between the lines when personal loyalties or personal traumas are reflected in poem. With a poet like Robert Frost, the poet's life story looms large in the background of the poetry—the struggle for acceptance, the impact of adversity, the recognition as a legendary poet-sage.

The Poet's Commitment   In the work of a politically committed poet, individual poems may be bulletins from an ongoing struggle. To relate to recurrent themes, we may have to understand the poet's sense of mission. We may have to understand the poet's social conscience, class consciousness, or solidarity with the oppressed. It would be hard to read poems by Gwendolyn Brooks while disregarding her involvement in the struggle of African Americans to achieve a place in the sun.

EMILY DICKINSON: THE POET'S VOICE

Surgeons must be very careful
When they take the knife!
Underneath their fine incisions
Stirs the culprit,—Life!
                    EMILY DICKINSON

Emily Dickinson (1830–1886) is the outstanding example of a poet with a distinctive voice that gradually came to be cherished by lovers of poetry everywhere. She led a withdrawn life and found practically no recognition in her day. She thought about success and fame ("Fame is a bee. / It has a song— / It has a sting— / Ah, too it has a wing"), but she ultimately had to settle for "fame of my mind"—recognition in her own mind.

Although she submitted over a hundred poems for publication, only a handful found their way into print in her lifetime. To editors, the bold experimental features of her poetry seemed "technical imperfections." When they did publish her poems, editors conventionalized them. They changed bold metaphorical words to dull ones; they changed her dashes to commas and periods; they made her off-rhymes and half-rhymes rhyme. A collection of over a hundred poems published shortly after Dickinson's death astonished her publishers by running through eleven editions in two years. Almost two thousand of her poems have since been found and published.

Much ink has flowed to create, embroider, and question the legend of Emily Dickinson as the mysterious lady in white living secluded in her father's house, embarked on her own private "journey into the interior." Who was the biographical person behind the persona—which she called the "supposed person"—that speaks to us in her poetry?

Dickinson "was born into a family that did everything for her but understand her" (Richard B. Sewall). Her father—a lawyer, judge, and member of Congress—practiced a stern Puritanical religion in the New England tradition. He led morning prayers for family and servants, reading scripture in what his daughter Emily called a "militant accent." At a time when questioning even minor points of doctrine was scandalous, Dickinson developed serious doubts about original sin. She stopped going to church by the time she was thirty. She decided to keep the sabbath at home, where, in her words, a "noted clergyman" (namely God) preached better and shorter sermons.

Suspicious of books that "joggle the mind," her father banned novels, which young Emily and her brother Austin had to smuggle into the house while the father was "too busy with his briefs to notice what we do." She read and admired the great woman writers of her day, from the Brontë sisters to Elizabeth Barrett Browning. In addition to the Bible, Shakespeare, and theological works, her reading included Charlotte Brontë's *Jane Eyre* and George Eliot's *Middlemarch,* each the record of the spiritual pilgrimage of a woman in search of an identity other than the role expected of her by society.

Dickinson attended Amherst Academy and for a year Mount Holyoke Female Seminary, one of the first women's colleges. Letters she wrote as a student show a young woman in love with exuberant word play and fired by youthful enthusiasm. Her quick wit and lively sense of irony never deserted her—in a poem written many years later, she said about a pompous fraud that "He preached upon 'Breadth' till it argued him narrow." However, she gradually withdrew from the outside world. One of her best-known poems begins "The Soul selects her own Society— / Then—Shuts the Door— / To her divine Majority— / Present no more."

She stayed in touch by letter with the few people who provided her with feedback for her poetry, including her sister-in-law Susan Gilbert Dickinson and Thomas Wentworth Higginson, the *Atlantic Monthly* editor whom she addressed as her mentor or "preceptor." Although Higginson had advanced ideas for his time, he was unable to come to terms with the strange and "wayward" poems she sent him. She in turn could not conform to the demands of the literary marketplace—to auction off "the Mind of Man" and to merchandise "Heavenly Grace" and the "Human Spirit."

Much literary detective work has probed psychological, social, or medical reasons for her increasing isolation. In poems and letters, she alludes to intense emotional attachments that ended in anguish and disappointment. Passionate, yearning letters to an unknown recipient survive, possibly addressed to a married minister. Feminist critics have focused on poems that hint at love and loss in a passionate relationship with another woman. Psychoanalysts have searched her relationship with an authoritarian father, an invalid mother, or an uncomprehending brother and sister for clues to the intense, disturbed emotions in some of her poems. She may have suffered from agoraphobia, a debilitating fear of public places.

What is the distinctive voice that makes her poems unmistakably hers? First of all, her poems remain fresh because of their intensely personal *perspective*. Her poems typically make us look at the world from an unexpected angle, thus forcing us to see something anew as if for the first time. She summed up her poetic credo in the following poem. (Numbers of poems refer to the numbering in Thomas H. Johnson's *The Collected Poems of Emily Dickinson*.)

Tell all the Truth but tell it slant   about 1868
J. 1129

Tell all the Truth but tell it slant—
Success in circuit lies
Too bright for our infirm Delight
The Truth's superb surprise

As Lightning to the Children eased   5
With explanation kind
The truth must dazzle gradually
Or every man be blind—

The truth is a "superb surprise," and it is too bright and dazzling for our infirm and weak capacity to absorb it. It must be presented "in circuit"—in a roundabout way. It must be allowed to dazzle and delight us "gradually." The way to tell the truth therefore is to tell it "slant"—not directly but aslant, so that it can approach us not head-on but from a slanted, nonthreatening angle.

The way Dickinson tells the truth "slant" is not to preach at us but to speak to us through startling graphic *images* and eye-opening metaphors. She looks at the world with a special alertness, marveling at what she finds, keeping alive in us the art of wondering. For people who notice birds only in passing, the following poem presents a series of striking visual images designed to surprise them into paying attention:

A Bird came down the Walk   about 1862
J. 328

A Bird came down the Walk—
He did not know I saw—
He bit an Angleworm in halves
And ate the fellow, raw,

And then he drank a Dew   5
From a convenient Grass—
And then hopped sidewise to the Wall
To let a Beetle pass—

He glanced with rapid eyes
That hurried all around—   10
They looked like frightened Beads, I thought—
He stirred his Velvet Head

Like one in danger. Cautious,
I offered him a Crumb   15
And he unrolled his feathers
And rowed him softer home—

Than Oars divide the Ocean,
Too silver for a seam—
Or Butterflies, off Banks of Noon
Leap, plashless° as they swim.   *without a splash*   20

    The opening lines give us a startling close-up view of the visitor that has come down from the air to go about essential bird business. We see the angleworm being bitten "in halves," then eaten raw, and washed down with dew drunk from a conveniently close blade of grass. We keep watching as the bird hops sidewise to get out of the way of a beetle. We get a glimpse of the beadlike eyes that are forever hurriedly glancing and shifting, looking for danger. At the approach of the human observer (who means no harm and offers a crumb), the bird returns to its natural airborne habitat, where he "rows him softer home" than an oar-propelled boat does in the ocean. We watch the striking transition from the comically hopping, restless, and anxious earthbound bird to the bird at home in the seamless air where it effortlessly glides. Does the transformation of the bird from its awkwardly hopping, frightened, grounded state to its serenely floating skyborne state have a symbolic meaning? Are our bodies stumbling awkwardly through life in our present earthbound existence? Will our souls float serenely upward, returning to their spiritual home, during a future state? The poem does not say. If this is the larger truth hinted at in the poem, the poet tells it "slant."

The Receptive Reader

    1. Dickinson's *wording* is often cryptic—compressing or telescoping meaning into short, puzzling phrases. When she talks about the "ocean" of air, what is the meaning of "too silver for a seam"? What is it about silver that keeps us from expecting to see seams? How would butterflies leap "off banks of noon"?

    2. Many people lay out money for photographs, paintings, or figurines of pretty birds. Is the bird in this poem pretty? Why or why not?

    3. What words and images in this poem make the natural creatures seem almost human? Which remind us that they are not? One student said after reading this poem, "We like to humanize animals, but we cannot communicate with

them. Sometimes we feel kinship with animals, and at other times we don't."
How would you sum up the poet's perspective on the animal world in this
poem?

A third feature of Dickinson's poetry is the deceptive *simplicity* of her
style. Her basic line is a sparse, irregular three-beat or four-beat line.
Lines are usually held loosely together by slant rhyme or half-rhyme in
a four-line stanza, reminding us of simple popular forms like hymns and
ballads. The absence of extraneous adornment highlights the importance of the individual word, the individual metaphor. In one of her last
letters, she wrote, "I hesitate which word to take, as I can take but a few
and each must be the chiefest."

What features of the following poem seem to illustrate the distinctive
Dickinson style? For instance, does it show her way of looking at the
world from a startling new perspective? Does it show her way of giving
concrete shape to abstract ideas? Does it seem simple on the surface?

Because I could not stop for Death   *about 1863*
J. 712

Because I could not stop for Death—
He kindly stopped for me—
The Carriage held but just Ourselves—
And Immortality.

We slowly drove—He knew no haste   5
And I had put away
My labor and my leisure too,
For His Civility—

We passed the School, where Children strove
At Recess—in the Ring—   10
We passed the Fields of Gazing Grain—
We passed the Setting Sun—

Or rather—He passed Us—
The Dews drew quivering and chill—
For only Gossamer, my Gown—   15
My Tippet—only Tulle°—   *scarf of lacelike material*

We paused before a House that seemed
A Swelling of the Ground—
The Roof was scarcely visible—
The Cornice°—in the Ground—   *ornamental strip,* 20
                                                usually high up

Since then—'tis Centuries—and yet
Feels shorter than the Day
I first surmised the Horses' Heads
Were toward Eternity—

The Receptive Reader

1. What is strange or different about the *attitude toward death* reflected in this poem? Can you sympathize with or relate to the feelings that seem to be mirrored in this poem?

2. What is the *symbolism* of the school, the fields, the setting sun, the house "that seemed / a Swelling in the Ground"?

POEMS FOR FURTHER STUDY

The following selection includes many of the most widely read of Dickinson's poems. What in each poem helps you recognize her personal voice? What are themes she returns to again and again? What is her characteristic way of treating them?

J. 67   *about 1859*

Success is counted sweetest
By those who ne'er succeed
To comprehend a nectar°   *drink of the gods*
Requires sorest need.

Not one of all the purple Host   5
Who took the Flag today
Can tell the definition
So clear of Victory

As he defeated—dying—
On whose forbidden ear   10
The distant strains of triumph
Burst agonized and clear!

J. 249   *about 1861*

Wild Nights—Wild Nights!
Were I with thee
Wild Nights should be
Our luxury!

Futile—the Winds—   5
To a Heart in port—
Done with the Compass—
Done with the Chart!

Rowing in Eden—
Ah, the Sea!   10
Might I but moor—Tonight—
In Thee!

J. 258

about 1861

There's a certain Slant of light,
Winter Afternoons—
That oppresses, like the Heft
Of Cathedral Tunes—

Heavenly Hurt, it gives us—   5
We can find no scar,
But internal difference,
Where the Meanings, are—

None may teach it—Any—
'Tis the Seal Despair—   10
An imperial affliction
Sent us of the Air—

When it comes, the Landscape listens—
Shadows—hold their breath—
When it goes, 'tis like the Distance   15
On the look of Death—

J. 288

about 1861

I'm Nobody! Who are you?
Are you—Nobody—Too?
Then there's a pair of us?
Don't tell! They'd advertise—you know!

How dreary—to be—Somebody!   5
How public—like a Frog—
To tell one's name—the livelong June—
To an admiring Bog!

J. 341

about 1862

After great pain, a formal feeling comes—
The Nerves sit ceremonious, like Tombs—
The stiff Heart questions was it He, that bore,
And Yesterday, or Centuries before?

The Feet, mechanical, go round—   5
Of Ground, or Air, or Ought°—   *anything*
A Wooden way
Regardless grown,
A Quartz contentment, like a stone—

This is the Hour of Lead—   10
Remembered, if outlived,
As Freezing persons, recollect the Snow—
First—Chill—then Stupor—then the letting go—

Facsimile of Emily Dickinson's original manuscript of J. 435. Courtesy The Houghton Library, Harvard University, Cambridge.

J. 435   *about 1862*

Much Madness is divinest Sense—
To a discerning Eye—
Much Sense—the starkest Madness—
'Tis the Majority
In this, as All, prevail—   5
Assent—and you are sane—
Demur°—you're straightway dangerous—   *disagree*
And handled with a Chain—

J. 579   *about 1862*

I had been hungry, all the Years—
My Noon had Come—to dine—
I trembling drew the Table near—
And touched the Curious Wine—

'Twas this on Tables I had seen—   5
When turning, hungry, Home
I looked in Windows, for the Wealth
I could not hope—for Mine—

I did not know the ample Bread—
'Twas so unlike the Crumb   10
The Birds and I, had often shared
In Nature's—Dining Room—

The Plenty hurt me—'twas so new—
Myself felt ill—and odd—
As Berry—of a Mountain Bush—   15
Transplanted—to the Road—

Nor was I hungry—so I found
That Hunger—was a way
Of Persons outside Windows—
The Entering—takes away—   20

J. 986   *about 1865*

A narrow fellow in the Grass
Occasionally rides—
You may have met him—did you not
His notice sudden is—

The grass divides as with a Comb—   5
A spotted shaft is seen—
And then it closes at your feet
And opens further on—

He likes a Boggy Acre°—   *swampy ground*
A Floor too cool for Corn—   10
Yet when a Boy, and Barefoot—
I more than once at Noon

Have passed, I thought, a Whiplash
Unbraiding in the Sun
When stooping to secure it   15
It wrinkled, and was gone—

Several of Nature's People
I know, and they know me—
I feel for them a transport°   *sudden impulsive feeling*
Of cordiality—   20

But never met this Fellow
Attended, or alone
Without a tighter breathing
And Zero at the bone—

J. 1732
about 1896

My life closed twice before its close—
It yet remains to see
If Immortality unveil
A third event to me
So huge, so hopeless to conceive   5
As these that twice befell
Parting is all we know of heaven,
And all we need of hell.

The Creative Dimension

From the poems by Dickinson you have read, choose a haunting image or a striking, puzzling detail that left a lasting impression. Write a passage in which you re-create the image or impression and follow the train of associations—of images, thoughts, or feelings—that it sets in motion in your mind.

Making Connections—For Discussion and Writing

For a library research project, search for books and articles that would provide material for a treatment of one of the following topics:

✗ A range of critical interpretations of the same Dickinson poem. How does the same poem look when read by different readers? Are there major areas of agreement? What are major differences in interpretation, and what might explain them?

✗ Several critics' treatment of a recurrent theme in Dickinson's poetry. What do different critics say about the poet's treatment of a central recurrent theme like death, nature, love, faith, or immortality?

✗ Several critics' discussion of a key feature of her style or personal voice.

Numberless discussions of Dickinson's poetry have appeared in periodicals ranging from the *Explicator* to *New Literary History*. You may be able to consult book-length sources like the following:

Albert Gelpi, *Emily Dickinson: The Mind of the Poet* (1965)
Ruth Miller, *The Poetry of Emily Dickinson* (1974)
Richard B. Sewall, *The Life of Emily Dickinson* (1974)
Susan Juhasz, *The Undiscovered Continent: Emily Dickinson and the Space of the Mind* (1983)
Susan Juhasz, ed., *Feminist Critics Read Emily Dickinson* (1983)
Jerome Loving, *Emily Dickinson: The Poet on the Second Story* (1986)
Helen McNeil, *Emily Dickinson* (1986)
Cynthia Griffin Wolff, *Emily Dickinson* (1986)
Christanne Miller, *Emily Dickinson: A Poet's Grammar* (1987)
Suzanne Juhasz, *Comic Power in Emily Dickinson* (1993)
Jamie Fuller, *The Diary of Emily Dickinson* (1993)

ROBERT FROST: POET AND PERSONA

If Robert Frost was much honored in his lifetime, it
was because a good many preferred to ignore his
darker truths.

JOHN F. KENNEDY

Robert Frost (1874–1963) became a living legend—the closest that twentieth-century America came to having a national poet. As with other legendary literary figures, biographers and critics have searched for the real-life person behind the legend. They have probed the relationship between the public persona of the adored poet-sage and the private demons of the poet's life.

In the early years, Frost struggled to make a living for himself and his family—as a farmer, a part-time teacher, a poet. He was born in San Francisco and spent his boyhood years in California. Frost's father, a southerner who had named the boy Robert Lee, died when Frost was eleven years old. His Scottish mother then took him to New England, where she had relatives. Frost attended Lawrence High School in Massachusetts, and he later married Elinor White, who had been his covaledictorian there. He attended first Dartmouth and then Harvard, but he walked out of both of them, deciding to learn not from teachers but from "writers who had written before me."

With help from his grandfather, Frost bought a farm in New Hampshire, the setting of many of his early poems. However, he was unable to make a living as a farmer and part-time teacher and unable to get more than a few poems accepted for publication. Frost and his wife then took their growing family to England, where he made friends with other aspiring young poets. He was first recognized as a poet while in England, where he published two volumes: *A Boy's Will* (1913) and *North of Boston* (1914).

When he returned to the United States, magazines started to print his poems, and he gradually became widely known as a poet and lecturer. Honors multiplied: four Pulitzer Prizes, honorary degrees from Oxford and Cambridge, travel abroad as a government-sponsored ambassador of good will. Prestigious teaching appointments included stints as "poet in residence" at Amherst College and later at the University of Michigan in Ann Arbor. He returned to Ann Arbor late in his life for the kind of poetry reading where he was adored and lionized by thousands of students.

As a poet, performer, and public figure, Frost played the role of the New England sage. He appeared "wide-shouldered, craggy, tough in texture, solid as New Hampshire granite" (Louis Untermeyer). He spoke as the voice of homely truths, keeping in touch with the simple realities of rural living, distancing himself from movements and trends.

In the following poem, Frost assumes the stance of the country sage: Something ordinary happens, related to the familiar chores of the country dweller. Some small happening raises a question in the poet's mind. Two different ways of looking at the issue suggest themselves. The speaker in the poem weighs simple alternatives, thinking the matter through. The tone is one of New England **understatement.** There is something here worth thinking about, without getting all bothered and excited.

The Tuft of Flowers   *1906*

I went to turn the grass once after one
Who mowed it in the dew before the sun.

The dew was gone that made his blade so keen
Before I came to view the leveled scene.

I looked for him behind an isle of trees;   5
I listened for his whetstone on the breeze.

But he had gone his way, the grass all mown,
And I must be, as he had been—alone.

"As all must be," I said within my heart,
"Whether they work together or apart."   10

But as I said it, swift there passed me by
On noiseless wing a bewildered butterfly,

Seeking with memories grown dim o'er night
Some resting flower of yesterday's delight.

And once I marked his flight go round and round,   15
As where some flower lay withering on the ground.

And then he flew as far as eye could see,
And then on tremulous wing came back to me.

I thought of questions that have no reply,
And would have turned to toss the grass to dry;   20

But he turned first, and led my eye to look
At a tall tuft of flowers beside a brook,

A leaping tongue of bloom the scythe had spared
Beside a reedy brook the scythe had bared.

The mower in the dew had loved them thus,   25
By leaving them to flourish, not for us,

Nor yet to draw one thought of ours to him,
But from sheer morning gladness at the brim.

The butterfly and I had lit upon,
Nevertheless, a message from the dawn,   30

That made me hear the wakening birds around,
And hear his long scythe whispering to the ground,

And feel a spirit kindred to my own;
So that henceforth I worked no more alone,

But glad with him, I worked as with his aid,   35
And weary, sought at noon with him the shade;

And dreaming, as it were, held brotherly speech
With one whose thought I had not hoped to reach.

"Men work together," I told him from the heart,
"Whether they work together or apart."   40

This poem has an almost childlike simplicity. Most of the stanzas are self-contained couplets in iambic pentameter, with little metrical variation. (Early and again in the last stanza, initial inversion—"WHETHer / they WORK"—alerts us to the key issue.) The stanzas tell the story step by step in simple "and-then" fashion. The speaker in the poem sees the grass that had been mown before and that is to be turned so it will dry in the sun. The mower is nowhere to be seen. The speaker in the poem thinks about the lonely fellow worker's morning labor, concluding that all workers work essentially alone, doing their jobs whether recognized by others or not. But the fluttering butterfly appears at the right time to guide us to the counterevidence: the tall tuft of flowers, the "leaping tongue of bloom," that the mower has left standing.

The Receptive Reader

How does noticing the tuft of flowers change the speaker's thinking? How and where does the poet line up the two contrasting points of view in parallel form?

Although Frost's best-loved poems are simple on the surface, they may turn out to be puzzlers. Frost once said that he liked to write poems that seem "altogether obvious" to the casual reader but that turn out to be subtle in unexpected ways. They disturb our set ways of thinking, making us ponder first one way of looking at things, then another. Some of Frost's most famous poems have been interpreted in radically different ways. For instance, different readers have read diametrically opposed meanings into the poem "Mending Wall." Is it true that "Good fences make good neighbors"? Or is this kind of territorial thinking the product of an obsolete, Stone Age mentality?

Mending Wall   *1914*

Something there is that doesn't love a wall,
That sends the frozen-ground-swell under it
And spills the upper boulders in the sun,
And makes gaps even two can pass abreast.
The work of hunters is another thing: 5
I have come after them and made repair
Where they have left not one stone on a stone,
But they would have the rabbit out of hiding,
To please the yelping dogs. The gaps I mean,
No one has seen them made or heard them made,   10
But at spring mending-time we find them there.
I let my neighbor know beyond the hill;
And on a day we meet to walk the line
And set the wall between us once again.
We keep the wall between us as we go.   15
To each the boulders that have fallen to each.
And some are loaves and some so nearly balls
We have to use a spell to make them balance:
"Stay where you are until our backs are turned!"
We wear our fingers rough with handling them.   20
Oh, just another kind of outdoor game,
One on a side. It comes to little more:
There where it is we do not need the wall:
He is all pine and I am apple orchard.
My apple trees will never get across   25
And eat the cones under his pines, I tell him.
He only says, "Good fences make good neighbors."
Spring is the mischief in me, and I wonder
If I could put a notion in his head:
"Why do they make good neighbors? Isn't it   30
Where there are cows? But here there are no cows.
Before I built a wall I'd ask to know
What I was walling in or walling out,
And to whom I was like to give offense.
Something there is that doesn't love a wall,   35
That wants it down." I could say "Elves" to him,
But it's not elves exactly, and I'd rather
He said it for himself. I see him there,
Bringing a stone grasped firmly by the top
In each hand, like an old-stone savage armed.   40
He moves in darkness as it seems to me,
Not of woods only and the shade of trees.
He will not go behind his father's saying,
And he likes having thought of it so well
He says again, "Good fences make good neighbors."   45

The Range of Interpretation

The two critical excerpts that follow continue the dialogue between the speaker in the poem and his neighbor. What side does the first reader take and why? How does he support his interpretation of the poem? What assumptions does the second reader bring to the poem? What evidence leads him to a very different conclusion? Which of the two readings do you agree with and why? Which of the two competing attitudes toward walls do you sympathize with and why?

1. Much of the public knows Frost by the phrase "Good fences make good neighbors." But the speaker in "Mending Wall" is saying just the opposite: that there is some mysterious force at work to break down barriers between human beings. "Elves," he calls it, in contrast to the matter-of-fact damage done by hunters (lines 5–11). But this is only a hint of what each person must discover for himself—companionship, respect, love, or the mystical togetherness of men who work.

The speaker's description of his neighbor makes the point even clearer (lines 38–42). The man and his ideas still belong to stone-age savagery. The darkness which surrounds him is not simply the natural darkness of the woods, but the primordial destructiveness in the heart of man. There is darkness also in the conventional mentality that makes a man repeat "Good fences make good neighbors" simply because his father said it (lines 43–44), when it does not fit the new situation at all (lines 30–31).

The poem, however, illustrates the difficulty of making a definite statement about any of Frost's ideas. The speaker does not agree with his neighbor in theory (lines 23–36); but in the fact of his labor, he is doing the same thing his neighbor is doing.

> From David A. Sohn and Richard H. Tyre, *Frost: The Poet and His Poetry*

2. Many general readers—and doubtless some stray sophisticated ones too—still see the poem as an argument against walls of all sorts, be they literal or metaphorical. To them walls are the divisive creations of selfish or shortsighted men who erect barriers to keep other people away. If only you will do away with useless, outmoded walls, they say, you will bring about a closer bond of fellowship—a deeper sense of community—among neighbors, in society at large, even among nations.

Generally, however, careful readers regard such views as hostile to the themes and attitudes they characteristically find in Frost. To them "Mending Wall" is Frost's finest expression of concern that in a world which doesn't seem to love a wall the individual may somehow get lost. To them the Yankee farmer, despite the scoffing questions that he puts to his neighbor, is the symbol of all those who love their privacy and their independence, and are resentful of those people—individuals or social planners—who would intrude upon that privacy. Or he is any individual who resents the levelers who would destroy walls and thus let others, even if friend or neighbor, infringe upon his right to be alone and to think his own thoughts after his own fashion. In short, despite the obvious warm appeal of the good neighborliness that wants walls down—even for the

Yankee individualist resentful of intrusions—walls are nonetheless the essential barriers that must exist between man and man if the individual is to preserve his own soul, and mutual understanding and respect are to survive and flourish. . . .

A wall is something more than the means for walling something visible in or out. If apple trees and pine cones were the only concern, then good fences would scarcely be worth the trouble it takes to keep them repaired. But in spite of all his scoffing the narrator knows that this is the least of the purposes that are served by good fences. This is why each spring it is he who takes the initiative and lets his neighbor know beyond the hill that once again it's time for mending wall. Good fences make good neighbors.

> From William S. Ward, "Lifted Pot Lids and Unmended Walls,"
> *College English,* February 1966

Frost took his readers from the neuroses of city living to a simpler rural world. In the words of Babette Deutsch in *Poetry in Our Time,* he wrote about the commonplace subjects of country life: "the steady caring for crops and creatures"; the "homely details of barn and farmhouse, orchard, pasture and wood lot"; apple-picking, haymaking, repairing orchard walls of loosely piled stones. He celebrated "the young life on and about the farm, be it a runaway colt, a young orchard threatened by false spring, a nestful of fledglings exposed by the cultivator."

Frost did not ignore the harsher side of farm life: the "drudgery and isolation"; ghastly accidents caused by machinery. However, only rarely do his best-known poems show the poet's darker and more pessimistic side. Donald Hall adored the older man when Hall himself was an aspiring young poet and befriended the aging poet toward the end of his career. Hall wrote about the anguish and sense of guilt that lay behind the public image of the "twinkling Yankee" of the Frost legend:

> To him—I learned over the years—his family background seemed precarious, dangerous; and his adult life cursed with tragedy, for which he took responsibility. His father was a sometime drunk, dead at an early age; his mother endured a bad marriage, was widowed young, and failed as a schoolteacher when she returned to her native Massachusetts; yet she was a fond mother, kind to her children—and she wrote poems. Her son felt dangerously close to her, and followed that fondness into devotion to one young woman, Elinor White, whom he courted extravagantly, romantically, and doggedly. Apparently losing her, he considered suicide; at least, he later dropped hints to friends that he had considered suicide. When Elinor and Robert finally married, they settled in Derry, New Hampshire, and lived in poverty, enduring an extraordinary series of family misfortunes.

> From *Remembering Poets: Reminiscences and Opinions,* 1977

Frost lost four of his children to fatal illness, insanity, death in childbirth, or suicide. His surviving daughter Lesley turned against him. The following late sonnet is the best-known of the poems in which Frost confronted "the anguish of existence and the presence of the malign" (Babette Deutsch).

Design   *1922*

I found a dimpled spider, fat and white,
On a white heal-all, holding up a moth
Like a white piece of rigid satin cloth—
Assorted characters of death and blight
Mixed ready to begin the morning right,   5
Like the ingredients of a witches' broth—
A snow-drop spider, a flower like a froth,
And dead wings carried like a paper kite.

What had that flower to do with being white,
The wayside blue and innocent heal-all?   10
What brought the kindred spider to that height,
Then steered the white moth thither in the night?
What but design of darkness to appall?—
If design govern in a thing so small.

Robert Frost was admired by critics and fellow poets while at the same time reaching a large popular audience. Critics and poets acclaimed him even though he was at odds with poetic fashions in the first half of the twentieth century. The most widely imitated poets of his time were poets like T. S. Eliot and Ezra Pound. They wrote difficult poems, filled with shifting images and obscure allusions, that made Frost's more accessible poems seem unsophisticated by comparison. Furthermore, Frost made himself the advocate of traditional form when the modern tendency was to reject traditional meter and rhyme as artificial and confining. He said on the role of form in our lives and in the world,

> Any psychiatrist will tell you that making a basket, or making a horse-shoe, or giving anything form gives you a confidence in the universe . . . that it has form, see. When you talk about your troubles and go to somebody about them, you're just a fool. The best way to settle them is to make something that has form, because all you want to do is get a sense of form.

POEMS FOR FURTHER STUDY

In reading these poems by Robert Frost, keep in mind questions like the following: Does the poem conform to the pattern of making a natural scene or an event real for you and then making you share in the reflections it inspires? Does the poem play off two different ways of looking at things? Which prevails and how? Is the poem in the "cool" New England voice? Or do you hear a more bitter, passionate, or questioning voice in the poem?

After Apple-Picking   *1914*

My long two-pointed ladder's sticking through a tree
Toward heaven still,
And there's a barrel that I didn't fill
Beside it, and there may be two or three
Apples I didn't pick upon some bough.   5
But I am done with apple-picking now.
Essence of winter sleep is on the night,
The scent of apples: I am drowsing off.
I cannot rub the strangeness from my sight
I got from looking through a pane of glass   10
I skimmed this morning from the drinking trough
And held against the world of hoary grass.
It melted, and I let it fall and break.
But I was well
Upon my way to sleep before it fell,   15
And I could tell
What form my dreaming was about to take.
Magnified apples appear and disappear,
Stem end and blossom end,
And every fleck of russet showing clear.   20
My instep arch not only keeps the ache,
It keeps the pressure of a ladder-round.
I feel the ladder sway as the boughs bend.
And I keep hearing from the cellar bin
The rumbling sound   25
Of load on load of apples coming in.
For I have had too much
Of apple-picking: I am overtired
Of the great harvest I myself desired.
There were ten thousand thousand fruit to touch,   30
Cherish in hand, lift down, and not let fall.
For all
That struck the earth,
No matter if not bruised or spiked with stubble,
Went surely to the cider-apple heap   35
As of no worth.
One can see what will trouble
This sleep of mine, whatever sleep it is.
Were he not gone,
The woodchuck could say whether it's like his   40
Long sleep, as I describe its coming on,
Or just some human sleep.

The Road Not Taken   *1915*

Two roads diverged in a yellow wood,
And sorry I could not travel both
And be one traveler, long I stood
And looked down one as far as I could
To where it bent in the undergrowth;   5

Then took the other, as just as fair,
And having perhaps the better claim,
Because it was grassy and wanted wear;
Though as for that, the passing there
Had worn them really about the same,   10

And both that morning equally lay
In leaves no step had trodden black.
Oh, I kept the first for another day!
Yet knowing how way leads on to way,
I doubted if I should ever come back.   15

I shall be telling this with a sigh
Somewhere ages and ages hence:
Two roads diverged in a wood, and I—
I took the one less traveled by,
And that has made all the difference.   20

Once by the Pacific   *1928*

The shattered water made a misty din.
Great waves looked over others coming in,
And thought of doing something to the shore
That water never did to land before.
The clouds were low and hairy in the skies,   5
Like locks blown forward in the gleam of eyes.
You could not tell, and yet it looked as if
The shore was lucky in being backed by cliff,
The cliff in being backed by continent;
It looked as if a night of dark intent   10
Was coming, and not only a night, an age.
Someone had better be prepared for rage.
There would be more than ocean-water broken
Before God's last *Put out the Light* was spoken.

The Oven Bird   *1916*

There is a singer everyone has heard,
Loud, a mid-summer and a mid-wood bird,
Who makes the solid tree trunks sound again.
He says that leaves are old and that for flowers
Mid-summer is to spring as one to ten.   5
He says the early petal-fall is past,

Once by the Pacific

The shattered water made a misty din.
Great waves looked over others coming in,
And thought of doing something to the shore
That water ~~...~~ had never done before.
The clouds were low and hairy in the skies,
Like locks blown forward in the gleam of eyes.
You could not tell, and yet it looked as if
The sand was lucky in being backed by cliff,
The cliff in being backed by continent.
It looked as if a night of dark intent
Was coming, and not only a night, an age.
Someone had better be prepared for rage.
There would be more than ocean water broken
Before God's last "Put out the light" was spoken.

Facsimile of Robert Frost's original manuscript of "Once by the Pacific." Courtesy Robert Frost Collection, Clifton Waller Barrett Library, Special Collections Department, Manuscripts, University of Virginia Library.

When pear and cherry bloom went down in showers
On sunny days a moment overcast;
And comes that other fall we name the fall.
He says the highway dust is over all.
The bird would cease and be as other birds   10
But that he knows in singing not to sing.
The question that he frames in all but words
Is what to make of a diminished thing.

Acquainted with the Night   *1928*

I have been one acquainted with the night.
I have walked out in rain—and back in rain.
I have outwalked the furthest city light.

I have looked down the saddest city lane.
I have passed by the watchman on his beat   5
And dropped my eyes, unwilling to explain.

I have stood still and stopped the sound of feet
When far away an interrupted cry
Came over houses from another street,

But not to call me back or say good-by;   10
And further still at an unearthly height,
One luminary clock against the sky

Proclaimed the time was neither wrong nor right.
I have been one acquainted with the night.

Neither Out Far Nor In Deep   *1936*

The people along the sand
All turn and look one way.
They turn their back on the land.
They look at the sea all day.

As long as it takes to pass   5
A ship keeps raising its hull;
The wetter ground like glass
Reflects a standing gull.

The land may vary more;
But wherever the truth may be—   10
The water comes ashore,
And the people look at the sea.

They cannot look out far.
They cannot look in deep.
But when was that ever a bar   15
To any watch they keep?

One Step Backward Taken   *1947*

Not only sands and gravels
Were once more on their travels,
But gulping muddy gallons
Great boulders off their balance
Bumped heads together dully   5
And started down the gully.
Whole capes caked off in slices.
I felt my standpoint shaken
In the universal crisis.
But with one step backward taken   10
I saved myself from going.
A world torn loose went by me.
Then the rain stopped and the blowing
And the sun came out to dry me.

The Night Light   *1947*

She always had to burn a light
Beside her attic bed at night.
It gave bad dreams and broken sleep,
But helped the Lord her soul to keep.
Good gloom on her was thrown away.   5
It is on me by night or day,
Who have, as I suppose, ahead
The darkest of it still to dread.

Making Connections—For Discussion or Writing

For a library research project, search for books and articles that would provide material for the treatment of one of the following topics:

✗ Several critical discussions of the same poem by Robert Frost. How does
the poem look from different critical perspectives? How much common ground
is there? What are significant differences, and how do you explain them?

✗ Several different perspectives on the private person behind the public legend. Books and articles have been written to defend Frost against what friends
and biographers considered unjustified attacks on the poet. What was involved
in these controversies?

Books you may be able to consult include the following:

Reginald L. Cook, *Robert Frost: A Living Voice* (1975)
Richard Poirier, *Robert Frost: The Work of Knowing* (1977)
John C. Kemp, *Robert Frost and New England: The Poet as Regionalist*
    (1979)
James L. Potter, *The Robert Frost Handbook* (1980)
William Pritchard, *Frost: A Literary Life Reconsidered* (1984)
John Evangelist Walsh, *Into My Own: The English Years of Robert Frost*
    (1988)
Judith Osper, *Toward Robert Frost the Reader and the Poet* (1992)
Katherine Kearns, *Robert Frost and a Poetics of Appetite* (1994)
Earl J. Wilcox, ed., *His Incalculable Influence on Others: Essays on Robert
    Frost in Our Time* (1994)
Jeffrey Myers, *Robert Frost: A Biography* (1996)

GWENDOLYN BROOKS: COMMITMENT AND UNIVERSALITY

*I am absolutely free of what any white critic might
say because I feel that it's going to be amazing if
any of them understand the true significance of
the struggle that's going on.*

GWENDOLYN BROOKS

Gwendolyn Brooks (born 1917) became known as the most power-ful and widely respected contemporary African-American poet. Her poems bring tremendous empathy to representative lives and people in the black community, especially the old and the very young. In the late sixties, she became part of the movement that explored sources of strength in the black heritage and in solidarity with fellow artists explor-ing the African past.

Gwendolyn Brooks was born in Topeka, Kansas, but she lived most of her life in Chicago, and she became Poet Laureate of the State of Illi-nois. She grew up in a closely knit, loving, traditional family ("no child abuse, no prostitution, no Mafia membership," she said in a 1984 self-interview). The Brooks house was filled with poetry, story, music, and song; she grew up in a "family-oriented" world with much visiting by and of relatives, traditional holiday feasts, family and church picnics. Her first poem was published in a children's magazine when she was ten; when in high school, she published several poems in the *Defender,* an African-American newspaper in Chicago. She received a Pulitzer Prize for poetry in 1950, the first black woman to receive the award. She has spent much of her time working with young people in colleges and schools and promoting workshops and awards for young poets.

The constant in Brooks's poetry has been her loyalty to characters trapped in an environment scarred by racial discrimination, poverty, and violence. She populated the imaginary community of Bronzeville with the human beings behind the stereotypes and government statistics. She chronicled their grey daily lives, their disillusionment and self-doubts, their defiance and futile rebellions. She observed with icy scorn the charitable rich who, from winters in Palm Beach and their world of "hostess gowns, and sunburst clocks, / Turtle soup, Chippendale" ven-ture forth in search of the "worthy poor," only to be appalled by the squalor of the slums. Her most famous poem is a poem of doomed youth—jaunty, defiant, lost:

We Real Cool   *1960*

THE POOL PLAYERS.
SEVEN AT THE GOLDEN SHOVEL.

We real cool. We
Left school. We

Lurk late. We
Strike straight. We

Sing sin. We   5
Thin gin. We

Jazz June. We
Die soon.

This poem, with its broken, syncopated, beboppy counter-rhythm ("We real cool. We / Left school"), is an anthem for doomed youth who act "cool" as a defensive armor. They have dropped out and find themselves in the slow lane to a dead end. They jazz up, or live up, June and will be dead soon after.

The Receptive Reader

Do you think you recognize the young people in the poem? What do you think is the poet's attitude toward them? How does she relate to them? How do you?

Brooks writes with special affection of young people who rebel against the narrow boundaries of their lives, adopting a stance of defiance or escaping into an intensely imagined fantasy world. The sense of being trapped and intensely imagined dreams of escape become recurrent themes in poems like "Hunchback Girl":

hunchback girl: she thinks of heaven   *1945*

My Father, it is surely a blue place
And straight. Right. Regular. Where I shall find
No need for scholarly nonchalance or looks
A little to the left or guards upon the
Heart to halt love that runs without crookedness   5
Along its crooked corridors. My Father,
It is a planned place surely. Out of coils,
Unscrewed, released, no more to be marvelous,
I shall walk straightly through most proper halls
Proper myself, princess of properness.   10

The poem is in the form of a passionate prayer, with the girl addressing "My Father" twice. The hunchbacked girl thinks of a future state where her burden will be lifted. In heaven ("surely a blue place / and straight"), she will no longer be stared or marveled at ("no more to be marvelous"). Everything that is crooked or coiled will there be straightened out, made right and regular and proper. She will walk "straightly through most proper halls," a very "princess of properness." She will no longer have to try hard to look nonchalant when being stared at; she will no longer have to avoid people's eyes.

The Receptive Reader

1. To judge from the poem, what is the girl's usual way of coping with her disability?
2. Some critics have noted the *ambiguity* of the words *marvel* and *marvelous*. These words may refer to something to be stared at in fear but also to

something arousing wonder or to be contemplated in awe. Does the poem bring into play either or both of these meanings?

3. Is it *paradoxical* that in the girl's heart love runs "without crookedness"—but that the corridors of the heart (hers? ours?) are themselves crooked? What did the poet have in mind? How do you explain the paradox?

4. One reader said that the irony underlying this poem is that "nothing in life is without its crookedness." What did she mean?

The Personal Response

Would *you* call the feelings expressed in this poem a mere dream? Have you or has someone you know well ever experienced similar feelings?

Brooks seems to speak most directly in her personal voice in poems of buried emotion, of humanity defeated by harsh reality. In the following sonnet, the "glory" of the pianist's music and the feeling of "proud delight" it calls up prevail for a time until they are drowned out by the unheard phantom cries of bitter men killed in war.

piano after war   *1945*

On a snug evening I shall watch her fingers,
Cleverly ringed, declining to clever pink,
Beg glory from the willing keys. Old hungers
Will break their coffins, rise to eat and thank.
And music, warily, like the golden rose   5
That sometimes after sunset warms the west,
Will warm that room, persuasively suffuse
That room and me, rejuvenate a past.
But suddenly, across my climbing fever
Of proud delight—a multiplying cry.   10
A cry of bitter dead men who will never
Attend a gentle maker of musical joy.
Then my thawed eye will go again to ice.
And stone will shove the softness from my face.

The music in this poem unfolds like a "golden rose," wakening long since buried capacities for joy. "Old hungers" break their coffins. The glow thaws the icy heart—but only for a time. Suddenly, the memory of the dead undercuts the feeling of gentleness and joy; their fate makes the glories of culture an unkept promise. However tempting, the blessings of traditional culture cannot really soften the bitterness left behind by disappointed hopes.

The Receptive Reader

1. What do you think are the "old hungers" aroused from "their coffins" in this poem?

2. How does this sonnet follow the traditional pattern of a *turning point* in the middle of a poem and of a concluding *couplet* that leaves the reader with a strong final impression?

3. Were you *surprised* by the turn the poem takes? Does the poem early strike a note of wariness, of ironic detachment?

Brooks writes with special empathy and understated tenderness about children, like the two girls in the following poem from *Bronzeville Boys and Girls:*

Mexie and Bridie   *1945*

A tiny tea-party
Is happening today.
Pink cakes, and nuts and bon-bons on
A tiny, shiny tray.

It's out within the weather,   5
Beneath the clouds and sun.
And pausing ants have peeked upon,
As birds and gods have done.

Mexie's in her white dress,
And Bridie's in her brown.   10
There are no finer ladies
Tea-ing in the town.

In the words of critic Gary Smith, the children in Brooks's poems live in a world of enclosed space—"alleyways, front and back yards, vacant lots, and back rooms. . . . Although trees, flowers, and grass poke through the concrete blocks of the urban environment, they are only reminders of a forbidden Eden." The "overwhelming desire for many of her children is the need to escape, to flee" to a world free of adults and oppression and "their unique ability to imagine this world—albeit on the wings of fantasy—distinguishes them from adults and creates some sense of hope."

Many of Brooks's poems were milestones in the spiritual journey of the black community from the goal of assimilation toward black pride and self-respect. For her, the years from 1967 to 1972 were years of awakening and moving toward "italicized black identity, solidarity, self-possession" and "vitally acknowledged African roots." In these years of "hot-breathing hope," she read books about the black experience from W. E. Burghardt Du Bois's *The Souls of Black Folk* to the novels of Zora Neale Hurston. She exchanged views with black writers from James Baldwin to Don L. Lee.

During the years of the civil rights movement, Brooks's work, like the work of many black writers and artists, became more committed and more political. One of her best-known poems takes stock of a reporter's foray to Little Rock, Arkansas, during the desegregation battle fought over the admission of the first nine black students to Central High. Backed by the Supreme Court's *Brown* decision outlawing segregated public schools, protected by federal troops called in by President Eisenhower, the students prevailed against the governor of the state, spitting and jeering mobs, and harassment and abuse from fellow students. (For a year, in a last-ditch stand, the governor closed all public schools.)

The Chicago Defender *Sends a Man to Little Rock*   *1960*

FALL, 1957

In Little Rock the people bear
Babes, and comb and part their hair
And watch the want ads, put repair
To roof and latch. While wheat toast burns
A woman waters multiferns.   5

Time upholds or overturns
The many, tight, and small concerns.

In Little Rock the people sing
Sunday hymns like anything,
Through Sunday pomp and polishing.   10

And after testament and tunes,
Some soften Sunday afternoons
With lemon tea and Lorna Doones.

I forecast
And I believe   15
Come Christmas Little Rock will cleave
To Christmas tree and trifle, weave,
From laugh and tinsel, texture fast.

In Little Rock is baseball; Barcarolle.
That hotness in July . . . the uniformed figures raw and implacable 20
And not intellectual,
Batting the hotness or clawing the suffering dust.
The Open Air Concert, on the special twilight green. . . .
When Beethoven is brutal or whispers to lady-like air.
Blanket-sitters are solemn, as Johann troubles to lean   25
To tell them what to mean. . . .

There is love, too, in Little Rock. Soft women softly
Opening themselves in kindness,
Or, pitying one's blindness,
Awaiting one's pleasure   30
In azure
Glory with anguished rose at the root. . . .

To wash away old semi-discomfitures.
They re-teach purple and unsullen blue.
The wispy soils go. And uncertain   35
Half-havings have they clarified to sures.

In Little Rock they know
Not answering the telephone is a way of rejecting life,
That it is our business to be bothered, is our business
To cherish bores or boredom, be polite   40
To lies and love and many-faceted fuzziness.

I scratch my head, massage the hate-I-had.
I blink across my prim and pencilled pad.
The saga I was sent for is not down.
Because there is a puzzle in this town.   45
The biggest News I do not dare
Telegraph to the Editor's chair:
"They are like people everywhere."
The angry Editor would reply
In hundred harryings of Why.   50

And true, they are hurling spittle, rock,
Garbage and fruit in Little Rock.
And I saw coiling storm a-writhe
On bright madonnas. And a scythe
Of men harrassing brownish girls.   55
(The bows and barrettes in the curls
And braids declined away from joy.)

I saw a bleeding brownish boy. . . .

The lariat lynch-wish I deplored.

The loveliest lynchee was our Lord.   60

    The people in this poem attend to their many large and small concerns—giving birth, baking, grooming, watering, tinkering, answering the telephone. They listen to operatic favorites (Offenbach's "Barcarolle") and Beethoven; sitting on blankets, they solemnly listen at the open-air concert to Johann (Sebastian Bach). They sing Sunday hymns "like anything," and come Christmas they will do it justice, tree and tinsel and all. The reporter from the *Chicago Defender* came to their city ready to hate and revile melodramatic villains. But the "biggest news" is: evil here is committed in a city of everyday people. The rock-throwing, spittle-hurling mob returns to everyday homes. We usually assume that evil people are monstrous creatures very different from ourselves. However, the people throwing the rocks and spitting on the "bright madonnas" are someone's Uncle Joe or Cousin Roy. Jesus was crucified in a city full of ordinary people.

The Receptive Reader

1. How do you think the people trying to block desegregation were seen by the civil rights workers at the time? How do you think the segregationists saw themselves? How is the poet's perspective different from either?

2. What use does she make of *religious references* at the end of the poem? With what effect?

3. Do you think the stand the poet takes on the events of the time is too strong or not strong enough?

POEMS FOR FURTHER STUDY

An editor and fellow poet said about Gwendolyn Brooks that she is "a woman who cannot live without her art, but who has never put her art above or before the people she writes about." In reading the following poems, pay special attention to the relation between content and form, between the poet's subject matter and her use of language.

when you have forgotten Sunday: the love story   *1945*

————And when you have forgotten the bright bedclothes on a
   Wednesday and a Saturday,
And most especially when you have forgotten Sunday—
When you have forgotten Sunday halves in bed,
Or me sitting on the front-room radiator in the limping afternoon
Looking off down the long street   5
To nowhere,
Hugged by my plain old wrapper of no-expectation
And nothing-I-have-to-do and I'm-happy-why?
And if-Monday-never-had-to-come—
When you have forgotten that, I say,   10
And how you swore, if somebody beeped the bell,
And how my heart played hopscotch if the telephone rang;
And how we finally went in to Sunday dinner,
That is to say, went across the front-room floor to the ink-spotted table
   in the southwest corner
To Sunday dinner, which was always chicken and noodles   15
Or chicken and rice
And salad and rye bread and tea
And chocolate chip cookies—
I say, when you have forgotten that,
When you have forgotten my little presentiment   20
That the war would be over before they got to you;
And how we finally undressed and whipped out the light and flowed
   into bed,
And lay loose-limbed for a moment in the week-end
Bright bedclothes,
Then gently folded into each other—   25

When you have, I say, forgotten all that,
Then you may tell,
Then I may believe
You have forgotten me well.

the preacher: ruminates behind the sermon   *1945*

I think it must be lonely to be God.
Nobody loves a master. No. Despite
the bright hosannas, bright dear-Lords, and bright
Determined reverence of Sunday eyes.

Picture Jehovah striding through the hall   5
Of His importance, creatures running out
From servant-corners to acclaim, to shout
Appreciation of his merit's glare.

But who walks with Him?—dares to take His arm,
To slap him on the shoulder, tweak His ear,   10
Buy Him a Coca-Cola or a beer,
Pooh-pooh his politics, call Him a fool?

Perhaps—who knows?—He tires of looking down.
Those eyes are never lifted. Never straight.
Perhaps sometimes he tires of being great   15
In solitude. Without a hand to hold.

the ballad of the light-eyed little girl   *1949*

Sweet Sally took a cardboard box,
And in went pigeon poor.
Whom she had starved to death but not
For lack of love, be sure.

The wind it harped as twenty men.   5
The wind it harped like hate.
It whipped our light-eyed little girl,
It made her wince and wait.

It screeched a hundred elegies
As it punished her light eyes   10
(Though only kindness covered these)
And it made her eyebrows rise.

"Now bury your bird," the wind it bawled,
"And bury him down and down
Who had to put his trust in one   15
So light-eyed and so brown.

"So light-eyed and so villainous,
Who whooped and who could hum

But could not find the time to toss
Confederate his crumb."   20

She has taken her passive pigeon poor,
She has buried him down and down.
He never shall sally to Sally
Nor soil any roofs of the town.

She has sprinkled nail polish on dead dandelions.   25
And children have gathered around
Funeral for him whose epitaph
Is "PIGEON—Under the ground."

The Boy Died in My Alley   *1975*

Without my having known.
Policeman said, next morning,
"Apparently died Alone."
"You heard a shot?" Policeman said.
Shots I hear and Shots I hear.   5
I never see the dead.

The Shot that killed him yes I heard
as I heard the Thousand shots before;
careening tinnily down the nights
across my years and arteries.   10

Policeman pounded on my door.
"Who is it?" "POLICE!" Policeman yelled.
"A boy was dying in your alley.
A boy is dead, and in your alley.
And have you known this Boy before?"   15

I have known this Boy before.
I have known this Boy before, who
ornaments my alley.
I never saw his face at all.
I never saw his futurefall.   20
But I have known this Boy.

I have always heard him deal with death.
I have always heard the shout, the volley.
I have closed my heart-ears late and early.
And I have killed him ever.   25

I joined the Wild and killed him
with knowledgeable unknowing.
I saw where he was going.
I saw him Crossed. And seeing,
I did not take him down.   30

He cried not only "Father!"
but "Mother!
Sister!
Brother!"
The cry climbed up the alley.   35
It went up to the wind.
It hung upon the heaven
for a long
stretch-strain of Moment.

The red floor of my alley   40
is a special speech to me.

Making Connections—For Discussion or Writing

For a library research project, search for books and articles that would provide material on one of the following topics:

✗ Gwendolyn Brooks's view of the social responsibility of the writer. What
is the relationship between protest and poetry in her work? What are her views
on the political responsibilities of the poet?

✗ Gwendolyn Brooks's relationship with or influence on other African-
American writers. What writer or writers did most to help shape her poetry or
her views? What has been her influence on other black poets?

✗ What has been the treatment of black men in her poetry? Has it changed
over the years?

Books you may be able to consult include the following:

Harry B. Shaw, *Gwendolyn Brooks* (1980)
Claudia Tate, *Black Women Writers at Work* (1983)
Mari Evans, ed., *Black Women Writers (1950–80): A Critical Evaluation* (1984)
R. Baxter Miller, ed., *Black American Poets between Worlds, 1940–60* (1986)
Marie Mootry and Gary Smith, eds., *A Life Distilled: Gwendolyn Brooks,
    Her Poetry and Fiction* (1987)
Haki Madhubuti, *Say That the River Turns: The Impact of Gwendolyn
    Brooks* (1987)
D. H. Melhem, *Gwendolyn Brooks: Poetry and the Heroic Voice* (1987)
George E. Kent, *A Life of Gwendolyn Brooks* (1990)
Stephen C. Wright, ed., *On Gwendolyn Brooks: Reliant Contemplation* (1995)

WRITING ABOUT LITERATURE

23   The Poet and the Critics (Documented Paper)

The Writing Workshop   For the projects outlined earlier in this chapter,
you will have to develop your own productive way of using library
resources. Your finished paper will differ from other papers you have

written in two major ways: you will be *integrating* material from a range of different sources. You will be *documenting* your sources, giving full information about the books and articles you have used.

Finding Promising Leads   To work up material for your paper, begin by checking in electronic or printed indexes for books, collections of critical articles, and individual articles in periodicals. For a writer like Dickinson, Frost, or Brooks, most college libraries will have a wide range of critical and scholarly sources. Often critical studies will include bibliographies alerting you to other promising leads.

Taking Notes   During your exploratory reading, you need to look sources over quickly, deciding whether they will be helpful. But you also have to slow down and close in when you hit upon promising materials. Remember:

✗ *Be a stickler for accuracy.*   Copy direct quotations accurately, word for word. Enclose all quoted material in quotation marks to show material copied verbatim. (Include the *closing* quotation mark to show where the quotation ends.)

✗ *Tag your notes.*   Start your notes with a tag or descriptor. (Indicate the subtopic or section of your paper where a quotation or piece of information will be useful.)

✗ *Record publishing information.*   On your first entry for any one source (or in a separate bibliography entry), record all data you will need later when you identify your source in a documented paper. Include exact page numbers for your quotations. (Also record inclusive page numbers for a whole article or story.) Sample notes might look like this:

Self-contained quotation

DICKINSON—SEXUAL IMAGERY

"Like her nature poetry, her use of female sexual imagery suggests . . . not the 'subversion' of an existing male tradition, nor the 'theft' of male power—but rather the assertion of a concept of female sexuality and female creativity."

Paula Bennett, *Emily Dickinson: Woman Poet* (Iowa City: U of Iowa P, 1990) 180

Paraphrase with partial direct quotation

DICKINSON—FREUDIAN PERSPECTIVE

The prime motive in D.'s life and poetry was fear created by a "bad child-parent relationship," specifically with her "cold and forbidding father." This relationship shaped her view of men, love, marriage, and religion. She viewed God as a forbidding father-figure who spurned her.

Clark Griffith, *The Long Shadow: Emily Dickinson's Tragic Poetry* (Princeton: Princeton UP, 1964) 78.

Distinguish clearly between paraphrase and direct quotation. When you paraphrase, you put someone else's ideas in your own words, highlighting what seems most important and condensing other parts. Even when you paraphrase, be sure to use quotation marks for striking phrases that you keep in the exact wording of the author.

Note finer points: use **single quotation marks** for a phrase that appears as a quote-within-a-quote. Use the **ellipsis**—three spaced periods—to show an omission (see Bennett quotation above). Use four periods when the periods include the period at the end of a sentence. **Square brackets** show that you have inserted material into the original quotation: "In this poem, based on the Emmett Till murder [1955], Brooks creates a surreal aura of hysteria and violence underlying an ostensibly calm domestic scene."

Pushing Toward a Thesis   Early in your note taking, begin to follow up tentative patterns and promising connections that you discover in your reading. Start looking for a unifying thread. Avoid a stitched-together pattern that goes from "one critic said this" to "another critic said that." Look for recurrent issues; look for a note that in your materials is struck again and again.

Suppose you are moving toward a paper showing how different critics have answered the question of Emily Dickinson's religious faith. The following might be a tentative thesis:

TRIAL THESIS: Emily Dickinson was not a believer or a skeptic but a poet always in search of the truth.

Using a Working Outline   To give direction to your reading and writing, sketch out a working outline as soon as you have a rough idea how your material is shaping up. At first, your plan might be very tentative. A working outline is not a final blueprint; its purpose is to help you visualize a possible pattern and to help you refine it as you go along. At an early stage, your working outline for the paper about Dickinson's faith might look like this:

WORKING OUTLINE: —poems of faith
—poems of despair
—poems of alienation
—poems of rebellion

Drafting and Revising   In your first draft, you are likely to concentrate on feeding into your paper the evidence you have collected. As always, feel free to work on later sections of the paper first—perhaps concentrating on key segments and filling in the connecting threads later. In your first draft, quotations are likely to be chunky, to be woven into the paper more tightly or more smoothly during revision. Often you will need to read a first draft back to yourself to see where major changes in strategy would be advisable. A reordering of major sections might be necessary to correct awkward backtrackings. You might need to strengthen the evidence for major points and play down material that tends to distract from your major arguments.

Documenting the Paper   When you draw on a range of sources—for instance, a range of critical interpretations of a poem—you may be asked to provide **documentation.** Remember that, in a documented paper, you fully identify your sources, furnishing complete publishing information and exact page numbers. Accurate documentation shows that your readers are welcome to go to the sources you have drawn on—to check your use of them and to get further information from them if they wish. As with other documented papers, follow the current style of the Modern Language Association (MLA) unless instructed otherwise. This current style no longer uses footnotes (though it still allows for **explanatory notes** at the end of a paper).

Remember three key features of the MLA style:

✗ *Identify your sources briefly in your text.*   Generally, introduce a quotation by saying something like the following:

In her article "Puns and Accordions: Emily Dickinson and the Unsaid," Mary Jo Salter says that Dickinson "has inspired a massive critical industry rivaling that devoted to Shakespeare and Milton."

✗ *Give page references in parentheses in your text.*   Usually, they will go at the end of the sentence and before the final period, for instance (89) or (89–90). If you have not mentioned the author, give his or her last name (Salter 192–93). If you are using more than one source by the same author, you may also have to specify briefly which one (Salter, "Puns" 192–93.) Remember to tag author or title in parentheses only if you have *not* already given the information in your running text.

✗ *Describe each source fully in a final alphabetical listing of Works Cited.*   Originally a bibliography (literally the "book list"), it now often includes **nonprint** sources—interviews, lectures, PBS broadcasts, videotapes, Internet sources, computer software. Here is a typical entry for an article in a critical journal. This entry includes volume number (a volume usually covers all issues for one year), year, and the complete page numbers for the whole article (not just the material you have quoted):

Morris, Timothy. "The Development of Dickinson's Style." *American Literature* 60 (1988): 26–42.

Study sample entries for your alphabetical listing of Works Cited. Remember a few pointers:

✗ Use <u>underlining</u> (or *italics* if preferred by your instructor) for the title of a whole publication—whether a book-length study, a collection or anthology of stories or essays, a periodical that prints critical articles, or a newspaper that prints reviews. However, use quotation marks for titles of poems or critical articles that are part of a collection.

✗ Leave *one* space after periods marking off chunks of information in the entry. Indent the second and following lines of each entry one-half inch or five typewriter spaces.

✗ Use ed. for editor; trans. for a translator.

✗ Abbreviate the names of publishing houses (Prentice for Prentice Hall, Inc; Southern Illinois UP for Southern Illinois University Press). Abbreviate the names of the months: Dec., Apr., Mar. Abbreviate the names of states when needed to locate a little-known place of publication: CA, NY, NJ.

Primary sources: Listing of poems, lectures, interviews

Brooks, Gwendolyn. *The World of Gwendolyn Brooks.* New York: Harper, 1971.
[Collected poems of the author. The publisher's name is short for Harper & Row.]

Colman, Cathy. "After Swimming in the Pacific." *New Poets: Women.* Ed. Terri Whetherby. Millbrae, CA: Les Femmes, 1976. 13.
[A poem printed in an anthology, with editor's name and with page number for the poem]

Johnson, Thomas H., ed. *The Complete Poems of Emily Dickinson.* Boston: Little, Brown, 1960.
[Editor's name first when editor's work of compiling or establishing texts is important]

Lorde, Audre. Interview. *Black Women Writers at Work.* Ed. Claudia Tate. Harpenden, Herts.: Oldcastle, 1985. 100–16.
[An interview with the poet, published in a collection of interviews]

Clifton, Lucille. Lecture. Visiting Poets Series. Tucson. 23 Feb. 1992.
[Talk by a poet as part of a lecture series]

Olsen, Tillie. Foreword. *Black Women Writers at Work.* Ed. Claudia Tate. Harpenden, Herts.: Oldcastle, 1985. ix–xxvi.
[Foreword by other than editor, with page numbers in small roman numerals for introductory material]

592 THREE POETS IN DEPTH

Secondary Sources: Listing of critical studies, articles, or reviews

Johnson, Thomas H. *Emily Dickinson: An Interpretive Biography.* Cambridge: Harvard UP, 1966.

[Biography with subtitle, published by a university press]

Rich, Adrienne. *On Lies, Secrets, and Silence: Selected Prose 1966–1978.* New York: Norton, 1975.

[Book with subtitle, with critical essays by the author]

Spillers, Hortense J. "Gwendolyn the Terrible: Propositions on Eleven Poems." *A Life Distilled: Gwendolyn Brooks, Her Poetry and Fiction.* Ed. Maria K. Mootry and Gary Smith. Urbana: U of Illinois P, 1987. 224–35.

[Article in a collection, with inclusive page numbers. Note "Ed." for the editors who assembled the collection.]

Morris, Timothy. "The Development of Dickinson's Style." *American Literature* 60 (1988): 26–42.

[Journal article, with volume number and inclusive page numbers. Note quotation marks for title of article; italics for title of publication.]

Monteiro, George. "Dickinson's 'We Thirst at First.'" *The Explicator* 48 (1990): 193–94.

[Title of poem (with single quotation marks) is cited in title of article (with double quotation marks).]

Jones, Rowena Revis. "'A Royal Seal': Emily Dickinson's Rite of Baptism." *Religion and Literature* 18.3 (1986): 29–51.

[Periodical with number of volume *and* issue. Number of issue may be needed when pages are not numbered consecutively throughout a single volume.]

Montgomery, Karen. "Today's Minimalist Poets." *New York Times* 22 Feb. 1992, late ed. , sec. 2: 1+.

[Newspaper article, with edition and section specified. Article starts on page 1 and continues not on the next page but later in the newspaper.]

Rev. of *The Penguin Book of Women Poets,* ed. Carol Cosman, Joan Keefe, and Kathleen Weaver. *Arts and Books Forum* May 1990: 17–19.

[Untitled, unsigned review]

Poets of Protest. Narr. Joan Moreno. Writ. and prod. Lorna Herold. KSBM, Los Angeles. 8 Feb. 1992.

[A television program with names of narrator and writer-producer. To be listed alphabetically under "Poets."]

Electronic Sources—Online, CD-ROM, e-mail

Guidelines for documenting electronic sources are being updated as new technology evolves. The following guidelines are based on the *MLA*

Style Manual (Second Edition, 1998). For most of your entries, start with as much of the usual publishing information as is available—including authors, titles, and dates. However, include the **access date**—the date you accessed the source or site. The date of access will often follow the date the material was published or posted. (The access date can tell your reader how recently the material was available.)

For material from the net, include the **Internet address**—the URL (named after the "uniform resource locator"). Put it between angled brackets. Typically, the electronic address will start with the access mode, usually **<http:// . . . .>.** (Other access modes include *telnet* and *ftp.*) The address will then go on to the relevant path and specific file names (often beginning with **www.** for the World Wide Web) Try to have the whole URL on the same line, or else try to have a break only after a period or slash. Make sure that dots, slashes, colons, capitals, and spacing are exactly right. (Do not add hyphens or final periods.)

For material from other electronic sources, specify the **medium,** such as CD-ROM, diskette, or magnetic tape. Here are sample entries:

Kaminsky, Rebecca. "An Unpublished Dickinson Letter." *New York Times on the Web* 28 Oct. 1996. 20 Apr.1997 <http://www.nytimes.com/web/doscroot/library/cyber/week/1028.html>
[Newspaper online]

Angelo, Gretchen V. Rev. of *The Book of the Body Politic,* by Christine de Pizan. *Bryn Mawr Medieval Review* 96.1.7 (1996). 26 Jan. 1997 <gopher://gopher.lib.virginia.edu/70/00/alpha/bmmr/v96/96-1-7>.
[Book review online]

"Dickinson." *Britannica Online.* Vers. 97.1.1. Mar. 1997. Encyclopaedia Britannica. 7 Apr. 1997. <http://www.eb.com/>
[Reference work online, with version number and date]

Garesca, Faith. "Dickinson and Agorophobia." *The Private World of Emily Dickinson.* CD-ROM. Boston: Femmes Press, 1999.
[Collection of Dickinson materials on CD-ROM]

Halfield, Frederica. E-mail to the author. 26 Mar. 2000.
[Give dates for e-mail to you or to others]

Sample Documented Paper

Study the following example of a documented paper. How well does the paper bring its subject into focus? How well does it support its main points? How clear and effective is its use of quotations from the poet and from the critics? Study the use of parenthetical documentation and the entries in the Works Cited; pay special attention to unusual situations or entries.

Emily Dickinson's Strange Irreverence

Religion in one guise or another pervades many of Dickinson's poems. It appears in the form of tender and not so tender prayers, skeptical questionings, and bitter confrontations. Critics have constructed a whole range of interpretations designed to provide a key to her changing, ambivalent religious attitudes. Some have cast her in the role of the rebel, rescuing her readers from the harshness of a rigid, con- stricted religious tradition, erecting for them a "citadel of art" and cultivating "the ego or consciousness" (Burbick 62). Others, however, see her as a "lone pilgrim" in the tradition of Puritan austerity and asceticism. She could not "allow herself the long luxury" of the evangelical movement of her own day, which was turning away from earlier, harsher versions of the Christian faith and promoting a sentimental atti- tude toward God as a "creature of caring, even motherly generosity" (Wolff 260). Still others attribute Dickinson's ambivalent, shifting religious attitudes to her need to keep her friends, to her "preoccupation with attachment" (Burbick 65). Some of Dickinson's dearest friends, to whom she wrote about her cherished hope for "one unbroken company in heaven," had experienced a religious conversion at Mt. Holyoke Seminary, and she felt she had to follow their example so that the bonds of friendship that were so precious to her would not be dissolved.

Perhaps the closest to a connecting thread is Denis Donoghue's discussion of her as a truth-seeker, who in life as in poetry was *looking* for the truth. As Donoghue says, "In a blunt paraphrase, many of her poems would contradict one another; but her answers are always provisional." Her answers are tentative; "only her questions are definitive" (13). Although there are in her poems many refer- ences to the Old and New Testaments, "nothing is necessarily believed" but may be entertained only as a poetic or symbolic truth (17).

Because of the elusive, ambivalent nature of Dickinson's relation to religion, each poem must be interpreted individually in the quest to plumb her heart. Several of her poems are direct affirmations of her faith in Christ. In poem 698 in the John- son edition ("Life—is what we make it"), she calls Christ a "tender pioneer," who blazed the trail of life and death for his "little Fellowmen":

> He—would trust no stranger—
> Others—could betray—
> Just his own endorsement—
> That—sufficeth me.
>
> All the other Distance
> He hath traversed first—
> No new mile remaineth—
> Far as Paradise—
>
> His sure foot preceding—
> Tender Pioneer—
> Base must be the Coward—
> Dare not venture—now— (333–34)

In other poems, however, the faith that is supposed to provide a bridge to the hereafter proves a bridge with "mouldering" or "brittle" piers. In a famous poem, "I heard a Funeral in my Brain" (280 in the Johnson edition), the promise of faith seems unable to counteract the sense of the nothingness at the end of life. The Christian teachings of resurrection and an afterlife here do not seem to avail against the "plunge" into despair:

And then I heard them lift a Box
And creak across my Soul
With those same Boots of Lead, again,
Then Space—began to toll,

As all the Heavens were a Bell,
And Being, but an Ear,
And I, and Silence, some strange Race
Wrecked, solitary, here—

And then a Plank in Reason, broke,
And I dropped down, and down—
And hit a World, at every plunge,
And Finished knowing—then (128–29)

Other poems seem to protest against the "ambiguous silence maintained by God" (Griffith 273). The following are the opening lines of poem 376 in Johnson's edition:

Of course—I prayed—
And did God Care?
He cared as much as on the Air
A Bird—had stamped her foot—
And cried "Give Me"— (179)

Many of her poems seem to mourn the absence of God, as does the following stanza from poem 502 in Johnson:

Thou settest Earthquake in the South—
And Maelstrom, In the Sea—
Say, Jesus Christ of Nazareth—
Hast thou no Arm for Me? (244)

In her most rebellious poems, she openly expresses defiance. She protests against the "tyranny" of God that forced Abraham to consent to offer his own son Isaac in sacrifice (Johnson 571). She rebels against commandments that keep us within a "magic prison," a limited and "constricted life," while we are within sight of the feast of happiness that is earthly pleasure—as if God were jealous of "the heaven on earth that is human happiness" (McNeil 60).

To read Emily Dickinson's poems is to see a poet's struggle for finding a meaning in her existence, rebelling at times against blind faith but also shrinking from complete doubt. She looked for evidence of the divine not in traditional revealed faith but in our earthly human existence. In a letter written several years before her death, she wrote: "To be human is more than to be divine . . . when Christ was divine he was uncontented until he had been human" (qtd. in Wolff 519).

Works Cited

Burbick, Joan. "'One Unbroken Company': Religion and Emily Dickinson." *New England Quarterly* 53 (1980): 62–75.
Donoghue, Denis. *Emily Dickinson.* U of Minnesota Pamphlets on American Writers. No. 81. 1969.
Griffith, Clark. *The Long Shadow: Emily Dickinson's Tragic Poetry.* Princeton: Princeton UP, 1964.

Johnson, Thomas H., ed. *The Complete Poems of Emily Dickinson*. Boston: Little,
    Brown, 1960.
McNeil, Helen. *Emily Dickinson*. New York: Pantheon, 1986.
Wolff, Cynthia Griffin. *Emily Dickinson*. Menlo Park, CA: Addison, 1988.

Questions

1. How does the writer succeed or fail in bringing the topic to life for you?
Does she spell out her *thesis* early in the paper? Does a key term or key concept
help sum up her point of view?

2. What are the major waystations in her overall *plan?* How convincing are
the major points the writer makes? At what points in the paper would you have
liked more explanation or support?

3. Does the *conclusion* merely recapitulate points already made?

4. Does the writer use a *range* of sources? Do her parenthetical documentation and her list of Works Cited show any major variations from routine identification or standard entries?

24 Perspectives

The Age of Theory

*Until we understand the assumptions in which we
are drenched we cannot know ourselves.*

ADRIENNE RICH

FOCUS ON CRITICAL PERSPECTIVES

Both poets and their readers are influenced by ideas about poetry. Poets may heed or they may rebel against critics who set critical standards. They may themselves turn critics, becoming trend makers, helping shape movements and countermovements. The modern age has been called the age of theory, with poets becoming very much self-aware, "self-reflective." At the same time, much attention has been paid to the reader's response—to the assumptions and expectations a reader brings to a poem.

Readers vary greatly in how much a critical perspective colors their response to poetry. Here are major perspectives that influence the perceptions of critical readers:

Biographical Criticism   Much critical analysis ties in discussion of the poet's work with biographical data—the poet's marital history or the poet's alienation from a materialistic society. Intensely personal poetry reveals but maybe also disguises or transforms the poet's personal experience. Much critical discussion, for instance, has focused on the relationship between Anne Sexton's poetry and the personal demons that bedeviled and finally destroyed her life.

Katha Pollitt

Anne Sexton: The Death Is Not the Life   1991

It seems oddly apt that Diane Wood Middlebrook's "Anne Sexton: A Biography," the first full-scale life of the poet, should already have attracted some of the same kind of scandalized attention as did Sexton herself. Most

597

readers will be aware of the debate surrounding the decision of Sexton's first long-term psychiatrist, Dr. Martin T. Orne, to give Ms. Middlebrook (a professor of English at Stanford University and herself a poet and literary critic) access to tapes of his therapy sessions with Sexton—tapes that Ms. Middlebrook, with the permission of Linda Gray Sexton, the poet's daughter and literary executor, extensively quotes. (Actually, debate is the wrong word, since nobody but the parties to the use of the tapes has risen to defend it. Thunderous condemnation is more like it.)

In view of the uproar, it seems important to say right up front that Ms. Middlebrook has written a wonderful book: just, balanced, insightful, complex in its sympathies and in its judgment of Sexton both as a person and as a writer. While she spares no detail of Sexton's pathology, her book is not, in any sense, what Joyce Carol Oates has called "a pathography." It is, rather, a deeply moving account of how one young woman—badly educated, marooned in the Boston suburbs and hampered at every turn by mental illness—managed to become, for a while, a poet of distinctive and original gifts.

When Sexton began seeing Dr. Orne in 1956, after the first of what would be many breakdowns and suicide attempts, she was almost 28 years old, a finishing-school dropout and, in her own view, a total failure as a wife to her businessman husband, Alfred Muller Sexton 2d (nicknamed Kayo), and as a mother to her two small daughters—who, indeed, spent much of their toddlerhood living with Kayo's mother. Sexton was obsessed with childhood traumas—her mother was cold and vain, her father rigid, alcoholic and abusive; her great-aunt Nana, who alone in the family had given her the affection she craved, had gone mad and died in a nursing home. When Dr. Orne asked her if there was anything she felt she could do well, the only answer she came up with was prostitution. He suggested writing instead: perhaps she could be of help to others who were suffering from mental illness.

Two years after writing her first sonnet—sparked by a program on educational television—Sexton had written the poems that were collected in her first book, "To Bedlam and Part Way Back," which was published in 1960. Within 10 years she was one of the most honored poets in America: a Pulitzer Prize winner, a fellow of the Royal Society of Literature, the first female member of the Harvard chapter of Phi Beta Kappa, the subject of a television documentary.

To Sexton's many fans—and with nearly half a million copies of her books sold in the United States alone, she has a huge audience among people who read little other poetry—her appeal, like that of Sylvia Plath, lies partly in her life and early death, with its inescapable feminist drama, and partly in the apparent candor of her self-presentation. Ms. Middlebrook carefully shows how simplistic this picture is.

Like other so-called confessional poets, Sexton reworked her life to suit artistic purposes. "I use the personal when I am applying a mask to my face," she wrote, "like a rubber mask that the robber wears." As her friend the British poet George MacBeth astutely noted, "She saw sincerity as a *technique,* the style that happened to fit what she wanted to say." Sexton made her debut, after all, as a formalist, with poems relentlessly pushed through 20 and 30 drafts and shaped by criticism in workshops with Robert Lowell and John Holmes—sessions attended by Plath, George Starbuck and Maxine Kumin, who became her lifelong friend and closest reader. Had Sexton merely been versifying her autobiography, she wouldn't have lasted two minutes in that crowd.

"How did a mad housewife become a star?" Ms. Middlebrook asks in her preface. Sexton's rise is a quintessential American success story, in which talent, ambition and staggering amounts of work (plus career smarts and a thoroughgoing refusal of domestic labor) triumph over seemingly insuperable obstacles: lack of formal education and family encouragement; treatment with mind-numbing drugs like Thorazine, which was first prescribed in 1964 and whose side effects she struggled against for the next eight years; an inability to go anywhere alone, even a bookstore or a supermarket.

Reading about how Sexton compensated for these disabilities (for she never overcame them) is a bit like reading about how an amputee became an Olympic athlete. She threw herself at teachers and mentors—including James Wright and W. D. Snodgrass—and became a "gaga student" of literature. She went off Thorazine to write (the drug, she joked, was "supposed to make the rhymer go away"), then endured the consequent mania. She enlisted friends, paid companions—and, at one point, even a prospective biographer—to travel with her when she had to give poetry readings. Certainly she was exploitative, narcissistic, impossibly demanding. But one is struck by how many people speak warmly of her in these pages: former lovers, neighbors, even her daughters, despite their hair-raising childhoods. "Annie gave as good as she got," Maxine Kumin told Ms. Middlebrook, and one feels she really did.

Unfortunately, Sexton's particularly American success led to a particularly American downfall—an urgent need for ever more attention and esteem, and an inability to reckon the cost. By the end of the 1960's, alcohol and pills were impairing her creativity, and the quest for fame had become an end in itself. When she started writing, Sexton had wanted to reach her fellow sufferers, but also what Maxine Kumin called the "vertical audience" of her poet peers and literary history. "In the field I have chosen, to be halfway is to be nothing," she told Dr. Orne. But increasingly she craved a kind of celebrity that can hardly ever be achieved in our time by words alone. . . .

How well do Sexton's poems hold up today? Rereading her work for this review, I was struck by the freshness, pathos and brio of many of her poems from the late 1950's and early 60's: "Music Swims Back to Me," "The Double Image" (her long and complex exploration of mothers and daughters), "The Starry Night," "The Touch." As Ms. Middlebrook points out, Sexton was writing for an audience that did not yet exist, for readers who wanted to hear women speaking in their own voices about their own lives. And in her strongest poems one can still feel the excitement of a writer who knows she is bringing into literature a range of human experience previously thought to be beneath its attention.

From *The New York Times Book Review*

The Receptive Reader

Why was the biographer's use of the psychiatrist's tapes controversial? (Do you have strong feelings about the point at issue?) What role does the American dream of success (or style of success) play in this discussion? What light does the reviewer shed on the relationship between the poet's struggle against illness and her writing?

Historical Criticism   Literary historians have charted the movements and countermovements that define major literary **periods** or period styles. For instance, **Romantic** poets rebelled against the neoclassical tradition of the eighteenth century, with its emphasis on the analytical intellect and artificial restraint. Outstanding among **neoclassical** poet-critics, Alexander Pope wrote his *Essay on Criticism* (1711) in polished closed couplets when the Age of Enlightenment was celebrating human reason as "one clear, unchanged, and universal light." It stressed the need for rational control over our impulses and emotions. Sound judgment was needed to guide the poetic imagination, with the poet pruning and revising first rough efforts. Pope saw poetic language and form as the vehicle for the poet's ideas—frequently ideas that were already part of the thinking of well-informed people:

> True wit is nature to advantage dressed,
> What oft was thought, but ne'er so well expressed;
> Something, whose truth convinced at sight we find,
> That gives us back the image of our mind.

Celebrating the creative imagination, the Romantic rebels exalted passion over reason. They warned that the unchecked analytical intellect would dry up the wellsprings of intuition, emotion, and inspiration. They believed that original genius could not be confined within the limits of rules and conventions. They turned to the healing influence of nature as the antidote to the neuroses of the Industrial Age. Like other Romantic poets, the English poet John Keats (1795–1821) believed that what we feel deeply and sincerely cannot be wrong. In a letter written in 1817, he said, "I am certain of nothing but of the holiness of the Heart's affections and the truth of Imagination—What the Imagination seizes as Beauty must be truth."

Modern critics have seen the Welsh poet Dylan Thomas as a latter-day Romantic—close to the Romantic "religion of nature." In one of Thomas's poems, the speaker wanders on the seashore, seeing everywhere signs of "blessed, unborn God and his Ghost, / And every soul his priest." Critics linking Thomas to the Romantics have pointed to his rich, sensuous language ("In My Craft and Sullen Art"), his love of nature and glorification of a rural childhood ("Fern Hill"), and his preoccupation with death ("Do Not Go Gentle into That Good Night"). In the follow-ing excerpt, a critic discusses Thomas's relationship to the Romantic tradition:

Alfred Kazin

Dylan Thomas and Romanticism   *1989*

All of Thomas's poetry shows the profound romantic need to intensify exis-tence, to make it all come alive as it is in personal consciousness. But where so many great poets—Blake, Wordsworth, Keats, even Whitman—have rec-ognized that their task is not to love their new vision of the commonplace world but to explain and to unite it to human existence, Thomas felt absurd and histrionic, acted like a man who in his heart thought himself a fake.

He was too humble. It is a strange thing to remember of anyone whose gift was so personal and sweeping, but he regarded his own gift as slightly absurd; he sheltered it, wouldn't have his poems discussed, because he couldn't admit that poetry is thought, and that what he said in his poems many of his contemporaries really believed and were most deeply grateful to a poet for saying again. He was left with his fantastic linguistic gift as if it were something to read from, to entertain with, but not, in the artistic sense, to practice as a criticism of life.

From "The Posthumous Life of Dylan Thomas"

Formalist Criticism   Much twentieth-century criticsm reacted against the late nineteenth-century Victorian poetry of uplift and ennobling sen-timent. Early moderns like Ezra Pound and T. S. Eliot insisted that poetry had its own language, its own challenging way of seeing. Criticism in the **New Critical,** or **formalist,** mode emphasized close reading and detailed formal analysis. The New Critics looked in poetry for the shap-ing and formal control needed to keep poetry from being a mere "turn-ing loose of emotion" (T. S. Eliot).

Readers influenced by the formalist traditions look in poetry for chal-lenge, for complexity. Poetry that is too regular, too smooth, has seemed to them simple-minded. Whatever ordering or shaping takes place should make us sense that jostling reality has been brought under con-trol. Many moderns have loved irony and paradox; they have looked for poets who do justice to mixed emotions and divided loyalties. They have looked for attempts to face and resolve ambiguities. They look for the breaks or counterrhythms that break up the te-DUM-te-DUM-te-DUM patterns of "jingle-poets."

"God's Grandeur" (1877) by Gerard Manley Hopkins, is one of the great poems of English literature. Its richness and complexity invite the kind of close reading that became a hallmark of formalistic analysis in the New Critical tradition.

The world is charged with the grandeur of God.
> It will flame out, like shining from shook foil;
> It gathers to a greatness, like the ooze of oil
Crushed. Why do men then now not reck his rod?
Generations have trod, have trod, have trod;
> And all is seared with trade; bleared, smeared with toil
> And wears man's smudge and shares man's smell: the soil
Is bare now, nor can foot feel, being shod.

And for all this, nature is never spent;
> There lives the dearest freshness deep down things;
And though the last lights off the black West went
> Oh, morning, at the brown brink eastward, springs—
Because the Holy Ghost over the bent
> World broods with warm breast and with ah! bright wings.

Does the following explication, or line-by-line explanation by an experienced reader, help you respond more fully to the richness of the poem?

J. R. Watson

A Close Reading of G. M. Hopkins' "God's Grandeur"   *1987*

The world is charged with the grandeur of God.

As a first line this is uncompromising. Its rhythm is confident and assured, and the full stop at the end of the line seems to emphasize the completeness and finality of the statement. The world is charged with God's grandeur, and that is that. Hopkins was so careful with line-endings and rhythms that this sentence within a line is evidently there for a purpose, to make the claim as strongly as possible. It does so especially because of the emphatic word "charged," which usefully has two meanings: "loaded," and "full of electricity" as a battery is when it has been charged. The world is therefore electric with God's grandeur, and loaded with it (which suggests that the grandeur is heavy and substantial): the image of electricity is carried on in the second line, when he senses that the grandeur of God will "flame out, like shining from shook foil." As foil, when shaken, gives off shining light, so the world, when looked at carefully, is full of the shining light of God Himself, leaping out like flames or sparks. Hopkins described it to Bridges as "I mean foil in its sense of leaf or tinsel, . . . Shaken gold foil gives off broad glares like sheet lightning, and this is true of nothing else, owing to its zigzag dints and creasings and network of small many cornered facets, a sort of fork lightning too" (L B 169). Its fullness is indicated by the next image

It gathers to a greatness, like the ooze of oil
Crushed.

Hopkins is here thinking of an olive press, with the oil oozing from the pressed fruit. It oozes from every part of the press, in a fine film, and then the trickles gather together to form a jar of oil. In the same way the grandeur of God is found everywhere, trickling from every simple thing in the created universe and accumulating to form a greatness, a grandeur that is perceived by the discerning mind of the Christian and poet. This is made clear in the lines that follow, which are a lament for the neglect and indifference shown by mankind. Once again the poetry is dense with metaphors: instead of saying "why do men take no notice?"' Hopkins writes

Why do men then now not reck his rod?

The rhythms and sounds are themselves awkward, like the question: "men then," "now not" and "reck his rod" (care for his rule: "reck" means "heed," occurring in ordinary speech in the word "reckless"). And these sounds continue, as if Hopkins is using the vocabulary and rhythms of his verse to act out, as well as describe, the situation:

Generations have trod, have trod, have trod;
    And all is seared with trade; bleared, smeared with toil;
    And wears man's smudge and shares man's smell: the soil
Is bare now, nor can foot feel, being shod.

Here the mechanical forces are captured in verse by the heavy accents. What is sometimes called the "daily grind" is a repetitive thump in which the feet of generations march on; and the "trod . . . trod . . . trod" sets up the three-beat ryhthm of the next line: "seared . . . bleared . . . smeared." The verbs themselves sprawl across the line, preventing any delicacy of feeling or perception. "Seared," for instance, means "dried up" or it can mean "rendered incapable of feeling": it is accomplished by "bleared" (blurred in inflammation of the eyes) and "smeared" (rubbed over with dirt). When we think of the minute attention to detail of Hopkins' drawings, these adjectives take on yet more force: they are part of the process of treading down, smudging, and generally spoiling nature. Because of this the soil is barren, and feet, being both shod with boots, cannot feel it. For Hopkins, the "foot feel" is but a part of the whole process of insensitivity: as a man's feet are encased in boots, so his whole soul is bound up, unfree. . . .

It is then that the sestet throws into the equation another mysterious force, the feeling of freshness and growth of nature that causes it to live on, to survive against all the neglect and exploitation of man, Its nature is in this way to be itself: to go on growing each year with its own process of generation and renewed life, so that against the unfeeling energies of man there is placed something greater, the inexhaustible forces of nature. Its spirit of growth is everywhere: it is as natural and inevitable as the coming of morning after nightfall. It is the "dearest freshness" deep down in things which ensures that "nature is never spent"; and in the final lines this inexhaustible quality is associated with the working of the Holy Ghost, the spirit of God who created all things and sustains them:

Because the Holy Ghost over the bent
    World broods with warm breast and with ah! bright wings.
                    From *The Poetry of Gerard Manley Hopkins*

The Receptive Reader

How does the critic show that the word *charged* is charged with meaning? What inside information does he use from the poet himself? Where and how does the critic show the meshing of content and form? What difficulties does this reading clear up for you? How does this excerpt change your understanding of and response to the poem?

Psychoanalytic Criticism   Critics indebted to Freudian psychoanalysis focus on the creative power of the unconscious mind. They treat the intellectual content of much poetry as surface rationalizations that mask the basic psychic conflicts of the individual. Freud himself, who wrote extensively about art and literature, had applied to poetry such basic psychoanalytic categories as repressed desire and the conflict between rebellious instinctual energies and control by the conscious rational mind—the conflict between the Id and the Ego. He inspired critics to look for fantasies of wish-fulfillment or for instances of sublimation—channeling sexual energy away from forbidden objects of desire into socially approved intellectual or artistic pursuits.

In richly symbolic poems by poets like William Blake or W. B. Yeats, critics schooled in Freudian psychology find much sexually charged imagery and the symbolic acting out of personal conflicts and confusions. In the following excerpt, two students of early modern critical crosscurrents discuss Freudian readings of Yeats's "The Second Coming." Earlier in the same chapter of their *The Muse of Fire,* they discuss Yeats's "long romance" with Maud Gonne, "whom he loved deeply and long," but who instead married John MacBride, a hero of the Irish nationalists who was executed in 1916. He alludes to her in poems speaking from his "embittered heart" to a soul enslaved by "fanaticism and hate." Rejected by her again, he found himself in love with Maud Gonne's adopted daughter Iseult, but eventually married another woman. Here are the opening lines of Yeats's "The Second Coming" (see Chapter 25 for the complete poem):

Turning and turning in the widening gyre°   *spiral*
The falcon cannot hear the falconer;
Things fall apart; the center cannot hold;
Mere anarchy is loosed upon the world,
The blood-dimmed tide is loosed, and everywhere
The ceremony of innocence is drowned;
The best lack all conviction, while the worst
Are full of passionate intensity.

H. Edward Richardson and Frederick B. Shroyer

Freudian Analysis and Yeats' "Second Coming"   1971

Yeats' feverish quest for marriage may suggest, on a broad level, a search for some kind of stability, or for love and wisdom, but its frantic circumstances indicate a desperate grasping for order within a life of chaos. In psychological terms, this would indicate a loss of ego control and an anarchy of the libido, which must have always been especially strong in Yeats.

If we accept Freud's thesis of an event of the present making "a strong impression on the writer," it would seem that Maud Gonne's "second coming" into Yeats' life would have been a sufficient causal agent to have "stirred up a memory of an earlier experience." If Yeats had indeed retreated far enough into his old memories, he may have stirred up a sexual fantasy for the Maud Gonne about whom, projecting his ego outward, he had often dreamed, and he may have then transmitted those dreams into poetry.

Within such a Freudian context, several images in "The Second Coming" take on sexual overtones. For example, the title may indicate, on one level, a significant "second" meeting, or on another, sexual orgasm; line 1, possibly, sexual intercourse; line 2, the lack of personal control or mastery of the ego over powerful unconscious desires; lines 3–5, a freely associated identity with the disintegrating world of order and propriety; line 6, a conscious awareness of guilt, the source of which may still be disguised, representing either the "ceremony" of his recent marriage, or his child about to be born, or both; lines 7–8, castigation of himself as "the best," perhaps a condemnation of Madame MacBride in the role of temptress as "the worst," although she still exudes for him her typical "passionate intensity.". . .

If we pursue the approach further, the final wish-fulfillment may be easy to explain in psychological terms, if one can imagine that Yeats' guilt and disillusionment in himself and in Madame MacBride were deep enough. The "rocking cradle" (perhaps the as-yet-unborn and innocent child) is an antipode to the probable consequences of this loss of control, this trammeling on innocence, this identity with disorder, chaos, and Dionysian revelry, and finally, to the ultimate destruction of the world. Why would Yeats choose such an antithetical image within the context of such annihilative violence? The answer may indicate Yeats' Protestant fear of breaking the Mosaic law— a real fear, deep in his unconscious, but functioning in such a way as to dominate his ego. Only the traditional summoning to judgment at the end of the world can lift the burden of what the ego can interpret only as tormenting shame. At this point, then, libido gives way to mortido, and life to death.

From *Muse of Fire: Approaches to Poetry*

The Receptive Reader

Many have read the opening lines of Yeats's poem as a prophetic vision of a modern world threatened by political and moral chaos. In how many ways does this account find possible personal meanings in these same lines? How does this account show the parallel between the traditional opposition of order and anarchy and the Freudian opposition of the ego and the id? (What is the role of the falcon image in these lines?)

Political Criticism   Politically engaged critics raise the question of the poet's social responsibility. Much traditional art or literature seems to them a retreat into a private sphere of art or beauty for its own sake. For critics indebted to Marxist thought, for instance, the key question has been: Does the poet collaborate in or oppose oppression by the state?

Marxist critics use recent history as a test of the poet's and the critic's political commitments. For instance, they fault poets and teachers of poetry for not dealing with the horrors of the Vietnam War and the role of American "corporate power" in the struggle of a third world country against the legacy of colonialism.

Even when not committed to a specific ideology, politically engaged poets and critics have seen poetry as a means for awakening the reader's social conscience and sense of injustice. The following poem is Jane Flanders's "The House That Fear Built: Warsaw 1943." The form of the poem is borrowed from a children's rhyme: "This is the house that Jack built." But the subject of the poem is far removed from child's play. The poem reminds readers of a haunting photograph taking during World War II: as the Nazi occupiers crush the Jewish resistance during the desperate uprising in the Warsaw ghetto, a group of Jewish civilians is led away by German soldiers. In the critical discussion that follows the poem, an editor who chose the poem for publication tries to explain why he was powerfully affected by the way this poem conveyed its message.

The purpose of poetry is to remind us
how difficult it is to remain just one person,
for our house is open, there are no keys in the
doors . . .   CZESLAW MILOSZ, FROM "ARS POETICA"

I am the boy with his hands raised over his head
in Warsaw.

I am the soldier whose rifle is trained
on the boy with his hands raised over his head
in Warsaw.

I am the woman with lowered gaze
who fears the soldier whose rifle is trained
on the boy with his hands raised over his head
in Warsaw.

I am the man in the overcoat
who loves the woman with lowered gaze
who fears the soldier whose rifle is trained
on the boy with his hands raised over his head
in Warsaw.

I am the stranger who photographs
the man in the overcoat

Women and children being led off by Nazi soldiers in the Warsaw ghetto, 1943. Main Commission for the Investigation of Nazi War Crimes, courtesy of the USHMM Photo Archives.

who loves the woman with lowered gaze
who fears the soldier whose rifle is trained
on the boy with his hands raised over his head
in Warsaw.

The crowd, of which I am each part, moves on
beneath my window, for I am the crone too
who shakes her sheets
over every street in the world
muttering
What's this? What's this?

Richard Foerster

Message and Means in Jane Flanders'
"The House That Fear Built"   *1990*

I remember enjoying initially the sound of this poem, the way it evoked
not only "The House That Jack Built," an eighteenth-century nursery rhyme
that some scholars believe is based on a sixteenth-century Hebrew chant,

but also Elizabeth Bishop's "Visits to St. Elizabeths." The incremental repetition of such poems has its roots in medieval ballads, in the plainspeak and melodies of communal entertainment, and I found myself responding to this ancient aural technique and the haunting mood it generated in counterpoint to the poem's World War II setting.

I was moved also by the poem's other sound effects, though I can't say I was conscious of them on first hearing. The labels come with hindsight. Now I detect an almost Anglo-Saxon use of alliteration and caesura to enhance the syntactic balance of many of the lines, such as:

who loves the woman   with lowered gaze
who fears the soldier   whose rifle is trained

Assonance and approximate rhymes thread through the stanzas, stitching together images and ideas:

stranger   gaze   trained   raised

and

beneath   sheets   streets

"The sound must seem an echo to the sense" is one Popean truism I find ignored by too many poets today. Flanders makes her sounds serve sense in a striking way. Like Eliot before her in "The Hollow Men" ("This is the way the world ends") and—to my mind—like Ravel in "La Valse," she uses traditional rhythms to overthrow tradition, to give us a glimpse of the deterioration of order. Against the ironic counterpoint of the innocent children's rhyme, Flanders unfolds a widening perspective of the horrors of twentieth-century war. Her rhythms and incremental repetitions undermine our initial expectations. The skipping rhythm introduced in the first stanza leads us to believe that the boy's arms might be raised in play. By the poem's end, however, we realize he is part of a gruesome, complex tableau of the Warsaw Ghetto Uprising of the spring of 1943. . . .

The progression of the poem's images and ideas seemed to me both surprising and inevitable; appropriately for a poem based on a photograph, they moved cinematically, from close-up to panorama, from boy to crowd to "every street in the world."

Seeing the typescript made clear for me the relationship between the epigraph and both the title and the subject of the poem. "Our house" I understood not only as Parnassus and the poet's ability to assume masks but also as the entire modern world, which seems increasingly invaded and controlled by fear. The poet/spectator of this drama is helpless to prevent herself from identifying with each of her characters. Unable "to remain just one person," as Milosz says, the poet becomes a part of each of them, shares in their fears, love, brutality, and indifference, and imparts these to us through craft. Reading the poem, I, too, found myself becoming each of the characters: boy/victim, soldier/victimizer, resigned woman, compassionate but equally helpless man, one of the crowd that "moves on," and finally the onlooking crone, who in traditional nursery rhymes shakes out the world's woes from her bedding. In Flanders' modern version, however, the crone cannot absolve herself of complicity by pretending not to understand the nature of the tragedy occurring beneath her window.

I also enjoyed the double-edged words that add to the poem's depth: *Warsaw* became in my mind a "war saw"; the soldier's rifle significantly is not aimed but *trained,* suggesting the political indoctrination that made young German men into instruments of the Nazi Reich, tools of the Final Solution; and finally the crone and her sheets. I imagine her not only attending to her domestic chores but also hiding behind the sheets of a newspaper, the way we overlook the world from our armchairs while muttering "What's this?" when certain headlines catch our eye.

From *Spreading the Word: Editors on Poetry*

The Receptive Reader

According to Foerster, why did the poet borrow the form of the children's rhyme? How does it serve as a "counterpoint" to the subject of the poem? What effect does it supposedly have on the reader? In reading this poem by Jane Flanders, were you too "helpless" to prevent yourself "from identifying with each of her characters"? (Why, or why not?) What, according to the critic, is the role of "the crone and her sheets"?

Feminist Criticism   Feminist writers have focused attention on how poetry deals with the basic issues in women's lives. They have questioned the traditional emphasis on formal analysis, and they have privileged the powerful expression of personal emotions. They have encouraged the poet to come out from behind the poetic persona, rehabilitating what has been called **confessional poetry,** devoted to personal revelation.

Feminist critics have paid special attention to the struggles of women to reconcile their mission as poets with traditional societal roles, as when Sylvia Plath says, "If I want to keep on being a triple-threat woman: wife, writer, and teacher . . . I can't be a drudge." They have sympathized with the struggle for self-realization and self-fulfillment, about which Plath said, "I am making a self, in great pain, often, as for a birth, but it is right that it should be so" and "By reforging my soul, I am a woman now the like of which I could never have dreamed" (*Letters Home*).

The following article is excerpted from a collection of feminist reevaluations of the life and work of Emily Dickinson, "the greatest woman poet in the English language" (Suzanne Juhasz). Feminist critics have revised a traditional view of Emily Dickinson as eccentric or quaint, showing her instead as a woman of genius in rebellion against "the nineteenth-century corseting of women's bodies, choices, and sexuality." From a feminist perspective, Dickinson's life was neither a flight from reality nor a sacrifice nor a substitution but a strategy for creating the kind of person she was; "it was a life deliberately organized on her terms" (Adrienne Rich). The following article reopens the much debated issue of Dickinson's emotional attachments to men or women.

Adelaide Morris

I see the better in the Dark—
I do not need a light—
The Love of Thee—a Prism be—
Excelling Violet

EMILY DICKINSON

A Feminist Reading of Emily Dickinson   1983

The list of Dickinson's possible attachments is long, and our confusion is augmented by the fact that many of her letters and no doubt many of her poems have been lost to us, both through carelessness and through deliberate destruction. Two significant sets of writing to those she loved remain, however. The letters to the man she called "Master" are, as Richard Sewall points out, "among the most intense and fervent love letters she ever wrote," and they are supplemented by dozens of poems with similar vocabulary, rhythm, imagery, and symbolic pattern. The other group, addressed to her friend, sister-in-law, and next-door neighbor, Susan Gilbert Dickinson, consists of 154 extant notes and letters and 276 identifiable poems and poem fragments, probably a mere fraction of a lifetime's whole. The biographical details are gone: we don't know who her "Master" was, we know almost nothing of her sensual experience, we don't even know if those she loved loved her back. A plentitude of verbal detail remains, however, to allow us to compare the two prisms these loves formed and the very different spectrums they cast.

The rhetoric that describes the two relationships is surprisingly, even suspiciously similar, as if Dickinson were writing to the Master and Sue out of some peculiarly elliptic book of pattern letters. Both correspondences are highly compressed and heavily revised: the Master letters exist in drafts that hesitate over each choice of diction, syntax, and symbol, and rough drafts remain for even the most casual of notes sent across the lawn to Sue. In both cases, the revisions make continuous minute adjustments between advance and evasion, excitement and control. Urgent and edgy, her writing teases, pleads, chides, jests, and sighs. The rhythms are by turns abrupt and sustained, gnomic and rhapsodic.

Both the Master and Sue evoke her passion; both are passionately solicited, courted with imagery chosen to convey their magnetic pull. Again and again she describes herself as bewitched, overwhelmed. The most revealing recurrence, however, is the linked imagery of sun, storms, volcanoes, and wounds that she uses in both sets of letters and poems. Sue is "an Avalanche of Sun!," a woman of "torrid Noons"; the Master becomes her

"man of noon . . . *mightier* than the morning." When the element of disturbance joins this imagery of huge heat and height, we have the thunderstorms described in so many poems sent to Sue. The setting is explosive,
even volcanic: a sky sealed with "A Cap of Lead" (1649), wind rocking the
grass (824), thunder piling and crumbling (1247), while

> Through fissures in
> Volcanic cloud
> The yellow lightning shone—
>
> [1694]

When explosion is withheld, Dickinson's image shifts from the thunderstorm to the silent, suppressed volcano vividly present in both sets of material. "Vesuvius dont talk—Etna—dont—," Dickinson reminds the Master, but
so intense is the repressed force, she continues, "one of them—said a syllable—a thousand years ago, and Pompeii heard it, and hid forever." This is
the dangerous "Vesuvius at Home" (1705), the deceptively domestic surface
she describes in a poem sent to Sue:

> On my volcano grows the Grass
> A meditative spot—
> An acre for a Bird to choose
> Would be the General thought—
>
> How red the Fire rocks below
> How insecure the sod
> Did I disclose
> Would populate with awe my solitude.
>
> [1677]

The red, rocking, inner fire of this poem is unreleased passion, passion that
endangers everything around it. The heat, intensity, and destructively deep
interiority this image stresses connect it with the last of the series: the image
of the profound inner wound. This is the hurt Dickinson describes to Sue as
a sting (156), a stab (238), the gash that "wantoned with a Bone" (479), and
to the Master as a stab, the "bullet" which "hit a Bird," the "Tomahawk in
my side.". . .

This is an intense—and intensely familiar—discourse. Sun, storms, volcanoes, wounds, rescue, redemption: all emerge from that catalogue of
romantic generalities Adrienne Rich calls "the language of love-letters, of
suicide notes." This language seems to fit so easily into both sets of letters
and poems that we might suppose it signifies a mode of loving Dickinson
solicited from men and women both. Such a suspicion is bolstered by the
existence of love poems with alternate sets of pronouns: in a particularly
apt example, one variant of poem 494 begins "Going to Him! Happy letter!"
while the other starts, "Going—to—Her!/Happy—Letter!" We would be
wrong, however, to conclude that similar rhetoric describes a similar sort of
love. The kind of love Dickinson desires and develops with a woman is
very different from the love she desires and develops with a man. The similarities in rhetoric mask deep dissimilarities of structure.

* * *

Romantic rhetoric permits only one set of relations, the paradigm of disturbance and idolatry that is everywhere consonant with the structures of her love for Sue. Western traditions offer no developed discourse for love between women and thus, in need of a precedent, Dickinson may have used conventional romantic rhetoric in the letters and poems to Sue as a linguistic formula signifying an intensity (love) rather than a structure (dominance/submission). The most intriguing aspect of the writing to Sue is the consistency with which the clichés of romantic love are undermined by a revolutionary revision of love's possibilities.

The differences in structure are coded into the names Dickinson assigned her lovers: a "Master" can exist only in a world of difference and hierarchy; a "Sister," on the other hand, inhabits a world of similarity and equality. The structures of the Master's world are predominantly vertical and its dramas are largely dramas of positioning: the prostration of the woman, the exaltation of the man. She is forever "a tiny courtier" as the pageant of his tremendous glory (151). By contrast, the structures of the sisters' world are horizontal, not a universe but a neighborhood. Its dramas detail the flexible push and pull, the coming and going of those who live day to day, side by side. Against the abstract dignity of stasis in the Master material, the two figures in the poems and letters to Sue demonstrate a scrappy spontaneity: they are alternately large and small, far and near, magisterial and coy.

In Suzanne Juhasz, ed., *Feminist Critics Read Emily Dickinson*

The Receptive Reader

How much does Morris rely on biographical data? How much on Dickinson's letters? How much on her poems? How, according to Morris, is Dickinson's rhetoric of love for men and for women "surprisingly, even suspiciously similar"? What difference in the two kinds of relationships is masked by this similarity?

Deconstructionism   In recent years, deconstructionist critics have read familiar classics from a radically new perspective. The following much-anthologized poem by a leader of the English Romantic movement is accompanied by a deconstructionist reading that clears away much of the apparent surface meaning of the poem. The critic then discovers a new and different dimension of meaning as the language used by the poet dances out its own significance.

The poem, as the critic says, is "a kind of epitaph," being part of the "Lucy poems," which commemorate a country girl who had died young. A "meta-epitaphic" poem would in some way go *beyond* the familiar conventions of an epitaph. Other words that are part of the critic's vocabulary here are *laconic* (very brief, using the fewest possible words) and *mimetic* (imitating or mirroring). The German word *aufgehoben,* used by the critic at a key point, means literally "taken up, lifted" but figuratively also "put up, preserved" and "taken off, canceled." Here is William Wordsworth's "A Slumber Did My Spirit Seal" (1800), followed by Geoffrey Hartman's critical reading:

A slumber did my spirit seal;
   I had no human fears:
She seemed a thing that could not feel
   The touch of earthly years.

No motion has she now, no force;
   She neither hears nor sees;
Rolled round in earth's diurnal° course,   *daily*
   With rocks, and stones, and trees.

Geoffrey Hartman

Deconstructing Wordsworth's "A Slumber Did My Spirit Seal"   *1987*

It does not matter whether you interpret the second stanza (especially its last line) as tending toward affirmation, or resignation, or a grief verging on bitterness. . . .

That [the poem] is a kind of epitaph is relevant, of course. We recognize, even if genre is not insisted on, that Wordsworth's style is laconic, even lapidary. There may be a mimetic or formal motive related to the ideal of epitaphic poetry. But the motive may also be, in a precise way, meta-epitaphic. The poem, first of all, marks the closure of a life that has never opened up: Lucy is likened in other poems to a hidden flower or the evening star. Setting overshadows rising, and her mode of existence is inherently inward, westering. I will suppose then, that Wordsworth was at some level giving expression to the traditional epitaphic wish: Let the earth rest lightly on the deceased. If so, his conversion of this epitaphic formula is so complete that to trace the process of conversion might seem gratuitous. The formula, a trite if deeply grounded figure of speech, has been catalyzed out of existence. Here it is formula itself, or better, the adjusted words of the mourner that lie lightly on the girl and everyone who is a mourner.

I come back, then, to the "aesthetic" sense of a burden lifted, rather than denied. A heavy element is made lighter. One may still feel that the term "elation" is inappropriate in this context; yet elation is, as a mood, the very subject of the first stanza. For the mood described is love or desire when it *eternizes* the loved person, when it makes her a star-like being that "could not feel / The touch of earthly years." This *naïve* elation, this spontaneous movement of the spirit upward, is reversed in the downturn or catastrophe of the second stanza. Yet this stanza does not close out the illusion; it preserves it within the elegiac form. The illusion is elated, in our use of the word: *aufgehoben* seems the proper term. For the girl is still, and all the more, what she seemed to be: beyond touch, like a star, if the earth in its daily motion is a planetary and erring rather than a fixed star, and if all on this star of earth must partake of its sublunar, mortal, temporal nature. . . .

To sum up: In Wordsworth's lyric the specific gravity of words is weighed in the balance of each stanza; and this balance is as much a judgment on speech in the context of our mortality as it is a meaningful response to the individual death. At the limit of the medium of words, and close to silence, what has been purged is not concreteness, or the empirical sphere of the emotions—shock, disillusion, trauma, recognition, grief, atonement—what has been purged is a series of flashy schematisms and false or partial mediations: artificial plot, inflated consolatory rhetoric, the coercive absolutes of logic or faith.

From "Elation in Hegel and Wordsworth,"
The Unremarkable Wordsworth

The Receptive Reader

What for you is the "surface meaning" of the poem? For you, does the poem as a whole tend "toward affirmation, or resignation, or grief verging on bitterness"? How or why does Hartman feel that the words of the poem have a lightening effect, producing a sense of a burden lifted? What, according to Hartman, has been "purged" by the poem?

Reader Response   "Central to the reading of every literary work is the interaction between its structure and its recipient," says Wolfgang Iser, leading exponent of **reader response** theory. The printed text is to our live response as the script of a play is to a live performance—in fact, to a live performance in which director and actors put their own strong personal imprint on the play.

Much of our response as readers depends on what we as readers bring to the poem. We see a poem through the lens of our own experience, our own preoccupations and preferences. One reader may say of a poem about a kid on a merry-go-round: "It brings back a sensitivity of my youth. It is the excitement and wonder and mouth-gaping curiosity found at a carnival. It is wild imagination bounded by mother's pessimism and the authority of the traffic cop" (Tom E. Knowlton). Another reader may be allergic to Sousa-music used for "colorful nostalgia" and find that the poem "never gets past cuteness" (Stanley Cooperman). Both readers are responding to the same poem, with the actual lived experience of the poem residing in the dynamic interchange between the objective text and the subjectivity of the reader.

POETS ON POETRY

A poet writes always of his personal life, in his finest work out of its tragedy, whatever it be, remorse, lost love, or mere loneliness.

WILLIAM BUTLER YEATS

Poets have often written *about* poetry. They have explained their work, defended their art, or revisited waystations in their poetic careers. Poets vary greatly in their writing habits and in how they explain their motives and procedures in writing poetry. They offer a range of perspectives on the relation between poetry and critical theory, poetry and politics, or poetry and the larger culture.

Dylan Thomas   *(1914–1953)*

Dylan Thomas became a poet because he "had fallen in love with words." Thomas was a Welsh poet who knew how to make his readers and listeners sense the sheer inspired exuberance of the creative act. The following excerpt is from "Notes on the Art of Poetry," which he wrote in response to a student's questions. A crowd-pleasing performer, he insisted that "a poem on a page is only half a poem," with the actual shared reading of a poem serving as the culminating acting out and interpretation of the written text.

Notes on the Art of Poetry   *1951*

I wanted to write poetry in the beginning because I had fallen in love with words. The first poems I knew were nursery rhymes, and before I could read them for myself I had come to love just the words of them, the words alone. What the words stand for, symbolized, or meant was of very secondary importance. What mattered was the sound of them as I heard them for the first time on the lips of the remote and incomprehensible grown-ups who seemed, for some reason, to be living in my world. And these words were, to me, as the notes of bells, the sounds of musical instruments, the noises of wind, sea, and rain, the rattle of milkcarts, the clopping of hooves on cobbles, the fingering of branches on a window pane, might be to someone, deaf from birth, who has miraculously found his hearing. I did not care what the words said, overmuch, nor what happened to Jack and Jill and the Mother Goose rest of them; I cared for the shapes of sound that their names, and the words describing their actions, made in my ears; I cared for the colors the words cast on my eyes. I realize that I may be, as I think all that way, romanticizing my reactions to the simple and beautiful words of those pure poems; but that is all I can honestly remember, however much time might have falsified my memory. I fell in love—that is the only expression I can think of—at once, and am still at the mercy of words, though sometimes now, knowing a little of their behavior very well, I think I can influence them slightly and have even learned to beat them now and then, which they appear to enjoy. I tumbled for words at once. And, when I began to read the nursery rhymes for myself, and, later, to read other verses and ballads, I knew that I had discovered the most important thing to me, that could be ever. There they were, seemingly lifeless, made only of black and white, but out of them, out of their own being, came love and terror and pity and pain and wonder and all the other vague abstractions that make our ephemeral lives dangerous, great, and bearable. Out of them came the gusts and grunts and hiccups and heehaws of common fun on the earth; and though what the words meant was, in its own way, often deliciously funny enough, so much funnier seemed to me, at that almost forgotten time, the shape and shade and size and noise of the words as they hummed, strummed, jugged and galloped along.

In James Scully, ed., *Modern Poetics*

The Receptive Reader

How would you describe this poet's relationship with words? In this selection, what are striking examples of Thomas's own wildly imaginative use of words?

Making Connections—For Discussion or Writing

Poems by Dylan Thomas reprinted in this volume include "In My Craft or Sullen Art" (Chapter 19), "Do Not Go Gentle into That Good Night" (Chapter 20), and "Fern Hill" (Chapter 17). How do they show the poet's love of language?

Richard Wilbur   *(born 1921)*

I have never been one to write by rule, even by my own rules.

T. S. ELIOT

Modern poets have debated whether or not the demands of traditional form are artificial and have a constraining effect on poetic expression. Richard Wilbur has written about how a poem might start with a close-up look at his herb patch, which reminded him of miniature Japanese gardens, which in turn reminded him of the ministanzas of the Japanese haiku. In the following excerpt, he explains how in his work a poem finds its form without the poet bringing ready-made formal patterns to the poem from without. Early in this excerpt, he pays tribute to the nineteenth-century American poet and essayist Ralph Waldo Emerson, who championed individualism and authentic self-expression.

Letting a Poem Find Its Form   *1987*

One thing I know is that I have never deliberately set about to "write heroic couplets" or "write a sonnet." Poetry is both art and craft, but I abominate formal exercises and am stuck with the Emersonian feeling that a poem is something which finds out what it has to say, and in the process discovers the form which will best stress its tone and meaning. It may seem improbable to some poets of the last thirty years that such a process could result in, let us say, a rondeau [repeating only two rhymes, with the opening words coming back as a refrain]; but that is because such poets are free-verse practitioners who lack my generation's instinctive sense—got both by reading and writing—of the capabilities of certain traditional forms.

Though I commonly work in meters, my way of going about a poem is very like the free-verse writer's; that is, I begin by letting the words find what line lengths seem right to them. Often this will result in a stanza of some sort, which (though the ensuing stanzas keep the metrical pattern) will still be flexible enough to permit the argument to move and speak as it likes. All of my poems, therefore, are formally *ad hoc;* quite a few are, so far as I know, without formal precedent, and none set out to fulfill the "rules" of some standard form.

In David Lehman, ed., *Ecstatic Occasions, Expedient Forms*

The Receptive Reader

How does Wilbur challenge the familiar assumption that poets using traditional forms fit content into ready-made patterns? What does Wilbur mean when he says that his poems are "formally *ad hoc*" and often "without formal precedent"?

Audre Lorde   *(1934–1992)*

For many women who are part of the women's movement, poetry has become a means of self-definition and self-assertion. Audre Lorde is an African American poet of West Indian heritage. What does she mean when she says that "poems are not luxuries"?

Poems Are Not Luxuries   *1977*

For each of us as women, there is a dark place within where hidden and growing our true spirit rises, "Beautiful and tough as chestnut / Stanchions against our nightmare of weakness" and of impotence. These places of possibility within ourselves are dark because they are ancient and hidden; they have survived and grown strong through darkness. Within these deep places, each one of us holds an incredible reserve of creativity and power, storehouse of unexamined and unrecorded emotion and feeling. The woman's place of power within each of us is neither white nor surface; it is dark, it is ancient, and it is deep.

When we view living, in the european mode, only as a problem to be solved, we rely solely upon our ideas to make us free, for these were what the white fathers told us were precious. But as we become more in touch with our own ancient, black, noneuropean view of living as a situation to be experienced and interacted with, we learn more and more to cherish our feelings, to respect those hidden sources of our power from where true knowledge and therefore lasting action comes. At this point in time, I believe that women carry within ourselves the possibility for fusion of these two approaches as a keystone for survival, and we come closest to this combination in our poetry. I speak here of poetry as the revelation or distillation of experience, not the sterile word play that, too often, the white fathers distorted the word *poetry* to mean—in order to cover their desperate wish for imagination without insight.

For women, then, poetry is not a luxury. It is a vital necessity of our existence. It forms the quality of the light within which we predicate our hopes and dreams toward survival and change, first made into language, then into idea, then into more tangible action. Poetry is the way we help give name to the nameless so it can be thought. The farthest external horizons of our hopes and fears are cobbled by our poems, carved from the rock experiences of our daily lives.

As they become known and accepted to ourselves, our feelings, and the honest exploration of them, become sanctuaries and fortresses and spawning ground for the most radical and daring of ideas, the house of difference so necessary to change and the conceptualization of any meaningful action. Right now, I could name at least ten ideas I would once have found intolerable or incomprehensible and frightening, except as they came after dreams and poems. This is not idle fantasy, but the true meaning of "It feels right to me." We can train ourselves to respect our feelings and to discipline (transpose) them into a language that catches those feelings so they can be shared.

In Donald Hall, ed., *Claims for Poetry*

The Receptive Reader

According to this poet, what is the role of poetry in women's struggle for change and survival? What is the difference between the European and the non-European mode?

Making Connections—For Discussion or Writing

Audre Lorde's poem "Coal" appears in Chapter 19 of this volume. How does it live up to the program sketched out in this selection?

In the following selections, two poets speak with exceptional candor about what makes them write. What inspired or motivated them as poets?

Diane Wakoski   *(born 1937)*

On Experience and Imagination   1974

It has always been a premise of mine in writing poetry that the poet has the same experiences everybody else does, but the technical challenge is to invent some imaginative way of talking about these problems, these realities so that they can be taken seriously. It does not really seem like a big deal to anyone else when you say a man or woman you loved betrayed you. So what? Everyone sometimes feels betrayed. However, that's precisely why it is so important for the poet to find a way to say it. I believe in the use of extravagant surrealist imagery, like the girl riding naked on a zebra wearing only diamonds, as a way of making the reader accept the specialness of the feelings of the speaker in the poem.

I write in the first person because I have always wanted to make my life more interesting than it was. So I created a Diane whose real experiences were dramatized and exaggerated, were presented as surrealist experiences or metaphysical ones, who involved herself with imaginary people who often had the characteristics of real people but were more interesting and mysterious. Perhaps I have always been the isolated lonely person living around dull or sad people, and the poems were a way of inventing myself into a new life. I do feel a strange connection with the worlds I have created and the people in them, though I do not feel they are me or my world. It had been my obsession to try to see and understand the world truly, but that means seeing it over and over again, with all its changes, its attendant contradictions. I am never satisfied with anything I see but must keep inventing and reinventing ways to understand it.

From the Introduction to Trilogy

The Receptive Reader

What, for Wakoski, is the relationship between common shared experience and imaginative creation? What, for her, is the relationship between "realism" and "surrealism"? What do you learn about the **persona** in those of her poems she likes best?

Pablo Neruda   *(1904–1973)*

Childhood and Poetry   *1954*

One time, investigating in the backyard of our house in Temuco the tiny objects and miniscule beings of my world, I came upon a hole in one of the boards of the fence. I looked through the hole and saw a landscape like that behind our house, uncared for, and wild. I moved back a few steps, because I sensed vaguely that something was about to happen. All of a sudden a hand appeared—a tiny hand of a boy about my own age. By the time I came close again, the hand was gone, and in its place there was a marvelous white sheep.

The sheep's wool was faded. Its wheels had escaped. All of this only made it more authentic. I had never seen such a wonderful sheep. I looked back through the hole but the boy had disappeared. I went into the house and brought out a treasure of my own: a pinecone, opened, full of odor and resin, which I adored. I set it down in the same spot and went off with the sheep.

I never saw either the hand or the boy again. And I have never again seen a sheep like that either. The toy I lost finally in a fire. But even now, in 1954, almost fifty years old, whenever I pass a toy shop, I look furtively into the window, but it's no use. They don't make sheep like that anymore.

I have been a lucky man. To feel the intimacy of brothers is a marvelous thing in life. To feel the love of people whom we love is a fire that feeds our life. But to feel the affection that comes from those whom we do not know, from those unknown to us, who are watching over our sleep and solitude, over our dangers and our weaknesses—that is something still greater and more beautiful because it widens out the boundaries of our being, and unites all living things.

That exchange brought home to me for the first time a precious idea: that all of humanity is somehow together. That experience came to me again much later; this time it sood out strikingly against a background of trouble and persecution.

It won't surprise you then that I attempted to give something resiny, earthlike, and fragrant in exchange for human brotherhood. Just as I once left the pinecone by the fence, I have since left my words on the door of so many people who were unknown to me, people in prison, or hunted, or alone.

From Robert Bly, ed., *Neruda and Vallejo: Selected Poems*

The Receptive Reader

What was the significance of the childhood incident for the poet? In what way did it become a motivating force for his poetry?

WRITING ABOUT LITERATURE

24　*The Essay Exam: Poetry (Preparing for Tests)*

The Writing Workshop　When you write about poetry as part of an essay exam, you need to be a quick, alert reader, and you need to think on your feet. Common types of essay questions will ask you to

✗ Interpret a poem without detailed questions to guide you. You are on your own, applying the critical skills you have learned.

✗ Do a close reading of a poem, responding to detailed questions focused on the formal features of the poem.

✗ Compare and contrast two poems, mapping similarities but also striking differences in such areas as form, theme, or point of view.

✗ Respond to the thematic implications of a poem. You may, for instance, be asked to compare the way a common theme is treated in a poem and in a related prose passage.

Study the following sample exam. How would you answer the questions? Compare your answers with the student responses that follow the questions.

Instructions　Study the following poem, one of John Donne's *Holy Sonnets* (Number 5). Then answer the questions that follow it.

I am a little world made cunningly°　　　　　　　　　　*skillfully*
Of elements and an angelic sprite;°　　　　　　　　　　*spirit*
But black sin hath betrayed to endless night
My world's both parts, and O, both parts must die.
You which° beyond that heaven which was most high　　*You who*　　5
Have found new spheres and of new lands can write,

Pour new seas in mine eyes, that so I might
Drown my world with my weeping earnestly,
Or wash it if it must be drowned no more.
But O, it must be burned! Alas, the fire   10
Of lust and envy have burnt it heretofore
And made it fouler; let their flames retire,
And burn me, O Lord, with a fiery zeal
Of thee and thy house, which doth in eating heal.

Questions

1. What is the sustained or organizing metaphor in the first four lines?

2. By Donne's time, the new science of astronomy had made people think of new reaches of space beyond the traditional heavenly spheres. Explorers and navigators like Columbus had discovered new worlds. What use does Donne make of these developments in this poem?

3. After Noah's flood, God had promised not ever to send floods again to drown sinful humanity. Where and how does the poet allude to this promise?

4. Sonnets often reach a turning point at or near the division between the opening octet and the concluding sestet. Does this sonnet follow this pattern?

5. The final lines of the poem make us imagine three different kinds of fire or flame. What are they?

6. What is paradoxical about the concluding couplet?

7. What is the prevailing tone of this sonnet? What are the dominant emotions? What kind of speaker does it make you imagine?

8. How does the poem as a whole develop or take shape? What is the overall movement or pattern that gives shape to the poem as a whole?

Compare your own answers with the following sample student responses:

Sample Student Responses

1. The sustained opening metaphor compares the speaker in the poem to the larger universe in which we live. A human being is a "little world" (a microcosm) made by the same creator that created the larger world outside. A human being is composed of earthly elements and an angelic, heavenly soul, just as the universe is composed of the earth and the heavens, inhabited by spirits or angels. Both the "little world" of the individual and the larger world (the macrocosm) will eventually be destroyed—the one at the end of our natural lives, the other on the eve of eternity.

2. Donne seems fascinated with geography, astronomy, and the other sciences. The opening up of new vistas in geography and astronomy gave his hyperbolical mind new areas in which to wander. In lines 5 and 6, he is turning to the new astronomers (who "have found new spheres") and to the discoverers of new continents (who can write "of new lands"). He asks them hyperbolically about newly discovered oceans that might replenish the reservoir of tears he has shed in weeping for his sins.

3. The speaker in the poem wants to "drown" his sinful "little world" with weeping, submerging it in tears. But God had promised Noah that He would not again allow humanity to be drowned; therefore, the speaker will use his tears merely to "wash" and cleanse rather than to drown (line 9).

4. There is a turning signaled by the word *but*, not exactly at the end of the octave but at the beginning of line 10. The tears of repentance alone will not be enough; the whole world will have to be destroyed by fire before we can enter into communion with God (no more floods—"the fire next time").

5. The first kind of fire is the physical fire that will destroy the world at the end. The second is the "fire of lust and envy" that leaves everything "foul" or scorched and besmirched. The third is the "fiery zeal" that cleanses us of sin.

6. It is paradoxical that Donne asks to be destroyed in order to be saved. The idea of a healing fire is paradoxical because the fire eats or devours what it consumes. But this fire "heals" by consuming only the infected part—it burns out sin.

7. The tone is paradoxical. The poem is somber and full of passionate remorse and despair, but it ends on a note of reaffirming the poet's faith. The speaker is a very intense person, passionately introspective, constantly dramatizing his own emotions.

8. The poem develops beautifully by first making us admire God's handiwork (the little world of the human body, "made cunningly" by God). But the poet almost immediately mourns its desperate condition after it has been "betrayed" by sin. The poet then asks for cleansing by water, then corrects himself in a rush of passion by asking for all-consuming fire. The poem proceeds by playing off polar opposites: the angelic spirit and the dark night of sin, water and fire.

25 Other Voices/Other Visions

A Gathering of Poets

Anonymous

Edward   *(traditional Scottish ballad)*

1
"Why does your brand sae drap wi' bluid,°   *sword so drip with blood*
    Edward, Edward,
Why does your brand sae drap wi' bluid,
    And why sae sad gang° ye, O?"   *so sadly go*
"O I ha'e killed my hawk sae guid,°   *good*   5
    Mither, mither,
O I ha'e killed my hawk sae guid,
    And I had nae mair° but he, O."   *no more*

2
"Your hawke's bluid was never sae reid,°   *red*
    Edward, Edward,   10
Your hawke's bluid was never sae reid,
    My dear son I tell thee, O."
"O I ha'e killed my reid-roan steed,
    Mither, mither,
O I ha'e killed my reid-roan steed,   15
    That erst was° sae fair and free, O."   *that once was*

3
"Your steed was auld, and ye ha'e gat mair,°   *more*
    Edward, Edward,
Your steed was auld, and ye ha'e gat mair,
    Some other dule ye drie,° O."   *other grief you suffer*   20
"O I ha'e killed my fader dear,
    Mither, mither,
O I ha'e killed my fader dear,
    Alas, and wae° is me, O!"   *woe*

4
"And whatten° penance wul ye drie for that,   *what sort of*   25
    Edward, Edward?
And whatten penance wul ye drie for that,
    My dear son, now tell me, O?"

623

"I'll set my feet in yonder boat,
          Mither, mither,   30
I'll set my feet in yonder boat,
     And I'll fare over the sea, O."

5
"And what wul ye do wi' your towers and your ha',°   *hall*
          Edward, Edward?
And what wul ye do wi' your towers and your ha',   35
     That were sae fair to see, O?"
"I'll let them stand tul they down fa',°   *fall*
          Mither, mither,
I'll let them stand tul they down fa',
     For here never mair maun° I be, O."   *never more must* 40

6
"And what wul ye leave to your bairns° and your wife,   *children*
          Edward, Edward?
And what wul ye leave to your bairns and your wife,
     Whan ye gang over the sea, O?"
"The warlde's° room, let them beg thrae° life,   *world's/through* 45
          Mither, mither,
The warlde's room, let them beg thrae life,
     For them never mair wul I see, O."

7
"And what wul ye leave to your ain mither dear,
          Edward, Edward?
And what wul ye leave to your ain mither dear,   50
     My dear son, now tell me, O?"
"The curse of hell frae me sall° ye bear,   *from me shall*
          Mither, mither,
The curse of hell frae me sall ye bear,   55
     Sic° counsels ye gave to me, O."   *such*

Aphra Behn   *(1640–1689)*

Song   *1676*

Love in fantastic triumph° sat,   *celebration of victory*
Whilst bleeding hearts around him flowed,
For whom fresh pains he did create,
And strange tyrannic power he showed.
From thy bright eyes he took his fire,   5
Which round about, in sport he hurled;
But 't was from mine he took desire,
Enough to undo the amorous° world.   *filled with love*

From me he took his sighs and tears,
From thee his pride and cruelty;   10
From me his languishments and fears,
And every killing dart from thee.
Thus thou and I, the god have armed,
And set him up a deity;°   *as a deity*
But my poor heart alone is harmed,   15
Whilst thine the victor is, and free.

John Berryman   *(1914–1972)*

Dream Song 14   *1964*

Life, friends, is boring. We must not say so.
After all, the sky flashes, the great sea yearns,
we ourselves flash and yearn,
and moreover my mother told me as a boy
(repeatingly) "Ever to confess you're bored   5
means you have no

Inner Resources." I conclude now I have no
inner resources, because I am heavy bored.
Peoples bore me,
literature bores me, especially great literature,   10
Henry bores me, with his plights & gripes
as bad as achilles,°   *mythical Greek warrior*
                                             invulnerable except in the heel

who loves people and valiant art, which bores me.
And the tranquil hills, & gin, look like a drag
and somehow a dog   15
has taken itself & its tail considerably away
into mountains or sea or sky, leaving
behind: me, wag.

William Blake   *(1757–1827)*

The Lamb   *1789*

    Little Lamb, who made thee?
    Dost thou know who made thee?
Gave thee life & bid thee feed,
By the stream & o'er the mead;°   *meadow*
Gave thee clothing of delight,   5
Softest clothing wooly bright;
Gave thee such a tender voice,
Making all the vales° rejoice!   *valleys*
    Little Lamb who made thee?
    Dost thou know who made thee?   10

Little Lamb I'll tell thee,
Little Lamb I'll tell thee!
He is callèd by thy name,
For he calls himself a Lamb:
He is meek & he is mild,   15
He became a little child:
I a child & thou a lamb,
We are callèd by his name.
    Little Lamb God bless thee.
    Little Lamb God bless thee.   20

Louise Bogan   *(1897–1970)*

Women   *1923*

Women have no wilderness in them,
They are provident° instead,   *frugal*
Content in the tight hot cell of their hearts
To eat dusty bread.

They do not see cattle cropping red winter grass,   5
They do not hear
Snow water going down under culverts
Shallow and clear.

They wait, when they should turn to journeys,
They stiffen, when they should bend.   10
They use against themselves that benevolence°   *good will*
To which no man is friend.

They cannot think of so many crops to a field
Or of clean wood cleft by° an axe.   *split by*
Their love is an eager meaninglessness
Too tense, or too lax.   15

They hear in every whisper that speaks to them
A shout and a cry.
As like as not, when they take life over their door-sills
They should let it go by.   20

Samuel Taylor Coleridge   *(1772–1834)*

Kubla Khan   *1798*
or a vision in a dream, a fragment

In Xanadu did Kubla Khan°   *13th-century Chinese ruler*
A stately pleasure dome decree:
Where Alph, the sacred river, ran

Through caverns measureless to man
    Down to a sunless sea.   5
So twice five miles of fertile ground
With walls and towers were girdled round:
And there were gardens bright with sinuous rills,°   *winding brooks*
Where blossomed many an incense-bearing tree;
And here were forests ancient as the hills,   10
Enfolding sunny spots of greenery.

But oh! that deep romantic chasm which slanted
Down the green hill athwart° a cedarn cover!   *across*
A savage place! as holy and enchanted
As ever beneath a waning moon was haunted   15
By woman wailing for her demon lover!
And from this chasm, with ceaseless turmoil seething,
As if this earth in fast thick pants were breathing,
A mighty fountain momently° was forced: *moment by moment*
Amid whose swift half-intermitted burst   20
Huge fragments vaulted like rebounding hail,
Or chaffy grain beneath the thresher's flail:
And 'mid these dancing rocks at once and ever
It flung up momently the sacred river.
Five miles meandering with a mazy motion   25
Through wood and dale° the sacred river ran,   *valley*
Then reached the caverns measureless to man,
And sank in tumult to a lifeless ocean:
And 'mid this tumult Kubla heard from far
Ancestral voices prophesying war!   30
    The shadow of the dome of pleasure
    Floated midway on the waves;
    Where was heard the mingled measure
    From the fountain and the caves.
It was a miracle of rare device,   35
A sunny pleasure dome with caves of ice!

    A damsel with a dulcimer°   *a stringed musical instrument*
    In a vision once I saw:
    It was an Abyssinian° maid,   *Ethiopian*
    And on her dulcimer she played,   40
    Singing of Mount Abora.
    Could I revive within me
    Her symphony and song,
    To such a deep delight 'twould win me,
That with music loud and long,   45
I would build that dome in air,
That sunny dome! those caves of ice!
And all who heard should see them there,
And all should cry, Beware! Beware!
His flashing eyes, his floating hair!   50

Weave a circle round him thrice,
And close your eyes with holy dread,
For he on honey-dew hath fed,
And drunk the milk of Paradise.

Chitra Divakaruni   *(born 1956)*

The Quilt   *1991*

The parrot flies to the custard-apple tree.
The bees are among the pomegranates.
I call and call you, little bride.
Why do you not speak?
                    BENGALI FOLK SONG

Blue and sudden as beginning,
a quilt at the bottom
of the small mahogany chest
which holds her things.

She died in childbirth,   5
this grandmother whose name
no one can tell me.

He married again,
a strong woman this time,
straight backed, wide-hipped   10
for boy-children.
In the portrait downstairs
she wears the family diamonds
and holds her fourth son.

There are no pictures   15
of the wife who failed.

Her quilt leaves on my fingers
satin dust
as from a butterfly wing.

I spread it against   20
the floor's darkness, see her fingers
working it into the world-design,
the *gul-mohur* tree
bright yellow against the blue,
the river winding through rice fields   25
into a horizon where men with swords
march to a war
or a wedding.

As the baby grew she stitched in
a drifting afternoon boat   30
with a peacock sail.
In the foreground, young grass.
A woman with a deer.
She is left unfinished,
no eyes, no mouth,   35
her face a smooth blankness
tilted up at birds
that fall like flames from the sky.

John Donne   *(1572–1631)*

Holy Sonnet 14   *1633*

Batter my heart, three-personed God; for You
As yet but knock, breathe, shine, and seek to mend;
That I may rise and stand, overthrow me, and bend
Your force to break, blow, burn, and make me new.
I, like an usurped town, to another due,   5
Labor to admit You, but Oh, to no end.
Reason, Your viceroy in me, me should defend,
But is captived, and proves weak or untrue.
Yet dearly I love You, and would be loved fain,°   *gladly*
But am betrothed unto Your enemy: 10
Divorce me, untie or break that knot again,
Take me to You, imprison me, for I,
Except You enthrall me,° never shall be free,   *unless you enslave me*
Nor ever chaste, except You ravish me.

T. S. Eliot   *(1888–1965)*

The Love Song of J. Alfred Prufrock   *1917*

S'io credesse che mia risposta fosse
A persona che mai tornasse al mondo,
Questa fiamma staria senza piu scosse.
Ma perciocche giammai di questo fondo
Non torno vivo alcun, s'i'odo il vero,
Senza tema d'infamia ti rispondo.

[From Dante's *Inferno:* "If I thought my answer were given / to anyone who would ever return to the world, / this flame would stand still
without moving any further. / But since never from this abyss has anyone ever returned alive, if what I hear is true, / without fear of infamy
I answer thee."]

Let us go then, you and I,
When the evening is spread out against the sky
Like a patient etherized upon a table;
Let us go, through certain half-deserted streets,
The muttering retreats   5
Of restless nights in one-night cheap hotels
And sawdust restaurants with oyster-shells:
Streets that follow like a tedious argument
Of insidious intent
To lead you to an overwhelming question . . .   10
Oh, do not ask, "What is it?"
Let us go and make our visit.

In the room the women come and go
Talking of Michelangelo.

The yellow fog that rubs its back upon the window-panes   15
The yellow smoke that rubs its muzzle on the window-panes
Licked its tongue into the corners of the evening,
Lingered upon the pools that stand in drains,
Let fall upon its back the soot that falls from chimneys,
Slipped by the terrace, made a sudden leap,   20
And seeing that it was a soft October night,
Curled once about the house, and fell asleep.

And indeed there will be time
For the yellow smoke that slides along the street,
Rubbing its back upon the window-panes;   25
There will be time, there will be time
To prepare a face to meet the faces that you meet;
There will be time to murder and create,
And time for all the works and days of hands
That lift and drop a question on your plate;   30
Time for you and time for me,
And time yet for a hundred indecisions,
And for a hundred visions and revisions,
Before the taking of a toast and tea.

In the room the women come and go   35
Talking of Michelangelo.

And indeed there will be time
To wonder, "Do I dare?" and, "Do I dare?"
Time to turn back and descend the stair,
With a bald spot in the middle of my hair—   40
(They will say: "How his hair is growing thin!")
My morning coat, my collar mounting firmly to the chin,
My necktie rich and modest, but asserted by a simple pin—
(They will say: "But how his arms and legs are thin!")
Do I dare   45

Disturb the universe?
In a minute there is time
For decisions and revisions which a minute will reverse.

For I have known them all already, known them all:
Have known the evenings, mornings, afternoons,   50
I have measured out my life with coffee spoons;
I know the voices dying with a dying fall
Beneath the music from a farther room.
       So how should I presume?

And I have known the eyes already, known them all—   55
The eyes that fix you in a formulated phrase,
And when I am formulated, sprawling on a pin,
When I am pinned and wriggling on the wall,
Then how should I begin
To spit out all the butt-ends of my days and ways?   60
      And how should I presume?

And I have known the arms already, known them all—
Arms that are braceleted and white and bare
(But in the lamplight, downed with light brown hair!)
Is it perfume from a dress   65
That makes me so digress?
Arms that lie along a table, or wrap about a shawl.
      And should I then presume?
      And how should I begin?

          . . . . .

Shall I say, I have gone at dusk through narrow streets   70
And watched the smoke that rises from the pipes
Of lonely men in shirt-sleeves, leaning out of windows? . . .

I should have been a pair of ragged claws
Scuttling across the floors of silent seas.

          . . . . .

And the afternoon, the evening, sleeps so peacefully!   75
Smoothed by long fingers,
Asleep . . . tired . . . or it malingers,
Stretched on the floor, here beside you and me.
Should I, after tea and cakes and ices,
Have the strength to force the moment to its crisis?   80
But though I have wept and fasted, wept and prayed,
Though I have seen my head (grown slightly bald) brought in upon a
    platter,
I am no prophet—and here's no great matter;
I have seen the moment of my greatness flicker,
And I have seen the eternal Footman hold my coat, and snicker,   85
And in short, I was afraid.

And would it have been worth it, after all,
After the cups, the marmalade, the tea,
Among the porcelain, among some talk of you and me,
Would it have been worth while,   90
To have bitten off the matter with a smile,
To have squeezed the universe into a ball
To roll it toward some overwhelming question,
To say: "I am Lazarus,° come from the dead,   *whom Jesus raised from the dead*
Come back to tell you all, I shall tell you all"—   95
If one, settling a pillow by her head,
        Should say: "That is not what I meant at all.
        That is not it, at all."

And would it have been worth it, after all,
Would it have been worth while,   100
After the sunsets and the dooryards and the sprinkled streets,
After the novels, after the teacups, after the skirts that trail along the
        floor—
And this, and so much more?—
It is impossible to say just what I mean!
But as if a magic lantern threw the nerves in patterns on a screen: 105
Would it have been worth while
If one, settling a pillow or throwing off a shawl,
And turning toward the window, should say:
        "That is not it at all,
        That is not what I meant, at all."   110

                              . . . . .

No! I am not Prince Hamlet, nor was meant to be;
Am an attendant lord, one that will do
To swell a progress, start a scene or two,
Advise the prince; no doubt, an easy tool,
Deferential, glad to be of use,   115
Politic, cautious, and meticulous;
Full of high sentence, but a bit obtuse;
At times, indeed, almost ridiculous—
Almost, at times, the Fool.

I grow old . . . I grow old . . .   120
I shall wear the bottoms of my trousers rolled.

Shall I part my hair behind? Do I dare to eat a peach?
I shall wear white flannel trousers, and walk upon the beach.
I have heard the mermaids singing, each to each.

I do not think that they will sing to me.   125

I have seen them riding seaward on the waves
Combining the white hair of the waves blown back
When the wind blows the water white and black.

We have lingered in the chambers of the sea
By sea-girls wreathed with seaweed red and brown   130
Till human voices wake us, and we drown.

Lawrence Ferlinghetti   *(born 1919)*

Constantly risking absurdity   *1958*

      Constantly risking absurdity
               and death
        whenever he performs
             above the heads
                of his audience   5
    the poet like an acrobat
          climbs on rime
             to a high wire of his own making
and balancing on eyebeams
           above a sea of faces   10
        paces his way
           to the other side of day
     performing *entrechats°*   *ballet leaps*
           and sleight-of-foot tricks
and other high theatrics   15
        and all without mistaking
    any thing
       for what it may not be
    For he's the super realist
         who must perforce perceive   20
    taut truth
        before the taking of each stance or step
  in his supposed advance
       toward that still higher perch
where Beauty stands and waits   25
       with gravity
         to start her death-defying leap
  And he
     a little charleychaplin man
        who may or may not catch   30
    her fair eternal form
       spreadeagled in the empty air
    of existence

Allen Ginsberg   *(1926–1997)*

A Supermarket in California   *1956*

    What thoughts I have of you tonight, Walt Whit-
man, for I walked down the sidestreets under the

trees with a headache self-conscious looking at the full moon.

In my hungry fatigue, and shopping for images, I went into the neon fruit supermarket, dreaming of your enumerations!° *cataloging of data*

What peaches and what penumbras!° Whole *partial shadows* families shopping at night! Aisles full of husbands! Wives in the avocados, babies in the tomatoes—and you, Garcia Lorca,° what were you doing down by *Spanish poet* the watermelons?

I saw you, Walt Whitman, childless, lonely old grubber, poking among the meats in the refrigerator and eyeing the grocery boys.

I heard you asking questions of each: Who   5 killed the pork chops? What price bananas? Are you my Angel?

I wandered in and out of the brilliant stacks of cans following you, and followed in my imagination by the store detective.

We strode down the open corridors together in our solitary fancy tasting artichokes, possessing every frozen delicacy, and never passing the cashier.

Where are we going, Walt Whitman? The doors close in an hour. Which way does your beard point tonight?

(I touch your book and dream of our odyssey in the supermarket and feel absurd.)

Will we walk all night through solitary streets?   10 The trees add shade to shade, lights out in the houses, we'll both be lonely.

Will we stroll dreaming of the lost America of love past blue automobiles in driveways, home to our silent cottage?

Ah, dear father, graybeard, lonely old courage-teacher, what America did you have when Charon° *mythical ferryman conveying* quit poling his ferry and you got out on a smoking *souls across River Styx to* bank and stood watching the boat disappear on the *Hades* black waters of Lethe?° *mythical underworld river of forgetfulness*

Louise Glück   *(born 1943)*

Gratitude   1975

Do not think I am not grateful for your small
kindness to me.
I like small kindnesses.

In fact I actually prefer them to the more
substantial kindness, that is always eyeing you,   5
like a large animal on a rug,
until your whole life reduces
to nothing but waking up morning after morning
cramped, and the bright sun shining on its tusks.

George Herbert   *(1593–1633)*

The Collar   *1633*

I struck the board° and cried, "No more;   table
      I will abroad!
What? shall I ever sigh and pine?
My lines and life are free, free as the road,
    Loose as the wind, as large as store.°   abundance   5
        Shall I be still in suit?°   begging favors
    Have I no harvest but a thorn
    To let me blood, and not restore
What I have lost with cordial° fruit?   life-giving
        Sure there was wine   10
    Before my sighs did dry it; there was corn
    Before my tears did drown it.
Is the year only lost to me?
    Have I no bays° to crown it,   laurel-wreaths symbolizing honor
No flowers, no garlands gay? All blasted?   15
        All wasted?
    Not so, my heart; but there is fruit,
        And thou hast hands.
    Recover all thy sigh-blown age
On double pleasures: leave thy cold dispute   20
Of what is fit and not. Forsake thy cage,
        Thy rope of sands,
Which petty thoughts have made, and made to thee
    Good cable, to enforce and draw,
        And be thy law,   25
    While thou didst wink and wouldst not see.
        Away! take heed;
        I will abroad.
Call in thy death's-head° there; tie up thy fears.   skull
        He that forbears   30
      To suit and serve his need,
        Deserves his load."
But as I raved and grew more fierce and wild
        At every word,
Methought I heard one calling, *Child!*   35
        And I replied, *My Lord.*

Edward Hirsch   *(born 1950)*

Fast Break   *1985*
(In Memory of Dennis Turner, 1946–1984)

A hook shot kisses the rim and
hangs there, helplessly, but doesn't drop,

and for once our gangly starting center
boxes out his man and times his jump

perfectly, gathering the orange leather   5
from the air like a cherished possession

and spinning around to throw a strike
to the outlet who is already shovelling

an underhand pass toward the other guard
scissoring past a flat-footed defender   10

who looks stunned and nailed to the floor
in the wrong direction, trying to catch sight

of a high, gliding dribble and a man
letting the play develop in front of him

in slow-motion, almost exactly   15
like a coach's drawing on the blackboard,

both forwards racing down the court
the way that forwards should, fanning out

and filling the lanes in tandem, moving
together as brothers passing the ball   20

between them without a dribble, without
a single bounce hitting the hardwood

until the guard finally lunges out
and commits to the wrong man

while the power-forward explodes past them   25
in a fury, taking the ball into the air

by himself now and laying it gently
against the glass for a lay-up,

but losing his balance in the process,
inexplicably falling, hitting the floor   30

with a wild, headlong motion
for the game he loved like a country

and swivelling back to see an orange blur
floating perfectly through the net.

Vicente Huidobro   *(1892–1948)*

Ars Poetica   *1963*

TRANSLATED BY DAVID M. GUSS

Let poetry be like a key
Opening a thousand doors.
A leaf falls; something flies by;
Let all the eye sees be created
And the soul of the listener tremble.   5

Invent new worlds and watch your word;
The adjective, when it doesn't give life, kills it.

We are in the age of nerves.
The muscle hangs,
Like a memory, in museums;   10
But we are not the weaker for it:
True vigor
Resides in the head.

Oh Poets, why sing of roses!
Let them flower in your poems;   15

For us alone
Do all things live beneath the Sun.

The poet is a little God.

Ben Jonson   *(1572–1637)*

Song: To Celia   *1616*

Drink to me only with thine eyes,
And I will pledge with mine;
Or leave a kiss but in the cup,
And I'll not look for wine.
The thirst that from the soul doth rise,   5
Doth ask a drink divine:
But might I of Jove's° nectar sup,   *Roman name of Zeus*
I would not change for thine.

I sent thee late° a rosy wreath,   *recently*
Not so much honoring thee,   10
As giving it a hope, that there
It could not withered be.
But thou thereon didst only breathe,
And sentst it back to me;
Since when it grows and smells, I swear,   15
Not of itself, but thee.

John Keats   *(1795–1821)*

Ode to a Nightingale   *1820*

1
My heart aches, and a drowsy numbness pains
        My sense, as though of hemlock° I had drunk,   *poison*
Or emptied some dull opiate to the drains
        One minute past, and Lethe-wards° had sunk: *toward Lethe, mythical under-*
'Tis not through envy of thy happy lot,   *world river of forgetfulness*   5
        But being too happy in thine happiness—
                That thou, light-wingèd Dryad° of the trees,   *wood nymph*
                In some melodious plot
        Of beechen green, and shadows numberless,
                Singest of summer in full-throated ease.   10

2
O, for a draught of vintage!° that hath been   *drink of wine*
        Cooled a long age in the deep-delvèd° earth,   *dug out deep*
Tasting of Flora° and the country green,   *Roman goddess of flowers*
        Dance, and Provençal song,° and sunburnt mirth!   *songs of Provence,*
O for a beaker full of the warm South,   *in southern France*   15
        Full of the true, the blushful Hippocrene,°   *fountain of the Muses in Greece*
                With beaded bubbles winking at the brim,
                And purple-stainèd mouth;
        That I might drink, and leave the world unseen,
                And with thee fade away into the forest dim: 20

3
Fade far away, dissolve, and quite forget
        What thou among the leaves hast never known,
The weariness, the fever, and the fret
        Here, where men sit and hear each other groan;
Where palsy shakes a few, sad, last gray hairs,   25
        Where youth grows pale, and specter-thin, and dies,
                Where but to think is to be full of sorrow
                And leaden-eyed despairs,
        Where Beauty cannot keep her lustrous° eyes,   *shining*
                Or new Love pine at them beyond tomorrow.   30

4
Away! away! for I will fly to thee,
        Not charioted by Bacchus and his pards,°   *god of wine and his leopards*
But on the viewless° wings of Poesy,   *invisible*
        Though the dull brain perplexes and retards:
Already with thee! tender is the night,   35
        And haply the Queen-Moon is on her throne,
                Clustered around by all her starry Fays;°   *fairies*
                But here there is no light,
        Save what from heaven is with the breezes blown

Through verdurous° glooms and winding   *filled with green vegetation*   40
    mossy ways.

5

I cannot see what flowers are at my feet,
    Nor what soft incense hangs upon the boughs,
But, in embalmed° darkness, guess each sweet   *perfumed*
    Wherewith the seasonable month endows
The grass, the thicket, and the fruit tree wild;   45
    White hawthorn, and the pastoral eglantine;°   *wood roses*
        Fast fading violets covered up in leaves;
            And mid-May's eldest child,
    The coming musk-rose, full of dewy wine,
        The murmurous haunt of flies on summer eves.   50

6

Darkling° I listen; and for many a time   *in darkness*
    I have been half in love with easeful Death,
Called him soft names in many a musèd rhyme,
    To take into the air my quiet breath;
Now more than ever seems it rich to die,   55
    To cease upon the midnight with no pain,
        While thou art pouring forth thy soul abroad
            In such an ecstasy!
    Still wouldst thou sing, and I have ears in vain—
        To thy high requiem become a sod.   60

7

Thou wast not born for death, immortal Bird!
    No hungry generations tread thee down;
The voice I hear this passing night was heard
    In ancient days by emperor and clown:°   *peasant*
Perhaps the selfsame song that found a path   65
    Through the sad heart of Ruth,° when, sick for home,   *of the biblical*
        She stood in tears amid the alien corn;   *Book of Ruth*
            The same that ofttimes hath
    Charmed magic casements, opening on the foam
        Of perilous seas, in faery lands forlorn.   70

8

Forlorn! the very word is like a bell
    To toll me back from thee to my sole self!
Adieu! the fancy cannot cheat so well
    As she is famed to do, deceiving elf.
Adieu! adieu! thy plaintive anthem fades   75
    Past the near meadows, over the still stream,
        Up the hill side; and now 'tis buried deep
            In the next valley-glades:
    Was it a vision, or a waking dream?
        Fled is that music:—Do I wake or sleep?   80

Maxine Kumin   *(born 1925)*

Woodchucks   *1971*

Gassing the woodchucks didn't turn out right.
The knockout bomb from the Feed and Grain Exchange
was featured as merciful, quick at the bone
and the case we had against them was airtight,
both exits shoehorned shut with puddingstone,   5
but they had a sub-sub-basement out of range.

Next morning they turned up again, no worse
for the cyanide than we for our cigarettes
and state-store Scotch, all of us up to scratch.
They brought down the marigolds as a matter of course   10
and then took over the vegetable patch
nipping the broccoli shoots, beheading the carrots.

The food from our mouths, I said, righteously thrilling
to the feel of the .22, the bullets' neat noses.
I, a lapsed pacifist fallen from grace   15
puffed with Darwinian pieties for killing,
now drew a bead on the littlest woodchuck's face.
He died down in the everbearing roses.

Ten minutes later I dropped the mother. She
flipflopped in the air and fell, her needle teeth   20
still hooked in a leaf of early Swiss chard.
Another baby next. O one-two-three
the murderer inside me rose up hard,
the hawkeye killer came on stage forthwith.

There's one chuck left. Old wily fellow, he keeps   25
me cocked and ready day after day after day.

Audre Lorde   *(1934–1992)*

Conversation in Crisis   *1985*

I speak to you as a friend speaks
or a true lover
not out of friendship or love
but for a clear meeting
of self upon self   5
in sight of our hearth
but without fire.

I cherish your words that ring
like late summer thunders
to sing without octave   10

and fade, having spoken the season.
But I hear the false heat of this voice
as it dries up the sides of your words
coaxing melodies from your tongue
and this curled music is treason.   15

Must I die in your fever—
or, as the flames was, take cover
in your heart's culverts
crouched like a stranger
under the scorched leaves of your other burnt loves   20
until the storm passes over?

Robert Lowell   *(1917–1977)*

Skunk Hour   *1959*
(for Elizabeth Bishop)

Nautilus Island's° hermit   *in Castine, Maine*
heiress still lives through winter in her Spartan cottage;
her sheep still graze above the sea.
Her son's a bishop. Her farmer
is first selectman° in our village;   *elected official*   5
she's in her dotage.°   *second childhood*

Thirsting for
the hierarchic privacy
of Queen Victoria's century,
she buys up all   10
the eyesores facing her shore,
and lets them fall.

The season's ill—
we've lost our summer millionaire,
who seemed to leap from an L. L. Bean°   *sporting goods company*   15
catalogue. His nine-knot yawl°   *boat*
was auctioned off to lobstermen.
A red fox stain covers Blue Hill.

And now our fairy
decorator brightens his shop for fall;   20
his fishnet's filled with orange cork,
orange, his cobbler's bench and awl;
there is no money in his work,
he'd rather marry.

One dark night,   25
my Tudor Ford climbed the hill's skull;
I watched for love-cars. Lights turned down,
they lay together, hull to hull,

Where the graveyard shelves on the town. . . .
My mind's not right.   30

A car radio bleats,
"Love, O careless Love. . . ." I hear
my ill-spirit sob in each blood cell,
as if my hand were at its throat. . . .
I myself am hell;   35
nobody's here—

only skunks, that search
in the moonlight for a bite to eat.
They march on their soles up Main Street:
white stripes, moonstruck eyes' red fire   40
under the chalk-dry and spar spire°   *pole used as a mast*
of the Trinitarian Church.

I stand on top
of our back steps and breathe the rich air—
a mother skunk with her column of kittens swills the garbage pail.   45
She jabs her wedge-head in a cup
of sour cream, drops her ostrich tail,
and will not scare.

Edna St. Vincent Millay   *(1892–1950)*

Pity Me Not Because the Light of Day   *1917*

Pity me not because the light of day
At close of day no longer walks the sky;
Pity me not for beauties passed away
From field and thicket as the years go by;
Pity me not the waning of the moon,   5
Nor that the ebbing tide goes out to sea,
Nor that man's desire is hushed so soon,
And you no longer look with love on me.
This have I known always: Love is no more
Than the wide blossom which the wind assails,   10
Than the great tide that treads the shifting shore,
Strewing fresh wreckage gathered in the gales:
Pity me that the heart is slow to learn
What the swift mind beholds at every turn.

John Milton   *(1608–1674)*

How Soon Hath Time   *1631*

How soon hath Time, the subtle thief of youth,
    Stoln on his wing my three and twentieth year!

My hasting days fly on with full career,°   *full speed*
But my late spring no bud or blossom shewth.°   *shows*
Perhaps my semblance° might deceive the truth,   *appearance*   5
    That I to manhood am arrived so near,
    And inward ripeness doth much less appear,
    That some more timely-happy spirits enduth.°   *endows*
Yet be it less or more, or soon or slow,
    It shall be still in strictest measure even   10
    To that same lot, however mean or high,
Toward which Time leads me, and the will of Heaven;
    All is, if I have grace to use it so,
    As ever in my great Taskmaster's eye.

Ezra Pound   *(1885–1972)*

The River-Merchant's Wife: A Letter   *1915*
(after Rihaku)°   *Japanese name for Li Po,*
                                                      an 8th-century Chinese poet

While my hair was still cut straight across my forehead
I played about the front gate, pulling flowers.
You came by on bamboo stilts, playing horse,
You walked about my seat, playing with blue plums.
And we went on living in the village of Chokan: 5
Two small people, without dislike or suspicion.

At fourteen I married My Lord you.
I never laughed, being bashful.
Lowering my head, I looked at the wall.
Called to, a thousand times, I never looked back.   10

At fifteen I stopped scowling,
I desired my dust to be mingled with yours
For ever and for ever and for ever.
Why should I climb the look out?

At sixteen you departed,   15
You went into far Ku-to-yen, by the river of swirling eddies,
And you have been gone five months.
The monkeys make sorrowful noise overhead.

You dragged your feet when you went out.
By the gate now, the moss is grown, the different mosses,   20
Too deep to clear them away!
The leaves fall early this autumn, in wind.
The paired butterflies are already yellow with August
Over the grass in the West garden;
They hurt me. I grow older,   25
If you are coming down through the narrows of the river Kiang,
Please let me know beforehand,

And I will come out to meet you
     As far as Cho-fu-Sa.

William Shakespeare   *(1564–1616)*

Sonnet 116   *1609*

Let me not to the marriage of true minds
Admit impediments. Love is not love
Which alters when it alteration finds,°   *when it encounters change*
Or bends with the remover to remove:°   *responds to inconstancy*
                                                          with inconstancy
Oh, no! it is an ever-fixèd mark,   5
That looks on tempests and is never shaken;
It is the star to every wandering bark,°   *boat*
Whose worth's unknown, although his height be taken.°   *although its elevation*
                                                          can be measured
Love's not Time's fool, though rosy lips and cheeks
Within his bending sickle's compass come;   10
Love alters not with his brief hours and weeks,
But bears it out even to the edge of doom.°   *Day of Judgment*
If this be error and upon me proved,
I never writ,° nor no man ever loved.   *wrote*

Percy Bysshe Shelley   *(1792–1822)*

To a Skylark   *1820*

Hail to thee, blithe Spirit!
     Bird thou never wert,
That from Heaven, or near it,
     Pourest thy full heart
In profuse strains° of unpremeditated art.   *melodies*   5

Higher still and higher
     From the earth thou springest
Like a cloud of fire;
     The blue deep thou wingest,
And singing still dost soar, and soaring ever singest.   10

In the golden lightning
     Of the sunken sun,
O'er which clouds are brightening,
     Thou dost float and run;
Like an unbodied joy whose race is just begun.   15

The pale purple even
     Melts around thy flight;
Like a star of Heaven,
     In the broad daylight
Thou are unseen, but yet I hear thy shrill delight,   20

Keen as are the arrows
    Of that silver sphere,°   *star*
Whose intense lamp narrows
    In the white dawn clear
Until we hardly see—we feel that it is there.   25

All the earth and air
    With thy voice is loud,
As, when night is bare,
    From one lonely cloud
The moon rains out her beams, and Heaven is overflowed.   30

What thou art we know not;
    What is most like thee?
From rainbow clouds there flow not
    Drops so bright to see
As from thy presence showers a rain of melody.   35

Like a Poet hidden
    In the light of thought,
Singing hymns unbidden,
    Till the world is wrought°   *moved*
To sympathy with hopes and fears it heeded not: 40

Like a high-born maiden
    In a palace tower,
Soothing her love-laden
    Soul in secret hour
With music sweet as love, which overflows her bower:°   *private chamber* 45

Like a glowworm golden
    In a dell° of dew,   *hideaway*
Scattering unbeholden
    Its aërial hue
Among the flowers and grass, which screen it from the view!   50

Like a rose embowered
    In its own green leaves,
By warm winds deflowered,
    Till the scent it gives
Makes faint with too much sweet those heavy-wingèd thieves: 55

Sound of vernal° showers   *spring*
    On the twinkling grass,
Rain-awakened flowers,
    All that ever was
Joyous, and clear, and fresh, thy music doth surpass: 60

Teach us, Sprite° or Bird,   *spirit*
    What sweet thoughts are thine:
I have never heard

        Praise of love or wine
That panted forth a flood of rapture so divine.   65

        Chorus Hymeneal°   *as for a wedding*
            Or triumphal chant,
        Matched with thine would be all
            But an empty vaunt,°   *boast*
A thing wherein we feel there is some hidden want.   70

        What objects are the fountains
            Of thy happy strain?
        What fields, or waves, or mountains?
            What shapes of sky or plain?
What love of thine own kind? what ignorance of pain?   75

        With thy clear keen joyance°   *joyful song*
            Languor° cannot be: *sluggishness*
        Shadow of annoyance
            Never came near thee:
Thou lovest—but never knew love's sad satiety.   80

        Waking or asleep,
            Thou of death must deem
        Things more true and deep
            Than we mortals dream,
Or how could thy notes flow in such a crystal stream?   85

        We look before and after,
            And pine° for what is not: *yearn*
        Our sincerest laughter
            With some pain is fraught;°   *burdened*
Our sweetest songs are those that tell of saddest thought.   90

        Yet if we could scorn
            Hate, and pride, and fear;
        If we were things born
            Not to shed a tear,
I know not how thy joy we ever should come near.   95

        Better than all measures
            Of delightful sound,
        Better than all treasures
            That in books are found,
Thy skill to poet were, thou scorner of the ground!   100

        Teach me half the gladness
            That thy brain must know,
        Such harmonious madness
            From my lips would flow
The world should listen then—as I am listening now.   105

Gary Snyder   *(born 1930)*

After Work   *1959*

The shack and a few trees
float in the blowing fog

I pull out your blouse,
warm my cold hands
        on your breasts.   5
you laugh and shudder
peeling garlic by the
        hot iron stove.
bring in the axe, the rake,
the wood   10

we'll lean on the wall
against each other
stew simmering on the fire
as it grows dark
                drinking wine.   15

Cathy Song   *(born 1955)*

Lost Sister   *1983*

1
In China,
even the peasants
named their first daughters
Jade—
the stone that in the far fields   5
could moisten the dry season,
could make men move mountains
for the healing green of the inner hills
glistening like slices of winter melon.

And the daughters were grateful: 10
They never left home.
To move freely was a luxury
stolen from them at birth.
Instead, they gathered patience;
learning to walk in shoes   15
the size of teacups,
without breaking—
the arc of their movements
as dormant as the rooted willow,
as redundant as the farmyard hens.   20

But they traveled far
in surviving,
learning to stretch the family rice,
to quiet the demons,
the noisy stomachs.   25

2
There is a sister
across the ocean,
who relinquished her name,
diluting jade green
with the blue of the Pacific.   30
Rising with a tide of locusts,
she swarmed with others
to inundate another shore.
In America,
there are many roads   35
and women can stride along with men.

But in another wilderness,
the possibilities,
the loneliness,
can strangulate like jungle vines.   40
The meager provisions and sentiments
of once belonging—
fermented roots, Mah-Jong° tiles and firecrackers—set but   *Chinese game*
a flimsy household
in a forest of nightless cities.   45
A giant snake rattles above,
spewing black clouds into your kitchen.
Dough-faced landlords
slip in and out of your keyholes,
making claims you don't understand,   50
tapping into your communication systems
of laundry lines and restaurant chains.

You find you need China:
your one fragile identification,
a jade link   55
handcuffed to your wrist.
You remember your mother
who walked for centuries,
footless—
and like her,   60
you have left no footprints,
but only because
there is an ocean in between,
the unremitting space of your rebellion.

Alfred, Lord Tennyson   *(1809–1892)*

Ulysses   *1833*

It little profits° that an idle king,   *it is little use*
By this still hearth, among these barren crags,
Matched with an agèd wife, I mete and dole°   *measure out*
Unequal laws unto a savage race,
That hoard, and sleep, and feed, and know not me.   5
I cannot rest from travel; I will drain
Life to the lees.° All times I have enjoyed   *dregs*
Greatly, have suffered greatly, both with those
That love me, and alone; on shore, and when
Through scudding drifts the rainy Hyades   10
Vexed the dim sea. I am become a name;
For always roaming with a hungry heart
Much have I seen and known—cities of men
And manners, climates, councils, governments,
Myself not least, but honored of them all—   15
And drunk delight of battle with my peers,
Far on the ringing plains of windy Troy.
I am a part of all that I have met;
Yet all experience is an arch wherethrough
Gleams that untraveled world whose margin fades   20
For ever and for ever when I move.
How dull it is to pause, to make an end,
To rust unburnished,° not to shine in use!   *unpolished*
As though to breathe were life! Life piled on life
Were all too little, and of one to me   25
Little remains; but every hour is saved
From that eternal silence, something more,
A bringer of new things; and vile it were°   *would be*
For some three suns to store and hoard myself,
And this gray spirit yearning in desire   30
To follow knowledge like a sinking star,
Beyond the utmost bound of human thought.
          This is my son, mine own Telemachus,
To whom I leave the scepter and the isle,—
Well-loved of me, discerning to fulfill   35
This labor, by slow prudence to make mild
A rugged people, and through soft degrees
Subdue them to the useful and the good.
Most blameless is he, centered in the sphere
Of common duties, decent not to fail   40
In offices of tenderness, and pay
Meet adoration to my household gods,
When I am gone. He works his work, I mine.
          There lies the port; the vessel puffs her sail;
There gloom the dark, broad seas. My mariners,   45

Souls that have toiled, and wrought, and thought with me,—
That ever with a frolic° welcome took   *cheerful*
The thunder and the sunshine, and opposed
Free hearts, free foreheads—you and I are old;
Old age hath yet his honor and his toil.   50
Death closes all; but something ere° the end,   *before*
Some work of noble note, may yet be done,
Not unbecoming men that strove with Gods.
The lights begin to twinkle from the rocks;
The long day wanes; the slow moon climbs; the deep   55
Moans round with many voices. Come, friends,
'Tis not too late to seek a newer world.
Push off, and sitting well in order smite°   *strike*
The sounding furrows; for my purpose holds
To sail beyond the sunset, and the baths   60
Of all the western stars, until I die.
It may be that the gulfs will wash us down;
It may be we shall touch the Happy Isles,
And see the great Achilles, whom we knew.
Though much is taken, much abides;° and though   *remains* 65
We are not now that strength which in old days
Moved earth and heaven, that which we are, we are,—
One equal temper of heroic hearts,
Made weak by time and fate, but strong in will
To strive, to seek, to find, and not to yield.   70

Miller Williams   *(born 1930)*

Thinking about Bill, Dead of AIDS   *1989*

We did not know the first thing about
how blood surrenders to even the smallest threat
when old allergies turn inside out,

the body rescinding all its normal orders
to all defenders of flesh, betraying the head,   5
pulling its guards back from all its borders.

Thinking of friends afraid to shake your hand,
we think of your hand shaking, your mouth set,
your eyes drained of any reprimand.

Loving, we kissed you, partly to persuade   10
both you and us, seeing what eyes had said,
that we were loving and were not afraid.

If we had had more, we would have given more.
As it was we stood next to your bed,
stopping, though, to set our smiles at the door.   15

Not because we were less sure at the last.
Only because, not knowing anything yet,
we didn't know what look would hurt you least.

William Butler Yeats   *(1865–1939)*

The Second Coming   *1921*

Turning and turning in the widening gyre°	*spiral*
The falcon cannot hear the falconer;	
Things fall apart; the center cannot hold;	
Mere anarchy is loosed upon the world,	
The blood-dimmed tide is loosed, and everywhere	5
The ceremony of innocence is drowned;	
The best lack all conviction, while the worst	
Are full of passionate intensity.	
Surely some revelation is at hand;	
Surely the Second Coming° is at hand;	*coming of Christ* 10
The Second Coming! Hardly are those words out	
When a vast image out of *Spiritus Mundi*°	*Spirit of the World*
Troubles my sight: somewhere in sands of the desert	
A shape with lion body and the head of a man,°	*sphinx*
A gaze blank and pitiless as the sun,	15
Is moving its slow thighs, while all about it	
Reel shadows of the indignant desert birds.	
The darkness drops again; but now I know	
That twenty centuries of stony sleep	
Were vexed to nightmare by a rocking cradle,	20
And what rough beast, its hour come round at last,	
Slouches towards Bethlehem to be born?	

Drama

There is a hunger to see the human presence acted out. As long as that need remains, people will find a way to do theater.

ZELDA FICHANDLER

26 Preview

The Magic of the Stage

On the stage is always now; *the personages are standing on that razor edge between the past and the future that is the essential character of conscious beings.*

ANATOLE BROYARD

FOCUS ON DRAMA

The magic of the stage makes us witness a live performance. The actors, handed the play as words on a page, bring it to life. We see their faces, hear their voices. We respond to the language of gestures, to the actors' body language. A successful performance draws us in; it carries us along. We participate in other lives. These may be more magnificent or drearier than our own. Or we may experience the shock of recognition, making us say, "That is exactly the way it is."

Reading a printed play, you translate the words on the page into action and dialogue the way directors and actors do. You are enacting the drama in the theater of the mind. How do the elements of a play—situation, character, dialogue, plot, style—work together to bring the play to life?

Situation   Where do we as spectators come in? The early scenes of a play answer basic questions in the spectators' minds: Where are we? What is the issue, or what is the problem? What past history explains the current situation? The early scenes of a play may give you important details of a family history. They may hint at skeletons in the family closet. There may be signs of quarrels of long standing. Sometimes, **flashbacks** to earlier days help you understand the characters' current predicaments.

Character   Who are these people? Dramatists create characters and set them in motion. Much of a playwright's task early in the play is feeding you the information that makes the characters come to life. You will learn much about the characters from what they say and do. They may

655

take you into their confidence in brief **asides** shared only with the audience. Or they might confide in you in lengthy solo speeches—**soliloquies.** (Sometimes a confidant—a close friend or trusted servant—may serve as a substitute or surrogate for the audience.) However, what truly defines major characters is their behavior in test situations—what they say and do when a major challenge puts them to the test. In addition, you will do well to listen to what *others* say about a central figure—this is often a major function of minor or supporting characters.

Dialogue   How much of the interaction takes place through words? Shakespeare's plays were acted on a wooden stage with little scenery and few props. He used words to conjure up throne rooms, battlefields, or a fog-shrouded heath. However, the chief function of **dialogue,** the verbal give-and-take between the characters, is to serve as the medium of human interaction in the play. Dialogue becomes **monologue** when one person for a time does all or most of the talking. Successful playwrights have an uncanny ear for how people talk. In Tennessee Williams's *The Glass Menagerie,* the mother speaks in a refined, genteel southern lady style that hides harsh realities behind euphemistic talk: "You just have a little defect . . . when people have a slight disadvantage like that, they cultivate other things to make up for it." Her alienated son talks back to her in the rough language of his street buddies: "Every time you come in yelling . . . 'Rise and Shine!' I say to myself, 'How lucky dead people are!'"

Plot   How are the events related? The **plot** of a play is the thread that leads us from initial tensions or problems, through complications, to climactic confrontations, to the windup or final resolution of a conflict. Plays differ greatly in what drives the plot and leads to the final resolution. Some plays build to a **climax,** preparing the audience for a high point or climactic event. The outcome may be happy—as in comedy. It may be unhappy—as in tragedy. Or it may be open-ended—as in many modern plays. The playwright may respond to the spectators' yearning for good news, for a happy end, if only as the result of a lucky coincidence. In some plays, parallel conflicts or **subplots** reinforce the central theme of a play.

Style   How does the playwright use language? The style of drama ranges from the ceremonial through the realistic to the surreal. Much traditional drama is in verse. In ancient Greek tragedy, the ceremonial chants of the chorus were written in elaborately crafted stanzas, or **odes.** At the opposite extreme, much modern drama is close to the freely moving rhythms of everyday speech. The language of the people in a play may be empty of poetry, or it may be alive with the soaring poetry of Shakespeare's Hamlet, to whom the star-spangled heavens are alternately "this majestical roof fretted with golden fire" and "a foul and pestilent congregation of vapors."

Susan Glaspell　　*(1876–1948)*

Glaspell was among the first writers to realize that it was not enough to present women at the center of the stage. If there were to be a radical break with plays of the past, women would have to exist in a world tailored to their persons and speak a language not borrowed from men.

ENOCH BRATER

Although the following play involves violent death, it is not a drama of violence or physical action. As in Greek tragedy, we witness none of the violent events directly—we merely hear about them. We gradually have to reconstruct what happened. Instead, the play focuses on the characters—their motives and their loyalties. What goes on in the minds of the characters? Why do they react to the events the way they do? We listen to them as they think through their responsibilities, bring their memories to bear, come to understand what happened, and take sides.

Susan Glaspell devoted much of her life to the theater. Educated at Drake University in Des Moines, Iowa, she worked for a time as a newspaper reporter and drew on her experiences as a journalist in her short stories, novels, and plays. She was a cofounder of the Provincetown Players, who performed many of the American playwright Eugene O'Neill's one-act plays and who performed her own one-act play *Trifles*. She acted and directed; she wrote a dozen plays; and she won the Pulitzer Prize for drama in 1931. As head of the Chicago bureau of a federal theater project, she reviewed hundreds of plays and helped in the production of important works by black playwrights. Although she did much of her work in the East, she said, "almost everything I write has its roots in the Middle West; I suppose because my own are there." She was a spiritual descendant of her pioneer ancestors who left "comfortable homes for unknown places." Many of her characters struggle against "fixity and stagnation," trying to move, as their pioneer forebears did, "into a new sphere, if not of place then of spirit" (Enoch Brater).

Glaspell's work was rediscovered by feminist critics who found in her plays a "woman's version" of events, created at a time when the theater was heavily dominated by male dramatists. Like her British contemporary Virginia Woolf, she has become an inspiration to women whose goal is "control over their own bodies and a voice with which to speak about it" (Susan Rubin Suleiman).

Trifles   *1916*

CHARACTERS

GEORGE HENDERSON, county attorney
HENRY PETERS, sheriff
LEWIS HALE, a neighboring farmer
MRS. PETERS
MRS. HALE

THE SETTING: *The kitchen in the now abandoned farmhouse of* JOHN WRIGHT.

SCENE: *The kitchen in the now abandoned farmhouse of* JOHN WRIGHT, *a gloomy kitchen, and left without having been put in order—unwashed pans under the sink, a loaf of bread outside the breadbox, a dish towel on the table—other signs of incompleted work. At the rear the outer door opens and the* SHERIFF *comes in followed by the* COUNTY ATTORNEY *and* HALE. *The* SHERIFF *and* HALE *are men in middle life, the* COUNTY ATTORNEY *is a young man; all are much bundled up and go at once to the stove. They are followed by the two women—the* SHERIFF'S *wife first; she is a slight wiry woman, a thin nervous face.* MRS. HALE *is larger and would ordinarily be called more comfortable looking, but she is disturbed now and looks fearfully about as she enters. The women have come in slowly, and stand close together near the door.*

COUNTY ATTORNEY (*rubbing his hands*): This feels good. Come up to the fire, ladies.

MRS. PETERS (*after taking a step forward*): I'm not—cold.

SHERIFF (*unbuttoning his overcoat and stepping away from the stove as if to mark the beginning of official business*): Now, Mr. Hale, before we move things about, you explain to Mr. Henderson just what you saw when you came here yesterday morning.

COUNTY ATTORNEY: By the way, has anything been moved? Are things just as you left them yesterday?

SHERIFF (*looking about*): It's just the same. When it dropped below zero last night I thought I'd better send Frank out this morning to make a fire for us—no use getting pneumonia with a big case on, but I told him not to touch anything except the stove—and you know Frank.

COUNTY ATTORNEY: Somebody should have been left here yesterday.

SHERIFF: Oh—yesterday. When I had to send Frank to Morris Center for that man who went crazy—I want you to know I had my hands full yesterday, I knew you could get back from Omaha by today and as long as I went over everything here myself—

COUNTY ATTORNEY: Well, Mr. Hale, tell just what happened when you came here yesterday morning.

HALE: Harry and I had started to town with a load of potatoes. We came along the road from my place and as I got here I said, "I'm going to see if I can't get John Wright to go in with me on a party telephone." I spoke to Wright about it once before and he put me off, saying folks talked too much anyway, and all he asked was peace and quiet—I guess you know about how much he talked himself; but I thought maybe if I went to the house and talked about it before his wife, though I said to Harry that I didn't know as what his wife wanted made much difference to John—

COUNTY ATTORNEY: Let's talk about that later, Mr. Hale. I do want to talk about that, but tell now just what happened when you got to the house.

HALE: I didn't hear or see anything; I knocked at the door, and still it was all quiet inside. I knew they must be up, it was past eight o'clock. So I knocked again, and I thought I heard somebody say, "Come in." I wasn't sure, I'm not sure yet, but I opened the door—this door (*indicating the door by which the two women are still standing*) and there in that rocker—(*pointing to it*) sat Mrs. Wright.

They all look at the rocker.

COUNTY ATTORNEY: What—was she doing?

HALE: She was rockin' back and forth. She had her apron in her hand and was kind of—pleating it.

COUNTY ATTORNEY: And how did she—look?

HALE: Well, she looked queer.

COUNTY ATTORNEY: How do you mean—queer?

HALE: Well, as if she didn't know what she was going to do next. And kind of done up.

COUNTY ATTORNEY: How did she seem to feel about your coming?

HALE: Why, I don't think she minded—one way or other. She didn't pay much attention. I said, "How do, Mrs. Wright, it's cold, ain't it?" And she said, "Is it?"—and went on kind of pleating at her apron. Well, I was surprised; she didn't ask me to come up to the stove, or to set down, but just sat there, not even looking at me, so I said, "I want to see John." And then she—laughed. I guess you would call it a laugh. I thought of Harry and the team outside, so I said a little sharp: "Can't I see John?" "No," she says, kind o' dull like. "Ain't he home?" says I. "Yes," says she, "he's home." "Then why can't I see him?" I asked her, out of patience. "'Cause he's dead," says she. *"Dead?"* says I. She just nodded her head, not getting a bit excited, but rockin' back and forth. "Why—where is he?" says I, not knowing what to say. She just pointed upstairs—like that (*himself pointing to the room above*). I got up, with the idea of going up there. I walked from there to here—then I says, "Why, what did he die of?" "He died of a rope round his neck," says she, and just went on pleatin' at her apron. Well, I went out and called Harry. I thought I might—need help. We went upstairs and there he was lyin'—

COUNTY ATTORNEY: I think I'd rather have you go into that upstairs, where you can point it all out. Just go on now with the rest of the story.

HALE: Well, my first thought was to get that rope off. It looked . . . (*stops, his face twitches*) . . . but Harry, he went up to him, and he said, "No, he's dead all right, and we'd better not touch anything." So we went back down stairs. She was still sitting that same way. "Has anybody been notified?" I asked. "No," says she, unconcerned. "Who did this, Mrs. Wright?" said Harry. He said it businesslike—and she stopped pleatin' of her apron. "I don't know," she says. "You don't *know?*" says Harry. "No," says she. "Weren't you sleepin' in the bed with him?" says Harry. "Yes," says she, "but I was on the inside." "Somebody slipped a rope round his neck and strangled him and you didn't wake up?" says Harry. "I didn't wake up," she said after him. We must 'a looked as if we didn't see how that could be, for after a minute she said, "I sleep sound." Harry was going to ask her more questions but I said maybe we ought to let her tell her story first to the coroner, or the sheriff, so Harry went fast as he could to Rivers' place, where there's a telephone.

COUNTY ATTORNEY: And what did Mrs. Wright do when she knew that you had gone for the coroner?

HALE: She moved from that chair to this one over here (*pointing to a small chair in the corner*) and just sat there with her hands held together and looking down. I got a feeling that I ought to make some conversation, so I said I had come in to see if John wanted to put in a telephone, and at that she started to laugh, and then she stopped and looked at me— scared. (*The* COUNTY ATTORNEY, *who has had his notebook out, makes a note.*) I dunno, maybe it wasn't scared. I wouldn't like to say it was. Soon Harry got back, and then Dr. Lloyd came, and you, Mr. Peters, and so I guess that's all I know that you don't.

COUNTY ATTORNEY (*looking around*): I guess we'll go upstairs first—and then out to the barn and around there. (*to the* SHERIFF) You're convinced that there was nothing important here—nothing that would point to any motive.

SHERIFF: Nothing here but kitchen things.

The COUNTY ATTORNEY, *after again looking around the kitchen, opens the door of a cupboard closet. He gets up on a chair and looks on a shelf. Pulls his hand away, sticky.*

COUNTY ATTORNEY: Here's a nice mess.

The women draw nearer.

MRS. PETERS (*to the other woman*): Oh, her fruit; it did freeze. (*to the* COUNTY ATTORNEY) She worried about that when it turned so cold. She said the fire'd go out and her jars would break.

SHERIFF: Well, can you beat the women! Held for murder and worryin' about her preserves.

COUNTY ATTORNEY: I guess before we're through she may have something more serious than preserves to worry about.

HALE: Well, women are used to worrying over trifles.

The two women move a little closer together.

COUNTY ATTORNEY (*with the gallantry of a young politician*): And yet, for all their worries, what would we do without the ladies? (*The women do not unbend. He goes to the sink, takes a dipperful of water from the pail and pouring it into a basin, washes his hands. Starts to wipe them on the roller towel, turns it for a cleaner place.*) Dirty towels! (*kicks his foot against the pans under the sink*) Not much of a housekeeper, would you say, ladies?

MRS. HALE (*stiffly*): There's a great deal of work to be done on a farm.

COUNTY ATTORNEY: To be sure. And yet (*with a little bow to her*) I know there are some Dickson county farmhouses which do not have such roller towels.

He gives it a pull to expose its full length again.

MRS. HALE: Those towels get dirty awful quick. Men's hands aren't always as clean as they might be.

COUNTY ATTORNEY: Ah, loyal to your sex, I see. But you and Mrs. Wright were neighbors. I suppose you were friends, too.

MRS. HALE (*shaking her head*): I've not seen much of her of late years. I've not been in this house—it's more than a year.

COUNTY ATTORNEY: And why was that? You didn't like her?

MRS. HALE: I liked her all well enough. Farmers' wives have their hands full, Mr. Henderson. And then—

COUNTY ATTORNEY: Yes—?

MRS. HALE (*looking about*): It never seemed a very cheerful place.

COUNTY ATTORNEY: No—it's not cheerful. I shouldn't say she had the home-making instinct.

MRS. HALE: Well, I don't know as Wright had, either.

COUNTY ATTORNEY: You mean that they didn't get on very well?

MRS. HALE: No, I don't mean anything. But I don't think a place'd be any cheerfuller for John Wright's being in it.

COUNTY ATTORNEY: I'd like to talk more of that a little later. I want to get the lay of things upstairs now.

He goes to the left, where three steps lead to a stair door.

SHERIFF: I suppose anything Mrs. Peters does'll be all right. She was to take in some clothes for her, you know, and a few little things. We left in such a hurry yesterday.

COUNTY ATTORNEY: Yes, but I would like to see what you take, Mrs. Peters, and keep an eye out for anything that might be of use to us.

MRS. PETERS: Yes, Mr. Henderson.

The women listen to the men's steps on the stairs, then look about the kitchen.

MRS. HALE: I'd hate to have men coming into my kitchen, snooping around and criticizing.

She arranges the pans under sink which the COUNTY ATTORNEY *had shoved out of place.*

MRS. PETERS: Of course it's no more than their duty.

MRS. HALE: Duty's all right, but I guess that deputy sheriff that came out to make the fire might have got a little of this on. (*gives the roller towel a pull*) Wish I'd thought of that sooner. Seems mean to talk about her for not having things slicked up when she had to come away in such a hurry.

MRS. PETERS (*who has gone to a small table in the left rear corner of the room, and lifted one end of a towel that covers a pan*): She had bread set.

Stands still.

MRS. HALE (*Eyes fixed on a loaf of bread beside the breadbox, which is on a low shelf at the other side of the room. Moves slowly toward it.*): She was going to put this in there. (*Picks up loaf, then abruptly drops it. In a manner of returning to familiar things.*) It's a shame about her fruit. I wonder if it's all gone. (*gets up on the chair and looks*) I think there's some here that's all right, Mrs. Peters. Yes—here; (*holding it toward the window*) this is cherries, too. (*looking again*) I declare I believe that's the only one. (*Gets down, bottle in her hand. Goes to the sink and wipes it off on the outside.*) She'll feel awful bad after all her hard work in the hot weather. I remember the afternoon I put my cherries last summer.

She puts the bottle on the big kitchen table, center of the room. With a sigh, is about to sit down in the rocking-chair. Before she is seated realizes what chair it is; with a slow look at it, steps back. The chair which she has touched rocks back and forth.

MRS. PETERS: Well, I must get those things from the front room closet. (*She goes to the door at the right, but after looking into the other room, steps back.*) You coming with me, Mrs. Hale? You could help me carry them.

They go in the other room; reappear, MRS. PETERS *carrying a dress and skirt,* MRS. HALE *following with a pair of shoes.*

MRS. PETERS: My, it's cold in there.

She puts the clothes on the big table, and hurries to the stove.

MRS. HALE (*examining the skirt*): Wright was close. I think maybe that's why she kept so much to herself. She didn't even belong to the Ladies Aid. I suppose she felt she couldn't do her part, and then you don't enjoy things when you feel shabby. She used to wear pretty clothes and be lively, when she was Minnie Foster, one of the town girls singing in the choir. But that—oh, that was thirty years ago. This all you was to take in?

MRS. PETERS: She said she wanted an apron. Funny thing to want, for there isn't much to get you dirty in jail, goodness knows. But I suppose just to make her feel more natural. She said they was in the top drawer in this cupboard. Yes, here. And then her little shawl that always hung behind the door. (*opens stair door and looks*) Yes, here it is.

Quickly shuts door leading upstairs.

MRS. HALE (*abruptly moving toward her*): Mrs. Peters?

MRS. PETERS: Yes, Mrs. Hale?

MRS. HALE: Do you think she did it?

MRS. PETERS (*in a frightened voice*): Oh, I don't know.

MRS. HALE: Well, I don't think she did. Asking for an apron and her little shawl. Worrying about her fruit.

MRS. PETERS (*Starts to speak, glances up, where footsteps are heard in the room above. In a low voice.*): Mr. Peters says it looks bad for her. Mr. Henderson is awful sarcastic in a speech and he'll make fun of her sayin' she didn't wake up.

MRS. HALE: Well, I guess John Wright didn't wake when they was slipping that rope under his neck.

MRS. PETERS: No, it's strange. It must have been done awful crafty and still. They say it was such a—funny way to kill a man, rigging it all up like that.

MRS. HALE: That's just what Mr. Hale said. There was a gun in the house. He says that's what he can't understand.

MRS. PETERS: Mr. Henderson said coming out that what was needed for the case was a motive; something to show anger, or—sudden feeling.

MRS. HALE (*who is standing by the table*): Well, I don't see any signs of anger around here. (*She puts her hand on the dish towel which lies on the table, stands looking down at table, one half of which is clean, the other half messy.*) It's wiped to here. (*Makes a move as if to finish work, then turns and looks at loaf of bread outside the breadbox. Drops towel. In that voice of coming back to familiar things.*) Wonder how they are finding things upstairs. I hope she had it a little more red-up up there. You know, it seems kind of *sneaking*. Locking her up in town and then coming out here and trying to get her own house to turn against her!

MRS. PETERS: But Mrs. Hale, the law is the law.

MRS. HALE: I s'pose 'tis. (*unbuttoning her coat*) Better loosen up your things, Mrs. Peters. You won't feel them when you go out.

MRS. PETERS takes off her fur tippet, goes to hang it on hook at back of room, stands looking at the under part of the small corner table.

MRS. PETERS: She was piecing a quilt.

She brings the large sewing basket and they look at the bright pieces.

MRS. HALE: It's log cabin pattern. Pretty, isn't it? I wonder if she was goin' to quilt it or just knot it?

Footsteps have been heard coming down the stairs. The SHERIFF enters followed by HALE and the COUNTY ATTORNEY.

SHERIFF: They wonder if she was going to quilt it or just knot it!

The men laugh; the women look abashed.

COUNTY ATTORNEY (*rubbing his hands over the stove*): Frank's fire didn't do much up there, did it? Well, let's go out to the barn and get that cleared up.

The men go outside.

MRS. HALE (*resentfully*): I don't know as there's anything so strange, our takin' up our time with little things while we're waiting for them to get the evidence. (*She sits down at the big table smoothing out a block with decision.*) I don't see as it's anything to laugh about.

MRS. PETERS (*apologetically*): Of course they've got awful important things on their minds.

Pulls up a chair and joins MRS. HALE at the table.

MRS. HALE (*examining another block*): Mrs. Peters, look at this one. Here, this is the one she was working on, and look at the sewing! All the rest of it has been so nice and even. And look at this! It's all over the place! Why, it looks as if she didn't know what she was about! (*After she has said this they look at each other, then start to glance back at the door. After an instant* MRS. HALE *has pulled at a knot and ripped the sewing.*)

MRS. PETERS: Oh, what are you doing, Mrs. Hale?

MRS. HALE (*mildly*): Just pulling out a stitch or two that's not sewed very good. (*threading a needle*) Bad sewing always made me fidgety.

MRS. PETERS (*nervously*): I don't think we ought to touch things.

MRS. HALE: I'll just finish up this end. (*suddenly stopping and leaning forward*) Mrs. Peters?

MRS. PETERS: Yes, Mrs. Hale?

MRS. HALE: What do you suppose she was so nervous about?

MRS. PETERS: Oh—I don't know. I don't know as she was nervous. I sometimes sew awful queer when I'm just tired. (MRS. HALE *starts to say something, looks at* MRS. PETERS, *then goes on sewing.*) Well, I must get these things wrapped up. They may be through sooner than we think. (*putting apron and other things together*) I wonder where I can find a piece of paper, and string.

MRS. HALE: In that cupboard, maybe.

MRS. PETERS (*looking in cupboard*): Why, here's a birdcage. (*holds it up*) Did she have a bird, Mrs. Hale?

MRS. HALE: Why, I don't know whether she did or not—I've not been here for so long. There was a man around last year selling canaries cheap, but I don't know as she took one; maybe she did. She used to sing real pretty herself.

MRS. PETERS (*glancing around*): Seems funny to think of a bird here. But she must have had one, or why would she have a cage? I wonder what happened to it.

MRS. HALE: I s'pose maybe the cat got it.

MRS. PETERS: No, she didn't have a cat. She's got that feeling some people have about cats—being afraid of them. My cat got in her room and she was real upset and asked me to take it out.

MRS. HALE: My sister Bessie was like that. Queer, ain't it?

MRS. PETERS (*examining the cage*): Why, look at this door. It's broke. One hinge is pulled apart.

MRS. HALE (*looking too*): Looks as if someone must have been rough with it.

MRS. PETERS: Why, yes.

She brings the cage forward and puts it on the table.

MRS. HALE: I wish if they're going to find any evidence they'd be about it. I don't like this place.

MRS. PETERS: But I'm awful glad you came with me, Mrs. Hale. It would be lonesome for me sitting here alone.

MRS. HALE: It would, wouldn't it? (*dropping her sewing*) But I tell you what I do wish, Mrs. Peters. I wish I had come over sometimes when *she* was here. I—(*looking around the room*)—wish I had.

MRS. PETERS: But of course you were awful busy, Mrs. Hale—your house and your children.

MRS. HALE: I could've come. I stayed away because it weren't cheerful—and that's why I ought to have come. I—I've never liked this place. Maybe because it's down in a hollow and you don't see the road. I dunno what it is, but it's a lonesome place and always was. I wish I had come over to see Minnie Foster sometimes. I can see now—

Shakes her head.

MRS. PETERS: Well, you mustn't reproach yourself, Mrs. Hale. Somehow we just don't see how it is with other folks until—something comes up.

MRS. HALE: Not having children makes less work—but it makes a quiet house, and Wright out to work all day, and no company when he did come in. Did you know John Wright, Mrs. Peters?

MRS. PETERS: Not to know him; I've seen him in town. They say he was a good man.

MRS. HALE: Yes—good; he didn't drink, and kept his word as well as most, I guess, and paid his debts. But he was a hard man, Mrs. Peters. Just to pass the time of day with him—(*shivers*) Like a raw wind that gets to the bone. (*pauses, her eye falling on the cage*) I should think she would 'a wanted a bird. But what do you suppose went with it?

MRS. PETERS: I don't know, unless it got sick and died.

She reaches over and swings the broken door, swings it again. Both women watch it.

MRS. HALE: You weren't raised 'round here, were you? (MRS. PETERS *shakes her head.*) You didn't know—her?

MRS. PETERS: Not till they brought her yesterday.

MRS. HALE: She—come to think of it, she was kind of like a bird herself—real sweet and pretty, but kind of timid and—fluttery. How—she—did—change. (*silence; then as if struck by a happy thought and relieved to get back to everyday things*) Tell you what, Mrs. Peters, why don't you take the quilt in with you? It might take up her mind.

MRS. PETERS: Why, I think that's a real nice idea, Mrs. Hale. There couldn't possibly be any objection to it, could there? Now, just what would I take? I wonder if her patches are in here—and her things.

They look in the sewing basket.

MRS. HALE: Here's some red. I expect this has got sewing things in it. (*brings out a fancy box*) What a pretty box. Looks like something somebody would give you. Maybe her scissors are in here. (*Opens box. Suddenly puts her hand to her nose.*) Why—(MRS. PETERS *bends nearer, then turns her face away.*) There's something wrapped up in this piece of silk.

MRS. PETERS: Why, this isn't her scissors.

MRS. HALE (*lifting the silk*): Oh, Mrs. Peters—it's—

MRS. PETERS *bends closer.*

MRS. PETERS: It's the bird.

MRS. HALE (*jumping up*): But, Mrs. Peters—look at it! Its neck! Look at its neck! It's all—other side *to.*

MRS. PETERS: Somebody—wrung—its—neck.

Their eyes meet. A look of growing comprehension, of horror. Steps are heard outside. MRS. HALE *slips box under quilt pieces, and sinks into her chair. Enter* SHERIFF *and* COUNTY ATTORNEY. MRS. PETERS *rises.*

COUNTY ATTORNEY (*as one turning from serious things to little pleasantries*): Well, ladies, have you decided whether she was going to quilt it or knot it?

MRS. PETERS: We think she was going to—knot it.

COUNTY ATTORNEY: Well, that's interesting, I'm sure. (*seeing the birdcage*) Has the bird flown?

MRS. HALE (*putting more quilt pieces over the box*): We think the—cat got it.

COUNTY ATTORNEY (*preoccupied*): Is there a cat?

MRS. HALE *glances in a quick covert way at* MRS. PETERS.

MRS. PETERS: Well, not *now*. They're superstitious, you know. They leave.

COUNTY ATTORNEY (*to* SHERIFF PETERS, *continuing an interrupted conversation*): No sign at all of anyone having come from the outside. Their own rope. Now let's go up again and go over it piece by piece. (*They start upstairs.*) It would have to have been someone who knew just the—

MRS. PETERS *sits down. The two women sit there not looking at one another, but as if peering into something and at the same time holding back. When they talk now it is in the manner of feeling their way over strange ground, as if afraid of what they are saying, but as if they cannot help saying it.*

MRS. HALE: She liked the bird. She was going to bury it in that pretty box.

MRS. PETERS (*in a whisper*): When I was a girl—my kitten—there was a boy took a hatchet, and before my eyes—and before I could get there— (*covers her face an instant*) If they hadn't held me back I would have—(*catches herself, looks upstairs where steps are heard, falters weakly*)—hurt him.

MRS. HALE (*with a slow look around her*): I wonder how it would seem never to have had any children around. (*pause*) No, Wright wouldn't like the bird—a thing that sang. She used to sing. He killed that, too.

MRS. PETERS (*moving uneasily*): We don't know who killed the bird.

MRS. HALE: I knew John Wright.

MRS. PETERS: It was an awful thing was done in this house that night, Mrs. Hale. Killing a man while he slept, slipping a rope around his neck that choked the life out of him.

MRS. HALE: His neck. Choked the life out of him.

Her hand goes out and rests on the birdcage.

MRS. PETERS (*with rising voice*): We don't know who killed him. We don't *know*.

MRS. HALE (*her own feeling not interrupted*): If there'd been years and years of nothing, then a bird to sing to you, it would be awful—still, after the bird was still.

MRS. PETERS (*something within her speaking*): I know what stillness is. When we homesteaded in Dakota, and my first baby died—after he was two years old, and me with no other then—

MRS. HALE (*moving*): How soon do you suppose they'll be through, looking for the evidence?

MRS. PETERS: I know what stillness is. (*pulling herself back*) The law has got to punish crime, Mrs. Hale.

MRS. HALE (*not as if answering that*): I wish you'd seen Minnie Foster when she wore a white dress with blue ribbons and stood up there in the choir and sang. (*a look around the room*) Oh, I *wish* I'd come over here once in a while! That was a crime! That was a crime! Who's going to punish that?

MRS. PETERS (*looking upstairs*): We mustn't—take on.

MRS. HALE: I might have known she needed help! I know how things can be—for women. I tell you, it's queer, Mrs. Peters. We live close together and we live far apart. We all go through the same things—it's all just a different kind of the same thing. (*brushes her eyes; noticing the bottle of fruit, reaches out for it*) If I was you I wouldn't tell her her fruit was gone. Tell her it *ain't*. Tell her it's all right. Take this in to prove it to her. She—she may never know whether it was broke or not.

MRS. PETERS (*Takes the bottle, looks about for something to wrap it in; takes petticoat from the clothes brought from the other room, very nervously begins winding this around the bottle. In a false voice.*): My, it's a good thing the men couldn't hear us. Wouldn't they just laugh! Getting all stirred up over a little thing like a—dead canary. As if that could have anything to do with—with—wouldn't they *laugh!*

The men are heard coming down stairs.

MRS. HALE (*under her breath*): Maybe they would—maybe they wouldn't.

COUNTY ATTORNEY: No, Peters, it's all perfectly clear except a reason for doing it. But you know juries when it comes to women. If there was some definite thing. Something to show—something to make a story about—a thing that would connect up with this strange way of doing it—

The women's eyes meet for an instant. Enter HALE *from outer door.*

HALE: Well, I've got the team around. Pretty cold out there.

COUNTY ATTORNEY: I'm going to stay here a while by myself. (*to the* SHERIFF) You can send Frank out for me, can't you? I want to go over everything. I'm not satisfied that we can't do better.

SHERIFF: Do you want to see what Mrs. Peters is going to take in?

The COUNTY ATTORNEY *goes to the table, picks up the apron, laughs.*

COUNTY ATTORNEY: Oh, I guess they're not very dangerous things the ladies have picked out. (*Moves a few things about, disturbing the quilt pieces which cover the box. Steps back.*) No, Mrs. Peters doesn't need supervising. For that matter, a sheriff's wife is married to the law. Ever think of it that way, Mrs. Peters?

MRS. PETERS: Not—just that way.

SHERIFF (*chuckling*): Married to the law. (*moves toward the other room*) I just want you to come in here a minute, George. We ought to take a look at these windows.

COUNTY ATTORNEY (*scoffingly*): Oh, windows!

SHERIFF: We'll be right out, Mr. Hale.

> HALE *goes outside. The* SHERIFF *follows the* COUNTY ATTORNEY *into the other room. Then* MRS. HALE *rises, hands tight together, looking intensely at* MRS. PETERS, *whose eyes make a slow turn, finally meeting* MRS. HALE'S. *A moment* MRS. HALE *holds her, then her own eyes point the way to where the box is concealed. Suddenly* MRS. PETERS *throws back quilt pieces and tries to put the box in the bag she is wearing. It is too big. She opens box, starts to take bird out, cannot touch it, goes to pieces, stands there helpless. Sound of a knob turning in the other room.* MRS. HALE *snatches the box and puts it in the pocket of her big coat. Enter* COUNTY ATTORNEY *and* SHERIFF.

COUNTY ATTORNEY (*facetiously*): Well, Henry, at least we found out that she was not going to quilt it. She was going to—what is it you call it, ladies?

MRS. HALE (*her hand against her pocket*): We call it—knot it, Mr. Henderson.

Curtain.

The Receptive Reader

1. Very early in the first scene, Hale, the neighbor, says in passing "I didn't know as what his wife wanted made much difference to John." How does this statement give you a first hint of the major *conflict* underlying the play?

2. Why does the playwright have the characters talk about the preserves? To wind up this discussion, Hale says, "Well, women are used to worrying over trifles." How does this statement point forward to a major *theme* of the play? What makes the use of the word here and in the title of the play ironic? How is the theme of the "little things" that matter to women taken up again in the discussion of the quilt?

3. How do you first gather that Mrs. Hale does not share the men's views but instead has a feeling of solidarity with Mrs. Wright? How do you begin to realize that in much of this you will be looking at events and issues from the women's *point of view?*

4. The men representing the law are asking about a *motive*—"something to show anger, or—sudden feeling." What are some of the first clues that point toward the answer the play gives to this question?

5. What clues and comments help you piece together your view of John Wright's *character* as the women talk mostly about other things? What is ironic about his being described as "a good man"?

6. What makes the bird a central *symbol* in this play? What makes you first realize that the women are going to close ranks behind Mrs. Wright? What are some of the things the playwright does to help you understand and sympathize with their decision?

7. What is the *irony* in Mrs. Peters's being "married to the law"?

8. The events of this play might have provided the material for a traditional detective story or an episode in a crime show. How is the treatment of the story in this play different from what you might expect in such a more conventional format?

The Creative Dimension

A major player in the events leading up to the events of the play—John, the husband—is no longer present to testify. What do you think he might say if he could come back among the living for a time to tell his side of the story? Or what do you think he might have said in a letter he left for a friend to be read after an untimely death?

WRITING ABOUT LITERATURE

26 Writing a Review (The Personal Response)

For playwrights and theater companies, reviewers act as audience surrogates. They alert author, director, and actors to strong positive and negative reactions, sometimes unexpected or highly personal. When you write your own review of a performance, you become part of the live interaction that through the centuries has often made the theater the center of a living culture. Write about a play reading, a live performance in a college theater or on a local stage, a showing of a videotaped play, or a movie version of a classic. Make your review a record of your growing interest in the theater.

In your review, you have a chance to answer questions like the following:

✘ *What major themes emerged strongly from the production?* A stage production is a collaboration. The playwright furnishes the script—often the result of much revision. Many contemporary dramatists revise their plays after tryouts and initial reviews. What do you think the playwright wanted you to see? What message or insight or puzzle is at the core of the play?

✘ *How did the director interpret or reinterpret the play?* A director (or perhaps a directorial committee) charts directions or develops a concept. For instance, a director might highlight the youthfulness of Shakespeare's Romeo and Juliet—their eagerness, their refusal to wait, their moving from heavenly joy to deadly despair in the course of a day. Strong directors reinterpret traditional plays for their time and audience. An experimental director might teleport Shakespeare's *Hamlet* from its original setting in Denmark to the antebellum mansion of a southern Senator named Claudius, whose wife is a southern belle named Gertrude, and whose financial adviser is a talkative old man named Polonius. Claudius's stepson (Hamlet), as in the original play, will be a young man alienated from his corrupt elders.

✘ *What were especially strong or weak performances by individual actors?* The performers take their cue (and sometimes dictatorial instructions) from the director. However, they may be as stubbornly independent as directors can be, and they bring a part to life in their own way. In a BBC production available on videotape in many college libraries, Ron Cook plays Shakespeare's evil Richard III less as the traditional sniggering and gloating hunchback and more like a conniving, corrupt bank vice president. This change makes the character more deadly and the threat more real, since audiences cannot simply laugh at him as a stage villain. The actor's conception of the character takes murder and deceit out of the world of stage melodrama and puts it into the real world.

✖ *How did the audience react?*   The theater cannot survive without the support of a live audience. You may want to discuss impact, audience appeal, audience reactions. Not all the action in the theater is on the stage. A major silent participant in the performance is you—the spectator. Without your collaboration, the stage will not work its magic. In the theater, you become part of a community embarked on a common venture. There is something contagious about the enthusiasm or laughter of a live audience. As a group, the members of the audience "act out" their reactions to the play: They sigh and gasp; they may watch in stunned silence; they express relief in a burst of happy laughter. When the chemistry is right, there is a special interaction between performers and spectators. Performers respond to a receptive audience, creating for the performance the heightened mood of a festive event.

✖ *What about the staging strongly influenced your reaction?*   The settings can create the right or the wrong atmosphere. You may want to talk about technical features that impressed or puzzled you: costuming, special effects, performers' authentic or fake British or southern accents.

Mamet's *Oleanna:* Men's and Women's Issues in the Raw

David Mamet is known as a playwright who knows how to stir the proverbial hornet's nest, and his play *Oleanna* is no exception. In the background notes for the current production at the Repertory theater, strong feminist Susan Brownmiller quotes a friend as saying that the play, although "powerful theater," is "a wicked denial of real rape and harassment." *Oleanna* is the story of a professor at a university and his female student. When she comes to his office seemingly for help, he says things that can be seen as innocent and supportive at the time but that are later construed as being intrusive and harassing. When he touches her on the shoulder in a gesture of support, the gesture later becomes unwanted physical contact leading up to a rape charge.

When I saw the production, women in the audience laughed and cheered when the student who was at first diffident and called herself "stupid" turned on the professor and challenged his condescending ways. The men clapped when the professor, losing his job and seeing his life disintegrate, finally turned on and attacked his tormentor. A reviewer for the local paper said that the performer playing the student did not make the transformation of Carol from a mousy confused student to the self-righteous avenger convincing, but I do not agree. A main point of the play is that how shy or assertive we are is part of our upbringing or of our culture. Women are trained to be meek and submissive; this does not mean that there is not a potentially independent aggressive human being under the surface.

The set for the play was a depressing sterile institutional office building, which created well the feeling of the professor being trapped, unable to extricate himself from the process that had been set in motion. I had mixed feelings about whose side to take in this play. The professor is the elitist male moving up in the academic world, about to be granted tenure. The student is the economically disadvantaged lower-class to middle-class female. I felt sorry for John because at first he was sincerely trying to help Carol. I could also see how she could perceive herself as the victim of a person who abused his power over her. However, when she turns the tables on him and destroys his reputation and his job, she uses her new found power to become exactly what she had detested in John.

Questions

Does this review make you want to see the play? Why or why not? Do you agree that "how shy or how assertive we are is part of our upbringing or our culture"? Have you seen audiences for a play, movie, or TV program split along male/female lines?

27 Conflict

The Heart of Drama

*We live in what is, but we find a thousand ways
not to face it. Great theater strengthens our faculty
to face it.*

THORNTON WILDER

FOCUS ON THE CENTRAL CONFLICT

Often, gripping drama focuses on opposites locked in a fateful struggle. People make fateful choices that alienate or antagonize others. In
the larger arena of society or politics, rival ambitions may put major
characters on a collision course. The play may oppose strong-willed
individuals. A clash of values may lead to a climactic meeting of mighty
opposites. Minor characters may have to take sides and are sometimes
ground up in the confrontation.

The Central Conflict   Powerful drama often centers on a **central conflict.** People who are part of the same family or who were brought
together by marriage may discover that they have different and irrecon-
cilable goals. Some of the great plays of world literature are family dramas, with a clash between the generations—father against son, father
against daughter, mother against son, mother against daughter. Spouses
may have become estranged, locked in a grueling contest for dominance or liberation. Antagonisms may have simmered under the surface,
and some fateful event brings them out into the open. An injustice or
slight from the past may have left festering resentments that erupt into
open conflict.

The Internal Conflict   Even in a play with much external action, the
central conflict may be an **internal conflict.** Shakespeare's *Macbeth* is
a play filled with violence: Macbeth murders his king, destroys people
who are in his way, and is finally defeated by an army raised by the dead
king's son. However, much of the time we focus on the internal conflict
in a mind divided against itself. With one part of his mind, Macbeth

672

yields to the siren song of ambition that makes him plot the assassination of King Duncan. But in another part of his mind, Macbeth is deeply troubled. He is haunted by his violated loyalty to his king and by a religion that teaches the abhorrence of murder.

The Clash of Ideas   The central conflict in a play is often a conflict between different ways of looking at the world. We experience the pull of divided loyalties as first the one side and then the other scores points. We are drawn into the **dialectic** of the play—the playing off of differing or opposite points of view. We share in the play of point and counterpoint. The Irish playwright George Bernard Shaw said about the characters in his plays that all of them were right *from their own point of view*—and that those who could not understand this vital point could not understand drama and indeed life.

Conflict and Resolution   How will the conflict be resolved? Sometimes a play seems to march single-mindedly to a foregone conclusion. In the tragedies of ancient Greece, we often sense that fate or the gods have already decided the outcome and that we are going to witness the slow unfolding of a story from which there is no escape. In other plays, the central conflict may set the stage for a climactic violent encounter. In a Shakespeare play, the outcome is often decided on the field of battle. In a truly dramatic play, the issue may be in doubt to the end. In an open-ended modern play, we may be left hanging, feeling that basic unresolved questions and contradictions stay with us as we leave the theater.

Henrik Ibsen   *(1828–1906)*

I thought the time had come when a few
boundaries ought to be moved.

HENRIK IBSEN

The Norwegian playwright Henrik Ibsen was a master at setting up and playing out the conflicts that are the heart of drama. His great plays—*A Doll's House, The Wild Duck, Hedda Gabler, Ghosts*—continue to remind theatergoers of his gift for asking questions to which they are still seeking the answers. His central characters are often in rebellion against the dominant middle-class morality of his time. He knew well the prosperous middle class of shopkeepers, industrialists, bank managers, and doctors who were *The Pillars of the Community* (the title of an Ibsen play). He attacked their self-righteousness—their belief that they stood for morality and law and order. In his plays, present prosperity often had its roots in shady business deals or the betrayal of friends. For all its

Claire Bloom and Anthony Hopkins as Nora and Torvald Helmer in *A Doll's House*. Courtesy of Photofest.

genteel trappings, the bourgeois society of the time was shown as ruthlessly competitive. The strong prospered while the weak went under. On the fringe of proper, well-to-do society were poor relations, business failures, and misfits who lived in genteel poverty, embittered by their lot.

Ibsen was one of the first great truth-tellers in the modern vein. He put on the stage businessmen who were unable to relate emotionally to their families, alienated from wife and children. They compensated for the sexual inhibitions of their time by furtive affairs with maids and prostitutes. Ibsen's most memorable characters were women—Nora Helmer in *A Doll's House* (1879), Hedda in *Hedda Gabler* (1892)—who were in rebellion against the role reserved for them in a man's world. They talked back to the domineering men in their lives; they rebelled against the stereotype of the woman whose duty was to husband and family. They refused to be the "little woman" who was humored and condescended to and never entrusted with real responsibility.

The truths that Ibsen told and that often outraged his early audiences were rooted in his own experience. His father, a lavish spender, went bankrupt when Henrik was six. Ibsen was at odds with his brothers and alienated from his father, and in later years he had contacts only with his sister Hedwig. Instead of studying to be a physician, as he had hoped, he spent miserable years as a pharmacist's apprentice. He had a child out of wedlock with an older servant and paid child support for many years. Determined to be a playwright, Ibsen eventually managed to have plays printed and performed, but he lived in what one of his translators calls "wretched poverty" for many years with his wife and son. Assisted by a government grant, Ibsen eventually left Norway to live for many years in self-imposed exile, writing many of his best-known plays abroad in Germany and Italy.

Among these plays, which later became known as **problem plays,** *A Doll's House* (1879) was the most spectacular and provocative. The play questioned the institution of marriage during an age when marriage was for life. The play was eventually performed in Germany, and in an adaptation, in England, creating much controversy and making Ibsen's reputation.

A Doll's House   *1879*

TRANSLATED BY PETER WATTS

The legal subordination of one sex to the other is wrong in itself and now one of the chief hindrances to human improvement.

JOHN STUART MILL

CHARACTERS

TORVALD HELMER, a lawyer
NORA, his wife
DR. RANK
NILS KROGSTAD, a barrister
MRS. LINDE
HELMER'S three small children
ANNA-MARIA, the nurse
A HOUSEMAID
A PORTER

The action takes place in HELMER'S *flat.*

Act One

A comfortable room, furnished inexpensively, but with taste. In the back wall there are two doors; that to the right leads out to a hall, the other, to the left, leads to HELMER'S *study. Between them stands a piano.*

In the middle of the left-hand wall is a door, with a window on its nearer side. Near the window is a round table with armchairs and a small sofa.

In the wall on the right-hand side, rather to the back, is a door, and farther forward on this wall there is a tiled stove with a couple of easy chairs and a rocking-chair in front of it. Between the door and the stove stands a little table.

There are etchings on the walls, and there is a cabinet with china ornaments and other bric-à-brac, and a small bookcase with handsomely bound books. There is a carpet on the floor, and the stove is lit. It is a winter day.

A bell rings in the hall outside, and a moment later the door is heard to open. NORA *comes into the room, humming happily. She is in outdoor clothes, and is carrying an armful of parcels which she puts down on the table to the right. Through the hall door, which she has left open, can be seen a* PORTER; *he is holding a Christmas tree and a hamper, and he gives them to the* MAID *who has opened the front door.*

NORA: Hide the Christmas tree properly, Helena. The children mustn't see it till this evening, when it's been decorated (*to the* PORTER, *taking out her purse*) How much is that?

PORTER: Fifty cents.

NORA: There's a crown. No, keep the change.

The PORTER *thanks her and goes.* NORA *shuts the door, and takes off her outdoor clothes, laughing quietly and happily to herself. Taking a bag of macaroons from her pocket, she eats one or two, then goes cautiously to her husband's door and listens.*

Yes, he's in. (*She starts humming again as she goes over to the table on the right.*)

HELMER (*from his study*): Is that my little skylark twittering out there?

NORA (*busy opening the parcels*): It is.

HELMER: Scampering about like a little squirrel?

NORA: Yes.

HELMER: When did the squirrel get home?

NORA: Just this minute. (*She slips the bag of macaroons in her pocket and wipes her mouth.*) Come in here, Torvald, and you can see what I've bought.

HELMER: I'm busy! (*A moment later he opens the door and looks out, pen in hand.*) Did you say "bought"? What, all that? Has my little featherbrain been out wasting money again?

NORA: But, Torvald, surely this year we can let ourselves go just a little bit? It's the first Christmas that we haven't had to economize.

HELMER: Still, we mustn't waste money, you know.

NORA: Oh, Torvald, surely we can waste a little now—just the teeniest bit? Now that you're going to earn a big salary, you'll have lots and lots of money.

HELMER: After New Year's Day, yes—but there'll be a whole quarter before I get paid.

NORA: Pooh, we can always borrow till then.

HELMER: Nora! (*He goes to her and takes her playfully by the ear.*) The same little scatterbrain. Just suppose I borrowed a thousand crowns today and you went and spent it all by Christmas, and then on New Year's Eve a tile fell on my head, and there I lay—

NORA (*putting a hand over his mouth*): Sh! Don't say such horrid things!

HELMER: But suppose something of the sort were to happen. . . .

NORA: If anything as horrid as that were to happen, I don't expect I should care whether I owed money or not.

HELMER: But what about the people I'd borrowed from?

NORA: Them? Who bothers about them? They're just strangers.

HELMER: Nora, Nora! Just like a woman! But seriously, Nora, you know what I think about that sort of thing. No debts, no borrowing. There's something constrained, something ugly even, about a home that's founded on borrowing and debt. You and I have managed to keep clear up till now, and we shall still do so for the little time that is left.

NORA (*going over to the stove*): Very well, Torvald, if you say so.

HELMER (*following her*): Now, now, my little songbird mustn't be so crestfallen. Well? Is the squirrel sulking? (*taking out his wallet*) Nora . . . guess what I have here!

NORA (*turning quickly*): Money!

HELMER: There! (*He hands her some notes.*) Good heavens, I know what a lot has to go on housekeeping at Christmas time.

NORA (*counting*): Ten—twenty—thirty—forty! Oh, thank you, Torvald, thank you! This'll keep me going for a long time!

HELMER: Well, you must see that it does.

NORA: Oh yes, of course I will. But now come and see all the things I've bought—so cheaply, too. Look, here's a new suit for Ivar, and a sword too. Here's a horse and a trumpet for Bob; and here's a doll and a doll's bed for Emmy. They're rather plain, but she'll soon smash them to bits anyway. And these are dress-lengths and handkerchiefs for the maids. . . . Old Nanny really ought to have something more. . . .

HELMER: And what's in *that* parcel?

NORA (*squealing*): No, Torvald! You're not to see that till this evening!

HELMER: Aha! And now, little prodigal, what do you think you want for yourself?

NORA: Oh, me? I don't want anything at all.

HELMER: Ah, but you must. Now tell me anything—within reason—that you feel you'd like.

NORA: No . . . I really can't think of anything. Unless . . . Torvald . . .

HELMER: Well?

NORA (*not looking at him—playing with his waistcoat buttons*): If you *really* want to give me something, you could—well, you could . . .

HELMER: Come along—out with it!

NORA (*in a rush*): You could give me money, Torvald. Only what you think you could spare—and then one of these days I'll buy something with it.

HELMER: But, Nora—

NORA: Oh, *do*, Torvald . . . please, please do! Then I'll wrap it in pretty gold paper and hang it on the Christmas tree. Wouldn't that be fun?

HELMER: What do they call little birds who are always making money fly?

NORA: Yes, I know—ducks-and-drakes! But let's do what I said, Torvald, and then I'll have time to think of something that I really want. Now, that's very sensible, isn't it?

HELMER (*smiling*): Oh, very. That is, it would be if you really kept the money I give you, and actually bought something for yourself with it. But if it goes in with the housekeeping, and gets spent on all sorts of useless things, then I only have to pay out again.

NORA: Oh, but, Torvald—

HELMER: You can't deny it, little Nora, now can you? (*putting an arm round her waist*) It's a sweet little bird, but it gets through a terrible amount of money. You wouldn't believe how much it costs a man when he's got a little songbird like you!

NORA: Oh, how *can* you say that? I really do save all I can.

HELMER (*laughing*): Yes, that's very true—"all you can." But the thing is, you *can't!*

NORA (*nodding and smiling happily*): Ah, if you only knew what expenses we skylarks and squirrels have, Torvald.

HELMER: What a funny little one you are! Just like your father—always on the look-out for all the money you can get, but the moment you have it, it seems to slip through your fingers and you never know what becomes of it. Well, I must take you as you are—it's in your blood. Oh yes, Nora, these things are hereditary.

NORA: I wish I'd inherited more of Papa's good qualities.

HELMER: And I wouldn't want you to be any different from what you are—just my sweet little songbird. But now I come to think of it, you look rather—rather—how shall I put it—rather as if you've been up to mischief today.

NORA: Do I?

HELMER: Yes, you certainly do. Look me straight in the face.

NORA (*looking at him*): Well?

HELMER (*wagging a finger at her*): Surely your sweet tooth didn't get the better of you in town today?

NORA: No . . . how could you think that?

HELMER: Didn't Little Sweet-Tooth just look in at the confectioner's?

NORA: No, honestly, Torvald.

HELMER: Not to taste one little sweet?

NORA: No, of course not.

HELMER: Not even to nibble a macaroon or two?

NORA: No, Torvald, really; I promise you.

HELMER: There, there, of course I was only joking.

NORA (*going to the table on the right*): I wouldn't do anything that you don't like.

HELMER: No, I know you wouldn't—besides, you've given me your word. (*going over to her*) Well, you keep your little Christmas secrets to yourself, Nora darling; I dare say I shall know them all this evening when the Christmas tree's lighted up.

NORA: Did you remember to invite Dr. Rank?

HELMER: No, but there's no need to—it's an understood thing that he dines with us. Still, I'll ask him when he looks in before lunch. I've ordered an excellent wine. . . . Oh, Nora, you can't imagine how much I'm looking forward to this evening.

NORA: So am I, Torvald—and how the children will love it.

HELMER: Oh, it's certainly wonderful to think that one has a good safe post and ample means. It's a very comforting thought, isn't it?

NORA: Oh, it's wonderful!

HELMER: Do you remember last Christmas? For three whole weeks beforehand you shut yourself up every evening till long after midnight, making flowers for the Christmas tree, and all the other wonderful surprises for us. Ugh, those were the most boring three weeks I've ever had to live through.

NORA: It wasn't the least bit boring for me.

HELMER (*smiling*): But there was so little to show for it, Nora!

NORA: Now, you mustn't tease me about that again. How could I help it if the cat got in and tore everything to bits?

HELMER: Poor little Nora—of course you couldn't. You did your best to please us—that's the main thing. But it's certainly good that the hard times are over.

NORA: Oh, it's really wonderful!

HELMER: Now I needn't sit here by myself and be bored, and you needn't tire your pretty eyes or your sweet little fingers—

NORA (*clapping her hands*): No, I needn't, need I? Not any more. Oh, it's really wonderful to know that. (*taking his arm*) Now I'll tell you how I've been thinking we ought to arrange things, Torvald. As soon as Christmas is over—

A bell rings in the hall.

Oh, that's the door! (*She tidies the room a little.*) It must be someone to see us—oh, that *is* tiresome!

HELMER: I'm not at home to callers, remember.

MAID (*at the door*): There's a lady to see you, Madam.

NORA: Well, show her in.

MAID (*to* HELMER): And the Doctor's here as well, sir.

HELMER: Has he gone straight to my study?

MAID: Yes, sir.

HELMER *goes to his study. The* MAID *shows in* MRS. LINDE, *who is in travelling clothes, and shuts the door after her.*

MRS. LINDE (*subdued and rather hesitant*): How do you do, Nora?

NORA (*doubtfully*): How do you do . . .

MRS. LINDE: You don't remember me.

NORA: No, I'm afraid I—Wait a minute . . . surely it's—(*impulsively*) Kristina! Is it really you?

MRS. LINDE: Yes, it really is.

NORA: Kristina! And to think I didn't know you! But how could *I?* (*more gently*) You *have* changed, Kristina.

MRS. LINDE: Yes, I have . . . nine years—nearly ten—it's a long time.

NORA: Is it really as long as that since we saw each other? Yes, I suppose it is. But you know, I've been so happy these last eight years! And now you've come to town too? How brave of you to travel all that way in the middle of winter.

MRS. LINDE: I arrived by steamer this morning.

NORA: In time to have a lovely Christmas. Oh, this is wonderful! We'll have a splendid time. But do take your things off—aren't you absolutely frozen? (*helping her*) There! Now come and sit by the stove where it's cosy. No, you have the armchair, I'll sit in the rocking-chair. (*taking her hands*) Yes, now you look like your old self again—it was just the first moment. . . . But you're paler, Kristina, and a little thinner, perhaps. . . .

MRS. LINDE: And a lot older, Nora.

NORA: A little older, perhaps—just a teeny bit—but certainly not a lot. (*suddenly checking herself and speaking seriously*) Oh, how thoughtless of me! Here I am, chattering away . . . dear sweet Kristina, can you ever forgive me?

MRS. LINDE: What do you mean, Nora?

NORA: Poor Kristina, you're a widow now.

MRS. LINDE: Yes . . . three years ago.

NORA: Yes, I know; I saw it in the papers. Oh, Kristina, I kept meaning to write to you, honestly I did, but something always cropped up and I put it off . . .

MRS. LINDE: Dear Nora, I do understand.

NORA: No, it was horrid of me. Oh, poor Kristina, what you must have gone through! And he didn't leave you anything to live on?

MRS. LINDE: No.

NORA: And no children?

MRS. LINDE: No.

NORA: Nothing at all?

MRS. LINDE: Not even any regrets to break my heart over.

NORA (*looking at her incredulously*): Oh, but Kristina, that can't be true.

MRS. LINDE (*stroking* NORA'S *hair with a sad smile*): It happens like that sometimes, Nora.

NORA: But to be so completely alone—that must be terribly sad for you. *I* have three lovely children; you can't see them just now, they're out with their Nanny. . . . But now you must tell me all about it.

MRS. LINDE: No, no, I want to hear about you.

NORA: No, you first—I mustn't be selfish today—I'm not going to think about anything but your troubles. I must just tell you one thing, though. Do you know, we've just had the most wonderful stroke of luck—only the other day.

MRS. LINDE: Oh? What was it?

NORA: Just think—my husband's been made Manager of the Savings Bank.

MRS. LINDE: Your husband? But that's wonderful.

NORA: Yes, it's magnificent! A barrister's life is such an uncertain one—especially when he won't touch any case that isn't absolutely respectable. Of course Torvald never would—and I quite agree with him. Well, you can imagine how delighted we are. He's to start at the Bank on New Year's Day, and he'll have a big salary and lots of commission. Oh, we shall be able to live quite differently from now on—to live as we'd like to. Oh,

Kristina, I'm so happy! It'll be really wonderful to have lots of money, and never need to worry, won't it?

MRS. LINDE: Yes, it must be pleasant to have everything you need.

NORA: Oh, not just what we need! Heaps and heaps of money!

MRS. LINDE (*with a smile*): Nora, Nora! Haven't you learned sense yet? Even at school you were a terrible spendthrift.

NORA (*laughing quietly*): Yes, Torvald says I still am. (*wagging her finger*) But "Nora, Nora" isn't as silly as you think. We simply hadn't the money for me to waste; we both had to work.

MRS. LINDE: You as well?

NORA: Yes, with odds and ends of needlework—crochet and embroidery and so on. (*casually*) And in other ways too. You see, when we married, Torvald gave up his government post—there wasn't any hope of promotion in his department, and of course he had to earn more money than before. But he overworked dreadfully that first year; you see, he had to take on all sorts of extra jobs, and he worked from morning till night. He couldn't stand it; he was dreadfully ill, and the doctors said he'd simply *have* to go to the south.

MRS. LINDE: Oh yes, you went to Italy for a whole year, didn't you?

NORA: Yes, we did. It wasn't easy to manage, I can tell you. It was just after Ivar was born, but of course we had to go. Oh, it was a wonderful trip—beautiful! And it saved Torvald's life. But it cost a terrible lot of money, Kristina!

MRS. LINDE: I'm sure it did.

NORA: Twelve hundred dollars—four thousand eight hundred crowns. That's a lot of money.

MRS. LINDE: Yes, at times like that, it's very lucky to have money.

NORA: Well, you see, we got it from Papa.

MRS. LINDE: Oh? Yes, I remember, your father died just about then.

NORA: Yes, just then. And just think, Kristina, I couldn't go and nurse him. I was expecting Ivar to arrive any day, and there was my poor Torvald, dreadfully ill, to look after. Dear, kind Papa—I never saw him again—that was the hardest thing I've had to bear in all my married life, Kristina.

MRS. LINDE: I know how fond of him you were. . . . And so you went to Italy?

NORA: Yes, we left a month later. We had the money then, and the doctors said there was no time to lose.

MRS. LINDE: And when you came back your husband was cured?

NORA: Fit as a fiddle!

MRS. LINDE: But the doctor . . . ?

NORA: What doctor?

MRS. LINDE: That man who arrived at the same time as I did—I thought your maid said he was the doctor?

NORA: Ah, that was Dr. Rank—but he doesn't come here professionally, he's our best friend, he always looks in at least once a day. No, Torvald's never had a day's illness since. And the children are well and strong, and so am I. (*jumping up and clapping her hands*) Oh Lord, Kristina, it's wonderful to be alive and happy! Oh, but how awful of me, I've just gone on talking about myself! (*She sits on a footstool beside* KRISTINA *and puts her arms on her knees.*) Now, you mustn't be angry with me. Tell me, is it really true that you didn't love your husband? Why did you marry him, then?

MRS. LINDE: My mother was still alive; she was bedridden and helpless, and I had my two younger brothers to look after—I didn't feel I *could* refuse his offer.

NORA: No, no, I suppose you couldn't. And he was rich in those days?

MRS. LINDE: I believe he was quite well off; but his business wasn't sound, and when he died it went to pieces and there wasn't anything left.

NORA: And you . . . ?

MRS. LINDE: Well, I just had to struggle along—I ran a little shop, then a small school, and anything else I could turn my hand to. These last three years I never seem to have stopped working. Still, that's all over now, Nora— poor Mother's gone, she doesn't need me any longer. Nor do the boys— they're working, and they can look after themselves.

NORA: How relieved you must feel.

MRS. LINDE: No . . . just unspeakably empty—I've no one to live for any more. (*She gets up restlessly.*) That's why I couldn't bear to stay in that little backwater any longer. It must be easier to find some sort of work here that'll keep me busy and take my mind off things. If only I could be lucky enough to find some office work . . .

NORA: But, Kristina, that's terribly tiring, and you look worn out already. It'd be much better for you to go for a holiday.

MRS. LINDE (*going over to the window*): I haven't a father to pay my fare, Nora.

NORA (*rising*): Oh, don't be angry with me.

MRS. LINDE (*going to her*): No, Nora, it's you who mustn't be angry with me. That's the worst of my sort of life—it makes you so bitter. There's no one to work for, yet you can never relax. You must live, so you become self-centered. Why, do you know, when you told me the news of your good fortune, I wasn't nearly so glad for your sake as for my own!

NORA: But . . . Oh, I see what you mean—you think perhaps Torvald might be able to do something for you.

MRS. LINDE: Yes, I thought he might.

NORA: Oh, he will, Kristina; just leave it to me. I'll bring the subject up very cleverly. . . . I'll think of some wonderful way to put him in a good mood. . . . Oh, I should so like to help you.

MRS. LINDE: It *is* kind of you, Nora, to want to do this for me . . . especially when *you* know so little about the troubles and hardships of life.

NORA: I? So little?

MRS. LINDE (*smiling*): Well, good heavens, a little bit of sewing and that sort of thing! You're only a baby, Nora!

NORA (*crossing the room with a toss of her head*): Don't be so superior.

MRS. LINDE: No?

NORA: You're like all the others—you none of you think I could do anything worthwhile. . . .

MRS. LINDE: Well?

NORA: And you think I've had an easy life, with nothing to contend with.

MRS. LINDE: But, Nora dear, you've just told me all your troubles.

NORA: Pooh, they were nothing. (*dropping her voice*) I haven't told you the really important thing.

MRS. LINDE: The important thing? What was that?

NORA: I expect you look down on me, Kristina, but you've no right to. You're proud because you worked so hard for your mother all those years.

MRS. LINDE: I don't look down on anyone; but of course I'm proud—and glad—to know that I was able to make Mother's last days a little easier.

NORA: And you're proud of what you did for your brothers.

MRS. LINDE: I think I have every right to be.

NORA: I quite agree. But now let me tell you something, Kristina; I've got something to be proud of, too.

MRS. LINDE: I'm sure you have; what is it?

NORA: Not so loud—suppose Torvald were to hear! I wouldn't have him find out for the world. No one must know about it—no one but you, Kristina.

MRS. LINDE: But what is it?

NORA: Come over here. (*pulling her down on the sofa beside her*) Oh yes, I've something to be proud of. It was I who saved Torvald's life.

MRS. LINDE: Saved his life? But how?

NORA: I told you about our trip to Italy. Torvald would never have got better if we hadn't gone there.

MRS. LINDE: Yes, but your father gave you the money you needed.

NORA (*smiling*): That's what Torvald thinks—and so does everyone else—but . . .

MRS. LINDE: Well?

NORA: Papa never gave us a penny. It was I who raised the money.

MRS. LINDE: You? All that money?

NORA: Twelve hundred dollars—four thousand eight hundred crowns. What do you think of that?

MRS. LINDE: But how could you, Nora? Did you win it in a lottery?

NORA (*contemptuously*): A lottery! (*with a snort*) Pooh—where would be the glory in *that?*

MRS. LINDE: Where did you get it then?

NORA (*with an enigmatic smile*): Aha! (*humming*) Tra-la-la!

MRS. LINDE: Because you certainly couldn't have borrowed it.

NORA: Oh? Why not?

MRS. LINDE: Because a wife can't borrow without her husband's consent.

NORA (*with a toss of her head*): Ah, yes she can—when it's a wife with a little flair for business—a wife who knows how to set about it . . .

MRS. LINDE: But, Nora, I don't see how—

NORA: There's no reason why you should. Besides, I never said anything about *borrowing* the money. There are all sorts of ways I might have got it. (*lying back on the sofa*) I might have got it from some admirer or other—after all, I'm quite attractive . . .

MRS. LINDE: Don't be so silly!

NORA: You know, you're simply dying of curiosity, Kristina!

MRS. LINDE: Now, Nora dear, listen to me—you haven't done anything rash, have you?

NORA (*sitting up*): Is it rash to save your husband's life?

MRS. LINDE: I think it's rash to do something without his knowing . . .

NORA: But I couldn't possibly let him know. Good heavens, don't you see?—it would never have done for him to realize how ill he was. It was to *me* that the doctors came; they said that his life was in danger and that the only way to save him was to take him to the south. Do you think I didn't try to wheedle him into it first? I told him how nice it would be for me to have a holiday abroad like all the other young wives. I tried tears and entreaties—I told him that he really ought to think about my condition—that he must be a dear and do what I asked. I hinted that he could easily borrow the money. But then, Kristina, he nearly lost his temper, he told me I was frivolous, and that it was his duty as a husband not to give in to what I believe he called my "whims and fancies." "All right," I thought, "but your life must be saved somehow." And then I thought of a way . . .

MRS. LINDE: But surely your father must have told him that the money didn't come from *him?*

NORA: No—it was just then that Papa died. I'd always meant to tell him about it and ask him not to give me away, but he was so ill . . . and I'm afraid in the end there was no need.

MRS. LINDE: And *you've* never told your husband?

NORA: Good heavens no, how could I? When he's so strict about that sort of thing. . . . Besides, Torvald has his pride—most men have—he'd be terribly hurt and humiliated if he thought he owed anything to me. It'd spoil everything between us, and our lovely happy home would never be the same again.

MRS. LINDE: Aren't you ever going to tell him?

NORA (*thoughtfully, with a little smile*): Well—one day, perhaps. But not for a long time. When I'm not pretty any more. No, you mustn't laugh. What I mean, of course, is when Torvald isn't as fond of me as he is now—when my dancing and dressing up and reciting don't amuse him any longer. It might be a good thing, then, to have something up my sleeve . . . (*breaking off*). But that's nonsense—that time'll never come. Well, Kristina, what do you think of my great secret? Am I still no use? What's more, you can take my word for it that it's all been a great worry to me—it hasn't been at all easy to meet all my obligations punctually. In business, you know, there are things called "quarterly payments" and "installments," and they're always dreadfully hard to meet, so you see, I've had to scrape together a little bit here and a little bit there, whenever I could. I couldn't save much out of the housekeeping money, because Torvald has to live properly, and I couldn't have the children looking shabby. I didn't feel I could touch the money that I had for my little darlings.

MRS. LINDE: So it all had to come out of your own pocket-money? Poor Nora.

NORA: Of course. After all, it was my own doing. So whenever Torvald gave me money for new dresses and things, I never spent more than half of it—I always bought the simplest, cheapest things. Thank goodness anything looks well on me, so Torvald never noticed. But, oh Kristina, it hasn't been at all easy, because it's so nice to be beautifully dressed, isn't it?

MRS. LINDE: It certainly is.

NORA: Then I've found other ways of earning money too. Last winter I was lucky enough to get a lot of copying to do, so I locked myself in and sat writing—often till after midnight. Oh, I was so tired sometimes . . . so tired. Still, it was really tremendous fun sitting there working and earning money. It was almost like being a man.

MRS. LINDE: But how much have you been able to pay off?

NORA: Well, I don't really know exactly. You see, with a thing like that, it's very difficult to keep accounts. All I know is that I've paid out every penny that I've been able to scrape together. Often I've been at my wits' end. . . . (*smiling*) Then I used to sit here and imagine that a rich old gentleman had fallen in love with me—

MRS. LINDE: Oh? Who was it?

NORA: Wait a minute—and that he died, and when they read his will, there it was, as large as life: "All my money is to go to the lovely Mrs. Nora Helmer—cash down."

MRS. LINDE: But, Nora dear, who was he?

NORA: Oh, good heavens, don't you see? There wasn't really any old gentleman, it was just something that I used to sit here and imagine—often and often—when I simply didn't know which way to turn for the money. But that's all over now; the silly old gentleman can stay where he is for all I care—I've finished with him and his will, my troubles are all over! (*jumping up*) Oh, goodness, Kristina, just think of it! No more worries! To be able to have no more worries at all! To be able to romp with the children, and to have all the lovely up-to-date things about the house that Torvald likes so much. . . . And then it'll soon be spring, and the sky'll be so blue, and perhaps we'll be able to go away for a bit. Perhaps I shall see the sea again. Oh, isn't it wonderful to be alive and happy?

The doorbell is heard from the hall.

MRS. LINDE (*getting up*): There's someone at the door—perhaps I'd better go.

NORA: No, stay. It'll be someone for Torvald, they won't come in here.

MAID (*at the hall door*): Excuse me, Madam, there's a gentleman to see the Lawyer—

NORA: The Bank Manager, you mean.

MAID: Yes, the Bank Manager. But I didn't know—seeing the Doctor's with him—

NORA: Who is it?

KROGSTAD (*in the doorway*): It's me, Mrs. Helmer.

MRS. LINDE *gives a start, then, collecting herself, turns away to the window.*

NORA (*tensely and in a low voice, taking a step toward him*): You? What is it? Why do you want to see my husband?

KROGSTAD: Bank business—in a way. I have a small post at the Savings Bank, and I hear your husband is to be our new Manager—

NORA: So it's only—

KROGSTAD: Only dull official business, Mrs. Helmer; nothing else whatever.

NORA: Well, you'll find him in his study. (*She bows perfunctorily and shuts the hall door. Then she goes over and attends to the stove.*)

MRS. LINDE: Nora . . . who was that man?

NORA: He's a lawyer named Krogstad.

MRS. LINDE: So it was really he . . .

NORA: Do you know him?

MRS. LINDE: I used to know him—years ago. He was once in a lawyer's office back at home.

NORA: Yes, so he was.

MRS. LINDE: How he's changed!

NORA: He's had a very unhappy married life.

MRS. LINDE: And now he's a widower?

NORA: With lots of children. There, that should burn up now.

> *She shuts the door of the stove and pushes the rocking-chair a little to one side.*

MRS. LINDE: He has a finger in all sorts of business, they say.

NORA: Really? Well, they may be right, I don't know anything about. . . . But don't let's talk about business—it's so boring.

> DR. RANK *comes out of* HELMER'S *room.*

RANK (*in the doorway*): No no, my dear fellow, I don't want to be in the way. Besides, I'd like to see your wife for a bit. (*As he shuts the door he notices* MRS. LINDE.) Oh, I'm sorry—I'm in the way here, too.

NORA: Not in the least. (*introducing them*) This is Dr. Rank—Mrs. Linde.

RANK: Ah, now that's a name that I'm constantly hearing in this house. I think I passed you on the stairs as I came up.

MRS. LINDE: Yes, I don't like stairs—I have to take them very slowly.

RANK: Ah, some little internal weakness?

MRS. LINDE: Only overwork, I think.

RANK: Is that all? So you've come to town for a rest—at all the parties?

MRS. LINDE: I've come here to look for work.

RANK: Is that a wise remedy for overwork?

MRS. LINDE: One must live, Doctor.

RANK: Yes, there seems to be a general impression that it's necessary.

NORA: Now, Dr. Rank, you know you want to live, too.

RANK: Yes, indeed I do. However wretched I may be, I always want to prolong the agony as long as possible. All my patients have the same idea. And it's the same with people whose sickness is moral, too. At this very moment there's a moral invalid in there with Helmer, and—

MRS. LINDE (*softly*): Ah.

NORA: Whom do you mean?

RANK: Oh, you wouldn't know him—it's a lawyer named Krogstad. He's rotten to the core, but the first thing he said—as if it were something really important—was that he must live.

NORA: Oh. What did he want to see Torvald about?

RANK: I don't really know; all I heard was that it was something to do with the Bank.

NORA: I didn't know that Krog—that this lawyer had anything to do with the Bank.

RANK: Yes, he has some sort of post there. (*to* MRS. LINDE) I don't know if it's the same where you live, but here there are people who grub around sniffing out moral corruption, and when they've found it they put it in a good job somewhere where they can keep an eye on it. The honest man probably finds himself left out in the cold.

MRS. LINDE: Well, I suppose the sick need looking after.

RANK (*shrugging his shoulders*): There you are! That's the sort of theory that's turning the community into a regular hospital!

NORA, *deep in her own thoughts, suddenly gives a quiet laugh and claps her hands.*

RANK: Why do you laugh at that? Do you really know what the community is?

NORA: What do I care for your dreary old community? I was laughing at something quite different—something frightfully funny. Tell me, Dr. Rank, do all the people who work at the Bank depend on Torvald now?

RANK: Is that what you found so "frightfully funny"?

NORA (*smiling and humming*): Ah, that's my business—that's my business! (*pacing around the room*) Yes, it really is frightfully funny to think that we—that Torvald has all that power over so many people. (*taking a bag from her pocket*) Won't you have a macaroon, Dr. Rank?

RANK: Macaroons? Now, now! I thought they were forbidden here!

NORA: Yes, but these are some that Kristina gave me.

MRS. LINDE: What? But I . . . ?

NORA: No, no, don't be frightened; you weren't to know that Torvald had forbidden them. The thing is, he's afraid I shall spoil my teeth with them. But pooh—just this once! That's right, isn't it, Dr. Rank? Here! (*She pops a macaroon into his mouth.*) And now you, Kristina. And I'll have one as well—just a little one. Or two at the most. (*pacing about again*) Oh, I'm really terribly happy! Now there's just one thing in the world that I want terribly badly.

RANK: Oh? What is it?

NORA: It's something that I've been wanting terribly to say in front of Torvald.

RANK: Then why can't you say it?

NORA: Oh, I daren't—it's very bad.

MRS. LINDE: Bad?

RANK: Then you'd better not say it. Though surely to *us* . . . What is it that you want so much to say in front of Torvald?

NORA: I terribly want to say—"Well I'm damned!"

RANK: You must be mad!

MRS. LINDE: But, good gracious, Nora—

RANK: Well, here he comes. Say it.

NORA (*hiding the macaroons*): Sh! Sh!

HELMER *comes out of his room with a coat over his arm and a hat in his hand.*

NORA (*going to him*): Well, so you got rid of him, Torvald dear?

HELMER: Yes, he's just gone.

NORA: Let me introduce you: this is Kristina—she's come to town.

HELMER: Kristina . . . ? I'm sorry, I'm afraid I don't—

NORA: Mrs. Linde, Torvald dear! Kristina Linde.

HELMER: Oh yes—surely you and my wife were girls together?

MRS. LINDE: Yes, we knew each other in the old days.

NORA: And just think, she's come all this way to see you!

HELMER: To see *me?*

NORA: Kristina's frightfully clever at office work, and she wants terribly to work under a really able man so that she can learn more still. . . .

HELMER: That's very wise of you, Mrs. Linde.

NORA: So when she heard that you'd been made a Bank Manager—they had a telegram about it—she came down here as quickly as she could. You'll be able to do something for her, Torvald, won't you? Just to please me?

HELMER: Well, it's not impossible. . . . I take it that you're a widow, Mrs. Linde?

MRS. LINDE: Yes.

HELMER: And you've had commercial experience?

MRS. LINDE: A certain amount, yes.

HELMER: Ah, then it's highly probable that I shall be able to find a post for you.

NORA (*clapping her hands*): There you are! You see!

HELMER: You've come at just the right moment, Mrs. Linde . . .

MRS. LINDE: I can't tell you how grateful I am.

HELMER: Oh, there's no need . . . (*putting on his overcoat*) But now you must excuse me. . . .

RANK: Wait, I'll come with you. (*He gets his fur coat from the hall and warms it at the stove.*)

NORA: Don't be long, Torvald dear.

HELMER: I shan't be more than about an hour.

NORA: Are you going too, Kristina?

MRS. LINDE (*putting on her outdoor things*): Yes, I must go and look for a room.

HELMER: Then perhaps we can all go down the street together.

NORA (*helping her*): How tiresome that we're so short of room here—we couldn't possibly—

MRS. LINDE: Oh no, you mustn't think of it. Good-bye, Nora dear—and thank you.

NORA: Good-bye for the present—you'll come back this evening, won't you? And you, too, Dr. Rank. What? "If you feel up to it"? Of course you will. Wrap up well, now!

They go out into the hall still talking: the CHILDREN'S *voices are heard on the stairs.*

NORA: Here they are! Here they are!

She runs out and opens the door; the nurse, ANNA-MARIA, *comes in with the* CHILDREN.

Come in, come in! (*She stoops down and kisses them.*) Oh, my little darlings! Look at them, Kristina, aren't they sweet?

RANK: Don't stand there chattering in the draught!

HELMER: Come along, Mrs. Linde, this is no place for anyone but a mother!

He and DR. RANK *and* MRS. LINDE *go down the stairs. The* NURSE *comes into the room with the* CHILDREN, *and* NORA *follows, shutting the hall door.*

NORA: How nice and healthy you look! Oh, what pink cheeks—like apples and roses!

The CHILDREN *keep chattering to her during the following:*

Did you enjoy yourselves? That's good. And so you gave Emmy and Bob a ride on your sledge? Both together? Well, fancy that! What a big boy you are, Ivar. Oh, let me take her for a minute, Nanny—my little baby dolly! (*She takes the youngest from the* NURSE *and dances with her.*) Yes, yes, Mummy'll dance with Bob too! What? You've been snowballing? Oh, I wish I'd been there. No, leave them, Nanny, I'll take their things off. Yes, let me do it, it's such fun. You look frozen—there's some hot coffee for you on the stove in the next room.

The NURSE *goes into the room on the left.* NORA *takes off the* CHILDREN'S *outdoor things, throwing them down anywhere, while the* CHILDREN *all talk at once.*

NORA: Well! So a great big dog ran after you? But he didn't bite you? No, dogs don't bite dear little baby dollies! No, don't look inside those parcels, Ivar. What's in them? Ah, wouldn't you like to know? No, no, it isn't anything nice at all! What, you want a game? What shall we play? Hide and seek? Yes, let's play hide and seek. Bob, you hide first. Me? All right, I'll hide first.

She and the CHILDREN *play, laughing and shouting, both in this room and the room on the right. At last,* NORA *hides under the table. The* CHILDREN *come rushing in to look for her but they can't find her. Then, hearing her smothered laughter, they run to the table, lift the cloth, and see her. Loud shouts. She comes out on all fours as if to frighten them. Fresh shouts. Meanwhile there has been knocking on the front door, but no one has noticed it. Now the door half opens, revealing* KROGSTAD. *He waits a little as the game continues.*

KROGSTAD: Excuse me, Mrs. Helmer . . .

NORA (*with a stifled cry she turns and half rises*): Oh! What do you want?

KROGSTAD: I'm sorry; the front door was open. Somebody must have forgotten to shut it.

NORA (*getting up*): My husband is out, Mr. Krogstad.

KROGSTAD: Yes, I know.

NORA: Then . . . what do you want here?

KROGSTAD: A word with you.

NORA: With . . . ? (*quietly, to the* CHILDREN) Go to Nanny. What? No, the strange man isn't going to hurt Mummy—directly he's gone, we'll go on with our game. (*She takes the* CHILDREN *out to the room on the left, shutting the door after them. Then, tense and wary.*) You want to see me?

KROGSTAD: Yes, I do.

NORA: Today? But it isn't the first of the month yet. . . .

KROGSTAD: No, it's Christmas Eve. It all depends on you whether you have a happy Christmas or not.

NORA: What do you want? I can't manage any today—

KROGSTAD: We'll talk about that later; this is something different. Can you spare a moment?

NORA: Well, yes . . . I can, but—

KROGSTAD: Good. I was sitting in Olsen's restaurant, and I saw your husband go down the street—

NORA: Well?

KROGSTAD: —with a lady.

NORA: What of it?

KROGSTAD: May I be so bold as to ask if the lady was a Mrs. Linde?

NORA: She was.

KROGSTAD: She's just arrived in town?

NORA: Today, yes.

KROGSTAD: She's a great friend of yours?

NORA: Yes, she is. But I don't see—

KROGSTAD: I knew her once, too.

NORA: Yes, I know.

KROGSTAD: Oh? So you know about it? I thought so. All right, then I can ask you straight out: is Mrs. Linde to have a post at the Bank?

NORA: How dare you question me, Mr. Krogstad—one of my husband's subordinates. But since you ask, I'll tell you. Yes, Mrs. Linde is to have a post, and it was I who recommended her, Mr. Krogstad. So now you know.

KROGSTAD: Yes, I guessed as much.

NORA (*walking up and down*): So it looks as if one has a *little* influence—just because one's a woman, it doesn't necessarily mean that—and people in subordinate positions, Mr. Krogstad, should be careful not to offend anyone who—well—

KROGSTAD: . . . who has influence?

NORA: Exactly.

KROGSTAD (*changing his tone*): Mrs. Helmer . . . would you please be good enough to use your influence on my behalf?

NORA: How? What do you mean?

KROGSTAD: Would you be so kind as to see that I keep my subordinate position at the Bank?

NORA: What do you mean? Who's trying to take it away?

KROGSTAD: Oh, you needn't pretend to *me* that you don't know. I can quite see that it wouldn't be pleasant for your friend to have to keep running into me. What's more, I know now whom I shall have to thank for getting me dismissed.

NORA: But I assure you—

KROGSTAD: Oh, of course, of course. But don't let's beat about the bush—I advise you, while there's still time, to use your influence to prevent it.

NORA: But, Mr. Krogstad, I haven't any influence.

KROGSTAD: No? I thought you said just now—

NORA: I didn't mean it like that, of course. I? How do you think I could influence my husband in that sort of thing?

KROGSTAD: Well . . . I've known your husband since his student days—I don't think our noble Bank Manager is more inflexible than any other husband.

NORA: If you speak disrespectfully of my husband I shall show you the door!

KROGSTAD: How brave of you!

NORA: I'm not afraid of you any more. After the New Year I shall very quickly be free of the whole thing.

KROGSTAD (*controlling himself*): Listen to me, Mrs. Helmer. If need be, I shall fight to keep my little post at the Bank as I'd fight for my life.

NORA: So it seems.

KROGSTAD: It's not just for the money—that's the least important thing about it. No, there's something else . . . Well, I might as well tell you—it's this: of course you know—everyone does—that I got into trouble a few years ago.

NORA: I believe I heard something of the sort.

KROGSTAD: It never came to court, but since then it's been as if every way was closed to me—that's why I took to the business that you know about. I had to live somehow, and I think I can claim that I haven't been as bad as some. But now I want to give up all that sort of thing. My sons are growing up, and in fairness to them I must try to win back as much respect as I can in the town. This post at the Bank was the first step for me—and now your husband's going to kick me off the ladder again, back into the mud.

NORA: But honestly, Mr. Krogstad, there's nothing that I can do to help you.

KROGSTAD: That's because you don't want to. But I have ways of making you.

NORA: You won't tell my husband that I owe you money?

KROGSTAD: Ah . . . suppose I did?

NORA: That would be a vile thing to do. (*with tears in her voice*) I've been so proud of my secret; I couldn't bear to have him hear it like that—brutally and clumsily—and from *you.* It would put me in a most unpleasant position.

KROGSTAD: Only unpleasant?

NORA (*impetuously*): All right, then—tell him! But it'll be the worse for you, because my husband will see what a brute you are, and then you'll certainly lose your post.

KROGSTAD: I asked you if it was only domestic unpleasantness that you were afraid of?

NORA: If my husband finds out, naturally he'll pay you whatever I still owe, and then we'll have nothing more to do with you.

KROGSTAD (*taking a step toward her*): Listen, Mrs. Helmer; either my memory isn't very good, or you don't know much about business. I shall have to make things a little clearer to you.

NORA: How?

KROGSTAD: When your husband was ill you came to me to borrow twelve hundred dollars.

NORA: I didn't know where else to go.

KROGSTAD: I promised to find you the money—

NORA: And you did find it.

KROGSTAD: I promised to find you the money on certain conditions. At the time you were so worried about your husband's illness, and so anxious to get the money for your journey, that I don't think you paid much attention to the details—so it won't be out of place if I remind you of them. Well . . . I promised to find you the money against a note of hand which I drew up.

NORA: Yes, and which I signed.

KROGSTAD: Exactly. But below that I'd added a few lines making your father surety for the money. Your father was to sign this clause.

NORA: Was to? But he did sign.

KROGSTAD: I'd left the date blank—that's to say, your father was to fill in the date when he signed the paper. Do you remember?

NORA: Yes, I think so . . .

KROGSTAD: Then I gave you the document so that you could post it to your father. Is that correct?

NORA: Yes.

KROGSTAD: And of course you sent it at once, because only five or six days later you brought it back to me with your father's signature . . . and I handed over the money.

NORA: Well? Haven't I paid it off regularly?

KROGSTAD: Yes, fairly regularly. But—to get back to the point—you were going through a trying time just then, Mrs. Helmer?

NORA: I certainly was.

KROGSTAD: Your father was ill, I believe?

NORA: He was dying.

KROGSTAD: He died soon afterwards?

NORA: Yes.

KROGSTAD: Tell me, Mrs. Helmer, do you happen to remember the day he died? The day of the month, I mean?

NORA: Papa died on the twenty-ninth of September.

KROGSTAD: That is correct—I've confirmed that for myself. And that brings us to a curious thing (*producing a paper*) which I'm quite unable to explain.

NORA: What curious thing? I don't know of any—

KROGSTAD: The curious thing, Mrs. Helmer, is that your father signed this note of hand three days after his death.

NORA: How? I don't understand.

KROGSTAD: Your father died on the twenty-ninth of September. But look at this—your father has dated his signature the second of October. Isn't that a curious thing, Mrs. Helmer?

NORA *is silent.*

Can you explain it?

NORA *is still silent.*

It's odd, too, that the words October the second and the year aren't in your father's handwriting, but in a writing that I think I know. Well, of course, that could be explained—your father might have forgotten to date his signature, and someone else might have guessed at the date before they knew of his death. There's nothing wrong in that. It's the signature that really matters. That *is* genuine, isn't it, Mrs. Helmer? It really was your father himself who wrote his name there?

NORA (*after a moment's pause, throwing her head back and looking defiantly at him*): No, it was not. *I* wrote Papa's name.

KROGSTAD: Look, Mrs. Helmer, you know that that's a very dangerous admission?

NORA: Why? You'll soon get your money.

KROGSTAD: May I ask you something? Why didn't you send the paper to your father?

NORA: I couldn't; he was far too ill. If I'd asked him for his signature, I should have had to tell him what the money was for—and when he was so ill himself, I couldn't tell him that my husband's life was in danger—I couldn't possibly.

KROGSTAD: Then it would have been better for you if you'd given up your trip abroad.

NORA: I couldn't do that. The journey was to save my husband's life—how could I give it up?

KROGSTAD: But didn't it occur to you that you were tricking me?

NORA: I couldn't worry about that—I wasn't thinking about you at all. I couldn't bear the way you were so cold-blooded—the way you made difficulties although you knew how desperately ill my husband was.

KROGSTAD: Mrs. Helmer, you obviously don't realize what you've been guilty of; but let me tell you that the thing that I once did that ruined my reputation was nothing more—and nothing worse—than that.

NORA: You? Are you trying to tell me that you would have done a brave deed to save your wife's life?

KROGSTAD: The law is not concerned with motives.

NORA: Then it must be a very stupid law.

KROGSTAD: Stupid or not, it's the law that you'll be judged by if I produce this paper in court.

NORA: I simply don't believe that. Hasn't a daughter the right to protect her dying father from worry and anxiety? Hasn't a wife the right to save her husband's life? I don't know much about the law, but I'm quite certain that it must say somewhere that things like that are allowed. Don't you, a lawyer, know that? You must be a very stupid lawyer, Mr. Krogstad.

KROGSTAD: Possibly. But you'll admit that I do understand business—the sort of business that you and I have been engaged in? Very well, you do as you please. But I tell you this—if I'm to be flung out for the second time, you'll keep me company! (*He bows and goes out through the hall.*)

NORA (*after a moment's thought, with a toss of her head*): What nonsense! Trying to frighten me like that! I'm not as silly as all that. (*She starts to busy herself by tidying the children's clothes, but soon stops.*) But . . . No, it isn't possible . . . I did it for love!

CHILDREN (*at the door to the left*): Mamma, the strange man's just gone out of the front door.

NORA: Yes . . . yes, I know. Now, you're not to tell anyone about the strange man, do you hear? Not even Papa.

CHILDREN: No, Mamma. Will you come and play with us again now?

NORA: No—not just now.

CHILDREN: But, Mamma, you promised!

NORA: Yes, but now I can't. Run along. I'm busy—run along, there's good children. (*She pushes them gently into the other room and shuts the door after them. She sits on the sofa and, picking up her needlework, she does a stitch or two but soon stops.*) No! (*She throws down the work and, rising, goes to the hall door and calls.*) Helena—bring me the tree, please. (*Going to the table on the left, she opens the drawer, then pauses again.*) No! It's simply not possible!

MAID (*with the Christmas tree*): Where shall I put it, Madam?

NORA: Here, in the middle of the room.

MAID: Is there anything else you want?

NORA: No, thank you, I've got all I want.

The MAID, *having put the tree down, goes out.*

NORA (*busily decorating the tree*): A candle here . . . and flowers here. . . . That horrible man! It's all nonsense . . . nonsense, there's nothing in it! We shall have a lovely tree—I'll do all the things you like, Torvald, I'll sing and dance—

HELMER *comes in with a bundle of papers under his arm.*

NORA: Oh, are you back already?

HELMER: Yes. Has there been anyone here?

NORA: Here? No.

HELMER: That's odd; I saw Krogstad coming out of the gate.

NORA: Did you? Oh yes, that's right; Krogstad *was* here for a moment.

HELMER: Nora, I can see by your face that he's been here begging you to put in a good word for him.

NORA: Yes.

HELMER: And you were to make it look as if it was your own idea. You weren't to let me know that he'd been here. That was what he asked, wasn't it?

NORA: Yes, Torvald, but—

HELMER: Nora, Nora, would you lend yourself to that sort of thing? Talking to a man like that—making him promises? And, worst of all, telling me a lie!

NORA: A lie?

HELMER: Didn't you say that no one had been here? (*shaking a finger at her*) My little songbird mustn't ever do that again. A songbird must have a clear voice to sing with—no false notes. (*putting his arm around her*) That's true, isn't it? Yes, I knew it was. (*letting her go*) Now we won't say any more about it. (*sitting by the stove*) Ah, this is nice and comfortable! (*He glances through his papers.*)

NORA (*after working at the Christmas tree for a little*): Torvald?

HELMER: Yes?

NORA: I'm terribly looking forward to the day after tomorrow—the fancy-dress party at the Stenborgs.

HELMER: And I'm "terribly" curious to see what surprise you're planning for me.

NORA: Oh, it's so silly . . .

HELMER: What is?

NORA: I can't think of anything that'll do. Everything seems so stupid and pointless.

HELMER: So little Nora's realized that?

NORA (*behind his chair, with her arms on the chair-back*): Are you very busy, Torvald?

HELMER: Well . . .

NORA: What are all those papers?

HELMER: Bank business.

NORA: Already?

HELMER: I've asked the retiring Manager to give me full authority to make some necessary changes in the staff, and the working arrangements—

that'll take me all Christmas week. I want to have everything ready by New Year's Day.

NORA: So that was why poor Krogstad—

HELMER: Hm!

NORA (*still leaning over the chair-back, and gently stroking his hair*): If you hadn't been so busy, Torvald, I'd have asked you a terribly great favor. . . .

HELMER: Well, what is it? Tell me.

NORA: No one has such good taste as you have, and I do so want to look nice at the fancy-dress party. Torvald, couldn't you take me in hand and decide what I'm to go as—what my costume's to be?

HELMER: Aha! So my little obstinate one's out of her depth, and wants someone to rescue her?

NORA: Yes, Torvald, I can't do anything without you to help me.

HELMER: Well, well . . . I'll think about it. We'll find something.

NORA: Oh, that *is* nice of you! (*She goes to the Christmas tree again. Pause.*) How pretty these red flowers look. . . . Tell me about this Krogstad—was it really so bad, what he did?

HELMER: He forged a signature. Have you any idea what that means?

NORA: Mightn't he have done it from dire necessity?

HELMER: Possibly—or, like so many others, from sheer foolhardiness. Oh, I'm not so hard-hearted that I'd condemn a man outright for just a single slip.

NORA: No, you wouldn't, would you, Torvald?

HELMER: Many a man can redeem his character if he freely confesses his guilt and takes his punishment.

NORA: Punishment . . . ?

HELMER: But Krogstad did nothing of the sort—he tried to wriggle out of it with tricks and subterfuges. That's what has corrupted him.

NORA: Do you think that would . . . ?

HELMER: Just think how a guilty man like that must have to lie and cheat and play the hypocrite with everyone. How he must wear a mask even with those nearest and dearest to him—yes, even with his own wife and children. Yes, even with his children—that's the most dreadful thing, Nora.

NORA: Why?

HELMER: Because an atmosphere of lies like that infects and poisons the whole life of a home. In a house like that, every breath that the children take is filled with the germs of evil.

NORA (*closer behind him*): Are you certain of that?

HELMER: Oh, my dear, as a lawyer I've seen it so often; nearly all young men who go to the bad have had lying mothers.

NORA: Why only mothers?

HELMER: It's generally the fault of the mother, though of course a father can have the same effect—as every lawyer very well knows. And certainly for years this fellow Krogstad has been going home and poisoning his own children with lies and deceit. That's why I call him a moral outcast. (*holding out his hands to her*) So my darling little Nora must promise me not to plead his cause. Let's shake hands on that. Now then, what's this? Give me your hand. . . . That's better; now it's a bargain. I tell you, it'd be quite impossible for me to work with him; when I'm near people like that, I actually feel physically ill.

NORA (*withdrawing her hand and going over to the far side of the Christmas tree*): How hot it is in here! And I have so much to see to.

HELMER (*rising and collecting his papers*): Yes, and I must try to look through a few of these before dinner. And I'll think about your fancy-dress, too. And perhaps I'll have something in gold paper to hang on the Christmas tree. (*taking her head in his hands*) My darling little songbird! (*He goes to his room, shutting the door behind him.*)

NORA (*in a hushed voice, after a moment*): Oh no! It can't be true. . . . No, it's not possible. It *can't* be possible!

NURSE (*at the door on the left*): The children want to come in to Mamma—they're asking so prettily.

NORA: No! No! Don't let them come near me! Keep them with you, Nanny.

NURSE: Yes Ma'am. (*She shuts the door.*)

NORA (*white with fear*): Corrupt my little children—poison my home? (*She pauses, then throws up her head.*) That's not true! It could never, never be true.

Act Two

The same room. In the corner by the piano stands the Christmas tree; it is stripped and dishevelled, with the stumps of burnt-out candles. NORA'S *outdoor clothes are on the sofa.*

NORA, *alone in the room, walks about restlessly. Eventually she stops by the sofa and picks up her cloak.*

NORA (*letting the cloak fall again*): Someone's coming! (*She goes to the door to listen.*) No—there's no one there. Of course no one would come today—not on Christmas Day. Nor tomorrow either. But perhaps . . . (*She opens the door and looks out.*) No, there's nothing in the letter-box—it's quite empty. (*coming back into the room*) What nonsense—he can't really have meant it. A thing like that *couldn't* happen. It isn't possible—I have three little children!

The NURSE *comes in from the room on the left, with a huge cardboard box.*

NURSE: I've found the box with the fancy-dress at last.

NORA: Thank you; put it on the table.

NURSE (*doing so*): But it's in a terrible state.

NORA: I should like to tear it all to pieces.

NURSE: Heaven forbid! It can soon be put right—it only needs a little patience.

NORA: Yes, I'll go and get Mrs. Linde to help me.

NURSE: You're not going out again—in this awful weather? You'll catch your death of cold, Miss Nora, Ma'am!

NORA: Well, there are worse things than that. How are the children?

NURSE: The poor little mites are playing with their presents, but—

NORA: Do they ask for me much?

NURSE: You see, they're so used to having their Mamma with them.

NORA: But, Nanny, I *can't* be with them like I used to.

NURSE: Oh well, young children'll get used to anything.

NORA: Do you think so? Do you think they'd forget their Mamma if she went away altogether?

NURSE: Went away altogether? But bless my soul . . . !

NORA: Tell me, Nanny . . . I've often wondered, how did you ever have the heart to hand over your child to strangers?

NURSE: But I had to, so that I could come and be Nanny to my little Nora.

NORA: Yes, but how could you *want* to?

NURSE: When I had the chance of such a good place? Any poor girl who'd got into trouble would be glad to. And that blackguard of a man never did a thing for me.

NORA: I suppose your daughter's quite forgotten you?

NURSE: No, indeed she hasn't. She wrote to me when she was confirmed, and again when she got married.

NORA (*putting her arms round her*): Dear old Nanny, you were a wonderful mother to me when I was little.

NURSE: Poor little Nora—she hadn't any other mother but me.

NORA: And if *my* babies hadn't any other mother, I know you'd . . . Oh, I'm talking nonsense. (*opening the box*) Go to them now; I must just—You'll see how fine I shall look tomorrow.

NURSE: I'm sure there won't be anyone in all the party as fine as you, Miss Nora, Ma'am. (*She goes out to the room on the left.*)

NORA (*starting to unpack the box, but soon pushing it away*): Oh, if only I dared go out! If I could be sure that no one would come—that nothing would happen here in the meantime. . . . Don't be so silly—no one will come. I just mustn't think about it. I'll brush the muff. Pretty, pretty gloves! Don't think about it—don't think! One . . . two . . . three . . . four . . . five . . . six—(*She screams.*) Ah, they're coming!

She starts for the door, but stands irresolute. MRS. LINDE *comes in from the hall, where she has left her street clothes.*

NORA: Oh, it's you, Kristina! There isn't anyone else out there? Oh, it was good of you to come!

MRS. LINDE: They told me you'd been over to ask for me.

NORA: Yes, I was just passing. Actually, there's something you could help me with. Come and sit on the sofa. Look, the people upstairs, the Stenborgs, are having a fancy-dress party tomorrow night, and Torvald wants me to go as a Neopolitan fisher-girl and dance the tarantella that I learned in Capri.

MRS. LINDE: I see, you're going to give a real performance?

NORA: Yes, Torvald says I ought to. Look, here's the costume—Torvald had it made for me when we were out there, but it's so torn now—I really don't know—

MRS. LINDE: Oh, we can easily put that right—it's just that some of the trimming's come undone in places. Have you got a needle and cotton? There, that's all we want.

NORA: Oh, this *is* kind of you.

MRS. LINDE (*as she sews*): So tomorrow you'll be all dressed up? I tell you what, Nora, I'll drop in for a moment and see you in all your finery. But I'm quite forgetting to thank you for a lovely evening yesterday.

NORA (*getting up and crossing the room*): Oh, yesterday . . . I didn't think it was as nice as usual. I wish you'd come up to town earlier, Kristina. Yes, Torvald certainly knows how to make a house attractive and comfortable.

MRS. LINDE: And so do you, if you ask *me,* or you wouldn't be your father's daughter. But tell me, is Dr. Rank always as depressed as he was last night?

NORA: No, it was worse than usual last night. But he's really very ill, poor man, he has consumption of the spine. The fact is, his father was a horrible man who had mistresses and that sort of thing, so, you see, the son's been delicate all his life.

MRS. LINDE (*putting down her sewing*): But, dearest Nora, how do you come to know about things like that?

NORA (*walking about*): Pooh—when you've had three children, you get visits from—from women with a certain amount of medical knowledge— and they gossip about these things.

MRS. LINDE (*after a short silence—sewing again*): Does Dr. Rank come here every day?

NORA: Oh yes, he and Torvald have been friends all their lives, and he's a great friend of mine too. Why, Dr. Rank's almost one of the family.

MRS. LINDE: But tell me, is he quite sincere? I mean doesn't he rather like saying things to please people?

NORA: Not in the least. Whatever makes you think that?

MRS. LINDE: Well, when you introduced us yesterday, he said he'd often heard my name in this house, but I noticed later that your husband had no idea who I was. So how could Dr. Rank . . . ?

NORA: Yes, that's quite right, Kristina. You see, Torvald's so incredibly fond of me that he wants to keep me all to himself, as he says. In the early days he used to get quite jealous if I even mentioned people I'd liked back at home, so of course I gave it up. But I often talk to Dr. Rank, because, you see, he likes to hear about them.

MRS. LINDE: Look, Nora, in lots of things you're still a child. I'm older than you in many ways and I've had a little more experience. There's something I'd like to say to you: you ought to stop all this with Dr. Rank.

NORA: What ought I to stop?

MRS. LINDE: Well . . . two things, I think. Yesterday you were talking about a rich admirer who was going to bring you money—

NORA: Yes, but he doesn't exist—unfortunately. But what about it?

MRS. LINDE: Is Dr. Rank rich?

NORA: Oh yes.

MRS. LINDE: And has no one to provide for?

NORA: No one; but—

MRS. LINDE: And he comes to the house every day?

NORA: Yes, I just said so.

MRS. LINDE: How can a man of his breeding be so tactless?

NORA: I simply don't know what you mean.

MRS. LINDE: Don't pretend, Nora. Do you think I don't know whom you borrowed that twelve hundred dollars from?

NORA: Have you gone completely mad? How could you think a thing like that? From a friend who comes here every single day? That would have been an absolutely impossible situation.

MRS. LINDE: It really wasn't him?

NORA: No, I promise you. Why, it would never have entered my head for a moment. Besides, in those days he hadn't the money to lend—he came into it later.

MRS. LINDE: Well, Nora dear, I think that was lucky for you.

NORA: No, it would never have entered my head to ask Dr. Rank. Though I'm quite sure that if I *were* to ask him . . .

MRS. LINDE: But of course you wouldn't.

NORA: Of course not. I can't imagine that there'd ever be any need. But I'm quite sure that if I told Dr. Rank—

MRS. LINDE: Behind your husband's back?

NORA: I must get clear of this other thing—that's behind his back too. I must get clear of that.

MRS. LINDE: Yes, that's what I was saying yesterday, but—

NORA (*pacing up and down*): A man can straighten out these things so much better than a woman . . .

MRS. LINDE: Her husband, yes.

NORA: Nonsense. (*coming to a halt*) When you've paid off everything you owe, you do get your bond back, don't you?

MRS. LINDE: Of course.

NORA: And you can tear it into little pieces and burn it—the horrid filthy thing?

MRS. LINDE (*giving her a penetrating look, she puts down her sewing and rises slowly*): Nora, you're hiding something from me.

NORA: Is it as obvious as all that?

MRS. LINDE: Something's happened to you since yesterday morning. Nora, what is it?

NORA (*going to her*): Kristina—(*listening*) Sh! Here's Torvald coming back. Look, go in and sit with the children for a bit—Torvald can't bear to see dressmaking. Let Nanny help you.

MRS. LINDE (*picking up a pile of things*): All right then; but I'm not going away till we've talked the whole thing over.

She goes out to the left as HELMER *comes in from the hall.*

NORA (*going to him*): Oh, Torvald dear, I've been so longing for you to come back.

HELMER: Was that the dressmaker?

NORA: No, it was Kristina—she's helping me to mend my costume. You know, I'm going to look so nice. . . .

HELMER: Now wasn't that a good idea of mine?

NORA: Splendid. But wasn't it nice of me to do as you said?

HELMER (*lifting her chin*): Nice? To do what your husband says? All right, little scatterbrain, I know you didn't mean it like that. But don't let me interrupt you—I know you'll be wanting to try it on.

NORA: I suppose you've got work to do?

HELMER: Yes (*showing her a bundle of papers*); look, I've been down to the Bank. (*He starts to go to his study.*)

NORA: Torvald . . .

HELMER (*stopping*): Yes?

NORA: If your little squirrel were to ask you very prettily for something . . .

HELMER: Well?

NORA: Would you do it?

HELMER: Well, naturally I should have to know what it is, first.

NORA: Your squirrel will scamper about and do all her tricks, if you'll be nice and do what she asks.

HELMER: Out with it, then.

NORA: Your skylark'll sing all over the house—up and down the scale . . .

HELMER: Oh well, my skylark does that anyhow!

NORA: I'll be a fairy and dance on a moonbeam for you, Torvald.

HELMER: Nora, you surely don't mean that matter you mentioned this morning?

NORA (*nearer*): Yes, Torvald, I really do beg you—

HELMER: I'm surprised at your bringing that up again.

NORA: Oh, but you must do as I ask—you must let Krogstad keep his place at the Bank.

HELMER: My dear Nora, it's his place that I'm giving to Mrs. Linde.

NORA: Yes, that's terribly nice of you. But you could dismiss some other clerk instead of Krogstad.

HELMER: Now, you're just being extremely obstinate. Because you're irresponsible enough to go and promise to put in a word for him, you expect me to—

NORA: No, it isn't that, Torvald—it's for your own sake. The man writes for the most scurrilous newspapers—you told me so yourself—there's no knowing what harm he could do you. I'm simply frightened to death of him. . . .

HELMER: Ah, now I understand; you remember what happened before, and that frightens you.

NORA: What do you mean?

HELMER: You're obviously thinking of your father.

NORA: Yes—yes, that's it. Just remember the wicked things they put in the papers about Papa—how cruelly they slandered him. I believe they'd have had him dismissed if the Ministry hadn't sent you to look into it, and if you hadn't been so kind and helpful to him.

HELMER: Dear little Nora, there's a considerable difference between your father and me. Your father's reputation as an official was not above suspicion—mine is, and I hope it will continue to be as long as I hold this position.

NORA: But you never know what harm people can do. We could live so happily and peacefully now, you and I and the children, Torvald, without a care in the world in our comfortable home. That's why I do implore you—

HELMER: But it's precisely by pleading for him that you make it impossible for me to keep him. They know already at the Bank that I mean to dismiss Krogstad; suppose it were to get about that the new Manager had let himself be influenced by his wife. . . .

NORA: Well, would that matter?

HELMER: No, of course not! So long as an obstinate little woman got her own way! So I'm to make a laughingstock of myself before the whole staff—with everybody saying that I can be swayed by all sorts of outside influences? I should soon have to face the consequences, I can tell you. Besides, there's one thing which makes it quite impossible for Krogstad to stay at the Bank so long as I'm Manager.

NORA: What?

HELMER: Perhaps at a pinch I might have overlooked his moral failings—

NORA: Yes, Torvald, couldn't you?

HELMER: And I hear that he's quite a good worker, too. But he was at school with me—it was one of those unfortunate friendships that one so often comes to regret later in life. I may as well tell you frankly that we were on Christian-name terms, and he's tactless enough to keep it up still—in front of everyone! In fact, he seems to think he has a *right* to be familiar with me, and out he comes with "Torvald this" and "Torvald that" all the time. I tell you, it's most unpleasant for me—he'll make my position in the Bank quite intolerable.

NORA: You surely can't mean that, Torvald!

HELMER: Oh? Why not?

NORA: Well—that's such a petty reason.

HELMER: What do you mean? Petty? Do you think I'm petty?

NORA: No, Torvald dear—far from it; that's just why—

HELMER: Never mind! You said my motives were petty, so I must be petty too. Petty! Very well, we'll settle this matter once and for all. (*He goes to the hall door and calls.*) Helena!

NORA: What are you going to do?

HELMER (*searching among his papers*): Settle things.

The MAID *comes in.*

Here, take this letter downstairs at once, find a messenger, and get him to deliver it. Immediately, mind. The address is on it. Wait—here's the money.

MAID: Yes, sir. (*She goes with the letter.*)

HELMER (*collecting his papers*): There, little Miss Stubborn!

NORA (*breathless*): Torvald . . . what was in that letter?

HELMER: Krogstad's notice.

NORA: Call it back, Torvald—there's still time. Oh Torvald, call it back, for my sake—for your own sake—for the children's sake. Listen, Torvald, you don't know what that letter can do to us all.

HELMER: It's too late.

NORA: Yes . . . it's too late.

HELMER: My dear Nora, I can forgive your anxiety—though actually it's rather insulting to me. Oh yes, it is. Isn't it insulting to believe that I could be afraid of some wretched scribbler's revenge? Still, it's a very touching proof of your love for me, so I forgive you. (*He takes her in his arms.*) Now, my own darling Nora, that's all settled. Whatever happens, when it comes to the point you can be quite sure that I shall have the necessary courage and strength. You'll see that I'm man enough to take it all on myself.

NORA (*horror-struck*): What do you mean?

HELMER: Exactly what I say.

NORA (*recovering*): You shall never never have to do that.

HELMER: Very well, Nora, then we shall share it as man and wife; that's what we'll do. (*caressing her*) Are you happy now? There—there—there— don't look like a little frightened dove—the whole thing's just sheer imagination. Now you must rehearse your tarantella—with the tambourine. I'll go and sit in the inner room and shut the doors, so you can make all the noise you like—I shan't hear a thing. (*turning in the doorway*) And when Dr. Rank comes, tell him where I am. (*Taking his papers, he gives her a nod and goes into his room, shutting the door behind him.*)

NORA (*half crazy with fear, she stands as if rooted to the spot and whispers*): He'd really do it—he'd do it! He'd do it in spite of everything. No—never in the world! Anything rather than that! There must be some way out— some help.

There is a ring at the door.

Dr. Rank! Yes, anything rather than that—anything—whatever it is.

Passing her hands over her face, she pulls herself together and goes and opens the hall door. DR. RANK *is standing there hanging up his fur coat. During the following scene it begins to grow dark.*

NORA: Good afternoon, Dr. Rank—I recognized your ring. But you mustn't go in to Torvald now, I think he's got some work to finish.

RANK: What about you?

NORA (*shutting the door after him as he comes into the room*): Oh, I always have time for you—you know that.

RANK: Thank you. I shall take advantage of that for as long as I'm able.

NORA: What do you mean by that? As long as you're able?

RANK: Yes . . . does that alarm you?

NORA: It seemed such an odd way to put it. Is anything going to happen?

RANK: Yes . . . something that I've been expecting for a long time—though I never really thought it'd come quite so soon.

NORA (*clutching his arm*): What have you just learned? Dr. Rank, you must tell me!

RANK (*sitting by the stove*): The sands are running out for me. . . . There's nothing to be done about it.

NORA (*with a sigh of relief*): Then it's *you* . . . !

RANK: Who else? There's no point in deceiving myself—I'm the most wretched of all my patients, Mrs. Helmer. These last few days I've been holding an audit of my internal economy. Bankrupt! In less than a month, perhaps, I shall lie rotting in the churchyard.

NORA: Oh no—that's a horrible thing to say.

RANK: The thing itself is damnably horrible. But worst of all is the horror that must be gone through first. There's still one more test to make, and when I've finished *that* I shall know pretty well when the final disintegration will begin. But there's something I want to say to you; Helmer's too sensitive to be able to face anything ugly—I won't have him in my sick-room.

NORA: But, Dr. Rank—

RANK: I won't have him there—not on any account. I shall lock the door against him. As soon as I'm quite certain that the worst has come, I shall send you my card with a black cross on it and then you'll know that my disgusting end has begun.

NORA: No, you're really being absurd today—and just when I so wanted you to be in a particularly good mood.

RANK: What, with death just round the corner? And when it's to pay for someone else's sins! Where's the justice in that? Yet in one way or another there isn't a single family where some such inexorable retribution isn't being exacted.

NORA (*stopping her ears*): Nonsense! Cheer up—cheer up!

RANK: Yes, indeed, the whole thing's nothing but a joke! My poor innocent spine must pay for my father's amusements as a gay young subaltern.

NORA (*by the table on the left*): He was too fond of asparagus and *foie gras*—isn't that it?

RANK: Yes, and truffles.

NORA: Truffles, yes. And oysters, too, I suppose?

RANK: Oysters? Oh yes, certainly oysters.

NORA: And then all that port and champagne. What a shame that all those nice things should attack the bones.

RANK: Especially when the unfortunate bones that they attack never had the least enjoyment out of them.

NORA: Yes, that's the saddest part of all.

RANK (*with a searching look at her*): Hm! . . .

NORA (*after a moment*): Why did you smile?

RANK: No, it's you who were laughing.

NORA: No, you smiled, Dr. Rank.

RANK (*getting up*): You're more of a rascal than I thought.

NORA: I'm in a ridiculous mood today.

RANK: So it seems.

NORA (*putting both hands on his shoulders*): Dear, dear Dr. Rank, you mustn't die and leave Torvald and me.

RANK: Oh, you'd soon get over it—those who go away are quickly forgotten.

NORA (*looking at him anxiously*): Do you believe that?

RANK: People make new friends, and then . . .

NORA: Who makes new friends?

RANK: You and Torvald will, when I'm gone. It looks to me as if *you're* starting already. What was that Mrs. Linde doing here last night?

NORA: Oh, surely you're not jealous of poor Kristina.

RANK: Yes, I am. She'll take my place in this house. After I've gone, I expect that woman will—

NORA: Sh! Not so loud—she's in there!

RANK: There you are! She's here again today.

NORA: Only to mend my dress. Good gracious, you *are* being absurd. (*sitting on the sofa*) Now be nice, Dr. Rank, and tomorrow you'll see how beautifully I shall dance, and you can tell yourself that it's all for you—and for Torvald too, of course. (*taking various things out of the box*) Come and sit here, Dr. Rank, and I'll show you something.

RANK: What is it?

NORA: Look here. Look.

RANK: Silk stockings.

NORA: Flesh colored—aren't they lovely? The light's bad in here now, but tomorrow . . . No, no, no, you must only look at the feet. Oh well, you may see the rest, too.

RANK: Hm . . .

NORA: Why are you looking so critical? Don't you think they'll fit?

RANK: I can't possibly give you an opinion on that.

NORA (*looking at him for a moment*): You ought to be ashamed of yourself! (*She flips him lightly on the cheek with the stockings.*) Take that! (*She rolls them up again.*)

RANK: What other pretty things have you to show me?

NORA: You shan't see another thing—you've been very naughty. (*She hums a little as she rummages among her things.*)

RANK (*after a short pause*): When I sit here like this talking to you so intimately, I can't imagine—no, I really can't—what would have become of me if I hadn't had this house to come to.

NORA (*smiling*): I believe you really do feel at home with us.

RANK (*more quietly, looking straight in front of him*): And to have to leave it all!

NORA: Nonsense, you're not going to leave us.

RANK (*as before*): Not to be able to leave behind even the smallest token of gratitude—hardly even a passing regret. Nothing but an empty place that the next person to come along will fill just as well.

NORA: Suppose I were to ask you for a . . . No . . .

RANK: For a what?

NORA: For a great proof of your friendship.

RANK: Yes.

NORA: No, I mean a terribly great favor.

RANK: I should be very happy if—just for once—you'd give me the chance.

NORA: Ah, but you don't know what it is.

RANK: Tell me, then.

NORA: No, Dr. Rank, I can't. It's something really enormous—not just advice or help, but a really great favor.

RANK: The greater the better. I can't think what it can be, so tell me. Don't you trust me?

NORA: There's no one else I'd trust more than you. I know you're my best, most faithful friend, so I'll tell you. . . . Well, Dr. Rank—it's something you must help me to stave off. You know how much—how incredibly deeply—Torvald loves me. He wouldn't hesitate for a moment to give his life for me.

RANK (*leaning nearer to her*): Nora . . . Do you think he's the only one?

NORA (*with a slight start*): The only one . . . ?

RANK: Who'd gladly give his life for you?

NORA (*sadly*): Ah . . .

RANK: I promised myself that I'd tell you before I went away, and I could never have a better opportunity. Well, Nora, now you know. And you know, too, that you can trust me—more than anyone else.

NORA (*calmly and evenly; rising*): I must go.

RANK (*making way for her, but still sitting*): Nora . . .

NORA (*in the hall doorway*): Helena, bring the lamp. (*going to the stove*) Oh, dear Dr. Rank, that was really horrid of you.

RANK (*rising*): To have loved you as deeply as anyone else—was that horrid?

NORA: No . . . but to go and tell me so. There was really no need to do that.

RANK: What do you mean? Did you know?

The MAID *brings in the lamp, puts it on the table, and goes again.*

RANK: Nora—Mrs. Helmer—I ask you: did you know?

NORA: Oh, how can I say if I knew or didn't know? I've really no idea. How could you be so clumsy, Dr. Rank? When everything was going so well. . . .

RANK: Well, at any rate you know that I'm at your service—body and soul. So won't you say what it is?

NORA (*looking at him*): After what's happened?

RANK: Please—please tell me what it is.

NORA: I can never tell you now.

RANK: Please. You mustn't punish me like this. If you'll let me, I promise to do anything for you that a man can.

NORA: There's nothing you can do for me now. Besides, I certainly don't need any help—it was all my imagination, really it was. Honestly. (*smiling*) You're a fine one, Dr. Rank! Aren't you ashamed of yourself, now that the lamp's come on?

RANK: No . . . not really. But perhaps I ought to go—for good.

NORA: No. You certainly mustn't do that—of course you must come here just as usual. You know Torvald couldn't get on without you.

RANK: But what about you?

NORA: Oh, I'm always tremendously glad to see you.

RANK: That's just what misled me. You're a mystery to me. . . . I've sometimes thought you'd as soon be with me as with Helmer.

NORA: You see, there are some people that one loves, and others that perhaps one would rather be with.

RANK: Yes, there's something in that.

NORA: When I lived at home, naturally I loved Papa best, but I always found it terribly amusing to slip into the servants' hall, because they always talked about such interesting things, and they never lectured me at all.

RANK: Ah, and now I've taken their place?

NORA (*jumping up and going over to him*): Oh, dear kind Dr. Rank, that isn't what I meant at all. But I'm sure you can see that being with Torvald is very like being with Papa.

The MAID *comes in from the hall.*

MAID: Excuse me, Madam. . . . (*She whispers to* NORA *as she hands her a card.*)

NORA (*glancing at the card*): Oh! (*She puts it in her pocket.*)

RANK: Is there anything wrong?

NORA: No, no, not in the least. It's only something . . . it's my new dress.

RANK: But . . . ? Surely your dress is out there?

NORA: Ah, that one, yes. But this is another one that I've ordered—I don't want Torvald to know. . . .

RANK: Aha! So *that's* your great secret?

NORA: Yes, of course. Go in to Torvald—he's in the inner room—keep him there till . . .

RANK: Don't worry, I shan't let him escape. (*He goes into* HELMER'S *room.*)

NORA (*to the* MAID): Is he waiting in the kitchen?

MAID: Yes, Madam, he came up the back stairs.

NORA: But didn't you tell him there was someone here?

MAID: Yes, but it wasn't any good.

NORA: He wouldn't go away?

MAID: No, he won't go till he's seen you, Madam.

NORA: Oh, all right, let him come in. Quietly, though. Helena, you mustn't mention this to anyone—it's a surprise for my husband.

MAID: Yes, I understand. (*She goes.*)

NORA: Oh, this is dreadful—it's going to happen after all. No, no, no, it *can't*—I won't let it!

She goes and pushes the bolt home on HELMER'S *door. The* MAID *opens the hall door to let* KROGSTAD *in, and shuts it after him. He is wearing travelling clothes, high boots, and a fur cap.*

NORA (*going to him*): Keep your voice down—my husband's at home.

KROGSTAD: What of it?

NORA: What do you want?

KROGSTAD: To find out something.

NORA: Be quick, then; what is it?

KROGSTAD: You know that I've been dismissed?

NORA: I couldn't stop it, Mr. Krogstad. I did absolutely everything I could for you, but it was no good.

KROGSTAD: Your husband can't love you very much, can he? He knows that I can expose you, and yet he dares to—

NORA: You surely don't imagine that he knows about it?

KROGSTAD: Well, no—I didn't really think so; it wouldn't be at all like our worthy Torvald Helmer to have so much courage.

NORA: Kindly show some respect for my husband, Mr. Krogstad.

KROGSTAD: But of course—all the respect he deserves. As you seem so anxious to keep things secret, I presume that you have a rather clearer idea than you had yesterday of what it is that you've actually done.

NORA: Clearer than you could ever make it.

KROGSTAD: Oh yes, I'm such a stupid lawyer!

NORA: What do you want?

KROGSTAD: Only to see how things stood with you, Mrs. Helmer. I've been thinking about you all day. Even a mere cashier, a scribbler, a—well, a man like me, has a certain amount of what is called "feeling," you know.

NORA: Then show it. Think of my little children.

KROGSTAD: Have you or your husband ever thought of mine? But never mind that; I only wanted to tell you that you needn't take all this too seriously—I shan't make any accusation for the present.

NORA: No, of course not—I didn't think you would.

KROGSTAD: It can all be settled quite amicably. Nothing need come out—it can just be arranged between us three.

NORA: My husband must never know anything about it.

KROGSTAD: How can you stop it? Unless, perhaps, you can pay off the rest of the debt.

NORA: Well, not at the moment.

KROGSTAD: Then perhaps you've found some way to raise the money within the next day or two.

NORA: No way that I'd use.

KROGSTAD: Well, it wouldn't have helped you, anyhow. Even if you were to stand there with a mint of money in your hand, you wouldn't get your bond back from me.

NORA: What are you going to do with it? Tell me.

KROGSTAD: Just keep it—have it in my possession. No one who isn't concerned need know anything about it. So if you have any desperate plan—

NORA: I have.

KROGSTAD: —If you've thought of running away from your home—

NORA: I have.

KROGSTAD: —or of anything worse—

NORA: How did you know?

KROGSTAD: —you'd better give up the idea.

NORA: How did you know that I'd thought of *that?*

KROGSTAD: Most of us think of that at first. I thought of it, too—only I hadn't the courage.

NORA (*dully*): Nor had I.

KROGSTAD (*relieved*): No, you haven't the courage either, have you?

NORA: No, I haven't—I haven't.

KROGSTAD: Besides, it would have been a very stupid thing to do. You've only got just one domestic storm to go through, then . . . I have a letter to your husband in my pocket.

NORA: Telling him everything?

KROGSTAD: In the gentlest possible way.

NORA (*quickly*): He must never see it. Tear it up. I'll get the money somehow.

KROGSTAD: Excuse me, Mrs. Helmer, but I believed I told you just now—

NORA: Oh, I don't mean the money I owe you. Tell me how much you're asking from my husband, and I'll get it.

KROGSTAD: I'm not asking your husband for any money.

NORA: What are you asking, then?

KROGSTAD: I'll tell you. I want to get back my standing in the world, Mrs. Helmer; I want to get on, and that's where your husband's going to help me. For the last eighteen months I haven't touched anything dishonest, and all that time I've been struggling against the most difficult conditions. I was prepared to work my way up step by step. Now I'm being thrown down again, and it's not going to be good enough for me to be taken back as a favor. I want to get on, I tell you; I want to get back into the Bank—and in a better job. Your husband must make one for me.

NORA: He'll never do that.

KROGSTAD: I know him—he'll do it! He daren't so much as murmur. And once I'm in there with him, then you'll see! Inside a year, I shall be the Manager's right-hand man. It'll be Nils Krogstad who runs the Bank, not Torvald Helmer.

NORA: That'll never happen as long as you live.

KROGSTAD: Do you mean that you'll—

NORA: Yes, I have the courage now.

KROGSTAD: Oh, you can't frighten me! A fine pampered lady like you—

NORA: You'll see—you'll see!

KROGSTAD: Under the ice, perhaps? Down into the cold black water? And then in the spring you'd float up to the top, ugly, hairless, unrecognizable—

NORA: You can't frighten me.

KROGSTAD: Nor can you frighten me. People don't do such things, Mrs. Helmer. And what good would it be, anyhow? I'd still have the letter in my pocket!

NORA: Still? Even if I weren't . . .

KROGSTAD: You forget that *then* your reputation would be in my hands.

NORA *stands speechless, looking at him.*

KROGSTAD: Yes, now you've been warned, so don't do anything stupid. I shall expect to hear from Helmer as soon as he gets my letter. And remember, it's your husband who's forced me to do this sort of thing again. I shall never forgive him for that. Good-bye, Mrs. Helmer. (*He goes out into the hall.*)

NORA (*going to the hall door and opening it a little to listen*): He's going! He hasn't left the letter. No, no, it couldn't happen! (*She opens the door inch by inch.*) Listen—he's standing just outside—he's not going down the stairs. . . . Has he changed his mind? Is he . . . ?

A letter falls into the box. KROGSTAD's *footsteps are heard fading away down the staircase.*

NORA (*With a stifled cry, runs over to the sofa table. A short pause.*): It's in the letter-box! (*creeping stealthily back to the hall door*) Yes, it's there. Oh, Torvald . . . Torvald—there's no hope for us now!

MRS. LINDE (*coming in from the left with the dress*): There—I don't think there's anything else that wants mending. Let's try it on.

NORA (*in a hoarse whisper*): Kristina, come here.

MRS. LINDE (*throwing the dress on the sofa*): What's the matter? What's upset you so?

NORA: Come here. Do you see that letter? There, look—through the glass of the letter-box.

MRS. LINDE: I can see it—Well?

NORA: That letter's from Krogstad.

MRS. LINDE: Nora . . . it was Krogstad who lent you the money!

NORA: Yes. And now Torvald'll find out everything.

MRS. LINDE: But, Nora, believe me, that'll be best for both of you.

NORA: There's something that you don't know. I forged a signature.

MRS. LINDE: Good heavens . . . !

NORA: There's just one thing I want to say, Kristina, and you shall be my witness.

MRS. LINDE: Witness? But what am I to—

NORA: If I were to go mad—as I easily might—

MRS. LINDE: Nora!

NORA: Or if anything else were to happen to me, so that I shouldn't be here—

MRS. LINDE: Nora, Nora, you must be out of your senses!

NORA: And in case there was someone else who tried to take it all on himself—all the blame, you understand—

MRS. LINDE: Yes . . . but how can you think . . . ?

NORA: —then, Kristina, you must bear witness that it isn't true. I'm perfectly sane, and I know exactly what I'm doing now, and I tell you this: no one else knew anything about it—I did it all by myself. Remember that.

MRS. LINDE: Of course I will. But I don't understand.

NORA: How could you understand this? We're going to see—a miracle.

MRS. LINDE: A miracle?

NORA: Yes, a miracle. But it's so dreadful. Kristina, it *mustn't* happen—not for anything in the world.

MRS. LINDE: I'm going straight round to talk to Krogstad.

NORA: No, don't go to him, he might do you some harm.

MRS. LINDE: There was a time when he would gladly have done anything for me.

NORA: Krogstad?

MRS. LINDE: Where does he live?

NORA: How should I know? Wait—(*feeling in her pocket*)—here's his card. But the letter—the letter . . . !

HELMER (*from inside his room, knocking on the door*): Nora!

NORA (*with a frightened cry*): What is it? What do you want?

HELMER (*off*): All right, there's nothing to be frightened of; we're not coming in. You've locked the door—are you trying on your dress?

NORA: Yes, I'm trying it on. I look so nice in it, Helmer.

MRS. LINDE (*having read the card*): He lives only just round the corner.

NORA: Yes, but it's no good; there's no hope for us now—the letter's in the box.

MRS. LINDE: And your husband has the key!

NORA: He always keeps it.

MRS. LINDE: Krogstad must ask for his letter back—unopened. He must find some excuse.

NORA: But this is just the time when Torvald always—

MRS. LINDE: Put him off. I'll be back as soon as I can. Go in to him now. (*She hurries out through the hall.*)

NORA (*going to* HELMER'S *door, unlocking it, and peeping in*): Torvald.

HELMER (*from the inner room*): Well, am I allowed in my own room again? Come along, Rank, now we're going to see—(*at the door*) But what's all this?

NORA: What, Torvald dear?

HELMER: Rank led me to expect a great transformation scene.

RANK (*at the door*): I certainly thought so—I must have been wrong.

NORA: No one's allowed to admire me in all my finery till tomorrow.

HELMER: But, Nora dear, you look tired out—have you been rehearsing too much?

NORA: No, I haven't rehearsed at all.

HELMER: Oh, but you should have.

NORA: Yes, I know I should have, but I can't do anything unless you help me, Torvald. I've forgotten absolutely everything.

HELMER: Oh, we'll soon polish it up again.

NORA: Yes, do take me in hand, Torvald—promise you will. I'm so nervous—all those people . . . You must give up the whole evening to me;

you mustn't do a scrap of business—not even pick up a pen! You'll do that, won't you, dear Torvald?

HELMER: I promise. This evening I'll be wholly and entirely at your service—you poor helpless little creature! Ah, but first, while I think of it, I must just—(*going toward the hall door*).

NORA: What do you want out there?

HELMER: I'm just seeing if the post's come.

NORA: No, no, Torvald—don't do that.

HELMER: Why not?

NORA: Please don't Torvald—there's nothing there.

HELMER: I'll just look. (*He starts to go.*)

NORA, *at the piano, plays the opening bars of the tarantella.*

HELMER (*stopping in the doorway*): Aha!

NORA: I shan't be able to dance tomorrow if I don't go over it with you.

HELMER (*going to her*): Nora dear, are you really so worried about it?

NORA: Yes, terribly worried. Let me rehearse it now—there's still time before dinner. Sit down and play for me, Torvald dear; criticize me, and show me where I'm wrong, the way you always do.

HELMER: I'd like to, if that's what you want. (*He sits at the piano.*)

NORA *pulls a tambourine out of the box, then a long particolored shawl which she quickly drapes round herself. Then, with a bound, she takes up her position in the middle of the floor, and calls:*

NORA: Now play for me, and I'll dance!

HELMER *plays and* NORA *dances.* DR. RANK *stands behind* HELMER *at the piano and looks on.*

HELMER (*as he plays*): Slower—slower!

NORA: I can only do it this way.

HELMER: Not so violently, Nora!

NORA: This is how it should go.

HELMER (*stops playing*): No, no, that's all wrong.

NORA (*laughing and brandishing her tambourine*): There! Didn't I tell you?

RANK: Let me play for her.

HELMER (*rising*): Yes, do; then I can show her better.

RANK *sits at the piano and plays.* NORA *dances more and more wildly.* HELMER, *taking up a position by the stove, gives her frequent directions as she dances. She seems not to hear them, her hair comes down and falls over her shoulders, but she goes on dancing without taking any notice.* MRS. LINDE *comes in.*

MRS. LINDE (*stopping spellbound in the doorway*): Ah!

NORA (*as she dances*): Oh, this is fun, Kristina!

HELMER: But, Nora darling, you're dancing as if your life depended on it!

NORA: So it does.

HELMER: Stop, Rank. This is sheer madness—stop, I tell you!

RANK *stops playing, and* NORA *comes to an abrupt halt.*

HELMER (*going to her*): I'd never have believed it—you've forgotten everything I taught you.

NORA (*throwing the tambourine aside*): There! You see.

HELMER: Well, you'll certainly need a lot of coaching.

NORA: Yes, you see how much I need. You must coach me up to the last minute—promise me you will, Torvald?

HELMER: You can rely on me.

NORA: All today and all tomorrow, you mustn't think of anything else but me. You mustn't open any letters—you mustn't even open the letter-box.

HELMER: Ah, you're still afraid of that man.

NORA: Oh yes, that as well.

HELMER: Nora, I can see by your face that there's a letter from him already.

NORA: There may be—I don't know. But you mustn't read anything like that now; we won't let anything horrid come between us till this is all over.

RANK (*quietly to* HELMER): You'd better not upset her.

HELMER (*putting his arm round her*): My baby shall have her own way. But tomorrow night, after you've danced—

NORA: Then you'll be free.

MAID (*at the door on the right*): Dinner is served, Madam.

NORA: We'll have champagne, Helena.

MAID: Very good, Madam. (*She goes.*)

HELMER: Well, well—so we're having a banquet!

NORA: A champagne supper—lasting till dawn. (*calling*) And some macaroons, Helena—lots and lots, just for once.

HELMER (*taking her hands*): Now, now, now! You mustn't be so wild and excitable. Be my own little skylark again.

NORA: Oh yes, I will. But go into the dining-room now—and you too, Dr. Rank. Kristina, you must help me put my hair straight.

RANK (*quietly as they go*): There isn't anything . . . ? I mean, she's not expecting . . . ?

HELMER: Oh no, my dear fellow. I've told you—she gets over-excited, like a child.

They go out to the right.

NORA: Well?

MRS. LINDE: He's gone out of town.

NORA: I saw it in your face.

MRS. LINDE: He'll be back tomorrow night; I left a note for him.

NORA: You should have let things alone—not tried to stop them. After all, it's a wonderful thing to be waiting for a miracle.

MRS. LINDE: What is it you're expecting?

NORA: You wouldn't understand. Go in and join the others—I'll come in a minute.

MRS. LINDE *goes into the dining-room.*

NORA (*standing for a moment as if to collect herself, then looking at her watch*): Seven hours till midnight. Then twenty-four hours till midnight tomorrow. Then the tarantella will be over. Twenty-four and seven . . . thirty-one hours to live.

HELMER (*at the door on the right*): But where's my little skylark?
NORA (*going to him with arms outstretched*): Here she is!

Act Three

The same scene. The table and chairs round it have been moved to the middle of the room; a lamp is alight on the table. The hall door is open and music for dancing can be heard from the flat above.

MRS. LINDE is sitting at the table, idly turning the pages of a book. She tries to read, but seems unable to concentrate. Once or twice she listens anxiously for the outer door.

MRS. LINDE (*looking at her watch*): Not here yet! There's not much more time—I do hope he hasn't—(*listening again*) Ah, here he is.

She goes out to the hall and carefully opens the front door. Soft footsteps are heard on the stairs. She whispers:

Come in—there's no one here.
KROGSTAD (*in the doorway*): I found a note from you at home. What's this about?
MRS. LINDE: I had to have a talk with you.
KROGSTAD: Oh? And did you have to have it in this house?
MRS. LINDE: I couldn't see you at the place where I'm staying—there's no separate entrance to my room. Come in, we're quite alone; the maid's asleep, and the Helmers are upstairs at the dance.
KROGSTAD (*coming into the room*): What? The Helmers at a dance tonight? Really?
MRS. LINDE: Yes. Why not?
KROGSTAD: True—why not?
MRS. LINDE: Well, Nils, let us have a talk.
KROGSTAD: Have you and I got anything more to talk about?
MRS. LINDE: A great deal.
KROGSTAD: I shouldn't have thought so.
MRS. LINDE: Well, you never really understood me.
KROGSTAD: Was there anything to understand—except what was so obvious to the whole world: a heartless woman throwing a man over when someone richer turns up?
MRS. LINDE: Do you really think I'm as heartless as all that? And do you think it was easy to break with you?
KROGSTAD: Wasn't it?
MRS. LINDE: Nils, did you really think that?
KROGSTAD: If it wasn't true, why did you write to me as you did at the time?
MRS. LINDE: What else could I do? I had to break with you, so it was up to me to kill any feeling that you might have had for me.
KROGSTAD (*clenching his hands*): So that was it? You did it—all of it—for the sake of the money?
MRS. LINDE: You mustn't forget that my mother was quite helpless, and that I had two small brothers. We couldn't wait for you, Nils—especially as you had no prospects in those days.

KROGSTAD: Even so, you had no right to throw me over for someone else.

MRS. LINDE: I've often asked myself if I had the right . . . I really don't know.

KROGSTAD (*softly*): When I lost you, it was just as if the very ground had given way under my feet. Look at me now—a shipwrecked man clinging to a spar.

MRS. LINDE: Help could be near.

KROGSTAD: It *was* near—until you came and got in the way.

MRS. LINDE: Without knowing it, Nils. I found out today that it's *your* place that I'm to have at the Bank.

KROGSTAD: I'll believe you if you say so. But now that you do know, aren't you going to give it up?

MRS. LINDE: No. You see, that wouldn't benefit you in the least.

KROGSTAD: "Benefit—benefit!" *I* would have done it.

MRS. LINDE: I've learned to think before I act. Life and bitter necessity have taught me that.

KROGSTAD: Life has taught me not to believe in fine speeches.

MRS. LINDE: Then life has taught you something valuable. But you must believe in deeds?

KROGSTAD: What do you mean by that?

MRS. LINDE: You said you were like a shipwrecked man clinging to a spar.

KROGSTAD: I had good reason to say so.

MRS. LINDE: I'm like a shipwrecked woman clinging to a spar—no one to cry over, and no one to care for.

KROGSTAD: It was your own choice.

MRS. LINDE: There was no other choice at the time.

KROGSTAD: Well?

MRS. LINDE: Nils . . . suppose we two shipwrecked people could join forces?

KROGSTAD: What do you mean?

MRS. LINDE: Two on one spar would be better off than each of us alone.

KROGSTAD: Kristina!

MRS. LINDE: Why do you suppose I came to town?

KROGSTAD: Were you really thinking of me?

MRS. LINDE: I must work or life isn't bearable. All my life, as long as I can remember, I've worked—that's been my one great joy. But now that I'm alone in the world I feel completely lost and empty. There's no joy in working for oneself. Nils . . . let me have something—and someone—to work for.

KROGSTAD: I don't trust that. It's nothing but a woman's exaggerated sense of nobility prompting her to sacrifice herself.

MRS. LINDE: Have you ever noticed anything exaggerated in me?

KROGSTAD: Could you really do it? Tell me, do you know all about my past?

MRS. LINDE: Yes.

KROGSTAD: And do you know my reputation here?

MRS. LINDE: You suggested just now that with me you might have been a different man.

KROGSTAD: I'm certain of it.

MRS. LINDE: Couldn't that still happen?

KROGSTAD: Kristina—have you really thought about what you're saying? Yes, you have—I see it in your face. And you really have the courage?

MRS. LINDE: I need someone to be a mother to, and your children need a mother. You and I need each other. I have faith in you—the real you—Nils, with you I could dare anything.

KROGSTAD (*grasping her hands*): Thank you—thank you, Kristina. Now I shall be able to set myself right in the eyes of the world too. Oh, but I'm forgetting—

MRS. LINDE (*listening*): Sh! The tarantella! Go—quickly.

KROGSTAD: Why? What is it?

MRS. LINDE: Don't you hear the dancing up there? As soon as this is over, they'll be coming back.

KROGSTAD: Yes—I'll go. But all this will come to nothing . . . you see, you don't know what I've done against the Helmers.

MRS. LINDE: Yes, Nils, I know about it.

KROGSTAD: And you still have the courage . . . ?

MRS. LINDE: I know only too well how far despair can drive a man like you.

KROGSTAD: Oh, if only I could undo it!

MRS. LINDE: You can—your letter's still in the box.

KROGSTAD: Are you sure?

MRS. LINDE: Quite sure—but . . .

KROGSTAD (*with a searching look at her*): You want to save your friend at any price—is that it? Tell me frankly—is it?

MRS. LINDE: Nils, when you've sold yourself once for the sake of others, you don't do it a second time.

KROGSTAD: I shall ask for my letter back.

MRS. LINDE: No, no!

KROGSTAD: But of course. I'll wait here till Helmer comes down, and I'll tell him that he must give me my letter back—that it's only about my dismissal, and that he's not to read it.

MRS. LINDE: No, Nils, you mustn't ask for your letter back.

KROGSTAD: But surely that was the very reason why you asked me to come here?

MRS. LINDE: Yes—in my first moment of panic. But now, a whole day's gone by and I've witnessed things in this house that I could hardly believe. Helmer must know the whole story. This wretched secret must be brought into the open so that there's complete understanding between them. That'd be impossible while there's so much concealment and subterfuge.

KROGSTAD: Very well—if you'll take the risk. . . . But there's one thing I can do—and it shall be done at once—

MRS. LINDE (*listening*): Go—quickly! The dance is over—we can't stay here a moment longer.

KROGSTAD: I'll wait for you downstairs.

MRS. LINDE: Yes, do. You must see me home.

KROGSTAD: Kristina, this is the most marvellous thing that's ever happened to me.

He goes out by the front door. The door between the room and the hall remains open.

MRS. LINDE (*tidying the room a little, and putting her hat and cape ready*): What a difference—what a difference! Someone to work for—and live for. A home to look after—and oh, I'll make it so comfortable. Oh, if they'd only hurry up and come! (*listening*) Ah, here they are—I'll put my things on.

She picks up her hat and cape. HELMER'S *and* NORA'S *voices are heard outside. A key turns, and* HELMER *pulls* NORA *almost forcibly into the room. She is in Italian costume with a great black shawl round herself; he is in a black domino which opens to show his evening dress underneath.*

NORA (*still in the doorway, struggling with him*): No, no, I don't want to go in—I want to go back upstairs. It's far too early to leave.

HELMER: But, my darling Nora—

NORA: Oh, please, Torvald—I do beg you. . . . Just one more hour!

HELMER: Not a single minute, Nora dear—you know what we agreed. Now come along in, you'll catch cold out here.

In spite of her resistance he brings her gently into the room.

MRS. LINDE: Good evening.

NORA: Kristina!

HELMER: Why, Mrs. Linde—here so late?

MRS. LINDE: Yes, forgive me, but I did want to see Nora in her costume.

NORA: Have you been sitting here waiting for me?

MRS. LINDE: Yes, I'm afraid I didn't get here in time—you'd already gone upstairs—and I felt I really couldn't go away without seeing you.

HELMER (*taking* NORA'S *shawl off*): Yes, just look at her! She's worth seeing, if you ask *me!* Isn't she lovely, Mrs. Linde?

MRS. LINDE: She certainly is.

HELMER: Remarkably lovely, isn't she? And that's what everybody at the dance thought, too. But this sweet little thing's dreadfully obstinate. What are we to do with her? You'd hardly believe it, but I practically had to use force to get her away.

NORA: You'll be very sorry you didn't let me stay, Torvald—even for just half an hour longer.

HELMER: Just listen to her, Mrs. Linde! She danced her tarantella; it was a huge success—and rightly so, even if it *was,* perhaps, a trifle too realistic—I mean, a little more so than was, strictly speaking, artistically necessary. . . . But never mind, it was a success—a huge success. Could I let her stay after that, and spoil the effect? No thank you; I put my arm round my lovely little Capri girl—I might almost say my *capricious* little Capri girl— we made a quick turn of the room, a bow all round, and then, as they say in the novels, the beautiful vision was gone! An exit should always be well-timed, Mrs. Linde; but that's something I simply cannot get Nora to see! Phew, it's warm in here. (*He throws his domino on a chair and opens the door to his room.*) Hullo, it's all dark! Oh yes, of course. . . . Excuse me—(*He goes in and lights the candles.*)

NORA (*in a rapid and breathless whisper*): Well?

MRS. LINDE (*softly*): I've had a talk with him.

NORA: Yes?

MRS. LINDE: Nora, you must tell your husband everything.

NORA (*dully*): I knew it.

MRS. LINDE: You've nothing to fear from Krogstad. But you *must* tell your husband.

NORA: I'll never tell him.

MRS. LINDE: Then the letter will.

NORA: Thank you, Kristina; now I know what I must do. . . . Sh!

HELMER (*coming in again*): Well, Mrs. Linde, you have been admiring her?

MRS. LINDE: Yes, indeed . . . and now I must say good night.

HELMER: What, already? Is this yours, this knitting?

MRS. LINDE (*taking it*): Oh yes, thank you—I nearly forgot it.

HELMER: So you knit?

MRS. LINDE: Oh yes.

HELMER: You know, it'd be much better if you did embroidery.

MRS. LINDE: Oh? Why?

HELMER: It's so much more graceful. I'll show you. You hold embroidery like this, in your left hand, and you work the needle with your right—in long easy sweeps. Isn't that so?

MRS. LINDE: Yes, I suppose so.

HELMER: But knitting's quite another matter—it can't help being ungraceful. Look here—arms held tightly in, needles going up and down—it has an almost Chinese effect. . . . That really was an excellent champagne they gave us tonight. . . .

MRS. LINDE: Well, good night. And Nora—don't be obstinate any longer.

HELMER: That's quite right, Mrs. Linde.

MRS. LINDE: Good night, Mr. Helmer.

HELMER (*seeing her to the door*): Good night—good night. I hope you get home safely. I'd be very glad to . . . but then you haven't far to go, have you? Good night—good night.

She goes. He shuts the door after her and comes back.

Well, I thought she'd never go—she's a terrible bore, that woman.

NORA: Aren't you tired out, Torvald?

HELMER: No, not in the least.

NORA: Not sleepy?

HELMER: Not a bit—in fact, I feel particularly lively. What about you? Yes, you do look tired out—why, you're half asleep.

NORA: Yes, I'm very tired—I could fall asleep here and now.

HELMER: There you are—there you are! You see how right I was not to let you stay any longer.

NORA: You're always right, Torvald, whatever you do.

HELMER (*kissing her on the forehead*): Now my little skylark's talking like a reasonable being. Did you notice how cheerful Rank was this evening?

NORA: Oh, was he? I didn't get a chance to talk to him.

HELMER: I hardly did; but I haven't seen him in such good spirits for a long time. (*He looks at* NORA *for a moment, then goes to her.*) Ah, it's wonderful to be back home again, all alone with you. . . . How fascinating you are, you lovely little thing.

NORA: Don't look at me like that, Torvald.

HELMER: Mayn't I look at my dearest treasure? At all the beauty that belongs to no one but me—that's all my very own?

NORA (*going round to the other side of the table*): You mustn't say things like that tonight.

HELMER (*following her*): I see you still have the tarantella in your blood—it makes you more enchanting than ever. Listen—the party's beginning to break up. (*softly*) Nora—soon the whole house'll be quiet . . .

NORA: Yes, I hope so.

HELMER: Yes, you do, don't you, my own darling Nora? I'll tell you something: when I'm out with you at a party, do you know why I hardly talk to you—don't come near you—and only steal a glance at you every now and then . . . do you know why? It's because I pretend that we're secretly in love—engaged in secret—and that no one dreams that there's anything between us.

NORA: Oh yes, yes, I know that you're always thinking of me.

HELMER: And when it's time to go, and I'm putting your shawl over your lovely young shoulders—round your exquisite neck—then I imagine that you're my little bride, that we've just come from the wedding, and that I'm bringing you back to my home for the first time—that for the first time I shall be alone with you—all alone with your young trembling loveliness. All the evening I've been longing for nothing but you. While I watched you swaying and beckoning in the tarantella, it set my blood on fire till I couldn't bear it any longer. That's why I brought you home so early—

NORA: No, Torvald, go away. Leave me alone—I don't want—

HELMER: What's all this? So my little Nora's playing with me! "Don't want"? I'm your husband, aren't I?

There is a knock on the front door.

NORA (*startled*): Listen!

HELMER (*going to the hall*): Who is it?

RANK (*outside*): It's I—may I come in for a moment?

HELMER (*angrily, under his breath*): Oh, what does he want now? (*aloud*) Wait a minute. (*He goes and opens the door.*) Ah, it's nice of you not to pass our door without looking in.

RANK: I thought I heard you talking, and I felt I'd like to see you. (*He lets his eye roam quickly round the room.*) Ah yes, this dear familiar place; you two must be very happy and comfortable here.

HELMER: It looked as if you were pretty happy upstairs, too.

RANK: Wonderfully—why not? Why shouldn't one enjoy everything the world has to offer—at any rate, as much as one can—and for as long as one can? The wine was superb!

HELMER: Especially the champagne.

RANK: You thought so too, did you? It's quite incredible the amount I managed to put away!

NORA: Torvald drank a good deal of champagne tonight, too.

RANK: Oh?

NORA: Yes, and that always puts him in high spirits.

RANK: Well, why shouldn't a man have a pleasant evening after a good day's work?

HELMER: A good day's work? I'm afraid I can't claim that.

RANK (*slapping him on the back*): Ah, but *I* can!

NORA: Dr. Rank . . . then you must have been working on a scientific test today?

RANK: Exactly.

HELMER: Well, well! Little Nora talking about scientific tests!

NORA: And am I to congratulate you on the result?

RANK: You may indeed.

NORA: It was good, then?

RANK: The best possible result—for doctor *and* patient. . . . Certainty.

NORA (*quickly, probing*): Certainty?

RANK: Complete certainty. So why shouldn't I give myself a jolly evening after that?

NORA: Yes, of course you must, Dr. Rank.

HELMER: I quite agree—as long as you don't have to pay for it the next morning.

RANK: Ah well, you don't get anything for nothing in this life.

NORA: Dr. Rank—you like fancy-dress parties, don't you?

RANK: Yes, when there are lots of pretty costumes.

NORA: Then tell me—what are you and I going to wear at our next?

HELMER: Little scatterbrain—thinking about the next dance already!

RANK: You and I? Yes, I can tell you—you shall be a mascot.

HELMER: Ah, but what costume would suggest *that?*

RANK: Your wife could go in what she wears every day . . .

HELMER: Very charmingly put. But don't you know what you'll wear?

RANK: Oh yes, my dear fellow, I'm quite certain about *that.*

HELMER: Well?

RANK: At the next fancy-dress party, I shall be invisible.

HELMER: What an odd idea!

RANK: There's a big black hat—you've heard of the Invisible Hat?—you put it on, and then no one can see you.

HELMER (*hiding a smile*): Well, perhaps you're right.

RANK: But I'm quite forgetting what I came for. Give me a cigar, Helmer— one of the black Havanas.

HELMER: With the greatest pleasure (*offering him the case*).

RANK (*taking one and cutting the end*): Thanks.

NORA (*striking a match*): Let me give you a light.

RANK: Thank you.

She holds the match while he lights the cigar.

And now—good-bye.

HELMER: Good-bye—good-bye, my dear fellow.

NORA: Sleep well, Dr. Rank.

RANK: Thank you for that wish.

NORA: Wish me the same.

RANK: You? Well, if you want me to. . . . Sleep well. And—thank you for the light. . . . (*With a nod to them both, he goes.*)

HELMER (*subdued*): He's had too much to drink.

NORA (*absently*): Perhaps.

HELMER, *taking his keys from his pocket, goes out to the hall.*

NORA: Torvald—what do you want out there?

HELMER: I must empty the letter-box, it's almost full; there won't be room for tomorrow's paper.

NORA: Are you going to work tonight?

HELMER: You know perfectly well I'm not. Here, what's this? Someone's been at the lock!

NORA: At the lock?

HELMER: Yes, they certainly have. What can this mean? I shouldn't have thought that the maid—Here's a broken hairpin—Nora, it's one of yours!

NORA (*quickly*): Perhaps the children . . .

HELMER: Then you must break them of that sort of thing. Ugh—ugh—There, I've got it open all the same. (*emptying the letter-box and calling into the kitchen*) Helena? Helena, put out the lamp at the front door. (*He shuts the front door and comes into the room with the letters in his hand.*) Look—just look what a lot there are! (*looking through them*) Whatever's this?

NORA (*at the window*): The letter! No, Torvald, no!

HELMER: Two visiting-cards—from Rank.

NORA: From Dr. Rank?

HELMER (*looking at them*): "S. Rank, M.D." They were on top—he must have put them in as he left.

NORA: Is there anything on them?

HELMER: There's a black cross over the name . . . look. What a gruesome idea—it's just as if he were announcing his own death.

NORA: That's what he's doing.

HELMER: What? Do you know about it? Has he told you something?

NORA: Yes, when these cards came, it would be to say good-bye to us; he's going to shut himself up to die.

HELMER: My poor old friend. Of course I knew that he wouldn't be with me much longer—but so soon . . . ! And to go away and hide, like a wounded animal . . .

NORA: If it *must* be, then it's best to go without a word, isn't it, Torvald?

HELMER (*pacing up and down*): He'd come to be so much a part of our lives. I can't realize that he's gone. With all his loneliness and suffering, he seemed like a background of clouds that set off the sunshine of our happiness. Well, perhaps it's all for the best—for him, at any rate. (*coming to a halt*) And maybe for us too, Nora, now that you and I have no one but each other. (*putting an arm round her*) Oh, my darling, I feel as if I can't hold you close enough. You know, Nora, I've often wished that you could be threatened by some imminent danger so that I could risk everything I had—even my life itself—to save you.

NORA (*freeing herself, and speaking firmly and purposefully*): Now you must read your letters, Torvald.

HELMER: No, no, not tonight. I want to be with my darling wife.

NORA: When your friend's dying . . . ?

HELMER: Yes, you're right—it's upset us both. Something ugly has come between us—the thought of death and decay. We must try to shake it off. . . . And until we do, let us keep apart.

NORA (*putting her arms round his neck*): Good night, Torvald—good night.

HELMER (*kissing her on the forehead*): Good night, Nora—sleep well, my little songbird. Now I'll go and read my letters. (*He takes the bundle into
his room, shutting the door behind him.*)

NORA (*Wild-eyed, groping round her she seizes* HELMER'S *domino and pulls it
round herself. She speaks in hoarse, rapid, broken whispers.*): I shall
never see him again! Never—never—never! (*She throws the shawl over
her head.*) And never see the children again either—never, never again.
The water's black, and cold as ice—and deep . . . so deep. . . . Oh, if only
it were all over! He has it now—he's reading it. . . . Oh no, no—not yet!
Good-bye, Torvald—good-bye, my children—

She is about to rush out through the hall, when HELMER *flings his door open
and stands there with the open letter in his hand.*

HELMER: Nora!

NORA (*with a loud cry*): Ah . . . !

HELMER: What is all this? Do you know what's in this letter?

NORA: Yes, I know. Let me go—let me out!

HELMER (*holding her back*): Where are you going?

NORA (*struggling to free herself*): You shan't save me, Torvald!

HELMER (*taken aback*): It's true! So what it says here is true? How terrible!
No, no, it's not possible—it *can't* be true.

NORA: It *is* true. I've loved you more than anything in the world.

HELMER: Now don't let's have any silly excuses.

NORA (*taking a step toward him*): Torvald . . . !

HELMER: You wretched woman—what have you done?

NORA: Let me go. You *shan't* take the blame—I won't let you suffer for me.

HELMER: We won't have any melodrama. (*locking the front door*) Here you
shall stay until you've explained yourself. Do you realize what you've
done? Answer me—do you realize?

NORA (*looking fixedly at him, her expression hardening as she speaks*): Yes,
now I'm beginning to realize everything.

HELMER (*pacing about the room*): What a terrible awakening! For these last
eight years you've been my joy and my pride—and now I find that you're
a liar, a hypocrite—even worse—a criminal! Oh, the unspeakable ugliness of it all! Ugh!

NORA *looks fixedly at him without speaking. He stops in front of her.*

I might have known that something of this sort would happen—I should
have foreseen it. All your father's shiftless character—Be quiet!—all your
father's shiftless character has come out in you. No religion, no morality,
no sense of duty . . . So this is what I get for condoning his fault! I did it
for your sake, and this is how you repay me!

NORA: Yes—like this.

HELMER: You've completely wrecked my happiness, you've ruined my
whole future! Oh, it doesn't bear thinking of. I'm in the power of a man
without scruples; he can do what he likes with me—ask what he wants
of me—order me about as he pleases, and I dare not refuse. And I'm
brought so pitifully low all because of a shiftless woman!

NORA: Once I'm out of the way, you'll be free.

HELMER: No rhetoric, please! Your father was always ready with fine phrases too. How would it help me if you were "out of the way," as you call it? Not in the least! He can still see that the thing gets about, and once he does, I may very well be suspected of having been involved in your crooked dealings. They may well think that I was behind it—that I put you up to it. And it's you that I have to thank for all this—and after I've cherished you all through our married life. *Now* do you realize what you've done to me?

NORA (*calm and cold*): Yes.

HELMER: It's so incredible that I can't grasp it. But we must try to come to some understanding. Take off that shawl—take it off, I tell you. Somehow or other I must try to appease him—the thing must be hushed up at all costs. As for ourselves—we must seem to go on just as before . . . but only in the eyes of the world of course. You will remain here in my house—that goes without saying—but I shall not allow you to bring up the children . . . I shouldn't dare trust you with them. Oh, to think that I should have to say this to someone I've loved so much—someone I still . . . Well, that's all over—it must be; from now on, there'll be no question of happiness, but only of saving the ruin of it—the fragments—the mere facade . . .

There is a ring at the front door.

HELMER (*collecting himself*): What's that—at this hour? Can the worst have— Could he . . . ? Keep out of sight, Nora—say that you're ill.

NORA *remains motionless.* HELMER *goes and opens the hall door.*

MAID (*at the door, half-dressed*): There's a letter for the Mistress.

HELMER: Give it to me. (*He takes the letter and shuts the door.*) Yes, it's from him. You're not to have it—I shall read it myself.

NORA: Yes, read it.

HELMER (*by the lamp*): I hardly dare—it may mean ruin for both of us. No, I *must* know! (*Tearing open the letter, he runs his eye over a few lines, looks at a paper that is enclosed, then gives a shout of joy.*) Nora!

She looks at him inquiringly.

Nora! Wait, I must just read it again. . . . Yes, it's true; I'm saved! Nora, I'm saved!

NORA: And I?

HELMER: You too, of course. We're both saved—both you and I. Look, he's sent you back your bond. He says that he regrets . . . and apologizes . . . a fortunate change in his life. . . . Oh, never mind what he says—we're saved, Nora, no one can touch you now. Oh Nora, Nora—Wait, first let me destroy the whole detestable business. (*casting his eye over the bond*) No, I won't even look at it—I shall treat the whole thing as nothing but a bad dream. (*Tearing the bond and the two letters in pieces, he throws them on the stove, and watches them burn.*) There! Now it's all gone. He said in his letter that since Christmas Eve you'd . . . Oh, Nora, these three days must have been terrible for you.

NORA: They've been a hard struggle, these three days.

HELMER: How you must have suffered—seeing no way out except . . . No, we'll put all those hateful things out of our minds. Now we can shout for joy, again and again: "It's all over—it's all over!" Listen, Nora—you don't seem to realize—it's all over. What's the matter? Such a grim face? Poor little Nora, I see what it is: you simply can't believe that I've forgiven you. But I have, Nora, I swear it—I've forgiven you everything. I know now that what you did was all for love of me.

NORA: That is true.

HELMER: You loved me as a wife *should* love her husband. It was just that you hadn't the experience to realize what you were doing. But do you imagine that you're any less dear to me for not knowing how to act on your own? No, no, you must simply rely on me—I shall advise you and guide you. I shouldn't be a proper man if your feminine helplessness didn't make you twice as attractive to me. You must forget all the hard things that I said to you in that first dreadful moment when it seemed as if the whole world was falling about my ears. I've forgiven you, Nora, I swear it—I've forgiven you.

NORA: Thank you for your forgiveness. (*She goes out through the door to the right.*)

HELMER: No, don't go. (*He looks in.*) What are you doing out there?

NORA (*off*): Taking off my fancy-dress.

HELMER (*at the open door*): Yes, do. Try to calm down and set your mind at peace, my frightened little songbird. You can rest safely, and my great wings will protect you. (*He paces up and down by the door.*) Oh, Nora, how warm and cosy our home is; it's your refuge, where I shall protect you like a hunted dove that I've saved from the talons of a hawk. Little by little, I shall calm your poor fluttering heart, Nora, take my word for it. In the morning you'll look on all this quite differently, and soon everything will be just as it used to be. There'll be no more need for me to tell you that I've forgiven you—you'll feel in your heart that I have. How can you imagine that I could ever think of rejecting—or even reproaching—you? Ah, you don't know what a real man's heart is like, Nora. There's something indescribably sweet and satisfying for a man to know deep down that he has forgiven his wife—completely forgiven her, with all his heart. It's as if that made her doubly his—as if he had brought her into the world afresh! In a sense, she has become both his wife and his child. So from now on, that's what you shall be to me, you poor, frightened, helpless, little darling. You mustn't worry about anything, Nora—only be absolutely frank with me, and I'll be both your will and your conscience. . . . Why, what's this? Not in bed? You've changed your clothes!

NORA (*in her everyday things*): Yes, Torvald, I've changed my clothes.

HELMER: But why? At *this* hour!

NORA: I shan't sleep tonight.

HELMER: But, my dear Nora—

NORA (*looking at her watch*): It's not so very late. Sit down here, Torvald—you and I have a lot to talk over. (*She sits down at one side of the table.*)

HELMER: Nora—what is all this? Why do you look so stern?

NORA: Sit down—this'll take some time. I have a lot to talk to you about.

HELMER (*sitting across the table from her*): Nora, you frighten me—I don't understand you.

NORA: No, that's just it—you don't understand me. And I've never understood you—until tonight. No, you mustn't interrupt—just listen to what I have to say. Torvald, this is a reckoning.

HELMER: What do you mean by that?

NORA (*after a short pause*): Doesn't it strike you that there's something strange about the way we're sitting here?

HELMER: No . . . what?

NORA: We've been married for eight years now. Don't you realize that this is the first time that we two—you and I, man and wife—have had a serious talk together?

HELMER: Serious? What do you mean by that?

NORA: For eight whole years—no, longer than that—ever since we first met, we've never exchanged a serious word on any serious subject.

HELMER: Was I to keep forever involving you in worries that you couldn't possibly help me with?

NORA: I'm not talking about worries; what I'm saying is that we've never sat down in earnest together to get to the bottom of a single thing.

HELMER: But, Nora dearest, what good would that have been to you?

NORA: That's just the point—you've never understood me. I've been dreadfully wronged, Torvald—first by Papa, and then by you.

HELMER: What? By your father and me? The two people who loved you more than anyone else in the world.

NORA (*shaking her head*): You've never loved me, you've only found it pleasant to be in love with me.

HELMER: Nora—what are you saying?

NORA: It's true, Torvald. When I lived at home with Papa, he used to tell me his opinion about everything, and so I had the same opinion. If I thought differently, I had to hide it from him, or he wouldn't have liked it. He called me his little doll, and he used to play with me just as I played with my dolls. Then I came to live in your house—

HELMER: That's no way to talk about our marriage!

NORA (*undisturbed*): I mean when I passed out of Papa's hands into yours. You arranged everything to suit your own tastes, and so I came to have the same tastes as yours . . . or I pretended to. I'm not quite sure which . . . perhaps it was a bit of both—sometimes one and sometimes the other. Now that I come to look at it, I've lived here like a pauper—simply from hand to mouth. I've lived by performing tricks for you, Torvald. That was how you wanted it. You and Papa have committed a grievous sin against me: it's your fault that I've made nothing of my life.

HELMER: That's unreasonable, Nora—and ungrateful. Haven't you been happy here?

NORA: No, that's something I've never been. I thought I had, but really I've never been happy.

HELMER: Never . . . happy?

NORA: No, only gay. And you've always been so kind to me. But our home has been nothing but a play-room. I've been your doll-wife here, just as at home I was Papa's doll-child. And the children have been my dolls in their turn. I liked it when you came and played with me, just as they liked it when I came and played with them. That's what our marriage has been, Torvald.

HELMER: There is some truth in what you say, though you've exaggerated and overstated it. But from now on, things will be different. Play-time's over, now comes lesson-time.

NORA: Whose lessons? Mine or the children's?

HELMER: Both yours and the children's, Nora darling.

NORA: Ah, Torvald, you're not the man to teach me to be a real wife to you—

HELMER: How can you say that?

NORA: —and how am I fitted to bring up the children?

HELMER: Nora!

NORA: Didn't you say yourself, a little while ago, that you daren't trust them to me?

HELMER: That was in a moment of anger—you mustn't pay any attention to that.

NORA: But you were perfectly right—I'm not fit for it. There's another task that I must finish first—I must try to educate myself. And you're not the man to help me with that; I must do it alone. That's why I'm leaving you.

HELMER (leaping to his feet): What's that you say?

NORA: I must stand on my own feet if I'm to get to know myself and the world outside. That's why I can't stay here with you any longer.

HELMER: Nora—Nora . . . !

NORA: I want to go at once. I'm sure Kristina will take me in for the night.

HELMER: You're out of your mind. I won't let you—I forbid it.

NORA: It's no good your forbidding me anything any longer. I shall take the things that belong to me, but I'll take nothing from you—now or later.

HELMER: But this is madness . . .

NORA: Tomorrow I shall go home—to my old home, I mean—it'll be easier for me to find something to do there.

HELMER: Oh, you blind, inexperienced creature . . . !

NORA: I must try to get some experience, Torvald.

HELMER: But to leave your home—your husband and your children. . . . You haven't thought of what people will say.

NORA: I can't consider that. All I know is that this is necessary for me.

HELMER: But this is disgraceful. Is this the way you neglect your most sacred duties?

NORA: What do you consider is my most sacred duty?

HELMER: Do I have to tell you that? Isn't it your duty to your husband and children?

NORA: I have another duty, just as sacred.

HELMER: You can't have. What duty do you mean?

NORA: My duty to myself.

HELMER: Before everything else, you're a wife and a mother.

NORA: I don't believe that any longer. I believe that before everything else I'm a human being—just as much as you are . . . or at any rate I shall try to become one. I know quite well that most people would agree with you, Torvald, and that you have warrant for it in books; but I can't be satisfied any longer with what most people say, and with what's in books. I must think things out for myself and try to understand them.

HELMER: Shouldn't you first understand your place in your own home? Haven't you an infallible guide in such matters—your religion?

NORA: Ah, Torvald, I don't really know what religion is.

HELMER: What's that you say?

NORA: I only know what Pastor Hansen taught me when I was confirmed. He told me that religion was this, that, and the other. When I get away from all this, and am on my own, I want to look into that too. I want to see if what Pastor Hansen told me was right—or at least, if it is right for me.

HELMER: This is unheard-of from a young girl like you. But if religion can't guide you, then let me rouse your conscience. You must have *some* moral sense. Or am I wrong? Perhaps you haven't.

NORA: Well, Torvald, it's hard to say; I don't really know—I'm so bewildered about it all. All I know is that I think quite differently from you about things; and now I find that the law is quite different from what I thought, and I simply can't convince myself that the law is right. That a woman shouldn't have the right to spare her old father on his deathbed, or to save her husband's life! I can't believe things like that.

HELMER: You're talking like a child; you don't understand the world you live in.

NORA: No, I don't. But now I mean to go into that, too. I must find out which is right—the world or I.

HELMER: You're ill, Nora—you're feverish. I almost believe you're out of your senses.

NORA: I've never seen things so clearly and certainly as I do tonight.

HELMER: Clearly and certainly enough to forsake your husband and your children?

NORA: Yes.

HELMER: Then there's only one possible explanation . . .

NORA: What?

HELMER: You don't love me any more.

NORA: No, that's just it.

HELMER: Nora! How can you say that?

NORA: I can hardly bear to, Torvald, because you've always been so kind to me—but I can't help it. I don't love you any more.

HELMER (*with forced self-control*): And are you clear and certain about that, too?

NORA: Yes, absolutely clear and certain. That's why I won't stay here any longer.

HELMER: And will you also be able to explain how I've forfeited your love?

NORA: Yes, I can indeed. It was this evening, when the miracle didn't happen—because then I saw that you weren't the man I'd always thought you.

HELMER: I don't understand that. Explain it.

NORA: For eight years I'd waited so patiently—for, goodness knows, I realized that miracles don't happen every day. Then this disaster overtook me, and I was completely certain that now the miracle would happen. When Krogstad's letter was lying out there, I never imagined for a moment that you would submit to his conditions. I was completely certain that you would say to him "Go and publish it to the whole world!" And when that was done . . .

HELMER: Well, what then? When I'd exposed my own wife to shame and disgrace?

NORA: When that was done, I thought—I was completely certain—that you would come forward and take all the blame—that you'd say *"I'm* the guilty one."

HELMER: Nora!

NORA: You think that I should never have accepted a sacrifice like that from you? No, of course I shouldn't. But who would have taken my word against yours? That was the miracle I hoped for . . . and dreaded. It was to prevent *that* that I was ready to kill myself.

HELMER: Nora, I'd gladly work night and day for you, and endure poverty and sorrow for your sake. But no man would sacrifice his *honor* for the one he loves.

NORA: Thousands of women have.

HELMER: Oh, you're talking and thinking like a stupid child.

NORA: Perhaps . . . But you don't talk or think like the man I could bind myself to. When your first panic was over—not about what threatened me, but about what might happen to *you*—and when there was no more danger, then, as far as you were concerned, it was just as if nothing had happened at all. I was simply your little songbird, your doll, and from now on you would handle it more gently than ever because it was so delicate and fragile. (*rising*) At that moment, Torvald, I realized that for eight years I'd been living here with a strange man, and that I'd borne him three children. Oh, I can't bear to think of it—I could tear myself to little pieces!

HELMER (*sadly*): Yes. I see—I see. There truly is a gulf between us. . . . Oh, but Nora, couldn't we somehow bridge it?

NORA: As I am now, I'm not the wife for you.

HELMER: I could change . . .

NORA: Perhaps—if your doll is taken away from you.

HELMER: But to lose you—to lose you, Nora! No, no, I can't even imagine it . . .

NORA (*going out to the right*): That's just why it *must* happen.

She returns with her outdoor clothes, and a little bag which she puts on a chair by the table.

HELMER: Nora! Not now, Nora—wait till morning.

NORA (*putting on her coat*): I couldn't spend the night in a strange man's house.

HELMER: But couldn't we live here as brother and sister?

NORA (*putting her hat on*): You know quite well that that wouldn't last. (*She pulls her shawl round her.*) Good-bye, Torvald. I won't see my children—I'm sure they're in better hands than mine. As I am now, I'm no good to them.

HELMER: But some day, Nora—some day . . . ?

NORA: How can I say? I've no idea what will become of me.

HELMER: But you're my wife—now, and whatever becomes of you.

NORA: Listen, Torvald: I've heard that when a wife leaves her husband's house as I'm doing now, he's legally freed from all his obligations to her.

Anyhow, *I* set you free from them. You're not to feel yourself bound in any way, and nor shall I. We must both be perfectly free. Look, here's your ring back—give me mine.

HELMER: Even that?

NORA: Even that.

HELMER: Here it is.

NORA: There. Now it's all over. Here are your keys. The servants know all about running the house—better than I did. Tomorrow, when I've gone, Kristina will come and pack my things that I brought from home; I'll have them sent after me.

HELMER: Over! All over! Nora, won't you ever think of me again?

NORA: I know I shall often think of you—and the children, and this house.

HELMER: May I write to you, Nora?

NORA: No . . . you must never do that.

HELMER: But surely I can send you—

NORA: Nothing—nothing.

HELMER: —or help you, if ever you need it?

NORA: No, I tell you, I couldn't take anything from a stranger.

HELMER: Nora—can't I ever be anything more than a stranger to you?

NORA (*picking up her bag*): Oh, Torvald—there would have to be the greatest miracle of all . . .

HELMER: What would that be—the greatest miracle of all?

NORA: Both of us would have to be so changed that—Oh, Torvald, I don't believe in miracles any longer.

HELMER: But I'll believe. Tell me: "so changed that . . ."?

NORA: That our life together could be a real marriage. Good-bye. (*She goes out through the hall.*)

HELMER (*sinking down on a chair by the door and burying his face in his hands*): Nora! Nora! (*He rises and looks round.*) Empty! She's not here any more! (*with a glimmer of hope*) "The greatest miracle of all . . ."?

From below comes the noise of a door slamming.

The Receptive Reader

1. In the early acts, Torvald Helmer holds forth on the role of the husband, standards of honesty or probity for dealing with money. Above all, in his talk and in many little ways, he demonstrates the role he has assigned to Nora in their household. What are revealing things he says and does? What portrait of him as a *major character* emerges in Acts 1 and 2? How do you react to him?

2. In what ways does Nora live up to the stereotype of the "little woman"? How does she conform to her husband's conception of her? What are telling details or patterns of behavior that make her the weaker partner in their marriage? What are revealing things she says or does in the early acts of the play?

3. When do you see the first signs that there might be another side to Nora's personality? When do you see signs that she might be a *complex* rather than a simple character? What are the first hints that Torvald and Nora are going to come into conflict?

4. In Acts 1 and 2, how does Mrs. Linde serves as a *foil* to Nora? How does Ibsen use her to remind the audience of the harsh economic realities facing women on the fringes of middle-class society? (What light do the comments of the Nurse throw on the role of lower-class women?)

5. Among the other *supporting characters,* what is the role of Dr. Rank, the physician? What role does he play in Nora's life? From what perspective does Rank see the major characters? How does Ibsen use him to throw added light on Nora and Torvald and their society?

6. What is Krogstad's central role in the *plot* of the play? How does he bring out into the open Helmer's (and his society's) standards about money, credit, and respectability? Why is the fact that at one time the two men were schoolmates an embarrassment to Helmer? What is the role of the relationship between Krogstad and Mrs. Linde in the play as a whole?

7. Krogstad at one point tells Nora that even "a man like me has a certain amount of what is called feeling." How do you react him? Is he a stage villain— someone all bad, whom the audience can hiss and despise?

8. What is the nature of Nora's dealings with Krogstad? How do they test her character and her view of the world? How do they make her change or grow? How do the revelations about the hushed-up events of the past change your view of Nora?

9. Torvald at the *climax,* or high point, of the play fails Nora—he fails to live up to her expectations. Why and how? What does she expect of him? How and why does she judge him? Do you concur in her judgment? In these climactic scenes in Act 3, what does Ibsen try to show about the workings of Torvald's kind of bourgeois morality? about Torvald's kind of person?

10. What questions does Nora raise about the nature of marriage in the final scenes? What answers does the play suggest? What is the meaning of Nora's concept of the "duty to myself"? What is her idea of a "real marriage"?

The Creative Dimension

To get his play performed in Germany, with opportunites for fame and fortune far beyond those of his native Norway, Ibsen rewrote the ending to make it more acceptable to the outraged forces of middle-class respectability. Gritting his teeth, he wrote a final scene in which Torvald makes Nora take a last look at her sleeping children:

> TORVALD: Tomorrow, when they wake up and call for their mother, they
>   will be . . . motherless!
> NORA (*trembling*): Motherless!
> TORVALD: As you once were.
> NORA: Motherless! (*After an inner struggle, she lets her bag fall, and says*)
>   Ah, though it is a sin against myself, I cannot leave them!

Choose one: Pretend you are a drama critic in Ibsen's time. Attack or defend the changed ending. Or do your own rewrite of the final page or pages for a current adaptation of the play—for instance, for a Hollywood movie or for an avant-garde production.

WRITING ABOUT LITERATURE

27   *Keeping a Drama Journal (Formats for Writing)*

The Writing Workshop   In reading or watching a play, you will ideally be carried along by the action that develops. Later, as you sort out your impressions, you will find it useful to keep a drama journal that allows you to record both your scene-by-scene reactions and your first thoughts about the play as a whole.

Different journal entries might explore topics like the following: Where does the play take us—what setting or context does it create? How do the characters come into focus? How do major issues shape up? Does a central conflict begin to give shape to the play as whole? Does a major theme begin to echo in key passages? What means does the dramatist use to steer the reactions of the audience or to create dramatic effects?

In form, your journal entries may vary greatly, ranging from reading notes (or viewing notes) to finished paragraphs and mini-essays. Study the following sample entries:

Running Commentary   Many readers find it useful to keep a **running commentary** on key developments and key passages in a play. Look at the way the following sample entries start recording queries and important evidence on key points in the opening scenes of Ibsen's *A Doll's House*. Note the amount of direct quotation for possible later use in a more formal paper:

> Torvald constantly uses what he thinks are terms of endearment that actually belittle Nora: "Is that my little skylark twittering out there?" "Scampering about like a little squirrel?" "Has my little featherbrain been out wasting money again?" "My little song bird mustn't be so crestfallen."
>
> Torvald gives lectures on not getting into debt:
>
> No debts, no borrowing. There's something constrained, something ugly even about a home that's founded on borrowing and debt. He calls Nora a "prodigal" who spends money "on all sorts of useless things."
>
> Nora's "sweet tooth" becomes an issue. She is treated like a child?

Focusing on Character   You may want to devote an entry to a major character, pulling together impressions that at first might have seemed contradictory or inconclusive. The following sample entry is a **character portrait** of a major character in the ancient Greek playwright Euripides' *The Women of Troy*. He wrote the play toward the end of the fifth century B.C., when his native Athens was reaching the end of a disastrous, long, drawn-out war. In the words of one student reader, the play "draws portraits of strong, independent, capable individuals, gathered together in the hours after the fall of Troy to the Greeks to mourn their dead and say goodbye to their homeland and to one another." Although the women are about to be taken into slavery, they speak up with great dignity and passion. A major source of strength to the other women is Hecabe, the newly widowed wife of King Priam, who with many of his sons and warriors has been killed in the fall of Troy.

> Euripides' women each have a unique personality, each dealing with her terrible fate as best she can. Hecabe, former wife of King Priam of Troy, is a truly pitiable tragic character of impressive stature. Early in the play, she says, "Lift your neck from the dust; up with your head! This is not Troy." She maintains this royal bearing and pride throughout the play, even when, "maddened and sick with horror," she awaits her fate. She bemoans aloud her fate of having to be a slave in Greece where she is likely to be a keeper of keys and answerer of doors, sleeping on the floor and wearing rags. The audience can share in her anguish when she finds that her daughter Polyxena has been offered as a human sacrifice at the grave of the Greek champion Achilles. She is also an extremely sympathetic character when she buries her little grandson Astyanax, killed by the Greeks to keep the boy from growing up to seek vengeance for the death of his father, Hector. However, Hecabe shows a vengeful or vindictive streak when she denounces Helen, whom she blames for much of what has befallen her city, in front of Helen's husband Menelaus. At a time when Helen is trying to save her life in the presence of the husband she had betrayed, Hecabe shows her thirst for vengeance and her unforgiving hatred of her enemies.

Focusing on Plot   Preparing a **plot summary** (of the play as a whole or perhaps of one climactic act) can give you a better sense of the flow of a play. When debating the larger questions about a play, you will often find it useful to go back to exactly what happens in an act or a scene. Ask yourself: Why are these plot developments important? For instance, your summary might trace major developments building up to a major turning point or to the final catastrophe. The following sample entry summarizes the action in the final scenes of Arthur Miller's *Death of a Salesman*. Willy Loman is losing his already weak grip on reality; his relationship with his alienated son, Biff, is coming to a head; Willy is hatching the scheme that will make up for his and Biff's lifetimes of failures:

> After leaving Willy "babbling in a toilet" at the restaurant, the boys go out on the town with their dates only to come home to be thoroughly castigated by their mother: "There isn't a stranger you would do that to!" Linda shouts. Meanwhile, Willy, retreating into his world of illusion, is planting vegetable seeds in the garden—in the middle of the night—while carrying on a conversation with the legendary Uncle Ben (who walked into the jungle and came back rich). At this point, we learn of Willy's plan to commit suicide, leaving the proceeds of his life insurance to Biff. "God, he'll be great yet." Willy explains to Ben. "And now with twenty-five thousand behind him." "It sounds like an interesting proposition, William," Ben concurs.

After Linda's bitter lecture to the boys, Biff tells his mother that he is no good and that he is leaving, never to return. He goes into the garden to bring his father into the kitchen where the climactic scene occurs. When Willy learns Biff is leaving, he is furious and denounces Biff for wasting his life. "Spite!" Willy screams. "Spite is the word of your undoing!" Ultimately, Biff breaks down, crying, "Let me go. Can't you see that I'm just no good? There's not spite in it anymore! I am just what I am." Willy, too, is overcome, although he still cannot let go of his illusion: "God, he'll be great yet."

Once everyone retires—Biff is to leave the following morning—Willy proceeds with his plan. But this is not the end of the play. We are in for yet another sad irony. The final scene is the funeral. Throughout the play, Willy prided himself on his popularity gained during all his years of selling; he had believed he was "well-liked." No one comes to his funeral—a bitter and tragic ending for one consumed by the "American Dream."

Focusing on an Issue   An entry may explore a major theme or issue in a play. It may look at pros and cons, presenting a **trial thesis** that could be argued more fully in a formal paper. The following entry takes on a key question raised by Ibsen's *A Doll's House:* Did Nora make the right decision at the end of the play?

"I am going to see if I can make out who is right, the world or I," Nora Helmer says near the end of Act 3 of *A Doll's House.* I know my reaction is based on hindsight, but a woman today might well urge Nora to be cautious in pitting herself against the world. In leaving her husband and children, she violates a social order larger and more powerful than herself. People like Torvald more often than not close ranks against the rebel who threatens the status quo and jealously guard their advantage. Women will not befriend her except for those who are themselves outside the order. Kristina, who is respectable as a widow, may or may not stand by her.

As it happens, the world is bigger, meaner, colder, and more ruthless than a single, isolated person such as Nora is likely to be. She should not refuse Torvald's help nor should she walk out taking only what she brought as a bride. Nora is likely to find that the world is manned by Torvalds. She is likely to be drawn to them and they to her, for it has been a lifetime pattern already deeply instilled. She has the natural gift to delight and charm men, and she has worked this gift down to a science as Ibsen shows us in the first two acts. It has been her vocation to be the perfect wife—charming and diverting on the surface and ruthlessly practical behind the scenes in arranging the loan and paying it back all these years.

Torvald's self-preoccupation, rage, and condemnation of her when he learns about the loan shatters Nora's illusion of him. Nora moves very quickly from focusing on what has happened in her relationship with Torvald—his selfishness and knee-jerk condemnation of her worth as a human being—to going into the world to find out who is right or wrong. The risks and variables of surviving in the world alone are large. She will need money and friends, and she may have neither because of her defiance of conventional, accepted behavior for women. She may not want to live a celibate life, either. Permanent relationships may offer the same kind of traps she is in with Torvald—maybe worse, temporary ones are fraught with danger, disease, unwanted pregnancy, further loss of status in the community.

In today's terms, Nora has no job skills, no money, no connections other than Christine and Krogstad. Today's feminists might urge her to see an attorney and get as much information as she can before she departs. Life may be rough at home, but it can be even worse alone and friendless in the cold, hard world.

The Personal Connection   A play will move us most strongly if it strikes a chord somewhere in our own experience, if at some level it relates to something we have strongly felt. In reading or watching a play, have you ever felt the kind of personal connection that is the subject of the following journal entry?

Shakespeare has a way of making the agony of a play intensely personal. Hamlet's anguish, I feel, is caused mainly by external difficulties, by people other than himself. He finds himself in a situation not of his own making, a situation over which he has no control. He says, "The world is out of joint. O cursed spite that I was born to set it right." Perhaps I relate to him strongly because I have had a traumatic experience of being at the mercy of other people's initiatives, with my own role being that of experiencing reactions rather than taking action. My parents each remarried shortly after their divorce ("o wicked speed"). I know what it feels like to be avoided, to be in the way. My father did not tell me that he got married until three weeks after the wedding. Of course, Hamlet's grievance was much stronger because he was a prince who had expected to follow his father to the crown. He struggled with the obligation to avenge his father. Today, instead of striking back, we are expected to work our way through the psychological upheaval. We are expected to "cope."

28 Greek Tragedy

The Embattled Protagonist

*The structure of a play is always the story of how
the birds come home to roost.*

ARTHUR MILLER

FOCUS ON GREEK DRAMA

The golden age of Greek drama takes us back 2,500 years to the Athens of the fifth century B.C. However, the great plays—*Antigone, Oedipus Rex, The Trojan Women*—are still gripping drama today. In Sophocles' *Antigone,* the characters speak to us across the gulf of time in terms we understand. In the first scene, Antigone speaks to an issue that has confronted many in our time: the powers that be command her to act in way that goes against her conscience. What the law requires offends her sense of what is right. The question is: Is there a higher law that the individual should obey? Can the individual defy the state?

In the Greek plays, recognizable human beings give voice to the hopes and fears, the dreams and nightmares, of our common humanity. True, the characters that occupy center stage are members of a privileged class. They are tribal chieftains or warlords and their spouses and the clans they represent. But their thoughts and feelings often mirror our own, although projected onto a larger screen. When they talk about their gods and myths, we may need the scholar to annotate references that have lost their meaning. But when they talk about their ambitions, their loyalties, and their jealousies, we often do not need an interpreter. We see a strong individual—man or woman—center stage, engaged in a fateful conflict with other human beings or with the gods.

Drama and Ritual   Greek drama—from the Greek for "doings" or "things done"—grew out of springtime festivals in honor of the god Dionysus. (To the Romans, he was Bacchus, the god of wine and revelry.) A statue of the god was close to the stage. The word *tragedy* originally meant "goat-song," from the goat that was offered to the god as a ritual sacrifice. Like the earlier religious rituals, the theater was a community affair,

733

The Theater of Epidauros, in Athens, dating from the fourth century B.C. Courtesy of Marburg-Art Resource, NY.

with as many as fifteen thousand people in attendance. Multitudes of spectators crowded a large semicircular outdoor theater, carved into the side of a hill, with steeply rising tiered stone seats.

Tragedy and Comedy   Plays were chosen during elaborately organized drama contests. The plays were usually performed in groups of three, with three playwrights competing for first prize. The major plays were **tragedies,** focused on famous calamities that had befallen the mighty. The basic fare of three serious plays was spiced with a satyr play (named after the goat-footed, oversexed satyrs of Greek mythology). This early kind of **comedy** featured coarse, suggestive humor and satirical jabs at greedy contemporaries and obtuse leaders.

Acting Conventions   Actors spoke through masks with exaggerated features—so that spectators on the periphery could see who was king, queen, servant, priest. With the spectators unable to read emotions in the face, the actors are likely to have used large sweeping gestures to express fear, hostility, defiance, and rage. In later periods, the actors wore high-soled boots (a kind of elevator shoe) that amplified their stature. As on Shakespeare's stage and in the Japanese Kabuki theater, male actors, it is assumed, played the female roles.

Actors and Chorus   Greek drama evolved from religious rituals using song and dance. As in the earlier rituals, the **chorus,** a group of performers, made solemn ceremonial entrances and exits. Led by the *choragos,* the chorus chanted and danced at regular intervals in the dramatic action. Before there were individual actors, the chorus, in song and dance, told the whole story. Gradually, individual actors (or soloists) began to act out the high points. Sophocles took an important step by having more than two actors interacting on the stage at one time. In his plays, the chorus reacts to and comments on the action. The chorus verbalizes for us what the reactions of a group of contemporary onlookers might have been.

Offstage Action   Greek drama stays in one place, such as the steps and open area in front of the king's palace. A familiar walk-on part in Greek tragedy is that of the **messenger:** news of key events comes to the central location through messages or eyewitness reports. As a result, there is little external action. The plays do not act out the violence found in the ancient stories. Assassinations, suicides, parricides (slayings of parents), fatal quarrels, the abandonment or exposure of infants—these are reported rather than enacted on the stage. The result is that the plays focus on *psychological* action—the characters' motives, loyalties, decisions, uncertainties—rather than on sensational physical violence.

Unity of Impact   Greek drama concentrates in single-minded fashion on the main action. There are no subplots, no comic interludes. A crisis or fateful conflict comes into focus; we are absorbed in how it came about and what will come of it. The concentrated effect comes from the celebrated **three unities:** unity of place, unity of time (a single day or at most a day and a half), unity of action.

THE DEFINITION OF TRAGEDY

The best-known Greek tragedies were traditional stories of terrible deeds among persons linked by close kinship. Later generations have brought to the tragedies expectations shaped by centuries of discussion of tragedy as a **genre,** or literary form.

Aristotle on Plot   The Greek philosopher Aristotle included guidelines for the ideal tragedy in his discussion of imaginative literature, the *Poetics* (330 B.C.). To Aristotle, the "life and soul" of tragedy was the plot, which had to be more than simply a sequence of disjointed episodes. He said, "The plot should be framed in such a way that even without seeing the events take place someone simply hearing the story should be moved to fear and pity." Aristotle distinguished two major phases:

first, setting up a problem or **complication** and then setting in motion the **denouement** (or unraveling) that resolves the issue. To Aristotle, the most powerful part of the plot was a sudden turn in the fortunes of the main character. This reversal (or **peripety**) was often brought on by an unexpected discovery. The turning point of the play might be the discovery of the true identity of the hero, or it might be the revelation of a long-forgotten incident from the past.

Catharsis and the Tragic Flaw   Aristotle said that it was in the nature of tragedy to "arouse pity and fear." The purpose was to bring about a cleansing or purging, or **catharsis,** of these feelings. To arouse these tragic emotions, the playwright needed a tragic hero neither totally good nor totally bad. To see an outstandingly good person overtaken by undeserved calamity would arouse not fear but indignation—rebellion against unjust punishment. To see a villain come to a well-deserved end would arouse not pity but satisfaction. The ideal character would be an "intermediate" kind of person—great or admirable in some way but in other ways more like us. The character's misfortune would be brought on by an "error of judgment" or an imbalance in the character's personality. Taking their clue from Aristotle, critics have looked in the personality of the hero for the **tragic flaw**—for instance, anger, self-righteousness, or indecision. In ancient Greek religion, the tragic flaw of arrogant humans was **hubris**—the overreaching pride that makes them forget their human limitations and makes them challenge the gods.

Tragedy and Pathos   The central heroic figure should not just be a victim who is ground into the dust and learns nothing from the experience. The mere passive experience of pain and misery would represent not tragedy but **pathos** (from the Greek word for "suffering").

SOPHOCLES AND THE GREEK STAGE

Fate leads the willing, drags the unwilling.
                              CLEANTHES

Sophocles wrote over a hundred plays for the drama festivals of ancient Athens. His *Antigone* (about 441 B.C.) is the first of three plays he based on the traditional story of Oedipus, king of Thebes, and his family. The doomed king had tried in vain to escape the fate marked out for him by the oracle of Apollo—

that I should lie with my own mother, breed
Children from whom all men would turn their eyes;
And that I should be my father's murderer.

Forewarned by the oracle, the parents of Oedipus—King Laius and Queen Jocasta of Thebes—had their newborn son exposed on a mountain to die, but the child was rescued by a shepherd and raised by the King of Corinth as his own son. When Oedipus was a young man, the oracle again sounded its prophecy of incest and parricide. In a vain attempt to thwart the oracle, Oedipus left his foster parents, whom he assumed to be his real parents. On a mountain highway, he became involved in a fatal quarrel and killed another traveler—unknown to him, this traveler was Laius, his real father. He cleared the Theban countryside of the rule of the monstrous Sphinx by solving her deadly riddle, and the grateful citizens of Thebes made him their king. He married their widowed queen Jocasta—unknown to him, his real mother.

In Sophocles' *Oedipus Rex,* Oedipus discovers his true identity and comes face to face with the unspeakable horror of incest. In the earlier *Antigone* play, Sophocles tells the story of the four children from Oedipus' incestuous union with Jocasta. Their father has died in exile, and their uncle Creon is now king of Thebes. Antigone is the more strong-willed and Ismene the more cautious of the two sisters. Of the two sons, one, Eteocles, has died fighting on the side of his native city in a war with neighboring Argos. But Polynices, the other brother, had turned traitor and fought on the side of Argos. He also has been killed in battle. Creon decrees that the corpse of the traitor be denied burial and be left to be devoured by dogs.

Creon's decree sets up the basic **conflict** of the play. On the one hand, loyalty to country—to the city-state (or *polis*)—was then as strong a force as patriotism, with the demands of the state for allegiance, is today. However, as in other early civilizations, burial customs and funeral rites were a cornerstone of Greek religion. Honoring its dead was a central duty of every family. Antigone is caught between these two conflicting loyalties. Should she obey the law of the gods and perform at least a symbolic burial for her dishonored brother? Her central role makes her the tragic **protagonist** in the play. Originally, *protagonist* meant the "first competitor," or first actor, initiating the action. However, today the term stands for a major force or principle of action in the play. Antigone is a powerfully motivated character who sets a fateful chain of events in motion. She is pitted against a worthy opponent, Creon, who is the **antagonist.** He is the counterforce that makes for a clash of powerful opposites.

Sophocles   *(496–406/5 B.C.)*

Sophocles was an honored public servant and military officer during the height of the power of Athens. He wrote over a hundred plays, seven of which have survived. He took first prize in the drama contests at Athens twenty-four times. He died shortly before Athens lost its long war against its chief rival, Sparta.

In reading the Antigone play, try to visualize the clash between protagonist and antagonist as they act out their fateful confrontation. (If you can, try to view the play on videotape.) Antigone and Creon are often face to face, trading pointed scornful remarks in the quick-fire exchanges the Greeks called *stichomythy*. You should also listen carefully to the supporting characters who are caught between the two mighty opposites. Ismene, Antigone's sister, provides a **foil** to Antigone by voicing the more cautious view. Haemon, Antigone's fiancé, is caught between his headstrong father and his strong-willed intended bride. As in the later *Oedipus* play, Tiresias, the blind priest and prophet, is a voice of warning heeded too late.

The characters in this play, and especially the chorus, use **allusions** to myths and legends familiar to Sophocles' audience. The chorus honors Dionysus, "god of many names" (Bacchus, Iacchus). He was the offspring of Zeus' union with a mortal (Semele). Other gods are mentioned: Aphrodite, goddess of love; Ares, god of war; and Demeter, goddess of the harvest. Antigone alludes to Niobe, who wept after losing all her numerous children (and in the end was turned to stone). The chorus compares Antigone's fate to that of Dana', another mortal lover of Zeus, and to the fate of Lycurgus, a king who was punished for trying to suppress the cult of Dionysus.

Antigone   *about 441* B.C.

TRANSLATED BY ROBERT FAGLES

Come out of the twilight
and walk before us a while
friendly, with the light step
of one whose mind is fully made up.
                    BERTOLT BRECHT, *ANTIGONE*

CHARACTERS

ANTIGONE, daughter of OEDIPUS and JOCASTA
ISMENE, sister of ANTIGONE
A CHORUS of old Theban citizens and their LEADER
CREON, king of Thebes, uncle of ANTIGONE and ISMENE
A SENTRY
HAEMON, son of CREON and EURYDICE
TIRESIAS, a blind prophet
A MESSENGER
EURYDICE, wife of CREON
Guards, attendants, and a boy

Prologue

TIME AND SCENE: *The royal house of Thebes. It is still night, and the invad-*
ing armies of Argos have just been driven from the city. Fighting on oppo-
site sides, the sons of Oedipus, Eteocles and Polynices, have killed each
other in combat. Their uncle, CREON, *is now king of Thebes.*

    Enter ANTIGONE, *slipping through the central doors of the palace. She*
motions to her sister, ISMENE, *who follows her cautiously toward an altar*
at the center of the stage.

ANTIGONE: My own flesh and blood—dear sister, dear Ismene,
    how many griefs our father Oedipus handed down!
    Do you know one, I ask you, one grief
    that Zeus will not perfect for the two of us
    while we still live and breathe? There's nothing,   5
    no pain—our lives are pain—no private shame,
    no public disgrace, nothing I haven't seen
    in your griefs and mine. And now this:
    an emergency decree, they say, the Commander
    has just now declared for all of Thebes.   10
    What, haven't you heard? Don't you see?
    The doom reserved for enemies
    marches on the ones we love the most.
ISMENE: Not I, I haven't heard a word, Antigone.
    Nothing of loved ones,   15
    no joy or pain has come my way, not since
    the two of us were robbed of our two brothers,
    both gone in a day, a double blow—
    not since the armies of Argos vanished,
    just this very night. I know nothing more,   20
    whether our luck's improved or ruin's still to come.
ANTIGONE: I thought so. That's why I brought you out here,
    past the gates, so you could hear in private.
ISMENE: What's the matter? Trouble, clearly . . .
    you sound so dark, so grim.   25
ANTIGONE: Why not? Our own brothers' burial!
    Hasn't Creon graced one with all the rites,
    disgraced the other? Eteocles, they say,
    has been given full military honors,
    rightly so—Creon has laid him in the earth   30
    and he goes with glory down among the dead.
    But the body of Polynices, who died miserably—
    why, a city-wide proclamation, rumor has it,
    forbids anyone to bury him, even mourn him.
    He's to be left unwept, unburied, a lovely treasure   35
    for birds that scan the field and feast to their heart's content.

    Such, I hear, is the martial law our good Creon
    lays down for you and me—yes, me, I tell you—

A modern production of *Antigone,* 1990. Photo: Robert A. Haller. From the film *Antigone / Rites of Passion*. Producer/director: Amy Greenfield. Actress: Janet Eilber. Distributed by Mystic Fire Video, Manhattan, and Filmmakers Cooperative.

and he's coming here to alert the uninformed
in no uncertain terms,   40
and he won't treat the matter lightly. Whoever
disobeys in the least will die, his doom is sealed:
stoning to death inside the city walls!

There you have it. You'll soon show what you are,
worth your breeding. Ismene, or a coward—   45
for all your royal blood.

ISMENE: My poor sister, if things have come to this,
    who am I to make or mend them, tell me,
    what good am I to you?
ANTIGONE: Decide.
    Will you share the labor, share the work?   50
ISMENE: What work, what's the risk? What do you mean?
ANTIGONE:

[*Raising her hands.*]

    Will you lift up his body with these bare hands
    and lower it with me?
ISMENE: What? You'd bury him—
    when a law forbids the city?
ANTIGONE: Yes!
    He is my brother and—deny it as you will—   55
    your brother too.
    No one will ever convict me for a traitor.
ISMENE: So desperate, and Creon has expressly—
ANTIGONE: No,
    he has no right to keep me from my own.
ISMENE: Oh my sister, think—   60
    think how our own father died, hated,
    his reputation in ruins, driven on
    by the crimes he brought to light himself
    to gouge out his eyes with his own hands—
    then mother . . . his mother and wife, both in one,   65
    mutilating her life in the twisted noose—
    and last, our two brothers dead in a single day,
    both shedding their own blood, poor suffering boys,
    battling out their common destiny hand-to-hand.

    Now look at the two of us, left so alone . . .   70
    think what a death we'll die, the worst of all
    if we violate the laws and override
    the fixed decree of the throne, its power—
    we must be sensible. Remember we are women,
    we're not born to contend with men. Then too,   75
    we're underlings, ruled by much stronger hands,
    so we must submit in this, and things still worse.

    I, for once, I'll beg the dead to forgive me—
    I'm forced, I have no choice—I must obey
    the ones who stand in power. Why rush to extremes?   80
    It's madness, madness.
ANTIGONE: I won't insist,
    no, even if you should have a change of heart,
    I'd never welcome you in the labor, not with me.
    So, do as you like, whatever suits you best—

I will bury him myself.   85
And even if I die in the act, that death will be a glory.
I will lie with the one I love and loved by him—
an outrage sacred to the gods! I have longer
to please the dead than please the living here:
in the kingdom down below I'll lie forever.   90
Do as you like, dishonor the laws
the gods hold in honor.
ISMENE: I'd do them no dishonor . . .
but defy the city? I have no strength for that.
ANTIGONE: You have your excuses. I am on my way,
I will raise a mound for him, for my dear brother.   95
ISMENE: Oh Antigone, you're so rash—I'm so afraid for you!
ANTIGONE: Don't fear for me. Set your own life in order.
ISMENE: Then don't, at least, blurt this out to anyone.
Keep it a secret. I'll join you in that, I promise.
ANTIGONE: Dear god, shout it from the rooftops. I'll hate you   100
all the more for silence—tell the world!
ISMENE: So fiery—and it ought to chill your heart.
ANTIGONE: I know I please where I must please the most.
ISMENE: Yes, if you can, but you're in love with impossibility.
ANTIGONE: Very well then, once my strength gives out   105
I will be done at last.
ISMENE: You're wrong from the start,
you're off on a hopeless quest.
ANTIGONE: If you say so, you will make me hate you,
and the hatred of the dead, by all rights,
will haunt you night and day.   110
But leave me to my own absurdity, leave me
to suffer this—dreadful thing. I will suffer
nothing as great as death without glory.

                                                    [*Exit to the side.*]

ISMENE: Then go if you must, but rest assured,
wild, irrational as you are, my sister,   115
you are truly dear to the ones who love you.

                                    [*Withdrawing to the palace.*]

[*Enter a* CHORUS, *the old citizens of Thebes, chanting as the sun begins to rise.*]

CHORUS: Glory!—great beam of the sun, brightest of all
that ever rose on the seven gates of Thebes,
          you burn through night at last!
                    Great eye of the golden day,   120
mounting the Dirce's banks you throw him back—
the enemy out of Argos, the white shield, the man of bronze—

he's flying headlong now
      the bridle of fate stampeding him with pain!

    And he had driven against our borders,   125
    launched by the warring claims of Polynices—
    like an eagle screaming, winging havoc
    over the land, wings of armor
    shielded white as snow,
    a huge army massing,   130
    crested helmets bristling for assault.

He hovered above our roofs, his vast maw gaping
closing down around our seven gates,
    his spears thirsting for the kill
        but now he's gone, look,   135
    before he could glut his jaws with Theban blood
    or the god of fire put our crown of towers to the torch.
    He grappled the Dragon none can master—Thebes—
        the clang of our arms like thunder at his back!

    Zeus hates with a vengeance all bravado,   140
    the mighty boasts of men. He watched them
    coming on in a rising flood, the pride
    of their golden armor ringing shrill—
    and brandishing his lightning
    blasted the fighter just at the goal,   145
    rushing to shout his triumph from our walls.
Down from the heights he crashed, pounding down on the earth!
And a moment ago, blazing torch in hand—
        mad for attack, ecstatic
he breathed his rage, the storm   150
    of his fury hurling at our heads!
But now his high hopes have laid him low
and down the enemy ranks the iron god of war
        deals his rewards, his stunning blows—Ares
        rapture of battle, our right arm in the crisis.   155

    Seven captains marshaled at seven gates
    seven against their equals, gave
    their brazen trophies up to Zeus,
    god of the breaking rout of battle,
    all but two: those blood brothers,   160
    one father, one mother—marched in rage,
    spears matched for the twin conquest—
    clashed and won the common prize of death.

But now for Victory! Glorious in the morning,
joy in her eyes to meet our joy   165
    she is winging down to Thebes,

our fleets of chariots wheeling in her wake—
     Now let us win oblivion from the wars,
thronging the temples of the gods
in singing, dancing choirs through the night!   170
     Lord Dionysus, god of the dance
     that shakes the land of Thebes, now lead the way!

Scene 1

[*Enter* CREON *from the palace, attended by his guard.*]

CHORUS: But look, the king of the realm is coming,
    Creon, the new man for the new day,
    whatever the gods are sending now . . .
    what new plan will he launch?
    Why this, this special session?   5
    Why this sudden call to the old men
    summoned at one command?
CREON: My countrymen,
    the ship of state is safe. The gods who rocked her,
    after a long, merciless pounding in the storm,
    have righted her once more.   10
                  Out of the whole city
    I have called you here alone. Well I know,
    first, your undeviating respect
    for the throne and royal power of King Laius.
    Next, while Oedipus steered the land of Thebes,
    and even after he died, your loyalty was unshakable,   15
    you still stood by their children. Now then,
    since the two sons are dead—two blows of fate
    in the same day, cut down by each other's hands,
    both killers, both brothers stained with blood—
    as I am next in kin to the dead,   20
    I now possess the throne and all its powers.

    Of course you cannot know a man completely,
    his character, his principles, sense of judgment,
    not till he's shown his colors, ruling the people,
    making laws. Experience, there's the test.   25
    As I see it, whoever assumes the task,
    the awesome task of setting the city's course,
    and refuses to adopt the soundest policies
    but fearing someone, keeps his lips locked tight,
    he's utterly worthless. So I rate him now,   30
    I always have. And whoever places a friend
    above the good of his own country, he is nothing:
    I have no use for him. Zeus my witness,
    Zeus who sees all things, always—

I could never stand by silent, watching destruction   35
march against our city, putting safety to rout,
nor could I ever make that man a friend of mine
who menaces our country. Remember this:
our country *is* our safety.
Only while she voyages true on course   40
can we establish friendships, truer than blood itself,
Such are my standards. They make our city great.

Closely akin to them I have proclaimed,
just now, the following decree to our people
concerning the two sons of Oedipus.   45
Eteocles, who died fighting for Thebes,
excelling all in arms: he shall be buried,
crowned with a hero's honors, the cups we pour
to soak the earth and reach the famous dead.

But as for his blood brother, Polynices,   50
who returned from exile, home to his father-city
and the gods of his race, consumed with one desire—
to burn them roof to roots—who thirsted to drink
his kinsmen's blood and sell the rest to slavery:
that man—a proclamation has forbidden the city   55
to dignify him with burial, mourn him at all.
No, he must be left unburied, his corpse
carrion for the birds and dogs to tear,
an obscenity for the citizens to behold!

These are my principles. Never at my hands   60
will the traitor be honored above the patriot.
But whoever proves his loyalty to the state—
I'll prize that man in death as well as life.
LEADER: If this is your pleasure, Creon, treating
our city's enemy and our friend this way . . .   65
The power is yours, I suppose, to enforce it
with the laws, both for the dead and all of us,
the living.
CREON: Follow my orders closely then,
be on your guard.
LEADER: We are too old.
Lay that burden on younger shoulders.
CREON: No, no,   70
I don't mean the body—I've posted guards already.
LEADER: What commands for us then? What other service?
CREON: See that you never side with those who break my orders.
LEADER: Never. Only a fool could be in love with death.
CREON: Death is the price—you're right. But all too often   75
the mere hope of money has ruined many men.

[*A* SENTRY *enters from the side.*]

SENTRY: My lord,
I can't say I'm winded from running, or set out
with any spring in my legs either—no sir,
I was lost in thought, and it made me stop, often,
dead in my tracks, wheeling, turning back,   80
and all the time a voice inside me muttering,
"Idiot, why? You're going straight to your death."
Then muttering, "Stopped again, poor fool?
If somebody gets the news to Creon first,
what's to save your neck?"
                                            And so,   85
mulling it over, on I trudged, dragging my feet,
you can make a short road take forever . . .
but at last, look, common sense won out,
I'm here, and I'm all yours,
and even though I come empty-handed   90
I'll tell my story just the same, because
I've come with a good grip on one hope,
what will come will come, whatever fate—
CREON: Come to the point!
What's wrong—why so afraid?   95
SENTRY: First, myself, I've got to tell you,
I didn't do it, didn't see who did—
Be fair, don't take it out on me.
CREON: You're playing it safe, soldier,
barricading yourself from any trouble.   100
It's obvious, you've something strange to tell.
SENTRY: Dangerous too, and danger makes you delay
for all you're worth.
CREON: Out with it—then dismiss!
SENTRY: All right, here it comes. The body—   105
someone's just buried it, then run off . . .
sprinkled some dry dust on the flesh,
given it proper rites.
CREON: What?
What man alive would dare—
SENTRY: I've no idea, I swear it.
There was no mark of a spade, no pickaxe there,   110
no earth turned up, the ground packed hard and dry,
unbroken, no tracks, no wheelruts, nothing,
the workman left no trace. Just at sunup
the first watch of the day points it out—
it was a wonder! We were stunned . . .   115
a terrific burden too, for all of us, listen:
you can't see the corpse, not that it's buried,
really, just a light cover of road-dust on it,
as if someone meant to lay the dead to rest
and keep from getting cursed.   120

Not a sign in sight that dogs or wild beasts
had worried the body, even torn the skin.

But what came next! Rough talk flew thick and fast,
guard grilling guard—we'd have come to blows
at last, nothing to stop it; each man for himself   125
and each the culprit, no one caught red-handed,
all of us pleading ignorance, dodging the charges,
ready to take up red-hot iron in our fists,
go through fire, swear oaths to the gods—
"I didn't do it, I had no hand in it either,   130
not in the plotting, not the work itself!"

Finally, after all this wrangling came to nothing,
one man spoke out and made us stare at the ground,
hanging our heads in fear. No way to counter him,
no way to take his advice and come through   135
safe and sound. Here's what he said:
"Look, we've got to report the facts to Creon,
we can't keep this hidden." Well, that won out,
and the lot fell to me, condemned me,
unlucky as ever, I got the prize. So here I am,   140
against my will and yours too, well I know—
no one wants the man who brings bad news.

LEADER: My king,
ever since he began I've been debating in my mind,
could this possibly be the work of the gods?

CREON: Stop—
before you make me choke with anger—the gods!   145
You, you're senile, must you be insane?
You say—why it's intolerable—say the gods
could have the slightest concern for that corpse?
Tell me, was it for meritorious service
they proceeded to bury him, prized him so? The hero   150
who came to burn their temples ringed with pillars,
their golden treasures—scorch their hallowed earth
and fling their laws to the winds.
Exactly when did you last see the gods
celebrating traitors? Inconceivable!   155

No, from the first there were certain citizens
who could hardly stand the spirit of my regime,
grumbling against me in the dark, heads together,
tossing wildly, never keeping their necks beneath
the yoke, loyally submitting to their king.   160
These are the instigators, I'm convinced—
they've perverted my own guard, bribed them
to do their work.
                    Money! Nothing worse

in our lives, so current, rampant, so corrupting.
Money—you demolish cities, root men from their homes,   165
you train and twist good minds and set them on
to the most atrocious schemes. No limit,
you make them adept at every kind of outrage,
every godless crime—money!
                        Everyone—
the whole crew bribed to commit this crime,   170
they've made one thing sure at least;
sooner or later they will pay the price.

[*Wheeling on the* SENTRY.]

                        You—
I swear to Zeus as I still believe in Zeus,
if you don't find the man who buried that corpse,
the very man, and produce him before my eyes,   175
simple death won't be enough for you,
not till we string you up alive
and wring the immorality out of you.
Then you can steal the rest of your days,
better informed about where to make a killing.   180
You'll have learned, at last, it doesn't pay
to itch for rewards from every hand that beckons.
Filthy profits wreck most men, you'll see—
they'll never save your life.
SENTRY: Please,
    may I say a word or two, or just turn and go?   185
CREON: Can't you tell? Everything you say offends me.
SENTRY: Where does it hurt you, in the ears or in the heart?
CREON: And who are you to pinpoint my displeasure?
SENTRY: The culprit grates on your feelings,
    I just annoy your ears.
CREON: Still talking?   190
    You talk too much! A born nuisance—
SENTRY: Maybe so,
    but I never did this thing, so help me!
CREON: Yes you did—
    what's more, you squandered your life for silver!
SENTRY: Oh it's terrible when the one who does the judging
    judges things all wrong.
CREON: Well now,   195
    you just be clever about your judgments—
    if you fail to produce the criminals for me,
    you'll swear your dirty money brought you pain.

                [*Turning sharply, reentering the palace.*]

SENTRY: I hope he's found. Best thing by far.
    But caught or not, that's in the lap of fortune: 200

I'll never come back, you've seen the last of me.
I'm saved, even now, and I never thought,
I never hoped—
dear gods, I owe you all my thanks!

[*Rushing out.*]

CHORUS: Numberless wonders
terrible wonders walk the world but none the match for man—   205
that great wonder crossing the heaving gray sea,
                    driven on by the blasts of winter
on through breakers crashing left and right,
        holds his steady course
and the oldest of the gods he wears away—   210
the Earth, the immortal, the inexhaustible—
as his plows go back and forth, year in, year out
        with the breed of stallions turning up the furrows.

And the blithe, lightheaded race of birds he snares,
and tribes of savage beasts, the life that swarms the depths—   215
                    with one fling of his nets
woven and coiled tight, he takes them all,
        man the skilled, the brilliant
He conquers all, taming with his techniques
the prey that roams the cliffs and wild lairs,   220
training the stallion, clamping the yoke across
        his shaggy neck, and the tireless mountain bull.

And speech and thought, quick as the wind
and the mood and mind for law that rules the city—
        all these he has taught himself   225
and shelter from the arrows of the frost
when there's rough lodging under the cold clear sky
and the shafts of lashing rain—
        ready, resourceful man!
                Never without resources   230
never an impasse as he marches on the future—
only Death, from Death alone he will find no rescue
but from desperate plagues he has plotted his escapes.

Man the master, ingenious past all measure
past all dreams, the skills within his grasp—   235
        he forges on, now to destruction
now again to greatness. When he weaves in
the laws of the land, and the justice of the gods
that binds his oaths together
        he and his city rise high—   240
                but the city casts out
that man who weds himself to inhumanity
thanks to the reckless daring. Never share my hearth
never think my thoughts, whoever does such things.

Scene 2

[*Enter* ANTIGONE *from the side, accompanied by the* SENTRY.]

CHORUS: Here is a dark sign from the gods—
    what to make of this? I know her,
    how can I deny it? That young girl's Antigone!
    Wretched, child of a wretched father,
    Oedipus. Look, is it possible?   5
    They bring you in like a prisoner—
    why? did you break the king's laws?
    Did they take you in some act of mad defiance?
SENTRY: She's the one, she did it single-handed—
    we caught her burying the body. Where's Creon?   10

[*Enter* CREON *from the palace.*]

LEADER: Back again, just in time when you need him.
CREON: In time for what? What is it?
SENTRY: My king,
    there's nothing you can swear you'll never do—
    second thoughts make liars of us all.
    I could have sworn I wouldn't hurry back   15
    (what with your threats, the buffeting I just took),
    but a stroke of luck beyond our wildest hopes,
    what a joy, there's nothing like it. So,
    back I've come, breaking my oath, who cares?
    I'm bringing in our prisoner—this young girl—   20
    we took her giving the dead the last rites.
    But no casting lots this time; this is *my* luck,
    my prize, no one else's.
                         Now, my lord,
    here she is. Take her, question her,
    cross-examine her to your heart's content.   25
    But set me free, it's only right—
    I'm rid of this dreadful business once for all.
CREON: Prisoner! Her? You took her—where, doing what?
SENTRY: Burying the man. That's the whole story.
CREON: What?
    You mean what you say, you're telling me the truth?   30
SENTRY: She's the one. With my own eyes I saw her
    bury the body, just what you've forbidden.
    There. Is that plain and clear?
CREON: What did you see? Did you catch her in the act?
SENTRY: Here's what happened. We went back to our post,   35
    those threats of yours breathing down our necks—
    we brushed the corpse clean of the dust that covered it,
    stripped it bare . . . it was slimy, going soft,
    and we took to high ground, backs to the wind

so the stink of him couldn't hit us;   40
jostling, baiting each other to keep awake,
shouting back and forth—no napping on the job,
not this time. And so the hours dragged by
until the sun stood dead above our heads,
a huge white ball in the noon sky, beating,   45
blazing down, and then it happened—
suddenly, a whirlwind!
Twisting a great dust-storm up from the earth,
a black plague of the heavens, filling the plain,
ripping the leaves off every tree in sight,   50
choking the air and sky. We squinted hard
and took our whipping from the gods.

And after the storm passed—it seemed endless—
there, we saw the girl!
And she cried out a sharp, piercing cry,   55
like a bird come back to an empty nest,
peering into its bed, and all the babies gone . . .
Just so, when she sees the corpse bare
she bursts into a long, shattering wail
and calls down withering curses on the heads   60
of all who did the work. And she scoops up dry dust,
handfuls, quickly, and lifting a fine bronze urn,
lifting it high and pouring, she crowns the dead
with three full libations.
                         Soon as we saw
we rushed her, closed on the kill like hunters,   65
and she, she didn't flinch. We interrogated her,
charging her with offenses past and present—
she stood up to it all, denied nothing. I tell you,
it made me ache and laugh in the same breath.
It's pure joy to escape the worst yourself,   70
it hurts a man to bring down his friends.
But all that, I'm afraid, means less to me
than my own skin. That's the way I'm made.
CREON:

[*Wheeling on* ANTIGONE.]

                                                      You,
with your eyes fixed on the ground—speak up.
Do you deny you did this, yes or no?   75
ANTIGONE: I did it. I don't deny a thing.
CREON:

[*To the* SENTRY.]

You, get out, wherever you please—
you're clear of a very heavy charge.

[*He leaves;* CREON *turns back to* ANTIGONE.]

You, tell me briefly, no long speeches—
were you aware a decree had forbidden this?   80
ANTIGONE: Well aware. How could I avoid it? It was public.
CREON: And still you had the gall to break this law?
ANTIGONE: Of course I did. It wasn't Zeus, not in the least,
    who made this proclamation—not to me.
    Nor did that Justice, dwelling with the gods   85
    beneath the earth, ordain such laws for men.
    Nor did I think your edict had such force
    that you, a mere mortal, could override the gods,
    the great unwritten, unshakable traditions.
    They are alive, not just today or yesterday: 90
    they live forever, from the first of time,
    and no one knows when they first saw the light.

    These laws—I was not about to break them,
    not out of fear of some man's wounded pride,
    and face the retribution of the gods.   95
    Die I must, I've known it all my life—
    how could I keep from knowing?—even without
    your death-sentence ringing in my ears.
    And if I am to die before my time
    I consider that a gain. Who on earth,   100
    alive in the midst of so much grief as I,
    could fail to find his death a rich reward?
    So for me, at least, to meet this doom of yours
    is precious little pain. But if I had allowed
    my own mother's son to rot, an unburied corpse—   105
    that would have been an agony! This is nothing.
    And if my present actions strike you as foolish,
    let's just say I've been accused of folly
    by a fool.
LEADER: Like father like daughter,
    passionate, wild . . .   110
    she hasn't learned to bend before adversity.
CREON: No? Believe me, the stiffest stubborn wills
    fall the hardest; the toughest iron,
    tempered strong in the white-hot fire,
    you'll see it crack and shatter first of all.   115
    And I've known spirited horses you can break
    with a light bit—proud, rebellious horses.
    There's no room for pride, not in a slave,
    not with the lord and master standing by.

    This girl was an old hand at insolence   120
    when she overrode the edicts we made public.
    But once she had done it—the insolence,

twice over—to glory in it, laughing,
mocking us to our face with what she'd done.
I am not the man, not now: she is the man   125
if this victory goes to her and she goes free.

Never! Sister's child or closer in blood
than all my family clustered at my altar
worshiping Guardian Zeus—she'll never escape,
she and her blood sister, the most barbaric death.   130
Yes, I accuse her sister of an equal part
in scheming this, this burial.

[*To his attendants.*]

                  Bring her here!
I just saw her inside, hysterical, gone to pieces.
It never fails: the mind convicts itself
in advance, when scoundrels are up to no good,   135
plotting in the dark. Oh but I hate it more
when a traitor, caught red-handed,
tries to glorify his crimes.
ANTIGONE: Creon, what more do you want
    than my arrest and execution?   140
CREON: Nothing. Then I have it all.
ANTIGONE: Then why delay? Your moralizing repels me,
    every word you say—pray god it always will.
    So naturally all I say repels you too.
                    Enough.
Give me glory! What greater glory could I win   145
than to give my own brother decent burial?
These citizens here would all agree,

[*To the* CHORUS.]

they would praise me too
if their lips weren't locked in fear.

[*Pointing to* CREON.]

Lucky tyrants—the perquisites of power!   150
    Ruthless power to do and say whatever pleases *them.*
CREON: You alone, of all the people in Thebes,
    see things that way.
ANTIGONE: They see it just that way
    but defer to you and keep their tongues in leash.
CREON: And you, aren't you ashamed to differ so from them?   155
    So disloyal!
ANTIGONE: Not ashamed for a moment,
    not to honor my brother, my own flesh and blood.

CREON: Wasn't Eteocles a brother too—cut down, facing him?

ANTIGONE: Brother, yes, by the same mother, the same father.

CREON: Then how can you render his enemy such honors,   160
    such impieties in his eyes?

ANTIGONE: He will never testify to that,
    Eteocles dead and buried.

CREON: He will—
    if you honor the traitor just as much as him.

ANTIGONE: But it was his brother, not some slave that died—   165

CREON: Ravaging our country!—
    but Eteocles died fighting in our behalf.

ANTIGONE: No matter—Death longs for the same rites for all.

CREON: Never the same for the patriot and the traitor.

ANTIGONE: Who, Creon, who on earth can say the ones below   170
    don't find this pure and uncorrupt?

CREON: Never. Once an enemy, never a friend,
    not even after death.

ANTIGONE: I was born to join in love, not hate—
    that is my nature.

CREON: Go down below and love,   175
    if love you must—love the dead! While I'm alive,
    no woman is going to lord it over me.

[Enter ISMENE *from the palace, under guard.*]

CHORUS: Look,
    Ismene's coming, weeping a sister's tears,
    loving sister, under a cloud . . .
    her face is flushed, her cheeks streaming.   180
    Sorrow puts her lovely radiance in the dark.

CREON: You—
    in my own house, you viper, slinking undetected,
    sucking my life-blood! I never knew
    I was breeding twin disasters, the two of you
    rising up against my throne. Come, tell me,   185
    will you confess your part in the crime or not?
    Answer me. Swear to me.

ISMENE: I did it, yes—
    if only she consents—I share the guilt,
    the consequences too.

ANTIGONE: No,
    Justice will never suffer that—not you,   190
    you were unwilling. I never brought you in.

ISMENE: But now you face such dangers . . . I'm not ashamed
    to sail through trouble with you,
    make your troubles mine.

ANTIGONE: Who did the work?
    Let the dead and the god of death bear witness!   195
    I have no love for a friend who loves in words alone.

ISMENE: Oh no, my sister, don't reject me, please,
   let me die beside you, consecrating
   the dead together.
ANTIGONE: Never share my dying,
   don't lay claim to what you never touched.   200
   My death will be enough.
ISMENE: What do I care for life, cut off from you?
ANTIGONE: Ask Creon. Your concern is all for him.
ISMENE: Why abuse me so? It doesn't help you now.
ANTIGONE: You're right—   205
   if I mock you, I get no pleasure from it,
   only pain.
ISMENE: Tell me, dear one,
   what can I do to help you, even now?
ANTIGONE: Save yourself. I don't grudge you your survival.
ISMENE: Oh no, no, denied my portion in your death?
ANTIGONE: You chose to live, I chose to die.
ISMENE: Not, at least,   210
   without every kind of caution I could voice.
ANTIGONE: Your wisdom appealed to one world—mine, another.
ISMENE: But look, we're both guilty, both condemned to death.
ANTIGONE: Courage! Live your life. I gave myself to death,
   long ago, so I might serve the dead.   215
CREON: They're both mad, I tell you, the two of them.
   One's just shown it, the other's been that way
   since she was born.
ISMENE: True, my king,
   the sense we were born with cannot last forever . . .
   commit cruelty on a person long enough   220
   and the mind begins to go.
CREON: Yours did,
   when you chose to commit your crimes with her.
ISMENE: How can I live alone, without her?
CREON: Her?
   Don't even mention her—she no longer exists.
ISMENE: What? You'd kill your own son's bride?
CREON: Absolutely: 225
   there are other fields for him to plow.
ISMENE: Perhaps,
   but never as true, as close a bond as theirs.
CREON: A worthless woman for my son? It repels me.
ISMENE: Dearest Haemon, your father wrongs you so!
CREON: Enough, enough—you and your talk of marriage!   230
ISMENE: Creon—you're really going to rob your son of Antigone?
CREON: Death will do it for me—break their marriage off.
LEADER: So, it's settled then? Antigone must die?
CREON: Settled, yes—we both know that.

   [*To the guards.*]

Stop wasting time. Take them in.   235
From now on they'll act like women.
Tie them up, no more running loose;
even the bravest will cut and run,
once they see Death coming for their lives.

[*The guards escort* ANTIGONE *and* ISMENE *into the palace.* CREON *remains
while the old citizens form their* CHORUS.]

CHORUS: Blest, they are the truly blest who all their lives   240
    have never tasted devastation. For others, once
    the gods have rocked a house to its foundations
        the ruin will never cease, cresting on and on
        from one generation on throughout the race—
like a great mounting tide   245
driven on by savage northern gales,
        surging over the dead black depths
roiling up from the bottom dark heaves of sand
and the headlands, taking the storm's onslaught full-force,
roar, and the low moaning
            echoes on and on
                and now   250
as in ancient times I see the sorrows of the house,
the living heirs of the old ancestral kings,
piling on the sorrows of the dead
    and one generation cannot free the next—
some god will bring them crashing down,   255
the race finds no release.
And now the light, the hope
        springing up from the late last root
in the house of Oedipus, that hope's cut down in turn
by the long, bloody knife swung by the gods of death   260
by a senseless word
        by fury at the heart.
                Zeus,
yours is the power, Zeus, what man on earth
can override it, who can hold it back?
Power that neither Sleep, the all-ensnaring
    no, nor the tireless months of heaven   265
can ever overmaster—young through all time,
mighty lord of power, you hold fast
    the dazzling crystal mansions of Olympus.
And throughout the future, late and soon
as through the past, your law prevails: 270
no towering form of greatness
    enters into the lives of mortals
        free and clear of ruin.
              True,
our dreams, our high hopes voyaging far and wide

bring sheer delight to many, to many others   275
  delusion, blithe, mindless lusts
and the fraud steals on one slowly . . . unaware
till he trips and puts his foot into the fire.
  He was a wise old man who coined
the famous saying: "Sooner or later   280
foul is fair, fair is foul
to the man the gods will ruin"—
  He goes his way for a moment only
    free of blinding ruin.

Scene 3

[*Enter* HAEMON *from the palace.*]

CHORUS: Here's Haemon now, the last of all you sons.
  Does he come in tears for his bride,
  his doomed bride, Antigone—
  bitter at being cheated of their marriage?
CREON: We'll soon know, better than seers could tell us.   5

[*Turning to* HAEMON.]

Son, you've heard the final verdict on your bride?
Are you coming now, raving against your father?
Or do you love me, no matter what I do?
HAEMON: Father, I'm your *son* . . . you in your wisdom
set my bearings for me—I obey you.   10
No marriage could ever mean more to me than you,
whatever good direction you may offer.
CREON: Fine, Haemon.
That's how you ought to feel within your heart,
subordinate to your father's will in every way.
That's what a man prays for: to produce good sons—   15
a household full of them, dutiful and attentive,
so they can pay his enemy back with interest
and match the respect their father shows his friend.
But the man who rears a brood of useless children,
what has he brought into the world, I ask you?   20
Nothing but trouble for himself, and mockery
from his enemies laughing in his face.
        Oh Haemon,
never lose your sense of judgment over a woman.
The warmth, the rush of pleasure, it all goes cold
in your arms, I warn you . . . a worthless woman   25
in your house, a misery in your bed.
What wound cuts deeper than a loved one
turned against you? Spit her out,

like a mortal enemy—let the girl go.
Let her find a husband down among the dead.   30

Imagine it: I caught her in naked rebellion,
the traitor, the only one in the whole city.
I'm not about to prove myself a liar,
not to my people, no, I'm going to kill her!
That's right—so let her cry for mercy, sing her hymns   35
to Zeus who defends all bonds of kindred blood.
Why, if I bring up my own kin to be rebels,
think what I'd suffer from the world at large.
Show me the man who rules his household well:
I'll show you someone fit to rule the state.   40
That good man, my son,
I have every confidence he and he alone
can give commands and take them too. Staunch
in the storm of spears he'll stand his ground,
a loyal, unflinching comrade at your side.   45

But whoever steps out of line, violates the laws
or presumes to hand out orders to his superiors,
he'll win no praise from me. But that man
the city places in authority, his orders
must be obeyed, large and small,   50
right and wrong.
                         Anarchy—
show me a greater crime in all the earth!
She, she destroys cities, rips up houses,
breaks the ranks of spearmen into headlong rout.
But the ones who last it out, the great mass of them   55
owe their lives to discipline. Therefore
we must defend the men who live by law,
never let some woman triumph over us.
Better to fall from power, if fall we must,
at the hands of a man—never be rated   60
inferior to a woman, never.
LEADER: To us,
unless old age has robbed us of our wits,
you seem to say what you have to say with sense.
HAEMON: Father, only the gods endow a man with reason,
the finest of all their gifts, a treasure.   65
Far be it from me—I haven't the skill,
and certainly no desire, to tell you when,
if ever, you make a slip in speech . . . though
someone else might have a good suggestion.

Of course, it's not for you,   70
in the normal run of things, to watch
whatever men say or do, or find to criticize.
The man in the street, you know, dreads your glance,

he'd never say anything displeasing to your face.
But it's for me to catch the murmurs in the dark,   75
the way the city mourns for this young girl.
"No woman," they say, "ever deserved death less,
and such a brutal death for such a glorious action.
She, with her own dear brother lying in his blood—
she couldn't bear to leave him dead, unburied,   80
food for the wild dogs or wheeling vultures.
Death? She deserves a glowing crown of gold!"
So they say, and the rumor spreads in secret,
darkly . . .
    I rejoice in your success, father—
nothing more precious to me in the world.   85
What medal of honor brighter to his children
than a father's growing glory? Or a child's
to his proud father? Now don't, please,
be quite so single-minded, self-involved,
or assume the world is wrong and you are right.   90
Whoever thinks that he alone possesses intelligence,
the gift of eloquence, he and no one else,
and character too . . . such men, I tell you,
spread them open—you will find them empty.
          No,
it's no disgrace for a man, even a wise man,   95
to learn many things and not to be too rigid.
You've seen trees by a raging winter torrent,
how many sway with the flood and salvage every twig,
but not the stubborn—they're ripped out, roots and all.
Bend or break. The same when a man is sailing: 100
haul your sheets too taut, never give an inch,
you'll capsize, and go the rest of the voyage
keel up and the rowing-benches under.

Oh give way. Relax your anger—change!
I'm young, I know, but let me offer this: 105
it would be best by far, I admit,
if a man were born infallible, right by nature.
If not—and things don't often go that way,
it's best to learn from those with good advice.
LEADER: You'd do well, my lord, if he's speaking to the point,   110
to learn from him,

[*Turning to* HAEMON.]

     and you, my boy, from him.
You both are talking sense.
CREON: So,
men our age, we're to be lectured, are we?—
schooled by a boy his age?

HAEMON: Only in what is right. But if I seem young,   115
  look less to my years and more to what I do.
CREON: Do? Is admiring rebels an achievement?
HAEMON: I'd never suggest that you admire treason.
CREON: Oh?—
  isn't that just the sickness that's attacked her?
HAEMON: The whole city of Thebes denies it, to a man.   120
CREON: And is Thebes about to tell me how to rule?
HAEMON: Now, you see? Who's talking like a child?
CREON: Am I to rule this land for others—or myself?
HAEMON: It's no city at all, owned by one man alone.
CREON: What? The city *is* the king's—that's the law!   125
HAEMON: What a splendid king you'd make of a desert island—
  you and you alone.
CREON:

[*To the* CHORUS.]

                      This boy, I do believe,
  is fighting on her side, the woman's side.
HAEMON: If you are a woman, yes—
  my concern is all for you.   130
CREON: Why, you degenerate—bandying accusations,
  threatening me with justice, your own father!
HAEMON: I see my father offending justice—wrong.
CREON: Wrong?
  To protect my royal rights?
HAEMON: Protect your rights?
  When you trample down the honors of the gods?   135
CREON: You, you soul of corruption, rotten through—
  woman's accomplice!
HAEMON: That may be,
  but you will never find me accomplice to a criminal.
CREON: That's what *she* is,
  and every word you say is a blatant appeal for her—   140
HAEMON: And you, and me, and the gods beneath the earth.
CREON: You will never marry her, not while she's alive.
HAEMON: Then she will die . . . but her death will kill another.
CREON: What, brazen threats? You go too far!
HAEMON: What threat?
  Combating your empty, mindless judgments with a word?   145
CREON: You'll suffer for your sermons, you and your empty wisdom!
HAEMON: If you weren't my father, I'd say you were insane.
CREON: Don't flatter me with Father—you woman's slave!
HAEMON: You really expect to fling abuse at me
  and not receive the same?
CREON: Is that so!   150
  Now, by heaven, I promise you, you'll pay—
  taunting, insulting me! Bring her out,

that hateful—she'll die now, here,
in front of his eyes, beside her groom!
HAEMON: No, no, she will never die beside me—   155
don't delude yourself. And you will never
see me, never set eyes on my face again.
Rage your heart out, rage with friends
who can stand the sight of you.

[*Rushing out.*]

LEADER: Gone, my king, in a burst of anger.   160
A temper young as his . . . hurt him once,
he may do something violent.
CREON: Let him do—
dream up something desperate, past all human limit!
Good riddance. Rest assured,
he'll never save those two young girls from death.   165
LEADER: Both of them, you really intend to kill them both?
CREON: No, not her, the one whose hands are clean—
you're quite right.
LEADER: But Antigone—
what sort of death do you have in mind for her?
CREON: I will take her down some wild, desolate path   170
never trod by men, and wall her up alive
in a rocky vault, and set out short rations,
just the measure piety demands
to keep the entire city free of defilement.
There let her pray to the one god she worships: 175
Death—who knows?—may just reprieve her from death.
Or she may learn at last, better late than never,
what a waste of breath it is to worship Death.

[*Exit to the palace.*]

CHORUS: Love, never conquered in battle
Love the plunderer laying waste the rich!   180
Love standing the night-watch
          guarding a girl's soft cheek,
you range the seas, the shepherds' steadings off in the wilds—
not even the deathless gods can flee your onset,
nothing human born for a day—   185
whoever feels your grip is driven mad.
                              Love!—
you wrench the minds of the righteous into outrage,
swerve them to their ruin—you have ignited this,
this kindred strife, father and son at war
          and Love alone the victor—   190
warm glance of the bride triumphant, burning with desire!
Throned in power, side-by-side with the mighty laws!

Irresistible Aphrodite, never conquered—
Love, you mock us for your sport.
        But now, even, I would rebel against the king,   195
        I would break all bounds when I see this—
        I fill with tears, I cannot hold them back,
        not any more . . . I see Antigone make her way
        to the bridal vault where all are laid to rest.

Scene 4

[ANTIGONE *is brought from the palace under guard.*]

ANTIGONE: Look at me, men of my fatherland,
        setting out on the last road
looking into the last light of day
the last I will ever see . . .
the god of death who puts us all to bed   5
takes me down to the banks of Acheron alive—
        denied my part in the wedding-songs,
no wedding-song in the dusk has crowned my marriage—
I go to wed the lord of the dark waters.
CHORUS: Not crowned with glory or with a dirge,   10
        you leave for the deep pit of the dead.
        No withering illness laid you low,
        no strokes of the sword—a law to yourself,
        alone, no mortal like you, ever, you go down
        to the halls of Death alive and breathing.   15
ANTIGONE: But think of Niobe—well I know her story—
        think what a living death she died,
Tantalus' daughter, stranger queen from the east:
there on the mountain heights, growing stone
binding as ivy, slowly walled her round   20
and the rains will never cease, the legends say
the snows will never leave her . . .
        wasting away, under her brows the tears
showering down her breasting ridge and slopes—
a rocky death like hers puts me to sleep.   25
CHORUS: But she was a god, born of gods,
        and we are only mortals born to die.
        And yet, of course, it's a great thing
        for a dying girl to hear, even to hear
        she shares a destiny equal to the gods,   30
        during life and later, once she's dead.
ANTIGONE: O you mock me!
Why, in the name of all my father's gods
why can't you wait till I am gone—
        must you abuse me to my face?
O my city, all your fine rich sons!   35

And you, you springs of the Dirce,
holy grove of Thebes where the chariots gather,
        you at least, you'll bear me witness, look,
unmourned by friends and forced by such crude laws
I go to my rockbound prison, strange new tomb—   40
      always a stranger, O dear god,
      I have no home on earth and none below,
        not with the living, not with the breathless dead.
CHORUS: You went too far, the last limits of daring—
      smashing against the high throne of Justice!   45
        Your life's in ruins, child—I wonder . . .
      do you pay for your father's terrible ordeal?
ANTIGONE: There—at last you've touched it, the worst pain
the worst anguish! Raking up the grief for father
        three times over, for all the doom   50
that's struck us down, the brilliant house of Laius.
O mother, your marriage-bed
the coiling horrors, the coupling there—
        you with your own son, my father—doomstruck mother!
Such, such were my parents, and I their wretched child.   55
I go to them now, cursed, unwed, to share their home—
        I am a stranger! O dear brother, doomed
      in your marriage—your marriage murders mine,
        your dying drags me down to death alive!

[*Enter* CREON.]

CHORUS: Reverence asks some reverence in return—   60
      but attacks on power never go unchecked,
        not by the man who holds the reins of power.
      Your own blind will, your passion has destroyed you.
ANTIGONE: No one to weep for me, my friends,
      no wedding-song—they take me away   65
      in all my pain . . . the road lies open, waiting.
      Never again, the law forbids me to see
      the sacred eye of day. I am agony!
      No tears for the destiny that's mine,
      no loved one mourns my death.
CREON: Can't you see?   70
If a man could wail his own dirge *before* he dies,
he'd never finish.

[*To the guards.*]

        Take her away, quickly!
Wall her up in the tomb, you have your orders.
Abandon her there, alone, and let her choose—
death or a buried life with a good roof for shelter.   75
As for myself, my hands are clean. This young girl—

dead or alive, she will be stripped of her rights,
her stranger's rights, here in the world above.
ANTIGONE: O tomb, my bridal-bed—my house, my prison
    cut in the hollow rock, my everlasting watch!   80
    I'll soon be there, soon embrace my own,
    the great growing family of our dead
    Persephone has received among her ghosts.
                                    I,

the last of them all, the most reviled by far,
go down before my destined time's run out.   85
But still I go, cherishing one good hope:
my arrival may be dear to father,
dear to you, my mother,
dear to you, my loving brother, Eteocles—
When you died I washed you with my hands,   90
I dressed you all, I poured the sacred cups
across your tombs. But now, Polynices,
because I laid your body out as well,
this, this is my reward. Nevertheless
I honored you—the decent will admit it—   95
well and wisely too.
                    Never, I tell you,
if I had been the mother of children
or if my husband had died, exposed and rotting—
I'd never have taken this ordeal upon myself,
never defied our people's will. What law,   100
you ask, do I satisfy with what I say?
A husband dead, there might have been another.
A child by another too, if I had lost the first.
But mother and father both lost in the halls of Death,
no brother could ever spring to light again.   105
For this law alone I held you first in honor.
For this, Creon, the king, judges me a criminal
guilty of dreadful outrage, my dear brother!
And now he leads me off, a captive in his hands,
with no part in the bridal-song, the bridal-bed,   110
denied all joy of marriage, raising children—
deserted so by loved ones, struck by fate,
I descend alive to the caverns of the dead.

What law of the mighty gods have I transgressed?
Why look to the heavens any more, tormented as I am?   115
Whom to call, what comrades now? Just think,
my reverence only brands me for irreverence!
Very well: if this is the pleasure of the gods,
once I suffer I will know that I was wrong.
But if these men are wrong, let them suffer   120
nothing worse than they mete out to me—
these masters of injustice!

LEADER: Still the same rough winds, the wild passion
  raging through the girl.
CREON:

[*To the guards.*]

                 Take her away.
You're wasting time—you'll pay for it too.   125
ANTIGONE: Oh god, the voice of death. It's come, it's here.
CREON: True. Not a word of hope—your doom is sealed.
ANTIGONE: Land of Thebes, city of all my fathers—
     O you gods, the first gods of the race!
     They drag me away, now, no more delay.   130
     Look on me, you noble sons of Thebes—
     the last of a great line of kings,
     I alone, see what I suffer now
     at the hands of what breed of men—
     all for reverence, my reverence for the gods!   135

[*She leaves under guard; the* CHORUS *gathers.*]

CHORUS: Danaë, Danaë—
  even she endured a fate like yours,
     in all her lovely strength she traded
  the light of day for the bolted brazen vault—
  buried within her tomb, her bridal-chamber,   140
  wed to the yoke and broken.
     But she was of glorious birth
           my child, my child
  and treasured the seed of Zeus within her womb,
  the cloudburst streaming gold!   145
      The power of fate is a wonder,
      dark, terrible wonder—
      neither wealth nor armies
      towered walls nor ships
      black hulls lashed by the salt   150
      can save us from that force.

The yoke tamed him too
  young Lycurgus flaming in anger
king of Edonia, all for his mad taunts
Dionysus clamped him down, encased   155
in the chain-mail of rock
  and there his rage
         his terrible flowering rage burst—
sobbing, dying away . . . at last that madman
came to know his god—   160
     the power he mocked, the power
     he taunted in all his frenzy

trying to stamp out
the women strong with the god—
the torch, the raving sacred cries—   165
enraging the Muses who adore the flute.

And far north where the Black Rocks
    cut the sea in half
and murderous straits
split the coast of Thrace   170
    a forbidding city stands
where once, hard by the walls
the savage Ares thrilled to watch
a king's new queen, a Fury rearing in rage
    against his two royal sons—   175
    her bloody hands, her dagger-shuttle
stabbing out their eyes—cursed, blinding wounds—
their eyes blind sockets screaming for revenge!

They wailed in agony, cries echoing cries
    the princes doomed at birth . . .   180
and their mother doomed to chains,
walled up in a tomb of stone—
    but she traced her own birth back
to a proud Athenian line and the high gods
and off in caverns half the world away,   185
born of the wild North Wind
    she sprang on her father's gales,
    racing stallions up the leaping cliffs—
child of the heavens. But even on her the Fates
the gray everlasting Fates rode hard   190
my child, my child.

Scene 5

[*Enter* TIRESIAS, *the blind prophet, led by a boy.*]

TIRESIAS: Lords of Thebes,
  I and the boy have come together,
  hand in hand. Two see with the eyes of one . . .
  so the blind must go, with a guide to lead the way.
CREON: What is it, old Tiresias? What news now?   5
TIRESIAS: I will teach you. And you obey the seer.
CREON: I will,
  I've never wavered from your advice before.
TIRESIAS: And so you kept the city straight on course.
CREON: I owe you a great deal, I swear to that.
TIRESIAS: Then reflect, my son: you are poised,   10
  once more, on the razor-edge of fate.

CREON: What is it? I shudder to hear you.
TIRESIAS: You will learn
   when you listen to the warnings of my craft.
   As I sat on the ancient seat of augury,
   in the sanctuary where every bird I know   15
   will hover at my hands—suddenly I heard it,
   a strange voice in the wingbeats, unintelligible,
   barbaric, a mad scream! Talons flashing, ripping,
   they were killing each other—that much I knew—
   the murderous fury whirring in those wings   20
   made that much clear!
               I was afraid,
   I turned quickly, tested the burnt-sacrifice,
   ignited the altar at all points—but no fire,
   the god in the fire never blazed.
   Not from those offerings . . . over the embers   25
   slid a heavy ooze from the long thighbones,
   smoking, sputtering out, and the bladder
   puffed and burst—spraying gall into the air—
   and the fat wrapping the bones slithered off
   and left them glistening white. No fire!   30
   The rites failed that might have blazed the future
   with a sign. So I learned from the boy here:
   he is my guide, as I am guide to others.
                 And it is you—
   your high resolve that sets this plague on Thebes.
   The public altars and sacred hearths are fouled,   35
   one and all, by the birds and dogs with carrion
   torn from the corpse, the doomstruck son of Oedipus!
   And so the gods are deaf to our prayers, they spurn
   the offerings in our hands, the flame of holy flesh.
   No birds cry out an omen clear and true—   40
   they're gorged with the murdered victim's blood and fat.
   Take these things to heart, my son, I warn you.
   All men make mistakes, it is only human.
   But once the wrong is done, a man
   can turn his back on folly, misfortune too,   45
   if he tries to make amends, however low he's fallen,
   and stops his bullnecked ways. Stubbornness
   brands you for stupidity—pride is a crime.
   No, yield to the dead!
   Never stab the fighter when he's down.   50
   Where's the glory, killing the dead twice over?

   I mean you well. I give you sound advice.
   It's best to learn from a good adviser
   when he speaks for your own good:
   it's pure gain.

CREON: Old man—all of you! So,   55
   you shoot your arrows at my head like archers at the target—
   I even have *him* loosed on me, this fortune-teller.
   Oh his ilk has tried to sell me short
   and ship me off for years. Well,
   drive your bargains, traffic—much as you like—   60
   in the gold of India, silver-gold of Sardis.
   You'll never bury that body in the grave,
   not even if Zeus's eagles rip the corpse
   and wing their rotten pickings off to the throne of god!
   Never, not even in fear of such defilement   65
   will I tolerate his burial, that traitor.
   Well I know, we can't defile the gods—
   no mortal has the power.
                 No,
   reverend old Tiresias, all men fall,
   it's only human, but the wisest fall obscenely   70
   when they glorify obscene advice with rhetoric—
   all for their own gain.
TIRESIAS: Oh god, is there a man alive
   who knows, who actually believes . . .
CREON: What now?
   What earth-shattering truth are you about to utter?   75
TIRESIAS: . . . just how much a sense of judgment, wisdom
   is the greatest gift we have?
CREON: Just as much, I'd say
   as a twisted mind is the worst affliction known.
TIRESIAS: You are the one who's sick, Creon, sick to death.
CREON: I am in no mood to trade insults with a seer.   80
TIRESIAS: You have already, calling my prophecies a lie.
CREON: Why not?
   You and the whole breed of seers are mad for money!
TIRESIAS: And the whole race of tyrants lusts for filthy gain.
CREON: This slander of yours—
   are you aware you're speaking to the king?   85
TIRESIAS: Well aware. Who helped you save the city?
CREON: You—
   you have your skills, old seer, but you lust for injustice!
TIRESIAS: You will drive me to utter the dreadful secret in my heart.
CREON: Spit it out! Just don't speak it out for profit.
TIRESIAS: Profit? No, not a bit of profit, not for you.   90
CREON: Know full well, you'll never buy off my resolve.
TIRESIAS: Then know this too, learn this by heart!
   The chariot of the sun will not race through
   so many circuits more, before you have surrendered
   one born of your own loins, your own flesh and blood,   95
   a corpse for corpses given in return, since you have thrust
   to the world below a child sprung for the world above,
   ruthlessly lodged a living soul within the grave—

then you've robbed the gods below the earth,
keeping a dead body here in the bright air,   100
unburied, unsung, unhallowed by the rites.

You, you have no business with the dead,
nor do the gods above—this is violence
you have forced upon the heavens.
And so the avengers, the dark destroyers late   105
but true to the mark, now lie in wait for you,
the Furies sent by the gods and the god of death
to strike you down with the pains that you perfected!

There. Reflect on that, tell me I've been bribed.
The day comes soon, no long test of time, not now,   110
when the mourning cries for men and women break
throughout your halls. Great hatred rises against you—
cities in tumult, all whose mutilated sons
the dogs have graced with burial, or the wild beasts
or a wheeling crow that wings the ungodly stench of carrion   115
back to each city, each warrior's hearth and home.

These arrows for your heart! Since you've raked me
I loose them like an archer in my anger,
arrows deadly true. You'll never escape
their burning, searing force.   120

[*Motioning to his escort.*]

Come, boy, take me home.
So he can vent his rage on younger men,
and learn to keep a gentler tongue in his head
and better sense than what he carries now.

[*Exit to the side.*]

LEADER: The old man's gone, my king—   125
    terrible prophecies. Well I know,
    since the hair on this old head went gray,
    he's never lied to Thebes.
CREON: I know it myself—I'm shaken, torn.
    It's a dreadful thing to yield . . . but resist now?   130
    Lay my pride bare to the blows of ruin?
    That's dreadful too.
LEADER: But good advice,
    Creon, take it now, you must.
CREON: What should I do? Tell me . . . I'll obey.
LEADER: Go! Free the girl from the rocky vault   135
    and raise a mound for the body you exposed.
CREON: That's your advice? You think I should give in?

LEADER: Yes, my king, quickly. Disasters sent by the gods
    cut short our follies in a flash.
CREON: Oh it's hard,
    giving up the heart's desire . . . but I will do it—   140
    no more fighting a losing battle with necessity.
LEADER: Do it now, go, don't leave it to others.
CREON: Now—I'm on my way! Come, each of you,
    take up axes, make for the high ground,
    over there, quickly! I and my better judgment   145
    have come round to this—I shackled her,
    I'll set her free myself. I am afraid . . .
    it's best to keep the established laws
    to the very day we die.

[*Rushing out, followed by his entourage.*]

[*The* CHORUS *clusters around the altar.*]

CHORUS: God of a hundred names!
                      Great Dionysus—   150
             Son and glory of Semele! Pride of Thebes—
Child of Zeus whose thunder rocks the clouds—
Lord of the famous lands of evening—
King of the Mysteries!
                 King of Eleusis, Demeter's plain
her breasting hills that welcome in the world—   155
Great Dionysus!
             Bacchus, living in Thebes
the mother-city of all your frenzied women—
                            Bacchus
    living along the Ismenus' rippling waters
standing over the field sown with the Dragon's teeth!

You—we have seen you through the flaring smoky fires,   160
    your torches blazing over the twin peaks
where nymphs of the hallowed cave climb onward
                fired with you, your sacred rage—
we have seen you at Castalia's running spring
and down from the heights of Nysa crowned with ivy   165
the greening shore rioting vines and grapes
       down you come in your storm of wild women
            ecstatic, mystic cries—
                      Dionysus—
down to watch and ward the roads of Thebes!

First of all cities, Thebes you honor first   170
you and your mother, bride of the lightning—
come Dionysus! now your people lie
in the iron grip of plague

come, in your racing, healing stride
                    down Parnassus' slopes   175
or across the moaning straits.
                              Lord of the dancing—
dance, dance the constellations breathing fire!
Great master of the voices of the night!
Child of Zeus, God's offspring, come, come forth!
Lord, king, dance with your nymphs, swirling, raving   180
arm-in-arm in frenzy through the night
          they dance you, Iacchus—
                              Dance, Dionysus
giver of all good things!

Scene 6

[*Enter a* MESSENGER *from the side.*]

MESSENGER: Neighbors,
    friends of the house of Cadmus and the kings,
    there's not a thing in this mortal life of ours
    I'd praise or blame as settled once for all.
    Fortune lifts and Fortune fells the lucky   5
    and unlucky every day. No prophet on earth
    can tell a man his fate. Take Creon:
    there was a man to rouse your envy once,
    as I see it. He saved the realm from enemies,
    taking power, he alone, the lord of the fatherland,   10
    he set us true on course—he flourished like a tree
    with the noble line of sons he bred and reared . . .
    and now it's lost, all gone.
                              Believe me,
    when a man has squandered his true joys,
    he's good as dead, I tell you, a living corpse.   15
    Pile up riches in your house, as much as you like—
    live like a king with a huge show of pomp,
    but if real delight is missing from the lot,
    I wouldn't give you a wisp of smoke for it,
    not compared with joy.
LEADER: What now?   20
    What new grief do you bring the house of kings?
MESSENGER: Dead, dead—and the living are guilty of their death!
LEADER: Who's the murderer? Who is dead? Tell us.
MESSENGER: Haemon's gone, his blood spilled by the very hand—
LEADER: His father's or his own?
MESSENGER: His own . . .   25
    raging mad with his father for the death—
LEADER: Oh great seer,
    you saw it all, you brought your word to birth!

MESSENGER: Those are the facts. Deal with them as you will.

[*As he turns to go,* EURYDICE *enters from the palace.*]

LEADER: Look, Eurydice. Poor woman, Creon's wife,
    so close at hand. By chance perhaps,   30
    unless she's heard the news about her son.
EURYDICE: My countrymen,
    all of you—I caught the sound of your words
    as I was leaving to do my part,
    to appeal to queen Athena with my prayers.
    I was just loosing the bolts, opening the doors,   35
    when a voice filled with sorrow, family sorrow,
    struck my ears, and I fell back, terrified,
    into the women's arms—everything went black.
    Tell me the news, again, whatever it is . . .
    sorrow and I are hardly strangers.   40
    I can bear the worst.
MESSENGER: I—dear, lady,
    I'll speak as an eye-witness. I was there.
    And I won't pass over one word of the truth.
    Why should I try to soothe you with a story,
    only to prove a liar in a moment?   45
    Truth is always best.
                        So,
    I escorted your lord, I guided him
    to the edge of the plain where the body lay,
    Polynices, torn by the dogs and still unmourned.
    And saying a prayer to Hecate of the Crossroads,   50
    Pluto too, to hold their anger and be kind,
    we washed the dead in a bath of holy water
    and plucking some fresh branches, gathering . . .
    what was left of him, we burned them all together
    and raised a high mound of native earth, and then   55
    we turned and made for that rocky vault of hers,
    the hollow, empty bed of the bride of Death.
    And far off, one of us heard a voice,
    a long wail rising, echoing
    out of that unhallowed wedding-chamber,   60
    he ran to alert the master and Creon pressed on,
    closer—the strange, inscrutable cry came sharper,
    throbbing around him now, and he let loose
    a cry of his own, enough to wrench the heart,
    "Oh god, am I the prophet now? going down   65
    the darkest road I've ever gone? My son—
    it's *his* dear voice, he greets me! Go, men,
    closer, quickly! Go through the gap,
    the rocks are dragged back—
    right to the tomb's very mouth—and look,   70

see if it's Haemon's voice I think I hear,
or the gods have robbed me of my senses."

The king was shattered. We took his orders,
went and searched, and there in the deepest,
dark recesses of the tomb we found her . . .   75
hanged by the neck in a fine linen noose,
strangled in her veils—and the boy,
his arms flung around her waist,
clinging to her, wailing for his bride,
dead and down below, for his father's crimes   80
and the bed of his marriage blighted by misfortune.
When Creon saw him, he gave a deep sob,
he ran in, shouting, crying out to him,
"Oh my child—what have you done? what seized you,
what insanity? what disaster drove you mad?   85
Come out, my son! I beg you on my knees!"
But the boy gave him a wild burning glance,
spat in his face, not a word in reply,
he drew his sword—his father rushed out,
running as Haemon lunged and missed!—   90
and then, doomed, desperate with himself,
suddenly leaning his full weight on the blade,
he buried it in his body, halfway to the hilt.
And still in his senses, pouring his arms around her,
he embraced the girl and breathing hard,   95
released a quick rush of blood,
bright red on her cheek glistening white.
And there he lies, body enfolding body . . .
he was won his bride at last, poor boy,
not here but in the houses of the dead.   100

Creon shows the world that of all the ills
afflicting men the worst is lack of judgment.

[EURYDICE *turns and reenters the palace.*]

LEADER: What do you make of that? The lady's gone,
     without a word, good or bad.
MESSENGER: I'm alarmed too
     but here's my hope—faced with her son's death   105
     she finds it unbecoming to mourn in public.
     Inside, under her roof, she'll set her women
     to the task and wail the sorrow of the house.
     She's too discreet. She won't do something rash.
LEADER: I'm not so sure. To me, at least,   110
     a long heavy silence promises danger,
     just as much as a lot of empty outcries.
MESSENGER: We'll see if she's holding something back,
     hiding some passion in her heart.

I'm going in. You may be right—who knows?   115
Even too much silence has its dangers.

[*Exit to the palace.*]

[*Enter* CREON *from the side, escorted by attendants carrying* HAEMON's *body
on a bier.*]

LEADER: The king himself! Coming toward us,
                 look, holding the boy's head in his hands.
                 Clear, damning proof, if it's right to say so—
                 proof of his own madness, no one else's,   120
                     no, his own blind wrongs
CREON: Ohhh,
                 so senseless, so insane . . . my crimes,
                 my stubborn, deadly—
                 Look at us, the killer, the killed,
                 father and son, the same blood—the misery!   125
                 My plans, my mad fanatic heart,
                 my son, cut off so young!
                 Ai, dead, lost to the world,
                 not through your stupidity, no, my own.
LEADER: Too late,
         too late, you see what justice means.
CREON: Oh I've learned   130
                 through blood and tears! Then, it was then,
                 when the god came down and struck me—a great weight
                 shattering, driving me down that wild savage path,
                 ruining, trampling down my joy. Oh the agony,
                     the heartbreaking agonies of our lives.

[*Enter the* MESSENGER *from the palace.*]

MESSENGER: Master,   135
         what a hoard of grief you have, and you'll have more.
         The grief that lies to hand you've brought yourself—

[*Pointing to* HAEMON's *body.*]

         the rest, in the house, you'll see it all too soon.
CREON: What now? What's worse than this?
MESSENGER: The queen is dead.
         The mother of this dead boy . . . mother to the end—   140
         poor thing, her wounds are fresh.
CREON: No, no,
                 harbor of Death, so choked, so hard to cleanse!—
                 why me? why are you killing me?
                 Herald of pain, more words, more grief?
                 I died once, you kill me again and again!   145

What's the report, boy . . . some news for me?
My wife dead? O dear god!
Slaughter heaped on slaughter?

[*The doors open; the body of* EURYDICE *is brought out on her bier.*]

MESSENGER: See for yourself:
now they bring her body from the palace.
CREON: Oh no,
    another, a second loss to break the heart.   150
    What next, what fate still waits for me?
    I just held my son in my arms and now,
    look, a new corpse rising before my eyes—
    wretched, helpless mother—O my son!
MESSENGER: She stabbed herself at the altar,   155
    then her eyes went dark, after she'd raised
    a cry for the noble fate of Megareus, the hero
    killed in the first assault, then for Haemon
    then with her dying breath she called down
    torments on your head—you killed her sons.
CREON: Oh the dread,   160
    I shudder with dread! Why not kill me too?—
    run me through with a good sharp sword?
    Oh god, the misery, anguish—
    I, I'm churning with it, going under.
MESSENGER: Yes, and the dead, the woman lying there,   165
    piles the guilt of all their deaths on you.
CREON: How did she end her life, what bloody stroke?
MESSENGER: She drove home to the heart with her own hand,
    once she learned her son was dead . . . that agony.
CREON: And the guilt is all mine—   170
    can never be fixed on another man,
    no escape for me. I killed you,
    I, god help me, I admit it all!

[*To his attendants.*]

    Take me away, quickly, out of sight.
    I don't even exist—I'm no one. Nothing.   175
LEADER: Good advice, if there's any good in suffering.
    Quickest is best when troubles block the way.
CREON:

[*Kneeling in prayer.*]

    Come, let it come!—that best of fates for me
    that brings the final day, best fate of all.
    Oh quickly, now—   180
    so I never have to see another sunrise.

LEADER: That will come when it comes;
　we must deal with all that lies before us.
　The future rests with the ones who tend the future.
CREON: That prayer—I poured my heart into that prayer!   185
LEADER: No more prayers now. For mortal men
　there is no escape from the doom we must endure.
CREON: Take me away, I beg you, out of sight.
　　　　　　A rash, indiscriminate fool!
　　　　　　I murdered you, my son, against my will—   190
　　　　　　you too, my wife . . .
　　　　　　　　　　Wailing wreck of a man,
　　　　whom to look to? where to lean for support?

[*Desperately turning from* HAEMON *to* EURYDICE *on their biers.*]

Whatever I touch goes wrong—once more
a crushing fate's come down upon my head!

[*The* MESSENGER *and attendants lead* CREON *into the palace.*]

CHORUS: Wisdom is by far the greatest part of joy,   195
　and reverence toward the gods must be safeguarded.
　The mighty words of the proud are paid in full
　with mighty blows of fate, and at long last
　those blows will teach us wisdom.

[*The old citizens exit to the side.*]

The Receptive Reader

Greek drama had continuous action with no formal division into acts and scenes. In this reprinting of the play, the scenes are numbered for the convenience of the reader. The rhythm of the play is set up by the alternation of the dramatic episodes with the chants (or **odes**) of the chorus. The following questions should help you respond to the flow of the play as the central conflict works itself out and proceeds to its seemingly inevitable conclusion.

1. (Prologue) How does the playwright set up the situation? How does he fill you in on the necessary background? What is your first impression of Antigone? Where does she most forcefully state her convictions? What is the relationship between the two sisters? Can you understand Ismene's position? What subject does the chorus talk about and what is its stance in its first appearance?

2. (Scene 1) What is your first impression of Creon? Does he seem an effective ruler? Or does he seem stubborn and wrong-headed to you? How does he deal with defiance or dissent? What stand does the chorus take as the challenge to Creon's authority unfolds?

3. (Scene 2) How does the contest of wills between protagonist and antagonist take shape in this scene? Where are the two polar opposites most clearly

defined? Is there any common ground? Are you surprised by the stand Ismene takes in this scene? (For a journal entry or a brief oral presentation, you may want to prepare a speech in which you enter into the *point of view* of the character whose motives and arguments you can most easily sympathize with or understand. Use the first person, on the "I, Creon, king of Thebes . . . " model.)

4. (Scene 3) How would you describe Haemon's initial stance toward his father? What is his strategy in trying to deal with his father? How does it work out and why? For you, which are the strongest arguments used by Creon and Haemon in this scene? What are striking examples of the rapid-fire trading of one-liners, or *stichomythy?* (Does this scene change or confirm your estimate of Creon's character?)

5. (Scene 4) What is the final impression you retain of Antigone in this last scene in which you see her? Antigone said about the chorus in Scene 2, that "these citizens" would all agree with her, that

they would praise me too
if their lips weren't locked in fear.

Is she right? In Scene 3, what side does the chorus seem to take in the confrontation between Creon and his son? What is the role and position of the chorus in Scene 4?

6. (Scene 5) The appearance of Tiresias, the blind prophet, signals the turning point, or *peripety,* of the play. What is the blind seer's intention and message? What causes Tiresias to reveal his horrible prophecy? What is Creon's reaction? (How does the playwright guide your reactions to the seer's prediction?)

7. (Scene 6) Greek tragedy often appeals to our sense of *irony* as we witness with a bitter smile the contrast between people's hopes and their actual fate. In what ways is Creon the victim or target of irony? The play concludes with orthodox warnings against **hubris,** the sin of arrogant pride. How does the play as a whole lead up to this conclusion?

The Whole Play—For Discussion or Writing

1. In Greek tragedy, we are often told that a person's *fate* was decreed by the gods. But we also see strong-willed individuals making fateful choices. To become great or admirable, the characters must not be mere pawns of fate but show evidence of strength of will. To what extent do both the major and the supporting characters in this play exercise free will—showing evidence of deliberate choice or independent judgment? To what extent do they seem to you victims of fate?

2. What attitude toward *women* does Creon reveal in his denunciation of Antigone? Is that attitude shared by others in the play? Is it shared by the playwright?

3. George Steiner, in a book on the influence of *Antigone* on Western culture, says that the drama brings into play all five major sources of *conflict* inherent in the human condition: the confrontation of men and women, of age and

youth, of society and individual, of the living and the dead, and of human beings and gods. Can you show what role each plays and how important it is in the play as a whole?

The Range of Interpretation

Creon says at the end, "The guilt is all mine." Do you agree? What is your final judgment of Antigone as the tragic heroine? The translator of this play questioned Antigone's "total indifference to the rights of the city" to protect itself against treason. He claimed that no one in the play really praises her, with the exception of her fiancé. She herself says that if the gods allowed her to suffer death for her stand she would know that she was wrong. Was she wrong? In your opinion, what in this play could or should have been done differently, and by whom?

The Creative Dimension

Much research has gone into reconstructing the original staging of the Greek plays—the use of masks; the movements and gesture language of the chorus; the nature of Greek music. (Recordings of reconstructed early Greek music are available.) Your class may want to initiate a research project leading to a mini-production of selected or adapted scenes from *Antigone*. The project should attempt to give your classmates a sense of the visual and auditory effects and of the overall impact of Greek drama.

Making Connections—For Discussion or Writing

✗ In Sophocles' *Antigone*, rival loyalties compete for the character's allegiance: loyalty to family, loyalty to country or state, loyalty to the laws of religion. Compare and contrast Sophocles' tragic heroine with Ibsen's Nora as heroines faced with divided loyalties. What is the nature of the conflict in each case? How does the heroine resolve it? What are important parallels or key differences?

✗ Compare and contrast Sophocles' *Antigone* and Ibsen's *A Doll's House* as plays centered on a conflict between a man and a woman.

WRITING ABOUT LITERATURE

28   Tracing a Central Conflict (Focusing Your Paper)

The Writing Workshop   A well-focused paper may target the central conflict in a play. Is an embattled protagonist locked in a struggle with a worthy antagonist? Is there a clash between two opposed forces or points of view? Does a central confrontation shape the play as a whole? The heart of Sophocles' *Antigone* is the conflict between Creon's insistence on loyalty to the state and Antigone's stubborn insistence on obeying the laws of the gods. Early in your thinking and writing, try to bring the central conflict into focus. You can then start the purposeful note taking that will give you ample evidence as you trace basic opposites and their ramifications.

Focused Note Taking   Look for details and quotations that help you line up the two sides in the central conflict. For instance, in Shakespeare's *Macbeth*, Lady Macbeth is committed to having her husband become king of Scotland through the murder of King Duncan. She early starts to prod and criticize her reluctant, hesitating partner in crime. She preaches the need for moving ahead swiftly and without scruples. Reading notes like the following will give you the ammunition needed to drive home the contrast in your paper:

> ✗ The key difference between the two shows in their different way of looking at ambition. To Macbeth, "o'ervaulting ambition" gives him pause (it leaps and falls on the other side); ambition represents his "deep and dark desires." Lady Macbeth early points to his problem: He is not ruthless enough; he wants to win the prize by honest means. She perceives him as ambitious but too sensitive, too kind:
>
> > Yet do I fear thy nature;
> > It is too full o' th' milk of human kindness
> > To catch the nearest way (1.5.17–19)
>
> ✗ When he falters, she shames her husband : "Art thou afeard / To be the same in thine own act and valor / As thou art in desire?" (1.7.39–41).
> ✗ As Macbeth is conscience-stricken over his deed, she keeps him focused and attends to the grisly coverup:
>
> > Infirm of purpose!
> > Give me the daggers. The sleeping and the dead
> > Are but as pictures. 'Tis the eye of childhood
> > That fears a painted devil. If he do bleed,
> > I'll gild the faces of the grooms withal,
> > For it must seem their guilt (2.2.51–56).

Clustering   **Cluster** a key character or key idea. Let associations and details branch out from a central core as they come to mind. Let your cluster help you map important associations and help you see them as part of a pattern. The following sample cluster brings into focus a range of ideas that will help you define one pole in the play of opposites in the *Macbeth* play:

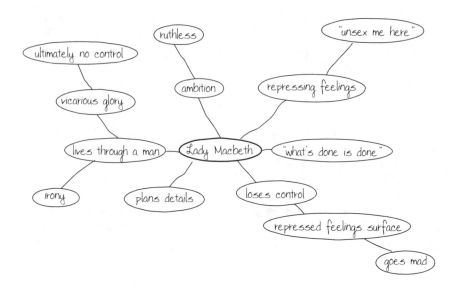

Here is the capsule portrait of Lady Macbeth that grew out of this cluster:

> Early in the play, Lady Macbeth seems to be the stronger of the two partners. She eggs on her husband and plans or supervises the details of the murder. She appears ruthless and bold, driven by overriding ambition. She represses any natural feelings of remorse or pity ("Unsex me here"). But the only way she has of realizing her ambitions is through her husband. She shares vicariously in his glory, and she has no control over an independent destiny. Her statement that "what's done is done" is ironic, because what she and her husband have done will destroy them both. The fears she had repressed or pushed down rise to the surface to destroy her, and she goes mad.

Focusing on Confrontations   Look for material that will help you highlight the central conflict. You may decide to pay special attention to climactic scenes in which two conflicting forces or views seem to clash head-on. In a famous scene in *A Doll's House,* a climactic exchange between Torvald and Nora brings into the open Nora's challenge to the traditional definition of a woman's duty:

HELMER: You haven't thought of what people will say.

NORA: I can't consider that. All I know is that this is necessary for me.

HELMER: But this is disgraceful. Is this the way you neglect your most sacred duties?

NORA: What do you consider is my most sacred duty?

HELMER: Do I have to tell you that? Isn't it your duty to your husband and children?

NORA: I have another duty, just as sacred.

HELMER: You can't have. What duty do you mean?
NORA: My duty to myself.

Focusing on Parallels   Often supporting characters or subplots echo and reinforce the major concerns of a play. Try to work into your paper exchanges that parallel in some way the major confrontations between protagonist and antagonist. For instance, in the initial exchange in *Antigone,* the heroine tests the loyalty of her sister Ismene, who has no wish "to dishonor the laws that the gods hold in honor" but who says: "Defy the city? I have no strength for that." The sisters' disagreement anticipates the later clashes between Antigone and Creon over the conflicting demands of religious law and of the state.

Focusing on the Resolution   How is the conflict resolved? In Shakespeare's *Macbeth,* Macbeth himself seems for a time the weaker partner. But in the end, Lady Macbeth crumbles, her mind diseased by "that perilous stuff / Which weighs upon the heart." The guilt feelings she has belittled or repressed surface and drive her insane. Macbeth, by contrast, is terribly lucid at the end. He recognizes that by denying all human ties and feelings he has isolated himself from all human contact.

Study the following sample student paper. How well does it bring the central conflict of the play into focus? How well does it trace the conflict into its ramifications? Does the writer adopt an independent view? Does the writer succeed in showing the appeal of the play to the modern audience?

Sample Student Paper

Antigone: A Contest of Wills

All ways of thinking contain their own blindnesses.
Marilyn French

In his tragedy *Antigone,* Sophocles sets up a classic conflict between two characters who are neither entirely in the right nor entirely in the wrong. Instead, both are sincere in their beliefs. Both are proud and self-righteous. The difference is that one turns out to be right in putting the law of the gods above human laws.

When Antigone's brother Polynices dies a traitor, King Creon orders that his body remain unburied. He wants the corpse to be "carion for the birds and dogs to tear, / an obscenity for the citizens to behold." Creon's decree serves a double purpose: it continues to punish Polynices even after death (his soul cannot go to heaven if he is not properly buried), and it is a reminder to the citizens of Thebes that the king's will is law. Anyone who defies the king defies the state, and is therefore a traitor. From Creon's point of view, there is no more deadly peril than disobedience. Even though Creon has declared that the penalty for defying his order is death, Antigone decides that the gods' law supersedes Creon's edict, and she buries her brother.

The striking feature of this play is that we see two strong-willed characters locked in battle. The trait that both Antigone and Creon have in common is their stubbornness—their unshakable conviction that they are right, their inability to change their minds until it is too late. However, American readers tend to view Antigone as the "righter" of the two characters, although perhaps for somewhat different reasons than the original Greek audience. We tend to rank the voice of the individual above that of society or the state. We tend to agree with Henry David Thoreau that a person who is in the right is in a majority of one already. As a result, we are predisposed to agree with Antigone when she says, "It wasn't Zeus, not in the least, / who made this proclamation." For her, "Justice, dwelling with the gods," has more force than the edict of "a mere mortal."

On the other hand, Antigone is totally unyielding, and her tremendous faith in her own righteousness can be seen as a flaw that helps bring disaster down on her and her lover and betrothed. She is totally contemptuous of her sister Ismene, who at first opts to take the practical, reasonable course: "to obey the ones who stand in power." Ismene says,

> we must be sensible. Remember we are women.
> We're not born to contend with men. Then too,
> we're underlings, ruled by much stronger hands.
> So we must submit in this, and things still worse.

The word *submit* is not in Antigone's vocabulary; she vows to reject Ismene's help "even if you should have a change of heart."

Creon speaks up for the safety of the "ship of state," and at first the chorus seems to honor his claim. The leader of the chorus says about Antigone: "Like father, like daugher, / passionate, wild . . . / she hasn't learned to bend before adversity." Later, the chorus tells Antigone, "attacks on power never go unchecked."

However, Creon doesn't get any more sympathy from a modern audience than he received from his advisors, his family, or, finally, his subjects. To us, he really does not seem to aim at serving his people; he does not profess to serve a higher power; he only serves himself. His image as a man is at stake: "There's no room for pride, not in a slave, / not with the lord and master standing by." Several characters try to point out to Creon that he is suffering from an excess of egotism, willfulness, and pride. But he's too self-absorbed to accept any of this criticism. His son provides us with an accurate sketch of Creon's character when he observes,

> Whoever thinks that he alone possesses intelligence,
> the gift of eloquence, he and no one else,
> and character too . . . such men, I tell you,
> spread them open—you will find them empty.

This self-righteousness, coupled with Creon's refusal to acknowledge the laws of heaven, leads him down the dark path of tragedy. It takes the death of his wife and son to convince him that he has been mistaken.

In the contest of wills, it is Antigone who stays the course. In the end, Antigone remains true to her principles; she chooses to die rather than acquiesce in an unjust civil law. It is Creon who capitulates (too late to save anyone but himself). It is Creon who changes his mind and admits, "it's best to keep the established laws/ to the very day we die." In the contest of wills, Antigone has perished, but her principles have prevailed.

Creon tried to coerce his subjects into being loyal by making the penalty for disobedience as severe as he could. He failed to take into account the fact that loyalty cannot be commanded into existence—or coerced into being. It must be given freely, or it can no longer be called loyalty; it becomes subjugation.

Questions

1. What is the *thesis* of this paper? Does it offer you a new or different perspective on the play? Do you agree with it, or would you take issue with it?

2. Where is the *central conflict* best summed up or described? Does the writer trace it into its ramifications? Does she look at the role of supporting characters?

3. What is the general *plan* or strategy of the paper? Is it easy or hard to outline?

4. Does the writer use sufficient *evidence?* What use does the writer make of firsthand quotation? Are any quotations especially telling or effective?

5. Does the paper leave you with any unanswered questions or loose ends?

6. Do you agree with the writer on the way a contemporary audience is likely to respond to the play?

29 Shakespearean Tragedy
The Inner Conflict

*Shakespeare himself was an actor, and the art of
acting is at the very root of his whole playwright-
ing art.*

FRANCIS FERGUSSON

FOCUS ON SHAKESPEARE'S STAGE

Shakespeare often makes spectators feel that he knows them better
than they know themselves. They hear characters on his stage voice
their own secret thoughts and feelings. Crossing cultural boundaries,
plays like *Romeo and Juliet, As You Like It, Hamlet, Macbeth, Othello,* or
King Lear act out for spectators the drama of human contact and interaction. Juliet and her Romeo, Portia and Shylock from *The Merchant of
Venice,* young Hamlet, and Lady Macbeth people the imagination of theatergoers around the world.

Nevertheless, Shakespeare's plays were part of a thriving contemporary culture and have deep roots in the politics and beliefs of his time.
They were part of a great flowering of the theater during the Elizabethan
age. Under Queen Elizabeth I of the house of Tudor, England had experienced prosperity, self-confidence, and national unity. The golden age
of the English stage lasted from the 1580s to the time the Puritans, hostile to worldly entertainment, closed the theaters in 1642.

Shakespeare and English History Shakespeare's first successes dramatized recent English history. Under Elizabeth and the Tudor monarchy,
England was leaving behind the fratricidal civil wars of the feudal Middle Ages. Feudalism had been a system of splintered authority. Powerful warlords owed allegiance and military service to the king, but often
they were his rivals for power. Shakespeare's history plays show a
nation trying to emerge from the "civic broils" that pitted brother against
brother, "blood against blood, Self against Self" (*Richard III,* 2.4.62–64).
A recurrent theme in these plays is the yearning for stable, legitimate
government, legitimized by true religion and "true descent."

784

The Elizabethan Stage   Modern directors have restored key features of the Elizabethan stage. Boy actors, it is true, no longer play the women's roles. But we often see Shakespeare performed, as in his time, on an open stage, with free-flowing action and no curtain coming down between acts or scenes. Shakespeare's audiences came to the theater for a spectacle with a large cast and a sprawling plot—often with the future of a kingdom at stake, with astonishing instances of loyalty and treachery, and with moments of high drama in climactic confrontations. The task of the playwright was to fill a commercial theater—"large, cheap, and popular"—several times a week (G. E. Bentley). Plays were at first performed in the courtyards of inns, which featured bear baitings and cockfights on other occasions. They gradually moved to specially constructed, wooden, open-roofed theaters holding several thousand spectators. There were special seats in "galleries," or roofed balconies, for the wealthy; there was standing room in the "yard" (surrounding the stage) for those Hamlet calls the "groundlings." The Globe Theater, most famous of the Elizabethan theaters, was built in 1599 on the other (south) side of the Thames River, beyond the reach of the restrictive city ordinances of London magistrates.

The Elizabethan Theatre of the Oregon Shakespeare Festival. Courtesy of Gregory Leiber.

The repertory changed with popular taste—with some plays, as Hamlet says to the players visiting his court, performed "not above once." Others enjoyed long runs. The plays, like Hollywood scripts, were often the result of collaboration. They were further adapted and modified by actors. Clowns, especially, as Hamlet says, were apt to speak "more than was set down for them" to get cheap laughs from a "quantity of barren spectators." When the plays were printed, the printer might use imperfect actors' copies. Modern editors have tried to reconstruct authentic texts of Shakespeare's plays by comparing early printings—the *quartos*—with the *folio*—texts collected and printed in 1623, seven years after the playwright's death. (The smaller quartos and the large folio are named after the size of the page.)

The Apprentice Playwright   The great successes of the early Elizabethan stage show what audiences came to see when Shakespeare arrived in London from his hometown, Stratford-on-Avon, to make his way as an actor and apprentice playwright. One spectacular success was Thomas Kyd's *The Spanish Tragedy,* a play of **intrigue,** of plotting and counterplotting, first written and acted about 1585. When Shakespeare wrote *Hamlet,* it was not the first time his audiences had seen a **revenge tragedy:** a play that starts with the ghost of the victim clamoring for revenge for a foul murder and ends with the avenger triumphing over his adversaries, taking them down with him to bloody death.

Blank Verse   Another popular long-running play was Christopher Marlowe's *Tamburlane the Great,* first performed in 1587. It was the spectacular story of an obscure Middle Eastern shepherd who by sheer force of ambition made himself emperor of the known world. Marlowe wrote *Tamburlane* in **blank verse**—the unrhymed iambic pentameter line that was to become the dominant medium of Shakespeare's serious plays. In the following sample passage, some lines are regular five-beat lines, with stress always on the second syllable of each foot: "UNTIL | we REACH | the RIP|est FRUIT | of ALL." Others play familiar variations on the underlying iambic beat. The next line starts with trochaic inversion, and it also has an unstressed or weakly stressed second syllable in the third foot: "NATure | that FRAMED | us of | four EL|eMENTS." (Notice how the departure from the regular beat makes the key word—*nature*—seem to stand out.) As later in Shakespeare, lines tend to combine in a verse paragraph that develops it own soaring rhythm:

Nature that framed us of four elements
Warring within our breasts for regiment,
Doth teach us all to have aspiring minds:
Our souls whose faculties can comprehend

The wondrous architecture of the world
And measure every wandering planet's course . . .
Wills us to wear ourselves and never rest
Until we reach the ripest fruit of all . . .
The sweet fruition of an earthly crown.

Religion and Mythology Playwright and audience shared religious beliefs, beliefs about ghosts, and popular superstitions—whether believed wholeheartedly or viewed more skeptically. Hamlet's good friend Horatio says about some of the spirit lore, "So have I heard and do in part believe it" (1.1.165). At the same time, the Elizabethan age was part of the European Renaissance, a time of revived interest in ancient Greek and Roman art and literature. Shakespeare is steeped in Greek legend and **mythology.** As a young man, he wrote *Venus and Adonis*—a long poem about Venus, the goddess of love, and her mortal lover. The dialogue of a Shakespeare play is shot through with allusions to playful Cupid, aiming his darts or arrows at lovers; or "plated Mars"— the armor-plated god of war. When Hamlet asks the itinerant player to recite a favorite speech about the death of King Priam, the playwright expects the audience to know the story of the Trojan War, the siege and fall of Troy. The player proceeds to raise a storm of passion over Queen Hecuba's witnessing the slaying of Priam, her husband and the father of the Trojan hero Hector.

Shakespeare's Language The language of Shakespeare's time was in transition from medieval English (or Middle English) to modern speech:

✗ There still were special pronouns (and matching verb forms) for talking to one rather than several persons: *thou art, thou wilt, thou canst,* and also *may it please thee* and *take what is thine.* Use of this familiar *thou* instead of the more formal *you* corresponded roughly to being on a first-name basis. *Methinks* and *methought* were still used for *I think* and *I thought.* Many of our modern auxiliaries or helping verbs are still missing: *Ride you tonight?* for *do you ride?; prepare we* for *let us prepare.*

✗ Word order often differs from ours. In modern English, "We will *our kingdom* give" has become "We will give *our kingdom.*" "Hamlet, thou hast *thy father* much offended" today would be "Hamlet, you have much offended *your father.*" (Objects now generally follow the complete verb.)

✗ Listeners and readers soon get used to frequently used words like *prithee* (please), *forsooth* (in truth), *anon* (presently, very soon), *aught* (anything), *ere* (before). *Would* is often used in the sense of *wish* or *want* ("*Would* it were true" for "*I wish* it were true").

In the following edition of *Hamlet,* the usual footnotes have been replaced by marginal glosses to help you read and study the play. These glosses give you suggested modern meanings close at hand and in the context of the line. Where the text is obscure or imperfect, these meanings represent the educated guesses of editors and scholars. As in other modern editions aimed at the general reader, spellings and sometimes word forms have been cautiously modernized.

THE ENIGMA OF HAMLET

In every actor is a Hamlet struggling to get out.
STEVEN BERKOFF

To many critics, *Hamlet* has been Shakespeare's most searching comment on life and human nature. "It is *we* who are Hamlet," said the Romantic critic William Hazlitt. Yet at the same time, *Hamlet* has proved Shakespeare's most challenging and mysterious play. A library of critical volumes has been written on the contest of wills between Prince Hamlet and his murderous stepfather Claudius; on Hamlet's relationship with his doting mother, Queen Gertrude (who "lives by his looks"); on his harsh treatment of Ophelia (whom he tells, "I loved you once"); and on his long-delayed revenge on Claudius, the "king of shreds and patches," who killed his father and married with his mother.

Although Hamlet is often accused of inaction, the play itself is a fast-moving spectacle, with much **stage business**—encounters with a ghost, a quarrel at a graveside, a climactic duel. Many scenes have long been audience favorites: Hamlet taunts the king's talky and slow-witted counselor (and Ophelia's father) Polonius. Hamlet talks with a group of itinerant, traveling players about his love of the theater. Hamlet plays cat and mouse with the king's spies, his former schoolmates Rosencrantz and Guildenstern. However, audiences and critics rivet their attention especially on the great **soliloquies** in which Hamlet bares his soul: "To be or not to be"; "O that this too too sullied flesh would melt."

As you read the play, keep in mind questions that audiences and critics have asked about Hamlet and his role in the play:

- How trustworthy is the *ghost?* Is the ghost of Hamlet's father, who spurs Hamlet on to revenge, a good or an evil spirit? Is he a "spirit of health or goblin damned"? Hamlet concludes that he is seeing and talking to an "honest ghost," and he reluctantly responds to the ghost's call for vengeance. But at least one modern critic has argued that, according to the spirit lore of Shakespeare's time, the ghost must have been an evil spirit, luring Hamlet on to damnation.

✗ What explains the *delay?* Why does it take Hamlet so long to accomplish his revenge, his "almost blunted purpose"? Are the reasons Hamlet gives for delaying his revenge merely pretexts? Is he temperamentally averse to decisive action? Is he too much the intellectual, forever debating, forever finding scruples and complications?

✗ What are the true sources of Hamlet's *melancholy?* Is he melancholy by temperament, illustrating one of the character types of the psychology of Shakespeare's time? (According to the psychology of "humors," excess of one such humor or bodily fluid would tilt a person toward melancholy, chronic anger, or cheerfulness.)

✗ How *mad* is Hamlet? He feigns madness to gain time to prepare his revenge. How close is the turmoil in his soul to driving him truly mad—instead of his just pretending to be insane to disorient the king?

✗ What is Hamlet's true relationship with his *mother?* Why is he so obsessed with lurid images of physical intimacy between her and the uncle? What evidence is there for or against his having Oedipal feelings toward his mother? (In some modern productions, these are acted out graphically in the bedroom scene.)

William Shakespeare   *(1564–1616)*

Hamlet   *1600–1601*

*Hamlet must be the best-known of all characters in
the theater of the world.*

                              BERNARD LOTT

CHARACTERS

CLAUDIUS, King of Denmark
HAMLET, nephew to the King
GERTRUDE, Queen of Denmark, mother to HAMLET
GHOST of HAMLET's father
POLONIUS, counselor to the King
LAERTES, son to POLONIUS
OPHELIA, daughter to POLONIUS
HORATIO, friend to HAMLET

And also:

VOLTEMAND
CORNELIUS
ROSENCRANTZ
GUILDENSTERN   } courtiers
OSRIC
A GENTLEMAN

MARCELLUS ⎫
BERNARDO   ⎬ soldiers
FRANCISCO ⎭
REYNALDO, servant to POLONIUS
FORTINBRAS, Prince of Norway
PLAYERS
Two CLOWNS, gravediggers
A Norwegian CAPTAIN
English Ambassadors
Lords, Ladies, Priests, Officers, Soldiers, Sailors, Messengers, Attendants

Act One

SCENE 1. Elsinore Castle. The platform of the guard.

[*Enter* BERNARDO *and* FRANCISCO, *two sentinels from opposite directions.*]

BERNARDO: Who's there?
FRANCISCO: Nay, answer me. Stand and unfold° yourself.   *identify*
BERNARDO: Long live the King!
FRANCISCO: Bernardo?
BERNARDO: He.   5
FRANCISCO: You come most carefully upon your hour.°   *at the exact time*
BERNARDO: 'Tis now struck twelve. Get thee to bed, Francisco.
FRANCISCO: For this relief much thanks. 'Tis bitter cold,
    And I am sick at heart.
BERNARDO: Have you had quiet guard?
FRANCISCO: Not a mouse stirring.   10
BERNARDO: Well, good night.
    If you do meet Horatio and Marcellus,
    The rivals° of my watch, bid them make haste.   *partners*

[*Enter* HORATIO *and* MARCELLUS.]

FRANCISCO: I think I hear them. Stand! Who's there?
HORATIO: Friends to this ground.
MARCELLUS: And liegemen to the Dane.°   *loyal Danish* 15
FRANCISCO: Give you good night.   *subjects*
MARCELLUS: O, farewell, honest soldier.
    Who hath relieved you?
FRANCISCO: Bernardo hath my place.
    Give you good night.

[*He leaves.*]

MARCELLUS: Holla, Bernardo!
BERNARDO: Say—
    What, is Horatio there?
HORATIO: A piece of him.
BERNARDO: Welcome, Horatio. Welcome, good Marcellus.   20

MARCELLUS: What, has this thing appeared again tonight?

BERNARDO: I have seen nothing.

MARCELLUS: Horatio says 'tis but our fantasy,
    And will not let belief take hold of him
    Touching this dreaded sight, twice seen of us.   25
    Therefore I have entreated him along,
    With us to watch the minutes of this night,
    That, if again this apparition come,
    He may approve our eyes° and speak to it.   *confirm what we saw*

HORATIO: Tush, tush, 'twill not appear.

BERNARDO: Sit down awhile,   30
    And let us once again assail your ears,
    That are so fortified against our story,
    What we two nights have seen.

HORATIO: Well, sit we down,
    And let us hear Bernardo speak of this.

BERNARDO: Last night of all,   35
    When yond same star that's westward from the pole
    Had made his° course to illume that part of heaven   *its*
    Where now it burns, Marcellus and myself,
    The bell then beating one—

[Enter GHOST.]

MARCELLUS: Peace! break thee off! Look where it comes
        again!   40

BERNARDO: In the same figure,° like the King that's dead.   *looking the same as*

MARCELLUS: Thou art a scholar; speak to it, Horatio.

BERNARDO: Looks it not like the King? Mark it, Horatio.

HORATIO: Most like. It harrows me with fear and wonder.

BERNARDO: It would be spoke to.

MARCELLUS: Question it, Horatio.   45

HORATIO: What art thou that usurpest this time of night
    Together with that fair and warlike form
    In which the majesty of buried Denmark°   *the buried Danish king*
    Did sometimes march? By heaven I charge thee speak!

MARCELLUS: It is offended.

BERNARDO: See, it stalks away!   50

HORATIO: Stay! Speak, speak! I charge thee speak!

[GHOST leaves.]

MARCELLUS: 'Tis gone and will not answer.

BERNARDO: How now, Horatio? You tremble and look pale.
    Is not this something more than fantasy?
    What think you on't?°   *do you think of it*   55

HORATIO: Before my God, I might not this believe
    Without the sensible and true avouch°   *concrete testimony*
    Of mine own eyes.

MARCELLUS: Is it not like the King?

HORATIO: As thou art to thyself.

    Such was the very armor he had on   60

    When he the ambitious Norway° combated;   *(king of Norway)*

    So frowned he once when, in an angry parle,°   *parley*

    He smote the sledded Polacks° on the ice.   *Poles in sleds*

    'Tis strange.

MARCELLUS: Thus twice before, and jump° at this dead hour,   *exactly* 65

    With martial stalk hath he gone by our watch.

HORATIO: In what particular thought to work I know not;

    But, in the gross and scope of my opinion,°   *in my general opinion*

    This bodes some strange eruption° to our state.   *means some strange*

MARCELLUS: Good now, sit down and tell me, he that   *upheaval*

    knows,   70

    Why this same strict and most observant watch

    So nightly toils the subject of the land,°   *makes our citizens toil*

    And why such daily cast of brazen cannon

    And foreign mart° for implements of war;   *shopping abroad*

    Why such impress° of shipwrights, whose sore task   *rushed hiring* 75

    Does not divide the Sunday from the week;

    What might be toward,° that this sweaty haste   *be in store*

    Doth make the night joint-laborer with the day?

    Who is't that can inform me?

HORATIO: That can I.

    At least, the whisper goes so. Our last King,   80

    Whose image even but now appeared to us,

    Was, as you know, by Fortinbras of Norway,

    Thereto pricked on by a most emulate° pride,   *envious*

    Dared to the combat; in which our valiant Hamlet°   *(Hamlet senior, the*

    (For so this side of our known world esteemed him)   *dead king)* 85

    Did slay this Fortinbras; who, by a sealed compact,°   *solemnly sealed treaty*

    Well ratified by law and heraldry,

    Did forfeit, with his life, all those his lands

    Which he stood seized of,° to the conqueror;   *which he held*

    Against the which a moiety competent°   *similar pledge* 90

    Was gaged by our King; which had° returned   *would have*

    To the inheritance of Fortinbras,

    Had he° been vanquisher, as, by the same comart°   *if he had/agreement*

    And carriage of the article designed,°   *meaning of the*

    His fell to Hamlet. Now, sir, young Fortinbras,   *stipulated article* 95

    Of unimproved mettle° hot and full,   *untested spirit*

    Hath in the skirts° of Norway, here and there,   *outskirts*

    Sharked up° a list of lawless resolutes,°   *drummed up/adventurers*

    For food and diet to some enterprise

    That hath a stomach in't;° which is no other,   *that takes courage* 100

    As it doth well appear unto our state,

    But to recover of us, by strong hand

    And terms compulsatory,° those foresaid lands   *(threatening terms)*

    So by his father lost; and this, I take it,

    Is the main motive of our preparations,   105

The source of this our watch, and the chief head°   main well-spring
Of this post-haste and romage° in the land.   commotion and turmoil
BERNARDO: I think it be no other but e'en so.
    Well may it sort° that this portentous figure   it fits well
    Comes armed through our watch, so like the King   110
    That was and is the question° of these wars.   cause
HORATIO: A mote° it is to trouble the mind's eye.   speck of dust
    In the most high and palmy state of Rome,
    A little ere the mightiest Julius fell,°   before Julius Caesar was killed
    The graves stood tenantless,° and the sheeted dead   without their occupants   115
    Did squeak and gibber in the Roman streets;
    As stars with trains of fire,° and dews of blood,   (meteors or comets)
    Disasters in the sun; and the moist star°   the moon (governing
    Upon whose influence Neptune's empire stands   the tides)
    Was sick almost to doomsday with eclipse.   120
    And even the like precurse° of fierce events,   forerunners
    As harbingers° preceding still the fates   messengers
    And prologue to the omen coming on,
    Have heaven and earth together demonstrated
    Unto our climatures° and countrymen.   area   125

[*Enter* GHOST *again.*]

    But soft! behold! Lo, where it comes again!
    I'll cross it,° though it blast me—Stay, illusion!   cross its path
    If thou hast any sound, or use of voice,
    Speak to me.
    If there be any good thing to be done,   130
    That may to thee do ease, and grace to me,
    Speak to me.
    If thou art privy to° thy country's fate,   if you have secret
    Which happily foreknowing may avoid,   knowledge of
    O, speak!   135
    Or if thou hast uphoarded in thy life
    Extorted treasure in the womb of earth
    (For which, they say, you spirits oft walk in death),

[*The cock crows.*]

    Speak of it! Stay, and speak!—Stop it, Marcellus!
MARCELLUS: Shall I strike at it with my partisan?°   weapon   140
HORATIO: Do, if it will not stand.
BERNARDO: 'Tis here!
HORATIO: 'Tis here!
MARCELLUS: 'Tis gone!

[GHOST *leaves.*]

    We do it wrong, being so majestical,
    To offer it the show of violence;
    For it is as the air, invulnerable,   145
    And our vain blows malicious mockery.

BERNARDO: It was about to speak, when the cock crew.
HORATIO: And then it started, like a guilty thing
    Upon a fearful summons. I have heard
    The cock, that is the trumpet to the morn,   150
    Doth with his lofty and shrill-sounding throat
    Awake the god of day; and at his warning,
    Whether in sea or fire, in earth or air,
    The extravagant and erring spirit hies°   *hurries back*
    To his confine;° and of the truth herein   *prison* 155
    This present object made probation.°   *showed proof*
MARCELLUS: It faded on the crowing of the cock.
    Some say that ever 'gainst that season comes
    Wherein our Savior's birth is celebrated,
    The bird of dawning singeth all night long;   160
    And then, they say, no spirit dare stir abroad,
    The nights are wholesome, then no planets strike,° *no evil influences of planets*
    No fairy takes, nor witch hath power to charm,
    So hallowed° and so gracious is the time.   *sacred*
HORATIO: So have I heard and do in part believe it.   165
    But look, the morn, in russet mantle clad,°   *in a reddish coat*
    Walks over the dew of yon high eastern hill.
    Break we our watch up;° and by my advice   *let us break up our watch*
    Let us impart what we have seen tonight
    Unto young Hamlet; for, upon my life,   170
    This spirit, dumb to us, will speak to him.
    Do you consent we shall acquaint him with it,
    As needful in our loves, fitting our duty?
MARCELLUS: Let's do't, I pray; and I this morning know
    Where we shall find him most conveniently.   175

                  [*They leave.*]

SCENE 2. Elsinore Castle. An audience chamber.

    [*Flourish of trumpets. Enter* CLAUDIUS, *King of Den-*
    mark, GERTRUDE *the Queen,* HAMLET, POLONIUS, LAERTES
    and his sister OPHELIA, *and attending lords.*]

KING: Though yet of Hamlet our dear brother's death
    The memory be green,° and that it us befitted   *is very recent*
    To bear our hearts in grief, and our whole kingdom
    To be contracted in one brow of woe,
    Yet so far hath discretion fought with nature   5
    That we with wisest sorrow think on him
    Together with remembrance of ourselves.
    Therefore our sometime sister,° now our queen,   *former sister-in-law*
    The imperial jointress° to this warlike state,   *partner*
    Have we, as 'twere with a defeated joy,   10
    With an auspicious,° and a dropping eye,   *happy*
    With mirth in funeral, and with dirge in marriage,

In equal scale weighing delight and dole,°   *grief*
Taken to wife; nor have we herein barred
Your better wisdoms,° which have freely gone   *wise advice*   15
With this affair along. For all, our thanks.
Now follows, that you know, young Fortinbras,
Holding a weak supposal° of our worth,   *estimate*
Or thinking by our late dear brother's death
Our state to be disjoint° and out of frame,   *weakened*   20
Colleagued with° this dream of his advantage,   *joined to*
He hath not failed to pester us with message
Importing° the surrender of those lands   *asking for*
Lost by his father, with all bands of law,°   *due formalities*
To our most valiant brother. So much for him.   25

[*Enter* VOLTEMAND *and* CORNELIUS.]

Now for ourself and for this time of meeting.
Thus much the business is: we have here writ°   *written*
To Norway,° uncle of young Fortinbras—   *(the king of Norway)*
Who, impotent and bedrid,° scarcely hears   *bedridden*
Of this his nephew's purpose—to suppress°   *stop*   30
His further gait herein, in that the levies,°   *proceedings*
The lists, and full proportions are all made
Out of his subject;° and we here dispatch   *from among his subjects*
You, good Cornelius, and you, Voltemand,
For bearers of this greeting to old Norway,   35
Giving to you no further personal power
To business° with the King, more than the scope   *to do business*
Of these dilated articles° allow.   *detailed points*

[*Gives a paper.*]

Farewell, and let your haste commend your° duty.   *show your sense of*
CORNELIUS, VOLTEMAND: In that, and all things, will we
    show our duty.   40
KING: We doubt it nothing.° Heartily farewell.   *not at all*

[VOLTEMAND *and* CORNELIUS *leave.*]

And now, Laertes, what's the news with you?
You told us of some suit.° What is't, Laertes?   *request*
You cannot speak of reason to the Dane°   *(the Danish king)*
And lose your voice.° What wouldst thou beg,   *speak in vain*
    Laertes,   45
That shall not be my offer, not thy asking?
The head is not more native° to the heart,   *akin*
The hand more instrumental to the mouth,
Than is the throne of Denmark to thy father.
What wouldst thou have, Laertes?
LAERTES: My dread lord,   50
Your leave° and favor to return to France,   *permission*
From whence° though willingly I came to Denmark   *from where*

To show my duty in your coronation,
Yet now I must confess, that duty done,
My thoughts and wishes bend again toward France   55
And bow them to your gracious leave and pardon.°   *submit to your*
                                                                    permission
KING: Have you your father's leave? What says Polonius?
POLONIUS: He hath, my lord, wrung from me my slow
        leave°   *reluctant approval*
    By laborsome petition, and at last
    Upon his will I sealed my hard consent.   60
    I do beseech you give him leave to go.
KING: Take thy fair hour,° Laertes. Time be thine,   *use the favorable hour*
    And thy best graces spend it at thy will!
    But now, my cousin Hamlet, and my son—
HAMLET [*aside*]: A little more than kin, and less than
        kind!°   *(a play on "one's kind"*   65
                                                                    and "being kind")
KING: How is it that the clouds still hang on you?
HAMLET: Not so, my lord. I am too much in the sun.
QUEEN: Good Hamlet, cast thy nighted color off,
    And let thine eye look like a friend on Denmark.°   *(the king of Denmark)*
    Do not for ever with thy vailèd° lids   *lowered*   70
    Seek for thy noble father in the dust.
    Thou know'st 'tis common,° all that lives must die,   *common experience*
    Passing through nature to eternity.
HAMLET: Ay, madam, it is common.
QUEEN: If it be,
    Why seems it so particular with thee?   75
HAMLET: Seems, madam? Nay, it is. I know not "seems."
    'Tis not alone my inky° cloak, good mother,   *ink-black*
    Nor customary suits of solemn black,
    Nor windy suspiration° of forced breath,   *heavy sighs*
    No, nor the fruitful river in the eye,   80
    Nor the dejected havior of the visage,°   *behavior of the face*
    Together with all forms, moods, shapes of grief,
    That can denote me truly. These indeed seem,
    For they are actions that a man might play;
    But I have that within which passeth show—   85
    These but the trappings and the suits of woe.
KING: 'Tis sweet and commendable in your nature,
        Hamlet,
    To give these mourning duties to your father;
    But you must know, your father lost a father;
    That father lost, lost his, and the survivor bound   90
    In filial obligation for some term
    To do obsequious sorrow.° But to persever   *to show downcast grief*
    In obstinate condolement° is a course   *stubborn grieving*
    Of impious stubbornness. 'Tis unmanly grief;
    It shows a will most incorrect° to heaven,   *rebellious*   95
    A heart unfortified, a mind impatient,

An understanding simple and unschooled;
For what we know must be, and is as common
As any the most vulgar° thing to sense,   *ordinary*
Why should we in our peevish opposition   100
Take it to heart? Fie! 'tis a fault to heaven,
A fault against the dead, a fault to nature,
To reason most absurd, whose common theme
Is death of fathers, and who still° hath cried,   *which always*
From the first corse° till he that died today,   *corpse* 105
"This must be so." We pray you throw to earth
This unprevailing woe, and think of us
As of a father; for let the world take note
You are the most immediate° to our throne,   *next in line*
And with no less nobility of love   110
Than that which dearest father bears his son
Do I impart toward you. For your intent
In going back to school in Wittenberg,
It is most retrograde to our desire;°   *the opposite of our wish*
And we beseech you, bend you to remain   115
Here in the cheer and comfort of our eye,
Our chiefest courtier, cousin, and our son.
QUEEN: Let not thy mother lose her prayers, Hamlet:
    I pray thee° stay with us, go not to Wittenberg.   *I ask you to*
HAMLET: I shall in all my best obey you, madam.   120
KING: Why, 'tis a loving and a fair reply.
    Be as ourself in Denmark. Madam, come.
    This gentle and unforced accord° of Hamlet   *consent*
    Sits smiling to my heart; in grace whereof,°   *in honor of which*
    No jocund health° that Denmark drinks today   *joyful toast* 125
    But the great cannon to the clouds shall tell,
    And the King's rouse the heaven shall bruit again,°   *the sky shall echo the*
                                                                        king's celebration
    Respeaking earthly thunder. Come away.

        [*Flourish of trumpets. All leave except* HAMLET.]

HAMLET: O that this too too sullied flesh would melt,
    Thaw, and resolve° itself into a dew!   *dissolve* 130
    Or that the Everlasting had not fixed
    His canon° 'gainst self-slaughter! O God! God!   *law*
    How weary, stale, flat, and unprofitable
    Seem to me all the uses of this world!
    Fie on't! ah, fie!° 'Tis an unweeded garden   *for shame* 135
    That grows to seed; things rank and gross in nature
    Possess it merely.° That it should come to this!   *have taken it over*
    But two months dead—nay, not so much, not two!
    So excellent a king, that was to this
    Hyperion to a satyr;° so loving to my mother   *like a god compared to a being half goat* 140
    That he might not beteem° the winds of   *allow*
        heaven

Visit her face too roughly. Heaven and earth!
Must I remember? Why, she would hang on him
As if increase of appetite had grown
By what it fed on; and yet, within a month—   145
Let me not think on't! Frailty, thy name is woman!—
A little month, or ere° those shoes were old   *before*
With which she followed my poor father's body
Like Niobe, all tears—why she, even she
(O God! a beast that wants discourse of reason°   *lacks reasoning power* 150
Would have mourned longer) married with my uncle;
My father's brother, but no more like my father
Than I to Hercules. Within a month,
Ere yet the salt of most unrighteous tears
Had left the flushing of her gallèd eyes,°   *stopped reddening her inflamed eyes* 155
She married. O, most wicked speed, to post°   *hurry*
With such dexterity° to incestuous sheets!   *agility*
It is not, nor it cannot come to good.
But break my heart, for I must hold my tongue!

[*Enter* HORATIO, MARCELLUS, *and* BERNARDO.]

HORATIO: Hail to your lordship!
HAMLET: I am glad to see you well.   160
    Horatio—or I do forget myself!
HORATIO: The same, my lord, and your poor servant ever.
HAMLET: Sir, my good friend—I'll change that name with
    you.
    And what make you from° Wittenberg, Horatio?   *are you doing away from*
    Marcellus?   165
MARCELLUS: My good lord!
HAMLET: I am very glad to see you.—[*to* BERNARDO] Good
    even, sir.—
    But what, in faith, make you from Wittenberg?
HORATIO: A truant disposition, good my lord.
HAMLET: I would not hear your enemy say so,   170
    Nor shall you do my ear that violence
    To make it truster of° your own report   *to make it trust*
    Against yourself. I know you are no truant.
    But what is your affair in Elsinore?
    We'll teach you to drink deep ere° you depart.   *before* 175
HORATIO: My lord, I came to see your father's funeral.
HAMLET: I prithee do not mock me, fellow student,
    I think it was to see my mother's wedding.
HORATIO: Indeed, my lord, it followed hard upon.°   *closely after*
HAMLET: Thrift, thrift, Horatio! The funeral baked meats   180
    Did coldly furnish forth° the marriage tables.   *served as cold cuts for*
    Would I° had met my dearest foe in heaven   *I wish I had*
    Or ever° I had seen that day, Horatio!   *before*
    My father—methinks I see my father.
HORATIO: O, where, my lord?

HAMLET: In my mind's eye, Horatio.   185
HORATIO: I saw him once. He was a goodly king.
HAMLET: He was a man, take him for all in all.
  I shall not look upon his like again.
HORATIO: My lord, I think I saw him yesternight.
HAMLET: Saw? who?   190
HORATIO: My lord, the King your father.
HAMLET: The King my
    father?
HORATIO: Season your admiration° for a while   *control your amazement*
  With an attent° ear, till I may deliver,   *attentive*
  Upon the witness of these gentlemen,
  This marvel to you.
HAMLET: For God's love let me hear!   195
HORATIO: Two nights together had these gentlemen
  (Marcellus and Bernardo) on their watch
  In the dead vast° and middle of the night   *vast emptiness*
  Been thus encountered. A figure like your father,
  Armed at point exactly, cap-a-pe,°   *head to foot* 200
  Appears before them and with solemn march
  Goes slow and stately by them. Thrice he walked
  By their oppressed and fear-surprisèd eyes,
  Within his truncheon's length; whilst they, distilled°   *changed*
  Almost to jelly with the act of fear,   205
  Stand dumb and speak not to him. This to me
  In dreadful secrecy impart they did,°   *they told*
  And I with them the third night kept the watch;
  Where, as they had delivered,° both in time,   *reported*
  Form of the thing, each word made true and good,   210
  The apparition comes. I knew your father:
  These hands are not more like.
HAMLET: But where was this?
MARCELLUS: My lord, upon the platform where we watched.
HAMLET: Did you not speak to it?
HORATIO: My lord, I did;
  But answer made it none. Yet once methought   215
  It lifted up its head and did address
  Itself to motion,° like as it would speak;   *prepared to move*
  But even then the morning cock crew° loud,   *crowed*
  And at the sound it shrunk in haste away
  And vanished from our sight.
HAMLET: 'Tis very strange.   220
HORATIO: As I do live, my honored lord, 'tis true;
  And we did think it writ down in our duty
  To let you know of it.
HAMLET: Indeed, indeed, sirs, but this troubles me.
  Hold you the watch tonight?   225
BOTH [MARCELLUS *and* BERNARDO]: We do, my lord.
HAMLET: Armed, say you?

BOTH: Armed, my lord.

HAMLET: From top to toe?

BOTH: My lord, from head to foot.

HAMLET: Then saw you not his face?   230

HORATIO: O, yes, my lord! He wore his beaver° up.   *the face cover of his helmet*

HAMLET: What, looked he frowningly?

HORATIO: A countenance more in sorrow than in anger.

HAMLET: Pale or red?

HORATIO: Nay, very pale.

HAMLET: And fixed his eyes upon you?   235

HORATIO: Most constantly.

HAMLET: I would I had° been there.   *wish I could have*

HORATIO: It would have much amazed you.

HAMLET: Very like,° very like. Stayed it long?   *very likely*

HORATIO: While one with moderate haste might tell a
    hundred.

BOTH: Longer, longer.   240

HORATIO: Not when I saw't.

HAMLET: His beard was grizzled—no?

HORATIO: It was, as I have seen it in his life,
    A sable silvered.°   *black with silver touches*

HAMLET: I will watch tonight.
    Perchance° 'twill walk again.   *perhaps*

HORATIO: I warrant it will.

HAMLET: If it assume my noble father's person,   245
    I'll speak to it, though hell itself should gape
    And bid me hold my peace.° I pray you all,   *tell me to be quiet*
    If you have hitherto concealed this sight,
    Let it be tenable in your silence still;°   *go on keeping it silent*
    And whatsoever else shall hap° tonight,   *happen* 250
    Give it an understanding but no tongue.°   *think but do not speak about it*
    I will requite° your loves. So, fare you well.   *reward*
    Upon the platform, 'twixt° eleven and twelve,   *between*
    I'll visit you.

ALL: Our duty to your honor.

HAMLET: Your loves, as mine to you. Farewell.   255

[All but HAMLET *leave.]*

My father's spirit—in arms? All is not well.
I doubt° some foul play. Would the night were come!   *suspect*
Till then sit still, my soul. Foul deeds will rise,
Though all the earth overwhelm them, to men's eyes.

[He leaves.]

SCENE 3. Elsinore. POLONIUS' house.

[Enter LAERTES *and* OPHELIA.]

LAERTES: My necessaries are embarked.° Farewell.   *luggage is on board*
    And, sister, as the winds give benefit

And convoy is assistant,° do not sleep,   *ships are available*
But let me hear from you.
OPHELIA: Do you doubt that?
LAERTES: For Hamlet, and the trifling of his favor,   5
   Hold it a fashion, and a toy in blood;°   *think of it as a fad and whim*
   A violet in the youth of primy nature,°   *nature at springtime*
   Forward,° not permanent; sweet, not lasting;   *fleeting*
   The perfume and suppliance° of a minute;   *aroma and pastime*
   No more.
OPHELIA: No more but so?
LAERTES: Think it no more.   10
   For nature crescent° does not grow alone   *a maturing person*
   In thews and bulk, but as this temple waxes,°   *not only in body, but as it grows*
   The inward service of the mind and soul
   Grows wide withal.° Perhaps he loves you now,   *along with it*
   And now no soil nor cautel° doth besmirch   *no stain or deceit*   15
   The virtue of his will; but you must fear,
   His greatness weighed,° his will is not his own,   *when his status is weighed*
   For he himself is subject to his birth.°   *the role he was born into*
   He may not, as unvalued persons do,
   Carve for himself, for on his choice depends   20
   The safety and health of his whole state,
   And therefore must his choice be circumscribed°   *limited*
   Unto the voice and yielding of that body
   Whereof he is the head. Then if he says he loves you,
   It fits your wisdom so far to believe it   25
   As he in his particular act and place
   May give his saying deed,° which is no further   *follow word with deed*
   Than the main voice of Denmark goes withal.°   *public opinion permits*
   Then weigh what loss your honor may sustain
   If with too credent ear you list° his songs,   *too willing ear you listen to*   30
   Or lose your heart, or your chaste treasure open
   To his unmastered importunity.°   *uncontrolled urging*
   Fear it, Ophelia, fear it, my dear sister,
   And keep you in the rear of your affection,
   Out of the shot° and danger of desire.   *out of firing range*   35
   The chariest° maid is prodigal° enough   *most careful/loose*
   If she unmask her beauty to the moon.
   Virtue itself scapes° not calumnious strokes.   *escapes*
   The canker galls the infants of the spring°   *worm ruins spring flowers*
   Too oft before their buttons be° disclosed,   *their buds are*   40
   And in the morn and liquid dew of youth
   Contagious blastments are most imminent.
   Be wary then; best safety lies in fear.
   Youth to itself° rebels, though none else near.   *by itself*
OPHELIA: I shall the effect of this good lesson keep   45
   As watchman to my heart. But, good my brother,
   Do not as some ungracious pastors° do,   *faithless priests*
   Show me the steep and thorny way to heaven,

Whiles, like a puffed and reckless libertine,°   *pleasure lover*
Himself the primrose path of dalliance treads   50
And recks not his own rede.°   *disregards his own counsel*
LAERTES: O, fear me not!°   *do not worry about me*

[*Enter* POLONIUS.]

I stay too long. But here my father comes.
A double blessing is a double grace;
Occasion smiles upon a second leave.°   *leave-taking*
POLONIUS: Yet here, Laertes? Aboard, aboard, for shame!   55
The wind sits in the shoulder of your sail,°   *wind is favorable*
And you are stayed for.° There—my blessing with thee!   *waited for*
And these few precepts in thy memory
Look thou character.° Give thy thoughts no tongue,   *make sure to record*
Nor any unproportioned thought his act.°   *its action*   60
Be thou familiar,° but by no means vulgar: *mingling with all*
Those friends thou hast, and their adoption tried,°   *after testing them*
Grapple them to thy soul with hoops of steel;
But do not dull thy palm° with entertainment   *wear out your hand*
Of each new-hatched, unfledged comrade. Beware   65
Of entrance to a quarrel; but being in,
Bear't that the opposed° may beware of thee.   *act so that the opponent*
Give every man thine ear, but few thy voice;
Take each man's censure, but reserve thy judgment.
Costly thy habit as thy purse can buy,°   *buy clothes you can afford*   70
But not expressed in fancy; rich, not gaudy;
For the apparel oft proclaims the man,
And they in France of the best rank and station
Are most select and generous, chief in that.
Neither a borrower nor a lender be;   75
For loan oft loses both itself and friend,
And borrowing dulls the edge of husbandry.°   *undermines good management*
This above all: to thine own self be true,
And it must follow, as the night the day,
Thou canst not then be false to any man.   80
Farewell. My blessing season this in thee!
LAERTES: Most humbly do I take my leave, my lord.
POLONIUS: The time invites you. Go, your servants tend.°   *wait*
LAERTES: Farewell, Ophelia, and remember well
  What I have said to you.
OPHELIA: 'Tis in my memory locked,   85
  And you yourself shall keep the key of it.
LAERTES: Farewell.

[*He leaves.*]

POLONIUS: What is't, Ophelia, he hath said to you?
OPHELIA: So please you, something touching the Lord Hamlet.
POLONIUS: Marry, well bethought!°   *good thinking*   90
  'Tis told me he hath very oft of late

Given private time to you, and you yourself
Have of your audience been most free and
   bounteous.°   *have been freely available*
If it be so—as so 'tis put on me,°   *as I've been told*
And that in way of caution—I must tell you   95
You do not understand yourself so clearly
As it behooves° my daughter and your honor.   *as is required of*
What is between you? Give me up the truth.
OPHELIA: He hath, my lord, of late made many tenders°   *given many signs*
Of his affection to me.   100
POLONIUS: Affection? Pooh! You speak like a green girl,
Unsifted° in such perilous circumstance.   *inexperienced*
Do you believe his tenders, as you call them?
OPHELIA: I do not know, my lord, what I should think.
POLONIUS: Marry, I will teach you! Think yourself a baby   105
That you have taken these tenders for true pay,
Which are not sterling.° Tender yourself more dearly,   *not true currency*
Or (not to crack the wind of the poor phrase,
Running it thus) you'll tender me° a fool.   *make me (or you) seem*
OPHELIA: My lord, he hath importuned me with love   110
In honorable fashion.
POLONIUS: Ay, fashion you may call it. Go to, go to!
OPHELIA: And hath given countenance to his speech, my lord,
With almost all the holy vows of heaven.
POLONIUS: Ay, springes to catch woodcocks!° I do know,   *traps for birds* 115
When the blood burns, how prodigal the soul
Lends the tongue vows. These blazes, daughter,
Giving more light than heat, extinct° in both   *ready to go out*
Even in their promise, as it is a-making,
You must not take for fire. From this time   120
Be somewhat scanter of your maiden presence.°   *make yourself scarcer*
Set your entreatments at a higher rate
Than a command to parley.° For Lord Hamlet,   *a mere summons to talk*
Believe so much in him, that he is young,
And with a larger tether may he walk   125
Than may be given you. In few,° Ophelia,   *in short*
Do not believe his vows; for they are brokers,
Not of that dye which their investments° show,   *appearances*
But mere implorators of unholy suits,°   *instigators of dishonest proposals*
Breathing like sanctified and pious bawds,°   *pimps* 130
The better to beguile. This is for all:
I would not, in plain terms, from this time forth
Have you so slander any moment° leisure   *so misuse any moment's*
As to give words or talk with the Lord Hamlet.
Look to't, I charge you. Come your ways.   135
OPHELIA: I shall obey, my lord.

[They leave.]

SCENE 4. Elsinore Castle. The platform of the guard.

[*Enter* HAMLET, HORATIO, *and* MARCELLUS.]

HAMLET: The air bites shrewdly; it is very cold.
HORATIO: It is a nipping and an eager air.
HAMLET: What hour now?
HORATIO: I think it lacks of° twelve.   *it's not quite*
MARCELLUS: No, it is struck.
HORATIO: Indeed? I heard it not. It then draws near the season°   *near the time*   5
    Wherein the spirit held his wont to walk.°   *used to walk*

[*A flourish of trumpets, and two cannons go off.*]

    What does this mean, my lord?
HAMLET: The King doth wake tonight and takes his rouse,°   *stays up to carouse*
    Keeps wassail, and the swaggering upspring reels,°   *drinks and dances*
    And, as he drains his draughts of Rhenish° down,   *Rhine wine*   10
    The kettledrum and trumpet thus bray out
    The triumph of his pledge.
HORATIO: Is it a custom?
HAMLET: Ay, marry, is't;
    But to my mind, though I am native here
    And to the manner born, it is a custom   15
    More honored in the breach° than the observance.   *in disregarding it*
    This heavy-headed revel east and west
    Makes us traduced and taxed of° other nations;   *defamed and blamed by*
    They call us drunkards and with swinish phrase
    Soil our addition;° and indeed it takes   *stain our reputation*   20
    From our achievements, though performed at height,
    The pith and marrow of our attribute.°   *the core of our good name*
    So oft it chances in particular men
    That for some vicious mole of nature in them,
    As in their birth—wherein they are not guilty,   25
    Since nature cannot choose his origin—
    By their overgrowth of some complexion,°   *some exaggerated trait*
    Oft breaking down the pales and forts° of reason,   *defenses*
    Or by some habit that too much overleavens
    The form of plausive° manners, that these men   *acceptable*   30
    Carrying, I say, the stamp of one defect,
    Being nature's livery,° or fortune's star—   *which nature has*
    Their virtues else (be they as pure as grace,   *dressed them in*
    As infinite as man may undergo)
    Shall in the general censure take corruption°   *in everyone's opinion be tarnished*   35
    From that particular fault. The dram° of evil   *drop*
    Doth all the noble substance often dout°   *drive out*
    To his own scandal.°   *its complete disgrace*

[*Enter* GHOST.]

HORATIO: Look, my lord, it comes!

HAMLET: Angels and ministers of grace defend us!
  Be thou° a spirit of health or goblin damned,   *whether you are*   40
  Bring with thee airs from heaven or blasts from hell,
  Be thy intents wicked or charitable,
  Thou com'st in such a questionable shape
  That I will speak to thee. I'll call thee Hamlet,
  King, father, royal Dane. O, answer me!   45
  Let me not burst in ignorance, but tell
  Why thy canonized° bones, hearsed in death,   *sanctified and duly buried*
  Have burst their cerements;° why the sepulchre   *left their burial shroud*
  Wherein we saw thee quietly inurned,
  Hath oped his° ponderous and marble jaws   *opened its*   50
  To cast thee up again. What may this mean
  That thou, dead corpse, again in complete steel,°   *in full armor*
  Revisits thus the glimpses of the moon,
  Making night hideous, and we fools of nature
  So horridly to shake our disposition°   *upset our reason*   55
  With thoughts beyond the reaches of our souls?
  Say, why is this? wherefore? What should we do?

  [GHOST *beckons* HAMLET.]

HORATIO: It beckons you to go away with it,
  As if it some impartment° did desire   *communication*
  To you alone.
MARCELLUS: Look with what courteous action   60
  It waves you to a more removed ground.
  But do not go with it!
HORATIO: No, by no means!
HAMLET: It will not speak. Then will I follow it.
HORATIO: Do not, my Lord!
HAMLET: Why, what should be the fear?
  I do not set my life at a pin's fee;°   *the price of a pin*   65
  And for my soul, what can it do to that,
  Being a thing immortal as itself?
  It waves me forth again. I'll follow it.
HORATIO: What if it tempt you toward the flood, my lord,
  Or to the dreadful summit of the cliff   70
  That beetles° over his base into the sea,   *juts out*
  And there assume some other, horrible form
  Which might deprive your sovereignty of reason°   *overthrow your*
  And draw you into madness? Think of it.   *sovereign reason*
  The very place puts toys of desperation,°   *desperate thoughts*   75
  Without more motive, into every brain
  That looks so many fathoms to the sea
  And hears it roar beneath.
HAMLET: It waves me still.
  Go on, I'll follow thee.
MARCELLUS: You shall not go, my lord.   80
HAMLET: Hold off your hands!

HORATIO: Be ruled, you shall not go.

HAMLET: My fate cries out
And makes each petty artery in this body
As hardy as the Nemean lion's nerve.°   *lion's sinews*

[GHOST *beckons*.]

Still am I called. Unhand me, gentlemen—
By heaven, I'll make a Ghost of him that lets° me!   *stops*   85
I say, away!—Go on, I'll follow thee.

[GHOST *and* HAMLET *leave*.]

HORATIO: He waxes° desperate with imagination.   *grows*
MARCELLUS: Let's follow; 'tis not fit thus to obey him.
HORATIO: Have after.° To what issue will this come?   *let's go after him*
MARCELLUS: Something is rotten in the state of Denmark.   90
HORATIO: Heaven will direct it.
MARCELLUS: Nay, let's follow him.

[*They leave.*]

SCENE 5. Same. Another part of the ramparts.

[*Enter* GHOST *and* HAMLET.]

HAMLET: Wither° wilt thou lead me? Speak, I'll go no further.   *where*
GHOST: Mark me.°   *listen carefully*
HAMLET: I will.
GHOST: My hour is almost come,
When I to sulphurous and tormenting flames
Must render up myself.
HAMLET: Alas, poor ghost!
GHOST: Pity me not, but lend thy serious hearing   5
To what I shall unfold.
HAMLET: Speak, I am bound to hear.
GHOST: So art thou to revenge, when thou shalt hear.
HAMLET: What?
GHOST: I am thy father's spirit,
Doomed for a certain term to walk the night,   10
And for the day confined to fast in fires,
Till the foul crimes done in my days of nature
Are burnt and purged away. But that I am forbid
To tell the secrets of my prison house,
I could a tale unfold whose lightest word   15
Would harrow up thy soul, freeze thy young blood,
Make thy two eyes, like stars, start from their spheres,
Thy knotted and combined locks to part,
And each particular hair to stand on end
Like quills upon the fretful porpentine.°   *angry porcupine*   20
But this eternal blazon° must not be   *this news of the*
To ears of flesh and blood. List, list, O, list! *supernatural world*
If thou didst ever thy dear father love—

HAMLET: O God!

GHOST: Revenge his foul and most unnatural murder.   25

HAMLET: Murder?

GHOST: Murder most foul, as in the best it is;
But this most foul, strange, and unnatural.

HAMLET: Hast me to know't, that I, with wings as swift
As meditation or the thoughts of love,   30
May sweep to my revenge.

GHOST: I find thee apt;
And duller shouldst thou be than the fat weed
That rots itself in ease on Lethe° wharf,   *river of oblivion*
Wouldst thou not stir° in this. Now, Hamlet, hear: *take action*
'Tis given out that, sleeping in my orchard,   35
A serpent stung me; so the whole ear of Denmark
Is by a forgèd process° of my death   *false account*
Rankly abused; but know, thou noble youth,
The serpent that did sting thy father's life
Now wears his crown.

HAMLET: O my prophetic soul!   40
My uncle?

GHOST: Ay, that incestuous, that adulterate beast,
With witchcraft of his wit, with traitorous gifts—
O wicked wit and gifts, that have the power
So to seduce!—won to his shameful lust   45
The will of my most seeming-virtuous queen.
O Hamlet, what a falling-off was there,
From me, whose love was of that dignity
That it went hand in hand even with the vow
I made to her in marriage, and to decline°   *to lower herself*   50
Upon a wretch whose natural gifts were poor
To those of mine!
But virtue, as it never will be moved,
Though lewdness court it in a shape of heaven,
So lust, though to a radiant angel linked,   55
Will sate itself° in a celestial bed   *will grow bored*
And prey on garbage.
But soft! methinks I scent the morning air.
Brief let me be. Sleeping within my orchard,
My custom always of the afternoon,   60
Upon my secure° hour thy uncle stole,   *thought to be safe*
With juice of cursed hebenon° in a vial,   *poison plant*
And in the porches of my ears did pour
The leperous distilment,° whose effect   *deadly liquid*
Holds such an enmity with° blood of man   *is so at war with* 65
That swift as quicksilver it courses° through   *runs*
The natural gates and alleys of the body,
And with a sudden vigor it doth posset°   *curdle*
And curd, like eager droppings° into milk,   *acid drops*
The thin and wholesome blood; so did it mine,   70

And a most instant tetter barked about,°   *sudden rash covered*
Most lazar-like,° with vile and loathsome crust   *like a leper*
All my smooth body.
Thus was I, sleeping, by a brother's hand
Of life, of crown, of queen, at once dispatched;   75
Cut off even in the blossoms of my sin,°   *with my sins in full flower*
Unhouseled, disappointed, unaneled,°   *without sacrament or*
No reckoning made, but sent to my account   *forgiveness of sins*
With all my imperfections on my head.
HAMLET: O, horrible! O, horrible! most horrible!   80
GHOST: If thou hast nature in thee, bear it not.
  Let not the royal bed of Denmark be
  A couch for luxury° and damnèd incest.   *bed for licentiousness*
  But, howsoever thou pursuest this act,
  Taint not thy mind, nor let thy soul contrive   85
  Against thy mother aught.° Leave her to heaven,   *anything against your mother*
  And to those thorns that in her bosom lodge
  To prick and sting her. Fare thee well at once,
  The glowworm shows the matin° to be near   *morning*
  And gins to pale his uneffectual fire.°   *begins to make it seem pale* 90
  Adieu, adieu, adieu! Remember me.

                   [He leaves.]

HAMLET: O all you host of heaven! O earth! What else?
  And shall I couple hell?° O fie! Hold, hold, my heart!   *shall I add hell*
  And you, my sinews, grow not instant old,
  But bear me stiffly up. Remember thee?   95
  Ay, thou poor ghost, while memory holds a seat
  In this distracted globe.° Remember thee?   *perturbed (globelike) head*
  Yea, from the table° of my memory   *record*
  I'll wipe away all trivial fond records,°   *foolish entries*
  All saws° of books, all forms, all pressures past   *wise sayings* 100
  That youth and observation copied there,
  And thy commandment all alone shall live
  Within the book and volume of my brain,
  Unmixed with baser matter. Yes, by heaven!
  O most pernicious woman!   105
  O villain, villain, smiling, damnèd villain!
  My tables, my tables!° Meet it is° I set it down   *note-keeping slates/it's right*
  That one may smile, and smile, and be a villain;
  At least I'm sure it may be so in Denmark.

  [Writes.]

  So, uncle, there you are. Now to my word: 110
  It is "Adieu, adieu! Remember me."
  I have sworn't.
HORATIO [*within*]: My lord, my lord!

  [Enter HORATIO *and* MARCELLUS.]

MARCELLUS: Lord Hamlet!

HORATIO: Heaven secure

him!°   *keep him safe*

HAMLET: So be it!

MARCELLUS: Illo, ho, ho, my lord!°   *(falconer's call)* 115

HAMLET: Hillo, ho, ho, boy! Come, bird, come.

MARCELLUS: How is't, my noble lord?

HORATIO: What news, my lord?

HAMLET: O, wonderful!

HORATIO: Good my lord, tell it.

HAMLET: No, you'll reveal it.

HORATIO: Not I, my lord, by heaven!

MARCELLUS: Nor I, my lord.   120

HAMLET: How say you then? Would heart of man once think it?
      But you'll be secret?

BOTH: Ay, by heaven, my lord.

HAMLET: There's never a villain dwelling in all Denmark
      But he's an arrant knave.°   *utter scoundrel*

HORATIO: There needs no ghost, my lord, come from the grave   125
      To tell us this.

HAMLET: Why, right! You are in the right!
      And so, without more circumstance° at all,   *ceremony*
      I hold it fit that we shake hands and part;
      You, as your business and desires shall point you,
      For every man hath business and desire,   130
      Such as it is; and for my own poor part,
      Look you, I'll go pray.

HORATIO: These are but wild and whirling words, my lord.

HAMLET: I am sorry they offend you, heartily;
      Yes, faith, heartily.

HORATIO: There's no offense, my lord.   135

HAMLET: Yes, by Saint Patrick, but there is, Horatio,
      And much offense too. Touching this vision here,
      It is an honest ghost,° that let me tell you.   *(not an evil spirit)*
      For° your desire to know what is between us,   *as for*
      O'ermaster't° as you may. And now, good friends,   *overcome it* 140
      As you are friends, scholars, and soldiers,
      Give° me one poor request.   *grant*

HORATIO: What is't, my lord? We will.

HAMLET: Never make known what you have seen tonight.

BOTH: My lord, we will not.

HAMLET: Nay, but swear't.

HORATIO: In faith,   145
      My lord, not I.

MARCELLUS: Nor I, my lord—in faith.

HAMLET: Upon my sword.

MARCELLUS: We have sworn, my lord, already.

HAMLET: Indeed, upon my sword, indeed.

[GHOST *cries under the stage.*]

GHOST: Swear.

HAMLET: Aha boy, say'st thou so? Art thou there, true-penny?   150
 Come on! You hear this fellow in the cellarage.
 Consent to swear.

HORATIO: Propose the oath, my lord.

HAMLET: Never to speak of this that you have seen.
 Swear by my sword.

GHOST [*beneath*]: Swear.   155

HAMLET: Hic et ubique?° Then we'll shift our ground. *(Latin) here and everywhere*
 Come hither, gentlemen,
 And lay your hands again upon my sword.
 Never to speak of this that you have heard:
 Swear by my sword.   160

GHOST [*beneath*]: Swear by his sword.

HAMLET: Well said, old mole! Canst work in the earth so fast?
 A worthy pioner!° Once more remove, good friends. *miner*

HORATIO: O day and night, but this is wondrous strange!

HAMLET: And therefore as a stranger give it welcome.   165
 There are more things in heaven and earth, Horatio,
 Than are dreamt of in your philosophy.
 But come!
 Here, as before, never, so help you mercy,
 How strange or odd soever° I bear myself *however strange or odd*   170
 (As I perchance hereafter shall think meet° *perhaps will think it right*
 To put an antic disposition on),° *to act very strange*
 That you, at such times seeing me, never shall,
 With arms encumbered° thus, or this head-shake, *folded*
 Or by pronouncing of some doubtful phrase,   175
 As "Well, well, we know," or "We could, an if we would,"
 Or "If we list° to speak," or "There be, an if they might," *if we wanted*
 Or such ambiguous giving out, to note
 That you know aught of me—this not to do,
 So grace and mercy at your most need help you,   180
 Swear.

GHOST [*beneath*]: Swear.

[*They swear.*]

HAMLET: Rest, rest, perturbèd spirit! So, gentlemen,
 With all my love I do commend me to you;
 And what so poor a man as Hamlet is   185
 May do to express his love and friending° to you, *friendship*
 God willing, shall not lack. Let us go in together;
 And still° your fingers on your lips, I pray. *always*
 The time is out of joint. O cursèd spite
 That ever I was born to set it right!   190
 Nay, come, let's go together.

[*They leave.*]

The Receptive Reader

1. (Act One, Scene l) Shakespeare treats the sighting of the ghost in carefully worked-out detail. Why do you think the playwright shows us that the guards are punctual for the changing of the watch? What picture do we get of Horatio here? What are his credentials? his attitude? Is he superstitious? How much of contemporary spirit lore can we reconstruct from this scene? (Why do you think the playwright kept Hamlet out of these first encounters with the ghost of his murdered father?)

2. (Act One, Scene 2) In this scene, what first impression do you form of Hamlet as the central character and *protagonist?* What different sides of his personality do you see in his interaction with the king and queen, in his soliloquies and asides, and in his interaction with Horatio? How does Hamlet react to his friends' reports of the ghost?

3. (Act One, Scene 3) What first impressions do you form of Polonius, Laertes, and Ophelia as major *supporting characters* in the play? How do Polonius and Laertes treat Ophelia, and how does she respond?

4. (Act One, Scenes 4 and 5) What are the major elements in the ghost's indictment of Claudius and Queen Gertrude? (How implicated or guilty do you think she is?) How do Hamlet's behavior and mood change as he first encounters the ghost, after he listens to the ghost's charges, and again when his associates rejoin him? How do you explain his irreverent behavior toward the ghost at the end of the scene? What does Hamlet say about the pretended madness that becomes a major strand in the play ? How does he begin to act out his "antic disposition"?

The Personal Dimension

Do you recognize any of the people in this play? Can you identify with or relate to any of them? Do you begin to understand their situation, their concerns, their motives?

Act Two

SCENE 1. Elsinore. POLONIUS' house.

[*Enter* POLONIUS *and* REYNALDO.]

POLONIUS: Give him this money and these notes, Reynaldo.
REYNALDO: I will, my lord.
POLONIUS: You shall do marvelous wisely, good Reynaldo,
   Before you visit him, to make inquire
   Of his behavior.
REYNALDO: My lord, I did intend it.   5
POLONIUS: Marry, well said, very well said. Look you, sir,
   Inquire me first what Danskers° are in Paris;   *Danish visitors*
   And how, and who, what means, and where they keep,
   What company, at what expense; and finding
   By this encompassment and drift of question°   *roundabout questioning* 10
   That they do know my son, come you more nearer

Than your particular demands will touch it.
Take you,° as 'twere, some distant knowledge of him;   *pretend*
As thus, "I know his father and his friends,
And in part him." Do you mark this, Reynaldo?   15
REYNALDO: Ay, very well, my lord.
POLONIUS: "And in part, him, but," you may say, "not well.
 But if't be he I mean, he's very wild,
 Addicted so and so"; and there put on him
 What forgeries° you please; marry,° none so rank *falsehoods/truly* 20
 As may dishonor him—take heed of that;
 But, sir, such wanton, wild, and usual slips
 As are companions noted and most known
 To youth and liberty.
REYNALDO: As gaming, my lord.
POLONIUS: Ay, or drinking, fencing, swearing, quarrelling,   25
 Drabbing.° You may go so far.   *running after*
                 loose women
REYNALDO: My lord, that would dishonor him.
POLONIUS: Faith, no, as you may season it in the charge.° *word it mildly*
 You must not put another scandal on him,
 That he is open to incontinency.°   *loose living* 30
 That's not my meaning. But breathe his faults so quaintly° *carefully*
 That they may seem the taints of liberty,
 The flash and outbreak of a fiery mind,
 A savageness in unreclaimèd blood,
 Of general assault.°   *commonly befalling*
REYNALDO: But, my good lord— *young people* 35
POLONIUS: Wherefore should you do this?
REYNALDO: Ay, my lord,
 I would know that.
POLONIUS: Marry, sir, here's my drift,
 And I believe it is a fetch of warrant.°   *permissible ploy*
 You laying these slight sullies on my son
 As 'twere a thing a little soiled in the working,   40
 Mark you,
 Your party in converse,° him you would sound, *conversation*
 Having ever seen in the prenominate° crimes *before-named*
 The youth you breathe of guilty, be assured
 He closes with you in this consequence:° *chimes in in this conclusion* 45
 "Good sir," or so, or "friend," or "gentleman"—
 According to the phrase or the addition° *proper way to address*
 Of man and country—
REYNALDO: Very good, my lord.
POLONIUS: And then, sir, does he this—he does—What was I
 about to say? By the mass, I was about to say some-   50
 thing! Where did I leave?
REYNALDO: At "closes in the consequence," at "friend or so,"
 and "gentleman."
POLONIUS: At "closes in the consequence"—Ay, marry!
 He closes thus: "I know the gentleman.   55

I saw him yesterday, or the other day,
Or then, or then, with such or such; and, as you say,
There was he gaming; there o'ertook in 's rouse;°   *overcome in his carousing*
There falling out at tennis"; or perchance,
"I saw him enter such a house of sale,"   60
Videlicet,° a brothel, or so forth.   *namely*
See you now—
Your bait of falsehood takes this carp of truth;
And thus do we of wisdom and of reach,
With windlasses and with assays of bias,°   *approaching it sideways*   65
By indirections find directions out.
So, by my former lecture and advice,
Shall you my son. You have° me, have you not?   *understand*
REYNALDO: My lord, I have.
POLONIUS: God be wi' you, fare you well!
REYNALDO: Good my lord!   70
POLONIUS: Observe his inclination in yourself.°   *for yourself*
REYNALDO: I shall, my lord.
POLONIUS: And let him ply his music.°   *do not interfere*
REYNALDO: Well, my lord.
POLONIUS: Farewell!

[REYNALDO *leaves*.]

[*Enter* OPHELIA.]

                    How now, Ophelia? What's the matter?
OPHELIA: O my lord, my lord, I have been so affrighted!°   *frightened*   75
POLONIUS: With what, in the name of God?
OPHELIA: My lord, as I was sewing in my closet,°   *private room*
    Lord Hamlet, with his doublet all unbraced,°   *jacket all loosened*
    No hat upon his head, his stockings fouled,°   *twisted*
    Ungartered, and down-gyvèd° to his ankle;   *coiled down*   80
    Pale as his shirt, his knees knocking each other,
    And with a look so piteous in purport°   *meaning*
    As if he had been loosèd out of hell
    To speak of horrors—he comes before me.
POLONIUS: Mad for thy love?
OPHELIA: My lord, I do not know,   85
    But truly I do fear it.
POLONIUS: What said he?
OPHELIA: He took me by the wrist and held me hard;
    Then goes he to the length of all his arm,
    And, with his other hand thus over his brow,
    He falls to such perusal° of my face   *study*   90
    As° he would draw it. Long stayed he so.   *as if*
    At last, a little shaking of mine arm,
    And thrice his head thus waving up and down,
    He raised a sigh so piteous and profound
    As it did seem to shatter all his bulk   95

And end his being. That done, he lets me go,
And with his head over his shoulder turned
He seemed to find his way without his eyes,
For out of doors he went without their help
And to the last bended their light on me.   100

POLONIUS: Come, go with me. I will go seek the King.
This is the very ecstasy° of love,   *the true madness*
Whose violent property° fordoes itself   *quality*
And leads the will to desperate undertakings
As oft as any passion under heaven   105
That does afflict our natures. I am sorry.
What, have you given him any hard words of late?

OPHELIA: No, my good lord; but, as you did command,
I did repel° his letters and denied   *reject*
His access to me.

POLONIUS: That hath made him mad.   110
I am sorry that with better heed and judgment
I had not quoted° him. I feared he did but trifle   *observed*
And meant to wrack° thee; but beshrew° my jealousy!   *ruin/curse*
By heaven, it is as proper to our age
To cast beyond ourselves in our opinions   115
As it is common for the younger sort
To lack discretion. Come, go we to the King.
This must be known; which, being kept close,° might   *if kept secret*
    move
More grief to hide than hate to utter love.°   *cause more grief to hide love than*
Come.   *it would cause hate to reveal it*   120

[They leave.]

SCENE 2. Elsinore. A room in the Castle.

[*Flourish of trumpets. Enter* KING *and* QUEEN, ROSENCRANTZ,
and GUILDENSTERN, *and others.*]

KING: Welcome, dear Rosencrantz and Guildenstern.
Moreover° that we much did long to see you,   *besides*
The need we have to use you did provoke
Our hasty sending. Something have you heard
Of Hamlet's transformation. So I call it,   5
Sith° nor the exterior nor the inward man   *since*
Resembles that it was. What it should be,
More than his father's death, that thus hath put him
So much from the understanding of himself,
I cannot dream of. I entreat you both   10
That, being of so young days° brought up with him,   *from your youngest days*
And since so neighbored° to his youth and havior,   *so close*
That you vouchsafe your rest° here in our court   *consent to stay*
Some little time; so by your companies
To draw him on to pleasures, and to gather   15

So much as from occasion you may glean,
Whether aught to us unknown afflicts him thus
That, opened,° lies within our remedy.   *when known*
QUEEN: Good gentlemen, he hath much talked of you,
And sure I am two men there are not living   20
To whom he more adheres.° If it will please you   *feels closer*
To show us so much gentry° and good will   *courtesy*
As to expend your time with us awhile
For the supply and profit of our hope,°   *so we may gain what we hope for*
Your visitation shall receive such thanks   25
As fits a king's remembrance.
ROSENCRANTZ: Both your Majesties
Might, by the sovereign power you have of us,
Put your dread pleasures° more into command   *wishes that we must treat with awe*
Than to entreaty.°   *polite request*
GUILDENSTERN: But we both obey,
And here give up ourselves, in the full bent,°   *to the fullest*   30
To lay our service freely at your feet,
To be commanded.
KING: Thanks, Rosencrantz and gentle Guildenstern.
QUEEN: Thanks, Guildenstern and gentle Rosencrantz.
And I beseech you instantly to visit   35
My too much changed son.—Go, some of you,
And bring these gentlemen where Hamlet is.
GUILDENSTERN: Heavens make our presence and our practices
Pleasant and helpful to him!
QUEEN: Ay, amen!

[ROSENCRANTZ *and* GUILDENSTERN *leave, with some attendants.*]

[*Enter* POLONIUS.]

POLONIUS: The ambassadors from Norway, my good lord,   40
Are joyfully returned.
KING: Thou still hast° been the father of good news.   *you always have*
POLONIUS: Have I, my lord? Assure you, my good liege,°   *overlord*
I hold my duty as I hold my soul,
Both to my God and to my gracious king;   45
And I do think—or else this brain of mine
Hunts not the trail of policy° so sure   *statecraft*
As it hath used to do—that I have found
The very cause of Hamlet's lunacy.
KING: O, speak of that! That do I long to hear.   50
POLONIUS: Give first admittance to the ambassadors,
My news shall be the fruit° to that great feast.   *come as dessert*
KING: Thyself do grace to them, and bring them in.

[POLONIUS *leaves.*]

He tells me, my dear Gertrude, he hath found
The head and source of all your son's distemper.°   *disturbed mind*   55

QUEEN: I doubt° it is no other but the main,°   *suspect/chief cause*
  His father's death and our overhasty marriage.
KING: Well, we shall sift° him.   *examine*

  [*Enter* POLONIUS, VOLTEMAND, *and* CORNELIUS.]

        Welcome, my good friends.
  Say, Voltemand, what from our brother Norway?
VOLTEMAND: Most fair return of greetings and desires.   60
  Upon our first, he sent out to suppress
  His nephew's levies,° which to him appeared   *warlike preparations*
  To be a preparation 'gainst the Polack,°   *against the Poles*
  But better looked into,° he truly found   *when he looked into it*
  It was against your Highness; whereat grieved,   65
  That so his sickness, age, and impotence°   *infirmity*
  Was falsely borne in hand,° sends out arrests°   *deceived/commands*
  On Fortinbras; which he, in brief, obeys,
  Receives rebuke from Norway, and, in fine,°   *finally*
  Makes vow before his uncle never more   70
  To give the assay of arms° against your Majesty.   *make war*
  Whereon old Norway, overcome with joy,
  Gives him three thousand crowns in annual fee°   *payment*
  And his commission to employ those soldiers,
  So levied as before, against the Polack;   75
  With an entreaty, herein further shown,

  [*Gives a paper.*]

  That it might please you to give quiet pass°   *grant the right to pass*
  Through your dominions for this enterprise,
  On such regards° of safety and allowance   *with such assurances*
  As therein are set down.
KING: It likes us well;°   *we like it*   80
  And at our more considered time we'll read,
  Answer, and think upon this business.
  Meantime we thank you for your well-took labor.
  Go to your rest; at night we'll feast together.
  Most welcome home!

      [*Ambassadors leave.*]

POLONIUS: This business is well ended.   85
  My liege, and madam, to expostulate
  What majesty should be, what duty is,
  Why day is day, night night, and time is time,
  Were nothing but to waste night, day, and time.
  Therefore, since brevity is the soul of wit,°   *intelligence*   90
  And tediousness the limbs and outward flourishes,
  I will be brief. Your noble son is mad.
  Mad call I it; for, to define true madness,
  What is't but to be nothing else but mad?
  But let that go.

QUEEN: More matter,° with less art.   *substance*   95
POLONIUS: Madam, I swear I use no art at all.
    That he is mad, 'tis true: 'tis true 'tis pity;
    And pity 'tis 'tis true. A foolish figure!°   *figure of speech*
    But farewell it, for I will use no art.
    Mad let us grant him then. And now remains   100
    That we find out the cause of this effect—
    Or rather say, the cause of this defect,
    For this effect defective comes by cause.
    Thus it remains, and the remainder thus.
    Perpend:°   *listen carefully*   105
    I have a daughter (have while she is mine),
    Who in her duty and obedience, mark,
    Hath given me this. Now gather, and surmise.

    [*Reads the letter.*]

      To the celestial, and my soul's idol, the most beautified
      Ophelia,—   110
    That's an ill phrase, a vile phrase; "beautified" is a vile
      phrase.
    But you shall hear. Thus:

    [*Reads.*]

      In her excellent white bosom, these, etc.
QUEEN: Came this from Hamlet to her?
POLONIUS: Good madam, stay awhile. I will be faithful.°   *patient*   115

    [*Reads.*]

      Doubt thou the stars are fire;
          Doubt that the sun doth move;
      Doubt truth to be a liar;
          But never doubt I love.

      O dear Ophelia, I am ill at these numbers;° I have   *not good at verse*   120
    not art to reckon my groans; but that I love thee best,
    O most best, believe it. Adieu.
          Thine evermore, most dear lady, whilst this
            machine° is to him, HAMLET.   *body*

    This, in obedience, hath my daughter shown me;°   *has reported to me*   125
    And more above, hath his solicitings,°   *pleas*
    As they fell out by time, by means, and place,
    All given to mine ear.
KING: But how hath she
    Received his love?
POLONIUS: What do you think of me?
KING: As of a man faithful and honorable.   130
POLONIUS: I would fain° prove so. But what might you think,   *gladly*
    When I had seen this hot love on the wing
    (As I perceived it, I must tell you that,

Before my daughter told me), what might you,
Or my dear Majesty your queen here, think,   135
If I had played the desk or table book,°   *mere passive recorder*
Or given my heart a winking, mute and dumb,
Or looked upon this love with idle sight?
What might you think? No, I went round to work
And my young mistress thus I did bespeak:°   *lecture*   140
"Lord Hamlet is a prince, out of thy star.°   *outside your sphere*
This must not be." And then I precepts gave her,
That she should lock herself from his resort,°   *company*
Admit no messengers, receive no tokens.
Which done, she took the fruits of my advice,   145
And he, repulsed, a short tale to make,
Fell into a sadness, then into a fast,
Thence to a watch, thence into a weakness,
Thence to a lightness, and, by this declension,°   *downward progression*
Into the madness wherein now he raves,   150
And all we mourn for.
KING: Do you think 'tis this?
QUEEN: It may be, very like.°   *very likely*
POLONIUS: Hath there been such a time—I would fain
    know that—
That I have positively said "'Tis so,"
When it proved otherwise?
KING: Not that I know.   155
POLONIUS [*points to his head and shoulder*]: Take this from
    this, if this be otherwise.
If circumstances lead me, I will find
Where truth is hid, though it were hid indeed
Within the center
KING: How may we try° it further?   *check*   160
POLONIUS: You know sometimes he walks four hours
    together
Here in the lobby.
QUEEN: So he does indeed.
POLONIUS: At such a time I'll loose° my daughter to him.   *release*
Be you and I behind an arras° then.   *tapestry curtain*
Mark the encounter. If he love her not,   165
And be not from his reason fallen° thereon,   *gone out of his mind*
Let me be no assistant for a state,°   *councilor of state*
But keep a farm and carters.°   *drivers of carts*
KING: We will try it.

[*Enter* HAMLET, *reading a book.*]

QUEEN: But look where sadly the poor wretch comes
    reading.
POLONIUS: Away, I do beseech you, both away!   170
I'll board° him presently. O, give me leave.   *approach*

[KING *and* QUEEN *leave, with attendants.*]

How does my good Lord Hamlet?

HAMLET: Well, God-a-mercy.

POLONIUS: Do you know me, my lord?

HAMLET: Excellent well. You are a fishmonger.   175

POLONIUS: Not I, my lord.

HAMLET: Then I would you were so honest a man.

POLONIUS: Honest, my lord?

HAMLET: Ay, sir. To be honest, as this world goes, is to
be one man picked out of ten thousand.   180

POLONIUS: That's very true, my lord.

HAMLET: For if the sun breed maggots in a dead dog,
being a god kissing carrion—Have you a daughter?

POLONIUS: I have, my lord.

HAMLET: Let her not walk in the sun. Conception is a   185
blessing, but not as your daughter may conceive.
Friend, look to't.

POLONIUS [*aside*]: How say you by that? Still harping
on my daughter. Yet he knew me not at first. He
said I was a fishmonger. He is far gone, far gone!   190
And truly in my youth I suffered much extremity
for love—very near this. I'll speak to him again.—
What do you read, my lord?

HAMLET: Words, words, words.

POLONIUS: What is the matter, my lord?   195

HAMLET: Between who?

POLONIUS: I mean, the matter that you read, my lord.

HAMLET: Slanders, sir; for the satirical rogue says here
that old men have grey beards; that their faces are
wrinkled; their eyes purging° thick amber and   *dripping* 200
plum-tree gum; and that they have a plentiful lack
of wit, together with most weak hams. All which,
sir, though I most powerfully and potently believe,
yet I hold it not honesty° to have it thus set down; *good manners*
for you yourself, sir, should be old as I am if, like   205
a crab, you could go backward.

POLONIUS [*aside*]: Though this be madness, yet there
is method in't.—Will you walk out of the air, my
lord?

HAMLET: Into my grave?   210

POLONIUS: Indeed, that is out of the air. [*aside*] How
pregnant° sometimes his replies are! a happiness   *meaningful*
that often madness hits on, which reason and san-
ity could not so prosperously be delivered of. I
will leave him and suddenly contrive the means   215
of meeting between him and my daughter.—My
honorable lord, I will most humbly take my leave
of you.

HAMLET: You cannot, sir, take from me anything that I will more willingly part withal°—except my life, except my life, except my life.

part with 220

[*Enter* ROSENCRANTZ *and* GUILDENSTERN.]

POLONIUS: Fare you well, my lord.
HAMLET: These tedious old fools!
POLONIUS: You go to seek the Lord Hamlet. There he is.
ROSENCRANTZ [*to* POLONIUS]: God save you, sir!

225

[POLONIUS *leaves.*]

GUILDENSTERN: My honored lord!
ROSENCRANTZ: My most dear lord!
HAMLET: My excellent good friends! How dost thou, Guildenstern? Ah, Rosencrantz! Good lads, how do ye both?

230

ROSENCRANTZ: As the indifferent° children of the earth.

ordinary

GUILDENSTERN: Happy in that we are not over-happy. On Fortune's cap we are not the very button.°

top

HAMLET: Nor the soles of her shoe?
ROSENCRANTZ: Neither, my lord.

235

HAMLET: Then you live about her waist, or in the middle of her favors?
GUILDENSTERN: Faith, her privates° we.

intimate friends

HAMLET: In the secret parts of Fortune? O, most true! she is a strumpet. What news?

240

ROSENCRANTZ: None, my lord, but that the world's grown honest.
HAMLET: Then is doomsday near! But your news is not true. Let me question more in particular. What have you, my good friends, deserved at the hands of Fortune that she sends you to prison hither?

245

GUILDENSTERN: Prison, my lord?
HAMLET: Denmark's a prison.
ROSENCRANTZ: Then is the world one.
HAMLET: A goodly one; in which there are many confines,° wards, and dungeons, Denmark being one of the worst.

250

cells

ROSENCRANTZ: We think not so, my lord.
HAMLET: Why, then 'tis none to you, for there is nothing either good or bad but thinking makes it so. To me it is a prison.

255

ROSENCRANTZ: Why, then your ambition makes it one. 'Tis too narrow for your mind.
HAMLET: O God, I could be bounded in a nutshell and count myself a king of infinite space, were it not that I have bad dreams.

260

GUILDENSTERN: Which dreams indeed are ambition; for the very substance of the ambitious is merely the shadow of a dream.

HAMLET: A dream itself is but a shadow.   265

ROSENCRANTZ: Truly, and I hold ambition of so airy and light a quality that it is but a shadow's shadow.

HAMLET: Then are our beggars bodies, and our monarchs and outstretched heroes the beggars' shadows. Shall we to the court? for, by my fay,° I cannot reason.   270   *faith*

BOTH: We'll wait upon you.

HAMLET: No such matter! I will not sort° you with the rest of my servants; for, to speak to you like an honest man, I am most dreadfully attended.° But in the beaten way of friendship, what make you at Elsinore?   *class*   275   *very poorly served*

ROSENCRANTZ: To visit you, my lord; no other occasion.

HAMLET: Beggar that I am, I am even poor in thanks; but I thank you; and sure, dear friends, my thanks are too dear° a halfpenny. Were you not sent for? Is it your own inclining? Is it a free visitation? Come, deal justly with me. Come, come! Nay, speak.   280   *too dear at (or by)*   285

GUILDENSTERN: What should we say, my lord?

HAMLET: Why, anything, but to the purpose.° You were sent for, and there is a kind of confession in your looks, which your modesties have not craft enough to color.° I know the good King and Queen have sent for you.   *point*   *not skill enough to disguise* 290

ROSENCRANTZ: To what end, my lord?

HAMLET: That you must teach me. But let me conjure you° by the rights of our fellowship, by the consonancy° of our youth, by the obligation of our ever-preserved love, and by what more dear a better proposer° could charge you withal, be even and direct with me, whether you were sent for or no.   *plead with you*   *harmony* 295   *talker*

ROSENCRANTZ [*aside to* GUILDENSTERN]: What say you?

HAMLET [*aside*]: Nay then, I have an eye of you.° If you love me, hold not off.   *I am on to you* 300

GUILDENSTERN: My lord, we were sent for.

HAMLET: I will tell you why, so shall my anticipation prevent your discovery,° and your secrecy to the King and Queen moult no feather.° I have of late—but wherefore I know not—lost all my mirth, forgone all custom of exercises;° and indeed, it goes so heavily with my disposition that this goodly frame, the earth, seems to me a sterile promontory;°   *your giving yourself away*   *not be damaged* 305   *all ordinary activities*   *barren outcropping*

this most excellent canopy, the air, look you, this   310
brave overhanging firmament, this majestical roof
fretted° with golden fire—why, it appeareth no   *ornamented*
other thing to me than a foul and pestilent congregation of vapors. What a piece of work is a
man! how noble in reason! how infinite in faculties!   315
in form and moving how express° and admirable!   *well made*
in action how like an angel! in apprehension° how   *understanding*
like a god! the beauty of the world, the paragon of
animals! And yet to me what is this quintessence°   *ultimate essence*
of dust? Man delights not me—no, nor woman   320
neither, though by your smiling you seem to
say so.
ROSENCRANTZ: My lord, there was no such stuff in my
thoughts.
HAMLET: Why did you laugh then, when I said "Man   325
delights not me"?
ROSENCRANTZ: To think, my lord, if you delight not in
man, what lenten entertainment° the players shall   *meager treatment*
receive from you. We coted° them on the way, and   *passed*
hither are they coming to offer you service.   330
HAMLET: He that plays the king shall be welcome—
his Majesty shall have tribute of me; the adventur-
ous knight shall use his foil and target;° the lover   *sword and shield*
shall not sigh gratis; the humorous man shall end
his part in peace; the clown shall make those   335
laugh whose lungs are tickle o' the sere;° and the   *quick on the trigger*
lady shall say her mind freely, or the blank verse
shall halt° for't. What players are they?   *stumble*
ROSENCRANTZ: Even those you were wont to° take   *you used to*
such delight in, the tragedians of the city.   340
HAMLET: How chances it they travel? Their residence,
both in reputation and profit, was better both ways.
ROSENCRANTZ: I think their inhibition° comes by the   *their being kept out*
means of the late innovation.°   *recent fad*
HAMLET: Do they hold the same estimation they did   345
when I was in the city? Are they so followed?
ROSENCRANTZ: No indeed are they not.
HAMLET: How comes it? Do they grow rusty?
ROSENCRANTZ: Nay, their endeavor keeps in the
wonted° pace; but there is, sir, an eyrie of chil-   *accustomed* 350
dren, little eyases,° that cry out on the top of ques-   *bird's brood of shrill little hawks*
tion and are most tyrannically clapped° for't. These   *wildly applauded*
are now the fashion, and so berattle the common
stages° (so they call them) that many wearing   *put down ordinary theaters*
rapiers are afraid of goosequills° and dare scarce   *fear the playwright's pen* 355
come thither.
HAMLET: What, are they children? Who maintains them?
How are they escoted?° Will they pursue the   *supported*

quality° no longer than they can sing? Will they *play this role*
not say afterwards, if they should grow themselves   360
to common players (as it is most like, if their means
are no better), their writers do them wrong to
make them exclaim against their own succession?° *future roles*

ROSENCRANTZ: Faith, there has been much to do on   365
both sides; and the nation holds it no sin to tarre
them° to controversy. There was, for a while, no *egg them on*
money bid for argument° unless the poet and the *for a new play*
player went to cuffs in the question.° *on this topic*

HAMLET: Is't possible?   370

GUILDENSTERN: O, there has been much throwing
about of brains.

HAMLET: Do the boys carry it away?

ROSENCRANTZ: Ay, that they do, my lord—Hercules
and his load° too. *Hercules carrying the globe (as* 375
on the Globe theater sign)

HAMLET: It is not very strange; for my uncle is King of
Denmark, and those that would make mows° at *faces*
him while my father lived give twenty, forty, fifty,
a hundred ducats apiece for his picture in little.° *miniature portrait*
'Sblood,° there is some thing in this more than nat- *by God's blood*
ural, if philosophy could find it out.   380

[*Flourish of trumpets for the* PLAYERS.]

GUILDENSTERN: There are the players.

HAMLET: Gentlemen, you are welcome to Elsinore.
Your hands, come! The appurtenance° of welcome *usual expression*
is fashion and ceremony. Let me comply with you
in this garb,° lest my extent° to the players (which *treat you in this fashion/* 385
welcome
I tell you must show fairly outwards) should more
appear like entertainment than yours. You are
welcome. But my uncle-father and aunt-mother
are deceived.

GUILDENSTERN: In what, my dear lord?   390

HAMLET: I am but mad north-north-west. When the
wind is southerly I know a hawk from a handsaw.

[*Enter* POLONIUS.]

POLONIUS: Well be with you, gentlemen!

HAMLET: Hark you, Guildenstern—and you too—at
each ear a hearer! That great baby you see there is   395
not yet out of his swaddling clouts.° *diapers*

ROSENCRANTZ: Happily he's the second time come to
them; for they say an old man is twice a child.

HAMLET: I will prophesy he comes to tell me of the
players. Mark it.—You say right, sir; a Monday   400
morning; 'twas so indeed.

POLONIUS: My lord, I have news to tell you.

HAMLET: My lord, I have news to tell you: when Roscius was an actor in Rome—

POLONIUS: The actors are come hither, my lord.   405

HAMLET: Buzz, buzz!

POLONIUS: Upon my honor—

HAMLET: Then came each actor on his ass—

POLONIUS: The best actors in the world, either for tragedy, comedy, history, pastoral, pastoral-comi-   410
cal, historical-pastoral, tragical-historical, tragical-comical-historical-pastoral; scene individable, or
poem unlimited.° Seneca cannot be too heavy, nor *plays classical or irregular*
Plautus° too light. For the law of writ and the lib-   *(Roman playwrights)*
erty, these are the only men.   415

HAMLET: O Jephthah,° judge of Israel, what a treasure   *(a biblical figure)*
hadst thou!

POLONIUS: What a treasure had he, my lord?

HAMLET: Why,

> One fair daughter, and no more,   420
> The which he loved passing well.

POLONIUS [*aside*]: Still on my daughter.

HAMLET: Am I not in the right, old Jephthah?

POLONIUS: If you call me Jephthah, my lord, I have a daughter that I love passing well.   425

HAMLET: Nay, that follows not.

POLONIUS: What follows then, my lord?

HAMLET: Why,

> As by lot, God wot,

and then, you know,   430

> It came to pass, as most like it was.

The first row° of the pious chanson will show you   *stanza*
more; for look where my abridgement° comes.   *interruption*

[*Enter four or five* PLAYERS.]

You are welcome, masters; welcome all.—I am
glad to see thee well.—Welcome, good friends.—   435
O, my old friend? Why, thy face is valanced° since I   *fringed*
saw thee last. Com'st thou to beard me in Den-
mark?—What, my young lady and mistress? By'r
Lady,° your ladyship is nearer to heaven than when   *by Our Lady*
I saw you last by the altitude of a chopine.° Pray   *the length of high heels* 440
God your voice, like a piece of uncurrent gold,° be   *defective coin*
not cracked° within the ring.—Masters, you are all   *do not crack (or change)*
welcome. We'll even to't° like French falconers, fly   *we'll go to it*
at anything we see. We'll have a speech straight.
Come, give us a taste of your quality.° Come, a   *talent* 445
passionate speech.

1. PLAYER: What speech, my good lord?

HAMLET: I heard thee speak me a speech once, but it
was never acted; or if it was, not above once; for
the play, I remember, pleased not the million,   450
'twas caviary to the general;° but it was (as I   *too choice for the many*
received it, and others, whose judgments in such
matters cried in the top of mine)° an excellent   *outweighed mine*
play, well digested° in the scenes, set down with   *arranged*
as much modesty as cunning.° I remember one   *moderation as skill* 455
said there were no sallets° in the lines to make the   *coarse jokes*
matter savory, nor no matter in the phrase that
might indict the author of affectation; but called it
an honest method, as wholesome as sweet, and by
very much more handsome than fine. One speech   460
in it I chiefly loved. 'Twas Æneas' tale to Dido,
and thereabout of it especially where he speaks of
Priam's slaughter. If it live in your memory, begin
at this line—let me see, let me see:

> The rugged Pyrrhus, like the Hyrcanian beast°—   *Asian tiger* 465

'Tis not so; it begins with Pyrrhus:

> The rugged Pyrrhus, he whose sable arms,°   *black-hued armor*
> Black as his purpose, did the night resemble
> When he lay crouched in the ominous horse,°   *hidden in the wooden*
> Hath now this dread and black complexion smeared   *Trojan horse* 470
> With heraldry more dismal. Head to foot
> Now is he total gules,° horridly tricked   *heraldic red*
> With blood of fathers, mothers, daughters, sons,
> Baked and impasted with the parching° streets,   *fire-parched*
> That lend a tyrannous and a damned light   475
> To their lord's murder. Roasted in wrath and fire,
> And thus oversized with coagulate gore,°   *smeared with clotted gore*
> With eyes like carbuncles,° the hellish Pyrrhus   *fiery-red stones*
> Old grandsire Priam seeks.

So, proceed you.   480

POLONIUS: Fore God, my lord, well spoken, with good
accent and good discretion.

1. PLAYER: Anon he finds him,
> Striking too short at Greeks. His antique sword,
> Rebellious to his arm, lies where it falls,   485
> Repugnant to command.° Unequal matched,   *refusing obedience*
> Pyrrhus at Priam drives, in rage strikes wide;
> But with the whiff and wind of his fell° sword   *deadly*
> The unnervèd father falls. Then senseless Ilium,°   *the unfeeling city*
> Seeming to feel this blow, with flaming top°   *with a tower on fire* 490
> Stoops to his base,° and with a hideous crash   *crashes to its base*
> Takes prisoner° Pyrrhus' ear. For lo! his sword,   *distracts*

Which was declining on the milky° head   milk-white
Of reverend Priam, seemed in the air to stick.
So, as a painted tyrant, Pyrrhus stood,   495
And, like a neutral to° his will and matter,   as if detached from
Did nothing.
But, as we often see, against some storm,
A silence in the heavens, the rack° stand still,   threatening clouds
The bold winds speechless, and the orb below   500
As hush as death—anon the dreadful thunder
Doth rend the region; so, after Pyrrhus' pause,
Aroused vengeance sets him new awork;
And never did the Cyclops' hammers fall
On Mars's armor, forged for proof eterne,°   made to last forever   505
With less remorse than Pyrrhus' bleeding sword
Now falls on Priam.
Out, out, thou strumpet Fortune! All you gods,
In general synod° take away her power;   council
Break all the spokes and fellies° from her wheel,   outer rim   510
And bowl the round nave° down the hill of heaven,   hub
As low as to the fiends!

POLONIUS: This is too long.

HAMLET: It shall to the barber's, with your beard.—Prithee
say on. He's for a jig or a tale of bawdry, or he sleeps.°   or else he falls asleep   515
Say on; come to Hecuba.

1. PLAYER: *But who, O who, had seen the mobled° queen—*   veiled

HAMLET: "The mobled queen"?

POLONIUS: That's good! "Mobled queen" is good.

1. PLAYER: *Run barefoot up and down, threatening the flames*   520
With bisson rheum;° a clout° upon that head   blinding tears/rag
Where late the diadem stood, and for a robe,
About her lank and all overteemed° loins,   worn out from childbirth
A blanket, in the alarm of fear caught up—
Who this had seen, with tongue in venom steeped   525
'Gainst Fortune's state would treason have
*   pronounced.*
But if the gods themselves did see her then,
When she saw Pyrrhus make malicious sport
In mincing with his sword her husband's limbs,
The instant burst of clamor that she made   530
(Unless things mortal move them not at all)
Would have made milch° the burning eyes of   moist with the milk of tears
*   heaven*
And passion in the gods.

POLONIUS: Look, whether he has not turned his color,
and has tears in his eyes. Prithee no more!   535

HAMLET: 'Tis well. I'll have thee speak out the rest of
this soon.—Good my lord, will you see the players
well bestowed?° Do you hear? Let them be well   accommodated
used; for they are the abstract° and brief chronicles   summary

of the time. After your death you were better have   540
a bad epitaph than their ill report while you live.

POLONIUS: My lord, I will use them according to their
desert.

HAMLET: God's bodykins, man, much better! Use every
man after his desert, and who should scape whip-   545
ping? Use them after your own honor and dignity.
The less they deserve, the more merit is in your
bounty.° Take them in.   *generosity*

POLONIUS: Come, sirs.

HAMLET: Follow him, friends. We'll hear a play   550
tomorrow.

[POLONIUS *and* PLAYERS *(except the first) leave.*]

Dost thou hear me, old friend? Can you play "The
Murder of Gonzago"?

1. PLAYER: Ay, my lord.

HAMLET: We'll have it tomorrow night. You could, for   555
a need, study a speech of some dozen or sixteen
lines which I would set down and insert in it,
could you not?

1. PLAYER: Ay, my lord.

HAMLET: Very well. Follow that lord—and look you   560
mock him not. [*First* PLAYER *leaves. To* ROSENCRANTZ.]
My good friends, I'll leave you till night. You are
welcome to Elsinore.

ROSENCRANTZ: Good my lord!

HAMLET: Ay, so, Good bye to you.

[ROSENCRANTZ *and* GUILDENSTERN *leave.*]

Now I am alone.   565
O, what a rogue and peasant slave am I!
Is it not monstrous that this player here,
But in a fiction, in a dream of passion,
Could force his soul so to his own conceit°   *imagination*
That, from her working, all his visage wanned,°   *his face paled* 570
Tears in his eyes, distraction in's aspect,°   *in his looks*
A broken voice, and his whole function suiting
With forms to his conceit? And all for nothing!
For Hecuba!
What's Hecuba to him, or he to Hecuba,   575
That he should weep for her? What would he do,
Had he the motive and the cue for passion
That I have? He would drown the stage with tears
And cleave the general ear° with horrid speech;   *split everyone's ear*
Make mad the guilty and appal the free,°   *innocent* 580
Confound the ignorant, and amaze indeed
The very faculties of eyes and ears.
Yet I,

A dull and muddy-mettled° rascal, peak°   *weak-souled/mope*
Like John-a-dreams, unpregnant of° my cause,   *unmoved by*   585
And can say nothing! No, not for a king,
Upon whose property and most dear life
A damned defeat was made.° Am I a coward?   *inflicted*
Who calls me villain? breaks my pate across?°   *cudgels my head*
Plucks off my beard and blows it in my face?   590
Tweaks me by the nose? gives me the lie in the throat°   *calls me a liar*
As deep as to the lungs? Who does me this, ha?
'Swounds,° I should take it! for it cannot be   *by God's wounds*
But I am pigeon-livered and lack gall
To make oppression bitter, or ere this°   *before now*   595
I should have fatted all the region kites°   *the vultures in the air*
With this slave's offal.° Bloody, bawdy, villain!   *rotting scraps*
Remorseless, treacherous, lecherous, kindless° villain!   *unnatural*
O, vengeance!
Why, what an ass am I! This is most brave,   600
That I, the son of a dear father murdered,
Prompted to my revenge by heaven and hell,
Must (like a whore) unpack my heart with words
And fall a-cursing like a very drab,°   *a true harlot*
A scullion!°   *kitchen wench*   605
Fie upon't! foh! About, my brain! I have heard
That guilty creatures, sitting at a play,
Have by the very cunning° of the scene   *ingenious arrangement*
Been struck so to the soul that presently
They have proclaimed their malefactions;°   *crimes*   610
For murder, though it have no tongue, will speak
With most miraculous organ. I'll have these players
Play something like the murder of my father
Before mine uncle. I'll observe his looks,
I'll tent° him to the quick; if he but blench,°   *test/turn pale*   615
I know my course. The spirit that I have seen
May be a devil; and the devil hath power
To assume a pleasing shape; yea, and perhaps
Out of my weakness and my melancholy,
As he is very potent with such spirits,°   *knows how to exploit such traits* 620
Abuses° me to damn me. I'll have grounds   *deceives*
More relative° than this. The play's the thing   *relevant*
Wherein I'll catch the conscience of the King.

[*He leaves.*]

The Receptive Reader

1. (Acts One and Two) One reviewer described Claudius in a new production as a king "who is disturbed, dishonest, and yet an ordinary respectable and
sensual stuffed-shirt politician" (Harold Clurman). What in Claudius's talk and
behavior in the first two acts lives up to this billing? What image do you get of

him in his dealings with Laertes, Polonius, Hamlet? How formidable an *antagonist* does he present for Hamlet?

2. (Act Two, Scene 1) Here and earlier, how silly or pompous does Polonius seem to you? Is he worthy of at least some respect? What kind of father is he for Laertes and Ophelia? How weak and submissive is Ophelia? Does she have any good lines?

3. (Act Two, Scene 2) In this scene, Hamlet starts his fencing and sparring with those in the service of the king. Is there a pattern in Hamlet's baiting of Polonius? (What makes Polonius say, "Though this be madness, yet there's method in't"?) How does Hamlet deal with Rosencrantz and Guildenstern? (Of what does he accuse them?) What side of Hamlet's character does his relationship with the actors bring out? (What do we learn here and in Act Three, Scene 2, indirectly about Shakespeare's views about the theater?)

4. Hamlet's "I have of late" speech is seen by many as a major *thematic passage.* What are the the polarities that help structure the speech? What is the keynote?

5. The concluding "O what a rogue and peasant slave" *soliloquy* is prime evidence for critics debating the question of Hamlet's delay or hesitation in pursuing his revenge. What occasions this speech? What is the keynote or prevailing tone? Does it lead anywhere?

Act Three

SCENE 1. Elsinore. A room in the Castle.

[*Enter* KING, QUEEN, POLONIUS, OPHELIA, ROSENCRANTZ, GUILDENSTERN, *and lords.*]

KING: And can you by no drift of circumstance°		*roundabout talk*
Get from him why he puts on this confusion,°		*acts in this disturbed fashion*
Grating so harshly all his days of quiet		
With turbulent and dangerous lunacy?		
ROSENCRANTZ: He does confess he feels himself distracted,	5	
But from what cause he will by no means speak.		
GUILDENSTERN: Nor do we find him forward to be sounded,°		*willing to be found out*
But with a crafty madness keeps aloof		
When we would bring him on to some confession		
Of his true state.		
QUEEN: Did he receive you well?	10	
ROSENCRANTZ: Most like a gentleman.		
GUILDENSTERN: But with much forcing of his disposition.°		*strained politeness*
ROSENCRANTZ: Niggard of question,° but of our demands		*asking few questions*
Most free in his reply.°		*answering freely*
QUEEN: Did you assay° him		*invite*
To any pastime?	15	
ROSENCRANTZ: Madam, it so fell out that certain players		
We overraught° on the way. Of these we told him,		*overtook*
And there did seem in him a kind of joy		

To hear of it. They are here about the court,
And, as I think, they have already order   20
This night to play before him.
POLONIUS: 'Tis most true;
And he beseeched me to entreat your Majesties
To hear and see the matter.
KING: With all my heart, and it doth much content me
To hear him so inclined.   25
Good gentlemen, give him a further edge
And drive his purpose on to these delights.
ROSENCRANTZ: We shall, my lord.

[ROSENCRANTZ *and* GUILDENSTERN *leave.*]

KING: Sweet Gertrude, leave us too;
For we have closely sent for Hamlet hither,
That he, as 'twere by accident, may here   30
Affront° Ophelia.   *encounter*
Her father and myself (lawful espials)°   *spies in a good cause*
Will so bestow ourselves that, seeing unseen,
We may of their encounter frankly judge
And gather° by him, as he is behaved,   *make up our minds*   35
If't be the affliction of his love, or no,
That thus he suffers for.
QUEEN: I shall obey you;
And for your part, Ophelia, I do wish
That your good beauties be the happy cause
Of Hamlet's wildness. So shall I hope your virtues   40
Will bring him to his wonted way° again,   *normal state*
To both your honors.
OPHELIA: Madam, I wish it may.

[QUEEN *leaves.*]

POLONIUS: Ophelia, walk you here.—Gracious, so please you,
We will bestow ourselves.°—[*To* OPHELIA.] Read on this   *take up our posts*
    book,
That show of such an exercise may color°   *may serve as an excuse for*   45
Your loneliness.—We are oft to blame in this,
'Tis too much proved, that with devotion's visage°   *with the façade of religion*
And pious action we do sugar over
The devil himself.
KING [*aside*]:   O, 'tis too true!
How smart a lash that speech doth give my conscience!   50
The harlot's cheek, beautied with plastering art,
Is not more ugly to the thing that helps it
Than is my deed to my most painted word.
O heavy burden!
POLONIUS: I hear him coming. Let's withdraw, my lord.   55

[KING *and* POLONIUS *leave.*]

[*Enter* HAMLET.]

HAMLET: To be, or not to be, that is the question:
Whether 'tis nobler in the mind to suffer
The slings and arrows of outrageous fortune
Or to take arms against a sea of troubles,
And by opposing end them.° To die—to sleep—   *end them by fighting them*   60
No more; and by a sleep to say we end
The heartache, and the thousand natural shocks
That flesh is heir to. 'Tis a consummation°   *crowning end result*
Devoutly to be wished. To die—to sleep.
To sleep—perchance to dream: ay, there's the rub!°   *that's what stops us*   65
For in that sleep of death what dreams may come
When we have shuffled off this mortal coil,°   *shell*
Must give us pause. There's the respect
That makes calamity of so long life.°   *makes misery so long-lived*
For who would bear the whips and scorns of time,   70
The oppressor's wrong, the proud man's contumely,°   *contempt*
The pangs of despised love, the law's delay,
The insolence of office, and the spurns°   *abuses*
That patient merit of the unworthy takes,
When he himself might his quietus° make   *ending for good*   75
With a bare bodkin?° Who would fardels° bear,   *dagger/burdens*
To grunt and sweat under a weary life,
But that the dread of something after death—
The undiscovered country, from whose bourn°   *border*
No traveler returns—puzzles the will,   80
And makes us rather bear those ills° we have   *evils*
Than fly to others that we know not of?
Thus conscience does make cowards of us all,
And thus the native hue of resolution
Is sicklied over° with the pale cast of thought,   *made to look sick*   85
And enterprises of great pitch and moment°   *great force and impact*
With this regard° their currents turn awry   *because of this*
And lose the name of action.—Soft you now!°   *now let me be quiet*
The fair Ophelia!—Nymph, in thy orisons°   *prayers*
Be all my sins remembered.
OPHELIA: Good my lord,   90
How does your honor for this many a day?
HAMLET: I humbly thank you; well, well, well.
OPHELIA: My lord, I have remembrances of yours°   *souvenirs from you*
That I have longed to redeliver.
I pray you, now receive them.
HAMLET: No, not I!   95
I never gave you aught.°   *anything*
OPHELIA: My honored lord, you know right well you did,
And with them words of so sweet breath composed
As made the things more rich. Their perfume lost,
Take these again; for to the noble mind   100

Rich gifts wax poor when givers prove unkind.°   *turn cheap*
There, my lord.

HAMLET: Ha, ha! Are you honest?°   *virtuous*

OPHELIA: My lord?

HAMLET: Are you fair?°   *beautiful* 105

OPHELIA: What means your lordship?

HAMLET: That if you be honest and fair, your honesty
should admit no discourse to° your beauty.   *should not talk to*

OPHELIA: Could beauty, my lord, have better commerce than with honesty?   110

HAMLET: Ay, truly; for the power of beauty will sooner
transform honesty from what it is to a bawd° than   *turn virtue into vice*
the force of honesty can translate beauty into his
likeness. This was sometime a paradox, but now
the time gives it proof. I did love you once.   115

OPHELIA: Indeed, my lord, you made me believe so.

HAMLET: You should not have believed me; for virtue
cannot so inoculate our old stock but we shall relish of it.° I loved you not.   *so change our sinful nature*

OPHELIA: I was the more deceived.   *that we no longer show it* 120

HAMLET: Get thee to a nunnery! Why wouldst thou be
a breeder of sinners? I am myself indifferent hon-
est,° but yet I could accuse me of such things that   *fairly virtuous*
it were better my mother had not borne me. I am
very proud, revengeful, ambitious; with more   125
offenses at my beck than I have thoughts to put
them in, imagination to give them shape, or time
to act them in. What should such fellows as I do,
crawling between earth and heaven? We are arrant
knaves° all; believe none of us. Go thy ways to a   *utter villains* 130
nunnery. Where's your father?

OPHELIA: At home, my lord.

HAMLET: Let the doors be shut upon him, that he may
play the fool nowhere but in's own house. Farewell.

OPHELIA: O, help him, you sweet heavens!   135

HAMLET: If thou dost marry, I'll give thee this plague°   *curse*
for thy dowry: be thou as chaste as ice, as pure as
snow, thou shalt not escape calumny. Get thee to
a nunnery. Go, farewell. Or if thou wilt needs°   *if you absolutely want to*
marry, marry a fool; for wise men know well   140
enough what monsters you make of them. To a
nunnery, go; and quickly too. Farewell.

OPHELIA: O heavenly powers, restore him!

HAMLET: I have heard of your paintings° too, well   *makeup*
enough. God hath given you one face, and you   145
make yourselves another. You jig, you amble, and
you lisp; you nickname° God's creatures and   *give fancy names to*
make your wantonness your ignorance.° Go to, I'll   *pretend you act wanton*
no more on't! it hath made me mad. I say, we will   *from ignorance*

have no more marriages. Those that are married   150
already—all but one—shall live; the rest shall
keep as they are. To a nunnery, go.

[*He leaves.*]

OPHELIA: O, what a noble mind is here o'erthrown!
The courtier's, soldier's, scholar's, eye, tongue, sword,
The expectancy° and rose of the fair state,   *hope* 155
The glass of fashion and the mould of form,
The observed of all observers—quite, quite down!
And I, of ladies most deject° and wretched,   *dejected*
That sucked the honey of his music vows,
Now see that noble and most sovereign reason,   160
Like sweet bells jangled, out of tune and harsh;
That unmatched form and feature of blown youth°   *youth in full bloom*
Blasted with ecstasy.° O, woe is me   *ruined by madness*
To have seen what I have seen, see what I see!

[*Enter* KING *and* POLONIUS.]

KING: Love? his affections do not that way tend;   165
Nor what he spoke, though it lacked form a little,
Was not like madness. There's something in his soul
Over which his melancholy sits on brood°   *brooding*
And I do doubt the hatch and the disclose°   *I fear the hatching and disclosure*
Will be some danger, which for to prevent,   *(of what was inside)* 170
I have in quick determination
Thus set it down: he shall with speed to England
For the demand of our neglected tribute.°   *tribute due but in arrears*
Haply° the seas, and countries different,   *perhaps*
With variable objects, shall expel   175
This something°-settled matter in his heart,   *somewhat*
Whereon his brains still beating puts him thus
From fashion of himself.° What think you on't?   *beside himself*
POLONIUS: It shall do well. But yet do I believe
The origin and commencement of his grief   180
Sprung from neglected love. How now, Ophelia?
You need not tell us what Lord Hamlet said,
We heard it all. My lord, do as you please;
But if you hold it fit, after the play
Let his queen mother all alone entreat him   185
To show his grief. Let her be round° with him;   *open*
And I'll be placed, so please you, in the ear°   *within earshot*
Of all their conference.° If she find him not,°   *talk/not find out about him*
To England send him; or confine him where
Your wisdom best shall think.
KING: It shall be so.   190
Madness in great ones must not unwatched go.

[*They leave.*]

SCENE 2. Elsinore. A hall in the Castle.

[*Enter* HAMLET *and three of the* PLAYERS.]

HAMLET: Speak the speech, I pray you, as I pronounced it to you, trippingly on the tongue. But if
you mouth it, as many of our players do, I had as
lief° the town crier spoke my lines. Nor do not saw   *as soon*
the air too much with your hand, thus, but use all   5
gently; for in the very torrent, tempest, and (as I
may say) whirlwind of your passion, you must
acquire and beget a temperance that may give it
smoothness. O, it offends me to the soul to hear a
robustious periwig-pated° fellow tear a passion to   *boisterous, bewigged*   10
tatters, to very rags, to split the ears of the ground-
lings, who (for the most part) are capable of° noth-   *who can take in*
ing but inexplicable dumb shows° and noise. I   *mimed action*
would have such a fellow whipped for overdoing
Termagant. It out-herods Herod.° Pray you avoid it.   *(bombastic stage characters)* 15
PLAYER: I warrant your honor.°   *I promise it*
HAMLET: Be not too tame neither; but let your own
discretion be your tutor. Suit the action to the
word, the word to the action; with this special
observance,° that you o'erstep not the modesty of   *rule*   20
nature: for anything so overdone is from the pur-
pose of playing, whose end, both at the first and
now, was and is, to hold, as 'twere, the mirror up
to nature; to show virtue her own feature, scorn
her own image, and the very age and body of the   25
time his form and pressure. Now this overdone, or
come tardy off,° though it make the unskilful°   *be badly done/uneducated*
laugh, cannot but make the judicious grieve; the
censure of the which one must in your allowance°   *judgment*
overweigh a whole theater of others. O, there be   30
players that I have seen play, and heard others
praise, and that highly (not to speak it profanely),° *speaking without offense*
that, neither having the accent of Christians, nor the
gait of Christian, pagan, nor man, have so strutted
and bellowed that I have thought some of Nature's   35
journeymen° had made men, and not made them   *day laborers*
well, they imitated humanity so abominably.
PLAYER: I hope we have reformed that indifferently°   *fairly well*
with us, sir.
HAMLET: Oh, reform it altogether! And let those that   40
play your clowns speak no more than is set down
for them. For there be of them that will themselves laugh, to set on some quantity of barren
spectators to laugh too, though in the mean time
some necessary question of the play be then to be   45
considered. That's villainous and shows a most

pitiful ambition in the fool that uses it. Go make
you ready.

[*The* PLAYERS *leave.*]

[*Enter* POLONIUS, ROSENCRANTZ, *and* GUILDENSTERN.]

How now, my lord? Will the King hear this piece
of work?   50
POLONIUS: And the Queen too, and that presently.
HAMLET: Bid the players make haste. [POLONIUS *leaves.*]
Will you two help to hasten them?
BOTH: We will, my lord.

[*Both leave.*]

HAMLET: What, ho, Horatio!   55

[*Enter* HORATIO.]

HORATIO: Here, sweet lord, at your service.
HAMLET: Horatio, thou art even° as just a man   *you are indeed*
As ever my conversation coped withal.°   *as I have ever met*
HORATIO: O, my dear lord!
HAMLET: Nay, do not think I flatter;
For what advancement may I hope from thee,   60
That no revenue° hast but thy good spirits   *income*
To feed and clothe thee? Why should the poor be flattered?
No, let the candied tongue lick absurd pomp,
And crook the pregnant° hinges of the knee   *bend the willing*
Where thrift may follow° fawning. Dost thou hear?   *profit may result from* 65
Since my dear soul was mistress of her choice
And could of men distinguish, her election°   *choice*
Hath sealed thee for herself.° For thou hast been   *has singled you out*
As one, in suffering all, that suffers nothing;
A man that Fortune's buffets° and rewards   *blows* 70
Hast taken with equal thanks; and blest are those
Whose blood and judgment° are so well commingled   *passion and reason*
That they are not a pipe for Fortune's finger
To sound what stop she please.° Give me that man   *(as on a flute)*
That is not passion's slave, and I will wear him   75
In my heart's core, ay, in my heart of heart,
As I do thee. Something too much of this.
There is a play tonight before the King.
One scene of it comes near the circumstance,°   *parallels the details*
Which I have told thee, of my father's death.   80
I prithee, when thou seest that act afoot,
Even with the very comment of thy soul
Observe my uncle. If his occulted° guilt   *hidden*
Do not itself unkennel in° one speech,   *reveal itself during*
It is a damnèd ghost that we have seen,   85
And my imaginations are as foul°   *dark and dirty*

As Vulcan's stithy.° Give him heedful note;   *the divine blacksmith's workshop*
For I mine eyes will rivet to his face,
And after we will both our judgments join
In censure of his seeming.°   *to judge his behavior*
HORATIO: Well, my lord.   90
If he steal aught the whilst this play is playing,
And scape detecting, I will pay the theft.°   *pay for the stolen item*

[*Flourish of trumpets. Trumpets and kettledrums play a Danish march. Enter* KING, QUEEN, POLONIUS, OPHELIA, ROSENCRANTZ, GUILDENSTERN, *and other lords, with the* KING's *guard carrying torches.*]

HAMLET: They are coming to the play: I must be idle.°   *play the fool*
Get you a place.
KING: How fares our cousin Hamlet?   95
HAMLET: Excellent, in faith, of the chameleon's dish:°   *food*
I eat the air, promise-crammed. You cannot feed
capons so.
KING: I have nothing with this answer, Hamlet. These
words are not mine.   100
HAMLET: No, nor mine now. [*to* POLONIUS] My lord, you
played once i' the university, you say?
POLONIUS: That did I, my lord, and was accounted a
good actor.
HAMLET: What did you enact?   105
POLONIUS: I did enact Julius Caesar; I was killed in the
Capitol; Brutus killed me.
HAMLET: It was a brute part of him to kill so capital° a   *outstanding*
calf there. Be the players ready?
ROSENCRANTZ: Ay, my lord. They stay upon your   110
patience.°   *await your permission*
QUEEN: Come hither, my dear Hamlet, sit by me.
HAMLET: No, good mother, here's metal more
attractive.°   *magnetic*
POLONIUS [*aside to the* KING]: O, ho! do you mark that?   115
HAMLET [*to* OPHELIA]: Lady, shall I lie in your lap?
OPHELIA: No, my lord.
HAMLET: I mean, my head upon your lap?
OPHELIA: Ay, my lord.
HAMLET: Do you think I meant country matters?°   *rustic horseplay* 120
OPHELIA: I think nothing, my lord.
HAMLET: That's a fair thought to lie between maids'
legs.
OPHELIA: What is, my lord?
HAMLET: Nothing.   125
OPHELIA: You are merry, my lord.
HAMLET: Who, I?
OPHELIA: Ay, my lord.

HAMLET: O God, your only jig-maker! What should a
man do but be merry? For look you how cheer-   130
fully my mother looks, and my father died within 's
two hours.°   *no more than two hours ago*

OPHELIA: Nay, 'tis twice two months, my lord.

HAMLET: So long? Nay then, let the devil wear black,
for I'll have a suit of sables.° O heavens! die two   *of rich dark cloth and fur* 135
months ago, and not forgotten yet? Then there's
hope a great man's memory may outlive his life
half a year. But, by'r Lady, he must build churches
then; or else shall he suffer not thinking on,° with   *not being remembered*
the hobby-horse, whose epitaph is "For O, for O,   140
the hobby-horse is forgot!"

[*Oboes play. The dumb show enters: Enter a King
and a Queen very lovingly; the Queen embracing
him. She kneels, and makes show of protestation
unto him. He takes her up, and declines his head
upon her neck. He lays him down upon a bank of
flowers. She, seeing him asleep, leaves him. Anon
comes in a fellow, takes off his crown, kisses it, pours
poison in the King's ears, and exits. The Queen
returns, finds the King dead, and makes passionate action. The Poisoner, with some two or three
Mutes, comes in again, seeming to lament with her.
The dead body is carried away. The Poisoner woos
the Queen with gifts; she seems loath and unwilling awhile, but in the end accepts his love.*]

[*They leave.*]

OPHELIA: What means this, my lord?

HAMLET: Marry, this is miching malicho;° it means   *bad trouble*
mischief.

OPHELIA: Belike° this show imports the argument° of   *probably/summarizes* 145
the play.   *the action*

[*Enter* PROLOGUE.]

HAMLET: We shall know by this fellow.° The players   *from what he says*
cannot keep counsel; they'll tell all.

OPHELIA: Will he tell us what this show meant?

HAMLET: Ay, or any show that you'll show him. Be not   150
you ashamed to show, he'll not shame to tell you
what it means.

OPHELIA: You are naught,° you are naught! I'll mark°   *wicked/pay attention to*
the play.

PROLOGUE: *For us, and for our tragedy,*   155
Here stooping to your clemency,
We beg your hearing patiently.

[*Leaves.*]

HAMLET: Is this a prologue, or the posy° of a ring?   *inscription*
OPHELIA: 'Tis brief, my lord.
HAMLET: As woman's love.   160

[*Enter two* PLAYERS *as King and Queen.*]

PLAYER KING: *Full thirty times hath Phoebus' cart gone round*
   Neptune's salt wash and Tellus' orbed ground,°   *the ocean and the*
   And thirty dozen moons with borrowed sheen   *round earth*
   About the world have times twelve thirties been,
   Since love our hearts, and Hymen° did our hands,   *(god of marriage)* 165
   Unite comutual° in most sacred bands.   *mutually*
PLAYER QUEEN: *So many journeys may the sun and moon*
   Make us again count over ere love be done!
   But woe is me! you are so sick of late,
   So far from cheer and from your former state,   170
   That I distrust you.° Yet, though I distrust,   *I fear for you*
   Discomfort you, my lord, it nothing must;
   For women's fear and love holds quantity,°   *go together*
   In neither aught, or in extremity.°   *either nonexistent or extreme*
   Now what my love is, proof hath made you know;   175
   And as my love is sized, my fear is so.
   Where love is great, the littlest doubts are fear;
   Where little fears grow great, great love grows there.
PLAYER KING: *Faith, I must leave thee, love, and shortly too;*
   My operant° powers their functions leave to do.° *vital/cease to do* 180
   And thou shalt live in this fair world behind,
   Honored, beloved, and haply one as kind
   For husband shalt thou—
PLAYER QUEEN: *O, confound the rest!*
   Such love must needs be treason in my breast.
   In second husband let me be accurst!   185
   None wed the second but who killed the first.
HAMLET [*aside*]: Wormwood, wormwood!°   *a bitter potion*
PLAYER QUEEN: *The instances that second marriage*
      move°   *the motives for marrying again*
   Are base respects of thrift,° but none of love.   *thoughts of property*
   A second time I kill my husband dead   190
   When second husband kisses me in bed.
PLAYER KING: *I do believe you think what now you speak;*
   But what we do determine oft we break.
   Purpose is but the slave to memory,
   Of violent birth, but poor validity;   195
   Which now, like fruit unripe, sticks on the tree,
   But fall unshaken when they mellow be.
   Most necessary 'tis that we forget
   To pay ourselves what to ourselves is debt.
   What to ourselves in passion we propose,   200
   The passion ending, doth the purpose lose.
   The violence of either grief or joy

Their own enactures° with themselves destroy.   acts
Where joy most revels, grief doth most lament;
Grief joys, joy grieves, on slender accident.   205
This world is not for aye,° nor 'tis not strange   forever
That even our loves should with our fortunes change;
For 'tis a question left us yet to prove,
Whether love lead fortune, or else fortune love.
The great man down, you mark his favorite flies,°   his protégé abandons him 210
The poor advanced makes° friends of enemies;   when the poor succeed, they make
And hitherto doth love on fortune tend,
For who not needs° shall never lack a friend,   who is not in need
And who in want a hollow friend doth try,
Directly seasons° him his enemy.   immediately makes 215
But, orderly to end where I begun,
Our wills and fates do so contrary run
That our devices° still are overthrown;   plans
Our thoughts are ours, their ends none of our own.
So think thou wilt no second husband wed;   220
But die thy thoughts° when thy first lord is dead.   your intentions will change
PLAYER QUEEN: *Nor earth° to me give food, nor heaven*   let the earth not . . .
  light,
Sport and repose lock from me day and night,
To desperation turn my trust and hope,
An anchor's cheer in prison be my scope,°   let a hermit's fare be my portion 225
Each opposite that blanks the face of joy
Meet what I would have well, and it destroy,
Both here and hence pursue me lasting strife,
If, once a widow, ever I be wife!
HAMLET: If she should break it now!   230
PLAYER KING: *'Tis deeply sworn. Sweet, leave me here awhile.*
  My spirits grow dull, and fain I would beguile
  The tedious day with sleep.
PLAYER QUEEN: *Sleep rock thy brain,*

[*He sleeps.*]

And never come mischance between us twain!

[*She leaves.*]

HAMLET: Madam, how like you this play?   235
QUEEN: The lady doth protest° too much, methinks.   advertise her feelings
HAMLET: O, but she'll keep her word.
KING: Have you heard the argument?° Is there no   plot
  offense in it?
HAMLET: No, no! They do but jest, poison in jest; no   240
  offense in the world.
KING: What do you call the play?
HAMLET: "The Mousetrap." Marry, how? Tropically.°   metaphorically
  This play is the image of a murder done in Vienna.
  Gonzago is the duke's name: his wife, Baptista.   245

You shall see anon. 'Tis a knavish° piece of work; but what of that? Your Majesty, and we that have free souls,° it touches us not. Let the galled jade° wince; our withers are unwrung.°

villainous

who are innocent/sore horse

our own necks are untouched

[*Enter* LUCIANUS.]

This is one Lucianus, nephew to the King.   250
OPHELIA: You are as good as a chorus, my lord.
HAMLET: I could interpret between° you and your love, if I could see the puppets dallying.°
OPHELIA: You are keen,° my lord, you are keen.
HAMLET: It would cost you a groaning to take off my   255
edge.
OPHELIA: Still better, and worse.
HAMLET: So you must take your husbands. Begin, murderer. Pox,° leave thy damnable faces, and begin! Come, the croaking raven doth bellow for   260
revenge.
LUCIANUS: *Thoughts black, hands apt, drugs fit, and*
    time agreeing;
Confederate season,° else no creature seeing;
Thou mixture rank, of midnight weeds collected,   265
With Hecate's ban thrice blasted, thrice infected,
Thy natural magic and dire property
On wholesome life usurp° immediately.

speak for

(as in a puppet show)

sharp

a plague on it

with the occasion conspiring

inflict

[*Pours the poison in his ears.*]

HAMLET: He poisons him in the garden for his estate; his name's Gonzago. The story is extant,° and writ° in choice Italian. You shall see anon how the murderer gets the love of Gonzago's wife.
OPHELIA: The King rises.
HAMLET: What, frighted with false fire?°
QUEEN: How fares my lord?
POLONIUS: Give over° the play.
KING: Give me some light! Away!
ALL: Lights, lights, lights!

exists 270

written

gunfire without bullets

275

stop

[*All leave but* HAMLET *and* HORATIO.]

HAMLET: Why, let the strucken deer go weep,
    The hart ungallèd° play;
For some must watch, while some must sleep:
    Thus runs the world away.
Would not this, sir, and a forest of feathers—if the rest of my fortunes turn Turk° with me—with two Provincial roses on my razed shoes, get me a fellowship in a cry of° players, sir?
HORATIO: Half a share.

uninjured deer 280

take a bad turn

285

a group of

HAMLET: A whole one I!
　　For thou dost know, O Damon dear,°   *(a faithful friend)*
　　　　This realm dismantled was   290
　　Of Jove himself; and now reigns here
　　　　A very, very—pajock.°   *(repulsive) peacock*
HORATIO: You might have rhymed.
HAMLET: O good Horatio, I'll take the ghost's word for
　　a thousand pound! Didst perceive?   295
HORATIO: Very well, my lord.
HAMLET: Upon the talk of the poisoning?
HORATIO: I did very well note him.
HAMLET: Aha! Come, some music! Come, the recorders!
　　For if the King like not the comedy,   300
　　Why then, belike he likes it not, perdy.
　　Come, some music!

[*Enter* ROSENCRANTZ *and* GUILDENSTERN.]

GUILDENSTERN: Good my lord, vouchsafe me a word
　　with you.
HAMLET: Sir, a whole history.   305
GUILDENSTERN: The King, sir—
HAMLET: Ay, sir, what of him?
GUILDENSTERN: Is in his retirement,° marvellous dis-   *private rooms*
　　tempered.°   *upset*
HAMLET: With drink, sir?   310
GUILDENSTERN: No, my lord; rather with choler.°   *anger*
HAMLET: Your wisdom should show itself more richer
　　to signify this to his doctor; for, for me to put him
　　to his purgation would perhaps plunge him into
　　far more choler.   315
GUILDENSTERN: Good my lord, put your discourse into
　　some frame, and start not so wildly from my affair.
HAMLET: I am tame, sir; pronounce.
GUILDENSTERN: The Queen, your mother, in most great
　　affliction of spirit hath sent me to you.   320
HAMLET: You are welcome.
GUILDENSTERN: Nay, good my lord, this courtesy is not
　　of the right breed. If it shall please you to make
　　me a wholesome° answer, I will do your mother's   *right kind of*
　　commandment; if not, your pardon and my return   325
　　shall be the end of my business.
HAMLET: Sir, I cannot.
GUILDENSTERN: What, my lord?
HAMLET: Make you a wholesome answer; my wit's
　　diseased. But, sir, such answer as I can make, you   330
　　shall command; or rather, as you say, my mother.
　　Therefore no more, but to the matter! My mother,
　　you say—

ROSENCRANTZ: Then thus she says: your behavior hath struck her into amazement and admiration.°   *wonder* 335

HAMLET: O wonderful son, that can so astonish a mother! But is there no sequel at the heels of this mother's admiration? Impart.°   *let me know*

ROSENCRANTZ: She desires to speak with you in her closet° ere you go to bed.   *private room* 340

HAMLET: We shall obey, were she° ten times our mother. Have you any further trade with us?   *even if she were*

ROSENCRANTZ: My lord, you once did love me.

HAMLET: And do still, by these pickers and stealers!°   *thieving hands*

ROSENCRANTZ: Good my lord, what is your cause of distemper? You do surely bar the door upon your own liberty,° if you deny your griefs to your friend.   *liberation from grief* 345

HAMLET: Sir, I lack advancement.

ROSENCRANTZ: How can that be, when you have the voice of the King himself for your succession in Denmark?   350

HAMLET: Ay, sir, but "while the grass grows"°—the proverb is something musty.   *("... the horse starves")*

[*Enter the* MUSICIANS *with recorders.*]

O, the recorders! Let me see one. To withdraw with you—why do you go about to recover the wind of° me, as if you would drive me into a toil?°   *to be downwind from* 355 / *trap*

GUILDENSTERN: O my lord, if my duty be too bold, my love is too unmannerly.°   *makes me forget good manners*

HAMLET: I do not well understand that. Will you play upon this pipe?°   *recorder* 360

GUILDENSTERN: My lord, I cannot.

HAMLET: I pray you.

GUILDENSTERN: Believe me, I cannot.

HAMLET: I do beseech you.

GUILDENSTERN: I know no touch of it, my lord.   365

HAMLET: It is as easy as lying. Govern these ventages° with your finger and thumb, give it breath with your mouth, and it will discourse° most eloquent music. Look you, these are the stops.   *control these openings* / *make*

GUILDENSTERN: But these cannot I command to any utterance of harmony. I have not the skill.   370

HAMLET: Why, look you now, how unworthy a thing you make of me! You would play upon me; you would seem to know my stops; you would pluck out the heart of my mystery; you would sound me from my lowest note to the top of my compass;° and there is much music, excellent voice, in this little organ,° yet cannot you make it speak. 'Sblood, do you think I am easier to be played on than a   375 / *range* / *instrument*

pipe? Call me what instrument you will, though   380
you can fret° me, you cannot play upon me.   *annoy (pun on preparing*
                                                                                                            an instrument)

[*Enter* POLONIUS.]

God bless you, sir!
POLONIUS: My lord, the Queen would° speak with   *wants to*
    you, and presently.
HAMLET: Do you see yonder cloud that's almost in   385
    shape of a camel?
POLONIUS: By the mass, and 'tis like a camel indeed.
HAMLET: Methinks° it is like a weasel.   *I think*
POLONIUS: It is backed like a weasel.
HAMLET: Or like a whale.   390
POLONIUS: Very like a whale.
HAMLET: Then will I come to my mother by-and-by.
    They fool me° to the top of my bent. I will come   *make me play the fool*
    by-and-by.
POLONIUS: I will say so.   395

[*He leaves.*]

HAMLET: "By-and-by" is easily said. Leave me, friends.

[*All but* HAMLET *leave.*]

'Tis now the very witching time of night,
When churchyards yawn, and hell itself breathes out
Contagion to this world. Now could I drink hot blood
And do such bitter business as the day   400
Would quake to look on. Soft! now to my mother!
O heart, lose not thy nature;° let not ever   *let me not be unnatural*
The soul of Nero° enter this firm bosom.   *(the bloody Roman emperor)*
Let me be cruel, not unnatural;
I will speak daggers to her, but use none.   405
My tongue and soul in this be hypocrites—
How in my words soever she be shent,°   *shamed*
To give them seals° never, my soul, consent!   *seal them with actions*

[*He leaves.*]

SCENE 3. A room in the Castle.

[*Enter* KING, ROSENCRANTZ, *and* GUILDENSTERN.]

KING: I like him not, nor stands it safe with us
    To let his madness range. Therefore prepare you;
    I your commission will forthwith dispatch,°   *right away draw up your orders*
    And he to England shall along° with you.   *shall travel*
    The terms of our estate° may not endure   *my position*   5
    Hazard° so near us as doth hourly grow   *extreme danger*
    Out of his lunacies.
GUILDENSTERN: We will ourselves provide.°   *will get ready*
    Most holy and religious fear it is

To keep those many many bodies safe
That live and feed upon your Majesty.   10
ROSENCRANTZ: The single and peculiar° life is bound   *private*
With all the strength and armor of the mind
To keep itself from noyance;° but much more   *harm*
That spirit upon whose weal° depends and rests   *welfare*
The lives of many. The cease of majesty°   *death of a king*   15
Dies not alone, but like a gulf° doth draw   *whirlpool*
What's near it with it. It is a massy wheel,
Fixed on the summit of the highest mount,
To whose huge spokes ten thousand lesser things
Are mortised° and adjoined; which when it falls,   *attached*   20
Each small annexment,° petty consequence,   *minor attachment*
Attends° the boisterous ruin. Never alone   *shares in*
Did the king sigh, but with a general groan.°   *sorrow for all the people*
KING: Arm you,° I pray you, to this speedy voyage;   *prepare yourselves*
For we will fetters put upon° this fear,   *will chain up*   25
Which now goes too free-footed.
BOTH: We will haste us.

                               [*They leave.*]

[*Enter* POLONIUS.]

POLONIUS: My lord, he's going to his mother's closet.
Behind the arras° I'll convey myself   *wall hanging*
To hear the process. I'll warrant she'll tax him home;°   *rebuke him sharply*
And, as you said, and wisely was it said,   30
'Tis meet° that some more audience than a mother,   *it's right*
Since nature makes them partial, should overhear
The speech, of vantage.° Fare you well, my liege.   *from a vantage point*
I'll call upon you ere you go to bed
And tell you what I know.
KING: Thanks, dear my lord.   35

                           [POLONIUS *leaves.*]

O, my offense is rank, it smells to heaven;
It hath the primal eldest° curse upon't,   *first and oldest*
A brother's murder! Pray can I not,
Though inclination be as sharp as will.
My stronger guilt defeats my strong intent,   40
And, like a man to double business bound,°   *who has to do two things*
I stand in pause° where I shall first begin,   *hesitate*
And both neglect. What if this cursèd hand
Were thicker than itself with brother's blood,
Is there not rain enough in the sweet heavens   45
To wash it white as snow? Whereto serves mercy
But to confront the visage of offense?°   *to battle with the face of guilt*
And what's in prayer but this twofold force,
To be forestalled ere we° come to fall,   *before we*

Or pardoned being down?° Then I'll look up; *when we have fallen* 50
My fault is past. But, O, what form of prayer
Can serve my turn? "Forgive me my foul murder"?
That cannot be; since I am still possessed
Of those effects for which I did the murder—
My crown, mine own ambition, and my queen. 55
May one be pardoned and retain the offense?° *the fruits of the crime*
In the corrupted currents of this world
Offense's gilded hand may shove by° justice, *push aside*
And oft 'tis seen the wicked prize itself
Buys out the law; but 'tis not so above. 60
There is no shuffling;° there the action lies° *no cheating/appears*
In his° true nature, and we ourselves compelled, *its*
Even to the teeth and forehead of our faults,
To give in evidence. What then? What rests?
Try what repentance can. What can it not? 65
Yet what can it when one cannot repent?
O wretched state! O bosom black as death!
O limèd° soul, that, struggling to be free, *trapped*
Art more engaged!° Help, angels! Make assay. *becomes more entangled*
Bow, stubborn knees; and heart with strings of steel, 70
Be soft as sinews of the new-born babe!
All may be well.

[*He kneels.*]

[*Enter* HAMLET.]

HAMLET: Now might I do it pat, now he is praying;
And now I'll do't. And so he goes to heaven,
And so am I revenged. That would be scanned.° *should be examined* 75
A villain kills my father; and for that,
I, his sole son, do this same villain send
To heaven.
Why, this is hire° and salary, not revenge! *reward*
He took my father grossly, full of bread,° *after a heavy meal* 80
With all his crimes broad blown,° as flush as May; *in full bloom*
And how his audit stands, who knows save heaven?
But in our circumstance and course of thought,° *according to common opinion*
'Tis heavy with him;° and am I then revenged, *he is in deep trouble*
To take him in the purging° of his soul, *cleansing* 85
When he is fit and seasoned for his passage?
No.
Up, sword, and know thou a more horrid hent.° *be ready for more horrible use*
When he is drunk asleep; or in his rage;
Or in the incestuous pleasure of his bed; 90
At gaming, swearing, or about some act
That has no relish of salvation in't—
Then trip him, that his heels may kick at heaven,
And that his soul may be as damned and black

As hell, whereto it goes. My mother stays.°   *waits*   95
This physic° but prolongs thy sickly days.   *medicine*

                                                                                                                   [*He leaves.*]

KING [*rises*]: My words fly up, my thoughts remain below;
    Words without thoughts never to heaven go.

                                                                                                                   [*He leaves.*]

SCENE 4. The QUEEN'S private chamber.

[*Enter* QUEEN *and* POLONIUS.]

POLONIUS: He will come straight. Look you lay home to him.°   *see that you*
    Tell him his pranks have been too broad to bear with,   *speak frankly*
    And that your Grace hath screened and stood between
    Much heat and him. I'll silence me even here.°   *I'll say no more*
    Pray you be round° with him.   *outspoken*   5
HAMLET [*within*]: Mother, mother, mother!
QUEEN: I'll warrant° you; fear me not. Withdraw;   *I promise*
    I hear him coming.

[POLONIUS *hides behind the arras.*]

[*Enter* HAMLET.]

HAMLET: Now, mother, what's the matter?
QUEEN: Hamlet, thou hast thy father much offended.   10
HAMLET: Mother, you have my father much offended.
QUEEN: Come, come, you answer with an idle tongue.
HAMLET: Go, go, you question with a wicked tongue.
QUEEN: Why, how now, Hamlet?
HAMLET: What's the matter now?
QUEEN: Have you forgot me?
HAMLET: No, by the rood,° not so!   *by the Cross*   15
    You are the Queen, your husband's brother's wife,
    And—would it were° not so—you are my mother.   *I wish it were*
QUEEN: Nay, then I'll set those to you° that can speak.   *I'll make you talk to those*
HAMLET: Come, come, and sit you down, you shall
    not budge!
    You go not till I set you up a glass°   *mirror*   20
    Where you may see the inmost part of you.
QUEEN: What wilt thou do? Thou wilt not murder me?
    Help, help, ho!
POLONIUS [*behind the arras*]: What, ho! help, help, help!
HAMLET [*draws his sword*]: How now? a rat? Dead for
    a ducat,° dead!   *(a gold coin)*   25

[*Stabs through the arras and kills* POLONIUS.]

POLONIUS: O, I am slain!
QUEEN: O me, what hast thou done?

HAMLET: Nay, I know not. Is it the King?
QUEEN: O, what a rash and bloody deed is this!
HAMLET: A bloody deed—almost as bad, good mother,
   As kill a king, and marry with his brother.   30
QUEEN: As kill a king?
HAMLET: Ay, lady, 'twas my word.

[*Pulls aside arras and sees* POLONIUS.]

Thou wretched, rash, intruding fool, farewell!
I took thee for thy better.° Take thy fortune.   *mistook you for your king*
Thou find'st to be too busy is some danger.
[*to his mother*] Leave° wringing of your hands.   *stop* 35
   Peace! sit you down
And let me wring your heart; for so I shall
If it be made of penetrable° stuff;   *that can be penetrated*
If damnèd custom have not brazed it so°   *force of habit has not made it so brazen*
That it is proof and bulwark against sense.°   *feeling* 40
QUEEN: What have I done that thou dar'st wag
   thy tongue
In noise so rude against me?
HAMLET: Such an act
   That blurs the grace and blush of modesty;
   Calls virtue hypocrite; takes off the rose
   From the fair forehead of an innocent love,   45
   And sets a blister° there; makes marriage vows   *brand of shame*
   As false as dicers'° oaths. O, such a deed   *gamblers'*
   As from the body of contraction° plucks   *marriage contract*
   The very soul, and sweet religion makes
   A rhapsody° of words! Heaven's face doth glow;°   *garbled string/blush* 50
   Yea, this solidity and compound mass,°   *this solid earth*
   With tristful visage,° as against the doom,°   *mournful face/on the eve of doom*
   Is thought-sick at the act.
QUEEN: Ay me, what act,
   That roars so loud and thunders in the index?°   *in your listing*
HAMLET: Look here upon this picture, and on this,   55
   The counterfeit presentment° of two brothers.   *painted likeness*
   See what a grace was seated on this brow;
   Hyperion's° curls; the front of Jove himself;   *(beautiful divine being)*
   An eye like Mars,° to threaten and command;   *(god of war)*
   A station° like the herald Mercury°   *bearing/(messenger of the gods)* 60
   New lighted° on a heaven-kissing hill: *having just landed*
   A combination and a form indeed
   Where every god did seem to set his seal
   To give the world assurance of a man.
   This was your husband. Look you now what follows.   65
   Here is your husband, like a mildewed ear°   *an infected ear of corn*
   Blasting° his wholesome brother. Have you eyes?   *spreading infection to*
   Could you on this fair mountain leave to feed,
   And batten on this moor?° Ha! have you eyes?   *feed greedily on a swamp*

You cannot call it love; for at your age   70
The heyday in the blood° is tame, it's humble,   *of physical passion*
And waits upon the judgment;° and what judgment   *is guided by reason*
Would step from this to this? Sense° sure you have,   *sensations*
Else could you not have motion; but sure that sense
Is apoplexed;° for madness would not err,   *paralyzed*   75
Nor sense to ecstasy was never so thralled°   *was never such a slave*
But it reserved some quantity of choice   *to madness*
To serve in such a difference. What devil was't
That thus hath cozened you at hoodman-blind?°   *cheated you at blindman's bluff*
Eyes without feeling, feeling without sight,   *(game with blindfolded player)*
Ears without hands or eyes, smelling sans° all,   80
Or but a sickly part of one true sense   *without*
Could not so mope.°   *blunder*
O shame! where is thy blush? Rebellious hell,
If thou canst mutiny in a matron's bones,   85
To flaming youth let virtue be as wax
And melt in her own fire. Proclaim no shame
When the compulsive ardor gives the charge,°   *passion leads the attack*
Since frost itself as actively doth burn,
And reason panders will.°   *panders to desire*
QUEEN: O Hamlet, speak no more!   90
Thou turn'st mine eyes into my very soul,
And there I see such black and grainèd° spots   *ingrained*
As will not leave their tint.°   *lose their color*
HAMLET: Nay, but to live
In the rank sweat of an enseamed° bed,   *greasy*
Stewed in corruption, honeying and making love   95
Over the nasty sty!
QUEEN: O, speak to me no more!
These words like daggers enter in mine ears.
No more, sweet Hamlet!
HAMLET: A murderer and a villain!
A slave that is not twentieth part the tithe°   *tenth share*
Of your precedent° lord; a vice° of kings;   *former/parody*   100
A cutpurse° of the empire and the rule,   *purse snatcher*
That from a shelf the precious diadem stole
And put it in his pocket!
QUEEN: No more!

[*Enter* GHOST.]

HAMLET: A king of shreds and patches—
Save me and hover over me with your wings,   105
You heavenly guards! What would your gracious figure?
QUEEN: Alas, he's mad!
HAMLET: Do you not come your tardy son to chide,
That, lapsed° in time and passion, lets go by   *negligent*
The important acting of your dread command?   110
O, say!

Mel Gibson and Glenn Close in the 1990 film version of *Hamlet.*
Courtesy of Photofest.

GHOST: Do not forget. This visitation
　Is but to whet thy almost blunted purpose.
　But look, amazement on thy mother sits.
　O, step between her and her fighting soul!　　　　　　　　　115
　Conceit° in weakest bodies strongest works.　　　　　　*imagination*
　Speak to her, Hamlet.
HAMLET:　　　　　　　　How is it with you, lady?
QUEEN: Alas, how is't with you,
　That you do bend your eye on vacancy,°　　　　　　　*vacant space*
　And with the incorporal° air do hold discourse?　　　　*bodiless* 120
　Forth at your eyes your spirits wildly peep;
　And, as the sleeping soldiers in the alarm,
　Your bedded hairs, like life in excrements,°　　　　*inert outgrowths*
　Start up and stand on end. O gentle son,
　Upon the heat and flame of thy distemper°　　　*your disturbed mind* 125
　Sprinkle cool patience! Whereon do you look?

HAMLET: On him, on him! Look you how pale he glares!
　His form and cause conjoined, preaching to stones,
　Would make them capable°—Do not look upon me,　*enable them to feel*
　Lest with this piteous action you convert　　　　　　　　　130
　My stern effects.° Then what I have to do　*my stern deeds*
　Will want° true color—tears perchance for blood.　*lack*
QUEEN: To whom do you speak this?
HAMLET:　　　　　　　　　Do you see nothing there?
QUEEN: Nothing at all; yet all that is I see.
HAMLET: Nor did you nothing hear?
QUEEN:　　　　　　　　No, nothing but ourselves.　　135
HAMLET: Why, look you there! Look how it steals away!
　My father, in his habit° as he lived!　*garment*
　Look where he goes even now out at the portal!

[GHOST *leaves.*]

QUEEN: This is the very coinage of your brain.
　This bodiless creation ecstasy°　*madness* 140
　Is very cunning in.°　*is very good at*
HAMLET:　　　　Ecstasy?
　My pulse as yours doth temperately keep time
　And makes as healthful music. It is not madness
　That I have uttered. Bring me to the test,
　And I the matter will reword, which madness　　　　145
　Would gambol from.° Mother, for love of grace,　*shy away from*
　Lay not that flattering unction° to your soul,　*soothing ointment*
　That not your trespass but my madness speaks.
　It will but skin and film° the ulcerous place,　*cover up*
　Whilst rank corruption, mining° all within,　*undermining* 150
　Infects unseen. Confess yourself to heaven;
　Repent what's past; avoid what is to come;
　And do not spread the compost on the weeds
　To make them ranker.° Forgive me this my virtue;　*grow wilder*
　For in the fatness of these pursy° times　*bloated* 155
　Virtue itself of vice must pardon beg—
　Yea, curb and woo for leave° to do him good.　*bow for permission*
QUEEN: O Hamlet, thou has cleft° my heart in twain.　*you have split*
HAMLET: O, throw away the worser part of it,
　And live the purer with the other half.　　　　　　　160
　Good night—but go not to my uncle's bed.
　Assume a virtue,° if you have it not.　*pretend to be virtuous*
　That monster, custom,° who all sense doth eat　*habit*
　Of habits evil, is angel yet in this,
　That to the use of actions fair and good　　　　　　　165
　He likewise gives a frock or livery,°　*an outward appearance*
　That aptly is put on. Refrain tonight,
　And that shall lend a kind of easiness
　To the next abstinence; the next more easy;

For use° almost can change the stamp of nature,   *force of habit* 170
And either master the devil, or throw him out
With wondrous potency. Once more, good night;
And when you are desirous to be blest,
I'll blessing beg of you.—For this same lord,
I do repent; but heaven hath pleased it so,   175
To punish me with this, and this with me,
That I must be their scourge and minister.
I will bestow him,° and will answer well   *dispose of him*
The death° I gave him. So again, good night.   *for the death*
I must be cruel, only to be kind;   180
Thus bad begins, and worse remains behind.°   *is yet to come*
One word more, good lady.
QUEEN: What shall I do?
HAMLET: Not this, by no means, that I bid you do:
Let the bloat King tempt you again to bed;
Pinch wanton on your cheek; call you his mouse;   185
And let him, for a pair of reechy° kisses,   *reeking*
Or paddling in your neck with his damned fingers,
Make you to ravel all this matter out,
That I essentially am not in madness,
But mad in craft.° 'Twere good you let him know;   *on purpose* 190
For who that's but a queen, fair, sober, wise,
Would from a paddock,° from a bat, a gib,°   *toad/tomcat*
Such dear concernings hide? Who would do so?
No, in despite of sense and secrecy,
Unpeg° the basket on the house's top,   *unfasten* 195
Let the birds fly, and like the famous ape,
To try conclusions,° in the basket creep   *make an experiment*
And break your own neck down.°   *fall down (while trying to fly)*
QUEEN: Be thou assured, if words be made of
          breath,
And breath of life, I have no life to breathe°   *reveal* 200
What thou hast said to me.
HAMLET: I must to England; you know that?
QUEEN: Alack,°   *alas*
I had forgot! 'Tis so concluded on.°   *so decided*
HAMLET: There's letters sealed; and my two
          schoolfellows,
Whom I will trust as I will adders fanged,   205
They bear the mandate;° they must sweep my way   *carry the instructions*
And marshal me to knavery. Let it work;
For 'tis the sport to have the enginer°   *engineer*
Hoist with his own petar;° and 't shall go hard   *blown up by his own bomb*
But I will delve° one yard below their mines   *dig* 210
And blow them at the moon. O 'tis most sweet
When in one line two crafts directly meet.°   *two plots converge*
This man shall set me packing:

I'll lug the guts into the neighbor room.
Mother, good night. Indeed, this counsellor   215
Is now most still, most secret, and most grave,
Who was in life a foolish prating knave.
Come, sir, to draw toward an end with you.
Good night, mother.

[*Both leave, with* HAMLET *dragging* POLONIUS.]

The Receptive Reader

1. (Act Three, Scene 1) By the end of this scene, how aware is the audience
of a plot of *intrigue?* How much has it seen of plotting and counterplotting on
the part of two major opposed parties?

2. The "To be or not to be" soliloquy is usually seen as Hamlet's debating the
pros and cons of suicide. (Some critics read the speech as a debate on "To act
or not to act"—whether to take decisive action against Claudius.) What are the
pros and cons? Does he seem to you to be in a highly disturbed or suicidal
frame of mind? How does this speech round out your understanding of Hamlet's character?

3. In his encounter with Ophelia, why does Hamlet deny having loved her
or having given her tokens of affection? What is the point of Hamlet's *satirical*
commentary on beauty, marriage, and offspring? Why does he direct it at Ophelia? Does Ophelia hold her own or is she the passive victim?

4. (Act Three, Scene 2) What does Hamlet's relationship with Horatio show
about his character? When Hamlet praises his friend, what are to him the ideal
qualities of an admirable person?

5. What is the tone or direction of Hamlet's running commentary during the
play-within-the-play? What is the upshot of Hamlet's "mousetrap" scheme? What
is Hamlet's frame of mind by the end of this scene?

6. What is sarcastic about remarks like "We will obey, were she ten times our
mother"? What other examples of Hamlet's *sarcastic tone* can you cite?

7. (Act Three, Scene 3) How does the prayer scene change your view of
Claudius as the villain of the play?

8. (Act Three, Scene 4) The killing of Polonius can be seen as a major turning point in the **plot** of the play. How and why? How does Hamlet explain his
killing of Polonius? What is his reaction; how does treat the dead body?

9. What are the major themes in his Hamlet's denunciation of his mother?
What picture does he paint of his dead father? of Claudius (his "father-uncle")?
of his mother? Is he in full control of his senses, as he claims, or profoundly disturbed? How does Queen Gertrude act in this *climactic* scene? What do you
conclude about her guilt—her implication in the murder? (What does the reappearance of the ghost add to this climactic scene?)

The Range of Interpretation

Hamlet's role in the prayer scene has been much debated. He refuses to kill
the king at prayer because in the state of repentance Claudius might be forgiven
his sin, with his soul going to heaven. To make the revenge complete, Claudius

should be sent to hell—killed when caught in some sinful act without a chance of repentance. Some critics have found this attitude too brutal and un-Christian to fit with their understanding of Hamlet's character. Is he more harsh and brutal in this thirst for revenge than you would expect? Or is his attitude here in keeping with his character as you understand it? Or is Hamlet perhaps using the king's praying as a pretext, as an excuse for further delaying his task? Or is the playwright perhaps signaling to the audience that Hamlet is not as admirable and virtuous as we might think—he himself is also infected by the moral corruption of his time?

Act Four

SCENE 1. Elsinore. A room in the Castle.

[*Enter* KING *and* QUEEN, *with* ROSENCRANTZ *and* GUILDENSTERN.]

KING: There's matter in these sighs. These profound heaves
    You must translate; 'tis fit we understand them.
    Where is your son?
QUEEN: Bestow this place on us° a little while.   *leave us alone*

[ROSENCRANTZ *and* GUILDENSTERN *leave.*]

    Ah, mine own lord, what have I seen tonight!   5
KING: What, Gertrude? How does Hamlet?
QUEEN: Mad as the sea and wind when both contend
    Which is the mightier. In his lawless fit,
    Behind the arras hearing something stir,
    Whips out his rapier, cries "A rat, a rat!"   10
    And in this brainish apprehension° kills   *brainsick fit*
    The unseen good old man.
KING: O heavy deed!
    It had been so with us,° had we been there.   *this would have happened to me*
    His liberty is full of threats to all—
    To you yourself, to us, to every one.   15
    Alas, how shall this bloody deed be answered?
    It will be laid to us,° whose providence   *we will be blamed*
    Should have kept short, restrained, and out of haunt°   *away from people*
    This mad young man. But so much was our love
    We would not understand what was most fit,   20
    But, like the owner of a foul disease,
    To keep it from divulging,° let it feed   *from being known*
    Even on the pith° of life. Where is he gone?   *essence*
QUEEN: To draw apart the body he hath killed,
    Over whom his very madness, like some ore°   *a more valuable vein* 25
    Among a mineral of metals base,
    Shows itself pure. He weeps for what is done.
KING: O Gertrude, come away!
    The sun no sooner shall the mountains touch
    But we will ship him hence; and this vile deed   30

We must with all our majesty and skill
Both countenance° and excuse. Ho, Guildenstern!   *sanction*

[*Enter* ROSENCRANTZ *and* GUILDENSTERN.]

Friends both, go join you with some further aid.
Hamlet in madness hath Polonius slain,
And from his mother's closet hath he dragged him.   35
Go seek him out; speak fair,° and bring the body   *talk to him politely*
Into the chapel. I pray you haste in this.

            [ROSENCRANTZ *and* GUILDENSTERN *leave*.]

Come, Gertrude, we'll call up our wisest friends
And let them know both what we mean to do
And what's untimely done. So haply° slander   *perhaps*   40
Whose whisper over the world's diameter,
As level as the cannon to his blank,°   *straight . . . to its target*
Transports his poisoned shot—may miss our name
And hit the woundless° air.—O, come away!   *which cannot be wounded*
My soul is full of discord and dismay.   45

                                    [*They leave*.]

SCENE 2. The same. A passage in the Castle.

[*Enter* HAMLET.]

HAMLET: Safely stowed.°   *hidden*
GENTLEMEN (*within*): Hamlet! Lord Hamlet!
HAMLET: But soft! What noise? Who calls on Hamlet?
O, here they come.

[*Enter* ROSENCRANTZ *and* GUILDENSTERN.]

ROSENCRANTZ: What have you done, my lord, with the   5
dead body?
HAMLET: Compounded° it with dust, whereto 'tis kin.   *mingled*
ROSENCRANTZ: Tell us where 'tis, that we may take it
thence. And bear it to the chapel.
HAMLET: Do not believe it.   10
ROSENCRANTZ: Believe what?
HAMLET: That I can keep your counsel,° and not mine   *secret*
own. Besides, to be demanded of° a sponge, what   *when questioned by*
replication° should be made by the son of a king?   *answer*
ROSENCRANTZ: Take you me for a sponge, my lord?   15
HAMLET: Ay, sir, that soaks up the King's counte-
nance,° his rewards, his authorities.° But such offi-   *looks/appointments*
cers do the King best service in the end. He keeps
them, like an ape, in the corner of his jaw; first
mouthed, to be last swallowed.° When he needs   *(like saving unswallowed*   20
what you have gleaned, it is but squeezing you   *food in one's cheeks)*
and, sponge, you shall be dry again.
ROSENCRANTZ: I understand you not, my lord.

HAMLET: I am glad of it: a knavish° speech sleeps in a   *wicked*
    foolish ear.   25
ROSENCRANTZ: My lord, you must tell us where the
    body is and go with us to the King.
HAMLET: The body is with the King, but the King is
    not with the body. The King is a thing—
GUILDENSTERN: A thing, my lord?   30
HAMLET: Of nothing. Bring me to him. Hide fox, and
    all after.

[They leave.]

SCENE 3. The same. A room as before.

[*Enter* KING.]

KING: I have sent to seek him and to find the body.
    How dangerous is it that this man goes loose!
    Yet must not we put the strong law on him.
    He's loved of the distracted multitude,°   *by the fickle crowds*
    Who like not in their judgment,° but their eyes;   *not by good judgment*   5
    And where 'tis so, the offender's scourge is
        weighed,°   *the penalty is questioned*
    But never the offense. To bear all° smooth and   *to make all seem*
        even,
    This sudden sending him away must seem
    Deliberate pause.° Diseases desperate grown   *like a well-weighed plan*
    By desperate appliance° are relieved,   *remedies*   10
    Or not at all.

[*Enter* ROSENCRANTZ.]

                How now? What hath befallen?
ROSENCRANTZ: Where the dead body is bestowed, my
        lord,
    We cannot get from him.
KING: But where is he?
ROSENCRANTZ: Without,° my lord; guarded, to know   *outside*
        your pleasure.
KING: Bring him before us.   15
ROSENCRANTZ: Ho, Guildenstern! Bring in my lord.

[*Enter* HAMLET *and* GUILDENSTERN *with attendants.*]

KING: Now, Hamlet, where's Polonius?
HAMLET: At supper.
KING: At supper? Where?
HAMLET: Not where he eats, but where he is eaten. A   20
    certain convocation of politic° worms are even at   *assembly of politically minded*
    him. Your worm is your only emperor for diet. We
    fat° all creatures else to fat us, and we fat ourselves   *fatten*
    for maggots. Your fat king and your lean beggar is

but variable service—two dishes, but to one table.   25
That's the end.
KING: Alas, alas!
HAMLET: A man may fish with the worm that hath eat of
a king, and eat of the fish that hath fed of that worm.
KING: What dost thou mean by this?   30
HAMLET: Nothing but to show you how a king may go
a progress° through the guts of a beggar.   *make his way*
KING: Where is Polonius?
HAMLET: In heaven. Send thither to see. If your mes-
senger find him not there, seek him in the other   35
place yourself. But indeed, if you find him not
within this month, you shall nose° him as you go   *smell*
up the stairs into the lobby.
KING [*to attendants*]: Go seek him there.
HAMLET: He will stay till you come.   40

                         [*Attendants leave.*]

KING: Hamlet, this deed, for thine especial safety—
Which we do tender° as we dearly grieve   *cherish*
For that which thou hast done—must send thee
    hence
With fiery quickness. Therefore prepare thyself.
The bark is ready and the wind at help,   45
The associates tend,° and everything is bent   *your companions are waiting*
For England.
HAMLET: For England?
KING: Ay, Hamlet.
HAMLET: Good.
KING: So is it, if thou knew'st our purposes.
HAMLET: I see a cherub° that sees them. But come, for   *an all-knowing angel*
England! Farewell, dear mother.   50
KING: Thy° loving father, Hamlet.   *I am your*
HAMLET: My mother! Father and mother is man and
wife; man and wife is one flesh; and so, my mother.
Come, for England!

                         [*He leaves.*]

KING: Follow him at foot; tempt° him with speed   *urge*   55
    aboard;
Delay it not, I'll have him hence° tonight.   *away from here*
Away! for everything is sealed and done
That else leans on° the affair. Pray you make haste.   *relates to*

              [ROSENCRANTZ *and* GUILDENSTERN *leave.*]

And, England, if my love thou hold'st at aught°—   *value my love at all*
As my great power thereof may give thee sense,°   *may impress it on you*   60
Since yet thy cicatrice° looks raw and red   *scar*
After the Danish sword, and thy free awe°   *you willingly out of fear*

Pays homage to us—thou mayst not coldly set°   *set aside*
Our sovereign process,° which imports at full,   *royal command*
By letters congruing to° that effect,   *pointing to*   65
They present° death of Hamlet. Do it, England;   *immediate*
For like the hectic° in my blood he rages,   *severe fever*
And thou must cure me. Till I know 'tis done,
However my haps,° my joys were never begun.   *whatever my fortunes*

[*Leaves.*]

SCENE 4. Near Elsinore Castle.

[*Enter* FORTINBRAS *with his army, marching across the stage.*]

FORTINBRAS: Go, Captain, from me greet the Danish king.
Tell him that by his license° Fortinbras   *permission*
Craves the conveyance° of a promised march   *requests safe conduct*
Over° his kingdom. You know the rendezvous.   *through*
If that his Majesty would aught with us,°   *wants to see us*   5
We shall express our duty in his eye;
And let him know so.
CAPTAIN: I will do't, my lord.
FORTINBRAS: Go softly on.

[*All but the* CAPTAIN *leave.*]

[*Enter* HAMLET, ROSENCRANTZ, GUILDENSTERN, *and others.*]

HAMLET: Good sir, whose powers° are these?   *forces*
CAPTAIN: They are of Norway, sir.   10
HAMLET: How purposed,° sir, I pray you?   *with what destination*
CAPTAIN: Against some part of Poland.
HAMLET: Who commands them, sir?
CAPTAIN: The nephew to old Norway, Fortinbras.
HAMLET: Goes it against the main° of Poland, sir,   *the central part*   15
Or for some frontier?
CAPTAIN: Truly to speak, and with no addition,
We go to gain a little patch of ground
That hath in it no profit° but the name.   *value*
To pay five ducats, five, I would not farm it;   20
Nor will it yield to Norway or the Pole
A ranker rate, should it be sold in fee.°   *a higher rate if sold outright*
HAMLET: Why, then the Polack never will defend it.
CAPTAIN: Yes, it is already garrisoned.
HAMLET: Two thousand soul and twenty thousand ducats   25
Will not debate the question of° this straw.   *settle the argument over*
This is the imposthume° of much wealth and peace,   *malignant growth*
That inward breaks, and shows no cause without°   *external cause*
Why the man dies—I humbly thank you, sir.
CAPTAIN: God be wi' you, sir.

[*He leaves.*]

ROSENCRANTZ: Will't please you go, my lord?   30
HAMLET: I'll be with you straight. Go a little before.

[*All but* HAMLET *leave.*]

How all occasions do inform against me°   *accuse me*
And spur my dull revenge! What is a man,
If his chief good and market of his time
Be but to sleep and feed? A beast, no more.   35
Sure he that made us with such large discourse,°   *far-ranging reasoning*
Looking before and after, gave us not
That capability and godlike reason
To fust° in us unused. Now, whether it be   *spoil*
Bestial oblivion, or some craven scruple°   *beastlike apathy or*   40
Of thinking too precisely on the event,—   *cowardly hesitation*
A thought which, quartered,° hath but one part wisdom   *when divided in four*
And ever three parts coward—I do not know
Why yet I live to say "This thing's to do,"
Sith° I have cause, and will, and strength, and means   *since*   45
To do't. Examples gross as° earth exhort me.   *as plain as*
Witness this army of such mass and charge,°   *and cost*
Led by a delicate and tender prince,
Whose spirit, with divine ambition puffed,
Makes mouths at the invisible event,°   *makes light of the outcome*   50
Exposing what is mortal and unsure
To all that fortune, death, and danger dare,
Even for an eggshell. Rightly to be great
Is not to stir without great argument,°   *take action without a great cause*
But greatly to find quarrel in a straw   55
When honor's at the stake. How stand I then,
That have a father killed, a mother stained,
Excitements° of my reason and my blood,   *incentives*
And let all sleep, while to my shame I see
The imminent death of twenty thousand men   60
That for a fantasy and trick of fame
Go to their graves like beds, fight for a plot
Whereon the numbers cannot try the cause,°   *decide the conflict*
Which is not tomb enough and continent°   *container*
To hide the slain? O, from this time forth,   65
My thoughts be bloody, or be nothing worth!

[*He leaves.*]

SCENE 5. Elsinore. A room in the Castle.

[*Enter* QUEEN, HORATIO, *and a* GENTLEMAN.]

QUEEN: I will not speak with her.
GENTLEMAN: She is importunate,° indeed distract;°   *insistent/distracted*
    Her mood will needs be° pitied.   *must be*

QUEEN: What would she have?°   *what is her wish*
GENTLEMAN: She speaks much of her father; says she hears
    There's tricks in the world, and hems, and beats her
       heart;   5
    Spurns enviously° at straws; speaks things in doubt,   *strikes out angrily*
    That carry but half sense. Her speech is nothing,
    Yet the unshaped use of it doth move
    The hearers to collection;° they aim at it,   *attention*
    And botch the words up fit to their own thoughts;   10
    Which, as her winks and nods and gestures yield them,
    Indeed would make one think there might be thought,
    Though nothing sure, yet much unhappily.°   *much that is sad*
HORATIO: 'Twere good she were spoken with; for she
    may strew
    Dangerous conjectures in ill-breeding° minds.   *thriving on bad news*   15
QUEEN: Let her come in.

                        [GENTLEMAN *leaves*.]

    [*aside*] To my sick soul (as sin's true nature is)
    Each toy° seems prologue to some great amiss.   *trifle*
    So full of artless jealousy° is guilt   *clumsy suspicion*
    It spills° itself in fearing to be spilt.   *reveals*   20

    [*Enter* OPHELIA *distracted*.]

OPHELIA: Where is the beauteous Majesty of Denmark?
QUEEN: How now, Ophelia?
OPHELIA [*sings*]:

    How should I your true-love know
        From another one?
    By his cockle hat° and staff   *pilgrim's hat (with a cockle shell)*   25
        And his sandal shoon.°   *shoes*

QUEEN: Alas, sweet lady, what imports° this song?   *what is the meaning of*
OPHELIA: Say you? Nay, pray you mark.°   *please listen*

    [*sings*] *He is dead and gone, lady,*
        He is dead and gone;   30
    At his head a grass-green turf,
        At his heels a stone.

    O, ho!
QUEEN: Nay, but Ophelia—
OPHELIA: Pray you mark.   35

    [*sings*] *White his shroud as the mountain snow*—

    [*Enter* KING.]

QUEEN: Alas, look here, my lord!

OPHELIA [*sings*]:

> Larded all with° sweet flowers;   *garnished with*
> Which bewept to the grave did not go
> With true-love showers.°   *showers of tears*   40

KING: How do you, pretty lady?

OPHELIA: Well, God 'ild you!° They say the owl was a   *God shield you*
baker's daughter. Lord, we know what we are, but
know not what we may be. God be at your table!

KING: Conceit upon° her father.   *she is thinking about*   45

OPHELIA: Pray let's have no words of this; but when
they ask you what it means, say you this:

> [*sings*] Tomorrow is Saint Valentine's day,
> All in the morning betime,°   *early*
> And I a maid at your window,   50
> To be your Valentine.

> Then up he rose and donned his clothes
> And dupped° the chamber door,   *opened*
> Let in the maid, that out a maid°   *as a virgin*
> Never departed more.   55

KING: Pretty Ophelia!

OPHELIA: Indeed, la, without an oath, I'll make an end on't!

> [*sings*] By Gis° and by Saint Charity,   *(by Jesus)*
> Alack, and fie for shame!
> Young men will do't if they come to't.   60
> By Cock,° they are to blame.   *weaker swearword for "by God"*

> Quoth she, "Before you tumbled me,
> You promised me to wed."

He answers:

> "So would I have done, by yonder sun,   65
> And thou hadst not° come to my bed."   *if you had not*

KING: How long hath she been thus?

OPHELIA: I hope all will be well. We must be patient;
but I cannot choose but weep to think they would
lay him in the cold ground. My brother shall know   70
of it; and so I thank you for your good counsel.
Come, my coach! Good night, ladies. Good night,
sweet ladies. Good night, good night.

[*She leaves.*]

KING: Follow her close; give her good watch, I pray you.

[HORATIO *leaves.*]

O, this is the poison of deep grief; it springs   75
All from her father's death. O Gertrude, Gertrude,

When sorrows come, they come not single spies,°   *not as single advance scouts*
But in battalions! First, her father slain;
Next, your son gone, and he most violent author
Of his own just remove;° the people muddied,   *deserved exile*   80
Thick and unwholesome in their thoughts and whispers
For good Polonius' death, and we have done but
    greenly°   *acted unthinkingly*
In hugger-mugger to inter° him; poor Ophelia   *in secrecy and disorder to bury*
Divided from herself and her fair judgment,
Without the which we are pictures or mere beasts;   85
Last, and as much containing as all these,
Her brother is in secret come from France;
Feeds on his wonder, keeps himself in clouds,
And wants not buzzers to infect his ear°   *does not lack talebearers*
With pestilent speeches of his father's death,   90
Wherein necessity, of matter beggared,°   *void of true substance*
Will nothing stick° our person to arraign   *will not hesitate*
In ear and ear.° O my dear Gertrude, this,   *in people's ears*
Like to a murdering piece,° in many places   *a cannon with scattered shot*
Gives me superfluous death.

[*A noise outside.*]

QUEEN: Alack, what noise is this?   95
KING: Where are my Switzers?° Let them guard the door.   *Swiss bodyguards*

[*Enter a* MESSENGER.]

What is the matter?
MESSENGER: Save yourself, my lord:
The ocean, overpeering of his list,°   *rising over its borders*
Eats not the flats° with more impetuous haste   *coastal flatlands*
Than young Laertes, in a riotous head,°   *heading a mob*   100
Overbears your officers. The rabble call him lord;
And, as the world were now but to begin,
Antiquity forgot,° custom not known,   *as if tradition were forgotten*
The ratifiers and props of every word,°   *pledge*
They cry "Choose we, Laertes shall be king!"   105
Caps, hands, and tongues applaud it to the clouds,
"Laertes shall be king! Laertes king!"

[*A noise outside.*]

QUEEN: How cheerfully on the false trail they cry!
    O, this is counter,° you false Danish dogs!   *on the wrong trail*
KING: The doors are broke.°   *forced open*   110

[*Enter* LAERTES *with others.*]

LAERTES: Where is this king?—Sirs, stand you all without.
ALL: No, let's come in!
LAERTES: I pray you give me leave.
ALL: We will, we will!

LAERTES: I thank you. Keep the door.

[His followers leave.]

O thou vile king,   115
Give me my father!

QUEEN: Calmly, good Laertes.

LAERTES: That drop of blood that's calm proclaims
    me bastard;°   *shows I am not my father's true son*
Cries cuckold to my father; brands the harlot   *(making the mother a whore)*
Even here between the chaste unsmirched brows
Of my true mother.

KING: What is the cause, Laertes,   120
That thy rebellion looks so giantlike?
Let him go, Gertrude. Do not fear our person.°   *don't be afraid on my behalf*
There's such divinity doth hedge° a king   *such divine sanction that protects*
That treason can but peep to what it would,°   *at its goal*
Acts little of his will.° Tell me, Laertes,   *acts out little of what it intends* 125
Why thou art thus incensed. Let him go, Gertrude.
Speak, man.

LAERTES: Where is my father?

KING: Dead.

QUEEN: But not by him!

KING: Let him demand his fill.°   *question freely*

LAERTES: How came he dead?° I'll not be juggled with: *how did he die* 130
To hell, allegiance! vows, to the blackest devil!
Conscience and grace, to the profoundest pit!
I dare damnation. To this point I stand,
That both the worlds I give to negligence,°   *write off both earth and heaven*
Let come what comes; only I'll be revenged   135
Most thoroughly for my father.

KING: Who shall stay° you?   *hinder*

LAERTES: My will,° not all the world.   *if I have my will*
And for my means, I'll husband° them so well   *use*
They shall go far with little.

KING: Good Laertes,
If you desire to know the certainty°   *actual facts* 140
Of your dear father's death, is't writ in your revenge
That swoopstake° you will draw both friend and foe,   *like a reckless gambler*
Winner and loser?

LAERTES: None but his enemies.

KING: Will you know them then?

LAERTES: To his good friends thus wide I'll open my arms   145
And, like the kind life-rendering pelican,
Repast them with my blood.°   *feed them with my own blood*

KING: Why, now you speak   *(as the pelican was thought*
Like a good child and a true gentleman.   *to feed its young)*
That I am guiltless of your father's death,
And am most sensibly° in grief for it,   *feelingly* 150

It shall as level to your judgment appear°   *strike your reason as directly*
As day does to your eye.

[*A noise outside: "Let her come in."*]

LAERTES: How now? What noise is that?

[*Enter* OPHELIA.]

O heat, dry up my brains! Tears seven times salt
Burn out the sense and virtue° of mine eye!   *faculty* 155
By heaven, thy madness shall be paid by weight
Till our scale turn the beam.° O rose of May!   *till the retribution outweighs the offense on the scale*
Dear maid, kind sister, sweet Ophelia!
O heavens! is't possible a young maid's wits
Should be as mortal as an old man's life?   160
Nature is fine in love, and where 'tis fine,
It sends some precious instance of itself
After the thing it loves.
OPHELIA [*sings*]:

They bore him barefaced on the bier
(Hey non nony, nony, hey nony)   165
And in his grave rained many a tear.

Fare you well, my dove!
LAERTES: Hadst thou thy wits, and didst persuade
revenge, it could not move thus.°   *not incite me the same way*
OPHELIA: You must sing "A-down, a-down," and you,   170
"Call him a-down-a." O, how the wheel becomes
it! It is the false steward, that stole his master's
daughter.
LAERTES: This nothing's more than matter.°   *these ramblings have more meaning than sane talk* 175
OPHELIA: There's rosemary, that's for remembrance.
Pray you, love, remember. And there is pansies,
that's for thoughts.
LAERTES: A document° in madness! Thoughts and   *lesson*
remembrance fitted.
OPHELIA: There's fennel for you, and columbines.   180
There's rue for you, and here's some for me. We
may call it herb of grace o' Sundays. O, you must
wear your rue with a difference! There's a daisy. I
would give you some violets, but they withered all
when my father died. They say he made a   185
good end.

[*sings*] *For bonny sweet Robin is all my joy.*

LAERTES: Thought and affliction, passion, hell itself,
She turns to favor° and to prettiness.   *charm*

OPHELIA [*sings*]:

And will he not come again?   190
And will he not come again?
  No, no, he is dead;
  Go to thy deathbed;
He never will come again.

His beard was as white as snow,   195
All flaxen was his poll.°   *head*
  He is gone, he is gone,
  And we cast away moan.
God have mercy on his soul!

And of all Christian souls, I pray God. God be wi' you.   200

                              [*Leaves.*]

LAERTES: Do you see this, O God?
KING: Laertes, I must commune with your grief,°   *talk to you in your grief*
  Or you deny me right.° Go but apart,   *what is my right*
  Make choice of whom your wisest friends you will,
  And they shall hear and judge 'twixt you and me.   205
  If by direct or by collateral° hand   *indirect*
  They find us touched,° we will our kingdom give,   *implicated*
  Our crown, our life, and all that we call ours,
  To you in satisfaction; but if not,
  Be you content to lend your patience to us,   210
  And we shall jointly labor with your soul
  To give it due content.
LAERTES: Let this be so.
  His means of death,° his obscure funeral—   *the way he died*
  No trophy, sword, nor hatchment° o'er his bones,   *coat of arms*
  No noble rite nor formal ostentation°—   *display* 215
  Cry to be heard, as 'twere from heaven to earth,
  That I must call't in question.°   *must raise questions*
KING: So you shall;
  And where the offense is let the great axe fall.
  I pray you go with me.

                              [*They leave.*]

SCENE 6. The same. Another room in the Castle.

  [*Enter* HORATIO *with an* ATTENDANT.]

HORATIO: What are they that would speak° with me?   *want to speak*
SERVANT: Sailors, sir. They say they have letters for you.
HORATIO: Let them come in.

                        [ATTENDANT *leaves.*]

  I do not know from what part of the world
  I should be greeted, if not from Lord Hamlet.   5

[*Enter* SAILORS.]

SAILOR: God bless you, sir.

HORATIO: Let him bless thee too.

SAILOR: He shall, sir, an't please him.° There's a letter   *if it pleases him*
for you, sir—it comes from the ambassador that
was bound for° England—if your name be Hora-   *headed for*   10
tio, as I am let to know it is.

HORATIO [*reads the letter*]: *Horatio, when thou shalt*
have overlooked this,° give these fellows some   *looked this over*
means° to the King. They have letters for him. Ere   *means of access*
we were two days old at sea, a pirate of very war-   15
like appointment° gave us chase. Finding ourselves   *equipment*
too slow of sail, we put on a compelled valor, and
in the grapple I boarded them. On the instant they
got clear of our ship; so I alone became their pris-
oner. They have dealt with me like thieves of mercy;   20
but they knew what they did: I am to do a good
turn for them. Let the King have the letters I have
sent, and repair thou to me° with as much speed as   *join me*
thou wouldst fly° death. I have words to speak in   *flee from*
thine ear will make thee dumb; yet are they much   25
too light for the bore° of the matter. These good fel-   *caliber*
lows will bring thee where I am. Rosencrantz and
Guildenstern hold their course for England. Of
them I have much to tell thee. Farewell.

He that thou knowest thine,° HAMLET.   *he who you know is yours*   30

Come, I will give you way° for these your letters,   *provide a channel*
And do it the speedier that you may direct me
To him from whom you brought them.

[*They leave.*]

SCENE 7. Another room in the Castle.

[*Enter* KING *and* LAERTES.]

KING: Now must your conscience my acquittance seal,°   *confirm my acquittal*
And you must put me in your heart for friend,
Sith° you have heard, and with a knowing ear,   *since*
That he which hath your noble father slain
Pursued my life.

LAERTES: It well appears. But tell me   5
Why you proceeded not against these feats°   *deeds*
So crimeful and so capital in nature,°   *so criminal and deserving death*
As by your safety, wisdom, all things else,
You mainly were stirred up.°   *were mightily impelled*

KING: O, for two special reasons,
Which may to you, perhaps, seem much unsinewed,°   *very weak*   10
But yet to me they are strong. The Queen his mother
Lives almost by his looks; and for myself—

My virtue or my plague, be it either which—
She's so conjunctive° to my life and soul   *so closely joined*
That, as the star moves not but in his sphere,   15
I could not but by her. The other motive
Why to a public count° I might not go   *accounting*
Is the great love the general gender° bear him,   *common people*
Who, dipping all his faults in their affection,
Would, like the spring that turneth wood to stone,   20
Convert his gyves° to graces; so that my arrows,   *prison chains*
Too slightly timbered° for so loud a wind,   *made of too flimsy wood*
Would have reverted to my bow again,
And not where I had aimed them.

LAERTES: And so have I a noble father lost;   25
A sister driven into desperate terms,°   *conditions*
Whose worth, if praises may go back again,°   *may go back to the past*
Stood challenger on mount of all the age°   *could challenge all rivals*
For her perfections. But my revenge will come.

KING: Break not your sleeps° for that. You must not think   *do not lose sleep*   30
That we are made of stuff so flat and dull
That we can let our beard be shook with danger,
And think it pastime. You shortly shall hear more.
I loved your father, and we love ourself,
And that, I hope, will teach you to imagine—   35

[*Enter a* MESSENGER *with letters.*]

How now? What news?

MESSENGER: Letters, my lord, from Hamlet:
This to your Majesty; this to the Queen.

KING: From Hamlet? Who brought them?

MESSENGER: Sailors, my lord, they say; I saw them not.
They were given me by Claudio; he received them   40
Of him that brought them.

KING: Laertes, you shall hear them.
Leave us.

                                          [MESSENGER *leaves.*]

[*reads*] *High and Mighty—You shall know I am set*
naked° on your kingdom. Tomorrow shall I beg leave to   *stripped of everything*
see your kingly eyes; when I shall (first asking your par-   45
don thereunto) recount the occasion of my sudden and
more strange return.

                                          HAMLET.

What should this mean? Are all the rest come back?
Or is it some abuse,° and no such thing?   *deception*   50

LAERTES: Know you the hand?°   *handwriting*

KING: 'Tis Hamlet's character.
"Naked!"

And in a postscript here, he says "alone."
Can you advise me?

LAERTES: I am lost in it, my lord. But let him come!   55
It warms the very sickness in my heart
That I shall live and tell him to his teeth,
"Thus did'st thou."

KING: If it be so, Laertes
(As how should it be so? how otherwise?),
Will you be ruled by me?

LAERTES: Ay, my lord,   60
So you will not overrule me to a peace.

KING: To thine own peace. If he be now returned,
As checking at° his voyage, and that he means   abandoning
No more to undertake it, I will work him
To an exploit now ripe in my device,°   now fully plotted by me   65
Under the which he shall not choose but fall;
And for his death no wind of blame shall breathe,
But even his mother shall uncharge the practice°   not allege wrongdoing
And call it accident.

LAERTES: My lord, I will be ruled;
The rather, if you could devise it so   70
That I might be the organ.°   instrument

KING: It falls right.
You have been talked of since your travel much,
And that in Hamlet's hearing, for a quality
Wherein they say you shine. Your sum of parts°   good qualities
Did not together pluck such envy from him   75
As did that one; and that, in my regard,
Of the unworthiest siege.°   of least importance

LAERTES: What part is that, my lord?

KING: A very riband° in the cap of youth—   a mere adornment
Yet needful too; for youth no less becomes°   no less fits
The light and careless livery° that it wears   clothing   80
Than settled age his sables and his weeds,°   its rich formal garments
Importing° health and graveness.° Two months since   showing/seriousness
Here was a gentleman of Normandy.
I have seen myself, and serve against, the French,
And they can well° on horseback; but this gallant   do well   85
Had witchcraft in it. He grew unto his seat,
And to such wondrous doing brought his horse
As had he been incorpsed and demi-natured°   made one body and
With the brave beast. So far he topped my thought   half of its nature
That I, in forgery of° shapes and tricks,   even in inventing   90
Come short of what he did.

LAERTES: A Norman was't?

KING: A Norman.

LAERTES: Upon my life, Lamound.

KING: The very same.

LAERTES: I know him well. He is the brooch° indeed   *chief ornament*
    And gem of all the nation.   95
KING: He made confession of you;°   *conceded your superior talent*
    And gave you such a masterly report
    For art and exercise in your defense,
    And for your rapier most especially,
    That he cried out 'twould be a sight indeed   100
    If one could match you. The scrimers° of their nation   *fencers*
    He swore had neither motion, guard, nor eye,
    If you opposed them. Sir, this report of his
    Did Hamlet so envenom with his envy
    That he could nothing do but wish and beg   105
    Your sudden coming over to play° with him.   *fence*
    Now, out of this—
LAERTES: What out of this, my lord?
KING: Laertes, was your father dear to you?
    Or are you like the painting of a sorrow,
    A face without a heart?
LAERTES: Why ask you this?   110
KING: Not that I think you did not love your father,
    But that I know love is begun by time,
    And that I see, in passages of proof,°   *by relevant examples*
    Time qualifies the spark and fire of it.
    There lives within the very flame of love   115
    A kind of wick or snuff that will abate it,°   *will put it out*
    And nothing is at a like goodness still;
    For goodness, growing to a plurisy,°   *malignant swelling*
    Dies in his own too-much. That we would do,
    We should do when we would;° for this "would"   *when we want to*
        changes,   120
    And hath abatements° and delays as many   *has obstacles*
    As there are tongues, are hands, are accidents;
    And then this "should" is like a spendthrift sigh,
    That hurts by easing. But to the quick of the ulcer!
    Hamlet comes back. What would you undertake   125
    To show yourself your father's son in deed
    More than in words?
LAERTES: To cut his throat in the church!
KING: No place indeed should murder sanctuarize;°   *give sanctuary to murder*
    Revenge should have no bounds.° But, good Laertes,   *know no boundaries*
    Will you do this? Keep close° within your chamber.   *stay inside* 130
    Hamlet, returned, shall know you are come home.
    We'll put on those shall praise° your excellence   *instigate people to praise*
    And set a double varnish on the fame
    The Frenchman gave you; bring you in fine° together   *at last*
    And wager on your heads. He, being remiss,°   *unsuspecting* 135
    Most generous, and free from all contriving,
    Will not peruse the foils;° so that with ease,   *check the weapons*
    Or with a little shuffling, you may choose

A sword unbated,° and, in a pass of practice,° *not blunted/treachery*
Requite him° for your father. *pay him back*
LAERTES: I will do't! 140
   And for that purpose I'll anoint my sword.
   I bought an unction of a mountebank,° *lotion from a quack*
   So mortal° that, but dip a knife in it, *lethal*
   Where it draws blood no cataplasm° so rare, *antidote*
   Collected from all simples° that have virtue *medicinal herbs* 145
   Under the moon, can save the thing from death
   That is but scratched withal.° I'll touch my point *with it*
   With this contagion,° that, if I gall° him slightly, *poison/scratch*
   It may be death.
KING: Let's further think of this,
   Weigh what convenience both of time and means 150
   May fit us to our shape. If this should fail,
   And that our drift look° through our bad *that our plan should show*
     performance,
   'Twere better not assayed.° Therefore this project *tried*
   Should have a back° for second, that might hold *backup*
   If this did blast in proof.° Soft! let me see. *fail when put to the test* 155
   We'll make a solemn wager on your cunnings°— *skills*
   I have it!
   When in your motion you are hot and dry—
   As made your bouts more violent to that end—
   And that he calls for drink, I'll have prepared him 160
   A chalice for the nonce;° whereon but sipping, *cup for that occasion*
   If he by chance escape your venomed stuck,° *thrust*
   Our purpose may hold° there.—But stay, what noise? *may still prevail*

[*Enter* QUEEN.]

   How now, sweet queen?
QUEEN: One woe doth tread upon another's heel, 165
   So fast they follow. Your sister's drowned, Laertes.
LAERTES: Drowned! O, where?
QUEEN: There is a willow grows aslant a brook,
   That shows his hoar° leaves in the glassy stream. *silvery-grey*
   There with fantastic garlands did she come 170
   Of crowflowers, nettles, daisies, and long purples,
   That liberal° shepherds give a grosser° name, *outspoken/coarser*
   But our cold maids° do dead men's fingers call them. *chaste maidens*
   There on the pendent boughs° her coronet weeds *hanging branches*
   Clambering to hang, an envious sliver° broke, *spiteful small branch* 175
   When down her weedy trophies and herself
   Fell in the weeping brook. Her clothes spread wide
   And, mermaid-like, awhile they bore her up;
   Which time she chanted snatches of old tunes,
   As one incapable of° her own distress, *unaware of* 180
   Or like a creature native and indued° *born there and used*
   Unto that element; but long it could not be

Till that her garments, heavy with their drink,
Pulled the poor wretch from her melodious lay°   *song*
To muddy death.
LAERTES: Alas, then she is drowned?   185
QUEEN: Drowned, drowned.
LAERTES: Too much of water hast thou, poor Ophelia,
And therefore I forbid my tears; but yet
It is our trick;° nature her custom holds,   *natural trait*
Let shame say what it will. When these are gone,   190
The woman will be out.° Adieu, my lord.   *the woman in me will disappear*
I have a speech of fire, that fain° would blaze   *gladly*
But that this folly douts it.°   *puts it out*

[*He leaves.*]

KING: Let's follow, Gertrude.
How much I had to do to calm his rage!
Now fear I this will give it start again;   195
Therefore let's follow.

[*They leave.*]

The Receptive Reader

1. (Act Four, Scenes 1–3) In these scenes, the plot thickens. What are the key developments here?

2. (Act Four, Scene 4) How does Fortinbras's expedition against Poland become for Hamlet an occasion "to spur my dull revenge"? Hamlet's *soliloquy* here is key evidence for critics debating Hamlet's delay in executing the ghost's command. What does Hamlet say about the delay? What is the tone of the soliloquy? What is Hamlet's train of thought? What is his definition of "greatness"? What is the conclusion or upshot of the soliloquy?

3. (Act Four, Scene 5) How does Ophelia's madness change the course of the play? Is it dramatically a digression or detour? Is Hamlet implicated in Ophelia's madness? How does it help make Laertes a major player in the final acts? Critics have listened to Ophelia's disjointed talk and songs for clues to a repressed or hidden personality. What kinds of clues do you think they might have found?

4. (Act Four, Scenes 6 and 7) What role does *chance* or sheer accident begin to play in the plot here? What impression do you get of Laertes as the king enlists his help in the king's plot? How does the king sway him?

The Creative Dimension

By the end of Act Four, some of the supporting characters—Polonius, Ophelia—have made their exit. Rosencrantz and Guildenstern will not return from their voyage to England; we will not see them again. Assume the role of one of the supporting characters in the play. Tell the story of your involvement in the events, looking at people and events from your own limited point of view. (You might want to start your story "I, Polonius, . . ." or "I, Ophelia, . . .")

Act Five

SCENE 1. Elsinore. A churchyard.

[*Enter two* CLOWNS, *with spades and pickaxes.*]

CLOWN: Is she to be buried in Christian burial that wilfully seeks her own salvation?

OTHER: I tell thee she is; therefore make her grave straight. The crowner hath sat on her,° and finds it Christian burial.   *coroner has examined her case*   5

CLOWN: How can that be, unless she drowned herself in her own defense?

OTHER: Why, 'tis found so.

CLOWN: It must be *se offendendo;*° it cannot be else. For here lies the point: if I drown myself wittingly, it argues an act; and an act hath three branches— it is to act, to do, and to perform; argal,° she drowned herself wittingly.   *"doing violence to herself"*   10   *(garbled for* ergo, *"therefore")*

OTHER: Nay, but hear you, Goodman Delver!

CLOWN: Give me leave. Here lies the water; good. Here stands the man; good. If the man go to this water and drown himself, it is, will he, nill he, he goes—mark you that. But if the water come to him and drown him, he drowns not himself. Argal, he that is not guilty of his own death shortens not his own life.   15   20

OTHER: But is this law?

CLOWN: Ay, marry,° is't—crowner's quest° law.   *yes indeed/inquest*

OTHER: Will you have the truth on't? If this had not been a gentlewoman, she should have been buried out o' Christian burial.°   *without religious rites*   25

CLOWN: Why, there thou say'st! And the more pity that great folk should have countenance° in this world to drown or hang themselves more than their even-Christian.° Come, my spade! There is no ancient gentlemen but gardeners, ditches, and grave-makers. They hold up° Adam's profession.   *more right*   *ordinary Christians*   30   *uphold*

OTHER: Was he a gentleman?

CLOWN: He was the first that ever bore arms.°   *(pun on arms and weapons)*

OTHER: Why, he had none.   35

CLOWN: What, art a heathen? How dost thou understand the Scripture? The Scripture says Adam digged. Could he dig without arms? I'll put another question to thee. If thou answerest me not to the purpose,° confess thyself—   *not to the point*   40

OTHER: Go to!

CLOWN: What is he that builds stronger than either the mason, the shipwright, or the carpenter?

OTHER: The gallows-maker; for that frame outlives a
thousand tenants.   45
CLOWN: I like thy wit well, in good faith. The gallows
does well. But how does it well? It does well to
those that do ill. Now, thou dost ill to say the gallows is built stronger than the church. Argal, the
gallows may do well to thee. To't again, come!   50
OTHER: Who builds stronger than a mason, a ship-
wright, or a carpenter?
CLOWN: Ay, tell me that, and unyoke.°   *quit for the day*
OTHER: Marry, now I can tell.
CLOWN: To't.   55
OTHER: Mass,° I cannot tell.   *by the Holy Mass*

[*Enter* HAMLET *and* HORATIO *afar off.*]

CLOWN: Cudgel thy brains no more about it, for your
dull ass° will not mend his pace with beating; and   *dim-witted donkey*
when you are asked this question next, say "a
grave-maker." The houses he makes lasts till   60
doomsday. Go, get thee to Yaughan; fetch me a
stoup° of liquor.   *cup*

                              [SECOND CLOWN *leaves.*]

[CLOWN *digs and sings.*]

In youth when I did love, did love,
*   Methought it was very sweet;*
To contract°—O—the time for—a—my behove,°   *to shorten/my benefit*   65
*   O, methought there—a—was nothing—a—*
meet.

HAMLET: Has this fellow no feeling of his business,
that he sings at grave-making?
HORATIO: Custom hath made it in him a property of
easiness.°   *habit has made it natural*   70
HAMLET: 'Tis e'en so. The hand of little employment
hath the daintier sense.°   *the little-used hand has*
CLOWN [*sings*]:   *the more sensitive touch*

But age with his stealing steps
*   Hath clawed me in his clutch,*
And hath shipped me intil the land,°   *put me in the ground*   75
*   As if I had never been such.*

[*Digs up a skull.*]

HAMLET: That skull had a tongue in it, and could sing
once. How the knave jowls° it to the ground, as if   *hurls*
'twere Cain's jawbone, that did the first murder!
This might be the pate of a politician, which this   80

ass now overreaches;° one that would circumvent°   *gets the better of/outwit*
God, might it not?

HORATIO: It might, my lord.

HAMLET: Or of a courtier, which could say "Good 85
morrow, sweet lord! How dost thou, good lord?"
This might be my Lord Such-a-one, that praised
my Lord Such-a-one's horse when he meant to
beg it°—might it not?   *beg for it*

HORATIO: Ay, my lord.

HAMLET: Why, even so! and now my Lady Worm's, 90
chapless,° and knocked about the mazzard° with a   *jawless/head*
sexton's spade. Here's fine revolution, if we had
the trick to see't. Did these bones cost no more the
breeding but to play at loggets with them?° Mine   *to throw them around like sticks*
ache to think on't. 95

CLOWN [*sings*]:

     A pickaxe and a spade, a spade,
       For and a shrouding sheet;
     O, a pit of clay for to be made
       For such a guest is meet.

[*Digs up another skull.*]

HAMLET: There's another. Why may not that be the 100
skull of a lawyer? Where be his quiddities now, his
quillets,° his cases, his tenures, and his tricks? Why   *quibbles and hair-splittings*
does he suffer this rude knave now to knock him
about the sconce° with a dirty shovel, and will not   *head*
tell him of his action of battery? Hum! This fellow 105
might be in's time a great buyer of land, with his
statutes, his recognizances, his fines, his double
vouchers, his recoveries. Is this the fine of his fines,°   *the final end of his fines*
and the recovery of his recoveries, to have his fine
pate full of fine dirt? Will his vouchers vouch him 110
no more of his purchases, and double ones too,
than the length and breadth of a pair of inden-
tures?° The very conveyances of his lands will   *contracts*
scarcely lie in this box; and must the inheritor himself have no more, ha? 115

HORATIO: Not a jot more, my lord.

HAMLET: Is not parchment made of sheepskins?

HORATIO: Ay, my lord, and of calveskins too.

HAMLET: They are sheep and calves which seek out
assurance in that. I will speak to this fellow. Whose 120
grave's this, sirrah?

CLOWN: Mine, sir.

[*sings*] *O, a pit of clay for to be made*
     For such a guest is meet.°   *just right*

HAMLET: I think it be thine indeed, for thou liest in't.   125
CLOWN: You lie out on't, sir, and therefore 'tis not
    yours. For my part, I do not lie in't, yet it is mine.
HAMLET: Thou dost lie in't, to be in't and say it is
    thine. 'Tis for the dead, not for the quick;° there-   *the living*
    fore thou liest.   130
CLOWN: 'Tis a quick lie, sir; 'twill away again from me
    to you.
HAMLET: What man dost thou dig it for?
CLOWN: For no man, sir.
HAMLET: What woman then?   135
CLOWN: For none neither.
HAMLET: Who is to be buried in't?
CLOWN: One that was a woman, sir; but, rest her soul,
    she's dead.
HAMLET: How absolute° the knave is! We must speak   *what a stickler*   140
    by the card,° or equivocation° will undo us. By the   *exactly/double meanings*
    Lord, Horatio, this three years I have taken note of
    it, the age is grown so picked° that the toe of the   *has become so sophisticated*
    peasant comes so near the heel of the courtier he
    galls his kibe.°—How long hast thou been a grave-   *rubs his sore heel*   145
    maker?
CLOWN: Of all the days in the year, I came to't that day
    that our last king Hamlet overcame Fortinbras.
HAMLET: How long is that since?
CLOWN: Cannot you tell that? Every fool can tell that.   150
    It was the very day that young Hamlet was born—
    he that is mad, and sent into England.
HAMLET: Ay, marry, why was he sent into England?
CLOWN: Why, because he was mad. He shall recover
    his wits there; or, if he do not, 'tis no great matter°   *does not matter much*   155
    there.
HAMLET: Why?
CLOWN: 'Twill not be seen in him there. There the
    men are as mad as he.
HAMLET: How came he mad?   160
CLOWN: Very strangely, they say.
HAMLET: How strangely?
CLOWN: Faith, even with losing his wits.
HAMLET: Upon what ground?
CLOWN: Why, here in Denmark. I have been sexton   165
    here, man and boy, thirty years.
HAMLET: How long will a man lie in the earth ere° he   *before*
    rot?
CLOWN: Faith, if he be not rotten before he die (as we
    have many pocky corses° now-a-days that will   *pox-riddled corpses*   170
    scarce hold the laying in),° he will last you some   *last till the burial*
    eight year or nine year. A tanner° will last you nine   *leather worker (preparing hides)*
    year.

Mel Gibson in the 1990 film version of *Hamlet.* Courtesy of Photofest.

HAMLET: Why he more than another?

CLOWN: Why, sir, his hide is so tanned with his trade   175
that he will keep out water a great while; and your
water is a sore decayer of your whoreson dead
body. Here's a skull now: this skull hath lain in the
earth three-and-twenty years.

HAMLET: Whose was it?   180

CLOWN: A whoreson mad fellow's it was. Whose do
you think it was?

HAMLET: Nay, I know not.

CLOWN: A pestilence on him for a mad rogue! He
poured a flagon of Rhenish° on my head once. This   *a pitcher of wine* 185
same skull, sir, was Yorick's skull, the King's jester.

HAMLET: This?

CLOWN: Even that.

HAMLET: Let me see. [*takes the skull*] Alas, poor Yorick!
I knew him, Horatio. A fellow of infinite jest, of   190
most excellent fancy. He hath borne me on his
back a thousand times. And now how abhorred in
my imagination it is! My gorge rises at it. Here
hung those lips that I have kissed I know not how
oft. Where be your gibes° now? your gambols? your   *barbs* 195
songs? your flashes of merriment that were wont
to set the table on a roar?° Not one now, to mock   *used to make the guests roar*

your own grinning? Quite chapfallen?° Now get you *down in the mouth*
to my lady's chamber, and tell her, let her paint an
inch thick, to this favor° she must come. Make her *look* 200
laugh at that. Prithee, Horatio, tell me one thing.
HORATIO: What's that, my lord?
HAMLET: Dost thou think Alexander° looked of this *(Alexander the Great)*
fashion in the earth?
HORATIO: Even so. 205
HAMLET: And smelt so? Pah!

[*Puts down the skull.*]

HORATIO: Even so, my lord.
HAMLET: To what base uses we may return, Horatio!
Why may not imagination trace the noble dust of
Alexander till he find it stopping a bunghole?° *tap hole of a barrel* 210
HORATIO: 'Twere to consider too curiously, to con-
sider so.
HAMLET: No, faith, not a jot; but to follow him thither
with modesty enough, and likelihood to lead it; as
thus: Alexander died, Alexander was buried, Alex- 215
ander returneth into dust; the dust is earth; of earth
we make loam; and why of that loam (whereto he
was converted) might they not stop a beer barrel?

  Imperious Caesar, dead and turned to clay,
  Might stop a hole to keep the wind away. 220
  O, that that earth which kept the world in awe
  Should patch a wall t' expel° the winter's flaw! *to keep out*

But soft! but soft! aside! Here comes the King—

[*Enter* KING, QUEEN, LAERTES, *and a coffin, with priests and lords.*]

The Queen, the courtiers. Who is this they follow?
And with such maimèd rites?° This doth betoken *minimal ceremony* 225
The corpse they follow did with desperate hand
Fordo its own life. 'Twas of some estate.° *of fairly high rank*
Couch we awhile,° and mark. *let us lie low*

[*Retires with* HORATIO.]

LAERTES: What ceremony else?° *additional ceremony*
HAMLET: That is Laertes,
A very noble youth. Mark. 230
LAERTES: What ceremony else?
PRIEST: Her obsequies° have been as far enlarged *funeral rites*
As we have warranty. Her death was doubtful;° *suspicious*
And, but that° great command oversways the order, *except that*
She should in ground unsanctified have
    lodged° *have been buried outside the churchyard* 235

Till the last trumpet. For° charitable prayers,   *instead of*
Shards, flints, and pebbles should be thrown on her.
Yet here she is allowed her virgin crants,°   *garlands*
Her maiden strewments,° and the bringing home   *strewn flowers*
Of bell and burial.   240
LAERTES: Must there no more be done?
PRIEST: No more be done.
We should profane the service of the dead
To sing a requiem and such rest to her
As to peace-parted souls.°   *those who died at peace*
LAERTES: Lay her i' the earth,
And from her fair and unpolluted flesh   245
May violets spring! I tell thee, churlish priest,
A ministering angel shall my sister be
When thou liest howling.°   *in hell*
HAMLET: What, the fair Ophelia?
QUEEN: Sweets to the sweet! Farewell.

[*Scatters flowers.*]

I hoped thou shouldst have been my Hamlet's wife;   250
I thought thy bride-bed to have decked,° sweet maid,   *strewn with flowers*
And not have strewed thy grave.
LAERTES: O, treble woe°   *three times woe*
Fall ten times treble on that cursèd head
Whose wicked deed thy most ingenious sense
Deprived thee of!° Hold off the earth awhile,   *deprived you of your fine mind* 255
Till I have caught° her once more in mine arms.   *taken*

[*Leaps in the grave.*]

Now pile your dust upon the quick° and dead   *the living*
Till of this flat a mountain you have made
To over top old Pelion or the skyish head
Of blue Olympus.°   *to be higher than the* 260
HAMLET [*advancing*]: What is he whose grief   *legendary Greek mountains*
Bears such an emphasis?° whose phrase of sorrow   *cries out so loud*
Conjures the wandering stars,° and makes them stand   *puts a spell on the planets*
Like wonder-wounded hearers? This is I,
Hamlet the Dane.

[*Leaps in after* LAERTES.]

LAERTES: The devil take thy soul!   265

[*Grappling with him.*]

HAMLET: Thou pray'st not well.
I prithee take thy fingers from my throat;
For, though I am not splenitive° and rash,   *bad-tempered*
Yet have I in me something dangerous,
Which let thy wisdom fear. Hold off thy hand!   270
KING: Pluck them asunder.

QUEEN: Hamlet, Hamlet!
ALL: Gentlemen!
HORATIO: Good my lord, be quiet.

[*Attendants part them, and they leave the grave.*]

HAMLET: Why, I will fight with him upon this theme°   *for this cause*
    Until my eyelids will no longer wag.
QUEEN: O my son, what theme?   275
HAMLET: I loved Ophelia. Forty thousand brothers
    Could not (with all their quantity of love)
    Make up my sum. What wilt thou do for her?
KING: O, he is mad, Laertes.
QUEEN: For love of God, forbear him!   280
HAMLET: 'Swounds, show me what thou't do.
    Woo't° weep? woo't fight? woo't fast? woo't tear thyself?   *will you*
    Woo't drink up eisell?° eat a crocodile?   *vinegar*
    I'll do't. Dost thou come here to whine?
    To outface me with leaping in her grave?   285
    Be buried quick° with her, and so will I.   *alive*
    And if thou prate of mountains, let them throw
    Millions of acres on us, till our ground,
    Singeing his pate against the burning zone,°   *its top burned by the sun*
    Make Ossa° like a wart! Nay, an thou'lt mouth,   *(a huge Greek mountain)* 290
    I'll rant as well as thou.
QUEEN: This is mere madness;
    And thus a while the fit will work on him.
    Anon,° as patient as the female dove   *soon*
    When that her golden couplets° are disclosed,   *the twin yellow hatchlings* 295
    His silence will sit drooping.
HAMLET: Hear you, sir!
    What is the reason that you use° me thus?   *treat*
    I loved you ever. But it is no matter.
    Let Hercules° himself do what he may,   *(legendary mighty Greek hero)*
    The cat will mew, and dog will have his day.   300

[*He leaves.*]

KING: I pray thee, good Horatio, wait upon him.

[HORATIO *leaves.*]

[*to* LAERTES] Strengthen your patience in our° last   *remembering our*
    night's speech.
We'll put the matter to the present push.°   *immediate test*
Good Gertrude, set some watch° over your son.   *guard*
This grave shall have a living° monument.   *lasting* 305
An hour of quiet shortly shall we see;
Till then in patience our proceeding be.

[*They leave.*]

SCENE 2. A hall in the Castle.

[*Enter* HAMLET *and* HORATIO.]

HAMLET: So much for this, sir; now shall you see the other.
    You do remember all the circumstance?
HORATIO: Remember it, my lord!
HAMLET: Sir, in my heart there was a kind of fighting
    That would not let me sleep. Methought° I lay   *I thought*   5
    Worse than the mutines in the bilboes.° Rashly—   *than shackled mutineers*
    (And praised be rashness for it) let us know,
    Our indiscretion sometime serves us well
    When our deep plots do pall.° And that should learn° us   *falter/teach*
    There's a divinity that shapes our ends,°   *that guides our path*   10
    Rough-hew them how we will°—   *no matter how roughly*
                                        we sketch it out
HORATIO: That is most certain.
HAMLET: Up from my cabin,
    My sea-gown scarfed about me,° in the dark   *wrapped in sailor's gown*
    Groped I to find out them, had my desire,
    Fingered° their packet, and in fine withdrew   *stole*   15
    To mine own room again, making so bold°   *becoming so bold as*
    (My fears forgetting manners) to unseal
    Their grand commission, where I found, Horatio
    (O royal knavery!), an exact command,
    Larded° with many several sorts of reasons,   *embellished*   20
    Importing° Denmark's health, and England's too,   *related to*
    With, ho! such bugs and goblins° in my life—   *such terrible deeds*
    That, on the supervise,° no leisure bated,°   *upon the reading/allowed*
    No, not to stay° the grinding of the axe,   *to wait for*
    My head should be struck off.
HORATIO: Is't possible?   25
HAMLET: Here's the commission;° read it at more leisure.   *instructions*
    But wilt thou hear me how I did proceed?
HORATIO: I beseech you.
HAMLET: Being thus benetted round° with villainies,   *trapped*
    Ere° I could make a prologue to my brains,   *before*   30
    They had begun the play. I sat me down;
    Devised a new commission; wrote it fair.
    I once did hold it, as our statists° do,   *officials*
    A baseness to write fair, and labored much
    How to forget that learning; but, sir, now   35
    It did me yeoman's service. Wilt thou know
    The effect of what I wrote?
HORATIO: Ay, good my lord.
HAMLET: An earnest conjuration° from the King,   *plea*
    As England was his faithful tributary,°   *payer of tribute*
    As love between them like the palm might flourish,   40
    As peace should still her wheaten garland wear
    And stand a comma° 'tween their amities,°   *as a link/friendships*
    And many such-like as's of great charge,

That, on the view and knowing of these contents,

Without debatement further, more or less,   45

He should the bearers° put to sudden death,   *bearers of these papers*

Not shriving time° allowed.   *no time for confession of sins*

HORATIO: How was this sealed?

HAMLET: Why, even in that was heaven ordinant.°   *heaven took charge*

I had my father's signet° in my purse,   *signet ring*

Which was the model of that Danish seal;   50

Folded the writ° up in the form of the other,   *document*

Subscribed it, gave't the impression, placed it safely,

The changeling° never known. Now, the next day   *substitution*

Was our sea-fight; and what to this was sequent°   *what followed*

Thou know'st already.   55

HORATIO: So Guildenstern and Rosencrantz go to't.

HAMLET: Why, man, they did make love to this employment.°   *pursued it eagerly*

They are not near my conscience;° their defeat   *on my conscience*

Does by their own insinuation grow.°   *results from their meddling*

'Tis dangerous when the baser nature comes   60

Between the pass and fell° incensèd points   *thrust and cruel*

Of mighty opposites.

HORATIO: Why, what a king is this!

HAMLET: Does it not, think'st thee, stand me now upon°—   *become my task*

He that hath killed my king, and whored my mother,

Popped in between the election° and my hopes,   *election to the throne* 65

Thrown out his angle° for my proper life,   *his fishhook*

And with such cozenage°—is't not perfect conscience   *trickery*

To quit him° with this arm? And is't not to be damned   *pay him back*

To let this canker° of our nature come   *blight*

In further evil?   70

HORATIO: It must be shortly known to him from England

What is the issue of the business there.

HAMLET: It will be short; the interim is mine,

And a man's life's no more than to say "one."

But I am very sorry, good Horatio,   75

That to Laertes I forgot myself;

For by the image of my cause I see

The portraiture of his. I'll court his favors.

But sure the bravery° of his grief did put me   *showy display*

Into a towering passion.

HORATIO: Peace!° Who comes here?   *quiet* 80

[*Enter young* OSRIC, *a courtier.*]

OSRIC: Your lordship is right welcome back to
Denmark.

HAMLET: I humbly thank you, sir. [*aside to* HORATIO]
Dost know this waterfly?

HORATIO [*aside to* HAMLET]: No, my good lord.

HAMLET [*aside to* HORATIO]: Thy state is the more gra-   85

cious;° for 'tis a vice to know him. He hath much   *soul is closer to grace*

land, and fertile. Let a beast be lord of beasts, and
his crib° shall stand at the king's mess. 'Tis a   *trough*
chough;° but, as I say, spacious in the possession   *chattering bird*
of dirt.   90
OSRIC: Sweet lord, if your lordship were at leisure, I
  should impart a thing to you from his Majesty.
HAMLET: I will receive it, sir, with all diligence of spirit.
  Put your bonnet to his right use, 'tis for the head.
OSRIC: I thank your lordship, it is very hot.   95
HAMLET: No, believe me, 'tis very cold; the wind is
  northerly.
OSRIC: It is indifferent cold,° my lord, indeed.   *fairly cold*
HAMLET: But yet methinks it is very sultry and hot for
  my complexion.   100
OSRIC: Exceedingly, my lord; it is very sultry, as
  'twere—I cannot tell how. But, my lord, his
  Majesty bade me signify to you that he has laid a
  great wager on your head. Sir, this is the matter—
HAMLET: I beseech you remember.   105

[HAMLET *moves him to put on his hat*.]

OSRIC: Nay, good my lord; for mine ease, in good
  faith. Sir, here is newly come to court Laertes;
  believe me, an absolute gentleman, full of most
  excellent differences, of very soft society and great
  showing. Indeed, to speak feelingly of him, he is   110
  the card or calendar° of gentry; for you shall find   *guide and index*
  in him the continent° of what part a gentleman   *sum*
  would see.
HAMLET: Sir, his definement suffers no perdition in
  you;° though, I know, to divide him inventorially   *(Hamlet is aping Osric's* 115
  would dozy the arithmetic of memory, and yet but   *precious and hyper-*
  yaw neither in respect of his quick sail. But, in the   *refined diction)*
  verity of extolment, I take him to be a soul of great
  article, and his infusion of such dearth and rare-
  ness as, to make true diction of him, his semblable   120
  is his mirror, and who else would trace him, his
  umbrage,° nothing more.   *shadow*
OSRIC: Your lordship speaks most infallibly of him.
HAMLET: The concernancy,° sir? Why do we wrap the   *point*
  gentleman in our more rawer breath?   125
OSRIC: Sir?
HORATIO [*aside to* HAMLET]: Is't not possible to under-
  stand in another tongue? You will do't, sir, really.
HAMLET: What imports the nomination of° this gentle-   *why do you name*
  man?   130
OSRIC: Of Laertes?
HORATIO [*aside*]: His purse is empty already; all's
  golden words are spent.

HAMLET: Of him, sir.

OSRIC: I know you are not ignorant— 135

HAMLET: I would you did, sir; yet, in faith, if you did, it would not much approve me. Well, sir?

OSRIC: You are not ignorant of what excellence Laertes is—

HAMLET: I dare not confess that, lest I should compare 140 with him in excellence; but to know a man well were to know himself.

OSRIC: I mean, sir, for his weapon; but in the imputation° laid on him by them, in his meed he's unfellowed.° 145

> imputation° *reputation*
> unfellowed° *his merit is unequaled*

HAMLET: What's his weapon?

OSRIC: Rapier and dagger.

HAMLET: That's two of his weapons—but well.

OSRIC: The King, sir, hath wagered with him six Barbary horses; against the which he has impawned,° 150 as I take it, six French rapiers and poniards,° with their assigns,° as girdle, hangers,° and so. Three of the carriages, in faith, are very dear to fancy, very responsive to the hilts, most delicate carriages, and of very liberal conceit.° 155

> impawned° *staked*
> poniards° *daggers*
> with their assigns° *with their gear/carrying straps*
> of very liberal conceit° *of rich design*

HAMLET: What call you the carriages?

HORATIO [*aside to* HAMLET]: I knew you must be edified by the margent° ere you had done.

> margent° *helped by notes in the margin (like readers of this text)*

OSRIC: The carriages, sir, are the hangers.

HAMLET: The phrase would be more germane° to the 160 matter if we could carry cannon by our sides. I would it might be hangers till then. But on! Six Barbary horses against six French swords, their assigns, and three liberal-conceited carriages: that's the French bet against the Danish. Why is this all 165 impawned, as you call it?

> germane° *suitable*

OSRIC: The King, sir, hath laid° that, in a dozen passes° between yourself and him, he shall not exceed you three hits; he hath laid on twelve for nine, and it would come to immediate trial° if your lordship 170 would vouchsafe the answer.°

> laid° *has bet*   passes° *bouts*
> trial° *test*
> vouchsafe the answer° *agree to respond*

HAMLET: How if I answer no?

OSRIC: I mean, my lord, the opposition of your person° in trial.

> person° *appearing in person*

HAMLET: Sir, I will walk here in the hall. If it please his 175 Majesty, it is the breathing time° of day with me. Let the foils° be brought, the gentleman willing, and the King hold his purpose,° I will win for him if I can; if not, I will gain nothing but my shame and the odd hits. 180

> breathing time° *exercise time*
> foils° *blunt fencing weapons*
> hold his purpose° *sticks to his intention*

OSRIC: Shall I redeliver you° even so?

> redeliver you° *bring back your answer*

HAMLET: To this effect, sir, after what flourish your
nature will.

OSRIC: I commend my duty to your lordship.

HAMLET: Yours, yours. [OSRIC *leaves*.] He does well to   185
commend it himself; there are no tongues else
for's turn.°   *to serve his turn*

HORATIO: This lapwing runs away with the shell on
his head.°   *newly hatched bird*

HAMLET: He did comply with his dug° before he sucked   *spoke politely to the nipple* 190
it. Thus has he, and many more of the same bevy
that I know the drossy° age dotes on, only got the   *silly*
tune of the time and outward habit of encounter—
a kind of yeasty° collection, which carries them   *frothy*
through and through the most fanned and win-   195
nowed opinions; and do but blow them to their
trial°—the bubbles are out.   *if you blow on them to test them*

[*Enter a* LORD.]

LORD: My lord, his Majesty commended him to you
by° young Osric, who brings back to him that you   *sent you greetings by*
attend him in the hall. He sends to know if your   200
pleasure hold to play° with Laertes, or that you   *fence*
will take longer time.

HAMLET: I am constant to my purposes; they follow the
King's pleasure. If his fitness speaks, mine is ready;
now or whensoever, provided I be so able as now.   205

LORD: The King and Queen and all are coming down.

HAMLET: In happy time.°   *at the right time*

LORD: The Queen desires you to use some gentle
entertainment° to Laertes before you fall to play.   *to speak courteously*

HAMLET: She well instructs me.   210

[LORD *leaves*.]

HORATIO: You will lose this wager, my lord.

HAMLET: I do not think so. Since he went into France
I have been in continual practice; I shall win at the
odds. But thou wouldst not think how ill all's here
about my heart. But it is no matter.   215

HORATIO: Nay, good my lord—

HAMLET: It is but foolery, but it is such a kind of gain-
giving° as would perhaps trouble a woman.   *misgiving*

HORATIO: If your mind dislike anything, obey it. I will
forestall their repair° hither and say you are not fit. *prevent their coming* 220

HAMLET: Not a whit, we defy augury;° there's a special   *let us ignore evil omens*
providence in the fall of a sparrow. If it be now,
'tis not to come; if it be not to come, it will be now;
if it be not now, yet it will come. The readiness is

all. Since no man has aught of what he leaves,°   *profits from what he*   225
what is't to leave betimes?° Let be.   *leaves behind/early*

[*Enter* KING, QUEEN, LAERTES, OSRIC, *and lords, with other
attendants with foils and daggers. A table and cups of
wine on it.*]

KING: Come, Hamlet, come, and take this hand from me.

[*He puts* LAERTES' *hand into* HAMLET'S.]

HAMLET: Give me your pardon, sir. I have done you wrong;
    But pardon't, as you are a gentleman.
    This presence° knows,   *assembled company*   230
    And you must needs have heard, how I am punished
    With sore distraction.° What I have done   *a severely disturbed mind*
    That might your nature, honor, and exception°   *disapproval*
    Roughly awake, I here proclaim was madness.
    Was't Hamlet wronged Laertes? Never Hamlet.   235
    If Hamlet from himself be taken away,
    And when he's not himself does wrong Laertes,
    Then Hamlet does it not. Hamlet denies it.
    Who does it, then? His madness. If't be so,
    Hamlet is of the faction that is wronged;   240
    His madness is poor Hamlet's enemy.
    Sir, in this audience,
    Let my disclaiming from a purposed evil°   *any evil done on purpose*
    Free me so far in your most generous thoughts
    That I have shot my arrow o'er the house   245
    And hurt my brother.
LAERTES: I am satisfied in nature,°   *my personal feelings*
    Whose motive in this case should stir me most
    To my revenge. But in my terms of honor
    I stand aloof,° and will no reconcilement   *I have to hold off*
    Till by some elder masters of known honor   250
    I have a voice and precedent° of peace   *confirmation of precedent*
    To keep my name ungored. But till that time   *for making peace*
    I do receive your offered love like love,
    And will not wrong it.
HAMLET: I embrace it freely,
    And will this brother's wager frankly play.°   *enter fully into the contest*   255
    Give us the foils. Come on.
LAERTES: Come, one for me.
HAMLET: I'll be your foil,° Laertes. In mine ignorance   *contrast setting off*
    Your skill shall, like a star in the darkest night,   *something precious*
    Stick fiery off indeed.°   *show fiery by contrast*
LAERTES: You mock me, sir.
HAMLET: No, by this hand.   260
KING: Give them the foils, young Osric. Cousin Hamlet,
    You know the wager?

HAMLET: Very well, my lord.
    Your Grace has laid the odds on the weaker side.
KING: I do not fear it,° I have seen you both;   *I am not worried*
    But since he is bettered,° we have therefore odds.   *has improved* 265
LAERTES: This is too heavy; let me see another.
HAMLET: This likes me well. These foils have all a length?

    [*They prepare to fence.*]

OSRIC: Ay, my good lord.
KING: Set me the stoups° of wine upon that table.   *cups*
    If Hamlet give the first or second hit,   270
    Or quit° in answer of the third exchange,   *hit back*
    Let all the battlements their ordnance° fire;   *cannon*
    The King shall drink to Hamlet's better breath,
    And in the cup an union° shall he throw   *a pearl*
    Richer than that which four successive kings   275
    In Denmark's crown have worn. Give me the cups;
    And let the kettle° to the trumpet speak,   *the kettledrum*
    The trumpet to the cannoneer without,
    The cannons to the heavens, the heaven to earth,
    "Now the King drinks to Hamlet." Come, begin.   280
    And you the judges, bear a wary eye.
HAMLET: Come on, sir.
LAERTES: Come, my lord.

    [*They fence.*]

HAMLET: One.
LAERTES: No.
HAMLET: Judgment!
OSRIC: A hit, a very palpable hit.
LAERTES: Well, again!
KING: Stay,° give me drink. Hamlet, this pearl is thine;   *wait*
    Here's to thy health.   285

    [*Drum; trumpets sound; a cannon goes off outside.*]

                 Give him the cup.
HAMLET: I'll play this bout first; set it by awhile.
    Come. [*They fight.*] Another hit. What say you?
LAERTES: A touch, a touch; I do confess.
KING: Our son shall win.
QUEEN: He's fat,° and scant of breath.   *sweaty*
    Here, Hamlet, take my napkin,° rub thy brows.   *handkerchief* 290
    The Queen carouses to thy fortune, Hamlet.
HAMLET: Good madam!
KING: Gertrude, do not drink.
QUEEN: I will, my lord; I pray you pardon me.

    [*She drinks.*]

KING [*aside*]: It is the poisoned cup; it is too late.
HAMLET: I dare not drink yet, madam; by-and-by.   295
QUEEN: Come, let me wipe thy face.
LAERTES: My lord, I'll hit him now.
KING: I do not think't.
LAERTES [*aside*]: And yet it is almost against my conscience.
HAMLET: Come for the third, Laertes! You but dally;
    I pray you pass with your best violence;   300
    I am afeard you make a wanton of me.°   *treat me like a child*
LAERTES: Say you so? Come on.

    [*They fence.*]

OSRIC: Nothing neither way.
LAERTES: Have at you now!

    [LAERTES *wounds* HAMLET; *then, in scuffling, they change rapiers,*
    and HAMLET *wounds* LAERTES.]

KING: Part them! They are incensed.°   *enraged*
HAMLET: Nay come! again!   305

    [*The* QUEEN *falls.*]

OSRIC: Look to the Queen there, ho!
HORATIO: They bleed on both sides. How is it, my lord?
OSRIC: How is't, Laertes?
LAERTES: Why, as a woodcock to mine own springe,°   *like a (decoy) bird*
    Osric.   *caught in my own trap*
    I am justly killed with mine own treachery.
HAMLET: How does the Queen?   310
KING: She swoons to see them bleed.
QUEEN: No, no! the drink, the drink! O my dear Hamlet!
    The drink, the drink! I am poisoned.

    [*She dies.*]

HAMLET: O villainy! Ho! let the door be locked.
    Treachery! Seek it out.

    [LAERTES *falls.*]

LAERTES: It is here, Hamlet. Hamlet, thou art slain;   315
    No medicine in the world can do thee good.
    In thee there is not half an hour of life.
    The treacherous instrument is in thy hand,
    Unbated° and envenomed. The foul practice°   *unchecked/vicious scheme*
    Hath turned itself on me. Lo, here I lie,   320
    Never to rise again. Thy mother's poisoned.
    I can no more. The King, the King's to blame.
HAMLET: The point envenomed too?
    Then, venom, to thy work.

[Hurts the KING.]

ALL: Treason! treason!   325
KING: O, yet defend me, friends! I am but hurt.
HAMLET: Here, thou incestuous, murderous, damned
        Dane,
    Drink off this potion! Is thy union here?°   *Is this the pearl you*
    Follow my mother.   *offered as a prize?*

[KING *dies.*]

LAERTES: He is justly served.
    It is a poison tempered by° himself.   *prepared by* 330
    Exchange forgiveness with me, noble Hamlet.
    Mine and my father's death come not upon thee,°   *you are not guilty of*
    Nor thine on me!

[Dies.]

HAMLET: Heaven make thee free° of it! I follow thee.   *may heaven clear you*
    I am dead, Horatio. Wretched queen, adieu!   335
    You that look pale and tremble at this chance,°   *mischance*
    That are but mutes° or audience to this act,   *silent spectators*
    Had I but time (as this fell sergeant,° Death,   *this cruel law officer*
    Is strict in his arrest) O, I could tell you—
    But let it be. Horatio, I am dead;   340
    Thou liv'st; report me and my cause aright
    To the unsatisfied.°   *those who do not know the truth*
HORATIO: Never believe it.
    I am more an antique Roman° than a Dane.   *(like a Roman believing in*
    Here's yet some liquor left.   *honorable suicide)*
HAMLET: As th'art a man,
    Give me the cup. Let go! By heaven, I'll have't.   345
    O good Horatio, what a wounded name
    (Things standing thus unknown) shall live behind me!
    If thou didst ever hold me in thy heart,
    Absent thee from felicity° awhile,   *turn your back on*
    And in this harsh world draw thy breath in pain,   *ultimate happiness* 350
    To tell my story.

[March afar off, and sound of cannon.]

                    What warlike noise is this?
OSRIC: Young Fortinbras, with conquest° come from Poland,   *after his conquest*
    To the ambassadors of England gives
    This warlike volley.
HAMLET: O, I die, Horatio!
    The potent poison quite overcrows° my spirit.   *overpowers (like a* 355
    I cannot live to hear the news from England,   *cock in a cockfight)*
    But I do prophesy the election lights
    On° Fortinbras. He has my dying voice.   *choice of a new king goes to*

So tell him, with the occurrents,° more and less,   *events*
Which have solicited°—the rest is silence.   *incited me*   360

[*Dies.*]

HORATIO: Now cracks a noble heart. Good night, sweet
        prince,
And flights of angels sing thee to thy rest!

[*Sound of marching outside.*]

Why does the drum come hither?

[*Enter* FORTINBRAS *and English ambassadors, with drum,
flags, and attendants.*]

FORTINBRAS: Where is this sight?
HORATIO: What is it you would see?
If aught° of woe or wonder, cease your search.   *anything*   365
FORTINBRAS: This quarry cries on havoc.° O proud   *these bodies call out*
        Death,   *for vengeance*
What feast is toward° in thine eternal cell   *ahead*
That thou so many princes at a shot
So bloodily hast struck?
AMBASSADOR: The sight is dismal;
And our affairs° from England come too late.   *news of our business*   370
The ears are senseless° that should give us hearing   *without life*
To tell him his commandment is fulfilled,
That Rosencrantz and Guildenstern are dead.
Where should we have our thanks?
HORATIO: Not from his° mouth,   *(Claudius')*
Had it the ability of life to thank you.   375
He never gave commandment for their death.
But since, so jump upon this bloody question,°   *right at the moment*
You from the Polack wars, and you from England,   *of bloodshed*
Are here arrived, give order that these bodies
High on a stage be placed to the view;   380
And let me speak to the yet unknowing world
How these things came about. So shall you hear
Of carnal, bloody, and unnatural acts;
Of accidental judgments, casual slaughters;°   *accidental killings*
Of deaths put on by cunning and forced cause;   385
And, in this upshot, purposes mistook°   *intentions badly carried out*
Fallen on the inventors' heads. All this can I
Truly deliver.
FORTINBRAS: Let us haste to hear it,
And call the noblest to the audience.
For me, with sorrow I embrace my fortune.   390
I have some rights of memory° in this kingdom,   *remembered claims*
Which now to claim my vantage° doth invite me.   *opportunity*
HORATIO: Of that I shall have also cause to speak,
And from his mouth whose voice will draw on more.

But let this same be presently performed,   395
Even while men's minds are wild, lest more mischance
On plots and errors happen.
FORTINBRAS: Let four captains
Bear Hamlet like a soldier to the stage;°   *platform*
For he was likely, had he been put on,°   *if he had been made king*
To have proved most royally; and for his passage   400
The soldiers' music and the rites of war
Speak loudly for him.
Take up the bodies. Such a sight as this
Becomes the field, but here shows much amiss.
Go, bid the soldiers shoot.   405

[*They leave marching, after which cannons are fired.*]

The Receptive Reader

1. (Act Five, Scene 1) The gravediggers' scene is an outstanding example of the *dark humor* Elizabethan audiences apparently expected and loved. What is the content and mode of the jests? Is the grim or macabre humor here mere comic relief or interlude, or is it related to the overall development of the play? (What kind of *foreshadowing* is going on here?)

2. How do Laertes and Hamlet behave at Ophelia's funeral? What side of either character comes to the fore here? What stance toward Ophelia's death is adopted by the church? by the other characters? Was her death suicide?

3. (Act Five, Scene 2) Hamlet's final exchanges with his *confidant* Horatio give the audience a glimpse of his frame of mind as he approaches the tragic conclusion (or *denouement*) of the play. What are his last words on life, on fate, on human nature? In Hamlet's return from the voyage, what was the role of his own inititative; what was the role of Providence? How does Hamlet react to the death of Rosencrantz and Guildenstern?

4. The precious Osric gives Hamlet a last opportunity to display his satirical wit. What makes Osric a prime target?

5. In preparing for the fencing contest, Hamlet treats Laertes with extreme courtesy. How and why? (How do you reconcile his behavior here with his extreme lack of courtesy in other situations?) Is the ending or denouement an example of happenstance—of confused accidental happenings that make a mockery of human planning? Is the ending an example of poetic justice, with the plotters finally getting their just deserts? Is the ending a triumph of *irony,* with the plot backfiring on the plotters, and with the "enginer hoist with his own petar"?

The Creative Dimension

Working with a group, make plans for a *miniproduction* that would focus on a major issue in the play, throw light on one of its puzzles, or look at part of it from a new or different perspective. Help the group with developing a concept and a script. You might want to transpose a scene or scenes to a modern setting, or you might want to rewrite a scene or scenes as seen through the eyes of a minor character. (In working with Shakespeare's *Macbeth,* one group of students staged "The Trial of Macbeth"—for killing King Duncan; another staged a miniproduction called "Ms. Beth," in which Lady Macbeth had become transformed into a ruthless corporate vice president plotting to take over the job of President Duncan.)

The Whole Play—For Discussion or Writing

1. Laertes' final verdict is, "The King, the King's to blame." Does guilt in this play rest mainly on a single individual? Is Claudius a *stereotypical villain?* What are the sources or what is the root cause of evil in this play?

2. Until recently, most critics did not question the validity of the *revenge ethic* preached by the ghost (an eye for an eye; a tooth for a tooth; a life for a life). Yet critics have also puzzled endlessly over Hamlet's apparent hesitation or delay in carrying out his dead father's command. How do you explain this paradox? Is Hamlet fully committed to the (pre-Christian) tradition of revenge or not?

3. Is Hamlet temperamentally unsuited for the task assigned him by the ghost? Did Shakespeare create a character too *introspective,* sensitive, or poetic for the initiative and effective action needed?

4. Is Hamlet a *tragic hero?* Does he have a tragic flaw? Does he progress toward self-realization—a fuller understanding of himself and his situation?

5. Is Hamlet's treatment of Ophelia and his mother harsh and unreasonable? Is it part of a pattern of misogyny deeply engrained in the culture he represents?

6. The English critic J. Dover Wilson has said that "there is a savage side" to Hamlet's character (shown for instance in his ruthless treatment of Rosencrantz and Guildenstern or of Polonius), but that it is not meant to "detract from our general sense of the nobility and greatness" of Hamlet. Do you agree?

7. Rebecca West said that "Hamlet was disgusted by his own kind." How profound or complete is Hamlet's *disillusionment* with humankind?

8. Some critics have seen poison as the master metaphor in this play. What is its role, literally and figuratively, in the play? For you, does it sum up a central theme?

WRITING ABOUT LITERATURE

29   Studying Character (Reading for Clues)

O brave new world that has such people in it!
SHAKESPEARE, *THE TEMPEST*

The Writing Workshop   The theater creates characters who often assume a life of their own, beyond the duration of the two-hour or three-hour play. Writing a paper about a central character or about several key characters in a play gives you a chance to sum up what you see in the mirror the play holds up to human nature. Is there a single clue or dominant trait that will help the audience understand the character? Or are there perhaps several major related traits, and do they form an understandable pattern? Can you take a close look at apparent contradictions in the character to see if they can be resolved?

When you write about a central character or the key characters in a play, consider the following general guidelines:

✗ *Be alert to clues provided by the playwright early in the play.*   For instance, watch for preliminary capsule descriptions of the character. Claudius says early in *Hamlet:*

There's something in his soul o'er which his melancholy sits on brood.

✗ *Be a patient listener.*   Quote revealing things a character says. In the theater, as in real life, language in many ways reveals (and sometimes betrays) people's thoughts. Look for clues to a character in what he or she says at key points—for instance, when defiantly talking back to an adversary, or when uttering last words. Listen to self-revelations of the character in **soliloquies** and confidential **asides;** in exchanges with **confidants**—trusted friends or associates:

Give me that man that is not passion's slave
And I'll wear him in my heart of hearts.

✗ *Listen to the testimony of others.*   However, remember who is talking. Consider the source. People who love and those who hate a character are likely to give conflicting accounts. Pay special attention when a consensus develops among different supporting characters. In Sophocles' *Antigone,* Creon is convicted of stubborn, unreasonable pride out of the mouth not only of the hostile prophet but also of his own son.

✗ *Pay special attention to test situations.*   What happens when a character is forced to make a decision or take a stand? In the *Antigone* play, for instance, what happens when Ismene is forced to take a stand or when Haimon faces his father? Listen to climactic confrontations that bring to the surface thoughts and feelings that until then may have been hidden under polite or cautious disguises. Hamlet had earlier said: "O break my heart, for I must hold my tongue." Now, at a **climax** or high point of the play, he is ready to indict his mother. When she reproaches him for having offended his (new) father, or stepfather, he charges her with her offense against his (real) father, her murdered husband. He reveals his righteous anger:

QUEEN: Hamlet, thou hast thy father much offended.
HAMLET: Mother, you have my father much offended.
QUEEN: Come, come, you answer with an idle tongue.
HAMLET: Go, go you question with a wicked tongue. (3.4. 10–13)

✗ *Bring together evidence from different parts of the play.*   What evidence can you bring together on Hamlet's true feelings about Ophelia? In spite of his harsh treatment of her, was he capable of love for her? To answer this question, you would have to look at a range of contradictory evidence. For instance, Ophelia says, looking back: "And I, of ladies most deject and wretched / That sucked the honey of his music vows . . . " / (3.1.158–159). Hamlet, fending her off, alternately affirms and denies his love for her:

> HAMLET: I did love you once.
> OPHELIA: Indeed, my lord, you made me believe so.
> HAMLET: You should not have believed me, for virtue cannot so inoculate our old stock but we shall relish of it. I loved you not. (3.1.115–119)

Hamlet aggressively vaunts his love for her at her grave, in his altercation with Laertes:

> I loved Ophelia. Forty thousand brothers
> Could not with all their quantity of love
> Make up my sum. What wilt thou do for her? (5.1.276–278)

✗ *Pay attention to nonverbal as well as verbal language.*   Look for meaning in gesture, revealing incidents, or recurrent symbols. What does the frantic tarantella symbolize that Nora dances at a climactic point in the Ibsen play?

The following student paper is focused on one aspect of Hamlet's multifaceted character.

Sample Student Paper

Playing for Time

Though this be madness, there is method in't.

Hamlet, Prince of Denmark: "unhinged mind" or master of intrigue? That this question continues to be asked after nearly four hundred years is testimony to the intriguing complexity of Hamlet's character. Samuel Taylor Coleridge, in *The Lectures of 1811–1812* (Lecture XII), regards Hamlet as

> an admirable and consistent character, deeply acquainted with his own feelings, painting them with such wonderful power and accuracy. . . . Such a mind as Hamlet's is near akin to madness.

How near? Most of the evidence points to the conclusion that Hamlet was fully in possession of his faculties. His behavior, while sometimes erratic or unpredictable, always has a rational motive behind it. It is true that he faces tremendous pressures. He is a victim of hostile circumstance. To Horatio he exclaims,

> The time is out of joint. O cursed spite,
> That ever I was born to set it right! (1.5.189–90)

However, throughout the play, Hamlet shows himself to be a perceptive, cogent observer of human nature and of his own inner being. He sees his mother's pretended grief. He recognizes Polonius' dishonesty. He sees through the hypocritical friendliness of Rosencrantz and Guildenstern. ("You were sent for, and there is a kind of confession in your looks" 2.2.275–76). The father's ghost reveals that he was murdered by his own brother and, although Hamlet questions the validity of the apparition, he gradually accepts the evidence of foul play. ("It is an honest ghost, that let me tell you" 1.5.138). With only a few exceptions, Hamlet conducts himself not as a madman, but as a man weighed down with the task of avenging his father's death, his own grief and anger, and his princely duties. As Laertes says to Ophelia

> his will is not his own.
> For he himself is subject to his birth. (1.3.17–18)

This statement speaks of obligations and knowledge beyond the grasp or experience of common humanity. Neither Hamlet nor his actions can be judged within the limited understanding that ordinary vision affords.

Hamlet himself consistently maintains that he is "mad in craft." In other words, he pretends to have an unhinged mind in order to be able to observe and thwart his enemies while confusing and disorienting them. For this purpose he warns his friends that he might see fit "to put an antic disposition on" (1.5.172). As he says later,

> I am but mad north-northwest: when the wind is southerly I know a hawk from a handsaw. (2.2.391–92)

His mother calls the ghost who speaks to him again in her bedroom "the very coinage of your brain" ("Alas, he's mad!" 3.4.107). Hamlet answers,

> My pulse as yours doth temperately keep time
> And makes as healthful music. It is not madness
> That I have uttered. . . .
> Lay not that flattering unction to your soul
> That not your trespass but my madness speaks. (3.4.142–48)

In assessing Hamlet's condition, we should remember that most of the discussion of his mental state comes from others' perceptions of his behavior. Ophelia, describing an encounter with Hamlet, tells her father that he came before her "as if he had been loosed out of hell" (2.1.83). Polonius, prime target of Hamlet's "wild and whirling words" (1.5.133), prides himself on having found "the very cause of Hamlet's lunacy" (2.2.49). In Act 4, as he returns from England, Hamlet hears the gravediggers talking about "Hamlet . . . he that is mad."

Modern psychoanalysts, like the Romantic poets before them, see Hamlet as flirting with the idea of suicide ("To be or not to be . . . "). Even in his morbid or depressed state, however, Hamlet manages to develop a brilliant strategy. No madman could have so fine-tuned his revenge as Hamlet does when he instructs the players in how to show the utmost restraint in playing the scene that he hopes will unhinge his mother and murderous uncle. He tells the players,

> in the very torrent, tempest and (as I may say) whirlwind of your passion, you
> must acquire and beget a temperance that may give it smoothness.
> (3.2.6–9)

Here Hamlet displays a keen grasp of situation and moment; he also invokes a treasured Renaissance ideal: temperance. Temperance is the opposite of the loss of control in a deranged mind. Hamlet shows this ideal in action as the play races toward its tragic conclusion. In the scene just before the duel between Laertes and Hamlet, both men enter into a refined, gentlemanly discourse, an amends-making, that could not have been executed by a man bereft of reason. His understanding of the harm he has done and his obvious remorse comes through when he tells Laertes,

> Let my disclaiming from a purposed evil
> Free me so far in your most generous thoughts
> That I have shot my arrow o'er the house
> And hurt my brother. (5.2.243–46)

Considering all that Hamlet faces and endures, much of which he abides with disarming grace, it hardly seems likely he was mad. That he would have known any other outcome is also unlikely, given the treachery and duplicity surrounding him. He is an extraordinary person in extraordinary circumstances. To judge him by conventional standards is to reduce the complexity of his character and situation to a trivial stature.

Questions

What is the author's thesis? Is it clearly and strategically presented? How is it reinforced and developed—what is the general plan of the paper? Which part of the argument or what evidence is most convincing? Can you think of contrary evidence that the student writer plays down? How important is the issue treated in this paper to our interpretation of the play?

30 Modern American Drama

The American Dream

*I am simply asking for a theater in which adults
who want to live can find plays that will heighten
their awareness of what living in our time involves.*
ARTHUR MILLER

FOCUS ON MODERN AMERICAN DRAMA

The modern American theater has given theatergoers a wide range of
choices: commercial and experimental, traditional and avant garde,
Broadway and off-Broadway and off-off-Broadway. One major strand in
modern American plays has been the tradition of realistic drama, which
harks back to the problem plays of Henrik Ibsen. This tradition has produced such slice-of-life plays as Arthur Miller's *All My Sons* and *Death of
a Salesman*, Tennessee Williams's *The Glass Menagerie* and *A Streetcar
Named Desire*, and Lorraine Hansberry's *A Raisin in the Sun*.

The Realistic Setting   Plays in the tradition of American **realism** place
ordinary people in ordinary settings. Ibsen had put on the stage the
small-town merchants and their servants and poor relations and alienated offspring that were part of everyday commonplace reality for many
of his contemporaries. Realism in an American play may mean lives in
tenement buildings or in once-prosperous southern towns; it may mean
jobs as sales reps and assistant managers and truck drivers. The basic
tenet of realism has been: Let historians glorify generals and warlords
and spectacular outlaws. In the meantime, ordinary people are worthy
of our attention and of our respect. "Attention," says the struggling,
defeated salesman's wife in Arthur Miller's classic *Death of a Salesman,*
"attention must be paid to such a person."

The Modern Antihero   Part of the definition of realism is the ordinariness of many of the characters. They are not people of heroic caliber.
They are not outstanding either in dedication and courage, or in
grandiose plans for evil. They are likely to be the modern antihero—

capable of pettiness and vindictiveness. Arthur Miller's Willy Loman became the archetypal salesman of the American gospel of success—of popularity, of easy money for those who know how to make the system work and are "well liked." But the story Miller's play tells is that Willy is falling behind in the rat race. The facts—about his age, his dwindling sales, and his alienated family—are catching up with him. Willy Loman is neither a good husband nor a model parent nor a leader in community affairs. He is not a great heroic figure but a fellow human being at the end of the line.

The Undercurrent of Determinism   In a modern play, the characters are often part of a web of human relationships, and they are often trapped in situations beyond their control. A recurrent theme in much modern American drama is invisible walls: the environment that hems the characters in. They are caught in a web of social and family ties. They are snared in patterns of social interaction that defeat them. What they can do may be in large part determined by how and where they live. In a deterministic worldview, what happens to us is already programmed for us from way back, no matter how we struggle. Even so, characters who struggle against their fate, like Miller's salesman or Hansberry's Mama—the black matriarch who is a tower of strength for her family—loom large.

Psychological Realism   While much modern drama re-creates for us the texture of everday reality, the plays often do not stay nailed down to the prosaic facts. Modern audiences expect **psychological realism.** We deal with the characters' *perception* of reality—their world made up of their personal memories, prejudices, and resentments. In the enormously successful plays of Tennessee Williams—*The Glass Menagerie, A Streetcar Named Desire, Cat on a Hot Tin Roof* among the best known— the suppressed desires and frustrations smouldering under the surface break through, derailing safe, established patterns of living and thinking.

The Death of Tragedy   Critics question whether true tragedy is still possible in the modern world. Are the characters in a modern play too much like us to develop into great tragic figures? Can the modern stage still present great characters worthy of our admiration? Much of the time, we may witness not the fall of the mighty but the slow slide of the lowly. We may, however, still feel pity and fear.

IN SEARCH OF THE AMERICAN DREAM

Lorraine Hansberry's *A Raisin in the Sun* appeals to the audience's belief in the American dream: people have the right to a decent place to live. They are entitled to a fair reward for hard work. They are entitled to recognition of their worth as human beings. Has the American dream become for many an unkept promise? Has it always been a mirage?

Lorraine Hansberry   *(1930–1965)*

One cannot live with sighted eyes and a feeling heart and not know and react to the miseries which afflict this world.

LORRAINE HANSBERRY

Lorraine Hansberry was the first African-American woman to have a play performed on Broadway (after she had raised the money for the out-of-town tryouts herself). Her *Raisin in the Sun,* a "milestone in the American theater" (Leonard Ashley), opened in New York in 1959 and ran for nineteen months.

Working as a journalist for a progressive paper, Hansberry met leading African-American intellectuals and artists like Paul Robeson, W. E. B. DuBois, and Langston Hughes, and she was friends with James Baldwin, author of *Notes of a Native Son* and *The Fire Next Time.* After watching her play in 1959, James Baldwin said, "it will demand a far less guilty and constricted people than the present-day Americans to be able to assess it . . . I had never in my life seen so many black people in the theater. And the reason was that never before, in the entire history of the American theater, had so much of the truth of black people's lives been seen on the stage." Hansberry quoted with admiration a speech made in 1879 by Susan B. Anthony, the early American feminist, who challenged the denial of a woman's right to vote as the denial of her "right of consent as one of the governed" and who called on "every man and woman in whose veins coursed a drop of human sympathy" to break the law that forbade offering a cup of water or a night's shelter to a fugitive slave.

Hansberry's *A Raisin in the Sun* is about what it means to be black in white America. Whether to hold on to the American dream or abandon it in disillusionment becomes a major issue in her play. Hansberry had witnessed the struggle against racial segregation at first hand. She was eight when her family moved into affluent and segregated Hyde Park in Chicago, where she encountered the curses, spitting, and brick throwing of "hellishly hostile" white neighbors. Her family was evicted from the house; her father, a real estate broker, worked with NAACP lawyers to carry his case all the way to the Supreme Court, which ruled in favor of the Hansberry family. Hansberry attributed her father's early death to this bitter struggle.

A Raisin in the Sun was part of the search for a new black identity and a new definition of the black role in society. Hansberry looked at the movement back to African roots and the challenge it presented to the traditional ideal of assimilation. She dramatized the role of the strong maternal female, or matriarch, in the black family, with the corresponding marginalization of the young black male. She shone a probing light into the workings of prejudice and tried to help people gain the spiritual strength to deal with it. Hansberry died young of cancer shortly after her second play, *The Sign in Sidney Brustein's Window,* opened on Broadway in 1964. After her death, her husband, Robert Nemiroff, edited and published several of her unpublished plays. In 1969, a dramatic adaptation of a biography drawing on her letters, journals, and plays was produced posthumously under the title *To Be Young, Gifted, and Black.* It became a long-running off-Broadway play and toured hundreds of college campuses.

A Raisin in the Sun   *1959*

What happens to a dream deferred?
Does it dry up
Like a raisin in the sun?
Or fester like a sore—
And then run?
Does it stink like rotten meat?
Or crust and sugar over—
Like a syrupy sweet?

Maybe it just sags
Like a heavy load.

Or does it explode?

LANGSTON HUGHES

CHARACTERS

RUTH YOUNGER
TRAVIS YOUNGER
WALTER LEE YOUNGER (BROTHER)
BENEATHA YOUNGER
LENA YOUNGER (MAMA)
JOSEPH ASAGAI
GEORGE MURCHISON
KARL LINDNER
BOBO
MOVING MEN

The action of the play is set in Chicago's Southside, sometime between World War II and the present.

Act One

SCENE 1:   *Friday morning.*
SCENE 2:   *The following morning.*

Act Two

SCENE 1:   *Later, the same day.*
SCENE 2:   *Friday night, a few weeks later.*
SCENE 3:   *Moving day, one week later.*

Act Three

An hour later.

Act One

SCENE 1

The YOUNGER *living room would be a comfortable and well-ordered room if it were not for a number of indestructible contradictions to this state of being. Its furnishings are typical and undistinguished and their primary feature now is that they have clearly had to accommodate the living of too many people for too many years—and they are tired. Still, we can see that at some time, a time probably no longer remembered by the family (except perhaps for* MAMA*), the furnishings of this room were actually selected with care and love and even hope—and brought to this apartment and arranged with taste and pride.*

That was a long time ago. Now the once loved pattern of the couch upholstery has to fight to show itself from under acres of crocheted doilies and couch covers which have themselves finally come to be more important than the upholstery. And here a table or a chair has been moved to disguise the worn places in the carpet; but the carpet has fought back by showing its weariness, with depressing uniformity, elsewhere on its surface.

Weariness has, in fact, won in this room. Everything has been polished, washed, sat on, used, scrubbed too often. All pretenses but living itself have long since vanished from the very atmosphere of this room.

Moreover, a section of this room, for it is not really a room unto itself, though the landlord's lease would make it seem so, slopes backward to provide a small kitchen area, where the family prepares the meals that are eaten in the living room proper, which must also serve as dining room. The single window that has been provided for these "two" rooms is located in this kitchen area. The sole natural light the family may enjoy in the course of a day is only that which fights its way through this little window.

At left, a door leads to a bedroom which is shared by MAMA *and her daughter,* BENEATHA*. At right, opposite, is a second room (which in the beginning of the life of this apartment was probably a breakfast room) which serves as a bedroom for* WALTER *and his wife,* RUTH*.*

TIME: *Sometime between World War II and the present.*
PLACE: *Chicago's Southside.*

AT RISE: *It is morning dark in the living room.* TRAVIS *is asleep on the make-down bed at center. An alarm clock sounds from within the bedroom at right, and presently* RUTH *enters from that room and closes the door behind her. She crosses sleepily toward the window. As she passes her sleeping son she reaches down and shakes him a little. At the window she raises the shade and a dusky Southside morning light comes in feebly. She fills a pot with water and puts it on to boil. She calls to the boy, between yawns, in a slightly muffled voice.*

RUTH *is about thirty. We can see that she was a pretty girl, even exceptionally so, but now it is apparent that life has been little that she expected, and disappointment has already begun to hang in her face. In a few years, before thirty-five even, she will be known among her people as a "settled woman."*

She crosses to her son and gives him a good, final, rousing shake.

RUTH: Come on now, boy, it's seven thirty! (*Her son sits up at last, in a stupor of sleepiness.*) I say hurry up, Travis! You ain't the only person in the world got to use a bathroom! (*The child, a sturdy, handsome little boy of ten or eleven, drags himself out of the bed and almost blindly takes his towels and "today's clothes" from drawers and a closet and goes out to the bathroom, which is in an outside hall and which is shared by another family or families on the same floor.* RUTH *crosses to the bedroom door at right and opens it and calls in to her husband.*) Walter Lee! . . . It's after seven thirty! Lemme see you do some waking up in there now! (*She waits.*) You better get up from there, man! It's after seven thirty I tell you. (*She waits again.*) All right, you just go ahead and lay there and next thing you know Travis be finished and Mr. Johnson'll be in there and you'll be fussing and cussing round here like a madman! And be late too! (*She waits, at the end of patience.*) Walter Lee—it's time for you to GET UP!

She waits another second and then starts to go into the bedroom, but is apparently satisfied that her husband has begun to get up. She stops, pulls the door to, and returns to the kitchen area. She wipes her face with a moist cloth and runs her fingers through her sleep-disheveled hair in a vain effort and ties an apron around her housecoat. The bedroom door at right opens and her husband stands in the doorway in his pajamas, which are rumpled and mismated. He is a lean, intense young man in his middle thirties, inclined to quick nervous movements and erratic speech habits—and always in his voice there is a quality of indictment.

WALTER: Is he out yet?

RUTH: What you mean *out?* He ain't hardly got in there good yet.

WALTER (*wandering in, still more oriented to sleep than to a new day*): Well, what was you doing all that yelling for if I can't even get in there yet? (*stopping and thinking*) Check coming today?

RUTH: They *said* Saturday and this is just Friday and I hopes to God you ain't going to get up here first thing this morning and start talking to me 'bout no money—'cause I 'bout don't want to hear it.

WALTER: Something the matter with you this morning?

RUTH: No—I'm just sleepy as the devil. What kind of eggs you want?

WALTER: Not scrambled. (RUTH *starts to scramble eggs.*) Paper come? (RUTH *points impatiently to the rolled up* Tribune *on the table, and he gets it and spreads it out and vaguely reads the front page.*) Set off another bomb yesterday.

RUTH (*maximum indifference*): Did they?

WALTER (*looking up*): What's the matter with you?

RUTH: Ain't nothing the matter with me. And don't keep asking me that this morning.

WALTER: Ain't nobody bothering you. (*reading the news of the day absently again*) Say Colonel McCormick is sick.

RUTH (*affecting tea-party interest*): Is he now? Poor thing.

WALTER (*sighing and looking at his watch*): Oh, me. (*He waits.*) Now what is that boy doing in that bathroom all this time? He just going to have to start getting up earlier. I can't be being late to work on account of him fooling around in there.

RUTH (*turning on him*): Oh, no he ain't going to be getting up no earlier no such thing! It ain't his fault that he can't get to bed no earlier nights 'cause he got a bunch of crazy good-for-nothing clowns sitting up running their mouths in what is supposed to be his bedroom after ten o'clock at night . . .

WALTER: That's what you mad about, ain't it? The things I want to talk about with my friends just couldn't be important in your mind, could they?

He rises and finds a cigarette in her handbag on the table and crosses to the little window and looks out, smoking and deeply enjoying this first one.

RUTH (*almost matter of factly, a complaint too automatic to deserve emphasis*): Why you always got to smoke before you eat in the morning?

WALTER (*at the window*): Just look at 'em down there . . . Running and racing to work . . . (*he turns and faces his wife and watches her a moment at the stove, and then, suddenly*) You look young this morning, baby.

RUTH (*indifferently*): Yeah?

WALTER: Just for a second—stirring them eggs. Just for a second it was—you looked real young again. (*He reaches for her; she crosses away. Then, drily.*) It's gone now—you look like yourself again!

RUTH: Man, if you don't shut up and leave me alone.

WALTER (*looking out to the street again*): First thing a man ought to learn in life is not to make love to no colored woman first thing in the morning. You all some eeeevil people at eight o'clock in the morning.

TRAVIS *appears in the hall doorway, almost fully dressed and quite wide awake now, his towels and pajamas across his shoulders. He opens the door and signals for his father to make the bathroom in a hurry.*

TRAVIS (*watching the bathroom*): Daddy, come on!

WALTER *gets his bathroom utensils and flies out to the bathroom.*

RUTH: Sit down and have your breakfast, Travis.

TRAVIS: Mama, this is Friday. (*gleefully*) Check coming tomorrow, huh?

RUTH: You get your mind off money and eat your breakfast.

TRAVIS (*eating*): This is the morning we supposed to bring the fifty cents to school.

RUTH: Well, I ain't got no fifty cents this morning.

TRAVIS: Teacher say we have to.

RUTH: I don't care what teacher say. I ain't got it. Eat your breakfast, Travis.

TRAVIS: I *am* eating.

RUTH: Hush up now and just eat!

The boy gives her an exasperated look for her lack of understanding, and eats grudgingly.

TRAVIS: You think Grandmama would have it?

RUTH: No! And I want you to stop asking your grandmother for money, you hear me?

TRAVIS (*outraged*): Gaaaleee! I don't ask her, she just gimme it sometimes!

RUTH: Travis Willard Younger—I got too much on me this morning to be—

TRAVIS: Maybe Daddy—

RUTH: *Travis!*

The boy hushes abruptly. They are both quiet and tense for several seconds.

TRAVIS (*presently*): Could I maybe go carry some groceries in front of the supermarket for a little while after school then?

RUTH: Just hush, I said. (*Travis jabs his spoon into his cereal bowl viciously, and rests his head in anger upon his fists.*) If you through eating, you can get over there and make up your bed.

The boy obeys stiffly and crosses the room, almost mechanically, to the bed and more or less folds the bedding into a heap, then angrily gets his books and cap.

TRAVIS (*sulking and standing apart from her unnaturally*): I'm gone.

RUTH (*looking up from the stove to inspect him automatically*): Come here. (*He crosses to her and she studies his head.*) If you don't take this comb and fix this here head, you better! (TRAVIS *puts down his books with a great sigh of oppression, and crosses to the mirror. His mother mutters under her breath about his "stubbornness."*) 'Bout to march out of here with that head looking just like chickens slept in it! I just don't know where you get your stubborn ways . . . And get your jacket, too. Looks chilly out this morning.

TRAVIS (*with conspicuously brushed hair and jacket*): I'm gone.

RUTH: Get carfare and milk money—(*waving one finger*)—and not a single penny for no caps, you hear me?

TRAVIS (*with sullen politeness*): Yes'm.

He turns in outrage to leave. His mother watches after him as in his frustration he approaches the door almost comically. When she speaks to him, her voice has become a very gentle tease.

RUTH (*mocking; as she thinks he would say it*): Oh, Mama makes me so mad sometimes, I don't know what to do! (*She waits and continues to his back as he stands stock-still in front of the door.*) I wouldn't kiss that woman good-bye for nothing in this world this morning! (*The boy finally turns around and rolls his eyes at her, knowing the mood has changed and he is vindicated; he does not, however, move toward her yet.*) Not for nothing in this world! (*She finally laughs aloud at him and holds out her arms to him and we see that it is a way between them, very old and practiced. He crosses to her and allows her to embrace him warmly but keeps his face fixed with masculine rigidity. She holds him back from her presently and looks at him and runs her fingers over the features of his face. With utter gentleness.*) Now—whose little old angry man are you?

TRAVIS (*The masculinity and gruffness start to fade at last.*): Aw gaalee—Mama . . .

RUTH (*mimicking*): Aw—gaaaaalleeeee, Mama! (*She pushes him, with rough playfulness and finality, toward the door.*) Get on out of here or you going to be late.

TRAVIS (*in the face of love, new aggressiveness*): Mama, could I *please* go carry groceries?

RUTH: Honey, it's starting to get so cold evenings.

WALTER (*coming in from the bathroom and drawing a make-believe gun from a make-believe holster and shooting at his son*): What is it he wants to do?

RUTH: Go carry groceries after school at the supermarket.

WALTER: Well, let him go . . .

TRAVIS (*quickly, to the ally*): I *have* to—she won't gimme the fifty cents . . .

WALTER (*to his wife only*): Why not?

RUTH (*simply, and with flavor*): 'Cause we don't have it.

WALTER (*to RUTH only*): What you tell the boy things like that for? (*reaching down into his pants with a rather important gesture*) Here, son—

He hands the boy the coin, but his eyes are directed to his wife's. TRAVIS *takes the money happily.*

TRAVIS: Thanks, Daddy.

He starts out. RUTH *watches both of them with murder in her eyes.* WALTER *stands and stares back at her with defiance, and suddenly reaches into his pocket again on an afterthought.*

WALTER (*without even looking at his son, still staring hard at his wife*): In fact, here's another fifty cents . . . Buy yourself some fruit today—or take a taxicab to school or something!

TRAVIS: Whoopee—

He leaps up and clasps his father around the middle with his legs, and they face each other in mutual appreciation; slowly WALTER LEE *peeks around the boy to catch the violent rays from his wife's eyes and draws his head back as if shot.*

WALTER: You better get down now—and get to school, man.

TRAVIS (*at the door*): O.K. Good-bye.

He exits.

WALTER (*after him, pointing with pride*): That's *my* boy. (*She looks at him in disgust and turns back to her work.*) You know what I was thinking 'bout in the bathroom this morning?

RUTH: No.

WALTER: How come you always try to be so pleasant!

RUTH: What is there to be pleasant 'bout!

WALTER: You want to know what I was thinking 'bout in the bathroom or not!

RUTH: I know what you thinking 'bout.

WALTER (*ignoring her*): 'Bout what me and Willy Harris was talking about last night.

RUTH (*immediately—a refrain*): Willy Harris is a good-for-nothing loudmouth.

WALTER: Anybody who talks to me has got to be a good-for-nothing loudmouth, ain't he? And what you know about who is just a good-for-nothing loudmouth? Charlie Atkins was just a "good-for-nothing loudmouth" too, wasn't he! When he wanted me to go in the dry-cleaning business with him. And now—he's grossing a hundred thousand a year. A hundred thousand dollars a year! You still call *him* a loudmouth!

RUTH (*bitterly*): Oh, Walter Lee . . .

She folds her head on her arms over the table.

WALTER (*rising and coming to her and standing over her*): You tired, ain't you? Tired of everything. Me, the boy, the way we live—this beat-up hole—everything. Ain't you? (*She doesn't look up, doesn't answer.*) So tired—moaning and groaning all the time, but you wouldn't do nothing to help, would you? You couldn't be on my side that long for nothing, could you?

RUTH: Walter, please leave me alone.

WALTER: A man needs for a woman to back him up . . .

RUTH: Walter—

WALTER: Mama would listen to you. You know she listen to you more than she do me and Bennie. She think more of you. All you have to do is just sit down with her when you drinking your coffee one morning and talking 'bout things like you do and—(*He sits down beside her and demonstrates graphically what he thinks her methods and tone should be.*)—you just sip your coffee, see, and say easy like that you been thinking 'bout that deal Walter Lee is so interested in, 'bout the store and all, and sip some more coffee, like what you saying ain't really that important to you—And the next thing you know, she be listening good and asking you questions and when I come home—I can tell her the details. This ain't no fly-by-night proposition, baby. I mean we figured it out, me and Willy and Bobo.

RUTH (*with a frown*): Bobo?

WALTER: Yeah. You see, this little liquor store we got in mind cost seventy-five thousand and we figured the initial investment on the place be 'bout thirty thousand, see. That be ten thousand each. Course, there's a couple of hundred you got to pay so's you don't spend your life just waiting for them clowns to let your license get approved—

RUTH: You mean graft?

WALTER (*frowning impatiently*): Don't call it that. See there, that just goes to show you what women understand about the world. Baby, don't *nothing* happen for you in this world 'less you pay *somebody* off!

RUTH: Walter, leave me alone! (*she raises her head and stares at him vigorously—then says, more quietly*) Eat your eggs, they gonna be cold.

WALTER (*straightening up from her and looking off*): That's it. There you are. Man say to his woman: I got me a dream. His woman say: Eat your eggs. (*sadly, but gaining in power*) Man say: I got to take hold of this here world, baby! And a woman will say: Eat your eggs and go to work. (*passionately now*) Man say: I got to change my life, I'm choking to death, baby! And his woman say—(*in utter anguish as he brings his fists down on his thighs*)—Your eggs is getting cold!

RUTH (*softly*): Walter, that ain't none of our money.

WALTER (*not listening at all or even looking at her*): This morning, I was lookin' in the mirror and thinking about it . . . I'm thirty-five years old; I been married eleven years and I got a boy who sleeps in the living room—(*very, very quietly*)—and all I got to give him is stories about how rich white people live . . .

RUTH: Eat your eggs, Walter.

WALTER (*slams the table and jumps up*): DAMN MY EGGS—DAMN ALL THE EGGS THAT EVER WAS!

RUTH: Then go to work.

WALTER (*looking up at her*): See—I'm trying to talk to you 'bout myself—(*shaking his head with the repetition*)—and all you can say is eat them eggs and go to work.

RUTH (*wearily*): Honey, you never say nothing new. I listen to you every day, every night and every morning, and you never say nothing new. (*shrugging*) So you would rather *be* Mr. Arnold than be his chauffeur. So—I would *rather* be living in Buckingham Palace.

WALTER: That is just what is wrong with the colored woman in this world . . . Don't understand about building their men up and making 'em feel like they somebody. Like they can do something.

RUTH (*drily, but to hurt*): There *are* colored men who do things.

WALTER: No thanks to the colored woman.

RUTH: Well, being a colored woman, I guess I can't help myself none.

She rises and gets the ironing board and sets it up and attacks a huge pile of rough-dried clothes, sprinkling them in preparation for the ironing and then rolling them into tight fat balls.

WALTER (*mumbling*): We one group of men tied to a race of women with small minds!

His sister BENEATHA *enters. She is about twenty, as slim and intense as her brother. She is not as pretty as her sister-in-law, but her lean, almost intellectual face has a handsomeness of its own. She wears a bright-red flannel nightie, and her thick hair stands wildly about her head. Her speech is a mixture of many things; it is different from the rest of the family's insofar as education has permeated her sense of English—and perhaps the Midwest rather than the South has finally—at last—won out in her inflection; but not altogether, because over all of it is a soft slurring and transformed use of vowels which is the decided influence of the Southside. She passes through the room without looking at either* RUTH *or* WALTER *and goes to the outside door and looks, a little blindly, out to the bathroom. She sees that it has been lost to the Johnsons. She closes the door with a sleepy vengeance and crosses to the table and sits down a little defeated.*

BENEATHA: I am going to start timing those people.

WALTER: You should get up earlier.

BENEATHA (*Her face in her hands. She is still fighting the urge to go back to bed.*): Really—would you suggest dawn? Where's the paper?

WALTER (*pushing the paper across the table to her as he studies her almost clinically, as though he has never seen her before*): You a horrible-looking chick at this hour.

BENEATHA (*drily*): Good morning, everybody.

WALTER (*senselessly*): How is school coming?

BENEATHA (*in the same spirit*): Lovely. Lovely. And you know, biology is the greatest. (*looking up at him*) I dissected something that looked just like you yesterday.

WALTER: I just wondered if you've made up your mind and everything.

BENEATHA (*gaining in sharpness and impatience*): And what did I answer yesterday morning—and the day before that?

RUTH (*from the ironing board, like someone disinterested and old*): Don't be so nasty, Bennie.

BENEATHA (*still to her brother*): And the day before that and the day before that!

WALTER (*defensively*): I'm interested in you. Something wrong with that? Ain't many girls who decide—

WALTER *and* BENEATHA (*in unison*): —"to be a doctor."

Silence.

WALTER: Have we figured out yet just exactly how much medical school is going to cost?

RUTH: Walter Lee, why don't you leave that girl alone and get out of here to work?

BENEATHA (*exits to the bathroom and bangs on the door*): Come on out of there, please!

She comes back into the room.

WALTER (*looking at his sister intently*): You know the check is coming tomorrow.

BENEATHA (*turning on him with a sharpness all her own*): That money belongs to Mama, Walter, and it's for her to decide how she wants to use it. I don't care if she wants to buy a house or a rocket ship or just nail it up somewhere and look at it. It's hers. Not ours—*hers*.

WALTER (*bitterly*): Now ain't that fine! You just got your mother's interest at heart, ain't you, girl? You such a nice girl—but if Mama got that money she can always take a few thousand and help you through school too—can't she?

BENEATHA: I have never asked anyone around here to do anything for me!

WALTER: No! And the line between asking and just accepting when the time comes is big and wide—ain't it!

BENEATHA (*with fury*): What do you want from me, Brother—that I quit school or just drop dead, which!

WALTER: I don't want nothing but for you to stop acting holy 'round here. Me and Ruth done made some sacrifices for you—why can't you do something for the family?

RUTH: Walter, don't be dragging me in it.

WALTER: You are in it—Don't you get up and go work in somebody's kitchen for the last three years to help put clothes on her back?

RUTH: Oh, Walter—that's not fair . . .

WALTER: It ain't that nobody expects you to get on your knees and say thank you, Brother; thank you, Ruth; thank you, Mama—and thank you, Travis, for wearing the same pair of shoes for two semesters—

BENEATHA (*dropping to her knees*): Well—I *do*—all right?—thank everybody! And forgive me for ever wanting to be anything at all! (*pursuing him on her knees across the floor*) FORGIVE ME, FORGIVE ME, FORGIVE ME!

RUTH: Please stop it! Your mama'll hear you.

WALTER: Who the hell told you you had to be a doctor? If you so crazy 'bout messing 'round with sick people—then go be a nurse like other women—or just get married and be quiet . . .

BENEATHA: Well—you finally got it said . . . It took you three years but you finally got it said. Walter, give up; leave me alone—it's Mama's money.

WALTER: *He was my father, too!*

BENEATHA: So what? He was mine, too—and Travis' grandfather—but the insurance money belongs to Mama. Picking on me is not going to make her give it to you to invest in any liquor stores—(*underbreath, dropping into a chair*)—and I for one say, God bless Mama for that!

WALTER (*to* RUTH): See—did you hear? Did you hear!

RUTH: Honey, please go to work.

WALTER: Nobody in this house is ever going to understand me.

BENEATHA: Because you're a nut.

WALTER: Who's a nut?

BENEATHA: You—you are a nut. Thee is mad, boy.

WALTER (*looking at his wife and his sister from the door, very sadly*): The world's most backward race of people, and that's a fact.

BENEATHA (*turning slowly in her chair*): And then there are all those prophets who would lead us out of the wilderness—(WALTER *slams out of the house.*)—into the swamps!

RUTH: Bennie, why you always gotta be pickin' on your brother? Can't you be a little sweeter sometimes? (*Door opens.* WALTER *walks in. He fumbles with his cap, starts to speak, clears throat, looks everywhere but at* RUTH. *Finally.*)

WALTER (*to* RUTH): I need some money for carfare.

RUTH (*looks at him, then warms; teasing, but tenderly*): Fifty cents? (*She goes to her bag and gets money.*) Here—take a taxi!

WALTER *exits.* MAMA *enters. She is a woman in her early sixties, full-bodied and strong. She is one of those women of a certain grace and beauty who wear it so unobtrusively that it takes a while to notice. Her dark-brown face is surrounded by the total whiteness of her hair, and, being a woman who has adjusted to many things in life and overcome many more, her face is full of strength. She has, we can see, wit and faith of a kind that keep her eyes lit and full of interest and expectancy. She is, in a word, a beautiful woman. Her bearing is perhaps most like the noble bearing of the women of the Hereros of Southwest Africa—rather as if she imagines that as she walks she still bears a basket or a vessel upon her head. Her speech, on the other hand, is as careless as her carriage is precise—she is inclined to slur everything—but her voice is perhaps not so much quiet as simply soft.*

MAMA: Who that 'round here slamming doors at this hour?

She crosses through the room, goes to the window, opens it, and brings in a feeble little plant growing doggedly in a small pot on the window sill. She feels the dirt and puts it back out.

RUTH: That was Walter Lee. He and Bennie was at it again.

MAMA: My children and they tempers. Lord, if this little old plant don't get more sun than it's been getting it ain't never going to see spring again. (*She turns from the window.*) What's the matter with you this morning, Ruth? You looks right peaked. You aiming to iron all them things? Leave some for me. I'll get to 'em this afternoon. Bennie honey, it's too drafty for you to be sitting 'round half dressed. Where's your robe?

BENEATHA: In the cleaners.

MAMA: Well, go get mine and put it on.

BENEATHA: I'm not cold, Mama, honest.

MAMA: I know—but you so thin . . .

BENEATHA (*irritably*): Mama, I'm not cold.

MAMA (*seeing the make-down bed as* TRAVIS *has left it*): Lord have mercy, look at that poor bed. Bless his heart—he tries, don't he?

She moves to the bed TRAVIS *has sloppily made up.*

RUTH: No—he don't half try at all 'cause he knows you going to come along behind him and fix everything. That's just how come he don't know how to do nothing right now—you done spoiled that boy so.

MAMA (*folding bedding*): Well—he's a little boy. Ain't supposed to know 'bout housekeeping. My baby, that's what he is. What you fix for his breakfast this morning?

RUTH (*angrily*): I feed my son, Lena!

MAMA: I ain't meddling—(*underbreath; busy-bodyish*) I just noticed all last week he had cold cereal, and when it starts getting this chilly in the fall a child ought to have some hot grits or something when he goes out in the cold—

RUTH (*furious*): I gave him hot oats—is that all right!

MAMA: I ain't meddling. (*pause*) Put a lot of nice butter on it? (RUTH *shoots her an angry look and does not reply.*) He likes lots of butter.

RUTH (*exasperated*): Lena—

MAMA (*To* BENEATHA. MAMA *is inclined to wander conversationally sometimes.*): What was you and your brother fussing 'bout this morning?

BENEATHA: It's not important, Mama.

She gets up and goes to look out at the bathroom, which is apparently free, and she picks up her towels and rushes out.

MAMA: What was they fighting about?

RUTH: Now you know as well as I do.

MAMA (*shaking her head*): Brother still worrying hisself sick about that money?

RUTH: You know he is.

MAMA: You had breakfast?

RUTH: Some coffee.

MAMA: Girl, you better start eating and looking after yourself better. You almost thin as Travis.

RUTH: Lena—

MAMA: Un-hunh?

RUTH: What are you going to do with it?

MAMA: Now don't you start, child. It's too early in the morning to be talking about money. It ain't Christian.

RUTH: It's just that he got his heart set on that store—

MAMA: You mean that liquor store that Willy Harris want him to invest in?

RUTH: Yes—

MAMA: We ain't no business people, Ruth. We just plain working folks.

RUTH: Ain't nobody business people till they go into business. Walter Lee say colored people ain't never going to start getting ahead till they start gambling on some different kinds of things in the world—investments and things.

MAMA: What done got into you, girl? Walter Lee done finally sold you on investing.

RUTH: No. Mama, something is happening between Walter and me. I don't know what it is—but he needs something—something I can't give him any more. He needs this chance, Lena.

MAMA (*frowning deeply*): But liquor, honey—

RUTH: Well—like Walter says—I spec people going to always be drinking themselves some liquor.

MAMA: Well—whether they drinks it or not ain't none of my business. But whether I go into business selling it to 'em *is,* and I don't want that on my ledger this late in life. (*stopping suddenly and studying her daughter-in-law*) Ruth Younger, what's the matter with you today? You look like you could fall over right there.

RUTH: I'm tired.

MAMA: Then you better stay home from work today.

RUTH: I can't stay home. She'd be calling up the agency and screaming at them, "My girl didn't come in today—send me somebody! My girl didn't come in!" Oh, she just have a fit . . .

MAMA: Well, let her have it. I'll just call her up and say you got the flu—

RUTH (*laughing*): Why the flu?

MAMA: 'Cause it sounds respectable to 'em. Something white people get, too. They know 'bout the flu. Otherwise they think you been cut up or something when you tell 'em you sick.

RUTH: I got to go in. We need the money.

MAMA: Somebody would of thought my children done all but starved to death the way they talk about money here late. Child, we got a great big old check coming tomorrow.

RUTH (*sincerely, but also self-righteously*): Now that's your money. It ain't got nothing to do with me. We all feel like that—Walter and Bennie and me—even Travis.

MAMA (*thoughtfully, and suddenly very far away*): Ten thousand dollars—

RUTH: Sure is wonderful.

MAMA: Ten thousand dollars.

RUTH: You know what you should do, Miss Lena? You should take yourself a trip somewhere. To Europe or South America or someplace—

MAMA (*throwing up her hands at the thought*): Oh, child!

RUTH: I'm serious. Just pack up and leave! Go on away and enjoy yourself some. Forget about the family and have yourself a ball for once in your life—

MAMA (*drily*): You sound like I'm just about ready to die. Who'd go with me? What I look like wandering 'round Europe by myself?

RUTH: Shoot—these here rich white women do it all the time. They don't think nothing of packing up they suitcases and piling on one of them big steamships and—swoosh!—they gone, child.

MAMA: Something always told me I wasn't no rich white woman.

RUTH: Well—what are you going to do with it then?

MAMA: I ain't rightly decided. (*Thinking. She speaks now with emphasis.*) Some of it got to be put away for Beneatha and her schoolin'—and ain't nothing going to touch that part of it. Nothing. (*She waits several seconds, trying to make up her mind about something, and looks at* RUTH *a little tentatively before going on.*) Been thinking that we maybe could meet the notes on a little old two-story somewhere, with a yard where Travis could play in the summertime, if we use part of the insurance for a down payment and everybody kind of pitch in. I could maybe take on a little day work again, few days a week—

RUTH (*studying her mother-in-law furtively and concentrating on her ironing, anxious to encourage without seeming to*): Well, Lord knows, we've put enough rent into this here rat trap to pay for four houses by now . . .

MAMA (*looking up at the words "rat trap" and then looking around and leaning back and sighing—in a suddenly reflective mood*): "Rat trap"—yes, that's all it is. (*smiling*) I remember just as well the day me and Big Walter moved in here. Hadn't been married but two weeks and wasn't planning on living here no more than a year. (*She shakes her head at the dissolved dream.*) We was going to set away, little by little, don't you know, and buy a little place out in Morgan Park. We had even picked out the house. (*chuckling a little*) Looks right dumpy today. But Lord, child, you should know all the dreams I had 'bout buying that house and fixing it up and making me a little garden in the back—(*She waits and stops smiling.*) And didn't none of it happen.

Dropping her hands in a futile gesture.

RUTH (*keeps her head down, ironing*): Yes, life can be a barrel of disappointments, sometimes.

MAMA: Honey, Big Walter would come in here some nights back then and slump down on that couch there and just look at the rug, and look at me and look at the rug and then back at me—and I'd know he was down then . . . really down. (*After a second very long and thoughtful pause; she is seeing back to times that only she can see.*) And then, Lord, when I lost that baby—little Claude—I almost thought I was going to lose Big Walter too. Oh, that man grieved hisself! He was one man to love his children.

RUTH: Ain't nothin' can tear at you like losin' your baby.

MAMA: I guess that's how come that man finally worked hisself to death like he done. Like he was fighting his own war with this here world that took his baby from him.

RUTH: He sure was a fine man, all right. I always liked Mr. Younger.

MAMA: Crazy 'bout his children! God knows there was plenty wrong with Walter Younger—hard-headed, mean, kind of wild with women—plenty wrong with him. But he sure loved his children. Always wanted them to have something—be something. That's where Brother gets all these notions, I reckon. Big Walter used to say, he'd get right wet in the eyes sometimes, lean his head back with the water standing in his eyes and say, "Seem like God didn't see fit to give the black man nothing but dreams—but He did give us children to make them dreams seem worth while." (*She smiles.*) He could talk like that, don't you know.

RUTH: Yes, he sure could. He was a good man, Mr. Younger.

MAMA: Yes, a fine man—just couldn't never catch up with his dreams, that's all.

BENEATHA *comes in, brushing her hair and looking up to the ceiling, where the sound of a vacuum cleaner has started up.*

BENEATHA: What could be so dirty on that woman's rugs that she has to vacuum them every single day?

RUTH: I wish certain young women 'round here who I could name would take inspiration about certain rugs in a certain apartment I could also mention.

BENEATHA (*shrugging*): How much cleaning can a house need, for Christ's sakes.

MAMA (*not liking the Lord's name used thus*): Bennie!

RUTH: Just listen to her—just listen!

BENEATHA: Oh, God!

MAMA: If you use the Lord's name just one more time—

BENEATHA (*a bit of a whine*): Oh, Mama—

RUTH: Fresh—just fresh as salt, this girl!

BENEATHA (*drily*): Well—if the salt loses its savor—

MAMA: Now that will do. I just ain't going to have you 'round here reciting the scriptures in vain—you hear me?

BENEATHA: How did I manage to get on everybody's wrong side by just walking into a room?

RUTH: If you weren't so fresh—

BENEATHA: Ruth, I'm twenty years old.

MAMA: What time you be home from school today?

BENEATHA: Kind of late. (*with enthusiasm*) Madeline is going to start my guitar lessons today.

MAMA *and* RUTH *look up with the same expression.*

MAMA: Your *what* kind of lessons?

BENEATHA: Guitar.

RUTH: Oh, Father!

MAMA: How come you done taken it in your mind to learn to play the guitar?

BENEATHA: I just want to, that's all.

MAMA (*smiling*): Lord, child, don't you know what to do with yourself? How long it going to be before you get tired of this now—like you got tired of that little play-acting group you joined last year? (*looking at* RUTH) And what was it the year before that?

RUTH: The horseback-riding club for which she bought that fifty-five-dollar riding habit that's been hanging in the closet ever since!

MAMA (*to* BENEATHA): Why you got to flit so from one thing to another, baby?

BENEATHA (*sharply*): I just want to learn to play the guitar. Is there anything wrong with that?

MAMA: Ain't nobody trying to stop you. I just wonders sometimes why you has to flit so from one thing to another all the time. You ain't never done nothing with all that camera equipment you brought home—

BENEATHA: I don't flit! I—I experiment with different forms of expression—

RUTH: Like riding a horse?

BENEATHA: —People have to express themselves one way or another.

MAMA: What is it you want to express?

BENEATHA (*angrily*): Me! (MAMA *and* RUTH *look at each other and burst into raucous laughter.*) Don't worry—I don't expect you to understand.

MAMA (*to change the subject*): Who you going out with tomorrow night?

BENEATHA (*with displeasure*): George Murchison again.

MAMA (*pleased*): Oh—you getting a little sweet on him?

RUTH: You ask me, this child ain't sweet on nobody but herself—(*underbreath*) Express herself!

They laugh.

BENEATHA: Oh—I like George all right, Mama. I mean I like him enough to go out with him and stuff, but—

RUTH (*for devilment*): What does *and stuff* mean?

BENEATHA: Mind your own business.

MAMA: Stop picking at her now, Ruth. (*She chuckles—then a suspicious sudden look at her daughter as she turns in her chair for emphasis.*) What DOES it mean?

BENEATHA (*wearily*): Oh, I just mean I couldn't ever really be serious about George. He's—he's so shallow.

RUTH: Shallow—what do you mean he's shallow? He's *Rich!*

MAMA: Hush, Ruth.

BENEATHA: I know he's rich. He knows he's rich, too.

RUTH: Well—what other qualities a man got to have to satisfy you, little girl?

BENEATHA: You wouldn't even begin to understand. Anybody who married Walter could not possibly understand.

MAMA (*outraged*): What kind of way is that to talk about your brother?

BENEATHA: Brother is a flip—let's face it.

MAMA (*to* RUTH, *helplessly*): What's a flip?

RUTH (*glad to add kindling*): She's saying he's crazy.

BENEATHA: Not crazy. Brother isn't really crazy yet—he—he's an elaborate neurotic.

MAMA: Hush your mouth!

BENEATHA: As for George. Well. George looks good—he's got a beautiful car and he takes me to nice places and, as my sister-in-law says, he is probably the richest boy I will ever get to know and I even like him sometimes—but if the Youngers are sitting around waiting to see if their little Bennie is going to tie up the family with the Murchisons, they are wasting their time.

RUTH: You mean you wouldn't marry George Murchison if he asked you someday? That pretty, rich thing? Honey, I knew you was odd—

BENEATHA: No I would not marry him if all I felt for him was what I feel now. Besides, George's family wouldn't really like it.

MAMA: Why not?

BENEATHA: Oh, Mama—The Murchisons are honest-to-God-real-*live*-rich colored people, and the only people in the world who are more snobbish than rich white people are rich colored people. I thought everybody knew that. I've met Mrs. Murchison. She's a scene!

MAMA: You must not dislike people 'cause they well off, honey.

BENEATHA: Why not? It makes just as much sense as disliking people 'cause they are poor, and lots of people do that.

RUTH (*A wisdom-of-the-ages manner. To* MAMA.): Well, she'll get over some of this—

BENEATHA: Get over it? What are you talking about, Ruth? Listen, I'm going to be a doctor. I'm not worried about who I'm going to marry yet—if I ever get married.

MAMA *and* RUTH: *If!*

MAMA: Now, Bennie—

BENEATHA: Oh, I probably will . . . but first I'm going to be a doctor, and George, for one, still thinks that's pretty funny. I couldn't be bothered with that. I am going to be a doctor and everybody around here better understand that!

MAMA (*kindly*): 'Course you going to be a doctor, honey, God willing.

BENEATHA (*drily*): God hasn't got a thing to do with it.

MAMA: Beneatha—that just wasn't necessary.

BENEATHA: Well—neither is God. I get sick of hearing about God.

MAMA: Beneatha!

BENEATHA: I mean it! I'm just tired of hearing about God all the time. What has He got to do with anything? Does He pay tuition?

MAMA: You 'bout to get your fresh little jaw slapped!

RUTH: That's just what she needs, all right!

BENEATHA: Why? Why can't I say what I want to around here, like everybody else?

MAMA: It don't sound nice for a young girl to say things like that—you wasn't brought up that way. Me and your father went to trouble to get you and Brother to church every Sunday.

BENEATHA: Mama, you don't understand. It's all a matter of ideas, and God is just one idea I don't accept. It's not important. I am not going out and be immoral or commit crimes because I don't believe in God. I don't even think about it. It's just that I get tired of Him getting credit for all the things the human race achieves through its own stubborn effort. There simply is no blasted God—there is only man and it is *he* who makes miracles!

MAMA *absorbs this speech, studies her daughter and rises slowly and crosses to* BENEATHA *and slaps her powerfully across the face. After, there is only silence and the daughter drops her eyes from her mother's face, and* MAMA *is very tall before her.*

MAMA: Now—you say after me, in my mother's house there is still God. (*There is a long pause and* BENEATHA *stares at the floor wordlessly.* MAMA *repeats the phrase with precision and cool emotion.*) In my mother's house there is still God.

BENEATHA: In my mother's house there is still God.

A long pause.

MAMA (*Walking away from* BENEATHA, *too disturbed for triumphant posture. Stopping and turning back to her daughter.*): There are some ideas we ain't going to have in this house. Not long as I am at the head of this family.

BENEATHA: Yes, ma'am.

MAMA *walks out of the room.*

RUTH (*almost gently, with profound understanding*): You think you a woman, Bennie—but you still a little girl. What you did was childish—so you got treated like a child.

BENEATHA: I see. (*quietly*) I also see that everybody thinks it's all right for Mama to be a tyrant. But all the tyranny in the world will never put a God in the heavens!

She picks up her books and goes out. Pause.

RUTH (*goes to* MAMA'S *door*): She said she was sorry.

MAMA (*coming out, going to her plant*): They frightens me, Ruth. My children.

RUTH: You got good children, Lena. They just a little off sometimes—but they're good.

MAMA: No—there's something come down between me and them that don't let us understand each other and I don't know what it is. One done almost lost his mind thinking 'bout money all the time and the other done commence to talk about things I can't seem to understand in no form or fashion. What is it that's changing, Ruth.

RUTH (*soothingly, older than her years*): Now . . . you taking it all too seriously. You just got strong-willed children and it takes a strong woman like you to keep 'em in hand.

MAMA (*looking at her plant and sprinkling a little water on it*): They spirited all right, my children. Got to admit they got spirit—Bennie and Walter. Like this little old plant that ain't never had enough sunshine or nothing—and look at it . . .

She has her back to RUTH, *who has had to stop ironing and lean against something and put the back of her hand to her forehead.*

RUTH (*trying to keep* MAMA *from noticing*): You . . . sure . . . loves that little old thing, don't you? . . .

MAMA: Well, I always wanted me a garden like I used to see sometimes at the back of the houses down home. This plant is close as I ever got to having one. (*She looks out of the window as she replaces the plant.*) Lord, ain't nothing as dreary as the view from this window on a dreary day, is there? Why ain't you singing this morning, Ruth? Sing that "No Ways Tired." That song always lifts me up so—(*She turns at last to see that* RUTH *has slipped quietly to the floor, in a state of semiconsciousness.*) Ruth! Ruth honey—what's the matter with you . . . Ruth!

Curtain.

SCENE 2

It is the following morning; a Saturday morning, and house cleaning is in progress at the YOUNGERS. *Furniture has been shoved hither and yon and* MAMA *is giving the kitchen-area walls a washing down.* BENEATHA, *in dungarees, with a handkerchief tied around her face, is spraying insecticide into the cracks in the walls. As they work, the radio is on and a Southside disk-jockey program is inappropriately filling the house with a rather exotic saxophone blues.* TRAVIS, *the sole idle one, is leaning on his arms, looking out of the window.*

TRAVIS: Grandmama, that stuff Bennie is using smells awful. Can I go downstairs, please?

MAMA: Did you get all them chores done already? I ain't seen you doing much.

TRAVIS: Yes'm—finished early. Where did Mama go this morning?

MAMA (*looking at* BENEATHA): She had to go on a little errand.

The phone rings. BENEATHA *runs to answer it and reaches it before* WALTER, *who has entered from bedroom.*

TRAVIS: Where?

MAMA: To tend to her business.

BENEATHA: Haylo . . . (*disappointed*) Yes, he is. (*She tosses the phone to* WALTER, *who barely catches it.*) It's Willie Harris again.

WALTER (*as privately as possible under* MAMA's *gaze*): Hello, Willie. Did you get the papers from the lawyer? . . . No, not yet. I told you the mailman doesn't get here till ten-thirty . . . No, I'll come there . . . Yeah! Right away. (*He hangs up and goes for his coat.*)

BENEATHA: Brother, where did Ruth go?

WALTER (*as he exits*): How should I know!

TRAVIS: Aw come on, Grandma. Can I go outside?

MAMA: Oh, I guess so. You stay right in front of the house, though, and keep a good lookout for the postman.

TRAVIS: Yes'm. (*He darts into bedroom for stickball and bat, reenters, and sees* BENEATHA *on her knees spraying under sofa with behind upraised. He edges closer to the target, takes aim, and lets her have it. She screams.)* Leave them poor little cockroaches alone, they ain't bothering you none! *(He runs as she swings the spraygun at him viciously and playfully.)* Grandma! Grandma!

MAMA: Look out there, girl, before you be spilling some of that stuff on that child!

TRAVIS *(safely behind the bastion of* MAMA*)*: That's right—look out, now! *(He exits.)*

BENEATHA *(drily)*: I can't imagine that it would hurt him—it has never hurt the roaches.

MAMA: Well, little boys' hides ain't as tough as Southside roaches. You better get over there behind the bureau. I seen one marching out of there like Napoleon yesterday.

BENEATHA: There's really only one way to get rid of them, Mama—

MAMA: How?

BENEATHA: Set fire to this building! Mama, where did Ruth go?

MAMA *(looking at her with meaning)*: To the doctor, I think.

BENEATHA: The doctor? What's the matter? *(They exchange glances.)* You don't think—

MAMA *(with her sense of drama)*: Now I ain't saying what I think. But I ain't never been wrong 'bout a woman neither.

The phone rings.

BENEATHA *(at the phone)*: Hay-lo . . . *(pause, and a moment of recognition)* Well—when did you get back! . . . And how was it? . . . Of course I've missed you—in my way . . . This morning? No . . . house cleaning and all that and Mama hates it if I let people come over when the house is like this . . . You *have?* Well, that's different . . . What is it—Oh, what the hell, come on over . . . Right, see you then. *Arrividerci.*

She hangs up.

MAMA *(who has listened vigorously, as is her habit)*: Who is that you inviting over here with this house looking like this? You ain't got the pride you was born with!

BENEATHA: Asagai doesn't care how houses look, Mama—he's an intellectual.

MAMA: *Who?*

BENEATHA: Asagai—Joseph Asagai. He's an African boy I met on campus. He's been studying in Canada all summer.

MAMA: What's his name?

BENEATHA: Asagai, Joseph. Ah-sah-guy . . . He's from Nigeria.

MAMA: Oh, that's the little country that was founded by slaves way back . . .

BENEATHA: No, Mama—that's Liberia.

MAMA: I don't think I never met no African before.

BENEATHA: Well, do me a favor and don't ask him a whole lot of ignorant questions about Africans. I mean, do they wear clothes and all that—

MAMA: Well, now, I guess if you think we so ignorant 'round here maybe you shouldn't bring your friends here—

BENEATHA: It's just that people ask such crazy things. All anyone seems to know about when it comes to Africa is Tarzan—

MAMA (*indignantly*): Why should I know anything about Africa?

BENEATHA: Why do you give money at church for the missionary work?

MAMA: Well, that's to help save people.

BENEATHA: You mean save them from *heathenism*—

MAMA (*innocently*): Yes.

BENEATHA: I'm afraid they need more salvation from the British and the French.

RUTH *comes in forlornly and pulls off her coat with dejection. They both turn to look at her.*

RUTH (*dispiritedly*): Well, I guess from all the happy faces—everybody knows.

BENEATHA: You pregnant?

MAMA: Lord have mercy, I sure hope it's a little old girl. Travis ought to have a sister.

BENEATHA *and* RUTH *give her a hopeless look for this grandmotherly enthusiasm.*

BENEATHA: How far along are you?

RUTH: Two months.

BENEATHA: Did you mean to? I mean did you plan it or was it an accident?

MAMA: What do you know about planning or not planning?

BENEATHA: Oh, Mama.

RUTH (*wearily*): She's twenty years old, Lena.

BENEATHA: Did you plan it, Ruth?

RUTH: Mind your own business.

BENEATHA: It is my business—where is he going to live, on the *roof?* (*There is silence following the remark as the three women react to the sense of it.*) Gee—I didn't mean that, Ruth, honest. Gee, I don't feel like that at all. I—I think it is wonderful.

RUTH (*dully*): Wonderful.

BENEATHA: Yes—really. (*There is a sudden commotion from the street and she goes to the window to look out.*) What on earth is going on out there? These kids. (*There are, as she throws open the window, the shouts of children rising up from the street. She sticks her head out to see better and calls out.*) TRAVIS! TRAVIS! . . . WHAT ARE YOU DOING DOWN THERE? (*She sees.*) Oh Lord, they're chasing a rat!

RUTH *covers her face with hands and turns away.*

MAMA (*angrily*): Tell that youngun to get himself up here, at once!

BENEATHA: TRAVIS . . . YOU COME UPSTAIRS . . . AT ONCE!

RUTH (*her face twisted*): Chasing a rat . . .

MAMA (*looking at* RUTH, *worried*): Doctor say everything going to be all right?

RUTH (*far away*): Yes—she says everything is going to be fine . . .

MAMA (*immediately suspicious*): "She"—What doctor you went to?

RUTH *just looks at* MAMA *meaningfully and* MAMA *opens her mouth to speak as* TRAVIS *bursts in.*

TRAVIS (*excited and full of narrative, coming directly to his mother*): Mama, you should of seen the rat . . . Big as a cat, honest! (*He shows an exaggerated size with his hands.*) Gaaleee, that rat was really cuttin' and Bubber caught him with his heel and the janitor, Mr. Barnett, got him with a stick—and then they got him in a corner and—BAM! BAM! BAM!—and he was still jumping around and bleeding like everything too—there's rat blood all over the street—

RUTH *reaches out suddenly and grabs her son without even looking at him and clamps her hand over his mouth and holds him to her.* MAMA *crosses to them rapidly and takes the boy from her.*

MAMA: You hush up now . . . talking all that terrible stuff . . . (TRAVIS *is staring at his mother with a stunned expression.* BENEATHA *comes quickly and takes him away from his grandmother and ushers him to the door.*)

BENEATHA: You go back outside and play . . . but not with any rats. (*She pushes him gently out the door with the boy straining to see what is wrong with his mother.*)

MAMA (*worriedly hovering over* RUTH): Ruth honey—what's the matter with you—you sick?

RUTH *has her fists clenched on her thighs and is fighting hard to suppress a scream that seems to be rising in her.*

BENEATHA: What's the matter with her, Mama?

MAMA (*working her fingers in* RUTH'S *shoulders to relax her*): She be all right. Women gets right depressed sometimes when they get her way. (*speaking softly, expertly, rapidly*) Now you just relax. That's right . . . just lean back, don't think 'bout nothing at all . . . nothing at all—

RUTH: I'm all right . . .

The glassy-eyed look melts and then she collapses into a fit of heavy sobbing. The bell rings.

BENEATHA: Oh, my God—that must be Asagai.

MAMA (*to* RUTH): Come on now, honey. You need to lie down and rest awhile . . . then have some nice hot food.

They exit, RUTH'S *weight on her mother-in-law.* BENEATHA, *herself profoundly disturbed, opens the door to admit a rather dramatic-looking young man with a large package.*

ASAGAI: Hello, Alaiyo—

BENEATHA (*holding the door open and regarding him with pleasure*): Hello . . . (*long pause*) Well—come in. And please excuse everything. My mother was very upset about my letting anyone come here with the place like this.

ASAGAI (*coming into the room*): You look disturbed too . . . Is something wrong?

BENEATHA (*still at the door, absently*): Yes . . . we've all got acute ghetto-itus. (*She smiles and comes toward him, finding a cigarette and sitting.*) So—sit down! No! Wait! (*She whips the spraygun off sofa where she had left it and puts the cushions back. At last perches on arm of sofa. He sits.*) So, how was Canada?

ASAGAI (*a sophisticate*): Canadian.

BENEATHA (*looking at him*): Asagai, I'm very glad you are back.

ASAGAI (*looking back at her in turn*): Are you really?

BENEATHA: Yes—very.

ASAGAI: Why?—you were quite glad when I went away. What happened?

BENEATHA: You went away.

ASAGAI: Ahhhhhhhh.

BENEATHA: Before—you wanted to be so serious before there was time.

ASAGAI: How much time must there be before one knows what one feels?

BENEATHA (*Stalling this particular conversation. Her hands pressed together, in a deliberately childish gesture.*): What did you bring me?

ASAGAI (*handing her the package*): Open it and see.

BENEATHA (*eagerly opening the package and drawing out some records and the colorful robes of a Nigerian woman*): Oh, Asagai! . . . You got them for me! . . . How beautiful . . . and the records too! (*She lifts out the robes and runs to the mirror with them and holds the drapery up in front of herself.*)

ASAGAI (*coming to her at the mirror*): I shall have to teach you how to drape it properly. (*He flings the material about her for the moment and stands back to look at her.*) Ah—*Oh-pay-gay-day, oh-gbah-mu-shay.* (*a Yoruba exclamation for admiration*) You wear it well . . . very well . . . mutilated hair and all.

BENEATHA (*turning suddenly*): My hair—what's wrong with my hair?

ASAGAI (*shrugging*): Were you born with it like that?

BENEATHA (*reaching up to touch it*): No . . . of course not.

She looks back to the mirror, disturbed.

ASAGAI (*smiling*): How then?

BENEATHA: You know perfectly well how . . . as crinkly as yours . . . that's how.

ASAGAI: And it is ugly to you that way?

BENEATHA (*quickly*): Oh, no—not ugly . . . (*more slowly, apologetically*) But it's so hard to manage when it's, well—raw.

ASAGAI: And so to accommodate that—you mutilate it every week?

BENEATHA: It's not mutilation!

ASAGAI (*laughing aloud at her seriousness*): Oh . . . please! I am only teasing you because you are so very serious about these things. (*He stands back from her and folds his arms across his chest as he watches her pulling at her hair and frowning in the mirror.*) Do you remember the first time you met me at school? . . . (*He laughs.*) You came up to me and you said—and I thought you were the most serious little thing I had ever seen—you said: (*He imitates her.*) "Mr. Asagai—I want very much to talk with you. About Africa. You see, Mr. Asagai, I am looking for my *identity!*"

He laughs.

BENEATHA (*turning to him, not laughing*): Yes—

Her face is quizzical, profoundly disturbed.

ASAGAI (*still teasing and reaching out and taking her face in his hands and turning her profile to him*): Well . . . it is true that this is not so much a profile of a Hollywood queen as perhaps a queen of the Nile—(*a mock dismissal of the importance of the question*) But what does it matter? Assimilationism is so popular in your country.

BENEATHA (*wheeling, passionately, sharply*): I am not an assimilationist!

ASAGAI (*The protest hangs in the room for a moment and* ASAGAI *studies her, his laughter fading.*): Such a serious one. (*There is a pause.*) So—you like the robes? You must take excellent care of them—they are from my sister's personal wardrobe.

BENEATHA (*with incredulity*): You—you sent all the way home—for me?

ASAGAI (*with charm*): For you—I would do much more . . . Well, that is what I came for. I must go.

BENEATHA: Will you call me Monday?

ASAGAI: Yes . . . We have a great deal to talk about. I mean about identity and time and all that.

BENEATHA: Time?

ASAGAI: Yes. About how much time one needs to know what one feels.

BENEATHA: You see! You never understood that there is more than one kind of feeling which can exist between a man and a woman—or, at least, there should be.

ASAGAI (*shaking his head negatively but gently*): No. Between a man and a woman there need be only one kind of feeling. I have that for you . . . Now even . . . right this moment . . .

BENEATHA: I know—and by itself—it won't do. I can find that anywhere.

ASAGAI: For a woman it should be enough.

BENEATHA: I know—because that's what it says in all the novels that men write. But it isn't. Go ahead and laugh—but I'm not interested in being someone's little episode in America or—(*with feminine vengeance*)—one of them! (ASAGAI *has burst into laughter again.*) That's funny as hell, huh!

ASAGAI: It's just that every American girl I have known has said that to me. White—black—in this you are all the same. And the same speech, too!

BENEATHA (*angrily*): Yuk, yuk, yuk!

ASAGAI: It's how you can be sure that the world's most liberated women are not liberated at all. You all talk about it too much!

MAMA *enters and is immediately all social charm because of the presence of a guest.*

BENEATHA: Oh—Mama—this is Mr. Asagai.

MAMA: How do you do?

ASAGAI (*total politeness to an elder*): How do you do, Mrs. Younger. Please forgive me for coming at such an outrageous hour on a Saturday.

MAMA: Well, you are quite welcome. I just hope you understand that our house don't always look like this. (*chatterish*) You must come again. I would love to hear all about—(*not sure of the name*)—your country. I think it's so sad the way our American Negroes don't know nothing about Africa 'cept Tarzan and all that. And all that money they pour into these churches when they ought to be helping you people over there drive out them French and Englishmen done taken away your land.

The mother flashes a slightly superior look at her daughter upon completion of the recitation.

ASAGAI (*taken aback by this sudden and acutely unrelated expression of sympathy*): Yes . . . yes . . .

MAMA (*smiling at him suddenly and relaxing and looking him over*): How many miles is it from here to where you come from?

ASAGAI: Many thousands.

MAMA (*looking at him as she would* WALTER): I bet you don't half look after yourself, being away from your mama either. I spec you better come 'round here from time to time to get yourself some decent homecooked meals . . .

ASAGAI (*moved*): Thank you. Thank you very much. (*they are all quiet, then*) Well . . . I must go. I will call you Monday, Alaiyo.

MAMA: What's that he call you?

ASAGAI: Oh—"Alaiyo." I hope you don't mind. It is what you would call a nickname, I think. It is a Yoruba word. I am a Yoruba.

MAMA (*looking at* BENEATHA): I—I thought he was from—(*uncertain*)

ASAGAI (*understanding*): Nigeria is my country. Yoruba is my tribal origin—

BENEATHA: You didn't tell us what Alaiyo means . . . for all I know, you might be calling me Little Idiot or something . . .

ASAGAI: Well . . . let me see . . . I do not know how just to explain it . . . The sense of a thing can be so different when it changes languages.

BENEATHA: You're evading.

ASAGAI: No—really it is difficult . . . (*thinking*) It means . . . it means One for Whom Bread—Food—Is Not Enough. (*He looks at her.*) Is that all right?

BENEATHA (*understanding, softly*): Thank you.

MAMA (*looking from one to the other and not understanding any of it*): Well . . . that's nice . . . You must come see us again—Mr.—

ASAGAI: Ah-sah-guy . . .

MAMA: Yes . . . Do come again.

ASAGAI: Good-bye.

He exits.

MAMA (*after him*): Lord, that's a pretty thing just went out here! (*insinuatingly, to her daughter*) Yes, I guess I see why we done commence to get so interested in Africa 'round here. Missionaries my aunt Jenny!

She exits.

BENEATHA: Oh, Mama! . . .

She picks up the Nigerian dress and holds it up to her in front of the mirror again. She sets the headdress on haphazardly and then notices her hair again and clutches at it and then replaces the headdress and frowns at herself. Then she starts to wriggle in front of the mirror as she thinks a Nigerian woman might. TRAVIS *enters and stands regarding her.*

TRAVIS: What's the matter, girl, you cracking up?

BENEATHA: Shut up.

She pulls the headdress off and looks at herself in the mirror and clutches at her hair again and squinches her eyes as if trying to imagine something. Then, suddenly, she gets her raincoat and kerchief and hurriedly prepares for going out.

MAMA (*coming back into the room*): She's resting now. Travis, baby, run next door and ask Miss Johnson to please let me have a little kitchen cleanser. This here can is empty as Jacob's kettle.

TRAVIS: I just came in.

MAMA: Do as you told. (*He exits and she looks at her daughter.*) Where you going?

BENEATHA (*halting at the door*): To become a queen of the Nile!

She exits in a breathless blaze of glory. RUTH *appears in the bedroom doorway.*

MAMA: Who told you to get up?

RUTH: Ain't nothing wrong with me to be lying in no bed for. Where did Bennie go?

MAMA (*drumming her fingers*): Far as I could make out—to Egypt. (RUTH *just looks at her.*) What time is it getting to?

RUTH: Ten twenty. And the mailman going to ring that bell this morning just like he done every morning for the last umpteen years.

TRAVIS *comes in with the cleanser can.*

TRAVIS: She say to tell you that she don't have much.

MAMA (*angrily*): Lord, some people I could name sure is tight-fisted! (*directing her grandson*) Mark two cans of cleanser down on the list there. If she that hard up for kitchen cleanser, I sure don't want to forget to get her none!

RUTH: Lena—maybe the woman is just short on cleanser—

MAMA (*not listening*): Much baking powder as she done borrowed from me all these years, she could of done gone into the baking business!

The bell sounds suddenly and sharply and all three are stunned—serious and silent—mid-speech. In spite of all the other conversations and distractions of the morning, this is what they have been waiting for, even TRAVIS, *who looks helplessly from his mother to his grandmother.* RUTH *is the first to come to life again.*

RUTH (*to* TRAVIS): *Get down them steps, boy!*

TRAVIS *snaps to life and flies out to get the mail.*

MAMA (*her eyes wide, her hand to her breast*): You mean it done really come?

RUTH (*excited*): Oh, Miss Lena!

MAMA (*collecting herself*): Well . . . I don't know what we all so excited about 'round here for. We known it was coming for months.

RUTH: That's a whole lot different from having it come and being able to hold it in your hands . . . a piece of paper worth ten thousand dollars . . . (TRAVIS *bursts back into the room. He holds the envelope high above his head, like a little dancer, his face is radiant and he is breathless. He moves to his grandmother with sudden slow ceremony and puts the envelope into her hands. She accepts it, and then merely holds it and looks at it.*) Come on! Open it . . . Lord have mercy, I wish Walter Lee was here!

TRAVIS: Open it, Grandmama!

MAMA (*staring at it*): Now you all be quiet. It's just a check.

RUTH: Open it . . .

MAMA (*still staring at it*): Now don't act silly . . . We ain't never been no people to act silly 'bout no money—

RUTH (*swiftly*): We ain't never had none before—OPEN IT!

MAMA *finally makes a good strong tear and pulls out the thin blue slice of paper and inspects it closely. The boy and his mother study it raptly over* MAMA's *shoulders.*

MAMA: Travis! (*She is counting off with doubt.*) Is that the right number of zeros?

TRAVIS: Yes'm . . . ten thousand dollars. Gaalee, Grandmama, you rich.

MAMA (*She holds the check away from her, still looking at it. Slowly her face sobers into a mask of unhappiness.*): Ten thousand dollars. (*She hands it to* RUTH.) Put it away somewhere, Ruth. (*She does not look at* RUTH; *her eyes seem to be seeing something somewhere very far off.*) Ten thousand dollars they give you. Ten thousand dollars.

TRAVIS (*to his mother, sincerely*): What's the matter with Grandmama—don't she want to be rich?

RUTH (*distractedly*): You go on out and play now, baby. (TRAVIS *exits.* MAMA *starts wiping dishes absently, humming intently to herself.* RUTH *turns to her, with kind exasperation.*) You've gone and got yourself upset.

MAMA (*not looking at her*): I spec if it wasn't for you all . . . I would just put that money away or give it to the church or something.

RUTH: Now what kind of talk is that. Mr. Younger would just be plain mad if he could hear you talking foolish like that.

MAMA (*stopping and staring off*): Yes . . . he sure would. (*sighing*) We got enough to do with that money, all right. (*She halts then, and turns and looks at her daughter-in-law hard;* RUTH *avoids her eyes and* MAMA *wipes her hands with finality and starts to speak firmly to* RUTH.) Where did you go today, girl?

RUTH: To the doctor.

MAMA (*impatiently*): Now, Ruth . . . you know better than that. Old Doctor Jones is strange enough in his way but there ain't nothing 'bout him make somebody slip and call him "she"—like you done this morning.

RUTH: Well, that's what happened—my tongue slipped.

MAMA: You went to see that woman, didn't you?

RUTH (*defensively, giving herself away*): What woman you talking about?

MAMA (*angrily*): That woman who—

WALTER *enters in great excitement.*

WALTER: Did it come?

MAMA (*quietly*): Can't you give people a Christian greeting before you start asking about money?

WALTER (*to* RUTH): Did it come? (RUTH *unfolds the check and lays it quietly before him, watching him intently with thoughts of her own.* WALTER *sits down and grasps it close and counts off the zeros.*) Ten thousand dollars—(*He turns suddenly, frantically to his mother and draws some papers out of his breast pocket.*) Mama—look. Old Willy Harris put everything on paper—

MAMA: Son—I think you ought to talk to your wife . . . I'll go on out and leave you alone if you want—

WALTER: I can talk to her later—Mama, look—

MAMA: Son—

WALTER: WILL SOMEBODY PLEASE LISTEN TO ME TODAY!

MAMA (*quietly*): I don't 'low no yellin' in this house, Walter Lee, and you know it—(WALTER *stares at them in frustration and starts to speak several times.*) And there ain't going to be no investing in no liquor stores.

WALTER: But, Mama, you ain't even looked at it.

MAMA: I don't aim to have to speak on that again.

A long pause.

WALTER: You ain't looked at it and you don't aim to have to speak on that again? You ain't even looked at it and *you* have decided—(*crumpling his papers*) Well, *you* tell that to my boy tonight when you put him to sleep on the living-room couch . . . (*turning to* MAMA *and speaking directly to her*) Yeah—and tell it to my wife, Mama, tomorrow when she has to go out of here to look after somebody else's kids. And tell it to *me*, Mama, every time we need a new pair of curtains and I have to watch *you* go out and work in somebody's kitchen. Yeah, you tell me then!

WALTER *starts out.*

RUTH: Where you going?

WALTER: I'm going out!

RUTH: Where?

WALTER: Just out of this house somewhere—

RUTH (*getting her coat*): I'll come too.

WALTER: I don't want you to come!

RUTH: I got something to talk to you about, Walter.

WALTER: That's too bad.

MAMA (*still quietly*): Walter Lee—(*She waits and he finally turns and looks at her.*) Sit down.

WALTER: I'm a grown man, Mama.

MAMA: Ain't nobody said you wasn't grown. But you still in my house and my presence. And as long as you are—you'll talk to your wife civil. Now sit down.

RUTH (*suddenly*): Oh, let him go on out and drink himself to death! He makes me sick to my stomach! (*She flings her coat against him and exits to bedroom.*)

WALTER (*violently flinging the coat after her*): And you turn mine too, baby! (*The door slams behind her.*) That was my biggest mistake—

MAMA (*still quietly*): Walter, what is the matter with you?

WALTER: Matter with me? Ain't nothing the matter with *me!*

MAMA: Yes there is. Something eating you up like a crazy man. Something more than me not giving you this money. The past few years I been watching it happen to you. You get all nervous acting and kind of wild in the eyes—(WALTER *jumps up impatiently at her words.*) I said sit there now, I'm talking to you!

WALTER: Mama—I don't need no nagging at me today.

MAMA: Seem like you getting to a place where you always tied up in some kind of knot about something. But if anybody ask you 'bout it you just yell at 'em and bust out the house and go out and drink somewheres. Walter Lee, people can't live with that. Ruth's a good, patient girl in her way—but you getting to be too much. Boy, don't make the mistake of driving that girl away from you.

WALTER: Why—what she do for me?

MAMA: She loves you.

WALTER: Mama—I'm going out. I want to go off somewhere and be by myself for a while.

MAMA: I'm sorry 'bout your liquor store, son. It just wasn't the thing for us to do. That's what I want to tell you about—

WALTER: I got to go out, Mama—

He rises.

MAMA: It's dangerous, son.

WALTER: What's dangerous?

MAMA: When a man goes outside his home to look for peace.

WALTER (*beseechingly*): Then why can't there never be no peace in this house then?

MAMA: You done found it in some other house?

WALTER: No—there ain't no woman! Why do women always think there's a woman somewhere when a man gets restless. (*picks up the check*) Do you know what this money means to me? Do you know what this money can do for us? (*puts it back*) Mama—Mama—I want so many things . . .

MAMA: Yes, son—

WALTER: I want so many things that they are driving me kind of crazy . . . Mama—look at me.

MAMA: I'm looking at you. You a good-looking boy. You got a job, a nice wife, a fine boy and—

WALTER: A job. (*looks at her*) Mama, a job? I open and close car doors all day long. I drive a man around in his limousine and I say, "Yes, sir; no, sir; very good, sir; shall I take the Drive, sir?" Mama, that ain't no kind of job . . . that ain't nothing at all. (*very quietly*) Mama, I don't know if I can make you understand.

MAMA: Understand what, baby?

WALTER (*quietly*): Sometimes it's like I can see the future stretched out in front of me—just plain as day. The future, Mama. Hanging over there at the edge of my days. Just waiting for me—a big, looming blank space—full of *nothing*. Just waiting for *me*. But it don't have to be. (*Pause. Kneeling beside her chair.*) Mama—sometimes when I'm downtown and I pass them cool, quiet-looking restaurants where them white boys are sitting back and talking 'bout things . . . sitting there turning deals worth millions of dollars . . . sometimes I see guys don't look much older than me—

MAMA: Son—how come you talk so much 'bout money?

WALTER (*with immense passion*): Because it is life, Mama!

MAMA (*quietly*): Oh—(*very quietly*) So now it's life. Money is life. Once upon a time freedom used to be life—now it's money. I guess the world really do change . . .

WALTER: No—it was always money, Mama. We just didn't know about it.

MAMA: No . . . something has changed. (*She looks at him.*) You something new, boy. In my time we was worried about not being lynched and getting to the North if we could and how to stay alive and still have a pinch of dignity too . . . Now here come you and Beneatha—talking 'bout things we ain't never even thought about hardly, me and your daddy. You ain't satisfied or proud of nothing we done. I mean that you had a home; that we kept you out of trouble till you was grown; that you don't have to ride to work on the back of nobody's streetcar—You my children—but how different we done become.

WALTER (*A long beat. He pats her hand and gets up.*): You just don't understand, Mama, you just don't understand.

MAMA: Son—do you know your wife is expecting another baby? (WALTER *stands, stunned, and absorbs what his mother has said.*) That's what she wanted to talk to you about. (WALTER *sinks down into a chair.*) This ain't for me to be telling—but you ought to know. (*She waits.*) I think Ruth is thinking 'bout getting rid of that child.

WALTER (*slowly understanding*): No—no—Ruth wouldn't do that.

MAMA: When the world gets ugly enough—a woman will do anything for her family. *The part that's already living.*

WALTER: You don't know Ruth, Mama, if you think she would do that.

RUTH *opens the bedroom door and stands there a little limp.*

RUTH (*beaten*): Yes I would too, Walter. (*pause*) I gave her a five-dollar down payment.

There is total silence as the man stares at his wife and the mother stares at her son.

MAMA (*presently*): Well—(*tightly*) Well—son, I'm waiting to hear you say something . . . (*She waits.*) I'm waiting to hear how you be your father's son. Be the man he was . . . (*Pause. The silence shouts.*) Your wife say she going to destroy your child. And I'm waiting to hear you talk like him and say we a people who give children life, not who destroys them—(*She rises*). I'm waiting to see you stand up and look like your daddy and say we done give up one baby to poverty and that we ain't going to give up nary another one . . . I'm waiting.

WALTER: Ruth—(*He can say nothing.*)

MAMA: If you a son of mine, tell her! (WALTER *picks up his keys and his coat and walks out. She continues, bitterly.*) You . . . you are a disgrace to your father's memory. Somebody get me my hat!

Curtain.

Act Two

SCENE 1

TIME: *Later the same day.*

AT RISE: RUTH *is ironing again. She has the radio going. Presently* BENEATHA'S *bedroom door opens and* RUTH'S *mouth falls and she puts down the iron in fascination.*

RUTH: What have we got on tonight!

BENEATHA (*emerging grandly from the doorway so that we can see her thoroughly robed in the costume Asagai brought*): You are looking at what a well-dressed Nigerian woman wears—(*She parades for* RUTH, *her hair completely hidden by the headdress; she is coquettishly fanning herself with an ornate oriental fan, mistakenly more like Butterfly than any Nigerian that ever was.*) Isn't it beautiful? (*She promenades to the radio and, with an arrogant flourish, turns off the good loud blues that is playing.*) Enough of this assimilationist junk! (RUTH *follows her with her eyes as she goes to the phonograph and puts on a record and turns and waits ceremoniously for the music to come up. Then, with a shout—*) OCOMOGOSIAY!

RUTH *jumps. The music comes up, a lovely Nigerian melody.* BENEATHA *listens, enraptured, her eyes far away—"back to the past." She begins to dance.* RUTH *is dumfounded.*

RUTH: What kind of dance is that?

BENEATHA: A folk dance.

RUTH (*Pearl Bailey*): What kind of folks do that, honey?

BENEATHA: It's from Nigeria. It's a dance of welcome.

RUTH: Who you welcoming?

BENEATHA: The men back to the village.

RUTH: Where they been?

BENEATHA: How should I know—out hunting or something. Anyway, they are coming back now . . .

RUTH: Well, that's good.

BENEATHA (*with the record*):

    Alundi, alundi
    Alundi alunya
    Jop pu a jeepua
    Ang gu soooooooooo

    Ai yai yae . . .
    Ayehaye—alundi . . .

WALTER *comes in during this performance; he has obviously been drinking. He leans against the door heavily and watches his sister, at first with distaste. Then his eyes look off—"back to the past"—as he lifts both his fists to the roof, screaming.*

WALTER: YEAH . . . AND ETHIOPIA STRETCH FORTH HER HANDS AGAIN! . . .

RUTH (*drily, looking at him*): Yes—and Africa sure is claiming her own tonight. (*She gives them both up and starts ironing again.*)

WALTER (*all in a drunken, dramatic shout*): Shut up! . . . I'm digging them drums . . . them drums move me! . . . (*He makes his weaving way to his wife's face and leans in close to her.*) In my *heart of hearts*—(*He thumps his chest.*)—I am much warrior!

RUTH (*without even looking up*): In your heart of hearts you are much drunkard.

WALTER (*coming away from her and starting to wander around the room, shouting*): Me and Jomo . . . (*Intently, in his sister's face. She has stopped dancing to watch him in this unknown mood.*) That's my man, Kenyatta. (*shouting and thumping his chest*) FLAMING SPEAR! HOT DAMN! (*He is suddenly in possession of an imaginary spear and actively spearing enemies all over the room.*) OCOMOGOSIAY . . .

BENEATHA (*to encourage* WALTER, *thoroughly caught up with this side of him*): OCOMOGOSIAY, FLAMING SPEAR!

WALTER: THE LION IS WAKING . . . OWIMOWEH! (*He pulls his shirt open and leaps up on the table and gestures with his spear.*)

BENEATHA: OWIMOWEH!

WALTER (*On the table, very far gone, his eyes pure glass sheets. He sees what we cannot, that he is a leader of his people, a great chief, a descendant of Chaka, and that the hour to march has come.*): Listen, my black brothers—

BENEATHA: OCOMOGOSIAY!

WALTER: —Do you hear the waters rushing against the shores of the coastlands—

BENEATHA: OCOMOGOSIAY!

WALTER: —Do you hear the screeching of the cocks in yonder hills beyond where the chiefs meet in council for the coming of the mighty war—

BENEATHA: OCOMOGOSIAY!

And now the lighting shifts subtly to suggest the world of WALTER'S *imagination, and the mood shifts from pure comedy. It is the inner* WALTER *speaking: the Southside chauffeur has assumed an unexpected majesty.*

WALTER: —Do you hear the beating of the wings of the birds flying low over the mountains and the low places of our land—

BENEATHA: OCOMOGOSIAY!

WALTER: —Do you hear the singing of the women, singing the war songs of our fathers to the babies in the great houses? Singing the sweet war songs! (*The doorbell rings.*) OH, DO YOU HEAR, MY *BLACK* BROTHERS!

BENEATHA (*completely gone*): We hear you, Flaming Spear—

RUTH *shuts off the phonograph and opens the door.* GEORGE MURCHISON *enters.*

WALTER: Telling us to prepare for the GREATNESS OF THE TIME! (*Lights back to normal. He turns and sees* GEORGE.) Black Brother!

He extends his hand for the fraternal clasp.

GEORGE: Black Brother, hell!

RUTH (*having had enough, and embarrassed for the family*): Beneatha, you got company—what's the matter with you? Walter Lee Younger, get down off that table and stop acting like a fool . . .

WALTER *comes down off the table suddenly and makes a quick exit to the bathroom.*

RUTH: He's had a little to drink . . . I don't know what her excuse is.

GEORGE (*to* BENEATHA): Look honey, we're going *to* the theatre—we're not going to be *in* it . . . so go change, huh?

BENEATHA *looks at him and slowly, ceremoniously, lifts her hands and pulls off the headdress. Her hair is close-cropped and unstraightened.* GEORGE *freezes mid-sentence and* RUTH'S *eyes all but fall out of her head.*

GEORGE: What in the name of—

RUTH (*touching* BENEATHA'S *hair*): Girl, you done lost your natural mind!? Look at your head!

GEORGE: What have you done to your head—I mean your hair!

BENEATHA: Nothing—except cut it off.

RUTH: Now that's the truth—it's what ain't been done to it! You expect this boy to go out with you with your head all nappy like that?

BENEATHA (*looking at* GEORGE): That's up to George. If he's ashamed of his heritage—

GEORGE: Oh, don't be so proud of yourself, Bennie—just because you look eccentric.

BENEATHA: How can something that's natural be eccentric?

GEORGE: That's what being eccentric means—being natural. Get dressed.

BENEATHA: I don't like that, George.

RUTH: Why must you and your brother make an argument out of everything people say?

BENEATHA: Because I hate assimilationist Negroes!

RUTH: Will somebody please tell me what assimila-who-ever means!

GEORGE: Oh, it's just a college girl's way of calling people Uncle Toms—but that isn't what it means at all.

RUTH: Well, what does it mean?

BENEATHA (*cutting* GEORGE *off and staring at him as she replies to* RUTH): It means someone who is willing to give up his own culture and submerge himself completely in the dominant, and in this case *oppressive* culture!

GEORGE: Oh, dear, dear, dear! Here we go! A lecture on the African past! On our Great West African Heritage! In one second we will hear all about the great Ashanti empires; the great Songhay civilizations; and the great sculpture of Bénin—and then some poetry in the Bantu—and the whole monologue will end with the word *heritage!* (*nastily*) Let's face it, baby, your heritage is nothing but a bunch of raggedy-assed spirituals and some grass huts!

BENEATHA: GRASS HUTS! (RUTH *crosses to her and forcibly pushes her toward the bedroom.*) See there . . . you are standing there in your splendid igno-rance talking about people who were the first to smelt iron on the face of the earth! (RUTH *is pushing her through the door.*) The Ashanti were performing surgical operations when the English—(RUTH *pulls the door to, with* BENEATHA *on the other side, and smiles graciously at* GEORGE. BENEATHA *opens the door and shouts the end of the sentence defiantly at*

GEORGE.)—were still tatooing themselves with blue dragons! (*She goes back inside.*)

RUTH: Have a seat, George. (*They both sit.* RUTH *folds her hands rather primly on her lap, determined to demonstrate the civilization of the family.*) Warm, ain't it? I mean for September. (*pause*) Just like they always say about Chicago weather: If it's too hot or cold for you, just wait a minute and it'll change. (*She smiles happily at this cliché of clichés.*) Everybody say it's got to do with them bombs and things they keep setting off. (*pause*) Would you like a nice cold beer?

GEORGE: No, thank you. I don't care for beer. (*He looks at his watch.*) I hope she hurries up.

RUTH: What time is the show?

GEORGE: It's an eight-thirty curtain. That's just Chicago, though. In New York standard curtain time is eight forty.

He is rather proud of this knowledge.

RUTH (*properly appreciating it*): You get to New York a lot?

GEORGE (*offhand*): Few times a year.

RUTH: Oh—that's nice. I've never been to New York.

WALTER *enters. We feel he has relieved himself, but the edge of unreality is still with him.*

WALTER: New York ain't got nothing Chicago ain't. Just a bunch of hustling people all squeezed up together—being "Eastern."

He turns his face into a screw of displeasure.

GEORGE: Oh—you've been?

WALTER: *Plenty* of times.

RUTH (*shocked at the lie*): Walter Lee Younger!

WALTER (*staring her down*): Plenty! (*pause*) What we got to drink in this house? Why don't you offer this man some refreshment. (*to* GEORGE) They don't know how to entertain people in this house, man.

GEORGE: Thank you—I don't really care for anything.

WALTER (*feeling his head; sobriety coming*): Where's Mama?

RUTH: She ain't come back yet.

WALTER (*looking* MURCHISON *over from head to toe, scrutinizing his carefully casual tweed sports jacket over cashmere V-neck sweater over soft eyelet shirt and tie, and soft slacks, finished off with white buckskin shoes*): Why all you college boys wear them faggoty-looking white shoes?

RUTH: Walter Lee!

GEORGE MURCHISON *ignores the remark.*

WALTER (*to* RUTH): Well, they look crazy as hell—white shoes, cold as it is.

RUTH (*crushed*): You have to excuse him—

WALTER: No he don't! Excuse me for what? What you always excusing me for! I'll excuse myself when I needs to be excused! (*a pause*) They look as funny as them black knee socks Beneatha wears out of here all the time.

RUTH: It's the college *style,* Walter.

WALTER: Style, hell. She looks like she got burnt legs or something!

RUTH: Oh, Walter—

WALTER (*an irritable mimic*): Oh, Walter! Oh, Walter! (*to* MURCHISON) How's your old man making out? I understand you all going to buy that big hotel on the Drive? (*He finds a beer in the refrigerator, wanders over to* MURCHISON, *sipping and wiping his lips with the back of his hand, and straddling a chair backwards to talk to the other man.*) Shrewd move. Your old man is all right, man. (*tapping his head and half winking for emphasis*) I mean he knows how to operate. I mean he thinks *big*, you know what I mean, I mean for a *home*, you know? But I think he's kind of running out of ideas now. I'd like to talk to him. Listen, man, I got some plans that could turn this city upside down. I mean think like he does. *Big*. Invest big, gamble big, hell, lose *big* if you have to, you know what I mean. It's hard to find a man on this whole Southside who understands my kind of thinking—you dig? (*He scrutinizes* MURCHISON *again, drinks his beer, squints his eyes and leans in close, confidential, man to man.*) Me and you ought to sit down and talk sometimes, man. Man, I got me some ideas . . .

MURCHISON (*with boredom*): Yeah—sometimes we'll have to do that, Walter.

WALTER (*understanding the indifference, and offended*): Yeah—well, when you get the time, man. I know you a busy little boy.

RUTH: Walter, please—

WALTER (*bitterly, hurt*): I know ain't nothing in this world as busy as you colored college boys with your fraternity pins and white shoes . . .

RUTH (*covering her face with humiliation*): Oh, Walter Lee—

WALTER: I see you all the time—with the books tucked under your arms—going to your (*British A—a mimic*) "clahsses." And for what! What the hell you learning over there? Filling up your heads—(*counting off on his fingers*)—with the sociology and the psychology—but they teaching you how to be a man? How to take over and run the world? They teaching you how to run a rubber plantation or a steel mill? Naw—just to talk proper and read books and wear them faggoty-looking white shoes . . .

GEORGE (*looking at him with distaste, a little above it all*): You're all wacked up with bitterness, man.

WALTER (*intently, almost quietly, between the teeth, glaring at the boy*): And you—ain't you bitter, man? Ain't you just about had it yet? Don't you see no stars gleaming that you can't reach out and grab? You happy?—You contented son-of-a-bitch—you happy? You got it made? Bitter? Man, I'm a volcano. Bitter? Here I am a giant—surrounded by ants! Ants who can't even understand what it is the giant is talking about.

RUTH (*passionately and suddenly*): Oh, Walter—ain't you with nobody!

WALTER (*violently*): No! 'Cause ain't nobody with me! Not even my own mother!

RUTH: Walter, that's a terrible thing to say!

BENEATHA *enters, dressed for the evening in a cocktail dress and earrings, hair natural.*

GEORGE: Well—hey—(*crosses to* BENEATHA; *thoughtful, with emphasis, since this is a reversal*) You look great!

WALTER (*seeing his sister's hair for the first time*): What's the matter with your head?

BENEATHA (*tired of the jokes now*): I cut it off, Brother.

WALTER (*coming close to inspect it and walking around her*): Well, I'll be damned. So that's what they mean by the African bush . . .

BENEATHA: Ha ha. Let's go, George.

GEORGE (*looking at her*): You know something? I like it. It's sharp. I mean it really is. (*helps her into her wrap*)

RUTH: Yes—I think so, too. (*She goes to the mirror and starts to clutch at her hair.*)

WALTER: Oh no! You leave yours alone, baby. You might turn out to have a pin-shaped head or something!

BENEATHA: See you all later.

RUTH: Have a nice time.

GEORGE: Thanks. Good night. (*Half out the door, he reopens it. To* WALTER.) Good night, Prometheus!

> BENEATHA *and* GEORGE *exit.*

WALTER (*to* RUTH): Who is Prometheus?

RUTH: I don't know. Don't worry about it.

WALTER (*in fury, pointing after* GEORGE): See there—they get to a point where they can't insult you man to man—they got to go talk about something ain't nobody never heard of!

RUTH: How do you know it was an insult? (*to humor him*) Maybe Prometheus is a nice fellow.

WALTER: Prometheus! I bet there ain't even no such thing! I bet that simple-minded clown—

RUTH: Walter—

> *She stops what she is doing and looks at him.*

WALTER (*yelling*): Don't start!

RUTH: Start what?

WALTER: Your nagging! Where was I? Who was I with? How much money did I spend?

RUTH (*plaintively*): Walter Lee—why don't we just try to talk about it . . .

WALTER (*not listening*): I been out talking with people who understand me. People who care about the things I got on my mind.

RUTH (*wearily*): I guess that means people like Willy Harris.

WALTER: Yes, people like Willy Harris.

RUTH (*with a sudden flash of impatience*): Why don't you all just hurry up and go into the banking business and stop talking about it!

WALTER: Why? You want to know why? 'Cause we all tied up in a race of people that don't know how to do nothing but moan, pray and have babies!

> *The line is too bitter even for him and he looks at her and sits down.*

RUTH: Oh, Walter . . . (*softly*) Honey, why can't you stop fighting me?

WALTER (*without thinking*): Who's fighting you? Who even cares about you?

> *This line begins the retardation of his mood.*

RUTH: Well—(*She waits a long time, and then with resignation starts to put away her things.*) I guess I might as well go on to bed . . . (*more or less to herself*) I don't know where we lost it . . . but we have . . . (*then, to him*) I—I'm sorry about this new baby, Walter. I guess maybe I better go on and do what I started . . . I guess I just didn't realize how bad things was with us . . . I guess I just didn't realize—(*She starts out to the bedroom and stops.*) You want some hot milk?

WALTER: Hot milk?

RUTH: Yes—hot milk.

WALTER: Why hot milk?

RUTH: 'Cause after all that liquor you come home with you ought to have something hot in your stomach.

WALTER: I don't want no milk.

RUTH: You want some coffee then?

WALTER: No, I don't want no coffee. I don't want nothing hot to drink. (*almost plaintively*) Why you always trying to give me something to eat?

RUTH (*standing and looking at him helplessly*): What *else* can I give you, Walter Lee Younger?

She stands and looks at him and presently turns to go out again. He lifts his head and watches her going away from him in a new mood which began to emerge when he asked her "Who cares about you?"

WALTER: It's been rough, ain't it, baby? (*She hears and stops but does not turn around and he continues to her back.*) I guess between two people there ain't never as much understood as folks generally thinks there is. I mean like between me and you—(*She turns to face him.*) How we gets to the place where we scared to talk softness to each other. (*He waits, thinking hard himself.*) Why you think it got to be like that? (*He is thoughtful, almost as a child would be.*) Ruth, what is it gets into people ought to be close?

RUTH: I don't know, honey. I think about it a lot.

WALTER: On account of you and me, you mean? The way things are with us. The way something done come down between us.

RUTH: There ain't so much between us, Walter . . . Not when you come to me and try to talk to me. Try to be with me . . . a little even.

WALTER (*total honesty*): Sometimes . . . sometimes . . . I don't even know how to try.

RUTH: Walter—

WALTER: Yes?

RUTH (*coming to him, gently and with misgiving, but coming to him*): Honey . . . life don't have to be like this. I mean sometimes people can do things so that things are better . . . You remember how we used to talk when Travis was born . . . about the way we were going to live . . . the kind of house . . . (*She is stroking his head.*) Well, it's all starting to slip away from us . . .

He turns her to him and they look at each other and kiss, tenderly and hungrily. The door opens and MAMA *enters—*WALTER *breaks away and jumps up. A beat.*

WALTER: Mama, where have you been?

MAMA: My—them steps is longer than they used to be. Whew! (*She sits down and ignores him.*) How you feeling this evening, Ruth?

RUTH *shrugs, disturbed at having been interrupted and watching her husband knowingly.*

WALTER: Mama, where have you been all day?

MAMA (*still ignoring him and leaning on the table and changing to more comfortable shoes*): Where's Travis?

RUTH: I let him go out earlier and he ain't come back yet. Boy, is he going to get it!

WALTER: Mama!

MAMA (*as if she has heard him for the first time*): Yes, son?

WALTER: Where did you go this afternoon?

MAMA: I went downtown to tend to some business that I had to tend to.

WALTER: What kind of business?

MAMA: You know better than to question me like a child, Brother.

WALTER (*rising and bending over the table*): Where were you, Mama? (*bringing his fists down and shouting*) Mama, you didn't go do something with that insurance money, something crazy?

The front door opens slowly, interrupting him, and TRAVIS *peeks his head in, less than hopefully.*

TRAVIS (*to his mother*): Mama, I—

RUTH: "Mama I" nothing! You're going to get it, boy! Get on in that bedroom and get yourself ready!

TRAVIS: But I—

MAMA: Why don't you all never let the child explain hisself.

RUTH: Keep out of it now, Lena.

MAMA *clamps her lips together, and* RUTH *advances toward her son menacingly.*

RUTH: A thousand times I have told you not to go off like that—

MAMA (*holding out her arms to her grandson*): Well—at least let me tell him something. I want him to be the first one to hear . . . Come here, Travis. (*The boy obeys, gladly.*) Travis—(*She takes him by the shoulder and looks into his face.*)—you know that money we got in the mail this morning?

TRAVIS: Yes'm—

MAMA: Well—what you think your grandmama gone and done with that money?

TRAVIS: I don't know, Grandmama.

MAMA (*putting her finger on his nose for emphasis*): She went out and she bought you a house! (*The explosion comes from* WALTER *at the end of the revelation and he jumps up and turns away from all of them in a fury.* MAMA *continues, to* TRAVIS.) You glad about the house? It's going to be yours when you get to be a man.

TRAVIS: Yeah—I always wanted to live in a house.

MAMA: All right, gimme some sugar then—(TRAVIS *puts his arms around her neck as she watches her son over the boy's shoulder. Then, to* TRAVIS, *after the embrace.*) Now when you say your prayers tonight, you thank God and your grandfather—'cause it was him who give you the house—in his way.

RUTH (*taking the boy from* MAMA *and pushing him toward the bedroom*): Now you get out of here and get ready for your beating.

TRAVIS: Aw, Mama—

RUTH: Get on in there—(*closing the door behind him and turning radiantly to her mother-in-law*) So you went and did it!

MAMA (*quietly, looking at her son with pain*): Yes, I did.

RUTH (*raising both arms classically*): PRAISE GOD! (*Looks at* WALTER *a moment, who says nothing. She crosses rapidly to her husband.*) Please, honey—let me be glad . . . you be glad too. (*She has laid her hands on his shoulders, but he shakes himself free of her roughly, without turning to face her.*) Oh, Walter . . . a home . . . *a home.* (*She comes back to* MAMA.) Well—where is it? How big is it? How much it going to cost?

MAMA: Well—

RUTH: When we moving?

MAMA (*smiling at her*): First of the month.

RUTH (*throwing back her head with jubilance*): *Praise God!*

MAMA (*tentatively, still looking at her son's back turned against her and* RUTH): It's—it's a nice house too . . . (*She cannot help speaking directly to him. An imploring quality in her voice, her manner, makes her almost like a girl now.*) Three bedrooms—nice big one for you and Ruth . . . Me and Beneatha still have to share our room, but Travis have one of his own—and (*with difficulty*) I figure if the—new baby—is a boy, we could get one of them double-decker outfits . . . And there's a yard with a little patch of dirt where I could maybe get to grow me a few flowers . . . And a nice big basement . . .

RUTH: Walter honey, be glad—

MAMA (*still to his back, fingering things on the table*): 'Course I don't want to make it sound fancier than it is . . . It's just a plain little old house—but it's made good and solid—and it will be *ours.* Walter Lee—it makes a difference in a man when he can walk on floors that belong to *him* . . .

RUTH: Where is it?

MAMA (*frightened at this telling*): Well—well—it's out there in Clybourne Park—

RUTH's *radiance fades abruptly, and* WALTER *finally turns slowly to face his mother with incredulity and hostility.*

RUTH: Where?

MAMA (*matter-of-factly*): Four o six Clybourne Street, Clybourne Park.

RUTH: Clybourne Park? Mama, there ain't no colored people living in Clybourne Park.

MAMA (*almost idiotically*): Well, I guess there's going to be some now.

WALTER (*bitterly*): So that's the peace and comfort you went out and bought for us today!

MAMA (*raising her eyes to meet his finally*): Son—I just tried to find the nicest place for the least amount of money for my family.

RUTH (*trying to recover from the shock*): Well—well—'course I ain't one never been 'fraid of no crackers, mind you—but—well, wasn't there no other houses nowhere?

MAMA: Them houses they put up for colored in them areas way out all seem to cost twice as much as other houses. I did the best I could.

RUTH (*Struck senseless with the news, in its various degrees of goodness and trouble, she sits a moment, her fists propping her chin in thought, and then she starts to rise, bringing her fists down with vigor, the radiance spreading from cheek to cheek again.*): Well—well!—All I can say is—if this is my time in life—MY TIME—to say good-bye—(*And she builds with momentum as she starts to circle the room with an exuberant, almost tearfully happy release.*)—to these Goddamned cracking walls!—(*She pounds the walls.*)—and these marching roaches!—(*She wipes at an imaginary army of marching roaches.*)—and this cramped little closet which ain't now or never was no kitchen! . . . then I say it loud and good, HALLELUJAH! AND GOOD-BYE MISERY . . . I DON'T NEVER WANT TO SEE YOUR UGLY FACE AGAIN! (*She laughs joyously, having practically destroyed the apartment, and flings her arms up and lets them come down happily, slowly, reflectively, over her abdomen, aware for the first time perhaps that the life therein pulses with happiness and not despair.*) Lena?

MAMA (*moved, watching her happiness*): Yes, honey?

RUTH (*looking off*): Is there—is there a whole lot of sunlight?

MAMA (*understanding*): Yes, child, there's a whole lot of sunlight.

Long pause.

RUTH (*collecting herself and going to the door of the room* TRAVIS *is in*): Well—I guess I better see 'bout Travis. (*to* MAMA) Lord, I sure don't feel like whipping nobody today!

She exits.

MAMA (*The mother and son are left alone now and the mother waits a long time, considering deeply, before she speaks.*): Son—you—you understand what I done, don't you? (WALTER *is silent and sullen.*) I—I just seen my family falling apart today . . . just falling to pieces in front of my eyes . . . We couldn't of gone on like we was today. We was going backwards 'stead of forwards—talking 'bout killing babies and wishing each other was dead . . . When it gets like that in life—you just got to do something different, push on out and do something bigger . . . (*She waits.*) I wish you say something, son . . . I wish you'd say how deep inside you think I done the right thing—

WALTER (*crossing slowly to his bedroom door and finally turning there and speaking measuredly*): What you need me to say you done right for? *You* the head of this family. You run our lives like you want to. It was your money and you did what you wanted with it. So what you need for me to say it was all right for? (*bitterly, to hurt her as deeply as he knows is possible*) So you butchered up a dream of mine—you—who always talking 'bout your children's dreams . . .

MAMA: Walter Lee—

He just closes the door behind him. MAMA *sits alone, thinking heavily.*

Curtain.

SCENE 2

TIME: *Friday night. A few weeks later.*

AT RISE: *Packing crates mark the intention of the family to move.* BENEATHA *and* GEORGE *come in, presumably from an evening out again.*

GEORGE: O.K. . . . O.K., whatever you say . . . (*They both sit on the couch. He tries to kiss her. She moves away.*) Look, we've had a nice evening; let's not spoil it, huh? . . .

He again turns her head and tries to nuzzle in and she turns away from him, not with distaste but with momentary lack of interest; in a mood to pursue what they were talking about.

BENEATHA: I'm *trying* to talk to you.

GEORGE: We always talk.

BENEATHA: Yes—and I love to talk.

GEORGE (*exasperated; rising*): I know it and I don't mind it sometimes . . . I want you to cut it out, see—The moody stuff, I mean. I don't like it. You're a nice-looking girl . . . all over. That's all you need, honey, forget the atmosphere. Guys aren't going to go for the atmosphere—they're going to go for what they see. Be glad for that. Drop the Garbo routine. It doesn't go with you. As for myself, I want a nice—(*groping*)—simple (*thoughtfully*)—sophisticated girl . . . not a poet—O.K.?

He starts to kiss her, she rebuffs him again and he jumps up.

BENEATHA: Why are you angry, George?

GEORGE: Because this is stupid! I don't go out with you to discuss the nature of "quiet desperation" or to hear all about your thoughts—because the world will go on thinking what it thinks regardless—

BENEATHA: Then why read books? Why go to school?

GEORGE (*with artificial patience, counting on his fingers*): It's simple. You read books—to learn facts—to get grades—to pass the course—to get a degree. That's all—it has nothing to do with thoughts.

A long pause.

BENEATHA: I see. (*He starts to sit.*) Good night, George.

GEORGE *looks at her a little oddly, and starts to exit. He meets* MAMA *coming in.*

GEORGE: Oh—hello, Mrs. Younger.

MAMA: Hello, George, how you feeling?

GEORGE: Fine—fine, how are you?

MAMA: Oh, a little tired. You know them steps can get you after a day's work. You all have a nice time tonight?

GEORGE: Yes—a fine time. A fine time.

MAMA: Well, good night.

GEORGE: Good night. (*He exits.* MAMA *closes the door behind her.*) Hello, honey. What you sitting like that for?

BENEATHA: I'm just sitting.

MAMA: Didn't you have a nice time?

BENEATHA: No.

MAMA: No? What's the matter?

BENEATHA: Mama, George is a fool—honest. (*She rises.*)

MAMA (*Hustling around unloading the packages she has entered with. She stops.*): Is he, baby?

BENEATHA: Yes.

BENEATHA *makes up* TRAVIS' *bed as she talks.*

MAMA: You sure?

BENEATHA: Yes.

MAMA: Well—I guess you better not waste your time with no fools.

BENEATHA *looks up at her mother, watching her put groceries in the refrigerator. Finally she gathers up her things and starts into the bedroom. At the door she stops and looks back at her mother.*

BENEATHA: Mama—

MAMA: Yes, baby—

BENEATHA: Thank you.

MAMA: For what?

BENEATHA: For understanding me this time.

She exits quickly and the mother stands, smiling a little, looking at the place where BENEATHA *just stood.* RUTH *enters.*

RUTH: Now don't you fool with any of this stuff, Lena—

MAMA: Oh, I just thought I'd sort a few things out. Is Brother here?

RUTH: Yes.

MAMA (*with concern*): Is he—

RUTH (*reading her eyes*): Yes.

MAMA *is silent and someone knocks on the door.* MAMA *and* RUTH *exchange weary and knowing glances and* RUTH *opens it to admit the neighbor,* MRS. JOHNSON,* *who is a rather squeaky wide-eyed lady of no particular age, with a newspaper under her arm.*

MAMA (*changing her expression to acute delight and a ringing cheerful greeting*): Oh—hello, there, Johnson.

JOHNSON (*This is a woman who decided long ago to be enthusiastic about* EVERYTHING *in life and she is inclined to wave her wrist vigorously at the height of her exclamatory comments.*): Hello there, yourself! H'you this evening, Ruth?

---

*This character and the scene of her visit were cut from the original production and early editions of the play.

RUTH (*not much of a deceptive type*): Fine, Mis' Johnson, h'you?

JOHNSON: Fine. (*reaching out quickly, playfully, and patting* RUTH'S *stomach*) Ain't you starting to poke out none yet! (*She mugs with delight at the over-familiar remark and her eyes dart around looking at the crates and packing preparation;* MAMA's *face is a cold sheet of endurance.*) Oh, ain't we getting ready round here, though! Yessir! Lookathere! I'm telling you the Youngers is really getting ready to "move on up a little higher!"—Bless God!

MAMA (*a little drily, doubting the total sincerity of the Blesser*): Bless God.

JOHNSON: He's good, ain't He?

MAMA: Oh yes, He's good.

JOHNSON: I mean sometimes He works in mysterious ways . . . but He works, don't He!

MAMA (*the same*): Yes, He does.

JOHNSON: I'm just soooooo happy for y'all. And this here child—(*about* RUTH) looks like she could just pop open with happiness, don't she. Where's all the rest of the family?

MAMA: Bennie's gone to bed—

JOHNSON: Ain't no . . . (*The implication is pregnancy.*) sickness done hit you—I hope . . . ?

MAMA: No—she just tired. She was out this evening.

JOHNSON (*All is a coo, an emphatic coo.*): Aw—ain't that lovely. She still going out with the little Murchison boy?

MAMA (*drily*): Ummmm huh.

JOHNSON: That's lovely. You sure got lovely children, Younger. Me and Isaiah talks all the time 'bout what fine children you was blessed with. We sure do.

MAMA: Ruth, give Mis' Johnson a piece of sweet potato pie and some milk.

JOHNSON: Oh honey, I can't stay hardly a minute—I just dropped in to see if there was anything I could do. (*accepting the food easily*) I guess y'all seen the news what's all over the colored paper this week . . .

MAMA: No—didn't get mine yet this week.

JOHNSON (*lifting her head and blinking with the spirit of catastrophe*): You mean you ain't read 'bout them colored people that was bombed out their place out there?

RUTH *straightens with concern and takes the paper and reads it.* JOHNSON *notices her and feeds commentary.*

JOHNSON: Ain't it something how bad these here white folks is getting here in Chicago! Lord, getting so you think you right down in Mississippi! (*with a tremendous and rather insincere sense of melodrama*) 'Course I thinks it's wonderful how our folks keeps on pushing out. You hear some of these Negroes round here talking 'bout how they don't go where they ain't wanted and all that—but not me, honey! (*This is a lie.*) Wilhemenia Othella Johnson goes anywhere, any time she feels like it! (*with head movement for emphasis*) Yes I do! Why if we left it up to these here crackers, the poor niggers wouldn't have nothing—(*She clasps her hand over her mouth.*) Oh, I always forgets you don't 'low that word in your house.

MAMA (*quietly, looking at her*): No—I don't 'low it.

JOHNSON (*vigorously again*): Me neither! I was just telling Isaiah yesterday when he come using it in front of me—I said, "Isaiah, it's just like Mis' Younger says all the time—"

MAMA: Don't you want some more pie?

JOHNSON: No—no thank you; this was lovely. I got to get on over home and have my midnight coffee. I hear some people say it don't let them sleep but I finds I can't close my eyes right lessen I done had that laaaast cup of coffee . . . (*She waits. A beat. Undaunted.*) My Goodnight coffee, I calls it!

MAMA (*with much eye-rolling and communication between herself and* RUTH): Ruth, why don't you give Mis' Johnson some coffee.

RUTH *gives* MAMA *an unpleasant look for her kindness.*

JOHNSON (*accepting the coffee*): Where's Brother tonight?

MAMA: He's lying down.

JOHNSON: MMmmmmm, he sure gets his beauty rest, don't he? Good-looking man. Sure is a good-looking man! (*reaching out to pat* RUTH'S *stomach again*) I guess that's how come we keep on having babies around here. (*She winks at* MAMA.) One thing 'bout Brother, he always know how to have a *good* time. And soooooo ambitious! I bet it was his idea y'all moving out to Clybourne Park. Lord—I bet this time next month y'all's names will have been in the papers plenty—(*holding up her hands to mark off each word of the headline she can see in front of her*) "NEGROES INVADE CLYBOURNE PARK—BOMBED!"

MAMA (*She and* RUTH *look at the woman in amazement.*): We ain't exactly moving out there to get bombed.

JOHNSON: Oh, honey—you know I'm praying to God every day that don't nothing like that happen! But you have to think of life like it is—and these here Chicago peckerwoods is some baaaad peckerwoods.

MAMA (*wearily*): We done thought about all that Mis' Johnson.

BENEATHA *comes out of the bedroom in her robe and passes through to the bathroom.* MRS. JOHNSON *turns.*

JOHNSON: Hello there, Bennie!

BENEATHA (*crisply*): Hello, Mrs. Johnson.

JOHNSON: How is school?

BENEATHA (*crisply*): Fine, thank you. (*She goes out.*)

JOHNSON (*insulted*): Getting so she don't have much to say to nobody.

MAMA: The child was on her way to the bathroom.

JOHNSON: I know—but sometimes she act like ain't got time to pass the time of day with nobody ain't been to college. Oh—I ain't criticizing her none. It's just—you know how some of our young people gets when they get a little education. (MAMA *and* RUTH *say nothing, just look at her.*) Yes— well. Well, I guess I better get on home. (*unmoving*) 'Course I can understand how she must be proud and everything—being the only one in the family to make something of herself. I know just being a chauffeur ain't never satisfied Brother none. He shouldn't feel like that, though. Ain't nothing wrong with being a chauffeur.

MAMA: There's plenty wrong with it.

JOHNSON: What?

MAMA: Plenty. My husband always said being any kind of a servant wasn't a fit thing for a man to have to be. He always said a man's hands was made to make things, or to turn the earth with—not to drive nobody's car for 'em—or—(*She looks at her own hands.*) carry they slop jars. And my boy is just like him—he wasn't meant to wait on nobody.

JOHNSON (*rising, somewhat offended*): Mmmmmmmmmmm. The Youngers is too much for me! (*She looks around.*) You sure one proud-acting bunch of colored folks. Well—I always thinks like Booker T. Washington said that time—"Education has spoiled many a good plow hand"—

MAMA: Is that what old Booker T. said?

JOHNSON: He sure did.

MAMA: Well, it sounds just like him. The fool.

JOHNSON (*indignantly*): Well—he was one of our great men.

MAMA: Who said so?

JOHNSON (*nonplussed*): You know, me and you ain't never agreed about some things, Lena Younger. I guess I better be going—

RUTH (*quickly*): Good night.

JOHNSON: Good night. Oh—(*thrusting it at her*) You can keep the paper! (*with a trill*) 'Night.

MAMA: Good night, Mis' Johnson.

MRS. JOHNSON *exits.*

RUTH: If ignorance was gold . . .

MAMA: Shush. Don't talk about folks behind their backs.

RUTH: You do.

MAMA: I'm old and corrupted. (BENEATHA *enters.*) You was rude to Mis' Johnson, Beneatha, and I don't like it at all.

BENEATHA (*at her door*): Mama, if there are two things we, as a people, have got to overcome, one is the Ku Klux Klan—and the other is Mrs. Johnson. (*She exits.*)

MAMA: Smart aleck.

The phone rings.

RUTH: I'll get it.

MAMA: Lord, ain't this a popular place tonight.

RUTH (*at the phone*): Hello—Just a minute. (*goes to door*) Walter, it's Mrs. Arnold. (*Waits. Goes back to the phone. Tense.*) Hello. Yes, this is his wife speaking . . . He's lying down now. Yes . . . well, he'll be in tomorrow. He's been very sick. Yes—I know we should have called, but we were so sure he'd be able to come in today. Yes—yes, I'm very sorry. Yes . . . Thank you very much. (*She hangs up.* WALTER *is standing in the doorway of the bedroom behind her.*) That was Mrs. Arnold.

WALTER (*indifferently*): Was it?

RUTH: She said if you don't come in tomorrow that they are getting a new man . . .

WALTER: Ain't that sad—ain't that crying sad.

RUTH: She said Mr. Arnold has had to take a cab for three days . . . Walter, you ain't been to work for three days! (*This is a revelation to her.*)

Where you been, Walter Lee Younger? (WALTER *looks at her and starts to laugh.*) You're going to lose your job.

WALTER: That's right . . . (*He turns on the radio.*)

RUTH: Oh, Walter, and with your mother working like a dog every day—

A steamy, deep blues pours into the room.

WALTER: That's sad too—Everything is sad.

MAMA: What you been doing for these three days, son?

WALTER: Mama—you don't know all the things a man what got leisure can find to do in this city . . . What's this—Friday night? Well—Wednesday I borrowed Willy Harris' car and I went for a drive . . . just me and myself and I drove and drove . . . Way out . . . way past South Chicago, and I parked the car and I sat and looked at the steel mills all day long. I just sat in the car and looked at them big black chimneys for hours. Then I drove back and I went to the Green Hat. (*pause*) And Thursday—Thursday I borrowed the car again and I got in it and I pointed it the other way and I drove the other way—for hours—way, way up to Wisconsin, and I looked at the farms. I just drove and looked at the farms. Then I drove back and I went to the Green Hat. (*pause*) And today—today I didn't get the car. Today I just walked. All over the Southside. And I looked at the Negroes and they looked at me and finally I just sat down on the curb at Thirty-ninth and South Parkway and I just sat there and watched the Negroes go by. And then I went to the Green Hat. You all sad? You all depressed? And you know where I am going right now—

RUTH *goes out quietly.*

MAMA: Oh, Big Walter, is this the harvest of our days?

WALTER: You know what I like about the Green Hat? I like this little cat they got there who blows a sax . . . He blows. He talks to me. He ain't but 'bout five feet tall and he's got a conked head and his eyes is always closed and he's all music—

MAMA (*rising and getting some papers out of her handbag*): Walter—

WALTER: And there's this other guy who plays the piano . . . and they got a sound. I mean they can work on some music . . . They got the best little combo in the world in the Green Hat . . . You can just sit there and drink and listen to them three men play and you realize that don't nothing matter worth a damn, but just being there—

MAMA: I've helped do it to you, haven't I, son? Walter I been wrong.

WALTER: Naw—you ain't never been wrong about nothing, Mama.

MAMA: Listen to me, now. I say I been wrong, son. That I been doing to you what the rest of the world been doing to you. (*She turns off the radio.*) Walter—(*She stops and he looks up slowly at her and she meets his eyes pleadingly.*) What you ain't never understood is that I ain't got nothing, don't own nothing, ain't never really wanted nothing that wasn't for you. There ain't nothing as precious to me . . . There ain't nothing worth holding on to, money, dreams, nothing else—if it means—if it means it's going to destroy my boy. (*She takes an envelope out of her handbag and puts it in front of him and he watches her without speaking or moving.*) I paid the man thirty-five hundred dollars down on the house. That leaves sixty-five hundred dollars. Monday morning I want you to take this money and take three thousand dollars and put it in a savings account for Beneatha's medical schooling. The rest you put in a checking account—with your name on it. And from now on any penny that come out of it or that go in it is for you to look after. For you to decide. (*She drops her hands a little helplessly.*) It ain't much, but it's all I got in the world and I'm putting it in your hands. I'm telling you to be the head of this family from now on like you supposed to be.

WALTER (*stares at the money*): You trust me like that, Mama?

MAMA: I ain't never stop trusting you. Like I ain't never stop loving you.

She goes out, and WALTER *sits looking at the money on the table. Finally, in a decisive gesture, he gets up, and, in mingled joy and desperation, picks up the money. At the same moment,* TRAVIS *enters for bed.*

TRAVIS: What's the matter, Daddy? You drunk?

WALTER (*sweetly, more sweetly than we have ever known him*): No, Daddy ain't drunk. Daddy ain't going to never be drunk again . . .

TRAVIS: Well, good night, Daddy.

The FATHER *has come from behind the couch and leans over, embracing his son.*

WALTER: Son, I feel like talking to you tonight.

TRAVIS: About what?

WALTER: Oh, about a lot of things. About you and what kind of man you going to be when you grow up . . . Son—son, what do you want to be when you grow up?

TRAVIS: A bus driver.

WALTER (*laughing a little*): A what? Man, that ain't nothing to want to be!

TRAVIS: Why not?

WALTER: 'Cause, man—it ain't big enough—you know what I mean.

TRAVIS: I don't know then. I can't make up my mind. Sometimes Mama asks me that too. And sometimes when I tell her I just want to be like you—she says she don't want me to be like that and sometimes she says she does . . .

WALTER (*gathering him up in his arms*): You know what, Travis? In seven years you going to be seventeen years old. And things is going to be very different with us in seven years, Travis . . . One day when you are seventeen I'll come home—home from my office downtown somewhere—

TRAVIS: You don't work in no office, Daddy.

WALTER: No—but after tonight. After what your daddy gonna do tonight, there's going to be offices—a whole lot of offices . . .

TRAVIS: What you gonna do tonight, Daddy?

WALTER: You wouldn't understand yet, son, but your daddy's gonna make a transaction . . . a business transaction that's going to change our lives . . . That's how come one day when you 'bout seventeen years old I'll come home and I'll be pretty tired, you know what I mean, after a day of conferences and secretaries getting things wrong the way they do . . . 'cause an executive's life is hell, man—(*The more he talks the farther away he gets.*) And I'll pull the car up on the driveway . . . just a plain black

Chrysler, I think, with white walls—no—black tires. More elegant. Rich people don't have to be flashy . . . though I'll have to get something a little sportier for Ruth—maybe a Cadillac convertible to do her shopping in . . . And I'll come up the steps to the house and the gardener will be clipping away at the hedges and he'll say, "Good evening, Mr. Younger." And I'll say, "Hello, Jefferson, how are you this evening?" And I'll go inside and Ruth will come downstairs and meet me at the door and we'll kiss each other and she'll take my arm and we'll go up to your room to see you sitting on the floor with the catalogues of all the great schools in America around you . . . All the great schools in the world! And—and I'll say, all right son—it's your seventeenth birthday, what is it you've decided? . . . Just tell me where you want to go to school and you'll *go*. Just tell me, what it is you want to be—and you'll *be* it . . . Whatever you want to be—Yessir! (*He holds his arms open for* TRAVIS.) You just name it, son . . . (TRAVIS *leaps into them.*) and I hand you the world!

WALTER'S *voice has risen in pitch and hysterical promise and on the last line he lifts* TRAVIS *high.*

(Blackout.)

SCENE 3

TIME: *Saturday, moving day, one week later.*

Before the curtain rises, RUTH'S *voice, a strident, dramatic church alto, cuts through the silence.*

It is, in the darkness, a triumphant surge, a penetrating statement of expectation: "Oh, Lord, I don't feel no ways tired! Children, oh, glory hallelujah!"

As the curtain rises we see that RUTH *is alone in the living room, finishing up the family's packing. It is moving day. She is nailing crates and tying cartons.* BENEATHA *enters, carrying a guitar case, and watches her exuberant sister-in-law.*

RUTH: Hey!

BENEATHA (*putting away the case*): Hi.

RUTH (*pointing at a package*): Honey—look in that package there and see what I found on sale this morning at the South Center. (RUTH *gets up and moves to the package and draws out some curtains.*) Lookahere—hand-turned hems!

BENEATHA: How do you know the window size out there?

RUTH (*who hadn't thought of that*): Oh—Well, they bound to fit something in the whole house. Anyhow, they was too good a bargain to pass up. (RUTH *slaps her head, suddenly remembering something.*) Oh, Bennie—I meant to put a special note on that carton over there. That's your mama's good china and she wants 'em to be very careful with it.

BENEATHA: I'll do it.

BENEATHA *finds a piece of paper and starts to draw large letters on it.*

RUTH: You know what I'm going to do soon as I get in that new house?

BENEATHA: What?

RUTH: Honey—I'm going to run me a tub of water up to here . . . (*with her fingers practically up to her nostrils*) And I'm going to get in it—and I am going to sit . . . and sit . . . and sit in that hot water and the first person who knocks to tell *me* to hurry up and come out—

BENEATHA: Gets shot at sunrise.

RUTH (*laughing happily*): You said it, sister! (*noticing how large* BENEATHA *is absent-mindedly making the note*) Honey, they ain't going to read that from no airplane.

BENEATHA (*laughing herself*): I guess I always think things have more emphasis if they are big, somehow.

RUTH (*looking up at her and smiling*): You and your brother seem to have that as a philosophy of life. Lord, that man—done changed so 'round here. You know—you know what we did last night? Me and Walter Lee?

BENEATHA: What?

RUTH (*smiling to herself*): We went to the movies. (*looking at* BENEATHA *to see if she understands*) We went to the movies. You know the last time me and Walter went to the movies together?

BENEATHA: No.

RUTH: Me neither. That's how long it been. (*smiling again*) But we went last night. The picture wasn't much good, but that didn't seem to matter. We went—and we held hands.

BENEATHA: Oh, Lord!

RUTH: We held hands—and you know what?

BENEATHA: What?

RUTH: When we come out of the show it was late and dark and all the stores and things was closed up . . . and it was kind of chilly and there wasn't many people on the streets . . . and we was still holding hands, me and Walter.

BENEATHA: You're killing me.

WALTER *enters with a large package. His happiness is deep in him; he cannot keep still with his new-found exuberance. He is singing and wiggling and snapping his fingers. He puts his package in a corner and puts a phonograph record, which he has brought in with him, on the record player. As the music, soulful and sensuous, comes up he dances over to* RUTH *and tries to get her to dance with him. She gives in at last to his raunchiness and in a fit of giggling allows herself to be drawn into his mood. They dip and she melts into his arms in a classic, body-melding "slow drag."*

BENEATHA (*regarding them a long time as they dance, then drawing in her breath for a deeply exaggerated comment which she does not particularly mean*): Talk about—olddddddddddd-fashioneddddddd—Negroes!

WALTER (*stopping momentarily*): What kind of Negroes?

He says this is fun. He is not angry with her today, nor with anyone. He starts to dance with his wife again.

BENEATHA: Old-fashioned.

WALTER (*as he dances with* RUTH): You know, when these *New Negroes* have their convention—(*pointing at his sister*)—that is going to be the chairman of the Committee on Unending Agitation. (*He goes on dancing, then stops.*) Race, race, race! . . . Girl, I do believe you are the first person in the history of the entire human race to successfully brainwash yourself. (BENEATHA *breaks up and he goes on dancing. He stops again, enjoying his tease.*) Damn, even the N double A C P takes a holiday sometimes! (BENEATHA *and* RUTH *laugh. He dances with* RUTH *some more and starts to laugh and stops and pantomimes someone over an operating table.*) I can just see that chick someday looking down at some poor cat on an operating table and before she starts to slice him, she says . . . (*pulling his sleeves back maliciously*) "By the way, what are your views on civil rights down there? . . ."

He laughs at her again and starts to dance happily. The bell sounds.

BENEATHA: Sticks and stones may break my bones but . . . words will never hurt me!

BENEATHA *goes to the door and opens it as* WALTER *and* RUTH *go on with the clowning.* BENEATHA *is somewhat surprised to see a quiet-looking middle-aged white man in a business suit holding his hat and a briefcase in his hand and consulting a small piece of paper.*

MAN: Uh—how do you do, miss. I am looking for a Mrs.—(*He looks at the slip of paper.*) Mrs. Lena Younger? (*He stops short, struck dumb at the sight of the oblivious* WALTER *and* RUTH.)
BENEATHA (*smoothing her hair with slight embarrassment*): Oh—yes, that's my mother. Excuse me. (*She closes the door and turns to quiet the other two.*) Ruth! Brother! (*Enunciating precisely but soundlessly: "There's a white man at the door!" They stop dancing,* RUTH *cuts off the phonograph,* BENEATHA *opens the door. The man casts a curious quick glance at all of them.*) Uh—come in please.
MAN (*coming in*): Thank you.
BENEATHA: My mother isn't here just now. Is it business?
MAN: Yes . . . well, of a sort.
WALTER (*freely, the Man of the House*): Have a seat. I'm Mrs. Younger's son. I look after most of her business matters.

RUTH *and* BENEATHA *exchange amused glances.*

MAN (*regarding* WALTER, *and sitting*): Well—My name is Karl Lindner . . .
WALTER (*stretching out his hand*): Walter Younger. This is my wife—(RUTH *nods politely.*)—and my sister.
LINDNER: How do you do.
WALTER (*amiably, as he sits himself easily on a chair, leaning forward on his knees with interest and looking expectantly into the newcomer's face*): What can we do for you, Mr. Lindner!
LINDNER (*some minor shuffling of the hat and briefcase on his knees*): Well— I am a representative of the Clybourne Park Improvement Association—
WALTER (*pointing*): Why don't you sit your things on the floor?
LINDNER: Oh—yes. Thank you. (*He slides the briefcase and hat under the chair.*) And as I was saying—I am from the Clybourne Park Improvement

Association and we have had it brought to our attention at the last meeting that you people—or at least your mother—has bought a piece of residential property at—(*He digs for the slip of paper again.*)—four o six Clybourne Street . . .

WALTER: That's right. Care for something to drink? Ruth, get Mr. Lindner a beer.

LINDNER (*upset for some reason*): Oh—no, really. I mean thank you very much, but no thank you.

RUTH (*innocently*): Some coffee?

LINDNER: Thank you, nothing at all.

BENEATHA *is watching the man carefully.*

LINDNER: Well, I don't know how much you folks know about our organization. (*He is a gentle man; thoughtful and somewhat labored in his manner.*) It is one of these community organizations set up to look after—oh, you know, things like block upkeep and special projects and we also have what we call our New Neighbors Orientation Committee . . .

BENEATHA (*drily*): Yes—and what do they do?

LINDNER (*turning a little to her and then returning the main force to* WALTER): Well—it's what you might call a sort of welcoming committee, I guess. I mean they, we—I'm the chairman of the committee—go around and see the new people who move into the neighborhood and sort of give them the lowdown on the way we do things out in Clybourne Park.

BENEATHA (*with appreciation of the two meanings, which escape* RUTH *and* WALTER): Uh-huh.

LINDNER: And we also have the category of what the association calls—(*He looks elsewhere.*)—uh—special community problems . . .

BENEATHA: Yes—and what are some of those?

WALTER: Girl, let the man talk.

LINDNER (*with understated relief*): Thank you. I would sort of like to explain this thing in my own way. I mean I want to explain to you in a certain way.

WALTER: Go ahead.

LINDNER: Yes. Well. I'm going to try to get right to the point. I'm sure we'll all appreciate that in the long run.

BENEATHA: Yes.

WALTER: Be still now!

LINDNER: Well—

RUTH (*still innocently*): Would you like another chair—you don't look comfortable.

LINDNER (*more frustrated than annoyed*): No, thank you very much. Please. Well—to get right to the point I—(*A great breath, and he is off at last.*) I am sure you people must be aware of some of the incidents which have happened in various parts of the city when colored people have moved into certain areas—(BENEATHA *exhales heavily and starts tossing a piece of fruit up and down in the air.*) Well—because we have what I think is going to be a unique type of organization in American community life— not only do we deplore that kind of thing—but we are trying to do something about it. (BENEATHA *stops tossing and turns with a new and quizzical interest to the man.*) We feel—(*gaining confidence in his mission because of the interest in the faces of the people he is talking to*)—we feel that most of the trouble in this world, when you come right down to it—(*He hits his knee for emphasis.*)—most of the trouble exists because people just don't sit down and talk to each other.

RUTH (*nodding as she might in church, pleased with the remark*): You can say that again, mister.

LINDNER (*more encouraged by such affirmation*): That we don't try hard enough in this world to understand the other fellow's problem. The other guy's point of view.

RUTH: Now that's right.

BENEATHA *and* WALTER *merely watch and listen with genuine interest.*

LINDNER: Yes—that's the way we feel out in Clybourne Park. And that's why I was elected to come here this afternoon and talk to you people. Friendly like, you know, the way people should talk to each other and see if we couldn't find some way to work this thing out. As I say, the whole business is a matter of *caring* about the other fellow. Anybody can see that you are a nice family of folks, hard working and honest I'm sure. (BENEATHA *frowns slightly, quizzically, her head tilted regarding him.*) Today everybody knows what it means to be on the outside of *something*. And of course, there is always somebody who is out to take advantage of people who don't always understand.

WALTER: What do you mean?

LINDNER: Well—you see our community is made up of people who've worked hard as the dickens for years to build up that little community. They're not rich and fancy people; just hard-working, honest people who don't really have much but those little homes and a dream of the kind of community they want to raise their children in. Now, I don't say we are perfect and there is a lot wrong in some of the things they want. But you've got to admit that a man, right or wrong, has the right to want to have the neighborhood he lives in a certain kind of way. And at the moment the overwhelming majority of our people out there feel that people get along better, take more of a common interest in the life of the community, when they share a common background. I want you to believe me when I tell you that race prejudice simply doesn't enter into it. It is a matter of the people of Clybourne Park believing, rightly or wrongly, as I say, that for the happiness of all concerned that our Negro families are happier when they live in their *own* communities.

BENEATHA (*with a grand and bitter gesture*): This, friends, is the Welcoming Committee!

WALTER (*dumfounded, looking at* LINDNER): Is this what you came marching all the way over here to tell us?

LINDNER: Well, now we've been having a fine conversation. I hope you'll hear me all the way through.

WALTER (*tightly*): Go ahead, man.

LINDNER: You see—in the face of all the things I have said, we are prepared to make your family a very generous offer . . .

BENEATHA: Thirty pieces and not a coin less!

WALTER: Yeah?

LINDNER (*putting on his glasses and drawing a form out of the briefcase*): Our association is prepared, through the collective effort of our people, to buy the house from you at a financial gain to your family.

RUTH: Lord have mercy, ain't this the living gall!

WALTER: All right, you through?

LINDNER: Well, I want to give you the exact terms of the financial arrangement—

WALTER: We don't want to hear no exact terms of no arrangements. I want to know if you got any more to tell us 'bout getting together?

LINDER (*taking off his glasses*): Well—I don't suppose that you feel . . .

WALTER: Never mind how I feel—you got any more to say 'bout how people ought to sit down and talk to each other? . . . Get out of my house, man.

He turns his back and walks to the door.

LINDNER (*looking around at the hostile faces and reaching and assembling his hat and briefcase*): Well—I don't understand why you people are reacting this way. What do you think you are going to gain by moving into a neighborhood where you just aren't wanted and where some elements—well—people can get awful worked up when they feel that their whole way of life and everything they've ever worked for is threatened.

WALTER: Get out.

LINDER (*at the door, holding a small card*): Well—I'm sorry it went like this.

WALTER: Get out.

LINDNER (*almost sadly regarding* WALTER): You just can't force people to change their hearts, son.

He turns and put his card on a table and exits. WALTER *pushes the door to with stinging hatred, and stands looking at it.* RUTH *just sits and* BENEATHA *just stands. They say nothing.* MAMA *and* TRAVIS *enter.*

MAMA: Well—this all the packing got done since I left out of here this morning. I testify before God that my children got all the energy of the *dead!* What time the moving men due?

BENEATHA: Four o'clock. You had a caller, Mama.

She is smiling, teasingly.

MAMA: Sure enough—who?

BENEATHA (*her arms folded saucily*): The Welcoming Committee.

WALTER *and* RUTH *giggle.*

MAMA (*innocently*): Who?

BENEATHA: The Welcoming Committee. They said they're sure going to be glad to see you when you get there.

WALTER (*devilishly*): Yeah, they said they can't hardly wait to see your face.

Laughter.

MAMA (*sensing their facetiousness*): What's the matter with you all?

WALTER: Ain't nothing the matter with us. We just telling you 'bout the gentleman who came to see you this afternoon. From the Clybourne Park Improvement Association.

MAMA: What he want?

RUTH (*in the same mood as* BENEATHA *and* WALTER): To welcome you, honey.

WALTER: He said they can't hardly wait. He said the one thing they don't have, that they just *dying* to have out there is a fine family of fine colored people! (*to* RUTH *and* BENEATHA) Ain't that right!

RUTH (*mockingly*): Yeah! He left his card—

BENEATHA (*handing card to* MAMA): In case.

> MAMA *reads and throws it on the floor—understanding and looking off as she draws her chair up to the table on which she has put her plant and some sticks and some cord.*

MAMA: Father, give us strength. (*knowingly—and without fun*) Did he threaten us?

BENEATHA: Oh—Mama—they don't do it like that any more. He talked Brotherhood. He said everybody ought to learn how to sit down and hate each other with good Christian fellowship.

> *She and* WALTER *shake hands to ridicule the remark.*

MAMA (*sadly*): Lord, protect us . . .

RUTH: You should hear the money those folks raised to buy the house from us. All we paid and then some.

BENEATHA: What they think we going to do—eat 'em?

RUTH: No, honey, marry 'em.

MAMA (*shaking her head*): Lord, Lord, Lord . . .

RUTH: Well—that's the way the crackers crumble. (*a beat*) Joke.

BENEATHA (*laughingly noticing what her mother is doing*): Mama, what are you doing?

MAMA: Fixing my plant so it won't get hurt none on the way . . .

BENEATHA: Mama, you going to take *that* to the new house?

MAMA: Un-huh—

BENEATHA: That raggedy-looking old thing?

MAMA (*stopping and looking at her*): It expresses ME!

RUTH (*with delight, to* BENEATHA): So there, Miss Thing!

> WALTER *comes to* MAMA *suddenly and bends down behind her and squeezes her in his arms with all his strength. She is overwhelmed by the suddenness of it and, though delighted, her manner is like that of* RUTH *and* TRAVIS.

MAMA: Look out now, boy! You make me mess up my thing here!

WALTER (*His face lit, he slips down on his knees beside her, his arms still about her.*): Mama . . . you know what it means to climb up in the chariot?

MAMA (*gruffly, very happy*): Get on away from me now . . .

RUTH (*near the gift-wrapped package, trying to catch* WALTER'S *eye*): Psst—

WALTER: What the old song say, Mama . . .

RUTH: Walter—Now?

> *She is pointing at the package.*

WALTER (*speaking the lines, sweetly, playfully, in his mother's face*):
> I got wings . . . you got wings . . .
> All God's Children got wings . . .

MAMA: Boy—get out of my face and do some work . . .

WALTER:

> *When I get to heaven gonna put on my wings,*
> *Gonna fly all over God's heaven . . .*

BENEATHA (*teasingly, from across the room*): Everybody talking 'bout heaven ain't going there!

WALTER (*to* RUTH, *who is carrying the box across to them*): I don't know, you think we ought to give her that . . . Seems to me she ain't been very appreciative around here.

MAMA (*eyeing the box, which is obviously a gift*): What is that?

WALTER (*taking it from* RUTH *and putting it on the table in front of* MAMA): Well—what you all think? Should we give it to her?

RUTH: Oh—she was pretty good today.

MAMA: I'll good you—

She turns her eyes to the box again.

BENEATHA: Open it, Mama.

She stands up, looks at it, turns and looks at all of them, and then presses her hands together and does not open the package.

WALTER (*sweetly*): Open it, Mama. It's for you. (MAMA *looks in his eyes. It is the first present in her life without its being Christmas. Slowly she opens her package and lifts out, one by one, a brand-new sparkling set of gardening tools.* WALTER *continues, prodding.*) Ruth made up the note—read it . . .

MAMA (*picking up the card and adjusting her glasses*): "To our own Mrs. Miniver—Love from Brother, Ruth and Beneatha." Ain't that lovely . . .

TRAVIS (*tugging at his father's sleeve*): Daddy, can I give her mine now?

WALTER: All right, son. (TRAVIS *flies to get his gift.*)

MAMA: Now I don't have to use my knives and forks no more . . .

WALTER: Travis didn't want to go in with the rest of us, Mama. He got his own. (*somewhat amused*) We don't know what it is . . .

TRAVIS (*racing back in the room with a large hatbox and putting it in front of his grandmother*): Here!

MAMA: Lord have mercy, baby. You done gone and bought your grand-mother a hat?

TRAVIS (*very proud*): Open it!

She does and lifts out an elaborate, but very elaborate, wide gardening hat, and all the adults break up at the sight of it.

RUTH: Travis, honey, what is that?

TRAVIS (*who thinks it is beautiful and appropriate*): It's a gardening hat! Like the ladies always have on in the magazines when they work in their gardens.

BENEATHA (*giggling fiercely*): Travis—we were trying to make Mama Mrs. Miniver—not Scarlett O'Hara!

MAMA (*indignantly*): What's the matter with you all! This here is a beautiful hat! (*absurdly*) I always wanted me one just like it!

She pops it on her head to prove it to her grandson, and the hat is ludi-crous and considerably oversized.

RUTH: Hot dog! Go, Mama!

WALTER (*doubled over with laughter*): I'm sorry, Mama—but you look like you ready to go out and chop you some cotton sure enough!

They all laugh except MAMA, *out of deference to* TRAVIS' *feelings.*

MAMA (*gathering the boy up to her*): Bless your heart—this is the prettiest hat I ever owned—(WALTER, RUTH *and* BENEATHA *chime in—noisily, festively and insincerely congratulating* TRAVIS *on his gift.*) What are we all standing around here for? We ain't finished packin' yet. Bennie, you ain't packed one book.

The bell rings.

BENEATHA: That couldn't be the movers . . . it's not hardly two good yet—

BENEATHA *goes into her room.* MAMA *starts for door.*

WALTER (*turning, stiffening*): Wait—wait—I'll get it.

He stands and looks at the door.

MAMA: You expecting company, son?

WALTER (*just looking at the door*): Yeah—yeah . . .

MAMA *looks at* RUTH, *and they exchange innocent and unfrightened glances.*

MAMA (*not understanding*): Well, let them in, son.

BENEATHA (*from her room*): We need some more string.

MAMA: Travis—you run to the hardware and get me some string cord.

MAMA *goes out and* WALTER *turns and looks at* RUTH. TRAVIS *goes to a dish for money.*

RUTH: Why don't you answer the door, man?

WALTER (*suddenly bounding across the floor to embrace her*): 'Cause sometimes it hard to let the future begin! (*stooping down in her face*)
    I got wings! You got wings!
    All God's children got wings!

He crosses to the door and throws it open. Standing there is a very slight little man in a not too prosperous business suit and with haunted frightened eyes and a hat pulled down tightly, brim up, around his forehead. TRAVIS *passes between the men and exits.* WALTER *leans deep in the man's face, still in his jubilance.*

    When I get to heaven gonna put on my wings,
    Gonna fly all over God's heaven . . .

        The little man just stares at him.

    Heaven—

        Suddenly he stops and looks past the little man into the empty hallway.

    Where's Willy, man?

BOBO: He ain't with me.

WALTER (*not disturbed*): Oh—come on in. You know my wife.

BOBO (*dumbly, taking off his hat*): Yes—h'you, Miss Ruth.

RUTH (*quietly, a mood apart from her husband already, seeing* BOBO): Hello, Bobo.

WALTER: You right on time today . . . Right on time. That's the way! (*He slaps* BOBO *on his back.*) Sit down . . . lemme hear.

RUTH *stands stiffly and quietly in back of them, as though somehow she senses death, her eyes fixed on her husband.*

BOBO (*his frightened eyes on the floor, his hat in his hands*): Could I please get a drink of water, before I tell you about it, Walter Lee?

WALTER *does not take his eyes off the man.* RUTH *goes blindly to the tap and gets a glass of water and brings it to* BOBO.

WALTER: There ain't nothing wrong, is there?

BOBO: Lemme tell you—

WALTER: Man—didn't nothing go wrong?

BOBO: Lemme tell you—Walter Lee. (*looking at* RUTH *and talking to her more than to* WALTER) You know how it was. I got to tell you how it was. I mean first I got to tell you how it was all the way . . . I mean about the money I put in, Walter Lee . . .

WALTER (*with taut agitation now*): What about the money you put in?

BOBO: Well—it wasn't much as we told you—me and Willy—(*He stops.*) I'm sorry, Walter. I got a bad feeling about it. I got a real bad feeling about it . . .

WALTER: Man, what you telling me about all this for? . . . Tell me what happened in Springfield . . .

BOBO: Springfield.

RUTH (*like a dead woman*): What was supposed to happen in Springfield?

BOBO (*to her*): This deal that me and Walter went into with Willy—Me and Willy was going to go down to Springfield and spread some money 'round so's we wouldn't have to wait so long for the liquor license . . . That's what we were going to do. Everybody said that was the way you had to do, you understand, Miss Ruth?

WALTER: Man—what happened down there?

BOBO (*a pitiful man, near tears*): I'm trying to tell you, Walter.

WALTER (*screaming at him suddenly*): THEN TELL ME, GODDAMMIT . . . WHAT'S THE MATTER WITH YOU?

BOBO: Man . . . I didn't go to no Springfield, yesterday.

WALTER (*halted, life hanging in the moment*): Why not?

BOBO (*the long way, the hard way to tell*): 'Cause I didn't have no reasons to . . .

WALTER: Man, what are you talking about!

BOBO: I'm talking about the fact that when I got to the train station yesterday morning—eight o'clock like we planned . . . Man—*Willy didn't never show up.*

WALTER: Why . . . where was he . . . where is he?

BOBO: That's what I'm trying to tell you . . . I don't know . . . I waited six hours . . . I called his house . . . and I waited . . . six hours . . . I waited in that train station six hours . . . (*breaking into tears*) That was all the extra money I had in the world . . . (*looking up at* WALTER *with tears running down his face*) Man, *Willy is gone.*

WALTER: Gone, what you mean Willy is gone? Gone where? You mean he went by himself. You mean he went off to Springfield by himself— to take care of getting the license—(*turns and looks anxiously at* RUTH) You mean maybe he didn't want too many people in on the business down there? (*looks to* RUTH *again, as before*) You know Willy got his own ways. (*looks back to* BOBO) Maybe you was late yesterday and he just went on down there without you. Maybe—maybe—he's been callin' you at home tryin' to tell you what happened or something. Maybe— maybe—he just got sick. He's somewhere—he's got to be somewhere. We just got to find him—me and you got to find him. (*grabs* BOBO *senselessly by the collar and starts to shake him*) We got to!

BOBO (*in sudden angry, frightened agony*): What's the matter with you, Walter! *When a cat take off with your money he don't leave you no road maps!*

WALTER (*turning madly, as though he is looking for* WILLY *in every room*): Willy! . . . Willy . . . don't do it . . . Please don't do it . . . Man, not with that money . . . Man, please, not with that money . . . Oh, God . . . Don't let it be true . . . (*He is wandering around, crying out for* WILLY *and looking for him or perhaps for help from God.*) Man . . . I trusted you . . . Man, I put my life in your hands . . . (*He starts to crumple down on the floor as* RUTH *just covers her face in horror.* MAMA *opens the door and comes into the room, with* BENEATHA *behind her.*) Man . . . (*He starts to pound the floor with his fists, sobbing wildly.*) THAT MONEY IS MADE OUT OF MY FATHER'S FLESH—

BOBO (*standing over him helplessly*): I'm sorry, Walter . . . (*Only* WALTER'S *sobs reply.* BOBO *puts on his hat.*) I had my life staked on this deal, too . . .

He exits.

MAMA (*to* WALTER): Son—(*She goes to him, bends down to him, talks to his bent head.*) Son . . . Is it gone? Son, I gave you sixty-five hundred dollars. Is it gone? All of it? Beneatha's money too?

WALTER (*lifting his head slowly*): Mama . . . I never . . . went to the bank at all . . .

MAMA (*not wanting to believe him*): You mean . . . Your sister's school money . . . you used that too . . . Walter? . . .

WALTER: Yessss! All of it . . . It's all gone . . .

There is total silence. RUTH *stands with her face covered with her hands;* BENEATHA *leans forlornly against a wall, fingering a piece of red ribbon from the mother's gift.* MAMA *stops and looks at her son without recognition and then, quite without thinking about it, starts to beat him senselessly in the face.* BENEATHA *goes to them and stops it.*

BENEATHA: Mama!

MAMA *stops and looks at both of her children and rises slowly and wanders vaguely, aimlessly away from them.*

MAMA: I seen . . . him . . . night after night . . . come in . . . and look at that rug . . . and then look at me . . . the red showing in his eyes . . . the veins moving in his head . . . I seen him grow thin and old before he was forty . . . working and working and working like somebody's old horse . . . killing himself . . . and you—you give it all away in a day—(*She raises her arms to strike him again.*)

BENEATHA: Mama—

MAMA: Oh, God . . . (*She looks up to Him.*) Look down here—and show me the strength.

BENEATHA: Mama—

MAMA (*folding over*): Strength . . .

BENEATHA (*plaintively*): Mama . . .

MAMA: Strength!

Curtain.

Act Three

TIME: *An hour later.*

At curtain, there is a sullen light of gloom in the living room, gray light not unlike that which began the first scene of Act One. At left we can see WAL-TER within his room, alone with himself. He is stretched out on the bed, his shirt out and open, his arms under his head. He does not smoke, he does not cry out, he merely lies there, looking up at the ceiling, much as if he were alone in the world.

In the living room BENEATHA sits at the table, still surrounded by the now almost ominous packing crates. She sits looking off. We feel that this is a mood struck perhaps an hour before, and it lingers now, full of the empty sound of profound disappointment. We see on a line from her brother's bedroom the sameness of their attitudes. Presently the bell rings and BENEATHA rises without ambition or interest in answering. It is ASAGAI, smiling broadly, striding into the room with energy and happy expectation and conversation.

ASAGAI: I came over . . . I had some free time. I thought I might help with the packing. Ah, I like the look of packing crates! A household in preparation for a journey! It depresses some people . . . but for me . . . it is another feeling. Something full of the flow of life, do you understand? Movement, progress . . . It makes me think of Africa.

BENEATHA: Africa!

ASAGAI: What kind of a mood is this? Have I told you how deeply you move me?

BENEATHA: He gave away the money, Asagai . . .

ASAGAI: Who gave away what money?

BENEATHA: The insurance money. My brother gave it away.

ASAGAI: Gave it away?

BENEATHA: He made an investment! With a man even Travis wouldn't have trusted with his most worn-out marbles.

ASAGAI: And it's gone?

BENEATHA: Gone!

ASAGAI: I'm very sorry . . . And you, now?

BENEATHA: Me? . . . Me? . . . Me, I'm nothing . . . Me. When I was very small . . . We used to take our sleds out in the wintertime and the only hills we had were the ice-covered stone steps of some houses down the street. And we used to fill them in with snow and make them smooth and slide down them all day . . . and it was very dangerous, you know . . . far too steep . . . and sure enough one day a kid named Rufus came down too fast and hit the sidewalk and we saw his face just split open right there in front of us . . . And I remember standing there looking at his bloody open face thinking that was the end of Rufus. But the ambulance came and they took him to the hospital and they fixed the broken bones and they sewed it all up . . . and the next time I saw Rufus he just had a little line down the middle of his face . . . I never got over that . . .

ASAGAI: What?

BENEATHA: That that was what one person could do for another, fix him up—sew up the problem, make him all right again. That was the most marvelous thing in the world . . . I wanted to do that. I always thought it was the one concrete thing in the world that a human being could do. Fix up the sick, you know—and make them whole again. This was truly being God . . .

ASAGAI: You wanted to be God?

BENEATHA: No—I wanted to cure. It used to be so important to me. I wanted to cure. It used to matter. I used to care. I mean about people and how their bodies hurt . . .

ASAGAI: And you've stopped caring?

BENEATHA: Yes—I think so.

ASAGAI: Why?

BENEATHA (*bitterly*): Because it doesn't seem deep enough, close enough to what ails mankind! It was a child's way of seeing things—or an idealist's.

ASAGAI: Children see things very well sometimes—and idealists even better.

BENEATHA: I know that's what you think. Because you are still where I left off. You with all your talk and dreams about Africa! You still think you can patch up the world. Cure the Great Sore of Colonialism—(*loftily, mocking it*) with the Penicillin of Independence—!

ASAGAI: Yes!

BENEATHA: Independence *and then what?* What about all the crooks and thieves and just plain idiots who will come into power and steal and plunder the same as before—only now they will be black and do it in the name of the new Independence—WHAT ABOUT THEM?!

ASAGAI: That will be the problem for another time. First we must get there.

BENEATHA: And where does it end?

ASAGAI: End? Who even spoke of an end? To life? To living?

BENEATHA: An end to misery! To stupidity! Don't you see there isn't any real progress, Asagai, there is only one large circle that we march in, around and around, each of us with our own little picture in front of us—our own little mirage that we think is the future.

ASAGAI: That is the mistake.

BENEATHA: What?

ASAGAI: What you just said—about the circle. It isn't a circle—it is simply a long line—as in geometry, you know, one that reaches into infinity. And because we cannot see the end—we also cannot see how it changes. And it is very odd but those who see the changes—who dream, who will not give up—are called idealists . . . and those who see only the circle— we call *them* the "realists"!

BENEATHA: Asagai, while I was sleeping in that bed in there, people went out and took the future right out of my hands! And nobody asked me, nobody consulted me—they just went out and changed my life!

ASAGAI: Was it your money?

BENEATHA: What?

ASAGAI: Was it your money he gave away?

BENEATHA: It belonged to all of us.

ASAGAI: But did you earn it? Would you have had it at all if your father had not died?

BENEATHA: No.

ASAGAI: Then isn't there something wrong in a house—in a world—where all dreams, good or bad, must depend on the death of a man? I never thought to see *you* like this, Alaiyo. You! Your brother made a mistake and you are grateful to him so that now you can give up the ailing human race on account of it! You talk about what good is struggle, what good is anything! Where are we all going and why are we bothering!

BENEATHA: AND YOU CANNOT ANSWER IT!

ASAGAI (*shouting over her*): I LIVE THE ANSWER! (*pause*) In my village at home it is the exceptional man who can even read a newspaper . . . or who ever sees a book at all. I will go home and much of what I will have to say will seem strange to the people of my village. But I will teach and work and things will happen, slowly and swiftly. At times it will seem that nothing changes at all . . . and then again the sudden dramatic events which make history leap into the future. And then quiet again. Retrogression even. Guns, murder, revolution. And I even will have moments when I wonder if the quiet was not better than all that death and hatred. But I look about my village at the illiteracy and disease and ignorance and I will not wonder long. And perhaps . . . perhaps I will be a great man . . . I mean perhaps I will hold on to the substance of truth and find my way always with the right course . . . and perhaps for it I will be butchered in my bed some night by the servants of empire . . .

BENEATHA: *The martyr!*

ASAGAI (*He smiles.*): . . . or perhaps I shall live to be a very old man, respected and esteemed in my new nation . . . And perhaps I shall hold office and this is what I'm trying to tell you, Alaiyo: Perhaps the things I believe now for my country will be wrong and outmoded, and I will not understand and do terrible things to have things my way or merely to keep my power. Don't you see that there will be young men and women—not British soldiers then, but my own black countrymen—to step out of the shadows some evening and slit my then useless throat? Don't you see they have always been there . . . that they always will be. And that such a thing as my own death will be an advance? They who might kill me even . . . actually replenish all that I was.

BENEATHA: Oh, Asagai, I know all that.

ASAGAI: Good! Then stop moaning and groaning and tell me what you plan to do.

BENEATHA: Do?

ASAGAI: I have a bit of a suggestion.

BENEATHA: What?

ASAGAI (*rather quietly for him*): That when it is all over—that you come home with me—

BENEATHA (*staring at him and crossing away with exasperation*): Oh— Asagai—at this moment you decide to be romantic!

ASAGAI (*quickly understanding the misunderstanding*): My dear, young creature of the New World—I do not mean across the city—I mean across the ocean: home—to Africa.

BENEATHA (*slowly understanding and turning to him with murmured amazement*): To Africa?

ASAGAI: Yes! . . . (*smiling and lifting his arms playfully*) Three hundred years later the African Prince rose up out of the seas and swept the maiden back across the middle passage over which her ancestors had come—

BENEATHA (*unable to play*): To—to Nigeria?

ASAGAI: Nigeria. Home. (*coming to her with genuine romantic flippancy*) I will show you our mountains and our stars; and give you cool drinks from gourds and teach you the old songs and the ways of our people— and, in time, we will pretend that—(*very softly*)—you have only been away for a day. Say that you'll come—(*He swings her around and takes her full in his arms in a kiss which proceeds to passion.*)

BENEATHA (*pulling away suddenly*): You're getting me all mixed up—

ASAGAI: Why?

BENEATHA: Too many things—too many things have happened today. I must sit down and think. I don't know what I feel about anything right this minute.

She promptly sits down and props her chin on her fist.

ASAGAI (*charmed*): All right, I shall leave you. No—don't get up. (*touching her, gently, sweetly*) Just sit awhile and think . . . Never be afraid to sit awhile and think. (*He goes to door and looks at her.*) How often I have looked at you and said, "Ah—so this is what the New World hath finally wrought . . ."

He exits. BENEATHA *sits on alone. Presently* WALTER *enters from his room and starts to rummage through things, feverishly looking for something. She looks up and turns in her seat.*

BENEATHA (*hissingly*): Yes—just look at what the New World hath wrought! . . . Just look! (*She gestures with bitter disgust.*) There he is! *Monsieur le petit bourgeois noir*—himself! There he is—Symbol of a Rising Class! Entrepreneur! Titan of the system! (WALTER *ignores her completely and continues frantically and destructively looking for something and hurling things to floor and tearing things out of their place in his search.* BENEATHA *ignores the eccentricity of his actions and goes on with the monologue of insult.*) Did you dream of yachts on Lake Michigan,

Brother? Did you see yourself on that Great Day sitting down at the Conference Table, surrounded by all the mighty bald-headed men in America? All halted, waiting, breathless, waiting for your pronouncements on industry? Waiting for you—Chairman of the Board! (WALTER *finds what he is looking for—a small piece of white paper—and pushes it in his pocket and puts on his coat and rushes out without ever having looked at her. She shouts after him.*) I look at you and I see the final triumph of stupidity in the world!

The door slams and she returns to just sitting again. RUTH *comes quickly out of* MAMA's *room.*

RUTH: Who was that?

BENEATHA: Your husband.

RUTH: Where did he go?

BENEATHA: Who knows—maybe he has an appointment at U.S. Steel.

RUTH (*anxiously, with frightened eyes*): You didn't say nothing bad to him, did you?

BENEATHA: Bad? Say anything bad to him? No—I told him he was a sweet boy and full of dreams and everything is strictly peachy keen, as the ofay kids say!

MAMA *enters from her bedroom. She is lost, vague, trying to catch hold, to make some sense of her former command of the world, but it still eludes her. A sense of waste overwhelms her gait; a measure of apology rides on her shoulders. She goes to her plant, which has remained on the table, looks at it, picks it up and takes it to the window sill and sits it outside, and she stands and looks at it a long moment. Then she closes the window, straightens her body with effort and turns around to her children.*

MAMA: Well—ain't it a mess in here, though? (*a false cheerfulness, a beginning of something*) I guess we all better stop moping around and get some work done. All this unpacking and everything we got to do. (RUTH *raises her head slowly in response to the sense of the line; and* BENEATHA *in similar manner turns very slowly to look at her mother.*) One of you all better call the moving people and tell 'em not to come.

RUTH: Tell 'em not to come?

MAMA: Of course, baby. Ain't no need in 'em coming all the way here and having to go back. They charges for that too. (*She sits down, fingers to her brow, thinking.*) Lord, ever since I was a little girl, I always remembers people saying, "Lena—Lena Eggleston, you aims too high all the time. You needs to slow down and see life a little more like it is. Just slow down some." That's what they always used to say down home—"Lord, that Lena Eggleston is a high-minded thing. She'll get her due one day!"

RUTH: No, Lena . . .

MAMA: Me and Big Walter just didn't never learn right.

RUTH: Lena, no! We gotta go. Bennie—tell her . . . (*She rises and crosses to* BENEATHA *with her arms outstretched.* BENEATHA *doesn't respond.*) Tell her we can still move . . . the notes ain't but a hundred and twenty-five a month. We got four grown people in this house—we can work . . .

MAMA (*to herself*): Just aimed too high all the time—

RUTH (*turning and going to* MAMA *fast—the words pouring out with urgency and desperation*): Lena—I'll work . . . I'll work twenty hours a day in all the kitchens in Chicago . . . I'll strap my baby on my back if I have to and scrub all the floors in America and wash all the sheets in America if I have to—but we got to MOVE! We got to get OUT OF HERE!!

MAMA *reaches out absently and pats* RUTH's *hand.*

MAMA: No—I sees things differently now. Been thinking 'bout some of the things we could do to fix this place up some. I seen a second-hand bureau over on Maxwell Street just the other day that could fit right there. (*She points to where the new furniture might go.* RUTH *wanders away from her.*) Would need some new handles on it and then a little varnish and it look like something brand-new. And—we can put up them new curtains in the kitchen . . . Why this place be looking fine. Cheer us all up so that we forget trouble ever come . . . (*to* RUTH) And you could get some nice screens to put up in your room round the baby's bassinet . . . (*She looks at both of them, pleadingly.*) Sometimes you just got to know when to give up some things . . . and hold on to what you got . . .

WALTER *enters from the outside, looking spent and leaning against the door, his coat hanging from him.*

MAMA: Where you been, son?
WALTER (*breathing hard*): Made a call.
MAMA: To who, son?
WALTER: To The Man. (*He heads for his room.*)
MAMA: What man, baby?
WALTER (*stops in the door*): The Man, Mama. Don't you know who The Man is?
RUTH: Walter Lee?
WALTER: *The Man.* Like the guys in the streets say—The Man. Captain Boss—Mistuh Charley . . . Old Cap'n Please Mr. Bossman . . .
BENEATHA (*suddenly*): Lindner!
WALTER: That's right! That's good. I told him to come right over.
BENEATHA (*fiercely, understanding*): For what? What do you want to see him for!
WALTER (*looking at his sister*): We going to do business with him.
MAMA: What you talking 'bout, son?
WALTER: Talking 'bout life, Mama. You all always telling me to see life like it is. Well—I laid in there on my back today . . . and I figured it out. Life just like it is. Who gets and who don't get. (*He sits down with his coat on and laughs.*) Mama, you know it's all divided up. Life is. Sure enough. Between the takers and the "tooken." (*He laughs.*) I've figured it out finally. (*He looks around at them.*) Yeah. Some of us always getting "tooken." (*He laughs.*) People like Willy Harris, they don't never get "tooken." And you know why the rest of us do? 'Cause we all mixed up. Mixed up bad. We get to looking 'round for the right and the wrong; and we worry about it and cry about it and stay up nights trying to figure out 'bout the wrong and the right of things all the time . . . And all the time, man, them takers is out there operating, just taking and taking. Willy Harris? Shoot—Willy Harris don't even count. He don't even count in the big

scheme of things. But I'll say one thing for old Willy Harris . . . he's taught me something. He's taught me to keep my eye on what counts in this world. Yeah—(*shouting out a little*) Thanks, Willy!

RUTH: What did you call that man for, Walter Lee?

WALTER: Called him to tell him to come on over to the show. Gonna put on a show for the man. Just what he wants to see. You see, Mama, the man came here today and he told us that them people out there where you want us to move—well they so upset they willing to pay us *not* to move! (*He laughs again.*) And—and oh, Mama—you would of been proud of the way me and Ruth and Bennie acted. We told him to get out . . . Lord have mercy! We told the man to get out! Oh, we was some proud folks this afternoon, yeah. (*He lights a cigarette.*) We were still full of that old-time stuff . . .

RUTH (*coming toward him slowly*): You talking 'bout taking them people's money to keep us from moving in that house?

WALTER: I ain't just talking 'bout it, baby—I'm telling you that's what's going to happen!

BENEATHA: Oh, God! Where is the bottom! Where is the real honest-to-God bottom so he can't go any farther!

WALTER: See—that's the old stuff. You and that boy that was here today. You all want everybody to carry a flag and a spear and sing some marching songs, huh? You wanna spend your life looking into things and trying to find the right and the wrong part, huh? Yeah. You know what's going to happen to that boy someday—he'll find himself sitting in a dungeon, locked in forever—and the takers will have the key! Forget it, baby! There ain't no causes—there ain't nothing but taking in this world, and he who takes most is smartest—and it don't make a damn bit of difference *how*.

MAMA: You making something inside me cry, son. Some awful pain inside me.

WALTER: Don't cry, Mama. Understand. That white man is going to walk in that door able to write checks for more money than we ever had. It's important to him and I'm going to help him . . . I'm going to put on the show, Mama.

MAMA: Son—I come from five generations of people who was slaves and sharecroppers—but ain't nobody in my family never let nobody pay 'em no money that was a way of telling us we wasn't fit to walk the earth. We ain't never been that poor. (*raising her eyes and looking at him*) We ain't never been that—dead inside.

BENEATHA: Well—we are dead now. All the talk about dreams and sunlight that goes on in this house. It's all dead now.

WALTER: What's the matter with you all! I didn't make this world! It was give to me this way! Hell, yes, I want me some yachts someday! Yes, I want to hang some real pearls 'round my wife's neck. Ain't she supposed to wear no pearls? Somebody tell me—tell me, who decides which women is suppose to wear pearls in this world. I tell you I am a *man*—and I think my wife should wear some pearls in this world!

This last line hangs a good while and WALTER *begins to move about the room. The word "Man" has penetrated his consciousness; he mumbles it to himself repeatedly between strange agitated pauses as he moves about.*

MAMA: Baby, how you going to feel on the inside?

WALTER: Fine! . . . Going to feel fine . . . a man . . .

MAMA: You won't have nothing left then, Walter Lee.

WALTER (*coming to her*): I'm going to feel fine, Mama. I'm going to look that son-of-a-bitch in the eyes and say—(*He falters.*)—and say, "All right, Mr. Lindner—(*He falters even more.*)—that's *your* neighborhood out there! You got the right to keep it like you want! You got the right to have it like you want! Just write the check and—the house is yours." And—and I am going to say—(*His voice almost breaks.*) "And you—you people just put the money in my hand and you won't have to live next to this bunch of stinking niggers! . . ." (*He straightens up and moves away from his mother, walking around the room.*) And maybe—maybe I'll just get down on my black knees . . . (*He does so; RUTH and BENNIE and MAMA watch him in frozen horror.*) "Captain, Mistuh, Bossman—(*groveling and grinning and wringing his hands in profoundly anguished imitation of the slow-witted movie stereotype*) A-hee-hee-hee! Oh, yassuh boss! Yasssssuh! Great white—(*Voice breaking, he forces himself to go on.*)—Father, just gi' ussen de money, fo' God's sake, and we's—we's ain't gwine come out deh and dirty up yo' white folks neighborhood . . ." (*He breaks down completely.*) And I'll feel fine! Fine! FINE! (*He gets up and goes into the bedroom.*)

BENEATHA: That is not a man. That is nothing but a toothless rat.

MAMA: Yes—death done come in this here house. (*She is nodding, slowly, reflectively.*) Done come walking in my house on the lips of my children. You what supposed to be my beginning again. You—what supposed to be my harvest. (*to BENEATHA*) You—you mourning your brother?

BENEATHA: He's no brother of mine.

MAMA: What you say?

BENEATHA: I said that that individual in that room is no brother of mine.

MAMA: That's what I thought you said. You feeling like you better than he is today? (BENEATHA *does not answer.*) Yes? What you tell him a minute ago? That he wasn't a man? Yes? You give him up for me? You done wrote his epitaph too—like the rest of the world? Well, who give you the privilege?

BENEATHA: Be on my side for once! You saw what he just did, Mama! You saw him—down on his knees. Wasn't it you who taught me to despise any man who would do that? Do what he's going to do?

MAMA: Yes—I taught you that. Me and your daddy. But I thought I taught you something else too . . . I thought I taught you to love him.

BENEATHA: Love him? There is nothing left to love.

MAMA: There is *always* something left to love. And if you ain't learned that, you ain't learned nothing. (*looking at her*) Have you cried for that boy today? I don't mean for yourself and for the family 'cause we lost the money. I mean for him: what he been through and what it done to him. Child, when do you think is the time to love somebody the most? When they done good and made things easy for everybody? Well then, you ain't through learning—because that ain't the time at all. It's when he's at his lowest and can't believe in hisself 'cause the world done whipped him so! When you starts measuring somebody, measure him right, child, measure him right. Make sure you done taken into account what hills and valleys he come through before he got to wherever he is.

TRAVIS *bursts into the room at the end of the speech, leaving the door open.*

TRAVIS: Grandmama—the moving men are downstairs! The truck just pulled up.

MAMA (*turning and looking at him*): Are they, baby? They downstairs?

She sighs and sits. LINDNER *appears in the doorway. He peers in and knocks lightly, to gain attention, and comes in. All turn to look at him.*

LINDNER (*hat and briefcase in hand*): Uh-hello . . .

RUTH *crosses mechanically to the bedroom door and opens it and lets it swing open freely and slowly as the lights come up on* WALTER *within, still in his coat, sitting at the far corner of the room. He looks up and out through the room to* LINDNER.

RUTH: He's here.

A long minute passes and WALTER *slowly gets up.*

LINDNER (*coming to the table with efficiency, putting his briefcase on the table and starting to unfold papers and unscrew fountain pens*): Well, I certainly was glad to hear from you people. (WALTER *has begun the trek out of the room, slowly and awkwardly, rather like a small boy, passing the back of his sleeve across his mouth from time to time.*) Life can really be so much simpler than people let it be most of the time. Well—with whom do I negotiate? You, Mrs. Younger, or your son here? (MAMA *sits with her hands folded on her lap and her eyes closed as* WALTER *advances.* TRAVIS *goes closer to* LINDNER *and looks at the papers curiously.*) Just some official papers, sonny.

RUTH: Travis, you go downstairs—

MAMA (*opening her eyes and looking into* WALTER'S): No. Travis, you stay right here. And you make him understand what you doing, Walter Lee. You teach him good. Like Willy Harris taught you. You show where our five generations done come to. (WALTER *looks from her to the boy, who grins at him innocently.*) Go ahead, son—(*She folds her hands and closes her eyes.*) Go ahead.

WALTER (*at last crosses to* LINDNER, *who is reviewing the contract*): Well, Mr. Lindner. (BENEATHA *turns away.*) We called you—(*There is a profound, simple groping quality in his speech.*)—because, well, me and my family (*He looks around and shifts from one foot to the other.*) Well—we are very plain people . . .

LINDNER: Yes—

WALTER: I mean—I have worked as a chauffeur most of my life—and my wife here, she does domestic work in people's kitchens. So does my mother. I mean—we are plain people . . .

LINDNER: Yes, Mr. Younger—

WALTER (*really like a small boy, looking down at his shoes and then up at the man*): And—uh—well, my father, well, he was a laborer most of his life . . .

LINDNER (*absolutely confused*): Uh, yes—yes, I understand. (*He turns back to the contract.*)

WALTER (*a beat; staring at him*): And my father—(*with sudden intensity*) My father almost *beat a man to death* once because this man called him a bad name or something, you know what I mean?

LINDNER (*looking up, frozen*): No, no, I'm afraid I don't—

WALTER (*A beat. The tension hangs; then* WALTER *steps back from it.*): Yeah. Well—what I mean is that we come from people who had a lot of *pride*. I mean—we are very proud people. And that's my sister over there and she's going to be a doctor—and we are very proud—

LINDNER: Well—I am sure that is very nice, but—

WALTER: What I am telling you is that we called you over here to tell you that we are very proud and that this—(*signaling to* TRAVIS) Travis, come here. (TRAVIS *crosses and* WALTER *draws him before him facing the man.*) This is my son, and he makes the sixth generation of our family in this country. And we have all thought about your offer—

LINDNER: Well, good . . . good—

WALTER: And we have decided to move into our house because my father— my father—he earned it for us brick by brick. (MAMA *has her eyes closed and is rocking back and forth as though she were in church, with her head nodding the Amen yes.*) We don't want to make no trouble for nobody or fight no causes, and we will try to be good neighbors. And that's *all* we got to say about that. (*He looks the man absolutely in the eyes.*) We don't want your money. (*He turns and walks away.*)

LINDNER (*looking around at all of them*): I take it then—that you have decided to occupy . . .

BENEATHA: That's what the man said.

LINDNER (*to* MAMA *in her reverie*): Then I would like to appeal to you, Mrs. Younger. You are older and wiser and understand things better I am sure . . .

MAMA: I am afraid you don't understand. My son said we was going to move and there ain't nothing left for me to say. (*briskly*) You know how these young folks is nowadays, mister. Can't do a thing with 'em! (*As he opens his mouth, she rises.*) Good-bye.

LINDER (*folding up his materials*): Well—if you are that final about it . . . there is nothing left for me to say. (*He finishes, almost ignored by the family, who are concentrating on* WALTER LEE. *At the door* LINDNER *halts and looks around.*) I sure hope you people know what you're getting into.

He shakes his head and exits.

RUTH (*looking around and coming to life*): Well, for God's sake—if the moving men are here—LET'S GET THE HELL OUT OF HERE!

MAMA (*into action*): Ain't it the truth! Look at all this here mess. Ruth, put Travis' good jacket on him . . . Walter Lee, fix your tie and tuck your shirt in, you look like somebody's hoodlum! Lord have mercy, where is my plant? (*She flies to get it amid the general bustling of the family, who are deliberately trying to ignore the nobility of the past moment.*) You all start on down . . . Travis child, don't go empty-handed . . . Ruth, where did I

put that box with my skillets in it? I want to be in charge of it myself . . .
I'm going to make us the biggest dinner we ever ate tonight . . .
Beneatha, what's the matter with them stockings? Pull them things up,
girl . . .

*The family starts to file out as two moving men appear and begin to carry
out the heavier pieces of furniture, bumping into the family as they move
about.*

BENEATHA: Mama, Asagai asked me to marry him today and go to Africa—
MAMA (*in the middle of her getting-ready activity*): He did? You ain't old
enough to marry nobody—(*seeing the moving men lifting one of her
chairs precariously*) Darling, that ain't no bale of cotton, please handle it
so we can sit in it again! I had that chair twenty-five years . . .

The movers sigh with exasperation and go on with their work.

BENEATHA (*girlishly and unreasonably trying to pursue the conversation*): To
go to Africa, Mama—be a doctor in Africa . . .
MAMA (*distracted*): Yes, baby—
WALTER: *Africa!* What he want you to go to Africa for?
BENEATHA: To practice there . . .
WALTER: Girl, if you don't get all them silly ideas out your head! You better
marry yourself a man with some loot . . .
BENEATHA (*angrily, precisely as in the first scene of the play*): What have you
got to do with who I marry!
WALTER: Plenty. Now I think George Murchison—
BENEATHA: *George Murchison!* I wouldn't marry him if he was Adam and I
was Eve!

WALTER *and* BENEATHA *go out yelling at each other vigorously and the anger
is loud and real till their voices diminish.* RUTH *stands at the door and
turns to* MAMA *and smiles knowingly.*

MAMA (*fixing her hat at last*): Yeah—they something all right, my children . . .
RUTH: Yeah—they're something. Let's go, Lena.
MAMA (*stalling, starting to look around at the house*): Yes—I'm coming.
Ruth—
RUTH: Yes?
MAMA (*quietly, woman to woman*): He finally come into his manhood today,
didn't he? Kind of like a rainbow after the rain . . .
RUTH (*biting her lip lest her own pride explode in front of* MAMA): Yes, Lena.

WALTER'S *voice calls for them raucously.*

WALTER (*off stage*): Y'all come on! These people charges by the hour, you
know!
MAMA (*waving* RUTH *out vaguely*): All right, honey—go on down. I be down
directly.

RUTH *hesitates, then exits.* MAMA *stands, at last alone in the living room,
her plant on the table before her as the lights start to come down. She looks
around at all the walls and ceilings and suddenly, despite herself, while*

the children call below, a great heaving thing rises in her and she puts her fist to her mouth to stifle it, takes a final desperate look, pulls her coat about her, pats her hat and goes out. The lights dim down. The door opens and she comes back in, grabs her plant, and goes out for the last time.

Curtain.

The Receptive Reader

1. How much does the playwright steer the director's and actors' interpretation of the characters in the *stage directions?* Prepare a capsule portrait of one or more of the characters as she sketches them out in these introductory descriptions.

2. What does Mama tell the younger generation about the history of her people and the history of her family? What makes Mama the strong *central character* in the play? What for you are the crucial confrontations where her strength is tested?

3. Would you agree that, among the characters in this play, Walter is the rebel? What are the sources of his hostility and rebellion? Where in the play do you most clearly see and understand his bitterness? How are Walter and his actions central to the *plot* of the play? (Some critics have asked how believable or plausible some of the key plot developments are in this play. Do you find them believable? Why or why not?)

4. What is the role of Ruth in the play? Does the confrontation between Walter and his mother make her a *minor character?* What is her relationship with her mother-in-law? What is her relationship with Walter?

5. What roles do the supporting characters play? What role does Murchison play? How does the playwright sketch the rejection by Beneatha and Asagai of the "melting pot" ideal of assimilation? How does Beneatha see the future? How does Asagai? (How does Beneatha provide a *foil* for Walter?)

6. Always in the background of the play is the world of "the Man." What role does it have in the play as a whole? What does Mr. Lindner as its emissary reveal about the working of prejudice or of segregation?

7. Does the play have a "happy ending"? Do you consider the play as a whole optimistic, pessimistic, or neither? What vision does the play as a whole present of the future for African Americans?

The Personal Response

✗ Do you see yourself anywhere in this play? Is there a character with whom you closely identify? Is there a character toward whom you feel strong antagonism? (With which of the characters do you think the author identified most closely?)

✗ Some critics have questioned Hansberry's treatment of the black matriarch as stereotyped or sentimental. Does Mama seem to you overidealized? Or does she seem a believable strong character to you?

✗ Do you think the author is too harsh toward or biased against Walter as the young black male in the family?

The Creative Dimension

As an exercise in **role playing,** prepare a brief monologue in which you assume the role of one of the characters in the play. Bring the character to life for your audience by talking about yourself in this assumed role: your background, your ties with other people, your hopes and aspirations.

WRITING ABOUT LITERATURE

30   The Play and the Critics (Documented Paper)

The Writing Workshop   The critical reception of a major play or of a challenging new playwright makes a good topic for a research paper. What makes a play a success or failure? What makes a major new playwright controversial? How receptive or wrong-headed are critics and reviewers? Why do some plays seem hits at the time but slowly fade from view? Why are others underrated when they first appear?

Finding Promising Leads   You are likely to begin by checking in electronic or printed indexes of periodical literature for reviews and critical appraisals in the year of the original production. Sometimes, a survey article or an appraisal of the playwright published years later may guide you to the original and later reviews. For instance, you might be investigating the critical reception of Lorraine Hansberry's *Raisin in the Sun.* You might come up with leads like the following:

Reviews of the original production:
Atkinson, Brooks. "The Theater: *Raisin in the Sun.*" *New York Times* 12 Mar. 1959. Reprinted in *New York Theatre Critics' Reviews,* 1959, p. 345.
Driver, Tom F. "Theater: *A Raisin in the Sun.*" *New Republic* 140 (13 Apr. 1959): 21.
Lewis, Theophilus. "Social Protest in *A Raisin in the Sun.*" *Catholic World* 190 (Oct. 1959): 31–35.

Reviews of the 1961 Columbia Pictures motion picture in *Commonweal* 74 (7 Apr. 1961); *Ebony* 16 (Apr. 1961: 53–56, *New Republic,* 20 Mar. 1961, p. 19; *New York Times,* 30 Mar. 1961, p. 24; *New Yorker* 8 Apr. 1961, p. 164; *Newsweek,* 10 Apr. 1961, p. 103.

Later assessments:
Brown-Guillory, Elizabeth. *Their Place on the Stage: Black Women Playwrights in America.* Westport: Greenwood P, 1988.
Ashley, Leonard R.N. "Lorraine Hansberry and the Great Black Way." June Schlueter ed. *Modern American Drama: The Female Canon.* Cranbury, NJ: Assoc. University Presses, 1990.

Taking Notes   Be alert for possibly useful material, such as evidence of the reluctance of white producers to produce Hansberry's play or of the compensating eagerness of others to support a black woman play-wright. Make sure to copy **direct quotations** exactly, word for word. Put all the quoted material in quotation marks to show material copied verbatim. Include all the publishing information you will need later when you identify your sources in a documented paper. Include exact page numbers. A sample note might look like this:

<u>Reluctance of white producers</u>
"*To Be Young, Gifted, and Black* was originally conceived not in its present form, but as a work for the stage. As had been the case with *A Raisin in the Sun,* however (and every other black play that I have ever heard of), estab-lished producers evinced skepticism—in this case that sufficient public inter-est would exist in the life of a deceased playwright whose entire reputation rested on two plays."
>   Robert Nemiroff. Postscript to *To Be Young, Gifted and Black:*
>   *Lorraine Hansberry in Her Own Words,* adapted by Robert Nemiroff
>   (Englewood Cliffs: Prentice, 1969), p. 263.

Distinguish clearly between **paraphrase** and direct firsthand quota-tion. When you paraphrase, you put someone else's ideas in your own words. You can thus highlight what seems most important to you and condense other parts. Even when you paraphrase, be sure to use quo-tation marks for striking phrases that you keep in the exact wording of the author. The following note might be your summing up of comments on the original casting of *Death of a Salesman* that Arthur Miller made in an article in *Theater Week* in 1991:

Miller admits he believes in typecasting, choosing the actor who looks right for the role, since no director really wants to make over an actor into some-thing he or she isn't. But although Miller wrote the part of Willy Loman origi-nally with a "small, feisty man" in mind, the original Willy Loman turned out to be Lee Cobb, "the closest thing in Equity to a hippo."

Here are related notes from a review by Lloyd Roe, titled "Lost in America," in the *Atlantic* for April 1984. Note the **single quotation marks** for the phrase "common man" that appears as a quote-within-a-quote. Note the use of the **ellipsis**—three spaced periods to show an omission (four when the periods include the period at the end of a sen-tence). Note the use of **square brackets** to show that material has been inserted into the original quotation.

"Big and slow-moving, with a suffering dignity in his thick face," Cobb "gave the lie to Miller's view of Willy as a 'common man.' Cobb's pain was outsized. He was like a huge, wounded animal . . . the real source of his agony was hidden and mute. Cobb rendered irrelevant the question of Willy's responsibility for his own defeat by making his sorrow too deep for the circumstances of his life."

"Hoffman [who played Willy Loman in the 1984 revival of the play] couldn't be more different from Cobb, both physically and technically, but he doesn't try for contrasts. . . . His Willy is freshly conceived—the characterization feels new, and there's a sense of discovery in it."

Pushing Toward a Thesis   Early during your exploratory reading and note taking, look for a unifying thread. Look for recurrent issues; look for a note that is sounded again and again. In reading contemporary reactions to Ibsen's plays, for instance, you are likely to be struck by their tendency to polarize the audience. Again and again, his defenders celebrate him as one of the pioneers of modern emancipated thinking. And also again and again, outraged champions of public morality target him as an enemy of decency and Western civilization. This recurrent pattern points toward a unifying **thesis:** Ibsen, in the words of an English director, "split the English theater in two." The following might be a tentative thesis:

TRIAL THESIS: Ibsen's plays were denounced as immoral by his outraged enemies and at the same time championed as ushering in a new
morality.

Using a Working Outline   As soon as you have a rough idea how your material is shaping up, sketch out a **working outline.** At first, your plan might be very tentative. The whole point of a working outline is to sketch a possible pattern and then refine it as you go along. At an intermediate stage in the Ibsen paper, the writer's working outline might look like this:

WORKING OUTLINE: —polarizing effect of Ibsen's plays
the "new" morality in his plays
the "old" morality of his contemporaries
—the attack on Ibsen
Scott's denunciation
Archer's collection of criticism
—Shaw's defense of the plays
—Ibsen's getting back at his critics
portrait of the moralist in his plays
Ibsen's letters

Documenting the Paper   **Documentation** identifies your sources, complete with publishing information and exact page numbers. Full documentation enables your readers to verify your sources and to get further information from them if they wish. Unless told differently by your instructor or editor, follow the style of documentation of the Modern Language Association (MLA). Use **parenthetical documentation**

in the running text of your paper (mostly to provide page numbers, but also to tag author and title as needed). Then give complete information about each source in a final alphabetical listing of **Works Cited.** (This was once the **bibliography,** or "book list," but it may now include non-print sources like Internet sources, videocassettes, radio and television programs, and computer software.)

Parenthetical documentation has done away with footnotes. (Numbered explanatory notes may still follow a paper or article.) If you have said that Susan Sontag in *Against Interpretation* speaks of the "volleying back and forth of clichés" in a typical play by Ionesco, all you need is the page number or numbers in parentheses (119). However, if you have merely said that a prominent critic used that phrase, you will have to include her name, so that the reader can find the source in the Works Cited (Sontag 119). If you plan to quote another book or article by Sontag, you will have to tag the first source here, using a shortened version of the title—if possible without interfering with alphabetical ordering later (Sontag, *Against Interpretation* 119). Remember to tag author or title in parentheses only if you have not already given the information in your running text.

For classics that are available in many different editions, show act, scene, and line in Arabic numerals instead of page numbers (3.2.46–49). Some prefer the traditional large and small Roman numerals for act and scene (III.ii.46–49).

Here are some standard entries for your alphabetical listing of Works Cited. Remember: underlining (or italics) for titles of separate publications; quotation marks for titles of articles or of plays that are part of a collection. Leave one space after periods marking off chunks of information in the entry. Remember to indent the second and following lines of each entry *five* typewriter spaces or half an inch.

Listing of a play

Wilson, August. *The Piano Lesson.* New York: Plume-NAL, 1990.
[Plume is an imprint, or special line of books, of New American Library.]

Beckett, Samuel. *Waiting for Godot: Tragicomedy in 2 Acts.* New York: Grove, 1954.
[Note underlined (italicized) subtitle]

Shakespeare, William. *The Tragedy of Hamlet.* Ed. Edward Hubler. New York: NAL: 1963.
[Special edition of a play]

Hubler, Edward, ed. *The Tragedy of Hamlet.* By William Shakespeare. New York: NAL, 1963.
[Editor's name first—editor's work important]

Hansberry, Lorraine. *A Raisin in the Sun. Black Theater: A Twentieth-Century Collection of the Work of Its Best Playwrights.* Ed. Lindsay Patterson. New York: Dodd, 1971. 221–76.

[Play in a collection, with complete page numbers for the play]

Aristophanes. *Lysistrata.* Trans. Donald Sutherland. *Classical Comedy Greek and Roman.* Ed. Robert W. Corrigan. New York: Applause, 1987. 11–68.

[Play in a collection (with page numbers); translator's name included]

Listing of a critical study or review

Lebowitz, Naomi. *Ibsen and the Great World.* Baton Rouge: Louisiana State UP, 1990.

[Book published by a university press]

Goodman, Charlotte. "The Fox's Cubs: Lillian Hellman, Arthur Miller, and Tennessee Williams." *Modern American Drama: The Female Canon.* Ed. June Schlueter. New York: Associated UP, 1990.

[Article in a collection]

Greeley, Andrew. "Today's Morality Play: The Sitcom." *New York Times* 17 May 1987, late ed. , sec. 2: 1+.

[Newspaper article, with edition and section specified. Article starts on page 1 and continues later in the newspaper.]

Lewis, Theophilus. "Social Protest in *Raisin in the Sun.*" *Catholic World* 190 (Oct. 1959): 31–35.

[Journal article, with volume number]

Davis, Ossie. "The Significance of Lorraine Hansberry." *Freedomways* 5, no. 3 (Summer 1965): 396–402.

[With number of volume and issue]

Driver, Tom F. Rev. of *A Raisin in the Sun,* by Lorraine Hansberry. *New Republic* 140 (13 Apr. 1959): 21.

[Untitled review]

Electronic sources—Online, CD-ROM, e-mail

Guidelines for documenting electronic sources keep changing to keep up with evolving new technology. The following guidelines are based on the *MLA Style Manual* (Second Edition, 1998). For most of your entries, start with as much of the usual publishing information as is available—including authors, titles, and dates. However, add the **access date**—the date you accessed the source or site. The date of access will often follow the date the material was published or posted. (The access date can tell your reader how recently the material was available.)

For material from the net, include the **Internet address**—the URL (for "uniform resource locator"). Put it between angled brackets. Typically,

the electronic address will start with the access mode, usually **<http://
. . . .>**. (Other access modes include *telnet* and *ftp.*) The address will
then go on to the relevant path and specific file names (often beginning
with **www.** for World Wide Web) Try to have the whole URL on the
same line, or else try to have a break only after a period or slash. Make
sure that dots, slashes, colons, capitals, and spacing are exactly right.
(Do not add hyphens or final periods.)

For material from other electronic sources, specify the **medium,** such
as CD-ROM, diskette, or magnetic tape. Here are sample entries:

"Actor Urges Film Conservation." *AP Online* 10 Mar. 1997. 12 Mar. 1997
<http://www.nytimes.com/aponline/e/James-Earl-Jones.html>
[News service online]

"August Wilson's *Seven Guitars* Sings the Blues." *Alley Theatre News* 6 Feb.
1998. 12 Oct. 1998 <http://www.alleytheatre.com/media/pr6.html>
[theater press release online]

"Hansberry." *Britannica Online.* Vers. 97.1.1. Mar. 1997. Encyclopaedia Britannica. 7 Apr. 1997. <http://www.eb.com/>
[Reference work online, with version number and date]

Aristotle. *The Complete Works of Aristotle: The Revised Oxford Translation.*
Ed. Jonathan Barnes. 2 vols. Princeton: Princeton UP, 1984. CD-ROM.
Clayton: Intelex, 1994.
[Complete works of a classic on CD-ROM]

Lincoln, Jonathan. E-mail to the author. 12 Mar. 2000.
[Give dates for e-mail to you or to others]

The following is an example of a documented paper. How successful
was the student author in finding contemporary sources? How well does
the paper support its main points? Study the use of parenthetical documentation and the entries in the Works Cited. Are there unusual situations or entries?

Sample Student Paper

The Furor over Ibsen

What did Henrik Ibsen do? According to Granville-Barker, "he split the English
theater in two" (24). Indeed, "as everyone knows, the introduction of Ibsen into
England was not a peaceful one. In its wake came one of those great outbursts of
critical frenzy and inflamed controversy which at regular intervals enliven literary
history" ("Retrospective" 199). In England, as in the rest of Europe, the public was
split into two factions: those who placed Ibsen on the blacklist as "immoral"; and
those who saw him as the champion of a new morality. A hundred years later, Ibsen
continues to stir the conscience of a later generation. In a recent study, Naomi
Lebowitz quotes a leading European intellectual on "the shame that overcomes the

descendant in the face of an earlier possibility that he has neglected to bring to fruition" (Theodor Adorno, qtd. in Lebowitz 2).

Ibsen's plays aroused both indignation and enthusiasm because he fought against maintaining appearances at the expense of happiness, or what he termed hypocrisy. Una Ellis-Fermor, a translator and lifelong student of Ibsen, said that he "took upon himself the task of exposing the makeshift morality of his contemporaries in private and public life":

> In *The Pillars of the Community,* he examines the lie in public life, the tragic struggle of Karsten Bernick to hide his sin and preserve his reputation at the expense of another man's good name. . . . In *A Doll's House* and *Ghosts* the subject is the lie in domestic life; the fist shows the destruction of a marriage by an unreal and insincere relationship between husband and wife, and the second the destruction of the lives and souls of the characters by the oppressive tyranny of convention. (Ibsen, *Three Plays* 9–11)

In *Ghosts,* a dutiful and unloving wife keeps up an elaborate façade of respectability for a profligate husband. She finds herself defeated when her cherished son returns home suffering incurably from the syphilis he has inherited from his father. According to Bernard Shaw, the play was "an uncompromising and outspoken attack on marriage as a useless sacrifice," the story of a woman who had wasted her life in manufacturing a "monstrous fabric of lies and false appearances" (86, 88).

Against the tyranny of middle-class standards, Ibsen pitted his own concept of individual integrity. He felt, according to Georg Brandes, that "the individuality of the human being is to be preserved for its own sake, not for the sake of higher powers; and since beyond all else the individual should remain free and whole, all concessions made to the world represent to Ibsen the foul fiend, the evil principle" (373). One of the main ideas fused into Ibsen's plays, according to a representative admiring article in the *Encyclopaedia Britannica,* is "the supreme importance of individual character, of personality: in the development and enrichment of the individual he saw the only hope for a really cultured and enlightened society" ("Drama" 65).

A Doll's House was particularly loaded with the "first duty to oneself" theme. Nora, in the last act, wakes to the fact that she is not worthy to be a good mother and wife because she has been merely a submissive servant and foil first for her father and then for her husband; she has been so protected and guided by them that she has no individual conception of life and its complexities. Nora realized that she did not know enough about the world and her place in it to be really "a reasonable human being," and she felt a duty to become one (Ibsen, *Four Plays* 65). Her life all at once seemed so artificial and meaningless to her that she felt like a doll living in a doll's house. Nora left her husband and children to try to gain an understanding of real life, and when she "banged the door of A Doll's House, the echo of that violence was heard across the continent" ("Drama" 600).

Ibsen wrote these plays at a time when people felt a general ferment, a "spirit of the age" or a "movement of the century" that had introduced everywhere a tendency toward change. Voices heralding the modern age referred to the "new phase into which humanity is passing" and expressed the conviction that "society must undergo a transformation or perish" (Goodwin 124, 122). But the voices resisting the clamor for "innovations" were equally strong. Their watchword was devotion to duty—toward God, country, one's family and husband. Self-denial for the sake of greater forces was the commendable action. The churches taught it was sinful to assert one's own wishes and desires. The people, especially the dominated wife with whom Ibsen frequently deals, were exhorted to live for the good of everyone but themselves. Advocates of the emancipation of women were told in the public press that "men are men and women women"; that "sex is a fact—no Act of Parliament can eliminate it"; and that "where two ride on a horse, one must needs ride behind" (Goodwin 103, 109). They were told that in women's hands "rests the keeping of a pure tone in society, of a high standard in morality, of a lofty devotion to duty in political life." If she were to enter openly into political conflict, she would "debase her sex" and "lower the ideal of womanhood amongst men" (Goodwin 103–4).

The old-fashioned moralists were shocked by the "Ibsenist" view that self-fulfillment is more important than the sanctity of marriage, one's duty to others, and even business success. According to Arthur Bingham Walkley, drama critic for the *London Times,* "Ibsen became a bogey to many worthy people who had never read or seen a single one of his plays." To these people, "Ibsenism was supposed vaguely to connote 'Woman's Rights,' Free Love, a new and fearful kind of wildfowl called 'Norwegian Socialism,' and generally, every manifestation of discontent with the existing order of things" (790). Clement Scott, a prominent drama critic, led such formidable opposition against Ibsen's dramas, especially *A Doll's House* and *Ghosts,* that they were actually banned for a time from English stages. "Ibsen fails," Scott says, "because he is, I suppose, an atheist, and has not realized what the great backbone of religion means to the English race." Scott continues, "He fails because his plays are nasty, dirty, impure, clever if you like, but foul to the last degree; and healthy-minded English people don't like to stand and sniff over an ash-pit" (qtd. in Granville-Barker 24).

Many of the people causing the uproar against Ibsen used similar language. William Archer, the first English translator of Ibsen, collected some of the attacks appearing in the English press when *Ghosts* was first produced. The play was called "disgusting," "loathsome," "gross," and "revoltingly suggestive and blasphemous." It was compared to "a dirty act done publicly" and was called "a piece to bring the stage into disrepute and dishonour with every right-thinking man and woman" (qtd. in Shaw 91–3).

Those who defended Ibsen—Shaw, Archer, Walkley—blamed his unpleasant reception in England on both his revolutionary themes and his new dramatic technique. I shall steer away from Ibsen's new dramatic technique and instead discuss the defense of Ibsenism as a new moral philosophy. Shaw himself has been called one of the men "who summon their generation to act by a new and higher standard." He made Ibsen his hero because Ibsen championed the view that Shaw made the basis for many of his own plays:

> By "morals" (or "ideals") Shaw means conventional, current standards. Because these standards are universal and inherited from the past, they often do not fit particular situations and present-day societies. Therefore good men—like some of Ibsen's characters—often choose to act "immorally," contrary to accepted morality. (Brower 687)

To Shaw, Ibsen became the first of the two types of pioneers classified by Shaw in *The Quintessence of Ibsenism.* This type of pioneer asserts "that it is right to do something hitherto regarded as infamous." Ibsen felt that it was right to think first of building himself and secondly of building the institutions of society. To Shaw, this change explained the unkindly reception of Ibsen's new thoughts in England: "So much easier is it to declare the right wrong than the wrong right. . . . a guilty society can more readily be persuaded that any apparently innocent act is guilty than that any apparently guilty act is innocent" (23–25). Shaw seems to feel that Ibsen would have had more success telling people it was wrong to work on Monday than he would have had saying it was right to work on Sunday. People could not accept the idea that the obligation of self-sacrifice could be removed from them—that it would be all right for them to consider a duty toward themselves first.

Shaw complained of the difficulty of finding "accurate terms" for Ibsen's new "realist morality." To Shaw, it was Ibsen's thesis that "the real slavery of today is slavery to ideals of goodness" (146–149). Ibsen had devoted himself to showing that "the spirit of man is constantly outgrowing the ideals," and the "thoughtless conformity" to them is constantly producing tragic results (152). Among those "ridden by current ideals," Ibsen's plays were bound to be denounced as immoral. But, Shaw concluded, there can be no question as to the effect likely to be produced on an individual by his conversion from the ordinary acceptance of current ideals as safe standards of conduct, to the vigilant open-mindedness of Ibsen. It must at once greatly deepen the sense of moral responsibility (154).

Ibsen himself knew well and satirized in his plays the moralists who inveighed against "the undermining of family life" and the "defiance of the most solemn truths." In *Ghosts,* Pastor Manders, who represents a timid regard for convention, warns people against books that he vaguely associates with "intellectual progress"—and that he has not read. Rörlund, the schoolmaster in *The Pillars of the Community,* sums up the position of the guardians of conventional morality when he says: "Our business is to keep society pure . . . to keep out all these experimental notions that an impatient age wants to force on us (Ibsen, *Three Plays* 27–28) Ironically, Rörlund provides a moral façade for "practical men of affairs" like the shipowner Bernick. Bernick, who talks about his "deep-rooted sense of decency," has abandoned the woman he loved in order to marry a wealthy girl and save the family business. He has abandoned to need and shame a married woman with whom he has had a secret affair. He has saved his own reputation in the community at the expense of having a younger friend blackened as a libertine and a thief. Bernick's defense of his conduct is that he lives in a community in which "a youthful indiscretion is never wiped out." The "community itself forces us into crooked ways" (97–98). But Ibsen's heroes are people who rebel against the "tyranny of custom and convention"; who hold that "the spirit of truth and the spirit of freedom" are the "true pillars of the community" (116, 137).

Ibsen was not intimidated by the controversy caused by his plays. In a letter to a friend he wrote in 1881, he said: "*Ghosts* will probably cause alarm in some circles. . . . If it didn't do that, there would have been no need to write it." In a letter written a year later, he said: "That my new play would produce a howl from the camp of those 'men of stagnation' was something I was quite prepared for" (*Ghosts* 126). Shortly afterward, he summed up his faith in the future in a letter that said in part:

> In time, and not before very long at that, the good people up home will get into their heads some understanding of *Ghosts*. But all those desiccated, decrepit individuals who pounced on this work, they will come in for devastating criticism in the literary histories of the future. People will be able to sniff out the nameless snipers and thugs who directed their dirty missiles at me from their ambush in Professor Goos's mouldy rag and other simlar places. My book holds the future. Yon crowd that roared about it haven't even any proper contact with their own genuinely vital age. (*Ghosts* 129–30)

It was Ibsen's assertion of man's duty to himself, against the tradition of conformity to custom and convention, that was the main grounds of significant controversy over Ibsen's works. In presenting this view in his plays, as a modern critic says, "Ibsen established realism as the ruling principle of modern drama." Problems of the day had been aired on the stage before, "but nobody before Ibsen had treated them without equivocation or without stressing secondary matters while ignoring primary ones." Because he was the first, "Henrik Ibsen . . . has long held the unofficial title of 'father of the modern drama'" (Gassner vii–viii).

Works Cited

Brandes, Georg. *Creative Spirits of the Nineteenth Century.* Trans. Rasmus B. Anderson. New York: Crowell, 1923.

Brower, Reuben A. "George Bernard Shaw." *Major British Writers.* Ed. G. B. Harrison. Vol 2. New York: Harcourt, 1959. 687. 2 vols.

"Drama." *Encyclopaedia Britannica.* 1958.

Gassner, John. Introduction. *Four Great Plays by Ibsen.* By Henrik Ibsen. New York: Dutton, 1959. i–x.

Goodwin, Michael, ed. *Nineteenth-Century Opinion: An Anthology (1877–1901).* Hammondsworth, Middlesex: Penguin, 1951.

Granville-Barker, Harley "When Ibsen Split the English Stage in Two." *Literary Digest* 28 (1928): 24–25.

Ibsen, Henrik. *Ghosts.* Trans. Kai Jurgensen and Robert Schenkkan. New York: Avon, 1965.

———. *Three Plays.* Trans. Una Ellis-Fermor. Hammondsworth, Middlesex: Penguin, 1950.

"Ibsen, Henrik Johan." *Encyclopaedia Britannica.* 1958.

"Inside Views of Ibsen in the Nineties." *Literary Digest* 12 (1928): 24.

Lebowitz, Naomi. *Ibsen and the Great World.* Baton Rouge: Louisiana State UP, 1990.

"A Retrospective Eye on Ibsen." *Theatre Arts Monthly* 12 (1928): 199–211.

Shaw, Bernard. *The Quintessence of Ibsenism.* 3rd ed. New York: Hill, 1957.

Walkley, A. B. "Ibsen in England." *Living Age* 12 (1901): 790.

Questions

Does the paper succeed in drawing you into the controversy? Why or why not? (Does it still have a meaning for today's reader?) What quotations do most to bring the two opposed factions to life? Does the writer do justice to both, or is one slighted? For what points does the writer choose to use extended quotations, printed as **block quotations** (indented ten typewriter spaces or one inch)? What questions remain in your mind as you read the paper?

31 Comedy

A Time for Laughter

Characters in a play don't always have to be big-
ger fools than in everyday life.

EUGÈNE IONESCO

FOCUS ON COMEDY

Comedy takes us into a golden world of liberating laughter. It is at
the opposite pole from tragedy. Tragedy makes us face our limits. It
brings men and women up against the boundaries of human hope and
endeavor. Comedy celebrates the renewal of hope. It reinforces our
belief that good things can happen; it tells us that we can laugh off some
of the things that bedevil us. At its best, comedy restores our faith in
good fortune, in young love, in generosity and changes of heart.

The Roots of Comedy Scholars have traced the roots of comedy to pre-
Christian Easter festivals celebrating the return of spring after the dead
of winter. Our remote ancestors celebrated the return of the sun and the
budding of new vegetation. They staged marriage festivals and fertility
rites that celebrated the bonding of love and the renewal of the community. Comedy helps us preserve the spirit of holiday—of merrymak-
ing, celebration, fiesta, festival, carnival, revelry.

Delight and Ridicule What makes audiences laugh? Critics early made
a distinction between two different kinds of laughter. The first kind
makes us respond to things that are congenial and desirable. We laugh
or more often smile when something delightful happens. The most basic
plot of traditional comedy has young people fall in love. They then meet
obstacles—greedy parents, lusting elders—but they overcome these in
the end. The second kind of laughter is the laughter of ridicule; it makes
us laugh at the opposite of what is desirable or agreeable to human
nature. We laugh at what is rigid, mechanical, or unnatural. People who
dance as if they were counting "one-two-three" in their heads; people

977

who are unbending in their religious or ideological or dietary views—
these are comic, to others if not to themselves.

Comedy and Satire   Comedy becomes a criticism of our everyday reality when it makes us laugh at attitudes that stand in the way of a more
humane world. Wielding humor as a weapon, the comic playwright
uses **satire** to do battle against callousness, stinginess, or hypocrisy.
Comedy satirizes traits that narrow life, forces that shut off possibility. It
mocks bullies and pompous idiots. The miser, the hypochondriac, and
the malcontent—forever dissatisfied with everything—have long been
stock characters that audiences delight in seeing on the stage.

Theories of Humor   A more hard-nosed theory holds that we laugh at
shortcomings that make us feel superior to others. People who are ham-
strung by their failings are no competition for us. We don't have to take
them seriously, and we laugh with relief. Thus, we laugh at bumblers,
clumsy lovers, waiters who drop heavy trays, and foreigners who wrestle with the English language. A more defensive theory looks at humor
as a shield, as a kind of armor. It is a mask we may put on to fend off
prying or pity. A character may always be wisecracking so as not to let
people see the hurt inside. The playwright Wendy Wasserstein has said
that "a lot of comedy is a deflection." She said about a character in one
of her plays that "she is *always* funny, so as not to say what she feels."

THE LANGUAGE OF COMEDY

The soul of comedy is often quick, witty dialogue. Audiences delight
in the **chase of wit,** with characters trading quick pointed remarks.
(Older man: "I had advanced ideas before you were born!" Younger
man: "I knew it was a long time ago.") Often comic dialogue is laced
with **word play** or verbal humor. Shakespeare's audiences loved
puns—they delighted in seeing a word put through its paces in a
quickly moving exchange:

DUKE (*offering money to the jester who has just finished a song*):
    There's for thy pains.
JESTER: No pains, sir. I take pleasure in singing, sir.
DUKE: I'll pay thy pleasure then.
CLOWN: Truly, sir, and pleasure will be paid one time or another.

Shakespeare, *Twelfth Night*

Oscar Wilde   *(1854–1900)*

*Humor is born in dark places of the soul, masking
anguish with a tilt toward absurdity.*

AL MARTINEZ

The Irish playwright Oscar Wilde was a master of fast-moving witty
dialogue. He was born and educated in Dublin before being transplanted to Oxford and becoming a thorn in the side of his earnest Victorian contemporaries. Displaying a flamboyant gay lifestyle, he became
a victim of a homophobic society, emerging from prison a broken man
after being sentenced for "gross indecency."

Wilde's *The Importance of Being Earnest* (1895) is a bravura piece still
brilliantly performed by modern theater companies. At a time when
society put the premium on serious effort, Wilde put on the stage frivolous young people finding excuses for trips to the country (or the city).
At a time when society prized respectability and the family name, one
of his heroes was a young man who at birth had been abandoned in a
handbag left at a railroad station.

In the following scene from *The Importance of Being Earnest,* Jack
Worthing is caught in a subterfuge of his own making: his excuse for
sneaking away to the city is that he claims to have a younger brother
there named Ernest, who needs supervision. Then, when he gets to the
city, Jack pretends to be Ernest. The following exchange between Jack
and Gwendolen, the young woman he adores, illustrate the witty come-
back, the unexpected twist on a cliché, and the parody of pomposity
that were hallmarks of Wilde's style.

A Proposal of Marriage   1895
From *The Importance of Being Earnest*

CHARACTERS

GWENDOLEN FAIRFAX
JACK WORTHING, known to GWENDOLEN as Ernest
LADY BRACKNELL, GWENDOLEN's mother

SCENE: *Algernon's apartment in London*

JACK: Charming day it has been, Miss Fairfax.

GWENDOLEN: Pray don't talk to me about the weather, Mr. Worthing. Whenever people talk to me about the weather, I always feel quite certain that
they mean something else. And that makes me so nervous.

JACK: I do mean something else.

GWENDOLEN: I thought so. In fact, I am never wrong.

JACK: And I would like to be allowed to take advantage of Lady Bracknell's temporary absence. . . .

GWENDOLEN: I would certainly advise you to do so. Mama has a way of coming back suddenly into a room that I have often had to speak to her about.

JACK (*nervously*): Miss Fairfax, ever since I met you I have admired you more than any girl . . . I have ever met since . . . I met you.

GWENDOLEN: Yes, I am quite aware of the fact. And I often wish that in public, at any rate, you had been more demonstrative. For me you have always had an irresistible fascination. Even before I met you I was far from indifferent to you. (*Jack looks at her in amazement.*) We live, as I hope you know, Mr. Worthing, in an age of ideals. The fact is constantly mentioned in the more expensive monthly magazines, and has reached the provincial pulpits, I am told; and my ideal has always been to love someone of the name of Ernest. There is something in that name that inspires absolute confidence. The moment Algernon first mentioned to me that he had a friend called Ernest, I knew I was destined to love you.

JACK: You really love me, Gwendolen?

GWENDOLEN: Passionately!

JACK: Darling! You don't know how happy you've made me.

GWENDOLEN: My own Ernest!

JACK: But you don't really mean to say that you couldn't love me if my name wasn't Ernest?

GWENDOLEN: But your name is Ernest.

JACK: Yes, I know it is. But supposing it was something else? Do you mean to say you couldn't love me then? Personally, darling, to speak quite candidly, I don't much care about the name of Ernest . . . I don't think the name suits me at all.

GWENDOLEN: It suits you perfectly. It is a divine name. It has a music of its own. It produces vibrations.

JACK: Well, really, Gwendolen, I must say that I think there are lots of other much nicer names. I think Jack, for instance, a charming name.

GWENDOLEN: Jack? . . . No, there is very little music in the name Jack, if any at all, indeed. It does not thrill. It produces absolutely no vibrations. . . . I have known several Jacks, and they all, without exception, were more than usually plain. Besides, Jack is a notorious domesticity for John! And I pity any woman who is married to a man called John. She would probably never be allowed to know the entrancing pleasure of a single moment's solitude. The only really safe name is Ernest.

JACK: Gwendolen, I must get christened at once—I mean we must get married at once. There is no time to be lost.

GWENDOLEN: Married, Mr. Worthing?

JACK (*astounded*): Well . . . surely. You know that I love you, and you led me to believe, Miss Fairfax, that you were not absolutely indifferent to me.

GWENDOLEN: I adore you. But you haven't proposed to me yet. Nothing has been said at all about marriage. The subject has not even been touched on.

JACK: Well . . . may I propose to you now?

GWENDOLEN: I think it would be an admirable opportunity. And to spare you any possible disappointment, Mr. Worthing, I think it only fair to tell you quite frankly beforehand that I am fully determined to accept you.

JACK: Gwendolen!

GWENDOLEN: Yes, Mr. Worthing, what have you got to say to me?

JACK: You know what I have got to say to you.

GWENDOLEN: Yes, but you don't say it.

JACK (*goes on his knees*): Gwendolen, will you marry me?

GWENDOLEN: Of course I will, darling. How long you have been about it! I am afraid you have had very little experience in how to propose.

JACK: My own one, I have never loved anyone in the world but you.

GWENDOLEN: Yes, but men often propose for practice. I know my brother Gerald does. All my girl friends tell me so. What wonderfully blue eyes you have, Ernest! I hope you will always look at me just like that, especially when there are other people present. (*Enter* LADY BRACKNELL.)

LADY BRACKNELL: Mr. Worthing! Rise, sir, from this semirecumbent posture. It is most indecorous.

GWENDOLEN: Mama! (*He tries to rise; she restrains him.*) I must beg you to retire. This is no place for you. Besides, Mr. Worthing has not quite finished yet.

LADY BRACKNELL: Finished what, may I ask?

GWENDOLEN: I am engaged to Mr. Worthing, Mama. (*They rise together.*)

LADY BRACKNELL: Pardon me, you are not engaged to anyone. When you do become engaged to someone, I, or your father, should his health permit him, will inform you of the fact. An engagement should come on a young girl as a surprise, pleasant or unpleasant, as the case may be. It is hardly a matter that she could be allowed to arrange for herself. . . . And now I have a few questions to put to you, Mr. Worthing. While I am making these inquiries, you, Gwendolen, will wait for me below in the carriage.

GWENDOLEN (*reproachfully*): Mama!

LADY BRACKNELL: In the carriage, Gwendolen! (GWENDOLEN *goes to the door. She and* JACK *blow kisses to each other behind* LADY BRACKNELL*'s back.* LADY BRACKNELL *looks vaguely about as if she could not understand what the noise was. Finally turns around.*) Gwendolen, the carriage!

GWENDOLEN: Yes, Mama. (*goes out looking back at* JACK)

LADY BRACKNELL (*sitting down*): You can take a seat, Mr. Worthing. (*looks in her pocket for notebook and pencil*)

JACK: Thank you, Lady Bracknell, I prefer standing.

LADY BRACKNELL (*pencil and notebook in hand*): I feel bound to tell you that you are not down on my list of eligible young men. However, I am quite ready to enter your name, should your answers be what a really affectionate mother requires. Do you smoke?

JACK: Well, yes, I must admit I smoke.

LADY BRACKNELL: I am glad to hear it. A man should always have an occupation of some kind. There are far too many idle men in London as it is. How old are you?

JACK: Twenty-nine.

LADY BRACKNELL: A very good age to be married at. I have always been of the opinion that a man who desires to get married should know either everything or nothing. Which do you know?

JACK (*after some hesitation*): I know nothing, Lady Bracknell.

LADY BRACKNELL: I am pleased to hear it. I do not approve of anything that tampers with natural ignorance. Ignorance is like a delicate exotic fruit; touch it and the bloom is gone. The whole theory of modern education is radically unsound. Fortunately in England, at any rate, education produces no effect whatsoever. If it did, it would prove a serious danger to the upper classes. What is your income?

JACK: Between seven and eight thousand pounds a year.

LADY BRACKNELL (*makes a note in her book*): In land or in investments?

JACK: In investments, chiefly.

LADY BRACKNELL: That is satisfactory. What between the duties expected of one during one's lifetime, and the duties exacted from one after one's death, land has ceased to be either a profit or a pleasure. It gives one position and prevents one from keeping it up. That's all that can be said about land.

JACK: I have a country house with some land, of course, attached to it, about fifteen hundred acres, I believe; but I don't depend on that for my real income. In fact, as far as I can make out, the poachers are the only people who make anything out of it.

LADY BRACKNELL: A country house! How many bedrooms? Well, that point can be cleared up afterward. You have a town house, I hope? A girl with a simple, unspoiled nature, like Gwendolen, could hardly be expected to reside in the country.

JACK: Well, I own a house in Belgrave Square.

LADY BRACKNELL: What number in Belgrave Square?

JACK: One hundred and forty nine.

LADY BRACKNELL (*shaking her head*): The unfashionable side. I thought there was something. However, that could easily be altered.

JACK: Do you mean the fashion, or the side?

LADY BRACKNELL (*sternly*): Both, if necessary, I presume. Are your parents living?

JACK: I have lost both my parents.

LADY BRACKNELL: To lose one parent, Mr. Worthing, may be regarded as a misfortune. To lose both looks like carelessness. Who was your father? He was evidently a man of some wealth. Was he born in what the Radical papers call the purple of commerce, or did he rise from the ranks of the aristocracy?

JACK: I am afraid I really don't know. The fact is, Lady Bracknell, I said I had lost my parents. It would be nearer the truth to say that my parents seem to have lost me. . . . I don't actually know who I am by birth. I was . . . well, I was found.

LADY BRACKNELL: Found!

JACK: The late Mr. Thomas Cardew, an old gentleman of a very charitable and kindly disposition, found me and gave me the name of Worthing, because he happened to have a first-class ticket for Worthing in his pocket at the time. Worthing is a place in Sussex. It is a seaside resort.

LADY BRACKNELL: Where did the charitable gentleman who had a first-class ticket for this seaside resort find you?

JACK (*gravely*): In a handbag.

LADY BRACKNELL: A handbag?

JACK (*very seriously*): Yes, Lady Bracknell. I was in a handbag—a somewhat large, black leather handbag, with handles to it—an ordinary handbag in fact.

LADY BRACKNELL: In what locality did this Mr. James, or Thomas, Cardew come across this ordinary handbag?

JACK: In the cloakroom at Victoria Station. It was given to him in mistake for his own.

LADY BRACKNELL: The cloakroom at Victoria Station?

JACK: Yes. The Brighton line.

LADY BRACKNELL: The line is immaterial. Mr. Worthing, I confess I feel somewhat bewildered by what you have just told me. To be born, or at any rate bred, in a handbag, whether it had handles or not, seems to me to display a contempt for the ordinary decencies of family life that reminds one of the worst excesses of the French Revolution. . . . As for the particular locality in which the handbag was found, a cloakroom at a railway station might serve to conceal a social indiscretion—has probably, indeed, been used for that purpose before now—but it could hardly be regarded as an assured basis for a recognized position in good society.

JACK: May I ask you then what you would advise me to do? I need hardly say I would do anything in the world to insure Gwendolen's happiness.

LADY BRACKNELL: I would strongly advise you, Mr. Worthing, to try and acquire some relations as soon as possible, and to make a definite effort to produce at any rate one parent, of either sex, before the season is quite over.

JACK: Well, I don't see how I could possibly manage to do that. I can produce the handbag at any moment. It is in my dressing room at home. I really think that should satisfy you, Lady Bracknell.

LADY BRACKNELL: Me, sir! What has it to do with me? You can hardly imagine that I and Lord Bracknell would dream of allowing our only daughter—a girl brought up with the utmost care—to marry into a cloakroom, and form an alliance with a parcel. Good morning, Mr. Worthing! (LADY BRACKNELL *sweeps out in majestic indignation.*)

The Receptive Reader

1. Wilde's comic characters in this scene are all talk. Describe each of the three characters and each character's way of talking. What makes Jack Worthing comic? What is hilarious about Gwendolen? What made Lady Bracknell immortal?

2. In his time, Wilde was notorious for witty sayings that stood some cliché or platitude on its head. Can you find examples in this scene?

3. What are the targets of Wilde's satire here—what traits or values does he make seem ridiculous? How serious and how effective is his satire?

4. As you look in the mirror the playwright holds up to human nature in this scene, do you see a reflection of yourself or of people you know?

5. Your class may want to have an audition for a Readers' Theater presentation of this scene. What traits and abilities would you look for in candidates for the three roles?

The Personal Response

Is Wilde's humor too frivolous for our day? Is it obsolete? Do we have more important things to worry about? Are we relapsing into the earnestness of the Victorians?

Wendy Wasserstein   *(born 1950)*

Wendy Wasserstein is a contemporary American playwright in whose comic sketches every satirical detail counts (and hurts). She was born in Brooklyn, studied creative writing at CCNY (City College of New York), and has done much of her writing in a Greenwich Village apartment. After her senior year in college, she went west to look for work writing for television and discovered that she "loathed" California. Several of her plays were successful Off Broadway. Her *Heidi Chronicles* (1988) moved on to Broadway and won a Pulitzer Prize, a Tony Award, and the prize of the New York Critics' Circle. She has written screenplays for television; she published a collection called *Bachelor Girls* in 1990.

The characters in Wasserstein's plays are often young, urban, and professional (in short, yuppies). Before she is through with them, the playwright has dissected their dating rituals, their attitudes toward their jobs, their food fetishes, their dependence on their psychiatrists or psychologists. Above all, she mimics the trendy way they talk—about places to be seen, about clothes with snob appeal, about food that is not ordinary, and about schools that are not public schools.

In the following one-act play, Wasserstein looks at the difficulties of communication between parent and offspring. What is sad and funny about this conversation between the father and his daughter?

Tender Offer   *1983*

SETTING: *A girl of around nine is alone in a dance studio. She is dressed in traditional leotards and tights. She begins singing to herself, "Nothing Could Be Finer Than to Be in Carolina." She maps out a dance routine, including parts for the chorus. She builds to a finale. A man, PAUL, around thirty-five, walks in. He has a sweet, though distant, demeanor. As he walks in, LISA notices him and stops.*

PAUL: You don't have to stop, sweetheart.
LISA: That's okay.
PAUL: Looked very good.
LISA: Thanks.

PAUL: Don't I get a kiss hello?

LISA: Sure.

PAUL: (*Embraces her.*) Hi, Tiger.

LISA: Hi, Dad.

PAUL: I'm sorry I'm late.

LISA: That's okay.

PAUL: How'd it go?

LISA: Good.

PAUL: Just good?

LISA: Pretty good.

PAUL: "Pretty good." You mean you got a lot of applause or "pretty good" you could have done better.

LISA: Well, Courtney Palumbo's mother thought I was pretty good. But you know the part in the middle when everybody's supposed to freeze and the big girl comes out. Well, I think I moved a little bit.

PAUL: I thought what you were doing looked very good.

LISA: Daddy, that's not what I was doing. That was tap-dancing. I made that up.

PAUL: Oh. Well it looked good. Kind of sexy.

LISA: Yuch!

PAUL: What do you mean "yuch?"

LISA: Just yuch!

PAUL: You don't want to be sexy?

LISA: I don't care.

PAUL: Let's go, Tiger. I promised your mother I'd get you home in time for dinner.

LISA: I can't find my leg warmers.

PAUL: You can't find your what?

LISA: Leg warmers. I can't go home till I find my leg warmers.

PAUL: I don't see you looking for them.

LISA: I was waiting for you.

PAUL: Oh.

LISA: Daddy.

PAUL: What?

LISA: Nothing.

PAUL: Where do you think you left them?

LISA: Somewhere around here. I can't remember.

PAUL: Well, try to remember, Lisa. We don't have all night.

LISA: I told you. I think somewhere around here.

PAUL: I don't see them. Let's go home now. You'll call the dancing school tomorrow.

LISA: Daddy, I can't go home till I find them. Miss Judy says it's not professional to leave things.

PAUL: Who's Miss Judy?

LISA: She's my ballet teacher. She once danced the lead in *Swan Lake,* and she was a June Taylor dancer.

PAUL: Well, then, I'm sure she'll understand about the leg warmers.

LISA: Daddy, Miss Judy wanted to know why you were late today.

PAUL: Hmmmmmmmmm?

LISA: Why were you late?

PAUL: I was in a meeting. Business. I'm sorry.

LISA: Why did you tell Mommy you'd come instead of her if you knew you had business?

PAUL: Honey, something just came up. I thought I'd be able to be here. I was looking forward to it.

LISA: I wish you wouldn't make appointments to see me.

PAUL: Hmmmmmmmm.

LISA: You shouldn't make appointments to see me unless you know you're going to come.

PAUL: Of course I'm going to come.

LISA: No, you're not. Talia Robbins told me she's much happier living without her father in the house. Her father used to come home late and go to sleep early.

PAUL: Lisa, stop it. Let's go.

LISA: I can't find my leg warmers.

PAUL: Forget your leg warmers.

LISA: Daddy.

PAUL: What is it?

LISA: I saw this show on television, I think it was WPIX Channel 11. Well, the father was crying about his daughter.

PAUL: Why was he crying? Was she sick?

LISA: No. She was at school. And he was at business. And he just missed her, so he started to cry.

PAUL: What was the name of this show?

LISA: I don't know. I came in in the middle.

PAUL: Well, Lisa, I certainly would cry if you were sick or far away, but I know that you're well and you're home. So no reason to get maudlin.

LISA: What's maudlin?

PAUL: Sentimental, soppy. Frequently used by children who make things up to get attention.

LISA: I am sick! I am sick! I have Hodgkin's disease and a bad itch on my leg.

PAUL: What do you mean you have Hodgkin's disease? Don't say things like that.

LISA: Swoosie Kurtz, she had Hodgkin's disease on a TV movie last year, but she got better and now she's on *Love Sidney*.

PAUL: Who is Swoosie Kurtz?

LISA: She's an actress named after an airplane. I saw her on *Live at Five*.

PAUL: You watch too much television; you should do your homework. Now, put your coat on.

LISA: Daddy, I really do have a bad itch on my leg. Would you scratch it?

PAUL: Lisa, you're procrastinating.

LISA: Why do you use words I don't understand? I hate it. You're like Daria Feldman's mother. She always talks in Yiddish to her husband so Daria won't understand.

PAUL: Procrastinating is not Yiddish.

LISA: Well, I don't know what it is.

PAUL: Procrastinating means you don't want to go about your business.

LISA: I don't go to business. I go to school.

PAUL: What I mean is you want to hang around here until you and I are late for dinner and your mother's angry and it's too late for you to do your homework.

LISA: I do not.

PAUL: Well, it sure looks that way. Now put your coat on and let's go.

LISA: Daddy.

PAUL: Honey, I'm tired. Really, later.

LISA: Why don't you want to talk to me?

PAUL: I do want to talk to you. I promise when we get home we'll have a nice talk.

LISA: No, we won't. You'll read the paper and fall asleep in front of the news.

PAUL: Honey, we'll talk on the weekend, I promise. Aren't I taking you to the theater this weekend? Let me look. (*He takes out appointment book.*) Yes. Sunday. *Joseph and the Amazing Technicolor Raincoat* with Lisa. Okay, Tiger?

LISA: Sure. It's Dreamcoat.

PAUL: What?

LISA: Nothing. I think I see my leg warmers. (*She goes to pick them up, and an odd-looking trophy.*)

PAUL: What's that?

LISA: It's stupid. I was second best at the dance recital, so they gave me this thing. It's stupid.

PAUL: Lisa.

LISA: What?

PAUL: What did you want to talk about?

LISA: Nothing.

PAUL: Was it about my missing your recital? I'm really sorry, Tiger. I would have liked to have been here.

LISA: That's okay.

PAUL: Honest?

LISA: Daddy, you're prostrastinating.

PAUL: I'm procrastinating. Sit down. Let's talk. So. How's school?

LISA: Fine.

PAUL: You like it?

LISA: Yup.

PAUL: You looking forward to camp this summer?

LISA: Yup.

PAUL: Is Daria Feldman going back?

LISA: Nope.

PAUL: Why not?

LISA: I don't know. We can go home now. Honest, my foot doesn't itch anymore.

PAUL: Lisa, you know what you do in business when it seems like there's nothing left to say? That's when you really start talking. Put a bid on the table.

LISA: What's a bid?

PAUL: You tell me what you want and I'll tell you what I've got to offer. Like Monopoly. You want Boardwalk, but I'm only willing to give you the

Railroads. Now, because you are my daughter I'd throw in Water Works and Electricity. Understand, Tiger?

LISA: No. I don't like board games. You know, Daddy, we could get Space Invaders for our home for thirty-five dollars. In fact, we could get an Osborne System for two thousand. Daria Feldman's parents . . .

PAUL: Daria Feldman's parents refuse to talk to Daria, so they bought a computer to keep Daria busy so they won't have to speak in Yiddish. Daria will probably grow up to be a homicidal maniac lesbian prostitute.

LISA: I know what that word *prostitute* means.

PAUL: Good. (*Pause.*) You still haven't told me about school. Do you still like your teacher?

LISA: She's okay.

PAUL: Lisa, if we're talking try to answer me.

LISA: I am answering you. Can we go home now, please?

PAUL: Damn it, Lisa, if you want to talk to me . . . Talk to me!

LISA: I can't wait till I'm old enough so I can make my own money and never have to see you again. Maybe I'll become a prostitute.

PAUL: Young lady, that's enough.

LISA: I hate you, Daddy! I hate you! (*She throws her trophy into the trash bin.*)

PAUL: What'd you do that for?

LISA: It's stupid.

PAUL: Maybe I wanted it.

LISA: What for?

PAUL: Maybe I wanted to put it where I keep your dinosaur and the picture you made of Mrs. Kimbel with the chicken pox.

LISA: You got mad at me when I made that picture. You told me I had to respect Mrs. Kimbel because she was my teacher.

PAUL: That's true. But she wasn't my teacher. I liked her better with the chicken pox. (*Pause.*) Lisa, I'm sorry. I was very wrong to miss your recital, and you don't have to become a prostitute. That's not the type of profession Miss Judy has in mind for you.

LISA: (*Mumbles.*) No.

PAUL: No. (*Pause.*) So Talia Robbins is really happy her father moved out?

LISA: Talia Robbins picks open the eighth-grade lockers during gym period. But she did that before her father moved out.

PAUL: You can't always judge someone by what they do or what they don't do. Sometimes you come home from dancing school and run upstairs and shut the door, and when I finally get to talk to you, everything is "okay" or "fine." Yup or nope?

LISA: Yup.

PAUL: Sometimes, a lot of times, I come home and fall asleep in front of the television. So you and I spend a lot of time being a little scared of each other. Maybe?

LISA: Maybe.

PAUL: Tell you what. I'll make you a tender offer.

LISA: What?

PAUL: I'll make you a tender offer. That's when one company publishes in the newspaper that they want to buy another company. And the company that publishes is called the Black Knight because they want to gobble up the poor little company. So the poor little company needs to be rescued. And then a White Knight comes along and makes a bigger and better offer so the shareholders won't have to tender shares to the Big Black Knight. You with me?

LISA: Sort of.

PAUL: I'll make you a tender offer like the White Knight. But I don't want to own you. I just want to make a much better offer. Okay?

LISA: (*Sort of understanding.*) Okay. (*Pause. They sit for a moment.*) Sort of. Daddy, what do you think about? I mean, like when you're quiet what do you think about?

PAUL: Oh, business usually. If I think I made a mistake or if I think I'm doing okay. Sometimes I think about what I'll be doing five years from now and if it's what I hoped it would be five years ago. Sometimes I think about what your life will be like, if Mount Saint Helen's will erupt again. What you'll become if you'll study penmanship or word processing. If you'll speak kindly of me to your psychiatrist when you are in graduate school. And how the hell I'll pay for your graduate school. And sometimes I try and think what it was I thought about when I was your age.

LISA: Do you ever look out your window at the clouds and try to see which kinds of shapes they are? Like one time, honest, I saw the head of Walter Cronkite in a flower vase. Really! Like look don't those kinda look like if you turn it upside down, two big elbows or two elephant trunks dancing?

PAUL: Actually still looks like Walter Cronkite in a flower vase to me. But look up a little. See the one that's still moving? That sorta looks like a whale on a thimble.

LISA: Where?

PAUL: Look up. To your right.

LISA: I don't see it. Where?

PAUL: The other way.

LISA: Oh, yeah! There's the head and there's the stomach. Yeah! (LISA *picks up her trophy.*) Hey, Daddy.

PAUL: Hey, Lisa.

LISA: You can have this thing if you want it. But you have to put it like this, because if you put it like that it is gross.

PAUL: You know what I'd like? So I can tell people who come into my office why I have this gross stupid thing on my shelf, I'd like it if you could show me your dance recital.

LISA: Now?

PAUL: We've got time. Mother said she won't be home till late.

LISA: Well, Daddy, during a lot of it I freeze and the big girl in front dances.

PAUL: Well, how 'bout the number you were doing when I walked in?

LISA: Well, see, I have parts for a lot of people in that one, too.

PAUL: I'll dance the other parts.

LISA: You can't dance.

PAUL: Young lady, I played Yvette Mimieux in a *Hasty Pudding Show.*

LISA: Who's Yvette Mimieux?

PAUL: Watch more television. You'll find out. (PAUL *stands up.*) So I'm ready. (*He begins singing.*) "Nothing could be finer than to be in Carolina."

LISA: Now I go. In the morning. And now you go. Dum-da.

PAUL: (*Obviously not a tap dancer.*) Da-da-dum.

LISA: (*Whines.*) Daddy!

PAUL: (*Mimics her.*) Lisa! Nothing could be finer . . .

LISA: That looks dumb.

PAUL: Oh, yeah? You think they do this better in *The Amazing Minkcoat?* No way! Now you go—da da da dum.

LISA: Da da da dum.

PAUL: If I had Aladdin's lamp for only a day, I'd make a wish . . .

LISA: Daddy, that's maudlin!

PAUL: I know it's maudlin. And here's what I'd say:

LISA *and* PAUL: I'd say that "nothing could be finer than to be in Carolina in the mooooooooooornin'."

The Receptive Reader

1. How does the gap between the generations show early in the way the two characters talk and look at things?

2. What is the source of tension between the two? Why is the daughter resentful? How does the father deal with her resentment? (Do you think they are a typical father-daughter pair? Why or why not?)

3. What lines seem funny to you? What are the sources of verbal humor in this scene?

4. In real life, scenes like this one can easily end on a note of conflict, bitterness, or estrangement. What makes the difference here? How does the playwright give the events a happy turn?

The Personal Response

From what perspective do you see the people in this play? With whom do you identify? (*At* whom are you laughing and *with* whom?)

The Creative Dimension

Wasserstein's plays often touch on topics of concern to feminists. Could this scene have been played out in a similar way if the two characters had been mother and son instead? Working with a group, you may want to help with a rewrite of the play along different gender lines.

WRITING ABOUT LITERATURE

31   Responding to Verbal Humor (Focus on Language)

The Writing Workshop   The dramatist's medium is words. Much critical study of imaginative literature takes a close look at the writer's language. In the comedies of writers from Shakespeare to Wilde and Wasserstein, spectators delight in the verbal fireworks. They respond to word play and verbal humor. They delight in the trading off of barbed comments and quick-witted answers, or repartee.

The following student paper takes a close look at the fast-moving language of a Shakespeare comedy. Study the way the student writer identifies major varieties of verbal humor. How successful is the paper in showing the role they play in the comedy as a whole?

Sample Student Paper

The Language of Comedy in *A Midsummer Night's Dream*

Love as infatuation is the foundation for the comedy of Shakespeare's *A Midsummer Night's Dream.* We laugh at the rash actions of the lovers as their affections change at a dizzy pace during an evening in the midsummer forest. We laugh at the way Puck, the mischievous sprite, manipulates the lovers. We laugh at the play the workmen perform, the "tragedy" of Pyramus and Thisby. But the humor in Shakespeare's play is derived from more than the play's plot, the characters' actions. Weaving witty responses, puns, repartee, and malapropisms through the play's plot, Shakespeare creates a humorous, clever world made of language.

This verbal universe makes us laugh and reveals the characters' personalities and social status. The group of craftsmen, for instance, represent low social standing. Thus, their verbal humor is of a "lower" form, such as vile puns and malapropisms—humorous misuse of words. Those of higher social standing—the lovers—also humorously play with words, but they do so intentionally. They make love the subject of clever remarks, often making it sound more like an intellectual game than a physical attraction or emotional bond. Shakespeare further sets apart the two types of humor by having the workmen speak in prose and the lovers speak in verse. The two groups are brought together in the final act, in which both forms of humor meet.

The lovers—Hermia, Lysander, Helena, and Demetrius—delight in the play of opposites that makes for clever, fast-moving love talk throughout the play. They play off diametrically opposed words by way of repartee—the spirited comebacks that require a quick wit. Hermia and Helena, for instance, have an exchange, in rhymed couplets about Demetrius. He loves Hermia—and is rejected by her; he rejects Helena, who loves him.

> Hermia: I frown upon him, yet he loves me still.
> Helena: O that your frowns would teach my smiles such skill!
> Hermia: I give him curses, yet he gives me love.
> Helena: O that my prayers could such affection move!
> Hermia: The more I hate, the more he follows me.
> Helena: The more I love, the more he hateth me. (1.1.194–99)

These characters are prone to punning, another form of verbal humor. In the dialogue, the same word often echoes again and again, often changing its meaning in the process. Hermia greets Helena, calling her beautiful ("fair") Helena: "God speed, fair Helena, whither away?" Helena responds: "Call you me fair? That fair again unsay. / Demetrius loves you fair. O happy fair!" (1.1.180–82) This kind of playing on a repeated word becomes outright punning when Lysander attempts to snuggle up to his love, Hermia. She says, "Nay, good Lysander, for my sake, my dear, / Lie further off, do not lie so near." Lysander assures her that his intentions are honorable; he is not a lying, deceiving seducer: "For lying so, Hermia, I do not lie" (2.2.41–52).

As Helena, obsessed with her love for Demetrius, follows him around, he harshly swears, "I am sick when I do look on thee." Helena responds, "And I am sick when I look not on you" (2.2.12). This harsh repudiation of Helena by Demetrius and her unflagging devotion are examples of the lovers' extreme statements occurring throughout the play. Much of the verbal humor results from the lovers' use of extremely exaggerated love talk that parodies the love poems of Shakespeare's time.

The hyperbolical, exaggerated language is especially hilarious when a lover swears undying passion after just having totally turned around, abandoning one love for another under the mischievous Puck's spell. We laugh at Lysander when his consummate love for Hermia suddenly becomes consummate love for Helena. In ryhming couplets he dramatically swears, "I do repent / The tedious minutes I with her [Hermia] have spent. / Not Hermia but Helena I love. / Who will not change a raven for a dove?" (3.1.111–14).

Demetrius, too, uses extreme flowery exaggeration after falling under the spell of the woods and swearing his love for the same Helena. She is perfect, a goddess. Compared with her, crystal is like mud:

> Oh Helen, goddess, nymph, perfect, divine!
> To what, my love, shall I compare thine eyne?
> Crystal is muddy. O, how ripe in show
> Thy lips, those kissing cherries, tempting grow! (3.3.137–41)

Because both men have so suddenly flip-flopped their affections, Helena is certain they, along with Hermia, are playing her for a fool. She calls Hermia a "counterfeit" and a "puppet." Hermia calls Helena a "juggler" and a "cankerblossom." Lysander swears at Hermia, calling her "thou cat, thou burr" and "you dwarf!" All this name-calling releases resentment and frustration that are usually bottled up in accordance with the requirement to be polite and mature. The exchange of insults in Act 3, Scene 2 creates a manic, humorous scene, leading Puck to exclaim, "Lord what fools these mortals be!"

The other mortals upon whom Puck eavesdrops and whom he manipulates are the honest but ignorant Athenian workmen, the characters of low comedy and low social class. These men, together in the forest on the same night as the lovers, are preparing a play to perform at the royal wedding. In prose, the workmen's verbal humor mainly focuses on malapropism—humorous misuses of words. We laugh at the unintentional blunders of these characters. For example, Quince intends to praise his friend Bottom by calling him a "paragon," a model. Instead, however, Quince says "paramour," a lover, and often an illicit or adulterous one.

Bottom constantly stumbles into the same kind of ridiculous verbal errors. Usually Bottom's mistakes stem from his desire to sound sophisticated, but his limited vocabulary leads him to unintentional humorous remarks. For example, after the craftsmen agree to meet in the woods, Bottom says, "We will meet, and there we may rehearse most obscenely and courageously." Later, instead of saying "to the same effect," he says, "to the same defect."

Often with his blunders, Bottom uses a word of opposite meaning or connotation to what he intends. Instead of "odorous [scented] savors sweet," Bottom says "odious [hateful] savors sweet." We laugh, but Bottom is not in on the joke. Also at his own expense are his puns: Like the lovers, he puns, but not intentionally or wittily. When the mischievous fairy Puck transforms Bottom's head into an ass's head, for example, he declares that his friends are making "an ass of him."

When Bottom and his entourage come together with the lovers and the royal couple at the end of the play, the low and high strands of comedy meet. Theseus, the duke, reads the description of the workmen's play:

"A tedious brief scene of young Pyramus
And his love Thisby; very tragical mirth." (5.1.56–57)

Here the "low" comics have created an oxymoronic, self-canceling description of their play, unaware of its absurd quality. The duke shows the absurdity with a witty retort:

Merry and tragical? Tedious and brief?
That is, hot ice and wondrous strange snow.
How shall we find the concord of this discord? (5.1.58–60)

Throughout the workmen's production, the aristocrats and lovers make clever punning remarks, at the expense of the "actors." When Quince errs in the prologue with punctuation blunders, Theseus says, "This fellow doth not stand upon points," which has a double meaning: Quince does not heed niceties, nor does he pay attention to punctuation in his reading. Lysander adds, "He hath rid his prologue like a rough colt; / he knows not the stop." The "stop" has two meanings: the stopping of a colt by reining it in, and the full stop, a period as a punctuation mark.

At first glance, one might assume that only the workmen are being ridiculed in this scene. Certainly they are inept and blundering, performing a play that the critic David Bevington has called "an absurdly bad play, full of lame epithets, bombastic alliteration, and bathos." But the bathos and exaggerated laments of the workmen's "lovers" sound suspiciously like the exchanges between the Athenian lovers:

O night, O night! Alack, alack, alack,
I fear my Thisby's promise is forgot.
And thou, O wall, O sweet, O lovely wall,
That stand'st between her father's ground and mine . . . (5.1.170–73)

Here Shakespeare invites us, the audience, to acknowledge that the exaggerated love talk invites parody. Just as the audience of Pyramus and Thisby laugh at the workmen, we laugh at *A Midsummer Night's Dream*. Who, then, may be laughing at us?

32 New Directions

Crossing the Boundaries

My characters have nothing. I'm working with impotence, ignorance, that whole zone of being that has always been set aside by artists as something unusable—something by definition incompatible with art.

SAMUEL BECKETT

FOCUS ON NEW DIRECTIONS

Much twentieth-century drama has been in rebellion against convention. Audiences have learned to expect experiment and innovation. Playwrights from George Bernard Shaw to Harold Pinter and Caryl Churchill have delighted in bourgeois-baiting, shocking the people in the good seats. Yet, after initial controversy, their plays have often become part of the established repertory. Some major movements have broken with the past more radically than others:

The Theater of the Absurd The **theater of the absurd** surfaced in the fifties to challenge the tradition of issue-oriented realistic plays and turn theater upside down. In 1954, Samuel Beckett, an Irish author living in Paris and writing mostly in French, wrote *Waiting for Godot,* one of the classics of the modern stage. It is a play about two homeless people waiting for Godot—a personage who never comes. The theater of the absurd mirrored the conviction that the "reality" acted out in most stage plays is artificial. It does not show the world in which most people live. Most people lead disjointed lives. They don't have grand plans. They don't have major crises; they stumble from one trivial crisis to another. They don't discuss the issues; instead they talk as if they were on automatic pilot, with language furnishing them a sheer endless supply of ready-made sayings and banalities.

Epic Theater Disciples of Bertolt Brecht used the label **epic theater** for his ideologically inspired plays that became a major influence on

994

critics, directors, and performers. Brecht was a German communist dramatist, driven into exile from Nazi Germany. His plays discarded theatrical conventions for a ballad-like storytelling, with the author often pointing the ideological moral. The heroine of *Mother Courage and Her Children* survives by selling supplies as a camp follower of the marauding armies of the Thirty Years' War while trying in vain to keep her children from being devoured by the war. (As one of the characters in the play says, "He who wants to dine with the devil needs a long spoon.")

Feminist Playwrights   In the last few decades, a major challenge to tradition has been the emergence of female playwrights challenging the domination of the theater by male dramatists. Audiences have witnessed a major effort to redefine and broaden the traditional canon of plays written by predominantly male writers. Feminist critics have reassessed the work and influence of playwrights like Susan Glaspell (*Trifles*), Lillian Hellman (*The Children's Hour,* 1934), and Clare Boothe Luce (*The Women,* 1937). Feminist critics have championed the work of women like ntozake shange, who wrote *for colored girls who have considered suicide/when the rainbow is enuf* (performed on Broadway in 1976) and who spoke of the "struggle to become all that is forbidden by our environment, forfeited by our gender, all that we have forgotten." Audiences are increasingly watching plays like Beth Henley's *The Wake of Jamey Foster* or *Crimes of the Heart* which reexamine human relationships from a woman's point of view (or women's points of view). Tina Howe has written comedies of life in the American nuclear family (*Birth and After Birth,* 1974; *Approaching Zanzibar,* 1988).

Multicultual Perspectives   Plays from outside the white mainstream have made their way into the established canon from minority sources and from other cultures. Luis Valdez's *The Shrunken Head of Pancho Villa* and other plays made their way into anthologies. In his *Los Vendidos,* white politicians shop for token representatives of minorities the way others shop for used cars. The American playwright August Wilson is making audiences rethink their stereotypes about black people. In *The Piano Lesson* (1990), he is teaching us to listen to authentic folk dialect as the natural expression of the exuberance and humanity of his characters rather than as the badge of poverty and illiteracy. Among world authors writing in English, the Nigerian playwright Wole Soyinka stands out. Intimately acquainted with the literary traditions of the West, he yet has remained rooted in and loyal to the culture of his own people. In his *Death and the King's Horseman,* he pays tribute to a tribal culture and tribal traditions that have survived centuries of colonialism and cultural myopia.

PSYCHOLOGICAL REALISM

For several decades, a major force on American and European stages has been drama that superficially could be classified as realistic theater. However, it probes deeper into the psychic hurts and existential frustrations of its characters. Audiences witness searing confrontations that bring to the surface buried hostilities. Verbal slugfests and lacerating self-revelations often leave the characters and the audience emotionally drained. Edward Albee is an American pioneer of this tradition of naturalistic, slice-of-life psychodrama. His blockbusting success *Who's Afraid of Virginia Woolf?* (1962) shows two married people destroying themselves in a relentless outpouring of recrimination and abuse. David Mamet—*Glengarry Glen Ross, Oleanna,* and a score of other plays—is the past master of the theater of confrontation, indictment, and self-laceration.

David Mamet   *(born 1947)*

David Mamet was born in Chicago. In his autobiographical *Memoir,* he writes about growing up in a loveless, harshly punitive family setting. He went on to become a wizard of the contemporary stage, turning out a succession of searing and immensely successful plays that at times seem bent on tearing the last shred of pretense from their characters. Plays like *Sexual Perversity in Chicago* (1974), *American Buffalo* (1975), and *Speed the Plow* (1988) made him a major force in today's American theater. His *Glengarry Glen Ross* (1983), a play about desperate, down-at-the-heels real estate agents, makes *Death of a Salesman* read like a tribute to an idyllic Golden Age of salesmanship. In *Oleanna* (1992), a female student who at first seems confused and in need of help slowly turns into the Avenger of women who have been belittled, condescended to, and denied access to the privileged upper layers of the academic world. Mamet has written screenplays for films, including *Homicide, House of Games,* and *The Verdict.*

Cryptogram was first produced in 1994. His most personal play, it takes the audience back to the archetypal nightmare fears of childhood. The play's title contains the Greek root *crypto-,* meaning "hidden" or "secret"; thus, a cryptogram is message written in code. Part of the loneliness and terror of childhood results from the discovery that the grownups are speaking in code, a code that the child may not be able to break. Like other Mamet plays, *Cryptogram* starts with apparently aimless routine conversation—in this play, involving a mother, a family friend, and a ten-year-old son. Gradually something disturbing or ominous comes into focus. For a time, the characters seem to be talking at cross purposes, having different agendas. We begin to sense that we are in for shattering revelations, watching a human tragedy unfold that we are helpless to head off.

The Cryptogram   *1994*
This play is dedicated to Gregory Mosher

Last night when you were all in bed Mrs. O'Leary
left a lantern in her shed

CAMPING SONG

CHARACTERS

DONNY, a woman in her late thirties
DEL, a man of the same age
JOHN, Donny's son, around ten

The action takes place in Donny's living room in 1959.

ACT ONE: *One evening*
ACT TWO: *The next night*
ACT THREE: *Evening, one month later*

Act One

A living room. One door leading off to the kitchen, one staircase leading up to the second floor. Evening. DEL *is seated on the couch.* JOHN *comes downstairs dressed in his pajamas.*

JOHN: I couldn't find 'em.
DEL: . . . couldn't find 'em.
JOHN: No.
DEL: What?
JOHN: Slippers.
DEL: Yes?
JOHN: They're packed.
DEL: . . . slippers are packed.
JOHN: Yes.
DEL: Why did you pack them?
JOHN: Take them along.
DEL: How are you going to use your slippers in the woods.
JOHN: To keep my feet warm.
DEL: Mmm.
JOHN: I shouldn't of packed them?
DEL: Well, put something on your feet.
JOHN: What?
DEL: Socks.
JOHN: Put something on my feet now.
DEL: Yes.

JOHN: "As long as I'm warm."

DEL: That's correct.

JOHN: I have 'em. (*Produces socks. Starts putting them on.*)

DEL: That's good. Think ahead.

JOHN: Why did you say "why did you pack them?"

DEL: I wondered that you'd taken them with.

JOHN: Why?

DEL: Out in the Woods?

JOHN: No, but to wear in the Cabin.

DEL: . . . that's right.

JOHN: Don't you think?

DEL: I do.

JOHN: I know I couldn't wear them in the woods.

DEL: No. No. That's right. Where were we?

JOHN: Issues of sleep.

DEL: . . . is . . .

JOHN: Issues of sleep.

DEL: No. I'm sorry. You were quite correct. To take your slippers. I spoke too quickly.

JOHN: That's alright.

DEL: Thank you. (*Pause.*) Where were we? Issues of Sleep.

JOHN: And last night either.

DEL: Mm . . . ?

JOHN: . . . I couldn't sleep.

DEL: So I'm told. (*Pause.*)

JOHN: Last night, either.

DEL: Fine. What does it mean "I could not sleep"?

JOHN: . . . what does it mean?

DEL: Yes. It means nothing other than the meaning you choose to assign to it.

JOHN: I don't get you.

DEL: I'm going to explain myself.

JOHN: Good.

DEL: A "Trip," for example, you've been looking forward to.

JOHN: A trip. Yes. Oh, yes.

DEL: . . . absolutely right.

JOHN: . . . that I'm excited.

DEL: . . . who wouldn't be?

JOHN: *Anyone* would be.

DEL: That's right.

JOHN: . . . to go in the *Woods*. . . ?

DEL: Well. You see? You've answered your own question.

JOHN: Yes. That I'm excited.

DEL: I can't blame you.

JOHN: You can't.

DEL: No. Do you see?

JOHN: That it's natural.

DEL: I think it is.

JOHN: Is it?

DEL: I think it absolutely is. To go with your *father*. . . ?

JOHN: Why isn't he home?

DEL: We don't know.

JOHN: . . . because it's something. To go out there.

DEL: I should say.

JOHN: In the Woods. . . ?

DEL: . . . I hope to tell you.

JOHN: Well, you *know* it is.

DEL: That I do.

And I will tell you: older people, too. Grown people.

You know what they do?

The night before a trip?

JOHN: What do they do?

DEL: Well, many times *they* cannot sleep. *They* will stay up that night.

JOHN: They will?

DEL: Oh yes.

JOHN: Why?

DEL: They can't sleep. No. Why?

Because their minds, you see, are full of thoughts.

JOHN: What are their thoughts of?

DEL: Their thoughts are of two things.

JOHN: Yes?

DEL: Of what they're *leaving.*

JOHN: . . . yes?

DEL: And what they're going *toward.* (*Pause.*) Just like you.

JOHN: . . . of what they're leaving . . .

DEL: . . . mmm . . . (*Pause.*)

JOHN: How do you know that?

DEL: Well, you know, they say we live and learn.

JOHN: They do?

DEL: That's what they say. And I'll tell you *another* thing . . .

(*A crash is heard offstage.*) (*Pause.*)

DONNY (*offstage*): . . . I'm alright . . .

DEL: . . . what?

DONNY (*offstage*): I'm alright . . .

DEL: . . . did . . .

DONNY (*offstage*): What? Did I what?

DEL: Are you . . .

DONNY (*offstage*): What?

I've spilt the tea.

DEL: What?

DONNY (*offstage*): I spilled the tea.

DEL: Do you want help?

DONNY (*offstage*): What?

JOHN: Do you want help he said.

DONNY (*offstage*): No.

DEL: You don't? (*To* JOHN.) Go help your mother.

DONNY (*offstage*) (*simultaneous with* "mother"): . . . I'm alright. I'm alright.

(*To self.*) Oh, hell . . .

DEL: What did you do?

DONNY (*offstage*): What?

DEL: . . . what did you do . . .

DONNY: I broke the pot, I broke the teapot. I'm alright. I broke the teapot. (*Pause.*)

DEL (*to* JOHN): Well, there you go. . . . a human *being* . . .

JOHN: . . . yes?

DEL: . . . cannot conceal himself.

JOHN: That's an example?

DEL: Well, hell, look at it: anything. When it is *disordered,* any, um, "Change," do you see. . . ?

JOHN: What is the change?

DEL: The trip.

JOHN: She ain't going.

DEL: No of course she's not. But *you* are. And your father is. It's an upheaval.

JOHN: It's a minor one.

DEL: Who is to say? (*Pause.*)

JOHN: But did *you* feel that?

DEL: Did I . . . ?

JOHN: Yes.

DEL: Feel what?

JOHN: Last week.

DEL: Feel. Last week.

JOHN: Thoughts on a trip.

DEL: . . . Did I . . . ?

JOHN: When you took *your* trip.

DONNY (*offstage*): It's going to be a minute.

JOHN: . . . when you took your trip.

DONNY (*offstage*): . . . hello . . . ?

DEL: We're alright.

DONNY (*offstage*): The tea is going to be a minute.

JOHN: We're alright in here.

DONNY (*entering*): I've put the . . . why aren't you asleep.

DEL: . . . did I feel "pressure"?

DONNY: . . . John . . . ?

JOHN: Yes.

DONNY: Why aren't you asleep?

DEL: Before my trip. No.

JOHN: No. Why?

DEL: Because, and this is important. Because people differ.

DONNY: What are you doing down here?

DEL: We're talking.

JOHN: . . . I came down.

DEL (*to* DONNY): I'm sorry. Are you alright?

DONNY: What? I dropped the teapot. What are you *doing* down . . .

JOHN: We're talking.

DEL: He came down, and I began a conversation.

DONNY: Alright, if you began it.

DEL: I did.

DONNY (*sighs*): We're going to have tea, and then you go upst . . . Where are your slippers?

JOHN: Packed.

DONNY: They're packed.

JOHN: For the trip.

DONNY: And then you go upstairs and you go to sleep.

JOHN: I want to wait till my father comes home.

DONNY: Well, yes, I'm sure you do. But you need your sleep. And if you don't get it, you're not going on the trip.

JOHN: Will he be home soon?

DONNY: Yes. He will.

JOHN: Where is he?

DONNY: I don't know. Yes, I do, yes. He's at the Office. And he'll be home soon.

JOHN: Why is he working late?

DONNY: I don't know. We'll find out when he comes home, John. Must we do this every night?

JOHN: I only want . . .

DEL: Do you know what?

JOHN: I didn't want to upset you, I only . . .

DEL: . . . could I . . . ?

JOHN: I only . . .

DEL (*simultaneous with* "only"): Could I make a suggestion? (*To* JOHN.) Why don't you busy yourself?

DONNY: He has to sleep.

DEL: . . . but he's not *going* to sleep. He's . . .

JOHN: That's right.

DONNY: . . . one moment.

JOHN: . . . If I had something to *do* . . .

DONNY (*simultaneous with* "do"): No. You're absolutely right.

JOHN: . . . something to do. If I had *that* . . .

DONNY: Alright.

DEL: Are you packed?

JOHN: I'm all packed.

DEL: . . . well . . .

JOHN: I, I My *Father* isn't packed, his . . .

DONNY: No . . .

JOHN: . . . I could pack *his* stuff.

DONNY: No, no, I'll tell you what you could do.

JOHN: What?

DONNY: Close up the attic.

JOHN: . . . close it up?

DONNY: Neaten it up. Yes.

JOHN: Is it disturbed?

DONNY: Mmm.

JOHN: Why?

DONNY: . . . after my "rummaging."

JOHN: Alright.

DONNY: . . . and . . .

JOHN: . . . alright.

DONNY: See if you find any things up there.

JOHN: Things.

DONNY: . . . you might need to take.

JOHN: . . . things I might need to take up.

DONNY: Mm.

JOHN: Or that *he* might need.

DONNY: That's right.

JOHN: . . . or that you forgot.

DONNY: Yes.

JOHN: To pack.

DONNY: Yes. Would you do that?

JOHN: Of course.

DONNY: Thank you, John.

DEL: Thank you.

DONNY: And perhaps you'd put on some clothing.

JOHN: Good.

DONNY: Very good. Off you go then.

JOHN: I will.

DEL: "My blessings on your House."

JOHN: That's what the Wizard said.

DEL: That's right.

JOHN: "And mine on yours."

DEL: "Until the whale shall speak."

JOHN: "Until the Moon shall Weep." Mother?

DONNY: I don't remember it . . . (*Pause.*)

JOHN: You don't remember it? (*Pause.*)

DEL: Well then, John. Alright then. Off you go to work.

JOHN (*exiting*): I will.

DEL: Off you go. (*Pause.*)

DONNY: No. I don't understand it.

DEL: Well . . .

DONNY: No.

DEL: He has trouble sleeping.

DONNY: Mm. No.

DEL: That's his nature.

DONNY: Is it?

DEL: Children . . .

DONNY: No. You see. It's grown into this minuet. Every night . . .

DEL: Well, yes. But this is *special,* he . . .

DONNY: No, No. He always has a reason. Some . . . every night . . .

DEL: Yes. Granted. But a Trip to the Woods . . .

DONNY: . . . he . . .

DEL: . . . with his Dad . . . ? It's an *event.* I think. What do I know? But, as his *friend* . . .

DONNY: . . . yes . . .

DEL: . . . as his *friend* . . .

DONNY: Yes. Yes. He Always has a Reason.

DEL: Yes, but I'm saying, in *spite* of . . . *I* don't know. I don't mean to intrude . . . but good. But *Good*. One sends him up to the Attic . . .

DONNY: Oh.

DEL: And that's "it." That's the solution.

DONNY: Oh. Oh . . .

DEL: To, um . . . to, um, what is the word . . . ?

DONNY: Look what I found.

DEL: To um . . . not "portray" . . . to um . . .

DONNY: Look what I found.

DEL: "Participate." That's the word. Is that the word? No. To, um . . .

DONNY: Del. Shut up.

DEL: To um . . .

DONNY (*simultaneous with* "To"): Shut up. Look what I found up in the attic.

(*She goes to a side table and brings back a small framed photograph and hands it to* DEL.)

DEL: (*Pause.*) When was this taken . . .

DONNY (*simultaneous with* "taken"): When I was packing for the trip.

DEL (*simultaneous with* "trip"): Mmm . . . No. When was this taken?

DONNY: Isn't it funny? Though? The things you find? (*Pause.*)

DEL: Huh . . .

DONNY: What?

DEL: I don't understand this photograph. (*Pause.*)

DONNY: What do you mean?

(JOHN *comes down onto the landing.*)

JOHN: Which coat? That's what I forgot. To pack my coat.

DONNY (*to* DEL): Which coat?

JOHN: That's what was on my mind.

DEL: Which coat should he take?

DEL (*looking up from the photograph*): Mm? When were you up there?

DONNY: Where?

DEL: Up in the attic?

DONNY (*simultaneous with* "attic"): In the attic today, cleaning up.

DEL (*of photo*) (*simultaneous with* "up"): . . . this is the damnedest thing . . .

DONNY: *Isn't* it . . . ?

DEL: When, when could this have been taken?

DONNY: And I found that old *Lap* robe.

DEL: The lap robe . . .

DONNY: The *stadium* blanket we . . .

JOHN: Which coat?

DONNY: Which?

JOHN: How cold is it up there yet?

DEL: . . . a lap robe . . .

DONNY: The *stadium* blanket.

JOHN: How cold was it last week? Del?

DONNY: Just bring your regular coat.

JOHN: My blue coat?

DONNY: The melton coat?

JOHN: What's melton?

DONNY: The blue coat. Your fabric coat.

JOHN: The *wool* one?

DONNY (*to* DEL): Is it too cold for that?

DEL: No.

DONNY: Then take it.

JOHN: My *blue* coat.

DONNY: Yes.

JOHN: Do I have any sweaters left?

DONNY: Up there?

JOHN: Yes.

DEL: I think so.

DONNY: I'm sure that you do.

JOHN: You think so?

DEL: They'd be in your bureau.

JOHN: And, the fishing stuff. Is it there?

DONNY: The fishing stuff. They brought back. Last week, John. It's all . . .

JOHN: . . . they brought it back.

DONNY: Yes. It's up in the attic . . .

JOHN (*simultaneous with* "attic"): You should have left it at the Cabin.

DONNY: It's in the attic. You'll see it up there.

DEL: . . . we were afraid . . .

DONNY: . . . they didn't want it to Get Stolen.

JOHN: And the fishing line. Do we have that good line?

DEL (*simultaneous with* "line"): . . . we were afraid it would get taken.

JOHN: . . . that good heavy line . . . ?

DONNY: . . . I'm sorry, John . . . ?

JOHN: The fishing line.

DONNY: I'm sure you. Yes. Fishing line. In the same box.

JOHN: Green? The green one?

DONNY: . . . I . . .

JOHN: The green line? In the Tackle Box? Because if not, we have to stop on the way, and . . .

DONNY: . . . I'm . . .

JOHN: Dad said that the Green line . . .

DEL: What's special about it?

DONNY: Open the box.

JOHN: . . . because if not . . .

DONNY: Find the box.

DEL: What's special about it?

JOHN: It's very strong.

DONNY: Find the box, open it, and check it out.

JOHN: Because that's how we'll know.

DONNY: That's what I'm telling you. (JOHN *exits, up the stairs.*)

DEL: Port out, starboard home.

DONNY: And put some clothing on. (*Pause.*)

DEL (*of photo*): . . . when was this taken?

DONNY: I swear. He's . . .

DEL: What? Well, he's having difficulty sleeping.

DONNY: It's all such a mystery.

DEL: Do you think?

DONNY: Yes. All our good intentions . . .

DEL: Big thing. Going in the Woods. Your Father . . .

DONNY: . . . mmm.

DEL: . . . big thing.

DONNY: Is it?

DEL: Hope to tell you.

DONNY: (*Pause.*) It goes so quickly.

DEL: Certain things remain.

DONNY: Yes?

DEL: (*Pause.*) *Friendship* . . . (*Pause.*) Certain habits.

DONNY: It goes so quickly . . . (*Pause.*)

DEL: Does it?

DONNY: Sometimes I wish I was a Monk.

DEL: Mmm . . . what's that?

DONNY: I wish I were a monk.

DEL: How would that go?

DONNY: An old man for example . . .

DEL: . . . mmm . . .

DONNY: (*Pause.*) . . . and all his sons are gone.

DEL: . . . an Oriental Fantasy.

DONNY: That's right.

DEL: "Mist" . . . "Mountains" . . . So on.

DONNY: . . . mmm . . .

DEL: And what does this man do?

DONNY: The monk.

DEL: Yes.

DONNY: Nothing. (*Pause.*) He sits; and gazes out at his . . .

DEL: Mm. Well, that's a form of meditation . . .

DONNY: Gazes out at his domain.

DEL: Well, I'm sure you'd be very good at it.

DONNY: You're very kind.

DEL: What? I'm very kind, yes. (*Pause.*) For *it's.* A *form.* Of meditation. (*Pause.*) As are they all.

DONNY: Mm.

DEL: The thing about photography is that it is very seductive.

DONNY: Because sometimes it seems the older I get, the less that I know.

DEL: Well, it's a mystery. The whole goddamned thing.

DONNY: Isn't it . . . ?

DEL: I think so. (*Pause.*) Goes fast. Goes quickly.

DONNY: Mmm.

DEL: . . . and then it is gone. (*Pause.*)

DONNY: No, I need a rest.

DEL (*of photograph*): Well, if we look here we see that the *tree* is gone. When would that have been?

DONNY (*to herself*): A fantasy of rest . . . (*Pause.*)

DEL: . . . Oh, oh, oh what are you doing this weekend . . . ?

DONNY: This weekend?

DEL: Yes.

DONNY: Well. I don't know.

DEL: You don't know what you're doing this weekend.

DONNY: I'm going to sit.

DEL: To sit here.

DONNY: Yes.

DEL: Do you want company?

(JOHN *reenters, wrapped in a plaid blanket.*)

DONNY: No. That's not clothing.

JOHN: . . . I . . .

DONNY: You put some clothing on right now. (*Pause.*) What? (*Pause.*)

JOHN: I tore it.

DONNY: You tore what?

JOHN: I tore the blanket. I'm sorry.

DONNY: You tore it?

JOHN (*simultaneous with* "tore"): I was opening the box. I think there was a
    nail sticking out. I heard something rip . . .

(*He shows the tear.*)

DONNY: You're saying you tore *that* blanket?

JOHN: I heard some . . .

DONNY: John . . .

JOHN: I was doing it too quickly. I know I heard.

DONNY (*simultaneous with* "heard"): John, that was torn so long ago.

JOHN: I heard it rip.

DONNY: No, it was torn years ago.

JOHN (*simultaneous with* "ago"): I didn't tear it?

DONNY: No.

JOHN: I heard it rip.

DEL: You may have heard it in your mind . . .

JOHN: . . . but . . .

DONNY: No we tore that long ago.

DEL: I think your mind is racing.

DONNY: It's alright, John. It's alright. Go upstairs. And you put on some
    clothing . . . (*Pause.*)

JOHN: It's tied with twine.

DONNY: I don't understand you.

JOHN: The *Tackle* box.

DONNY: Box . . .

JOHN: . . . with the fishing line . . .

DONNY: . . . well, *untie* it. And . . .

JOHN: I can't untie it. That's what I'm saying. I tried to pull the twine off,
    but . . .

DEL (*Takes out knife. Of knife.*): This'll do it.

JOHN: I can't . . .

DEL: . . . is it alright . . . ?

DONNY: . . . If you don't get some rest, before . . .

DEL (*to* DONNY): Is it alright?

DONNY: What?

DEL: Can he have the knife?

DONNY: . . . to have the knife . . .

DEL: . . . to use. To cut the twine . . .

DONNY (*simultaneous with* "twine"): What would your father say?

JOHN: It's alright.

DONNY: He would?

JOHN: Yes.

DONNY: It's alright for you . . .

JOHN: . . . yes. Oh, yes.

DONNY: . . . to have the knife.

JOHN: Yes.

DONNY (*simultaneous with* "Yes"): I hardly think so.

JOHN: No he *would.*

DEL: Then there you go. (*Hands* JOHN *the knife.*)

JOHN: Where did you get the knife, though?

DONNY: Good *Lord,* John . . . calm *down* tonight.

JOHN: No.

DONNY: What?

JOHN: I can't.

DONNY: . . . why not?

JOHN: The Tea, the Blanket . . . ?

DONNY: I don't understand.

JOHN: I'm *waiting* for it.

DEL: You're waiting for what?

JOHN: "The Third Misfortune."

DEL: "The Third Misfortune."

DONNY: Third . . . ?

JOHN: I'm waiting to see "What is the Third Misfortune?" (*Pause.*)

DONNY: What does he mean?

JOHN: It's in the book.

DEL: Misfortunes come in threes.

DONNY: Where *is* that book, by the way?

JOHN: Misfortunes come in threes.

DONNY: The third misfortune. I remember. Yes.

JOHN: It's in the book.

DONNY: Wait. How long since we've seen that book?

JOHN: A long time.

DONNY: Ha. And you remembered it?

JOHN: Of course I remember it.

DONNY: Isn't that odd?

JOHN: "When we think of sickness, sickness is approaching," said the Wizard.

DEL: . . . That's what the Wizard said.

DONNY: Where *is* that book?

DEL: It will turn up someday.

DONNY: No, did we leave it at the lake?

JOHN: Misfortunes come in threes.

DONNY: Alright, what are the three misfortunes?

JOHN: The Lance, and the Chalice; The Lance was broken by the Lord of Night, the Chalice was burnt . . .

DONNY: Yes. No. Not in the book, here.

JOHN: What are the others here?

DONNY: The Three Misfortunes.

JOHN: *Here.*

DONNY: Yes.

JOHN: Alright. One: The Pot, The Teapot broke.

DONNY: That's one, yes. And?

JOHN: The blanket.

DEL: . . . the blanket.

DONNY: What about it?

JOHN: . . . torn . . .

DONNY: No, but it *wasn't* torn. That happened long ago.

JOHN: I *thought* I tore it now.

(*Sound of teakettle,* DONNY *exits.*)

DONNY (*offstage*): It was torn long ago. You can absolve yourself.

JOHN: . . . I *thought* that I tore it.

DEL: But, you see, in reality, things unfold . . . independent of our fears of them.

JOHN: I don't know what you mean.

DEL: Because we *think* a thing is one way does not mean that this is the way that this thing must be.

JOHN: The blanket was torn long ago?

DEL: That's what your mother said.

JOHN: How?

DEL: Well . . .

JOHN: Did you see my hat?

DEL: . . . did?

JOHN: At the Cabin?

DEL: Which hat is that?

JOHN: The grey cap.

DEL: Like mine, except grey?

JOHN: Yes.

DEL: I don't remember.

JOHN: Not like yours, actually, it's . . .

DEL: I don't remember.

JOHN: No, it's not actually like yours, it's . . .

DEL: How is it different?

JOHN: It's. I steered you wrong. It's not like yours at all.

DEL: Then I don't know which one you mean.

JOHN: My *Grey* hat. It was on the peg.

DEL: The peg . . .

JOHN: . . . Near the door. At the cabin.

DEL: I don't remember.

JOHN: You don't? Why?

DEL: Because I wasn't looking for it. (*Pause.*) Do you know. I'm going to tell you a game.

JOHN: A game?

DEL: A game you can play.

You and your father. Up there. Eh?

To "sharpen your skills." (*Pause.*) To "aid your camping."

JOHN: Me and my father.

DEL: Yes.

JOHN: Does he know this game?

DEL: I think that he may.

JOHN: Did he teach it to you?

DEL: No. I learned it independently.

JOHN: Um.

DEL: And. If he does not know it, you can teach it to *him*.

JOHN: Good.

DEL: Yes? You think so?

JOHN: Well, I think so. You have to tell me the game.

DEL: Here it is: . . . you write down . . .

JOHN: ". . . to sharpen our skills . . ."

DEL: You write down your *recollections*.

Of the things you've seen. During the day.

Then you compare them.

JOHN: I don't understand.

DEL: To see who has observed the best.

You observe things during the day. Then, at night you write them down. To test your observation. (*Pause.*) Things in the Cabin, for instance. Or the woods. And, then, you see whose recollection was more accurate. (*Pause.*) You see?

JOHN: See who was more accurate.

DEL: That's correct. (*Pause.*)

JOHN: And why is this game useful?

DEL: If you were lost it could assist you to orient yourself.

JOHN: Would it be things which we *decided before* to observe? Or things . . .

DEL: . . . it could be both.

JOHN: . . . both things we *decided* to observe, and things we decided, later on, we should remember.

DEL: That's right.

JOHN: But something could have been the Third Misfortune, even though it had happened quite long ago. (*Pause.*)

DEL: How could that be?

JOHN: It could be if the "Third Misfortune" happened long ago. If, when it *happened,* no one *noticed,* or . . .

DEL: "at the *time* . . ."

JOHN: Yes, or neglected to *count* it . . .

DEL: . . . I . . .

JOHN: . . . until we recognized it *now* . . . And also, what could we pick. To observe, beside the Cabin?

DEL: What? *Anything.* The *pond,* the . . .

JOHN: . . . where did you get the knife?

DEL: The knife.

JOHN: Yes.

DEL: I told you. Your father gave it to me.

JOHN: He gave you his war knife.

DEL: Yes.

JOHN: His *pilot's* knife . . . ?

DEL: Yes. (*Pause.*)

JOHN: But we couldn't choose the pond.

DEL: Why not?

JOHN: Because it's changing. (*Pause.*) When?

DEL: . . . when what?

JOHN: Did he give it to you?

DEL: Aha.

JOHN: When?

DEL: Last week. When we went camping.

JOHN: Oh.

DEL: Does that upset you?

JOHN: No.

DEL: Aha.

JOHN: What do you mean?

DEL: Nothing.

JOHN: Why did you say "aha."

DEL: Something occurred to me.

JOHN: What?

DEL: Something. (*Pause.*)

JOHN: We couldn't choose the pond.

DEL: The pond?

JOHN: To observe.

DEL: No? Why not?

JOHN: Because it's changing. (DONNY *reenters with tea mugs.*)

DEL: Well, then you choose something else.

JOHN: What should I choose?

DEL: Something that doesn't change. (*Of photo.*) Who, who, what *is* this?

DONNY: It's the Lake.

DEL: No, please, I know where it is, I just don't . . .

DONNY: . . . what?

DEL: . . . I don't remember it.

DONNY: . . . you've seen that photo so . . .

DEL: . . . Well. I don't remember it.

JOHN: You have a strange expression on your face. *Mother:* doesn't . . .

DONNY: Calm down. John.

DEL: . . . I do?

JOHN: You're grinning. (*To* DONNY.) I am calm.

DEL: . . . when was this taken? (DONNY *looks at photo.*)

DONNY: Well, the boathouse is still up . . .

DEL (*to* JOHN): It's strange I'm grinning?

DONNY: . . . so it's . . .

JOHN: It looks unlike you.

DONNY (*of photo, to* DEL): You don't remember this?

DEL: No.

DONNY: *Truly?*

DEL: No. When was it taken?

DONNY (*simultaneous with* "taken"): Well, alright: the boathouse is up, so, I can tell you what *year* it is: The boathouse is up, but the birch is down, so: it's before the War . . .

DEL: . . . it would have to be before the War . . .

DONNY (*simultaneous with* "war"): Wait a moment . . . (JOHN *yawns. Sits on the couch.*) Oh, John; are you getting sleepy?

JOHN: When is Dad coming home?

DONNY: He'll be here when he gets here, I think.

JOHN: . . . I want to tell him this game.

DEL (*of photograph*): I remember the shirt.

DONNY: . . . he'll be home soon, John.

DEL: . . . is this Robert's shirt?

DONNY: What?

DEL: That I'm wearing.

DONNY: In the photo . . .

DEL: Yes . . .

DONNY: . . . I . . . (*Pause.*)

DEL: Do you see my problem? (*Pause.*)

DONNY: Alright.

DEL: Because I remember neither the occasion nor the photograph.

DONNY: . . . Do you have his *shirt* on . . .

DEL: Yes.

DONNY: Why *would* you?

DEL: Well, that's what I'm saying.

DONNY: Can you make the pattern out?

DEL: He's asleep.

DONNY: *Finally.* (*Pause.*) He thought that he tore the blanket.

DEL: I believe that this Trip has a "meaning" for him.

DONNY: Del, he's always had this problem.

DEL: No, I've had a "clue."

DONNY: No, you're ten years too late. You know, Robert always said: we disagreed about it. From the first. And his theory was "let the child cry."

DEL: . . . let him cry . . .

DONNY: To teach him to . . .

DEL: No, this trip . . .

DONNY: Del, He Always Has a Reason . . .

DEL: He's a sensitive kid . . . ?

DONNY: . . . whatever that means.

DEL: I think it means . . . Well, in *this* case he *told* me, in effect.

DONNY: . . . yes?

DEL: In *this* case it means he's *jealous.*

DONNY: Jealous.

DEL: Of my trip. Last week with Robert.

DONNY: He was jealous?

DEL: That's right.

DONNY: But why does that come out *now?*

    And I'll tell you one other thing.

    Let him be jealous. What if he was? Yes. I think he needs to spend more time with his father; and, yes, I think that he has to learn the world does not revolve around him. (*Pause.*)

Oh, Lord. I'll tell you. No. You're right. It's guilt.

It's guilt. I'm guilty. I get to spend one weekend on my own. And I'm consumed with guilt.

DEL (*of photo*): Who took this picture? (*Pause.* DONNY *looks at it.*)

DONNY: I don't know.

DEL: Eh? Who could have taken it?

DONNY: Huh. (*Pause.*) I don't . . .

DEL: Do you see? If we're all in it? (*Pause.*)

That's why I don't remember it.

DONNY: I . . . (*Pause.*) Isn't that funny . . . ?

DEL: That's why I don't remember it. (*Pause.*) I knew there was a reason. (*Pause.*)

DONNY: Lord, I found so much *stuff* up there.

DEL: . . . up . . . ?

DONNY: In the attic. The *stadium* blanket, the . . .

DEL: I recognized that.

DONNY: The blanket. Well I hope so.

DEL: How could he think he tore it?

DONNY: . . . I . . .

DEL: He'd seen it for years.

DONNY: . . . so long ago . . .

DEL: Isn't it . . . ? (*Pause.*)

Do you know, at the Hotel. I collect things. I'm amazed. I clean my room out. Every few months. I'm amazed. I always think I've kept it *bare*. But when I clean it out. I find this mass of *things* I have accumulated.

DONNY: They, what are they, mostly?

DEL: Papers. (*Pause.*)

DONNY: I went to the Point.

DEL: You did?

DONNY: I walked down there. Yes.

DEL: Recently?

DONNY: Yes. (*Pause.*)

And I remembered. When the Three of us would go.

Late at night. Before the war.

DEL: I remember.

DONNY: And *Robert* and I. Would make love under a blanket. And I wondered. After all this time, why it never occurred to me. I don't know. But I wondered. Did you *hear* us; and, if you did. If it upset you. (*Pause.*)

DEL: And you've thought about it all this time.

DONNY: That's right.

DEL: Oh, Donny.

DONNY: Did it upset you?

DEL: Aren't you sweet . . . aren't you sweet to worry.

DONNY: Did it?

DEL: Well. I . . .

JOHN (*waking*): What did they say? What?

DONNY: Go to sleep, John.

JOHN: I was going there. But you said to bring the, bring . . . (*Pause.*) Bring them the . . . (*Pause.*)

DONNY: John:

JOHN: . . . huh . . .

DONNY: It's alright.

JOHN: What did they talk about?

DONNY: John . . .

JOHN: I don't like it. I don't like it. No.

DONNY: John . . .

JOHN: I . . . What? No. No. I don't want to. (*Pause.*) Is my father back yet?

DONNY: No. Why don't you go and get in bed . . .

JOHN: When is he coming back?

DONNY: Very soon, I think.

JOHN: He is?

DONNY: Yes. Is that alright?

JOHN (*of photograph*): You asked if the shirt you're wearing is his shirt.

DEL: What?

JOHN: . . . in the photograph.

DEL: Is that His Shirt.

JOHN: You asked that.

DEL: Yes.

JOHN: Well, does it *look* like his shirt?

DEL: It's hard to tell. The picture is old . . .

JOHN (*to* DONNY): I didn't tear the blanket?

DONNY: No.

JOHN: You're certain.

DONNY: We've had it for years.

JOHN: I don't remember it.

DONNY: Yes. You would. If you thought about it.

JOHN: What was it?

DONNY: What? Go to sleep.

JOHN: What did you use it for?

DONNY: What did I use it for?
    A coverlet.

JOHN: To keep you warm.

DONNY: That's right.

JOHN: A coverlet.

DONNY: Yes.

JOHN: Where did it come from? The blanket.

DONNY: Where? In England.

JOHN: England.

DONNY: Yes. From an Arcade.

JOHN: Arcade . . .

DONNY: With stores on either side.

JOHN: Did you buy it together?

DONNY: No. I bought it when he was away.

JOHN: Away.

DONNY: Yes. One day.

JOHN: Away in the War.

DONNY: That's right. (*Pause.*)

JOHN: Did you miss him when he was gone?

DONNY: Yes, I did.

JOHN: What did you think about?

DONNY: (*Pause.*) Many things.

JOHN: What things did you think of?

DONNY: I don't know. *Many* things.

JOHN: Were you frightened for him?

DONNY: Yes. I was.

JOHN: Did you tell him?

DONNY: We used to go out. To the Country, you know . . .

JOHN: Is it wool . . .

DONNY: When he'd come back. Walk in a *field,* or . . .

JOHN: Is it wool?

DONNY: I'm sorry?

JOHN: Is it wool. The blanket.

DONNY: Do you know. When you were small. *You* slept in it. All of the time. We covered you.

JOHN: Why did you stop using it.

DONNY: We put it away.

JOHN: Why?

DONNY: It was torn. (*Pause.*) And now you go to sleep.

JOHN: Mother—Do you ever think you hear singing?

DONNY: I don't know what you mean.

JOHN: *Singing.*

DONNY: I don't know what you mean, John.

JOHN: At night. When you are asleep. Before you go to sleep.

DONNY: I don't know.

JOHN: . . . and you hear . . .

DONNY: . . . it's time for bed, now . . .

JOHN: . . . or you think you hear a *radio* . . .

DONNY: . . . a radio . . .

JOHN: Playing *music.* And you think. "Yes. I know. That's a radio." And you listen. But then, you say: "It's just in my head." But you can *listen* to it. It goes on. (*Pause.*) Or *voices.*

DONNY: You hear voices?

JOHN: Just before you go to sleep. Do you ever do that? (*Pause.*) I hear them. Outside my room.

DONNY: What are they saying?

JOHN: Do you ever do that?

DONNY: I don't know.

DEL: What are your voices saying?

JOHN (*simultaneous with* "saying"): Tell me how the blanket was torn.

DONNY: You go to sleep now, John.

JOHN: I want to see my father.

DONNY: Yes. But now you go to sleep.

JOHN: It's time to go to sleep.

DONNY: That's right.

JOHN: Is that right?

DONNY: You have a big . . .

JOHN: *Tomorrow.*

DONNY: Yes.

JOHN: I'm going, you know, I'm going to do that thing.

DONNY: What thing is that?

JOHN: The Game.

DONNY: . . . the Game.

JOHN: To remember. With him.

DONNY: The game. Yes. (JOHN *starts upstairs.*) You take the blanket.

JOHN: To observe.

DONNY: Mmm . . .

JOHN: . . . but it would have to be some thing that would surprise us.

DONNY: That's right.

JOHN: When we look around.

(*He continues up the stairs. Stops to lean over the landing. Looking down at the mantelpiece.*)

So, I'll ask my Dad. First thing. "You tell me the name of an *object.*" Or a "*collection* of things" . . . you know what I mean . . .

DEL: . . . that's right.

JOHN: "As we approach the Cabin."

DONNY: Mm . . .

JOHN: "To test our skills."

DONNY: . . . mm.

JOHN: But it doesn't have to be the Cabin.

DEL: No . . .

JOHN: It could be *anywhere* . . .

DEL: That's right.

JOHN: It could be anywhere at all.

DEL: That's right. As long as it's some *thing.* You have determined to observe.

JOHN: Yes. It could be right here . . .

DEL: That's absolutely right.

DONNY (*goes to him with the blanket*) (*simultaneous with* "and"): . . . and take the blanket . . .

DEL: Goodnight. John.

(JOHN *picks up white envelope.*)

DONNY (*of envelope*): What have you got?

JOHN: Goodnight.

DONNY: . . . what is that?

JOHN: It's a letter . . . It's a note for you. (*She takes it, opens it.*) And it could be something right here, anything that, that, it would have to be some-thing *new* . . . something that would . . .

DONNY: . . . that's right . . .

JOHN: . . . *surprise* us.

DONNY: . . . when did this get here . . . ?

JOHN: . . . you see?

DONNY: John. Go to bed. Now. Yes.

JOHN: Do you see?

DONNY: Go to bed.

JOHN: Alright. I understand. I'm going.

DEL: Goodnight, John. (JOHN *exits*.)

DEL: What is it?

DONNY: It's a letter to me. (*Pause*.)

DEL: A letter. (*Pause*.) What does it say?

DONNY: My husband's leaving me.

DEL: He's leaving you. (*Pause*.) Why would he want to do that . . . ?

Act Two

The next night.

JOHN, *in his bathrobe, and* DONNY.

JOHN: I thought that maybe there was nothing there. (*Pause*.) I thought that nothing was *there*. Then I was looking at my *book*. I thought "Maybe there's nothing *in* my book." It talked about the *buildings*. Maybe there's nothing *in* the buildings. And . . . or on my *globe*. You know my globe? You know my globe?

DONNY: Yes.

JOHN: Maybe there's nothing on the thing that it is of. We don't know what's there. *We* don't know that those things are there.

DONNY: I've been there. To many of them.

JOHN: Or in *buildings* we have not been in. Or in *history*. In the *history* of things. Or *thought*. (*Pause*.) I was *lying* there, and maybe there is no such thing as *thought*. Who *says* there is? Or human beings. And we are a dream. Who knows we are here? No one knows we are. We are a dream. We are just *dreaming*. I *know* we are. Or else . . . or else . . . (*Pause*.) . . . and how do we *know* the things we know? We don't know what's real. And all we do is *say* things. (*Pause*.) Where do we *get* them from? And, or that things, go on forever. (*Pause*.) Or that we're *born*. Or that dead people moan. Or that, or that there's *hell*. And maybe we are there. Maybe there are people who've *been* there. Or, or else why should we *think* it? That's what I don't know. And maybe *everything* is true. Maybe it's true that I'm *sitting* here . . .

DONNY: Johnnie.

JOHN: What . . . ?

DONNY: I think . . .

JOHN: . . . don't you think?

DONNY: . . . you have to . . .

JOHN: No, I don't.

DONNY: Please, please do, though.

JOHN: I don't want to, though. (DEL *enters*.) (*Of* DEL.) That's what I mean. I don't want to . . . didn't you, mother. Mother . . .

DONNY (*to* DEL): Did you . . .

DEL (*simultaneous with* "you"): No.

DONNY: Did you find him?

DEL (*to* JOHN): How are you? (*To* DONNY.) No.

JOHN: I'm fine.

DONNY: Where did you look?

DEL: The *Windemere,* and then I stopped at Jimmy's.

DONNY: Did you try The Eagle?

DEL: No. (*Unpacking his paper bag.*) How has he . . .

DONNY: Why *not?* Why *not?*

DEL: I'm sorry . . . why not what?

DONNY (*simultaneous with* "what"): Why didn't you go to the . . .

DEL: . . . I thought you were going to call them.

DONNY: Why should I call them, if they'll say he wasn't *there?* Even if he *is* there . . . ?

DEL (*simultaneous with* "there"): I thought you were going to call them.

DONNY (*simultaneous with* "call"): No. I never said that.

DEL: Well, then, I made a mistake. (*He is preparing syrup from medicine bottle.*)

DONNY: How much was it?

DEL: I told them to charge it to you. (*Holding spoon.*) (*To* JOHN.) Open your mouth.

JOHN: I don't want to take that stuff.

DONNY: You're going to take it and you're going to *sleep.*

JOHN: No. I'm not sleepy.

DONNY: Take the medicine. Did you *hear* me? You're *sick,* and you're going to *bed.*

JOHN: I can't *sleep.*

DEL: . . . that's why . . .

JOHN: Every time I go to sleep I *see* things . . .

DONNY: You must . . .

DEL: That's, that's why you have to take the medicine, John.

JOHN (*simultaneous with* "John"): No. I'm not tired.

DONNY: Do you want to go to the Hospital?

JOHN: No.

DONNY: No? Did you hear what The Doctor said?

JOHN: No.

DEL: . . . what did he say?

DONNY: I want you to go to bed *now.*

DEL: You heard your mother.

JOHN: No. No.

DONNY: Johnnie . . .

JOHN: No one understands. You think that I'm *in* something . . . You don't know what I'm feeling.

DEL: What are you feeling? (*Pause.*) Are you afraid to go to bed?

JOHN: Yes.

DONNY: Why?

DEL: What are you afraid of in there?

JOHN: I don't know.

DONNY: I . . . I . . . I know it *frightens* you . . .

JOHN: I don't want to go to sleep.

DEL: Alright, alright, I'm going to *promise* you . . . look at me. John. I'm going to *promise* you if you take this and . . . you take this and go upstairs then you won't be afraid. I promise. (*Pause.*) I promise you. (*Pause.*)

JOHN: I sweat through the sheets . . .

DEL: We'll change . . .

JOHN: . . . the *bed* is wet.

DEL: We'll change, we'll change the sheets, you don't have to worry.

DONNY: You go lie down in my bed.

DEL: . . . you lie down in your mother's bed. (*Pause.*) You go lie down there.

JOHN: I'm going to sweat them.

DEL: That's alright. Do you hear what I'm telling you . . . ? (*Pause.*)

JOHN: Maybe I'll just . . . maybe I'll just go there . . . maybe I'll just go there and lie down.

DONNY: Yes. You go and lie down now. You take this, now. (DEL *gives* JOHN *his medicine.*)

JOHN: Do you know why I took it, 'cause I'm tired.

DEL: I'm sure you are.

JOHN: . . . 'cause I've been *up* all day . . .

DEL: I know you have. And I know how that feels.

JOHN: I . . . I . . .

DONNY: . . . you go to bed now.

DEL: John? "My blessings on this house . . . ," the Wizard said.

JOHN: When is my father coming for me . . . ?

DONNY: Shhhh.

JOHN: . . . No. I don't understand.

DONNY: Shh. It's alright.

JOHN: What's happening to me . . . ?

DONNY (*embracing him*): It's alright. Hush. You go to bed. It's alright. John. Shh. You've only got a fever. Shhh . . .

DEL: . . . you're fine . . .

DONNY: You go upstairs now. Shhh. You go upstairs now, John . . . (*She starts him upstairs. Comes down.*)

DEL: . . . I looked every place I thought that he would *be* . . .

DONNY: I'm sorry.

DEL: But I couldn't find him. (*Pause.*) Do you want a drink?

DONNY: No. (*Pause.*)

DEL: I'm sorry that I couldn't find him. (*Pause.*) Would you like me to go out again?

DONNY: No. (*Pause.*)

DEL: Would you like to play Casino?

DONNY: No.

DEL: No, you're right, that's stupid. Oh God, oh God, that's *stupid*. (*Pause.*) Would you like to play Gin?

DONNY: Del . . .

DEL: Yeah. Do you see what I mean when I talk about myself? (*Pause.*) But would you like to?

DONNY: Let's have a drink.

DEL: Well. I know I know I'm limited.

(DEL *goes to the liquor cabinet, examines bottles.*)

There's only a new one.

DONNY: That's alright, open it. Enough. Enough for one day. I don't care. (*Pause.*) I don't care anymore. I swear to God.

(DEL *takes out bottle, takes out his knife, opens it.*)

DEL (*of bottle*): I think that this is good for you. (*Pause.*) You know why . . . ? Because it's a ceremony. To, to *delimit* umm . . .

DONNY: A ceremony.

DEL: Of . . . of what? Of, of *inebriation,* certainly, of, of of well, of *together-ness* . . . I don't know. (*He goes to the kitchen, comes out with two glasses and the bottle.*) (*Pours two glasses.*)

DONNY: Thank you.

DEL: Uh . . . Days May Come and Days May Go . . . (*Pause.*) Well, *that's* true enough.

DONNY: Isn't it?

DEL: I think so. (*Pause.*) Days May Come and Go.

DONNY: And May we Always be as . . .

DEL: Yes.

DONNY: As . . .

DEL: Unified . . .

DONNY: Well, let's pick something more moving than that.

DEL: Alright . . . be . be . be . be-*nighted?* No, that's not the word I want to use . . . be-*trothed . . .* ? No.

DONNY: Close . . .

DEL: Yes.

DONNY: Close to each other.

DEL: As we happen to be right now. (*Pause.*)

DONNY: Fine.

DEL: (*Pause.*) And . . . May the Spirit of Friendship . . . (*Pause.*) oh, the hell with it. I mean, can't people just have a drink . . . for the love of God? (*They drink.*) Bec, because I swear, because I think there's just too much. In *trial* . . . in *adversity* . . . (*Pause*) and you can't, you can't go always look . . .

DONNY: Go Looking for *answers* . . .

DEL: No.

DONNY: . . . you're absolutely right . . .

DEL: In intro*spec*tion. (*Pause.*)
You know, at times of *trial* . . .

DONNY: hmm . . .

DEL: Do you hear what I'm telling you?

DONNY: Yes.

DEL: . . . and they come for us all.

DONNY: . . . Oh, Lord.

DEL: Yes. They do. Then many times the answer comes. In reaching out. Or, do you know what? In getting drunk.

DONNY: . . . in drinking.

DEL: Be. Because, you know? Then you forget. (*Pause.*) And I don't *give* a damn. (*Pause.*) In this *shithole.* (*Pause.*) Well. I'm not going to *dwell* upon it. (*Pause.*) You drink, and then, when you *remember* again—this is the good part—when you *remember* again . . . (*Pause.*) It's later on. And time has dulled your, your . . . you know, for whatever portion of time that, that you for*got*. (*Pause.*)

DONNY: "You should get married."

DEL: "It would have to be someone nice."

DONNY: "We'll find them for you."

DEL: "Would you?" (*Pause.*) Although we joke about it. (*Sighs.*) Do you want me to go and look at John?

DONNY: He's going to be alright.

DEL: Are *you* alright, though?

DONNY: Yes.

DEL: I'm sorry that I didn't find Robert.

DONNY (*simultaneous with* "find"): . . . That's

DEL: I *looked* for him, but . . .

DONNY: That's al . . .

DEL: I Didn't find him. I suppose I thought that—in, you know, in addition to the things I said—that it wasn't a good *idea* to have him come here. But what business is that of *mine?* (*Pause.*) None. None, really.

DONNY: That's alright.

DEL: None at all. But I *looked* for him. (*Pause.*)

DONNY: (*Long pause.*) Well . . .

DEL: Worse things have happened, I suppose. (*Pause.*)

DONNY: . . . mmm.

DEL: It's such a shock.

DONNY: However much we . . .

DEL: What?

DONNY: I'm sorry?

DEL: However much . . . ?

DONNY: We could have anticipated it.

DEL: How could we?

DONNY: He tried to tell you.

DEL: What do you mean?

DONNY: He gave you the knife.

DEL: I don't understand.

DONNY: The Odd Gesture. (*Pause.*) Isn't it.

DEL: I don't understand.

DONNY: You don't understand the Gesture?

DEL: No.

DONNY: It was his going-away present. (*Pause.*) Going away. (*Pause.*) Big German knife. His war memento. Do you know the Meaning of it?

DEL: . . . meaning . . .

DONNY: You know what it's for.

DEL: The knife.

DONNY: Yes.

DEL: (*Pause.*) To cut things.

DONNY: I mean the specific . . .

DEL: The specific *purpose?* No. No. I mean, *no.*

DONNY: It's a *pilot's* knife . . .

DEL: . . . yes. I know that . . .

DONNY: If he was forced to *parachute* . . .

DEL: Yes.

DONNY: The pilot would use it to cut the *cords*. If his parachute snagged.

DEL: Huh. If it snagged. On, on what?

DONNY: On a tree.

DEL: Oh, you mean when he landed.

DONNY: Yes.

DEL: Huh. (*Pause.*)

DONNY: And that's the meaning. (*Pause.*)

DEL: . . . yes . . .

DONNY: When he was forced to abandon . . .

DEL: Yes. (*Pause.*) When he was forced to *abandon* his . . . (*Pause.*) He looked for *safety,* and the knife, it cut . . . It "released" him.

DONNY: Yes. That's right.

DEL: . . . as *any* tool . . .

DONNY: And he gave it to you.

DEL: He can be very generous. Is that alright? To . . .

DONNY: Yes. No. He can. (*Pause.*)
. . . what am I going to do? You tell me. Yes. He could be generous. *I* don't know.

DEL: . . . he was opening a can. With it. And I said . . . actually, he saw me looking at the knife. And he wiped it. And gave it to me. (*Pause.*)

DONNY: When you were at the Camp. Last week.

DEL: That's right—(*Pause.*)

DONNY: Tell me what you talked about.

DEL: What we talked about. In the Woods.

DONNY: Yes.

DEL: We talked about you.

DONNY: About *me* . . . ?

DEL: Yes. (*Pause.*)

DONNY: What did he say?

DEL: How happy he had been.

DONNY: Really.

DEL: That's what he said.

DONNY: How can you understand that. (*Pause.*) How in the world . . .

DEL: I'm so sorry.

DONNY: Did you know he was leaving me?

DEL: No.

DONNY: Did you think that he was?

DEL: No.

DONNY: No? You didn't?

DEL: How could I?

DONNY: . . . he didn't . . . ?

DEL: No. He didn't what . . . ?

DONNY: Give you a sign . . . ?

DEL: A sign. No.

DONNY: How can we understand . . . how . . . *men,* you know. How . . . men . . .

DEL: I'm going to *tell* you something.

It's funny for two grown men to go camping anyway. (*Pause.*) I don't care. (*Pause.*) Huh. I was born a *city* boy. (*Pause.*) (*He displays knife.*) And now I'm a Forester. (*Pause.*) I'm a Ranger . . . did you know there's a Fraternal Group called the Catholic Order of Foresters?

DONNY: Yes.

DEL: You knew that?

DONNY: Yes. Sure.

DEL: I wonder what they do. (*Pause.*)

DONNY: Did you say he gave that knife to you when you went camping?

DEL: Yes. (*Pause.*)

DONNY: When the two of you went camping. Last . . .

DEL: Last week. That's right. (*Pause.*)

DONNY: He gave the knife to you.

DEL: Yes. He was opening a can of . . . (*Pause.*) Why? (*Pause.*) Why did you ask?

DONNY: I saw it in the attic. When I went up there. To put the things away.

DEL: (*Pause.*) What things?

DONNY: When I took the camping things up. Last week. (*Pause.*) After your trip. When you came back.

DEL: I don't understand.

DONNY: When you came back, last week, Robert and you.

DEL: . . . yes . . .

DONNY: From your Trip.

I went up. To put his things away. And the knife was up there. (*Pause.*) It was already in the attic.

DEL: Well, maybe he went up there first, to put it back.

DONNY: . . . What?

DEL: I'm saying, maybe Robert went there first to put it back. When we came back. When we came back from *camping*. (*Pause.*) I'm sure that's what occurred. (*Pause.*)

DONNY: You're saying that he went upstairs to put it back.

DEL: Yes. Because it was precious to him.

DONNY: I don't understand.

DEL: It was a *war* memento. I'm saying that it was so *precious* to him that he went, and *left* the stuff . . . for *you* to put away, but went upstairs and put the *knife* into the trunk himself. (*Pause.*)

DONNY: Then how did *you* get it? (*Pause.*)

DEL: What?

DONNY: How did you get the knife?

DEL: He gave it to me.

DONNY: I don't understand.

DEL: He gave it to me.

DONNY: How could he give it to you?

DEL: What?

DONNY: You said he gave it to you when you were camping. (*Pause.*) How could he give it to you when you were *camping*, when it was here in the trunk when you both came back? (*Pause.*)

DEL: There must be two knives. (*Pause.*)

DONNY: I . . . I don't understand.

DEL: There must be two knives.

DONNY: What?

DEL: I bet if you went in the trunk to look right now you'd see. There was another knife.

DONNY: Yes. No. Wait . . . When did Robert give the knife to you?

DEL: I *thought* . . . isn't it funny? I was sure he gave the knife to me while we were camping. I guess I'm mistaken. (*Pause.*) Huh. (*Pause.*) Unless, no . . . Huh! . . . I . . . I don't know. (*Pause.*) It's a mystery to me. Unless . . .

DONNY: *Wait!*

DEL: What?

DONNY: He came upstairs. He came up. To the attic!

DEL: Who?

DONNY: I was putting the things away. He said. Yes. "Leave the trunk open." (*Pause.*) He *got* it from the trunk. When you came back. He didn't *put* it there. He went up there to *get* it. (*Pause.*)

DEL: That could happen.

DONNY: What do you mean?

DEL: Well, that, that's not so unusual.

DONNY: What isn't.

DEL: . . . for someone to do that. (*Pause.*)

DONNY: Did he do that?

DEL: It's possible. I think he did. Yes. I think *that's*. Um, that's *exactly* what he did. I *think*. (*Pause.*)

DONNY: Why did you lie to me?

DEL: I didn't lie. It was a slip of memory.

DONNY: Why did you lie?

DEL: If I did I *assure* you, it was, um, *you* know . . .

DONNY: What?

DEL: It was . . .

DONNY: You didn't go camping.

DEL: Who?

DONNY: You and Robert.

DEL: That's ridiculous!

DONNY: You never went.

DEL: That's . . .

DONNY: . . . Yes . . . ?

DEL: Be, because, be . . . what are you *saying* to me? Am, am I to be *accused* of this!

DONNY: Of what?

DEL: Well, that's my point.

DONNY: What did you do?

DEL: I. Why do you say *that?* For god*sake!*

DONNY: What did you do? I'll ask Robert.

DEL: You can't find him!

DONNY: What do you mean?

DEL: He won't tell you. (*Pause.*) Alright. (*Pause.*) But: I want to *tell* you something: I knew that I should not take that knife.

DONNY: Why did you take it?

DEL: Be, because he *gave* it to me.

DONNY: Why? (*Pause.*)

DEL: Huh. Well, that's the *question.* (*Pause.*) *That's* what you'd like to *know.* (*Pause.*) *Isn't* it? Yes. So you could say, "Old Del, who we thought was so Loyal" . . . I know what you mean. Be*lieve* me. (*Pause.*) Believe me.

DONNY: Why did he give the knife to you?

DEL: You don't want to know.

DONNY: I do.

DEL: *Believe* me, you don't. (*Pause.*) To shut me up. Alright? There. Are you *happy?* I told you you wouldn't be.

DONNY: To shut you up about what? (*Pause.*)

DEL: Because we didn't go.

DONNY: What?

DEL: We didn't *go!* Do I have to *shout* it for you . . . ? We stayed *home.* What do you *think?* He'd traipse off in the *wilds* . . . with *me* . . . ? To talk about *life?* Are you *stupid?* Are you *blind?* He wouldn't spend a *moment* with me. Some poor geek . . . "Here's my Old Friend Del . . ." You're *nuts,* you're *stupid* if you think that's what went on. (*Pause.*) He used my *room,* alright? He said, "Del, can I Use Your Room?" Is that so weird? There. Now I've told you. Now you can sleep easier. I *told* you not to ask. Don't tell me I didn't tell you. (*Pause.*)

DONNY: He used your room.

DEL: That's absolutely right.

DONNY: Why? (*Pause.*)

DEL: To go there with a woman. (*Pause.*) And now, and now you know the truth, How weak I am. How "Evil" I am. He said, "I have some things to do," "I want it to seem like I'm gone." *I* spent the week, *I* slept in the, in my, my nook in the *library.* In *fishing* clothes . . . and don't you think *that* looked stupid! (*Pause.*) I . . . I, actually, I've been waiting for this. I knew that I should tell you. This is the only bad thing I have ever done to you. I'm sorry that it came out like this. Indeed I am. (*Pause.*) But we can't always choose the, um . . . (*Pause.*)

DONNY: Get out. (*Pause.*) Get out.

(DEL *exits.*) (*Pause.*)

(DONNY *starts to cry.*)

DONNY: (*Pause.*) Bobby. Bobby. Bobby. (JOHN *appears in bathrobe.*) (*Pause.*)

JOHN: Are you dead?

DONNY: What?

JOHN: Are you dead? (*Pause.*)

DONNY: Why do you say that?

JOHN (*simultaneous with* "that"): I heard you calling.

DONNY: Go back to bed, John.

JOHN: I heard voices . . .

DONNY: . . . you should go back to bed.

JOHN: . . . and I thought they were you. (*Pause.*)

DONNY: It was me.

JOHN: And so I said, ". . . there's someone troubled." And I walked around. Did you hear walking?

DONNY: No.

JOHN: . . . and so I went outside. I saw a candle. In the dark.

DONNY: Where was this?

JOHN: In my room. It was burning there.

I said, "I'm perfectly alone." This is what I was saying to myself: "I'm perfectly alone." And I think I was saying it a long time. 'Cause I didn't have a pen. Did that ever happen to you?

DONNY: I don't know, John.

JOHN: So I came downstairs to write it down. I know that there *are* pens up there. But I don't want to look for them.

(DONNY *goes to him and cradles him.*)

Do you think that was right?

DONNY: Shhh.

JOHN: Do you think that I was right?

DONNY: Go to bed.

JOHN: Mother? (*Pause.*)

DONNY: What?

JOHN: Do you think that I was right.

DONNY: I don't know, John.

JOHN: I saw a candle in my room.

Act Three

Evening. One month later.

The room is denuded. Various packing boxes are seen. JOHN *is sitting on one of them.* DONNY *comes downstairs carrying a box. She puts it down and starts for the kitchen.*

JOHN: Where were you?

DONNY: I'll put the kettle on.

JOHN (*simultaneous with* "on"): Where were you?

DONNY: I went up for your bag.

JOHN: The movers will take it.

DONNY: There were some things I thought that you might like to have.

JOHN: What things?

DONNY: For the first few nights.

(*Pause.*) Until the boxes come. (*She starts into the kitchen.*)

JOHN: Mother.

DONNY (*offstage*): . . . yes . . .

JOHN: Do you ever think things? (*Pause.*) Mother . . . ?

DONNY (*offstage, simultaneous with* "mother"): What? (*Pause.*) What, John? (DONNY *reenters.*) What did you say?

JOHN: I asked you. Do you think things.

DONNY: What things, John? (*Pause.*)

JOHN: Do you ever wish that you could die? (*Pause.*)

DONNY: . . . do I wish I could die?

JOHN: Yes. (*Pause.*)

DONNY: I don't know.

JOHN: Yes, you do.

DONNY: No, I don't know, John.

JOHN: Yes you do. You can tell me. (*Pause.*)
It's not such a bad feeling. (*Pause.*) Is it?

DONNY: I don't know.

JOHN: Yes. You do. (*Pause.*) I think you do.

DONNY: John: Things occur. In our lives. And the meaning of them . . . the *meaning* of them . . . is not clear.

JOHN: . . . the meaning of them . . .

DONNY: That's correct. At the time. But we assume they have a meaning. We must. And we don't know what it is.

JOHN: Do you ever wish you could die?
(*Pause.*) Would you tell me?

DONNY: Do I wish that I could die?

JOHN: You can tell me. You won't frighten me.

DONNY: (*Pause.*) How can I *help* you? Do you see? (*Pause.*) Do you see?

JOHN: No.

DONNY: At some point . . . there are things that have occurred I cannot help you with . . . that . . .

JOHN: I can't sleep.

DONNY: Well. It's an unsettling time.

JOHN: . . . I want . . .

DONNY: Yes?

JOHN: I would like to go to the Cabin.

DONNY: . . . well . . .

JOHN: I want to go to the Lake.

DONNY: Well, no, John, we can't. You know we can't.

JOHN: I don't know that.

DONNY: No. We can't.

JOHN: That's why I can't sleep.

DONNY: What do you want me to do? John? I am not God. I don't control the World. If you could think what it is I could do for you . . . If I could help you . . . (*Sound of kettle, offstage.*)

JOHN: Do you ever wish you could die? (*Pause.*)
It's not such a bad feeling. Is it?

DONNY: I know that you're frightened. I know you are. But at some point, do you see . . . ? (*Pause. Exits.*) (*Offstage.*) John, everyone has a story. Did you know that? In their lives. This is yours. (DEL *enters.*) And finally . . . finally . . . you are going to have to learn how you will deal with it. You understand? I'm going to speak to you as an adult: At some point . . . At some point, we have to learn to face ourselves . . . what kind of tea . . .

DEL: Hello.

JOHN: Hello.

DEL: How are you today?

JOHN: I'm fine.

DONNY (*offstage*): What kind of tea?

DEL: That's good.

DONNY (*offstage*): John?

JOHN: What did my mother say?

DEL: I came to talk to you.

JOHN (*simultaneous with* "you"): . . . what did my mother say?

DEL (*simultaneous with* "say"): She wanted to know what kind of tea . . .

DONNY (*offstage*): John . . . ?

DEL: . . . what sort of tea you wanted. What sort of tea *do* you want? (JOHN *rises to exit.*)

JOHN: I don't know.

DEL: I'd like to talk to you, John.

JOHN: About what?

DEL: Several things.

JOHN: When is my father coming?

DEL: I have something that I'd like to say.

JOHN: I have to go upstairs.

DEL: Could you wait a moment?

(JOHN *exits.*)

DEL: John . . .

DONNY (*offstage*): Do you see? One has to go on. That's all we can say. I'm speaking to you as an adult.

(*She enters, with a tea tray. Pause.*)

DONNY: Where's my son?

DEL: I don't know. He went upstairs. (*Pause.*)

DONNY: Mm.

DEL: That's right.

DONNY: How is my husband.

DEL: I don't see him.

DONNY: No . . . ?

DEL: I came to talk to you. And to the boy.

DONNY: Well, it seems that he's gone upstairs.

DEL: Aha.

DONNY: What do you need to say? (*Pause.*)

DEL: I'm sorry what I did. (*Pause.*) Aren't we a funny race? The things we do. (*Pause.*) And then what we say about them. You'd think, if there were a "Deity" we would all burn. (*Pause.*) Swine that we are. But we go on. (*Pause.*) I brought something for you.

DONNY: You did?

DEL: (*Produces book.*) As you see.

DONNY: And that's supposed to put you back in my good graces?

DEL: What would do that?

DONNY: Nothing you've brought.

DEL: Well. (*Pause.*) Here is a book. It's your book, by the way. I've kept it. All these years. Perhaps that's what rotted my soul. Do you know, they say: it is not the sins we commit that destroy us, but how we act after we've committed them. Is that a useful bit of lore? (*Pause.*) I've found it so. (*Pause.*) And here is the German Pilot's Knife. I was obsessed to bring it. I thought, "But why would she want it?" But, of course, it's not for you. It's a propitiation. To the boy.

DONNY: To the boy . . .

DEL: Yes. Well, he should have it. Shouldn't he?

DONNY: Should he?

DEL: Yes.

DONNY: Why?

DEL: Because I've wronged him.

DONNY: You've wronged him.

DEL: I have.

DONNY: Haven't you wronged me?

DEL: What was I going to bring you, Flowers?

DONNY: But you brought the boy the knife.

DEL: That's right.

DONNY: No, you puzzle me.

DEL: *I* don't deserve it. It's his father's, um, what do they call it? "War" memento. A "combat" trophy. I brought you the bbb . . .

DONNY: . . . it's not a "combat" . . .

DEL: I brought you the *book* . . .

DONNY: It's not a combat trophy.

DEL: Well, well, it's a *War* memen . . .

DONNY: It's not a Combat Trophy.

DEL: *Whatever* it is.

DONNY: It's not . . .

DEL: Alright. He won it in the War. I didn't want to deprive the boy of . . .

DONNY: He didn't win it in the war.

DEL: *Really.*

DONNY: No.

DEL: No. The German Knife.

DONNY: No.

DEL: Well, of *course* he did.

DONNY: Not in the "fighting."

DEL: Oh. He didn't . . . ?

DONNY: No. Not in the "fighting." No.

DEL: He didn't get it in the fighting.

DONNY: No.

DEL: Well, yes, he did.

DONNY: How could he?

DEL: Well, you tell me. How could he *not?* It's a *war* mem . . .

DONNY: He was a flier. Do you see?

DEL: No.

DONNY: He was a flier.

DEL: I don't see.

DONNY: He was in the *air.* Could he capture the knife in the Air?

DEL: I don't understand.

DONNY: Could he get it in the Air? You "fairy"? Could he capture the knife from the other man in the Air? You fool.

DEL: (*Pause.*) Then how did he obtain it?

DONNY: How do you think?

DEL: I don't know.

DONNY: But how do you think?

DEL: I don't know. That's why I ask.

DONNY: He bought it.

DEL: He bought the knife.

DONNY: That's right.

DEL: The Combat knife.

DONNY: Mm.

DEL: . . . he gave me.

DONNY: Yes.

DEL: Where?

DONNY: From a man. On the street. In London.

DEL: Huh. (*Pause.*) You're saying he bought the knife. And you thought that would hurt me. (*Pause.*) And you're right of course.

DONNY: . . . to hurt you.

DEL: Well, you knew it would.

DONNY: Why would that hurt you?

DEL: Oh, you didn't know that.

DONNY: No.

DEL: Then why did you say it?

DONNY: I . . .

DEL: Why did you say it, then? Excuse me, that the souvenir that he gave me, as a War Memento, with "associations," that it had no meaning for him. And what would *I* know about the war? I live in a *Hotel.* (*Pause.*)

DONNY: I didn't mean to hurt you.

DEL: Oh, if we could speak the truth, do you see, for one instant. Then we would be free. (*Pause.*) I should have chucked it anyway. (*Pause.*) How could a knife be a suitable gift for a child? No, but we know it can't. We bring our . . . our little "gifts." And take your book. It's your goddam book. I've had it at the hotel. All these years. I borrowed it and never brought it back. How about that. Eh? Years ago. That's how long I've had it. Was ever anyone so false? Take it. I hate it. I hate the whole fucking progression. Here. Take the cursed thing. (*Hands her the book.*)

DONNY: It's your copy.

DEL: It is?

DONNY: Yes.

DEL: How do you know?

DONNY: It's got your name in it. (*Pause.*)

DEL: Where? (*She shows him.*) (*Of book.*) This *is* my copy . . . isn't that funny? (*Pause.*) Because I'd *wondered* what I'd done with it. Do you know how long I've been *looking* for this? (*Pause.*) (*Reads.*) "May you always be as . . ."

DONNY: Aren't you funny.

DEL: I'm pathetic. I know that. You don't have to tell me. The life that I lead is trash. I hate myself. Oh well. (*Pause.*) But I would like to talk to you. (*Pause.*) If I might. (*Pause.*) In spite of . . .

DONNY: In spite of . . .

DEL: What has occurred. (*Pause.*)

DONNY: Why?

DEL: Because there are things. I have been longing to say. To, um . . . "say," for a long . . . And perhaps this is what it takes. Isn't it funny? If you'd permit me. Alright. Thank you. For a long while . . .

(JOHN *appears on the stairs.*)

DONNY: (*Pause.*) Yes? Yes, John . . . ?

JOHN: I'm cold. I'm sorry. (*Pause.*) I'm cold.
My *mind* is racing. I . . .

DONNY: You what? (*Pause.*)

JOHN: . . . I think . . .

DONNY: . . . what can I do about it?

JOHN: I . . .

DONNY: What can I *do* about it, John?

JOHN: I don't know.

DONNY: What do you expect me to do?

JOHN: I don't know.

DONNY: Well.

DEL: . . . may I speak to him?

JOHN: I don't, I'm afraid. I know that I should not *think* about certain things, but . . .

DEL (*to* DONNY): May . . . ?

JOHN: . . . but I . . .

DONNY: John: John: I'd like to help you; now: you have to go to sleep. You must go to sleep.
If you do *not* sleep, *lay* there. Lay in bed. What you think about there is your concern. No one can help you. Do you understand? *Finally, each* of us.

JOHN: Where is the blanket?

DONNY: I . . . *Each* of us . . .

JOHN: . . . I want the blanket.

DONNY: Is alone.

JOHN: . . . the *stadium* blanket.

DONNY (*simultaneous with* "stadium"): I've put it away.

JOHN: No: Mother . . .

DEL: May I speak to him?

JOHN: I want it.

DONNY: I've put it away, John.

JOHN: I'm cold. Could I have it, please.

DONNY: It's packed away.

JOHN: Where?

DONNY: A box. Up in the attic, I believe . . .

DEL (*simultaneous with* "believe"): It's in the attic, John.

JOHN: I need it. I'm cold.

DONNY: John . . . Alright, now.

JOHN: I . . .

DEL (*to* DONNY): Perhaps he . . .

DONNY: It's packed in a box.

DEL: But couldn't he get it, though?

DONNY: No. It's waiting for the *movers.*

DEL: But might he have it?

DONNY: It's wrapped up.

JOHN: I could undo it.

DONNY: Fine. Then it's in the attic. In the large brown box.

DEL: You see?

JOHN: Yes.

DONNY: With the new address on it.

JOHN: And I can open it. The box?

DONNY: If you will go to sleep. You must go to sleep. Do you hear me?

DEL: That is the point, do you see? John?

DONNY: You can unwrap it if you go to sleep.

DEL: . . . that's right.

DONNY: But you must . . .

DEL: We're talking to you like a man.

DONNY: But you must promise . . .

JOHN: . . . I promise.

DONNY: . . . Because . . .

JOHN: I understand. I promise. (*Pause.*) I promise.

DONNY: Do you understand?

JOHN: Yes. Yes. I promise.

DEL: Good, then, John. Goodnight.

DONNY: Goodnight. (JOHN *exits.*) (*Pause.*) Lucky boy. To have a protector. (*Pause.*)

DEL: Well . . .

DONNY: Don't you think?

DEL: Donny, I . . .

DONNY: Do you know. If I could find one man in my life. Who would not betray me. (*Pause.*)

DEL: I'm sorry.

DONNY: That's what I mean.

DEL: I'm sorry I betrayed you.

DONNY: Isn't that sweet. Aren't you sweet. How could one be miffed with you? The problem must be *mine*.

DEL: I'm sorry I betrayed you.

DONNY: Just like the rest of them. All of you are.

DEL: I'm sorry.

DONNY: Can you explain it to me, though? Why? (*Pause.*) You see? That's what baffles me. I try to say "human nature" . . .

DEL: . . . I know . . .

DONNY: I don't know what our nature is. If I do, then it's bad.

DEL: . . . I know . . .

DONNY: If I do, then it's filthy. No, you don't know. You have no idea. All the men I ever met . . .

DEL: And I'm so sorry. To have added one *iota*, in my stupid . . .

DONNY: . . . in this cesspool.

DEL: Could I . . .

DONNY: (*Pause.*) No. I don't care anymore.

DEL: Could I talk to you? Who am I? Some poor Queen. Lives in a hotel. Some silly old Soul Who loves you.

DONNY: Oh, please.

DEL: No—I need you to forgive me.

DONNY: Why would I do that?

DEL: You should do that if it would make you happy.

DONNY: No, look here: don't tell me I'm going to make a sacrifice for you, and it's for my own good.

Do you see? Because every man I ever met in this shithole . . . Don't you dare come in my house and do that. You faggot. Every man I ever met in my life . . .

DEL: *Well, why does it happen?*

DONNY: Excuse me . . . ?

DEL: Why does it happen? Is it chance? Do you think it's some mystery? What you encounter? What you provoke . . . ?

DONNY: What I *provoke* . . . ?

DEL: That's right.

DONNY: What are you saying?

DEL: Well . . .

DONNY: You might as well say it.

DEL: Are you sure?

DONNY: Oh. Don't "tease" me . . . mmm? For God's sake: don't "tease" me, lad . . .

DEL: . . . No.

DONNY: You came to say your little piece—go on.

DEL: Alright. For some time, for quite a long time I've watched you.

DONNY: *Have* you?

DEL: I have . . .

DONNY: You've *watched* me.

DEL: . . . and I've thought about you. And the boy. Quite a long time.

DONNY: Well . . .

DEL: Alright. Here is what I think: (*Pause.*)

(JOHN *appears at the head of the stairs.*) (*Pause.*)

DONNY: Yes. Yes, John, What?

JOHN: I . . .

DONNY: What? What? You promised. Did you promise?

JOHN: . . . I . . .

DONNY: . . . It's not a small *thing.* You . . .

JOHN: I only . . .

DONNY: Yes, *What? What?* "You Only . . ." You prom . . .

JOHN: . . . I only . . .

DONNY: I DON'T CARE. Do You Know What It Means To Give . . .

JOHN: . . . I . . .

DONNY: . . . to give your word? I DON'T CARE.

JOHN: I . . .

DONNY: I don't care. Do you hear? I don't care. You *promised* me that you would stay upstairs.

JOHN: . . . I . . .

DONNY: I don't care. Go away. You lied.

DEL: Donny . . .

DONNY: I love you, but I can't like you.

DEL: Donny . . .

DONNY: Do you know why? You lied.

DEL: Let me . . . Let me . . . John: Here. Go to bed. Take the book. This is the book, John. We were talking about. It was my copy. It's yours now. "That's what the Wizard said." It's yours. Off you go. If you can't sleep . . .

JOHN: . . . I . . .

DEL: F'you can't sleep, you read it. It's alright now. You go to bed. S'alright. Off you go.

(*Pause.*)

JOHN: I have to cut the twine.

DONNY: The twine.

JOHN: On the box.

DONNY: I don't understand.

JOHN: To get to the blanket. It's tied.

DEL: Alright, go to the kitchen, take, no, they're packed. Are they packed? They're put away, John. The knives are put away. (*Pause.*)

JOHN: You said I could have the blanket.

DEL: Well,

JOHN: You said that.

DEL: Well, you'll have to do without. But you'll be fine, I promise you. We'll . . .

DONNY: Goodnight, John.

DEL: You understand. You'll be fine. Goodnight, now.

JOHN: You said I could have the blanket.

DEL: Goodnight, Jjjj . . .

(JOHN *starts to exit.*)

DONNY: John? Del said "goodnight" to you. (*Pause.*) Did you hear him?

DEL: It's alright.

DONNY: John . . . ?

DEL: It's alr . . .

DONNY: No. It isn't alright. I'm speaking to you. Come back here. John? The man said goodnight to you. Come back down and tell the man you're sorry.

DEL: It's alright, Donny.

DONNY: John? I'm *speaking* to you. What must I do?

DEL: Donn . . .

DONNY: What must I do that you treat me like an animal?

DEL: It's . . .

DONNY: Don't you tell me it's alright, for the love of God. Don't you *dare* to dispute me.

DEL: The child . . .

DONNY: Don't you *dare* to dispute me in my home. Now, I'm *speaking* to you, John. Don't stand there so innocently. I've asked you a question. Do you want me to go mad? Is that what you want? Is that what you want?

DEL: Your mother's speaking to you, John.

DONNY: Is that what you want?

DEL: She asked you a question.

DONNY: Can't you see that I need comfort? Are you blind? For the love of God . . .

JOHN: I hear voices.

DEL: John: Your mother's waiting for you to . . .

JOHN: Before I go to sleep.

DEL: Your mother's waiting, John. What does she want to hear?

JOHN: . . . before I go to sleep.

DEL: What does she want to hear you say?

JOHN: I don't know.

DEL: I think that you do. (*Pause.*) What does she want to hear you say. (*Pause.*)

JOHN: "I'm sorry."

DEL: What?

JOHN: I'm sorry.

DEL: Alright, then.

JOHN: You told me I could have the blanket.

DONNY: Goodnight, John.

JOHN: You told me I could have the blanket.

DEL: Yes. You can.

JOHN: It's wrapped up.

DEL: Take the knife. When you're done . . . (*Hands the boy the knife.*)

JOHN: I can't fall asleep.

DEL: That's up to you, now.

JOHN: I hear voices. They're calling to me. (*Pause.*)

DONNY: Yes I'm sure they are.

JOHN: They're calling me.

DEL: Take the knife and go.

JOHN: They're calling my name. (*Pause.*) Mother. They're calling my name.

The Receptive Reader

1. As you listen to the characters in the opening scene or scenes, what do you learn about the situation? Who are the characters, and how do they relate? When do you first sense that something is wrong?

2. People reacting to this play disagree on whether John is a convincing ten-year-old. Do you understand who and what he is? Why is his inability or unwillingness to sleep such an issue in the play?

3. In this play, the stereotypical emotionally absent father is literally absent. How does he gradually become more central as the play develops?

4. The ripped blanket, the broken teakettle, and the knife are all darkly symbolic. What is their symbolic meaning? What is their role in the play?

5. What is Del's role in the play? When or how do you learn that Del is gay? Does it make any difference to his role in the play?

6. Betrayal becomes a powerful central theme as the play approaches its end. Who betrays whom? Which of the betrayals is the most basic or the most shattering?

7. John is waiting for the "Third Misfortune," having read in a book that misfortunes come in threes. What was the first? What was the second? What is the third? Which of the misfortunes is most ominous? What do they all have in common?

The Personal Response

Who are you in this play? With which of the characters can you identify most directly or most strongly? Why?

The Creative Dimension

Psychiatrist Sheldon Kopp wrote that "childhood is a nightmare." This observation contradicts a common belief that childhood is the best time of life, free from trouble. In a small group or with the class as a whole, discuss which view of childhood you believe to be more nearly true. Turning to your own childhood memories, write a vignette, or snapshot, of some dramatic or traumatic scene that bears out your perspective on childhood. Your class may decide to collect these autobiographical vignettes for a class publication.

THE SEARCH FOR ROOTS

I discovered that you have no respect for what you
do not understand.
    WOLE SOYINKA, *DEATH AND THE KING'S HORSEMAN*

Advocates of a multicultural perspective see a recognition and acceptance of diversity as the essential clue to an understanding of American history and American culture. They see it as the only hope for a world threatened by a relapse into tribalism, "ethnic cleansing," and paranoid, xenophobic nationalism. In a world with a global economy and a worldwide youth culture, the theater can serve its ancient function as a moral force by helping us cross narrow traditional boundaries.

August Wilson   *(born 1945)*

August Wilson is a black American playwright whose endlessly talkative and articulate characters speak black English. What features of it do you recognize? How would you react to it as a theatergoer or reader? The following excerpt is from Wilson's *The Piano Lesson,* a play first staged by the Yale Repertory Theatre in 1988. Bill Moyers, interviewing Wilson, asked, "I was going to ask you, don't you grow weary of thinking black, writing black, being asked questions about being black?" Wilson replied, "How could one grow weary of that? Whites don't get tired of thinking white or being who they are. I'm just who I am. You never transcend who you are. Black is not limiting. There's no idea in the world that is not contained by black life. I could write forever about the black experience in America."

How Avery Got to Be a Preacher   1987

BOY WILLIE: How you get to be a preacher, Avery? I might want to be a preacher one day. Have everybody call me Reverend Boy Willie.

AVERY: It come to me in a dream. God called me and told me he wanted me to be a shepherd for his flock. That's what I'm gonna call my church . . . The Good Shepherd Church of God in Christ.

DOAKER: Tell him what you told me. Tell him about the three hobos.

AVERY: Boy Willie don't want to hear all that.

LYMON: I do. Lots a people say your dreams can come true.

AVERY: Naw. You don't want to hear all that.

DOAKER: Go on. I told him you was a preacher. He didn't want to believe me. Tell him about the three hobos.

AVERY: Well, it come to me in a dream. See . . . I was sitting out in this railroad yard watching the trains go by. The train stopped and these three hobos got off. They told me they had come from Nazareth and was on their way to Jerusalem. They had three candles. They gave me one and told me to light it . . . but to be careful that it didn't go out. Next thing I knew I was standing in front of this house. Something told me to go knock on the door. This old woman opened the door and said they had been waiting on me. Then she led me into this room. It was a big room and it was full of all kinds of different people. They looked like anybody else except they all had sheep heads and was making noise like sheep make. I heard somebody call my name. I looked around and there was these same three hobos. They told me to take off my clothes and they give me a blue robe with gold thread. They washed my feet and combed my hair. Then they showed me these three doors and told me to pick one.

   I went through one of them doors and that flame leapt off that candle and it seemed like my whole head caught fire. I looked around and there was four or five other men standing there with these same blue robes on. Then we heard a voice tell us to look out across this valley. We looked out and saw the valley was full of wolves. The voice told us that these sheep people that I had seen in the other room had to go over to the other side of this valley and somebody had to take them. Then I heard another voice say, "Who shall I send?" Next thing I knew I said, "Here I am. Send me." That's when I met Jesus. He say, "If you go, I'll go with you." Something told me to say, "Come on. Let's go." That's when I woke up. My head still felt like it was on fire . . . but I had a peace about myself that was hard to explain. I knew right then that I had been filled with the Holy Ghost and called to be a servant of the Lord. It took me a while before I could accept that. But then a lot of little ways God showed me that it was true. So I became a preacher.

LYMON: I see why you gonna call it the Good Shepherd Church. You dreaming about them sheep people. I can see that easy.

Act One, Scene 1

The Receptive Reader

1. A reviewer in the *New York Times* said about *The Piano Lesson* that "the play's real music is in the language." What did he mean?

2. In the past, regional or cultural varieties of English have often been ridiculed. Do you think college audiences of your generation are ready to accept the use of language in this play? Why or why not?

3. What role do language differences—for example, southern speech, British accents, street language—play in American popular culture today? Do you think their role has changed over the years?

David Henry Hwang   *(born 1957)*

David Henry Hwang, a Chinese-American playwright, explores the lives of Asian Americans, who had seldom been seen on the American stage. He made a dramatic bid for recognition with his *M. Butterfly* (1988), which mocked the stereotype of the meek, submissive, self-sacrificing Asian woman immortalized in Puccini's opera *Madame Butterfly*. The Italian composer had set to lush music the story of the geisha girl who is abandoned by the American naval officer she loved. She hands their love child over to the officer's wife and then commits suicide. Hwang's Madame Butterfly is a male Chinese opera singer playing women's roles and working for the Chinese government as a spy.

The short play that follows is a dialogue between two of the immigrants who came from starving villages in China to build the transcontinental railroad. One of the characters is a familiar type in Hwang's plays—the FOB, the immigrant "fresh off the boat," who still believes much of what Americans or earlier immigrants tell him. The other is keeping alive his ties with a thousand-year-old Chinese tradition of opera and dance. Hwang sets his play at the time of the Chinese railroad workers' strike of 1867. He says, "So often, 'coolie' laborers have been characterized in America as passive and subservient, two stereotypes often attached to Asians. The strike is important because it reminds us that in historical fact these were assertive men who stood up for their rights in the face of great adversity."

The Dance and the Railroad   *1981*

CHARACTERS

LONE, twenty years old, ChinaMan railroad worker.
MA, eighteen years old, ChinaMan railroad worker.

PLACE: *A mountaintop near the transcontinental railroad.*

TIME: *June, 1867.*

SYNOPSIS OF SCENES
    SCENE 1: *Afternoon.*
    SCENE 2: *Afternoon, a day later.*
    SCENE 3: *Late afternoon, four days later.*
    SCENE 4: *Late that night.*
    SCENE 5: *Just before the following dawn.*

Scene 1

> *A mountaintop.* LONE *is practicing opera steps. He swings his pigtail around like a fan.* MA *enters, cautiously, watches from a hidden spot.* MA *approaches* LONE.

LONE: So, there are insects hiding in the bushes.
MA: Hey, listen, we haven't met, but—
LONE: I don't spend time with insects.

> (LONE *whips his hair into* MA's *face;* MA *backs off;* LONE *pursues him, swiping at* MA *with his hair*)

MA: What the—? Cut it out!

> (MA *pushes* LONE *away*)

LONE: Don't push me.
MA: What was that for?
LONE: Don't ever push me again.
MA: You mess like that, you're gonna get pushed.
LONE: Don't push me.
MA: You started it. I just wanted to watch.
LONE: You "just wanted to watch." Did you ask my permission?
MA: What?
LONE: Did you?
MA: C'mon.
LONE: You can't expect to get in for free.
MA: Listen. I got some stuff you'll wanna hear.
LONE: You think so?
MA: Yeah. Some advice.
LONE: Advice? How old are you, anyway?
MA: Eighteen.
LONE: A child.
MA: Yeah. Right. A child. But listen—
LONE: A child who tries to advise a grown man—
MA: Listen, you got this kind of attitude.
LONE: —is a child who will never grow up.
MA: You know, the ChinaMen down at camp, they can't stand it.
LONE: Oh?
MA: Yeah. You gotta watch yourself. You know what they say? They call you "Prince of the Mountain." Like you're too good to spend time with them.

LONE: Perceptive of them.

MA: After all, you never sing songs, never tell stories. They say you act like your spit is too clean for them, and they got ways to fix that.

LONE: Is that so?

MA: Like they're gonna bury you in the shit buckets, so you'll have more to clean than your nails.

LONE: But I don't shit.

MA: Or they're gonna cut out your tongue, since you never speak to them.

LONE: There's no one here worth talking to.

MA: Cut it out, Lone. Look, I'm trying to help you, all right? I got a solution.

LONE: So young yet so clever.

MA: That stuff you're doing—it's beautiful. Why don't you do it for the guys at camp? Help us celebrate?

LONE: What will "this stuff" help celebrate?

MA: C'mon. The strike of course. Guys on a railroad gang, we gotta stick together, you know.

LONE: This is something to celebrate?

MA: Yeah. Yesterday, the weak-kneed ChinaMen, they were running around like chickens without a head: "The white devils are sending their soldiers! Shoot us all!" But now, look—day four, see? Still in one piece. Those soldiers—we've never seen a gun or a bullet.

LONE: So you're all warrior-spirits, huh?

MA: They're scared of us, Lone—that's what it means.

LONE: I appreciate your advice. Tell you what—you go down—

MA: Yeah?

LONE: Down to the camp—

MA: Okay.

LONE: To where the men are—

MA: Yeah?

LONE: Sit there—

MA: Yeah?

LONE: And wait for me.

MA: Okay. (*Pause*) That's it? What do you think I am?

LONE: I think you're an insect interrupting my practice. So fly away. Go home.

MA: Look, I didn't come here to get laughed at.

LONE: No, I suppose you didn't.

MA: So just stay up here. By yourself. You deserve it.

LONE: I do.

MA: And don't expect any more help from me.

LONE: I haven't gotten any yet.

MA: If one day, you wake up and your head is buried in the shit can—

LONE: Yes?

MA: You can't find your body, your tongue is cut out—

LONE: Yes.

MA: Don't worry, 'cuz I'll be there.

LONE: Oh.

MA: To make sure your mother's head is sitting right next to yours.

(MA *exits.*)

LONE: His head is too big for this mountain.

(*Returns to practicing*)

Scene 2

Mountaintop. Next day. LONE *is practicing.* MA *enters.*

MA: Hey.

LONE: You? Again?

MA: I forgive you.

LONE: You . . . what?

MA: For making fun of me yesterday. I forgive you.

LONE: You can't—

MA: No. Don't thank me.

LONE: You can't forgive me.

MA: No. Don't mention it.

LONE: You—! I never asked for your forgiveness.

MA: I know. That's just the kinda guy I am.

LONE: This is ridiculous. Why don't you leave? Go down to your friends and play soldiers, sing songs, tell stories.

MA: Ah! See? That's just it. I got other ways I wanna spend my time. Will you teach me the opera?

LONE: What?

MA: I wanna learn it. I dreamt about it all last night.

LONE: No.

MA: The dance, the opera—I can do it.

LONE: You think so?

MA: Yeah. When I get outa here, I wanna go back to China and perform.

LONE: You want to become an actor?

MA: Well, I wanna perform.

LONE: Don't you remember the story about the three sons whose parents send them away to learn a trade? After three years, they return. The first one says, "I have become a coppersmith." The parents say, "Good. Second son, what have you become?" "I've become a silversmith." "Good— and youngest son, what about you?" "I have become an actor." When the parents hear that their son has become only an actor, they are very sad. The mother beats her head against the ground until the ground, out of pity, opens up and swallows her. The father is so angry he can't even speak, and the anger builds up inside him until it blows his body to pieces—little bits of his skin are found hanging from trees days later. You don't know how you endanger your relatives by becoming an actor.

MA: Well, I don't wanna become an "actor." That sounds terrible. I just wanna perform. Look, I'll be rich by the time I get out of here, right?

LONE: Oh?

MA: Sure. By the time I go back to China, I'll ride in gold sedan chairs, with twenty wives fanning me all around.

LONE: Twenty wives? This boy is ambitious.

MA: I'll give out pigs on New Year's and keep a stable of small birds to give to any woman who pleases me. And in my spare time, I'll perform.

LONE: Between your twenty wives and your birds, where will you find a free moment?

MA: I'll play Gwan Gung and tell stories of what life was like on the Gold Mountain.

LONE: Ma, just how long have you been in "America"?

MA: Huh? About four weeks.

LONE: You are a big dreamer.

MA: Well, all us ChinaMen here are—right? Men with little dreams—have little brains to match. They walk with their eyes down, trying to find extra grains of rice on the ground.

LONE: So, you know all about "America"? Tell me, what kind of stories will you tell?

MA: I'll say, "We laid tracks like soldiers. Mountains? We hung from cliffs in baskets and the winds blew us like birds. Snow? We lived underground like moles for days at a time. Deserts? We—"

LONE: Wait. Wait. How do you know these things after only four weeks?

MA: They told me—the other ChinaMen on the gang. We've been telling stories ever since the strike began.

LONE: They make it sound like it's very enjoyable.

MA: They said it is.

LONE: Oh? And you believe them?

MA: They're my friends. Living underground in winter—sounds exciting, huh?

LONE: Did they say anything about the cold?

MA: Oh, I already know about that. They told me about the mild winters and the warm snow.

LONE: Warm snow?

MA: When I go home, I'll bring some back to show my brothers.

LONE: Bring some—? On the boat?

MA: They'll be shocked—they never seen American snow before.

LONE: You can't. By the time you get snow to the boat, it'll have melted, evaporated, and returned as rain already.

MA: No.

LONE: No?

MA: Stupid.

LONE: Me?

MA: You been here awhile, haven't you?

LONE: Yes. Two years.

MA: Then how come you're so stupid? This is the Gold Mountain. The snow here doesn't melt. It's not wet.

LONE: That's what they told you?

MA: Yeah. It's true.

LONE: Did anyone show you any of this snow?

MA: No. It's not winter.

LONE: So where does it go?

MA: Huh?

LONE: Where does it go, if it doesn't melt? What happens to it?

MA: The snow? I dunno. I guess it just stays around.

LONE: So where is it? Do you see any?

MA: Here? Well, no, but . . . (*Pause*) This is probably one of those places where it doesn't snow—even in winter.

LONE: Oh.

MA: Anyway, what's the use of me telling you what you already know? Hey, c'mon—teach me some of that stuff. Look—I've been practicing the walk—how's this? (*Demonstrates*)

LONE: You look like a duck in heat.

MA: Hey—it's a start, isn't it?

LONE: Tell you what—you want to play some *die siu?*

MA: *Die siu?* Sure.

LONE: You know, I'm pretty good.

MA: Hey, I play with the guys at camp. You can't be any better than Lee—he's really got it down.

(LONE *pulls out a case with two dice*)

LONE: I used to play till morning.

MA: Hey, us too. We see the sun start to rise, and say, "Hey, if we got to sleep now, we'll never get up for work." So we just keep playing.

LONE (*holding out dice*): *Die* or *siu?*

MA: *Siu.*

LONE: You sure?

MA: Yeah!

LONE: All right. (*He rolls.*) *Die!*

MA: *Siu!*

(*They see the result*)

MA: Not bad.

(*They continue taking turns rolling through the following section;* MA *always loses*)

LONE: I haven't touched these in two years.

MA: I gotta practice more.

LONE: Have you lost much money?

MA: Huh? So what?

LONE: Oh, you have gold hidden in all your shirt linings, huh?

MA: Here in "America"—losing is no problem. You know—End of the Year Bonus?

LONE: Oh, right.

MA: After I get that, I'll laugh at what I lost.

LONE: Lee told you there was a bonus, right?

MA: How'd you know?

LONE: When I arrived here, Lee told me there was a bonus, too.

MA: Lee teach you how to play?

LONE: Him? He talked to me a lot.

MA: Look, why don't you come down and start playing with the guys again?

LONE: "The guys."

MA: Before we start playing, Lee uses a stick to write "Kill!" in the dirt.

LONE: You seem to live for your nights with "the guys."

MA: What's life without friends, huh?

LONE: Well, why do *you* think I stopped playing?

MA: Hey, maybe you were the one getting killed, huh?

LONE: What?

MA: Hey, just kidding.

LONE: Who's getting killed here?

MA: Just a joke.

LONE: That's not a joke, it's blasphemy.

MA: Look, obviously you stopped playing 'cause you wanted to practice the opera.

LONE: Do you understand that discipline?

MA: But, I mean, you don't have to overdo it either. You don't have to treat 'em like dirt. I mean, who are you trying to impress?

(*Pause.* LONE *throws dice into the bushes*)

LONE: Ooooops. Better go see who won.

MA: Hey! C'mon! Help me look!

LONE: If you find them, they are yours.

MA: You serious?

LONE: Yes.

MA: Here.

(*Finds the dice*)

LONE: Who won?

MA: I didn't check.

LONE: Well, no matter. Keep the dice. Take them and go play with your friends.

MA: Here. (*He offers them to* LONE) A present.

LONE: A present? This isn't a present!

MA: They're mine, aren't they? You gave them to me, right?

LONE: Well, yes, but—

MA: So now I'm giving them to you.

LONE: You can't give me a present. I don't want them.

MA: You wanted them enough to keep them two years.

LONE: I'd forgotten I had them.

MA: See, I know, Lone. You wanna get rid of me. But you can't. I'm paying for lessons.

LONE: With my dice.

MA: Mine now. (*He offers them again*) Here.

(*Pause.* LONE *runs* MA*'s hand across his forehead*)

LONE: Feel this.

MA: Hey!

LONE: Pretty wet, huh?

MA: Big deal.

LONE: Well, it's not from playing *die siu.*

MA: I know how to sweat. I wouldn't be here if I didn't.

LONE: Yes, but are you willing to sweat after you've finished sweating? Are you willing to come up after you've spent the whole day chipping half an inch off a rock, and punish your body some more?

MA: Yeah. Even after work, I still—

LONE: No, you don't. You want to gamble, and tell dirty stories, and dress up like women to do shows.

MA: Hey, I never did that.

LONE: You've only been here a month. (*Pause*) And what about "the guys"? They're not going to treat you so well once you stop playing with them. Are you willing to work all day listening to them whisper, "That one— let's put spiders in his soup"?

MA: They won't do that to me. With you, it's different.

LONE: Is it?

MA: You don't have to act that way.

LONE: What way?

MA: Like you're so much better than them.

LONE: No. You haven't even begun to understand. To practice every day, you must have a fear to force you up here.

MA: A fear? No—it's 'cause what you're doing is beautiful.

LONE: No.

MA: I've seen it.

LONE: It's ugly to practice when the mountain has turned your muscles to ice. When my body hurts too much to come here, I look at the other ChinaMen and think, "They are dead. Their muscles work only because the white man forces them. I live because I can still force my muscles to work for me." Say it. "They are dead."

MA: No. They're my friends.

LONE: Well, then, take your dice down to your friends.

MA: But I want to learn—

LONE: This is your first lesson.

MA: Look, it shouldn't matter—

LONE: It does.

MA: It shouldn't matter what I think.

LONE: Attitude is everything.

MA: But as long as I come up, do the exercises—

LONE: I'm not going to waste time on a quitter.

MA: I'm not!

LONE: Then say it.—"They are dead men."

MA: I can't.

LONE: Then you will never have the dedication.

MA: That doesn't prove anything.

LONE: I will not teach a dead man.

MA: What?

LONE: If you can't see it, then you're dead too.

MA: Don't start pinning—

LONE: Say it!

MA: All right.

LONE: What?

MA: All right. I'm one of them. I'm a dead man too.

(*Pause*)

LONE: I thought as much. So, go. You have your friends.
MA: But I don't have a teacher.
LONE: I don't think you need both.
MA: Are you sure?
LONE: I'm being questioned by a child.

(LONE *returns to practicing. Silence*)

MA: Look, Lone, I'll come up here every night—after work—I'll spend my time practicing, okay? (*Pause*) But I'm not gonna say that they're dead. Look at them. They're on strike; dead men don't go on strike, Lone. The white devils—they try and stick us with a ten-hour day. We want a return to eight hours and also a fourteen-dollar-a-month raise. I learned the demon English—listen: "Eight hour a day good for white man, all same good for ChinaMan." These are the demands of live ChinaMen, Lone. Dead men don't complain.
LONE: All right, this is something new. No one can judge the ChinaMen till after the strike.
MA: They say we'll hold out for months if we have to. The smart men will live on what we've hoarded.
LONE: A ChinaMan's mouth can swallow the earth. (*He takes the dice*) While the strike is on, I'll teach you.
MA: And afterwards?
LONE: Afterwards—we'll decide then whether these are dead or live men.
MA: When can we start?
LONE: We've already begun. Give me your hand.

Scene 3

LONE *and* MA *are doing physical exercises.*

MA: How long will it be before I can play Gwan Gung?
LONE: How long before a dog can play the violin?
MA: Old Ah Hong—have you heard him play the violin?
LONE: Yes. Now, he should take his violin and give it to a dog.
MA: I think he sounds okay.
LONE: I think he caused that avalanche last winter.
MA: He used to play for weddings back home.
LONE: Ah Hong?
MA: That's what he said.
LONE: You probably heard wrong.
MA: No.
LONE: He probably said he played for funerals.
MA: He's been playing for the guys down at camp.
LONE: He should play for the white devils—that will end this stupid strike.
MA: Yang told me for sure—it'll be over by tomorrow.

LONE: Eight days already. And Yang doesn't know anything.

MA: He said they're already down to an eight-hour day and five-dollar raise at the bargaining sessions.

LONE: Yang eats too much opium.

MA: That doesn't mean he's wrong about this.

LONE: You can't trust him. One time—last year—he went around camp looking in everybody's eyes and saying, "Your nails are too long. They're hurting my eyes." This went on for a week. Finally, all the men clipped their nails, made a big pile, which they wrapped in leaves and gave to him. Yang used the nails to season his food—he put it in his soup, sprinkled it on his rice, and never said a word about it again. Now tell me—are you going to trust a man who eats other men's fingernails?

MA: Well, all I know is we won't go back to work until they meet all our demands. Listen, teach me some Gwan Gung steps.

LONE: I should have expected this. A boy who wants to have twenty wives is the type who demands more than he can handle.

MA: Just a few.

LONE: It takes years before an actor can play Gwan Gung.

MA: I can do it. I spend a lot of time watching the opera when it comes around. Every time I see Gwan Gung, I say, "Yeah. That's me. The god of fighters. The god of adventurers. We have the same kind of spirit."

LONE: I tell you, if you work very hard, when you return to China, you can perhaps be the Second Clown.

MA: Second Clown?

LONE: If you work hard.

MA: What's the Second Clown?

LONE: You can play the *p'i p'a,* and dance and jump all over.

MA: I'll buy them.

LONE: Excuse me?

MA: I'm going to be rich, remember? I'll buy a troupe and force them to let me play Gwan Gung.

LONE: I hope you have enough money, then, to pay audiences to sit through your show.

MA: You mean, I'm going to have to practice here every night—and in return, all I can play is the Second Clown?

LONE: If you work hard.

MA: Am I that bad? Maybe I shouldn't even try to do this. Maybe I should just go down.

LONE: It's not you. Everyone must earn the right to play Gwan Gung. I entered opera school when I was ten years old. My parents decided to sell me for ten years to this opera company. I lived with eighty other boys and we slept in bunks four beds high and hid our candy and rice cakes from each other. After eight years, I was studying to play Gwan Gung.

MA: Eight years?

LONE: I was one of the best in my class. One day, I was summoned by my master, who told me I was to go home for two days because my mother had fallen very ill and was dying. When I arrived home, Mother was standing at the door waiting, not sick at all. Her first words to me, the son away for eight years, were, "You've been playing while your village has starved. You must go to the Gold Mountain and work."

MA: And you never returned to school?

LONE: I went from a room with eighty boys to a ship with three hundred men. So, you see, it does not come easily to play Gwan Gung.

MA: Did you want to play Gwan Gung?

LONE: What a foolish question!

MA: Well, you're better off this way.

LONE: What?

MA: Actors—they don't make much money. Here, you make a bundle, then go back and be an actor again. Best of both worlds.

LONE: "Best of both worlds."

MA: Yeah!

(LONE *drops to the ground, begins imitating a duck, waddling and quacking*)

MA: Lone? What are you doing? (LONE *quacks*) You're a duck? (LONE *quacks*) I can see that. (LONE *quacks*) Is this an exercise? Am I supposed to do this? (LONE *quacks*) This is dumb. I never seen Gwan Gung waddle. (LONE *quacks*) Okay. All right. I'll do it. (MA *and* LONE *quack and waddle*) You know, I never realized before how uncomfortable a duck's life is. And you have to listen to yourself quacking all day. Go crazy! (LONE *stands up straight*) Now, what was that all about?

LONE: No, no. Stay down there, duck.

MA: What's the—

LONE (*prompting*): Quack, quack, quack.

MA: I don't—

LONE: Act your species!

MA: I'm not a duck!

LONE: Nothing worse than a duck that doesn't know his place.

MA: All right. (*Mechanically*) Quack, quack.

LONE: More.

MA: Quack.

LONE: More!

MA: Quack, quack, quack!

(MA *now continues quacking, as* LONE *gives commands*)

LONE: Louder! It's your mating call! Think of your twenty duck wives! Good! Louder! Project! More! Don't slow down! Put your tail feathers into it! They can't hear you!

(MA *is now quacking up a storm.* LONE *exits, unnoticed by* MA)

MA: Quack! Quack! Quack! Quack. Quack . . . quack. (*He looks around*) Quack . . . quack . . . Lone? . . . Lone? (*He waddles around the stage looking*) Lone, where are you? Where'd you go? (*He stops, scratches his left leg with his right foot*) C'mon—stop playing around. What is this? (LONE *enters as a tiger, unseen by* MA) Look, let's call it a day, okay? I'm getting hungry. (MA *turns around, notices* LONE *right before* LONE *is to bite him*) Aaaaah! Quack, quack, quack!

*(They face off, in character as animals. Duck-*MA *is terrified)*

LONE: Grrrr!

MA *(as a cry for help)*: Quack, quack, quack!

*(*LONE *pounces on* MA. *They struggle, in character.* MA *is quacking madly, eyes tightly closed.* LONE *stands up straight.* MA *continues to quack)*

LONE: Stand up.

MA *(eyes still closed)*: Quack, quack, quack!

LONE *(louder)*: Stand up!

MA *(opening his eyes)*: Oh.

LONE: What are you?

MA: Huh?

LONE: A ChinaMan or a duck?

MA: Huh? Gimme a second to remember.

LONE: You like being a duck?

MA: My feet fell asleep.

LONE: You change forms so easily.

MA: You said to.

LONE: What else could you turn into?

MA: Well, you scared me—sneaking up like that.

LONE: Perhaps a rock. That would be useful. When the men need to rest, they can sit on you.

MA: I got carried away.

LONE: Let's try . . . a locust. Can you become a locust?

MA: No. Let's cut this, okay?

LONE: Here. It's easy. You just have to know how to hop.

MA: You're not gonna get me—

LONE: Like this.

(He demonstrates)

MA: Forget it, Lone.

LONE: I'm a locust.

(He begins jumping toward MA)

MA: Hey! Get away!

LONE: I devour whole fields.

MA: Stop it.

LONE: I starve babies before they are born.

MA: Hey, look, stop it!

LONE: I cause famines and destroy villages.

MA: I'm warning you! Get away!

LONE: What are you going to do? You can't kill a locust.

MA: You're not a locust.

LONE: You kill one, and another sits on your hand.

MA: Stop following me.

LONE: Locusts always trouble people. If not, we'd feel useless. Now, if you became a locust, too . . .

MA: I'm not going to become a locust.

LONE: Just stick your teeth out!

MA: I'm not gonna be a bug! It's stupid!

LONE: No man who's just been a duck has the right to call anything stupid.

MA: I thought you were trying to teach me something.

LONE: I am. Go ahead.

MA: All right. There. That look right?

LONE: Your legs should be a little lower. Lower! There. That's adequate. So how does it feel to be a locust?

(LONE *gets up*)

MA: I dunno. How long do I have to do this?

LONE: Could you do it for three years?

MA: Three years? Don't be—

LONE: You couldn't, could you? Could you be a duck for that long?

MA: Look, I wasn't born to be either of those.

LONE: Exactly. Well, I wasn't born to work on a railroad, either. "Best of both worlds." How can you be such an insect!

(*Pause*)

MA: Lone . . .

LONE: Stay down there! Don't move! I've never told anyone my story—the story of my parents' kidnapping me from school. All the time we were crossing the ocean, the last two years here—I've kept my mouth shut. To you, I finally tell it. And all you can say is, "Best of both worlds." You're a bug to me, a locust. You think you understand the dedication one must have to be in the opera? You think it's the same as working on a railroad.

MA: Lone, all I was saying is that you'll go back too, and—

LONE: You're no longer a student of mine.

MA: What?

LONE: You have no dedication.

MA: Lone, I'm sorry.

LONE: Get up.

MA: I'm honored that you told me that.

LONE: Get up.

MA: No.

LONE: No?

MA: I don't want to. I want to talk.

LONE: Well, I've learned from the past. You're stubborn. You don't go. All right. Stay there. If you want to prove to me that you're dedicated, be a locust till morning. I'll go.

MA: Lone, I'm really honored that you told me.

LONE: I'll return in the morning.

(*Exits*)

MA: Lone? Lone, that's ridiculous. You think I'm gonna stay like this? If you do, you're crazy. Lone? Come back here.

Scene 4

Night. MA, *alone, as a locust.*

MA: Locusts travel in huge swarms, so large that when they cross the sky, they block out the sun, like a storm. Second Uncle—back home—when he was a young man, his whole crop got wiped out by locusts one year. In the famine that followed, Second Uncle lost his eldest son and his second wife—the one he married for love. Even to this day, we look around before saying the word "locust," to make sure Second Uncle is out of hearing range. About eight years ago, my brother and I discovered Second Uncle's cave in back of the stream near our house. We saw him come out of it one day around noon. Later, just before the sun went down, we sneaked in. We only looked once. Inside, there must have been hundreds—maybe five hundred or more—grasshoppers in huge bamboo cages—and around them—stacks of grasshopper legs, grasshopper heads, grasshopper antennae, grasshoppers with one leg, still trying to hop but toppling like trees coughing, grasshoppers wrapped around sharp branches rolling from side to side, grasshoppers legs cut off grasshopper bodies, then tied around grasshoppers and tightened till grasshoppers died. Every conceivable kind of grasshopper in every conceivable stage of life and death, subject to every conceivable grasshopper torture. We ran out quickly, my brother and I—we knew an evil place by the thickness of the air. Now, I think of Second Uncle. How sad that the locusts forced him to take out his agony on innocent grasshoppers. What if Second Uncle could see me now? Would he cut off my legs? He might as well. I can barely feel them. But then again, Second Uncle never tortured actual locusts, just weak grasshoppers.

Scene 5

Night. MA *still as a locust.*

LONE: (*Off, singing*)
Hit your hardest
Pound out your tears
The more you try
The more you'll cry
At how little I've moved
And how large I loom
By the time the sun goes down
MA: You look rested.
LONE: Me?
MA: Well, you sound rested.
LONE: No, not at all.
MA: Maybe I'm comparing you to me.
LONE: I didn't even close my eyes all last night.
MA: Aw, Lone, you didn't have to stay up for me. You coulda just come up here and—

LONE: For you?

MA: —apologized and everything woulda been—

LONE: I didn't stay up for you.

MA: Huh? You didn't?

LONE: No.

MA: Oh. You sure?

LONE: Positive. I was thinking, that's all.

MA: About me?

LONE: Well . . .

MA: Even a little?

LONE: I was thinking about the ChinaMen—and you. Get up, Ma.

MA: Aw, do I have to? I've gotten to know these grasshoppers real well.

LONE: Get up. I have a lot to tell you.

MA: What'll they think? They take me in, even though I'm a little large, then they find out I'm a human being. I stepped on their kids. No trust. Gimme a hand, will you? (LONE *helps* MA *up, but* MA's *legs can't support him*) Aw, shit. My legs are coming off.

(*He lies down and tries to straighten them out*)

LONE: I have many surprises. First, you will play Gwan Gung.

MA: My legs will be sent home without me. What'll my family think? Come to port to meet me and all they get is two legs.

LONE: Did you hear me?

MA: Hold on. I can't be in agony and listen to Chinese at the same time.

LONE: Did you hear my first surprise?

MA: No. I'm too busy screaming.

LONE: I said, you'll play Gwan Gung.

MA: Gwan Gung?

LONE: Yes.

MA: Me?

LONE: Yes.

MA: Without legs?

LONE: What?

MA: That might be good.

LONE: Stop that!

MA: I'll become a legend. Like the blind man who defended Amoy.

LONE: Did you hear?

MA: "The legless man who played Gwan Gung."

LONE: Isn't this what you want? To play Gwan Gung?

MA: No, I just wanna sleep.

LONE: No, you don't. Look. Here. I brought you something.

MA: Food?

LONE: Here. Some rice.

MA: Thanks, Lone. And duck?

LONE: Just a little.

MA: Where'd you get the duck?

LONE: Just bones and skin.

MA: We don't have duck. And the white devils have been blockading the food.

LONE: Sing—he had some left over.

MA: Sing? That thief?

LONE: And something to go with it.

MA: What? Lone, where did you find whiskey?

LONE: You know, Sing—he has almost anything.

MA: Yeah. For a price.

LONE: Once, even some thousand-day-old eggs.

MA: He's a thief. That's what they told me.

LONE: Not if you're his friend.

MA: Sing don't have any real friends. Everyone talks about him bein' tied in to the head of the klan in San Francisco. Lone, you didn't have to do this. Here. Have some.

LONE: I had plenty.

MA: Don't gimme that. This cost you plenty, Lone.

LONE: Well, I thought if we were going to celebrate, we should do it as well as we would at home.

MA: Celebrate? What for? Wait.

LONE: Ma, the strike is over.

MA: Shit, I knew it. And we won, right?

LONE: Yes, the ChinaMen have won. They can do more than just talk.

MA: I told you. Didn't I tell you?

LONE: Yes. Yes, you did.

MA: Yang told me it was gonna be done. He said—

LONE: Yes, I remember.

MA: Didn't I tell you? Huh?

LONE: Ma, eat your duck.

MA: Nine days, we civilized the white devils. I knew it. I knew we'd hold out till their ears started twitching. So that's where you got the duck, right? At the celebration?

LONE: No, there wasn't a celebration.

MA: Huh? You sure? ChinaMen—they look for any excuse to party.

LONE: But I thought *we* should celebrate.

MA: Well, that's for sure.

LONE: So you will play Gwan Gung.

MA: God, nine days. Shit, it's finally done. Well, we'll show them how to party. Make noise. Jump off rocks. Make the mountain shake.

LONE: We'll wash your body, to prepare you for the role.

MA: What role?

LONE: Gwan Gung. I've been telling you.

MA: I don't wanna play Gwan Gung.

LONE: You've shown the dedication required to become my student, so—

MA: Lone, you think I stayed up last night 'cause I wanted to play Gwan Gung?

LONE: You said you were like him.

MA: I am. Gwan Gung stayed up all night once to prove his loyalty. Well, now I have too. Lone, I'm honored that you told me your story.

LONE: Yes . . . That is like Gwan Gung.

MA: Good. So let's do an opera about *me*.

LONE: What?

MA: You wanna party or what?

LONE: About you?

MA: You said I was like Gwan Gung, didn't you?

LONE: Yes, but—

MA: Well, look at the operas he's got. I ain't even got one.

LONE: Still, you can't—

MA: You tell me, is that fair?

LONE: You can't do an opera about yourself.

MA: I just won a victory, didn't I? I deserve an opera in my honor.

LONE: But it's not traditional.

MA: Traditional? Lone, you gotta figure any way I could do Gwan Gung wasn't gonna be traditional anyway. I may be as good a guy as him, but he's a better dancer. (*Sings*)

> Old Gwan Gung, just sits about
> Till the dime-store fighters have had it out
> Then he pitches his peach pit
> Combs his beard
> Draws his sword
> And they scatter in fear

LONE: What are you talking about?

MA: I just won a great victory. I get—whatcha call it?—poetic license. C'mon. Hit the gongs. I'll immortalize my story.

LONE: I refuse. This goes against all my training. I try and give you your wish and—

MA: Do it. Gimme my wish. Hit the gongs.

LONE: I never—I can't.

MA: Can't what? Don't think I'm worth an opera? No, I guess not. I forgot— you think I'm just one of those dead men.

(*Silence.* LONE *pulls out a gong.* MA *gets into position.* LONE *hits the gong. They do the following in a mock-Chinese-opera style*)

MA: I am Ma. Yesterday, I was kicked out of my house by my three elder brothers, calling me the lazy dreamer of the family. I am sitting here in front of the temple trying to decide how I will avenge this indignity. Here comes the poorest beggar in this village. (*He cues* LONE) He is called Flea-man because his body is the most popular meeting place for fleas from around the province.

LONE: (*Singing*)

> Fleas in love,
> Find your happiness
> In the gray scraps of my suit

MA: Hello, Flea—

LONE: (*Continuing*)

> Fleas in need,
> Shield your families
> In the gray hairs of my beard

MA: Hello, Flea—

(LONE *cuts* MA *off, continues an extended improvised aria*)

MA: Hello, Fleaman.
LONE: Hello, Ma. Are you interested in providing a home for these fleas?
MA: No!
LONE: This couple here—seeking to start a new home. Housing today is so hard to find. How about your left arm?
MA: I may have plenty of my own fleas in time. I have been thrown out by my elder brothers.
LONE: Are you seeking revenge? A flea epidemic on your house? (*To a flea*) Get back there. You should be asleep. Your mother will worry.
MA: Nothing would make my brothers angrier than seeing me rich.
LONE: Rich? After the bad crops of the last three years, even the fleas are thinking of moving north.
MA: I heard a white devil talk yesterday.
LONE: Oh—with hair the color of a sick chicken and eyes round as eggs? The fleas and I call him Chicken-Laying-an-Egg.
MA: He said we can make our fortunes on the Gold Mountain, where work is play and the sun scares off snow.
LONE: Don't listen to chicken-brains.
MA: Why not? He said gold grows like weeds.
LONE: I have heard that it is slavery.
MA: Slavery? What do you know, Fleaman? Who told you? The fleas? Yes, I will go to Gold Mountain.

(*Gongs.* MA *strikes a submissive pose to* LONE)

LONE: "The one hundred twenty-five dollars passage money is to be paid to the said head of said Hong, who will make arrangements with the coolies, that their wages shall be deducted until the debt is absorbed."

(MA *bows to* LONE. *Gongs. They pick up fighting sticks and do a water-crossing dance. Dance ends. They stoop next to each other and rock*)

MA: I have been in the bottom of this boat for thirty-six days now. Tang, how many have died?
LONE: Not me. I'll live through this ride.
MA: I didn't ask how you are.
LONE: But why's the Gold Mountain so far?
MA: We left with three hundred and three.
LONE: My family's depending on me.
MA: So tell me, how many have died?
LONE: I'll be the last one alive.
MA: That's not what I wanted to know.
LONE: I'll find some fresh air in this hole.
MA: I asked, how many have died.
LONE: Is that a crack in the side?
MA: Are you listening to me?
LONE: If I had some air—
MA: I asked, don't you see—?

LONE: The crack—over there—
MA: Will you answer me, please?
LONE: I need to get out.
MA: The rest here agree—
LONE: I can't stand the smell.
MA: That a hundred eighty—
LONE: I can't see the air—
MA: Of us will not see—
LONE: And I can't die.
MA: Our Gold Mountain dream.

(LONE/TANG *dies;* MA *throws his body overboard. The boat docks.* MA *exits, walks through the streets. He picks up one of the fighting sticks, while* LONE *becomes the mountain*)

MA: I have been given my pickax. Now I will attack the mountain.

(MA *does a dance of labor.* LONE *sings*)

LONE:

Hit your hardest
Pound out your tears
The more you try
The more you'll cry
At how little I've moved
And how large I loom
By the time the sun goes down.

(*Dance stops*)

MA: This mountain is clever. But why shouldn't it be? It's fighting for its life, like we fight for ours.

(*The* MOUNTAIN *picks up a stick.* MA *and the* MOUNTAIN *do a battle dance. Dance ends*)

MA: This mountain not only defends itself—it also attacks. It turns our strength against us.

(LONE *does* MA*'s labor dance, while* MA *plants explosives in midair. Dance ends*)

MA: This mountain has survived for millions of years. Its wisdom is immense.

(LONE *and* MA *begin a second battle dance. This one ends with them working the battle sticks together.* LONE *breaks away, does a warrior strut*)

LONE: I am a white devil! Listen to my stupid language. "Wha che doo doo blah blah." Look at my wide eyes—like I have drunk seventy-two pots of tea. Look at my funny hair—twisting, turning, like a snake telling lies. (*To* MA) Bla bla doo doo tee tee.
MA: We don't understand English.
LONE (*angry*): Bla bla doo doo tee tee!
MA (*with Chinese accent*): Please you-ah speak-ah Chinese?

LONE: Oh. Work—uh—one—two—more—work—two—

MA: Two hours more? Stupid demons. As confused as your hair. We will strike!

(*Gongs.* MA *is on strike*)

MA (*in broken English*): Eight hours day good for white man, all same good for ChinaMan.

LONE: The strike is over! We've won!

MA: I knew we would.

LONE: We forced the white devil to act civilized.

MA: Tamed the Barbarians!

LONE: Did you think—

MA: Who woulda thought?

LONE: —it could be done?

MA: Who?

LONE: But who?

MA: Who could tame them?

MA *and* LONE: Only a ChinaMan!

(*They laugh*)

LONE: Well, c'mon.

MA: Let's celebrate!

LONE: We have.

MA: Oh.

LONE: Back to work.

MA: But we've won the strike.

LONE: I know. Congratulations! And now—

MA: —back to work?

LONE: Right.

MA: No.

LONE: But the strike is over.

(LONE *tosses* MA *a stick. They resume their stick battle as before, but* MA *is heard over* LONE'*s singing*)

LONE:	MA:
Hit your hardest	Wait.
Pound out your tears	I'm tired of this!
The more you try	How do we end it?
The more you'll cry	Let's stop now, all right?
At how little I've moved	Look, I said enough!
And how large I loom	
By the time the sun goes down	

(MA *tosses his stick away, but* LONE *is already aiming a blow toward it, so that* LONE *hits* MA *instead and knocks him down*)

MA: Oh! Shit . . .

LONE: I'm sorry! Are you all right?

MA: Yeah. I guess.

LONE: Why'd you let go? You can't just do that.

MA: I'm bleeding.

LONE: That was stupid—where?

MA: Here.

LONE: No.

MA: Ow!

LONE: There will probably be a bump.

MA: I dunno.

LONE: What?

MA: I dunno why I let go.

LONE: It was stupid.

MA: But how were we going to end the opera?

LONE: Here. (*He applies whiskey to* MA*'s bruise*) I don't know.

MA: Why didn't we just end it with the celebration? Ow! Careful.

LONE: Sorry. But Ma, the celebration's not the end. We're returning to work. Today. At dawn.

MA: What?

LONE: We've already lost nine days of work. But we got eight hours.

MA: Today? That's terrible.

LONE: What do you think we're here for? But they listened to our demands. We're getting a raise.

MA: Right. Fourteen dollars.

LONE: No. Eight.

MA: What?

LONE: We had to compromise. We got an eight-dollar raise.

MA: But we wanted fourteen. Why didn't we get fourteen?

LONE: It was the best deal they could get. Congratulations.

MA: Congratulations? Look, Lone, I'm sick of you making fun of the ChinaMen.

LONE: Ma, I'm not. For the first time. I was wrong. We got eight dollars.

MA: We wanted fourteen.

LONE: But we got eight hours.

MA: We'll go back on strike.

LONE: Why?

MA: We could hold out for months.

LONE: And lose all that work?

MA: But we just gave in.

LONE: You're being ridiculous. We got eight hours. Besides, it's already been decided.

MA: I didn't decide. I wasn't there. You made me stay up here.

LONE: The heads of the gangs decide.

MA: And that's it?

LONE: It's done.

MA: Back to work? That's what they decided? Lone, I don't want to go back to work.

LONE: Who does?

MA: I forgot what it's like.

LONE: You'll pick up the technique again soon enough.

MA: I mean, what it's like to have them telling you what to do all the time. Using up your strength.

LONE: I thought you said even after work, you still feel good.

MA: Some days. But others . . . (*Pause*) I get so frustrated sometimes. At the rock. The rock doesn't give in. It's not human. I wanna claw it with my fingers, but that would just rip them up. I wanna throw myself head first onto it, but it'd just knock my skull open. The rock would knock my skull open, then just sit there, still, like nothing had happened, like a faceless Buddha. (*Pause*) Lone, when do I get out of here?

LONE: Well, the railroad may get finished—

MA: It'll never get finished.

LONE: —or you may get rich.

MA: Rich. Right. This is the Gold Mountain. (*Pause*) Lone, has anyone ever gone home rich from here?

LONE: Yes. Some.

MA: But most?

LONE: Most . . . do go home.

MA: Do you still have the fear?

LONE: The fear?

MA: That you'll become like them—dead men?

LONE: Maybe I was wrong about them.

MA: Well, I do. You wanted me to say it before. I can say it now: "They are dead men." Their greatest accomplishment was to win a strike that's gotten us nothing.

LONE: They're sending money home.

MA: No.

LONE: It's not much, I know, but it's something.

MA: Lone, I'm not even doing that. If I don't get rich here, I might as well die here. Let my brothers laugh in peace.

LONE: Ma, you're too soft to get rich here, naïve—you believed the snow was warm.

MA: I've got to change myself. Toughen up. Take no shit. Count my change. Learn to gamble. Learn to win. Learn to stare. Learn to deny. Learn to look at men with opaque eyes.

LONE: You want to do that?

MA: I will. 'Cause I've got the fear. You've given it to me.

(*Pause*)

LONE: Will I see you here tonight?

MA: Tonight?

LONE: I just thought I'd ask.

MA: I'm sorry, Lone. I haven't got time to be the Second Clown.

LONE: I thought you might not.

MA: Sorry.

LONE: You could have been a . . . fair actor.

MA: You coming down? I gotta get ready for work. This is gonna be a terrible day. My legs are sore and my arms are outa practice.

LONE: You go first. I'm going to practice some before work. There's still time.

MA: Practice? But you said you lost your fear. And you said that's what brings you up here.

LONE: I guess I was wrong about that, too. Today, I am dancing for no reason at all.

MA: Do whatever you want. See you down at camp.

LONE: Could you do me a favor?

MA: A favor?

LONE: Could you take this down so I don't have to take it all?

(LONE *points to a pile of props*)

MA: Well, okay. (*Pause*) But this is the last time.

LONE: Of course, Ma. (MA *exits*) See you soon. The last time. I suppose so.

(LONE *resumes practicing. He twirls his hair around as in the beginning of the play. The sun begins to rise. It continues rising until* LONE *is moving and seen only in shadow*)

Curtain

The Receptive Reader

1. How do the two *characters* take shape in the early scenes? What kind of person is each character? What clues does the playwright provide in the way they talk and act?

2. How do the two characters *interact?* Is one a foil to the other? Does their relationship change or evolve?

3. Do you see any *connection* between the workers' strike and Lone's devotion to his art?

4. Why can the phrase "best of both worlds" be seen as a *key phrase* in this play? Who uses it and who echoes it, and with what effect?

The Personal Response

Do you think a spectator would have to be Asian or be a member of a minority group to get fully into the spirit of this play?

The Creative Dimension

With a group, you may want to work on a presentation designed to *pantomime*—act out without words—some of the action and especially the animal characters in this play.

JUXTAPOSITIONS

A Modern Everyman

It is always ourselves that we see upon the stage.
WILLIAM BUTLER YEATS

Some plays focus on the outstanding heroic individual, others on the Everyman or Everywoman who represents our common humanity. The church of the Middle Ages taught that all were equal in the sight of God and that Death was no respecter of persons. Whether peasant, beggar, merchant, emperor, or pope, all would be summoned to a final reckoning. ("People, in the beginning / Look well ahead to the ending" says the Messenger at the beginning of the *Everyman* play.) The struggle in the soul of Everyman and Everywoman mirrored the struggle between the forces of good and evil in the larger world. The basic conflict in each individual was the battle between sin and righteousness, with the outcome determining salvation or perdition. The two selections that follow ask you to compare the medieval conception of Everyman with a more modern Everyman—a Chicano GI being sent to Vietnam in a play by the Mexican-American playwright Luis Valdez.

In the European Middle Ages, **morality plays** acted out basic teachings of the church, putting on the stage personified virtues and vices as part of a religious **allegory.** The best known (and in its time most widely acted) is the anonymous *Everyman* play, written about 1485. A modern adaptation by the Austrian playwright Hugo von Hoffmansthal is still performed each year in front of Salzburg Cathedral. Like much of the teaching literature of the Middle Ages, *Everyman* translates the theology of the church into simple teachings for the common people. In a classroom reading or in a miniproduction, the play can still make the modern audience shudder at the sudden summons of incorruptible Death experienced by medieval Christians.

Everyman   *1485*
A Modern Abridgment

TRANSLATED BY HANS P. GUTH

Scene 1

MESSENGER: I ask you all in the audience
    To hear our play with reverence:
    The Summoning of Everyman it is called
    It shows our lives and how they end,
    And how quickly our time passes on this earth.   5
    The topic of our play is most serious,
    But the lesson is more precious
    And sweet to carry away.
    The story says: People, in the beginning
    Look well ahead to the ending—   10
    No matter how carefree you are.
    Sin in the beginning seems most sweet,
    But in the end it causes the soul to weep,
    When the body has returned to dust.
    Here you shall see how Fellowship and Jollity,   15
    And Strength, Pleasure, and Beauty,

Will fade away like a flower in May.
And you will hear how our heavenly King
Will call Everyman to a general reckoning.
Now listen to what he will say.   20

The MESSENGER *leaves and* GOD *speaks to the audience.*

GOD: I see here in my majesty
How people forget the love they owe me.
They live without fear in worldly prosperity
And worldly riches is all they think about.
They do not fear the sharp rod of my righteousness.   25
Pride, greed, and every other deadly sin
Have become acceptable in the world.
People think only of their own pleasure.
The more I show them kindness,
The more they live in wickedness.   30
They have forgotten the meaning of charity.
Therefore, I will in all haste
Have a reckoning of Everyman's conduct.
I offered the people great riches of mercy,
But there are few who sincerely seek it.   35
The time has come to pronounce justice
On Everyman living without fear.
Where are you, Death, my mighty messenger?

DEATH *enters.*

DEATH: Almighty God, I am here at your bidding
To fulfill your every commandment.   40
GOD: Go now to Everyman,
And tell him, in my name,
That he must go on a pilgrimage
Which he may in no way avoid,
And tell him to bring a sure accounting   45
Without excuse or any delay.
DEATH: Lord, I will go forth into the world
And search out cruelly both great and small.

GOD *leaves.*

Scene 2

DEATH: I will find Everyman who lives like a beast,
Ignoring God's laws, and sunk in folly.
I will strike down those who love riches,
To dwell in hell for time without end,
Unless Good Deeds prove their friend.   5
Lo, yonder I see Everyman walking—
No way does he expect my coming!

His mind is on the joys of the flesh and treasure,
And great pain it shall cause him to endure
Before the Lord, Heaven's king.   10

EVERYMAN *enters.*

Everyman, stand still! Where are you going
So merrily? Have you forgotten your Maker?
EVERYMAN: Why do you ask?
Who wants to know?
DEATH: That I will tell you: 15
In great haste I am sent
From God in His Majesty.
EVERYMAN: What! Sent to me?
DEATH: Most certainly.
Though you have forgotten Him here,   20
He thinks of you in His heavenly sphere,
As, before we depart, you shall know.
EVERYMAN: What does God want from me?
DEATH: That I will tell you:
He must have a speedy reckoning   25
Without any delay.
EVERYMAN: To make a reckoning, I'll need more time.
This sudden summons catches me unprepared.
DEATH: The time has come to take a long journey.
And be sure to bring your book of accounts,   30
For there is no way you could go back for it.
And be sure your reckoning is straight and true—
Showing much bad, and good deeds but a few;
How you have spent your life, in what wise
Before the Chief Lord of Paradise.   35
Make yourself ready to take that road,
For you can send none in your place.
EVERYMAN: Who are you to ask me for this accounting?
DEATH: I am Death, and I fear no one.
I summon all and spare no creature,   40
For God has decreed
That all must obey my call.
EVERYMAN: O Death, you come when I least expected you.
You have the power to save me—
If you spare me, I will give you great reward;   45
Yea, a thousand pounds will be yours
If you put off this matter till another day!
DEATH: Everyman, it cannot be.
I care nothing for gold, silver, or riches,
Or for pope, emperor, king, duke, or princes,   50
For if I were to accept gifts,
I could have all the treasure of this world.
But such is quite contrary to my custom.
I brook no delay. Make ready to depart!

EVERYMAN: Alas! Is there no escape?   55
  I may say Death gives no warning.
  To think about you makes me sick at the heart,
  For my book of accounts is not ready at all.
  If I could have just a dozen more years,
  I would clear my accounts in such a way   60
  That a reckoning would not frighten me.
DEATH: In vain it is to cry, weep, or pray—
  In all haste you must go on your journey.
  Now you can put your friends to the test!
  For, know well, time waits for no one,   65
  And every living creature in the world
  Must pay the price of death for the sin of Adam.
EVERYMAN: O gracious God, have mercy on me in my need!
  And may I have any company as I leave this earth,
  And have my acquaintance lead the way?   70
DEATH: Yes—if any be so bold
  To go with you and share your voyage.
  Too long you have thought your life and treasure were yours.
EVERYMAN: I thought so indeed!
DEATH: No, no—these were merely lent for a time!   75
  For as soon as you are gone,
  Another will have them for a while, and then
  Leave them behind, even as you have done.
  Everyman, how foolish you are! You have your five wits,
  But you did not use them to better your life—   80
  For suddenly I come.
EVERYMAN: O wretch that I am! How can I flee
  And escape from endless sorrow?
  Now, kind Death, spare me till tomorrow,
  And give me time to think.   85
DEATH: No, I cannot agree,
  Nor grant a delay to any.
  But I strike suddenly to the heart
  Without warning.
  And now I will leave you for a time—   90
  See that you be ready shortly,
  For this is the appointed day
  That no living person can escape.

                              DEATH *leaves.*

Scene 3

EVERYMAN: Alas! I may well weep with deep sighs:
  Now I have no kind of company
  To help me and comfort me in my journey.
  And also my reckoning is quite unready.

What shall I say to excuse me?   5
The time passes—God help me, that made all!
It does me no good to grieve,
For the day passes and is almost gone.
To whom can I tell my troubles?
What if I talked to Fellowship   10
And told him this sudden news?
For he is quite in my confidence.
We have in the world on many a day
Been good friends in sport and play.
I see him yonder, certainly.   15
I trust that he will keep me company.
Therefore I will speak to him to ease my sorrow.

FELLOWSHIP *enters*.

Well met, good Fellowship, and good morrow!
FELLOWSHIP: Everyman, good morrow, and good day!
   Why, friend, do you look so distraught?   20
   If anything is amiss, you will let me know
   So that I may help bring the remedy.
EVERYMAN: Good Fellowship, I am in great danger.
FELLOWSHIP: My true friend, tell me what is on your mind.
   I will not forsake you to my life's end   25
   And provide you good company.
EVERYMAN: That was well spoken, and lovingly!
FELLOWSHIP: Sir, I must know the cause of your sorrow.
   I feel pity to see you in any distress.
   If any have wronged you, we shall have revenge,   30
   Though it should cost me my life.
EVERYMAN: I thank you most sincerely, Fellowship!
FELLOWSHIP: Ah—do not worry about thanking me:
   Tell me what is wrong and say no more.
EVERYMAN: But if I should open my heart to you,   35
   And you then turn away from my grief
   And offer me no comfort when I speak,
   Then should I be ten times more sorry.
FELLOWSHIP: Sir, I will do as I say, indeed.
EVERYMAN: Then you are a good friend in time of need,   40
   As I have found you a true friend before.
FELLOWSHIP: And so we shall be forevermore.
   For truly, if you were headed for hell,
   I would not let you go alone on your way.
EVERYMAN: You speak like a good friend, and I believe you.   45
   I will prove worthy of your friendship, you may be sure.
FELLOWSHIP: No need to prove anything between us two!
   For those who will promise and not keep their word
   Do not deserve to live in good company.
   Therefore tell me the sorrow in your mind   50
   As to a friend most loving and kind.

EVERYMAN: I shall show you how it is:
   I am commanded to go on a journey—
   A long way, hard and dangerous—
   And to render strict accounts, without delay,   55
   Before the highest judge of all.
   Therefore I beg of you to keep me company,
   As you have promised, on this journey.
FELLOWSHIP: Here is trouble indeed! A promise is a promise,
   But if I should set out on such a voyage,   60
   I know well it would cause me great grief,
   And I feel fear in my heart.
   Let us consider this matter most carefully,
   For your words would frighten the strongest man.
EVERYMAN: But you said that in my need   65
   You would never forsake me, dead or alive—
   Yes, even on the road to hell!
FELLOWSHIP: So I said, certainly.
   But this is no time for pleasant talk!
   If we took such a journey,   70
   When would we come back again?
EVERYMAN: Truly, never again, till the day of doom!
FELLOWSHIP: By my faith, then I will not go there.
   Who brought you this evil news?
EVERYMAN: It was Death, indeed, who came to see me.   75
FELLOWSHIP: Now by God that redeemed us all,
   If Death was the messenger,
   I will not go on that hated journey
   For any man living today—
   Not for the father that raised me from a child!   80
EVERYMAN: You promised otherwise, that's certain.
FELLOWSHIP: Of that I am well aware.
   And yet, if you wanted to eat, drink, and be merry,
   Or spend the pleasant hours in women's company,
   I would stay with you the livelong day—   85
   For that you may trust me!
EVERYMAN: Yes indeed—then you would be ready!
   Your mind is set on mirth, pleasure, and play,
   And you would sooner attend to such folly
   Than keep me company in my long journey.   90
FELLOWSHIP: I cannot go—that is the truth.
EVERYMAN: Dear Friend, help me in my hour of need.
   Loyal love has long linked us—
   And now, sweet Fellowship, remember me!
FELLOWSHIP: Love or no love, I cannot go!   95
EVERYMAN: But at least do this much for me:
   In the name of charity, see me off at the city gate
   As I set out on the highway!
FELLOWSHIP: For love or money, I will not budge!
   If you could stay—then I would be your friend!   100

But as it is, good luck in your journey!
And now I must take my leave.
EVERYMAN: Don't leave me, Fellowship! Will you abandon me?
FELLOWSHIP: I must go. And may God look after you!

FELLOWSHIP leaves.

EVERYMAN: Farewell, sweet Fellowship! Is this the end,   105
   Never to meet again?
   And not a word of comfort at the parting?
   Now where can I turn?
   Friends crowd around us in prosperity
   That will prove faithless in adversity.   110
   Now I must turn to family and kin,
   Asking them for help in my dire need.
   For your kin will befriend you when others shut their door.
   Yonder I see them walking—
   Now I will try their loyalty.   115

KINSHIP *and* COUSIN *come in.*

Scene 4

KINSHIP: Here we are, at your service.
   Tell us everything that is on your mind,
   And hold nothing back.
COUSIN: Yes, Everyman, and let us know
   What your errand is or your goal,   5
   For, as you know, we will live and die together.
KINSHIP: We will be with you in good luck and bad,
   For no one may turn down his kinfolk in need.
EVERYMAN: Many thanks, my kind friends.
   Now I shall tell you what grieves me.   10
   I received orders from a messenger
   That is the chief officer of a high king:
   He bade me start out on a pilgrimage, without fail,
   From which I know I shall never return.
   I must bring a strict accounting.   15
   And along the way, the great enemy of our souls
   Lies in wait to do me fatal harm.
   Therefore I ask you to be by my side
   And help me in the name of holy charity.
COUSIN: We should be by your side—is that what you ask?   20
   No, Everyman, I would rather fast
   And live on bread and water for five years!
KINSHIP: I hope you do not take it amiss,
   But as for me, you shall go alone!
EVERYMAN: Alas, that ever I was born!   25
   Cousin, will you not come with me?

COUSIN: No, by our Lady! I have a cramp in my toe.
  Do not rely on me, for, so help me,
  You are deceived!
KINSHIP: There is no way you can sway us—   30
  But I have a maid who loves to travel,
  To dance and go to feasts and gad about:
  I will give her leave to go with you on that journey,
  If you and she can agree.
EVERYMAN: Now tell me truly: 35
  Will you go with me or stay behind?
KINSHIP: Stay behind? Yes, that I will and shall!
  Therefore farewell until another day.

                                        KINSHIP *leaves.*

EVERYMAN: This makes me sad:
  People flatter me with fair promises,   40
  But they forsake me when I need them most.
COUSIN: Cousin Everyman, I bid you farewell,
  For truly I will not go with you.
  It troubles me to think of my own accounting—
  Therefore I will stay and make ready my own reckoning.   45

                                        COUSIN *leaves.*

Scene 5

EVERYMAN: Is this what I have come to?
  Those who trust fair words are fools.
  Kinship like Fellowship flees from me,
  And all their promises were empty words.
  Where now do I turn for a helping hand?   5
  One thing I do remember:
  All my life I have loved riches.
  If my Worldly Goods could now help me,
  It would set my mind at ease.
  Where are you, my Worldly Goods and riches of this world?   10

  The voice of WORLDLY GOODS *is heard from inside.*

WORLDLY GOODS: Who calls me? Everyman? What is your hurry?
  I lie here inside, trussed and piled so high,
  And locked securely in strong chests,
  Or packed into bags—I cannot stir,
  As you may see with your own eye.   15
EVERYMAN: Come here, Worldly Goods, and make haste,
  For I need your advice.

  WORLDLY GOODS *enters.*

WORLDLY GOODS: Sir, for any sorrow or adversity in this world,
   I can provide a speedy remedy.
EVERYMAN: My troubles are not of this world.   20
   I must go quite another way
   And give a strick reckoning
   Before the highest judge of all.
   All my life, you have been my pleasure and my joy.
   Therefore, I ask you to come with me,   25
   For it might be that before God Almighty
   You could help me balance my accounts.
   Certainly you have heard it said
   That money can set right many a wrong.
WORLDLY GOODS: No, Everyman—I sing a different song: 30
   I never follow anyone on such an errand.
   For, if I went along,
   You would fare much the worse for my presence.
   Because you always had me in mind,
   Your account is weighed down with many debts   35
   That will count heavily in the balance.
   For your love of me you will have to pay dearly.
EVERYMAN: Alas, I have loved you truly and had great pleasure
   All my life in worldly goods and treasure.
WORLDLY GOODS: That was your downfall—I tell no lie.   40
   For the love of me is contrary to Love Everlasting.
   But if you had loved me with moderation
   And given part of me to the poor,
   Then you would not be in this sorrowful state.
EVERYMAN: False friend that you are,   45
   And traitor to God, you have deceived me
   And caught me in a deadly snare!
WORLDLY GOODS: You have only yourself to blame.
   Your sorrows make me laugh—
   Why should I be sad?   50
EVERYMAN: I gave you all that should have been the Lord's.
   Now will you not come with me, indeed?
   Tell me the truth!
WORLDLY GOODS: I will not follow you, by God!
   Therefore farewell.   55

                    WORLDLY GOODS *leaves*.

Scene 6

EVERYMAN: Oh, whom now can I trust
   To go with me on that fearful journey?
   First, Fellowship promised to go with me;
   His words were pleasing and sweet,

But afterward he deserted me.   5
Then I turned to my Kin in despair;
They also answered with words most fair—
But they too forsook me in the end.
Then I turned to my Worldly Goods that I loved,
Hoping to find comfort; but it was not to be—   10
He told me in sharp words
That he has delivered many unto hell.
Now do I feel remorse and shame;
I know I am worthy of blame.
Who is left to counsel me?   15
I think I shall fare badly
Unless I visit my Good Deeds—
But alas! she is most weak;
She can neither walk nor speak.
And yet I must ask her for help.   20
My Good Deeds, where are you?

   GOOD DEEDS *speaks, huddled on the ground.*

GOOD DEEDS: Here I lie, on the cold ground.
   Your sins have left me so weak
   That I cannot stir.
EVERYMAN: O Good Deeds, I am sore afraid.   25
   You must counsel me,
   For now help would be most welcome.
GOOD DEEDS: Everyman, I understand
   You have been summoned to a reckoning
   Before the King of the Heavenly Jerusalem.   30
   If you heed my words, I will share in your journey.
EVERYMAN: That indeed was my hope—
   That you would keep me company.
GOOD DEEDS: I most gladly would go, though I can hardly stand.
EVERYMAN: Why, has anything hurt you?   35
GOOD DEEDS: Yes—your heedless neglect!
   Here look at the record of your deeds.

   She shows him a book of accounts.

   Here is a sorry reckoning, all blotted and defaced,
   That spells eternal danger to your soul!
EVERYMAN: Good Deeds, I pray for your help,   40
   Or else I am damned forever!
   Therefore help me with my reckoning
   Before the King that is and was and ever will be.
GOOD DEEDS: Everyman, I pity you in your plight,
   And will help you as much as I can.   45
   And though my feet might not carry me farther,
   I have a sister who will also go with you:
   True Knowledge she is called, to keep with you

And help you face that dreaded judgment.

TRUE KNOWLEDGE *enters*.

TRUE KNOWLEDGE: Everyman, I will go with you and be your guide,   50
  In your hour of need to stay by your side.
EVERYMAN: Now do my fortunes mend,
  For which I thank my Creator.
GOOD DEEDS: She will bring you to the place
  Where you will be healed of your grief.   55
EVERYMAN: I thank you from my heart, Good Deeds!
  Your sweet words make me glad.
TRUE KNOWLEDGE: Now let us go together lovingly
  To Confession, that cleansing river.

TRUE KNOWLEDGE *leads* EVERYMAN *to* CONFESSION.

Scene 7

TRUE KNOWLEDGE: Here, this is Confession: kneel down and ask for mercy.
  For his counsel is well esteemed by God Almighty.

EVERYMAN *kneels*.

EVERYMAN: O glorious fountain that washes away all uncleanness,
  Clear me of the spots of unclean vices.
  I come with True Knowledge for my redemption,   5
  Sorry from the heart for my sins.
CONFESSION: I know your sorrow well, Everyman.
  Because you have come to me with True Knowledge,
  I will comfort you as well as I can.
  And I will give you a precious jewel   10
  Called Penance, that wards off misfortune.
  Through it, your body will be chastised
  With abstinence and perseverance in God's service.
  Here you shall receive this scourge from me,
  As a sign of harsh penance that you must endure,   15
  To remind you that your Savior was lashed for your sake
  With sharp scourges, and suffered patiently.
  So in turn you must suffer patiently to save your soul.
  And if you stay on the right road,
  Your Good Deeds will be with you,   20
  And you will be sure of mercy.

[*In a section of the play left out in this adaptation,* EVERYMAN *punishes his
body for the sins of the flesh and puts on the garment of sorrow. He then
takes leave of* BEAUTY, STRENGTH, DISCRETION, *and* THE FIVE WITS *as he read-
ies himself for the final stage of his journey.* GOOD DEEDS *stays with him to
the end.*]

Scene 8

EVERYMAN: Alas! I must be on my way
 To present my reckoning and pay my debts,
 For all the time that I had is now spent.
 Remember well, all you who followed my story,
 How they that I loved best abandoned me,   5
 And only Good Deeds stayed with me to the end.
GOOD DEEDS: All the things of this earth are mere vanity.
 Beauty, Strength, and Discretion fade away.
 Foolish friends and heedless next of kin—
 All flee from you, except Good Deeds.   10
EVERYMAN: Have mercy on me, Almighty God!
GOOD DEEDS: Do not fear, I will speak for you.

 EVERYMAN *and* GOOD DEEDS *descend into the grave.*

TRUE KNOWLEDGE: Now he has suffered what we must all endure.
 Good Deeds will offer him safe conduct.
 Now that the end has come   15
 I hear angels singing with great joy
 Bidding welcome to the soul of Everyman.
 Remember: After death no one can make amends,
 And mercy and pity then do not avail.
 If the final reckoning is faulty,   20
 The sinner will burn in everlasting fire.
 But if your accounting is whole and sound,
 You will be crowned high in heaven.

The Receptive Reader

1. How does this play make audiences think or feel about death? How does the perspective on death compare with more modern perspectives?

2. Purposeful insistent repetition, or **reiteration,** was a favorite teaching technique in medieval didactic literature. Is there a recurrent pattern in Everyman's encounters with the different allegorical characters? Are there other examples of repetition?

3. *Allegory* is sometimes described as lifeless or mechanical. Do the characters become human for you? Did the author have a sense of humor?

4. A familiar problem with didactic literature is that the good characters sometimes seem lifeless compared with the bad. Is that true in this play?

The Personal Response

Does the spectator have to be religious to respond to this play? What, to you, is the central message of the play? How do you relate to it as a modern reader?

The Creative Dimension

This translation and abridgment of the play is suitable for a *readers' theater* presentation (where different readers read their parts) or other kind of classroom adaptation. One group of students rewrote the play for a miniproduction with *Everywoman* as the updated title. Work with a group of fellow students to prepare a miniproduction or adaptation of the play.

Luis Valdez   *(born 1940)*

If you can sing, dance, walk, march, hold a picket sign, play a guitar or harmonica or any other instrument, you can participate! No acting experience required.

FROM A RECRUITING LEAFLET FOR
THE TEATRO CAMPESINO

Luis Valdez is the founder of the Teatro Campesino, which has performed and been honored throughout the United States and in Europe. He is a prolific writer, organizer, director, teacher, and promoter of Chicano drama. The dialogue in his plays, like the speech of many Mexican Americans, shifts easily from English to Spanish and back. The Teatro he founded in 1965 began by performing *actos*—short one-act plays—in community centers, church halls, and the fields in California. The plays were designed to raise the political consciousness of field workers struggling to make a living and preserve their dignity in a system rigged against them. (A *campesino* is someone who works in the fields.) Valdez has a lively sense of the tragedy and comedy of the lives of ordinary people. He also has a gift for cutting satire: at the beginning of his play *Los Vendidos* (*"The Sellouts,"* 1967) a secretary from the governor's office comes to Honest Sancho's Used Mexican Lot to look for a not-too-dark Chicano to become a token Mexican American at social functions in the state capital.

Valdez himself started to work in the fields at age six, with the much-interrupted schooling of the children of America's migrant workers. He eventually accepted a scholarship at San Jose State University and graduated with a B.A. in English in 1964. Much of his early experience in the theater was with the San Francisco Mime Troupe, which practiced improvisational theater. Under his leadership, the Teatro Campesino explored the lives of urban Chicano youth, Mexican Indian legend and mythology, and materials from Third World sources. In 1987, Valdez wrote and directed the movie *La Bamba,* a biography of the Chicano rock 'n' roll singer Ritchie Valens. His PBS production of *Corridos: Tales of Passion and Revolution,* with Linda Ronstadt, won the Peabody Award.

Soldado Razo, or *The Buck Private,* was first performed by the Teatro Campesino in 1971. What makes the private a modern Everyman?

The Buck Private
From Soldado Razo

CHARACTERS

JOHNNY
THE FATHER
DEATH
THE MOTHER
CECILIA
THE BROTHER

DEATH (*enters singing*): I'm taking off as a private, I'm going to join the ranks . . . along with the courageous young men who leave behind beloved mothers, who leave their girlfriends crying, crying, crying their farewell. Yeah! How lucky for me that there's a war. How goes it, bro? I am death. What else is new? Well, don't get paranoid because I didn't come to take anybody away. I came to tell you a story. Sure, the story of the Buck Private. Maybe you knew him, eh? He was killed not too long ago in Vietnam.

JOHNNY *enters, adjusting his uniform.*

DEATH: This is Johnny, the Buck Private. He's leaving for Vietnam in the morning, but tonight—well, tonight he's going to enjoy himself, right? Look at his face. Know what he's thinking? He's thinking (JOHNNY *moves his lips.*) "Now, I'm a man!"

THE MOTHER *enters.*

DEATH: This is his mother. Poor thing. She's worried about her son, like all mothers. "Blessed be God," she's thinking; (THE MOTHER *moves her mouth.*) "I hope nothing happens to my son." (THE MOTHER *touches* JOHNNY *on the shoulder.*)
JOHNNY: Is dinner ready, mom?
MOTHER: Yes, son, almost. Why did you dress like that? You're not leaving until tomorrow.
JOHNNY: Well, you know. Cecilia's coming and everything.
MOTHER: Oh, my son. You're always bringing girlfriends to the house but you never think about settling down.
JOHNNY: One of these days I'll give you a surprise, ma. (*He kisses her forehead. Embraces her.*)
DEATH: Oh, my! What a picture of tenderness, no? But, watch the old lady. Listen to what she's thinking. "Now, my son is a man. He looks so handsome in that uniform."
JOHNNY: Well, mom, it's getting late. I'll be back shortly with Cecilia, okay?
MOTHER: Yes, son, hurry back. (*He leaves.*) May God take care of you, mom's pride and joy.

JOHNNY *reenters and begins to talk.*

DEATH: Out in the street, Johnny begins to think about his family, his girl, his neighborhood, his life.

JOHNNY: Poor mom. Tomorrow it will be very difficult for her. For me as well. It was pretty hard when I went to boot camp, but now? Vietnam! It's a killer, man. The old man, too. I'm not going to be here to help him out. I wasn't getting rich doing fieldwork, but it was something. A little help, at least. My little brother can't work yet because he's still in school. I just hope he stays there. And finishes. I never liked that school stuff, but I know my little brother digs it. He's smart too—maybe he'll even go to college. One of us has got to make it in this life. Me—I guess I'll just get married to Cecilia and have a bunch of kids. I remember when I first saw her at the Rainbow Ballroom. I couldn't even dance with her because I had had a few beers. The next week was pretty good, though. Since then. How long ago was that? June . . . no, July. Four months. Now I want to get hitched. Her parents don't like me, I know. They think I'm a good for nothing. Maybe they'll feel different when I come back from Nam. Sure, the War Veteran! Maybe I'll get wounded and come back with tons of medals. I wonder how the dudes around here are going to think about that? Damn neighborhood—I've lived here all my life. Now I'm going to Vietnam. (*taps and drum*) It's going to be a drag, man. I might even get killed. If I do, they'll bring me back here in a box, covered with a flag . . . military funeral like they gave Pete Gomez . . . everybody crying . . . the old lady—(*stops*) What the hell am I thinking, man? Damn fool! (*He freezes.*)

DEATH *powders* JOHNNY's *face white during the next speech.*

DEATH: Foolish, but not stupid, eh? He knew the kind of funeral he wanted and he got it. Military coffin, lots of flowers, American flag, women crying, and a trumpet playing taps with a rifle salute at the end. Or was it goodbye? It doesn't matter, you know what I mean. It was first class all the way. Oh, by the way, don't get upset about the makeup I'm putting on him, eh? I'm just getting him ready for what's coming. I don't always do things in a hurry, you know. Okay, then, next scene. (JOHNNY *exits.*)

JOHNNY *goes on to* CECILIA's *and exits.*

DEATH: Back at the house, his old man is just getting home.

THE FATHER *enters.*

FATHER: Hey, old lady, I'm home. Is dinner ready?

THE MOTHER *enters.*

MOTHER: Yes, dear. Just wait till Juan gets home. What did you buy?
FATHER: A sixpack of Coors.
MOTHER: Beer?
FATHER: Well, why not? Look—This is my son's last night.
MOTHER: What do you mean, his last night? Don't speak like that.
FATHER: I mean his last night at home, woman. You understand—hic.
MOTHER: You're drunk, aren't you?

FATHER: And if I am, what's it to you? I just had a few beers with my buddy and that's it. Well, what is this, anyway . . . ? It's all I need, man. My son's going to war and you don't want me to drink. I've got to celebrate, woman!

MOTHER: Celebrate what?

FATHER: That my son is now a man! And quite a man, the twerp. So don't pester me. Bring me some supper.

MOTHER: Wait for Juan to come home.

FATHER: Where is he? He's not here? Is that so-and-so loafing around again? Juan? Juan?

MOTHER: I'm telling you he went to get Cecilia, who's going to have dinner with us. And please don't use any foul language. What will the girl say if she hears you talking like that?

FATHER: To hell with it! Who owns this damn house, anyway? Aren't I the one who pays the rent? The one who buys the food? Don't make me get angry, huh? Or you'll get it. It doesn't matter if you already have a son who's a soldier.

MOTHER: Please. I ask you in your son's name, eh? Calm down. (*She exits.*)

FATHER: Calm down! Just like that she wants me to calm down. And who's going to shut my trap? My son the soldier? My son . . .

DEATH: The old man's thoughts are racing back a dozen years to a warm afternoon in July. Johnny, eight years old, is running toward him between the vines, shouting: "Paaa, I already picked 20 trays, paaapá!"

FATHER: Huh. Twenty trays. Little bugger.

THE BROTHER *enters*.

BROTHER: Pa, is Johnny here?

DEATH: This is Johnny's little brother.

FATHER: And where are you coming from?

BROTHER: I was over at Polo's house. He has a new motor scooter.

FATHER: You just spend all your time playing, don't you?

BROTHER: I didn't do anything.

FATHER: Don't talk back to your father.

BROTHER (*shrugs*): Are we going to eat soon?

FATHER: I don't know. Go ask your mother.

THE BROTHER *exits*.

DEATH: Looking at his younger son, the old man starts thinking about him. His thoughts spin around in the usual hopeless cycle of defeat, undercut by more defeat.

FATHER: That boy should be working. He's already fourteen years old. I don't know why the law forces them to go to school till they're sixteen. He won't amount to anything, anyway. It's better if he starts working with me so that he can help the family.

DEATH: Sure, he gets out of school and in three or four years, I take him the way I took Johnny. Crazy, huh?

JOHNNY *returns with* CECILIA.

JOHNNY: Good evening, pa.

FATHER: Son! Good evening! What's this? You're dressed as a soldier?

JOHNNY: I brought Cecilia over to have dinner with us.

FATHER: Well, have her come in, come in.

CECILIA: Thank you very much.

FATHER: My son looks good, doesn't he?

CECILIA: Yes, sir.

FATHER: Damn right. He's off to be a buck private. (*pause*) Well, let's see . . . uh, son, would you like a beer?!

JOHNNY: Yes, sir, but couldn't we get a chair first? For Cecilia?

FATHER: But, of course. We have all the modern conveniences. Let me bring one. Sweetheart? The company's here! (*He exits.*)

JOHNNY: How you doing?

CECILIA: Okay. I love you.

DEATH: This, of course, is Johnny's girlfriend. Fine, ha? Too bad he'll never get to marry her. Oh, he proposed tonight and everything—and she accepted, but she doesn't know what's ahead. Listen to what she's thinking. (CECILIA *moves her mouth.*) "When we get married I hope Johnny still has his uniform. We'd look so good together. Me in a wedding gown and him like that. I wish we were getting married tomorrow!"

JOHNNY: What are you thinking?

CECILIA: Nothing.

JOHNNY: Come on.

CECILIA: Really.

JOHNNY: Come on, I saw your eyes. Now come on, tell me what you were thinking.

CECILIA: It was nothing.

JOHNNY: Are you scared?

CECILIA: About what?

JOHNNY: My going to Vietnam.

CECILIA: No! I mean . . . yes, in a way, but I wasn't thinking that.

JOHNNY: What was it?

CECILIA (*pause*): I was thinking I wish the wedding was tomorrow.

JOHNNY: Really?

CECILIA: Yes.

JOHNNY: You know what? I wish it was too. (*He embraces her.*)

DEATH: And, of course, now he's thinking too. But it's not what she was thinking. What a world!

THE FATHER *and* THE BROTHER *enter with four chairs.*

FATHER: Here are the chairs. What did I tell you? (*to* THE BROTHER) Hey, you, help me move the table, come on.

JOHNNY: Do you need help, pa?

FATHER: No, son, your brother and I'll move it. (*He and* THE BROTHER *move imaginary table into place.*) There it is. And your mom says you should start sitting down because dinner's ready. She made tamales, can you believe that!

JOHNNY: Tamales?

BROTHER: They're Colonel Sanders, eeehh.

FATHER: You shut your trap! Look . . . don't pay attention to him, Cecilia; this little bugger, uh, this kid is always saying stupid things, uh, silly things. Sit down.

MOTHER (*entering with imaginary bowl*): Here come the tamales! Watch out because the pot's hot, okay? Oh, Cecilia, good evening.

CECILIA: Good evening, ma'am. Can I help you with anything?

MOTHER: No, no, everything's ready. Sit down, please.

JOHNNY: Ma, how come you made tamales? (DEATH *begins to put some more makeup on* JOHNNY's *face.*)

MOTHER: Well, because I know you like them so much, son.

DEATH: A thought flashes across Johnny's mind: "Too much, man. I should go to war every day." Over on this side of the table, the little brother is thinking: "What's so hot about going to war—tamales?"

BROTHER: I like tamales.

FATHER: Who told you to open your mouth? Would you like a beer, son?

JOHNNY (*nods*): Thanks, dad.

FATHER: And you, Cecilia?

CECILIA (*surprised*): No, sir, uh, thanks.

MOTHER: Juan, don't be so thoughtless. Cecilia's not old enough to drink. What are her parents going to say? I made some Kool-Aid, sweetheart; I'll bring the pitcher right out. (*She exits.*)

DEATH: You know what's going through the little brother's mind? He is thinking: "He offered her a beer! She was barely in the eighth grade three years ago. When I'm 17 I'm going to join the service and get really drunk."

FATHER: How old are you, Cecilia?

CECILIA: Eighteen.

DEATH: She lied, of course.

FATHER: Oh, well, what the heck, you're already a woman! Come on son, don't let her get away.

JOHNNY: I'm not.

MOTHER (*reentering*): Here's the Kool-Aid and the beans.

JOHNNY: Ma, I got an announcement to make. Will you please sit down?

MOTHER: What is it?

FATHER (*to* THE BROTHER): Give your chair to your mother.

BROTHER: What about my tamale?

MOTHER: Let him eat his dinner.

FATHER (*to* THE BROTHER): Get up!

JOHNNY: Sit down, Mom.

MOTHER: What is it, son? (*She sits down.*)

DEATH: Funny little games people play, ha? The mother asks, but she already knows what her son is going to say. So does the father. And even little brother. They are all thinking: "He is going to say: Cecilia and I are getting married!"

JOHNNY: Cecilia and I are getting married!

MOTHER: Oh, son!

FATHER: You don't say!

BROTHER: Really?

MOTHER: When, son?

JOHNNY: When I get back from Vietnam.

DEATH: Suddenly a thought is crossing everybody's mind: "What if he doesn't come back?" But they shove it aside.

MOTHER: Oh, darling! (*She hugs* CECILIA.)

FATHER: Congratulations, son. (*He hugs* JOHNNY.)

MOTHER (*hugging* JOHNNY): My boy! (*She cries.*)

JOHNNY: Hey, mom, wait a minute. Save that for tomorrow. That's enough, ma.

FATHER: Daughter. (*He hugs* CECILIA *properly.*)

BROTHER: Heh, Johnny, why don't I go to Vietnam and you stay here for the wedding? I'm not afraid to die.

MOTHER: What makes you say that, child?

BROTHER: It just came out.

FATHER: You've let out too much already, don't you think?

BROTHER: I didn't mean it! (THE BROTHER *exits.*)

JOHNNY: It was an accident, pa.

MOTHER: You're right; it was an accident. Please, sweetheart, let's eat in peace, ha? Juan leaves tomorrow.

DEATH: The rest of the meal goes by without any incidents. They discuss the wedding, the tamales, and the weather. Then it's time to go to the party.

FATHER: Is it true there's going to be a party?

JOHNNY: Just a small dance, over at Sapo's house.

MOTHER: Which Sapo, son?

JOHNNY: Sapo, my friend.

FATHER: Don't get drunk, okay?

JOHNNY: Oh, come on, dad, Cecilia will be with me.

FATHER: Did you ask her parents for permission?

JOHNNY: Yes, sir. She's got to be home by eleven.

FATHER: Okay. (JOHNNY *and* CECILIA *rise.*)

CECILIA: Thank you for the dinner, ma'am.

MOTHER: You're very welcome.

CECILIA: The tamales were really good.

JOHNNY: Yes, ma, they were terrific.

MOTHER: Is that right, son? You liked them?

JOHNNY: They were great. (*He hugs her.*) Thanks, eh?

MOTHER: What do you mean thanks? You're my son. Go then, it's getting late.

FATHER: Do you want to take the truck, son?

JOHNNY: No thanks, pa. I already have Cecilia's car.

CECILIA: Not mine. My parents' car. They loaned it to us for the dance.

FATHER: It seems like you made a good impression, eh?

CECILIA: He sure did. They say he's more responsible now that he's in the service.

DEATH (*to audience*): Did you hear that? Listen to her again.

CECILIA (*repeats sentence, exactly as before*): They say he's more responsible now that he's in the service.

DEATH: That's what I like to hear!

FATHER: That's good. Then all you have to do is go ask for Cecilia's hand, right, sweetheart?

MOTHER: God willing.

JOHNNY: We're going, then.

CECILIA: Good night.

FATHER: Good night.

MOTHER: Be careful on the road, children.

JOHNNY: Don't worry, mom. Be back later.

CECILIA: Bye!

> JOHNNY *and* CECILIA *exit.* THE MOTHER *stands at the door.*

FATHER (*sitting down again*): Well, old lady, little Johnny has become a man. The years fly by, don't they?

DEATH: The old man is thinking about the Korean War. Johnny was born about that time. He wishes he had some advice, some hints, to pass on to him about war. But he never went to Korea. The draft skipped him, and somehow, he never got around to enlisting. (THE MOTHER *turns around.*)

MOTHER (*she sees* DEATH): Oh, my God! (*exit*)

DEATH (*ducking down*): Damn, I think she saw me.

FATHER: What's wrong with you? (THE MOTHER *is standing frozen, looking toward the spot where* DEATH *was standing.*) Answer me, what's up? (*pause*) Speak to me! What am I, invisible?

MOTHER (*solemnly*): I just saw Death.

FATHER: Death? You're crazy.

MOTHER: It's true. As soon as Juan left, I turned around and there was Death, standing—smiling! (THE FATHER *moves away from the spot inadvertently.*) Oh, Blessed Virgin Mary, what if something happens to Juan.

FATHER: Don't say that! Don't you know it's bad luck?

They exit. DEATH *reenters.*

The Greyhound Bus Depot.

DEATH: The next day, Johnny goes to the Greyhound Bus Depot. His mother, his father, and his girlfriend go with him to say goodbye. The Bus Depot is full of soldiers and sailors and old men. Here and there, a drunkard is passed out on the benches. Then there's the announcements: THE LOS ANGELES BUS IS NOW RECEIVING PASSENGERS AT GATE TWO, FOR KINGS-BURG, TULARE, DELANO, BAKERSFIELD AND LOS ANGELES, CONNECTIONS IN L.A. FOR POINTS EAST AND SOUTH.

> JOHNNY, FATHER, MOTHER, *and* CECILIA *enter.* CECILIA *clings to* JOHNNY.

FATHER: It's been several years since I last set foot at the station.

MOTHER: Do you have your ticket, son?

JOHNNY: Oh, no, I have to buy it.

CECILIA: I'll go with you.

FATHER: Do you have money, son?

JOHNNY: Yes, pa, I have it.

> JOHNNY *and* CECILIA *walk over to* DEATH.

JOHNNY: One ticket, please.

DEATH: Where to?

JOHNNY: Vietnam. I mean, Oakland.

DEATH: Round trip or one way?

JOHNNY: One way.

DEATH: Right. One way. (*applies more makeup*)

> JOHNNY *gets his ticket and he and* CECILIA *start back toward his parents.* JOHNNY *stops abruptly and glances back at* DEATH, *who has already shifted positions.*

CECILIA: What's wrong?

JOHNNY: Nothing. (*They join the parents.*)

DEATH: For half an hour then, they exchange small talk and trivialities, repeating some of the things that have been said several times before. Cecilia promises Johnny she will be true to him and wait until he returns. Then it's time to go: THE OAKLAND-VIETNAM EXPRESS IS NOW RECEIVING PASSENGERS AT GATE NUMBER FOUR. ALL ABOARD PLEASE.

JOHNNY: That's my bus.

MOTHER: Oh, son.

FATHER: Take good care of yourself then, okay, son?

CECILIA: I love you, Johnny. (*She embraces him.*)

DEATH: THE OAKLAND-VIETNAM EXPRESS IS IN THE FINAL BOARDING STAGES. PASSENGERS WITH TICKETS ALL ABOARD PLEASE. AND THANKS FOR GOING GREYHOUND.

JOHNNY: I'm leaving, now.

> *Embraces all around, weeping, last goodbyes, etc.* JOHNNY *exits. Then parents exit.* THE MOTHER *and* CECILIA *are crying.*

DEATH (*sings*): *Goodbye, Goodbye*
> *Star of my nights*
> *A soldier said in front of a window*
> *I'm leaving, I'm leaving*
> *But don't cry, my angel*
> *For tomorrow I'll be back . . .*

So Johnny left for Vietnam, never to return. He didn't want to go and yet he did. It never crossed his mind to refuse. How can he refuse the government of the United States? How could he refuse his family? Besides, who wants to go to prison? And there was the chance he'd come back alive . . . wounded maybe, but alive. So he took a chance—and lost. But before he died he saw many things in Vietnam; he had his eyes opened. He wrote his mother about them.

> JOHNNY *and* THE MOTHER *enter at opposite sides of the stage.* JOHNNY *is in full battle gear. His face is now a skull.*

JOHNNY: Dear mom.

MOTHER: Dear son.

JOHNNY: I am writing this letter.

MOTHER: I received your letter.

JOHNNY: To tell you I'm okay.

MOTHER: And I thank the heavens you're all right.

JOHNNY: How's everybody over there?

MOTHER: Here, we're all doing fine, thank God.

JOHNNY: Ma, there's a lot happening here that I didn't know about before. I don't know if I'm allowed to write about it, but I'm going to try. Yesterday we attacked a small village near some rice paddies. We had orders to kill everybody because they were supposed to be V-C's, communists. We entered the small village and my buddies started shooting. I saw one of them kill an old man and an old lady. My sergeant killed a small boy about seven years old, then he shot his mother or some woman that came running up crying. Blood was everywhere. I don't remember what happened after that but my sergeant ordered me to start shooting. I think I did. May God forgive me for what I did, but I never wanted to come over here. They say we have to do it to defend our country.

MOTHER: Son what you are writing to us makes me sad. I talked to your father and he also got very worried, but he says that's what war is like. He reminds you that you're fighting communists. I have a candle lit and every day I ask God to take good care of you wherever you are and that he return you to our arms healthy and in one piece.

JOHNNY: Ma, I had a dream the other night. I dreamed I was breaking into one of the hooches, that's what we call the Vietnamese's houses. I went in firing my M-16 because I knew that the village was controlled by the gooks. I killed three of them right away, but when I looked down it was my pa, my little brother and you, mother. I don't know how much more I can stand. Please tell Sapo and all the dudes how it's like over here. Don't let them . . .

DEATH *fires a gun, shooting* JOHNNY *in the head. He falls.* THE MOTHER *screams without looking at* JOHNNY.

DEATH: Johnny was killed in action November 1965 at Chu Lai. His body lay in the field for two days and then it was taken to the beach and placed in a freezer, a converted portable food locker. Two weeks later he was shipped home for burial.

DEATH *straightens out* JOHNNY'S *body. Takes his helmet, rifle, etc.* THE FATHER, THE MOTHER, THE BROTHER, *and* CECILIA *file past and gather around the body. Taps plays.*

The Receptive Reader

1. The central conflict in the medieval *Everyman* was between sin and virtue. What is the central conflict in *The Buck Private?*

2. To judge from this excerpt, does this play have a universal appeal transcending the appeal to a particular ethnic group? In what ways is the buck private a modern Everyman?

3. How does the role of Death compare in the two plays? How does the role of Kinship compare in the two plays?

The Personal Response

What is the central statement this selection makes about the war in Vietnam?

The Creative Dimension

Like the traditional *Everyman,* Valdez's modern Everyman play lends itself well to adaptation for a miniproduction designed to help an audience get into the spirit of the play. One class production changed the GI in the Valdez play to a young woman in the Desert Storm war against Iraq. You and your classmates may want to stage your own reenactment of the Valdez play.

WRITING ABOUT LITERATURE

32   Branching Out (Independent Reading or Viewing)

The Writing Workshop   The test of what you have learned about drama comes when you encounter a new play or an unfamiliar classic on your own. As a theatergoer, you sooner or later start trusting your own judgment. What made a play like Peter Shaffer's *Equus* or *Amadeus* a huge audience success? Why did Samuel Becket's *Waiting for Godot* run for three hundred consecutive performances in Paris? Why was it translated into Swedish, Japanese, and many other languages and produced around the world? What did audiences see in Beth Henley's *Crimes of the Heart*—the play and the movie? What made a new black playwright like August Wilson—*Joe Turner's Come and Gone* (1988), *The Piano Lesson* (1987)—a major figure in American drama?

Consider the following guidelines when you write about your independent reading, viewing, or playgoing:

✘ *If possible, give yourself a head start.*   For instance, choose a play that was the subject of a much-discussed local production. Or choose a play that was made into a movie with a stellar cast (and perhaps with modifications and adaptations that split the critical community). Or decide to study a modern classic that you have often seen mentioned but never came to know.

✘ *Check out the critics' reactions.*   What have knowledgeable people said about this play? How have they reacted? What questions have the critics raised? Remember not to let the critics answer all your questions for you. You are the spectator (or reader).

✘ *If you can, quote insiders or people in the know.*   Look at comments by author, director, or actors. What perspective or guidance for interpretation do they offer? Draw on their comments to give your paper the insider's touch.

✘ *Give the new and difficult the benefit of the doubt.*   Remember that early audiences considered the operas of Wagner a hoax and that Van Gogh sold now-priceless paintings for the price of a lunch.

✗ *Push toward a central question or unifying theme.* For instance, a play from the theater of the absurd may at first sound or read like inspired nonsense. Does it perhaps actually raise serious questions about society? Does it hold the mirror up to human nature after all— even though we might not like the reflection we see?

✗ *Anchor your judgments to the actual text of the play.* Make extensive use of short, apt quotations. Highlight revealing key quotes. Weave a rich tapestry of firsthand references to the play.

The following sample paper was first published in a student literary magazine. What are strong features that may have moved the editors to print the paper?

Sample Student Paper

Karen Traficante

In Defense of The American Dream

Robert Brustein, in his attempt to discredit Edward Albee's play *The American Dream,* claimed there was an "absence of any compelling theme, commitment, or sense of life." Are these accusations true? And if so, do they classify the play as a "fumble"? Harold Clurman's review of the play in the *Nation* advised that Albee "stick closer to the facts of life so his plays may remain humanly and socially relevant." How far does Albee stray?

In order for this play to have a "compelling theme, commitment, or sense of life," a struggle or conflict is needed. But no struggle is found. There is no "man against society" here. The conventional Mommy and Daddy are relatively content with their lives. It does not matter to them that they are living conformities. There are no carrots in their family tree of apples. Mommy and Daddy are typical Jonathan apples. And they don't care. They carry their dull lives to an extreme. Everything about them points to their lack of originality. Their apartment shows no personality. The hideous gilded furniture and frames with no pictures point to their lack of individualism. Socially accepted Mrs. Barker is actually a "dreadful woman"; however, realizing that she is a professional woman and that one is expected to like such elite people, Mommy goes on and explains, "but she is chairman of our woman's club, so naturally I'm terribly fond of her." Naturally! No attempts are made to struggle against society and its conformities here either. And thus, with no struggle, no theme. But the play doesn't need a "theme." It is a parable and a parody. It makes its readers question, struggle, and laugh at the absurdity of their human freedoms. It gives its readers a theme to live by: that is, man against society, mechanization, conformity. The play is not a "fumble"; it is a successful defensive play.

Albee's characters and their lives are exaggerated examples of human mass existence and experience. But he does not deviate that far from the truth. Daniel Bell, in an article on the "Theory of Mass Society," said, "The sense of a radical dehumanization of life which has accompanied events of the past several decades has given rise to the theory of 'mass society.'" And this present mass society has lessened the possiblity for "persons of achieving a sense of individual self in our mechanized society." There exists a majority of conventional Mommies and Daddies, and their dull lives are common to many. The uninventive apartment of the play is similar to some modern flats of our society: the rugs blend with the walls which in turn fuse with the upholstery which is highlighted by the paintings on the walls. Why do people tend to buy expensive pictures merely because the wood frame matches their fruitwood cocktail table and the artist's pigments match the color scheme of the room? Paintings are not a part of the furniture. They are unique expressions; they are art.

Mommy and Daddy are overjoyed with the arrival of the new "bumble." He a "Clean-cut midwest farm boy type, almost insultingly good-looking in a typically American way. . ." And don't most parents look for these traits in their own off-spring? They not only conform, but expect their child to fit the mold as well. Mommy and Daddy's first bumble would not concede, and so he was chopped up and thrown away. Mommy and Daddy wanted only another Jonathan apple. Realistically, modern Mommies and Daddies do not chop up their undesired youth. They may, however, smother their children's individualism or simply break ties with them. Brabantio abandoned his lovely daughter Desdemona in Shakespeare's Othello. Why? Because she deviated from his hopes and from society's ideals as well. And so it is true of our modern Mommies and Daddies; unmarried pregnant daughters are banned from their homes; interracial and inter-religious marriages cause conflict or rejection. So Albee is not straying far from the truth when his Mommy and Daddy throw away their stubborn bumble.

A predominant condition which exists in our world is an inability to communicate. Mommy and Daddy, though married, are essentially strangers. Their daily conversations are vacuums filled with clichés, small talk, and trivialities. Daddy avoids really talking to Mommy. He simply responds with "Have they!" or "Yes . . . yes . . . ," barely recognizing what she is saying. Their marriage exists only in custom. There is no love bond established because they lack the communication necessary to understand one another and thus to love.

Mrs. Barker and Mommy also make some fruitless attemps at social intercourse. With their automatic replies, however, they miss the true substance of what seem to be urbanities: "My, what an unattractive apartment you have!" "Yes, but you don't know what a trouble it is."

Without a "compelling theme, commitment, or sense of life," Albee successfully brings his readers' attentions to the paralysis of conformity, the failure of communication, and a vision of a future world. The vision is exaggerated to the point of humor and horror. But by its existence, it points out the urgency for alterations, struggle, and reform.

Questions

What, according to this paper, accounted for the critics' hostility or lack of comprehension? What are the major points in the student writer's defense of the play? How convincing is her interpretation? How well supported is it? What are some of her most telling points? Does she make you want to see this kind of play?

Plays for Independent Reading

Edward Albee	*The American Dream, The Zoo Story*
Imamu Amiri Baraka	*The Dutchman*
Samuel Beckett	*Waiting for Godot, Endgame*

Bertolt Brecht	*Mother Courage, Galileo, The Good Woman of Szechuan*
Caryl Churchill	*Top Girls, Objections to Sex and Violence*
Brian Friel	*Translations*
Beth Henley	*Crimes of the Heart*
Eugène Ionesco	*The Bald Soprano, The Chairs, The Lesson*
David Mamet	*American Buffalo, Glengarry Glen Ross, Oleanna*
Sean O'Casey	*Juno and the Paycock, Red Roses for Me*
Harold Pinter	*The Homecoming, The Birthday Party*
Jean-Paul Sartre	*No Exit, Dirty Hands, The Flies*
Peter Shaffer	*Equus, Amadeus*
ntozake shange	*for colored girls who have considered suicide/ when the rainbow is enuf*
Tom Stoppard	*Rosencrantz and Guildenstern Are Dead, The Real Thing, Arcadia*
Luis Valdez	*Zoot Suit, The Shrunken Head of Pancho Villa, Los Vendidos*
Wendy Wasserstein	*The Heidi Chronicles*
August Wilson	*Joe Turner's Come and Gone, The Piano Lesson, Guitars*

33 Perspectives

The Range of Interpretation

Just as artists seek to communicate their experi-
ence of life through the use of the raw materials
and the specific means of their art, so critics, con-
fronting the resultant creation, shed a new light
on it, enhance our understanding of it, and finally
end by making their own sense of life significant to
their readers. At best, the critic is an artist whose
point of departure is another artist's work.

HAROLD CLURMAN

FOCUS ON CRITICAL PERSPECTIVES

A successful dramatist lives with critical attention, wanted or not.
There are reviews of tryouts, reviews on opening night, and reviews of
a play having a successful run. Often plays are revised (or scuttled) in
response to influential criticism. There are critical assessments of an
established play, critical reassessments on the occasion of new productions, and critical assessments of a playwright's influence on others.
Here are currents and countercurrents of critical theory that strongly
influence discussions of drama:

Historical/Biographical Criticism   Literary historians remind us that a
playwright's work has roots in contemporary social arrangements and
systems of belief. For example, many of Shakespeare's contemporaries
believed in ghosts. (Hamlet tells his friend Horatio: "There are more
things in heaven and earth, Horatio, / Than are dreamt of in your philosophy.") The ghost in *Hamlet* is seen and verified by competent, sober
observers, so it cannot be, as Queen Gertrude claims, "the very coinage
of your brain"—the product of Hamlet's mad imaginings. When Hamlet
overhears Claudius at prayer and postpones killing him, many of Shakespeare's contemporaries are likely to have shared the belief that a repen-
tant sinner, praying for forgiveness, had a chance to go to heaven. (That

1086

was indeed the point of repentance.) Better wait until the sinner could be caught in the act of sin. Shakespeare's audiences were likely to take seriously the question whether the ghost was a good spirit or an evil influence—a "spirit of health or goblin damned." One modern literary historian has argued that the ghost is indeed an evil spirit, leading Hamlet to damnation.

Psychoanalytic Criticism   Psychoananalytic critics have seen a major source of dramatic conflict in the struggle between our overt rational motives and the repressed subconscious impulses revealed in our dreams. Modern depth psychology, or psychoanalysis, has looked in dreams for clues to deep hidden desires and traumas of human beings. Sigmund Freud (1865–1939), in *The Interpretation of Dreams,* went beyond the surface action of Sophocles' *Oedipus* to probe for a deeper underlying meaning that would explain the hold the play has on the human imagination. Art and literature, to the psychoanalyst, are like dreams in that much of their deeper meaning is repressed, hidden in the subconscious, acted out in disguises to protect them from condemnation by our moral selves. Seen in this light, Oedipus becomes a symbol of one of the oldest patterns in the collective experience of the human race: the son, as a very young child, depends on and responds with all his being to the overpowering mother love that makes the mother the sun of the child's universe. The father, grudging the undivided attention lavished by the mother on the child, becomes the rival for the mother's affection—and, in the Freudian mythology, a deadly enemy. Secretly, unconsciously, the son comes to wish the father dead. Since the conscious, moral, rational self condemns this parricidal desire with horror, the result is a tortured conscience, self-loathing.

Myth Criticism   Greek drama, like the later drama of the Middle Ages, grew out of religious ritual. Critics tracing the roots of drama in myth and ritual have often called attention to the echoes of mythical significance in later plays. In an influential book, the drama critic Francis Fergusson linked Greek tragedy generally to the form of ancient ceremonies enacting the ritual sacrifice of a seasonal god. In such rituals, found in many early cultures, the quasi-divine hero-king fights with a rival, is slain and dismembered, but then rises again with the coming of spring. In Sophocles' *Oedipus* play, Oedipus' struggle, his fall, and his final acceptance of his fate roughly parallel this pattern of death and rebirth. As the culprit who is identified as the source of pollution, Oedipus also fits the mythical figure of the scapegoat driven out of the city into the desert, carrying with it the sins and corruptions of the community, bringing about a cleansing or purgation.

Feminist Criticism   With the theater long dominated by male play-wrights, feminist critics have made a special effort to listen to women's voices or to characters who look at the world from a woman's point of view. In *Shakespeare's Division of Experience,* Marilyn French discusses gender principles that she sees as basic to traditional male perceptions of the world. The masculine principle is associated with power, control, purposefulness, ownership, individualism; it "values action over feeling, thought over sensation." The feminine principle is associated with nature, sensuality, nurturing, pleasure. A major turning point in the history of Western culture was reached when the feminine principle was subdivided into two—benign and malign, represented by the images of the madonna and the whore. For French, this schizophrenic view of womanhood explains Hamlet's attitude toward his mother, which leads him to a general indictment of the female sex.

Deconstructionism   Deconstructionists reacted against the traditional assumption of "organic unity" in a successful literary work. Seen from their perspective, a Shakespeare play is not a finished, integrated piece in which every detail and comma is deliberate and part of the larger whole, informed by an integrating overall intention. The surface text may disguise underlying tensions, with elements in a precarious unstable balance. The surface plot may mask real underlying agendas. We may need to read "against the grain"; we may have to listen between the lines. The playwright may be sending coded insider's messages going counter to the overt surface meaning. While Hamlet on the literal level seems to accept unquestioningly the need for revenge, his own long delays and "almost blunted purpose" may be intended as a signal that the author is not endorsing the traditional revenge ethic without question.

New Historicism   The rewriting of history from a postimperial or post-colonial perspective has brought about a revaluation of the politics of traditional authors. Critics representing the **New Historicism** put renewed emphasis on an author's social context—the way literature reflects and comments on the assumptions governing contemporary society. For example, in Shakespeare's play *The Tempest,* we see Europeans in exile or shipwrecked on an exotic island. Caliban, the only remaining native inhabitant, is made to fetch and carry for his white masters. (His name plays on the indigenous word *carib* that survives in *Carribean* and *cannibal.*) He says, "You taught me language, and my profit on't is I know how to curse." A critic representing the New Historicism may remind us that Shakespeare knew the writings of his French contemporary Montaigne, an early critic of European colonialism. Montaigne denounced the destruction of ancient cultures and the massacres and enslavement of whole populations that followed the European discovery of the New World. Contemporary Spanish sources "presented cases against the enslavement of the Indians and against the claim to imperial possession of the Americas" (Stephen Greenblatt). Readers of the play may sense a strange undertow of sympathy for the underdog defying established authority and conventional morality.

THE RANGE OF INTERPRETATION

The richer a play, the more likely different readers are to find in it elements that have a special meaning for them. Successive generations have read Shakespeare's plays from the perspective of their times. Readers with different political commitments have stressed in Ibsen's plays elements related to their political agendas.

Samuel Taylor Coleridge   *(1772–1834)*

Different schools of thought focus on different dimensions of Hamlet's multifaceted, complex character. The **Romantic** poets revered Shakespeare, initiating the modern Shakespeare cult. The Romantics rejected the eighteenth-century view of Shakespeare as an untutored natural genius, who wrote irregular, uneven plays with flashes of brilliance. To Samuel Taylor Coleridge and other Romantics, Shakespeare's work showed the creative imagination at its most sublime. Every detail in a play was subordinated to an overriding purpose that gave "organic unity" to the whole. For Coleridge and other Romantic poets and critics, that overriding purpose in *Hamlet* was to explore a temperament akin to their own. The Romantic Hamlet is the melancholy, solitary, introspective Hamlet. He is forever musing; his "powers of action have been eaten up by thought." Coleridge, who said "I have a smack of Hamlet myself," frequently returned to the topic of Hamlet's character in his lecture notes and critical essays.

The Romantic Hamlet   *1818*

In Hamlet, [Shakespeare] seems to have wished to exemplify the moral necessity of a due balance between our attention to the objects of our senses and our meditations on the working of our minds—an *equilibrium* between the real and imaginary worlds. In Hamlet, this balance is disturbed: his thoughts, and the images of his fancy, are far more vivid than his actual perceptions, and his very perceptions, instantly passing through the medium of his contemplations, acquire, as they pass, a form and a color not naturally their own. Hence, we see a great, an almost enormous, intellectual activity, and a proportionate aversion to real action. . . . This character Shakespeare places in circumstances under which it is obliged to act on the spur of the moment: Hamlet is brave and careless of death; but he vacillates from sensibility, and procrastinates from thought, and loses the power of action in the energy of resolve. Thus it is that this tragedy presents a direct contrast to that of Macbeth; the one proceeds with the utmost slowness, the other with a crowded and breathless rapidity.

The effect of the overbalance of the imaginative power is beautifully illustrated in the everlasting broodings and superfluous activities of Hamlet's mind, which, unseated from its healthy relation, is constantly occupied with the world within and abstracted from the world without—giving substance to shadows and throwing a mist over all commonplace actualities.

The Receptive Reader

1. What scenes in the play best bear out the Romantic conception of the solitary, melancholy Hamlet, "sicklied o'er by the pale cast of thought"?

2. Coleridge said that Hamlet "delays action till action is of no use and dies the victim of mere circumstance and accident." Is this view borne out by your reading of the final scenes of the play?

Elmer Edgar Stoll

Literary history keeps us from taking a play out of its original time frame and seeing it from an anachronistic, modern point of view. In the historical context of the author's time, Hamlet is a Renaissance prince— "a lord of the Renaissance, and loves name and fame" (E. E. Stoll). In Ophelia's words, he is a courtier, a soldier, and a scholar. Fortinbras says at the end that Hamlet would have made a truly kingly ruler: "he was likely, had he been put on, / To have proved most royal." The Renaissance ideal was not a solitary, withdrawn individual but a person functioning easily and competently in society. Hamlet is a trusting friend to Horatio; he is a courteous, generous host to the wandering players; he is fully in control when playing cat and mouse with Polonius or the king's spies. Edgar Elmer Stoll tries to show that Hamlet's self-image, and the image of him mirrored in the words of other characters, are very different from that of the indecisive, hesitating Romantic Hamlet.

The Renaissance Hamlet   *1933*

By his tone and bearing, likewise, and a conduct that is (if we be not cavilling) irreproachable, and a reputation that is stainless, is Hamlet to be judged. Even early in the play—as, in the soliloquy "O what a rogue," he looks forward to the Mousetrap—the tone is exactly the same that we notice when he is looking forward to the fencing match:

I'll tent him to the quick; if he but blench,
I know my course.

Such accents (unless I be utterly blind to the finer shades of expression, and deaf to the differences in rhythm of verse and speech) are not meant for those of irresolution or shiftiness, apathy, or frailty. . . .

In the form and fashion of Hamlet's speech, there is no trace of uncertainty or fatuity, as there is no trace of suspiciousness or childishness, before he falls into the human devils' clutches, in Othello. And after one's ear (for are we not at the theater?) one's simple wits. In this case [the killing of Polonius], as at the fencing match and on the trip to England, and in the same way, he makes his previous words good; for he kills the man he thinks to be the king. What is plainer still, he thus makes good the words he had uttered as he withheld his hand from the fratricide [of the king at prayer] a minute or so before. Here, indeed, is the "more horrid hent"—to "trip him as his heels may kick at heaven," as he catches the murderer spying on him. And these plain and tangible things, this record of promise and fulfilment, the audience would notice, and were meant to notice; and if a few of them stopped to think that in keeping the great deed to the last he was like the heroes of all revenge tragedies they knew of, they were used to that, and would instinctively approve of it. It is both the traditional form and the natural procedure; obviously, the deed done, the tragedy is over.

From *Art and Artifice in Shakespeare*

The Receptive Reader

1. Can you find and cite other passages in which Hamlet sounds determined or resolute?

2. For critics in the Romantic tradition, scenes like Hamlet's deciding not to kill the king at prayer are mere *pretexts* or excuses for continued inaction. What side do you incline to after rereading the scene?

3. Do you think both the sensitive, meditative side of Hamlet's character stressed by the Romantics and the aggressive, determined side stressed by Stoll could be parts of the same character?

Ernest Jones

Twentieth-century **psychoanalytic criticism** focused on Hamlet's inner turmoil as evidence of a profoundly disturbed, "unhinged" mind. What explains his misogyny—his harsh, abusive treatment of the innocent Ophelia and his hateful comments about women in general? Psychoanalysts, trained to trace severe maladjustments to the workings of sexual repression, looked for buried, unacknowledged desires as the source of Hamlet's "near madness." Ernest Jones, a British follower of Freud, tried to show in the play detailed evidence of the Oedipus complex: intense jealousy and resentment directed at the mother (seen as having betrayed the son's love); hatred of the mother's husband (Claudius) as the successful rival for the mother's affection; inability to overcome the fixation on the mother and transfer love or sexual desire to a younger woman (Ophelia). Jones saw in Hamlet's idealized picture of his dead father the result of the conscious mind adopting the teachings of society. These teachings cause the overlay of dutiful respect and filial piety covering up the repressed resentment and sexual jealousy against the father that still lurk in the subconscious.

The Psychoanalytic Hamlet   *1947*

His [Hamlet's] resentment against women is still further inflamed by the hypocritical prudishness with which Ophelia follows her father and brother in seeing evil in his natural affection, an attitude which poisons his love in exactly the same way that the love of his childhood, like that of all children, must have been poisoned. He can forgive a woman neither her rejection of his sexual advances nor, still less, her alliance with another man. Most intolerable of all to him, as Bradley well remarks, is the sight of sensuality in a quarter from which he had trained himself ever since infancy vigorously to exclude it. The total reaction culminates in the bitter misogyny of his outburst against Ophelia, who is devastated at having to bear a reaction so wholly out of proportion to her own offense and has no idea that in reviling her Hamlet is really expressing his bitter resentment against his mother. The identification is further demonstrated in the course of the play by Hamlet's killing the men who stand between him and his mother and Ophelia (Claudius and Polonius). On only one occasion does he for a moment escape from the sordid implication with which his love has been impregnated and achieve a healthier attitude toward Ophelia, namely at the open grave when in remorse he breaks out at Laertes for presuming to pretend that his feeling for her could ever equal that of her lover.

The intensity of Hamlet's repulsion against women in general, and Ophelia in particular, is a measure of the powerful repression to which his sexual feelings are being subjected. The outlet for those feelings in the direction of his mother has always been firmly dammed, and now that the narrower channel in Ophelia's direction has also been closed the increase in the original direction consequent on the awakening of early memories tasks all his energy to maintain the represssion. His pent up feelings find a partial vent in other directions. The petulant irascibility and explosive outbursts called forth by his vexation at the hands of Guildenstern and Rosencrantz, and especially of Polonius, are evidently to be interpreted in this way, as also is in part the burning nature of his reproaches to his mother. Indeed toward the end of his interview with his mother the thought of her misconduct expresses itself in that almost physical disgust which is so characteristic a manifestation of intensely repressed sexual feeling.

Let the bloat king tempt you again to bed;
Pinch wanton on your cheek; call you his mouse;

And let him, for a pair of reechy kisses,
Or paddling in your neck with his damned fingers,
Make you to ravel all this matter out . . . (III.iv)

From the introduction to *Hamlet, Prince of Denmark*

The Receptive Reader

For you, does this excerpt throw new light on Hamlet's anger and hostility? What scenes or details from the play does Jones make you reconsider? How persuasive is Jones's explanation of Hamlet's misogyny? What are other possible explanations?

Sandra K. Fischer

Some **feminist criticism** has focused on those of Shakespeare's female characters who exhibit in varying degrees "independence, self-control, and, frequently, defiance": "By creating confident, attractive, independent women whom we like, he questions the wisdom of a power structure that insists they relinquish personal freedom" (Irene G. Dash). Other feminists have focused on those of Shakespeare's women who seem defeated by a patriarchal society. The author of the following excerpt said that the two essential steps toward a feminist approach to the play were (1) to notice how much in *Hamlet* is "based on a stereotyped judgment of women as *others*," and (2) "to read female characters in as real and serious a fashion as the males—as grappling with their identities, needing outlets for their conflicts, and trying to articulate their truths" when denied full voice. In the following excerpt, the author tries to hear one of the "quieter and less powerful voices" almost drowned out by Hamlet's assertive rhetoric.

The Feminist's Hamlet: Hearing Ophelia   1990

Ophelia's debut is with Laertes, who bids her farewell by solidifying her role as object and by squelching any effort on her part for mutual perspective and adult interchange. Polonius and Laertes, father and son, both treat her like a child who lacks self-knowledge and apprehension about the ways of the world. As Polonius speaks his truisms to Laertes, so Laertes gives his platitudinous wisdom to Ophelia, establishing a chain of cultural dissemination and control. Remarkably missing in this scene is an outside audience or any sense of commentary on the action. In contradistinction, Hamlet's entrance reveals "the privileges of the Self . . . attributed to the masculine hero. The hero is, to begin with, *concerned* with himself; the first privilege of the Self is to have an *extra* Self who comments on or is simply aware of the original one. The tragic hero explains and justifies himself, he finds fault with himself, he insists on himself, he struggles to be true to himself" (Linda

Bamber). In Ophelia's discourse, these functions are completely externalized: she finds herself explained, faulted, and struggled over by rival authorities outside herself.

Ophelia's language is an index to her enforced silence and circumscribed self. With Laertes, her familiar, she is allowed mostly half-lines and questions that are codes of acquiescence without the gesture of assent. They actually invite further commands: "Do you doubt that? . . . No more but so?" (I.iii,4, 10). Her allowed discourse with Polonius is even more frightening. First, in the course of thirteen lines she breaks her promise of secrecy to Laertes by relating to her father the gist of their conversation. Moreover, her speeches here are marked by phrases of self-effacing obeisance: "So please you . . . my lord . . . I do not know, my lord, what I should think. . . . I shall obey, my lord" (89–136).

In his intervening scene, I.iv, Hamlet again is afforded the medium of intimate and leisurely dialogue that establishes and cements his sense of self. Here is the camaraderie of the watch and the comforting mirror of Horatio; here as well is discourse with the ghost, which is remarkably similar to soliloquy. Ophelia's link with Hamlet's mission from the ghost is to be the recipient of his first attempt at an antic disposition. The prologue to her description of his madness is in her usual tentative form—"O my lord, my lord, I have been so affrighted. . . . My lord, I do not know, / But truly I do fear it" (II.i.75,85–86). As she describes to Polonius what she has witnessed, she depicts herself throughout as the passive object of Hamlet's actions: he holds her wrist; stares at her face; shakes her arm; nods, sighs; leaves while staring at her still. To obedience, acquiescence, and obeisance is now added negative objectification. The cause of this treatment has not been Ophelia's self, but rather her absence: "No, my good lord, but as you did command, / I did repel his letters and denied / His access to me" (II.i.108–10). Ophelia's closet scene is remarkable for acting as a discursive pivot. Here the characters embarked on parallel tragic courses are alone together, yet the chance for dialogue is missed, and each begins a path toward a stunning isolation. Ophelia loses all interlocutors as Polonius objectifies her further, "loosing" her (in the sense of unlocking or offering for mating) to probe the depths of Hamlet's self. Hamlet, meanwhile, complains of his isolation, yet he is constantly allowed confrontations that permit him to shape his changing sense of identity: with Polonius, with Rosencrantz and Guildenstern, and with the Players. As Belsey notes, "since meaning is plural, to be able to speak is to be able to take part in the contest for meaning which issues in the production of new subject-positions, new determinations of what it is possible to be." These exchanges result in Hamlet's second soliloquy, beginning "Now I am alone" (II.ii.565). Yet it is Ophelia whose linguistic isolation is the most profound, and she is offered no means to vent her confusion. Her confrontation with Hamlet in III.i, with Polonius and Claudius as silent observers, is a mistimed parody of what might have ensued in the closet scene. Both are aware of their audience. Ophelia tries her usual speech forms, half-lines, and questions, in addition to cautious and polite assertions of a changed reality, but Hamlet refuses to communicate, judging her the bait in the trap of his selfhood.

From *Renaissance and Reformation* 26, Winter 1990

The Receptive Reader

This article focuses on functions of language other than merely communicating information. What are some of these functions? What is their meaning or symbolic significance? What are striking illustrations from the play? Do they alert you to striking differences between the roles of Hamlet and Ophelia? How does this article change your thinking about sex roles or gender roles in the play?

Joan Templeton

Ibsen's *Doll's House* was seen by many as a feminist manifesto and inspired furious denunciation by its enemies and spirited defense by its admirers. Ibsen admired women who fought the battle for women's right to vote. Calling their female contemporaries "morally disabled," they advanced the ideal of an independent, educated New Woman taking her place in the world of work and politics. In 1884, Ibsen joined with the president of the Norwegian Women's Rights League and with fellow writers in signing a petition supporting a proposed law establishing property rights for married women. He advised legislators against consulting men on this topic: "To consult men in such a matter is like asking wolves if they desire better protection for the sheep."

Ibsen and Feminism *1989*

Ibsen's contemporaries, the sophisticated as well as the crude, recognized *A Doll's House* as the clearest and most substantial expression of the "woman question" that had yet appeared. In Europe and America, from the 1880's on, the articles poured forth: "Der Noratypus" [The Nora Type], "Ibsen und die Frauenfragen" [Ibsen and the Women's Questions], "Ibsen et la femme," "La réprésentation féministe et sociale d'Ibsen," "A Prophet of the New Womanhood," "Ibsen as a Pioneer of the Woman Movement." These are a small sampling of titles from scholars and journalists who agreed with their more famous contemporaries Lou Andréas Salomé, Alla Nazimova, Georg Brandes, and August Strindberg, along with every other writer on Ibsen, whether in the important dailies and weeklies or in the highbrow and lowbrow reviews, that the theme of *A Doll's House* was the subjection of women by men.

Havelock Ellis, filled with a young man's dreams and inspired by Nora, proclaimed that she held out nothing less than "the promise of a new social order." In 1890, eleven years after Betty Hennings as Nora first slammed the shaky backdrop door in Copenhagen's Royal Theatre, he summarized what *A Doll's House* meant to the progressives of Ibsen's time:

> The great wave of emancipation which is now sweeping across the civilized world means nominally nothing more than that women should have the right to education, freedom to work, and political enfranchisement— nothing in short but the bare ordinary rights of an adult human creature in a civilized state.

Profoundly disturbing in its day, *A Doll's House* remains so still because, in James Huneker's succinct analysis, it is "the plea for woman as a human being, neither more nor less than man, which the dramatist made." . . .

A Doll's House is a natural development of the play Ibsen had just written, the unabashedly feminist *Pillars of Society;* both plays reflect Ibsen's extremely privileged feminist education, which he shared with few other nineteenth-century male authors and which he owed to a trio of extraordinary women: Suzannah Thoresen Ibsen, his wife; Magdalen Thoresen, his colleague at the Norwegian National Theatre in Bergen, who was Suzannah's stepmother and former governess; and Camilla Wergeland Collett, Ibsen's literary colleague, valued friend, and the founder of Norwegian feminism.

Magdalen Thoresen wrote novels and plays and translated the French plays Ibsen put on as a young stage manager at the Bergen theater. She was probably the first "New Woman" he had ever met. She pitied the insolvent young writer, took him under her wing, and brought him home. She had passed her strong feminist principles on to her charge, the outspoken and irrepressible Suzannah, who adored her strong-minded stepmother and whose favorite author was George Sand [pen name of Lucile Dudevant]. The second time Ibsen met Suzannah he asked her to marry him. Hjordis, the fierce shield-maiden of *The Vikings at Helgeland,* the play of their engagement, and Svanhild, the strong-willed heroine of *Love's Comedy,* the play that followed, owe much to Suzannah Thoresen Ibsen. Later, Nora's way of speaking would remind people of Suzannah's.

The third and perhaps most important feminist in Ibsen's life was his friend Camilla Collett, one of the most active feminists in nineteenth-century Europe and founder of the modern Norwegian novel. Fifteen years before Mill's *Subjection of Women,* Collett wrote *Amtmandens Døttre* (The Governor's Daughters). Faced with the choice of a masculine *nom de plume* [pen name] or no name at all on the title page, Collett brought out her novel anonymously in two parts in 1854 and 1855, but she nonetheless became widely known as the author. Its main argument, based on the general feminist claim that women's feelings matter, is that women should have the right to educate themselves and to marry whom they please. In the world of the governor's daughters, it is masculine success that matters. Bought up to be ornaments and mothers, women marry suitable men and devote their lives to their husbands' careers and to their children. The novel, a cause célèbre, made Collett famous overnight.

Collett regularly visisted the Ibsens in their years of exile in Germany, and she and Suzannah took every occasion to urge Ibsen to take up the feminist cause. They had long, lively discussions in the years preceding *A Doll's House,* when feminism had become a strong movement and the topic of the day in Scandinavia. Collett was in Munich in 1877, when Ibsen was hard at work on *Pillars of Society,* and Ibsen's biographer Koht speculates that Ibsen may have deliberately prodded her to talk about the women's movement in order to get material for his dialogue. . . .

It is foolish to apply the formalist notion that art is never sullied by argument to Ibsen's middle-period plays, written at a time when he was an outspoken and direct fighter in what he called the "mortal combat between two epochs." . . . While it is true that Ibsen never reduced life to "ideas," it is equally true that he was passionately interested in the events and ideas of his day. He was as deeply anchored in his time as any writer has been before or since.

From "The *Doll House* Backlash: Criticism, Feminism, and Ibsen"

The Receptive Reader

One school of critics has seen Nora's search for her own true self as transcending sex roles. The play is "a metaphor for individual freedom" generally (Robert Brustein). Nora is Everyman trying to find himself or herself. However, feminist critics have stressed Nora's identity as a "nineteenth-century married woman." *A Doll's House* "is not about Everybody's struggle to find himself or herself" but "about Everywoman's struggle against Everyman" (Joan Templeton). Which of these two views is closer to your own reading of the play?

Errol Durbach

Ibsen wrote at the time of the first stirrings of socialism and communism that foreshadowed the revolutionary upheavals of the twentieth century. He helped turn drama into a political force, inspiring disciples like the Irish playwright George Bernard Shaw, whose plays were manifestos and at the same time highly successful drama. American admirers drew the parallel between Ibsen's provincial bourgeois society and small-town American middle-class life, seeing him as a champion of the "victories of self-assertion over the oppression of society, and of naked truth over conventional shams" (Edwin Slosson). The following selection focuses on the impact Ibsen had on avant-garde intellectuals in England.

Ibsen and Marxism   1991

For the English Ibsenites, the Norwegian Master was full of ideological fervor, a champion of political causes from Marxism and Fabianism to secularism, hedonism, and atheism. Eleanor Marx played Nora to Aveling's Torvald, roles that they acted with the utter conviction that the "miracle" had already taken place in their pleasant house in Great Russell Street. The couple had just published an article called "The Woman Question: From a Socialist Point of View" in which they argued that when the revolution came—and Eleanor believed that *A Doll's House* was its harbinger—men and women would be joined in free contract, mind to mind, as a whole and completed entity. For Marxists, *A Doll's House* envisioned the emancipation of men and women from the capitalist system with the abolition of class rule serving as a prerequisite for the abolition of sex rule, and because, for Eleanor Marx, the status of women in society was directly analogous to that of the proletariat, she submerged all interest in sectarian feminism into the larger issues of social change through revolutionary action. For her, Nora's predicament was a metaphor for the oppression and exploitation of the working classes, and marriage in Ibsen's play symbolized the last bastion of serfdom recognized by law. The resounding door slam was viewed as the first rumble of momentous social rebellion, and if Ibsen's play ends on a note of tenuous possibility that some secular "miracle" might transform Christmas into a celebration of cultural renewal, for Eleanor Marx that "miracle" was socialism, which would bring economic and intellectual emancipation for women and workers alike.

From *A Doll's House: Ibsen's Myth of Transformation*

The Receptive Reader

Can you see why for socialist readers of Ibsen's play "the status of women in society was directly analogous to that of the proletariat"? Would you use the term *oppression* for Nora's situation in the play? Why or why not?

PLAYWRIGHTS AND CRITICS

Some critical assessments become classics in their own right. They serve as programmatic statements providing guidelines for converts and followers. The theory of tragedy that Aristotle formulated in his *Poetics* became a code for future playwrights to honor or to break. Through the centuries, it guided critical reactions and shaped audience expectations in ways that dramatists found hard to ignore. Modern playwrights have often taken an active part in critical controversies swirling around their craft. The Irish playwright George Bernard Shaw published a famous defense of Ibsen's plays in *The Quintessence of Ibsenism,* celebrating the Norwegian playwright's mirroring of the human spirit as it moved beyond the past in quest of new ideals. Playwrights from Arthur Miller to ntozake shange have spoken up to explain and defend their work.

Aristotle   *(384–322 B.C.)*

Aristotle, the encyclopedic philosopher of classical antiquity, wrote his *Poetics* a century after the height of classical Greek drama. His discussion of tragedy is a spectacular example of **critical theory** read as gospel by many. Although Aristotle developed his theories after the fact, based on plays he loved, his followers in later centuries set them up as rules for future playwrights to follow. In times of classical revival, his *Poetics* became the bible for **neoclassical** critics. The following excerpt from Aristotle's theory of tragedy includes his discussion of **hamartia,** or the tragic flaw. A few references to plays lost or little known have been omitted.

On the Perfect Plot

330 B.C.

TRANSLATED BY INGRAM BYWATER

We assume that, for the finest form of tragedy, the plot must be not simple but complex; and further, that it must imitate actions arousing fear and pity, since that is the distinctive function of this kind of imitation. It follows, therefore, that there are three forms of plot to be avoided. (1) A good man must not be seen passing from happiness to misery, or (2) a bad man from misery to happiness. The first situation is not fear-inspiring or piteous, but simply odious to us. The second is the most untragic that can be; it has not one of the requisites of tragedy; it does not appeal either to the human feeling in us, or to our pity, or to our fears. Nor, on the other hand, should (3) an extremely bad man be seen falling from happiness into misery. Such a story may arouse the human feeling in us, but it will not move us to either pity or fear; pity is occasioned by undeserved misfortune, and fear by that of one like ourselves; so that there will be nothing either piteous or fear-inspiring in the situation.

There remains, then, the intermediate kind of person, a man not pre-eminently virtuous and just, whose misfortune, however, is brought upon him not by vice and depravity but by some error of judgment **[hamartia],** of the number of those in the enjoyment of great reputation and prosperity; for example, Oedipus, Thyestes, and the men of note of similar families. The perfect plot, accordingly, must have a single, and not (as some tell us) a double issue; the change in the hero's fortunes must be not from misery to happiness, but on the contrary from happiness to misery; and the cause of it must lie not in any depravity, but in some great error on his part; the man himself being either such as we have described, or better, not worse, than that. Fact also confirms our theory. Though the poets began by accepting any tragic story that came to hand, in these days the finest tragedies are always on the story of some few houses, on that of Alcmeon, Oedipus, Orestes, Meleager, Tyestes, Telephus, or any others that may have been involved, as either agents or sufferers, in some deed of horror. The theoretically best tragedy, then, has a plot of this description. The critics, therefore, are wrong who blame Euripides for taking this line in his tragedies, and giving many of them an unhappy ending. It is, as we have said, the right line to take. The best proof is this: on the stage, and in the public performances, such plays, properly worked out, are seen to be the most truly tragic; and Euripides, even if his execution be faulty in every other point, is seen to be nevertheless the most tragic certainly of the dramatists.

After this comes the construction of plot which some rank first, one with a double story . . . and an opposite issue for the good and the bad characters. It is ranked as first only through the weakness of the audiences; the poets merely follow their public, writing as its wishes dictate. But the pleasure here is not that of tragedy. It belongs rather to comedy, where the bitterest enemies in the piece . . . walk off good friends at the end, with no slaying of anyone by anyone.

The tragic fear and pity may be aroused by the spectacle; but they may also be aroused by the very structure and incidents of the play—which is the better way and shows the better poet. The plot in fact should be so framed that, even without seeing the things take place, he who simply hears the account of them shall be filled with horror and pity at the incidents; which is just the effect that the mere recital of the story in *Oedipus* would have on one. To produce this same effect by means of the spectacle is less artistic, and requires extraneous aid. Those, however, who make use of the spectacle to put before us that which is merely monstrous and not productive of fear, are wholly out of touch with tragedy; not every kind of pleasure should be required of a tragedy, but only its own proper pleasure.

The tragic pleasure is that of pity and fear, and the poet has to produce it by a work of imitation; it is clear, therefore, that the causes should be included in the incidents of the story. Let us see, then, what kinds of incident strike one as horrible, or rather as piteous. In a deed of this description the parties must necessarily be either friends, or enemies, or indifferent to one another. Now when enemy does it on enemy, there is nothing to move us to pity either in his doing or in his meditating the deed, except so far as the actual pain of the sufferer is concerned; and the same is true when the parties are indifferent to one another. Whenever the tragic deed, however, is done within the family—when the murder or the like is done or meditated by brother on brother, by son on father, by mother on son, or son on mother—these are the situations the poet should seek after. The traditional stories, accordingly, must be kept as they are, for instance, the murder of Clytaemnestra by Orestes. At the same time even with these there is something left to the poet himself; it is for him to devise the right way of treating them.

Let us explain more clearly what we mean by "the right way." The deed of horror may be done by the doer knowingly and consciously, as in the old poets, and in Medea's murder of her children in Euripides. Or he may do it, but in ignorance of his relationship, and discover that afterwards, as does the Oedipus in Sophocles. . . . A third possibility is for one meditating some deadly injury to another, in ignorance of his relationship, to make the discovery in time to draw back. These exhaust the possibilities, since the deed must necessarily be either done or not done, and either knowingly or unknowingly.

The worst situation is when the character is with full knowledge on the point of doing the deed, and leaves it undone. It is odious and also (through the absence of suffering) untragic; hence it is that no one is made to act thus except in some few instances, e.g., Haemon and Creon in *Antigone*. Next after this comes the actual perpetration of the deed meditated. A better situation than that, however, is for the deed to be done in ignorance, and the relationship discovered afterwards, since there is nothing odious in it, and the discovery will serve to astound us. But the best of all is the last; what we have in *Cresphontes*, for example, where Merope, on the point of slaying her son, recognizes him in time, and in *Iphigenia*, where sister and brother are in a like position.

From Poetics

The Receptive Reader

1. Aristotle throughout focuses on the effect a play has on the *audience*. How does this concern with audience reaction show in his discussion of the ideal tragic hero?

2. Does Aristotle's definition of the *tragic flaw* fit Antigone? Does it fit Hamlet?

Esther Cohen

Esther Cohen conducted her interview with Wendy Wasserstein after being challenged by the editor of *Women's Studies* to write an article on women writers and humor in the theater. Cohen had met the playwright while working as a stage manager for a production of one of Wasserstein's plays. In the following excerpts, Cohen elicits responses that sound casual and funny but that also shed light on the challenges facing women writing comedy today.

Uncommon Woman: Interview with Wendy Wasserstein   *1988*

ESTHER: I guess my first question is, when did you decide you liked to write? When did writing become something that you liked to do?

WENDY: I remember as a child thinking that my family was very funny. I think this was because my mother was somewhat eccentric. And I do remember watching shows like "Make Room for Daddy" and thinking that those kids were pretty boring. And I actually thought, like Rusty Hammer and Angela Cartwright, they are such good kids, and I thought "no one's family is really like this." And actually I thought our family was far more entertaining than that. So I think partially from that, though I didn't really write those things.

I wrote in high school. I went to school in New York City at Calhoun, and I figured out that one of the ways I could get out of gym was if I wrote something called the Mother-Daughter Fashion Show. I know very little about fashion, but they used to have this Mother-Daughter Fashion Show once a year at the Plaza Hotel, and you got to leave school to go to the fashion show. But if you wrote it you didn't have to go to gym for like two or three weeks, it was fantastic. So, I started writing those. . . .

E: Do you find, as you're writing, that your humor comes more out of the situation you're writing about, or are the characters themselves funny?

W: Sometimes the characters are funny. I mean, sometimes I like to do bright colors, and then they can be quite funny. Sometimes, you know—I haven't learned to use a computer, so I still type, and it's such a pain in the neck—sometimes I just retype scenes and start putting in things. I couldn't believe it—I'm writing a play right now about twenty years of people's lives, and this girl is telling this boy how unhappy she is, and for some reason I started writing Yasser Arafat jokes. For no reason. Because it's so boring retyping this stupid thing. But, you know sometimes it's funny to see. I think for myself, I'm slightly shy actually, and sometimes it's fun for me to write some character who's larger than life. Who would say things I would never say but I know they're funny. And I like to do that a lot. And I also think, to get further into humor and women, that a lot of comedy is a deflection. If you look at "Isn't It Romantic?," Janie Blumberg is *always* funny, so as not to say what she feels. And so, I think you use it—you use it to get a laugh, but you use it deliberately too. I mean the best is when you use it deliberately.

E: Do you think that your women characters are more prone to doing in that way—using their humor as a deflection?
W: Sometimes, yes, the women use it more as a defense, I think.

E: Do you think that—among your friends, people you know—do women use their humor in different ways than the men do?
W: Yes, I think they do. I think sometimes, men sometimes top each other. Women don't do that. Women know how to lay back and have a good time, you know, and the gossip is great. Great!. . . .

E: I think that—certainly in my relationships with my women friends—life is just funny between us, and we share those sorts of humorous moments. We're not always telling each other jokes.
W: No, and I don't even know how to tell a joke. But, you know, if you come home from a bad date, or something's happened, you know, and you've been fired—you know, you've just lost your job to some 21-year-old girl who's blond and can't do anything, but the boss. . . . You know that if you go home and tell your story to somebody, you will make it funny. And it will release the pain from you of whatever it is. Because you can't take that nonsense seriously. . . .

E: How about writing for a nonperformance medium? Like articles. Do you have a different emotional reaction to writing those than to writing something that's being performed?
W: I've been writing for a magazine called *New York Woman* recently. And it's fun. It's different though. You know what it is? I remember as a kid someone once told me that I had to learn to postpone gratification. And the thing about magazines is it gets published pretty quickly. I mean, a play you can write and two years from then maybe you'll work it out. And I think in a magazine, because it's a shorter form, you can get—like I just wrote an article about manicures. I'd never write a play, a two-hour play about manicures unless you could do it quite artistically I guess with dancing fingers and stuff. . . .

E: Does your humor translate the same way in each of these different media?

w: It depends. I mean, the magazine I wrote for sent me off to meet Philipe de Montebello at the Met. It was pretty funny. But in these magazine things I always use "I," first person, and there's a persona that I elect to use. You know, there's an "I" that's always talking about how I wish I wore leather miniskirts and I hate pantyhose and things like that. I don't do that so much in the plays. I mean, what's fun about plays is you can divide yourself into a lot of characters and hide yourself in different places.

E: Even though you're not on the stage, do you enjoy that audience feedback?
w: I do. I mean, when it works, it's great. When a production goes wrong, it is hell. It's really hell, it's so painful. That's the other thing. I mean, so you write an article and people don't like it. Or you write an article and they never call you again and they don't publish it. It's not the same pain, it's really not. From the word go, from the no actors are available to the director doesn't show up, to the show doesn't work and no one's laughing, to you pick up some terrible review—I mean, all of that is devastating. It's just terrible. It's enough to give you a sense of humor. I mean, it's really awful! I'm writing this play here and I can't even think about all that stuff. It's just too awful.

E: Well, it's such a process.
w: It's a real process. And you don't know what's going to happen. You just don't know.

E: It's true, it's not just your input that will make it in the end. There are so many other factors and people involved. . . . Do you think it's hard for women to get started? To get funding, to get. . . .
w: You know what's hard? It's hard to keep one's confidence. It's hard to keep yourself in the middle, not to be a nice girl and not to be a tough girl, you know, but somehow to be yourself. That's hard. And as soon as you start playacting in your writing or in your life, there's trouble, a little bit. Especially in your writing. Because what works is going to be whatever's honest to you. So I think in that way, yes, there's somewhat of a problem. But, I mean, I think the most important thing is that decent women write and get those plays out. I think that's very important.

From *Women's Studies*

The Receptive Reader

1. What does Wasserstein mean when she says much comedy "is a deflection"?

2. What difference does she see between male and female humor? (Have you observed similar differences?) Where else in the interview does Wasserstein see things from a female perspective?

3. What differences does she see between her writing in her magazine pieces and her work as a playwright? What do you learn from this interview about the playwright's relation with her audience?

David D. Cooper

At the end of the following reexamination, David D. Cooper quotes Robert Nemiroff as calling Hansberry's *Raisin in the Sun* one of the plays that at the deepest level are not about a specific situation but about "the human condition"—so that "in each generation we recognize ourselves in them anew."

Idealism and Fatalism in **A Raisin in the Sun**   *1993*

When duty whispers low, "Thou Must"
The youth replies, "I can!"
RALPH WALDO EMERSON

Few modern American plays better capture the essence of Emerson's claim for moral exuberance that galvanizes youthful idealism than Lorraine Hansberry's *A Raisin in the Sun*. Set against a backdrop of overt racism and pervasive housing discrimination in the 1950s, Hansberry's play manages to recover and sustain ethical idealism amid conditions, personal and societal, that would make fatalistic surrender understandable. It does so without sentimentality and in spite of the unresolved conflicts and uncertainties that are left over at the play's end, which remain Hansberry's legacy to the continuing struggle for racial justice and decency in America. It is a play about distress, futility, and tragedy, but also about hope and pride and what kind of conviction and commitment it takes to bring hope out of hopelessness, courage out of fear, and idealism out of fatalism. Robert Coles speaks of the black family—the Youngers—and their ordeal of trying to move out of a segregated Chicago borough as a "continual tension between hope and despair in people who have had such a rough time and whose prospects are by no means cheerful" (60). Nowhere in the play is that tension more gripping than in the penultimate scene between Asagai and Beneatha Younger, a scene that Robert Nemiroff, who produced and adapted many of Hansberry's works, describes as capturing "the larger statement of the play—and the ongoing struggle it portends" (Hansberry x).

After Beneatha's brother Walter Lee squanders, on an ill-advised investment, the life insurance money set aside for Beneatha's medical education, she gives in to despair, even cynicism, watching her dream of becoming a doctor seemingly go up in smoke. Beneatha had always pinned her personal aspirations and her hopes for a more equitable and compassionate society on the prospect of becoming a doctor, reflecting Hansberry's belief that social idealism—the commitment to a better society—is intimately tied to individual moral obligation: that social justice is the collective expression of idealism deeply felt by individuals. "I always thought," Beneatha says to Asagai, that being a doctor "was the one concrete thing in the world that a human being could do. Fix up the sick, you know—and make them whole again."

Once the fragile bond of commitment between her aspirations and society's common welfare is broken, however, Beneatha quickly retrenches into cynicism. "I wanted to cure," Beneatha explains to Asagai. "It used to be so important to me. . . . I used to care. I mean about people and how their bodies hurt. . . ." When Asagai asks her to explain why she stopped caring, Beneatha comes of age, so to speak, morally. "Because [doctoring] doesn't seem deep enough, close enough to what ails mankind! It was a child's way of seeing things—or an idealist's."

At just this point, the play pivots delicately on the moral fulcrum that Coles positions between hope and despair or, put in a socioethical idiom, between idealism and fatalism. Asagai, a patriot for an independent Africa, steps forward to defend hope and idealism. "Children," he reminds Beneatha, "see things very well sometimes—and idealists even better." Beneatha counters, bitterly fatalistic: "You with all your talk and dreams about [a free] Africa! You still think you can patch up the world. Cure the Great Sore of Colonialism—with the Penicillin of Independence—! . . . What about all the crooks and thieves and just plain idiots who will come into power and steal and plunder the same as before—only now they will be black . . . —WHAT ABOUT THEM?!"

Hansberry quickly synthesizes the moral dilemma into two very precise images:

> BENEATHA: Don't you see there isn't any real progress, Asagai, there is only one large circle that we march in, around and around, each of us with our own little picture in front of us—our own little mirage that we think is the future.
> ASAGAI: It isn't a circle—it is simply a long line—as in geometry, you know, one that reaches into infinity. And because we cannot see the end—we also cannot see how it changes. And it is very odd but those who see the changes—who dream, who will not give up—are called idealists . . . and those who see only the circle—we call *them* the "realists." (134)

How one imagines the shape of the future—whether as another version of the present or as a limitless plain of possibilities for personal and societal change—dictates one's solution to the central problem of moral life and whether one draws upon the resources of idealism or "realism"—as Asagai defines it here—insofar as moral action and ethical commitment are concerned. Hansberry makes her choice. Beneatha decides to become a doctor—in Africa. The Younger family reaches down for the courage to integrate a white neighborhood. Without addressing the important complexities and ambivalence of those decisions, they represent the courage and moral resourcefulness that were both instrumental in, and essential to, the successes of the following decade's Civil Rights struggles. Among white liberals, for example, the Youngers' decision to move becomes the essence of what liberalism stood for during that time, namely, that racial integration was simultaneously the empowerment of black Americans and the salvation of white America. In his commentary on *A Raisin in the Sun,* Robert Nemiroff lifts the play to this higher level of sociomoral analysis.

> For at the deepest level it is not a specific situation but the human condition, human aspiration and human relationship—the persistence of

dreams, of the bonds and conflicts between men and women, parents and children, old ways and new, and the endless struggle against human oppression, whatever the forms it may take, and for individual fulfillment, recognition, and liberation—that are at the heart of such plays. It is not surprising therefore that in each generation we recognize ourselves in them anew. (Hansberry xvii–xviii)

From *The Explicator*

The Receptive Reader
Why does Cooper select Beneatha and Asagai as key characters in the play? How does he trace Beneatha's journey between idealism and cynicism? What is the symbolism of the circle and the line in the key passage that Cooper quotes?

The Personal Response
Who for you is the key or pivotal character in *Raisin in the Sun?*

WRITING ABOUT LITERATURE

33   Defining a Critical Term (Focus on Definition)

The Writing Workshop   We would find it hard to talk about drama without terms like *tragedy, protagonist, tragicomedy, subplot,* or *theater of the absurd.* Such critical terms focus our attention and guide our expectations. They help us put into words important similarities and differences. They enable us to formulate our standards, to explain our preferences and aversions.

When you define an important critical term, you stake out the territory it covers. You spell out what it covers and what it fences out. In writing a definition paper, try to find a term that *needs* definition. For instance, you might focus on a term with a rich and confusing history and try to clear up basic ambiguities. Or you might zero in on a trendy term whose meaning is still fuzzy in many people's minds. Consider the following when trying to find a topic that fills a need or presents a challenge:

The History of a Term   Important terms may change their meanings as they serve the agendas of different schools of critical thought. Terms that once had negative connotations may become terms of praise and vice versa. For instance, followers of the classical tradition have tended to frown on mixed genres. They have objected to the mingling of the tragic and the comic, being suspicious of "mongrel tragicomedy" (Sir Philip Sidney). But tragicomedy has appealed to the modern temper, which welcomes irony and paradox. What is it about this genre that has appealed to modern audiences?

Drawing the Line   It may prove hard to draw a clear line between often paired terms. Most definitions of comedy sooner or later contrast it with tragedy. They stress the contrast between ordinary or low-life characters and the exalted personages of the tragic muse. Or they show the difference between the marvelous arrival of good fortune in comedy and the tragic defeat of the tragic hero. What are the key differences? Where do the two genres shade over into each other?

Initiating the Reader   You may want to help the reader become more knowledgeable about modern trends. Your paper might set out to define Bertolt Brecht's epic theater; the theater of the absurd as practiced by Ionesco, Beckett, or Albee; existential drama; feminist drama as defined by leading feminist critics or written by leading feminist playwrights; the art of the mime; dramatic happenings.

In working on a definition paper, consider the following guidelines:

✘ *Be aware of traditional or conventional definitions.*   Reckon with the received wisdom—what everybody knows or "what oft was thought" (Alexander Pope). Although dictionary definitions can alert you to important dimensions, you will generally do well not to quote them in your actual paper. Dictionary or encyclopedia entries tend to sound too dry and neutral to get your readers involved in the dialectic of living literature. Consider quoting a critic, a playwright, or a reviewer instead.

✘ *Pull together and spell out your own definition.*   Writing a definition paper, like writing other worthwhile papers, should be a voyage of discovery. However, try to sum up somewhere in your paper what continent you have found. Often, you will want to present your overall definition as a preview or **thesis** at the end of a short introduction. For instance, let your readers know that your definition of tragedy comes in three parts. You might want to make it clear that three essential requirements, or criteria, qualify a play as a true tragedy:

CRITERION 1   A true tragedy arouses the tragic emotions of pity and fear.
CRITERION 2   The tragic hero or heroine exhibits a tragic flaw.
CRITERION 3   The play moves toward insight or self-realization.

Using an alternate strategy, you might start with a trial definition and then proceed to modify it in the light of important evidence. You will be taking your reader along *in search of* a more adequate definition. (In such an **inductive** paper—which works *toward* a general conclusion—transitions and overall direction need to be especially clear to keep the reader moving along to the destination.)

✘ *Use ample supporting examples.*   Bridge the gap between theory and practice. Show that your general criteria actually apply to the characters on the stage, to the things they say and do. Definitions easily remain too neat and unrealistic when they remain abstract.

✗ *Use comparison and contrast with related terms.* A term often becomes clearer as you explain what it does *not* mean. Clarify your key term by marking it off from related terms—whether near synonyms or opposites. For instance, a definition of tragedy can become more meaningful when tragedy is clearly distinguished from melodrama or from pathos—two forms that in the eyes of the critics tend to play the role of its poor relations.

Study the following sample student paper on a classic of the modern American stage. How clear and workable is its definition of the key term?

Model Student Paper

Death of a Salesman—a Modern Tragedy?

Ever since Willy Loman trudged into his living room and set down his heavy sample satchel in the first stage production of *Death of a Salesman,* critics have been arguing whether or not Arthur Miller's creation is a tragedy. Some maintain the play is a tragedy of the ordinary person, with Willy Loman as the tragic hero. The author himself said in his "Tragedy and the Common Man" that the "common man is as apt a subject for tragedy in its highest sense as kings were." Others hold that the play does not fit the requirements of true tragedy and that Willy Loman is incapable of being a tragic hero—or indeed any other type of hero at all. Ultimately, the truth may be that Willy Loman fails to become a tragic hero, not because he is modern or because he is common, but because of basic and obvious limitations of his character.

Since Aristotle, critics have tended to agree on the first criterion of true tragedy: It should arouse the tragic emotions of pity and fear. Aristotle used the term *catharsis*—a cleansing or purgation—to describe the emotional experience of the audience. The pity the audience feels for the tragic hero is not patronizing or condescending. Instead it implies a sense of equality, a sharing of grief. The word *fear* is not restricted to fright or abject terror but implies anxious concern, awe, reverence, and apprehension.

Critics have with almost equal unanimity emphasized the second criterion: The tragic hero or heroine should have some tragic flaw that shapes the character's action and helps bring about the eventual downfall. We need to assume that the hero has free will; and we look in his or her character for a flaw that begins the chain of events leading to ruin. Some fatal blindness or weakness in an otherwise admirable person helps explain the tragic course of events.

A third criterion is less universally stressed, but it seems to do much to help the hero or heroine achieve true tragic stature. In the agony, humiliation, and suffering of defeat, the hero reaches a point of increased self-awareness. The hero or heroine is able to look back and see the steps leading to disaster. Or at least the hero or heroine shows an understanding of what is happening. Shakespeare's Macbeth, bitter and pessimistic at the end, begins to see with terrifying clarity his total isolation: "honor, love, obedience, troops of friends / I must not look to have"

(5.3. 25–26). Othello, in his last words, asks the audience to remember him as one "who loved not wisely, but too well" (5.2. 344).

How do these criteria apply to Willy Loman? Miller certainly achieves the effects of pity and fear on his audience. Audiences today as much as ever can sympathize with Willy's terrifying underlying insecurity in a dog-eat-dog system. In Willy's world, as in ours, there is for many people no real safety net. Linda appeals to our sympathy when she says, "You cannot eat the fruit and throw the peel away." Her plea for "attention" is the author's plea for pity for a struggling character whom we saw in the process of going under.

Certainly, Willy possesses a tragic flaw, if not several. But this flaw is perhaps not so much a personal characteristic, a failing in an otherwise great and admirable person. It is more a burden put on him by society. Willy believed in the American dream because he was brought up to do so. He seems too gullible, too credulous. He is too much of a victim to be a great but flawed individual. Much of the play seems to illustrate pathos—the helpless suffering of someone victimized—rather than tragedy.

Willy, finally, never seems to progress toward the self-realization that should be part of true tragedy. If the play were tragic, Willy himself would realize in the last act that, as Biff says, "he had the wrong dreams. All, all, wrong." But this conception remained beyond Willy. He died dreaming another daydream, thinking of himself worth more dead than he was alive, fantasizing about the insurance money that none of his family are likely to see. He dies, as he lived, in a world of illusion, dreaming of Biff as finally a success—"Can you imagine that magnificence with twenty-thousand dollars in his pocket?"

Although Miller's play powerfully stirs the tragic emotions of pity and fear, Willy Loman lacks the stature of a tragic hero. The true tragic effect cannot be achieved without the tragic hero's bitter recognition of his true self.

Questions

How does this student writer's three-point definition of tragedy structure the paper as a whole? Do the three parts of the definition become clear and convincing? Where and why would you take issue with the student writer?

34 Other Voices/Other Visions

The Magic of the Stage

Tennessee Williams   *(1911–1983)*

*I have found it easier to identify with the charac-
ters who verge upon hysteria, who were frightened
of life, who were desperate to reach out to another
person.*

TENNESSEE WILLIAMS

Much of Tennessee Williams's work shows his fascination with characters facing lonely struggles in emotionally starved environments. Much
of his work has biographical roots, harking back to his own family's
atmosphere of repression and anger, evoked through characterizations
of psychologically vulnerable women and domineering men. Williams
began writing in high school; during his college years, he wrote one-act
plays. In 1945, *The Glass Menagerie* won the Drama Critics' Circle
Award. It was also a spectacular commercial success, the beginning of a
series of theatrical triumphs including *A Streetcar Named Desire* (1947),
The Rose Tattoo (1950), *Cat on a Hot Tin Roof* (1955), *Suddenly Last
Summer* (1958), and *The Night of the Iguana* (1961). Many of his plays
were made into movies, including the classic *Streetcar* with Vivien Leigh
as Blanche and Marlon Brando as Kowalski. *Cat on a Hot Tin Roof*
starred Elizabeth Taylor and Paul Newman.

In his memoirs, Williams called *The Glass Menagerie,* with its burden
of guilt and cruelty, "the big one—close to the marrow of my being."
This play, in which Laura retreats to the private world of her glass animals and Tom leaves while carrying with him an obsession with the
past, has its roots in Williams's actual relationship with his sister, Rose,
whom he felt he failed in her greatest need. He writes: It's not very
pleasant to look back on [1937] and to know that Rose knew she was
going mad and to know, also, that I was not too kind to my sister." In a
moment of fury, he hissed at her, "I hate the sight of your ugly old face!"
He said about this experience, "This is the cruelest thing I have done
in my life, I suspect, and one for which I can never properly atone."
After he left home, his parents permitted the performance of a frontal

lobotomy on Rose. These traumatic events left the playwright with a deep sense that love leads inevitably to loss and betrayal.

Tennessee Williams's theater typically takes his audiences to a southern setting, made intensely real by his command of southern speech and manners. His poetic and symbolic drama goes beyond the realistic surface of life to probe the complex psychological intermeshings of "love, pity, regret, guilt, self-lacerating ruthlessness, posing, and bravado" (Brian Parker).

The Glass Menagerie   *1945*

CHARACTERS

AMANDA WINGFIELD, the mother. A little woman of great but confused vitality clinging frantically to another time and place. Her characterization must be carefully created, not copied from type. She is not paranoiac, but her life is paranoia. There is much to admire in AMANDA, and as much to love and pity as there is to laugh at. Certainly she has endurance and a kind of heroism, and though her foolishness makes her unwittingly cruel at times, there is tenderness in her slight person.

LAURA WINGFIELD, her daughter. AMANDA, having failed to establish contact with reality, continues to live vitally in her illusions, but LAURA's situation is even graver. A childhood illness has left her crippled, one leg slightly shorter than the other, and held in a brace. This defect need not be more than suggested on the stage. Stemming from this, LAURA's separation increases till she is like a piece of her own glass collection, too exquisitely fragile to move from the shelf.

TOM WINGFIELD, her son, and the narrator of the play. A poet with a job in a warehouse. His nature is not remorseless, but to escape from a trap he has to act without pity.

JIM O'CONNOR, the gentleman caller. A nice, ordinary, young man.

SCENE: *An alley in St. Louis.*

PART I: *Preparation for a gentleman caller.*

PART II: *The gentleman calls.*

TIME: *Now and the past.*

AUTHOR'S PRODUCTION NOTES

Being a "memory play," *The Glass Menagerie* can be presented with unusual freedom of convention. Because of its considerably delicate or tenuous material, atmospheric touches and subtleties of direction play a particularly important part. Expressionism and all other unconventional techniques in drama have only one valid aim, and that is a closer approach to truth. When a play employs unconventional techniques, it is not, or certainly shouldn't be, trying to escape its responsibility of dealing with reality, or interpreting experience, but is actually or should be attempting to find a closer approach, a more penetrating and vivid expression of things as they are. The straight realistic play with its genuine frigidaire and authentic ice-cubes, its characters that speak exactly as its audience speaks, corresponds to the academic landscape and has the same virtue of a photographic likeness. Everyone should know nowadays the unimportance of the photographic in art: that truth, life, or reality is an organic thing which the poetic imagination can represent or suggest, in essence, only through transformation, through changing into other forms than those which were merely present in appearance.

These remarks are not meant as a preface only to this particular play. They have to do with a conception of a new, plastic theatre which must take the place of the exhausted theatre of realistic conventions if the theatre is to resume vitality as a part of our culture.

The Screen Device: There is *only one important difference between the original and acting version of the play* and that is the *omission* in the latter of the device which I tentatively included in my *original* script. This device was the use of a screen on which were projected magic-lantern slides bearing images or titles. I do not regret the omission of this device from the present Broadway production. The extraordinary power of Miss Taylor's performance made it suitable to have the utmost simplicity in the physical production. But I think it may be interesting to some readers to see how this device was conceived. So I am putting it into the published manuscript. These images and legends, projected from behind, were cast on a section of wall between the front-room and dining-room areas, which should be indistinguishable from the rest when not in use.

The purpose of this will probably be apparent. It is to give accent to certain values in each scene. Each scene contains a particular point (or several) which is structurally the most important. In an episodic play, such as this, the basic structure or narrative line may be obscured from the audience; the effect may seem fragmentary rather than architectural. This may not be the fault of the play so much as a lack of attention in the audience. The legend or image upon the screen will strengthen the effect of what is merely allusion in the writing and allow the primary point to be made more simply and lightly than if the entire responsibility were on the spoken lines. Aside from this structural value, I think the screen will have a definite emotional appeal, less definable but just as important. An imaginative producer or director may invent many other uses for this device than those indicated in the present script. In fact the possibilities of the device seem much larger to me than the instance of this play can possibly utilize.

The Music: Another extra-literary accent in this play is provided by the use of music. A single recurring tune, "The Glass Menagerie," is used to give emotional emphasis to suitable passages. This tune is like circus music, not when you are on the grounds or in the immediate vicinity of the parade, but when you are at some distance and very likely thinking of something else. It seems under those circumstances to continue almost interminably and it weaves in and out of your preoccupied consciousness; then it is the lightest, most delicate music in the world and perhaps the saddest. It expresses the surface vivacity of life with the underlying strain of immutable and inexpressible sorrow. When you look at a piece of delicately spun glass you think of two things: how beautiful it is and how easily it can be broken. Both of those ideas should be woven into the recurring tune, which dips in and out of the play as if it were carried on a wind that changes. It serves as a thread of connection and allusion between the narrator with his separate point in time and space and the subject of his story. Between each episode it returns as reference to the emotion, nostalgia, which is the first condition of the play. It is primarily LAURA's music and therefore comes out most clearly when the play focuses upon her and the lovely fragility of glass which is her image.

The Lighting: The lighting in the play is not realistic. In keeping with the atmosphere of memory, the stage is dim. Shafts of light are focused on selected areas or actors, sometimes in contradistinction to what is the apparent center. For instance, in the quarrel scene between TOM and AMANDA, in which LAURA has no active part, the clearest pool of light is on her figure. This is also true of the supper scene, when her silent figure on the sofa should remain the visual center. The light upon LAURA should be distinct from the others, having a peculiar pristine clarity such as light used in early religious portraits of female saints or madonnas. A certain correspondence to light in religious paintings, such as El Greco's, where the figures are radiant in atmosphere that is relatively dusky, could be effectively used throughout the play. (It will also permit a more effective use of the screen.) A free, imaginative use of light can be of enormous value in giving a mobile, plastic quality to plays of a more or less static nature.

T. W.

Scene 1

The Wingfield apartment is in the rear of the building, one of those vast hive-like conglomerations of cellular living-units that flower as warty growths in overcrowded urban centers of lower middle-class population and are symptomatic of the impulse of this largest and fundamentally enslaved section of American society to avoid fluidity and differentiation and to exist and function as one interfused mass of automatism.

The apartment faces an alley and is entered by a fire-escape, a structure whose name is a touch of accidental poetic truth, for all of these huge buildings are always burning with the slow and implacable fires of human desperation. The fire-escape is included in the set—that is, the landing of it and steps descending from it.

The scene is memory and is therefore nonrealistic. Memory takes a lot of poetic license. It omits some details; others are exaggerated, according to the emotional value of the articles it touches, for memory is seated and predominantly in the heart. The interior is therefore rather dim and poetic.

At the rise of the curtain, the audience is faced with the dark, grim rear wall of the Wingfield tenement. This building, which runs parallel to the footlights, is flanked on both sides by dark, narrow alleys which run into murky canyons of tangled clotheslines, garbage cans and the sinister lattice work of neighboring fire-escapes. It is up and down these side alleys that exterior entrances and exits are made, during the play. At the end of TOM's opening commentary, the dark tenement wall slowly reveals (by means of a transparency) the interior of the ground floor Wingfield apartment.

Downstage is the living room, which also serves as a sleeping room for LAURA, *the sofa unfolding to make her bed. Upstage, center, and divided by a wide arch or second proscenium with transparent faded portieres (or second curtain), is the dining room. In an old-fashioned what-not in the living room are seen scores of transparent glass animals. A blown-up photograph of the father hangs on the wall of the living room, facing the audience, to the left of the archway. It is the face of a very handsome young man in a dough-boy's First World War cap. He is gallantly smiling, ineluctably smiling, as if to say, "I will be smiling forever."*

The audience hears and sees the opening scene in the dining room through both the transparent fourth wall of the building and the transparent gauze portieres of the dining-room arch. It is during this revealing scene that the fourth wall slowly ascends, out of sight. This transparent exterior wall is not brought down again until the very end of the play, during TOM'S *final speech.*

The narrator is an undisguised convention of the play. He takes whatever license with dramatic convention as is convenient to his purposes.

TOM *enters dressed as a merchant sailor from alley, stage left, and strolls across the front of the stage to the fire-escape. There he stops and lights a cigarette. He addresses the audience.*

TOM: Yes, I have tricks in my pocket, I have things up my sleeve. But I am the opposite of a stage magician. He gives you illusion that has the appearance of truth. I give you truth in the pleasant disguise of illusion. To begin with, I turn back time. I reverse it to that quaint period, the thirties, when the huge middle class of America was matriculating in a school for the blind. Their eyes had failed them, or they had failed their eyes, and so they were having their fingers pressed forcibly down on the fiery Braille alphabet of a dissolving economy. In Spain there was revolution. Here there was only shouting and confusion. In Spain there was Guernica. Here there were disturbances of labor, sometimes pretty violent, in otherwise peaceful cities such as Chicago, Cleveland, Saint Louis . . . This is the social background of the play.

(Music.)

The play is memory. Being a memory play, it is dimly lighted, it is sentimental, it is not realistic. In memory everything seems to happen to music. That explains the fiddle in the wings. I am the narrator of the play, and also a character in it. The other characters are my mother, Amanda, my sister, Laura, and a gentleman caller who appears in the final scenes. He is the most realistic character in the play, being an emissary from a world of reality that we were somehow set apart from. But since I have a poet's weakness for symbols, I am using this character also as a symbol; he is the long delayed but always expected something that we live for. There is a fifth character in the play who doesn't appear except in this larger-than-life-size photograph over the mantel. This is our father who left us a long time ago. He was a telephone man who fell in love with long distances; he gave up his job with the telephone company and skipped the light fantastic out of town . . . The last we heard of him was a picture post-card from Mazatlan, on the Pacific coast of Mexico, containing a message of two words—"Hello—Good-bye!" and no address. I think the rest of the play will explain itself. . . .

> AMANDA's *voice becomes audible through the portieres.*
>   (*Legend on screen: "Où sont les neiges."*)
>   *He divides the portieres and enters the upstage area.*
>   AMANDA *and* LAURA *are seated at a drop-leaf table. Eating is indicated by gestures without food or utensils.* AMANDA *faces the audience.* TOM *and* LAURA *are seated in profile.*
>   *The interior has lit up softly and through the scrim we see* AMANDA *and* LAURA *seated at the table in the upstage area.*

AMANDA (*calling*): Tom?

TOM: Yes, Mother.

AMANDA: We can't say grace until you come to the table!

TOM: Coming, Mother. (*He bows slightly and withdraws, reappearing a few moments later in his place at the table.*)

AMANDA (*to her son*): Honey, don't *push* with your *fingers.* If you have to push with something, the thing to push with is a crust of bread. And chew—chew! Animals have sections in their stomachs which enable them to digest food without mastication, but human beings are supposed to chew their food before they swallow it down. Eat food leisurely, son, and really enjoy it. A well-cooked meal has lots of delicate flavors that have to be held in the mouth for appreciation. So chew your food and give your salivary glands a chance to function!

> TOM *deliberately lays his imaginary fork down and pushes his chair back from the table.*

TOM: I haven't enjoyed one bite of this dinner because of your constant directions on how to eat it. It's you that make me rush through meals with your hawk-like attention to every bite I take. Sickening—spoils my appetite—all this discussion of—animals' secretion—salivary glands—mastication!

AMANDA (*lightly*): Temperament like a Metropolitan star! (*He rises and crosses downstage.*) You're not excused from the table.

TOM: I'm getting a cigarette.

AMANDA: You smoke too much.

> LAURA *rises.*

LAURA: I'll bring in the blanc mange.

> *He remains standing with his cigarette by the portieres during the following.*

AMANDA (*rising*): No, sister, no, sister—you be the lady this time and I'll be the darky.

LAURA: I'm already up.

AMANDA: Resume your seat, little sister—I want you to stay fresh and pretty—for gentlemen callers!

LAURA: I'm not expecting any gentlemen callers.

AMANDA (*Crossing out to kitchenette. Airily.*): Sometimes they come when they are least expected! Why, I remember one Sunday afternoon in Blue Mountain—(*enters kitchenette*)

TOM: I know what's coming!

LAURA: Yes. But let her tell it.

TOM: Again?

LAURA: She loves to tell it.

AMANDA *returns with bowl of dessert.*

AMANDA: One Sunday afternoon in Blue Mountain—your mother received—*seventeen!*—gentlemen callers! Why, sometimes there weren't chairs enough to accommodate them all. We had to send the nigger over to bring in folding chairs from the parish house.

TOM (*remaining at portieres*): How did you entertain those gentlemen callers?

AMANDA: I understood the art of conversation!

TOM: I bet you could talk.

AMANDA: Girls in those days *knew* how to talk, I can tell you.

TOM: Yes?

(*Image:* AMANDA *as a girl on a porch, greeting callers.*)

AMANDA: They knew how to entertain their gentlemen callers. It wasn't enough for a girl to be possessed of a pretty face and a graceful figure—although I wasn't slighted in either respect. She also needed to have a nimble wit and a tongue to meet all occasions.

TOM: What did you talk about?

AMANDA: Things of importance going on in the world! Never anything coarse or common or vulgar. (*She addresses* TOM *as though he were seated in the vacant chair at the table though he remains by portieres. He plays this scene as though he held the book.*) My callers were gentlemen—all! Among my callers were some of the most prominent young planters of the Mississippi Delta—planters and sons of planters!

TOM *motions for music and a spot of light on* AMANDA.
Her eyes lift, her face glows, her voice becomes rich and elegiac.
(*Screen legend: "Où sont les neiges."*)

There was young Champ Laughlin who later became vice-president of the Delta Planters Bank. Hadley Stevenson who was drowned in Moon Lake and left his widow one hundred and fifty thousand in Government bonds. There were the Cutrere brothers, Wesley and Bates. Bates was one of my bright particular beaux! He got in a quarrel with that wild Wainwright boy. They shot it out on the floor of Moon Lake Casino. Bates was shot through the stomach. Died in the ambulance on his way to Memphis. His widow was also well-provided for, came into eight or ten thousand acres, that's all. She married him on the rebound—never loved her—carried my picture on him the night he died! And there was that boy that every girl in the Delta had set her cap for! That beautiful, brilliant young Fitzhugh boy from Greene County!

TOM: What did he leave his widow?

AMANDA: He never married! Gracious, you talk as though all of my old admirers had turned up their toes to the daisies!

TOM: Isn't this the first you've mentioned that still survives?

AMANDA: That Fitzhugh boy went North and made a fortune—came to be known as the Wolf of Wall Street! He had the Midas touch, whatever he touched turned to gold!

And I could have been Mrs. Duncan J. Fitzhugh, mind you! But—I picked your *father!*

LAURA (*rising*): Mother, let me clear the table.

AMANDA: No, dear, you go in front and study your typewriter chart. Or practice your shorthand a little. Stay fresh and pretty!—It's almost time for our gentlemen callers to start arriving. (*She flounces girlishly toward the kitchenette.*) How many do you suppose we're going to entertain this afternoon?

TOM *throws down the paper and jumps up with a groan.*

LAURA (*alone in the dining room*): I don't believe we're going to receive any, Mother.

AMANDA (*reappearing, airily*): What? No one—not one? You must be joking! (LAURA *nervously echoes her laugh. She slips in a fugitive manner through the half-open portieres and draws them gently behind her. A shaft of very clear light is thrown on her face against the faded tapestry of the curtains.*) (*Music: "The Glass Menagerie" under faintly.*) (*lightly*) Not one gentleman caller? It can't be true! There must be a flood, there must have been a tornado!

LAURA: It isn't a flood, it's not a tornado, Mother. I'm just not popular like you were in Blue Mountain. . . . (TOM *utters another groan.* LAURA *glances at him with a faint, apologetic smile. Her voice catching a little.*) Mother's afraid I'm going to be an old maid.

(*The scene dims out with "Glass Menagerie" music.*)

Scene 2

"Laura, Haven't You Ever Liked Some Boy?"

On the dark stage the screen is lighted with the image of blue roses.
Gradually LAURA'S *figure becomes apparent and the screen goes out. The music subsides.*
LAURA *is seated in the delicate ivory chair at the small claw-foot table. She wears a dress of soft violet material for a kimono—her hair tied back from her forehead with a ribbon.*
She is washing and polishing her collection of glass.
AMANDA *appears on the fire-escape steps. At the sound of her ascent,* LAURA *catches her breath, thrusts the bowl of ornaments away and seats herself stiffly before the diagram of the typewriter keyboard as though it held her spellbound.*

Something has happened to AMANDA. *It is written in her face as she climbs to the landing: a look that is grim and hopeless and a little absurd.*

She has on one of those cheap or imitation velvety-looking cloth coats with imitation fur collar. Her hat is five or six years old, one of those dreadful cloche hats that were worn in the late twenties and she is clasping an enormous black patent-leather pocketbook with nickel clasps and initials. This is her full-dress outfit, the one she usually wears to the D.A.R.

Before entering she looks through the door.

She purses her lips, opens her eyes very wide, rolls them upward and shakes her head.

Then she slowly lets herself in the door. Seeing her mother's expression LAURA *touches her lips with a nervous gesture.*

LAURA: Hello, Mother, I was—(*She makes a nervous gesture toward the chart on the wall.* AMANDA *leans against the shut door and stares at* LAURA *with a martyred look.*)

AMANDA: Deception? Deception? (*She slowly removes her hat and gloves, continuing the sweet suffering stare. She lets the hat and gloves fall on the floor—a bit of acting.*)

LAURA (*shakily*): How was the D.A.R. meeting? (AMANDA *slowly opens her purse and removes a dainty white handkerchief which she shakes out delicately and delicately touches to her lips and nostrils.*) Didn't you go to the D.A.R. meeting, Mother?

AMANDA (*faintly, almost inaudibly*): —No.—No. (*then more forcibly*) I did not have the strength—to go to the D.A.R. In fact, I did not have the courage! I wanted to find a hole in the ground and hide myself in it forever! (*She crosses slowly to the wall and removes the diagram of the typewriter keyboard. She holds it in front of her for a second, staring at it sweetly and sorrowfully—then bites her lips and tears it in two pieces.*)

LAURA (*faintly*): Why did you do that, Mother? (AMANDA *repeats the same procedure with the chart of the Gregg Alphabet.*) Why are you—

AMANDA: Why? Why? How old are you, Laura?

LAURA: Mother, you know my age.

AMANDA: I thought that you were an adult; it seems that I was mistaken. (*She crosses slowly to the sofa and sinks down and stares at* LAURA.)

LAURA: Please don't stare at me, Mother.

AMANDA *closes her eyes and lowers her head. Count ten.*

AMANDA: What are we going to do, what is going to become of us, what is the future?

Count ten.

LAURA: Has something happened, Mother? (AMANDA *draws a long breath and takes out the handkerchief again. Dabbing process.*) Mother, has—something happened?

AMANDA: I'll be all right in a minute, I'm just bewildered—(*count five*)—by life. . . .

LAURA: Mother, I wish that you would tell me what's happened!

AMANDA: As you know, I was supposed to be inducted into my office at the D.A.R. this afternoon. (*Image: A swarm of typewriters.*) But I stopped off at Rubicam's business college to speak to your teachers about your having a cold and ask them what progress they thought you were making down there.

LAURA: Oh. . . .

AMANDA: I went to the typing instructor and introduced myself as your mother. She didn't know who you were. Wingfield, she said. We don't have any such student enrolled at the school! I assured her she did, that you had been going to classes since early in January. "I wonder," she said, "if you could be talking about that terribly shy little girl who dropped out of school after only a few days' attendance?" "No," I said, "Laura, my daughter, has been going to school every day for the past six weeks!" "Excuse me," she said. She took the attendance book out and there was your name, unmistakably printed, and all the dates you were absent until they decided that you had dropped out of school. I still said, "No, there must have been some mistake! There must have been some mix-up in the records!" And she said, "No—I remember her perfectly now. Her hands shook so that she couldn't hit the right keys! The first time we gave a speed-test, she broke down completely—was sick at the stomach and almost had to be carried into the wash-room! After that morning she never showed up any more. We phoned the house but never got any answer—while I was working at Famous and Barr, I suppose, demonstrating those—Oh!" I felt so weak I could barely keep on my feet! I had to sit down while they got me a glass of water! Fifty dollars' tuition, all of our plans—my hopes and ambitions for you—just gone up the spout, just gone up the spout like that. (LAURA *draws a long breath and gets awkwardly to her feet. She crosses to the victrola and winds it up.*) What are you doing?

LAURA: Oh! (*She releases the handle and returns to her seat.*)

AMANDA: Laura, where have you been going when you've gone out pretending that you were going to business college?

LAURA: I've just been going out walking.

AMANDA: That's not true.

LAURA: It is. I just went walking.

AMANDA: Walking? Walking? In winter? Deliberately courting pneumonia in that light coat? Where did you walk to, Laura?

LAURA: All sorts of places—mostly in the park.

AMANDA: Even after you'd started catching that cold?

LAURA: It was the lesser of two evils, Mother. (*Image: Winter scene in the park.*) I couldn't go back up. I—threw up—on the floor!

AMANDA: From half past seven till after five every day you mean to tell me you walked around in the park, because you wanted to make me think that you were still going to Rubicam's Business College?

LAURA: It wasn't as bad as it sounds. I went inside places to get warmed up.

AMANDA: Inside where?

LAURA: I went in the art museum and the bird-houses at the Zoo. I visited the penguins every day! Sometimes I did without lunch and went to the movies. Lately I've been spending most of my afternoons in the Jewel-box, that big glass house where they raise the tropical flowers.

AMANDA: You did all this to deceive me, just for deception? (LAURA *looks down.*) Why?

LAURA: Mother, when you're disappointed, you get that awful suffering look on your face, like the picture of Jesus' mother in the museum!

AMANDA: Hush!

LAURA: I couldn't face it.

Pause. A whisper of strings.
(*Legend: "The Crust of Humility."*)

AMANDA (*hopelessly fingering the huge pocketbook*): So what are we going to do the rest of our lives? Stay home and watch the parades go by? Amuse ourselves with the glass menagerie, darling? Eternally play those worn-out phonograph records your father left as a painful reminder of him? We won't have a business career—we've given that up because it gave us nervous indigestion! (*laughs wearily*) What is there left but dependency all our lives? I know so well what becomes of unmarried women who aren't prepared to occupy a position. I've seen such pitiful cases in the South—barely tolerated spinsters living upon the grudging patronage of sister's husband or brother's wife!—stuck away in some little mouse-trap of a room—encouraged by one in-law to visit another—little birdlike women without any nest—eating the crust of humility all their life! Is that the future that we've mapped out for ourselves? I swear it's the only alternative I can think of! It isn't a very pleasant alternative, is it? Of course—some girls *do marry.* (LAURA *twists her hands nervously.*) Haven't you ever liked some boy?

LAURA: Yes. I liked one once. (*rises*) I came across his picture a while ago.

AMANDA (*with some interest*): He gave you his picture?

LAURA: No, it's in the year-book.

AMANDA (*disappointed*): Oh—a high-school boy.

(*Screen image:* JIM *as high-school hero bearing a silver cup.*)

LAURA: Yes. His name was Jim. (LAURA *lifts the heavy annual from the claw-foot table.*) Here he is in *The Pirates of Penzance.*

AMANDA (*absently*): The what?

LAURA: The operetta the senior class put on. He had a wonderful voice and we sat across the aisle from each other Mondays, Wednesdays and Fridays in the Aud. Here he is with the silver cup for debating! See his grin?

AMANDA (*absently*): He must have had a jolly disposition.

LAURA: He used to call me—Blue Roses.

(*Image: Blue roses.*)

AMANDA: Why did he call you such a name as that?

LAURA: When I had that attack of pleurosis—he asked me what was the matter when I came back. I said pleurosis—he thought that I said Blue Roses! So that's what he always called me after that. Whenever he saw me, he'd holler, "Hello, Blue Roses!" I didn't care for the girl that he went out with. Emily Meisenbach. Emily was the best-dressed girl at Soldan.

She never struck me, though, as being sincere . . . It says in the Personal Section—they're engaged. That's—six years ago! They must be married by now.

AMANDA: Girls that aren't cut out for business careers usually wind up married to some nice man. (*gets up with a spark of revival*) Sister, that's what you'll do!

LAURA *utters a startled, doubtful laugh. She reaches quickly for a piece of glass.*

LAURA: But, Mother—
AMANDA: Yes? (*crossing to photograph*)
LAURA (*in a tone of frightened apology*): I'm—crippled!

(*Image: Screen.*)

AMANDA: Nonsense! Laura, I've told you never, never to use that word. Why, you're not crippled, you just have a little defect—hardly noticeable, even! When people have some slight disadvantage like that, they cultivate other things to make up for it—develop charm—and vivacity—and—*charm!* That's all you have to do! (*She turns again to the photograph.*) One thing your father had *plenty of*—was *charm!*

TOM *motions to the fiddle in the winds.*

(*The scene fades out with music.*)

Scene 3

(*Legend on screen: "After the Fiasco—"*)
TOM *speaks from the fire-escape landing.*

TOM: After the fiasco at Rubicam's Business College, the idea of getting a gentleman caller for Laura began to play a more and more important part in Mother's calculations. It became an obsession. Like some archetype of the universal unconscious, the image of the gentleman caller haunted our small apartment. . . . (*Image: Young man at door with flowers.*) An evening at home rarely passed without some allusion to this image, this spectre, this hope. . . . Even when he wasn't mentioned, his presence hung in Mother's preoccupied look and in my sister's frightened, apologetic manner—hung like a sentence passed upon the Wingfields! Mother was a woman of action as well as words. She began to take logical steps in the planned direction. Late that winter and in the early spring—realizing that extra money would be needed to properly feather the nest and plume the bird—she conducted a vigorous campaign on the telephone, roping in subscribers to one of those magazines for matrons called *The Home-maker's Companion,* the type of journal that features the serialized sublimations of ladies of letters who think in terms of delicate cup-like breasts, slim, tapering waists, rich, creamy thighs, eyes like wood-smoke in autumn, fingers that soothe and caress like strains of music, bodies as powerful as Etruscan sculpture.

(*Screen image: Glamor magazine cover.*)

AMANDA *enters with phone on long extension cord. She is spotted in the dim stage.*

AMANDA: Ida Scott? This is Amanda Wingfield! We *missed* you at the D.A.R. last Monday! I said to myself: She's probably suffering with that sinus condition! How is that sinus condition? Horrors! Heaven have mercy!— You're a Christian martyr, yes, that's what you are, a Christian martyr! Well, I just now happened to notice that your subscription to the *Companion's* about to expire! Yes, it expires with the next issue, honey!—just when that wonderful new serial by Bessie Mae Hopper is getting off to such an exciting start. Oh, honey, it's something that you can't miss! You remember how *Gone With the Wind* took everybody by storm? You simply couldn't go out if you hadn't read it. All everybody *talked* was Scarlett O'Hara. Well, this is a book that critics already compare to *Gone With the Wind*. It's the *Gone With the Wind* of the post–World War generation!—What?—Burning?—Oh, honey, don't let them burn, go take a look in the oven and I'll hold the wire! Heavens—I think she's hung up!

(*Dim out.*)

(*Legend on screen: "You think I'm in love with continental shoemakers?"*)

Before the stage is lighted, the violent voices of TOM *and* AMANDA *are heard. They are quarreling behind the portieres. In front of them stands* LAURA *with clenched hands and panicky expression.*

A clear pool of light on her figure throughout this scene.

TOM: What in Christ's name am I—
AMANDA (*shrilly*): Don't you use that—
TOM: Supposed to do!
AMANDA: Expression! Not in my—
TOM: Ohhh!
AMANDA: Presence! Have you gone out of your senses?
TOM: I have, that's true, *driven* out!
AMANDA: What is the matter with you, you—big—big—IDIOT!
TOM: Look—I've got *no thing,* no single thing—
AMANDA: Lower your voice!
TOM: In my life here that I can call my own! Everything is—
AMANDA: Stop that shouting!
TOM: Yesterday you confiscated my books! You had the nerve to—
AMANDA: I took that horrible novel back to the library—yes! That hideous book by that insane Mr. Lawrence. (TOM *laughs wildly.*) I cannot control the output of diseased minds or people who cater to them—(TOM *laughs still more wildly.*) BUT I WON'T ALLOW SUCH FILTH BROUGHT INTO MY HOUSE! No, no, no, no, no!
TOM: House, house! Who pays rent on it, who makes a slave of himself to—
AMANDA (*fairly screeching*): Don't you DARE to—
TOM: No, no, *I* mustn't say things! *I've* got to just—
AMANDA: Let me tell you—
TOM: I don't want to hear any more! (*He tears the portieres open. The upstage area is lit with a turgid smoky red glow.*)

AMANDA'S *hair is in metal curlers and she wears a very old bathrobe, much too large for her slight figure, a relic of the faithless Mr. Wingfield.*

An upright typewriter and a wild disarray of manuscripts is on the drop-leaf table. The quarrel was probably precipitated by AMANDA'S *interruption of his creative labor. A chair lying overthrown on the floor.*

Their gesticulating shadows are cast on the ceiling by the fiery glow.

AMANDA: You *will* hear more, you—

TOM: No, I won't hear more, I'm going out!

AMANDA: You come right back in—

TOM: Out, out, out! Because I'm—

AMANDA: Come back here, Tom Wingfield! I'm not through talking to you!

TOM: Oh, go—

LAURA (*desperately*): —*Tom!*

AMANDA: You're going to listen, and no more insolence from you! I'm at the end of my patience! (*He comes back toward her.*)

TOM: What do you think I'm at? Aren't I supposed to have any patience to reach the end of, Mother? I know, I know. It seems unimportant to you, what I'm *doing*—what I *want* to do—having a little *difference* between them! You don't think that—

AMANDA: I think you've been doing things that you're ashamed of. That's why you act like this. I don't believe that you go every night to the movies. Nobody goes to the movies night after night. Nobody in their right minds goes to the movies as often as you pretend to. People don't go to the movies at nearly midnight, and movies don't let out at two A.M. Come in stumbling. Muttering to yourself like a maniac! You get three hours' sleep and then go to work. Oh, I can picture the way you're doing down there. Moping, doping, because you're in no condition.

TOM (*wildly*): No, I'm in no condition!

AMANDA: What right have you got to jeopardize your job? Jeopardize the security of us all? How do you think we'd manage if you were—

TOM: Listen! You think I'm crazy *about the warehouse?* (*He bends fiercely toward her slight figure.*) You think I'm in love with the Continental Shoemakers? You think I want to spend fifty-five *years* down there in that—*celotex interior!* with—*fluorescent—tubes!* Look! I'd rather somebody picked up a crowbar and battered out my brains—than go back mornings! I *go!* Every time you come in yelling that God damn *"Rise and Shine!"* *"Rise and Shine!"* I say to myself, "How *lucky dead* people are!" But I get up. I *go!* For sixty-five dollars a month I give up all that I dream of doing and being *ever!* And you say self—*self's* all I ever think of. Why, listen, if self is what I thought of, Mother, I'd be where he is—GONE! (*pointing to father's picture*) As far as the system of transportation reaches! (*He starts past her. She grabs his arm.*) Don't grab at me, Mother!

AMANDA: Where are you going?

TOM: I'm going to the *movies!*

AMANDA: I don't believe that lie!

TOM (*Crouching toward her, overtowering her tiny figure. She backs away, gasping.*): I'm going to opium dens! Yes, opium dens, dens of vice and criminals' hang-outs, Mother. I've joined the Hogan gang, I'm a hired assassin, I carry a tommy-gun in a violin case! I run a string of cat-houses in the Valley! They call me Killer, Killer Wingfield, I'm leading a double-life, a simple, honest warehouse worker by day, by night a dynamic *czar* of the *underworld, Mother.* I go to gambling casinos, I spin away fortunes on the roulette table! I wear a patch over one eye and a false mustache, sometimes I put on green whiskers. On those occasions they call me—*El Diablo!* Oh, I could tell you things to make you sleepless! My enemies plan to dynamite this place. They're going to blow us all sky-high some night! I'll be glad, very happy, and so will you! You'll go up, up on a broomstick, over Blue Mountain with seventeen gentlemen callers! You ugly—babbling old—*witch*. . . . (*He goes through a series of violent, clumsy movements, seizing his overcoat, lunging to the door, pulling it fiercely open. The women watch him, aghast. His arm catches in the sleeve of the coat as he struggles to pull it on. For a moment he is pinioned by the bulky garment. With an outraged groan he tears the coat off again, splitting the shoulder of it, and hurls it across the room. It strikes against the shelf of* LAURA'S *glass collection, there is a tinkle of shattering glass.* LAURA *cries out as if wounded.*)

(*Music. Legend: "The Glass Menagerie."*)

LAURA (*shrilly*): My glass!—menagerie. . . . (*She covers her face and turns away.*)

But AMANDA *is still stunned and stupefied by the "ugly witch" so that she barely notices this occurrence. Now she recovers her speech.*

AMANDA (*in an awful voice*): I won't speak to you—until you apologize! (*She crosses through portieres and draws them together behind her.* TOM *is left with* LAURA. LAURA *clings weakly to the mantel with her face averted.* TOM *stares at her stupidly for a moment. Then he crosses to shelf. Drops awkwardly on his knees to collect the fallen glass, glancing at* LAURA *as if he would speak but couldn't.*)

"The Glass Menagerie" steals in as

(*The scene dims out.*)

Scene 4

The interior is dark. Faint light in the alley.

A deep-voiced bell in a church is tolling the hour of five as the scene commences.

TOM *appears at the top of the alley. After each solemn boom of the bell in the tower, he shakes a little noise-maker or rattle as if to express the tiny spasm of man in contrast to the sustained power and dignity of the Almighty. This and the unsteadiness of his advance make it evident that he has been drinking.*

As he climbs the few steps to the fire-escape landing light steals up inside. LAURA *appears in night-dress, observing* TOM'S *empty bed in the front room.*

TOM *fishes in his pockets for door-key, removing a motley assortment of articles in the search, including a perfect shower of movie-ticket stubs and an empty bottle. At last he finds the key, but just as he is about to insert it, it slips from his fingers. He strikes a match and crouches below the door.*

TOM (*bitterly*): One crack—and it falls through!

LAURA *opens the door.*

LAURA: Tom! Tom, what are you doing?

TOM: Looking for a door-key.

LAURA: Where have you been all this time?

TOM: I have been to the movies.

LAURA: All this time at the movies?

TOM: There was a very long program. There was a Garbo picture and a Mickey Mouse and a travelogue and a newsreel and a preview of coming attractions. And there was an organ solo and a collection for the milk-fund—simultaneously—which ended up in a terrible fight between a fat lady and an usher!

LAURA (*innocently*): Did you have to stay through everything?

TOM: Of course! And, oh, I forgot! There was a big stage show! The head-liner on this stage show was Malvolio the Magician. He performed wonderful tricks, many of them, such as pouring water back and forth between pitchers. First it turned to wine and then it turned to beer and then it turned to whiskey. I know it was whiskey it finally turned into because he needed somebody to come up out of the audience to help him, and I came up—both shows! It was Kentucky Straight Bourbon. A very generous fellow, he gave souvenirs. (*He pulls from his back pocket a shimmering rainbow-colored scarf.*) He gave me this. This is his magic scarf. You can have it, Laura. You wave it over a canary cage and you get a bowl of gold-fish. You wave it over the gold-fish bowl and they fly away canaries. . . . But the wonderfullest trick of all was the coffin trick. We nailed him into a coffin and he got out of the coffin without removing one nail. (*He has come inside.*) There is a trick that would come in handy for me—get me out of this 2 by 4 situation! (*flops onto bed and starts removing shoes*)

LAURA: Tom—Shhh!

TOM: What're you shushing me for?

LAURA: You'll wake up Mother.

TOM: Goody, goody! Pay 'er back for all those "Rise an' Shines." (*lies down, groaning*) You know it don't take much intelligence to get yourself into a nailed-up coffin, Laura. But who in hell ever got himself out of one without removing one nail?

As if in answer, the father's grinning photograph lights up.
    (*Scene dims out.*)
    Immediately following: The church bell is heard striking six. At the sixth stroke the alarm clock goes off in AMANDA'S *room, and after a few moments we hear her calling: "Rise and Shine! Rise and Shine! Laura, go tell your brother to rise and shine!"*

TOM (*sitting up slowly*): I'll rise—but I won't shine.

The light increases.

AMANDA: Laura, tell your brother his coffee is ready.

LAURA *slips into front room.*

LAURA: Tom!—It's nearly seven. Don't make Mother nervous. (*He stares at her stupidly. Beseechingly.*) Tom, speak to Mother this morning. Make up with her, apologize, speak to her!

TOM: She won't to me. It's her that started not speaking.

LAURA: If you just say you're sorry she'll start speaking.

TOM: Her not speaking—is that such a tragedy?

LAURA: Please—please!

AMANDA (*calling from kitchenette*): Laura, are you going to do what I asked you to do, or do I have to get dressed and go out myself?

LAURA: Going, going—soon as I get on my coat! (*She pulls on a shapeless felt hat with nervous, jerky movement, pleadingly glancing at* TOM. *Rushes awkwardly for coat. The coat is one of* AMANDA'S, *inaccurately made-over, the sleeves too short for* LAURA.) Butter and what else?

AMANDA (*entering upstage*): Just butter. Tell them to charge it.

LAURA: Mother, they make such faces when I do that.

AMANDA: Sticks and stones can break our bones, but the expression on Mr. Garfinkel's face won't harm us! Tell your brother his coffee is getting cold.

LAURA (*at door*): Do what I asked you, will you, will you, Tom?

He looks sullenly away.

AMANDA: Laura, go now or just don't go at all!

LAURA (*rushing out*): Going—going! (*A second later she cries out.* TOM *springs up and crosses to door.* AMANDA *rushes anxiously in.* TOM *opens the door.*)

TOM: Laura?

LAURA: I'm all right. I slipped, but I'm all right.

AMANDA (*peering anxiously after her*): If anyone breaks a leg on those fire-escape steps, the landlord ought to be sued for every cent he possesses! (*She shuts door. Remembers she isn't speaking and returns to other room.*)

As TOM *enters listlessly for his coffee, she turns her back to him and stands rigidly facing the window on the gloomy gray vault of the areaway. Its light on her face with its aged but childish features is cruelly sharp, satirical as a Daumier print.*

(*Music under: "Ave Maria."*)

TOM *glances sheepishly but sullenly at her averted figure and slumps at the table. The coffee is scalding hot; he sips it and gasps and spits it back in the cup. At his gasp,* AMANDA *catches her breath and half turns. Then catches herself and turns back to window.*

TOM *blows on his coffee, glancing sidewise at his mother. She clears her throat.* TOM *clears his. He starts to rise. Sinks back down again, scratches his head, clears his throat again.* AMANDA *coughs.* TOM *raises his cup in both hands to blow on it, his eyes staring over the rim of it at his mother for several moments. Then he slowly sets the cup down and awkwardly and hesitantly rises from the chair.*

TOM (*hoarsely*): Mother. I—I apologize, Mother. (AMANDA *draws a quick, shuddering breath. Her face works grotesquely. She breaks into childlike tears.*) I'm sorry for what I said, for everything that I said, I didn't mean it.

AMANDA (*sobbingly*): My devotion has made me a witch and so I make myself hateful to my children!

TOM: *No,* you *don't.*

AMANDA: I worry so much, don't sleep, it makes me nervous!

TOM (*gently*): I understand that.

AMANDA: I've had to put up a solitary battle all these years. But you're my right-hand bower! Don't fall down, don't fail!

TOM (*gently*): I try, Mother.

AMANDA (*with great enthusiasm*): Try and you will SUCCEED! (*The notion makes her breathless.*) Why, you—you're just *full* of natural endowments! Both of my children—they're *unusual* children! Don't you think I know it? I'm so—*proud!* Happy and—feel I've—so much to be thankful for but—Promise me one thing, Son!

TOM: What, Mother?

AMANDA: Promise, son, you'll—never be a drunkard!

TOM (*turns to her grinning*): I will never be a drunkard, Mother.

AMANDA: That's what frightened me so, that you'd be drinking! Eat a bowl of Purina!

TOM: Just coffee, Mother.

AMANDA: Shredded wheat biscuit?

TOM: No. No, Mother, just coffee.

AMANDA: You can't put in a day's work on an empty stomach. You've got ten minutes—don't gulp! Drinking too-hot liquids makes cancer of the stomach. . . . Put cream in.

TOM: No, thank you.

AMANDA: To cool it.

TOM: No! No, thank you, I want it black.

AMANDA: I know, but it's not good for you. We have to do all that we can to build ourselves up. In these trying times we live in, all that we have to cling to is—each other. . . . That's why it's so important to—Tom, I—I sent out your sister so I could discuss something with you. If you hadn't spoken I would have spoken to you. (*sits down*)

TOM (*gently*): What is it, Mother, that you want to discuss?

AMANDA: *Laura!*

TOM *puts his cup down slowly.*
 (*Legend on screen: "Laura."*)
 (*Music: "The Glass Menagerie."*)

TOM: —Oh.—Laura . . .

AMANDA (*touching his sleeve*): You know how Laura is. So quiet but—still water runs deep! She notices things and I think she—broods about them. (TOM *looks up.*) A few days ago I came in and she was crying.

TOM: What about?

AMANDA: You.

TOM: Me?

AMANDA: She has an idea that you're not happy here.

TOM: What gave her that idea?

AMANDA: What gives her any idea? However, you do act strangely. I—I'm not criticizing, understand *that!* I know your ambitions do not lie in the warehouse, that like everybody in the whole wide world—you've had to—make sacrifices, but—Tom—Tom—life's not easy, it calls for—Spartan endurance! There's so many things in my heart that I cannot describe to you! I've never told you but I—*loved* your father. . . .

TOM (*gently*): I know that, Mother.

AMANDA: And you—when I see you taking after his ways! Staying out late—and—well, you *had* been drinking the night you were in that—terrifying condition! Laura says that you hate the apartment and that you go out nights to get away from it! Is that true, Tom?

TOM: No. You say there's so much in your heart that you can't describe to me. That's true of me, too. There's so much in my heart that I can't describe to *you!* So let's respect each other's—

AMANDA: But, why—*why,* Tom—are you always so *restless?* Where do you *go* to, nights?

TOM: I—go to the movies.

AMANDA: Why do you go to the movies so much, Tom?

TOM: I go to the movies because—I like adventure. Adventure is something I don't have much of at work, so I go to the movies.

AMANDA: But, Tom, you go to the movies *entirely* too much!

TOM: I like a lot of adventure.

> AMANDA *looks baffled, then hurt. As the familiar inquisition resumes he becomes hard and impatient again.* AMANDA *slips back into her querulous attitude toward him.*
>
> (*Image on screen: Sailing vessel with Jolly Roger.*)

AMANDA: Most young men find adventure in their careers.

TOM: Then most young men are not employed in a warehouse.

AMANDA: The world is full of young men employed in warehouses and offices and factories.

TOM: Do all of them find adventure in their careers?

AMANDA: They do or they do without it! Not everybody has a craze for adventure.

TOM: Man is by instinct a lover, a hunter, a fighter, and none of those instincts are given much play at the warehouse!

AMANDA: Man is by instinct! Don't quote instinct to me! Instinct is something that people have got away from! It belongs to animals! Christian adults don't want it!

TOM: What do Christian adults want, then, Mother?

AMANDA: Superior things! Things of the mind and the spirit! Only animals have to satisfy instincts! Surely your aims are somewhat higher than theirs! Than monkeys—pigs—

TOM: I reckon they're not.

AMANDA: You're joking. However, that isn't what I wanted to discuss.

TOM (*rising*): I haven't much time.

AMANDA (*pushing his shoulders*): Sit down.

TOM: You want me to punch in red at the warehouse, Mother?

AMANDA: You have five minutes. I want to talk about Laura.

(*Legend: "Plans and Provisions."*)

TOM: All right! What about Laura?

AMANDA: We have to be making some plans and provisions for her. She's older than you, two years, and nothing has happened. She just drifts along doing nothing. It frightens me terribly how she just drifts along.

TOM: I guess she's the type that people call home girls.

AMANDA: There's no such type, and if there is, it's a pity! That is unless the home is hers, with a husband!

TOM: What?

AMANDA: Oh, I can see the handwriting on the wall as plain as I see the nose in front of my face! It's terrifying! More and more you remind me of your father! He was out all hours without explanation!—Then *left! Good-bye!* And me with the bag to hold. I saw that letter you got from the Merchant Marine. I know what you're dreaming of. I'm not standing here blindfolded. Very well, then. Then *do* it! But not till there's somebody to take your place.

TOM: What do you mean?

AMANDA: I mean that as soon as Laura has got somebody to take care of her, married, a home of her own, independent—why, then you'll be free to go wherever you please, on land, on sea, whichever way the wind blows you! But until that time you've got to look out for your sister. I don't say me because I'm old and don't matter! I say for your sister because she's young and dependent. I put her in business college—a dismal failure! Frightened her so it made her sick at the stomach. I took her over to the Young People's League at the church. Another fiasco. She spoke to nobody, nobody spoke to her. Now all she does is fool with those pieces of glass and play those worn-out records. What kind of a life is that for a girl to lead?

TOM: What can I do about it?

AMANDA: Overcome selfishness! Self, self, self is all that you ever think of! (TOM *springs up and crosses to get his coat. It is ugly and bulky. He pulls on a cap with earmuffs.*) Where is your muffler? Put your wool muffler on! (*He snatches it angrily from the closet and tosses it around his neck and pulls both ends tight.*) Tom! I haven't said what I had in mind to ask you.

TOM: I'm too late to—

AMANDA (*Catching his arm—very importunately. Then shyly.*): Down at the warehouse, aren't there some—nice young men?

TOM: No!

AMANDA: There *must* be—some . . .

TOM: Mother—

Gesture.

AMANDA: Find out one that's clean-living—doesn't drink and—ask him out for sister!

TOM: What?

AMANDA: For *sister!* To *meet!* Get *acquainted!*

TOM (*stamping to door*): Oh, my *go-osh!*

AMANDA: Will you? (*He opens door. Imploringly.*) Will you? (*He starts down.*) Will you? *Will* you, dear?

TOM (*calling back*): YES!

> AMANDA *closes the door hesitantly and with a troubled but faintly hopeful expression.*
> (*Screen image: Glamor magazine cover.*)
> *Spot* AMANDA *at phone.*

AMANDA: Ella Cartwright? This is Amanda Wingfield! How are you, honey? How is that kidney condition? (*count five*) Horrors! (*count five*) You're a Christian martyr, yes, honey, that's what you are, a Christian martyr! Well, I just now happened to notice in my little red book that your subscription to the *Companion* has just run out! I knew that you wouldn't want to miss out on the wonderful serial starting in this new issue. It's by Bessie Mae Hopper, the first thing she's written since *Honeymoon for Three.* Wasn't that a strange and interesting story? Well, this one is even lovelier, I believe. It has a sophisticated, society background. It's all about the horsey set on Long Island!

(*Fade out.*)

Scene 5

> (*Legend on screen: "Annunciation."*) *Fade with music.*
> It is early dusk of a spring evening. Supper has just been finished in the Wingfield apartment. AMANDA and LAURA in light-colored dresses are removing dishes from the table, in the upstage area, which is shadowy, their movements formalized almost as a dance or ritual, their moving forms as pale and silent as moths.
> TOM, in white shirt and trousers, rises from the table and crosses toward the fire-escape.

AMANDA (*as he passes her*): Son, will you do me a favor?

TOM: What?

AMANDA: Comb your hair! You look so pretty when your hair is combed! (TOM *slouches on sofa with evening paper. Enormous caption "Franco Triumphs."*) There is only one respect in which I would like you to emulate your father.

TOM: What respect is that?

AMANDA: The care he always took of his appearance. He never allowed himself to look untidy. (*He throws down the paper and crosses to fire-escape.*) Where are you going?

TOM: I'm going out to smoke.

AMANDA: You smoke too much. A pack a day at fifteen cents a pack. How much would that amount to in a month? Thirty times fifteen is how much, Tom? Figure it out and you will be astounded at what you could save. Enough to give you a night-school course in accounting at Washington U! Just think what a wonderful thing that would be for you, Son!

TOM *is unmoved by the thought.*

TOM: I'd rather smoke. (*He steps out on landing, letting the screen door slam.*)
AMANDA (*sharply*): I know! That's the tragedy of it. . . . (*Alone, she turns to look at her husband's picture.*)

(*Dance music: "All the world is waiting for the sunrise!"*)

TOM (*to the audience*): Across the alley from us was the Paradise Dance Hall. On evenings in spring the windows and doors were open and the music came outdoors. Sometimes the lights were turned out except for a large glass sphere that hung from the ceiling. It would turn slowly about and filter the dusk with delicate rainbow colors. Then the orchestra played a waltz or a tango, something that had a slow and sensuous rhythm. Couples would come outside, to the relative privacy of the alley. You could see them kissing behind ash-pits and telephone poles. This was the compensation for lives that passed like mine, without any change or adventure. Adventure and change were imminent in this year. They were waiting around the corner for all these kids. Suspended in the mist over Berchtesgaden, caught in the folds of Chamberlain's umbrella— In Spain there was Guernica! But here there was only hot swing music and liquor, dance halls, bars, and movies, and sex that hung in the gloom like a chandelier and flooded the world with brief, deceptive rainbows. . . . All the world was waiting for bombardments!

AMANDA *turns from the picture and comes outside.*

AMANDA (*sighing*): A fire-escape landing's a poor excuse for a porch. (*She spreads a newspaper on a step and sits down, gracefully and demurely as if she were settling into a swing on a Mississippi veranda.*) What are you looking at?
TOM: The moon.
AMANDA: Is there a moon this evening?
TOM: It's rising over Garfinkel's Delicatessen.
AMANDA: So it is! A little silver slipper of a moon. Have you made a wish on it yet?
TOM: Um-hum.
AMANDA: What did you wish for?
TOM: That's a secret.
AMANDA: A secret, huh? Well, I won't tell mine either. I will be just as mysterious as you.
TOM: I bet I can guess what yours is.
AMANDA: Is my head so transparent?
TOM: You're not a sphinx.

AMANDA: No, I don't have secrets. I'll tell you what I wished for on the moon. Success and happiness for my precious children! I wish for that whenever there's a moon, and when there isn't a moon, I wish for it, too.

TOM: I thought perhaps you wished for a gentleman caller.

AMANDA: Why do you say that?

TOM: Don't you remember asking me to fetch one?

AMANDA: I remember suggesting that it would be nice for your sister if you brought home some nice young man from the warehouse. I think that I've made that suggestion more than once.

TOM: Yes, you have made it repeatedly.

AMANDA: Well?

TOM: We are going to have one.

AMANDA: *What?*

TOM: A gentleman caller!

(*The annunciation is celebrated with music.*)
    AMANDA *rises.*
    (*Image on screen: Caller with bouquet.*)

AMANDA: You mean you have asked some nice young man to come over?

TOM: Yep. I've asked him to dinner.

AMANDA: You really did?

TOM: I did!

AMANDA: You did, and did he—*accept?*

TOM: He did!

AMANDA: Well, well—well, well! That's—lovely!

TOM: I thought that you would be pleased.

AMANDA: It's definite, then?

TOM: Very definite.

AMANDA: Soon?

TOM: Very soon.

AMANDA: For heaven's sake, stop putting on and tell me some things, will you?

TOM: What things do you want me to tell you?

AMANDA: *Naturally* I would like to know when he's *coming!*

TOM: He's coming tomorrow.

AMANDA: *Tomorrow?*

TOM: Yep. Tomorrow.

AMANDA: But, Tom!

TOM: Yes, Mother?

AMANDA: Tomorrow gives me no time!

TOM: Time for what?

AMANDA: Preparations! Why didn't you phone me at once, as soon as you asked him, the minute that he accepted? Then, don't you see, I could have been getting ready!

TOM: You don't have to make any fuss.

AMANDA: Oh, Tom, Tom, Tom, of course I have to make a fuss! I want things nice, not sloppy! Not thrown together. I'll certainly have to do some fast thinking, won't I?

TOM: I don't see why you have to think at all.

AMANDA: You just don't know. We can't have a gentleman caller in a pig-sty! All my wedding silver has to be polished, the monogrammed table linen ought to be laundered! The windows have to be washed and fresh curtains put up. And how about clothes? We have to *wear* something, don't we?

TOM: Mother, this boy is no one to make a fuss over!

AMANDA: Do you realize he's the first young man we've introduced to your sister? It's terrible, dreadful, disgraceful that poor little sister has never received a single gentleman caller! Tom, come inside! (*She opens the screen door.*)

TOM: What for?

AMANDA: I want to ask you some things.

TOM: If you're going to make such a fuss, I'll call it off, I'll tell him not to come!

AMANDA: You certainly won't do anything of the kind. Nothing offends people worse than broken engagements. It simply means I'll have to work like a Turk! We won't be brilliant, but we will pass inspection. Come on inside. (TOM *follows, groaning.*) Sit down.

TOM: Any particular place you would like me to sit?

AMANDA: Thank heavens I've got that new sofa! I'm also making payments on a floor lamp I'll have sent out! And put the chintz covers on, they'll brighten things up! Of course I'd hoped to have these walls re-papered. . . . What is the young man's name?

TOM: His name is O'Connor.

AMANDA: That, of course, means fish—tomorrow is Friday! I'll have that salmon loaf—with Durkee's dressing! What does he do? He works at the warehouse?

TOM: Of course! How else would I—

AMANDA: Tom, he—doesn't drink?

TOM: Why do you ask me that?

AMANDA: Your father *did!*

TOM: Don't get started on that!

AMANDA: He *does* drink, then?

TOM: Not that I know of!

AMANDA: Make sure, be certain! The last thing I want for my daughter's a boy who drinks!

TOM: Aren't you being a little bit premature? Mr. O'Connor has not yet appeared on the scene!

AMANDA: But will tomorrow. To meet your sister, and what do I know about his character? Nothing! Old maids are better off than wives of drunkards!

TOM: Oh, my God!

AMANDA: Be still!

TOM (*leaning forward to whisper*): Lots of fellows meet girls whom they don't marry!

AMANDA: Oh, talk sensibly, Tom—and don't be sarcastic! (*She has gotten a hairbrush.*)

TOM: What are you doing?

AMANDA: I'm brushing that cow-lick down! What is this young man's position at the warehouse?

TOM (*submitting grimly to the brush and the interrogation*): This young man's position is that of a shipping clerk, Mother.

AMANDA: Sounds to me like a fairly responsible job, the sort of a job *you* would be in if you just had more *get-up*. What is his salary? Have you any idea?

TOM: I would judge it to be approximately eighty-five dollars a month.

AMANDA: Well—not princely, but—

TOM: Twenty more than I make.

AMANDA: Yes, how well I know! But for a family man, eighty-five dollars a month is not much more than you can just get by on. . . .

TOM: Yes, but Mr. O'Connor is not a family man.

AMANDA: He might be, mightn't he? Some time in the future?

TOM: I see. Plans and provisions.

AMANDA: You are the only young man that I know of who ignores the fact that the future becomes the present, the present the past, and the past turns into everlasting regret if you don't plan for it!

TOM: I will think that over and see what I can make of it.

AMANDA: Don't be supercilious with your mother! Tell me some more about this—what do you call him?

TOM: James D. O'Connor. The D. is for Delaney.

AMANDA: Irish on *both* sides! *Gracious!* And doesn't drink?

TOM: Shall I call him up and ask him right this minute?

AMANDA: The only way to find out about those things is to make discreet inquiries at the proper moment. When I was a girl in Blue Mountain and it was suspected that a young man drank, the girl whose attentions he had been receiving, if any girl *was,* would sometimes speak to the minister of his church, or rather her father would if her father was living, and sort of feel him out on the young man's character. That is the way such things are discreetly handled to keep a young woman from making a tragic mistake!

TOM: Then how did you happen to make a tragic mistake?

AMANDA: That innocent look of your father's had everyone fooled! He *smiled*—the world was *enchanted!* No girl can do worse than put herself at the mercy of a handsome appearance! I hope that Mr. O'Connor is not too good-looking.

TOM: No, he's not too good-looking. He's covered with freckles and hasn't too much of a nose.

AMANDA: He's not right-down homely, though?

TOM: Not right-down homely. Just medium homely, I'd say.

AMANDA: Character's what to look for in a man.

TOM: That's what I've always said, Mother.

AMANDA: You've never said anything of the kind and I suspect you would never give it a thought.

TOM: Don't be so suspicious of me.

AMANDA: At least I hope he's the type that's up and coming.

TOM: I think he really goes in for self-improvement.

AMANDA: What reason have you to think so?

TOM: He goes to night school.

AMANDA (*beaming*): Splendid! What does he do, I mean study?

TOM: Radio engineering and public speaking!

AMANDA: Then he has visions of being advanced in the world! Any young man who studies public speaking is aiming to have an executive job some day! And radio engineering? A thing for the future! Both of these facts are very illuminating. Those are the sort of things that a mother should know concerning any young man who comes to call on her daughter. Seriously or—not.

TOM: One little warning. He doesn't know about Laura. I didn't let on that we had dark ulterior motives. I just said, why don't you come and have dinner with us? He said okay and that was the whole conversation.

AMANDA: I bet it was! You're eloquent as an oyster. However, he'll know about Laura when he gets here. When he sees how lovely and sweet and pretty she is, he'll thank his lucky stars he was asked to dinner.

TOM: Mother, you mustn't expect too much of Laura.

AMANDA: What do you mean?

TOM: Laura seems all those things to you and me because she's ours and we love her. We don't even notice she's crippled any more.

AMANDA: Don't say crippled! You know that I never allow that word to be used!

TOM: But face facts, Mother. She is and—that's not all—

AMANDA: What do you mean "not all"?

TOM: Laura is very different from other girls.

AMANDA: I think the difference is all to her advantage.

TOM: Not quite all—in the eyes of others—strangers—she's terribly shy and lives in a world of her own and those things make her seem a little peculiar to people outside the house.

AMANDA: Don't say peculiar.

TOM: Face the facts. She is.

(*The dance-hall music changes to a tango that has a minor and somewhat ominous tone.*)

AMANDA: In what way is she peculiar—may I ask?

TOM (*gently*): She lives in a world of her own—a world of—little glass ornaments, Mother. . . . (*Gets up.* AMANDA *remains holding brush, looking at him, troubled.*) She plays old phonograph records and—that's about all—(*He glances at himself in the mirror and crosses to door.*)

AMANDA (*sharply*): Where are you going?

TOM: I'm going to the movies. (*out screen door*)

AMANDA: Not to the movies, every night to the movies! (*follows quickly to screen door*) I don't believe you always go to the movies! (*He is gone.* AMANDA *looks worriedly after him for a moment. Then vitality and optimism return and she turns from the door. Crossing to portieres.*) Laura! Laura! (LAURA *answers from kitchenette.*)

LAURA: Yes, Mother.

AMANDA: Let those dishes go and come in front! (LAURA *appears with dish towel. Gaily.*) Laura, come here and make a wish on the moon!

(*Screen image: Moon.*)

LAURA (*entering*): Moon—moon?

AMANDA: A little silver slipper of a moon. Look over your left shoulder, Laura, and make a wish! (LAURA *looks faintly puzzled as if called out of sleep.* AMANDA *seizes her shoulders and turns her at an angle by the door.*) Now! Now, darling, *wish!*

LAURA: What shall I wish for, Mother?

AMANDA (*her voice trembling and her eyes suddenly filling with tears*): Happiness! Good fortune!

(*The violin rises and the stage dims out.*)

Scene 6

(*Image: High school hero.*)

TOM: And so the following evening I brought Jim home to dinner. I had known Jim slightly in high school. In high school Jim was a hero. He had tremendous Irish good nature and vitality with the scrubbed and polished look of white chinaware. He seemed to move in a continual spotlight. He was a star in basketball, captain of the debating club, president of the senior class and the glee club and he sang the male lead in the annual light operas. He was always running or bounding, never just walking. He seemed always at the point of defeating the law of gravity. He was shooting with such velocity through his adolescence that you would logically expect him to arrive at nothing short of the White House by the time he was thirty. But Jim apparently ran into more interference after his graduation from Soldan. His speed had definitely slowed. Six years after he left high school he was holding a job that wasn't much better than mine.

(*Image: Clerk.*)

He was the only one at the warehouse with whom I was on friendly terms. I was valuable to him as someone who could remember his former glory, who had seen him win basketball games and the silver cup in debating. He knew of my secret practice of retiring to a cabinet of the wash-room to work on poems when business was slack in the warehouse. He called me Shakespeare. And while the other boys in the warehouse regarded me with suspicious hostility, Jim took a humorous attitude toward me. Gradually his attitude affected the others, their hostility wore off and they also began to smile at me as people smile at an oddly fashioned dog who trots across their path at some distance.

I knew that Jim and Laura had known each other at Soldan, and I had heard Laura speak admiringly of his voice. I didn't know if Jim remembered her or not. In high school Laura had been as unobtrusive as Jim had been astonishing. If he did remember Laura, it was not as my sister, for when I asked him to dinner, he grinned and said, "You know, Shakespeare, I never thought of you as having folks!" He was about to discover that I did. . . .

(*Light up stage.*)

(*Legend on screen: "The Accent of a Coming Foot."*)

Friday evening. It is about five o'clock of a late spring evening which comes "scattering poems in the sky."

A delicate lemony light is in the Wingfield apartment.

AMANDA *has worked like a Turk in preparation for the gentleman caller. The results are astonishing. The new floor lamp with its rose-silk shade is in place, a colored paper lantern conceals the broken light fixture in the ceiling, new billowing white curtains are at the windows, chintz covers are on chairs and sofa, a pair of new sofa pillows make their initial appearance.*

Open boxes and tissue paper are scattered on the floor.

LAURA *stands in the middle with lifted arms while* AMANDA *crouches before her, adjusting the hem of the new dress, devout and ritualistic. The dress is colored and designed by memory. The arrangement of* LAURA'S *hair is changed; it is softer and more becoming. A fragile, unearthly prettiness has come out in* LAURA: *she is like a piece of translucent glass touched by light, given a momentary radiance, not actual, not lasting.*

AMANDA (*impatiently*): Why are you trembling?

LAURA: Mother, you've made me so nervous!

AMANDA: How have I made you nervous?

LAURA: By all this fuss! You make it seem so important!

AMANDA: I don't understand you, Laura. You couldn't be satisfied with just sitting home, and yet whenever I try to arrange something for you, you seem to resist it.

She gets up.

Now take a look at yourself. No, wait! Wait just a moment—I have an idea!

LAURA: What is it now?

AMANDA *produces two powder puffs which she wraps in handkerchiefs and stuffs in* LAURA'S *bosom.*

LAURA: Mother, what are you doing?

AMANDA: They call them "Gay Deceivers"!

LAURA: I won't wear them!

AMANDA: You will!

LAURA: Why should I?

AMANDA: Because, to be painfully honest, your chest is flat.

LAURA: You make it seem like we were setting a trap.

AMANDA: All pretty girls are a trap, a pretty trap, and men expect them to be. (*Legend: "A Pretty Trap."*) Now look at yourself, young lady. This is the prettiest you will ever be! I've got to fix myself now! You're going to be surprised by your mother's appearance! (*She crosses through portieres, humming gaily.*)

LAURA *moves slowly to the long mirror and stares solemnly at herself.*

A wind blows the white curtains inward in a slow, graceful motion and with a faint, sorrowful sighing.

AMANDA (*off stage*): It isn't dark enough yet. (*She turns slowly before the mirror with a troubled look.*)

(*Legend on screen: "This Is My Sister: Celebrate Her with Strings!" Music.*)

AMANDA (*laughing, off*): I'm going to show you something. I'm going to make a spectacular appearance!

LAURA: What is it, Mother?

AMANDA: Possess your soul in patience—you will see! Something I've resurrected from that old trunk! Styles haven't changed so terribly much after all. . . . (*She parts the portieres.*) Now just look at your mother! (*She wears a girlish frock of yellowed voile with a blue silk sash. She carries a bunch of jonquils—the legend of her youth is nearly revived. Feverishly.*) This is the dress in which I led the cotillion. Won the cakewalk twice at Sunset Hill, wore one spring to the Governor's ball in Jackson! See how I sashayed around the ballroom, Laura? (*She raises her skirt and does a mincing step around the room.*) I wore it on Sundays for my gentlemen callers! I had it on the day I met your father—I had malaria fever all that spring. The change of climate from East Tennessee to the Delta—weakened resistance—I had a little temperature all the time—not enough to be serious—just enough to make me restless and giddy!—Invitations poured in—parties all over the Delta!—"Stay in bed," said Mother, "you have fever!"—but I just wouldn't.—I took quinine but kept on going, going!—Evenings, dances!—Afternoons, long, long rides! Picnics—lovely!—So lovely, that country in May.—All lacy with dogwood, literally flooded with jonquils!—That was the spring I had the craze for jonquils. Jonquils became an absolute obsession. Mother said, "Honey, there's no more room for jonquils." And still I kept on bringing in more jonquils. Whenever, wherever I saw them, I'd say, "Stop! Stop! I see jonquils!" I made the young men help me gather the jonquils! It was a joke, Amanda and her jonquils! Finally there were no more vases to hold them, every available space was filled with jonquils. No vases to hold them? All right, I'll hold them myself! And then I—(*She stops in front of the picture. Music.*) met your father! Malaria fever and jonquils and then—this—boy. . . . (*She switches on the rose-colored lamp.*) I hope they get here before it starts to rain. (*She crosses upstage and places the jonquils in bowl on table.*) I gave your brother a little extra change so he and Mr. O'Connor could take the service car home.

LAURA (*with altered look*): What did you say his name was?

AMANDA: O'Connor.

LAURA: What is his first name?

AMANDA: I don't remember. Oh, yes, I do. It was—Jim!

LAURA *sways slightly and catches hold of a chair.*
(*Legend on screen: "Not Jim!"*)

LAURA (*faintly*): Not—Jim!

AMANDA: Yes, that was it, it was Jim! I've never known a Jim that wasn't nice!

(*Music: Ominous.*)

LAURA: Are you sure his name is Jim O'Connor?

AMANDA: Yes. Why?

LAURA: Is he the one that Tom used to know in high school?

AMANDA: He didn't say so. I think he just got to know him at the warehouse.

LAURA: There was a Jim O'Connor we both knew in high school—(*then, with effort*) If that is the one that Tom is bringing to dinner—you'll have to excuse me, I won't come to the table.

AMANDA: What sort of nonsense is this?

LAURA: You asked me once if I'd ever liked a boy. Don't you remember I showed you this boy's picture?

AMANDA: You mean the boy you showed me in the year book?

LAURA: Yes, that boy.

AMANDA: Laura, Laura, were you in love with that boy?

LAURA: I don't know, Mother. All I know is I couldn't sit at the table if it was him!

AMANDA: It won't be him! It isn't the least bit likely. But whether it is or not, you will come to the table. You will not be excused.

LAURA: I'll have to be, Mother.

AMANDA: I don't intend to humor your silliness, Laura. I've had too much from you and your brother, both! So just sit down and compose yourself till they come. Tom has forgotten his key so you'll have to let them in, when they arrive.

LAURA (*panicky*): Oh, Mother—*you* answer the door!

AMANDA (*lightly*): I'll be in the kitchen—busy!

LAURA: Oh, Mother, please answer the door, don't make me do it!

AMANDA (*crossing into kitchenette*): I've got to fix the dressing for the salmon. Fuss, fuss—silliness!—over a gentleman caller!

> *Door swings shut.* LAURA *is left alone.*
> (*Legend: "Terror!"*)
> *She utters a low moan and turns off the lamp—sits stiffly on the edge of the sofa, knotting her fingers together.*
> (*Legend on screen: "The Opening of a Door!"*)
> TOM *and* JIM *appear on the fire-escape steps and climb to landing. Hearing their approach,* LAURA *rises with a panicky gesture. She retreats to the portieres.*
> *The doorbell.* LAURA *catches her breath and touches her throat. Low drums.*

AMANDA (*calling*): Laura, sweetheart! The door!

> LAURA *stares at it without moving.*

JIM: I think we just beat the rain.

TOM: Uh-huh. (*He rings again, nervously.* JIM *whistles and fishes for a cigarette.*)

AMANDA (*very, very gaily*): Laura, that is your brother and Mr. O'Connor! Will you let them in, darling?

> LAURA *crosses toward kitchenette door.*

LAURA (*breathlessly*): Mother—you go to the door!

AMANDA *steps out of kitchenette and stares furiously at* LAURA. *She points imperiously at the door.*

LAURA: Please, please!

AMANDA (*in a fierce whisper*): What is the matter with you, you silly thing?

LAURA (*desperately*): Please, you answer it, *please!*

AMANDA: I told you I wasn't going to humor you, Laura. Why have you chosen this moment to lose your mind?

LAURA: Please, please, please, you go!

AMANDA: You'll have to go to the door because I can't!

LAURA (*despairingly*): I can't either!

AMANDA: *Why?*

LAURA: I'm *sick!*

AMANDA: I'm sick, too—of your nonsense! Why can't you and your brother be normal people? Fantastic whims and behavior! (TOM *gives a long ring.*) Preposterous goings on! Can you give me one reason—(*calls out lyrically*) COMING! JUST ONE SECOND!—why you should be afraid to open a door? Now you answer it, Laura!

LAURA: Oh, oh, oh . . . (*She returns through the portieres. Darts to the victrola and winds it frantically and turns it on.*)

AMANDA: Laura Wingfield, you march right to that door!

LAURA: Yes—yes, Mother!

A faraway, scratchy rendition of "Dardanella" softens the air and gives her strength to move through it. She slips to the door and draws it cautiously open.

   TOM enters with the caller, JIM O'CONNOR.

TOM: Laura, this is Jim. Jim, this is my sister, Laura.

JIM (*stepping inside*): I didn't know that Shakespeare had a sister!

LAURA (*retreating stiff and trembling from the door*): How—how do you do?

JIM (*heartily extending his hand*): Okay!

   LAURA *touches it hesitantly with hers.*

JIM: Your hand's *cold,* Laura!

LAURA: Yes, well—I've been playing the victrola. . . .

JIM: Must have been playing classical music on it! You ought to play a little hot swing music to warm you up!

LAURA: Excuse me—I haven't finished playing the victrola. . . . (*She turns awkwardly and hurries into the front room. She pauses a second by the victrola. Then catches her breath and darts through the portieres like a frightened deer.*)

JIM (*grinning*): What was the matter?

TOM: Oh—with Laura? Laura is—terribly shy.

JIM: Shy, huh? It's unusual to meet a shy girl nowadays. I don't believe you ever mentioned you had a sister.

TOM: Well, now you know. I have one. Here is the *Post Dispatch*. You want a piece of it?

JIM: Uh-huh.

TOM: What piece? The comics?

JIM: Sports! (*glances at it*) Ole Dizzy Dean is on his bad behavior.

TOM (*disinterest*): Yeah? (*lights cigarette and crosses back to fire-escape door*)

JIM: Where are *you* going?

TOM: I'm going out on the terrace.

JIM (*goes after him*): You know, Shakespeare—I'm going to sell you a bill of goods!

TOM: What goods?

JIM: A course I'm taking.

TOM: Huh?

JIM: In public speaking! You and me, we're not the warehouse type.

TOM: Thanks—that's good news. But what has public speaking got to do with it?

JIM: It fits you for—executive positions!

TOM: Awww.

JIM: I tell you it's done a helluva lot for me.

(*Image: Executive at desk.*)

TOM: In what respect?

JIM: In every! Ask yourself what is the difference between you an' me and men in the office down front? Brains?—No!—Ability?—No! Then what? Just one little thing—

TOM: What is that one little thing?

JIM: Primarily it amounts to—social poise! Being able to square up to people and hold your own on any social level!

AMANDA (*off stage*): Tom?

TOM: Yes, Mother?

AMANDA: Is that you and Mr. O'Connor?

TOM: Yes, Mother.

AMANDA: Well, you just make yourselves comfortable in there.

TOM: Yes, Mother.

AMANDA: Ask Mr. O'Connor if he would like to wash his hands.

JIM: Aw, no—no—thank you—I took care of that at the warehouse. Tom—

TOM: Yes?

JIM: Mr. Mendoza was speaking to me about you.

TOM: Favorably?

JIM: What do you think?

TOM: Well—

JIM: You're going to be out of a job if you don't wake up.

TOM: I am waking up—

JIM: You show no signs.

TOM: The signs are interior.

(*Image on screen: The sailing vessel with Jolly Roger again.*)

TOM: I'm planning to change. (*He leans over the rail speaking with quiet exhilaration. The incandescent marquees and signs of the first-run movie houses light his face from across the alley. He looks like a voyager.*) I'm right at the point of committing myself to a future that doesn't include the warehouse and Mr. Mendoza or even a night-school course in public speaking.

JIM: What are you gassing about?

TOM: I'm tired of the movies.

JIM: Movies!

TOM: Yes, movies! Look at them—(*a wave toward the marvels of Grand Avenue*) All of those glamorous people—having adventures—hogging it all, gobbling the whole thing up! You know what happens? People go to the *movies* instead of *moving!* Hollywood characters are supposed to have all the adventures for everybody in America, while everybody in America sits in a dark room and watches them have them! Yes, until there's a war. That's when adventure becomes available to the masses! *Everyone's* dish, not only Gable's! Then the people in the dark room come out of the dark room to have some adventures themselves— Goody, goody!—It's our turn now, to go to the South Sea Island—to make a safari—to be exotic, far-off!—But I'm not patient. I don't want to wait till then. I'm tired of the *movies* and I am *about* to *move!*

JIM (*incredulously*): Move?

TOM: Yes.

JIM: When?

TOM: Soon!

JIM: Where? Where?

(*Theme three music seems to answer the question, while* TOM *thinks it over. He searches among his pockets.*)

TOM: I'm starting to boil inside. I know I seem dreamy, but inside—well, I'm boiling!—Whenever I pick up a shoe, I shudder a little thinking how short life is and what I am doing!—Whatever that means, I know it doesn't mean shoes—except as something to wear on a traveler's feet! (*finds paper*) Look—

JIM: What?

TOM: I'm a member.

JIM (*reading*): The Union of Merchant Seamen.

TOM: I paid my dues this month, instead of the light bill.

JIM: You will regret it when they turn the lights off.

TOM: I won't be here.

JIM: How about your mother?

TOM: I'm like my father. The bastard son of a bastard! See how he grins? And he's been absent going on sixteen years!

JIM: You're just talking, you drip. How does your mother feel about it?

TOM: Shhh!—Here comes Mother! Mother is not acquainted with my plans!

AMANDA (*enters portieres*): Where are you all?

TOM: On the terrace, Mother.

They start inside. She advances to them. TOM *is distinctly shocked at her appearance. Even* JIM *blinks a little. He is making his first contact with girlish Southern vivacity and in spite of the night-school course in public speaking is somewhat thrown off the beam by the unexpected outlay of social charm.*

Certain responses are attempted by JIM *but are swept aside by* AMANDA'S *gay laughter and chatter.* TOM *is embarrassed but after the first shock* JIM *reacts very warmly. Grins and chuckles, is altogether won over.*
(*Image:* AMANDA *as a girl.*)

AMANDA (*coyly smiling, shaking her girlish ringlets*): Well, well, well, so this is Mr. O'Connor. Introductions entirely unnecessary. I've heard so much about you from my boy. I finally said to him, Tom—good gracious!—why don't you bring this paragon to supper? I'd like to meet this nice young man at the warehouse!—Instead of just hearing him sing your praises so much! I don't know why my son is so stand-offish—that's not Southern behavior! Let's sit down and—I think we could stand a little more air in here! Tom, leave the door open. I felt a nice fresh breeze a moment ago. Where has it gone to? Mmm, so warm already! And not quite summer, even. We're going to burn up when summer really gets started. However, we're having—we're having a very light supper. I think light things are better fo' this time of year. The same as light clothes are. Light clothes an' light food are what warm weather calls fo'. You know our blood gets so thick during th' winter—it takes a while fo' us to *adjust* ou'selves!—when the season changes . . . It's come so quick this year. I wasn't prepared. All of a sudden—heavens! Already summer!—I ran to the trunk an' pulled out this light dress— Terribly old! Historical almost! But feels so good—so good an' co-ol, y' know. . . .

TOM: Mother—

AMANDA: Yes, honey?

TOM: How about—supper?

AMANDA: Honey, you go ask Sister if supper is ready! You know that Sister is in full charge of supper! Tell her you hungry boys are waiting for it. (*to* JIM) Have you met Laura?

JIM: She—

AMANDA: Let you in? Oh, good, you've met already! It's rare for a girl as sweet an' pretty as Laura to be domestic! But Laura is, thank heavens, not only pretty but also very domestic. I'm not at all. I never was a bit. I never could make a thing but angel-food cake. Well, in the South we had so many servants. Gone, gone, gone. All vestige of gracious living! Gone completely! I wasn't prepared for what the future brought me. All of my gentlemen callers were sons of planters and so of course I assumed that I would be married to one and raise my family on a large piece of land with plenty of servants. But man proposes—and woman accepts the proposal!—To vary that old, old saying a little bit—I married no planter! I married a man who worked for the telephone company!—That gallantly smiling gentleman over there! (*points to the picture*) A telephone man who—fell in love with long-distance!—Now he travels and I don't even know where!—But what am I going on for about my—tribulations? Tell me yours—I hope you don't have any! Tom?

TOM (*returning*): Yes, Mother?

AMANDA: Is supper nearly ready?

TOM: It looks to me like supper is on the table.

AMANDA: Let me look—(*She rises prettily and looks through portieres.*) Oh, lovely!—But where is Sister?

TOM: Laura is not feeling well and she says that she thinks she'd better not come to the table.

AMANDA: What?—Nonsense—Laura? Oh, Laura!

LAURA (*off stage, faintly*): Yes, Mother.

AMANDA: You really must come to the table. We won't be seated until you come to the table! Come in, Mr. O'Connor. You sit over there, and I'll— Laura? Laura Wingfield! You're keeping us waiting, honey! We can't say grace until you come to the table!

The back door is pushed weakly open and LAURA *comes in. She is obviously quite faint, her lips trembling, her eyes wide and staring. She moves unsteadily toward the table.*
    (*Legend: "Terror!"*)
    Outside a summer storm is coming abruptly. The white curtains billow inward at the windows and there is a sorrowful murmur and deep blue dusk.
    LAURA *suddenly stumbles—she catches at a chair with a faint moan.*

TOM: Laura!

AMANDA: Laura! (*There is a clap of thunder.*) (*Legend: "Ah!"*) (*despairingly*) Why, Laura, you *are* sick, darling! Tom, help your sister into the living room, dear! Sit in the living room, Laura—rest on the sofa. Well! (*to the gentleman caller*) Standing over the hot stove made her ill!—I told her that it was just too warm this evening, but—(TOM *comes back in.* LAURA *is on the sofa.*) Is Laura all right now?

TOM: Yes.

AMANDA: What *is* that? Rain? A nice cool rain has come up! (*She gives the gentleman caller a frightened look.*) I think we may—have grace— now . . . (TOM *looks at her stupidly.*) Tom, honey—you say grace!

TOM: Oh . . . "For these and all thy mercies—" (*They bow their heads,* AMANDA *stealing a nervous glance at* JIM. *In the living room* LAURA, *stretched on the sofa, clenches her hand to her lips, to hold back a shuddering sob.*) God's Holy Name be praised—

(*The scene dims out.*)

Scene 7

A Souvenir.

Half an hour later. Dinner is just being finished in the upstage area which is concealed by the drawn portieres.
    As the curtain rises LAURA *is still huddled upon the sofa, her feet drawn under her, her head resting on a pale blue pillow, her eyes wide and mysteriously watchful. The new floor lamp with its shade of rose-colored silk gives a soft, becoming light to her face, bringing out the fragile, unearthly prettiness which usually escapes attention. There is a steady murmur of*

rain, but it is slackening and stops soon after the scene begins; the air out-side becomes pale and luminous as the moon breaks out.

A moment after the curtain rises, the lights in both rooms flicker and go out.

JIM: Hey, there, Mr. Light Bulb!

AMANDA *laughs nervously.*
(*Legend: "Suspension of a Public Service."*)

AMANDA: Where was Moses when the lights went out? Ha-ha. Do you know the answer to that one, Mr. O'Connor?

JIM: No, Ma'am, what's the answer?

AMANDA: In the dark! (JIM *laughs appreciatively.*) Everybody sit still. I'll light the candles. Isn't it lucky we have them on the table? Where's a match? Which of you gentlemen can provide a match?

JIM: Here.

AMANDA: Thank you, sir.

JIM: Not at all, Ma'am!

AMANDA: I guess the fuse has burnt out. Mr. O'Connor, can you tell a burnt-out fuse? I know I can't and Tom is a total loss when it comes to mechanics. (*Sound: Getting up: Voices recede a little to kitchenette.*) Oh, be careful you don't bump into something. We don't want our gentleman caller to break his neck. Now wouldn't that be a fine howdy-do?

JIM: Ha-ha! Where is the fuse-box?

AMANDA: Right here next to the stove. Can you see anything?

JIM: Just a minute.

AMANDA: Isn't electricity a mysterious thing? Wasn't it Benjamin Franklin who tied a key to a kite? We live in such a mysterious universe, don't we? Some people say that science clears up all the mysteries for us. In my opinion it only creates more! Have you found it yet?

JIM: No, Ma'am. All these fuses look okay to me.

AMANDA: Tom!

TOM: Yes, Mother?

AMANDA: That light bill I gave you several days ago. The one I told you we got the notices about?

(*Legend: "Ha!"*)

TOM: Oh.—Yeah.

AMANDA: You didn't neglect to pay it by any chance?

TOM: Why, I—

AMANDA: Didn't! I might have known it!

JIM: Shakespeare probably wrote a poem on that light bill, Mrs. Wingfield.

AMANDA: I might have known better than to trust him with it! There's such a high price for negligence in this world!

JIM: Maybe the poem will win a ten-dollar prize.

AMANDA: We'll just have to spend the remainder of the evening in the nine-teenth century, before Mr. Edison made the Mazda lamp!

JIM: Candlelight is my favorite kind of light.

AMANDA: That shows you're romantic! But that's no excuse for Tom. Well, we got through dinner. Very considerate of them to let us get through dinner before they plunged us into everlasting darkness, wasn't it, Mr. O'Connor?

JIM: Ha-ha!

AMANDA: Tom, as a penalty for your carelessness you can help me with the dishes.

JIM: Let me give you a hand.

AMANDA: Indeed you will not!

JIM: I ought to be good for something.

AMANDA: Good for something? (*Her tone is rhapsodic.*) *You?* Why, Mr. O'Connor, nobody, *nobody's* given me this much entertainment in years—as you have!

JIM: Aw, now, Mrs. Wingfield!

AMANDA: I'm not exaggerating, not one bit! But Sister is all by her lonesome. You go keep her company in the parlor! I'll give you this lovely old candelabrum that used to be on the altar at the church of the Heavenly Rest. It was melted a little out of shape when the church burnt down. Lightning struck it one spring. Gypsy Jones was holding a revival at the time and he intimated that the church was destroyed because the Episcopalians gave card parties.

JIM: Ha-ha.

AMANDA: And how about you coaxing Sister to drink a little wine? I think it would be good for her! Can you carry both at once?

JIM: Sure. I'm Superman!

AMANDA: Now, Thomas, get into this apron!

The door of kitchenette swings closed on AMANDA'S *gay laughter; the flickering light approaches the portieres.*

LAURA sits up nervously as he enters. Her speech at first is low and breathless from the almost intolerable strain of being alone with a stranger.

(The legend: "I Don't Suppose You Remember Me at All!")

In her first speeches in this scene, before JIM'S *warmth overcomes her paralyzing shyness,* LAURA'S *voice is thin and breathless as though she has just run up a steep flight of stairs.*

JIM'S *attitude is gently humorous. In playing this scene it should be stressed that while the incident is apparently unimportant, it is to* LAURA *the climax of her secret life.*

JIM: Hello, there, Laura.

LAURA (*faintly*): Hello. (*She clears her throat.*)

JIM: How are you feeling now? Better?

LAURA: Yes. Yes, thank you.

JIM: This is for you. A little dandelion wine. (*He extends it toward her with extravagant gallantry.*)

LAURA: Thank you.

JIM: Drink it—but don't get drunk! (*He laughs heartily.* LAURA *takes the glass uncertainly; laughs shyly.*) Where shall I set the candles?

LAURA: Oh—oh, anywhere . . .

JIM: How about here on the floor? Any objections?

LAURA: No.

JIM: I'll spread a newspaper under to catch the drippings. I like to sit on the floor. Mind if I do?

LAURA: Oh, no.

JIM: Give me a pillow?

LAURA: What?

JIM: A pillow!

LAURA: Oh . . . (*hands him one quickly*)

JIM: How about you? Don't you like to sit on the floor?

LAURA: Oh—yes.

JIM: Why don't you, then?

LAURA: I—will.

JIM: Take a pillow! (LAURA *does. Sits on the other side of the candelabrum.* JIM *crosses his legs and smiles engagingly at her.*) I can't hardly see you sitting way over there.

LAURA: I can—see you.

JIM: I know, but that's not fair, I'm in the limelight. (LAURA *moves her pillow closer.*) Good! Now I can see you! Comfortable?

LAURA: Yes.

JIM: So am I. Comfortable as a cow! Will you have some gum?

LAURA: No, thank you.

JIM: I think that I will indulge, with your permission. (*musingly unwraps it and holds it up*) Think of the fortune made by the guy that invented the first piece of chewing gum. Amazing, huh? The Wrigley Building is one of the sights of Chicago.—I saw it summer before last when I went up to the Century of Progress. Did you take in the Century of Progress?

LAURA: No, I didn't.

JIM: Well, it was quite a wonderful exposition. What impressed me most was the Hall of Science. Gives you an idea of what the future will be in America, even more wonderful than the present time is! (*Pause. Smiling at her.*) Your brother tells me you're shy. Is that right, Laura?

LAURA: I—don't know.

JIM: I judge you to be an old-fashioned type of girl. Well, I think that's a pretty good type to be. Hope you don't think I'm being too personal— do you?

LAURA (*hastily, out of embarrassment*): I believe I *will* take a piece of gum, if you—don't mind. (*clearing her throat*) Mr. O'Connor, have you—kept up with your singing?

JIM: Singing? Me?

LAURA: Yes. I remember what a beautiful voice you had.

JIM: When did you hear me sing?

(*Voice off stage in the pause.*)

VOICE (*off stage*): O blow, ye winds, heigh-ho,
        A-roving I will go!
        I'm off to my love
        With a boxing glove—
        Ten thousand miles away!

JIM: You say you've heard me sing?

LAURA: Oh, yes! Yes, very often . . . I—don't suppose—you remember me—at all?

JIM (*smiling doubtfully*): You know I have an idea I've seen you before. I had that idea soon as you opened the door. It seemed almost like I was about to remember your name. But the name that I started to call you—wasn't a name! And so I stopped myself before I said it.

LAURA: Wasn't it—Blue Roses?

JIM (*springs up, grinning*): Blue Roses!—My gosh, yes—Blue Roses! That's what I had on my tongue when you opened the door! Isn't it funny what tricks your memory plays? I didn't connect you with high school some-how or other. But that's where it was; it was high school. I didn't even know you were Shakespeare's sister! Gosh, I'm sorry.

LAURA: I didn't expect you to. You—barely knew me!

JIM: But we did have a speaking acquaintance, huh?

LAURA: Yes, we—spoke to each other.

JIM: When did you recognize me?

LAURA: Oh, right away!

JIM: Soon as I came in the door?

LAURA: When I heard your name I thought it was probably you. I knew that Tom used to know you a little in high school. So when you came in the door—Well, then I was—sure.

JIM: Why didn't you *say* something, then?

LAURA (*breathlessly*): I didn't know what to say, I was—too surprised!

JIM: For goodness' sakes! You know, this sure is funny!

LAURA: Yes! Yes, isn't it, though . . .

JIM: Didn't we have a class in something together?

LAURA: Yes, we did.

JIM: What class was that?

LAURA: It was—singing—Chorus!

JIM: Aw!

LAURA: I sat across the aisle from you in the Aud.

JIM: Aw.

LAURA: Mondays, Wednesdays and Fridays.

JIM: Now I remember—you always came in late.

LAURA: Yes, it was so hard for me, getting upstairs. I had that brace on my leg—it clumped so loud!

JIM: I never heard any clumping.

LAURA (*wincing at the recollection*): To me it sounded like—thunder!

JIM: Well, well, well, I never even noticed.

LAURA: And everybody was seated before I came in. I had to walk in front of all those people. My seat was in the back row. I had to go clumping all the way up the aisle with everyone watching!

JIM: You shouldn't have been self-conscious.

LAURA: I know, but I was. It was always such a relief when the singing started.

JIM: Aw, yes, I've placed you now! I used to call you Blue Roses. How was it that I got started calling you that?

LAURA: I was out of school a little while with pleurosis. When I came back you asked me what was the matter. I said I had pleurosis—you thought I said Blue Roses. That's what you always called me after that!

JIM: I hope you didn't mind.

LAURA: Oh, no—I liked it. You see, I wasn't acquainted with many—people. . . .

JIM: As I remember you sort of stuck by yourself.

LAURA: I—I—never have had much luck at—making friends.

JIM: I don't see why you wouldn't.

LAURA: Well, I—started out badly.

JIM: You mean being—

LAURA: Yes, it sort of—stood between me—

JIM: You shouldn't have let it!

LAURA: I know, but it did, and—

JIM: You were shy with people!

LAURA: I tried not to be but never could—

JIM: Overcome it?

LAURA: No, I—I never could!

JIM: I guess being shy is something you have to work out of kind of gradually.

LAURA (*sorrowfully*): Yes—I guess it—

JIM: Takes time!

LAURA: Yes—

JIM: People are not so dreadful when you know them. That's what you have to remember! And everybody has problems, not just you, but practically everybody has got some problems. You think of yourself as having the only problems, as being the only one who is disappointed. But just look around you and you will see lots of people as disappointed as you are. For instance, I hoped when I was going to high school that I would be further along at this time, six years later, than I am now—You remember that wonderful write-up I had in *The Torch?*

LAURA: Yes! (*She rises and crosses to table.*)

JIM: It said I was bound to succeed in anything I went into! (LAURA *returns with the annual.*) Holy Jeez! *The Torch!* (*He accepts it reverently. They smile across it with mutual wonder.* LAURA *crouches beside him and they begin to turn through it.* LAURA's *shyness is dissolving in his warmth.*)

LAURA: Here you are in *The Pirates of Penzance!*

JIM (*wistfully*): I sang the baritone lead in that operetta.

LAURA (*raptly*): So—*beautifully!*

JIM (*protesting*): Aw—

LAURA: Yes, yes—beautifully—beautifully!

JIM: You heard me?

LAURA: All three times!

JIM: No!

LAURA: Yes!

JIM: All three performances?

LAURA (*looking down*): Yes.

JIM: Why?

LAURA: I—wanted to ask you to—autograph my program.

JIM: Why didn't you ask me to?

LAURA: You were always surrounded by your own friends so much that I never had a chance to.

JIM: You should have just—

LAURA: Well, I—thought you might think I was—

JIM: Thought I might think you was—what?

LAURA: Oh—

JIM (*with reflective relish*): I was beleaguered by females in those days.

LAURA: You were terribly popular!

JIM: Yeah—

LAURA: You had such a—friendly way—

JIM: I was spoiled in high school.

LAURA: Everybody—liked you!

JIM: Including you?

LAURA: I—yes, I—I did, too—(*She gently closes the book in her lap.*)

JIM: Well, well, well!—Give me that program, Laura. (*She hands it to him. He signs it with a flourish.*) There you are—better late than never!

LAURA: Oh, I—what a—surprise!

JIM: My signature isn't worth very much right now. But some day—maybe—it will increase in value! Being disappointed is one thing and being discouraged is something else. I am disappointed but I am not discouraged. I'm twenty-three years old. How old are you?

LAURA: I'll be twenty-four in June.

JIM: That's not old age!

LAURA: No, but—

JIM: You finished high school?

LAURA (*with difficulty*): I didn't go back.

JIM: You mean you dropped out?

LAURA: I made bad grades in my final examinations. (*She rises and replaces the book and the program. Her voice strained.*) How is—Emily Meisenbach getting along?

JIM: Oh, that kraut-head!

LAURA: Why do you call her that?

JIM: That's what she was.

LAURA: You're not still—going with her?

JIM: I never see her.

LAURA: It said in the Personal Section that you were—engaged!

JIM: I know, but I wasn't impressed by that—propaganda!

LAURA: It wasn't—the truth?

JIM: Only in Emily's optimistic opinion!

LAURA: Oh—

> (*Legend: "What Have You Done Since High School?"*)
> JIM *lights a cigarette and leans indolently back on his elbows smiling at* LAURA *with a warmth and charm which lights her inwardly with altar candles. She remains by the table and turns in her hands a piece of glass to cover her tumult.*

JIM (*after several reflective puffs on a cigarette*): What have you done since high school? (*She seems not to hear him.*) Huh? (LAURA *looks up.*) I said what have you done since high school, Laura?

LAURA: Nothing much.

JIM: You must have been doing something these six long years.

LAURA: Yes.

JIM: Well, then, such as what?

LAURA: I took a business course at business college—

JIM: How did that work out?

LAURA: Well, not very—well—I had to drop out, it gave me—indigestion—

JIM *laughs gently.*

JIM: What are you doing now?

LAURA: I don't do anything—much. Oh, please don't think I sit around doing nothing! My glass collection takes up a good deal of time. Glass is something you have to take good care of.

JIM: What did you say—about glass?

LAURA: Collection I said—I have one—(*She clears her throat and turns away again, acutely shy.*)

JIM (*abruptly*): You know what I judge to be the trouble with you? Inferiority complex! Know what that is? That's what they call it when someone low-rates himself! I understand it because I had it, too. Although my case was not so aggravated as yours seems to be. I had it until I took up public speaking, developed my voice, and learned that I had an aptitude for science. Before that time I never thought of myself as being outstanding in any way whatsoever! Now I've never made a regular study of it, but I have a friend who says I can analyze people better than doctors that make a profession of it. I don't claim that to be necessarily true, but I can sure guess a person's psychology, Laura! (*takes out his gum*) Excuse me, Laura. I always take it out when the flavor is gone. I'll use this scrap of paper to wrap it in. I know how it is to get it stuck on a shoe. Yep—that's what I judge to be your principal trouble. A lack of confidence in yourself as a person. You don't have the proper amount of faith in yourself. I'm basing that fact on a number of your remarks and also on certain observations I've made. For instance that clumping you thought was so awful in high school. You say that you even dreaded to walk into class. You see what you did? You dropped out of school, you gave up an education because of a clump, which as far as I know was practically nonexistent! A little physical defect is what you have. Hardly noticeable even! Magnified thousands of times by imagination! You know what my strong advice to you is? Think of yourself as *superior* in some way!

LAURA: In what way would I think?

JIM: Why, man alive, Laura! Just look about you a little. What do you see? A world full of common people! All of 'em born and all of 'em going to die! Which of them has one-tenth of your good points! Or mine! Or anyone else's, as far as that goes—Gosh! Everybody excels in some one thing. Some in many! (*unconsciously glances at himself in the mirror*) All you've got to do is discover in *what!* Take me, for instance. (*He adjusts his tie at the mirror.*) My interest happens to lie in electrodynamics. I'm taking a course in radio engineering at night school, Laura, on top of a fairly responsible job at the warehouse. I'm taking that course and studying public speaking.

LAURA: Ohhhh.

JIM: Because I believe in the future of television! (*turning back to her*) I wish to be ready to go up right along with it. Therefore I'm planning to get in on the ground floor. In fact I've already made the right connections and all that remains is for the industry itself to get under way! Full steam— (*His eyes are starry.*) *Knowledge*—zzzzzp! *Money*—zzzzzzp!—*Power!* That's the cycle democracy is built on! (*His attitude is convincingly dynamic.* LAURA *stares at him, even her shyness eclipsed in her absolute wonder. He suddenly grins.*) I guess you think I think a lot of myself!

LAURA: No—o-o-o, I—

JIM: Now how about you? Isn't there something you take more interest in than anything else?

LAURA: Well, I do—as I said—have my—glass collection—

A peal of girlish laughter from the kitchen.

JIM: I'm not right sure I know what you're talking about. What kind of glass is it?

LAURA: Little articles of it, they're ornaments mostly! Most of them are little animals made out of glass, the tiniest little animals in the world. Mother calls them a glass menagerie! Here's an example of one, if you'd like to see it! This one is one of the oldest. It's nearly thirteen. (*Music: "The Glass Menagerie."*) (*He stretches out his hand.*) Oh, be careful—if you breathe, it breaks!

JIM: I'd better not take it. I'm pretty clumsy with things.

LAURA: Go on, I trust you with him! (*places it in his palm*) There now— you're holding him gently! Hold him over the light, he loves the light! You see how the light shines through him?

JIM: It sure does shine!

LAURA: I shouldn't be partial, but he is my favorite one.

JIM: What kind of a thing is this one supposed to be?

LAURA: Haven't you noticed the single horn on his forehead?

JIM: A unicorn, huh?

LAURA: Mmm-hmmm!

JIM: Unicorns, aren't they extinct in the modern world?

LAURA: I know!

JIM: Poor little fellow, he must feel sort of lonesome.

LAURA (*smiling*): Well, if he does he doesn't complain about it. He stays on a shelf with some horses that don't have horns and all of them seem to get along nicely together.

JIM: How do you know?

LAURA (*lightly*): I haven't heard any arguments among them!

JIM (*grinning*): No arguments, huh? Well, that's a pretty good sign! Where shall I set him?

LAURA: Put him on the table. They all like a change of scenery once in a while!

JIM (*stretching*): Well, well, well, well—Look how big my shadow is when I stretch!

LAURA: Oh, oh, yes—it stretches across the ceiling!

JIM (*crossing to door*): I think it's stopped raining. (*opens fire-escape door*) Where does the music come from?

LAURA: From the Paradise Dance Hall across the alley.

JIM: How about cutting the rug a little, Miss Wingfield?

LAURA: Oh, I—

JIM: Or is your program filled up? Let me have a look at it. (*grasps imaginary card*) Why, every dance is taken! I'll just have to scratch some out. (*Waltz music: "La Colondrina."*) Ahhh, a waltz! (*He executes some sweeping turns by himself then holds his arms toward* LAURA.)

LAURA (*breathlessly*): I—can't dance!

JIM: There you go, that inferiority stuff!

LAURA: I've never danced in my life!

JIM: Come on, try!

LAURA: Oh, but I'd step on you!

JIM: I'm not made out of glass.

LAURA: How—how—how do we start?

JIM: Just leave it to me. You hold your arms out a little.

LAURA: Like this?

JIM: A little bit higher. Right. Now don't tighten up, that's the main thing about it—relax.

LAURA (*laughing breathlessly*): It's hard not to.

JIM: Okay.

LAURA: I'm afraid you can't budge me.

JIM: What do you bet I can't? (*He swings her into motion.*)

LAURA: Goodness, yes, you can!

JIM: Let yourself go, now, Laura, just let yourself go.

LAURA: I'm—

JIM: Come on!

LAURA: Trying!

JIM: Not so stiff—Easy does it!

LAURA: I know but I'm—

JIM: Loosen th' backbone! There now, that's a lot better.

LAURA: Am I?

JIM: Lots, lots better! (*He moves her about the room in a clumsy waltz.*)

LAURA: Oh, my!

JIM: Ha-ha!

LAURA: Oh, my goodness!

JIM: Ha-ha-ha! (*They suddenly bump into the table.* JIM *stops.*) What did we hit on?

LAURA: Table.

JIM: Did something fall off it? I think—

LAURA: Yes.

JIM: I hope that it wasn't the little glass horse with the horn!

LAURA: Yes.

JIM: Aw, aw, aw. Is it broken?

LAURA: Now it is just like all the other horses.

JIM: It's lost its—

LAURA: Horn! It doesn't matter. Maybe it's a blessing in disguise.

JIM: You'll never forgive me. I bet that was your favorite piece of glass.

LAURA: I don't have favorites much. It's no tragedy, Freckles. Glass breaks so easily. No matter how careful you are. The traffic jars the shelves and things fall off them.

JIM: Still I'm awfully sorry that I was the cause.

LAURA (*smiling*): I'll just imagine he had an operation. The horn was removed to make him feel less—freakish! (*They both laugh.*) Now he will feel more at home with the other horses, the ones that don't have horns. . . .

JIM: Ha-ha, that's very funny! (*suddenly serious*) I'm glad to see that you have a sense of humor. You know—you're—well—very different! Surprisingly different from anyone else I know! (*His voice becomes soft and hesitant with a genuine feeling.*) Do you mind me telling you that? (LAURA *is abashed beyond speech.*) I mean it in a nice way . . . (LAURA *nods shyly, looking away.*) You make me feel sort of—I don't know how to put it! I'm usually pretty good at expressing things, but—This is something that I don't know how to say! (LAURA *touches her throat and clears it—turns the broken unicorn in her hands.*) (*even softer*) Has anyone ever told you that you were pretty? (*Pause: Music.*) (LAURA *looks up slowly, with wonder, and shakes her head.*) Well, you are! In a very different way from anyone else. And all the nicer because of the difference, too. (*His voice becomes low and husky.* LAURA *turns away, nearly faint with the novelty of her emotions.*) I wish that you were my sister. I'd teach you to have some confidence in yourself. The different people are not like other people, but being different is nothing to be ashamed of. Because other people are not such wonderful people. They're one hundred times one thousand. You're one times one! They walk all over the earth. You just stay here. They're common as—weeds, but—you—well, you're—*Blue Roses!*

(*Image on screen: Blue roses.*)
(*Music changes.*)

LAURA: But blue is wrong for—roses . . .

JIM: It's right for you!—You're—pretty!

LAURA: In what respect am I pretty?

JIM: In all respects—believe me! Your eyes—your hair—are pretty! Your hands are pretty! (*He catches hold of her hand.*) You think I'm making this up because I'm invited to dinner and have to be nice. Oh, I could do that! I could put on an act for you, Laura, and say lots of things without being very sincere. But this time I am. I'm talking to you sincerely. I happened to notice you had this inferiority complex that keeps you from feeling comfortable with people. Somebody needs to build your confidence up and make you proud instead of shy and turning away and—blushing—Somebody—ought to—Ought to—*kiss* you, Laura! (*His hand slips slowly up her arm to her shoulder.*) (*Music swells tumultuously.*) (*He suddenly turns her about and kisses her on the lips. When he releases her,* LAURA *sinks on the sofa with a bright, dazed look.* JIM *backs away and fishes in his pocket for a cigarette.*) (*Legend on screen: "Souvenir."*) Stumble-john! (*He lights the cigarette, avoiding her look. There is a peal of girlish laughter from* AMANDA *in the kitchen.* LAURA *slowly raises and opens her hand. It still contains the little broken glass animal. She looks at it with a tender, bewildered expression.*) Stumble-john! I shouldn't have done that—That was way off the beam. You don't smoke, do you? (*She looks up, smiling, not hearing the question. He sits beside her a little gingerly.*

She looks at him speechlessly—waiting. He coughs decorously and moves a little farther aside as he considers the situation and senses her feelings, dimly, with perturbation.) (gently) Would you—care for a—mint? *(She doesn't seem to hear him but her look grows brighter even.)* Peppermint—LifeSaver? My pocket's a regular drug store—wherever I go . . . *(He pops a mint in his mouth. Then gulps and decides to make a clean breast of it. He speaks slowly and gingerly.)* Laura, you know, if I had a sister like you, I'd do the same thing as Tom. I'd bring out fellows and—introduce her to them. The right type of boys of a type to—appreciate her. Only—well—he made a mistake about me. Maybe I've got no call to be saying this. That may not have been the idea in having me over. But what if it was? There's nothing wrong about that. The only trouble is that in my case—I'm not in a situation to—do the right thing. I can't take down your number and say I'll phone. I can't call up next week and—ask for a date. I thought I had better explain the situation in case you—misunderstood it and—hurt your feelings. . . . *(pause) (Slowly, very slowly,* LAURA'S *look changes, her eyes returning slowly from his to the ornament in her palm.)* *(*AMANDA *utters another gay laugh in the kitchen.)*

LAURA *(faintly)*: You—won't—call again?

JIM: No, Laura, I can't. *(He rises from the sofa.)* As I was just explaining, I've—got strings on me. Laura, I've—been going steady! I go out all of the time with a girl named Betty. She's a home-girl like you, and Catholic, and Irish, and in a great many ways we—get along fine. I met her last summer on a moonlight boat trip up the river to Alton, on the *Majestic*. Well—right away from the start it was—love! *(Legend: Love!)* *(*LAURA *sways slightly forward and grips the arm of the sofa. He fails to notice, now enrapt in his own comfortable being.)* Being in love has made a new man of me! *(Leaning stiffly forward, clutching the arm of the sofa,* LAURA *struggles visibly with her storm. But* JIM *is oblivious, she is a long way off.)* The power of love is really pretty tremendous! Love is something that—changes the whole world, Laura! *(The storm abates a little and* LAURA *leans back. He notices her again.)* It happened that Betty's aunt took sick, she got a wire and had to go to Centralia. So Tom—when he asked me to dinner—I naturally just accepted the invitation, not knowing that you—that he—that I— *(He stops awkwardly.)* Huh—I'm a stumble-john! *(He flops back on the sofa.)* *(The holy candles in the altar of* LAURA'S *face have been snuffed out. There is a look of almost infinite desolation.)* *(*JIM *glances at her uneasily.)* I wish that you would—say something. *(She bites her lip which was trembling and then bravely smiles. She opens her hand again on the broken glass ornament. Then she gently takes his hand and raises it level with her own. She carefully places the unicorn in the palm of his hand, then pushes his fingers closed upon it.)* What are you—doing that for? You want me to have him?—Laura? *(She nods.)* What for?

LAURA: A—souvenir . . .

She rises unsteadily and crouches beside the victrola to wind it up.
   (Legend on screen: "Things Have a Way of Turning Out So Badly!")
   (Or image: "Gentleman Caller Waving Good-bye!—Gaily.")

At this moment AMANDA *rushes brightly back in the front room. She bears a pitcher of fruit punch in an old-fashioned cut-glass pitcher and a plate of macaroons. The plate has a gold border and poppies painted on it.*

AMANDA: Well, well, well! Isn't the air delightful after the shower? I've made you children a little liquid refreshment. (*turns gaily to the gentleman caller*) Jim, do you know that song about lemonade?
  "Lemonade, lemonade
  Made in the shade and stirred with a spade—
  Good enough for any old maid!"

JIM (*uneasily*): Ha-ha! No—I never heard it.

AMANDA: Why, Laura! You look so serious!

JIM: We were having a serious conversation.

AMANDA: Good! Now you're better acquainted!

JIM (*uncertainly*): Ha-ha! Yes.

AMANDA: You modern young people are much more serious-minded than my generation. I was so gay as a girl!

JIM: You haven't changed, Mrs. Wingfield.

AMANDA: Tonight I'm rejuvenated! The gaiety of the occasion, Mr. O'Connor! (*She tosses her head with a peal of laughter. Spills lemonade.*) Oooo! I'm baptizing myself!

JIM: Here—let me—

AMANDA (*setting the pitcher down*): There now. I discovered we had some maraschino cherries. I dumped them in, juice and all!

JIM: You shouldn't have gone to that trouble, Mrs. Wingfield.

AMANDA: Trouble, trouble? Why, it was loads of fun! Didn't you hear me cutting up in the kitchen? I bet your ears were burning! I told Tom how outdone with him I was for keeping you to himself so long a time! He should have brought you over much, much sooner! Well, now that you've found your way, I want you to be a very frequent caller! Not just occasional but all the time. Oh, we're going to have a lot of gay times together! I see them coming! Mmm, just breathe that air! So fresh, and the moon's so pretty! I'll skip back out—I know where my place is when young folks are having a—serious conversation!

JIM: Oh, don't go out, Mrs. Wingfield. The fact of the matter is I've got to be going.

AMANDA: Going, now? You're joking! Why, it's only the shank of the evening, Mr. O'Connor!

JIM: Well, you know how it is.

AMANDA: You mean you're a young workingman and have to keep workingmen's hours. We'll let you off early tonight. But only on the condition that next time you stay later. What's the best night for you? Isn't Saturday night the best night for you workingmen?

JIM: I have a couple of time-clocks to punch, Mrs. Wingfield. One at morning, another one at night!

AMANDA: My, but you *are* ambitious! You work at night, too?

JIM: No, Ma'am, not work but—Betty! (*He crosses deliberately to pick up his hat. The band at the Paradise Dance Hall goes into a tender waltz.*)

AMANDA: Betty? Betty? Who's—Betty! (*There is an ominous cracking sound in the sky.*)

JIM: Oh, just a girl. The girl I go steady with! (*He smiles charmingly. The sky falls.*)

(*Legend: "The Sky Falls."*)

AMANDA (*a long-drawn exhalation*): Ohhhh . . . Is it a serious romance, Mr. O'Connor?

JIM: We're going to be married the second Sunday in June.

AMANDA: Ohhhh—how nice! Tom didn't mention that you were engaged to be married.

JIM: The cat's not out of the bag at the warehouse yet. You know how they are. They call you Romeo and stuff like that. (*He stops at the oval mirror to put on his hat. He carefully shapes the brim and the crown to give a discreetly dashing effect.*) It's been a wonderful evening, Mrs. Wingfield. I guess this is what they mean by Southern hospitality.

AMANDA: It really wasn't anything at all.

JIM: I hope it don't seem like I'm rushing off. But I promised Betty I'd pick her up at the Wabash depot, an' by the time I get my jalopy down there her train'll be in. Some women are pretty upset if you keep 'em waiting.

AMANDA: Yes, I know—The tyranny of women! (*extends her hand*) Good-bye, Mr. O'Connor. I wish you luck—and happiness—and success! All three of them, and so does Laura!—Don't you, Laura?

LAURA: Yes!

JIM (*taking her hand*): Good-bye, Laura. I'm certainly going to treasure that souvenir. And don't you forget the good advice I gave you. (*raises his voice to a cheery shout*) So long, Shakespeare! Thanks again, ladies—Good night!

He grins and ducks jauntily out.

Still bravely grimacing, AMANDA *closes the door on the gentleman caller. Then she turns back to the room with a puzzled expression. She and* LAURA *don't dare to face each other.* LAURA *crouches beside the victrola to wind it.*

AMANDA (*faintly*): Things have a way of turning out so badly. I don't believe that I would play the victrola. Well, well—well—Our gentleman caller was engaged to be married! Tom!

TOM (*from back*): Yes, Mother?

AMANDA: Come in here a minute. I want to tell you something awfully funny.

TOM (*enters with macaroon and a glass of the lemonade*): Has the gentleman caller gotten away already?

AMANDA: The gentleman caller has made an early departure. What a wonderful joke you played on us!

TOM: How do you mean?

AMANDA: You didn't mention that he was engaged to be married.

TOM: Jim? Engaged?

AMANDA: That's what he just informed us.

TOM: I'll be jiggered! I didn't know about that.

AMANDA: That seems very peculiar.

TOM: What's peculiar about it?

AMANDA: Didn't you call him your best friend down at the warehouse?

TOM: He is, but how did I know?

AMANDA: It seems extremely peculiar that you wouldn't know your best friend was going to be married!

TOM: The warehouse is where I work, not where I know things about people!

AMANDA: You don't know things anywhere! You live in a dream; you manufacture illusions! (*He crosses to door.*) Where are you going?

TOM: I'm going to the movies.

AMANDA: That's right, now that you've had us make such fools of ourselves. The effort, the preparations, all the expense! The new floor lamp, the rug, the clothes for Laura! All for what? To entertain some other girl's fiancé! Go to the movies, go! Don't think about us, a mother deserted, an unmarried sister who's crippled and has no job! Don't let anything interfere with your selfish pleasure! Just go, go, go—to the movies!

TOM: All right, I will! The more you shout about my selfishness to me the quicker I'll go, and I won't go to the movies!

AMANDA: Go, then! Then go to the moon—you selfish dreamer!

> TOM *smashes his glass on the floor. He plunges out on the fire-escape, slamming the door.* LAURA *screams—cut by door.*
>
> *Dance-hall music up.* TOM *goes to the rail and grips it desperately, lifting his face in the chill white moonlight penetrating the narrow abyss of the alley.*
>
> (*Legend on screen: "And So Good-bye . . ."*)
>
> TOM'S *closing speech is timed with the interior pantomime. The interior scene is played as though viewed through soundproof glass.* AMANDA *appears to be making a comforting speech to* LAURA *who is huddled upon the sofa. Now that we cannot hear the mother's speech, her silliness is gone and she has dignity and tragic beauty.* LAURA'S *dark hair hides her face until at the end of the speech she lifts it to smile at her mother.* AMANDA'S *gestures are slow and graceful, almost dancelike, as she comforts the daughter. At the end of her speech she glances a moment at the father's picture—then withdraws through the portieres. At close of* TOM'S *speech,* LAURA *blows out the candles, ending the play.*)

TOM: I didn't go to the moon, I went much further—for time is the longest distance between two places—Not long after that I was fired for writing a poem on the lid of a shoe-box. I left Saint Louis. I descended the steps of this fire-escape for a last time and followed, from then on, in my father's footsteps, attempting to find in motion what was lost in space— I traveled around a great deal. The cities swept about me like dead leaves, leaves that were brightly colored but torn away from the branches. I would have stopped, but I was pursued by something. It always came upon me unawares, taking me altogether by surprise. Perhaps it was a familiar bit of music. Perhaps it was only a piece of transparent glass— Perhaps I am walking along a street at night, in some strange city, before I have found companions. I pass the lighted window of a shop where perfume is sold. The window is filled with pieces of colored glass, tiny transparent bottles in delicate colors, like bits of a shattered rainbow. Then all at once my sister touches my shoulder. I turn around and look into her eyes . . . Oh, Laura, Laura, I tried to leave you behind me, but I am more faithful than I intended to be! I reach for a cigarette, I cross the street, I run into the movies or a bar, I buy a drink, I speak to the nearest stranger—anything that can blow your candles out! (LAURA *bends over the candles.*)—for nowadays the world is lit by lightning! Blow out your candles, Laura—and so goodbye . . . (*She blows the candles out.*)

(*The scene dissolves.*)

The Receptive Reader

1. What is the difference between a stereotype and an archetype? Is Amanda the stereotpye of the southern belle? Is she the archetype of the fading beauty? Is the playwright's portrayal of Amanda cruel?

2. Is Tom an archetypal representative of adolescent rebellion?

3. Symbols are plentiful in this play. What about the typewriter? Could Laura have been taking harpsichord lessons instead of typing lessons? What is significant about the victrola? the glass animals Laura collects? the unicorn and the loss of its horn?

4. The play of light and darkness becomes a recurrent symbolic pattern in the play. (The lights go out because Tom has not paid the electric bill; Amanda "brightens" and darkens; it is a world of "the blind"; Laura "blows the candles out.") Look for other passages that reflect not only literal darkness but also the darkness of extinguished hopes.

5. Tennessee Williams crafted his plays carefully, with much connection between and echoing of images, phrases, symbols, and other elements. With a classmate or in a small group, trace one continuing strand that helps braid all or part of the play into a cohesive whole. Share your findings with the class.

6. If Laura's escape is her glass menagerie, what is Tom's escape? What is Amanda's? How successful are they?

7. What is the role of Laura's physical disability in the play? To what extent is it symbolic?

The Whole Play—For Discussion or Writing

Traditionally, critics have used the term **pathos** instead of *tragedy* when a central character in a play is an example of passive suffering. To you, is Laura a tragic character or merely pathetic?

Biographies of Poets

Maya Angelou   (born 1928) is an autobiographer, poet, playwright, composer, screen and stage producer, performer, and singer. She wrote and read the poem "On the Pulse of Morning" at President Bill Clinton's inauguration in 1993. Of her several autobiographies, *I Know Why the Caged Bird Sings* (1969) is her best known. Of Angelou's first collection of poetry, *I Shall Not Be Moved* (1990), Gloria Hull writes: "As I listen, what I hear in her open colloquial poems is racial wit and earthy wisdom, honest black female pain and strength, humor, passion, and rhetorical force."

Matthew Arnold   (1822–1888)—English critic, educator, and poet—graduated from Oxford and served as inspector of the British schools for most of his life. As a poet, Arnold was inspired by Greek tragedies, Keats, and Wordsworth. In 1857 he began to teach poetry at Oxford and to publish numerous books of literary criticism. In much of his writing, Arnold took the position of the agnostic unable to accept traditional faith, wishing to replace doctrines that had become doubtful with great literature as a source of inspiration and moral guidance. His prose writings helped define the nineteenth-century ideal of high culture, which he saw as a synthesis of Judeo-Christian ethics and the classical dedication to reason and form.

Margaret Atwood   (born 1939) has said, "My life really has been writing since the age of sixteen; all other decisions I made were determined by that fact." Born in Ottawa, Canada, Atwood resides in Toronto but has lived all over Canada as well as in the United States and England. She studied at the University of Toronto and Harvard, and has taught and lectured widely. In addition to two collections of short stories and seven volumes of poetry, Atwood has published six novels, including *The Edible Woman* (1969), *Cat's Eye* (1989), *The Robber Bride* (1993), and *Alias Grace* (1996). Her chilling portrayal of a nightmarish dystopian future, *The Handmaid's Tale* (1985), won a *Los Angeles Times* award for best

1161

fiction and was made into a movie. A feminist, Atwood explains that she had confronted issues related to growing up female and sex-role changes long before they were popularized by the women's movement.

W. H. Auden (1907–1973) was well versed in science, history, politics, philosophy, psychology, art, music, and literature. As a result his poetry "is full of knowledge and wisdom and ideas" (Kenneth Koch). Wystan Hugh Auden believed that "living is always thinking." Born in the ancient city of York, he graduated from Oxford University and became an important voice for the radical criticism of established society by the Marxist left. After serving on the Loyalist side of the Spanish Civil War, he emigrated to America in 1939 and became a U.S. citizen. His first collection of poetry, *Poems,* appeared in 1930. In 1948 he won the Pulitzer Prize for his collection *The Age of Anxiety,* an expression he coined to describe the 1930s. Auden saw poetry "as a game of knowledge, a bringing to consciousness, by naming them, of emotions and their hidden relationships."

Wendell Berry (born 1934) is a poet, novelist, and essayist who was educated at the University of Kentucky, where he also has taught for many years. Although Berry deals primarily with Kentucky and its people, "one would be hard-pressed to dismiss him as a mere regionalist. . . . his work is rooted in the land and in the values of an older America" (Jonathan Yardly). Among his many titles are *The Broken Ground* (1964), *Findings* (1969), *To What Listens* (1975), and *Clearing* (1977). About the archetypal nature of poetry and song, Berry writes: "Song is natural; we have it in common with animals. . . . The rhythm of a song or a poem rises, no doubt, in reference to the pulse and breath of the poet . . . [but] it rises also in reference to daily and seasonal—and surely even longer—rhythms in the life of the poet and in the life that surrounds him. . . . Song, then, is the testimony of the singer's inescapable relation to the world, to the human community, and also to tradition."

Elizabeth Bishop (1911–1979), who said, "There's nothing more embarrassing than being a poet," was born in Massachusetts. Only four years old when her father died, she was taken to live with her grandmother after her mother suffered a mental breakdown. After graduating from Vassar, Bishop planned to enter Cornell Medical School, but poet Marianne Moore persuaded her to become a writer. She served as a poetry consultant to the Library of Congress (1949–1950) and taught poetry writing at Harvard. She received numerous awards, including a Pulitzer Prize (1956). Bishop's poetry has been called "both precise and suggestive . . . fantastic yet fanciful" (Louis Untermeyer).

William Blake (1757–1827), a forerunner of the English Romantic movement, "could transmit his basic consciousness and communicate it to somebody else after he was dead—in other words, build a time machine," said poet Allen Ginsberg. Born in London, Blake was apprenticed at the age of fourteen to an engraver; his engravings illustrated many popular books of his day as well as his own poems. He began to write his richly symbolic, mystical poetry in his youth, and with the financial assistance of his friends published his first collection of poems, *Poetical Sketches,* in 1783. However, efforts to find a publisher for his second manuscript, *Songs of Innocence,* were unsuccessful. The last twenty-five years of his life were marked by extreme poverty; it remained for later audiences to appreciate the complex symbolism of his mystical, enigmatic poetry.

Louise Bogan   (1897–1970), born in Livermore Falls, Maine, was educated at Boston University. She served as consultant in poetry to the Library of Congress, taught at a number of universities in the United States and Austria, and served for over twenty years as a poetry critic for the *New Yorker.* Her books of poetry include *Body of This Death* (1923), *Dark Summer, The Blue Estuaries,* and *Collected Poems, 1923–1953* (1954), which won the Bollingen Prize in poetry.

Anne Bradstreet   (about 1612–1672), author of the first volume of original poetry written in the British colonies of North America, had sailed for America from her native England after marrying at the age of sixteen. Her father, Thomas Dudley, became a governor of the Massachusetts Bay Colony, as did her husband, Simon Bradstreet. The mother of eight children, Bradstreet also wrote an autobiography entitled *Religious Experiences.*

Gwendolyn Brooks   (born 1917) was the first African American woman to achieve widespread critical acclaim as a poet. Brooks began writing poetry as a child in Chicago and had her first poem published at age ten in a children's magazine. In high school, she saw several of her poems published in *Defender,* a Chicago newspaper. In the early 1940s she won prizes for her poetry and published her first poetry collection in 1945. The first African American woman to be so honored, Brooks won a Pulitzer Prize for poetry in 1950 for her second collection, *Annie Allen.* Other works include *The Bean Eaters* (1960), *In the Mecca* (1980), and *To Disembark* (1981). Not only a major force in the movement to define black identity and to foster black pride, she has also been poet laureate for the state of Illinois and poetry consultant to the Library of Congress. In 1989 she received the National Endowment for the Arts Lifetime Achievement Award, and in 1990 became the only American to receive, from the University of Thessaloniki, Greece, the Society for Literature Award.

Elizabeth Barrett Browning   (1806–1861), who wrote that "grief may be joy misunderstood," had a difficult young life. Born into a well-to-do family in Durham, England, as the oldest of eleven children, Barrett was reading Greek at the age of eight and writing poems that imitated her favorite authors. At fifteen she suffered a spinal injury when she fell from a pony and was a partial invalid when she met the poet Robert Browning in 1845. The two fell in love immediately, but she had to elope to escape from her obsessively jealous father. Because of her health, the couple went to live in Italy. Her most famous collection, *Sonnets from the Portuguese,* love poems written to her husband, was published in 1850.

Robert Browning   (1812–1889) was born in Camberwall, England. He decided to become a poet at age seventeen and after setbacks became one of the best known and most influential poet-sages of Victorian England. He was still receiving financial support from his family when in 1845 he met and fell in love with Elizabeth Barrett, one of the leading poets of the day. *The Ring and the Book,* a series of dramatic monologues based on a seventeenth-century murder, appeared in 1869 and finally brought him popular acclaim. His metrically rough and intellectually challenging poetry secured him a following of dedicated admirers; Browning Societies survive to this day.

Robert Burns   (1759–1796)—born in a small cottage in Alloway, Scotland, to a family of poor tenant farmers—knew poverty and exploitation firsthand. He was steeped in the traditional ballads and songs of his country, and he became for the Romantic poets the embodiment of untutored, spontaneous, original genius throwing off artificial conventions. After years of trying unsuccessfully to earn a living as a farmer, he was offered a job as an overseer in Jamaica. To pay for his passage, he published in 1786 a collection of poems and songs entitled *Poems Chiefly in the Scottish Dialect.* Because of its tremendous success, he was able to give up his Jamaica project. Like the Romantic poets after him, he was fired with generous enthusiasm for the aims of the French Revolution, envisioning a world in which the aristocracy would be swept away and brotherhood and human dignity would prevail.

Lorna Dee Cervantes   (born 1954) discovered the world of books in the homes that her mother cleaned. "We were so poor . . . We were brilliant at wishing," she wrote in her poem "To My Brother." Born in San Francisco of Mexican descent, Cervantes published her first poetry collection, *Emplumada,* in 1981. Educated at San José State University, she is the founder of Mango Publications, a small press that publishes books and a literary magazine.

Lucille Clifton   (born 1936) has said, "I am a Black woman poet, and I sound like one." Born in Depew, New York, and educated at Howard University, Clifton has taught at several colleges, worked as a claims clerk in the New York State Division of Employment, and was a literature assistant in the Office of Education in Washington, D.C. Her first collection of poetry, *Good Times,* was selected as one of the ten best books of 1969 by the *New York Times.* Among her awards are the University of Massachusetts Press Juniper Prize for Poetry, an Emmy Award, and creative writing fellowships from the National Endowment for the Arts. In 1979 she was named Maryland's poet laureate.

Juana Inés de la Cruz   (1651–1695) was a childhood prodigy, learning to read at age three and primarily educating herself. Renowned for her intelligence, beauty, wit, and learning, she served as a lady-in-waiting at the New Spanish court and later retired to become a nun, insisting that only monastic life gave her the chance to carry on her intellectual pursuits. In addition to writing poetry she studied literature, history, music, science, and theology. She became known as the Tenth Muse. She wrote a letter considered "a defining work in feminist literature" when authorities of the Catholic Church disapproved of her studies, and she pleaded for equal educational opportunities for women.

Countee Cullen   (1903–1946) was a moving force in the Harlem Renaissance of the 1920s and 1930s, which made the work of poets like Claude McKay, Langston Hughes, and Helene Johnson known to a large public. Cullen's poetry, traditional in form, deals memorably with the joys and sorrows of African Americans. Born and raised in New York City, Cullen graduated from New York University in 1925 and received a master's degree from Harvard the following year. His first three collections of poetry—*Color, Copper Sun,* and *The Ballad of a Brown Girl*—were published in the mid-1920s. His only novel, *One Way to Heaven,* a description of life in Harlem, appeared in 1932. A selection of his own favorite poems, *On These I Stand,* appeared a year after his death.

e. e. cummings   (1894–1962) believed that "poetry is being, not doing." One of the most provocative and unconventional of modern poets, cummings was born in Cambridge, Massachusetts, and educated at Harvard. During World War I, he served as a volunteer ambulance driver and was held briefly as a prisoner of war. After the war he spent several years in Paris, studying art. A talented painter, he often exhibited his artwork. His first volume of poetry, *Tulips and Chimneys* (1923), was both criticized and praised for its unusual use of language and punctuation, which is reflected in the unorthodox use of lowercase letters in his name. "The effect of this experimentation is not to take the meaning away but to add or emphasize a certain kind of meaning. His way of writing seems to call attention to the sense of each word, so that each word counts and is important in the poem" (Kenneth Koch). The centennial edition of his *Complete Poems: 1904–1962* (1994) is part of an ongoing reassessment of cummings' contribution to literature. Writes George J. Firmage, "Combining Thoreau's controlled belligerence with the brash abandon of an uninhibited Bohemian, cummings, together with Pound,

Eliot, and William Carlos Williams, helped bring about the twentieth-century revolution in literary expression." Richard Kostelanetz considers him "the major American poet of the middle-twentieth century."

Reuel Denney   (born 1913) has said, "When I learned to write, I chalked criticisms of the household on the tile entry of the house. For example, slogans taken from fairy tales such as the Little Tailor's lampoon against the castle holding him prison: 'Too much potatoes and not enuff meat.' Instead of being told that some children somewhere in the world didn't even have potatoes . . . I was praised for my literacy. This was the start of my writing, but I was not published until later, at sixteen or so." Born in New York, Denney was educated at Dartmouth. He lives in Honolulu, Hawaii, where he writes "for three to fifteen hours a week."

Countess of Dia   (born about 1140) was one of the women troubadours of the Provençal courts in southern France, who provided counterpoint to the usually male-oriented tradition of courtly love.

Emily Dickinson   (1830–1886) is now considered one of the greatest American poets, but only a few of her poems were published—and those in edited and conventionalized versions—in her lifetime. After attending Amherst Academy and spending a year in a female seminary, she spent her life and died in the same house in Amherst, Massachusetts. In 1862, she wrote to Thomas Wentworth Higginson, editor of the *Atlantic* magazine, enclosing some poems and asking his opinion. Unable to deal with her strange, provocative poetry, he encouraged her to make her poetry more "regular." After her death 1,775 poems were discovered in a dresser drawer in her bedroom. "She did in her poetry what she could never have done out loud," writes Louise Bernikow. "She found a voice both original and strange in which to speak with the kind of honesty that exists in no other poet of her time."

Chitra Divakaruni   (born 1956) was born in India and came to the United States when she was nineteen years old. Having received her Ph.D. from Berkeley, she now teaches at Foothill College in northern California. Her two volumes of poetry are *The Reason for Nasturtiums* (1990) and *Black Candle* (1991). She has recently published a book of short stories entitled *Arranged Marriage* (1996). Very involved in women's issues, Divakaruni is one of the founders of MAITRI, a service that helps South Asian women in distress. Of the importance of writing—and reading—she says, "When you open yourself to writing as a writer or a reader, it changes your life."

John Donne   (1572–1631), English poet, preacher, and religious prose writer, was born in London. He enrolled in Oxford; after converting from Roman Catholicism to the Anglican Church, he was ordained into its priesthood in 1614. In 1621 he became dean of St. Paul's Cathedral in

London, a position he held as an influential and compelling preacher until his death. When he was very ill in 1623, he wrote a series of essays called *Meditations*. His early love poems were probably written before 1614; his later religious poems were published in *Poems* in 1633. In recent decades, Donne's poetry and that of other metaphysical poets of the seventeenth century have been the object of much critical discussion. His poems appeal strongly to modern readers who prefer the challenging to the conventional, the complex to the superficial, the ironic to the sentimental.

Rita Dove   (born 1952), the first black U.S. poet laureate, has been described as a quiet leader who, while she does not avoid race issues, does not make them her central focus: "As a black woman I am concerned with race. . . . I cannot run from, I won't run from any kind of truth." Critic Helen Vendler observed of the Pulitzer Prize–winning *Thomas and Beulah* (1987), whose main characters are based on Dove's maternal grandparents, that "though the photograph, and the chronology of the lives of Thomas and Beulah might lead one to suspect that Dove is a poet of simple realism [it] is far from the case. Dove has learned how to make a biographical fact the buried bone of an imagined edifice." Critic A. L. Nielson finds that the poems in *Grace Notes* (1989) "abound in unforgettable details of family character. [Dove] is one of those rare poets who approach common experience with the same sincerity with which the objectivist poets of an earlier generation approached the things of our world." Dove published a novel, *Through the Ivory Gate,* in 1992.

Richard Eberhart   (born 1904), critically acclaimed American poet, was educated at Cambridge and has worked as a tutor to the son of the king of Siam, a businessman, a naval officer, a cultural adviser, and a professor. His numerous books of poetry include *Gifts of Being* (1968) and *Selected Poems, 1930–1965* (1976).

T. S. Eliot   (1888–1965) was a chief architect of modern poetic theory and one of the twentieth century's most influential poets. Born in St. Louis, Missouri, he studied at Harvard and then settled in London in 1915, becoming a British citizen thirteen years later. His poetry departed dramatically from familiar conventions and techniques, notably in "The Love Song of J. Alfred Prufrock" and the epochal *The Waste Land,* which he dedicated to Ezra Pound. Eliot's later works include *Four Quartets* (1943); his plays *Murder in the Cathedral* (1935) and *The Family Reunion* (1939); and poems for cat lovers, which inspired a triumphantly successful musical. He won the Nobel Prize for literature in 1948.

Louise Erdrich   (born 1954) writes about American Indian traditions in her novels *The Beet Queen* and *Love Medicine,* as well as in her shorter works. Part Chippewa Indian, Erdrich is intensely involved in Native

American land claims and other issues concerning Native Americans. Born in Little Falls, Minnesota, she spent much of her youth on the North Dakota reservation where her father taught school. She was educated at Dartmouth and Johns Hopkins. She has collaborated with her husband, Michael Dorris, on a nonfiction book, *Broken Chord,* about fetal alcohol syndrome among American Indians, from which his adopted son suffered. They also coauthored the novel *The Crown of Columbus* (1991). Erdrich's newest volume of poetry is *Baptism of Desire* (1991).

Martín Espada (born 1957) was raised in a Brooklyn housing project and became an attorney and a poet, using the "power of the word to fight against what I consider to be wrong." He won the 1991 Peterson Poetry Prize for *Rebellion Is the Circle of a Lover's Hands.* Espada's poetry has often been recited or published with the work of his father— photographer Frank Espada. Both have a deep need to document the social and political conditions in the urban United States. Espada not only loves to write poetry, but also loves to perform it, organizing workshops in the Boston area. In his role as lawyer, Espada defends the civil rights of immigrants.

Donald Finkel (born 1929) "is one of the few Americans," says Peter Meinke, "trying to extend poetry past the internal into the external world." Much of Finkel's work has been praised by the critics for its startling images and "comic extravagance." A New York native, Finkel has taught at the University of Iowa, Washington University, and Princeton. His numerous awards include the National Book Award for his 1979 poetry collection *The Garbage Wars.* Joseph Bennet wrote in the *New York Times Book Review* that Finkel is "so gifted he does not need subjects for his poems. . . . He has, above all, the gift of wonderment."

Robert Frost (1874–1963), born in San Francisco, moved to New England at age ten upon his father's death, and his poetry is closely linked with rural Vermont and New Hampshire. After briefly attending Dartmouth and Harvard, Frost worked as a shoemaker, schoolteacher, editor, and farmer. Unable to make a living, he took his family to England, where his first poetry collection, *A Boy's Will,* appeared in 1913. By 1914 his reputation had become firmly established through the publication of *North of Boston,* a collection containing what were to become some of his most popular poems, including "Mending Wall" and "The Death of the Hired Man." Frost won Pulitzer Prizes for poetry in 1924, 1931, 1937, and 1943. He developed a legendary reputation as America's best-known poet; he read "The Gift Outright" at John F. Kennedy's inauguration in 1960.

Dana Gioia (born 1950), whose surname is pronounced "Joy ah," was born in Los Angeles to a cab driver and a telephone operator. Educated at Stanford and Harvard universities, Gioia has said, "Though most of my poems use rhyme or meter, they rarely follow 'traditional' patterns. I love traditional forms, but I find them slightly dangerous. Their music can become so seductive that one loses touch with contemporary speech, which is, to my judgment, the basis for all genuine poetry."

Louise Glück   (born 1943) was born in New York City and studied at both Sarah Lawrence College and Columbia University. Her books of poems include *Firstborn* (1969), *The House on Marshland* (1975), *Descending Figure* (1980), *The Triumph of Achilles* (1985), and *Ararat* (1990). The common denominator in Glück's poetry, alternately sensuous and spare, is that "to be human is to love, to long, to suffer, and to know you will die" (A. Poulin, Jr.).

Judy Grahn   (born 1940), born in Chicago, graduated from San Francisco State University. She has published eight books of poetry, including *The Work of a Common Woman* and *The Queen of Swords,* which was performed in San Francisco. She has also written books about poetry and language, as well as a novel, *Mundane's World.* The winner of several grants and awards, Grahn founded the Women's Press Collective in 1970 and has taught writing and mythology.

Thomas Hardy   (1840–1928)—a major British novelist (*Tess of the D'Urbervilles, The Mayor of Casterbridge*)—produced eleven novels and three collections of stories before he finally abandoned prose for his first love, poetry, in his sixtieth year. He produced delicately bittersweet poems until he was almost ninety. Thinking his power had waned, critics did not take his poetry seriously until he published his epic, *The Dynasts* (1903, 1906, 1908), which established his reputation as a poet. The young poet Siegfried Sassoon wrote that Hardy recorded life with "microscopic exactitude . . . and a subtle ironic sense" of the tragic in human existence: "But his despair is mitigated by tenderness and pity for his fellows. With a wistful understanding he surveys the human scene." As an octogenarian, Hardy published *Late Lyrics and Earlier* (1922); his posthumous *Winter Words in Various Moods and Metres* (1928) was arranged by him before his death. Louis Untermeyer observed that, although his syntax was often clumsy, his poetry is "as disciplined as it is original."

Joy Harjo   (born 1951) is a major Native American voice who builds on jazz, story, and prayer in her work. About one of her volumes of poetry, *The Woman Who Fell from the Sky* (1994), Harjo writes: "I believe the word *poet* is synonymous with the word *truth teller.* So this collection tells a bit of the truth of what I have seen since my coming of age in the late sixties." Harjo was born in Tulsa, Oklahoma and is a member of the Muskogee Tribe. Her earlier books include *She Had Some Horses* (1983), *Secrets from the Center of the World* (1989), and *In Mad Love and War* (1990). She not only writes poetry but performs it, in addition to playing saxophone with her band, Poetic Justice. Poet Adrienne Rich has written: "I turn and return to Harjo's poetry for her heartbreaking, complex witness and for her world-remaking language: precise, unsentimental, miraculous." Teacher as well as visionary and spiritual poet, Harjo is a professor at the University of New Mexico.

Jeffrey Harrison   (born 1957) believes that "poetry is the lens through which the soul looks at the world, thereby keeping the soul alive." Harrison, an Ohio native who lives in Cincinnati, is author of the poetry collection *The Singing Underneath* and a contributor to many magazines. Educated at Columbia University and the University of Iowa, Harrison has taught English in Japan and has worked as a researcher in Washington, D.C.

Robert Hayden   (1913–1980), born in Detroit, Michigan, graduated from Wayne State University in Detroit and did graduate work at the University of Michigan. He later joined the faculty of Fisk University. *Heart-shape in the Dust,* his first poetry collection, appeared in 1940. His 1963 collection, *A Ballad of Remembrance,* received the grand prize at the World Festival of Negro Arts. Hayden called his work "a form of prayer—a prayer of illumination, perfection."

Seamus Heaney   (born 1939) was born to a rural Catholic family in Northern Ireland, received a B.A. from Queen's University in Belfast in 1961, and taught in secondary schools and universities. His first published book, *Death of a Naturalist* (1966), set his reputation as a powerful "rural poet," a label he addresses in these lines: "Between my fingers and my thumb / The squat pen rests. / I'll dig with it." Heaney's poetry is steeped in Irish lore and history and noted for its "inventive language and sharp, immediate physical imagery." More than simply portraying the Irish countryside and folklore, however, Heaney is concerned with the poet's political role, seeing poets as "both helpless witnesses and accomplices in the fratricidal battles" of Ireland. Inevitably, Heaney is favorably compared with the great Irish poet William Butler Yeats. Of his own creative process he writes: "One thing I try to avoid ever saying at readings is 'my poem' because that sounds like a presumption. The poem *came, it came.* I didn't go and fetch it. To some extent you can wait for it, you coax it in the door when it gets there. I prefer to think of myself as a host to the thing rather than a big game hunter."

John Heaviside   published his poem in the *Olivetree Review,* a publication devoted to student work and published at Hunter College of the City University of New York.

H. D.   (1886–1961), pseudonym of Hilda Doolittle, took on the "prophet's mantle in poetry, anticipating the spirit of the current feminist movement by a good half century" (Tom Clark). Born in Bethlehem,

Pennsylvania, H. D. attended Bryn Mawr. In 1911 she went to Europe, where she lived most of her life. The publishing of her work began when in 1913 Ezra Pound sent some of her poems to Harriet Monroe, editor of *Poetry* magazine. H. D. soon became known as one of the leaders of the imagist poets. She published six poetry collections, wrote several novels, and translated Greek literature.

George Herbert   (1593–1633), a younger son of a wealthy aristocratic English family, began writing religious verse while an undergraduate at Cambridge University. Until the death of King James in 1625, Herbert enjoyed royal favor and participated in the life of the court. Undecided for a time between the uncertain promise of a career in public office and a career as a churchman, he eventually became an Anglican priest. His collected poems were published after his death in a volume entitled *The Temple*. Like other metaphysical poets of his time, Herbert introduced into religious poetry complex imagery and intense personal emotion.

Robert Herrick   (1591–1674) addressed light, conventional poems about love to imaginary Corinnas and Julias while leading a quiet life as a country priest. Born in London, Herrick was apprenticed as a young man to his uncle, a wealthy goldsmith. Later Herrick entered Cambridge, and at some point before 1627 he was ordained an Anglican priest. Two years later the king appointed him to a rural parish in a location he hated at first but grew to love. His *Hesperion,* published in 1648, contains 1,200 poems.

Gerard Manley Hopkins   (1844–1889) saw none of his poems published during his lifetime. Born in London, this English poet earned a degree from Oxford in 1867, one year after he had converted to Roman Catholicism. He then entered the Society of Jesus and was ordained a Jesuit priest. Troubled by what he saw as a conflict between his life as a priest and as a poet, he burned all his poems when he entered the Jesuit order but began to write poetry again in 1875. His complete poetic works were published nineteen years after Hopkins' death by his friend, the poet Robert Bridges. Modern poets and critics soon provided a receptive audience for its complex diction, startling imagery, and intense religious emotion. His poems defied convention and are marked by what one of his editors called "a kind of creative violence."

Langston Hughes   (1902–1967) was a central figure of the Harlem Renaissance of the 1920s, a movement that examined and celebrated American black life and its African heritage. Hughes focused on what it was like to be black in America, a thread that runs through his work as poet, editor, and biographer. Born in Joplin, Missouri, Hughes attended high school in Cleveland, and his first published poems appeared in the school's literary magazine. He attended New York's Columbia University for a year and graduated from Lincoln University in Pennsylvania. His first poetry collection, *The Weary Blues,* appeared in 1926. In addition to numerous collections of poetry, Hughes wrote novels, short stories, plays, radio and motion picture scripts, and nonfiction. In his frequent lecture appearances at black colleges throughout the South, Hughes encouraged others to write. He also translated into English the poetry of black writers from other parts of the world. His own poetry has been translated into many other languages.

Marie Luise Kaschnitz   (1902–1974), like many German artists and writers, was censored and driven into exile by Hitler. Born in Karlsruhe, she was honored with some of the most prestigious German literary prizes after the war. In addition to writing short stories, essays, and poetry, Kaschnitz produced several radio plays. Her reflections of an aging woman in *Tage, Tage, Jahre (Days, Days, Years)* "define the high point of her literary achievement" (Marilyn Sibley Fries).

John Keats   (1795–1821) died at age twenty-six from tuberculosis and became for later generations a symbol of the sensitive artist destroyed by a harsh world. Born in London, Keats gave up studying medicine for writing when thirty-three of his poems were published. He produced some of his finest poetry in 1818 and 1819, including "La Belle Dame sans Merci" and "Ode on a Grecian Urn." Admired for the rich sensuous imagery of his poetry, Keats was passionately concerned with the relationship between emotion and knowledge, between beauty and truth. He expressed a conviction shared by many Romantic writers when he wrote, "I am certain of the heart's affections and the truth of imagination—What the imagination seizes as beauty must be truth."

Yusef Komunyakaa   (born 1947), a Pulitzer Prize winner, confesses that he "never really approached [poetry] from the perspective of making a living. It was simply a need." A war correspondent in Vietnam during the conflict, Komunyakaa has written a number of poems on Vietnam. Critic Leonard Moore, in reviewing *Neon Vernacular: New and Selected Poems,* writes, "A master at interweaving memory and history to shape his experiences into narratives, Komunyakaa, an African American, defines a culture with striking imagery that is often misunderstood by mainstream readers." He has published ten books of poems. Even when writing about emotionally wrenching events about his tour of duty in Vietnam or his relationship with his abusive father, Komunyakaa paradoxically evokes feelings of tenderness.

Maxine Kumin   (born 1925) was born in Philadelphia, Pennsylvania. She earned her B.A. and M.A. degrees from Radcliffe and lives on a farm in New Hampshire. She published her first collection of poetry in 1961 and won the Pulitzer Prize in 1974 for her collection of poems entitled *Up Country.* She has written a number of novels and numerous successful children's books, several in collaboration with her friend, poet Anne

Sexton. She has lectured at the University of Massachusetts, Columbia, Brandeis, and Princeton. May Swenson has called Kumin's work "large-hearted, articulate, and acute."

Melvin Walker La Follette   (born 1930) "believes in the sensuous body of the world," wrote Richard Eberhart, adding, "He finds his feelings of the greatest richness of life in three areas . . . youth, the love of small animals," and "the devotion to the idea of saints and sainthood." La Follette was born in Evansville, Indiana. He received his B.A. in creative writing at the University of Washington. He taught for many years at colleges in California, Canada, and Oregon. He also spent time in forestry work in various parts of the Pacific Northwest.

Denise Levertov   (1923–1997) has said she grew up in "a house full of books and everyone in the family engaged in some literary activity." The family's vast library and the diverse visitors to the house—"Jewish book-sellers, German theologians, Russian priests from Paris, and Viennese opera singers"—were her education. Her father, a biblical scholar and Anglican priest, harbored the lifelong hope of the unification of Judaism and Christianity. Born in Essex, England, Levertov was a civilian nurse in London during World War II, then settled in New York in 1948 with her American husband. The influence of the American poet William Carlos Williams helped her to develop "from a British Romantic with almost Victorian background to an American poet of . . . vitality." Her best-known book of poetry, *The Sorrow Dance* (1967), reflects her feelings of rage over the Vietnam War and the death of her older sister. Her most recent books, dealing with loneliness and personal pilgrimage, include *Evening Train* (1992) and *New and Selected Essays* (1992).

Audre Lorde   (1934–1992) described herself as a "black lesbian feminist warrior poet." Born in New York City of West Indian parents, Lorde attended Hunter College and Columbia. She worked as a librarian and then taught at several colleges before becoming a professor of English at Hunter College in New York City. She lived on Staten Island with her companion and her two children. Her first poetry collection, *The First Cities* (1968), chronicles the effects of racism on African Americans. A more recent work, *Zami: A Nevo Spelling of My Name,* Lorde called her "biomythography." In what Claudia Tate calls "stunning figurative language," Lorde "outlines the progress of her unyielding struggle for the human rights of all people."

Andrew Marvell   (1621–1678) was known in his day for satirical commentary on political events; his poetry was not published until after his death. Today his "To His Coy Mistress" is one of the best-known poems in the English language. Twentieth-century critics rediscovered Marvell and other metaphysical poets (John Donne, George Herbert), championing their love of irony and paradox and their blend of intellectual vigor and passionate intensity. Born in Yorkshire, Marvell entered Oxford at the age of twelve. When the civil war broke out, he was appointed assistant to John Milton in the Cromwell government. After the monarchy was restored, he served in Parliament until his death.

John Masefield   (1878–1967), a native of Herefordshire, England, was a young boy when his father, a lawyer, died. At age fourteen Masefield was indentured to work on a merchant ship and became a wanderer for a few years. Staying for a time in New York, he took odd jobs before returning to England at age nineteen. After Masefield read Chaucer, he was determined to become a poet. Not until the 1911 publication of *The Everlasting Mercy* did he become famous. In addition to his poetry, he wrote more than a dozen plays, a book on Shakespeare, twelve volumes of essays, books for youths, and adventure novels.

Peter Meinke   (born 1932) was born in Brooklyn, New York. He served in the U.S. Army and received a B.A. from Hamilton College, an M.A. from the University of Michigan, and a Ph.D. from the University of Minnesota. Meinke's reviews, poems, and stories have appeared in periodicals such as the *Atlantic,* the *New Yorker,* and the *New Republic.* His collection of short stories, *The Piano Tuner,* won the 1986 Flannery O'Connor Award. *Scars,* published in 1996, is his newest book of poems.

W. S. Merwin   (1927–1995), one of the most prolific poets and translators of his generation, was born the son of a Presbyterian minister in New York City. Educated at Princeton, Merwin was influenced by poet Robert Graves, whose son he tutored in Majorca, Spain. Merwin has translated widely from Spanish, Portuguese, Latin, French, and Russian, in both conventional forms and free verse. He has received numerous fellowships and awards, including a Pulitzer Prize in 1971 for his collection *A Carrier of Ladders.* He went to live in Hawaii in 1968.

Edna St. Vincent Millay   (1892–1950) began writing poetry as a child in Camden, Maine, encouraged by her mother, who had left her father when Millay was eight years old. While a rebellious student at Vassar, Millay dared the president to expel her, and he explained that he didn't want a "banished Shelley on my doorstep." She supposedly replied, "On those terms, I think I can continue to live in this hellhole." She graduated in 1917, the same year her first book of poems was published. In 1923 she won a Pulitzer Prize for her poetry collection *The Harp-Weaver.* In addition to over twenty volumes of verse, she published three verse plays, wrote a libretto for an opera, and translated Baudelaire. Neglected for a time by critics who thought her poetry too traditional in form and too frankly emotional, she has recently been rediscovered by feminist critics as an early champion of feminist themes.

Vassar Miller   (born 1924) calls poetry "an act of love." Born in Houston, Texas, Miller was educated at the University of Houston. She has published several poetry collections, including *Wage War on Silence*. Afflicted with cerebral palsy from birth, Miller has dedicated herself to poetry "and has demonstrated . . . that craftsmanship, religious fervor, and personal joy and agony can produce major poetry" (Chad Walsh).

John Milton   (1608–1674) was a poet deeply involved in the political and religious turmoil of his time. Born in Cheapside, London, he was steeped in classical literature and wrote some of his early poems in Latin and Italian. After graduating from Cambridge, Milton traveled the Continent, returning to England shortly before the civil war. Milton was an ardent supporter of the Puritan cause. He joined in the vigorous polemics of the time and published aggressive prose tracts on subjects including censorship. After the overthrow of King Charles I, Milton became Latin secretary in charge of diplomatic correspondence under the dictator Cromwell. He escaped death as a traitor to the crown after the restoration of the monarchy, publishing his monumental religious epic *Paradise Lost* in 1667. By this time he was completely blind and living in poverty. "Lycidas," the best known of his shorter poems, appeared in 1637.

Janice Mirikitani   (born 1938), who lives on the West Coast, has been an outspoken poet of political issues. Her images juxtapose the terrors of Vietnam with the indignities of World War II relocation camps. An early proponent of multicultural awareness, Mirikitani insisted that the language of the Third World was "universal, freeing, connective." She co-edited *Third World Women* (1973), *Time to Greez* (1975), and *Ayumi: The Japanese American Anthology* (1979).

N. Scott Momaday   (born 1934) is a Kiowa whose writing explores the history and culture of his people. Momaday was born in Lawton, Oklahoma. He graduated from the University of New Mexico in 1958 and received master's and doctoral degrees from Stanford. He began his academic career teaching English at the University of California, Santa Barbara, in 1973. He told the story of his rediscovery of his heritage in *The Journey of Tai-me* (1968)—republished with illustrations by his father, Al Momaday, under the title *The Way to Rainy Mountain*. His novel *The House Made of Dawn* won a Pulitzer Prize in 1969.

Ogden Nash   (1902–1971) gave pleasure to untold readers with a steady stream of irreverent light verse. Born in Rye, New York, Nash attended Harvard and worked as a teacher, a bond salesperson, and an editor for Doubleday Publishers in New York City. Later he joined the editorial staff of the *New Yorker*. His collected poems, *I Wouldn't Have Missed It*, appeared in 1975.

Thomas Nashe (1567–1601), the son of a minister, was born in Lowestoft, England. After graduating from Cambridge, Nashe toured France and Italy and by 1588 was a professional writer living in London. Nashe wrote pamphlets to defend the Anglican Church against attacks by the Puritans. He also wrote several plays and in 1594 published an adventure novel, *The Unfortunate Traveler.*

Howard Nemerov (born 1920), American poet and literary critic, was born and raised in New York City. He graduated from Harvard and served in World War II with a fighter squadron in the British Royal Air Force. He has taught at Bennington College in Vermont and George Washington University in St. Louis. Known for its clarity and simplicity, his poetry sings the praises of nature and the simple life. In 1988 Nemerov became U.S. poet laureate, succeeding Richard Wilbur and later succeeded by Mark Strand in 1989.

Sharon Olds (born 1942) has said, "One of the hardest tasks as a poet is to believe in oneself—or to act as if we do!" A self-described "late bloomer," Olds says she was thirty before she found her voice, her ability "to embody on the page thinking about an actual self." Born in San Francisco, Olds earned a B.A. from Stanford and a Ph.D. from Columbia. Winner of many awards, she has taught and given numerous readings at colleges and universities. Her poetry books are *Satan Says* (1980), *The Dead and the Living* (1982), *The Gold Cell* (1987), *The Father* (1992), and, most recently, *The Wellspring* (1995). This sequence of poems takes us back to the womb, on to childhood, to sexual awakening, to the drama of childbirth, to the amazements of parenthood, and to mature love. Always she writes with astonishing frankness and authentic emotion about being a child, a woman, and a mother. Michael Ondaatje observed that Sharon Olds' poems "are pure fire in the hands—risky, on the verge of falling, and in the end leaping up. I love the roughness and humor and brag and tenderness and completion in her work as she carries the reader through rooms of passion and loss."

Mary Oliver (born 1935) was born in Cleveland, Ohio, and attended both Ohio State and Vassar. She worked as a secretary to the sister of poet Edna St. Vincent Millay. Her first collection of poetry, *No Voyage and Other Poems,* appeared in 1963 and then again in 1965 with nineteen additional poems. Her second collection, *The River Styx, Ohio, and Other Poems,* appeared in 1972. In 1991 Oliver won a pair of awards for *House of Light* and, in 1992, the National Book Award for poetry for *New and Selected Poems.* These recent works reflect a shift to self and a pervasive tone of amazement. Susan Reynolds describes her work as having a "Blake-eyed revelatory quality." In the poem "When Death Comes," Oliver writes: "When it's over I want to say: all my life / I was a bride married to amazement."

Wilfred Owen   (1893–1918) wrote powerful antiwar poems during World War I—poems that are a lasting memorial and tribute to a generation destroyed in the trenches of Flanders and northern France. Owen was killed in action at age twenty-five, one week before the armistice. Born in Shropshire, England, into a devout, relatively poor family, Owen was educated at London University and enlisted in military service when England entered the war. In late 1917 he was wounded and sent to a military hospital. There he met the poet Siegfried Sassoon, who edited and published Owen's poems after Owen's death.

Dorothy Parker   (1893–1967) has been called "the quintessential New York wit, known as much for what she said as for what she wrote." Parker often wrote bitter satire and showed empathy toward suffering. "The humorist has never been happy, anyhow," she once said. "Today he's whistling past worse graveyards to worse tunes." In addition to writing for the *New Yorker* and *Vanity Fair,* Parker wrote screenplays for Hollywood.

Linda Pastan   (born 1932) was born in New York City and studied at Brandeis and Radcliffe. Her first poetry collection, *A Perfect Circle of Sun,* appeared in 1971. Other collections include *Five Stages of Grief* (1978), *AM/PM* (1982), *Imperfect Paradise* (1988), and *Heroes in Disguise* (1991). Poet laureate of the state of Maryland, she has been honored with fellowships from the National Endowment for the Arts. The *Washington Post* noted that Pastan "writes with a music of her own—reinforced by overtones of Yeats and Frost."

Francesco Petrarca   (1304–1374) was a humanist of the early Italian Renaissance, participating in the rediscovery of the learning and literature of classical antiquity. His *Canzoniere,* a collection of songs (*canzoni*) and sonnets, started the vogue of Petrarchan love poetry that dominated lyric poetry in Europe for centuries.

Marge Piercy   (born 1936) was born in poverty in Detroit during the Depression. She was the first in her family to go to college and "took five years to recover." She has published eight novels, including *Woman on the Edge of Time* (1976), a science fiction work in which she experiments with a "woman's language." She has also written a play, essays, and nine volumes of poetry, including *Available Light* (1988). When she is not giving readings and conducting workshops throughout the country, she writes in her Cape Cod home.

Christine de Pisan   (about 1364–1430), called "France's first woman of letters" by biographer Charity Cannon Willard, lived and wrote at the end of the Middle Ages. Born in Venice, Italy, she moved to Paris, France, at age four. There her family became part of the royal court, for her father, a scientist, was employed by King Charles V. At age fifteen she married but was widowed after ten years. Her first poetry collection, published by 1402, marked the beginning of a long literary career, during which de Pisan wrote lyrical and allegorical poetry, biographies of important political figures (including Charles V), textbooks, and books about women and government. She is also known for her role in a debate over contemporary negative attitudes toward women and for her championing of women's rights.

Sylvia Plath   (1932–1963) was born near Boston, of an Austrian-born father who was an instructor at Boston University and an expert on bees. She began writing early and sold several stories and poems to *Seventeen* magazine. A 1955 summa cum laude graduate in English from Smith, Plath earned an M.A. at Cambridge as a Fulbright scholar. In 1956 she married English poet Ted Hughes. *The Colossus,* published in 1960, was her only poetry collection to appear before she committed suicide. *The Bell Jar,* a quasi-autobiographical novel, chronicles the struggles of a brilliant young woman radically alienated from her environment who suffers bouts of suicidal depression. Critic David Young says Plath "lived on a knife-edge, in the presence of a tremendous attraction to death and nothingness." Since her death, her powerful and disturbing poetry has been widely discussed and anthologized.

Ezra Pound   (1885–1972) was one of the great innovators and nonconformists of early modern poetry. He championed or inspired writers like Marianne Moore, T. S. Eliot, Robert Frost, William Carlos Williams, Ernest Hemingway, and James Joyce. Pound was born in Idaho and educated at Hamilton College and the University of Pennsylvania. Associated with the imagist poets, Pound translated Chinese, Latin, Japanese, German, French, Italian, Greek, Anglo-Saxon, and Provençal (thirteenth-century French) poetry. In 1945 he was arrested for treason because of his radio broadcasts of Fascist propaganda in Italy during World War II. Found unfit for trial by reason of insanity, he was committed to St. Elizabeth's Hospital in Washington, D.C., where he spent over ten years. His most ambitious and complex work is *The Cantos,* a vast, richly allusive collection of poems he worked on in depth while in a prisoner of war camp near Pisa, Italy; he continued to work on them throughout his life, and they were left unfinished at the time of his death.

Leroy V. Quintana   (born 1944) has said, "In many ways, I'm still basically a small-town New Mexico boy carrying on the oral tradition." Born in Albuquerque, Quintana was raised by his grandparents, who told him *cuentos*—traditional Mexican folktales—and stories of life in the Old West. "I seem to be tied to a sense of the past," he said. "My work reflects the 'sense of place' evoked by New Mexico. I hope I am worthy of portraying the land and its people well." Quintana, a graduate of the University of New Mexico, won the American Book Award for poetry in

1982 for *Sangre*. His other titles include *Hijo del Pueblo: New Mexico Poems* (1976) and *The Reason People Don't Like Mexicans* (1984).

Henry Reed (1914–1986), poet and playwright, was born in Birmingham, England. After earning a B.A. from the University of Birmingham in 1937, he worked as a teacher and freelance writer. He served a stint in the British army and wrote poetry about his experience in cadet training, as well as about political events of the time. His only collection of poetry, *A Map of Verona,* appeared in 1946. Soon thereafter, he began writing radio plays, including the popular BBC "Hilda Tablet" series, a parody of British society in the 1930s.

Adrienne Rich (born 1929) was educated by her parents in their Baltimore, Maryland, home until fourth grade, when she entered public school. A 1951 Phi Beta Kappa graduate of Radcliffe, Rich won the Yale Younger Poets competition that same year for her collection *A Change of World*. Since then she has been awarded the prestigious Bollingen Prize and in 1974 was a cowinner with Allen Ginsberg of the National Book Award for poetry. She has published more than half a dozen books of poetry, including *Diving into the Wreck* (1973) and *The Dream of a Common Language: Poems 1974–1977*. An inspiration to feminist poets and critics, Rich collected some of her incisive, thought-provoking prose in *On Lies, Secrets, and Silence* (1979). Her most recent collections of poems are *Your Native Land, Your Life* (1986) and *An Atlas of the Difficult World* (1992). Through her poetry Rich has encouraged the questioning of conventional beliefs on issues such as homosexuality, her Jewish heritage, and the politics of oppression. Observes Willard Spiegelman, "Rich is our only poet who understands heroism and grandeur as the other side of degradation and suffering, and who, even in her most personal lyrics, stretches all human activities on the frame of social and political consciousness." And Alice Ostriker sees this predilection as a difficult issue: "Whatever distresses me in Rich—the joylessness, the self-pity, the self-righteousness, exists also within myself and within others." And in Rich's work, the male of the species is an overwhelming negative: "Men . . . are depicted universally and exclusively as parasitic on women, emotionally threatened by them, brutal . . . and undeserving of pity. 'His' mind is a nightmare of possessiveness, conquest, and misogyny." Francine du Plessix Gray echoes Ostriker when she writes that "it is vexing to see such a dedicated feminist playing the dangerous game of using the oppressor's tactics. Going from mythologization of history to remythologizing of male and female character traits, Rich indulges in stereotypes throughout."

Rainer Maria Rilke (1875–1926), perhaps the most widely admired and translated of the twentieth-century German poets, was born in Prague to German-speaking parents. In 1898 he went to Russia, where he met Leo

Tolstoy, author of *War and Peace*. In 1905 in France, Rilke served as secretary for the famous French sculptor Rodin, and the influence of this experience can be seen in his collection *New Poems* (1907). When World War I broke out, Rilke moved to Switzerland, where he wrote *Sonnets to Orpheus* (1923) and *The Duino Elegies* (1923). Critic Kenneth Koch has said of Rilke's power as a poet: "When Rilke writes about a subject, it is as if nothing were known about it, as if he started from the very beginning in order to understand deeply, for himself, the power or purpose or beauty of it."

Alberto Rios (born 1952) was born in Arizona to an English mother and a Mexican American father. He is a professor of creative writing and director of the creative writing program at Arizona State University. He has won a number of awards, including the Pushcart Prize IX, the Governor of Arizona Arts Award, and the Walt Whitman Award of the Academy of American Poets (1981). Rios' poetry has appeared in all of the major poetry reviews in the United States, and he has published several books of poetry, among them *Whispering to Fool the Wind* (1982) and *The Lima Orchard Woman* (1990).

Theodore Roethke (1908–1963) grew up in Saginaw, Michigan, where his father and uncle owned a greenhouse; greenhouses would serve as prominent images in his poetry. He studied at the University of Michigan and Harvard, and he taught and coached tennis at a number of colleges. He sold his first poems for a dollar, but shortly thereafter his poetry appeared in several widely read magazines. He won a Pulitzer Prize in 1954 for *The Waking: Poems 1933–1953,* which was followed by the Bollingen Prize in 1959 for *Words or the Wind* and two National Book Awards. Abrasive in his criticism of contemporary culture and fellow poets, Roethke looked to the world of nature for sources of spiritual renewal.

Christina Rossetti (1830–1894), whose father had come to England as a political refugee from his native Italy, was born in London in a poor neighborhood. Rossetti had no formal education but was taught to read by her mother. From her earliest days she loved to write, and her grandfather had a number of her poems privately printed when she was twelve. Her first collection of poetry, *Goblin Market and Other Poems,* appeared in 1862.

Sappho (about 620–550 B.C.), called "the tenth muse" by Plato, lived on the Greek island of Lesbos, where she wrote passionate love poems addressed to younger women she may have taught. She was an aristocrat involved in controversial political activities that led to her being exiled twice. She married a rich merchant and bore a daughter. In A.D. 1073, a large collection of her verse was publicly burned by church dignitaries of Rome and Constantinople. However, some of her writing—as well as her legendary reputation—has remained intact.

Anne Sexton (1928–1974) encouraged writers to "put your ear close down to your soul and listen hard." Born in Newton, Massachusetts, she studied at Boston University and Brandeis. At age twenty-eight, a suburban housewife, she suffered a nervous breakdown. Her therapist encouraged her to write, and she soon became a successful poet. She claimed that when she began to write she was reborn, for "suicide is the opposite of the poem." She wrote eight books of poetry; *Live or Die* won the 1967 Pulitzer Prize. Sexton lived a troubled life, punctuated by suicide attempts and hospitalizations, until she finally took her life in 1974, mourned by fellow poets who thought of her as one of the great poetic talents of our time. "When I'm writing, I know I'm doing the thing I was born to do," she said. "I guess I listen for my melody. When it comes, I just turn . . . like a little dancer." A 1991 biography of Anne Sexton made the *New York Times* best-seller list.

William Shakespeare (1564–1616) is the foremost English dramatist of the reigns of Queen Elizabeth and King James I. Shakespeare was actor, playwright, and shareholder in a theatrical company at a time when the English stage enjoyed both royal patronage and popular support. He wrote some thirty-five plays for an audience that liked spectacle and was used to keen competition among theatrical companies and to rapid changes in dramatic fashions. A vast literature of comment, analysis, background information, and textual study has grown up around his works. His great tragedies—*Romeo and Juliet, Hamlet, Othello, King Lear, Macbeth*—probe the paradoxes of our human nature and destiny. Little is known about his life: He was born in the small town of Stratford-on-Avon, and his formal studies ended with grammar school. At age eighteen he married Anne Hathaway. He retired to his hometown at the end of his career.

Percy Bysshe Shelley (1792–1822), most iconoclastic of the younger Romantic poets, was born in Sussex, England, the eldest son of a conservative country squire. He went to Oxford but was expelled for publishing a pamphlet that advocated atheism. This was but the first of many rebellions against convention and established institutions that marked his brief life. Shelley spent most of his adult life in Italy; many of his shorter and more famous lyric poems, such as "To a Skylark" and "Ode to the West Wind," he wrote in Pisa in 1819. One of his last poems is the elegy written to mourn the death of his close friend John Keats. Shelley himself, who had written "How wonderful is Death, / Death and his brother Sleep," died in a boating accident at age thirty.

Gary Soto (born 1952), award-winning Mexican American poet, believes that "writing makes the ordinary stand out, thus enabling us to build in some kind of metaphorical meaning." Much of Soto's writing includes the ordinary events of his childhood in Fresno, California. In addition to the prose memoir *Living up the Street,* Soto has published five books of poetry, including *Home Course in Religion* (1991). An alumnus of Fresno State and the University of California, Irvine, he joined the faculty at Berkeley. Soto says that literature "reshapes experience—both real and invented—to help us see ourselves—our foibles, failures, potential, beauty, pettiness. In short, literature helps define the world for us."

William Stafford   (1914–1992) grew up in small towns of central Kansas, hunting, camping, and fishing in the countryside. He earned a doctorate in English from Iowa State. A member of the United Brethren, Stafford became a conscientious objector during World War II. He worked in labor camps, an experience recorded in a prose memoir, *Down in My Heart.* In 1947 his first collection of poems appeared, and the next year he joined the faculty at Lewis and Clark College in Oregon. His third poetry collection, *Traveling through the Dark,* received the National Book Award in 1963. His poems often explore commonplace events; critics note, however, that on closer examination, Stafford proves to be "a very elusive poet with a distinctive private vision that slips through our grasp when we try to identify, summarize, or paraphrase it" (David Young).

Wallace Stevens   (1879–1955), who commanded a large, loyal following among readers dedicated to the cause of poetry, believed "the poem refreshes the world." Born in Reading, Pennsylvania, Stevens attended Harvard University and New York Law School. He began practicing law in 1904 and then joined the legal department of a Connecticut insurance company, retiring as vice president of the firm. His challenging, complex poetry appeared in journals as early as 1914; his first collection, *Harmonium,* appeared in 1923. His second collection, *Ideas of Order,* was published thirteen years later.

Sir John Suckling   (1609–1642), who has been called "the most skeptical and libertine of the Cavaliers," was born the son of the secretary of state to King James I. Suckling studied at Cambridge and then traveled throughout Europe. A courtier with a reputation of brilliant wit, Suckling wrote four plays and a number of lyric poems. He became embroiled in political intrigue, committing suicide in 1642.

May Swenson   (1919–1989), a child of immigrant Swedish parents, was born in Logan, Utah. After graduating from Utah State University, she came to New York City and worked as an editor. She has received many awards for her poetry, which is noted for its freshness of perspective and experimental form. Some of her poetry collection titles are *Another Animal* (1954), *Iconographs* (1970), and *Poems to Solve* (1966), a volume for children.

Alfred, Lord Tennyson   (1809–1892), poet laureate of Victorian England, gave voice to characteristic assumptions and aspirations of his contemporaries. Born the son of a clergyman, Tennyson was educated at Cambridge. His first published poems appeared in 1830; in 1842 he published two volumes that included "Morte d'Arthur" and "Ulysses." His *In Memoriam* (1850), written after the death of a close friend, mirrored the religious doubts and earnestness of his time. His "Idylls of the King" (1859) became required reading for generations of high school students.

Dylan Thomas   (1914–1953) called his poetry a record of his "struggle from darkness toward some measure of light." Born in Wales, Thomas had his only formal education in grammar school. When his first poetry collection appeared in 1932, he was hailed as a leading modern poet. His radio work in England and his numerous poetry readings at American college campuses made him a popular figure on both sides of the Atlantic. His passionate, visionary tone and wild flights of the imagination appealed to readers starved for mysticism and emotion. Alcoholism and lung ailments precipitated his early death. Thomas once said that his poems, "with all their crudities, doubts, and confusions, are written for the love of man and in Praise of God, and I'd be a damn fool if they weren't."

David Wagoner   (born 1926), "a master technician" (Daniel Halpern), was born in Ohio and educated at Penn State and Indiana University. An award-winning poet and novelist, Wagoner taught English at several colleges and made his home in Seattle. He has been praised for his witty and deep perceptions, as well as his "skillful manipulation of language" (Halpern).

Alice Walker   (born 1944) has said, "All of my poems . . . are written when I have successfully pulled myself out of a completely numbing despair, and stand again in the sunlight." Born in the small town of Eatonsville, Georgia, Walker received her bachelor's degree in 1965 from Sarah Lawrence College. After graduating, she taught at several universities and worked for voter registration and welfare rights. Her novel *The Color Purple* (1982) made her the best-known black writer of her generation. In 1983, she published the essay collection *In Search of Our Mothers' Gardens*. Using language as catharsis and potential for growth is essential to Walker, who said, "No person is your friend (or kin) who demands your silence, or denies your right to grow and be perceived as fully blossomed as you were intended. Or who belittles in any fashion the gifts you labor so to bring into the world."

Bethlyn Madison Webster   (born 1964) is an artist, poet, and part-time teacher of English at the college level, working on her M.F.A. at California State University, Fresno. Her poem "Stamps" was recently nominated for a Pushcart Prize.

Walt Whitman (1819–1892), a giant of American and world literature, successfully created a public persona as the poet of democracy and the voice of an expansive vision of America. Son of a carpenter and farmer, he spent much of his life as a journalist in Brooklyn, Manhattan, and Long Island. In 1855, he published the first edition of *Leaves of Grass,* a milestone of nineteenth-century American literature. He celebrated the varied scene of contemporary America: the steamers and railroads and ferries, the carpenters and pilots and farmers, the cities and plains and mountains. He once said, "The United States themselves are essentially the greatest poem." His use of rhythm as a fluid instrument of poetic structure went far beyond the conventional meter of the day. His work has symphonic qualities, based on repeated yet highly suggestive motifs. He dropped conventional poetic figures, drawing on his own experience for new metaphors. A private printing of *Leaves of Grass* was not widely received partly because it was a half-century ahead of its time. Although he remained relatively poor, the last decade of Whitman's life brought him wide recognition. Gay Wilson Allen notes that Whitman's poetry has been translated into every major language and that he had great influence on poets such as William Carlos Williams, Wallace Stevens, and Allen Ginsberg, "who was inspired by Whitman's bold treatment of sexuality."

Richard Wilbur (born 1921) had won the first of two Pulitzer Prizes by the time he published his third volume of poetry. Born in New York City, he went to Amherst and to Harvard, becoming a professor of English at Wesleyan University. Wilbur has been called the thinking poet, and we cannot read his poems lightly. For him a poem is not just a vehicle for communicating but rather it is a created object having its own life: "The poem," he says, is an effort to express a knowledge imperfectly felt, to articulate relationships not quite seen, to make or discover some pattern in the world." Richard Wilbur respects the strictness of form: "The strength of the genie comes of his being confined in a bottle." Yet at the same time he is known for his play with sound by a daring originality of language. Appointed U.S. poet laureate in 1987, Wilbur also won a Pulitzer Prize for *Things of This World* (1956).

Miller Williams (born 1930), born in Hoxie, Arkansas, and educated in the sciences, is described as a "poet who has entirely secured his own line and his own idiom. He has a lively eye, wit and analytic intelligence. His style is lean and spare, streamlined to add up a welter of fresh images and impressions at a remarkable velocity" (Laurence Lieberman). Among his numerous books of poems are titles such as *A Circle of Stones* (1964) and *Why God Permits Evil: Poems* (1977). In 1986 Williams published a prose work, *Patterns of Poetry: An Encyclopedia of Forms.* Joel Conarroe calls him "funny as hell . . . a rare phenomenon."

William Carlos Williams (1883–1963), writer of fiction, essays, and poetry, also had a full-time career as a physician. Born in Rutherford, New Jersey, Williams attended preparatory schools in New York and Switzerland and studied medicine at the University of Pennsylvania, where he met Ezra Pound. With Pound's encouragement, Williams began publishing poetry. Winner of many prestigious awards, including a National Book Award and a Pulitzer Prize, Williams worked in New Jersey as both a poet and a doctor until his death. Radically experimental in technique and form, his mature work was influenced by the imagist movement in its rejection of sentimentality and its reliance on the language of common speech, concrete, sensory experience, and emotional restraint.

William Wordsworth (1770–1850), in collaboration with his friend Samuel Taylor Coleridge, published the collection *Lyrical Ballads* in 1798. The poems in this volume and its programmatic preface broke with the poetic conventions of the eighteenth century and signaled the beginning of the English Romantic movement. Wordsworth, born in Westmoreland, England, was educated at Cambridge. He for a time was caught up in the revolutionary fervor of the French Revolution but became a voice of conservatism in his later years. He is best remembered for his poems that turn to the healing influence of nature as the antidote to the ills of city civilization.

Sir Thomas Wyatt (1503–1541) was the first to introduce into England Petrarch's sonnets of frustrated love, which started the sonnet vogue of the Elizabethan age. Born in Kent, England, Wyatt was educated at Cambridge. His father was a joint constable with the father of Anne Boleyn, who was to become the second wife of Henry VIII and the mother of Elizabeth, the future queen. Wyatt was assigned his first diplomatic mission by Henry VIII in 1525 and led a busy life as a courtier and diplomat.

William Butler Yeats (1865–1939) became known for poems drawing on the heritage of Irish myth and legend and developed a rich symbolic language in his later poetry. Yeats, who won the Nobel Prize for literature in 1923, is widely recognized as one of the most outstanding poets of the English-speaking world. An Irish dramatist and poet, he was born in Dublin. In the 1890s he became involved in the developing revolution against British rule in Ireland. Cofounder of the Irish Literary Theatre, he wrote plays for its stage. From 1922—the year of the Proclamation of the Irish Free State—until 1928 he was a member of the Irish Senate. Poet Seamus Heaney says that "a Yeats poem gives the feeling of being empowered and thrilled."

Glossary of Literary Terms

Abstraction A broad, general label or umbrella term for an idea like happiness, freedom, or honor. Abstractions often label important areas of human experience or thought, but they run the danger of becoming mere words if they are not anchored to concrete experience. See *concrete*.

Absurd See *theater of the absurd*.

Alexandrine A twelve-syllable line made up of six iambic feet (iambic hexameter). The Elizabethan poet Edmund Spenser used the alexandrine in his Spenserian stanza, which is composed of eight pentameter lines followed by an alexandrine. See *iamb*.

Allegory A work in which related symbols work together, with characters, events, or settings representing ideas or moral qualities. The characters of an allegory are often *abstractions* personified. Famous allegories include Spenser's *The Faerie Queene* and Bunyan's *The Pilgrim's Progress.*

Alliteration The repetition of the same sound (or similar sound) at the beginning of successive words, as in Tennyson's "He Clasps the Crag with Crooked hands." Alliteration was widely used in the Germanic epic and in Middle English poetry before end rhyme gradually took its place.

Allusion A brief mention that calls a character, event, or idea to the reader's mind. An allusion taps into associations and meanings already in the reader's memory. Poets and playwrights through the ages have used allusions to Greek mythology and to the Bible.

Ambiguity Intentional or unintentional double meanings. Intentional ambiguity can leave a poem or story open-ended. Formalist critics made multiple layers of possible meaning a major criterion of challenging poetry.

Anapest Two unaccented syllables followed by an accented one, as in New ROCHELLE. The following lines from Percy Bysshe Shelley's "The

Cloud" are anapestic: "Like a CHILD from the WOMB, like a GHOST from the TOMB, / I ARISE and unBUILD it aGAIN."

Antagonist   Originally, the second major character in early Greek plays. The antagonist is the worthy opponent or counterforce that sets up a central conflict in a play or story, doing battle with or trying to thwart the *protagonist.*

Antithesis   A playing off of opposites or a balancing of one term against another, as in the point/counterpoint statement, "Man proposes, God disposes." *Thesis* and *antithesis* in the original Greek mean "statement" and "counterstatement."

Antonym   A word with the opposite or nearly the opposite meaning of another word. *Order* is an antonym of *chaos.* See *synonym.*

Apostrophe   A solemn or dignified invocation addressing a divine being or a personified abstraction like Liberty or Justice.

Archaic language   Language that is no longer in common use. Unlike *obsolete language,* archaic words and phrases have survived but have an old-fashioned flavor, as for instance *brethren* and *paramour.* Used intentionally, archaisms can re-create a past style or evoke a vanished era.

Archetype   A recurrent image that brings into play deep-seated associations anchored in universal patterns of experience. The Swiss psychoanalyst Carl Jung saw archetypes as rising from the collective unconscious of the human species; his followers trace the central role of archetypes in myth, religion, dream, and imaginative literature.

Assonance   Repetition of similar internal vowel sounds of final syllables, as in *break/fade, mice/flight, told/woe.* See *consonance.*

Autobiographical "I"   The personal voice through which poets share their personal experiences and feelings. Confessional poets use the autobiographical "I" to make public their private, often painful, experiences and observations. The first person pronoun in poetry or fiction is not always the autobiographical "I." The "I" may be a *persona* or assumed identity. See *confessional poetry, point of view,* and *speaker.*

Author biography   The study of an author's life for clues to the meaning of a literary work or for insight into the creative process. Much modern literary biography probes the traumas or dilemmas behind the public persona.

Ballad   A songlike narrative poem traditionally characterized by a recurring refrain and four-line stanzas rhyming *abcb.* Anonymous folk ballads were originally sung as the record of a notable exploit or calamity. From *balar,* "to dance," ballads are created both by individual composers and through communal activity. See *literary ballad.*

Blank verse   Unrhymed iambic pentameter. Marlowe's "mighty line" and the prevailing metrical form of Shakespeare's greatest plays. Also used for long poems by poets over the ages from Marlowe to Words-worth to Frost.

Byplay An action or gesture which takes place apart from the main action of the play, as in an aside, and which can prepare the audience for future conflict.

Caesura A strong pause or a break within a line of verse, often creating a counter rhythm. From the Latin for "a cutting off."

Caricature A comic distortion exaggerating key traits to make them ridiculous. From the Italian for "exaggeration," a caricature often focuses on mannerisms and physical qualities.

Carpe diem Latin for "seize the day." A poetic convention urging us to make use of the passing day, to live for the moment. This theme was common in sixteenth- and seventeenth-century love lyrics, as in Robert Herrick's lines, "Gather ye rosebuds while ye may / Old Time is still a-flying, / And this same flower that smiles today, / Tomorrow will be dying."

Character The representation of a person in a play, story, novel, or poem. A character who has a one-track personality, or who repre-sents a stereotype, is often referred to as *flat*. A character who dis-plays a realistically complex combination of traits—including mixed emotions, conflicting motivations, and divided loyalties—is often called *round*.

Characterization The way in which an author portrays a character for the reader. Characterization can occur through author exposition about a character as well as through the character's actions, speech, and thoughts. In drama a character's thoughts can be revealed through *soliloquy*.

Chorus In ancient Greek drama, a group of onlookers or citizens that comment on the action and serve as guides or interpreters for the audience. The chorus chants and dances at set intervals in the play. In Elizabethan drama, a single actor sometimes serves as a one-person chorus, reciting the prologue and epilogue and commenting between acts.

Circumlocution Indirect, roundabout phrasing, such as calling a "home" a "primary residence." A circumlocution "takes the long way around."

Cliché A term that has lost its freshness through overuse, such as "strong as an ox," "tip of the iceberg," and "American as apple pie." Overused situations or plot elements also can be regarded as clichés.

Climax The highest point of interest or intensity in a literary work, reached after a series of preparatory steps. The climax is often the point in a story where the fortunes of the protagonist take an important turn.

Closure A satisfying conclusion or sense of completion at the end of a work.

Comedy The traditional genre that provides the alternative to the tragic view of life. Audiences for comedy expect happy endings, good fortune, and young love triumphing over obstacles. **High comedy** creates a spirit of mirth and festival; it delights in love talk and love dilemmas; it features high-spirited, quick-witted dialogue. **Low comedy** tends toward horseplay, pratfalls, and bawdry. See *comedy of manners, farce,* and *romantic comedy.*

Comedy of manners A comedy that satirizes the stylized fashions and manners of sophisticated society. This type of comedy is characterized by jabs at convention and witty dialogue, or repartee. Some typical comedies of manners include Oliver Goldsmith's *She Stoops to Conquer,* Oscar Wilde's *The Importance of Being Earnest,* and Philip Barry's *The Philadelphia Story.* See *comedy.*

Comic relief A moment of humor in a serious work. Comic relief provides a temporary break from emotional intensity and may, paradoxically, heighten the seriousness of the story. Shakespeare, for example, employed comic relief in the gravedigger scene in *Hamlet* (Act 5, Scene 1).

Conceit An extended, ingenious imaginative comparison tracing the same metaphor—spring, the garden, the ship—into many related details or applications. Poets from Petrarch to Shakespeare and Donne wrote love poetry using elaborate conceits.

Concrete Concrete images are vivid, graphic images that appeal strongly to the senses, as opposed to *abstractions.*

Concrete poetry Poems that use the physical arrangement of words on a page to mirror meaning (for example, a poem about a bell that is bell-shaped). Concrete poetry takes advantage of the visible shapes of letters and words to create a picture.

Confessional poetry Poetry that employs the *autobiographical "I"* as the poem's speaker for an often painful, public display of personal, private matters. During the 1960s and 1970s, confessional poets such as Anne Sexton, John Berryman, and Sylvia Plath began to provide an alternative to the detached ironic poetry that had long been fashionable. Although confessional poetry is most often associated with contemporary poets, poets over the ages, such as the ancient Greek poet Sappho, for instance, have employed confessional techniques.

Conflict Conflict creates tension and suspense and is the heart of drama. For instance, a central character may be in conflict with another person, with a system of beliefs or values, with the gods, or with natural forces (**external conflict**). A character may be at war with himself or herself, with divided loyalties or contradictory motives pulling the character in different directions (**internal conflict**).

Connotation   The associations and attitudes called up by a word, as opposed to its *denotation* or straight, literal meaning. For instance, the words *scent* and *odor* both denote smell, but advertisers uses the different connotations of the words to make us buy either perfume or deodorant.

Consonance   Repetition of similar sounds in the final syllables of words, as in *torn/burn, add/read, heaven/given*. See *assonance*.

Context   The phrase, sentence, or passage in which a word occurs; the situation that helps give meaning to actions or behavior. Words, gestures, and actions have different meanings in different contexts.

Convention   The customary or established way of talking, writing, or behaving. Writers may follow the conventions of their time, but they may also give them a strong personal twist or rebel against them altogether.

Counterpoint   A counterstatement or countercurrent. A strong direct rejoinder pushing a trend or argument in the opposite direction. (In music, counterpoint is a countermelody played off against the dominant original melody.)

Couplet   Two rhymed lines of verse. If set aside or self-contained, the two rhymed lines are called a *closed couplet*.

Criticism   The systematic analysis of works of imaginative literature. Contemporary critical theory is an active and diverse field, with *formalist, psychoanalytic, feminist, Marxist,* and *deconstructionist* critics among others advancing rival views of literature.

Cumulative repetition   See *repetition*.

Dactyl   One stressed syllable followed by two unstressed syllables, as in BALtimore.

Dark humor   A paradoxical, sardonic form of humor that makes us see catastrophe, illness, or other events that usually defeat people in a comic light.

Deconstructionism   A fashionable postmodern critical perspective that goes beyond the surface structure or surface meanings of a work, lifting the disguises that may obscure its true dynamics or built-in contradictions.

Denotation   The literal definition of a word; its stripped-down meaning devoid of emotional overtones or *connotations*.

Dénouement   French for "untying," the *dénouement* is the wrapping up of major plot elements at the end of a play. The term implies an ingenious, satisfying outcome—for instance, the solution to a central dilemma.

Deus ex machina   Latin for "god from a machine." In the ancient Greek theater a contraption lowered a god or goddess onto the stage to intervene in the action and to work a last-minute solution. Thus, the phrase refers to any device, character, or event introduced suddenly to resolve a conflict in a literary work.

Dialectic   The playing off of opposing forces or points of view.

Dialects   The regional variations of a common language that are still mutually intelligible, although some actually border on becoming separate languages.

Dialogue   Verbal exchange between two or more people. In a literary work, dialogue may help establish the situation, delineate character, or focus attention on major themes.

Diction   The writer's choice and use of words.

Didacticism   Heavy reliance on ideas meant to instruct or improve the reader. The term is often used for overt or heavy-handed preaching or editorializing in a literary work.

Dramatic irony   Audience awareness of the meaning of words or actions unknown to one or more characters. Dramatic irony occurs when we are "in on" an event a character is not in on. In *Oedipus Rex,* the readers or viewers know that Oedipus has killed his father and married his mother, a situation Oedipus remains unaware of until the last scene.

Dramatic monologue   A lengthy first-person speech which enlightens the reader about the setting, the speaker's identity, and the dramatic situation.

Elegy   A poem of mourning and lamentation. Elegies are most often sustained, formal poems with a meditative, solemn mood. Walt Whitman's "When Lilacs Last in the Dooryard Bloomed" was an elegy on the death of President Lincoln.

Elizabethan Age   The English literary period named after Queen Elizabeth and lasting from 1558 until 1642, the year of the closing of the theaters. This "golden age" saw such literary figures as Shakespeare develop the beginnings of modern drama and saw an outburst of lyric poetry. Other notable names of the period include Sidney, Spenser, Marlowe, and Jonson.

Empathy   Imaginative sympathy that allows us to identify with the experience, situation, feelings, or motives of another.

End rhyme   The echo effect that makes the last words of two or more lines of poetry rhyme, as in Gwendolyn Brooks' "My last deFENSE / Is the present TENSE." See also *internal rhyme.*

End-stopped line   A line of poetry that ends with a period, colon, or semicolon. See *enjambment.*

Enjambment   The continuation of a sentence in a poem so that it spills over from one line to the next. "How like a winter has my absence been / From thee . . . (Shakespeare, Sonnet 97). See *end-stopped line.*

Epic poem   A long narrative poem that speaks to the listener in an elevated style and often embodies the central values of a civilization. The traditional epic celebrated the exploits of the tribe or nation and often focused on charismatic heroic leaders. Among epics rooted in age-old oral tradition are Homer's *Iliad* and *Odyssey,* the Old English *Beowulf,* the Spanish *El Cid,* and Virgil's *Aeneid.*

Epigram   A concise, cleverly worded remark making a pointed, witty statement. From the Greek for "inscription," an epigram may play off antithetical ideas, as in "Man proposes, God disposes."

Epiphany   A sudden flash of intuitive understanding when the true meaning of things and events is revealed. The term was used by James Joyce, and epiphanies appear at the end of many of his stories, including "Araby."

Euphemism   From the Greek for "beautiful words." The use of pleasant-sounding language for harsh realities, often with the intention of sounding less offensive or more refined. Examples of euphemisms are calling garbage disposal "waste management" or calling death a "passing away."

Existentialism   An influential, pervasive twentieth-century philosophy that denies the existence of transcendent meanings and places the burden of giving meaning to their lives on individual human beings. French philosopher, playwright, and novelist Jean-Paul Sartre and French novelist Albert Camus were among prominent disseminators of existentialist thought.

Explication   The line-by-line explanation of a literary text. Explication differs from interpretation in that it usually refers to a literal, step-by-step scrutiny of the language of a work, as opposed to a broader, more subjective look at its overall significance.

Exposition   The part of a play or story that establishes setting and situation and that often introduces important characters and themes.

Extended (or sustained) metaphor   A metaphor traced into several related details, often becoming the central metaphor of a poem.

External evidence   Evidence outside a piece of literature itself, examined in an attempt to understand a work's meaning. Characteristic themes in the author's other works or information found in the author's letters or interviews are common forms of external evidence.

Farce   An exaggerated kind of low comedy that derives its humor from crude jokes, pratfalls and ineptitude, and rambunctious horseplay. See *comedy.*

Feminine (or double) rhyme   Two-syllable rhyme, with the first syllable stressed and the second unstressed, as in *ocean/motion, started/parted.* See also *masculine rhyme.*

Feminist criticism   Feminist critics have a special interest in how imaginative literature reflects the lives of women. Feminist scholars have rediscovered and reevaluated women writers of the past; they have focused on how women are marginalized or trivialized in much traditional literature written from a male perspective.

Figurative language   Language using imaginative comparison rather than literal statement. See *metaphor, simile.*

Flashback   A shifting back to events that took place at an earlier time, allowing the writer to break up straight chronological order by playing off memories of the past against the present.

Foil   A character who serves as a contrast to a main character, thus highlighting or underscoring distinctive features of the other.

Folklore   Traditional material—stories, legends, proverbs, riddles, charms, spells, folk songs, ballads—reflecting the customs and beliefs of a culture. Echoes of prehistoric myths and rituals often survive in the folklore of a people.

Foot   The smallest unit of verse, usually made up of one stressed and one or more unstressed syllables. For different types of metric feet, see *iamb, trochee, dactyl, anapest,* and *spondee.*

Foreshadowing   A hint pointing forward to a future development. For instance, foreshadowing may take the form of a mood created by the setting, of ominous hints concerning unsolved problems, of a sense of foreboding expressed by a character, or of frequent focus on an object fraught with symbolic meaning.

Formalist criticism   Formalism in the tradition of the New Critics of the forties and fifties reacted against approaches that shifted attention too routinely from the literary work to author biography, author psychology, or the sociological context. The New Critics insisted on close reading of the work itself, focusing on how features of form—image, metaphor, symbol, point of view, irony, paradox—gave shape to a poem or work of fiction as a whole.

Frame story   A narrative which frames the main series of events, often by setting up an occasion for the narrator to tell the main story.

Free verse   Poetry freed from the restraints of strong, regular meter and rhyme, developing instead its own individual pattern and free-flowing rhythm.

Freudian criticism   See *psychoanalytic criticism.*

Genre   A French word for "type" or "kind," used by critics to mark off traditional subdivisions of imaginative literature. Fiction, poetry, and drama are the three major traditional genres; subgenres include the novel, the short story, the epic, the lyric (further subdivided into categories like elegy, satire, or pastoral), tragedy, and comedy.

Traditionalists used to set up rules or conventions for each genre; they objected to mixed genres like tragicomedy.

Ghazal   A traditional Persian (Iranian) poetic form made up of sequences of five to fifteen related couplets.

Grotesque   A mixed genre combining the frightening and the ridiculous. The grotesque in literature or art caters to a taste for the bizarre, fantastic, and ominous.

Haiku   A widely practiced traditional Japanese poetic form of three lines of five, seven, and five syllables each. The haiku captures a moment in time, allowing a thought or image to linger in the memory.

Half-rhymes   Words that do not rhyme but distantly sound alike.

High comedy   See *comedy.*

Hubris   The overreaching pride of humans that leads to their tragic downfall. The word *hubris* comes from the Greek for "insolence" or "outrage." Hubris makes human beings forget their limitations and makes them challenge the gods. Oedipus, for example, challenged the gods by believing he could escape their prophecy.

Hyperbole   Extreme exaggeration, common in the love poetry of earlier centuries and the opposite of modern understatement. From the Greek for "excess." "Ah, she doth teach the torches to burn bright," says Shakespeare's hyperbolical Romeo.

Iamb   A two-syllable foot with the stress on the last syllable, as in DETROIT. Over the centuries, iambic meter with four or five beats to the line (iambic tetrameter and iambic pentameter) became the most common meter in poetry written in English.

Idiom   The characteristic, natural language of a group, or a phrase or way of expressing an idea that is an example of natural speech.

Image   Not just a vivid visual impression but more generally any concrete detail that speaks directly and vividly to our senses of sight, hearing, smell, taste, or touch. See *concrete.*

Incongruity   Things that clash or violate decorum. The metaphysical poets of the seventeenth century yoked incongruous, discordant elements to compel attention—mixing, for instance, the language of love with the technical language of map making. See also *paradox.*

Interlude   A short, humorous performance presented in the intervals between more serious dramatic entertainment.

Internal rhyme   Two or more words rhyming within a line of poetry rather than at the end of lines. Sometimes occur in combination with *end rhyme.*

Interpretation   Moving beyond line-by-line explication of a text to examine its major themes or larger meanings.

Intruding author   The distinctive feature of a narrative style that allows the author or an authorial persona to step into the story to interrupt the narrative and chat with the reader—for instance, to offer explanations, witty asides, or philosophical reflections. Nineteenth-century readers of fiction were used to the friendly presence of the author taking them into his or her confidence.

Inversion   The reversal of normal word order in a sentence (*"that* I will never do") or the reversal of the rhythmic stress in a poem, for instance by starting a line of iambic pentameter with a trochaic foot.

Irony   A wry, humorous effect produced when an overt or surface meaning is negated by a different meaning representing the writer's or speaker's true intention. ("Easier availability of assault weapons is just what this country needs.") *Verbal irony* refers to a deliberate contrast between what is said and what is meant. *Irony of situation* refers to a contrast between what we expected to happen and what really happened, especially when we should have known better. See also *dramatic irony.*

Jungian criticism   See *myth criticism.*

Literary ballad   A poem written by a poet reviving or imitating the style of the traditional anonymous folk ballad.

Low comedy   See *comedy.*

Lyric   Now a general label for a fairly short poem expressing personal thought and emotion, as contrasted with *narrative poetry* or the traditional *epic.*

Malapropism   An inadvertent and often hilarious misuse of a word. The practice is named after Mrs. Malaprop, in Sheridan's play *The Rivals,* who said things like *"illiterate* him . . . from your memory."

Marxist criticism   Marxist and other politically engaged critics focus on how literature reflects the social and political arrangements that shape people's lives. They call attention to how writers show their origin from or allegiance to a social class, to how writers serve or challenge the interests of the power structure, and to how writers ignore or critique patterns of exploitation and oppression.

Masculine (or single) rhyme   A rhyme that makes only the final accented syllables of two or more words rhyme—for instance, *high/sky, leave/ grieve, renown/gown.* Different from *feminine rhyme.*

Melodrama   A wildly popular kind of drama or fiction pitting good against evil and employing sensational plot twists and tear-jerking devices. Traditional melodramas present good and evil stock characters, with the audience weeping over the persecution of wronged innocence, hissing dyed-in-the-wool malefactors, and cheering when the villains are brought to justice. See also *sentimentality.*

Metaphor   An imaginative, often bold or thought-provoking comparison treating one thing as if it were another, without the use of *like* or *as,* as in these Emily Dickinson lines: "Hope is the thing with feathers / That perches in the soul." See *extended metaphor, organizing metaphor,* and *simile.*

Metaphysical poets   Poets of the seventeenth century known for their bold imagery, complex demanding form, and abundant reliance on incongruity, paradox, and irony. Metaphysical poets including John Donne, Andrew Marvell, and George Herbert were rediscovered early in the twentieth century by moderns rebelling against jingle poets, Victorian uplift, and versified sentimentality.

Meter   The underlying beat that in much traditional poetry regularizes the natural rhythms of speech. *Trimeter* is meter with three stressed syllables to the line, *tetrameter* has four stressed syllables, *pentameter* has five, and *hexameter* has six.

Metonymy   A figure of speech that makes a term closely related to something serve as its substitute. For instance, the word *sword* by extension means "military career" in the line "He abandoned the sword." See also *synechdoche.*

Minimalism   A contemporary style of writing that tries to eliminate all rhetoric and emotion or at least to reduce these elements to bare essentials. Minimalist writers include Anne Beattie and Raymond Carver.

Modernism   A movement of the early twentieth century that rebelled against self-approving Victorian earnestness in the arts or literature generally and against versified noble sentiments in poetry in particular. In their search for new contemporary modes of expression, the modernists rejected flowery artificial language and began using experimental techniques, including *stream of consciousness* in fiction and *free verse* in poetry. Pioneering early modernists included James Joyce, Ernest Hemingway, Virginia Woolf, Ezra Pound, and T. S. Eliot. See also *postmodernism.*

Monologue   An extended solo speech by a character in a play (or sometimes a poem). A monologue, since it is typically heard by or directed at other characters, may be less of a private revelation of personal thought and feeling than a *soliloquy.*

Mood   A pervasive emotional quality or psychological cast of a work, which may be created by literary devices including *tone, imagery,* and *setting.*

Morality play   A medieval form of religious drama, with personified abstractions such as Shame, Mercy, and Conscience teaching religious and moral lessons. See also *allegory.*

Myth criticism   Myth critics in the tradition of Jung and his followers see imaginative literature as growing out of age-old rituals that acted out the myths or invoked the archetypes wired into the collective unconscious of the human species.

Narrator   The person speaking to us in a story or telling the story. Twentieth-century critics have paid close attention to the role of the narrator in contemporary fiction. See *point of view, reflector,* and *speaker.*

Naturalism   A literary movement in the late nineteenth and early twentieth centuries that went beyond realism to give readers unvarnished portrayals of nature in the raw. Naturalists set out to right the balance by providing frank portrayals of harsh realities; these were glossed over in more genteel or euphemistic literature. Widely read and influential representatives of the naturalistic movement include the French novelist Émile Zola and the Americans Jack London, Stephen Crane, and John Steinbeck.

Neoclassicism   A dominant eighteenth-century style turning to the art and literature of classical Greek and Roman work for models and inspiration. Neoclassical writers preached that sound judgment should guide and restrain the poetic imagination. They prized order, clarity, economic wording, logic, refinement, and decorum. Theirs was an age of rationalism, wit, and satire. High priests of the neo-classical spirit in literature were Alexander Pope and Samuel Johnson.

New Critics   See *formalist criticism.*

Novel   A work of narrative prose fiction, generally considerably longer and more complex than a short story, with a central character or group of characters whose experiences the reader may follow through a lifetime. The novel, often published in installments in magazines, began to build up a large reading audience in the eighteenth and nineteenth centuries, with favorite authors such as Jane Austen and Charles Dickens eventually read by millions around the world.

Novella   A pointed story shorter than a full-length novel but longer than a traditional short story.

Obsolete language   Words, or meanings of words, that are no longer in use, like *fond* in the sense of "foolish."

Octave   A set of eight lines, such as the first eight lines linked by inter-lacing rhymes in the traditional sonnet.

Ode   An elaborately crafted, stately poem fit for solemn subjects, often written in imitation of ancient Greek models.

Onomatopoeia   The use of words that seem to sound out their meanings, such as *pop, hiss,* or *buzz.*

Open form   A poetic form abandoning the constraints of regular rhyme, meter, line length, or stanza form.

Oral history   A cultural tradition of passing spoken stories from one generation to the next, often combining myth, history, and current events.

Organizing (or controlling) metaphor   A single extended metaphor that gives shape to a poem as a whole.

Ottava rima   From the Italian for "eighth rhyme." A finely crafted stanza consisting of eight iambic pentameter lines with the rhyme pattern *abababcc*.

Pantomime   Acting that relies solely on gestures or body language rather than words to communicate a story.

Paradox   An apparent contradiction that, on second thought, illuminates a truth. See also *incongruity, irony*.

Parallelism   The repetition of similar or identical structures to emphasize connections between related ideas ("I came, I saw, I conquered").

Paraphrase   Restating someone else's ideas in your own words.

Para-rhyme   See *slant rhyme*.

Parody   A humorous, sometimes affectionate and sometimes mocking imitation, exaggerating or aping characteristic features.

Pastoral   A poetic tradition offering harried city dwellers a nostalgic vision of the idealized simplicity and leisure of country life. Pastorals were first written by the Greeks and continue to be written today. Traditional pastorals dwelled on the love games of make-believe shepherds and shepherdesses but often also became a vehicle for social criticism.

Pathos   A quality in literature or art that arouses pity, sympathy, tenderness, or sorrow. From the Greek for "suffering" and "passion," pathos usually applies to a helpless character who suffers passively.

Peripety   A sudden reversal of fortune for a protagonist, brought on for instance by an unexpected discovery of a long hidden or ignored truth. From the Greek for "to change suddenly."

Persona   The assumed identity the writer presents when speaking to us in poetry or fiction. The persona may be close to the real-life personality of the writer, but it may also be far removed from it, serving perhaps as a mask or disguise.

Personification   Figurative language that endows something nonhuman with human qualities, as in "the trees *whispered* in the wind."

Petrarchan sonnet   A dominant Italian form of the sonnet practiced by Petrarch and imitated by his English translators and admirers. The Petrarchan sonnet tends to have a turning point, or turn, after the first two quatrains before the concluding sestet.

Plot   The chain of events in fiction or drama. A plot may be tightly structured, with a chain of cause and effect leading to a seemingly inevitable conclusion. However, it may also keep readers or spectators in suspense or surprise them with unexpected twists and turns. Plots of traditional novels were often leisurely, with the author exploring byways or indulging in detours, following the slow meandering rhythm of life. Twentieth-century writers have often broken up traditional plot structure with flashbacks, free association, or broken-mirror effects. See also *flashback, subplot.*

Poetic diction   Poetic language more elevated and refined than ordinary speech. Often used for an artificial eighteenth-century style tending toward euphemism and circumlocution.

Point of view   The vantage point from which we see the events of a story; the angle from which a story is told. With a **first-person** point of view, one of the characters narrates the story, seeing and knowing only what that individual can observe from his or her limited point of view. With a **third-person omniscient** point of view, the writer may write as an "all-seeing" author, knowing not only the behavior but also the private thoughts and feelings of the characters. With a **third-person limited** point of view, the writer focuses on the actions and thoughts of only some of the characters. With a **third-person objective** point of view, the writer acts as the impartial observer, offering little or no editorial comment.

Polarity   The setting up and playing off of polar opposites as a major organizing element in our perception of reality and in the patterning of imaginative literature.

Postmodernism   An umbrella term for critical approaches that discount surface meaning and look in a literary work for instance for an implied critique of the limitations of language or the writer's craft.

Problem play   A play in the tradition of the Norwegian playwright Henrik Ibsen, making the audience confront contemporary social problems or issues and often challenging conventional thinking and social mores.

Prose poem   A passage printed like prose but using poetic imagery or asking for concentrated attention like a poem.

Protagonist   The lead actor or principal figure in drama or fiction. The confrontation between the protagonist and the antagonist, the second most important character, is often at the heart of the dramatic conflict in a play. See *antagonist.*

Psychoanalytic criticism   Psychoanalytic critics in the tradition of Freud and his followers look in literature for a reflection of deep-seated psychic conflicts, typically resulting from the repression of our instinctual selves. The symbolic action of a poem or play may show the interplay of the id (the anarchic repressed unconscious self), the ego (the overlay of conscious moral rules and inhibitions), and the superego (the society or moral system as a whole).

Pun A type of word play, exploiting the similar sense or sound of words or sometimes different meanings of the same word, as when a punster calls a congested bridge the "car-strangled spanner."

Quatrain A set of four lines, like the two sets of four lines that form the opening part of a Petrarchan sonnet.

Reader response Reader response criticism calls special attention to what readers bring to the reading of a poem, a story, a play. A poem does not exist as dead letters on a page; it comes to life as its readers decode the text, relating it to their own world of experience and meanings.

Realism A late-nineteenth-century literary movement that reacted against both the Romantic idealizing of nature and Victorian moral uplift. It emphasized instead the faithful rendering of ordinary human experience. Pioneers included the Norwegian playwright Henrik Ibsen and the British novelists George Eliot (Marian Evans) and Thomas Hardy. Playwrights like Arthur Miller continued the tradition of realistic drama.

Recurrence The reappearance of themes or key elements, serving to echo issues and concerns introduced earlier.

Reflector A person through whose eyes we see the events of a story. Although this is often the narrator, it can also be a character within the story if important information is communicated through his or her perceptions or thoughts.

Refrain In much folk song or ballad, a line (or group of lines) that comes back or echoes at intervals in a poem, often at the end of each stanza.

Reiteration Purposeful, insistent repetition in poetry or prose to reinforce a basic point.

Repartee The quick exchange of pointed, witty remarks, with characters trading clever quips or barbed personal comments.

Repetition Recurrence of the same word or phrase used to highlight or emphasize something in a poem or story. Poets often use purposeful cumulative repetition to build up to a climactic effect.

Revenge tragedy A form of tragedy going back to the Roman playwright Seneca and popular in Shakespeare's time. The play may start with the ghost of a murdered victim clamoring for revenge, lead into a plot of intrigue revolving around plots and counterplots, and end with the avenger taking the perpetrators down with him to bloody death. Shakespeare's *Hamlet* fits key criteria of the traditional revenge tragedy.

Rhetoric Traditionally, the effective use of language for purposes of persuasion, especially in politics and law. The early Greek philosopher Aristotle published a first major influential treatise on the art of rhetoric, or effective public speech. The term is now used for the study and practice of effective language both spoken and written. The term has acquired a pejorative alternative meaning as the result of the abuse of language by windbags and manipulators.

Rhyme   The echo effect produced when a writer repeats the same sounds at the ends of words: *moon/June, delighted/indicted*. See *end rhyme, feminine rhyme, half-rhyme, internal rhyme, masculine rhyme, sight rhyme, slant rhyme,* and *triple rhyme.*

Romantic comedy   A type of comedy focusing on love as a chief element of the plot. Romantic comedies may play with the obstacles in the path of young love but tend to culminate in easy reconciliations, happy endings, and multiple marriages.

Romanticism   An artistic revolt against the conventions of the fashionable formal, civilized, and refined neoclassicism of the eighteenth century. Whereas Neoclassicism stressed the "order in beauty," Romanticism stresses the "strangeness in beauty" (Walter Pater). The Romantics dropped conventional poetic diction and forms in favor of freer forms and bolder language. They preached a return to nature, elevated sincere feeling over the dry intellect, and often shared in the revolutionary fervor of the late eighteenth century. Blake, Coleridge, Wordsworth, Keats, Shelley, and Byron are prominent in the pantheon of English Romantic poets.

Sarcasm   A bitter or cutting form of verbal irony.

Satire   The use of humor and often sharp biting wit to critique human misconduct or ridicule stupidity, vice, and folly. Offenders are measured against an implied standard of humane behavior.

Scansion   A system for charting the underlying beat, or meter, of a literary work.

Sentimentality   Working on the emotions of an audience, for instance through exploiting sympathy for helpless victims and through self-righteous indignation at dastardly villains. Sentimentality allows people to bask in the warm glow of self-approving emotions.

Sestet   A six-line poetic stanza.

Setting   Place and time, often providing more than a mere backdrop for the action of a story or play.

Shakespearean sonnet   The typical Shakespearean sonnet has three quatrains followed by a concluding couplet. See *sonnet.*

Sight rhyme   Words that coincide in spelling but not in sound, like *come* and *home.*

Simile   An imaginative comparison signaled by such words as *like, as,* or *as if:* "My love is like a red, red rose." Unlike the implied comparison of a metaphor, a simile says outright that something is like something else.

Slang   Extremely, often aggressively informal language suggesting complete disregard for polite conventions.

Slant (or para-) rhyme   The near rhyming of words that distantly sound alike. See *assonance* and *consonance*.

Soliloquy   A solo speech a character makes in a drama revealing his or her feelings and inner conflicts. During a soliloquy, a character usually stands alone on stage, talking without addressing another character. See *monologue*.

Sonnet   An elaborately crafted fourteen-line poem in iambic pentameter. The Petrarchan sonnet starts with an eight-line segment, or octave, with an interlaced *abbaabba* rhyme scheme, followed by a sestet (six-line segment) of *cdcdee* or *cdecde*. The octave often raises a question or states a predicament or proposition that is answered in the sestet. The Shakespearean sonnet generally is arranged as three quatrains (four-line segments) and a couplet (two lines), with the typical rhyme scheme of *abab/cdcd/efef/gg*. The Spenserian sonnet uses three quatrains and a couplet like the Shakespearean sonnet but employs a linking rhyme scheme more similar to the Petrarchan sonnet: *abab/bcbc/cdcd/ee*. See *sonnet sequence*.

Sonnet sequence   A group of sonnets exploring related themes, often centering originally on the sorrows of unrequited love. Petrarch, Sidney, Spenser, and Shakespeare are among sonneteers who wrote extended sonnet sequences or "cycles." A once widely read, later sonnet sequence is Elizabeth Barrett Browning's *Sonnets from the Portuguese*.

Speaker   The voice speaking in a poem or story, as distinct from the author as a person. Also called "persona."

Spenserian sonnet   See *sonnet*.

Spenserian stanza   A nine-line stanza used by Edmund Spenser. It follows the rhyming pattern *ababbcbcc;* the first eight lines are pentameter and the last is an alexandrine (iambic with six stresses).

Spondee   A rare metrical foot of two stressed syllables, as in one possible pronunciation of HONG KONG.

Sprung rhythm   An irregular, syncopated rhythmic pattern developed by Gerard Manley Hopkins, with stressed syllables followed by a varying number of unstressed syllables.

Stanza   A grouping of related lines with a characteristic metrical and rhyme scheme to be repeated or varied in subsequent stanzas.

Stress   Accent or emphasis that makes one syllable stand out from the others in a word or phrase.

Stream of consciousness   A narrative technique mirroring the flow of sensations, thought, and feelings in our minds—a kaleidoscopic mix of fleeting images, bodily sensations, memories, and half-finished trains of thought.

Stock character   A conventional, easily recognizable character; a stereotype. Stock characters of traditional comedy include the skinflint, the grouch, the hypochondriac, and the amorous old man. In popular modern plays, stock characters may include the meddling in-laws, the oversolicitous ethnic mother, or the studious "nerd."

Style   At its best, an author's unmistakable personal way of using language, looking at the world, and giving shape to a work of literature. (An author's style may however also be imitative, colorless, or impersonal.)

Subplot   Secondary story lines or conflicts that run parallel to the main plot. A subplot may reinforce a work's central theme, such as filial ingratitude in Shakespeare's *King Lear*—the betrayal of a loyal parent by disloyal offspring.

Symbol   An object or action that has acquired a meaning beyond itself. Traditional symbols carry a range of familiar associations, but writers may develop their own language of private symbols that readers have to respond to and decode.

Synecdoche   A figure of speech that uses the part to stand for the whole, or the whole to stand for the part: *wheels* to mean "car" and *hired hands* to mean "hired people." See also *metonymy*.

Synonym   A word that has the same or nearly the same meaning as another, such as *liberty* and *freedom*. See also *antonym*.

Tercet   A set of three lines.

Theater of the Absurd   Drama pioneered by playwrights like Eugène Ionesco, Samuel Beckett, and Edward Albee, rejecting the linear, logical surface of realistic plays as artificial. Absurdist plays mirror the tragicomic gropings of moderns doomed to disappointment in the search for meaning. "Conceived in perplexity and spiritual anguish, the theater of the absurd portrays not a series of connected incidents telling a story but a pattern of images presenting people as bewildered beings in an incomprehensible universe" (Hugh Holman).

Theme   A recurring, unifying subject, idea, or motif—like the breakdown of the family, or the alienation of young people from their parents. However, more specifically and pointedly, the term *theme* may stand for the answer that a literary work as a whole seems to give to the questions it raises (what the work as a whole seems to say *about* family, or alienation). Twentieth-century writers have generally been reluctant to spell out a thematic message in so many words, preferring to let readers ponder implied or suggested meanings.

Thesis   In expository prose, a concise, memorable summing up of what a writer is trying to say or setting out to prove. A thesis statement often appears toward the beginning of a paper or article as a preview or program, setting directions and steering the attention of the reader. However, in a more inductive kind of writing the writer may build toward the thesis and present it as a justified conclusion at the end.

Tone   The human quality or emotional coloring that reveals a writer's attitude toward the subject and toward the reader, ranging from light-hearted or frivolous to bitter or gloomy.

Tragedy   One of the two traditional Greek dramatic genres. Growing out of rituals honoring the god Dionysos, ancient Greek tragedy drama-tized stories about lethal conflicts, often among persons closely linked by kinship or marriage. The traditional tragedy recounts the fall of heroes or persons of high degree, as in the fall of a king in Sophocles' *Oedipus Rex* and Shakespeare's *Macbeth*. Modern stu-dents of tragedy have focused on such topics as the fateful choices faced by tragic protagonists, the journey toward self-awareness, or archetypal patterns of experience acted out by the tragic hero. See also *revenge tragedy* and *tragic flaw*.

Tragic flaw   A fatal flaw or shortcoming in an otherwise admirable tragic hero. Critics following the lead of the early Greek philosopher Aris-totle (in his *Poetics*) use the tragic flaw to explain or justify the down-fall of an otherwise outstanding individual. This flaw may be anything from impious pride to uncontrollable anger, jealousy, or indecision. See *hubris*.

Tragicomedy   A mixed genre in which the tragic and comedic elements contend. A tragicomedy, for instance, may take the audience to the brink of tragic events but then end happily, like a comedy. It is likely to have noble and lowlife characters mingle, moving from elevated sentiments to coarse humor.

Transition   A link that smoothly moves the reader from one stanza, para-graph, or idea to the next.

Triple rhyme   Rhyme that makes the whole of a three-syllable word (or phrase) rhyme. The rhyming stressed syllable is followed by two unstressed syllables, as in *moralities/realities* or *meticulous/ridiculous*.

Trochee   A two-syllable metrical foot with the stress on the first syllable (BOSTON). The following example of trochaic meter is from Coleridge: "TROchee TRIPS from LONG to SHORT."

Understatement   A deliberate playing down of the significance and emo-tional impact of events. Many twentieth-century writers, suspicious of arm-waving and emoting, have cultivated an understated, detached, "cool" modern style. See *tone*.

Vignette   A sketch or brief narrative that focuses on a character or event. It may be a separate whole or serve as a sidelight in a larger work.

Word play   Witty or clever use of words. See also *pun*.

Acknowledgments

FICTION

Toni Cade Bambara   "The Lesson" from *Gorilla, My Love*. Copyright © 1972 by Toni Cade Bambara. Reprinted with the permission of Random House, Inc. Excerpts from "Trying to Stay Centered" from *Black Women Writers at Work*, edited by Claudia Tate (New York: Continuum, 1983). Reprinted with the permission of the Audrey Wolf Literary Agency.

Raymond Carver   "The Third Thing That Killed My Father Off" (originally titled "Dummy") from *Furious Seasons*. Copyright © 1977 by Raymond Carver. Reprinted with the permission of Capra Press, Santa Barbara, California.

Anton Chekhov   "Vanka" from *The Portable Chekhov*, edited by Avrahm Yarmolinsky. Copyright 1947, © 1968 by Viking Penguin, Inc.; renewed © 1975 by Avrahm Yarmolinsky. Reprinted with the permission of Viking Penguin, a division of Penguin Putnam, Inc.

Sandra Cisneros   "Mericans" from *Woman Hollering Creek and Other Stories* (New York: Random House, 1991). Copyright © 1991 by Sandra Cisneros. Reprinted with the permission of Susan Bergholz Literary Services, New York. All rights reserved.

Louise Erdrich   "The Red Convertible" from *Love Medicine*, new and expanded version. Copyright © 1984 by Louise Erdrich. Reprinted with the permission of Henry Holt and Company, Inc.

William Faulkner   "A Rose for Emily" from *Collected Stories of William Faulkner*. Copyright 1930, 1950, and renewed © 1958 by William Faulkner, © 1977 by Jill Faulkner Summers. Reprinted with the permission of Random House, Inc.

Richard Giannone   "The Mystery of Love" from *Flannery O'Connor and the Mystery of Love*. Copyright © 1989 by Richard Giannone. Reprinted with the permission of the University of Illinois Press.

Sandra M. Gilbert and Susan Gubar   "Enclosure and Escape: Gilman's 'The Yellow Wallpaper'" from *The Madwoman in the Attic: The Woman Writer and the Nineteenth Century Literary Imagination*. Copyright © 1979 by Yale University; renewed © 1984 by Sandra M. Gilbert and Susan Gubar. Reprinted with the permission of Yale University Press.

Wilfred L. Guerin   Excerpt from "'Young Goodman Brown': Id versus Superego" from *Handbook of Critical Approaches to Literature*, 3rd ed. Copyright © 1992 by Oxford University Press, Inc. Reprinted with the permission of the publishers.

Ernest Hemingway   "Hills like White Elephants" from *Men Without Women*. Copyright 1927 by Charles Scribner's Sons, renewed © 1955 by Ernest Hemingway. Excerpt from "Big Two-Hearted River" from *The Complete Short Stories of Ernest Hemingway*. Copyright 1925 by Charles Scribner's Sons; renewed 1953 by Ernest Hemingway. Both reprinted with the permission of Scribner, a division of Simon & Schuster.

Shirley Jackson   "The Lottery" from *The Lottery and Other Stories*. Copyright 1948, 1949 by Shirley Jackson, renewed © 1976, 1977 by Laurence Hyman, Barry Hyman, Mrs. Sarah Webster, and Mrs. Joanne Schnurer. Reprinted with the permission of Farrar, Straus & Giroux, Inc.

1207

Alice Walker   "Everyday Use" from *In Love and Trouble: Stories of Black Women*. Copyright © 1973 by Alice Walker. "Beyond the Peacock: The Reconstruction of Flannery O'Connor" from *In Search of Our Mothers' Gardens*. Copyright © 1975 by Alice Walker. Both reprinted with the permission of Harcourt Brace and Company.

POETRY

Maya Angelou   "Phenomenal Woman" from *And Still I Rise*. Copyright © 1978 by Maya Angelou. Reprinted with the permission of Random House, Inc.

Margaret Atwood   "Dreams of the Animals" from *Selected Poems 1965–1975*. Reprinted in *Selected Poems 1966–1984*. Copyright © 1976, 1990 by Margaret Atwood. Reprinted with the permission of Houghton Mifflin Company and Oxford University Press Canada.

W. H. Auden   "The Unknown Citizen" from *W. H. Auden: Collected Poems,* edited by Edward Mendelson. Copyright 1940 and renewed © 1968 by W. H. Auden. Reprinted with the permission of Random House, Inc.

Wendell Berry   "The Peace of Wild Things" from *The Collected Poems, 1957–1982*. Copyright © 1987 by Wendell Berry. Reprinted with the permission of North Point Press, a division of Farrar, Straus & Giroux, Inc.

John Berryman   "Dream Song 14" from *The Dream Songs*. Copyright © 1969 by John Berryman. Reprinted with the permission of Farrar, Straus & Giroux, Inc.

Elizabeth Bishop   "The Fish" from *The Complete Poems 1927–1979*. Copyright © 1979, 1983 by Alice Helen Methfessel. Reprinted with the permission of Farrar, Straus & Giroux, Inc.

Louise Bogan   "Cassandra," "The Dream," and "Women" from *The Blue Estuaries: Poems 1923–1968*. Copyright © 1968 by Louise Bogan. Reprinted with the permission of Farrar, Straus & Giroux, Inc.

Gwendolyn Brooks   "truth," "We Real Cool," "hunchback girl: she thinks of heaven," "piano after war," "The Chicago *Defender* Sends a Man to Little Rock," "when you have forgotten Sunday: the love story," "the preacher: ruminates behind the sermon," "the ballad of the light-eyed little girl, " and "The Bean Eaters" from *Blacks* (Chicago: Third World Press, 1987). Copyright © 1987 by Gwendolyn Brooks Blakely. Reprinted with the permission of the author. "Mexie and Bridie" from *Bronzeville Boys and Girls* (New York: Harper & Row, 1956). Copyright © 1956 by Gwendolyn Brooks Blakely. Reprinted with the permission of HarperCollins Publishers, Inc. "The Boy Died in My Alley" from *Beckonings*. Copyright © 1975 by Gwendolyn Brooks Blakeley. Reprinted with the permission of Broadside Press.

Lorna Dee Cervantes   "Freeway 280" from *Latin American Literary Review* 15 (1977). Copyright © 1977. Reprinted with the permission of the publishers. Excerpt from "Refugee Ship" from *A Decade of Hispanic Literature: An Anniversary Anthology*. Reprinted with the permission of Arte Publico Press, University of Houston. Excerpt from "Poem for the Young White Man Who Asked Me How I, an Intelligent, Well-Read Person, Could Believe in the War between Races" from *Emplumada*. Copyright © 1981 by Lorna Dee Cervantes. Reprinted with the permission of University of Pittsburgh Press.

Lucille Clifton   "my mama moved among the days" from *good woman: poems and a memoir 1969–1980*. Copyright © 1987 by Lucille Clifton. Reprinted with the permission of BOA Editions, Ltd., 92 Park Avenue, Brockport, N.Y. 14420.

Robert Creeley   Excerpt from "Ballad of the Despairing Husband" from *Collected Poems of Robert Creeley, 1945–1975*. Copyright © 1983 by The Regents of the University of California. Reprinted with the permission of the University of California Press.

Juana Inés de la Cruz   "Ignorant Men" from "A Satirical Romance," translated by Judith Thurman, from *I Became Alone: Five Women Poets* by Judith Thurman with drawings by James and Ruth McCrea (New York: Atheneum Publishers, 1975). Translation copyright © 1975 by Judith Thurman. Reprinted with the permission of Marian Reiner Literary Agent for the author.

Countee Cullen   "For My Grandmother" and "Saturday's Child" from *Color*. Copyright 1925 by Harper & Brothers; renewed 1953 by Ida M. Cullen. Reprinted with the permission of, and copyrights administered by, Thompson and Thompson, New York, N.Y.

e. e. cummings   "in Just-" and "Buffalo Bill's" from *Complete Poems 1904–1962,* edited by George J. Firmage. Copyright 1923, 1925, 1926, 1931, 1935, 1938, 1939, 1940, 1941, 1945, 1946, 1947, 1948, 1949, 1950, 1951, 1952, 1953, 1954, 1955, 1956, 1957, 1958, 1959, 1960, 1961, 1962, 1963, 1966, 1967, 1968, 1972, 1973, 1974, 1975, 1976, 1977, 1978, 1979, 1980, 1981, 1982, 1983, 1984, 1985, 1986, 1987, 1989, 1990, 1991 by the Trustees for the E. E. Cummings Trust. Copyright © 1973, 1976, 1978, 1979, 1981, 1983, 1985, 1991 by George James Firmage. Reprinted with the permission of Liveright Publishing Corporation.

Reuel Denney   "Fixer of Midnight" from *In Praise of Adam* (Chicago: University of Chicago Press, 1961). Copyright © 1961 by Reuel Denney. Reprinted with the permission of the author.

Christine de Pisan   "Marriage Is a Lovely Thing," translated by Joanna Bankier, from *Women Poets of the World,* edited by Joanna Bankier and Deirdre Lashgari. Copyright © 1983 by Macmillan Publishing Company, Inc. Reprinted with the permission of the translator.

Emily Dickinson   67 ("Success is counted sweetest!"), excerpt from 108 ("Surgeons must be very careful"), 249 ("Wild Nights—Wild Nights!"), 258 ("There's a certain Slant of light"), 288 ("I'm Nobody! Who are you?"), 303 ("The Soul selects her own Society"), 328 ("A Bird came down the Walk"), 341 ("After great pain a formal feeling comes"), 435 ("Much Madness is divinest Sense—"), 579 ("I had been hungry, all the Years"), excerpt (4 lines) from 611 ("I see thee better—in the Dark—"), 712 ("Because I could not stop for Death"), 764 ("Presentiment"), 986 ("A narrow Fellow in the Grass"), 1129 ("Tell all the Truth but tell it slant"), 1624 ("Apparently with no surprise"), 1732 ("My life closed twice before its close—"), excerpt (4 lines) from 1763 ("Fame is a bee"), and excerpt from 1770 ("Experiment escorts us last—") from *The Complete Poems of Emily Dickinson,* edited by Thomas H. Johnson. Copyright 1929 by Martha Dickinson, renewed © 1957 Mary L. Hampson. Copyright 1951, © 1955, 1979, 1983 by the President and Fellows of Harvard College. Reprinted with the permission of The Belknap Press of Harvard University Press.

Chitra Divakaruni   "The Quilt" from *Black Candle.* Copyright © 1991 by Chitra Banerjee Divakaruni. Reprinted with the permission of CALYX Books.

H. D. (Hilda Doolittle)   "Helen" from *Collected Poems 1912–1944,* edited by Louis L. Martz. Copyright © 1962 by The Estate of Hilda Doolittle. Reprinted with the permission of New Directions Publishing Corporation.

Rita Dove   "Silos" and "Flash Cards" from *Grace Notes.* Copyright © 1989 by Rita Dove. Reprinted with the permission of the author and W. W. Norton & Company., Inc.

Bob Dylan   excerpt from "It's Alright Ma (I'm Only Bleeding)." Copyright © 1985 by Warner Bros. Music; renewed © 1993 by Special Rider Music. All rights reserved. International copyright secured. Reprinted with the permission of Special Rider Music.

Richard Eberhart   "The Fury of Aerial Bombardment" from *Collected Poems 1930–1986.* Copyright © 1988 by Richard Eberhart. Reprinted with the permission of Oxford University Press, Inc.

T. S. Eliot   "Preludes" and "The Love Song of J. Alfred Prufrock" from *T. S. Eliot: The Complete Poems and Plays 1909–1962.* Reprinted with the permission of Faber and Faber, Ltd.

Louise Erdrich   "Indian Boarding School: The Runaways" from *Love Medicine,* new and expanded version. Copyright © 1993 by Louise Erdrich. Reprinted with the permission of Henry Holt and Company, Inc.

Martín Espada   "Latin Night at the Pawnshop" from *Rebellion is the Circle of a Lover's Hands.* Copyright © 1987 by Martín Espada. Reprinted with the permission of Curbstone Press.

John Fandel   Excerpt from "Tribute." Copyright © 1979 by John Fandel. Reprinted with the permission of the author.

Lawrence Ferlinghetti   "Constantly Risking Absurdity" from *A Coney Island of the Mind.* Copyright © 1958 by Lawrence Ferlinghetti. Reprinted with the permission of New Directions Publishing Corporation.

Donald Finkel   "The Sirens" from *The Clothing's New Emperor* (New York: Charles Scribner's Sons, 1959). Copyright © 1959 by Donald Finkel. Reprinted with the permission of the author.

Jane Flanders   "The House That Fear Built: Warsaw 1943" from *Timepiece.* Copyright © 1988 by Jane Flanders. Reprinted with the permission of the University of Pittsburgh Press.

Richard Foerster   "Message and Means in Jane Flanders' 'The House That Fear Built'" from *Spreading the Word: Editors on Poetry,* edited by Warren Slesinger (Columbia, S.C.: Bench Press, 1990). Reprinted with the permission of the author.

Robert Frost   "Stopping by Woods on a Snowy Evening," "Fire and Ice," "Dust of Snow," "The Tuft of Flowers," "Mending Wall," "Design," "After Apple-Picking," "The Road Not Taken," "The Oven Bird," "Acquainted with the Night," "Once by the Pacific," "Neither Out Far Nor In Deep," "The Night Light," "One Step Backward Taken" and excerpt (3 lines) from "Pertinax" from *The Poetry of Robert Frost,* edited by Edward Connery Lathem. Copyright 1936, 1942, 1944, 1951, © 1956, 1958, 1962 by Robert Frost. Copyright © 1964, 1967, 1970, 1975 by Leslie Frost Ballantine. Copyright 1916, 1923, 1928, 1930, 1934, 1939, 1947, © 1969 by Henry Holt and Company. Reprinted with the permission of the publishers.

Allen Ginsberg   "A Supermarket in California" from *Collected Poems 1947–1980.* Copyright © 1955 by Allen Ginsberg. Reprinted with the permission of HarperCollins Publishers, Inc.

Dana Gioia   "California Hills in August" from *Daily Horoscope.* Originally published in *The New Yorker* (1982). Copyright © 1982 by Dana Gioia. Reprinted with the permission of Graywolf Press, St. Paul, Minn.

Louise Glück   "Gratitude" from *The House on the Marshland.* Copyright © 1971, 1972, 1973, 1974, 1975 by Louise Glück. Reprinted with the permission of The Ecco Press.

Paul Goodman   "Haiku" from *Collected Poems,* edited by Taylor Stoehr (New York: Random House, 1973). Copyright © 1973 by the Estate of Paul Goodman. Reprinted with the permission of Sally Goodman.

Judy Grahn   "They Say She Is Veiled" and excerpt from "Helen in Hollywood" from *The Queen of Wands.* Copyright © 1982 by Judy Grahn. Reprinted with the permission of The Crossing Press, Freedom, Calif.

Donald Hall   Excerpt from *Remembering Poets: Reminiscences and Opinions* (New York: Harper & Row, 1978). Copyright © 1977, 1978 by Donald Hall. Reprinted with the permission of the author.

Joy Harjo   "Leaving" from *She Had Some Horses.* Copyright © 1983 by Thunder's Mouth Press. Reprinted with the permission of the publisher.

Jeffrey Harrison   "Bathtubs, Three Varieties" and "Reflection on the Vietnam War Memorial" from *The Singing Underneath* (New York: E. P. Dutton, 1988). Copyright © 1987 by Jeffrey Harrison. Reprinted with the permission of the author.

Geoffrey Hartman   Excerpt from "Elation in Hegel and Wordsworth" from *The Unremarkable Wordsworth.* Copyright © 1987 by the University of Minnesota. Reprinted with the permission of the University of Minnesota Press.

Robert Hayden   "Those Winter Sundays" and "Frederick Douglass" from *Angle of Ascent: New and Collected Poems.* Copyright © 1966 by Robert Hayden. Reprinted with the permission of Liveright Publishing Corporation.

Seamus Heaney   "Valediction" from *Poems, 1965–1975.* Copyright © 1987 by Seamus Heaney. Reprinted with the permission of Farrar, Straus & Giroux, Inc. and Faber and Faber Ltd.

John Heaviside   "A Gathering of Deafs" from *Olivetree Review* 8 (Fall 1989). Reprinted with the permission of the author.

Calvin C. Hernton   Excerpt from "The Distant Drum" from *The Medicine Man: Collected Poems* (New York: Reed, Cannon & Johnson, 1976). Copyright © 1976 by Calvin Hernton. Reprinted with the permission of the author.

Edward Hirsch   "Fast Break" from *Wild Gratitude* by Edward Hirsch. Copyright © 1985 by Edward Hirsch. Reprinted by permission of Alfred A. Knopf, Inc.

Langston Hughes   "Harlem (A Dream Deferred)" from *The Collected Poems of Langston Hughes,* edited by Arnold Rampersad and David Roessel. Copyright © 1994 by the Estate of Langston Hughes. Reprinted with the permission of Alfred A. Knopf, Inc.

Vicente Huidobro   "Ars Poetica," translated by David M. Guss, from *The Selected Poetry of Vicente Huidobro.* Copyright © 1963 by Empreza Editoria Zig Zag, S.A. Copyright © 1981 by David Guss. Reprinted with the permission of New Directions Publishing Corporation.

Elizabeth Jennings Excerpt from "Song for a Birth or a Death" and excerpt from "Answers" from *Collected Poems* (Manchester: Carcanet Press, 1985). Copyright © 1979, 1985 by Elizabeth Jennings. Reprinted with the permission of David Higham Associates.

Marie Luise Kaschnitz "Women's Program," translated by Lisel Müller, from *Selected Later Poems of Marie Luise Kaschnitz*. Copyright © 1980 by Princeton University Press. Reprinted with the permission of the publishers.

Alfred Kazin Excerpt from "The Posthumous Life of Dylan Thomas" from *The Atlantic Monthly* (1957). Copyright © 1957 by Alfred Kazin. Reprinted with the permission of the author.

Yusef Komunyakaa "My Father's Love Letters" from *Magic City* (Middletown, Conn.: Wesleyan University Press, 1992). Copyright © 1992 by Yusef Komunyakaa. Reprinted with the permission of the University Press of New England.

Maxine Kumin "Woodchucks" from *Selected Poems 1960–1990*. Copyright © 1972 by Maxine Kumin. Reprinted with the permission of W. W. Norton & Company, Inc.

Melvin Walker La Follette "The Ballad of Red Fox" from *The New Yorker* (1952). Copyright 1952, © 1980. Reprinted with the permission of The New Yorker Magazine, Inc.

John Lennon and Paul McCartney Excerpt from "Lucy in the Sky with Diamonds." Words and music by John Lennon and Paul McCartney. Copyright © 1967; renewed © 1995 by Sony/ATV Songs LLC. All rights controlled and administered by EMI Blackwood Music, Inc. Under license from SONY/ATV Songs LLC (BMI). All rights reserved. International copyright secured. Reprinted with the permission of EMI Music Publishing.

Denise Levertov "To One Steeped in Bitterness" from *Breathing the Water*. Copyright © 1987 by Denise Levertov. "In Mind," "What Were They Like?" and "The Mutes" from *Poems 1960–1967*. Copyright © 1964, 1966 by Denise Levertov Goodman. All reprinted with the permission of New Directions Publishing Corporation.

Audre Lorde "Coal" from *Collected Poems*. Copyright © 1968, 1970, 1973 by Audre Lorde. Reprinted with the permission of W. W. Norton & Company Inc. "Poems Are Not Luxuries" from *Claims for Poetry*, edited by Donald Hall (Ann Arbor: University of Michigan Press, 1982). Copyright © 1982 by Audre Lorde. Reprinted with the permission of Charlotte Sheedy Literary Agency, Inc. Excerpt from "Conversation in Crisis" from *Black Women Writers at Work*, edited by Claudia Tate (New York: Continuum, 1983). Reprinted with the permission of Audrey Wolf Literary Agency.

Robert Lowell "Skunk Hour" from *Life Studies*. Copyright © 1956, 1959 by Robert Lowell, renewed 1987 by Harriet W. Lowell, Sheridan Lowell, and Caroline Lowell. Reprinted with the permission of Farrar, Straus & Giroux, Inc.

John Masefield "Cargoes" from *Ballads and Poems* (New York: The Macmillan Company, 1910). Copyright 1910 by Macmillan Publishing Company, renewed 1938 by John Masefield. Reprinted with the permission of The Society of Authors as the literary representative of the Estate of John Masefield.

Peter Meinke "Sunday at the Apple Market" from *Inlet* (Norfolk, Virginia: Virginia Wesleyan College). Reprinted by permission. Excerpt from "When I With You" from *The Night Train and the Golden Bird*. Copyright © 1977 by Peter Meinke. Reprinted with the permission of The University of Pittsburgh Press.

W. S. Merwin "Separation" from *The Moving Target* (New York: Atheneum Publishers, 1963). Copyright © 1960, 1961, 1962, 1963 by W. S. Merwin. Reprinted with the permission of Georges Borchardt, Inc. on behalf of the author.

Edna St. Vincent Millay "Pity Me Not Because the Light of Day," "I, Being Born a Woman, and Distressed," and "An Ancient Gesture" from *Collected Poems* (New York: Harper & Row, Publishers, 1967). Copyright 1923, 1934, 1951, 1954, © 1962, 1982 by Edna St. Vincent Millay and Norma Millay Ellis. Reprinted with the permission of Elizabeth Barnett, Literary Executor for the Edna St. Vincent Millay Society.

Vassar Miller "The New Icarus" from *Wage War on Silence* (Middletown, Conn.: Wesleyan University Press, 1960). Copyright © 1960 by Vassar Miller. Reprinted with the permission of the University Press of New England.

Janice Mirikitani "For My Father" from *Shedding Silence*. Copyright © 1987 by Janice Mirikitani. Reprinted with the permission of Celestial Arts, P.O. Box 7123, Berkeley, Calif. 94707.

H. Edward Richardson and Frederick B. Shroyer   "Freudian Analysis and Yeats' 'Second Coming'" from *The Muse of Fire: Approaches to Poetry*. Copyright © 1971 by Alfred A. Knopf, Inc. Reprinted with the permission of the publishers.

Rainer Maria Rilke   "The Panther" from *Selected Poems of Rainer Maria Rilke*, edited and translated by Robert Bly. Copyright © 1981 by Robert Bly. Reprinted with the permission of HarperCollins Publishers, Inc.

Alberto Ríos   "The Vietnam Wall" from *The Lime Orchard Woman*. Copyright © 1988 by Alberto Ríos. Reprinted with the permission of Sheep Meadow Press.

Theodore Roethke   "My Papa's Waltz" from *The Collected Poems of Theodore Roethke*. Copyright © 1943 by Modern Poetry Association. Copyright 1953, 1954, by Theodore Roethke. Reprinted with the permission of Doubleday, a division of Random House, Inc.

Sappho   "Letter to Anaktoria" and excerpt (6 lines) from "Invocation to Aphrodite" from *Greek Lyrics,* translated by Richard Lattimore. Copyright 1949, © 1955, 1960 by Richard Lattimore. Reprinted with the permission of The University of Chicago Press.

Anne Sexton   "Ringing the Bells" and "Her Kind" from *To Bedlam and Part Way Back*. Copyright © 1960 by Anne Sexton, renewed 1988 by Linda G. Sexton. "To a Friend Whose Work Has Come to Triumph" from *All My Pretty Ones*. Copyright © 1962 by Anne Sexton, renewed 1990 by Linda G. Sexton. All reprinted with the permission of Houghton Mifflin Company. All rights reserved.

Gary Snyder   "After Work" from *The Back Country*. Copyright © 1995 by Gary Snyder. Reprinted with the permission of New Directions Publishing Corporation.

David A. Sohn and Richard H. Tyre   Excerpt from *Frost: The Poet and His Poetry*. Copyright © 1967. Reprinted with the permission of Holt, Rinehart and Winston.

Cathy Song   "Lost Sister" from *The Picture Bride*. Copyright © 1983 by Cathy Song. Reprinted with the permission of Yale University Press.

Gary Soto   "Oranges" from *New and Selected Poems*. Copyright © 1995 by Gary Soto. Reprinted with the permission of Chronicle Books.

William Stafford   "Traveling through the Dark," "At the Bomb Testing Site," "One Home," and "Freedom" from *Stories That Could Be True: New and Collected Poems*. Copyright © 1960, 1969 by William Stafford. Reprinted with the permission of the Estate of William Stafford.

Wallace Stevens   "The Disillusionment of Ten O'Clock" from *The Collected Poems of Wallace Stevens*. Copyright © 1923, 1936, 1942, 1947, 1954 by Wallace Stevens, renewed 1951 by Wallace Stevens, © 1964, 1970, 1975, 1982 by Holly Stevens. Reprinted with the permission of Alfred A. Knopf, Inc.

May Swenson   "Question" from *New and Selected Things Taking Place*. Copyright 1954 and renewed © 1982 by May Swenson. Reprinted with the permission of The Literary Estate of May Swenson.

Dylan Thomas   "Fern Hill," "In My Craft or Sullen Art," and "Do Not Go Gentle into That Good Night" from *The Poems of Dylan Thomas*. Copyright 1952 by the Trustees for the Copyrights of Dylan Thomas. Reprinted with the permission of New Directions Publishing Corporation and David Higham Associates, London as agents for the Trustees of the Copyrights of Dylan Thomas. Excerpt from "Notes on the Art of Poetry" from *Texas Quarterly* (1961). Copyright © 1961 by the University of Texas, renewed © 1989 by Stuart Thomas and Wynford Vaughan Thomas. Reprinted with the permission of Harold Ober Associates.

Charles Tomlinson   Excerpt from "The View" from *Collected Poems*. Copyright © 1985 by Charles Tomlinson. Reprinted with the permission of Oxford University Press, Inc.

David Wagoner   "The Other House" from *First Light*. Originally published in *Slackwater Review*. Copyright © 1983 by David Wagoner. Reprinted with the permission of Little, Brown and Company. "The Return of Icarus" from *Collected Poems 1956–1976* (Bloomington: Indiana University Press, 1976). Copyright © 1976 by David Wagoner. Reprinted with the permission of the author.

John Wain   Excerpt from "Apology for Understatement" from *Weep before God* (New York: St. Martin's Press, 1961). Copyright © 1961 by John Wain. Reprinted with the permission of Curtis Brown Ltd.

Diane Wakoski   Excerpt from "Meeting an Astronomer" and "On Experience and Imagination" from the Introduction to *Trilogy*. Copyright © 1962, 1966, 1967, 1974 by Diane Wakoski. Reprinted with the permission of Doubleday, a division of Random House, Inc.

Alice Walker   "Women" from *Revolutionary Petunias & Other Poems*. Copyright © 1970, 1973 by Alice Walker. Reprinted with the permission of Harcourt Brace & Company.

William S. Ward   Excerpt from "Lifted Pot Lids and Unmended Walls" from *College English* (February 1966). Copyright © 1966 by the National Council of Teachers of English. Reprinted with the permission of the publisher.

J. R. Watson   "A Close Reading of G. M. Hopkins' 'God's Grandeur'" from *The Poetry of Gerard Manley Hopkins*. Copyright © 1987 by J. R. Watson. Reprinted with the permission of Penguin Books, Ltd.

Bethlyn Madison Webster   "Stamps" from *bite to eat place*, edited by Andrea Adolph et al. (Oakland, Calif.: Redwood Coast Press, 1995). Reprinted with the permission of the author.

Richard Wilbur   Excerpt from "Letting a Poem Find Its Form" from *Ecstatic Occasions, Expedient Forms*, edited by David Lehman (New York: Macmillan Publishing Company, 1987). Copyright © 1987 by Richard Wilbur. Reprinted with the permission of the author.

C. K. Williams   Excerpts from "Hood" from *Poems 1963–1983*. Copyright © 1988 by C. K. Williams. Reprinted with the permission of Farrar, Straus & Giroux, Inc.

Miller Williams   "Thinking about Bill, Dead of AIDS" from *Living on the Surface: New and Selected Poems*. Copyright © 1989 by Miller Williams. Reprinted with the permission of Louisiana State University Press.

William Carlos Williams   "Landscape with the Fall of Icarus" from *The Collected Poems of William Carlos Williams*, vol. 2, *1939–1962*. Copyright © 1962 by William Carlos Williams. "This Is Just to Say," "Between Walls," "The Dance," and "The Red Wheelbarrow" from *The Collected Poems of William Carlos Williams*, vol. 1, *1909–1939*. Copyright 1938, 1944, 1945 by William Carlos Williams. All reprinted with the permission of New Directions Publishing Corporation.

William Butler Yeats   "Sailing to Byzantium," "Leda and the Swan," "The Second Coming," and excerpt from "The White Birds" from *The Poems of W. B. Yeats: A New Edition*, edited by Richard J. Finneran. Copyright 1928 by Macmillan Publishing Company. Copyright 1924 by Macmillan Publishing Company, renewed 1952, © 1956 by Bertha Georgie Yeats. Reprinted with the permission of Simon & Schuster.

DRAMA

Esther Cohen   Excerpt from "Uncommon Woman: An Interview with Wendy Wasserstein" from *Women's Studies* 15 (1988). Reprinted with the permission of Gordon and Breach Publishers.

David D. Cooper   "Idealism and Fatalism in *A Raisin in the Sun*" from *The Explicator* 52, no. 1 (Fall 1993). Copyright © 1993 by the Helen Dwight Reid Educational Foundation. Reprinted with the permission of Heldref Publications and the Helen Dwight Read Educational Foundation.

Errol Durbach   "Ibsen and Marxism" from *A Doll's House: Ibsen's Myth of Transformation*. Copyright © 1991 by G. K. Hall & Co. Reprinted with the permission of Twayne Publishers, an imprint of Simon & Schuster.

Sandra K. Fischer   Excerpt from "The Feminist Hamlet: Hearing Ophelia" from *Renaissance and Reformation* 26 , no. 1 (Winter 1990). Reprinted with the permission of the publisher.

Lorraine Hansberry   *A Raisin in the Sun*. Copyright © 1958 by Robert Nemiroff as an unpublished work. Copyright © 1959, 1966 and 1984 by Robert Nemiroff. Reprinted with the permission of Random House, Inc.

David Henry Hwang   "The Dance and the Railroad" from *FOB and Other Plays*. Copyright © 1981 by David Henry Hwang. Reprinted with the permission of Dutton Signet, a division of Penguin Putnam, Inc.

Henrik Ibsen   "A Doll's House," translated by Peter Watts, from *A Doll's House and Other Plays*. Copyright © 1965 by Peter Watts. Reprinted with the permission of Penguin Books Ltd.

Ernest Jones   Excerpt from Introduction to *Hamlet, Prince of Denmark* by William Shakespeare. Reprinted with the permission of Vision Press Ltd.

David Mamet   *The Cryptogram.* Copyright © 1995 by David Mamet. Reprinted with the permission of Vintage Books, a division of Random House, Inc.

Lloyd Rose   Excerpt from "Lost in America" from *The Atlantic Monthly* (April 1984). Copyright © 1984 by Lloyd Rose. Reprinted with the permission of the author.

Sophocles   *Antigone* from *Three Theban Plays,* translated by Robert Fagles. Copyright © 1982 by Robert Fagles. Reprinted with the permission of Viking Penguin, a division of Penguin Putnam, Inc.

Elmer Edgar Stoll   "The Renaissance Hamlet" from *Art and Artifice in Shakespeare.* Reprinted with the permission of Routledge.

Joan Templeton   Excerpt from "The *Doll House* Backlash: Criticism, Feminism, and Ibsen" from *PMLA,* 104 (January 1989). Copyright © 1989 by the Modern Language Association of America. Reprinted with the permission of the publishers.

Luis Valdez   Excerpt from *Soldado Razo (The Buck Private).* Reprinted with the permission of the author.

Wendy Wasserstein   *Tender Offer.* Copyright © 1991 by Wendy Wasserstein. No part of this material may be reproduced in whole or in part without the express permission of the author or her agent. Reprinted with the permission of Rosenstone Wender.

Tennessee Williams   "The Glass Menagerie." Copyright 1945 by Tennessee Williams and Edwina D. Williams, renewed © 1973 by Tennessee Williams. Reprinted with the permission of Random House, Inc.

August Wilson   "How Avery Got to Be Preacher" from *The Piano Lesson.* Copyright © 1988, 1990 by August Wilson. Reprinted with the permission of Dutton Signet, a division of Penguin Putnam, Inc.

Index of Authors, Titles, and First Lines

Subject Index